St. Joseph
Springfield
Indianapolis
Leavenworth
Lexington
12-20 SEP 61
Topeka
Jefferson City
St. Louis
Louisville
CURTIS
Evansville
LYON
Bowling Green
Baxter Springs
Springfield
Wilson's Cr.
10 AUG 61
Ironton
Cape Girardeau
FOOTE
GRANT
Cairo
Belmont - 7 NOV 61
Paducah
PRICE and McCULLOCH
New Madrid
13 MAR 62
Columbus
BUELL
Tahlequah
Pea Ridge
6-7 MAR 62
Island Ten
8 APR 62
Forts Henry and Donelson
6 FEB 62 & 16 FEB 62
Nashville
OCCUPIED
23 FEB 62
VAN DORN
DAVIS
Plum Run Bend
10 MAY 62
Murfreesboro
Ft. Smith
Ft. Pillow
EVAC. 4 JUN 62
Jackson
HALLECK
Tullahoma
Little Rock
Corinth
3-4 OCT 62
Shiloh
6-7 APR 62
Memphis
6 JUN 62
Iuka - 20 SEP 62
St. Charles
17 JAN 62
Helena
Decatur
Federal
Confederate
GRANT
Tupelo
BUELL
Napoleon
Grenada
BRAGG
LEFT 24 JULY 62
Tuscaloosa
Tyler
Shreveport
Monroe
Meridian
Selma
The "Arkansas"
15 JUL 62
Montgomery
Miles   100
Vicksburg
26-29 JUN 62
Jackson
BRECKINRIDGE
Alexandria
Natchez
"Arkansas"
BLOWN UP
5 AUG 62
Port Hudson
Mobile
Baton Rouge
5 AUG 62
Pass Christian
Pensacola
10 MAY 62
Beaumont
Biloxi - APR 62
FARRAGUT
Ship I.
17 SEP 61
Galveston
5 OCT 62
N
New Orleans
Ft. St. Philip
24 APR 62
FARRAGUT & BUTLER
Ft. Jackson
Head of Passes
12 OCT 61
Gulf of Mexico

Wheeling

McCLELLAN

Carrick's Ford
13 JUL 61

STUART

Baltimore

Philippi
3 JUN 61

McCLELLAN
(2)

Washington

Cincinnati

Buckhannon

Rich Mountain
11 JUL 61

JACKSON

Dover

McCLELLAN
(1)

McDOWELL

POPE

Frankfort
4 OCT 62
INAUGURAL DISRUPTED

FOR DETAILS
SEE BACK
ENDPAPER

Staunton

Fredericksburg

LEE'

Richmond
30 AUG 62

Pikeville

Lynchburg

Richmond

Norfolk

erryville
8 OCT 62
afordville
SEP 62

Roanoke

Danville

Suffolk

Elizabeth City
10 FEB
62

Mill
Springs
19 JAN 62

Abingdon

Cumberland Gap
EVAC. 18 JUN 62

Weldon

Roano
Isla
8 FEB

LEFT 19 AUG
RET. 24 OCT
62

KIRBY
SMITH

Greensboro

Sparta

BRAGG

Knoxville

Asheville

Raleigh

Goldsboro

Pamlito Sd.

LEFT 28
AUG

Fayetteville

New Bern
14 MAR 62

Cape
Hatteras
29 AUG

Chattanooga

Greenville

Spartanburg

Charlotte

Ft. Macon
25 APR 62

LOCOMOTIVE
CHASE
12 APR 62

Rome

Athens

Columbia

Florence

Wilmington
Ft. Fisher

Atlanta

lladega

Augusta

Milledgeville

Charleston

Ft. Sumter
12 APR 61

Macon

Pocotaligo
22 OCT 62

Secessionville
16 JUN 62

Columbus

Savannah

Port Royal
7 NOV 61

Ft. Pulaski
11 APR 62

Atlantic Ocean

rt
ames

Albany

Brunswick
9 MAR 62

Fernandina
4 MAR 62

Jacksonville
9 APR 62

Tallahassee

St. Augustine
11 MAR 62

Apalachicola
2 APR 62

Theater of War
1861 ~ 1862

Wheeling

Carrick's Ford
13 JUL 61

McCLELLAN

Philippi
3 JUN 61

STUART

Baltimore

McCLELLAN (2)

Washington

Dover

Buckhannon

Rich Mountain
11 JUL 61

JACKSON

McDOWELL
McCLELLAN (1)
POPE

Cincinnati

FOR DETAILS
SEE BACK
ENDPAPER

Staunton

Fredericksburg

Frankfort
4 OCT 62
INAUGURAL DISRUPTED

Richmond
30 AUG 62

Pikeville

Lynchburg

Richmond

LEE

Norfolk

erryville
8 OCT 62
fordville
62

Roanoke

Suffolk

Abingdon

Danville

Weldon

Elizabeth City
10 FEB 62

Mill
Springs
19 JAN 62

Cumberland Gap
EVAC. 18 JUN 62

Greensboro

Roano
Island
8 FEB

LEFT 14 AUG
RET. 24 OCT
62

KIRBY
SMITH

Raleigh

Goldsboro

Pamlico Sd.

Sparta

Knoxville

Asheville

Fayetteville

New Bern
14 MAR 62

Cape
Hattera
29 AUG

BRAGG
LEFT
28
AUG

Ft. Macon
25 APR 62

Chattanooga

Greenville

Spartanburg

Charlotte

Wilmington
Ft. Fisher

LOCOMOTIVE
CHASE
12 APR 62

ome

Columbia

Florence

ladega

Atlanta

Athens

Augusta

Charleston

Milledgeville

Ft. Sumter
12 APR 61

Macon

Pocotaligo
22 OCT 62

Secessionville
16 JUN 62

Columbus

Savannah

Port Royal
7 NOV 61

Ft. Pulaski
11 APR 62

rt
aines

Albany

Brunswick
9 MAR 62

Fernandina
4 MAR 62

Atlantic Ocean

Tallahassee

Jacksonville
9 APR 62

Apalachicola
2 APR 62

St. Augustine
11 MAR 62

Theater of War
1861 ~ 1862

THE CIVIL WAR - 1

Although he now makes his home in Memphis, Tennessee, Shelby Foote comes from a long line of Mississippians. He was born in Greenville, Mississippi, and attended school there until he entered the University of North Carolina. During the Second World War, he served in Europe as a captain of field artillery. He has written six novels: *Tournament, Follow Me Down, Love in a Dry Season, Shiloh, Jordan County* and *September, September.* While writing *The Civil War: A Narrative* (Pimlico, 3 volumes) he was awarded three Guggenheim fellowships.

THE CIVIL WAR

A Narrative

1 Fort Sumter to Perryville

SHELBY FOOTE

PIMLICO

PIMLICO

20 Vauxhall Bridge Road, London SW1V2SA

London Melbourne Sydney Auckland Johannesburg
and agencies throughout the world

First published in Great Britain by The Bodley Head
1991
Pimlico edition 1992
Reprinted 1993
Reprinted 1994
Reprinted 2000
© Shelby Foote 1958 and renewed by
Shelby Foote 1986

Printed and bound in the USA

ISBN 0-7126-9802-7 (volume 1)
0-7126-9807-8 (volume 2)
0-7126-9812-4 (volume 3)

TABLE OF CONTENTS

★ ✗ ☆

Prologue – The Opponents

★ ✗ ☆

☞ IT WAS A MONDAY IN WASHINGTON, January 21; Jefferson Davis rose from his seat in the Senate. South Carolina had left the Union a month before, followed by Mississippi, Florida, and Alabama, which seceded at the rate of one a day during the second week of the new year. Georgia went out eight days later; Louisiana and Texas were poised to go; few doubted that they would, along with others. For more than a decade there had been intensive discussion as to the legality of secession, but now the argument was no longer academic. A convention had been called for the first week in February, at Montgomery, Alabama, for the purpose of forming a confederacy of the departed states, however many there should be in addition to the five already gone. As a protest against the election of Abraham Lincoln, who had received not a single southern electoral vote, secession was a fact — to be reinforced, if necessary, by the sword. The senator from Mississippi rose. It was high noon. The occasion was momentous and expected; the galleries were crowded, hoop-skirted ladies and men in broadcloth come to hear him say farewell. He was going home.

By now he was one of the acknowledged spokesmen of secession, though it had not always been so. By nature he was a moderate, with a deep devotion to the Union. He had been for compromise so long as he believed compromise was possible; he reserved secession as a last resort. Yet now they were at that stage. In a paper which he had helped to draft and which he had signed and sent as advice to his state in early December, his position had been explicit. "The argument is exhausted," it declared. "All hope of relief in the Union . . . is extinguished." At last he was for disunion, with a southern confederacy to follow.

During the twelve days since the secession of Mississippi he had remained in Washington, sick in mind and body, waiting for the news to reach him officially. He hoped he might be arrested as a traitor, thereby gaining a chance to test the right of secession in the federal courts. Now the news had been given him officially the day before, a Sunday, and he stayed to say goodbye. He had never doubted the right of secession. What he doubted was its wisdom. Yet now it was no longer a question even of wisdom; it was a question of necessity — meaning Honor. On the day before Lincoln's election, Davis had struck an organ tone that brought a storm of applause in his home state. "I glory in Mississippi's star!" he cried. "But before I would see it dishonored I would tear it from its place, to be set on the perilous ridge of battle as a sign around which her bravest and best shall meet the harvest home of death."

Thus he had spoken in November, but now in January, rising to say farewell, his manner held more of sadness than defiance. For a long moment after he rose he struck the accustomed preliminary stance of the orators of his day: high-stomached, almost sway-backed, the knuckles of one hand braced against the desk top, the other hand raised behind him with the wrist at the small of his back. He was dressed in neat black broadcloth, cuffless trouser-legs crumpling over his boots, the coat full-skirted with wide lapels, a satin waistcoat framing the stiff white bosom of his shirt, a black silk handkerchief wound stockwise twice around the upturned collar and knotted loosely at the throat. Close-shaven except for the tuft of beard at the jut of the chin, the face was built economically close to the skull, and more than anything it expressed an iron control by the brain within that skull. He had been sick for the past month and he looked it. He looked in fact like a man who had emerged from a long bout with a fever; which was what he was, except that the fever had been a generation back, when he was twenty-seven, and now he was fifty-two. Beneath the high square forehead, etched with the fine criss-cross lines of pain and overwork, the eyes were deep-set, gray and stern, large and lustrous, though one was partly covered by a film, a result of the neuralgia which had racked him all those years. The nose was aquiline, finely shaped, the nostrils broad and delicately chiseled. The cheeks were deeply hollowed beneath the too-high cheekbones and above the wide, determined jaw. His voice was low, with the warmth of the Deep South in it.

"I rise, Mr President, for the purpose of announcing to the Senate that I have satisfactory evidence that the State of Mississippi, by a solemn ordinance of her people in convention assembled, has declared her separation from the United States. Under these circumstances, of course, my functions terminate here. It has seemed to me proper, however, that I should appear in the Senate to announce that fact to my associates, and I will say but very little more."

His voice faltered at the outset, but soon it gathered volume and rang clear — "like a silver trumpet," according to his wife, who sat in the gallery. "Unshed tears were in it," she added, "and a plea for peace permeated every tone." Davis continued:

"It is known to senators who have served with me here, that I have for many years advocated, as an essential attribute of State sovereignty, the right of a State to secede from the Union.... If I had thought that Mississippi was acting without sufficient provocation ... I should still, under my theory of government, because of my allegiance to the State of which I am a citizen, have been bound by her action."

He foresaw the founding of a nation, inheritor of the traditions of the American Revolution. "We but tread in the paths of our fathers when we proclaim our independence and take the hazard ... not in hostility to others, not to injure any section of the country, not even for our own pecuniary benefit, but from the high and solemn motive of defending and protecting the rights we inherited, and which it is our duty to transmit unshorn to our children." England had been a lion; the Union might turn out to be a bear; in which case, "we will invoke the God of our fathers, who delivered them from the power of the lion, to protect us from the ravages of the bear; and thus, putting our trust in God and in our own firm hearts and strong arms, we will vindicate the right as best we may."

Davis glanced around the chamber, then continued. "I see now around me some with whom I have served long. There have been points of collision; but whatever of offense there has been to me, I leave here. I carry with me no hostile remembrance.... I go hence unencumbered by the remembrance of any injury received, and having discharged the duty of making the only reparation in my power for any injury received." He then spoke the final sentence to which all the rest had served as prologue. "Mr President and Senators, having made the announcement which the occasion seemed to me to require, it remains only for me to bid you a final adieu."

For a moment there was silence. Then came the ovation, the sustained thunder of applause, the flutter of handkerchiefs and hum of comment. Davis shrank from this, however, or at any rate ignored it. As he resumed his seat he lowered his head and covered his face with his hands. Some in the gallery claimed his shoulders shook; he was weeping, they said. It may have been so, though he was not given to public tears. If so, it could have been from more than present tension. His life was crowded with glory, as a soldier, as a suitor, as a statesman; yet the glory was more than balanced by personal sorrow as a man. He had known tears in his time.

He was born in Christian County, Kentucky, within a year and a hundred miles of the man whose election had brought on the present furor. Like that man, he was a log-cabin boy, the youngest of ten chil-

dren whose grandfather had been born in Philadelphia in 1702, the
son of an immigrant Welshman who signed his name with an X. This
grandfather moved to Georgia, where he married a widow who bore
him one son, Samuel. Samuel raised and led an irregular militia company
in the Revolution. After the war he married and moved northwest to
south-central Kentucky, where he put up his own log house, farmed
six hundred acres of land by the hard agronomy of the time, and supplied himself with children, naming the sons out of the Bible — Joseph,
Samuel, Benjamin, and Isaac — until the tenth child, born in early June
of 1808, whom he named for the red-headed President then in office, and
gave him the middle name Finis in the belief, or perhaps the hope, that
he was the last; which he was.

By the time the baby Jefferson was weaned the family was on the
move again, south one thousand miles to Bayou Teche, Louisiana, only
to find the climate unhealthy and to move again, three hundred miles
northeast to Wilkinson County, Mississippi Territory, southeast of
Natchez and forty miles from the Mississippi River. Here the patriarch
stopped, for he prospered; he did not move again, and here Jefferson
spent his early childhood.

The crop now was cotton, and though Samuel Davis had slaves,
he was his own overseer, working alongside them in the field. It was a
farm, not a plantation; he was a farmer, not a planter. In a region where
the leading men were Episcopalians and Federalists, he was a Baptist and
a Democrat. Now his older children were coming of age, and at their
marriages he gave them what he could, one Negro slave, and that was
all. The youngest, called Little Jeff, began his education when he was
six. For the next fifteen years he attended one school after another, first
a log schoolhouse within walking distance of home, then a Dominican
institution in Kentucky, Saint Thomas Aquinas, where he was still called
Little Jeff because he was the smallest pupil there. He asked to become
a Roman Catholic but the priest told him to wait and learn, which he
did, and either forgot or changed his mind. Then, his mother having
grown lonesome for her last-born, he came home to the Mississippi
schoolhouse where he had started.

He did not like it. One hot fall day he rebelled; he would not go.
Very well, his father said, but he could not be idle, and sent him to the
field with the work gang. Two days later Jeff was back at his desk. "The
heat of the sun and the physical labor, in conjunction with the implied
equality with the other cotton pickers, convinced me that school was the
lesser evil." Thus he later explained his early decision to work with his
head, not his hands. In continuation of this decision, just before his four-
teenth birthday he left once more for Kentucky, entering Transylvania
University, an excellent school, one of the few in the country to live up
to a high-sounding name. Under competent professors he continued his

studies in Latin and Greek and mathematics, including trigonometry, and explored the mysteries of sacred and profane history and natural philosophy — meaning chemistry and physics — with surveying and oratory thrown in for good measure. While he was there his father died and his oldest brother, Joseph, twenty-four years his senior, assumed the role of guardian.

Not long before his death, the father had secured for his youngest son an appointment to West Point, signed by the Secretary of War, and thus for the first time the names were linked: Jefferson Davis, John C. Calhoun. Joseph Davis by now had become what his father had never been — a planter, with a planter's views, a planter's way of life. Jefferson inclined toward the University of Virginia, but Joseph persuaded him to give the Academy a try. It was in the tradition for the younger sons of prominent southern families to go there; if at the end of a year he found he did not like it he could transfer. So Davis attended West Point, and found he liked it.

Up to now he had shown no special inclination to study. Alert and affectionate, he was of a mischievous disposition, enjoyed a practical joke, and sought the admiration of his fellows rather more than the esteem of his professors. Now at the Academy he continued along this course, learning something of tavern life in the process. "O Benny Haven's, O!" he sang, linking arms and clinking tankards. He found he liked the military comradeship, the thought of unrequited death on lonely, far-off battlefields:

> "*To our comrades who have fallen, one cup before we go;*
> *They poured their life-blood freely out pro bono publico.*
> *No marble points the stranger to where they rest below;*
> *They lie neglected — far away from Benny Haven's, O!*"

Brought before a court martial for out-of-bounds drinking of "spirituous liquors," he made the defense of a strict constructionist: 1) visiting Benny Haven's was not *officially* prohibited in the regulations, and 2) malt liquors were not "spirituous" in the first place. The defense was successful; he was not dismissed, and he emerged from the scrape a stricter constructionist than ever. He also got to know his fellow cadets. Leonidas Polk was his roommate; Joseph E. Johnston was said to have been his opponent in a fist fight over a girl; along with others, he admired the open manliness of Albert Sidney Johnston, the high-born rectitude of Robert E. Lee.

Davis himself was admired, even liked. Witnesses spoke of his well-shaped head, his self-esteem, his determination and personal mastery. A "florid young fellow," he had "beautiful blue eyes, a graceful figure." In his studies he did less well, receiving his lowest marks in mathematics and deportment, his highest in rhetoric and moral philosophy, including constitutional law. But the highs could not pull up the lows. He stood well below the middle of his class, still a private at the close of his senior year, and graduated in 1828, twenty-third in a class of thirty-four.

As a second lieutenant, U.S. Army, he now began a seven-year adventure, serving in Wisconsin, Iowa, Illinois, Missouri, where he learned to fight Indians, build forts, scout, and lead a simple social existence. He had liked West Point; he found he liked this even better. Soon he proved himself a superior junior officer, quick-witted and resourceful — as when once with a few men he was chased by a band of Indians after scalps; both parties being in canoes, he improvised a sail and drew away. In a winter of deep snow he came down with pneumonia, and though he won that fight as well, his susceptibility to colds and neuralgia dated from then. He was promoted to first lieutenant within four years, and when Black Hawk was captured in 1832, Davis was appointed by his colonel, Zachary Taylor, to escort the prisoner to Jefferson Barracks.

Thus Colonel Taylor, called "Old Rough and Ready," showed his approval of Davis as a soldier. But as a son-in-law, it developed, he wanted no part of him. The lieutenant had met the colonel's daughter, sixteen-year-old Knox Taylor, brown-haired and blue-eyed like himself, though later the color of his own eyes would deepen to gray. Love came quickly, and his letters to her show a man unseen before or after. "By my dreams I have been lately almost crazed, for they were of you," he wrote to her, and also thus: "Kind, dear letter; I have kissed it often and often, and it has driven away mad notions from my brain." The girl accepted his suit, but the father did not; Taylor wanted no soldier son-in-law, apparently especially not this one. Therefore Davis, who had spent the past seven years as a man of action, proposed to challenge the colonel to a duel. Dissuaded from this, he remained a man of action still. He resigned his commission, went straight to Louisville, and married the girl. The wedding was held at the home of an aunt she was visiting. "After the service everybody cried but Davis," a witness remarked, adding that they "thought this most peculiar."

As it turned out, he was reserving his tears. The young couple did not wait to attempt a reconciliation with her father; perhaps they depended on time to accomplish this. Instead they took a steamboat south to Davis Bend, Mississippi, below Vicksburg, where Joseph Davis, the guardian elder brother, had prospered on a plantation called The Hurricane. He presented them with an adjoining 800-acre place and fourteen slaves on credit. Davis put in a cotton crop, but before the harvest time came round they were both down with fever. They were confined to separate rooms, each too sick to be told of the other's condition, though Davis managed to make it to the door of his bride's room in time to see her die. She had been a wife not quite three months, and as she died she sang snatches of "Fairy Bells," a favorite air; she had had it from her mother. Now those tears which he had not shed at the wedding came to scald his eyes. He was too sick to attend the funeral; the doctor believed he would not be long behind her.

The doctor was wrong, though Davis never lost the drawn, gaunt look of a fever convalescent. He returned to the plantation; then, finding it too crowded with recent memories, left for Cuba, thought to be a fine climate and landscape for restoring broken hearts. The sea bathing at least did his health much good, and he returned by way of New York and Washington, renewing acquaintances with old friends now on the rise and gaining some notion of how much he had missed on the frontier. Then he came home to Mississippi. He would be a planter and, at last, a student.

He found a ready tutor awaiting him. Joseph Davis had got a law degree in Kentucky, had set up practice in Natchez, and, prospering, had bought the land which in that section practically amounted to a patent of nobility. By now, in his middle fifties, he was the wealthiest planter in the state, the "leading philosopher" — whatever that meant — and the possessor of the finest library, which he gladly made available to his idolized younger brother. Davis soon had the Constitution by heart and went deeply into *Elliot's Debates*, theories of government as argued by the framers. He read John Locke and Adam Smith, *The Federalist* and the works of Thomas Jefferson. Shakespeare and Swift lent him what an orator might need of cadenced beauty and invective; Byron and Scott were there at hand, along with the best English magazines and the leading American newspapers. He read them all, and discussed them with his brother.

Also there was the plantation; Brierfield, he called it. Here too he worked and learned, making certain innovations in the labor system. The overseer was a Negro, James Pemberton. No slave was ever punished except after a formal trial by an all-Negro jury, Davis only reserving the right to temper the severity of the judgment. James was always James, never Jim; "It is disrespect to give a nickname," Davis said, and the overseer repaid him with frankness, loyalty, and efficiency. Once when something went amiss and the master asked him why, James replied: "I rather think, sir, through my neglect."

Davis gained all this from his decade of seclusion and study; but he gained something else as well. Up to now, his four years at West Point, brief and interrupted as they were, had been the longest period he had spent at any one place in his life. His school years had been various indeed, with instructors ranging from log-cabin teachers to Catholic priests and New England scholars. When a Virginian or a Carolinian spoke of his "country," he meant Virginia or Carolina. It was not so with Davis. Tennessee and Kentucky were as familiar to him as Mississippi; the whole South, as a region, formed his background; he was thirty before he knew a real home in any real sense of the word. Now at last he had this, too, though still with a feeling of being somewhat apart. Like his brother Joseph and his father before him, he was a Democrat, and while this was true of the majority of the people in his state, it was by no means true of the majority in his class, who were Federalists or Whigs.

Then history intervened for him and solved this problem too. Previously the cotton capitalists had thought their interests coincided with the interests of capitalists in general. Now anti-slavery and pro-tariff agitation was beginning to teach them otherwise. In 1844, the year when Davis emerged from seclusion, the upheaval was accomplished. Repudiating Jefferson and Jackson, the Democrats went over to the Whigs, who came to meet them, creating what Calhoun had been after from the start: a solid South. Davis caught the movement at its outset.

Before that, however, in the previous December, his brother produced one more item from the horn of plenty. He had a lawyer friend, W. B. Howell of Natchez, son of an eight-term governor of New Jersey. Howell had married a Kempe of Virginia and moved south to cotton country. Joseph Davis was an intimate of their house; their first son was named for him, and their seventeen-year-old daughter Varina called him Uncle Joe. Now he wrote to the girl's parents, inviting her to visit The Hurricane. She arrived by steamboat during the Christmas season, having just completed an education in the classics. She did not stay at The Hurricane; she stayed at his sister's plantation, fourteen miles away. Presently a horseman arrived with a message. He dismounted to give it to her, lingered briefly, then excused himself and rode off to a political meeting in Vicksburg. That night Varina wrote to her mother, giving her first impression of the horseman.

> Today Uncle Joe sent, by his younger brother (did you know he had one?), an urgent invitation to me to go at once to The Hurricane. I do not know whether this Mr Jefferson Davis is young or old. He looks both at times; but I believe he is old, for from what I hear he is only two years younger than you are. He impresses me as a remarkable kind of man, but of uncertain temper, and has a way of taking for granted that everybody agrees with him when he expresses an opinion, which offends me; yet he is most agreeable and has a peculiarly sweet voice and a winning manner of asserting himself. The fact is, he is the kind of person I should expect to rescue one from a mad dog at any risk, but to insist upon a stoical indifference to the fright afterward. I do not think I shall ever like him as I do his brother Joe. Would you believe it, he is refined and cultivated, and yet he is a Democrat!

This last was the principal difficulty between them. Varina was a Natchez girl, which meant not only that her background was Federalist, but also that she had led a life of gaiety quite unlike the daily round in the malarial bottoms of Davis Bend. The Christmas season was a merry one, however, and Joseph proved an excellent matchmaker, although a rather heavy-handed one. "By Jove, she is as beautiful as Venus!" he told his brother, adding: "As well as good looks, she has a mind that will fit her for any sphere that the man to whom she is married will feel proud to reach." Jefferson agreed, admiring the milk-pale skin, the raven hair, the generous mouth, the slender waist. "She is beautiful and she has a fine mind," he admitted, with some caution at the outset.

In the evenings there were readings from historians and orators, and the brothers marveled at the ease with which the girl pronounced and translated the Latin phrases and quotations that studded the texts. The conquest was nearly complete; there remained only the political difference. In the course of these discussions Varina wore a cameo brooch with a Whig device carved into the stone, a watchdog crouched by a strongbox. Then one day she appeared without it, and Davis knew he had won.

He left The Hurricane in late January, engaged. In February of the following year, 1845, they were married. Davis was thirty-six, Varina half that. They went to New Orleans on the wedding tour, enjoyed a fashionable Creole interlude, and returned after a few weeks to Brierfield.

The house they moved into was a one-story frame twin-wing structure; Davis had planned and built it himself, with the help of James Pemberton. It had charm, but he and his young wife had little time to enjoy it. By then he had emerged from his shell in more ways than one. In 1843 he had run for the state legislature against Sergeant S. Prentiss, famous as an orator, a Whig in an overwhelmingly Whig district. Davis was defeated, though with credit and a growing reputation. The following year, taking time off from courtship, he stumped the state as an elector for James K. Polk. In the year of his marriage, Whigs and Democrats having coalesced, he was elected to Congress as representative-at-large. In Washington, his first act was to introduce a resolution that federal troops be withdrawn from federal forts, their posts to be taken by state recruits. It died in committee, and his congressional career was ended by the outbreak of the Mexican War.

Davis resigned his seat and came home to head a volunteer regiment, the Mississippi Rifles. Under the strict discipline of their West Point colonel, who saw to it that they were armed with a new model rifle, they were the crack outfit of Zachary Taylor's army, fighting bravely at Monterey and saving the day at Buena Vista, where Davis formed them in a V that broke the back of a Mexican cavalry charge and won the battle. He was wounded in the foot, came home on crutches, and at victory banquets in New Orleans and elsewhere heard himself proclaimed a military genius and the hero of the South. Hunched upon his crutches, he responded to such toasts with dignified modesty. Basically his outlook was unchanged. When Polk sent him a commission as a brigadier general of volunteers, Davis returned it promptly, remarking that the President had no authority to make such an appointment, that power inhering in the states alone. Perhaps all these honors were somewhat anticlimactic anyhow, coming as they did after the words General Taylor was supposed to have spoken to him at Buena Vista: "My daughter, sir, was a better judge of men than I was."

Honors fell thickly upon him now. Within sixty days the governor appointed him to the U.S. Senate. At a private banquet tendered before he left, he stood and heard the toasts go round: "Colonel Jeff Davis, the Game Cock of the South!" "Jeff Davis, the President of the Southern Confederacy!" Davis stood there, allowing no change of expression, no flush of emotion on his face. He took this stiffness, this coldness up to Washington and onto the floor of the Senate.

He would not unbend; he would engage in no log-rolling. In a cloakroom exchange, when he stated his case supporting a bill for removing obstructions from the river down near Vicksburg, another senator, who had his pet project too, interrupted to ask, "Will you vote for the Lake appropriations?" Davis responded: "Sir, I make no terms. I accept no compromises. If when I ask for an appropriation, the object shall be shown to be proper and the expenditure constitutional, I defy the gentleman, for his conscience' sake, to vote against it. If it shall appear to him otherwise, then I expect his opposition, and only ask that it shall be directly, fairly, and openly exerted. The case shall be presented on its single merit; on that I wish to stand or fall. I feel, sir, that I am incapable of sectional distinction upon such subjects. I abhor and reject all interested combinations." He would hammer thus at what he thought was wrong, and continue to hammer, icy cold and in measured terms, long after the opposition had been demolished, without considering the thoughts of the other man or the chance that he might be useful to him someday.

He was perhaps the best informed, probably the best educated, and certainly the most intellectual man in the Senate. Yet he too had to take his knocks. Supporting an army pay-increase bill, he remarked in passing that "a common blacksmith or tailor" could not be hired as a military engineer; whereupon Andrew Johnson of Tennessee — formerly a tailor — rose from his desk shouting that "an illegitimate, swaggering, bastard, scrub aristocracy" took much credit to itself, yet in fact had "neither talents nor information." Hot words in a Washington boarding house led to a fist fight between Davis and Henry S. Foote, his fellow senator from Mississippi. An Illinois congressman, W. H. Bissell, said in a speech that Davis' command had been a mile and a half from the blaze of battle at Buena Vista. Davis sent an immediate challenge, and Bissell, having the choice of weapons, named muskets loaded with ball and shot at fifteen paces, then went home, wrote his will, and said he would be ready in the morning. Friends intervening, Bissell explained that he had been referring to another quarter of the field and had not meant to question Davis' personal bravery anyhow; the duel was canceled. Davis made enemies in high places, as for example when he claimed that General Winfield Scott had overcharged $300 in mileage expenses. Scott later delivered himself of a judgment as to Davis: "He is not a cheap Judas. I do not think he would have sold the Saviour for thirty shillings. But for the successorship to Pontius Pilate he would have betrayed Christ and the Apostles and the whole Christian church." Sam Houston of Texas, speaking more briefly, declared that Davis was "ambitious as Lucifer and cold as a lizard."

Out of the rough-and-tumble of debate and acrimony, a more or less accepted part of political life at the time, Davis was winning a position as a leader in the Senate. Successor to Calhoun, he had become the spokesman for southern nationalism, which in those days meant not independence but domination from within the Union. This movement had been given impetus by the Mexican War. Up till then the future of the country pointed north and west, but now the needle trembled and suddenly swung south. The treaty signed at Guadalupe Hidalgo brought into the Union a new southwestern domain, seemingly ripe for slavery and the southern way of life: not only Texas down to the Rio Grande, the original strip of contention, but also the vast sun-cooked area that was to become Arizona, New Mexico, Nevada, Utah, part of Colorado, and California with its new-found gold. Here was room for expansion indeed, with more to follow; for the nationalists looked forward to taking what was left of Mexico, all of Central America south to Panama, and Yucatan and Cuba by annexation. Yet the North, so recently having learned the comfort of the saddle, had no intention of yielding the reins. The South would have to fight for this; and this the South was prepared to do, using States Rights for a spear and the Constitution for a shield. Jefferson Davis, who had formed his troops in a V at Buena Vista and continued the fight with a boot full of blood, took a position, now as then, at the apex of the wedge.

He lost the fight, and lost it quickly — betrayed, as he thought, from within his ranks. The North opposed this dream of southern expansion by opposing the extension of slavery, without which the new southwestern territory would be anything but southern. Attracted by the hope of so much gain, and goaded by the fear of such a loss, Davis and his cohorts adopted more drastic actions, including threats of secession. To give substance to this threat, he called the Nashville Convention of June 1850, and in conjunction with Albert Gallatin Brown of Mississippi, William Lowndes Yancey of Alabama, and Robert Barnwell Rhett of South Carolina, informed the North quite plainly that unless slavery was extended to the territories, the South would leave the Union. It was at this point that Davis was "betrayed," meaning that he discovered that he had outrun his constituents. Henry Clay proposed his Compromise, supported by Daniel Webster, and both houses of Congress gladly accepted it. California came in as a free state and the question of slavery was left to be settled by the various other territories at the time when they should apply for admission into the Union.

What was worse from Davis' point of view, the voters seemed to approve. All over the nation, even in Mississippi, there was rejoicing that disunion and war had been avoided. Davis could scarcely believe it; he must test it at the polls. So he resigned his seat in the Senate and went home to run for governor against Henry S. Foote, the senator with whom he had exchanged first tart remarks and finally blows. Now the issue was clearly drawn, for his opponent was a Unionist Whig of Natchez and had voted consistently against Davis, from the beginning down to the Compromise itself; the voters could make a clear-cut choice before all the world. This they did — repudiating Davis.

It was bad enough to be vanquished as the champion of secession, but to receive defeat at the hands of a man he detested as much as he detested Foote was gall and wormwood. At forty-three, in the hour of his glory and at the height of his prime, he was destroyed; or so he thought. At any rate he was through. He came home to Brierfield to plant cotton.

Then history intervened again, as history always seemed to do for him. This time the muse took the form of Franklin Pierce, who in organizing a cabinet reached down from New Hampshire, all the way to Mississippi, and chose Jefferson Davis as his Secretary of War. They had been fellow officers in Mexico, friends in Congress, and shared a dislike of abolitionists. Whatever his reasons, Pierce chose well. Davis made perhaps the best War Secretary the country ever had, and though it included such capable men as William L. Marcy of New York and Caleb Cushing of Massachusetts, he dominated the cabinet in a time of strain and doubt.

Yet the man who returned to public life in 1853 was somewhat different from the man who had left it in 1851 at the behest of the voters. Rather chastened — though he kept his southern nationalism and clung to the spear of States Rights, the shield of the Constitution — he left the fire-eaters Yancey and Rhett behind him. He was no longer the impetuous champion of secession; he believed now that whatever was to be gained might best be accomplished within the Union. He strengthened the army, renovated the Military Academy, and came out strong for un-Jeffersonian internal improvements, including a Pacific Railway along a southern route through Memphis or Vicksburg, to be financed by a hundred-million-dollar federal appropriation. The Gadsden Purchase was a Davis project, ten million paid for a strip of Mexican soil necessary for the railroad right-of-way. Nor was his old imperialism dead. He still had designs on what was left of Mexico and on Central America, and he shocked the diplomats of Europe with a proclamation of his government's intention to annex Cuba. Above all, he was for the unlimited extension of slavery, with a revival of the slave trade if need be.

Returned to the Senate in 1857, he continued to work along these lines, once more a southern champion, not as a secessionist, but as a believer that the destiny of the nation pointed south. It was a stormy time, and much of the bitterness between the sections came to a head on the floor of the Senate, where northern invective and southern arrogance necessarily met. Here Texas senator Louis T. Wigfall, a duelist of note, would sneer at his northern colleagues as he told them, "The difficulty between you and us, gentlemen, is that you will not send the right sort of people here. Why will you not send either Christians or gentlemen?" Here, too, the anti-slavery Massachusetts senator Charles Sumner had his head broken by Congressman Preston Brooks of South Carolina, who, taking exception to remarks Sumner had made on the floor of the Senate regarding a kinsman, caned him as he sat at his desk. Brooks explained that he attacked him sitting because, Sumner being the larger man, he would have had to shoot him if he had risen, and he did not want to kill him, only maim him. Sumner lay bleeding in the aisle among the gutta-percha fragments of the cane, and his enemies stood by and watched him bleed. Southern sympathizers sent Brooks walking sticks by the dozen, recommending their use on other abolitionists, and through the years of Sumner's convalescence Massachusetts let his desk stand empty as a reproach to southern hotheads, though these were in fact more likely to see the vacant seat as a warning to men like Sumner.

During this three-year furor, which led in the end to the disintegration of the Democratic Party and the resultant election of a Republican President, Davis remained as inflexible as ever. But his arguments now did not progress toward secession. They ended instead against a hard brick wall. He did not even claim to know the answers beyond debate. In 1860, speaking in Boston's Faneuil Hall while he and Mrs Davis were up there vacationing for his health — he was a chronic dyspeptic by now, racked by neuralgia through sleepless nights and losing the sight of one eye — he stated his position as to slavery and southern nationalism, but announced that he remained opposed to secession; he still would not take the logical next step. He was much admired by the people of Massachusetts, many of whom despised the abolitionists as much as he did; but the people of Mississippi hardly knew what to make of him. "Davis is at sea," they said.

Then he looked back, and saw that instead of outrunning his constituents, this time he had let them outrun him. He hurried South, made his harvest-home-of-death speech on the eve of Lincoln's election, and returned to Washington, at last reconverted to secession. South Carolina left the Union, then Mississippi and the others, and opinion no longer mattered. As he said in his farewell, even if he had opposed his state's action, he still would have considered himself "bound."

Having spoken his adieu, he left the crowded chamber and, head lowered, went out into the street. That night Mrs Davis heard him pacing the floor. "May God have us in His holy keeping," she heard him say over and over as he paced, "and grant that before it is too late, peaceful councils may prevail."

Such was Davis' way of saying farewell to his colleagues, speaking out of sadness and regret. It was not the way of others: Robert Toombs of Georgia, for example, whose state had seceded two days before Davis spoke. Two days later Toombs delivered his farewell. "The Union, sir, is dissolved," he told the Senate. A large, slack-mouthed man, he tossed his head in shaggy defiance as he spoke. "You see the glittering bayonet, and you hear the tramp of armed men from yon Capitol to the Rio Grande. It is a sight that gladdens the eye and cheers the hearts of other men ready to second them." In case there were those of the North who would maintain the Union by force: "Come and do it!" Toombs cried. "Georgia is on the war path! We are as ready to fight now as we ever shall be. Treason? Bah!" And with that he stalked out of the chamber, walked up to the Treasury, and demanded his salary due to date, plus mileage back to Georgia.

Thus Toombs. But Davis, having sent his wife home with their three children — Margaret aged six, Jeff three, and the year-old baby named for the guardian elder brother Joseph at Davis Bend — lingered in Washington another week, ill and confined to his bed for most of the time, still hoping he might be arrested as a traitor so as to test his claims in the federal courts, then took the train for Jackson, where Governor J. J. Pettus met him with a commission as major general of volunteers. It was the job Davis wanted. He believed there would be war, and he advised the governor to push the procurement of arms.

"The limit of our purchases should be our power to pay," he said. "We shall need all and many more than we can get."

"General," the governor protested, "you overrate the risk."

"I only wish I did," Davis said.

Awaiting the raising of his army, he went to Brierfield. In Alabama, now in early February, a convention was founding a Southern Confederacy, electing political leaders and formulating a new government. He was content, however, to leave such matters to those who were there. He considered his highest talents to be military and he had the position he wanted, commander of the Mississippi army, with advancement to come along with glory when the issue swung to war.

Then history beckoned again, assuming another of her guises. February 10; he and Mrs Davis were out in the garden, cutting a rose bush in the early blue spring weather, when a messenger approached with a telegram in his hand. Davis read it. In that moment of painful silence he seemed stricken; his face took on a look of calamity. Then he read the message to his wife. It was headed "Montgomery, Alabama," and dated the day before.

> Sir:
> We are directed to inform you that you are this day unanimously elected President of the Provisional Government of the Confederate States of America, and to request you to come to Montgomery immediately. We send also a special messenger. Do not wait for him.
>
> > R. Toombs,
> > R. Barnwell Rhett...

He spoke of it, Mrs Davis said, "as a man might speak of a sentence of death." Yet he wasted no time. He packed and left next day.

The train made many stops along the line and the people were out to meet him, in sunlight and by the glare of torches. They wanted a look at his face, the thin lips and determined jaw, the hollow cheeks with their jutting bones, the long skull behind the aquiline nose; "a wizard physiognomy," one called it. He brought forth cheers with confident words, but he had something else to say as well — something no one had told them before. He advised them to prepare for the long war that lay ahead. They did not believe him, apparently. Or if they did, they went on cheering anyhow.

He reached Montgomery Sunday night, February 17, and was driven from the station in a carriage, down the long torch-lit avenue to the old Exchange Hotel. The crowd followed through streets that had been decked as for a fair; they flowed until they were packed in a mass about the gallery of the hotel in time to see Davis dismount from the carriage and climb the steps; they cheered as he turned and looked at them. Then suddenly they fell silent. William Lowndes Yancey, short and rather seedy-looking alongside the erect and well-groomed Davis, had raised one hand. They cheered again when he brought it down, gesturing toward the tall man beside him, and said in a voice that rang above the expectant, torch-paled faces of the crowd: "The man and the hour have met."

★ ★ ★

The day that Davis received the summons in the rose garden was Abraham Lincoln's last full day in Springfield, Illinois. He would be leaving tomorrow for Washington and his inauguration, the same day that Davis left for Montgomery and his. During the three months since the election, Springfield had changed from a sleepy, fairly typical

western county seat and capital into a bustling, cadging hive of politicians, office seekers, reporters, committees representing "folks back
home," and the plain downright curious with time on their hands, many
of whom had come for no other reason than to breathe the same air
with a man who had his name in all the papers. Some were lodged in
railway cars on sidings; boarding houses were feeding double shifts.

All of these people wanted a look at Lincoln, and most of them
wanted interviews, which they got. "I can't sleep nights," he was saying.
His fingers throbbed from shaking hands and his face ached from smiling. He had leased the two-story family residence, sold the cow and
the horse and buggy, and left the dog to be cared for by a neighbor; he
and his wife and children were staying now at the Chenery House,
where the President-elect himself had roped their trunks and addressed
them to "A. Lincoln, The White House, Washington D.C." He was by
nature a friendly man but his smile was becoming a grimace. "I am sick
of office-holding already," he said on this final day in Illinois.

Change was predominant not only in Springfield; the Union appeared to be coming apart at the seams. Louisiana and Texas had
brought the total of seceded states to seven. Banks and business firms
were folding; the stock market declined and declined. James Buchanan,
badly confused, was doing nothing in these last weeks of office. Having
stated in his December message to Congress that while a state had no
lawful right to secede, neither had the federal government any right to
prevent it, privately he was saying that he was the last President of the
United States.

North and South, Union men looked to Lincoln, whose election
had been the signal for all this trouble. They wanted words of reassurance, words of threat, anything to slow the present trend, the drift
toward chaos. Yet he said nothing. When a Missouri editor asked him
for a statement, something he could print to make men listen, Lincoln
wrote back: "I could say nothing which I have not already said, and
which is in print and accessible to the public. . . . I am not at liberty to
shift my ground; that is out of the question. If I thought a repetition
would do any good I would make it. But my judgment is it would do
positive harm. The secessionists, *per se* believing they had alarmed me,
would clamor all the louder."

People hardly knew what to make of this tall, thin-chested, raw-
boned man who spoke with the frontier in his voice, wore a stove-pipe
hat as if to emphasize his six-foot four-inch height, and walked with a
shambling western slouch, the big feet planted flat at every step, the
big hands dangling from wrists that hung down out of the sleeves of
his rusty tailcoat. Mr Lincoln, they called him, or Lincoln, never "Abe"
as in the campaign literature. The seamed, leathery face was becoming
familiar: the mole on the right cheek, the high narrow forehead with
the unruly, coarse black shock of hair above it, barely grizzled: the

pale gray eyes set deep in bruised sockets, the broad mouth somewhat quizzical with a protruding lower lip, the pointed chin behind its recent growth of scraggly beard, the wry neck — a clown face; a sad face, some observed on closer inspection, perhaps the saddest they had ever seen. It was hard to imagine a man like this in the White House, where Madison and Van Buren had kept court. He had more or less blundered into the Republican nomination, much as his Democratic opponents had blundered into defeat in the election which had followed. It had all come about as a result of linking accidents and crises, and the people, with their accustomed championing of the underdog, the dark horse, had enjoyed it at the time. Yet now that the nation was in truth a house divided, now that war loomed, they were not so sure. Down South, men were hearing speeches that fired their blood. Here it was not so; for there was only silence from Abraham Lincoln. Congressman Horace Maynard, a Tennessee Unionist, believed he knew why. "I imagine that he keeps silence," Maynard said, "for the good and sufficient reason that he has nothing to say."

It was true that he had nothing to say at the time. He was waiting; he was drawing on one of his greatest virtues, patience. Though the Cotton South had gone out solid, the eight northernmost slave states remained loyal. Delaware and Maryland, Virginia and North Carolina, Kentucky and Tennessee, Missouri and Arkansas were banked between the hotheads, north and south, a double buffer, and though Lincoln had not received a single electoral vote from this whole area, he counted on the sound common sense of the people there. What was more — provided he did nothing to alienate the loyalty of the border states — he counted on Union sentiment in the departed states to bring them back into the family.

He had had much practice in just this kind of waiting. One of these days, while he was sitting in his office with a visitor, his son Willie came clattering in to demand a quarter. "I can't let you have a quarter," Lincoln said; "I can only spare five cents." He took five pennies from his pocket and stacked them on a corner of the desk. Willie had not asked for a nickel; he wanted a quarter. He sulked and went away, leaving the pennies on the desk. "He will be back after that in a few minutes," Lincoln told the visitor. "As soon as he finds I will give him no more, he will come and get it." They went on talking. Presently the boy returned, took the pennies from the desk, and quietly left. Patience had worked, where attempts at persuasion might have resulted in a flare-up. So with the departed states; self-interest and family ties might bring them back in time. Meanwhile Lincoln walked as softly as he could.

In this manner he had gotten through three of the four anxious months that lay between the election and inauguration, and on this final afternoon in Springfield he went down to his law office to pick up some books and papers and to say goodbye to his partner, William L. Herndon. Nine years his junior, Herndon was excitable, apt to fling off at a tangent, and Lincoln would calm him, saying, "Billy, you're too rampant." There had been times, too, when the older man had gone about collecting fees to pay the fine when his partner was about to be jailed for disorderly conduct on a spree. Now the two sat in the office, discussing business matters. Then came an awkward silence, which Lincoln broke by asking: "Billy, there's one thing I have for some time wanted you to tell me. . . . I want you to tell me how many times you have been drunk." Flustered, Herndon stammered, and Lincoln let it pass. This was the closest he ever came to delivering a temperance lecture.

They rose, walked downstairs, and paused on the boardwalk. Lincoln glanced up at the weathered law shingle: LINCOLN & HERNDON. "Let it hang there undisturbed," he said. "Give our clients to under-stand that the election of a President makes no change in the firm of Lincoln and Herndon. If I live I'm coming back some time, and then we'll go right on practicing law as if nothing ever happened." Again there was an awkward pause. Lincoln put his hand out. "Goodbye," he said, and went off down the street.

Herndon stood and watched him go, the tall, loose-jointed figure with the napless stove-pipe hat, the high-water pantaloons, the ill-fitting tailcoat bulging at the elbows from long wear. This junior partner was one of those who saw the sadness in Lincoln's face. "Melancholy dripped from him as he walked," he was to write. Herndon knew something else as well, something that had not been included in the campaign literature: "That man who thinks that Lincoln sat calmly down and gathered his robes about him, waiting for the people to call him, has a very erroneous knowledge of Lincoln. He was always calculating, and always planning ahead. His ambition was a little engine that knew no rest."

That day, as the sun went down and he returned to the Chenery House for his last sleep in Illinois, there were few who knew this side of him. There were gaps in the story that even Herndon could not fill, and other gaps that no one could fill, ever, though writers were to make him the subject of more biographies and memoirs, more brochures and poems than any other American. On the face of it the facts were simple enough, as he told a journalist who came seeking information about his boyhood years for a campaign biography: "Why, Scripps, it is a great piece of folly to attempt to make anything out of my early life. It can all be condensed into a single sentence, and that sentence you will find in Gray's *Elegy:* 'The short and simple annals of the poor.' "

He was born in the Kentucky wilderness of Daniel Boone, mid-February of 1809, in a one-room dirt-floor cabin put up that same win-ter by his father, Thomas Lincoln, a thick-chested man of average height, who passed on to Abraham only his coarse black hair and dark complexion. Originally from Virginia, Thomas was a wanderer like the Lincolns before him, who had come down out of New Jersey and Pennsylvania, and though in early manhood he could sign his name when necessary, later he either forgot or else he stopped taking the trouble; he made his X-mark like his wife, born Nancy Hanks.

In after years when Lincoln tried to trace his ancestry he could go no further back than his father's father, also named Abraham, who had been killed from ambush by an Indian. That was on his father's side. On his mother's he discovered only that she had been born out of wedlock to Lucy Hanks who later married a man named Sparrow. Nancy died of the milksick when Abraham was nine, and her body lay in another of those one-room cabins while her husband knocked together a coffin in the yard.

They were in Indiana by then, having come to the big woods after a previous move to Knob Creek, south of Louisville and beside the Cumberland Trail, along which pioneers with many children and few livestock marched northwestward. Thomas Lincoln joined them for the move across the Ohio, and when his wife died took another the following year: Sarah Bush Johnston, a widow with three children. She was called Sally Bush Lincoln now, tall and hard-working, a welcome addition to any frontier family, especially this one, which had been without a woman for almost a year. She brought to Abraham all the love and affection she had given her own. The boy returned it, and in later years, when his memory of Nancy Hanks Lincoln had paled, referred to the one who took her place as "my angel mother," saying: "All that I am I owe to my angel mother."

For one thing, she saw to it that the boy went to school. Previously he had not gone much deeper into learning than his ABC's, and only then at such times as his father felt he could spare him from his chores. Now at intervals he was able to fit in brief weeks of schooling, amounting in all to something under a year. They were "blab" schools, which meant that the pupils studied aloud at their desks and the master judged the extent of their concentration by the volume of their din. Between such periods of formal education he studied at home, ciphering on boards when he had no slate, and shaving them clean with a knife for an eraser. He developed a talent for mimicry, too, mounting a stump when out with a work gang and delivering mock orations and sermons. This earned him the laughter of the men, who would break off work to watch him, but his father disapproved of such interruptions and would speak to him sharply or cuff him off the stump.

He grew tall and angular, with long muscles, so that in his early teens he could grip an ax one-handed at the end of the helve and hold it out, untrembling. Neighbors testified to his skill with this implement, one saying: "He can sink an ax deeper into wood than any man I ever saw," and another: "If you heard him felling trees in a clearing, you would say there was three men at work by the way the trees fell." However, though he did his chores, including work his father hired him out to do, he developed no real liking for manual labor. He would rather be reading what few books he got his hands on: Parson Weems's *Life of Washington, Pilgrim's Progress, Æsop's Fables, Robinson Crusoe,* Grimshaw's *History of the United States,* and *The Kentucky Preceptor.* Sometimes he managed to combine the two, for in plowing he would stop at the end of a row, reading while he gave the horse a breather.

From a flatboat trip one thousand miles downriver to New Orleans, during which he learned to trim a deck and man a sweep, he returned in time for his twenty-first birthday and another family migration, from Indiana out to central Illinois, where he and a cousin hired out to split four thousand rails for their neighbors. Thus he came to manhood, a rail-splitter, wilderness-born and frontier-raised. He was of the West, the new country out beyond the old, a product of a nation fulfilling a manifest destiny. It was in his walk, in his talk and in his character, indelibly. It would be with him wherever he went, along with the knowledge that he had survived in a region where "the Lord spared the fitten and the rest He seen fitten to let die."

He had never had much fondness for his father, and now that he was legally independent he struck out on his own. The family moved once more, deeper into Illinois, but Lincoln did not go with them. He took instead another flatboat trip down to New Orleans, and then came back to another kind of life. This was prairie country, with a rich soil and a future. Lincoln got a job clerking in a New Salem store at fifteen dollars a month plus a bed to sleep in. He defeated the leader of the regional toughs in a wrestling match, and when the leader's friends pitched in, Lincoln backed against a wall and dared them to come at him one by one; whereupon they acknowledged him as their new leader.

This last was rather in line with the life he had led before, but he found something new as well. He attended the New Salem Debating Society, and though at first the charter members snickered at his looks and awkwardness, presently they were admiring the logic and conciseness of his arguments. "All he lacked was culture," one of them said. Lincoln took such encouragement from his success that in the spring of 1832 he announced as a candidate for the state legislature.

The Black Hawk War interrupting his campaign, he enlisted and was elected captain by his fellow volunteers. Discipline was not strong among them; the new commander's first order to one of his men brought the reply, "You go to hell." They saw no action, and Lincoln afterwards joked about his military career, saying that all the blood he lost was to mosquitoes and all his charges were against wild-onion beds. When the company's thirty-day enlistment expired he reënlisted for another twenty days as a private, then came home and resumed his campaign for the legislature, two weeks remaining until election day. His first political speech was made at a country auction. Twenty-three years old, he stood on a box, wearing a frayed straw hat, a calico shirt, and pantaloons held up by a single-strap suspender. As he was about to speak, a fight broke out in the crowd. Lincoln stepped down, broke up the fight, then stepped back onto the box.

"Gentlemen and fellow citizens," he said, "I presume you all know who I am: I am humble Abraham Lincoln. I have been solicited by many friends to become a candidate for the legislature. My politics are short and sweet, like the old woman's dance. I am in favor of a national bank. I am in favor of the internal-improvements system and a high protective tariff. These are my sentiments and political principles. If elected, I shall be thankful; if not, it will be all the same."

Election day he ran eighth in a field of thirteen, but he received 277 of the 300 votes in the New Salem precinct.

It was probably then that Lincoln determined to run for the same office next time around. Meanwhile there was a living to earn. He could always split rails and do odd jobs. These he did, and then went into partnership in a grocery store that failed, leaving him a debt beyond a thousand dollars; "the National Debt," he called it ruefully, and worked for years to pay it off. He became village postmaster, sometimes carrying letters in his hat, which became a habit. He studied surveying and worked a while at that. He also began the study of law, reading Blackstone and Chitty, and improved his education with borrowed books. His name was becoming more widely known; he was winning popularity by his great strength and his ability at telling funny stories, but mostly by his force of character. Then in the spring of 1834, when another legislature race came round, he conducted an all-out full-time campaign and was elected.

With borrowed money he bought his first tailor-made suit, paying sixty dollars for it, and left for the first of his four terms in the state law-making body, learning the rough-and-tumble give-and-take of western politics. Two years later he was licensed as an attorney, and soon afterwards moved to Springfield as a partner in a law firm. He said goodbye to the manual labor he had been so good at, yet had never really liked; from now on he would work with his head, as a leader of men. His ambition became what Herndon later called "a little engine."

Springfield was about to be declared the state capital, moved there from Vandalia largely through Lincoln's efforts in the legislature, and here he began to acquire that culture which the New Salem intellectuals had said was "all he lacked." The big, work-splayed hands were losing their horn-hard calluses. He settled down to the law, becoming in time an excellent trial lawyer and a capable stump debater at political rallies, even against such opponents as Stephen A. Douglas, the coming Little Giant. Socially, however, he was slow in getting started. About a month after his arrival he wrote in a letter: "I have been spoken to by but one woman since I've been here, and should not have been by her, if she could have avoided it." He was leery of the ladies, having once remarked, half-jokingly, "A woman is the only thing I am afraid of that I know will not hurt me." Nevertheless, by the time he was elected to his fourth term in the legislature, Lincoln was courting Mary Todd, a visitor from Lexington, Kentucky, and in early November of 1842 he married her.

It was an attraction of opposites, and as such it was stormy. At one point they broke off the engagement; she left Illinois and Lincoln had to go to Kentucky for a reconciliation before she would return to Springfield and marry him in her sister's parlor. If "culture" was what he was after, still, Lincoln again had moved in the proper direction. His wife, the great-granddaughter of a Revolutionary general, had attended a private academy in Lexington, where she learned to speak French, read music after a fashion, paint on china, and dance the sedate figures of the time. At twenty-four she was impulsive and vivacious, short and rather plump, looking especially so alongside her long lean husband, who was thirty-three. Lincoln seemed to take it calmly enough. Five days after the wedding he wrote to a lawyer friend: "Nothing new here, except my marrying, which to me is matter of profound wonder."

Their first child, Robert Todd, called Bob, was born the following year. Three others came in the course of the next decade, all sons: Edward and William and Thomas, called Eddy, Willie, Tad. Eddy died before he was five, and Tad had a cleft palate; he spoke with a lisp. The Lincolns lived a year in rented rooms, then moved into the $1500 white frame house which remained their home. They took their place in Springfield society, and Lincoln worked hard at law, riding the Eighth Judicial Circuit in all kinds of weather, a clean shirt and a change of underwear in his saddlebag, along with books and papers and a yellow flannel nightshirt. Fees averaged about five dollars a case, sometimes paid in groceries, which he was glad to get, since the cost of the house represented something beyond one year's total earnings.

Home life taught him patience, for his wife was high-strung as well as high-born. He called her Mother and met her fits of temper with forbearance, which must have been the last thing she wanted at the time. When her temper got too hot he would walk off to his office and stay until it cooled. Accustomed to Negro house slaves in Kentucky, Mary Lincoln could not get along with Illinois hired girls, who were inclined to answer back. Lincoln did what he could here too, slipping the girls an extra weekly dollar for compensation. Once after a particularly bitter scene between mistress and maid, when Mrs Lincoln had left the room he patted the girl on the shoulder and gave her the same advice he had given himself: "Stay with her, Maria. Stay with her."

His law practice grew; he felt prepared to grow in other directions. Having completed his fourth term in the state legislature, he was ready to move on up the political ladder. He wrote to Whig associates in the district, "Now if you should hear anyone say that Lincoln don't want to go to Congress, I wish you as a personal friend of mine would tell him you have reason to believe he is mistaken. The truth is, I would like to go very much." In the backstage party scramble, however, he lost the nomination in 1842 and again in 1844. It was 1847 before he got to Congress. From a back row on the Whig side of the House he came to know the voices and faces of men he would know better, Ashmun of Massachusetts, Rhett of South Carolina, Smith of Indiana, Toombs and Stephens of Georgia, while a visit to the Senate would show him the elder statesmen Webster and Calhoun, along with newer men of note, such as Cameron of Pennsylvania and Davis of Mississippi.

The Mexican War had ended by then, and though Lincoln voted for whatever army supply bills came before the House, like most Whigs he attacked the motives behind the war, which now was being spoken of, by northern Whigs at least, as "infamous and wicked," an imperialist attempt to extend the slavery realm. This got him into trouble back home, where the Democratic papers began calling him a latter-day Benedict Arnold and the people read and noted all he did as a slur against the volunteers of his state. When Congress convened for his second session, Lincoln was the only Whig from Illinois. It was a hectic session anyhow, with tempers flaring over the question of slavery in the territories. He came home with no chance for reëlection, and did not try. He gave up politics, refusing even a spoils offer of the governorship of Oregon Territory, and returned to the practice of law, once more riding the circuit. Disheartened, he paused now to restore his soul through work and meditation.

Though he did not believe at the outset that it would necessarily ever reach an end — indeed, he believed it would not; otherwise it could never have done for him what it did — this five-year "retreat," coming as it did between his fortieth and his forty-fifth years, 1849 to 1854, was his interlude of greatest growth. Like many, perhaps most, men of genius, Lincoln developed late.

It was a time for study, a time for self-improvement. He went back and drilled his way through the first six books of Euclid, as an exercise to discipline his mind. Not politics but the law was his main interest now. Riding the circuit he talked less and listened more. Together with a new understanding and a deeper reading of Shakespeare and the Bible, this brought him a profounder faith in people, including those who had rejected him and repudiated what he had to offer as a leader. Here, too, he was learning. This was the period in which he was reported to have said, "You can fool some of the people all the time, and all the people some of the time, but you can't fool all the people all the time."

Nonparticipation in public affairs did not mean a loss of interest in them. Lincoln read the papers more carefully now than he had ever done before, learning from them of the deaths of Calhoun, Clay, and Webster, whose passing marked the passing of an era. When the 1850 Compromise — as he and most men believed, including Clay who engineered it shortly before his death — settled the differences that had brought turmoil to the nation and fist fights to the floors of Congress while Lincoln himself was there, he breathed easier. But not for long. The conflict soon was heading up again. *Uncle Tom's Cabin* came from the presses in a stream; southern nationalists were announcing plans for the annexation of Cuba; the case of the slave Dred Scott, suing for his freedom, moved by legal osmosis through the courts; the Whigs seemed lost and the Democrats were splitting. Then Lincoln's old stump opponent, Stephen A. Douglas, who was four years younger than Lincoln but who had suffered no setback in political advancement, filling now his second term in the Senate, brought the crisis to a head.

Scarcely taller than Napoleon, but with all that monarch's driving ambition and belief in a private star, Douglas moved to repeal that part of the Missouri Compromise which served to restrict the extension of slavery. This came as a result of his championing a northern route for the proposed Pacific railway. A southern route was also proposed and Douglas sought to effect a swap, reporting a bill for the organization of two new territories, Kansas and Nebraska, with the provision that the people there should determine for themselves as to the admission or exclusion of slavery, despite the fact that both areas lay well north of the 36°30' line drawn by the Compromise, which had guaranteed that the institution would be kept forever south of there. The Southerners were glad to abandon their New Mexico route for such a gain, provided the repeal was made not only implicit but explicit in the bill. Douglas was somewhat shocked (he brought a certain naivety to even his deepest plots) but soon agreed, and Secretary of War Jefferson Davis persuaded Franklin Pierce to make the bill an Administration issue. "Popular sovereignty," Douglas called it; "Squatter sovereignty," his opponents considered a better name. "It will raise a hell of a storm," Douglas predicted. It did indeed, though the Democrats managed to ram it through by late May of 1854, preparing the ground for Bleeding Kansas and the birth of the Republican Party that same year.

Another effect of the Kansas-Nebraska Bill was that it brought Lincoln out of retirement. It had raised even more of a storm than Douglas predicted, and not only in Congress. For when the senator came home to Illinois he saw through the train window his effigy being burned in courthouse squares, and when he came to explain his case before eight thousand people in Chicago, they jeered him off the rostrum He left, shaking his fist in their faces, and set out to stump the state with a speech that confounded opposition orators and won back many of the voters. Then in early October he came to Springfield, packing the hall of the House of Representatives. After the speech — which had been as successful here as elsewhere in turning the jeers to cheers — the crowd filed out through the lobby and saw Abraham Lincoln standing on the staircase, announcing that he would reply to Douglas the following day and inviting the senator to be present, to answer if he cared.

Next day they were there, close-packed as yesterday; Douglas had a front-row seat. It was hot and Lincoln spoke in shirt sleeves, wearing no collar or tie. His voice was shrill as he began, though presently it settled to lower tones, interrupted from time to time by crackles and thunders of applause. Wet with sweat, his shirt clung to his shoulders and big arms. He had written his speech out beforehand, clarifying in his own mind his position as to slavery, which he saw as the nub of the issue — much to the discomfort of Douglas, who wanted to talk about "popular sovereignty," keeping the issue one of self-government, whereas Lincoln insisted on going beyond, making slavery the main question. Emerging from his long retirement, having restored his soul, he was asking himself and all men certain questions. And now the Lincoln music began to sound.

"The doctrine of self-government is right, absolutely and eternally right; but it has no just application, as here attempted. Or perhaps I should rather say that whether it has such just application depends upon whether a Negro is not or is a man. If he is not a man, why in that case he who is a man may, as a matter of self-government, do just as he pleases with him. But if the Negro is a man, is it not to that extent a total destruction of self-government to say that he too shall not govern himself? When the white man governs himself, that is self-government; but when he governs himself and also governs another man, that is more than self-government; that is despotism. If the Negro is a man, why then my ancient faith teaches me that 'all men are created equal,' and that there can be no moral right in connection with one man's making a slave of another."

He believed that it was a moral wrong; he had not come to believe that it was a legal wrong, though he believed that too would be clarified in time. The words of his mouth came like meditations from his heart: "Slavery is founded in the selfishness of man's nature, opposition to it in his love of justice. These principles are an eternal antagonism, and when brought into collision so fiercely as slavery extension brings them, shocks and throes and convulsions must ceaselessly follow. Repeal the Missouri Compromise, repeal all compromises; repeal the

Declaration of Independence, repeal all past history — you still cannot repeal human nature. It still will be the abundance of man's heart that slavery extension is wrong, and out of the abundance of his heart his mouth will continue to speak."

This, in part, was the speech that caused his name to be recognized throughout the Northwest, though personally he was still but little known outside his state. He repeated it twelve days later in Peoria, where shorthand reporters took it down for their papers, and continued to speak in central Illinois and in Chicago. Winning reëlection to the legislature, he presently had a chance at a seat in the U.S. Senate. His hopes were high and he resigned from the legislature to be eligible, but at the last minute he had to throw his votes to an anti-Nebraska Democrat to defeat the opposition.

Again he had failed, and again he regretted failing. Yet this time he was not despondent. He kept working and waiting. His law practice boomed; he earned a five-thousand-dollar fee on a railroad case, and was retained to assist a high-powered group of big-city lawyers on a patents case in Cincinnati, but when they saw him come to town, wearing his usual rusty clothes and carrying a ball-handled blue cotton umbrella, they would scarcely speak to him. One of the attorneys, Edwin M. Stanton of Pittsburgh, was downright rude; "Where did that long-armed creature come from?" he asked within earshot. Lincoln went his way, taking no apparent umbrage.

Politically he was wary, too, writing to a friend: "Just now I fear to do anything, lest I do wrong." He had good cause for fear, and so had all men through this time of "shocks and throes and convulsions." Popular sovereignty was being tested in Kansas in a manner Douglas had not foreseen. Missouri border ruffians and hired abolitionist gunmen were cutting each other's throats for votes in the coming referendum; the Mormons were resisting federal authority in the West, and while a ruinous financial panic gripped the East, the Know-Nothing Party was sweeping New England with anti-foreigner, anti-Catholic appeals. The Whigs had foundered, the Democrats had split on all those rocks. Like many men just now, Lincoln hardly knew where he stood along party lines.

"I think I am a Whig," he wrote, "but others say there are no Whigs, and that I am an Abolitionist. . . . I am not a Know-Nothing. That is certain. How could I be? How can anyone who abhors the oppression of Negroes be in favor of degrading classes of white people? Our progress in degeneracy appears to me to be pretty rapid."

He was waiting and looking. And then he found the answer.

It was 1856, a presidential election year. Out of the Nebraska crisis, two years before, the Republican Party had been born, a coalition of foundered Whigs and disaffected northern Democrats, largely abolitionist at the core. They made overtures to Lincoln but he dodged them at the time, not wanting a Radical tag attached to his name. Now, however, seeking to unify the anti-Nebraska elements in Illinois, he came to meet them. As a delegate to the state convention he caught fire and made what may have been the greatest speech of his career, though no one would ever really know, since the heat of his words seemed to burn them from men's memory, and in that conglomerate mass of gaping, howling old-line Whigs and bolted Democrats, Know-Nothings, Free Soilers and Abolitionists, even the shorthand reporters sat enthralled, forgetting to use their pencils. From now on he was a Republican; he would take his chances with the Radical tag.

At the national convention in Philadelphia he received 110 votes on the first ballot for the vice-presidential nomination, yielding them on the second to a New Jersey running mate for John C. Frémont of California. Lincoln had not favored Frémont, but he worked hard for him in the campaign that saw the election of the Democratic nominee James Buchanan, an elderly bachelor whose main advantage lay in the fact that he was the least controversial candidate, having been out of the country as Minister to England during the trying past three years. The Republicans were by no means dispirited at running second. They sniffed victory down the wind, in the race four years from now — provided only that the turmoil and sectional antagonism should continue, which seemed likely.

At this point the United States Supreme Court handed down a decision which appeared to cut the ground from under all their feet. The test case of the slave Dred Scott, suing for freedom on a plea that his master had taken him into a territory where slavery was forbidden by the Missouri Compromise, had at last reached the high court. In filing the majority opinion, Chief Justice Roger B. Taney dismissed Scott's lawyer's claim. A Negro, he said, was not a citizen of the United States, and therefore had no right to sue in a federal court. This was enough to enrage the Abolitionists, who secretly had sponsored the suit. But Taney went even further. The Missouri Compromise itself was void, he declared; Congress had no power over territories except to prepare for their admission to the Union; slaves being private property, Congress had no right to exclude them anywhere. According to this decision, "popular sovereignty" went into the discard, since obviously whatever powers Congress lacked would be lacked by any territorial legislature created by Congress.

The reaction was immediate and uproarious. Secession, formerly the threat of the South, now came as a cry from the North, particularly New England, where secessionist meetings were held in many towns. Douglas, on the other hand, digested the bitter dose as best he could, then announced that the decision was in fact a vindication of his repeal of the Compromise two years before, as well as a confirmation of the principles of popular sovereignty, since slavery, whether legal or not, could never thrive where the people did not welcome it. Lincoln did not mask his disappointment. He believed the decision was erroneous and harmful, but he respected the judgment of the Court and urged his followers to work toward the time when the five-four decision would be reversed. Meanwhile, during the off-year 1857, he prepared to run for the Senate against Douglas, whose third term would expire the following year.

Just then, unexpectedly, Douglas split with the Administration over the adoption of a constitution for Kansas. Threatened with expulsion from his party, he swung over to the Republicans on the issue, bringing many Democrats along with him. The Republicans were surprised and grateful, and it began to look as if Lincoln would be passed over again when nominating time came round. However, they were too accustomed to fighting the Little Giant to break off hostilities now. They nominated Lincoln at the state convention in mid-June. Lincoln was ready, and more than ready. He had not only prepared his acceptance, but now for the first time he read a speech from manuscript, as if to emphasize his knowledge of the need for precision. It was at this point that Lincoln's political destiny and the destiny of the nation became one. The first paragraph once more summed up his thinking and struck the keynote for all that was to follow:

"If we could first know where we are, and whither we are tending, we could better judge what to do, and how to do it. We are now far into the fifth year since a policy was initiated with the avowed object and confident promise of putting an end to slavery agitation. Under the operation of that policy, that agitation has not only not ceased, but has constantly augmented. In my opinion it will not cease until a crisis shall have been reached and passed. 'A house divided against itself cannot stand.' I believe this government cannot endure permanently half slave and half free. I do not expect the Union to be dissolved — I do not expect the house to fall — but I do expect it will cease to be divided. It will become all one thing, or all the other. Either the opponents of slavery will arrest the further spread of it, and place it where the public mind shall be at rest in the belief that it is in the course of ultimate extinction, or its advocates will push it forward till it shall have become alike lawful in all the states, old as well as new, North as well as South."

Seizing upon this as proof of Lincoln's radicalism, and declaring that it proved him not only a proponent of sectional discord but also a reckless prophet of war, Douglas came home and launched an all-out campaign against the Republicans and the Democrats who had not walked out with him. He spoke in Chicago to a crowd that broke into frenzies of cheers, then set out to stump the state, traveling with a retinue of secretaries, stenographers, and influential admirers in a gaily bannered private car placed at his disposal by George B. McClellan, chief engineer of the Illinois Central, who also provided a flatcar mounting a brass cannon to boom the announcement that the Little Giant was coming down the line. Traveling unaccompanied on an ordinary ticket, Lincoln moved in his wake, sometimes on the same train, addressing the crowds attracted by the Douglas panoply. At last he made the arrangement formal, challenging his opponent to a series of debates. Douglas, with nothing to gain, could not refuse. He agreed to meet Lincoln once in each of the seven congressional districts where they had not already spoken.

Thus the colorful Douglas-Lincoln debates got under way, the pudgy, well-tailored Douglas with his scowl, his luxurious mane of hair, gesturing aggressively as his voice wore to a froggy croak, and Lincoln in his claw-hammer coat and straight-leg trousers, tall and earnest, with a shrill voice that reached the outer edges of the crowd, bending his knees while he led up to a point, then straightening them with a jerk, rising to his full height as he made it. Crowds turned out, ten to fifteen thousand strong, thronging the lonesome prairie towns. At Freeport, Lincoln threw Douglas upon the horns of a dilemma, asking: "Can the people of a United States Territory, in any lawful way ... exclude slavery from its limits prior to the formation of a State Constitution?" If Douglas answered No he would offend the free-soil voters of Illinois. If he answered Yes he would make himself unacceptable to the South in the 1860 presidential campaign, toward which his ambition so clearly pointed. He made his choice; Yes, he said, defying both the Supreme Court and the South, and thereby cinched the present election and stored up trouble for the future.

Approaching fifty, Lincoln again took defeat in his stride, turning once more to the practice of law to build up a flattened bank account. He was known throughout the nation now as a result of the cross-state debates. In his mail and in the newspapers there began to appear suggestions that he was presidential timber — to which he replied, sometimes forthrightly: "I must, in candor, say I do not think I am fit for the Presidency," sometimes less forthrightly: "I shall labor faithfully in the ranks, unless, as I think not probable, the judgment of the party shall assign me a different position." Through the long hot summer of 1859, past fifty now, he wrote letters and made speeches and did in general what he could to improve the party strategy, looking toward next year's elections.

Then in mid-October the telegraph clacked a message that drove all such thoughts from men's minds. John Brown, called Osawatomie Brown after a massacre staged in Kansas, had seized the federal arsenal at Harpers Ferry, Virginia, as the first step in leading a slave insurrection. His army counted eighteen men, including five Negroes; "One man and God can overturn the universe," he said. Captured by United States

Marines under Colonel Robert E. Lee, U.S. Army, he was tried in a Virginia court and sentenced to be hanged in early December. He had the backing of several New England Abolitionists; they spent an anxious six weeks while the old fanatic kept their secret, close-mouthed behind his long gray beard. Seated on his coffin while he rode in a wagon to the gallows, he looked out at the hazy Blue Ridge Mountains. "This *is* a beautiful country," he said. "I never had the pleasure of really seeing it before." After the hanging the jailor unfolded a slip of paper Brown had left behind, a prophecy: "I John Brown am now quite certain that the crimes of this guilty land; will never be purged away; but with blood."

This too was added to the issues men were split on; John Brown's soul went marching, a symbol of good or evil, depending on the viewer. Douglas, back in Washington, was quick to claim that such incidents of lawlessness and bloodshed were outgrowths of the House Divided speech, and Lincoln's name was better known than ever. In late February, just past his fifty-first birthday, Lincoln traveled to New York for a speech at Cooper Union. The city audience thought him strange as he stood there, tall and awkward in a new broadcloth suit that hung badly from having been folded in a satchel for the train ride. "Mr Cheerman," he began. Presently, however, the awkwardness was dropped, or else they forgot it. He spoke with calm authority, denying that the Republican Party was either sectional or radical, except as its opponents had made it so. Slavery was the issue, North and South, he said, probing once more for the heart of the matter.

"All they ask, we could readily grant, if we thought slavery right; all we ask, they could as readily grant, if they thought it wrong. Their thinking it right, and our thinking it wrong, is the precise fact upon which depends the whole controversy. Thinking it right, as they do, they are not to blame for desiring its full recognition as being right; but thinking it wrong, as we do, can we yield to them? Can we cast our votes with their view and against our own? In view of our moral, social, and political responsibilities can we do this?" He thought not. "If our sense of duty forbids this, then let us stand by our duty fearlessly and effectively.... Neither let us be slandered from our duty by false accusations against us, nor frightened from it by menaces of destruction to the government nor of dungeons to ourselves. Let us have faith that right makes might, and in that faith let us, to the end, dare to do our duty as we understand it."

That was the peroration, and the listeners surged from their seats to applaud him, waving handkerchiefs and hats as they came forward to wring his hand. Four New York newspapers printed the speech in full next morning, and Lincoln went on into New England, making a series of addresses there before returning to Springfield much enhanced. The time for presidential nominations was drawing close. When a friend asked if he would allow his name to be entered, Lincoln admitted: "The taste *is* in my mouth a little."

Chicago was the scene of the Republican national convention, the result of a political maneuver toward the close of the previous year by one of Lincoln's supporters, who, poker-faced, had suggested the western city as an ideal neutral site, since Illinois would have no candidate of her own. Now in mid-May, however, as the delegates converged upon the raw pine Wigwam put up to accommodate ten thousand in an atmosphere of victory foreseen, they found that Illinois had a candidate indeed, and something beyond the usual favorite son. Alongside such prominent men as William H. Seward of New York, Salmon P. Chase of Ohio, Edward Bates of Missouri, and Simon Cameron of Pennsylvania, Lincoln was comparatively unknown. Yet this had its advantages, since the shorter the public record a candidate presented, the smaller the target he would expose to the mud that was sure to be flung. Each of these men had disadvantages; Seward had spoken too often of the "irrepressible conflict," Chase had been too radical, Bates was tainted by Know-Nothingism, and Cameron was said to be a crook. Besides all this, Lincoln came from the critical Northwest, where the political scale was likely to be tipped.

His managers set up headquarters and got to work behind the scenes, giving commitments, making deals. Then, on the eve of balloting, they received a wire from Springfield: "I authorize no bargains and will be bound by none." "Lincoln aint here and don't know what we have to meet," the managers said, and went on dickering right and left, promising cabinet posts and patronage, printing counterfeit admission tickets to pack the Wigwam nomination morning. The Seward yell was met by the Lincoln yawp. The New Yorker led on the first ballot. On the second there were readjustments as the others jockeyed for position; Lincoln was closing fast. On the third he swept in. The Wigwam vibrated with shouts and cheers, bells and whistles swelling the uproar while the news went out to the nation.

"Just think of such a sucker as me being President," Lincoln had said. Yet in Springfield when his friends came running, those who were not already with him in the newspaper office, they were somewhat taken aback at the new, calm, sure dignity which clothed him now like a garment.

Lincoln himself did not campaign. No presidential candidate ever had, such action being considered incommensurate with the dignity of the office. Nor did two of his three opponents. But Douglas, the only one of the four who seemed to believe that the election might bring war, set forth to stump the country. All four were running on platforms that called for the preservation of the Union. The defeat of

Lincoln depended solely on Douglas, however, since neither of the others could hope to carry the free states. Knowing this, Douglas worked with all his strength. Wherever he went he was met by Lincoln men, including Seward, Chase, and Bates. The Republican campaign for "Honest Abe, the Rail Splitter" was a colorful one, with pole raisings, barbecues, and torchlight parades. Douglas kept fighting. Then in August, when Lincoln supporters carried local elections in Maine and Vermont, and in October when Pennsylvania and Ohio followed suit, Douglas saw what was coming. He told his secretary, "Mr Lincoln is the next President. We must try to save the Union. I will go South."

He did go South in a final attempt to heal the three-way Democratic split, but there men would not listen either. On election day, November 6, though he ran closest to Lincoln in popular votes, he had the fewest electoral votes of all.

That night Lincoln sat in the Springfield telegraph office, watching the tabulations mount to a climax: Bell, 588,879; Breckinridge, 849,781; Douglas, 1,376,957; Lincoln, 1,866,452. The combined votes of his opponents outnumbered his own by almost a million; he would be a minority President, like the indecisive Buchanan now in office. He had carried none of the fifteen southern states, receiving not a single popular ballot in five of them, even from a crank, and no electoral votes at all. Yet he had carried all of the northern states except New Jersey, which he split with Douglas, so that the final electoral vote had a brighter aspect: Lincoln 180, Breckinridge 72, Bell 39, Douglas 12. Even if all the opposing popular votes had been concentrated on a single candidate, he would have received but eleven fewer electoral votes, which still would have left him more than he needed to win. Any way men figured it, North or South, barring assassination or an act of God, Abraham Lincoln would be President of the United States in March.

How many states would remain united was another question. South Carolina had warned that she would secede if Lincoln was elected. Now she did, and within three of the four months that lay between the election and the inauguration, six others followed her out. Lincoln in Springfield gave no assurance that he would seek a compromise or be willing to accept one. "Stand firm," he wrote privately to an Illinois senator. "The tug has to come, and better now than any time hereafter." "Hold firm, as with a chain of steel," he wrote to a friend in the House.

He had troubles enough, right there at home. "No bargains," he had wired his managers at the convention, but they had ignored him out of necessity. Now the claimants hedged him in, swarming into his home and office, plucking at his coat sleeve on the street.

The week before his departure for Washington he made a trip down to Coles County to say goodbye to Sally Bush Lincoln, the step-mother who had done for him all she could. When his father had died there, nine years back, Lincoln had not attended the funeral; but he took time out for this. He kissed her and held her close, then came back to Springfield, closed his office the final day, said goodbye to his partner Herndon, and went to the Chenery House for his last sleep in Illinois.

Next morning dawned cold and drizzly; 8 o'clock was leaving time. Lincoln and his party of fifteen, together with those who had come to say goodbye, assembled in the waiting room of the small brick depot. They felt unaccountably depressed; there was a gloom about the gathering, no laughter and few smiles as people came forward for hand-shakes and farewells. When the stub, funnel-stack locomotive blew the all-aboard they filed out of the station. The President-elect, and those who were going with him, boarded the single passenger car; those who were staying collected about the back platform, the rain making a steady murmur against the taut cotton or silk of their umbrellas. As he stood at the rail, chin down, Lincoln's look of sadness deepened. Tomorrow he would be fifty-two, one of the youngest men ever to fill the office he had won three months ago. Then he raised his head, and the people were hushed as he looked into their faces.

"My friends," he said quietly, above the murmur of the rain, "no one not in my situation can appreciate my feeling of sadness at this part-ing. To this place and the kindness of these people I owe everything. Here I have lived for a quarter of a century, and have passed from a young to an old man. Here my children have been born, and one is buried. I now leave, not knowing when, or whether ever, I may return, with a task before me greater than that which rested upon Washington. Without the assistance of that Divine Being who ever attended him, I cannot succeed. With that assistance I cannot fail. Trusting in Him who can go with me and remain with you and be everywhere for good, let us confidently hope that all will yet be well. To His care commending you, as I hope in your prayers you will commend me, I bid you an affectionate farewell."

The train pulled out and the people stood and watched it go, some with tears on their faces. Four years and two months later, still down in Coles County, Sally Bush Lincoln was to say: "I knowed when he went away he wasn't ever coming back alive."

✗ 2 ✗

Throughout the twelve days of his roundabout trip to Washington, traversing five states along an itinerary that called for twenty speeches and an endless series of conferences with prominent men who boarded the train at every station, Lincoln's resolution to keep silent on the vital issues was made more difficult if not impossible. Determined to withhold his plans until the inauguration had given him the authority to act as well as declare, he attempted to say nothing even as he spoke. And in this he was surprisingly successful. He met the crowds with generalities and the dignitaries with jokes — to the confusion and outrage of both. He told the Ohio legislature, "There is nothing going wrong. It is a consoling circumstance that when we look out there is nothing that really hurts anybody. We entertain different views upon political questions, but nobody is suffering anything."

With seven states out of the Union, arsenals and mints seized along with vessels and forts, the Mississippi obstructed, the flag itself fired upon, this man could say there was nothing going wrong. His listeners shrugged and muttered at his ostrich policy. They had come prepared for cheers, and they did cheer him loudly each time he seemed ready to face the issue, as when he warned in New Jersey that if it became necessary "to put the foot down firmly" they must support him. Even so, his appearance was not reassuring to the Easterners. In New York he offended the sensibilities of many by wearing black kid gloves to the opera and letting his big hands dangle over the box rail. Taken in conjunction with the frontier accent and the shambling western gait, it made them wonder what manner of man they had entrusted with their destinies. Hostile papers called him "gorilla" and "baboon," and as caricature the words seemed unpleasantly fitting.

In Philadelphia, raising a flag at Independence Hall, he felt his breath quicken as he drew down on the halyard and saw the bright red and rippling blue of the bunting take the breeze. Turning to the crowd he touched a theme he would return to. "I have often inquired of myself what great principle or idea it was that kept this confederacy so long together. It was not the mere matter of the separation of the colonies from the mother land, but that something in the Declaration giving liberty, not alone to the people of this land, but hope to the world for all future time. It was that which gave promise that in due time the weights should be lifted from the shoulders of all men, and that all should have an equal chance." Men stood and listened with upturned faces, wanting fire for the tinder of their wrath, not ointment for their fears, and the music crept by them. It was not this they had come to hear.

So far Lincoln had seemed merely inadequate, inept, at worst a bumpkin; but now the trip was given a comic-opera finish, in which he was called to play the part not only of a fool but of a coward. Baltimore, the last scheduled stop before Washington, would mark his first entry into a slavery region as President-elect. The city had sent him no welcome message, as all the others had done, and apparently had made no official plans for receiving him or even observing his presence while he passed through. Unofficially, however, according to reports, there awaited him a reception quite different from any he had been given along the way. Bands of toughs, called Blood Tubs, roamed the streets, plotting his abduction or assassination. He would be stabbed or shot, or both; or he would be hustled aboard a boat and taken South, the ransom being southern independence. All this was no more than gossip until the night before the flag-raising ceremony in Philadelphia, when news came from reliable sources that much of it was fact. General Winfield Scott, head of the armed forces, wrote warnings; Senator Seward, slated for Secretary of State, sent his son with documentary evidence; and now came the railroad head with his detective, Allan Pinkerton, whose operatives had joined such Maryland bands, he said, and as members had taken deep and bloody oaths. Such threats and warnings had become familiar over the past three months, but hearing all this Lincoln was disturbed. The last thing he wanted just now was an "incident," least of all one with himself as a corpse to be squabbled over. His friends urged him to cancel the schedule and leave for Washington immediately. Lincoln refused, but agreed that if, after he had spoken at Philadelphia the next morning and at Harrisburg in the afternoon, no Baltimore delegation came to welcome him to that city, he would by-pass it or go through unobserved.

Next afternoon, when no such group had come to meet him, he returned to his hotel, put on an overcoat, stuffed a soft wool hat into his pocket, and went to the railroad station. There he boarded a special car, accompanied only by his friend Ward Hill Lamon, known to be a good man in a fight. As the train pulled out, all telegraph wires out of Harrisburg were cut. When the travelers reached Philadelphia about 10 o'clock that night, Pinkerton was waiting. He put them aboard the Baltimore train; they had berths reserved by a female operative for her "invalid brother" and his companion. At 3.30 in the morning the sleeping-car was drawn through the quiet Baltimore streets to Camden Station. While they waited, Lincoln heard a drunk bawling "Dixie" on the quay. Lamon, with his bulging eyes and sad frontier mustache, sat clutching four pistols and two large knives. At last the car was picked up by a train from the west, and Lincoln stepped onto the Washington platform at 6 o'clock in the morning. "You can't play that on me," a man said, coming forward. Lamon drew back his fist. "Don't strike him!" Lincoln cried, and caught his arm, recognizing Elihu Washburn, an Illinois congressman. They went to Willard's Hotel for breakfast.

Such was the manner in which the new leader entered his capital to take the oath of office. Though the friendly press was embarrassed to explain it, the hostile papers had a field day, using the basic facts of the incident as notes of a theme particularly suited for variations. The overcoat became "a long military cloak," draping the lanky form from heels to eyes, and the wool hat became a Scotch-plaid cap, a sort of tam-o'-shanter. Cartoonists drew "fugitive sketches" showing Lincoln with his hair on end, the elongated figure surrounded by squiggles to show how he quaked as he ran from the threats of the Blood Tubs. "Only an attack of ager," they had his friends explaining. Before long, the Scotch-plaid pattern was transferred from the cap to the cloak, which at last became a garment he had borrowed from his wife, whom he left at the mercy of imaginary assassins. In the North there was shame behind the laughter and the sighs. Elation was high in the South, where people found themselves confirmed in their decision to leave a Union which soon would have such a coward for its leader. Certainly no one could picture Jefferson Davis fleeing from threats to his safety, in a plaid disguise and surrounded by squiggles of fear.

Mrs Lincoln and the children arrived that afternoon, and the family moved into Parlor 6, Willard's finest, which between now and the inauguration became a Little White House. To Parlor 6 came the public figures, resembling their photographs except for a third-dimensional grossness of the flesh, and the office seekers, importunate or demanding, oily or brash, as they had come to Springfield. Here as there, Lincoln could say of the men who had engineered his nomination in Chicago, "They have gambled me all around, bought and sold me a hundred times. I cannot begin to fill all the pledges made in my name."

The card-writing stand in the lobby offered a line of cockades for buttonholes or hatbands, "suitable for all shades of political sentiment," while elsewhere in the rambling structure a Peace Convention was meeting behind closed doors, the delegates mostly old men who talked and fussed, advancing the views of their twenty-one states — six of them from the buffer region, but none from the Cotton South — until at last they gave up and dispersed, having come to nothing. Washington was a southern city, surrounded by slave states, and the military patrolled the streets, drilled and paraded and bivouacked in vacant lots, so that townspeople, waking to the crash of sunrise guns and blare of bugles, threw up their windows and leaned out in nightcaps, thinking the war had begun. Congress was into its closing days, and finally in early March adjourned, having left the incoming President no authority to assemble the militia or call for volunteers, no matter what emergency might arise.

Inauguration day broke fair, but soon a cold wind shook the early flowers and the sky was overcast. Then this too yielded to a change. The wind scoured the clouds away and dropped, so that by noon, when President Buchanan called for Lincoln at Willard's, the sky was clear and summer-blue. Along streets lined with soldiers, including riflemen posted at upper-story windows and cannoneers braced at attention beside their guns, the silver-haired sixty-nine-year-old bachelor and his high-shouldered successor rode in sunshine to the Capitol. From the unfinished dome, disfigured by scaffolds, a derrick extended a skeleton arm. A bronze Freedom lay on the grass, the huge figure of a woman holding a sword in one hand and a wreath in the other, awaiting the dome's completion when she would be hoisted to its summit. In the Senate chamber Buchanan and Lincoln watched the swearing-in of Vice President Hannibal Hamlin of Maine, so dark-skinned that campaign rumors had had him a mulatto; then proceeded to a temporary platform on the east portico, where they gazed out upon a crowd of ten thousand.

Lincoln wore new black clothes, a tall hat, and carried a gold-headed ebony cane. As he rose to deliver the inaugural address, Stephen Douglas leaned forward from among the dignitaries and took the hat, holding it while Lincoln adjusted his spectacles and read from a manuscript he took out of his pocket. A first draft had been written at Springfield; since then, by a process of collaboration, it had been strengthened in places and watered down in others. Now, after months of silence and straddling many issues, he could speak, and his first words were spoken for southern ears.

"I have no purpose, directly or indirectly, to interfere with the institution of slavery in the states where it exists. I believe I have no lawful right to do so, and I have no inclination to do so." However, he denied that there could be any constitutional right to secession. "It is safe to assert that no government proper ever had a provision in its organic law for its own termination.... No state upon its own mere motion can lawfully get out of the Union." Then followed sterner words. "I shall take care, as the Constitution itself expressly enjoins upon me, that the laws of the Union be faithfully executed in all the states. Doing this I deem to be only a simple duty on my part; and I shall perform it, so far as practicable, unless my rightful masters, the American people, shall withhold the requisite means, or in some authoritative manner direct the contrary.... The power confided in me will be used to hold, occupy and possess the property and places belonging to the government, and to collect the duties and imposts."

Having clarified this, he returned to the question of secession, which he considered not only unlawful, but unwise. "Physically speaking, we cannot separate.... A husband and wife may be divorced, and go out of the presence and beyond the reach of each other; but the different parts of our country cannot do this. They cannot but remain face to face, and intercourse, either amicable or hostile, must continue between them." War, too, would be unwise. "Suppose you go to war, you cannot fight always; and when, after much loss on both sides and no gain on either, you cease fighting, the identical old questions as to terms of intercourse are again upon you." The issue lay as in a balance, which they could tip if they chose. "In your hands, my dissatisfied fellow countrymen, and not in mine, is the momentous issue of civil war. The government will not assail you. You can have no conflict without being yourselves the aggressors. You have no oath registered in heaven to destroy the government, while I shall have the most solemn one to 'preserve, protect and defend' it."

He then read the final paragraph, written in collaboration with Seward. "I am loath to close. We are not enemies, but friends. We must not be enemies. Though passion may have strained, it must not break our bonds of affection. The mystic chords of memory, stretching from every battlefield and patriot grave to every living heart and hearthstone all over this broad land, will yet swell the chorus of the Union when again touched, as surely they will be, by the better angels of our nature."

Chief Justice Taney, tall and cave-chested, sepulchral in his flowing robes — "with the face of a galvanized corpse," one witness said — stepped forward and performed the function he had performed eight times already for eight other men. Extending the Bible with trembling hands, he administered the oath of office to Abraham Lincoln as sixteenth President of the United States, and minute guns began to thud their salutes throughout the city.

★ ★ ★

Reactions to this address followed in general the preconceptions of its hearers, who detected what they sought. Extremists at opposite ends found it diabolical or too mild, while the mass of people occupying the center on both sides saw in Lincoln's words a confirmation of all that they were willing to believe. He was conciliatory or cunning, depending on the angle he was seen from. Southerners, comparing it to the inaugural delivered by Jefferson Davis in Montgomery two weeks before, congratulated themselves on the results; for Davis had spoken with the calmness and noncontention of a man describing an established fact, seeking neither approval nor confirmation among his enemies.

Standing on the portico of the Alabama capital, in the heart of the slave country, he did not mention slavery: an omission he had scarcely committed in fifteen years of public speaking. Nor did he waste breath on the possibility of reconciliation with the old government, remarking merely that in the event of any attempt at coercion "the suffering of millions will bear testimony to the folly and wickedness" of those who tried it. He spoke, rather, of agriculture and the tariff, both in Jeffersonian terms, and closed with the calm confidence of his beginning: "It is joyous in the midst of perilous times to look around upon a people united in heart, where one purpose of high resolve animates and actuates the whole, where the sacrifices to be made are not weighed in the balance against honor and right and liberty and equality. Obstacles may retard, but they cannot long prevent the progress of a movement sanctified by its justice and sustained by a virtuous people. Reverently let us invoke the God of our fathers to guide and protect us in our efforts to perpetuate the principles which by His blessing they were able to vindicate, establish, and transmit to their posterity. With the continuance of His favor, ever gratefully acknowledged, we may hopefully look forward to success, to peace, and to prosperity."

He had been chosen over such fire-eaters as Rhett and Yancey, Toombs and Howell Cobb, partly for reasons of compromise, but mainly on grounds that as a moderate he would be more attractive and less alarming to the people of the border states, still hanging back, conservative and easily shocked. Yet whatever their reasons for having chosen him, the people of the Deep South, watching him move among them, his lithe, rather boyish figure trim and erect in a suit of slate-gray homespun, believed they had chosen well. "Have you seen our President?" they asked, and the visitor heard pride in their tone. Charmed by the music of his oratory, the handsomeness of his clear-cut features, the dignity of his manner, they were thankful for the providence of history, which apparently gave every great movement the leader it deserved.

Such doubts as he had he kept to himself, or declared them only to his wife still back at Brierfield, writing to her two days after the inauguration: "The audience was large and brilliant. Upon my weary heart were showered smiles, plaudits, and flowers; but beyond them, I saw troubles and thorns innumerable.... We are without machinery, without means, and threatened by a powerful opposition; but I do not despond, and will not shrink from the task imposed upon me.... As soon as I can call an hour my own, I will look for a house and write you more fully."

Somehow he found both the time and the house, a plain two-story frame dwelling, and Mrs Davis and the children came to join him. "She is as witty as he is wise," one witness said. She was a great help at the levées and the less formal at-homes, having become in their senatorial years a more accomplished political manager than her husband, who had little time for anything but the exactions of his office. The croakers had already begun their chorus, though so far they were mostly limited to disappointed office seekers. Arriving, Mrs Davis had found him careworn, but when she expressed her concern, Davis told her plainly: "If we succeed we shall hear nothing of these malcontents. If we do not, then I shall be held accountable by friends as well as foes. I will do my best."

Rising early, he worked at home until breakfast, then went to his office, where he often stayed past midnight. He had need for all this labor, founding like Washington a new government, a new nation, except that whereas the earlier patriot had worked in a time of peace, with his war for independence safely won, Davis worked in a hurry against time, with possibly a harder war ahead. Like Washington, too, he lived without ostentation or pomp. His office was upstairs in the ugly red brick State House on a downtown corner, "The President"

handwritten across a sheet of foolscap pasted to the door. He made himself accessible to all callers, and even at his busiest he was gracious, much
as Jefferson had been.

Such aping of the earlier revolutionists was considered by the
Confederates not as plagiarism, but simply as a claiming of what was
their own, since most of those leaders had been southern in the first
place, especially the ones who set the tone, including four of the first
five, seven of the first ten, and nine of the first fifteen Presidents. In
adopting a national standard, the present revolutionists' initial thought
was to take the old flag with them, and the first name proposed for the
new nation was The Southern United States of America. Except for
certain elucidations, the lack of which had been at the root of the recent
trouble, the Confederate Constitution was a replica of the one its framers
had learned by heart and guarded as their most precious heritage. "We,
the people of the United States," became "We, the people of the Confederate States, each state acting in its sovereign and independent character," and they assembled not "to form a more perfect Union," but
"to form a permanent Federal government." There was no provision as
to the right of secession. The law-makers explained privately that there
was no need for this, such a right being as implicit as the right to
revolution, and to have included such a provision would have been to
imply its necessity.

One important oversight was corrected, however. Where the
founding fathers, living in a less pious age of reason, had omitted any
reference to the Deity, the modern preamble invoked "the favor and
guidance of Almighty God." Nor were more practical considerations
neglected. The President and Vice President were elected to a six-
year term, neither of them eligible for reëlection. Congress was forbidden to pass a protective tariff or to appropriate money for internal improvements. Cabinet officers were to be given seats on the floor of Congress. Each law must deal with only one subject, announced in its title,
and the President had the right to veto separate items in appropriation
bills. Instead of requiring a three-fourths majority, amendments could
be ratified by two-thirds of the states. While the newer document expressly prohibited any revival of the slave trade, those chattels referred
to in the old one as "persons" now became outright "slaves," and in all
territory acquired by the Confederacy, slavery was to be "recognized
and protected" by both the federal and territorial governments.

Thus the paperwork foundation had been laid; the Confederacy
was a going concern, one of the nations of earth. Whether it would
remain so depended in a large part on the events of March and April,
following the two inaugurals, particularly as these events affected the
sympathies of the eight states in the two- to four-hundred-mile-deep
neutral region which lay between the two countries. Davis knew this,
of course, and knew as well that it would be the opposition's strategy to

maneuver him into striking the first blow. This he was willing to do, provided the provocation to strike it was great enough to gain him the approval of the buffer states and the European powers. Actually, the odds were with him, for the neutral states were slave states, bound to the South by ties of history and kinship, and it was to the interests of the nations of Europe to see a growing competitor split in two. Meanwhile what was needed was patience, which Davis knew was not his dominant virtue, and indeed was hardly a southern virtue at all. Therefore, though his people were united, as he said, by "one purpose of high resolve," he could also speak of his "weary heart" and "troubles and thorns innumerable."

Lincoln up in Washington had most of these troubles, including the problem of holding the border states, and a greater one as well. Having first made up his mind, he must then unite the North before he could move to divide and conquer the South. He had made up his mind; he had stated his position; "The Union is unbroken," he had said. Yet while Europe applauded the forthright manner in which the Confederacy had set itself in motion, Lincoln was confronted with division even among the states that had stayed loyal. New Jersey was talking secession; so was California, which along with Oregon was considering the establishment of a new Pacific nation; so, even, was New York City, which beside being southern in sentiment would have much to gain from independence. While moderates were advising sadly, "Let the erring sisters depart in peace," extremists were violently in favor of the split: "No union with slaveholders! Away with this foul thing! . . . The Union was not formed by force, nor can it be maintained by force."

On the other hand, whatever there was of native Union persuasion was sustained by economic considerations. Without the rod of a strong protective tariff, eastern manufacturers would lose their southern markets to the cheaper, largely superior products of England, and this was feared by the workers as well as the owners. The people of the Northwest remained staunchly pro-Union, faced as they were with loss of access to the lower Mississippi, that outlet to the Gulf which they had had for less than fifty years. Then too, following Lincoln's inaugural address, there was a growing belief that separation would solve no problems, but rather would add others of an international character, with the question of domination intensified. In early April the New York *Times* stated the proposition: "If the two sections can no longer live together, they can no longer live apart in quiet till it is determined which is master. No two civilizations ever did, or can, come into contact as the North and South threaten to do, without a trial of strength, in which the weaker goes to the wall. . . . We must remain master of the occasion and the dominant power on this continent." Reading this, there were men who faced responsibility; they believed they must accept it as members of a generation on trial. "A collision is inevitable," one said.

"Why ought not we test our government instead of leaving it" —
meaning the testing — "to our children?"

Walking the midnight corridors of the White House after the
day-long din of office seekers and divided counsels, Lincoln knew that
his first task was to unite all these discordant elements, and he knew, too,
that the most effective way to do this was to await an act of aggression
by the South, exerting in the interim just enough pressure to provoke
such an action, without exerting enough to justify it. He had good cause
to believe that he would not have long to wait. The longer the border
states remained neutral, the less they were ashamed of their neutrality
in the eyes of their sisters farther south; the Confederates were urged to
force the issue. Roger Pryor, a smooth-shaven Virginian with long
black hair that brushed his shoulders, a fire-eater irked that his state hung
back, was speaking now from a Charleston balcony, advising the South
Carolinians how to muster Virginia into their ranks "in less than an
hour by Shrewsbury clock: Strike a blow!"

What Pryor had in mind was Fort Sumter, out in Charleston
harbor, one of the four Federal forts still flying the Union flag in Confederate territory. Lincoln also had it in mind, along with the other
three, all Florida forts: Pickens off Pensacola Bay, Taylor at Key West,
and Jefferson in the Dry Tortugas. The crowd was delighted with
Pryor's advice. So would Lincoln have been if he had heard him, for
by now he saw Sumter as the answer to his need for uniting the North.

The garrison at Fort Sumter had originally occupied the more
vulnerable Fort Moultrie on Sullivan's Island, but the night after Christmas, six days after South Carolina seceded, Major Robert Anderson
removed his eighty-two men to the stronger fortress three miles out in
the harbor. South Carolina protested to Washington, demanding as one
nation to another that the troops return to Moultrie. Instead, Buchanan
sent an unarmed merchant steamer, the *Star of the West*, with men and
supplies to reinforce the fort; but when the Charleston gunners took her
under fire, union jack and all, she turned back. That was that. Though
they ringed the harbor with guns trained on Sumter and no longer
allowed the garrison to buy food at local markets, the Carolinians fired
no shot against the fort itself, nor did the Confederate authorities when
they took over in March. Buchanan, with his after-me-the-deluge policy,
left the situation for his successor to handle as he saw fit, including the
question of whether to swallow the insult to the flag. On the day after
his inauguration Lincoln received dispatches from Anderson announcing
that he had not food enough to last six weeks, which meant that Lincoln
had something less than that period of time in which to make up his
mind whether to send supplies to the fort or let it go.

During this period, while Lincoln was making up his mind and
seemed lost in indecision, there was played in Washington a drama of

cross-purposes involving backstairs diplomacy and earnest misrepresentation. Secretary of State William H. Seward, leader of the Republican Party and a man of wide experience in public life, saw the new President as well-meaning but incompetent in such matters, a prairie lawyer fumbling toward disaster, and himself as the Administration's one hope to forestall civil war. He believed that if the pegs that held men's nerves screwed tight could somehow be loosened, or at any rate not screwed still tighter, the crisis would pass; the neutral states would remain loyal, and in time even the seceded states would return to the fold, penitent and convinced by consideration. He did not believe that Sumter should be reinforced or resupplied, since this would be exactly the sort of incident likely to increase the tension to the snapping point.

In this he was supported by most of his fellow cabinet members, for when Lincoln polled them on the issue — "Assuming it to be possible to now provision Fort Sumter, under all the circumstances is it wise to attempt it?" — they voted five-to-two to abandon the fort. The Army, too, had advised against any attempt at reinforcement, estimating that 20,000 troops would be required, a number far beyond its present means. Only the Navy seemed willing to undertake it. Lincoln himself, in spite of his inaugural statement that he would "hold, occupy and possess the property and places belonging to the government," seemed undecided or anyhow did not announce his decision. Seward believed he would come around in time, especially in the light of the odds among his counselors. Meanwhile he, Seward, would do what he could to spare the Southerners any additional provocation.

Three of them were in Washington now, sent there from Montgomery as commissioners to accomplish "the speedy adjustment of all questions growing out of separation, as the respective interests, geographical contiguity, and future welfare of the two nations may render necessary." They had much to offer and much to ask. The Confederate Congress having opened the navigation of the lower Mississippi to the northern states, they expected to secure in return the evacuation of Sumter and the Florida forts, along with much else. Lincoln, however, would not see them. To have done so would have been to give over the constitutional reasoning that what was taking place in Alabama was merely a "rebellion" by private persons, no more entitled to send representatives to the rightful government than any other band of outlaws. Being also an official person, Seward of course could not see them either, no matter how much good he thought would proceed from a face-to-face conciliatory talk. Yet he found a way at least to show them the extent to which he believed the government would go in proving it meant no harm in their direction.

On March 15, the day Lincoln polled his cabinet for its views on Sumter, U.S. Supreme Court Justice John A. Campbell of Alabama, who had not yet gone South, came into Seward's office to urge him to receive the Southerners. The Secretary regretfully declined, then added: "If Jefferson Davis had known the state of things here, he would not have sent those commissioners. The evacuation of Sumter is as much as the Administration can bear."

Justice Campbell was alert at once. Here was Seward, guaranteeing for the government, whose Secretary of State he was, the main concession the commissioners were seeking. To make this even more definite, Campbell remarked that he would write to Davis at once. "And what shall I say to him on the subject of Fort Sumter?"

"You may say to him that before that letter reaches him —— How far is it to Montgomery?"

"Three days."

"You may say to him that before that letter reaches him, the telegraph will have informed him that Sumter will have been evacuated."

Lincoln was still either making up his mind or reinforcing whatever decision he had already made. In this connection he sent three men down to Charleston to observe the situation and report on what they saw. The first two, both southern-born, were Illinois law associates. Both reported reconciliation impossible, and one — the faithful Lamon, who had come through Baltimore on the sleeping-car with Lincoln — went so far as to assure South Carolina's Governor Pickens that Sumter would be evacuated. The third, a high-ranking naval observer who secured an interview with Anderson at the fort, returned to declare that a relief expedition was feasible. Lincoln ordered him to assemble the necessary ships and to stand by for sailing orders; he would use him or not, depending on events. At the same time, in an interview with a member of the Virginia state convention — which had voted against leaving the Union, but remained in session, prepared to vote the other way if the Administration went against the grain of its sense of justice — Lincoln proposed a swap. If the convention would adjourn *sine die*, he would evacuate Sumter. "A state for a fort is no bad business," he said.

Nothing came of this, but at the end of March, when Lincoln again polled the cabinet on the question, the vote was three-to-three, one member being absent. Seward by now had begun to see that he might well have gone too far in his guarantees to the Confederate commissioners. When Justice Campbell returned on April 1 to ask why his promise of two weeks before had not been carried out, Seward replied with the straight-faced solemnity of a man delivering an April Fool pronouncement: "I am satisfied the government will not undertake to supply Fort Sumter without giving notice to Governor Pickens."

"What does this mean?" Campbell asked, taken aback. This was something quite different from the Secretary's former assurances. "Does the President design to supply Sumter?"

"No, I think not," Seward said. "It is a very irksome thing to him to surrender it. His ears are open to everyone, and they fill his head with schemes for its supply. I do not think he will adopt any of them. There is no design to reinforce it."

Campbell reported these developments to the Confederate commissioners, who saw them in a clearer light than Seward himself had done. Restating them in sterner terms, the following day they telegraphed their government in Montgomery: "The war wing presses on the President; he vibrates to that side.... Their form of notice to us may be that of a coward, who gives it when he strikes."

This, or something like this, was what followed; for though Lincoln himself had practiced no deception (at least not toward the Confederates) Seward's well-meant misrepresentations had led exactly to that effect. By now Lincoln was ready. On April 6 he signed an order dispatching the naval expedition to Fort Sumter. Yet Seward was still not quite through. The following day, when Justice Campbell asked him to confirm or deny rumors that such a fleet was about to sail, Seward replied by note: "Faith as to Sumter fully kept. Wait and see." Campbell thought that this applied to the original guarantee, whereas Seward only meant to repeat that there would be no action without warning; and this, too, was taken for deception on the part of the Federal government. For on the day after that, April 8, there appeared before Governor Pickens an envoy who read him the following message: "I am directed by the President of the United States to notify you to expect an attempt will be made to supply Fort Sumter with provisions only, and that if such an attempt be not resisted, no effort to throw in men, arms, or ammunition will be made without further notice, or in case of an attack upon the fort."

Pickens could only forward the communication to the Confederate authorities at Montgomery. Lincoln had maneuvered them into the position of having either to back down on their threats or else to fire the first shot of the war. What was worse, in the eyes of the world, that first shot would be fired for the immediate purpose of keeping food from hungry men.

Davis assembled his cabinet and laid the message before them. Their reactions were varied. Robert Toombs, the fire-eater, was disturbed and said so: "The firing on that fort will inaugurate a civil war greater than any the world has yet seen, and I do not feel competent to advise you." He paced the room, head lowered, hands clasped beneath his coattails. "Mr President, at this time it is suicide, murder, and you will lose us every friend at the North. You will wantonly strike a hornets' nest which extends from mountains to ocean. Legions now quiet will swarm out and sting us to death. It is unnecessary. It puts us in the wrong. It is fatal."

Davis reasoned otherwise, and made his decision accordingly. It was not he who had forced the issue, but Lincoln, and this the world would see and know, along with the deception which had been practiced. Through his Secretary of War he sent the following message to General P. G. T. Beauregard, commanding the defenses at Charleston harbor:

> If you have no doubt as to the authorized character of the agent who communicated to you the intention of the Washington government to supply Fort Sumter by force, you will at once demand its evacuation, and, if this is refused, proceed in such manner as you may determine to reduce it.

Beauregard sent two men out to Sumter in a rowboat flying a flag of truce. They tendered Major Anderson a note demanding evacuation and stipulating the terms of surrender: "All proper facilities will be afforded for the removal of yourself and command, together with company arms and property, and all private property, to any post in the United States which you may select. The flag which you have upheld so long and with so much fortitude, under the most trying circumstances, may be saluted by you on taking it down."

Anderson received it sorrowfully. He was a Kentuckian married to a Georgian, and though he had been the military hero of the North since his exploit in the harbor the night after Christmas, he was torn between his love for the Union and his native state. If Kentucky seceded he would go to Europe, he said, desiring "to become a spectator of the contest, and not an actor." Approaching fifty-six, formerly Beauregard's artillery instructor at West Point, he had made the army his life; so that what he did he did from a sense of duty. The Confederates knew his thoughts, for they had intercepted his reply to Lincoln's dispatch informing him that Sumter would be relieved. "We shall strive to do our duty," he had written, "though I frankly say that my heart is not in the war, which I see is to be thus commenced." Therefore he read Beauregard's note sorrowfully, and sorrowfully replied that it was "a demand with which I regret that my sense of honor, and of my obligations to my government, prevent my compliance." Having written this, however, he remarked as he handed the note to the two aides, "Gentlemen, if you do not batter us to pieces, we shall be starved out in a few days."

Beauregard, hearing this last, telegraphed it immediately to Montgomery. Though he knew that it was only a question of time until the navy relief expedition would arrive to add the weight of its guns to those of the fort, and in spite of the danger that hot-headed South Carolina gunners might take matters in their own hands, Davis was glad to defer the opening shot. The Secretary of War wired back instructions for Beauregard to get Anderson to state a definite time for the surrender. Otherwise, he repeated, "reduce the fort."

It was now past midnight, the morning of April 12; there could be no delay, for advance units of the relief expedition had been sighted off the bar. This time four men went out in the white-flagged boat, empowered by Beauregard to make the decision without further conferences, according to Anderson's answer. He heard their demand and replied that he would evacuate the fort "by noon of the 15th instant" unless he received "controlling instructions from my government, or additional supplies." This last of course, with the relief fleet standing just outside the harbor — though Anderson did not know it had arrived — made the guarantee short-lived at best and therefore unacceptable to the aides, who announced that Beauregard would open fire "in one hour from this time." It was then 3.20 a.m. Anderson, about to test his former gunnery student in a manner neither had foreseen in the West Point classroom, shook the hands of the four men and told them in parting: "If we do not meet again in this world, I hope we may meet in the better one." Without returning to Beauregard's headquarters, they proceeded at once to Cummings Point and gave the order to fire.

One of the four was Roger Pryor, the Virginian who had spoken from a Charleston balcony just two days ago. "Strike a blow!" he had urged the Carolinians. Now when he was offered the honor of firing the first shot, he shook his head, his long hair swaying. "I could not fire the first gun of the war," he said, his voice as husky with emotion as Anderson's had been, back on the wharf at the fort. Another Virginian could and would — white-haired Edmund Ruffin, a farm-paper editor and old-line secessionist, sixty-seven years of age. At 4.30 he pulled a lanyard; the first shot of the war drew a red parabola against the sky and burst with a glare, outlining the dark pentagon of Fort Sumter.

Friday dawned crimson on the water as the siege got under way. Beauregard's forty-seven howitzers and mortars began a bombardment which the citizens of Charleston, together with people who had come from miles around by train and buggy, on horseback and afoot to see the show, watched from rooftops as from grandstand seats at a fireworks display, cheering as the gunnery grew less ragged and more accurate, until at last almost every shot was jarring the fort itself. Anderson had forty guns, but in the casemates which gave his cannoneers protection from the plunging shells of the encircling batteries he could man only flat-trajectory weapons firing nonexplosive shot. Beauregard's gunners got off more than 4000 rounds. As they struck the terreplein and rooted into the turf of the parade, their explosions shook the fort as if by earthquakes. Heated shot started fires, endangering the magazine. Presently the casemates were so filled with smoke that the cannoneers hugged the ground, breathing through wet handkerchiefs. Soon they were down to six guns. The issue was never in doubt; Anderson's was no more than a token resistance. Yet he continued firing, if for no other purpose than to prove that the defenders were still there. The flag was shot from its staff; a sergeant nailed it up again. Once, after a lull —

which at first was thought to be preparatory to surrender — when the Union gunners resumed firing, the Confederates rose from behind their parapets and cheered them. Thus it continued, all through Friday and Friday night and into Saturday. The weary defenders were down to pork and water. Then at last, the conditions of honor satisfied, Anderson agreed to yield under the terms offered two days ago.

So far there had been no casualties on either side. The casualties came later, during the arrangement of the particulars of surrender and finally during the ceremony itself. The first was Roger Pryor, who apparently had recovered from his reluctance and was sent to the fort as one of Beauregard's emissaries. Sitting at a table in the unused hospital while the formal terms were being put to paper, he developed a thirst and poured himself a drink from a bottle which he found at his right hand. When he had tossed it off he read the label, and discovered that it was iodine of potassium. The Federal surgeon took him outside, very pale, his long hair hanging sideways, and laid him on the grass to apply the stomach pump that saved his life.

A second mishap, this time in the Unionist ranks and far more serious, occurred at 4 o'clock Sunday afternoon. While Anderson, in accordance with the capitulation terms, was firing a fifty-gun salute to his flag, an ember fell into some powder. One man was killed in the explosion and five were injured. Private Daniel Hough thus became the first fatality of the war, before a man had fallen in combat. The scorched and shot-torn flag was lowered and given to Anderson, who packed it among his effects — intending, he said, to have it wrapped about him as a winding sheet on his burying day — then marched his men, with flying colors and throbbing drums, to the wharf where they boarded a steamer from the relief expedition which had observed rather than shared their fight, but which at least could perform the service of taking them home once it was over.

As the weary artillerymen passed silently out of the harbor, Confederate soldiers lining the beaches removed their caps in salute. There was no cheering.

★   ★   ★

Lincoln soon had cause to believe he had judged correctly. Sumter did indeed unite and electrify the North. That Sunday, when the news arrived by telegraph of the surrender in Charleston harbor, the White House was besieged by callers anxious to assure the President of their loyalty and support. Among them were senators and congressmen who pledged the resources of their states; their people, they said, would stand by the Union through fire and bloodshed. Among them was Stephen Douglas, who rose from his sickbed, the pallor of death already on his face, "to preserve the Union, maintain the government, and defend the capital." Thus he reported his pledge to the people afterwards, more than a million of whom had voted for him for President, never suspecting that he would be dead by early June. Now in mid-April Lincoln met him with outstretched hands and a smile.

Douglas was one among many throughout the nation. It was a time for oratory and easy promises. Businessmen formerly opposed to war as economically unsound now switched their line. They wanted it, now — as bloody as need be, so long as it was short and vigorous. In Pittsburgh, hangman's nooses dangled from lampposts inscribed "Death to Traitors!" Here as in other northern cities, secession sympathizers were bayed by angry crowds until they waved Union banners from their windows. Down in Knoxville, Tennessee, the loyal newspaper editor William G. Brownlow declared that he would "fight the Secession leaders till Hell froze over, and then fight them on the ice."

That same Sunday, in such a heady atmosphere of elation and indignation, Lincoln assembled his cabinet to frame a proclamation calling on the states for 75,000 militia to serve for ninety days against "combinations too powerful to be suppressed by the ordinary course of judicial proceedings." Technically it was not a declaration of war; only Congress could declare war, and Congress was not in session — a fact for which Lincoln was duly thankful, not wanting to be hampered. Though he called a special session for July 4, he expected to have the situation in hand by then. Meanwhile he proceeded unmolested, having determined in his own mind that extraordinary events called for extraordinary measures. The militia draft was issued the following day, April 15, to all the states and territories except the rebellious seven, apportioning the number of troops to be forwarded by each.

Here too, at first, the reply was thunderous. The northern states quickly oversubscribed their quotas; governor after northern governor wired forthright encouragement, asking only to be informed of the Administration's needs. Then Lincoln met a check. As he raised a pontifical hand, commanding "the persons composing the combinations aforesaid to disperse and retire peacefully to their respective abodes," he was given cause to think that he had perhaps outgeneraled himself. It soon became more or less obvious that, just as Davis had united the North by firing on Sumter, so had Lincoln united the South by issuing this demand for troops to be used against her kinsmen. This was true not only in the cotton states, where whatever remained of Union sentiment now vanished, but also in the states of the all-important buffer region, where Lincoln believed the victory balance hung. Telegram after telegram arrived from governors of the previously neutral states, each one bristling with moral indignation at the enormity of the proclamation, rather as if it had been in fact an invitation to fratricide or incest.

Governor Letcher of Virginia replied that since Lincoln had "chosen to inaugurate civil war," he would be sent no troops from Old

Dominion. "The people of this Commonwealth are freemen, not slaves," Governor Rector answered for Arkansas, "and will defend to the last extremity their honor, lives, and property, against Northern mendacity and usurpation." Governor Ellis of North Carolina declared that his state would "be no party to this wicked violation of the laws of the country and this war upon the liberties of a free people." "Tennessee will furnish not a single man for the purpose of coercion," Governor Harris told Lincoln, "but fifty thousand if necessary for the defense of our rights and those of our Southern brothers."

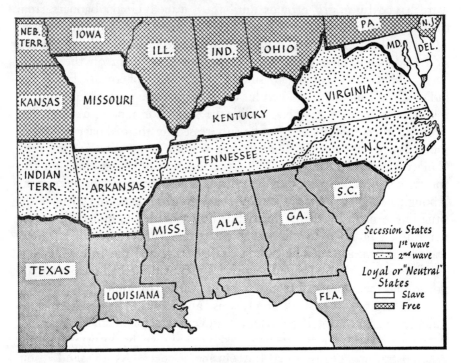

In such hard words did these four governors reply to the call for troops. And their people backed them up. Virginia seceded within two days, followed by the other three, Arkansas and Tennessee and finally North Carolina. East of the Mississippi the area of the Confederacy was doubled, and her flag, which now could claim eleven stars, flew along a boundary that had leapfrogged northward two to four hundred miles, across soil that had been Union.

Four slave states still dangled in the balance, Delaware and Maryland, Kentucky and Missouri. The first two were cautious; Governor Burton of Delaware reported that his state had no militia and therefore could not comply with the call for troops, while Governor Hicks of Maryland replied that he would forward soldiers only for the defense of Washington. Lincoln was somewhat reassured by their cautiousness, which at least indicated that there would be no precipitate action on their part. He could take no such consolation from the other two wires he received. "I say, emphatically," Governor Magoffin responded, "Kentucky will furnish no troops for the wicked purpose of subduing her sister Southern states." Governor Jackson of Missouri sent the harshest reply of all: "Your requisition is illegal, unconstitutional, revolutionary, inhuman, diabolical, and cannot be complied with."

These were frets with which Lincoln would have to deal through the coming months, particularly the problem of holding onto his native state, Kentucky, with its critical location, its rivers and manpower, its horses and bluegrass cattle. "I think to lose Kentucky is nearly the same as to lose the whole game," he said. "Kentucky gone, we cannot hold Missouri, nor, as I think, Maryland. These all against us, and the job on our hands is too large for us. We would as well consent to separation at once, including the surrender of this capital."

Maryland compassed the District on three sides, while on the fourth, across the Potomac, lay hostile Virginia, whose troops were already on the march, their campfires gleaming on the southern bank. They had seized the arsenal at Harpers Ferry and the Norfolk navy yard, and now the Richmond *Examiner* proclaimed "one wild shout of fierce resolve to capture Washington City, at all and every human hazard. That filthy cage of unclean birds must and will be purified by fire." It seemed possible, even probable. Many of the army's best officers were resigning, going South along with hundreds of civil workers from the various departments.

The day of the proclamation passed, then another, and still another; not a volunteer arrived. The city was defenseless. On April 18, five hundred Pennsylvanians showed up, unarmed, untrained. They had met cold stares in Baltimore, but the troops who arrived next day, the 6th Massachusetts, met something worse. A crowd of southern sympathizers threw bricks and stones and fired into their ranks as they changed trains. They returned the fire, killing twelve citizens and wounding many more, then packed their four dead in ice for shipment north, and came on into Washington, bearing their seventeen wounded on stretchers. Three days later, when a Baltimore committee called on the President to protest the "pollution" of Maryland soil, Lincoln replied that he must have troops to defend the capital. "Our men are not moles, and cannot dig under the earth," he told them. "They are not birds, and cannot fly through the air. There is no way but to march across, and that they must do." So the Baltimore delegation went back and clipped the telegraph lines, tore up railroad tracks, and wrecked the bridges. Washington was cut off from the outside world.

It was now a deserted city, the public buildings barricaded with sandbags and barrels of flour, howitzers frowning from porticoes. The Willard's thousand guests had shrunk to fifty, its corridors as empty as the avenues outside. Many among the few who remained flaunted secession badges, preparing to welcome their southern friends. Virginia's Colonel T. J. Jackson had 8000 men at Harpers Ferry, while Beauregard, the conqueror of Sumter, was reported nearing Alexandria with 15,000 more. If they effected a junction, all Lincoln had to throw in their path was the handful from Pennsylvania and Massachusetts, five companies of the former, a regiment of the latter, quartered in the House of Representatives and the Senate Chamber.

They had arrived on Thursday and Friday. Saturday and Sunday passed, then Monday, and still there was no further sign of the 75,000 Lincoln had called for. "Why don't they come? Why don't they come?" he muttered, pacing his office, peering out through the window. Tuesday brought a little mail, the first in days, and also a few newspapers telling of northern enthusiasm and the dispatching of troops to Washington: Rhode Islanders and New York's 7th Regiment. Lincoln could scarcely credit these reports, and Wednesday when officers and men who had been wounded in the Baltimore fracas called at the White House he thanked them for their presence in the capital, then added: "I don't believe there is any North! The 7th Regiment is a myth; Rhode Island is not known in our geography any longer. You are the only northern realities!"

Then on Thursday, April 25, the piercing shriek of a locomotive broke the noonday stillness of the city. The 7th New York arrived, followed by 1200 Rhode Island militiamen and an equal number from Massachusetts, whose volunteer mechanics had repaired a crippled engine and relaid the torn-up Annapolis track. A route had been opened to the north.

By the end of the month, Washington had 10,000 troops for its defense, with more on the way. Lincoln could breathe easier. An iron hand was laid on Baltimore, securing Maryland to the Union. Major Robert Anderson, the returned hero of Sumter, was promoted to brigadier general and sent to assert the Federal claim to his native Kentucky. Major General John C. Frémont, the California Pathfinder and the Republican Party's first presidential candidate, was sent to perform a like function in Missouri. Before long, Lincoln could even assume the offensive.

Harpers Ferry was recaptured, Arlington Heights and Alexandria occupied. Confederate campfires no longer gleamed across the Potomac; the fires there now were Federal. Fortress Monroe, at the tip of the York-James peninsula, was reinforced, and an attack was launched against western Virginia, across the Ohio. Within another month, so quickly had despair been overcome and mobilization completed, there began to be heard in the North a cry that would grow familiar: "On to Richmond!"

✳ ✳ ✳

That city was the southern capital now, moved there from Montgomery toward the end of May at the climax of the fervor following Sumter and the northern call for troops. Vice President Alexander H. Stephens voiced the defiance of the Confederacy, crying: "Lincoln may bring his 75,000 troops against us. We fight for our homes, our fathers and mothers, our wives, brothers, sisters, sons, and daughters! ... We can call out a million of peoples if need be, and when they are cut down we can call another, and still another, until the last man of the South finds a bloody grave."

Davis, with a sidelong glance at Europe and what history might say, reinforced the defensive character of these words in a message to Congress, called into extra session on April 29. Though desirous of peace "at any sacrifice, save that of honor and independence," he said, the South would "meet" — not *wage* — the war now launched by Lincoln. "All we ask is to be let alone," he added. Spoken before the assembly, the words had a defiant ring like those of Stephens. Read off the printed page, however, they sounded somewhat plaintive.

When Congress voted to accept Virginia's invitation to transfer the national capital to Richmond, Davis at first opposed the move. In the event of all-out war, which he expected, the strategic risk would be less disconcerting in the Deep South area, where the revolution had had its birth, than on the frontier, near the jar of battle. Yet when he was overruled by the politicians, who were finding Montgomery uncomfortable and dull, he acceded gracefully, even cheerfully, and made the two-day train trip without ceremony or a special car. He took instead a seat in the rear coach of a regular train and remained unrecognized by his fellow passengers until he was called to their attention by cheers from station platforms along the way.

In Richmond the Virginians, offering something more of pomp, met him at the station with a carriage drawn by four white horses. When a tossed bouquet fell into the street during the ride to the hotel, the President ordered the vehicle stopped, dismounted to pick up the flowers, and handed them to a lady in the carriage before signaling the coachman to drive on. This was noted with approval by the Virginians, already won by the dignified simplicity of his manner, which was tested further at luncheon in the hotel dining room, when a group of ladies stood around the table and fanned him while he ate. Davis proved equal even to this, and afterwards at the Fair Grounds, having gotten through the ordeal of a handshaking ceremony more exhausting than the two-day train ride, he made a short informal speech in which he called his listeners "the last best hope of liberty." "The country relies upon you," he told them. "Upon you rest the hopes of our people; and I have only to say, my friends, that to the last breath of my life I am wholly your own."

Here as in Montgomery — also a city of seven hills; Our Rome,

Virginians called their capital — the people congratulated themselves on having inherited such a President. At St Paul's, the first Sunday after secession, the words of the First Lesson had come with all the force of a prophecy: "I will remove far off from you the northern army, and will drive him into a land barren and desolate ... and his stink shall come up, and his ill savour." Now they seemed to have found the man to lead them through its accomplishment. Originally they had had doubts, wondering how a Westerner could head a people so conscious of having furnished the best leaders of the past, but now that they had seen him they were reassured. Daily he rode out to inspect the training camps, sometimes with his staff, more often with a single aide. "Mr Davis rode a beautiful gray horse," a witness wrote of one of these excursions. "His worst enemy will allow that he is a consummate rider, graceful and easy in the saddle."

He devoted most of his energy to organizing an army: work for which his years at West Point and in Mexico, as well as his experience as Pierce's capable Secretary of War, had prepared him well. War was an extension of statecraft, to be resorted to when diplomacy failed its purpose; but Davis took the aphorism one step further, believing that a nation's military policy should logically duplicate its political intentions. Lincoln had more or less maneuvered him into firing the first shot, and while Davis did not regret his action in the case of Sumter, he did not intend to give his opponent another chance to brand him an aggressor in the eyes of history and Europe. "All we ask is to be let alone," he had announced. Therefore, while Lincoln was gathering the resources and manpower of the North in response to the shout, "On to Richmond," Davis chose to meet the challenge by interposing troops where they blocked the more obvious paths of invasion.

All this time, men were being forwarded to Richmond by the states. By mid-July he had three small armies in the Virginia theater: Beauregard, with 23,000 northward beyond the important rail junction at Manassas, facing a Union army of 35,000; Joseph E. Johnston with 11,000 near the Potomac end of the Shenandoah Valley, facing the 14,000 who had retaken Harpers Ferry; and J. B. Magruder, with about 5000 down on the York-James peninsula, facing 15,000 at Fortress Monroe, which the North could reinforce by sea. Outnumbered at every point, with just under 40,000 opposing well over 60,000 troops, the Confederates yet held the interior lines and could thereby move reinforcements from army to army, across any arc of the circle, in much less time than the Federals beyond the long perimeter would require.

Already there had been clashes of arms. Down the Peninsula — at Big Bethel, northwest of Newport News — Major General Benjamin F. Butler attacked one of Magruder's outposts, seven Union regiments against 1400 Confederates. The attackers became confused, firing into one another's ranks until artillery drove them back. Casualties

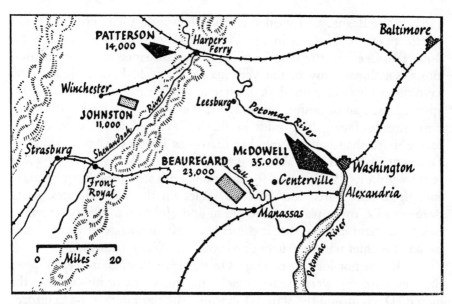

were 76 for the Federals, eight for the Confederates; which, the latter felt, came within a hair of proving their claim that one southern fighting man was worth ten Yankee hirelings. Yet there had been reverses, too. Johnston had abandoned Harpers Ferry in mid-June: a strategic withdrawal, he called it, under pressure from superior numbers. But when the Union commander, Major General Robert Patterson, a sixty-nine-year-old veteran of the War of 1812, crossed the river in early July there was a sharp clash at Falling Waters, casualties being about a dozen on each side, not including fifty Northerners taken prisoner. This too was felt to be a credit to southern arms, considering the odds, even though more of Virginia's "sacred soil" had been yielded to the invader. At the far-off western end of the state the advantage was clearly with the enemy, but this was blamed on bungling and mismanagement of brave troops. All in all, the Confederates were confident and saw far more reasons for pride than despair in the odds. The victories were glorious; the reverses were explicable. Besides, it was said in discussions on the home front, all this was mere jockeying for position, West Pointism, preliminaries leading up to the one big fight that would end the war and establish southern independence for all time.

The first Confederate council of war was held July 14 in the parlor of the Spotswood Hotel, where Davis had temporary quarters. Beauregard, as became the popular conqueror of Sumter, sent an aide down from Manassas to propose a plan of Napoleonic simplicity and brilliance. Reinforced by 20,000 men from Johnston, he would fall upon and shatter the Union army to his front; this accomplished, he would send the reinforcements, plus 10,000 of his own men, back to Johnston, who then could crush the smaller army facing him in the Valley and march through Maryland against Washington from the

north, while Beauregard assailed it from the south; together they would
dictate peace to Lincoln in the White House. This was opposed by
Robert E. Lee, the President's military assistant since the consolidation
into the national army of the Virginia forces he had commanded. The
handsome Virginian, his dark mustache and hair touched with gray,
opposed such an offensive, not only on the obvious grounds that Johnston, already facing long odds in the Valley, had in his whole army
barely more than half the number of troops Beauregard was asking to
have sent eastward, but also on grounds that the Federal army would
retire within its Washington fortifications until it had built up strength
enough to sally forth and turn the tables on the Confederates, using
Beauregard's own plan against him and Johnston. Davis accepted
Lee's judgment, finding that it coincided with his own, and sent the aide
back to his chief with instructions to await the Federal advance.

It was not long in coming. On the 17th Beauregard telegraphed
that his outposts were under attack; the northern army was on the
march. Davis promptly wired Johnston, suggesting that he reinforce
Beauregard at Manassas by giving Patterson the slip; which Johnston
did, arriving by noon of the 20th with the leading elements of his
army while the rest were still en route. The first big battle of the war
was about to be fought.

✗ 3 ✗

Christmas Eve of the year before, William Tecumseh Sherman, superintendent of the Louisiana State Military Academy, was having supper
in his quarters with the school's professor of Latin and Greek, a Virginian named Boyd, when a servant entered with an Alexandria newspaper that told of the secession of South Carolina. Sherman was an
Ohioan, a West Pointer and a former army officer, forty years old,
red-bearded, tall and thin, with sunken temples and a fidgety manner.
He had come South because he liked it, as well as for reasons of health,
being twenty pounds underweight and possibly consumptive; the room
had a smell of niter paper, which he burned for his asthma. Rapidly he
read the story beneath the black headline announcing the dissolution
of the Union, then tossed it into Boyd's lap and strode up and down the
room while the professor read it. Finally he stopped pacing and stood in
front of his friend's chair, shaking a bony finger in the Virginian's face
as if he had the whole fire-eating South there in the room.

"You people of the South don't know what you are doing," he
declared. "This country will be drenched in blood, and God only knows
how it will end. It is all folly, madness, a crime against civilization! You
people speak so lightly of war; you don't know what you're talking
about. War is a terrible thing!" He resumed his pacing, still talking.

"You mistake, too, the people of the North. They are a peaceable people but an earnest people, and they will fight, too. They are not going to let this country be destroyed without a mighty effort to save it. . . . Besides, where are your men and appliances of war to contend against them? The North can make a steam engine, locomotive or railway car; hardly a yard of cloth or a pair of shoes can you make. You are rushing into war with one of the most powerful, ingeniously mechanical and determined people on earth — right at your doors." Then he delivered a prophecy. "You are bound to fail. Only in your spirit and determination are you prepared for war. In all else you are totally unprepared, with a bad cause to start with. At first you will make headway, but as your limited resources begin to fail, shut out from the markets of Europe as you will be, your cause will begin to wane. If your people will but stop and think, they must see that in the end you will surely fail."

In February he resigned from the academy and came north, stopping off in Washington to see his brother John, a senator, who took him for a visit with the President. It was late March by then; Lincoln was at his busiest, harried by office seekers and conflicting counsels on Sumter. When the senator introduced his brother as a competent witness just arrived from the South, Lincoln said, "Ah. How are they getting along down there?"

"They think they are getting along swimmingly," Sherman told him. "They are preparing for war."

"Oh, well," Lincoln said, "I guess we'll manage to keep house."

Sherman left in disgust. In reply to his brother's plea that he stay and resume his military career, Sherman flung out against him and all politicians: "You have got things in a hell of a fix, and you may get them out as best you can!"

He went to St Louis and accepted a position as head of a streetcar company. However, when Sumter was fired on he returned to Washington, and after refusing a brigadier's commission — saying, to Lincoln's amazement, that he would rather work up to such rank — accepted command of one of the newly organized regiments of regulars. As he came down the White House steps he met a West Point friend and fellow Ohioan, Irvin McDowell, wearing stars on his shoulder straps.

"Hello, Sherman," McDowell said. "What did you ask for?"

"A colonelcy."

"What? You should have asked for a brigadier general's rank. You're just as fit for it as I am."

"I know it," Sherman snapped.

In his anguished tirade on Christmas Eve, comparing the resources of the two regions about to be at war, the waspish Ohio colonel had made a strong case, mostly within the bounds of truth. Yet he could have made a still stronger case, entirely within such bounds, by the use of statistics from the 1860 census. According to this, the southern population was nine million, the northern twenty million, and in the disparity of available manpower for the armies the odds were even longer, rising from better than two-to-one to almost four-to-one. White males between the ages of fifteen and forty numbered 1,140,000 in the South, compared to 4,070,000 in the North: a difference mainly due to the fact that more than three and one-half million out of the total southern population were Negroes. While these of course would contribute to the overall strength, by service as agricultural workers and diggers of intrenchments, their value was about offset by the fact that the North would be open to immigration — particularly from Germany and Ireland, both of which would furnish men in considerable numbers — as well as by the additional fact that the Negroes themselves would constitute a recruitable body for the invaders; 186,017, nearly all of them southern, were to enroll in the northern armies before the finish.

Sherman, however, had underrated the manufacturing capacity of the South. For the past decade the Tredegar Iron Works in Richmond had been building locomotives for domestic and foreign use, as well as projectiles and cannon for the U.S. Navy, and only the previous year a steam fire engine produced for the Russian government had been exhibited in the North before being shipped abroad. All the same, the colonel was mainly right. It was in just this field that the odds were longest. The North had 110,000 manufacturing establishments, the South 18,000 — 1,300,000 industrial workers, compared to 110,000 — Massachusetts alone producing over sixty percent more manufactured goods than the whole Confederacy, Pennsylvania nearly twice as much, and New York more than twice. Only in land area — and only then in a special sense — could the South, with its eleven states, out-statistic the twenty-two states of the North: 780,000 square miles as opposed to 670,000 in the area including Texas and the first tier of states west of the Mississippi. Yet this was a doubtful advantage at best, as might be seen by comparing the railway systems. The South had 9000 miles, the North 22,000, in both cases about a mile of track to every thousand persons. The North, with better than double the mileage in an area somewhat smaller, was obviously better able to move and feed her armies.

Statistically, therefore, Sherman had solid ground for his judgment, "You are bound to fail." Yet wars were seldom begun or even waged according to statistics. Nor were they always won on such a basis. The South had the proud example of the American Revolution, where the odds were even longer against those in rebellion. Now as then, she could reason, the nations of Europe, hungry for produce for their mills, would welcome the establishment of a new, tariff-free market for their goods, as well as the crippling of a growing competitor. And now among the nations offering aid there would be not only France, as in the earlier war for independence, but also the former adversary England, who was most powerful in just those directions where the Confederacy was statistically most weak.

What was more, aside from the likelihood of foreign intervention, there were other advantages not listed in those tables dribbling decimals down the pages. Principal among these, in the southern mind at any rate, was the worth of the individual soldier. The Southerner, being accustomed to command under the plantation system, as well as to the rigors of outdoor living and the use of horse and gun, would obviously make the superior trooper or infantryman or cannoneer. If the North took pride in her million-odd industrial workers, the South could not see it so; "pasty-faced mechanics," she called such, and accounted them a downright liability in any army, jumpy and apt to run from the first danger.

Such beliefs, though in fact they appeared to be borne out in the opening days of the conflict, were mostly prejudices and as such might be discounted by an opponent. There were other considerations, more likely to appeal to a professional soldier such as Sherman. Strategically, the South would fight a defensive war, and to her accordingly would proceed all the advantages of the defensive: advantages which had been increasing in ratio to the improvement of modern weapons, until now it was believed and taught that the attacking force on any given field should outnumber the defenders in a proportion of at least two-to-one; three-to-one, some authorities insisted, when the defenders had had time to prepare, which surely would be the case in the matter at hand. A study of the map would show additional difficulties for the North, particularly in the theater lying between the two capitals, where the rivers ran east and west across the line of march, presenting a series of obstacles to the invader. (In the West it would be otherwise; there the rivers ran north and south for the most part, broad highways for invasion; but few were looking westward in those days.) The northern objective, announced early in the war by the man who would be her leading general, was "unconditional surrender." Against this stern demand, southern soldiers would fight in defense of their homes, with all the fervor and desperation accompanying such a position.

The contrast, of course, would be as true on the home front as in the armies, together with the additional knowledge on both sides that the North could stop fighting at any time, with no loss of independence or personal liberty: whereas the South would lose not only her national existence, but would have to submit, in the course of peace, to any terms the victor might exact under a government that would interpret, and even rewrite, the Constitution in whatever manner seemed most to its advantage. Under such conditions, given the American pride and the American love of liberty and self-government, it seemed certain that the South would fight with all her strength. Whether the North, driven by no such necessities, would exert herself to a similar extent in a war of conquest remained to be seen.

All this, or something like it, must have occurred to Sherman in the months after he left Louisiana for Washington, where he heard Lincoln say with a shrug, "Oh well, I guess we'll manage to keep house." So far had he revised his opinion since that Christmas Eve in his rooms with Professor Boyd, that before the new year was out he informed the Secretary of War that 200,000 troops would be required to put down the rebellion in the Mississippi Valley alone. And it must have gone to convince him even further of a lack of northern awareness and determination when, under suspicion of insanity, he was removed from command of troops for this remark.

★　★　★

On the eve of the great battle for which both North and South were now preparing, Lincoln declared in his July message to Congress: "So large an army as the government now has on foot was never before known, without a soldier in it but who has taken his place there of his own free choice. But more than this, there are many single regiments whose members, one and another, possess full practical knowledge of all the arts, sciences, professions, and whatever else, whether useful or elegant, is known to the world; and there is scarcely one from which there could not be selected a President, a Cabinet, a Congress, and perhaps a Court, abundantly competent to administer the government itself. Nor do I say this is not true also in the army of our late friends, now adversaries in this contest."

This estimate of the American volunteer, though pleasant to contemplate before the shock of battle, was discovered to be far beyond the mark, North and South, especially by drill instructors charged with teaching him the manual of arms and parade ground evolutions of the line — in the course of which it often appeared that, far from being the paragon Lincoln discerned, he did not know his left foot from his right, nor his backside from his front. He took cold easily, filling the nighttime barracks and tent camps with the racking uproar of his coughs. He was short-winded and queasy in the stomach, littering the roadsides in the course of conditioning marches, like so many corpses scattered along the way. What was worse, he showed a surprising bewilderment in learning to handle his rifle.

Yet these were but the shortcomings of recruits throughout the world and down the ages, back to the time of the crossbow and the spear. New problems were encountered, peculiar to the two opposing armies. The soldiers of a northern outfit, sleeping for the first time in the open, had their democratic sensibilities offended when their officers rolled themselves in their blankets a few paces apart from the line of enlisted men. On the other hand, accustomed as they were to instances of caste in civilian life, Southerners had no objections to such privileges of rank. The outrage was intensified, however, when a former social relationship was upset, so that an overseer or a storekeeper, say, was placed above a planter in the army hierarchy. "God damn you, I own niggers up the country!" might be the reply to a distasteful order, while officers were sometimes called to account because of the tone in which they gave commands to certain highborn privates.

Such problems were individual, and as such would be solved by time or cease to matter. Even at the outset it was clear to the discerning eye that the two armies were more alike than different. For all the talk of States Rights and the Union, men volunteered for much the same reasons on both sides: in search of glory or excitement, or from fear of being thought afraid, but mostly because it was the thing to do. The one characteristic they shared beyond all others was a lack of preparedness and an ignorance of what they had to face. Arming themselves with bowie knives and bullet-stopping Bibles, they somehow managed at the same time to believe that the war would be bloodless. Though it was in Boston, it might have been in New Orleans or Atlanta that a mother said earnestly to the regimental commander as the volunteers entrained for the journey south: "We look to you, Colonel Gordon, to bring all of these young men back in safety to their homes."

All shared a belief that the war would be short, and some joined in haste, out of fear that it would be over before they got there. Uniforms were at first a matter of personal taste or the availability of materials, resulting in the following exchange:

"Who's that chap?"

"Guess he's the colonel."

"What sort of a way is that for a colonel to rig himself?"

"Morphodite rig, I guess."

"He aint no colonel; he's one of those new brigadier generals that aint got his uniform yet."

"Half general and half minister."

"Well, I said he was a morphodite."

They were not yet cynical; the soldiers of that war earned their cynicism. They were sentimental, and their favorite songs were sad ones that answered some deep-seated need: "The Dew is on the Blossom," "Lorena," "Aura Lea," "The Girl I Left Behind Me," and the tender "Home, Sweet Home." Yet they kept a biting sense of the ridiculous, which they directed against anything pompous. Northern troops, for example, could poke fun at their favorite battle hymn:

Mary had a little lamb,
Its fleece was white as snow,
Shouting the Battle-Cry of Freedom!
And everywhere that Mary went
The lamb was sure to go,
Shouting the Battle-Cry of Freedom!

Some of their other marching songs were briefer, more sardonic, pretending to a roughness which they had not yet acquired:

Saw my leg off,
Saw my leg off,
Saw my leg off
SHORT!!!

Confederates hardly needed to parody their favorite, "Dixie." The verses were already rollicksome enough:

Old Missus marry Will de Weaver,
William was a gay deceiver —
Look away, look away, look away,
Dixie land!
But when he put his arm around 'er
He smile as fierce as a forty pounder;
Look away, look away, look away,
Dixie land!

Northern troops, however, had a stanza of their own for the southern tune:

I wish I was in Saint Law County,
Two years up and I had my bounty,
Away! Look away! Dixie land!

Southern soldiers objected to such onerous details as guard duty; they had joined the army to fight Yankees, not walk a post and miss their sleep. Similarly, Northerners were glad of a chance to move against the Rebels, yet on practice marches they claimed the right to break ranks for berry-picking along the roadside. At this time there was no agreement in either army as to what the war was about, though on both sides there was a general feeling that each was meeting some sort of challenge flung out by the other. They were rather in the position of two men who, having reached that stage of an argument where one has said to the other, "Step outside," find that the subject of dispute has faded into the background while they concern themselves with the actual fight at hand.

Perhaps the best definition of the conflict was given in conversation by a civilian, James M. Mason of Virginia: "I look upon it then, sir, as a war of sentiment and opinion by one form of society against another form of society." No soldier would have argued with this; but few would have found it satisfactory. They wanted something more immediate and less comprehensive. The formulation of some such definition and identification became the problem of opposing statesmen. Meanwhile, perhaps no soldier in either army gave a better answer — one more readily understandable to his fellow soldiers, at any rate — than a ragged Virginia private, pounced on by the Northerners in a retreat.

"What are you fighting for anyhow?" his captors asked, looking at him. They were genuinely puzzled, for he obviously owned no slaves and seemingly could have little interest in States Rights or even Independence.

"I'm fighting because you're down here," he said.

Chief among the statesmen seeking a more complex definition men could carry into battle were the two leaders, Davis in Richmond and Lincoln in Washington. At the outset it was the former who had the advantage in this respect, for in the southern mind the present contest was a Second American Revolution, fought for principles no less high, against a tyranny no less harsh. In the Confederate capital stood the white frame church where Patrick Henry had said, "Give me liberty or give me death," and eighty-five years later another Virginian, Colonel T. J. Jackson, commanding at Harpers Ferry, could voice the same thought no less nobly: "What is life without honor? Degradation is worse than death. We must think of the living and of those who are to come after us, and see that by God's blessing we transmit to them the freedom we have ourselves inherited."

The choice, then, lay between honor and degradation. There could be no middle ground. Southerners saw themselves as the guardians of the American tradition, which included the right to revolt, and therefore they launched a Conservative revolution. Davis in his inaugural had said, "Our present condition ... illustrates the American idea that government rests upon the consent of the governed. ... The declared purpose of the compact of union from which we have withdrawn was 'to establish justice, insure domestic tranquillity, provide for the common defense, promote the general welfare, and secure the blessings of liberty to ourselves and posterity'; and when, in the judgment of the sovereign States now composing this Confederacy, it had been perverted from the purposes for which it was established, a peaceful appeal to the ballot box declared that, so far as they were concerned, the government created by that compact should cease to exist." For him, as for most Southerners, even those who deplored the war that was now upon them, there was no question of seeing the other side of the proposition. There was no other side. Mrs Davis had defined this outlook long ago: "If anyone disagrees with Mr Davis he resents it and ascribes the difference to the perversity of his opponent."

Afterwards in Richmond he repeated, "All we ask is to be let alone," a remark which the Virginia private was to translate into combat terms when he told his captors, "I'm fighting because you're down here." Davis knew as well as Lincoln that after the balance sheet was struck, after the advantages of the preponderance of manpower and matériel had been weighed against the advantages of the strategical defensive, what would decide the contest was the people's will to resist, on the home front as well as on the field of battle. Time after time he declared that the outcome could not be in doubt. Yet now, as he walked the capital streets, to and from the Spotswood and his office, or rode out to the training camps that ringed the seven-hilled city, though his step was lithe on the pavement and his figure erect in the saddle, he was showing the effects of months of strain.

Men looked at him and wondered. They had been of various minds about him all along, both North and South. Back at the outset, when he first was summoned to Montgomery, while the far-north Bangor *Democrat* was calling him "one of the very, very few gigantic minds which adorn the pages of history," old General Winfield Scott, commander-in-chief of all the Union armies, received the news of Davis' election with words of an entirely different nature. Perhaps recalling their squabble over a mileage report, Scott declared: "I am amazed that any man of judgment should hope for the success of any cause in which Jefferson Davis is a leader. There is contamination in his touch."

Lincoln, too, was careworn. A reporter who had known him during the prairie years, visiting the White House now, found "the same fund of humorous anecdote," but not "the old, free, lingering laugh." His face was seamed, eroded by responsibilities and disappointments, fast becoming the ambiguous tragedy mask of the Brady photographs. Loving the Union with what amounted in his own mind to a religious mysticism, he had overrated that feeling in the South; Sumter had cost him more than he had been prepared to pay for uniting the North. Through these months his main concern had been to avoid offending any faction — "My policy is to have no policy," he told his secretary — with the result that he offended all. Yet this was behind him now; Sumter at least had gained him that, and this perhaps was the greatest gain of all. He was free to evolve and follow a policy at last.

Unlike Davis, in doing this he not only did not find a course of action already laid out for him, with his only task being one of giving it the eloquence of words and the dignity of a firm example; he could not even follow a logical development of his own beliefs as he had announced them in the past, but must in fact reverse himself on certain tenets which he had expressed in words that returned to plague him now and in the years to come. At the time of the Mexican War he had spoken plainly for all to hear: "Any people anywhere being inclined and having the power have the right to rise up and shake off the existing government and form a new one that suits them better. This is a most valuable, a most sacred right — a right which we hope and believe is to liberate the world. Nor is this right confined to cases in which the whole people of an existing government may choose to exercise it. Any portion of such people that can may revolutionize and make their own so much of the territory as they inhabit."

He must raze before he could build, and this he was willing to do. Presently some among those who had criticized him for doing nothing began to wail that he did too much. And with good and relevant cause; for now that the issue was unalterably one of arms, Lincoln took unto himself powers far beyond any ever claimed by a Chief Executive. In late April, for security reasons, he authorized simultaneous raids on every telegraph office in the northern states, seizing the originals and copies of all telegrams sent or received during the past year. As a result of this and other measures, sometimes on no stronger evidence than the suspicions of an informer nursing a grudge, men were taken from their homes in the dead of night, thrown into dungeons, and held without explanation or communication with the outside world. Writs of habeas corpus were denied, including those issued by the Supreme Court of the United States. By the same authority, or in the absence of it, he took millions from the treasury and handed them to private individuals, instructing them to act as purchasing agents for procuring the implements of war at home and abroad. In early May, following the call for 75,000 militiamen, still without congressional sanction, he issued a proclamation increasing the regular army by more than 20,000, the navy by 18,000, and authorizing 42,034 three-year volunteers. On Independence Day, when Congress at last convened upon his call, he explained such extraordinary steps in his message to that body: "It became necessary for me to choose whether I should let the government fall into ruin, or whether . . . availing myself of the broader powers conferred by the Constitution in cases of insurrection, I would make an effort to save it."

Congress bowed its head and agreed. Though Americans grew pale in prison cells without knowing the charges under which they had been snatched from their homes or places of employment, there were guilty men among the innocent, and a dungeon was as good a place as any for a patriot to serve his country through a time of strain. Meanwhile the arsenals were being stocked and the ranks of the armed forces were being filled. By July 6, within three months of the first shot fired in anger, the Secretary of War could report that 64 volunteer regiments of 900 men each, together with 1200 regulars, were in readiness around Washington. These 60,000, composing not one-fourth of the men then under arms in the North, were prepared to march in all their might against the cockpit of the rebellion whenever the Commander in Chief saw fit to order the advance.

For Lincoln, as for "our late friends, now adversaries" to the south, this was a Second American Revolution; but by a different interpretation. The first had been fought to free the new world from the drag of Europe, and now on the verge of her greatest expansion the drag was being applied again, necessitating a second; the revolution, having been extended, must be secured once more by arms against those who would retard and roll it back. This was a war for democracy, for popular government, not only in a national but also in a universal sense. In that same Europe — though France had sold her revolutionary birthright, first for the starry glitter of one Napoleon, and again for the bourgeois security of a second — other nations were striving toward the freedom goal, and as they strove they looked across the water. Here the birthright had not been sold nor the experiment discontinued; here the struggle still went on, until now it faced the greatest test of all. Lincoln saw his country as the keeper of a trust.

On July 4 he said to Congress: "This is essentially a People's war. On the side of the Union it is a struggle for maintaining in the world that form and substance of government whose leading object is to elevate the condition of man, to lift artificial weights from all shoulders, to clear the paths of laudable pursuit for all, to afford all an unfettered start and a fair chance in the race of life. . . . Our popular government has often been called an experiment. Two points in it our people have already settled, the successful establishing and the successful administering of it. One still remains — its successful maintenance against a formidable attempt to overthrow it. It is now for them to demonstrate to the world that those who can fairly carry an election can also suppress a rebellion, that ballots are the rightful and peaceful successors of bullets, and that when ballots have fairly and constitutionally decided, there can be no successful appeal except to ballots themselves at succeeding elections. Such will be a great lesson of peace, teaching men that what they cannot take by an election, neither can they take by war — teaching all the folly of being the beginners of a war."

In early May he had said to his young secretary, "For my part I consider the central idea pervading this struggle is the necessity that is upon us of proving that popular government is not an absurdity. We must settle this question now, whether in a free government the minority have the right to break up the government whenever they choose. If we fail it will go far to prove the incapacity of the people to govern themselves." Two months later, addressing Congress, he developed this theme, just as he was to continue to develop it through the coming months and years, walking the White House corridors at night, speaking from balconies and rear platforms to upturned faces, or looking out over new cemeteries created by this war: "The issue embraces more than the fate of these United States. It presents to the whole family of man the question whether . . . a government of the people, by the same people, can or cannot maintain its territorial integrity against its own domestic foes."

★ ★ ★

These days the military news was mostly good; Lincoln could take pride in the fact that so much had been done so quickly, the armies being strengthened and trained and permanent gains already being made. From northwest Virginia the news was not only good, it was spectacular. Here the contest was between Ohio and Virginia, and the advantage was all with the former. The Federal army had only to cross the Ohio and penetrate the settled river valleys, while the Confederates had to make long marches across the almost trackless Allegheny ridges: 8000 loyal troops against 4000 rebels in an area where the people wanted no part of secession. It was an ideal setting for the emergence of a national hero, and such a hero soon appeared.

At thirty-four, Major General George Brinton McClellan, commanding the Ohio volunteers, had earned both a military and a business reputation in the fifteen years since his graduation near the top of his Academy class, as a distinguished Mexican War soldier, official observer of the Crimean War, designer of the McClellan saddle, superintendent of the Illinois Central, and president of the Ohio & Mississippi Railroad. In late May, directing operations from Cincinnati, he sent troops to Grafton, east of Clarksburg on the B & O, who then marched southward thirty miles against Philippi, where they surprised the Confederates with a night attack, June 3; "the Philippi Races," it was called, for the rebels were demoralized and retreated through rain and darkness to the fastness of the mountains. Then McClellan came up.

"Soldiers!" he announced, in an address struck off on the portable printing press which was part of his camp equipment, "I have heard there was danger here. I have come to place myself at your head and share it with you. I fear now but one thing — that you will not find foemen worthy of your steel."

Seeking such foemen, he pressed the attack. When the southern commander, Brigadier General Robert S. Garnett, retreating up the Tygart Valley, divided his army to defend the passes at Rich Mountain and Laurel Hill, McClellan divided his army, too. Advancing one force to hold Garnett at the latter place, he swung widely to the right with the main body, marching by way of Buckhannon against the rebel detachment on Rich Mountain. Before that place he again divided his forces, sending Brigadier General William S. Rosecrans around by a little-used wagon trail to strike the enemy on the flank. "No prospect of a brilliant victory," he explained, "shall induce me to depart from my intention of gaining success by maneuvering rather than by fighting. I will not throw these raw men of mine into the teeth of artillery and intrenchments if it is possible to avoid it."

Either way, it was brilliant. The flanking column made a rear attack and forced the surrender of the detachment, which in turn rendered Garnett's positon on Laurel Hill untenable; he retreated northward and, having got the remnant of his army across Cheat River, was killed with the rear guard at Carrick's Ford, the first general officer to die in battle on either side. By mid-July the "brief but brilliant campaign," as McClellan called it in his report, was over. He telegraphed Washington: "Our success is complete, and secession is killed in this country." To his troops he issued an address beginning, "Soldiers of the Army of the West! I am more than satisfied with you." It was indeed brilliant, just as the youthful general said, and more; it was Napoleonic. The North had found an answer to the southern Beauregard.

In Lincoln's mind, this western Virginia campaign also served to emphasize a lack of aggressiveness nearer Washington. Patterson had taken Harpers Ferry. Down on the James peninsula Ben Butler at least had shown fight; Big Bethel was better than nothing. But McDowell, with his army of 35,000 around Washington, had demonstrated no such spirit. In late June, responding to a request, he had submitted a plan to General Scott. While Patterson held Johnston fast in the Valley, McDowell proposed "to move against Manassas with a force of thirty thousand of all arms, organized into three columns, with a reserve of ten thousand." Though he warned that his new regiments were "exceedingly raw and the best of them, with few exceptions, not over steady in line," he added that he believed there was every chance of success "if they are well led."

Thus far, nothing had come of this; the old General-in-Chief did not believe in what he called "a little war by piecemeal." Lincoln, however — aware that the time of the three-month volunteers was about to expire before any more than a fraction of them had had a chance to fire a shot at anything in gray — saw in the plan exactly what he had been seeking. At a cabinet meeting, called soon afterwards, General Scott was overruled. McDowell was told to go forward as he proposed.

At first he intended to move on Monday, July 8, but problems of supply and organization delayed him until Tuesday, eight days later, when he issued his march order to the alerted regiments. "The troops will march to the front this afternoon," it began, and included warnings: "The three following things will not be pardonable in any commander: 1st. To come upon a battery or breastwork without a knowledge of its position. 2d. To be surprised. 3d. To fall back. Advance guards, with vedettes well in front and flankers and vigilance, will guard against the first and second."

So they set out, fifty regiments of infantry, ten batteries of field artillery, and one battalion of cavalry, shuffling the hot dust of the Virginia roads. This marching column of approximately 1450 officers and 30,000 men, the largest and finest army on the continent, was led by experienced soldiers and superbly equipped. All five of the division commanders and eight of the eleven brigade commanders were regular army men, and over half of the 55 cannon were rifled. Light marching order was prescribed and Fairfax Courthouse was the immediate march objective, thirteen miles from Arlington, the point of departure. The start had been too late for the army to reach Fairfax that first day, but orders were that it would be cleared by 8 a.m. Wednesday, Centerville being the day's objective, another nine miles down the road and within striking distance of Manassas Junction, where the Confederates were massing.

Perhaps because the warning in the march order had made the leaders meticulous and over-ambush-conscious, and certainly because of the inexperience of the troops, no such schedule could be kept. Accordion-action in the column caused the men to have to trot to keep up, equipment clanking, or stand in the stifling heat while the dust set tled; they hooted and complained and fell out from time to time for berry-picking, just as they had done on practice marches. It was all the army could do to reach Fairfax Wednesday night, and at nightfall Thursday the column was just approaching Centerville, 22 miles from the starting point after two and one-half days on the road, stop and go but mostly stop. Then it was found that the men did not have in their haversacks the cooked rations McDowell's order had said "they must have." Friday was spent correcting this and other matters; Saturday was used up by reconnaissance, studying maps and locating approaches to and around the enemy assembled at Manassas. Beauregard thus had been presented with two days of grace, by which time McDowell heard a rumor that Johnston, out in the Valley, had given Patterson the slip and was at hand. He took the news with what calmness he had left, forwarded it to Washington, and set about completing his battle plan. Johnston or no Johnston, the attack was scheduled for first light, Sunday morning.

Lincoln in Washington and Davis in Richmond, one hundred miles apart, now were exposed for the first time to the ordeal of waiting for news of the outcome of a battle in progress between the two capitals. The northern President took it best. When McDowell had asked for a little more time for training, Lincoln told him, "You are green, it is true; but they are green also. You are all green alike." Now that the armies were arrayed and the guns were speaking, Lincoln kept this calmness. The Sunday morning news was reassuring; even old General Scott saw victory in the telegrams from Virginia. Lincoln attended church, came back for lunch and more exultant telegrams, and went for a carriage drive in the late afternoon, believing the battle won.

Davis, being more in the dark, experienced more alarm. Beauregard's wire on the 17th had told him, "The enemy has assailed my outposts in heavy force. I have fallen back on the line of Bull Run, and will make a stand at Mitchell's Ford." He spoke of retiring farther, possibly all the way to the Rappahannock, and closed with a plea for reinforcements for his 29 regiments and 29 guns, only nine of which were rifled. Davis sent what he could, including three regiments and a battery from Fredericksburg, and directed Johnston to move his army to Manassas "if practicable." Johnston's 18 regiments and 20 smooth-bore guns, even if they all arrived in time, would not bring Beauregard up to the reported strength of the Federals, for of the fifty regiments thus assembled to meet the fifty of the enemy, 1700 of the Valley soldiers — the equivalent of two regiments — were down with the measles. Presently, however, it seemed not to matter, or to be no more than a lost academic possibility. For that same Wednesday afternoon in Richmond another telegram arrived from Beauregard: "I believe this proposed movement of General Johnston is too late. Enemy will attack me in force tomorrow morning."

Thursday came and passed, and there was no attack. Then Friday came, and still the wire brought no word of battle. Davis kept busy, forwarding every corporal's guard he could lay hands on. At noon Saturday Johnston reached Manassas with the van of his army, the rest coming along behind as fast as the overworked railroad could transport them. Sunday came and Davis, a soldier himself, could wait no longer. He took a special northbound train.

In mid-afternoon, as it neared the Junction, there were so many signs of a defeat that the conductor would not permit the train to proceed, fearing it would be captured. But Davis was determined to go on. The engine was uncoupled and the President mounted the cab, riding toward the boom of guns and, now, the clatter of musketry. Beyond the Junction he secured a horse and continued north. Fugitives streamed around and past him, the wounded and the ones who had lost nerve. "Go back!" he told them. "Do your duty and you can save the day." Most of the powder-grimed men did not bother to answer the tall, clean civilian riding into the smoky uproar they had just come out of. Others shouted warnings of disaster. The battle had been lost, they cried; the army had been routed. Davis rode on toward the front.

First Blood; New Conceptions

★ ✗ ☆

IRVIN McDOWELL HAD COME A LONG WAY since he said to Sherman on the White House steps in April, "You should have asked for a brigadier general's rank. You're just as fit for it as I am." Now perhaps not even Sherman, still a colonel, commanding a brigade in his fellow Ohioan's army, would have replied as he did then. A West Pointer, in his early forties — he and Beauregard had been classmates — McDowell was six feet tall and heavy-set, with dark brown hair and a grizzled beard worn in the French style. He had attended military school in France and later spent a year's leave of absence there, so that, in addition to wearing a distinctive beard, he was one of the few regular army officers with a first-hand knowledge of the classical tactics texts, mostly French. His manner was modest and friendly in the main, but this was marred from time to time by a tendency to be impulsive and dogmatic in conversation, which offended many people. Some were appalled as well by his gargantuan appetite, one witness telling how he watched in dismay while McDowell, after a full meal, polished off a whole watermelon for dessert and pronounced it "monstrous fine!" He had a strong will along certain lines, as for instance in his belief that alcohol was an evil. Once when his horse fell on him and knocked him out, the surgeon who tried to administer some brandy found his teeth so firmly clamped that they could not be pried apart, and McDowell was proud that, even unconscious, he would not take liquor.

Now, indeed, marching at the head of an army whose fitness for testing under fire he himself had doubted, he had need to clamp his teeth still tighter and call on all his self-control. Since setting out, prodded into motion by a civilian President who discounted the unpreparedness by remarking that the men of both armies were "green alike" — which did not at all take into account that one of them (McDowell's) would

be required to execute a tactical march in the presence of the enemy —
he had watched his fears come true. While congressmen and other members of Washington society, some of them accompanied by ladies with
picnic hampers, harried the column with buggies and gigs, the troops
went along with the lark, lending the march the holiday air of an outing.
They not only broke ranks for berry-picking; they discarded their
packs and "spare" equipment, including their cumbersome cartridge
boxes, and ate up the rations intended to carry them through the fighting.

Re-issuing ammunition and food had cost him a day of valuable
time, in addition to the one already lost in wretched marching, and
now as he spent another day with his army brought up short at Centerville while he explored the roads and fords leading down to and
across Bull Run, where the rebels were improving their position, the
worst of his fears was rumored to be fact: Johnston had reached
Manassas, leaving Patterson holding the bag out in the Valley. As he
rose before daylight Sunday morning, having completed his reconnaissance, issued the orders for attack, and eaten his usual oversized supper
the night before, it was no wonder he was experiencing the discomfort
of an upset digestion. Even McDowell's iron stomach had gone back on
him, cramping his midriff with twinges of pain and tightening the tension on his nerves.

Despite the twinges as he waited for the roar of guns to announce that the attack was rolling, there was confidence in his bearing.
He felt that his tactical plan, based as it was on careful preparations,
was a sound one. A study of the map had shown a battlefield resembling
a spraddled X. Bull Run flowed from the northwest to the southeast
to form one cross-member; Warrenton Turnpike ran arrow straight,
southwest-northeast, to form the other. The stream was steep-banked,
dominated by high ground and difficult to cross except at fords above
and below a stone bridge spanning the run where the turnpike intersected it. McDowell had planned to attack on the left, that flank affording the best approach to Richmond; but when reconnaissance showed
that the fords below the bridge were strongly held by rebel infantry
and artillery, he looked to his right. Upstream, out the western arm
of the X, he found what he was seeking. Cavalry patrols reported good
crossings lightly held in that direction: one at Sudley Springs, all the
way out the western arm, and another about halfway out. Both were
suitable for wheeled vehicles, the troopers reported, which meant that
the main effort, launched by way of these two crossings, could be supported by the superior Federal artillery. Now McDowell had his attack
plan, and he committed it to paper.

Of his four divisions, each with about 8000 men, two would
demonstrate against the run, while the other two executed a turning
movement against the Confederate left flank. The First Division, under

Brigadier General Daniel Tyler, would move "toward the stone bridge . . . to feint the main attack upon this point." The Fourth Division, under Colonel D. S. Miles, would be held in reserve near Centerville, at the tip of the eastern arm of the X, but one of its brigades would make a "false attack" on Blackburn's Ford, halfway down the eastern leg and midway between Centerville and Manassas. As the Second and Third Divisions, under Colonels David Hunter and S. P. Heintzelman, having made their turning movement and launched their attack, swept down the south bank of the stream, crumpling the Confederate line of battle, they would uncover the bridge and the fords, permitting the First and Fourth Divisions to cross the run and strengthen the main effort with fresh troops. This time there were no admonitions as to what would "not be pardonable"; the troops were to drive right through, with more of savagery than caution. Richmond lay beyond the roll of the southern horizon.

Sound as the plan was, it was also complicated, involving two feints by half the army and a flank attack by the other half, with the main effort to be made at right angles to the line of advance. McDowell knew that much depended on soldierly obedience to orders. Yet his commanders were regulars, and despite their clumsy performance on the long march, he felt that he could count on them for a short one. As a professional soldier he also knew that much would depend on luck, good and bad, but in this connection all he could do was hope for the former and guard against the latter. For one thing, to forestall delay he could order an early start, and this he did. The holding divisions were to leave their camps by 3 a.m. to open the demonstrations at Stone Bridge and Blackburn's Ford, while the turning column was to set out even earlier, at 2 o'clock, in order to clear Sudley Springs by 7 at the latest.

And so it was. The troops lurched into motion on schedule, some having had but very little sleep, others having had no sleep at all, and now again it was stop and go but mostly stop, just as on the other march, except that now there was the added confusion of darkness and bone-deep weariness as they stumbled over logs and roots and were stabbed at by branches in the woods, clanking as they ran to catch up or stood stock-still to breathe the thick dust of the "sacred soil." About 9.30 — two and one-half hours behind schedule — the head of the column reached Sudley Springs, where the men were halted to rest and drink. Away downstream, opposite the stone bridge and the ford, the guns of the other two divisions had been booming with false aggressiveness for more than three hours now.

Beauregard at Manassas, midway between the straddled feet of the X, had no intention of awaiting his classmate's pleasure. When Johnston had joined him Saturday with about half of his 9000 men, the rest being due to arrive in the night, the Creole general's spirits rose. Now that his army was about to be almost equal to the enemy's, he would attack. He made his dispositions accordingly, concentrating his regiments along the eastern leg of the X, from Stone Bridge down to Union Mills Ford, where the crossing would be made in force to envelop the Federal left and crush it while he marched on Centerville.

Thus Beauregard and McDowell, on opposite sides of Bull Run, had more or less identical plans, each intending to execute a turning movement by the right flank to strike his opponent's left. If both had moved according to plan, the two armies might have grappled and spun round and round, like a pair of dancers clutching each other and twirling to the accompaniment of cannon. However, this could only happen if both moved on schedule. And late as McDowell was, Beauregard was later.

In the first place there was trouble on the railroad from Manassas Gap, and though some of Johnston's men had been assigned a share in the forward movement, the remainder of them did not arrive that night. In the second place, the attack order was ambiguous and vague. There was to be an advance across the run, then an advance on Centerville, and though each section of the plan ended: "The order to advance will be given by the commander in chief," it was not clear to the brigade commanders just which advance was meant. They took it to mean the advance on the crossing, whereas Beauregard intended it to mean the second advance, after the crossing had been forced. Accordingly, early Sunday morning at Manassas, while Beauregard listened for the roar of guns, there was only silence from the right.

Then there arrived from Mitchell's Ford, two miles below Stone Bridge, a messenger who reported that the enemy had appeared in strength to the left front of that position; and as if to reinforce this information there came a sound of firing from the vicinity of the bridge. To guard against a crossing, Beauregard sent his reserve brigades, under Brigadier Generals Barnard Bee and T. J. Jackson, to strengthen the few troops he had stationed there, on the left flank of his army. All this time he listened for the boom of cannon to indicate that his attack was underway on the right. From that direction, all he heard was silence; but northward, from the direction of the bridge, the cannonade was swelling to a roar. At 8 o'clock Beauregard left his office at Manassas Junction to establish field headquarters on Lookout Hill, in the rear of Mitchell's Ford.

From there, of course, the roar of guns was louder, coming from both the left and right, Stone Bridge and Blackburn's Ford, but still there were no signs of an advance across the run. By 9 o'clock Beauregard had begun to suspect that the Federal main body was elsewhere, probably on one of his flanks, preparing to surprise him. Just then, as if in substantiation of his fears, a message arrived from a signal officer:

> I see a body of troops crossing Bull Run about two miles above the Stone Bridge. The head of the column is in the woods on this side. The rear of the column is in the woods on the other side. About a half-mile of its length is visible in the open ground between. I can see both infantry and artillery.

Beauregard reacted fast. While a dust cloud floated up from that direction to show the enemy in force, he sent couriers after Bee and Jackson, instructing them to march above the bridge, and ordered Colonel Wade Hampton, just arrived from Richmond with 600 South Carolinians, also to proceed to the exposed flank. When these commands joined the brigade of Colonel N. G. Evans, already posted near the bridge, he would have about 6500 men on the left: barely one-fourth of his army. Still, in spite of a rumor that the mystery column raising its ominous dust cloud might be Patterson, arrived from the Valley with 30,000 men, Beauregard was hoping that somehow the long overdue attack on the enemy left might have smashed through for a counterstroke. Then a message arrived from Brigadier General R. S. Ewell at Union Mills Ford. He had waited all this time for orders; now he was going forward without them. Beauregard despaired. This late, the attack could do no good; it would serve only to make those troops unavailable to help stem whatever success the enemy might achieve on the left. With his army so scattered, it hardly seemed possible to organize any sort of effective resistance. "My heart for a moment failed me," he said later.

Johnston was also there on Lookout Hill, the ranking Confederate, though so far he had left the dispositions in Beauregard's hands, being himself unfamiliar with the terrain. He watched with increasing concern as things went from bad to worse, the dust cloud spreading on the left while Beauregard did what he could to meet the challenge, recalling from across the run the brigades of Ewell, D. R. Jones, and James Longstreet. By 11 o'clock the fury beyond Stone Bridge was approaching crescendo. The tearing clatter of musketry swelled the uproar of the guns, and powdersmoke boiled up dead-white out of the dust. Johnston, chafing under his self-imposed inaction, at last could bear it no longer. "The battle is there," he told Beauregard; "I am going!" And he went.

Beauregard was not far behind him. Remaining only long enough to order Brigadier General T. H. Holmes and Colonel Jubal Early to march their brigades to the left, he overtook Johnston soon after noon, the Virginian having paused to send a couple of unemployed batteries into action, and the two went on together, accompanied by their staffs.

They rode past wounded and frightened men, dazed and blood-stained
stragglers from the fight which they could hear but could not see until,
climbing a wooded hill, they reached the crest at about 12.30, to find
the battle raging below them, a panorama of jetting smoke and furious
movement.

A few gray regiments were in action, their muskets flashing pink
in the swirl of smoke. Others, shattered by the blue onslaught, were
streaming for the rear. Across the line of their retreat a fresh Confederate brigade stood just behind the crest of a ridge adjoining the hill the
generals watched from. Their ranks aligned steadily on both sides of a
battery whose six guns were firing rapidly into the advancing mass of
Federals, these troops had the determined, steadfast appearance of veterans. Otherwise the field had a look of impending disaster.

McDowell at last had got his flanking divisions over the run at
Sudley Springs, doubling the column to speed the crossing. It was
smartly done, the blue ranks closely packed, water squelching in their
shoes after their splash across the creek. But as they emerged from the
woods about a mile south of the ford, Colonel Ambrose Burnside's
Rhode Islanders heading the advance, they ran into fire from two Confederate regiments drawn up to meet them with two smooth-bore six-
pounders barking aggressively on the flank. These were South Carolinians and Louisianians; their commander, Colonel Evans, charged with
defending the stone bridge, had soon determined that the cannonade
there was no more than a feint. Evans — called "Shanks" because of the
thinness of his legs — was an old line soldier, resentful at having been
stationed far to the left of where the main effort was intended. When
he observed the dust cloud to the northwest, beyond the flank of the
army, he saw his opportunity and acted on his own initiative. Leaving
a handful to guard the bridge, he marched his thousand men upstream
to block the path of 13,000 Federals.

The meeting engagement was sudden and furious, the gray troops
having the advantage of firing the first volley. As they were beginning
to come apart under pressure, they were joined by the Mississippians,
Alabamians and Georgians in the brigade of General Bee, who like
Evans had marched without orders toward the point of danger. All
the cotton states were represented, presently reinforced by Hampton's
Legion, which also came onto the field at a critical time. Then, as the
tide turned again, the Federals exerting the pressure of their numbers, in
war as in peace the fire-eaters looked to Virginia. On a ridge to their
rear — as Johnston and Beauregard had observed, arriving at this moment — Jackson's Virginians were staunchly aligned on their guns.

"There is Jackson standing like a stone wall!" Bee shouted. "Let
us determine to die here, and we will conquer."

Jackson too had arrived at a critical moment, but instead of rushing into the melee on the plain, he had formed his troops on the reverse slope of the ridge, protected from artillery and ready for whatever moved against them. When an officer came crying, "General! the day is going against us!" the stern-lipped Jackson calmly replied: "If you think so, sir, you had better not say anything about it." Another reported, "General, they are beating us back!" "Sir, we'll give them the bayonet," Jackson said.

Over the crest and down the hill, high on the western leg of the X, the battle raged around a small frame house where the eighty-year-old widow Judith Henry lay dying. When the Union troops came pounding south from Sudley Springs her invalid sons carried her on a mattress to the shelter of a ravine, but she begged so piteously to be allowed to die in her own bed that they brought her back, and there she had her wish. A shell killed her the instant they laid her down, and her body was riddled with bullets as the house began to flame.

In a dense blue mass, avenging the months of rebel boasting and insults to the flag, the Federal infantry roared to the attack. The advance had cleared the stone bridge now; Tyler's division poured across, adding its weight to the charge. Bee fell, shot as he rallied his men, who leaderless gave back before the cheering ranks of Federal attackers. On they came, their battle flags slanting forward in the sunlight, up the hill and over the crest, where Jackson's men stood sighting down their muskets. For a moment the blue soldiers were outlined black against the sky, and then it was as if the earth exploded in their faces. One volley struck them, then another, and the survivors stumbled back down the slope, where their officers were shouting for them to reform.

By now there were 18,000 Union troops on this quarter of the field. Supported by well-served rifled guns, the men who had been repulsed closed ranks and presently they charged again, up the slope and over the crest where the Virginians were waiting. But it was too late; the crisis had passed. Johnston and Beauregard had come down off the adjoining hill, Beauregard to ride along the battle line, replacing fallen commanders with members of his staff and making at intervals a speech in which, he said, he "sought to infuse into the hearts of my officers and men the confidence and determined spirit of resistance to this wicked invasion of the homes of a free people," while Johnston established a command post to the rear, at a road intersection where troops from the right and reinforcements from the Valley could be rushed to where the issue was in doubt. As fast as they came within reach he spurred them toward the fight on Henry Hill. There, while the battle raged on the forward slope — disintegrated by now into a strung-out, seemingly disconnected series of hand-to-hand skirmishes by knots of men clustered about their shot-ripped flags, each man fighting as if the outcome of the whole battle depended on himself alone — Beauregard used them to strengthen the line along the crest and to extend the left, where McDowell was attempting to envelop the Confederate defense.

The Union commander advanced two batteries of rifled guns, intending to support them with a regiment of New York Fire Zouaves. As these men in baggy trousers were forming off to the right, Colonel J. E. B. Stuart mistook them for an Alabama outfit, similarly clad, which he thought was facing rear, about to retreat. "Don't run, boys; we're here!" he cried, riding toward them at the head of his cavalry regiment. By the time he saw his mistake, it was too late to turn back. So he charged, his troopers slashing at the white turbans of the men in blue and scarlet, who panicked and scattered in gaudy confusion, leaving the eleven guns unsupported, and a Virginia infantry regiment ran forward to deliver at seventy yards a volley that toppled every cannoneer. The guns were out of action.

Back on the crest, having watched all this, the Confederates were cheering. Jackson rode up and down his line. "Steady, men; all's well," he kept saying. Then, as the Federal infantry pushed forward again, he gave his troops instructions: "Hold your fire until they're on you. Then fire and give them the bayonet. And when you charge, yell like furies!"

By now Beauregard had what he had been building toward. Johnston had been feeding him men, including Brigadier General Kirby Smith's brigade from the Valley army, just off the cars from Manassas Gap, and Beauregard had built a solid line along both flanks of Jackson, extending the left westward until it not only met the threat from that direction, but overlapped the Federal right. The general was ready and so were his men, heartened by their recent success and the arrival of reinforcements. About 3.30, as if by signal, the gray line surged forward. "Yell like furies," Jackson had told his soldiers, and now they did. From flank to flank, for the first time in the war, the weird halloo of the rebel yell went up, as if twenty thousand foxhunters were closing on a quarry.

The Federals had watched the rebel line as it thickened and lengthened to their front and on their flank. Now the opposing forces were roughly equal. But the blue troops did not know this; they only knew that the enemy was receiving reinforcements, while they themselves got none. "Where are *our* reserves?" they asked in consternation after the scattering of the zouaves and the loss of their two most effective batteries near the center of the field. Wearied by thirteen hours of marching on dusty roads at night and fighting under a July sun, they began to reason that they had been too thoroughly mismanaged for mere incompetence to account for all the blunders. They were angry and dismayed, and from point to point along the front a strange cry broke out: "Betrayed! We are betrayed! Sold out!" When the long gray line sprang at them, bayonets snapping and glinting in the sunlight as the shrill, unearthly quaver of the rebel yell came surging down the slope, they faltered. Then they broke. They turned and fled past officers on horseback flailing the smoke with sabers while screaming for them to stand. They ran and they kept on running, many of them throwing down their rifles in order to travel lighter and run faster. "Betrayed! Sold out!" some shouted hoarsely as they fled, explaining — as all men apparently always must — the logic behind their fear.

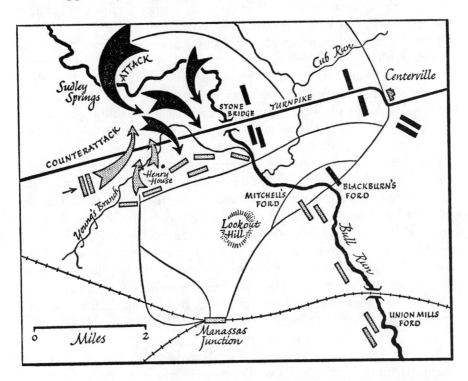

So far the retreat was mainly sullen, with more grim anger than panic in the ranks. It had not yet become a rout, though the Southerners were doing what they could to make it one. Kirby Smith had ridden down the line as his troops came off the cars to form for battle within the sound of guns and the sight of smoke boiling over the northward ridge. "This is the signal, men," he cried, the back of his hand to the bill of his cap; "the watchword is Sumter!" It didn't make much sense but it sounded fine, and the Valley soldiers cheered him riding past. He was wounded as soon as he reached the field; Colonel Arnold Elzey took command. Coming presently into sight of a mass of infantry drawn across the road ahead — whether Union or Confederate none could tell with the naked eye — Elzey halted the column. As he raised his binoculars a breeze stirred the drifting smoke; flags rippled stiffly from their staffs. "Stars and Stripes! Stars and Stripes! Give it to them, boys!" he yelled, and led his regiments forward at a run. Early's brigade had come up, too, their cheers swelling the din on the left as the whole gray line, curving away northeastward along the crest of Henry Hill, came whooping down upon the startled men in blue.

While his flanking column fell back over the run, McDowell did what he could to save the day. Two brigades, withdrawn from the fords below Stone Bridge, along with the one reserve brigade and some regiments just arrived from Alexandria, were combined to form a rally line near Centerville, in hopes that the retreaters from the crushed right flank would fall in here to challenge the Confederate counterattack. But it was no use. Anger was fast giving way to panic as the retreat gathered momentum. These men were bound for the Potomac, along a road that had been traveled prophetically that morning by a regiment of infantry and a battery of field artillery; their enlistments expiring today, they had declined any share in the battle, and deaf alike to pleas and jeers had returned to Washington for discharge. Panic was contagious. Troops from the proposed rally line fell in with the skulkers going past, and now the more or less sullen retreat became a rout, the column once more harried by the carriages and victorias of the junketing politicians who had driven out to see the Union reëstablished. Now, somehow, across the run and down the western leg of that spraddled X, in a roiling cauldron of dust and smoke with fitful, pinkish-yellow stabs of fire mixed in, the carefree lark had been transmuted into something out of a nightmare. "Turn back! Turn back! We are whipped!" the civilians heard the soldiers shout as they came surging up the pike. Darkness spread and the moon came out: a full moon like the one that had flooded the landscape two months ago, when the Grand Army crossed the Potomac to take potshots at an occasional scampering rebel.

Disorderly as the column was, it made good time. In that one night, returning north, McDowell's army covered more distance than it had managed to cover in three days of southward marching the week before.

On the Confederate side there was disorganization, too. It was of a different kind, however, proceeding from the elation of victory rather than from the depression of defeat. The two were strangely alike. Belief that the battle was won produced very much the same effect, as far as concerted action went, as belief that the battle was lost. In either case it was over, and southern leaders could accomplish no more toward organizing pursuit along the turnpike than their northern counterparts could accomplish toward organizing a rally line across it. On the left, above Stone Bridge, the regiments were halted for realignment, all possibility of control being gone; while on the right, where the brigades had forced their way across the fords below the bridge, pursuit was abandoned and the men recalled to the south bank of the run to meet a false alarm of an attack at Union Mills. One brigadier, Longstreet — he had already crossed and recrossed the stream five times that day — was commanded to fall back just as he gave the order for his batteries to open fire on the retreating Federal column. Stuart's cavalry, swinging wide around Sudley Springs, should have been free to accomplish most; but the troopers soon were burdened with so many prisoners picked up along the way that they lost all mobility, and presently they dwindled to a squad. It was the same all along the line. Little could be done to gather the potential fruits of victory.

Even Jefferson Davis, braced for disaster as he rode from Manassas Junction through the backwash of the army, lost some measure of his self-control in the sudden release from anxiety when he emerged to find the Union soldiers fleeing from the charging men in gray. Meeting Colonel Elzey he conferred the first battlefield promotion of the war: "General Elzey, you are the Blücher of the day!" He joined the horseback chase toward Sudley Springs, and everywhere he encountered rejoicing and elation. In the gathering dusk, coming upon a body of men he thought were stragglers, he began a speech to rally them, only to learn that they were Jackson's Virginians, who had done so much to win the battle. Their commander was in a nearby dressing station, having a wounded finger bandaged. "Give me ten thousand men," he was saying, "and I would be in Washington tomorrow."

Davis rather thought so, too. He rode back to see Johnston and Beauregard at the latter's Manassas headquarters. The generals were as elated as their men; but when the President asked what forces were pushing the beaten enemy, they replied that the troops were confused and hungry and needed rest; pursuit had ended for the night. Davis was unwilling to reconcile himself to this, but presently a slow rain came on, turning the dust to mud all over eastern Virginia, and there was no longer even a question of the possibility of pursuit. Out on the field, along the turnpike and the run and in the angles of the X they formed, the drizzle soaked the dead and fell upon the wounded of both armies.

Among them was Major Roberdeau Wheat, commander of the Louisiana Tigers, who had opened the fight alongside Evans above Stone Bridge. He was a lawyer and had been a soldier of fortune, fighting with Carravajal in Mexico, Walker in Nicaragua, and Garibaldi in Sicily; but now a Union bullet had gone through both of his lungs and a surgeon told him he must die.

"I don't feel like dying yet," Wheat said.

The doctor insisted: "There is no instance on record of recovery from such a wound."

"Well, then," the lawyer-soldier replied, "I will put my case on record."

Next morning at breakfast Davis wrote out for Beauregard, subject to the approval of Congress, a promotion to full general. Then he returned to Richmond, where the bodies of General Bee and other leaders killed on yesterday's field were to lie in state, with honor guards and fitting obsequies. In spite of such causes for individual grief, the people in the capital were as elated as the soldiers around Manassas. Here as there, the feeling was that the Yankees had been shown for once and for all. The war was won. Independence was a fact beyond all doubt. Even the casualty lists, the source of their sorrow, reinforced their conviction of superiority to anything the North could bring against them.

The Confederates had lost almost two thousand, but the Union army had lost more than three thousand; 387 were dead in gray, 481 in blue. Only among the wounded were the Northerners outnumbered, 1582 to 1124, and this in itself was interpreted as a credit to the South; what, they asked, could be nobler than for a soldier to bleed for his country? However, they found the principal support for their opinion in the amount of captured equipment and the number of prisoners taken. Fifteen hundred Yankees had thrown down their arms and submitted to being marched away to prison, while in the Confederate ranks only eight were listed as missing, and no one believed that even these had surrendered. Equipment captured during the battle, or garnered from the field when the fighting was over, included 28 artillery pieces, 17 of them rifled, as well as 37 caissons, half a million rounds of small-arms ammunition, 500 muskets, and nine flags.

Later in the week, while southern outpost riders once more gazed across the Potomac at the spires of Washington, the wounded were brought to Richmond to be cared for — including Rob Wheat, who had put his case on record. The ladies turned out with an enthusiasm which sometimes tried the patience of the men. Asked if he wanted his face washed, one replied: "Well, ma'am, it's been washed twenty times already. But go ahead, if you want to." Prisoners came to Richmond, too, where a three-story tobacco warehouse had been hurriedly converted into a military prison. From the sidewalk, citizens tried to bribe the guards for a glimpse at a real live Yankee: especially New York Congressman Alfred Ely, who had strolled too near the scene of battle just as the lines gave way and was discovered trying to hide behind a tree. President Davis sent him two fine white wool blankets to keep him warm in the warehouse prison, and the people in general approved of such chivalry. They felt that they could afford to be magnanimous, now that the war was won.

Lincoln, who had gone out for his Sunday drive believing the battle a Union victory, returned at sundown to find that the Secretary of State had come looking for him, white and shaky, and had left a message that McDowell had been whipped and was falling back. Hurrying to the War Department, he read a telegram confirming the bad news: "General McDowell's army in full retreat through Centerville. The day is lost. Save Washington and the remnants of this army." He returned to the White House and spent the night on a sofa in the cabinet room while bedraggled politicians, with the startled expressions of men emerging from nightmares, brought him eye-witness accounts of the disaster. Next morning, through windows lashed by rain, he watched his soldiers stagger up the streets, many of them so exhausted that they stumbled and slept in yards and on the steps of houses, oblivious to the pelting rain and the women who moved among them offering coffee.

General Scott and others with long faces soon arrived. "Sir, I am the greatest coward in America," Scott told one of them. "I deserve removal because I did not stand up, when my army was not in condition for fighting, and resist it to the last." Lincoln broke in: "Your conversation seems to imply that I forced you to fight this battle." The old general hesitated. He believed this was quite literally true, but he would not be rude. "I have never served a President who has been kinder to me than you have been," he said evasively, leaving Lincoln to draw from this what solace he could.

While Davis was soaring from anxiety to elation and Lincoln was moving in the opposite direction, downhill from elation to anxiety, others around the country and the world were reacting according to their natures. Horace Greeley, who had clamored for invasion, removed the banner "Forward to Richmond!" from the masthead of his New York *Tribune*, and after what he called "my seventh sleepless night — yours, too, doubtless" — wrote to Lincoln: "On every brow sits sullen, scorching, black despair. If it is best for the country and for mankind that we make peace with the rebels at once and on their own terms, do not shrink even from that." Tecumseh Sherman, reassembling his scattered brigade, wrote privately: "Nobody, no man, can save the country. Our men are not good soldiers. They brag, but don't perform, complain sadly if they don't get everything they want, and a march of a few miles uses them up. It will take a long time to overcome these things, and what is in store for us in the future I know not." One English journalist at least believed he could guess what was in store. "So short lived has been the American Union," the London *Times* observed, "that men who saw its rise may live to see its fall."

Allowing for journalistic license, "sullen, scorching, black despair" was scarcely an overstatement. All along the troubled line, from Missouri to the Atlantic, the gloom was lighted at only one point. In western Virginia, scene of the Philippi Races and the rout at Carrick's Ford, there was a commander with a Napoleonic flair who lifted men's hearts and brought cheers. Lincoln looked in that direction, the long sad face grown longer and sadder in the past few hours, and there he believed he found his man of destiny. On that same Monday, while fugitives from Sunday's battle still limped across Long Bridge and slept in the rain, he summoned him by telegraph:

> General George B. McClellan
> Beverly, Virginia:
>   Circumstances make your presence here necessary. Charge Rosecrans or some other general with your present department and come hither without delay.

⚔ 2 ⚔

Lincoln was already dealing with two men of destiny: Robert Anderson, the hero of Sumter, and John Charles Frémont, the California Pathfinder. They were to save Kentucky and Missouri for the Union, both having ties in the states to which they had been sent. Anderson was a Bluegrass native, and Frémont, though Georgia-born, had made important Missouri connections by eloping with the daughter of old Thomas Hart Benton, who lived long enough to be reconciled to the match.

In Kentucky the contest was political, swinging around the problem of the state's declared neutrality. Her sympathies were southern but her interests lay northward, beyond the Ohio, Lincoln having guaranteed the inviolability of her property in slaves. What was more, her desire for peace was reinforced by the knowledge that her "dark and bloody ground," as it was called, would be the scene of bitterest fighting if war came. Therefore, after the furor of Sumter and the departure into Confederate ranks of the eastern border states and Tennessee, the governor and both houses of the legislature announced that Kentucky would defend her borders, north and south, against invaders from either direction, and the people signified their approval in the special congressional election of late June, when nine out of the ten men sent to Washington were Unionists, and again in the August legislature races, which also were overwhelming Union victories.

Meanwhile Kentucky had become a recruiting ground for agents of both armies. The state militia, under Simon Bolivar Buckner, a West Pointer and a wealthy Kentucky aristocrat, was the largest and probably the best-drilled body of nonregular troops in the country. Its 10,000 members were pro-Confederate, but this threat was countered by the Home Guard, swiftly organized under William Nelson, a six-foot five-inch, three-hundred-pound U.S. Navy lieutenant who distributed 10,000 "Lincoln rifles" among men of strong pro-Union beliefs. Whatever caution their political leaders might show, Kentuckians did not stand aside from individual bloodshed; 35,000 would fight for the South before the war was over, while more than twice that many would fight for the

North, including 14,000 of her Negroes. Here the conflict was quite literally "a war of brothers." Senator John J. Crittenden typified the predicament of his state; he who had done so much for peace had two sons who became major generals in the opposing armies. Likewise Henry Clay, that other great compromiser, had three grandsons who fought to preserve the Union and four who enlisted on the other side. All over the state, instances such as these were reproduced and multiplied. Fathers and sons, brothers and cousins were split on issues that split the nation. Kentucky was in truth a house divided. The question was in which direction the house would fall.

Commissioned a brigadier after the public acclaim that greeted him when he landed in New York from Fort Sumter, Anderson was sent west in late August. He had said that his heart was not in the struggle, that if Kentucky seceded he would go to Europe and wait the war out. But now that his native state expressed intentions of holding firm, he determined to take the field. Frail and aged beyond his fifty-six years, he was warned by his physicians that he might break under the stress of active duty: to which, according to a Washington newspaper interview, he replied that "the Union men of Kentucky were calling on him to lead them and that he must and would fall in a most glorious cause."

Out of respect for his state's declared neutrality, and despite his official designation as commander of the Military Department of Kentucky, he established headquarters in Cincinnati, just across the Ohio, and attempted to direct operations from there. He did little, for there was little he could do; which gave the impression that he was biding his time, waiting for the Bluegrass leaders to evolve their own decisions unmolested. Considering their touchy sensibilities — so violently in favor of peace that they were willing to fight for it — this was the best he could possibly have done. It was more, at any rate, than his opponent Leonidas Polk could do.

Polk was a West Pointer who had gone into the ministry and done well. Aged fifty-five at the outbreak of the war, he was Episcopal Bishop of Louisiana. Visiting Richmond in June he dropped by to see his Academy schoolmate Jefferson Davis, and when he emerged from the President's office he held, to his surprise, the commission of a Confederate major general and appointment to the command of troops in the Mississippi Valley. Northerners expressed horror at such sacrilege, but Southerners were delighted with this transfer from the Army of the Lord. Polk himself, considering his new duty temporary, did not resign his bishopric. He felt, he said, "like a man who has dropped his business when his house is on fire, to put it out; for as soon as the war is over I will return to my proper calling."

Just now, however, the bishop-general was alarmed at the development of events in Kentucky, which had gone from bad to worse from the Confederate point of view. Not only was the legislature pro-

Unionist, but in mid-July, feeling that his position was somehow dishonorable or anyhow equivocal, Buckner resigned as head of the militia, which then disbanded, its guns and equipment passing into the hands of the Home Guard. At this rate Kentucky would soon be irretrievably gone. One of the first things Polk did when he arrived at his Memphis headquarters was to order a concentration of Confederate troops at Union City, in northwest Tennessee, prepared to cross the border and occupy Columbus, Kentucky — which Polk saw as the key to the upper Mississippi — whenever some Federal act of aggression made such a movement plausible.

Anderson, marking time in Cincinnati, would give him no such provocation, but Frémont, across the way, was more precipitate. On August 28 he instructed Brigadier General Ulysses S. Grant to take command of "a combined forward movement" and "to occupy Columbus, Ky. as soon as possible." That city's pro-southern citizens had already petitioned the Confederates to march to their defense, and now that he had an excuse Polk moved quickly. Not waiting to deal with an accomplished act of aggression, but hastening to forestall one, he ordered his troops to cross the border. They occupied Columbus on September 4, the day before the Federals were scheduled to arrive. Grant, thus checked, countered by crossing the border and occupying Paducah, strategically located at the junction of the Ohio and the Tennessee. Now both Confederate and Union soldiers, in rapid sequence, had violated Kentucky's declared neutrality.

The reaction, which was immediate, was directed mainly against the Southerners, since they had entered first and could make a less effective show of moral indignation. Anderson left Cincinnati at last, transferring his headquarters to Frankfort, where he appeared before the legislature on September 7 and was given an ovation. Four days later, though it sent no such angry communication to Grant or Frémont, this body issued a formal demand that the Confederacy withdraw its troops. When this injunction was not obeyed, it passed on the 18th an act creating a military force to expel them.

Neutrality was over. Politically, Kentucky had chosen the Union. She had a star in the Confederate flag and a secessionist legislature at Russellville, but these represented hardly anything more than the Kentuckians in the southern army. If she was to be reclaimed, if the northern boundary of the new nation was to reach the natural barrier of the Ohio, it would have to be accomplished by force of arms.

Much of the credit was due Anderson, who had waited. He had spoken of glory on setting out, but there had been little of that for him in his native Kentucky; he had said goodbye to glory in Charleston harbor. And now his physician's prediction came true. His health broke and he was given indefinite sick leave, Sherman replacing him in mid-October. Thus the Union's first man of destiny left the scene. Afterwards brevetted a major general and retired, he spent the war years in New York City, pointed out on the avenue as he took his daily constitutional, still the hero of Sumter, wearing a long military cloak across his shoulders to hide his stars. He read the war news in the papers and took a particular pride in the career of Sherman, who had served under him as a junior lieutenant in the peacetime army; "One of my boys," he called him.

★ ★ ★

Lincoln's second man of destiny was quite different from the first, as indeed he had need to be. In Missouri the secession question had long since passed the political stage. Here there was bloodshed from the outset, and all through the last half of the opening year it was touch and go, a series of furious skirmishes, marches and countermarches by confused commanders, occupations, evacuations, and several full-scale battles. Jesse James studied tactics here, and Mark Twain skedaddled.

Whatever talents Frémont might show, and he was reputed to have many, the ability to wait and do nothing was not one of them. Heading westward on the day of McDowell's defeat on the plains of Manassas, he fell into Missouri's seething cauldron toward the end of July, when he established headquarters in St Louis. Apprised of the situation — disaffection throughout the state, bands of marauders roaming at will, Confederates massed along the southern border — he sent telegrams in all directions, from Washington D.C. out to California, calling for reinforcements. None were forthcoming, but apparently relieved just by the effort of having tried, Frémont settled down at once to making plans for the future.

Something of a mystic, he was a man of action, too, and within the widening circle of his glory he had a magnetism that drew men to him. With the help of such guides as Kit Carson he had explored and mapped the Rocky Mountain passes through which settlers came west. Under his leadership — the Pathfinder, they called him — they broke California loose from Mexico and joined her to the Union, rewarding Frémont by making him one of her first two senators, as well as one of her first millionaires, and subsequently the Republican Party's first presidential nominee. He was in France at the outbreak of war, but he came straight to Washington, where Lincoln made him a major general and sent him westward. His slender yet muscular body evidenced a youthfulness which the touches of gray in his hair and beard only served to emphasize by contrast, as if they represented not so much his forty-eight years, but rather the width of experience and adventure he had packed into them. His features were regular, his glance piercing. There was drama in his gestures, and his voice had overtones of music.

"I have given you carte blanche. You must use your own judgment, and do the best you can," Lincoln had told him, saying goodbye on the portico of the White House. And now in Missouri Frémont took him at his word.

While the news from Manassas dampened Unionist spirits, he continued to exorcise dismay with works and projects. After ordering intrenchments thrown around St Louis to secure it from attack, he occupied and fortified Cape Girardeau, above Cairo, as well as the railheads at Ironton and Rolla and the state capital at Jefferson City. Such actions were mainly defensive, but Frémont had offensive conceptions as well, and of these such occupations were a part. Poring over strategic maps in his headquarters, which he saw as the storm center of events, he looked beyond the present crisis and evolved a master plan for Federal efforts in the West. Whoever controlled the trunk controlled the tree; whoever held the Mississippi Valley, he discerned from his coign of vantage, "would hold the country by the heart." Missouri was only a starting point, elemental but essential to the plan, "of which the great object was the descent of the Mississippi River." With Memphis and Vicksburg lopped off, and finally New Orleans, the Confederacy would wither like a tree with a severed taproot.

Cairo was the key, and having secured it he went ahead. He began construction of 38 mortar boats and two gunboats to scour the rivers, and ordered Grant to seize Columbus, or, as it turned out — since Polk moved first, and thereby won the race and lost Kentucky — Paducah, which served as well. Whatever fit the plan got full attention; whatever did not fit got brushed aside. Some, in fact, found him too vague and exalted for their taste — Grant, for example, who recorded: "He sat in a room in full uniform with his maps before him. When you went in he would point out one line or another in a mysterious manner, never asking you to take a seat. You left without the least idea of what he meant or what he wanted you to do."

It was true that he was difficult to get at. To protect his privacy from obscure brigadiers like Grant while he worked eighteen hours a day in the three-story St Louis mansion which served as headquarters, he had a bodyguard of 300 men, "the very best material Kentucky could afford; average height 5 feet 11½ inches, and measuring 40½ inches around the breast." Resplendent in feathers and loops of the gold braid known locally as "chicken guts," his personal staff included Hungarians and Italians with titles such as "adlatus to the chief" and names that were hardly pronounceable to a Missouri tongue; Emavic, Meizarras, Kalamaneuzze were three among many. The list ran long, causing one of his Confederate opponents to remark as he read it, "There's too much tail to that kite."

Whether he would soar or not, Frémont kept his gaze on far horizons. Down in the southwest corner of the state he had a compact, well-drilled army of 6000, including 1200 regulars and several batteries of artillery. Its commander, Brigadier General Nathaniel Lyon, had been active against rebellion from the start. Back in May, disguised in women's clothes, including a bonnet and veil to hide his red hair and whiskers, he had ridden in an open carriage to reconnoiter a secessionist camp. Afterwards he surrounded the place, forced its surrender under the muzzles of his guns, and marched the would-be Confederates off to prison, shooting down two dozen civilians when a crowd on the streets of St Louis attempted to interfere. By similar forthright action he had saved for the Union the arms in the Federal arsenal there. He was a hard-bitten, capable New Englander, forty-three years old, well acquainted with violence and well adapted for countering that particular brand of it being met with in Missouri. "I was born among the rocks," he once remarked.

So far, however, Lyon had no part in the plan Frémont was spending long hours evolving. In June he had led his troops southwest, intending to secure that section of the state and then move into Arkansas, with Little Rock as his goal. By early August he was beyond Springfield, near the border, but breakdowns along his line of supply had made his army ragged, ill-shod, low on ammunition, and disheartened. Frémont, intent on his master plan, could send no reinforcements. What was worse, the Confederates encamped to Lyon's front around Cowskin Prairie were growing stronger every day. He estimated their strength at 20,000; it was "impractical to advance." On August 4 he reported: "I am under the painful necessity of retreating, and can at most only hope to make my retreat good. I am in too great haste to explain more fully." On the 6th he fell back to a position around Springfield, and the Confederates came on after him, pausing a few miles south before making the final pounce.

They were not as formidable as Lyon thought, and for several reasons. Though they numbered about 12,000 — twice the size of the Union force — for the most part they were miserably equipped and poorly organized, under commanders who were divided in their counsels and ambitions. The majority were Missouri militia led by Sterling Price, a fifty-two-year-old Virginia-born ex-governor who thought so little of West Pointers that he inserted a notice in the papers, indignantly quashing a rumor that he had received a formal military education. His men had neither uniforms nor tents; many had no arms at all, while others had only shotguns or 1812-style flintlocks, and as substitutes for artillery projectiles they had laid in a stock of smooth stones, rusty chains, and iron rods to be shot from their eight antiquated cannon. The remainder, under Ben McCulloch of Tennessee, forty years old and a former Texas Ranger, were somewhat better equipped, being regular Confederate troops.

Price was a major general, McCulloch a brigadier, both veterans of the Mexican War; but the latter, who held his commission directly from Richmond, did not feel that the former should outrank him, and refused to combine the two forces unless the Missourian would yield command. Price, called Old Pap by his men — they asserted that their general had "won more battles in Mexico than McCulloch ever witnessed" — was so anxious to fall upon Lyon that he agreed to the stipulation. As soon as Lyon began his retreat, McCulloch led the combined forces after him. They went into camp along Wilson's Creek, ten miles short of Springfield, where the Federals had halted. McCulloch drew up plans for attack. The movement began on August 9, but was called off because of threatening rain; the troops returned to camp and settled down to sleep, not bothering to put out pickets. At dawn the storm of Lyon's attack exploded in their rear.

The red-haired Federal was also a veteran of Mexico, where he had won promotion for valor, capturing three guns at Cerro Gordo. In the spirit of those days, instead of waiting to receive attack or risking being struck while in motion, he had decided to deliver a blow that would permit him to retreat unmolested. The fact that he was outnumbered two to one — three to one, as he thought — did not discourage this, but rather — in Lyon's eyes, at any rate — demanded it. He felt that his army would do a better job of delivering an attack than of standing to receive one. With his men somewhat heartened by a day's rest and the arrival of shoes from the railhead at Rolla, he distributed the shoes on the afternoon of the 9th and set out south for Springfield. Soon after midnight, the Confederates having averted a meeting engagement by turning back in the face of lowering weather, he had his troops within striking distance of the rebel camp on Wilson's Creek.

He had not minded the rain, and he counted the darkness a positive advantage. Under its cover he disposed his army for one of those complicated envelopments so popular in the early days of the war, when the generals and the soldiers they commanded were least capable of executing them. One column, under Colonel Franz Sigel — two regiments of infantry, two troops of cavalry, and a six-gun battery of artillery — was sent on a wide swing to hit the enemy rear, while Lyon struck in front with the main body, southward down the western bank where most of the rebels lay snug in their blankets. He detached one regiment of regulars — First Infantry, U.S. Army: about as regular as troops could be — sending them beyond the creek to handle whatever Confederates might have pitched their camps on that side.

Sigel set out; Lyon waited in the darkness. Nothing stirred in the rebel camp. As dawn paled the rising ground beyond the creek, the limbs of trees coming black against the sky, there was a sudden spatter of musketry — the skirmishers had opened fire — then the roar and flash of guns like summer lightning on the far horizon: Sigel had come up from the south and was in action, on time and in place. Lyon ordered the main body forward, east and west of the creek, closing the upper jaw of his tactical vise.

Everything was moiling confusion in the camps along the creek-bed, guns booming north and south as men came out of their blankets in various stages of undress, tousle-haired, half asleep, and badly frightened. Under the stress of that first panic many fled. Some returned, rather shamefaced. Others ran, and kept on running, right out of the war. Yet those who stood were hard-core men from Arkansas and Louisiana, Texas and Missouri, wanting only to be told what to do. McCulloch and his aides soon established a line of resistance, and these men fell in eagerly. Price had yielded the command, but he was there, too, his white hair streaming in the wind as he rode up and down the line of his rallied Missourians, shouting encouragement. Under such leadership, the Southerners assembled in time to meet the attack from both directions. The battle that followed set the pattern for all such encounters in the West.

Few of the romantic preconceptions as to brilliant maneuver and individual gallantry were realized. Fighting at close quarters because of the short-range Confederate flintlocks and muzzle-loading fowling pieces, a regiment would walk up to the firing line, deliver a volley, then reload and deliver another, continuing this until it dissolved and was replaced by another regiment, which repeated the process, melting away in the heat of that furnace and being in turn replaced. No fighting anywhere ever required greater courage, yet individual gallantry seemed strangely out of place. A plume in a man's hat, for example, accom-

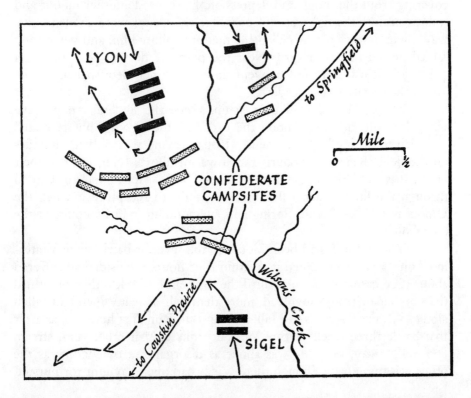

plished nothing except to make him a more conspicuous target. Nor did
the rebel yell ring out on the banks of Wilson's Creek. There was little
cheering on either side; for a cheer seemed as oddly out of place as a
plume. The men went about their deadly business of firing and reloading
and melting away in a grim silence broken only by the rattling crash of
musketry and the deeper roar of guns, with the screams of the injured
sometimes piercing the din. Far from resembling panoplied war, it was
more like reciprocal murder.

In such a battle the weight of numbers told. Sigel's surprise attack
from the south became a rout almost as soon as he encountered resistance.
His men broke, stampeded, and did not stop till they got back to Springfield, having abandoned their colors and all but one of their guns. To the
north, Lyon's men were wavering, too. East of the creek the regulars,
lacking reinforcements, were blasted off the field. The main body, west
of the creek, stood manfully to their work for a while; but presently, the
Confederates clustering thicker and thicker to their front, new regiments arriving after their success in dealing with other columns of attack, the Federals began to look back over their shoulders, apprehensive. Lyon rode among them, calling for them to stand firm in the face
of gathering resistance. As he sought thus to rally them, a bullet creased
his scalp. A second struck his thigh, a third his ankle. His horse was shot
and fell dead under him. Stunned, Lyon limped slowly toward the rear,
shaking his head. "I fear the day is lost," he said. Presently, though, recovering from the shock and depression, he secured another mount and
rode again into the fight, at a place where the troops were about to give
way. Swinging his hat he called for them to follow him, and when they
rallied he led them forward. Near the point of deepest penetration, a
bullet struck his heart and he went down. His men fled, shaken by the
loss of their red-bearded leader.

It was Manassas all over again. Once the Federal troops gave
way, they did not stand upon the order of their going, but retreated
pell-mell to Springfield and then to Rolla, leaving their fallen comrades
on the field: Kansas, Missouri, and Iowa farmboys, lying dead in their
new shoes, and the brave Lyon, whose body McCulloch forwarded
through the lines under a flag of truce, only to recapture it when the
Unionists fell back from Springfield, abandoning it in its coffin in the
courthouse.

The fighting had been bloody; "the severest battle since Waterloo," one participant called it. Within four hours each side had suffered
about 1200 casualties. In one-third the time, and with less than one-third
the number of troops involved, more than half as many men had fallen
along Wilson's Creek as had fallen along Bull Run. Yet here too, as after
that battle three weeks before, on the banks of that other rural stream
800 miles away, one side was about as disorganized by victory as the
other was by defeat. Though there was broad open daylight for pursuit,

the Confederates could not be put into column to press the retreating Federals. All the same, the battle was taken as further proof, if such was needed, of the obvious superiority of the southern fighting man, and in Missouri as in Virginia there was the feeling that, now that the Yankees had been shown what they were up against, there was no real need for giving chase.

In Richmond, President Davis announced the victory in much the same tone of quiet exultation he had used for the announcement in July. Then, out of respect for Missouri's "neutrality," he ordered McCulloch to return to Arkansas with his Confederate troops, awaiting an invitation from the secessionist legislature soon to assemble in Neosho, Lyon having scattered them from Jefferson City in July. Price and his native militiamen followed slowly as the Federals fell back. The battle was therefore inconclusive in results, since Lyon had been retreating anyhow.

One thing it did, at any rate. It removed Frémont's transfixed gaze from far horizons. The lopping descent of the Mississippi could never be accomplished without Missouri under control. Galvanized by reports of the battle, which indicated that he was in danger of losing his starting-point, he reacted first according to pattern, wiring the Secretary of War for reinforcements: "Let the governor of Ohio be ordered forthwith to send me what disposable force he has; also governors of Illinois, Indiana, and Wisconsin. Order the utmost promptitude." This done — though nothing came of it — he sent five regiments to strengthen the defeated men at Rolla, and declared martial law in St Louis. Other rebel columns were reported to be advancing, however, and all over the northern portion of the state, guerillas were coming out of hiding, emboldened by Confederate successes.

As the month wore on, Frémont realized that something had to be done to stem the tide. The week before the battle, Congress had passed a confiscation act prescribing certain penalties against persons in rebellion. Now Frémont issued a proclamation of his own, with real teeth in it, written in one night and printed for distribution the following morning. Drawing a line from Fort Leavenworth to Cape Girardeau, he directed that any unauthorized person found under arms north of this line would be tried by court martial, the sentence being death before a firing squad. In addition he announced as confiscated the property, real and personal, of all Missourians who should be "proved to have taken an active part with their enemies in the field." Nor was that all. "And their slaves, if any they have," he added, "are hereby declared freemen."

Emancipation: feared or hoped for, the word had been spoken at last. The reaction came from several directions: first from down in the southeast corner of the state, where the Missouri brigadier, M. Jeff Thompson, issued a proclamation of his own. "For every member of the Missouri State Guard, or soldier of our allies the Confederate States, who shall be put to death in pursuance of said order of General Frémont," he avowed, "I will *Hang, Draw* and *Quarter* a minion of said Abraham Lincoln . . . so help me God!" Throughout the North, on the other hand, antislavery radicals were delighted. They had wanted a proclamation such as Frémont's all along, and now they had a champion who said plainly, "War consists not only in battles, but in well-considered movements which bring the same results." In Kentucky the reaction was otherwise. A Unionist volunteer company threw down its arms on receiving the news, and the legislature balked on the verge of landing the state officially in the Federal camp. Lincoln thus was caught between two fires, having to offend either the abolitionist wing of his own party, which clamored for emancipation, or the loyal men of the border states, who had been promised nonintervention on the slavery question. Three of the latter wired from Louisville: "There is not a day to be lost in disavowing emancipation, or Kentucky is gone over the mill dam."

Lincoln was circumspect, threading his way. He wrote to Frémont "in a spirit of caution, and not of censure," explaining the predicament and requesting that the Pathfinder modify the edict so as to conform to the recent act of Congress. As for the use of firing squads, he reminded the general that the Confederates would retaliate "man for man, indefinitely," and directed that no shootings were to take place without presidential approval. Frémont waited six days, then replied that he would not "change or shade it. It was worth a victory in the field," he earnestly maintained. As Commander in Chief, Lincoln could *order* it modified; otherwise, the proclamation stood.

This letter was entrusted to no ordinary courier, but was taken to Washington by Jessie Benton Frémont, an illustrious father's ambitious daughter, who had been at her husband's elbow all the while. She arrived after two days and nights on the cars, and, despite the late hour at which she checked into Willard's, sent a note to the White House, asking when she might deliver the message. A card was brought: "Now, at once. A. Lincoln." She had not had time to rest or change her clothes, but she went immediately. The President was waiting. "Well?" he said.

She found his manner "hard," she later declared, and when she handed him the letter he smiled "with an expression not agreeable." When she attempted to reinforce her husband's defense of the proclamation, enlarging upon his explanation that the war must be won by more than the force of arms and that Europe would cheer a blow struck at slavery, Lincoln interrupted her lecture by remarking, "You are quite a female politician." At this she lost her temper and reminded Lincoln that the Pathfinder was beyond the ordinary run of soldiers. If the President wanted to "try titles," he would find Frémont a worthy adversary. "He is a man and I am his wife!" she added hotly. Lincoln had not doubted that Frémont was a man, or that Jessie was his wife; but having stirred up this hornets' nest, he mustered what tact he could to try to calm her. It was not enough. She "left in anger," he said afterwards, "flaunting her handkerchief before my face."

Returning westward she traveled in the wake of a letter addressed to her husband in St Louis. Signed "Your Obt Servt A Lincoln," it began: "Yours of the 8th, in answer to mine of the 2d instant, is just received," and remarked that while the President "perceived in general no objection" to the proclamation, he could not allow an Act of Congress to be overridden; therefore he would assume responsibility for revoking so much of Frémont's edict as failed to conform to that Act. "Your answer ... expresses the preference on your part that I should make an open order for the modification, which I very cheerfully do." Thus he drew the teeth of the proclamation for the sake of the border Unionists, while for the sake of the abolitionists he explained that this was done, not because of its policy — to which he "perceived in general no objection" — but simply because it was unlawful, interfering as it did with the prerogative of Congress, where the most vociferous of the abolitionists sat.

Such wary action pacified the conservatives, but the antislavery radicals were by no means satisfied. In this first open break within his party Lincoln was assailed on the floor of the Senate, in the press, and from the pulpit. Protests were especially loud among the German emigrants in Missouri — "the St Louis Dutch," their enemies called them — whose devotion to the general was redoubled. Jessie Frémont's threat that her husband might set up for himself and try titles with the President began to seem quite possible.

Meanwhile, alarming reports of a different kind were arriving from the West, where $12,000,000 had gone down the drain for steamboats, fortifications, uniforms, food, and ice for sherry cobblers. Graft and extravagances were charged against the men surrounding Frémont — "a gang of California robbers and scoundrels," the head of a congressional investigating committee called them, adding that while the general refused to confer with men of honor and wisdom, these boodlers "rule, control and direct everything." Lincoln wrote to Major General David Hunter, who had commanded the flanking column at Manassas, saying of Frémont: "He needs to have by his side a man of large experience. Will you not, for me, take that place? Your rank is one grade too high to be ordered to it, but will you not serve the country and oblige me by taking it voluntarily?" Hunter knew well enough what was meant. He also knew an opportunity when he saw one; and he set out at once for St Louis.

There was a need for military wisdom and alertness, for bushwhackers were plundering the state while Price moved northward with his 15,000 militia, their shortage of arms somewhat repaired by 3000 Union rifles picked up after the fight at Wilson's Creek. At Lexington they besieged Mulligan's Irish Guard, 2800 men intrenched on the campus of the Masonic College. Price was low on percussion caps, but when a supply arrived in mid-September he attacked, keeping his casualties down by advancing his men behind water-soaked bales of hemp which they jimmied along as a sort of sliding breastwork. The Irish surrendered, and Price, with 3000 more rifles and a single-handed victory to his credit, issued a call for his fellow Missourians to flock to his standard: "Do I hear your shouts? Is that your war-cry which echoes through the land? Are you coming? Fifty thousand men! Missouri shall move to victory with the tread of a giant. Come on, my brave boys, 50,-000 heroic, gallant, unconquerable, Southern men! We await your coming."

Once more Frémont was galvanized. "I am taking the field myself," he telegraphed Washington. "Please notify the President immediately." He assembled five divisions, 38,000 men, and set out after Price. He had not lost sight of his goal, however. "My plan is New Orleans straight," he wrote his wife, October 7 from Tipton, adding: "I think it can be done gloriously."

It might be done gloriously, but not by Frémont; Lincoln had marked him for destruction. Having found that the Pathfinder would not hesitate to embarrass him politically, the President sent observers to investigate his competence in other matters. In addition to the rumors of graft, the Adjutant General and the Secretary of War had both reported the general unfit for his post: an opinion shared by Brigadier General Samuel Curtis in St Louis, who wrote that Frémont lacked "the intelligence, the experience, and the sagacity necessary to his command." Such reports, in themselves, justified removal; but Jessie Frémont's threat, reinforced by warnings from observers — "[Frémont] does not intend to yield his command at your bidding," one flatly declared — made the problem of procedure a difficult one, and Lincoln continued to exercise caution. On October 28 he sent General Curtis two orders for delivery: one relieving Frémont, the other appointing Hunter in his place. Curtis was told to deliver them only on condition that Frémont had not won a battle or was not about to fight one; Lincoln would not risk the clamor that would follow the dismissal of a general on the eve of an engagement or the morrow of a victory.

News of the order had leaked to the press, however, and Frémont, in camp southwest of Springfield, surrounded by his bodyguard and army, was forewarned. Disguised as a farmer with information about the rebels, a captain detailed by Curtis to deliver Lincoln's order got past Frémont's pickets at 5 a.m., November 1. At headquarters he was told that he could not see the general in person but that his information would be passed on. The captain declined, saying he would wait.

He waited hours on end, and then at last was ushered into the presence. Removing the order from the lining of his coat, he handed it to the general. Frémont read it, then frowned. "Sir," he said, trembling with anger, "how did you get admission into my lines?"

There was one chance. A victory would abrogate the order and vindicate his generalship. He placed the disguised captain in arrest to prevent the spread of news of his relief, stirred up the camp, and prepared to fall upon the enemy to his front. But there was no enemy to his front. Undetected, Price had fallen back beyond his reach, recruits and all, and the captain-messenger, having overheard the password, had escaped. Next morning, rounding out one hundred days of glory, Frémont issued a farewell address, beginning: "Soldiers! I regret to leave you," and requesting loyalty to his successor. Then he set out for St Louis to join his wife, who remarked when she received the news of his downfall: "Oh, if my husband had only been more positive! But he never did assert himself enough. That was his greatest fault."

★ ★ ★

While these two men of destiny rose and fell, a third was rising fast, and he kept rising. On the day Frémont received his dismissal, McClellan was appointed to head all the armies of the nation, superseding his old chieftain Winfield Scott. Much had been done in the three months since his arrival, five days after the Bull Run disaster. The army of 50,000 which he then found waiting for him — "a mere collection of regiments cowering on the banks of the Potomac," he called it — had grown to 168,000 well-trained, spirited men, superbly equipped and worshipful of the commander who had accomplished their transformation.

Out in western Virginia when he received the telegram ordering him to "come hither without delay," he rode sixty miles on horseback to the nearest railway station and caught the train for the capital. Given command of the Washington army on the day after his arrival, he found the city "almost in condition to have been taken by a dash of a regiment of cavalry," and himself looked up to from all sides as the deliverer. "I find myself in a new and strange position here," he wrote his wife that evening; "President, cabinet, Gen. Scott, and all deferring to me. By some strange operation of magic I seem to have become the power of the land." With a strong belief in his ability to set things straight, he had gone to work at once. "I see already the main causes of our recent failure," he declared; "I am sure that I can remedy these, and am confident that I can lead these armies of men to victory."

Employing two regiments of regulars as military police — hard-faced men who had stood fast, taking up position after rear-guard position during the Bull Run retreat — he cleared the bars and hotel lobbies of stragglers and shirkers, requiring officers and men alike to show passes

authorizing their absence from their outfits. The crests of the hills ringing the city were fortified, the slopes whitened overnight by tent camps
that sprang up as the three-year volunteers arrived in answer to Lincoln's call for 400,000 on the morrow of Manassas. Soon the men within
the encampments far outnumbered the population of the city they encircled. The clatter of musketry came from the firing ranges, a ragged
uproar punctuated by the cries of sergeants on the drill fields: "Your
left! Your *left!* Now you've *got* it; damn you, *hold* it! *Left!*" Thus Mc-
Clellan set about restoring order, securing the defenses of the capital as
a prelude to the offensive, which he intended to launch as soon as possible. "I shall carry this thing *en grand*," he wrote, "and crush the rebels
in one campaign."

Rigid discipline was the order of the day, and the commander
himself was on hand to see it inforced. Something new had come into
the war; Little Mac, the soldiers called this man who had transformed
them from a whipped mob into a hot-blooded army that seemed never
to have known the taste of defeat. He brought out the best in them and
restored their pride, and they hurrahed whenever he appeared on horseback, which he frequently did, accompanied by his staff, a glittering
cavalcade that included two genuine princes of the blood: the Comte de
Paris, pretender to the throne of France, and the Duc de Chartres,
known respectively to their fellow officers as Captain Parry and Captain Chatters. There was also an American prince among them, John
Jacob Astor, who lived in a style that outshone the Europeans, served by
his own valet, steward, chef, and female companions whom he took
driving four-in-hand, at once the glory and the despair of Washington
society.

Yet even in such company as this, of foreign and domestic roy-
alty, McClellan was dominant. The fame that had preceded him was enhanced by his arrival, and unlike Frémont, whose brilliant first impression soon wore thin, McClellan improved with acquaintance. He did not
seem young; he *was* young, with all the vigor and clear-eyed forcefulness that went with being thirty-four. His eyes were blue, unclouded by
suspicion, his glance direct. He wore his dark auburn hair parted far on
the left and brushed straight across, adding a certain boyish charm to his
air of forthright manliness. Clean-shaven save for a faint goatee and a
heavy, rather straggly mustache which hid his mouth except when he
threw back his head to laugh, he had strong, regular features that gave
cartoonists little to catch hold of. He was of average height, five feet
nine and one-half inches, yet was so robust and stockily built — his chest
massive, his well-shaped head set firmly on a muscular neck; "a neck such
as not one man in ten thousand possesses," an admirer wrote — that he
seemed short. The Young Napoleon, journalists had begun to call him,
and photographers posed him standing with folded arms, frowning into
the lens as if he were dictating terms for the camera's surrender.

Galloping twelve hours a day or poring over paperwork by lamplight, he had in fact the Napoleonic touch. Men looking at him somehow saw themselves as they would have liked to be, and he could therefore draw on their best efforts. He could be firm or he could temper justice. When two regiments mutinied, declaring that their time was up and they were leaving, McClellan handled each in a different way. The ringleaders of one were sent to the Dry Tortugas to serve out their enlistments at hard labor. In the other case he merely took away the regimental colors and kept them in the hall of his headquarters until the mutineers should earn by good behavior the right to have them back, which they presently did. Both regiments soon cheered him to the echo whenever he came riding through their camps.

Within ten days of his arrival he could write, "I have restored order completely." Training now entered a new phase, with emphasis on the development of unit pride, as the men learned to polish equipment to new degrees of brightness and step to parade-ground music. Reviews were staged, the massed columns swinging past reviewing stands, eyes-right, guidons snapping, where the generals and distinguished civilians stood and ladies in hoop skirts watched from under parasols. Then, for climax, McClellan himself rode down the line, his charger Dan Webster setting a pace that made the staff string out behind, the rather desperate faces of the junior officers at the rear affording much amusement to the men in ranks. Yet even they, who had sat up half the night, scrubbing and polishing cloth and leather, could see the purpose behind the panoply and the results that purpose yielded. The young general had an eye for everything. A dingy cartridge box or a special gleam on a pair of shoes could bring a sudden frown or a smile of pride, and the men were disconsolate or happy, depending on which expression flickered across the youthful face. They cheered him riding past, and when he acknowledged the cheers with his jaunty salute, they cheered again. Even the salute was something special. He "gave his cap a little twirl," one witness wrote, "which with his bow and smile seemed to carry a little of personal good fellowship even to the humblest private soldier. If the cheer was repeated he would turn in the saddle and repeat the salute." It was reciprocal. Between them they felt that they were forging the finest army the world had ever seen.

Yet all was not as confident in McClellan's mind as the soldiers judged from his manner on parade. In the small hours of the night, alone in his quarters, musing upon the example of McDowell, whose army had been wrecked on the very plains where the Confederates were still massing under the same victorious commanders, he took counsel of his fears. Soon after his arrival, in the flush of early confidence, he had written: "I flatter myself that Beauregard has gained his last victory." Now he wrote, "I have scarcely slept one moment for the last three nights, knowing well that the enemy intend some movement and fully recognizing our own weakness. If Beauregard does not attack to-night I shall look upon it as a dispensation of Providence. He ought to do it." The dispensation was granted, but that did not keep McClellan from complaining: "I am here in a terrible place. The enemy have from three to four times my force."

Such figures were not guesswork. They came from his chief of intelligence, Allan Pinkerton, the railroad detective who had herded Lincoln through Baltimore on the eve of inauguration, and they were detailed and explicit, based on reports from agents planted behind the rebel lines. Earlier in August, Pinkerton had shown his chief that the forces around Manassas amounted to beyond 100,000 men. This estimate grew steadily as the agents grew more industrious, until by early October, as the days drew in and shadows lengthened, McClellan was reporting: "The enemy have a force on the Potomac not less than 150,000 strong, well drilled and equipped, ably commanded, and strongly intrenched."

What was worse — or was at least more irritating — it seemed to him that he not only had to contend with the threat of overwhelming numbers across the river, but there was a Virginian here in Washington against whom he must also fight his way: Lieutenant General Winfield Scott, second only to the Father of his Country on the list of the nation's military heroes and the first person McClellan had called on to pay his respects when he arrived. Scott had been a great man in his day, six feet four and a quarter inches tall, resplendent in epaulets of solid gold and wearing an aura of victory through two wars. Yet now, as he said himself, "broken down by many particular hurts, besides the general infirmities of age," he could no longer mount a horse and had to be assisted out of his chair before he could rise. When he would indicate troop positions on a wall map, an aide stood by to wield the pointer. "I have become an incumbrance to the Army as well as to myself," he confessed, with pain to his enormous pride.

McClellan's original feelings of veneration and pity ("It made me feel a little strangely when I went into the President's last evening with the old general leaning on me; I could see that many marked the contrast") had turned to resentment and exasperation as Scott continued to get in the way of his plans. Regular army officers commanding companies and battalions of regulars should not be transferred to lead brigades and divisions of volunteers; a hard core of trained regulars, officered by regulars, was needed. Divisions should not even be created; the brigade had been the largest unit in the army he took to Mexico, where he had accomplished maneuvers that now were described in the history books and tactics manuals. Ensconced between McClellan and Lincoln, and between McClellan and the War Department, Scott advanced these views and delayed the reorganization. Worst of all, the old general put little stock in the Pinkerton reports. Regardless of what was set down in black and white, he would not believe the Union army was outnumbered. When McClellan reported his fears for the safety of the capital, Scott protested: "Relying upon our numbers, our forts, and the Potomac River, I am confident in the opposite direction."

"He understands nothing, appreciates nothing," McClellan declared on August 8, and on the 9th: "Gen. Scott is the great obstacle. He will not comprehend the danger. I have to fight my way against him." Five days later he was saying outright, "Gen. Scott is the most dangerous antagonist I have." Plainly, the old general had to go. As McClellan had already told his wife, "The people call upon me to save the country. I must save it, and I cannot respect anything that is in the way." It was not his doing, he wrote. "I was called to it; my previous life seems to have been unwittingly directed to this great end."

With military acumen, he attacked where his adversary was weakest: in his pride. Snubbing him in public and differing with him abruptly in private councils, he goaded him into such trembling fury that the old man requested to be placed on the retired list as soon as possible, "to seek the palliatives of physical pain and exertion." Lincoln felt he could not spare him yet, however, and asked him to stay on, which Scott reluctantly agreed to do. McClellan kept at him, and at last in early October at a War Department meeting Scott turned heavily in his chair, addressing McClellan who lounged in the doorway: "You were called here by my advice. The times require vigilance and activity. I am not active and never shall be again. When I proposed that you should come here to aid, not supersede me, you had my friendship and confidence. You still have my confidence."

A week before, there had been an incident which seemed to support the old man's opinion that the force across the river might not be as powerful as McClellan claimed. About halfway between Washington and Fairfax Courthouse, less than ten miles from the former, was Munson's Hill, the nearest enemy outpost, from which Confederate pickets could look out and see the unfinished dome of the Capitol itself. On the last day of August, on his own responsibility — partly because the rebels had been taking potshots, but mostly because he could no longer abide the impudence of their dominating an area where his men were learning to drill — a New Jersey colonel pushed his regiment forward against the height. This took courage, for the graybacks had a gun up there, black against the skyline. After a few shots and the fall of a few New Jersey boys, though the cannon itself was providently silent, the colonel fell back, with at least the satisfaction of having protested. A month later, September 28, Johnston apparently having decided that the outpost could be captured or destroyed by a more determined push, the Federals woke to find the hill unoccupied. They went up somewhat cautiously, for the gun was still in position and it seemed unlikely that the rebels would abandon ordinance. Then the revelation came. The cannon was not iron but wood, a peeled log painted black, a Quaker gun.

There was general indignation as the newspapers spread word of how McClellan had been tricked, held at bay by the frown of a wooden cannon. Sightseers, riding out to Munson's Hill to be amused and to exercise their wit, could not see what was clear to army Intelligence: that if Johnston hadn't wanted them to think he was equipped with wooden guns he would never have left one in position when he drew back. With the swift, uncluttered logic of civilians, all they could see was the painted log itself, complete with a pair of rickety wagon wheels, and the fact that the Confederates had fallen back unpushed. Mutterings began to be heard against the Young Napoleon, especially among senators and businessmen, who wanted a short quick fight no matter how bloody. The daily bulletin, "All quiet along the Potomac," which had given the war its first indigenous popular song and which had been so reassuring through the weeks of unease that followed defeat, was greeted now with derision.

Then suddenly, as if to reinforce the army's caution, that quiet was shattered by proof that the rebels on the southern bank had something more than wooden ordinance.

In late October, when the leaves were turning and a brisk promise of winter came down the wind, McClellan received word that Johnston was preparing to evacuate Leesburg, up the Potomac about two-thirds of the way to Harpers Ferry. This time he acted. If Old Joe was ready to fall back, Little Mac at least would give him a nudge to hasten his going.

First, though, he must determine if Johnston was really ready to leave. One division was sent up the Virginia shore to investigate, and another, training in Maryland opposite where the Confederates were reported to be sending their baggage to the rear, was told that it might have a share in the reconnaissance. The Union general across the river halted at Dranesville, ten miles short of Leesburg, content to do his observing from there. The commander on the Maryland side, however — Brigadier General Charles P. Stone, who read his instructions as permission to push things — believed that the best way to discover the enemy's strength was to provoke him into showing it. Accordingly, a couple of regiments were put across the Potomac at Edwards Ferry, while others were sent on a night march to complete the envelopment by crossing at Harrison's Island, three miles upstream.

Here the operation was necessarily slow, being made in three small boats with a combined capacity of 25 men. By dawn, one regiment was on the island, looking out across the other half of the river at the wooded Virginia bank. It reared up tall there, over a hundred feet, steep and mean-looking; Ball's Bluff, it was called, and from beyond its rim they heard a nervous popping of musketry, each shot as flat and distinct as a handclap, only more so. They were Massachusetts boys, and they looked at one another, wondering. No one had told them on the drill field or in bivouac that the war might be like this. They continued the crossing, still in groups of 25, herded by their officers, and took a meandering cow path up the bluff toward the hollow-sounding spatter of rifle fire.

At the top, in explanation of the firing — it had a sharper sound up here, less mysterious but considerably more deadly, with the occasional twang of a ricochet mixed in — they found another Massachusetts outfit drawn up in a glade, returning shots that were coming at them from beyond the brush and timber at the far end of the clearing. These men had crossed the river during the night; their colonel, a Boston lawyer, had taken a patrol almost to Leesburg without uncovering the rebel camp; but presently, coming under fire from scouts or pickets, he had drawn back to the glade above the bluff and assembled his troops to meet the threat that seemed to be building up beyond the brush. He and his men were glad to see their sister Bay State regiment arrive as reinforcements from the island, and he sent word to General Stone of what had happened. In reply the general instructed him to hold what he had: Colonel Edward D. Baker was crossing with his Pennsylvania regiment, and would take command when he arrived.

Baker was someone special, not only a colonel but a full-fledged senator, a one-time Illinois lawyer and an intimate friend of Abraham Lincoln, whose second son had been named for him. Veteran of the Mexican War and the California gold rush, in 1860 he had moved to Oregon at the invitation of the people, who promptly elected him to the U.S. Senate. There he became the Administration's chief far-western spokesman, riding in the presidential carriage on inauguration day and introducing Lincoln for the inaugural address. He welcomed the nation's angry reaction to Sumter; "I want sudden, bold, forward, determined war," he told the Senate, and personally raised a Philadelphia regiment. He did not resign his Senate seat, however, and would not accept a major general's commission from his friend the Commander in Chief, since by law this would have required his resignation from Congress. From time to time he would return from the field, appearing in full uniform on the floor of the Senate, where he would unbuckle his sword, lay it across his desktop, and launch an oratorical attack upon those of his fellow lawmakers who appeared to favor any compromise with secession. At fifty he was clean-shaven and handsome, with a high forehead and a fondness for declaiming poetry. "Press where ye see my white plume shine amidst the ranks of war," he quoted as he took the field.

Now on this October 21, coming up the bluff with his Pennsylvanians, he was happy to be where bullets were flying. "I congratulate you, sir, on the prospect of a battle," he told the Massachusetts colonel, shaking hands as he assumed command. In point of fact, it was more than a prospect; he had a battle on his hands already, as he soon found out.

He had managed to get two guns across the river, and now he put them into action, shelling the brush from which the rebel sniping was getting more vicious all the time. Then he went back to the lip of the bluff and, peering down, saw a New York outfit known as the Tammany Regiment toiling up the cow path. This would make a total of four Union regiments on the field. Baker felt confident and expansive. Spotting the colonel at the head of the climbing column, he waved gaily and greeted him with a quotation from "The Lady of the Lake":

> *"One blast upon your bugle horn*
> *Is worth a thousand men."*

Reaching the top of the bluff, the New York colonel — a West Pointer and the only professional soldier on a field in charge of lawyers and politicians — was amazed to find Baker so confident and buoyant over a situation in which, to the military eye at any rate, the danger in front was exceeded only by the confusion in the rear. The Confederates, holding high ground beyond the brush and timber where their snipers were picking off men in the glade almost at will, obviously were building up to launching an attack; whereas the Federals, backed up to the rim of a steep drop with an unfordable river one hundred feet below, were doing little more than dodging bullets and listening to their senator-colonel sing out quotations from Walter Scott.

About this time, one of the two guns recoiled sharply and top-pled backward off the bluff; the other was already silent, its cannoneers dropped or driven away by snipers. It seemed to the New Yorker that events were moving swiftly toward disaster. Suddenly Baker seemed to realize it, too. He hurried along the wavering line, calling for his soldiers to stand fast. Perhaps he had some counter-movement in mind. If so, no one ever learned it. For just then, by way of climax, he who had called for sudden, bold, forward, determined war received it in the form of a bullet through the brain, which left him not even time for a dying quotation.

The Confederates out in the brush were Mississippians and Virginians, three regiments of the former and one of the latter, brigaded under Shanks Evans, who had marched above the stone bridge at Bull Run to meet McDowell's flank attack head-on. Evans was not here to-day, but his men had absorbed what he had taught them. Maneuvering on familiar ground, they had allowed the Yankees to penetrate almost to their Leesburg camp, then had taken them under fire and followed them back to the bluff. There, while the Federals drew into a compact mass in the ten-acre glade above the river, with reinforcements coming up to render the mass even more compact and the target plumper, the

Southerners kept up a galling fire, some of them even climbing trees to do so. All this while, two of the four regiments returning from a march to meet the empty threat downriver, their battle line was forming in the timber. There was no hurry. By now they saw clearly that the Yanks were too rattled to organize a charge, and they were enjoying their advantage thoroughly; particularly the Mississippians, who were reminded of turkey-shoots down home. It was late afternoon before the gray line was ready. Then their officers led them forward, and the rebel yell quavered above the crash of snapping brush and trampled saplings.

What followed was pandemonium. Colonel Baker had just fallen, and the troops drawn up to meet the onslaught were demoralized when a group of soldiers carried the colonel's body to the rear. They thought it was the beginning of a retreat. As it turned out, they were right. Remembering the limited capacity of the boats, each man wanted to be in the first wave heading for the Maryland shore and no man wanted to be among the last, with all those screeching fiends in gray concentrating their fire on him. "A kind of shiver ran through the huddled mass upon the brow of the cliff," a Confederate later wrote. Then, as he watched, "it gave way; rushed a few steps; then, in one wild, panic-stricken herd, rolled, leaped, tumbled over the precipice." The descent was steep, with jagged rocks, but they would not wait to take the roundabout cowpath. They leaped and kept on leaping, some still clutching their muskets, and tumbled onto the heads and bayonets of the men below, with resultant screams of pain and terror. Presently, the witness added, "the side of the bluff was worn smooth by the number sliding down."

Some Confederates hesitated in pursuit, horrified at the results of the panic they had just been doing their utmost to create. They shook this off, however, and running to the rim of the bluff they fired into the huddled, leaping rout of blue-clad men as fast as they could manipulate ramrods and triggers. On the narrow bank and in the water — lashed by bullets until the surface boiled "as white as in a great hail storm," one declared — the scene was worse than the one back on the summit. The wounded had been coming down all day, to be ferried across for medical care and safety. Just as two such boatloads were leaving, their comrades came hurtling down the bluff. Making straight for the loaded boats, they filled them till they swamped and went all the way under, and those of the wounded too badly hurt to swim were swept away and drowned. A flatboat Colonel Baker had horsed out of a nearby canal, using it to get his guns across, was scrambled into until it was almost awash. The fugitives set out in this, but presently, live men ducking and dodging and shot men falling heavily on the gunwales, it capsized and thirty or forty were drowned. One skiff remained, a sheet-metal lifeboat, which soon was so riddled by bullets that it sank, and that left none.

It was dusk by now, the pearly gunsmoke turning blue, the pink stabs of muzzle-flashes deepening to scarlet as they stitched the lip of the bluff overhead. Marooned, many of the fugitives surrendered. A few removed their clothes and swam to safety across the bullet-lashed Potomac. Still others discovered a neck-deep ford leading over to Harrison's Island and got away in the darkness.

Confederate casualties were negligible, but Union losses approached 1000 — over 200 shot and more than 700 captured. Prominent men were among them, including a grandson of Paul Revere, a son of Oliver Wendell Holmes, and a nephew of James Russell Lowell. Most prominent of all, however, was the senator from Oregon, Edward D. Baker, called Ned by his friend the President. Back in Washington, Lincoln was at army headquarters while the telegraph clicked off news of the disaster. When the death of Ned Baker came over the wire, Lincoln sat for five minutes, stunned, then made his way unaccompanied through the anteroom, breast heaving, tears streaming down his cheeks. As he stepped out into the street he stumbled, groping blindly, and almost fell. Orderlies and newspapermen jumped to help him, but he recovered his balance and went on alone, leaving them the memory of a weeping President.

Thus Lincoln received the news, with sorrow and tears. Baker's fellow congressmen received it otherwise. Their breasts heaved, too, but with quite different emotions. Men who had squirmed with impatience at the army's over-cautiousness in coming to grips with the rebels now raged against a rashness which had snuffed out one of the Senate's brightest stars. Someone had blundered and blundered badly, and they were out to fix the blame, determined to revenge their martyred colleague. And their rage brought out of this clash on the bluff above the Potomac a new influence, a new force to shape the character of the conflict: the Joint Committee on the Conduct of the War. Senator Ben Wade of Ohio was its chairman, an all-out abolitionist with keen little jet-black eyes and bulldog flews, the upper lip overhanging the lower one at the corners of his mouth, a figure to frighten the disloyal or the inefficient or the merely unlucky. Congress was voting a million dollars a day for war expenses, and now they were out to get their money's worth, in the form of at least a share in its prosecution. "We must stir ourselves," Wade said, "on account of the expense."

Star Chamber-like, the committee's meeting room was in the Capitol basement, and here the military were summoned to answer accusations without being faced by their accusers or even being allowed to learn their names. General Stone was the first. It was Stone who had ordered Baker across the river; whatever had happened there was clearly his fault. He was suspect anyhow. Back in September he had issued general orders admonishing his men "not to incite and encourage insubordination among the colored servants in the neighborhood of the camps." That in itself was enough for Wade; but further investigation turned up all sorts of things. There had been strange bonfires, mysterious messengers passing between the lines, and much else. Before long it became clear to the committee that Stone had sent those men across the river to get them butchered, probably after prearrangement with the enemy. He was called up, confronted with the evidence, such as it was — but not with the ones who gave it — and when he protested that he was the man who had guarded the capital through the dark week following Sumter ("I could have surrendered Washington," he reminded them) they were unimpressed. He was relieved of his command, placed in a cell at Fort Lafayette in New York harbor, and kept there under lock and key, an example to all who dared the wrath of the joint committee.

All this took time, a matter of months. The man they were really after was McClellan, who had Democratic leanings — it was true he had voted only once, but that once had been for Douglas — in addition to being a "soft war" man, with a concern for rebel property rights, including slaves. Beyond McClellan was Lincoln, who had some of the same attributes, and if they were not precisely after Lincoln's scalp — he had too many votes behind him for that — they intended at least to put some iron in his backbone. Stone was merely an opportunity that popped up, a chance to install the machine and test it, too, even as it was being installed. The trial run had worked out fine, with Stone lodged in a prison cell beyond the help of Lincoln or McClellan. Now they would pass on to bigger things. Ben Wade and his colleagues were out to make this fight a war to the knife, and Stone was their warning to anyone who might think otherwise.

McClellan was aware of this, of course, and was on guard. "I have a set of men to deal with unscrupulous and false," he told his wife. "If possible they will throw whatever blame there is on my shoulders, and I do not intend to be sacrificed by such people." It made him wary, coupled as it was with a belief that he was outnumbered by the enemy to his front. Ball's Bluff had reinforced that belief, and he felt a deep-down sadness.

"There is many a good fellow that wears the shoulder-straps going under the sod before this thing is over," he told Lincoln soon after they received word of Baker's death. Then he added, by way of consolation: "There is no loss too great to be repaired. If I should get knocked on the head, Mr President, you will put another man into my shoes."

"I want you to take care of yourself," Lincoln said.

Presently there was more cause than ever for him to want Little Mac to take care of himself. Within eleven days of the Ball's Bluff fiasco, General Scott having at last broken completely under the pointed snubs and contradictions, McClellan was given command of all the Union armies. The old Virginian's renewed application for retirement was accepted November 1. "Wherever I may spend my little remainder of life," he wrote, "my frequent and latest prayer will be, 'God save the

Union.'" The same day, McClellan was appointed to fill his place, in addition to remaining in command of the Washington army.

Lincoln was worried that the young general might feel overburdened by the increased responsibility. So that evening — while out in Missouri the captain disguised as a farmer was being held incommunicado, having delivered the order relieving Frémont — Lincoln went to McClellan's headquarters to see how he was bearing up.

He found him in high spirits, glad to be out from under the dead weight of General Scott. Lincoln was pleased to find him so, but he wondered whether McClellan was fully aware of how much he was undertaking. After expressing his pleasure that the change had been made, the President added: "I should be perfectly satisfied if I thought this vast increase of responsibility would not embarrass you."

"It is a great relief, sir!" McClellan answered. "I feel as if several tons were taken from my shoulders today. I am now in contact with you and the Secretary. I am not embarrassed by intervention."

"Well," Lincoln said, "draw on me for all the sense I have, and all the information." Still wondering, however, if McClellan was as aware of the weight that had been added as he was of the weight that had been taken away, he returned to the point: "In addition to your present command, the supreme command of the Army will entail a vast labor upon you."

"I can do it all," McClellan told him.

✕ 3 ✕

After a few hours' sleep the following night, McClellan and his staff got out of their beds at 4 o'clock in the morning, mounted their horses, and, accompanied by a squadron of cavalry, escorted General Scott to the railway station. It was rainy and pitch dark. On the depot platform the gaslight glittered blackly on the officers' rain-suits, so that they seemed clad in lacquered armor.

Touched by this show of respect, as well as by a general order McClellan had issued that day in his praise — "let us do nothing that can cause him to blush for us," it ended; "let no defeat of the army he has so long commanded embitter his last years, but let our victories illuminate the close of a life so grand"— the old warrior was cordial to the man who had made his final weeks in Washington a torment. He sent his regards to the young general's wife and baby, and added that his sensations were "very peculiar" on leaving active duty. Then, the clank of sabers and chink of spur-chains somewhat muffled under the rubberized suits, he received his goodbye salute and boarded the train, which then pulled out.

McClellan returned to his quarters and his bed. Rising for the second time that morning, he found his mind so impressed by the fare-well at the depot a few hours ago that he took time to describe it in a letter to his wife. After forwarding Scott's greetings to her and the new baby, he philosophized on what he had seen: "The sight of this morn-ing was a lesson to me which I hope not soon to forget. I saw there the end of a long, active, and industrious life, the end of the career of the first soldier of his nation; and it was a feeble old man scarce able to walk; hardly anyone there to see him off but his successor. Should I ever become vainglorious and ambitious, remind me of that spectacle."

The old soldier had faded away — had gone, in fact, to live for a time at Delmonico's in New York, where he could get his fill of ter-rapin; "the best food vouchsafed by Providence to man," he called it, admiring a steaming forkful held six inches above his plate. Yet he had left a great deal more behind him than the memory of that final scene from which his young successor drew a moral. In the '40s, command-ing in Mexico, he had conducted, on a live-ammunition training ground, a postgraduate course in the art of war for officers who, having fought against Mexicans, would find a broader scope for their talents when they fought against each other in the '60s. Landing at Vera Cruz, out-flanking Cerro Gordo, cutting loose from his base in hostile country to reduce Chapultepec and occupy Mexico City, he had established models for operations that would be repeated, time and again, on a larger scale, so that to list the men who received their baptism of fire under his direc-tion was practically to call the roll of army commanders and generals-in-chief, both North and South, in the war that was building toward a climax at the time of his retirement. All this was much, but he had done still more. He had provided a plan for total war: Scott's Anaconda.

As a Virginian, older than the capital he was defending, he be-lieved he knew the temper of the people across the Potomac and the Ohio. Their love for the Union was as deep as his own, he believed, and in time — provided they could be made to feel the dull reality of war against a more powerful opponent, without being pricked in their hot-blooded pride by the bayonets of a penetrating army — they would see the error of their angry choice and renounce the men who had led them into a wilderness, away from the direction in which their devotion and true interests lay. Out of this belief he evolved his plan, though what was called an anaconda might better have been described as a water serpent.

All down the eastern seaboard, from Chesapeake Bay to the Florida Keys, thence along the shores of the Gulf, counter-clockwise from the Keys to Matamoros, he would establish a deep-water naval blockade to wall the Confederacy off from Europe and whatever aid might come from that direction. Meanwhile, down the length of the Mississippi, from Cairo past New Orleans, he would send an army of 60,000 "rough-vigor fellows" backed by gunboats, thus cutting the

Southerners off from the cattle and cereals of Texas, as well as from such foreign help as might be forwarded through the neutral ports of Mexico. Having seized all this he would hold on tight, neither advancing nor yielding ground, and within those constricting coils the South would become in very fact a political and economic wilderness, the awful hug of the serpent producing results which bursting shells and prodding bayonets could never bring about. The flame of rebellion, so difficult to stamp out — as an experienced military leader, Scott was thoroughly aware of all the problems of subduing a hostile and determined people — would die from lack of fuel or be smothered by sheer boredom. Unionist sentiment, unprovoked, would reassert itself. The people would come to their senses and force their hot-headed wrong-minded leaders to sue for peace and readmission to the Union, which they never should have left.

Such was Scott's Anaconda. From the outset, it came in for a considerable measure of ridicule — especially from cartoonists, who confused the metaphor by sketching the old general in a turban, sitting cross-legged as he tried to charm the southern cobra with a flute — as well as violent opposition from such spokesmen as Senator-Colonel Baker, who demanded bold and forward war and would not see that either of these adjectives could be applied to the so-called anaconda plan. Also it was believed to have overrated Unionist sentiment in the South, though whether this was so or not was presently removed to the realm of conjecture; McDowell's march on Manassas, which Scott opposed, applied the goad which the plan would have avoided. It certainly ran against the grain of McClellan's expressed intention to "crush the rebels in one campaign" by an overland march on Richmond. Yet in other respects, of all the plans evolved by many men, right up to the end, it was the first to recognize and utilize the North's tremendous advantage of numbers and material, and it was the first to emphasize the importance of the Mississippi Valley in an over-all view of the war.

Lincoln, at any rate, welcomed it, studied it, and acted on those parts of it which seemed to him most feasible at that stage of the contest. On April 19 — the day the 6th Massachusetts was mobbed in Baltimore and the Friday after the Friday whose dawn saw Sumter under fire in Charleston harbor — he proclaimed a blockade of the southern coast. Proclaiming and enforcing were two different things, however, especially considering the size of the fleet charged with transferring the blockade from dry paper to salt water. At that date the Union navy, scattered over the seven seas, included 42 ships, 555 guns, and 7600 sailors, and though by the end of the year this had been consolidated and increased to 264 ships, 2557 guns, and 22,000 sailors, the magnitude of the task ahead made a navy of almost any size seem small.

The anaconda was required to hug a circumference of about five thousand miles, two-fifths dry land and rivers and the remaining three-fifths shoreline. This 3000-mile coastal portion, belly and crotch of the continent, bisected by the phallic droop of the Florida peninsula, was doubled along much of its length, both in the Atlantic and the Gulf, by intricate mazes of sandbars, lagoons, and outlying islands, which, though less forbidding at first glance than the rocky shores of New England, were obviously at second glance much harder to patrol. Nassau and Havana were less than 700 miles, respectively, from Charleston and New Orleans, while Bermuda was but slightly farther from Wilmington. Such good harbors were few, but each had many entrances and outlets. It would be a slow ship, conned by a clumsy skipper indeed, that could not come and go by the dark of the moon, undetected in making its run to or from the safety of those neutral ports.

Knowing all this, Southerners laughed at the anaconda, much as the northern cartoonists were doing, especially that portion of it covered by the blockade proclamation, and predicted — quite accurately, as it turned out — that when Yankee sailors began patrolling the swampy littoral they would discover that even the mosquitoes had enlisted in the resistance. Besides, there was an economic consideration beyond all this, by which the blockade might be reckoned a positive good from the southern point of view, a reinforcement of one of the most powerful weapons in the Confederate arsenal. Cotton, the raw material of Great Britain's second leading industry, as well as the answer to France's feverish quest for prosperity, was the white gold key that would unlock and swing ajar the door through which foreign intervention would come marching. Remembering the effectiveness of Jefferson's embargo on tobacco, of which the Colonies had not controlled the world supply, the South could expect much greater results from an embargo on cotton, on which she held a world monopoly. Going without tobacco had been unpleasant for Europeans, but they would find it downright impossible to manage without cotton. Unfortunately, there had been a bumper crop the year before; French and English warehouses were bulging with the surplus. But that only lengthened the time factor. When the reserve dwindled and the white stream that fed the jennies and looms and the workers who tended them was shut off, Europe would come knocking at Jefferson Davis' door, offering recognition and the goods of war, the might of the British navy and the use of armies that had blasted Napoleon himself clean off the pages of military history. For all these reasons the South could laugh at and even welcome the proposed blockade, which would strengthen one of her strongest weapons in ratio to its own effectiveness. There was much that was amusing, too, in the contemplation of northern ships patrolling the southern coast to inforce a southern embargo. Few sailors and no ships at all had come over voluntarily to the Confederate side when the nation split in two.

Now, belatedly and paradoxically, they would cross over, under orders from their own Commander in Chief.

At the outset the Confederate government, having almost no regular navy, determined to create an irregular one which would function while the other was being built. The Declaration of Paris, an agreement between the European powers five years back, had defined privateering as illegal; but the United States, remembering the success of independent Yankee vessels against the British merchant marine in the War of 1812 — and not knowing, moreover, when she might be engaged in such a war again — had refused to sign the document. So now the Richmond Congress, recalling such successes, too, authorized the issue of letters of marque to the captains of whatever ships might apply. It was characteristic of the current southern opinion of northern morals that they expected many such applications to come from New England skippers attracted by a chance at easy dollars.

These were not forthcoming, but before long about twenty vessels were on the high seas, privateering in the American tradition. Lincoln declared them outright pirates and announced that the crews would be treated as such when captured, with hanging as the penalty after conviction in the courts. Davis, never the man to decline a challenge of any sort, replied that for every Confederate sailor so hanged he would hang a Union soldier of corresponding rank, chosen by lot from among the thousands of prisoners in the Richmond tobacco warehouse.

Thus it stood, threat countering threat, until presently the world was given what appeared to be a chance to see which President had the courage of his convictions. The privateer *Savannah* was taken in June, its crew lodged in a common jail awaiting trial for piracy. Despite the clamor throughout the North in favor of dancing the defendants at a rope end, when the trial was held the New York jury could not agree on a verdict, and thus the crisis passed. Later in the year, however, when the privateer *Jeff Davis* was taken, the crew brought to trial in Philadelphia, convicted of piracy and sentenced to be hanged, Lincoln showed every sign of going ahead: whereupon Davis reinforced his counterthreat by causing lots to be drawn among the Union prisoners. The short-straw men — including that grandson of Paul Revere, captured at Ball's Bluff — were placed in condemned cells to await the action of Abraham Lincoln in reviewing the sentence of the men condemned to death in the City of Brotherly Love.

Lincoln paused and considered; and having reconsidered, he backed down. Though he thus exposed himself to charges of indecision and cowardice, declining to engage in a hanging match with Jefferson Davis, he saved the lives of Union soldiers and Confederate sailors — Americans both — and thereby saved the nation a blot on its record. North and South, however, many persons saw only that Davis had taken the measure of his opponent.

Whatever apparent moral advantage the Confederates gained from this clash of presidential wills, they soon found their bloodless victory offset by three sudden hammer blows struck by the Federal navy — two on the Atlantic coast and one in the Gulf of Mexico: Cape Hatteras and Port Royal, off North and South Carolina, and Ship Island, near New Orleans.

These objectives were the choice of a joint three-man strategy board composed of Army, Navy, and Coast Survey officers appointed to make "a thorough investigation of the coast and harbors, their access and defenses." The fleet was far too small for the enormous job of patrolling the 189 harbor and river openings along the 3549 miles of shoreline between the Potomac and the Rio Grande, and what there was of it was badly in need of ports of refuge, especially along the stormy South Atlantic. Out of this double necessity the blockade gained a new dimension, one in which the army would have a share. Not only could harbor entrances be patrolled; the harbors themselves might be seized, thus reducing the number of points to be guarded and at the same time freeing ships for duty elsewhere. Now, as the summer of the opening year of the war merged into the drawn-out southern fall, it was the task of the strategy board, with its three-headed knowledge of "the coast and harbors, their access and defenses," to select likely targets for the proposed amphibious operations.

The first was modest in scope but effective in execution. Off North Carolina the wide shallows of Pamlico and Albemarle Sounds, inclosed by a barrier of islands and reefs, afforded an ideal anchorage for raiders and blockade runners. Here if anywhere was the place at which the board should point its finger. Off that stormy cape the sea was frequently too rough for a fleet to be able to keep station. The only way to block it was to take it. At Hatteras Inlet, the break in the barrier, the Confederates had built two forts on opposite sides of the passage, Clark and Hatteras. Whoever held these forts held Pamlico Sound, and on August 26 an expedition of fourteen vessels under Flag Officer Silas H. Stringham sailed from Hampton Roads to take them. Among the ships were four transports carrying 860 men under Ben Butler, who thus was given a chance to redeem his blunders at Big Bethel.

This he did, and easily, for the army had almost nothing to do. Stringham, with superior ordinance, stood just outside the range of the rebel guns and for two days threw shells into the forts at will, suffering no hurt himself. Butler's men, put ashore well north of the forts — 300 of them, anyhow; for the surf staved in the landing-boats by the time that many got ashore — marched down the island, wet and hungry, their ammunition ruined by the surf, and arrived in time to watch their general share with Stringham the honor of receiving the surrender of Fort Hatteras, Fort Clark having run up its white flag the day before. Most of the soldiers and three of the ships were left to hold what had been won, while the rest returned to Fortress Monroe with their 615 prisoners. The navy had taken its first Confederate stronghold, and in doing so had reduced its blockade task.

The second offensive operation, down in the Gulf in mid-September, was even simpler, requiring not even the token assistance of troops. Here the lower delta of the many-mouthed Mississippi posed a problem much like Hatteras, with raiders and blockade runners entering and leaving the great port of New Orleans almost at will. Though the threat of storms was not as constant, a tropical hurricane was something a man had to see to believe, and sandbars lurked as dangerous as reefs. All in all, the strategy board perceived that here, too, the only way to block the port effectively was to seize it. The navy was by no means prepared to undertake such an assignment just yet, but the board believed it was ready to make a beginning. Ship Island, off the Mississippi coast, would provide an excellent station for patrolling the eastern delta outlets and the passes down out of Lake Pontchartrain, as well as an ideal base from which to launch the attack on New Orleans itself, if and when the opportunity came. So the board instructed the navy: Take it. And the navy did, together with its uncompleted fortifications, before the Confederates were prepared to fire a shot in its defense. Thus the Union secured its second foothold along the secession coast.

The third and final operation of the year was far more ambitious than the others, neither of which had given the fleet the large, deep-water harbor it needed in order to maintain a year-round blockade of such busy ports as Wilmington, Charleston, and Savannah. About one-third of the way up the palmetto-studded hundred miles of South Carolina littoral lying between the latter two cities, the strategy board found what it was seeking. Port Royal, the finest natural harbor on the southern coast, would float the navies of the world. Obviously, however, though they had no real need for it themselves, having almost no navy, the Confederates were thoroughly aware of what covetous eyes the Union navy was casting in that direction. If it was to be undertaken, the job must be done in strength, after preparation in great secrecy. Both were provided for; the board took no chances it could avoid. The naval member himself, Captain Samuel F. Du Pont, was appointed to head the expedition of 74 vessels, including transports for a land force of 12,000 men. In late October, sailing under sealed orders, this fleet put out from Hampton Roads, considerable pains having been taken to conceal its destination.

Almost at once, Du Pont was struck a double blow by fate — in the form of Confederate intelligence and the weather. He not only lost the advantages of secrecy; he came close to losing his fleet as well. On the day he put out, the Richmond government alerted its coastal defenses, giving warning that the force had sailed. Three days later, November 1, the defenders of the fleet's objective received a specific telegram: "The enemy's expedition is intended for Port Royal." On the same day, the fleet ran into a gale off Hatteras. The wind approaching hurricane strength, two of the ships went down and the crew of a third had to heave her guns into the sea to keep from foundering. By dawn of the following day, November 2, the fleet was so scattered that Du Pont could sight but one sail from the deck of his flagship, the *Wabash*. He continued southward, however, and in clear weather two days later dropped anchor off the bar at Port Royal. Twenty-five of his ships had rejoined by then, together with reinforcements from the Charleston squadron, and others kept bobbing up along the horizon. He spent another two days replacing the rebel-destroyed channel markers, crossing the bar — a dangerous business for the deep-draft *Wabash* — completing his attack plan, and finally holding a conference at which he outlined for his captains the order of battle. At last he was ready, and at 8 o'clock the following morning, November 7, the attack got under way.

He knew what his wooden ships would encounter. At the entrance to Port Royal Sound the enemy held Fort Beauregard, mounting 20 guns on Bay Point to the north, and Fort Walker, mounting 23 guns on Hilton Head to the south. Less than three miles apart, both of these forts were strongly built, their gunners alerted for a week, awaiting the opportunity Du Pont was about to offer them. Somewhere beyond them, too, was a Confederate flotilla of three tugs, mounting one gun each, and a converted river steamer under Commodore Josiah Tattnall, whom Du Pont knew to be a bold and capable officer, having messed with him in what was already known as "the old navy." The forts were Du Pont's main concern, however, and in attempting their reduction he would have no help from the three brigades of soldiers in the transports. Not only were these landsmen still somewhat green about the gills as a result of their experience off Hatteras, but in that storm, along with much else, they had lost nearly all their landing craft. It was to be a job for the naval force alone. In fact, Du Pont preferred it so. The most he would ask of the army was that it stand by to help pick up the pieces.

To accomplish the double reduction he had evolved a novel plan of attack, an order of battle which divided his fighting force into a main squadron of nine of the heaviest frigates and sloops, ranged in line ahead, and a flanking squadron of five gunboats. They would enter the sound in parallel columns, the lighter squadron ranged to starboard, and pass midway between the forts, receiving and returning the fire of both. At a point about two miles beyond the entrance, the main force was to round by the south and come back west, moving slowly past Fort Walker, maintaining the heaviest possible fire, then round to the north and head back east, slowing again as it passed Fort Beauregard.

The flanking squadron, meanwhile, was to peel off and engage the Confederate flotilla or whatever targets of opportunity the rebels might afford, while the main force kept both forts under fire, widening the elliptical attack so as to bring its guns in closer on every turn.

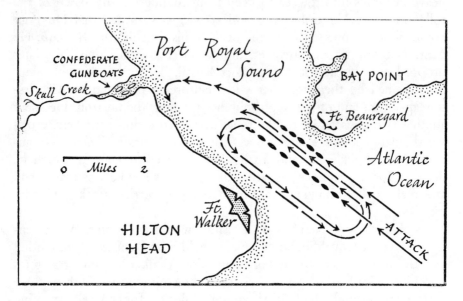

And so it was. At the signal from the commander on the *Wabash*, leading the way across the sunlit water, the fleet steamed forward, two columns in close order. A flash and a roar shot out from Fort Walker, echoed at once by Beauregard. The ships took up the challenge and the fight was on. As they neared the turning point, Tattnall brought his four makeshift warships down the sound, and from a raking position let go several broadsides at the *Wabash* as soon as she came within range. The gunboats gave him their attention then; whereupon the Confederate, with fourteen Union men-of-war to his immediate front, discreetly came about and made a swift, flat-bottomed retreat up Skull Creek, three miles northwest of the fort on Hilton Head. He was out of the fight for good, bottled up by the gunboats, which took station off the creek mouth. According to a Savannah newspaper published five days later, Tattnall dipped his pennant three times in jaunty salute to his old messmate, "regretting his inability to return the highflown compliments of Flag Officer Du Pont in a more satisfactory manner."

By then the Federal captain was busy elsewhere, with little time for compliments, highflown or otherwise. As the main column turned south, beginning its first eastward run, each ship opened with its forward pivot against Fort Walker's northern flank, which Du Pont had learned from reconnaissance was its weakest. The cannon being lodged on the parapet — which, if it increased their range, also increased their vulnerability — several were violently dismounted, others lost their crews, and the gunners, taken thus by enfilade from a direction in which they had not expected to fight, were dismayed. A British correspondent on one of the Union ships saw tall columns of dust spring up from the fort to mark the hits the fleet was scoring, and it looked to him "as if we had suddenly raised from the dust a grove of poplars."

Not that the rebel gunnery had been very effective in the first place. The enemy ships, moving along their elliptical course, with constant changes in speed, range, and deflection, were extremely hard to hit. What was more, the defenders had not wasted their scant powder on anything as unprofitable as target practice, and now that it came to bloody work they found that many of the shells would not fit, the powder was inferior, and the crews became exhausted within an hour of opening fire. All of which, sad as it was in Confederate eyes, was really quite beside the point. Fort Walker — to which Fort Beauregard, across the water, was merely adjunct — had been built to be defended only from dead ahead, against a force moving straight in from the sea. When this became apparent, it became apparent, too, that the fight had been lost from the moment Du Pont conceived his plan of attack. The only conditions left to be satisfied were those of honor.

Erratic or deadly, the firing continued, and as the main squadron steamed slowly past Fort Walker, delivering broadsides at point-blank range, the flanking squadron, maintaining its watch over the mouth of the creek up which Tattnall had retreated, added the weight of its guns to the pressure against the vulnerable northern flank, its shells bowling down the line of metal on the parapet. Assailed from both directions by naval crews who worked with coolness and precision — more guns were dismounted; more men fell — the defenders fired even more wildly. The main squadron completed its first pass, closing upon Fort Beauregard, then swept down and around again, coming within less than 600 yards of the fort on Hilton Head, which had but three guns left in working order by the time the ships completed their second run. The *Wabash* was just rounding to the south, leading the way into a third ellipse, when Du Pont received a message that Fort Walker had been abandoned. At 2.20 a naval landing party raised the Union flag above ramparts that were pocked and battered, strewn with wreckage left by men who would not sweat to keep from bleeding, and then had wound up doing both at once. Army transports now put in. By nightfall, troops had occupied the works. Across the way, Fort Beauregard hauled down its flag at sunset, and early next morning the troops crossed over and occupied it too.

The victory was complete, and by it the Federal navy gained an excellent harbor in the very heart-land of secession. Nor was that all. Within the next three days the victors moved up the rivers and inlets and occupied the colonial towns of Beaufort and Port Royal, bringing under their control some of the finest old plantations in the South and thereby affording an opportunity not to be neglected by their abolitionist brethren, who presently arrived and began conducting uplift experiments among the Negro fieldhands. The battle itself had not been without its romantic aspect, for one of the defenders had been Brigadier General Thomas F. Drayton, C.S.A., whose brother, Captain Percival Drayton, U.S.N., commanded one of the attacking frigates; the South Carolina island for which they fought had been their boyhood home.

Satisfying as all this was to supporters of the Union — the loyal brother having won, Federal guns and Federal notions were now in operation within fifty airline miles of Charleston, where secession had had its birth eleven months before — there emerged from the battle another fact which had, for those who understood its implications, more weight than all the other facts combined, heart-warming and romantic though they were. Against stiffer resistance, this third hammer blow had been even more successful than the other two, and nowhere had the fleet failed to seize any objective assigned by the strategy board. Some standard theories were going to have to be revised: the belief that one gun on land was equal to four on water, for example. Steam had changed all that, removing the restrictions of wind and current, and making possible such maneuvers as Du Pont's expanding ellipse. From now on, apparently, the board had only to select its targets, concentrate the might of the fleet, and blast them into submission. Naval power was going to be a dominant factor in this war.

✗ 4 ✗

Coming as it did in the wake of defeats along Bull Run and Wilson's Creek, near opposite ends of the thousand-mile-long fighting line, this triple victory hammered out by the Federal navy did much to revive the flagging martial spirit of the North. There was no corresponding depression in the South, however, the odds in all three of these naval engagements having been too one-sided to give much cause for doubting the proved superiority of Confederate arms. It had been more or less obvious all along that the enemy could concentrate and strike with superior force at almost any point along the perimeter; that had been one of the conditions accepted by Davis when he chose the strategic defensive. When the pressure elsewhere was relieved, when the advantage shifted so that the South would be doing the concentrating and striking, the world would find out whether the North would be able to hold what it had won. Yet now, since that policy involved the dispersal of force to meet attacks from all directions, as the drawn-out fall wore on and the year was rounding toward a close, Southerners began to discover the price they would have to pay, in the hard cash of lost chances, for the advantages that accrued to the defensive.

In late September, after Hatteras and Ship Island had been lost and a third such operation was probably already into the planning stage, Davis went up to Fairfax Courthouse for a conference with the victors of Manassas. While the blasted oaks on the battlefield to their rear turned red in the fine clear weather of early fall, the men who had won that battle lay idle, watching the blue-clad host to their front grow stronger every day. At this stage, Federal troops were joining at the rate of 40,000 a month — about the total effective strength of Johnston's army. Pinkerton, with his tabulated lists compiled by operatives in Richmond, had misled his employer badly. Yet McClellan had been right in his fears that he might be brought to battle before his soldiers were ready: Beauregard was planning an offensive.

Though volunteering had fallen off to such an extent that the men arriving barely replaced those lost by the expiration of short-term enlistments and a liberal granting of furloughs, and though the army was crippled by a shortage of arms and supplies — food as well as munitions — he believed that the northern army, still in something of a state of shock from the whipping it had taken two months back, had perhaps now merely reached that stage of crystallization at which a smartly administered rap would cause it to fly apart again. In reply to the Federal threat to divide and conquer the South by a descent of the Mississippi, Beauregard wanted to make a sudden thrust across the Potomac and divide the Union, east and west, by seizing the strip of territory lying between Pittsburgh and Lake Erie. When the Yankee army came out from behind its Washington intrenchments he would administer the rap that would accomplish its disintegration, then go about his business of division and conquest. The odds were long, he admitted, but they were shorter than they were likely to be at any time hereafter, especially if the Confederates remained passive and continued to allow the growing enemy host time in which to regain its confidence.

Such was his plan, and as Davis listened to it on the first day of October, closeted with the generals at their Fairfax headquarters, within twenty miles of Washington itself, Beauregard expounding and Johnston nodding approval, he could see its advantages, in spite of its abrogation of his claim that "all we ask is to be let alone." Then came the rub. Beauregard declared that he would undertake the movement with 50,000 men, while Johnston held out for 60,000; which meant that Davis would have the problem of finding 10- to 20,000 reinforcements for the invasion.

The Federal navy, having launched its first two amphibious operations, now was preparing a third, whose objective could only be guessed at. Every general in every department along the Atlantic and the Gulf —

and, what was worse, every governor of every state that touched salt water; which included all but two of the eleven — not only believed that the blow would be struck, but was convinced that it would be aimed straight at him. They were calling loudly for help, and Davis could foresee the clamor that would follow any request that they forward troops to fatten the army now lying idle in northern Virginia. And with good cause; for in practically every case the political clamor would be followed by a military disaster. Down in North Carolina, for example, the loss of Hatteras had exposed New Bern, and the loss of New Bern would mean the loss of the Weldon railroad, the only supply line between Richmond and the South Atlantic states. Without that line the Virginia army not only could not hope to mount an invasion, it could not even be maintained in its present position beyond ten days. On the Gulf the situation was almost as critical. The army being assembled and drilled at Pensacola might be considered available, but the recent seizure of Ship Island had exposed the nation's tender underbelly to assault, and that army was all that stood in a position to blunt the point of such a stab. Wherever Davis looked, the situation was such that to strip one area for the removal of troops to another would be to exchange possible success for probable disaster.

Beauregard urged in vain that the length of the odds was an argument for, not against, the risk; that desperate men must take desperate chances, and that whatever was lost in the interim could be retaken after a victory on northern soil. Davis shook his head. No reinforcements could be sent, he said, without "a total disregard for the safety of other threatened positions."

The Creole could only shrug, while Johnston sat resigned, not being exactly a forward, cut-and-slash sort of commander in the first place. That ended all talk of a fall offensive, either along the Virginia line or elsewhere. For this year at least, the nation was committed to the dispersed defensive, and Davis took the cars back to Richmond.

He had troubles enough to vex him there, what with the day-to-day frets of office, the long nights rendered sleepless by neuralgia, and the fire-eaters shouting angrily that he had no policy that could even hinder, let alone halt, the southward crunch of the gigantic war machine the North was building unmolested. The cabinet he had assembled with such concern for political expediency had already begun to come apart at the seams. The brilliant and unpredictable Toombs, after hesitating to recommend the firing of the opening shot at Sumter, had bridled, once the shot had been fired, at being desk-bound while other men were learning the glad companionship of service in the field. On the day of Manassas, the issue being still in doubt in Richmond, where all that was known was that the guns were booming, he could abide it no longer. He submitted his resignation, as of that day, and left his post as head of the State Department to enter the army as

a Georgia brigadier. Within another two months War Secretary Leroy
P. Walker had done likewise, though for quite different reasons. Instead
of feeling left out or insufficiently employed, the Alabamian had been
employed beyond his capabilities, and he knew it. Swamped with work,
trussed up in yards of red tape, he too departed for the field, where
a man had only the comparatively simple frets of being killed or mangled. They would be missed, especially Toombs, but their going gave
Davis a double — or in fact, as he worked it out, a triple — opportunity.

As Attorney General, Judah P. Benjamin was largely wasting his
talents, since the Justice Department no more had courts than the Postal
Department, in the early months, had stamps. The War Office, which
Walker had left in such a snarl, seemed the perfect field for Benjamin's administrative abilities. Accordingly, Davis shifted him there.
This still left two vacancies, and in filling them the President corrected another shortcoming. The all-important border states had come
into the Confederacy in April, and all this time had been without
representation in the cabinet, there having been no vacancy. Now that
there were two such, Davis filled them with men of distinction from
Virginia and North Carolina: Robert M. T. Hunter of the former and
Thomas Bragg of the latter. The Virginian went in as head of the State
Department and the North Carolinian was given Benjamin's post as Attorney General. How Davis would get along with them remained to be
seen. Like most of the old cabinet members, neither of the new ones
had been intimate friends of his in private life before the war; nor were
they now.

At any rate he had his family with him, established at last in
what was called the White House of the Confederacy, not because it
was white (it wasn't; it was gray) but because the President's residence
had been called that under the old flag: a handsome, high-ceilinged mansion on the brow of a hill at the eastern end of Clay Street, with a
garden to the rear, downhill, shaded by poplars and sycamores and the
horse-chestnuts his wife loved. Though the Virginia ladies looked askance
and called her "a western belle" behind their fans, Mrs Davis, already
heavy with the child she had conceived in Montgomery and would bear
in Richmond in December, assumed her social duties with grace and
charm. She was a credit to her position and a comfort to her husband.
Yet even with her there to minister to his mental and bodily ills, the
long hours and the constant strain were telling on his health and on his
temper, both highly frangible in the first place.

Twenty years of public life had not thickened his skin against
the pricks of criticism, and the past seven months had even thinned it.
At times he was like a flayed man in a sandstorm. His wife could overlook the sidelong glances of the FFVs, but to Davis any facial tic of disagreement became at once a frown of disapproval. He had lost none
of the gracious manner by which he could charm an opponent into

glad agreement, yet now he scorned to employ it, and turned snap-pishly upon any man who crossed him. Smarting under the goads of office, he fell out with whoever did not yield to him in all things, and any difference was immediately made personal.

It had been thus even in the case of the two generals he had counseled with at Fairfax. Though nothing in their words or manner had shown this at the conference itself — all three being gentlemen and patriots who, in any given situation for which they had had time to steel their tempers, could place the national good above personal bias — Davis had shared a sort of running quarrel-by-courier with both of the ranking heroes of Manassas. Beauregard with his bloodhound eyes and swarthy complexion, his hair brushed forward at the temples, Napoleonic in aspect and conception, eager for glory, Gallic and ex-pansive, and Johnston with his prim, high-colored, wedge-shaped face, his balding head, his gray-shot sideburns and goatee, Virginia-proud, Virginia-genial when he wanted to be, cunctative as Fabius Maximus yet jaunty as a gamecock: these two had known the quick wrath and the withering scorn of the intellectual Davis in dispatches that were alternately hot or icy, but which in either case, when designed to sting, performed that function all too well. Gone was the glad comrade-ship they had shared on the field of Manassas, born of relief and exulta-tion in that July twilight while the Union flood ran backward up the roads to Washington. Since then, both men had fallen from presidential favor.

Beauregard fell first. The man who had shown much modesty on his arrival at Richmond, with the laurels of Sumter still green on his brow, became a different man entirely when he took up his pen in the seclusion of his tent. After Manassas, talk had grown rife that the Presi-dent had prevented any pursuit of the routed enemy: so rife, indeed, that Davis took the unusual step of asking his generals to deny the rumor officially. This Beauregard was glad to do, and promptly. But in his report on the battle, which unfortunately got to the newspapers before it reached the presidential desk, he reverted to his original scheme for combining the armies to crush the Union forces in detail — the plan which had been outlined by one of his aides at the first Confederate war council, held at the Spotswood a week before the battle — with the implication that its having been rejected was the reason why the southern army was not in the northern capital now.

Davis would not let this pass. "With much surprise, I found that the newspaper statements were sustained by the text of your report," he wrote, and took the general to task. His last letter to the Louisianian had begun "My dear General" and ended "Very truly, your friend." This one opened with a frigid "Sir" and closed with an ambiguous "Very respectfully, yours &c."

The breach widened as the general's friends took up the cudgel. At last, in early November, Beauregard himself aired the grievance in a letter to the Richmond *Whig*. Headed "within hearing of the enemy's guns," it referred to the "unfortunate controversy now going on," and said in part: "I entreat my friends not to trouble themselves about refuting the slanders and calumnies aimed at me. . . . If certain minds cannot understand the difference between *patriotism*, the highest civic virtue, and *office-seeking*, the lowest civic occupation, I pity them from the bottom of my heart." However, the reaction was quite different from what he had anticipated. In reference to the "unique" heading, for example, a rival paper asked: "Are we expected to give special credit to the general's lucubrations by reason of a fact certainly not very unusual in military operations?" The public, too, was disenchanted; a star had lost its luster. If Davis himself had chosen the words and directed the actions, the general could not have played more neatly into his hands.

The Creole was unhappy anyhow. He felt cramped, no more than a supernumerary, now that his army was merely a corps in Johnston's command. Practically overnight his dark hair was shot with gray: a phenomenon for which the different factions offered different explanations. Friends said that this was the result of overwork and heavy responsibility. Others attributed it to the blockade, which had cut him off from accustomed shipments of French hair dye. Whatever caused his graying, before the end of the year it was plain that he would have to go. Davis was considering sending him West, where he would find problems of such complexity that even his active mind would be kept busy and there would be ample opportunity for him to exercise his talents, both with the sword and the pen.

Trouble with Johnston had begun even sooner — all the way back in their West Point days, some said, when he and Davis were alleged to have had a fist fight over the favors of Benny Haven's daughter. Johnston won both the fight and the girl, rumor added; which might or might not have been true. At any rate, whatever had gone before, anger flared in considerable heat soon after the last day of August, when Davis forwarded to the Senate the names of five men to be given the rank of full general, lately provided for by law. The Senate confirmed them promptly, and in the order proposed. Adjutant-General Samuel Cooper headed the list, a sixty-six-year-old New Yorker who had married South and crossed over from the old army, in which he had held the same position. Next came Albert Sidney Johnston, still on the way from California after resigning his U.S. commission, a Kentucky-born Texan whom Davis and many others considered the first soldier of the Confederacy. Third was Robert E. Lee, mobilizer and former commander of all the Virginia forces, now campaigning in the

Alleghenies, charged with regaining what had been lost out there. Near the bottom of the list came Joseph E. Johnston himself, followed only by P. G. T. Beauregard, who came fifth.

When notice of these promotions reached Johnston he was outraged in his sense of equity and wounded in his pride. In the old army he had outranked them all, having been appointed Quartermaster-General, with a staff commission as a brigadier, while they were only colonels. He saw no justice in Davis' assumption that seniority for line command must be based exclusively on line service, in which both Lee and the other Johnston had held their commissions. All he saw was that he had been passed over.

Accordingly, while his wrath still smoked, he sat down and wrote a six-page letter of protest addressed to Jefferson Davis as the author of his woes. After expressing his "surprise and mortification," he wrote: "I now and here declare my claims, that notwithstanding these nominations by the President and their confirmation by Congress I still rightfully hold the rank of first general of the Armies of the Southern Confederacy." The order of names on the list, he added, "seeks to tarnish my fair fame as a soldier and a man, earned by more than thirty years of laborious and perilous service. I had but this, the scars of many wounds, all honorably taken in my front and in the front of battle, and my father's Revolutionary sword. It was delivered to me from his venerated hand, without a stain of dishonor. Its blade is still unblemished as when it passed from his hand to mine"; and much else, in much the same vein of outraged virtue. He waited two days before sending it. Then, finding his anger still uncooled, and remaining convinced of the trenchancy of his arguments and the fitness of the words he had used to advance them, he forwarded the letter unrevised.

Davis read it with a wrath that quickly rose to match the sender's. This Virginian, rattling his father's sword between lines that spoke of his "fair fame" and his wounded front, outdid even Beauregard. In composing his reply, however, Davis employed not a foil but a cutlass. Rejecting the nimble parry and riposte of rhetoric and logic, at both of which he was a master, he delivered instead one quick slash of scorn:

> Sir: I have just received and read your letter of the 12th instant. Its language is, as you say, unusual; its arguments and statements utterly one sided, and its insinuations as unfounded as they are unbecoming.
> I am, &c.
>
> Jeff'n Davis.

Knowing Johnston he knew the effect this letter would have. He knew that it would never be forgotten or forgiven and that it must necessarily underlie a relationship involving the fortune, if not the very being, of their new nation. In writing and sending this reply it was therefore as if he deliberately threw off-center a vital gear in a machine which had been delivered into his care and was his whole concern. Yet his reasons, his motivations, were basic. Loving his country he was willing to give it all he owned, including his life; but he would not sacrifice his prerogative or his pride, since in his mind that would have been to sacrifice not only his life but his existence. There was a difference. It was not only that he would not. He could not. Without his prerogative, he would not be President; without his pride, he would not even be Davis.

Men interpreted him as they saw him, and for the most part they considered him argumentative in the extreme, irascible, and a seeker after discord. A Richmond editor later wrote, for all to read, that Davis was "ready for any quarrel with any and everybody, at any time and all times; and the suspicion goes that rather than not have a row on hand with the enemy, he would make one with the best friend he had on earth."

Since Davis seldom chose to explain his actions — such explanations not fitting his conception of the dignity of his office — all too often the editor's charge seemed true. It appeared to be quite literally true in one case which came up about this time. He received from a general in the field a confidential report that a subordinate must be dismissed. This officer was an old friend of Davis', and when he received the presidential order of dismissal he came to Richmond to plead his case before the man who had signed it. "You know me," he said. "How could I ever hold my head up under the implied censure from you, my old friend?" Davis would give him no explanation. Choosing rather to alienate a friend than to betray a confidence, or even infer that there was a confidence he could not betray, he told him: "You have, I believe, your orders. I can suggest nothing but obedience." And neither the friend nor the editor, nor for that matter the parlor gossips in Richmond, ever learned why this was done; nor that Davis came home that evening, suffering from the dyspepsia which was with him a symptom of nervous upset, and went to his room without eating.

In this dark autumn, while Beauregard and Johnston chafed and politicians grew bitter at having to accept disproof of their prediction that the war would be a ninety-day excursion, Davis was disappointed by another general from whom he had expected much. Robert E. Lee's failure, however, came not because he was self-seeking or insubordinate — Lee was never either — but seemingly because he was incompetent in the field. The harshness of this judgment was emphasized by the contrast between what was done and what had been expected.

When Garnett fell in western Virginia and his army scattered before the skillful combinations of McClellan, it became necessary for Davis to send someone out there to put the pieces back together. Lee was the obvious choice. A man of considerable handsomeness and moral grandeur, hero of the Mexican War, he was Virginia's first soldier. Though it was not widely known that he had been tendered command of the U.S. forces before his resignation to go with his state, it was a matter of general knowledge that his rapid mobilization of Virginia's troops had made possible the victory at Manassas. One week after that battle he started west, taking with him the expectations of the President and the southern people.

Federal military successes in the region had reinforced an earlier political maneuver. Back in April, when the Richmond convention voted for secession, the western members crossed the mountains and assembled in Wheeling, where — on grounds that by voting for secession the other members had committed treason and thereby placed themselves outside the law — they drew up a new constitution, elected a new governor, and petitioned Washington for recognition as the lawful government of the state. Lincoln, of course, welcomed them, and presently their representatives were occupying the Virginia seats in Congress and laying the groundwork for the creation of the loyal state of West Virginia. Nothing was more galling to Confederate Virginians than the presence of these men in Washington, and one of the things expected of Lee was that he would abolish the rump government which had sent them there.

Strategically, too, the region was of great importance. Along its far edge ran the Ohio River, which not only was the traditional natural barrier of the new nation, but also flowed down toward the heart of Kentucky. Through its northern counties ran two vital supply lines, the Baltimore & Ohio Railroad and the Chesapeake & Ohio Canal. These severed, Washington would have to find a roundabout route for drawing men and supplies from the West. Still more important, with only a one-hundred-mile neck of land dividing the northward jut of its tiny panhandle from the shores of Lake Erie, it was the best location from which to launch an offensive such as the one proposed by Beauregard at Fairfax. That narrow isthmus also divided the Union, east and west; to seize it would be to split the North in two. When Lee left Richmond, all these opportunities lay before him in the western mountains, and no one went on record then as doubting that he would accomplish everything to which he put his hand.

What the public did not know was that he did not go out there to command but to advise, to coördinate the operations of four small independent "armies" whose commanders included one professional soldier, one scholarly ex-diplomat, and two high-tempered politicians. The campaign was to be conducted seventy miles from the nearest railhead, in an area whose population was largely hostile and whose principal "crop" was mountain laurel, so that supplies had to be brought up over roads made bottomless by rain that seldom slacked. "It rained thirty-*two* days in August," one veteran asserted. The troops were hungry and ragged, cowed by the defeats of the past month, half of them down with measles or mumps and the other half lacking confidence in their leaders. It was here in the mountains that Lee encountered for the first time a new type of animal: the disaffected southern volunteer. "They are worse than children," he declared, "for the latter can be forced."

Nevertheless, with such material and under such conditions, he now tried to work with the first pair in his highly diversified quartet of brigadiers. The soldier, W. W. Loring, who had been there only a week, resented Lee's arrival as a sign that the government did not trust him, and the diplomat, Henry R. Jackson, though willing, was inexperienced; with the result that when Lee attempted to trap the Federals on Cheat Mountain by an involved convergence of five columns from the two commands, the soldier balked, the diplomat blundered, and nothing was accomplished except to warn the Union troops of the movement, which had to be called off. Failing here, Lee looked south, where the two politicians were independently arrayed.

They were John B. Floyd and Henry A. Wise, both one-time governors of Virginia, the latter having occupied that office during the John Brown raid and the former having gone on to become Secretary of War in Buchanan's cabinet. Floyd had shown a tendency to grow flustered under pressure, and Wise had indicated what manner of soldier he was by ordering a battery commander to open fire in woods so thick that he could see no target and could therefore do no execution. "Damn the execution, sir!" Wise replied when the artillerist protested. "It's the *sound* that we want."

These shortcomings were nothing, though, compared to the relationship that Lee discovered existing between the commanders when he arrived. With an eye for past rivalries, and for possible future ones as well, the two ex-governors seemed more intent on destroying each other than they were on injuring the enemy to their front. Wise had raised an independent Legion, and when Floyd, who outranked him, came into the district, he telegraphed Richmond: "I solemnly protest that my force is not safe under his control." Floyd, enjoying the advantages of such rank, countered by offering to swap Wise's Legion for any three regiments of infantry, sight unseen. It was obvious that neither of these generals, intent as they were on mutual destruction — for which Floyd was perhaps the better equipped, having three newspaper editors on his staff — would be anxious, or maybe even willing, to coöperate in any venture which might bring credit to his adversary.

Yet Lee did what he could. He designed another combined operation, this time up the Kanawha Valley, and finally got the two commands in motion: whereupon, at the critical moment, with the enemy before them, the rivals took up separate positions, twelve miles apart, and, each declaring his own position superior, refused to march to join the other. Lee, whose primary reaction to the situation was embarrassment, was spared the ultimate necessity for sternness, however, when a War Department courier arrived with a dispatch instructing Wise to report immediately to Richmond. Wise pondered mutiny, but then, advised by Lee, decided against it and left, muttering imprecations.

With his problem thus reduced at least by half, Lee assembled the forces and took up a strong defensive position, planning destruction for the Federals. He hoped they would attack; if not, then he would launch an attack himself. For three days he waited. On the fourth he found the woods in front of him vacant, the enemy having pulled back out of reach, unobserved. All Lee could do, with winter closing in, was pull back, too. The three-month campaign was over, and he followed Wise to Richmond.

It was over and he had accomplished none of those things the public had expected. He had kept the advancing Federals off the Virginia Central and the Virginia & Tennessee Railroads, but this was generally ignored in the shadow of the darker fact that, with all those bright prospects before him, he had not even fought a battle. A Richmond journalist reviewed the operation thus: "The most remarkable circumstance of this campaign was, that it was conducted by a general who had never fought a battle, who had a pious horror of guerillas, and whose extreme tenderness of blood induced him to depend exclusively upon the resources of strategy to essay the achievement without the cost of life."

Lee had already written his wife, "I am sorry ... that the movements of our armies cannot keep pace with the expectations of the editors. ... I know they can arrange things satisfactory to themselves on paper. I wish they could do so in the field." And yet there was justice in the charge. Lee *had* been tender of bloodshed, designing complicated envelopments to avoid it — none of which had worked. Above all, he had shown himself incapable of jamming discipline down insubordinate throats. Besides, the journalist was reflecting general opinion. The public saw Lee now as a theorist, an engineer, a desk soldier, one who must fight by the book if he fought at all, and those who had watched with pride as he set out, expecting satisfaction for their hopes, now prepared looks of scorn for his return.

They did not use them to his face, however. Three months of adversity in the mountains had given him an austerity that would not permit familiarity, not even the familiarity of scorn. At fifty-four he had grown a beard; it came out gray, and people looked at him in awe. But beyond the influence of his presence, they sneered and called him Granny Lee and Evacuating Lee and wondered what use could be made of a soldier who would not fight.

Davis found a use for him as soon as he returned in early November. Having learned in private the details of the campaign — details which the public did not know, since Lee's delicacy, even toward men whose bickering had wrecked his reputation, would not allow him to include them in a report for the record — the President sent him to the South Atlantic coast, where his engineering abilities would be useful in improving the defenses. Hatteras Inlet and Ship Island had been lost, and a third blow seemed about to land. It landed, in fact, the day Lee got there. He arrived just in time to hear the guns at Port Royal and meet the fugitives streaming rearward from that fight. The Virginian could scarcely be blamed for this, yet a South Carolina matron wrote of him in her diary next day: *"Preux chevalier,* booted and bridled and gallant rode he, but so far his bonnie face had only brought us ill luck."

He believed more in work, however, than in luck. Having studied the situation, he strengthened some forts, abandoned others, and redrew the defenses, shifting them back from the sounds and rivers so that the invaders would have to fight beyond range of their gunboats. This called for digging, which Lee ordered done, and this in turn brought a storm of protest. His soldiers, especially the native South Carolinians, found the order doubly onerous. Digging wasn't fit work for a white man, they complained, and a brave man wouldn't hide behind earthworks in the first place. He put them at it anyhow, and as they dug they coined a new name for him: King of Spades.

Granny Lee, Evacuating Lee, the King of Spades, was one of several ranking Confederates who found their loyalty to Davis repaid in kind. Risking, sometimes losing, the affection and confidence of large segments of the people for their sakes, Davis sustained them through adversity and unpopularity, whether the public reaction seemed likely to reach an end or not. Obviously this had its drawbacks. Then and down the years, depending on the critic's estimate of the bolstered individual, it was the quality for which he was at once most highly praised and most deeply blamed. Yet one advantage it clearly had for southern leaders, with a value greatly enhanced by the fact that it was seldom available to their opposite northern numbers: No man, knowing that Davis trusted him and knowing what that trust entailed, ever had to glance back over his shoulder, wondering whether the government — meaning Davis — would support him against the clamor of the disgruntled or sacrifice him on grounds of political expediency. And if this was clear to the generals thus sustained, it was even clearer to the politicians, who knew that Davis would do his duty as he saw it. When legislation which they knew was bad for the country came before them, they did not hesitate to pass the measure if it was popular with the folks back home, knowing that Davis would exercise his veto. (He employed it thirty-nine times in the course of the war, while his opponent used it thrice, and only in one case was it overridden.) Thus in dignified silence he shouldered the blame for men who called him obstinate and argumentative and did their worst to swell the chorus of abuse.

His tenure was no longer merely provisional. On the first Wednesday in November he and Stephens were elected, without opposition, to six-year terms of office. Inauguration ceremonies were scheduled for Washington's birthday, which seemed a fitting date for the formal launching of the permanent government established by the Second American Revolution. That this government *was* permanent, in fact as well as name, Davis had no doubt. "If we husband our means and make a judicious use of our resources," he assured the Provisional Congress at its final session, November 18, "it would be difficult to fix a limit to the period during which we could conduct a war against the adversary whom we now encounter."

For that adversary, whose leader styled the southern revolution a "rebellion" and whose people now were submitting meekly to indignities no American had ever encountered without fight, he expressed contempt. "If instead of being a dissolution of a league, it were indeed a rebellion in which we are engaged, we might find ample vindication for the course we have adopted in the scenes which are now being enacted in the United States. Our people now look with contemptuous astonishment on those with whom they had been so recently associated. They shrink with aversion from the bare idea of renewing such a connection. When they see a President making war without the assent of Congress; when they behold judges threatened because they maintain the writ of *habeas corpus* so sacred to freedom; when they see justice and law trampled under the armed heel of military authority, and upright men and innocent women dragged to distant dungeons upon the mere edict of a despot; when they find all this tolerated and applauded by a people who had been in the full enjoyment of freedom but a few months ago — they believe that there must be some radical incompatibility between such a people and themselves. With such a people we may be content to live at peace, but the separation is final, and for the independence we have asserted we will accept no alternative."

Yet even as he spoke, thus stigmatizing his opponent across the Potomac, Davis was faced with the necessity for emulating his "tyrannous" example. Two days after the first-Wednesday election an insurrection exploded in the loyalist mountain region of East Tennessee. Bridges were burned and armed men assembled to assist the expected advance of a Union army through Cumberland Gap.

Though undeveloped industrially, the area was of considerable economic value as a grain and cattle country, offsetting the one-crop cotton agronomy farther south, and of even greater strategic importance because of the Virginia & Tennessee Railroad running through

Knoxville and Chattanooga, westward to Memphis and the Transmississippi. The insurrection confronted Davis with a problem much like the one that had confronted Lincoln in Maryland immediately after Sumter, and Davis met it with measures even sterner. Troops were sent at once from Memphis and Pensacola. Resistance was quashed and a considerable number of Unionists arrested. Habeas corpus, "so sacred to freedom," went by the board. When the Confederate commander in Knoxville asked what he should do with these men, Davis had the Secretary of War reply that those insurrectionists not actually known to be bridge burners were to be held as prisoners of war. As for the burners themselves, they were "to be tried summarily by drumhead court martial, and, if found guilty, executed on the spot by hanging. It would be well," the Secretary added, "to leave their bodies hanging in the vicinity of the burned bridges."

Five were so hanged, and others were held, including that William G. Brownlow who earlier had said that he would fight secession on the ice in hell. Admittedly the leader of regional resistance, he was editor of the Knoxville *Whig* and formerly had been a Methodist circuit rider; wherefore he was called Parson. An honest, fearless, vociferous man who neither smoked nor drank nor swore, he had courted only one girl in his life "and her I married." Though he was mysteriously absent from home on the night of the burnings, his actual complicity could not be established. He was held in arrest — for a time, at least, until his presence proved embarrassing in the light of Davis' complaint about "upright men ... dragged to distant dungeons" in the North. Again through the Secretary of War, under the theory that it was better for "the most dangerous enemy" to escape than for the honor and good faith of the Confederate government to be "impugned or even suspected," Davis directed that the parson-editor be released to enter the Union lines. Though he was thus denied the chance to recite the speech he had memorized for delivery on the gallows, Brownlow went rejoicing. "Glory to God in the highest," he exclaimed as he crossed over, "and on earth peace, good will toward all men, except a few hell-born and hell-bound rebels in Knoxville."

Under his reek of fire and brimstone there was much that was amusing about Brownlow. But there was nothing laughable about what he represented. Least of all was there anything comical about the situation he and his followers had created in the mountains of Tennessee. Now it had come to this, that Americans danced at rope ends as a consequence of actions proceeding from their political convictions. The harshest irony of all was that they were hanged by the direction of Jefferson Davis, who loved liberty and justice above all things, and who as a grown man, in a time of sickness, halted a reading of the child's story "Babes in the Woods" (it was characteristic that he had never heard it) because he would not endure the horror of the tale. The operation on his high-strung nature of such incidents as these in Tennessee caused him to remark long afterward, concerning his northern opponent's fondness for anecdotes and frontier humor, that he could not "conceive how a man so oppressed with care as Mr Lincoln was could have any relish for such pleasantries."

He was afflicted, however, by troubles both nearer and farther than the stern, unpleasant necessity for jailing, banishing, and hanging insurrectionists in eastern Tennessee. Fire-eaters in Richmond and the Deep South, their claim to the spoils of higher offices denied, their policy of bold aggression rejected, were everywhere disaffected. Vocal in their disaffection, they had now begun to raise a multivoiced outcry like the frantic babble of a miscued chorus. Charging that Davis had "no policy whatever," they represented him as "standing in a corner telling his beads and relying on a miracle to save the country." As caricature, the likeness was not too far-fetched, and the fact that the no-policy charge was true, or nearly true, did not make the barbs of criticism sting one whit the less.

His critics would have had him strip the troops from threatened points and send them marching forthwith against the North, staking everything on one assault. To Davis, this not only seemed inconsistent with his repeated claim that the South was merely defending herself against aggression, it seemed unnecessarily risky. That way the war might be quickly won, as Beauregard had pointed out; but it also might be quickly lost that way. Davis preferred to watch and wait. He believed that time was with him and he planned accordingly, not yet by any means aware that what he was waiting for would require a miracle. At this stage, in Davis' mind at any rate, nothing seemed more likely, more inevitable, than foreign intervention; as had been shown by his first action in attempting to secure it.

Back in the Montgomery days, a month before Sumter, Barnwell Rhett, chairman of the foreign affairs committee, reported a bill to Congress providing for the dispatch of a three-man mission to secure the recognition of the Confederacy by the European powers. Rhett had certain notions as to what these men should do over there, but he could not give instructions to such emissaries; the making of treaties rested with the President, who seemed to believe that nothing more would be needed than a polite call on the various proper statesmen across the water, whereupon those dignitaries would spread their arms to welcome a new sister bringing a dowry of precious cotton into the family of nations. This belief was emphasized by the fact that the man appointed to head the mission was William L. Yancey, the fieriest fire-eater of them all. For fifteen years the southern answer to the most outspoken of northern abolitionists, the Georgia-born Alabamian extended his defense of the "peculiar institution" to include a proposed reopening of the African slave trade — with the result that his name was anathema to every liberal on earth. In selecting Yancey to represent her, it was as if the South said plainly to all Europe: "To get cotton you must swallow slavery."

Nothing in his personality had shown that he would be armed with patience against discouragement or with coolness against rebuff, or indeed that he was in any way suited to a diplomatic post. Discouragement was not expected, however, let alone rebuff. Besides, Yancey having declined the minor cabinet job of Attorney General, the appointment solved the problem of what to do with him. Since that February evening on the gallery of the Exchange Hotel, when he presented "the man and the hour" to the crowd, no fitting use for his talents had been found. Now there was this — though some declared that he was being hustled off the scene as a possible rival before the election of a permanent President came round.

However that might have been, when he and his associates, Pierre A. Rost and A. Dudley Mann, received their instructions from the State Department, something came over Yancey that seemed to come over all fire-eaters when they were abruptly saddled with the responsibility for using more than their lungs and tongues — something akin to the sinking sensation that came over Roger Pryor, for example, when he was offered the honor of firing the first shot of the war. Returning from the conference, Yancey went to Rhett and told him of the instructions. They had agreed at the outset that the power to make commercial treaties was necessary to the success of the mission. However, the commissioners had not been given such power. All they were to do was explain the conflict in terms of the rightness of the southern cause, point out the Confederacy's devotion to low tariffs and free trade, and make a "delicate allusion" to the probable stoppage of cotton shipments if the war continued without European intervention. Hearing this, Rhett shared his friend's dismay. "Then," he told Yancey, "if you will take my advice as your friend, do not accept the appointment. For if you have nothing to propose and nothing to treat about, you must necessarily fail. Demand of the President the powers essential to your mission, or stay at home."

Whatever his qualms and misgivings, Yancey did not take his friend's advice. Sailing on the eve of Sumter, the commissioners reached England in late April to discover that the nation they represented was in the process of being increased from seven states to eleven, doubled in size east of the Mississippi and more than doubled in wealth and population. Soon afterwards, May 3, they secured an interview with Lord John Russell, Secretary of State for Foreign Affairs, who had replied to their request for an audience that he would be pleased to hear them, but that "under present circumstances. I shall have but little to say."

The interview was as one-sided as his lordship predicted. Having heard the envoys out, he replied — without committing his government in the slightest — that the Confederacy's request for recognition would be placed before the Cabinet at an early date. Six days later there was a second, briefer meeting; and that was all. In Paris, Napoleon III was more genial and less forthright, though he did make it clear in the end that, however much he wished to intervene, France could not act without England. So Yancey and Mann, leaving Rost to watch Napoleon, returned to London to try again.

Their hopes were higher now, and with good cause. When Lincoln announced a blockade of the southern coast, Britain — in accordance with international law, since obviously no nation would blockade its own ports — issued in mid-May a proclamation of neutrality, granting the Confederacy the rights of a belligerent, and the other European powers followed suit. That was much, and when more followed, Manassas enhancing the dignity of southern arms, Yancey thought the time was ripe for recognition. Accordingly, another note was sent to Russell, requesting another interview. The reply came back: "Earl Russell presents his compliments to Mr W. L. Yancey, Mr A. Dudley Mann, and would be obliged to them if they would put in writing any communications they wish to make to him."

This was something of a shock; yet they smothered their anger and complied, writing at length and basing their claims for recognition on recent Confederate triumphs. The reply to this was a bare acknowledgment of receipt; which in turn was another shock, for they knew that an English gentleman was never rude except on purpose. Again they swallowed their pride, however, and, Rost having recrossed the channel to lend what weight he could, continued to send letters until early December, when the Foreign Secretary added the last straw: "Lord Russell presents his compliments to Mr Yancey, Mr Rost and Mr Mann. He has had the honour to receive their letters of the 27th and 30th of November, but in the present state of affairs he must decline to enter into any official communication with them."

That broke the camel's back, for Yancey anyhow, whose pride had been subjected to a good deal more than it could bear. He resigned and sailed for home. Arriving he went straight to Rhett, whose advice he had not taken. "You were right, sir," he declared. "I went on a fool's errand."

Davis might continue to comfort despair with hope; Yancey himself had none. "While the war which is waged to take from us the right of self-government can never attain that end," Davis asserted at the final session of the Provisional Congress — knowing the "delicate allusion" would be heard across the Atlantic — "it remains to be seen how far it may work a revolution in the industrial system of the world, which may carry suffering to other lands as well as our own." It did not remain to be seen as far as Yancey was concerned. He had been there; he had seen already. He put no faith in anything that might happen in those nations whose statesmen had galled his pride.

Speaking in New Orleans in the spring, soon after his return, he told the people outright what he had told Davis earlier in private: "You have no friends in Europe.... The sentiment of Europe is anti-slavery, and that portion of public opinion which forms, and is represented by, the government of Great Britain, is abolition. They will never recognize our independence until our conquering sword hangs dripping over the prostrate heads of the North.... It is an error to say, 'Cotton is King.' It is not. It is a great and influential factor in commerce, but not its dictator. The nations of Europe will never raise the blockade until it suits their interests."

Thus Yancey, who had failed. How much his words were influenced by the fact that he had failed, his pride having been injured in the process, Davis could not know. At any rate, having spoken from the outset scarcely a public word that was not designed for foreign as well as domestic ears, the southern President had banked too heavily on European intervention to turn back now. The pinch of a cotton shortage not yet having been felt, the jennies and looms were running full-speed in England and France, and whether such a pinch, even if it eventually came, would "work a revolution," as Davis remarked in his mid-November speech, "remain[ed] to be seen."

Nor for that matter could he know how much of this initial failure had been due to ineptness. Yancey was many things, including a brilliant orator, but he was obviously no diplomat. Even before the final rebuff, which prompted his departure, Davis had moved to replace him, and the other two commissioners as well. Yancey would be recalled, his talents given a fitter scope, and Mann and Rost "disunited," one being sent to Spain and one to Belgium, their places to be taken at London and Paris by men whose gifts and reputations were more in keeping with the weight of their assignments: James M. Mason and John Slidell, former U.S. senators from Virginia and Louisiana.

The Virginian was the more prominent of the two. Grandson of George Mason of Gunston Hall (framer of the Bill of Rights) and withal an able statesman on his own, at sixty-three he had rather a ferocious aspect, with "burning" eyes and a broad, fleshy nose, a mouth drawn down at the corners, and brown, gray-shot hair bushed out around a large, pale, smooth-shaven face. His name, like Yancey's, was anathema to abolitionists, for he was the author of the Fugitive Slave Law and also of a public letter eulogizing Preston Brooks for caning their common adversary Sumner. Though he had got both his schooling and his wife in Philadelphia, Mason was an ardent secessionist and disapproved in general of things northern. He had been to New England once, to dedicate a monument, and found it quite distasteful. Invited to return, he replied that he would never visit that shore again, "except as an ambassador." Which was what he was now, in effect: on his way to the Court of St James's, however, not to the northern republic.

His companion Slidell was five years older and looked it, with narrowed eyes and a knife-blade nose, his mouth twisted bitterly awry and his pink scalp shining through lank white locks that clamped the upper half of his face like a pair of parentheses. He was New York–born, the son of a candlemaker who had risen, but he had removed to New Orleans as a young man to escape the consequences of debt and a duel with a theatrical manager over the affections of an actress. Importing the methods of Tammany Hall, he prospered in Louisiana politics. Though not without attendant scandal, he won himself a fortune in sugar, a Creole bride, three terms in Congress — one in the House and two in the Senate — and an appointment as Minister to Mexico on the eve of war with that nation, which event prevented his actual service in that capacity. He was aptly named, being noted for his slyness. At the outbreak of hostilities, back in the spring, an English journalist called him "a man of iron will and strong passions, who loves the excitement of combinations and who in his dungeon, or whatever else it may be, would conspire with the mice against the cat rather than not conspire at all." Possessing such qualities, together with the ability to converse in French, New Orleans–style, and also in Spanish, Empress Eugénie's native tongue, Slidell seemed as particularly well suited for the atmosphere of the City of Light as Mason, with his rectitude and cavalier descent, was for London.

Davis and the nation expected much from this second attempt at winning foreign recognition and assistance. By early October the two were in Charleston with their secretaries and Slidell's wife and daughters, awaiting a chance to run the blockade. At first they intended to take the Confederate cruiser *Nashville*, being outfitted there as a commerce raider. That would have been to arrive in a style which the British, as a naval people, could appreciate. Unwilling to wait, however, they booked passage instead an a small private steamer, the *Gordon*, and at 1 o'clock in the morning, October 12, slipped out of the harbor and crossed the bar in a driving rain, bound for Nassau. From there, having found no steamer connection with England, the *Gordon* sailed for St Thomas, a regular port for transatlantic packets. Running low on coal, her captain put into Cárdenas, on the north coast of Cuba, whence the commissioners made their way overland to Havana. November 7 they boarded the British mail steamer *Trent*, which cleared for Southampton that same day. Thus, the blockade having been run without incident, themselves securely quartered on a ship that flew the ensign of the mightiest naval power in the world, the risky leg of the journey was behind them.

So they thought until noon of the following day, when the

Trent, steaming through the Bahama Passage, 240 miles out of Havana, sighted an armed sloop athwart her course at a point where the channel narrowed to fifteen miles. The *Trent* broke out her colors and continued on her way; whereupon the sloop ran up the union jack — and put a shot across her bow. After a second shot, which was closer, the *Trent* stopped engines.

"What do you mean by heaving my vessel to in this way?" the British captain shouted through a trumpet.

For answer the sloop put out two boats, which as they drew nearer were seen to be loaded with sailors, armed marines, and a naval officer who identified himself as he came aboard: Lieutenant D. MacNeill Fairfax of the screw sloop *San Jacinto*, Captain Charles Wilkes, U.S.N., commanding. Having information that Confederate Commissioners James M. Mason and John Slidell were aboard, he demanded the passenger list. At this, Slidell came forward. "I am Mr Slidell. Do you want to see me?" Mason stepped up, too, but no introduction was necessary, he and the lieutenant having met some years ago. (For that matter, Slidell and Captain Wilkes, waiting now aboard the sloop, had been boyhood friends in the old First Ward, back in their New York days, though they had had a falling out before Slidell's departure.) Their identities thus established, together with those of their secretaries, Lieutenant Fairfax informed the British captain, who all this time had scarcely ceased objecting, that he was seizing the four men for return to the United States and trial as traitors. When the captain continued to object — "Pirates! Villains!" some of the passengers were crying; "Throw the damned fellow overboard!" — the lieutenant indicated the *San Jacinto*, whose guns were bearing on the unarmed *Trent*. The captain yielded, still protesting; Mason and Slidell and their secretaries were taken over the side.

"Goodbye, my dear," the Louisianian told his wife on parting. "We shall meet in Paris in sixty days."

The two ships drew apart and continued on their separate courses, northward and northeastward toward their two countries, bearing their respective emotional cargoes of exultation and outrage: cargoes in each case large enough, and fervent enough, to be shared by all the people who, off on those different points of the compass, awaited their arrival all unknowing.

Davis in Richmond was scantly braced for such a smile of fortune. After so many disappointments, he hardly presumed even to hope for such news as this which now was coming his way across the water. Here was a ready-made, bona fide international incident, brought about not by the machinations of cloak-and-dagger agents sent out by the Confederate secret service, but by a responsible northern naval officer who had taken unto himself the interpretation of law on the high seas and who in his rashness had inforced that interpretation against the flag which admittedly ruled those seas.

The news would be no less welcome for being unexpected; Davis was badly in need of encouragement at this point. At the outset he had predicted a long war. Now he was showing the erosive effects of living with the fulfillment of his prediction. He was thinner, almost emaciated; "gaunted" was the southern word. His features were sharper, the cheeks more hollow, the blind left eye with its stone-gray pupil in contrast to the lustrous gleam of the other — a "wizard physiognomy," indeed. The lips were compressed and the square jaw was even more firmly set to express determination, as if this quality might prove contagious to those around him. Under the wide brim of a planter's hat, his face had lost all signs of youth. It had become austere, a symbol; so that a North Carolina soldier, seeing him thus on the street one day, walking unaccompanied as was his custom, stopped him and asked doubtfully, "Sir, mister, be'ent you Jefferson Davis?" And when Davis, employing the careful courtesy which was habitual, admitted his identity: "Sir, that is my name" — "I thought so," the soldier said. "You look so much like a Confederate postage stamp."

★ ★ ★

Lincoln, too, was showing the strain, but unlike Davis he found his worries concentrated mostly on one man: Major General George B. McClellan. Since saying that he could "do it all," McClellan had found that "all" involved a great deal more than he had intended or suspected at the time. It included, for instance, the task of pacifying Ben Wade and Zachariah Chandler, members of the joint committee investigating the Ball's Bluff fiasco: men whom the youthful general considered "unscrupulous and false," but who, regardless of what he thought of them, were determined to have a voice in how the war was fought before they would vote the money needed to fight it.

They did not like the way it was being fought at present; or, rather, the way it was not being fought at all. Above Harpers Ferry the Confederates had cut the B & O, one of the main arteries of supply, while down the Potomac they had established batteries denying the capital access to the sea. "For God's sake," Wade cried, infuriated by such effrontery, "at least push back the defiant traitors!" It did no good to explain that such outposts would crumble of their own accord, once the main attack was launched, and that meanwhile, undeterred by incidentals, the proper course was to concentrate on building up the force with which to launch it. The congressmen saw only that the rebels were holding such positions unmolested. Or if McClellan's thesis was true, as to what the rebel reaction would be, they wanted to see it demonstrated. They had had enough of delay.

A Massachusetts Adams declared in August, "We have now gone

through three stages of this great political disease. The first was the cold fit, when it seemed as if nothing would start the country. The second was the hot one, when it seemed almost in the highest continual delirium. The third is the process of waking to the awful reality before it. I do not venture to predict what the next will be."

McClellan had already ventured a prediction: "I shall . . . crush the rebels in one campaign." That was still his intention. Yet now, with the war still in the waking stage, all that he was truly sure of was that he did not want this phase to end as the first two had done, at Sumter and Bull Run. In spite of which, to his dismay — with those examples of unpreparedness stark before him — he was being prodded by rash counselors to commit the selfsame errors. Adams had seen the nation struggling for its life as if in the throes of breakbone fever; the war was "this great political disease," attacking the whole organism. But McClellan, who was a soldier, not a politician or a diplomat, could not or would not see that the contest was political as well as military, that the two had merged, that men like Wade and Chandler were as much a part of it as men like Johnston and Beauregard — or McClellan himself, for that matter. Given the time, he believed he could get over or around the enemy intrenched across the Potomac; he could "crush" them. He could never get over or around men like Wade and Chandler, let alone crush them, and he knew it. And knowing it he turned bitter. He turned peevish.

"The people think me all-powerful," he wrote in one of the nightly letters to his wife. "Never was there a greater mistake. I am thwarted and deceived . . . at every turn." At first it was the politicians: "I can't tell you how disgusted I am becoming with these wretched politicians." Next it was the Administration itself: "I am becoming daily more disgusted with this Administration — perfectly sick of it. If I could with honor resign I would quit the whole concern tomorrow." "It is sickening in the extreme, and makes me feel heavy at heart, when I see the weakness and unfitness of the poor beings who control the destinies of this great country." "I was obliged to attend a meeting of the cabinet at 8 p.m., and was bored and annoyed. There are some of the greatest geese in the cabinet I have ever seen — enough to tax the patience of Job."

So far, the President was not included in the indictment. McClellan wrote, "I enclose a card just received from 'A. Lincoln'; it shows too much deference to be seen outside." Having come to know Lincoln better, he found he liked him, or at any rate thought him amusing. One day as he was writing he had callers, and when he resumed his letter he wrote, "I have just been interrupted here by the President and Secretary Seward, who had nothing very particular to say, except some stories to tell, which were, as usual, very pertinent, and some pretty good. I never in my life met anyone so full of anecdote as our friend."

It was not all anecdote. One day a division commander came to see the general and found Lincoln with him, poring over a map of Virginia and making operational suggestions, to which McClellan listened respectfully but with obvious amusement. At last the amateur strategist left. Returning from seeing him to the door, McClellan looked back over his shoulder and smiled. "Isn't he a rare bird?" he said.

Lincoln had been boning on the science of war, borrowing military treatises from the Library of Congress and reading them in the small hours of the night. He took a particular pleasure in discussing strategy with his young general-in-chief, who had been so good at such studies himself. McClellan saw no harm in all this. He viewed Lincoln's efforts with that air of amused tolerance reserved by professionals for amateurs, and the visits afforded relaxation from the daily round. Besides, such studies and discussions were leading the President toward a better comprehension of the military problem: especially of the necessity for protecting the commanding general from the interference of politicians.

"I intend to be careful and do as well as possible," McClellan said earnestly one night as they parted after such a conference. "Don't let them hurry me, is all I ask."

"You shall have your own way in the matter, I assure you," Lincoln told him.

Whereupon — as if, having gotten what he wanted in the way of assurance, he could move on now to other things; or perhaps because his tolerance or his capacity for amusement was exhausted — McClellan changed his tone. Now he wrote, "I have not been at home for some three hours, but am concealed at Stanton's to dodge all enemies in the shape of 'browsing' presidents, etc."

The friend affording sanctuary was Edwin M. Stanton, the attorney who had snubbed Lincoln four years ago when the gangling Springfield lawyer came to Chicago to assist in a patents case. Irascible and sharp-tongued, a leading Democrat, Stanton was even more important now. Having served as Attorney General during Buchanan's last four months, he had gone on to become chief legal adviser to the present Secretary of War. His first impression of "that long-armed creature" had not changed, but now at least he took the trouble to exercise his wit at his expense. Du Chaillu, for example, had not needed to go all the way to the Congo in search of the missing link; there was an excellent specimen here in Washington. "The original gorilla," he called Lincoln, and McClellan took up the phrase in letters to his wife. They laughed together at a perspiration splotch on the back of Lincoln's shirt, Stanton remarking that it resembled a map of Africa.

If he noticed this at all, Lincoln took it calmly. He was accustomed to being laughed at, and had even been known to encourage laughter at his own expense. Such friends as he cared about had a deep appreciation of humility, and he could afford to let the others go. Attracted, however, as so many were, by McClellan's forthright air of youthful manliness, he did not want to lose him as a friend. Then one mid-November night he drew the rebuke humility must always draw from pride. He and Seward, accompanied by Lincoln's young secretary John Hay, went over to McClellan's house. When the servant told them the general was attending a wedding but would be back presently, they said they would wait. They had waited about an hour when McClellan returned. The servant told him the President and the Secretary of State were there, but he seemed bemused as he went past the door of the room where they were waiting. They waited another half hour, then once more sent the servant to inform the general that they were there. The answer came — "coolly," Hay recorded — that McClellan had gone to bed.

On the way home, when the secretary broke out angrily against what he called the "insolence of epaulets," Lincoln, though he was saddened by this final indication that he had lost a friend, quietly remarked that this was no time for concern over points of etiquette and personal dignity. "I will hold McClellan's horse if he will only bring us success," he said soon afterward. But Hay observed with satisfaction that from then on, when the President wanted to see McClellan, he summoned him to the White House.

The Young Napoleon had changed. "We shall strike them there," he used to say, gesturing toward the eastern end of the rebel lines at Centerville when he rode out on inspection. After inching some troops forward "by way of getting elbow-room," he gaily told his wife: "The more room I get the more I want, until by and by I suppose I shall be so insatiable as to think I cannot do with less than the whole state of Virginia." He did not talk that way now, or write that way either. That was in the past. Bored, annoyed, disgusted, sick, thwarted and deceived at every turn, he no longer gestured aggressively toward the Centerville-Manassas lines. According to Pinkerton, 90,000 gray-clad soldiers, superbly equipped and thirsty for blood, with one Manassas victory already blazoned on their battleflags, were behind those earthworks praying for McClellan's army to advance and be wrecked, like McDowell's, on those same plains. All that stood between the army and catastrophe was Little Mac, resisting the unscrupulous men who would hurl it into the furnace of combat before the mold had set.

By now, though, more than the frock-coated congressmen were urging him forward against his will. While the clear bright days of autumn declined and the hard roads leading southward were about to dissolve into mud, the public was getting restless, too, wondering at the army's inaction. The soldiers loved and trusted him as much as ever; Our George, they called him still. But to the public he seemed overcautious, like a finicky dandy hesitating to blood a bright new sword, either because he did not want to spoil its glitter, or else because he did not trust its temper. Horace Greeley, the journalistic barometer, had recovered from his fright and recommenced his Forward-to-Richmond chant. Other voices swelled the chorus, while shriller cries came through its pulse to accuse the young commander of vacillation. McClellan was reduced to finding consolation in the approval of his horse, Dan Webster: writing, "He, at least, had full confidence in his master."

Affairs were progressing no better in the West. Politically, though the storm still raged from point to point and fugitive secessionist legislatures were assembling, Missouri and Kentucky had been secured to the Union. Militarily, however, little had been done since Wilson's Creek and Frémont's feverish southward march into the vacuum created by that explosion. Assuming the supreme command on the day the Pathfinder received Lincoln's order deposing him, McClellan promptly reorganized that vast, conglomerate area into two departments.

The first, Frémont's old Department of the West, to which was added that part of Kentucky west of the Cumberland River, was under Henry W. Halleck; while the second, the Department of the Ohio, including the rest of Kentucky and Tennessee, had Don Carlos Buell for commander. Both were responsible to McClellan, but neither was accountable to the other. Each in fact saw the other as his rival for the future command of the whole. And therein lay the seeds of much mischief. Admittedly, ambition and rivalry were the stimuli that made the military organism tick. But in this case, with McClellan racked by problems of his own in Washington, the result was that there was not only little coördination of effort between theaters, East and West; there was also little coöperation between the armies resting flank to flank on opposite banks of the Cumberland.

A major general at forty-six, three years older and one rank higher than his rival, Halleck had the advantage at the outset. Buell was generally considered one of the best officers in the service, particularly as an organizer and disciplinarian; yet Halleck was not only senior in age and grade, he was by far the more distinguished in previous accomplishments. Author of *Elements of Military Art and Science*, a highly respected volume issued fifteen years before, translator of Jomini's *Napoleon*, authority on international law, on which he had published a treatise just before the war began, he was called Old Brains by his fellow officers, not altogether jokingly. In the shadow of all this, even as a result of it, Buell had one not inconsiderable advantage: Halleck had been McClellan's rival for the post of general-in-chief — old Winfield Scott had favored him, for one — and Little Mac, perhaps somewhat influenced by this, considered Buell the superior in practical ability as a soldier in the field. That was arbitrary, though, or anyhow problematical, since the two West Pointers had been promoted equally for gallantry in the Mexican War and had had no such opportunity for distinction since.

In another direction, there was little room for doubt. Both were more impressive in the abstract than prepossessing in the flesh; but here the advantage clearly passed to the junior, if only by default. Of average height, inclined toward fat and flabbiness, Halleck had an unmilitary aspect. Balding, he wore gray mutton-chop side whiskers and looked considerably older than his years. The olive-tinted flesh of his face hung so loosely that it quivered when he moved, particularly his double chin, and he had a strangely repellent habit of crossing his arms on his lower chest to scratch his elbows when he was worried or plunged in thought. In manner he was irritable and sometimes harsh, not inclined to allow for the smaller brains of lesser men. Interviewed, he would hold his head sideways and stare fishily, directing one goggle eye toward a point somewhere beyond his interviewer. This caused one disconcerted officer to remark that conversing with Halleck was like talking to someone over your shoulder.

No one ever said this about Buell. His glance was piercing and direct: too much so, perhaps, for he was even harsher in manner than Halleck. Dark-skinned, with a scraggly, gray-shot beard, close-set eyes, and a hawk-beak nose, Buell maintained an icy reserve, engaged in no small talk, and brooked no difference of opinion from subordinates. Despite his operatic name, Don Carlos, there was nothing flamboyant in his nature. Like McClellan he was an excellent disciplinarian, robust of physique, and a hard, methodical worker round the clock; but he had scarcely a vestige of McClellan's charm, none of his glamor, and therefore none of his popularity, either. He never expressed the least regret at this, however. Apparently he never believed that popularity could be a useful factor in turning farmboys into soldiers. Or if so, not by him; he never sought it.

Instructions given the two commanders on setting out were similar as to policy. Both were told to hold firmly onto all that had been gained in Missouri and Kentucky, meanwhile impressing on the people of the area that the army's purpose was the restoration of the Union, not the abolition of slavery, which was not even incidentally on the agenda. In addition, Halleck was to assemble his troops "on or near the Mississippi, prepared for such ulterior operations as the public interests may demand," while Buell massed for an advance into the loyalist mountain region of eastern Tennessee. The former plan had reference to Frémont's dream of a lopping descent of the Father of Waters. The latter was Lincoln's fondest project. He hoped that Buell would accomplish there what McClellan had accomplished in western Virginia under similar conditions, the people having voted five-to-one against secession back in June. Nothing vexed the President more than the fact that this Union stronghold was in southern hands. "My distress," he wrote, "is that our friends in East Tennessee are being hanged and driven to despair, and even more, I fear, are thinking of taking rebel arms for the sake of personal protection." Besides, he saw great strategic profit in an advance through Cumberland Gap, since taking Knoxville would cut the northernmost east-west Confederate railroad, thus coming between the secessionists and what Lincoln called their "hog and hominy."

Buell, who had helped to frame his own instructions, saw it that way, too, on setting out. Soon after he reached Louisville, however, peering southeast across the barrens in the direction of the Gap, which he saw now as a natural fortress straddled athwart his path, he changed his mind. For him, as for McClellan — whom he addressed as "My dear Friend" in official dispatches — obstacles loomed more starkly at close range. Features that seemed innocuous on a two-dimensional map could dominate a three-dimensional landscape. Even the absence of some feature, whether natural or man-made, could prove ruinous: as for instance a railroad. From his base on the Ohio he observed that there were no railroads by which he could haul supplies to feed and equip an army moving directly upon East Tennessee. He would have to depend on a wagon train, grinding weary distances over wretched roads and vulnerable to raiders throughout its length. The more he looked the more impossible it seemed, until presently he abandoned it altogether.

He did not abandon his offensive plans, however. Buell was nothing if not thorough. Turning his mind's eye westward along a sixty-degree arc, he perceived that Nashville, the Tennessee capital on the Cumberland, a manufacturing center and a transportation nexus, was not only closer than Knoxville, it was even a bit closer than Cumberland Gap. The way led through a land far richer in supplies, with no natural fortress at the end, and best of all there was a railroad all the way. Nashville taken, the Confederates defending East Tennessee would be outflanked; when they fell back he could march in unopposed. This might take a bit longer, but it was surer. As for the Unionists awaiting his advance into the mountains, Buell believed their constancy would "sustain them until the hour of deliverance." Thus he wrote in mid-December, by which time five had already been "sustained" by the necks after drumhead trials for arson.

Before occupying Nashville he would have to cross the Cumberland River, but he did not consider this a drawback. He counted it a positive advantage, since it meant that he could secure the coöperation of Union gunboats on that stream. This in turn meant securing the coöperation of Halleck, and now that his mind had turned that way, Buell went on to essay grand strategy. He proposed nothing less than an all-out concerted drive by both Kentucky armies, with Nashville as the objective: Halleck to advance from the northwest in "two flotilla columns up the Tennessee and the Cumberland," and himself from the northeast, down the railroad. The result would be to penetrate, and thereby outflank, the whole Confederate line; whereupon the Federals could occupy not only East Tennessee, his original objective, but the entire state, along with whatever parts of Kentucky remained in enemy hands. In his enthusiasm, which somewhat resembled the elation of a poet just delivered of an ode, he wrote McClellan of his plan, remarking incidentally that he feared no advance by the rebels at Bowling Green ("I should almost as soon expect to see the Army of the Potomac marching up the road") and closing with a light-hearted request for a few high-ranking officers, "not my seniors," to assist him in carrying out his plan: "If you have any unoccupied brigadiers . . . send six or eight, even though they should be no better than marked poles."

Far from being elated, or even amused, McClellan was chagrined and upset by the proposal. He saw the soundness of this substitute plan — which, moreover, had the sort of strategic brilliance he admired — yet he hated to lose the advantages of the first. Invading eastern Tennessee, Buell's army would not only sever one of the arteries supplying the Confederates in northern Virginia; it would also be poised on their flank, and could then be angled forward to maneuver them out of their intrenched position and assist in the taking of Richmond. For this reason, as well as the political ones, McClellan replied that he still considered "a prompt movement on eastern Tennessee imperative," but "if there are causes which render this course impossible," he regretfully allowed, "we must submit to the necessity." All the same, he did not submit without frequent backward glances. By the end of November he was hoping Buell would attempt both movements, one on East Tennessee, "with say 15,000 men," and one on Nashville "with, say, 50,000 men." He added, by way of encouragement, "I will at once take the necessary steps to carry out your views as to the rivers."

This meant that he would urge Halleck to undertake the advance from western Kentucky. When he did so, in a telegram sent December 5, Halleck replied from St Louis the following day: "I assure you, General, this cannot be done with safety at present. Some weeks hence I hope to have a large disposable force for other points; but now, destitute as we are of arms, organization, and discipline, it seems to me madness to remove any of our troops from this State."

In all conscience, McClellan had to admit that Old Brains had his hands full already. Charged with restoring order to the chaos Frémont left — "a system of reckless expenditure and fraud, perhaps unheard of before in the history of the world," his instructions warned him — he had to attend at once to the guerilla bands marauding in his rear, to Price and McCulloch, reported marching against his front, as well as to the enormous task of preparing for the descent of the Mississippi. As if all this was not enough, he was having to deal at the same time with a mentally upset brigadier, red-haired Tecumseh Sherman, who was bombarding headquarters with reports of rebel advances from all directions. "Look well to Jefferson City and the North Missouri Railroad," Sherman would wire; "Price aims at both."

Succeeding Anderson when the Sumter hero's health broke, Sherman earnestly told the Secretary of War that 200,000 troops would be needed to put down the rebellion in the Mississippi Valley alone, and when this "evidence of insanity" was reinforced by other alarming symptoms reported in the papers — a brooding melancholy broken only by intermittent fits of rage and fright — he was relieved of his command. Superseded by Buell, he was sent to serve under Halleck in Missouri, where his fidgety manner and tocsin-shrill dispatches presently served to verify the suspicions which had followed him from Kentucky. He appeared thoroughly demoralized: "stampeded," Halleck called it, but McClellan put it simpler, saying, "Sherman's gone in the head." In hopes that a few weeks' rest would restore his faculties, Halleck gave an indefinite leave of absence to the distraught Ohioan, whose wife then came down and took him home.

Not all of Halleck's personnel problems could be handled so easily. As a sort of counterbalance to the highly nervous Sherman, he had another brigadier who seemed to have no nerves at all. The trouble with U.S. Grant was that, for all Halleck knew, he might have no brains either.

There were indications of such a lack. Grant was a West Pointer and had been commended for bravery in Mexico, but since then his reputation had gone downhill. Stationed out in California, he had had to resign his captain's commission because of an overfondness for the bottle, and in the seven following years he had been signally unsuccessful as a civilian. Commissioned a colonel of Illinois volunteers, he had won promotion to brigadier by a political fluke, his congressman claiming it for him as a due share of the spoils. Since then he had done well enough in a straightforward, soldierly way; he had not panicked under pressure, and best of all he had worked with what he had instead of calling for help in each emergency. Aware of his unsavory past, however, Halleck could never be sure when a relapse might come, exposing the basic instability of Grant's character and leaving the army commander to take the blame for having reposed the nation's trust in such a man.

Despite his seedy appearance (he was five feet eight inches tall and weighed 135 pounds; one eye was set a trifle lower than the other, giving his face a somewhat out-of-balance look; he walked with a round-shouldered slouch, pitching forward on his toes, and paid as scant attention to the grooming of his beard as he did to the cut and condition of his clothes) Grant had proved himself a fighter. But that could have its drawbacks when it included, as it seemed to do in this case, a large element of rashness. Halleck did not want to be embarrassed by Grant, the way Frémont had been embarrassed by the ill-fated Lyon: with whom, for that matter, in spite of his lack of surface fire, the thirty-nine-year-old Illinois brigadier had shown a disturbing degree of kinship. Wilson's Creek had come within three weeks of Bull Run, and had been fought to the same pattern. Then on the eve of Halleck's arrival, within three weeks of Ball's Bluff, came Belmont. Even apart from the balanced chronology, East and West, the resemblance was much too close for comfort.

Though Bishop Polk had won the race for Columbus, Grant had been by no means willing to admit that this gave the Confederates any permanent claim to the place. Within the week, having occupied Paducah, he had written Frémont: "If it were discretionary with me, with a little addition to my present force I would take Columbus." The Pathfinder made no reply to this, but when he took the field at last, marching against the victors of Wilson's Creek, he had his adjutant order Grant to feint against Polk to prevent that general from reinforcing Price. In doing this Grant was to make a show of aggression along both sides of the Mississippi, keeping his troops "constantly moving back and forward ... without, however, attacking the enemy." Also in accordance with orders, on November 3 — the day Frémont left Springfield, relieved of command, and Winfield Scott left Washington, retired — Grant sent a column southward, west of the river, to assist in an attempt to bag or destroy a force under M. Jeff Thompson, reported down near the Missouri boot-heel, in the St Francis River area. Two days later a dispatch informed him that Polk was definitely sending reinforcements to Price. Marching "back and forward" not having sufficed to immobilize the bishop, Grant now was ordered to make a demonstration against Columbus itself.

Accordingly, on the 6th he loaded five infantry regiments, supported by two cavalry troops and a six-gun battery, onto four transports — 3114 men in all — and steamed down the river, protected by two gunboats. Nine miles below Cairo, tied up for the night against the eastern bank, he received a report that Polk had ordered a strong column to cut off and destroy the troops Grant had sent to do the same to Thompson. The message arrived at 2 o'clock in the morning, and within the hour Grant made his decision. Instead of a mere demonstration, he would launch a direct, all-out attack on Belmont, the steamboat landing opposite Columbus, where the enemy column was reported to be assembling.

At dawn the downstream approach got under way, the troops experiencing the qualms and elation of facing their first test under fire. Their emotions perhaps would have been less mixed, though probably no less violent, if they had known that none of the conditions their commander assumed existing at or near Columbus was true. Polk had no intention of reinforcing Price, nor was he preparing a column to bag the force that supposed itself to be pursuing Thompson, who for that matter had retired from the field by now. Far from being a staging area, Belmont was only an observation post, a low-lying, three-shack hamlet dominated by the guns on the tall bluff across the river and manned by one regiment of infantry — half of which was on the sick list — one battery of artillery, and a scratch collection of cavalry. Unaware that the drama in which they were taking part was in fact an Intelligence comedy of errors, Grant's men came off their transports at 8 o'clock, three miles above Belmont, their debarkation concealed by a skirt of timber. While the gunboats continued downstream to engage the batteries on the Columbus bluff, the troops formed a line of battle and marched southward toward the landing, skirmishers out. Presently, the guns of the naval engagement booming hollow across the water to their left, they came under heavy musket fire from out in front.

By now there was more to oppose them than one half-sick infantry regiment. Polk, having learned of the attack, had reinforced the Belmont garrison with four regiments under Brigadier General Gideon Pillow, the Tennessean who had preceded him in command. Ferried across the river, they hurried northward from the landing, scorning the protection of previously constructed fortifications, and took position in the path of Grant's advance. It was hard, stand-up fighting, the forces being about equal, five regiments on each side, each force being supported by a battery of light artillery. The Federals had the initiative, however, and also they had Grant, who was something rare in that or any war: a man who could actually learn from experience. Three months before, he had made a similar advance against an enemy position reported held by Colonel Thomas Harris and his command, and as Grant drew closer, mounting the ridge that masked the camp, "my heart kept getting higher and higher until it felt to me as though it was in my throat." He kept his men going, he said, because "I had not the moral courage to halt and consider what to do." Then, topping the rise, he found the camp deserted, the enemy gone. "My heart resumed its place. It occurred to me at once that Harris had been as much afraid of me as I had been of him. This was a view of the question I had never taken before; but I never forgot it afterwards."

He did not forget it now. Leaving five companies near the transports as rear guard, he put the rest in line and pushed straight forward, his six guns barking busily all the while. Under such pressure, the Confederates gave ground stubbornly — until, after about two hours of fighting, the Federals roaring down upon them in the vicinity of the camp, they broke, giving way completely, and took off for the rear in headlong panic. Here, on a narrow mud-flat left by the falling river and protected by a steep low bank, they found shelter from the humming bullets. "Don't land! Don't land!" they called out to reinforcements arriving by boat from Columbus. "We are whipped! Go back!"

They spoke too soon. Grant's men, having overrun the camp, had stopped to loot, and their officers, elated by the rout, "galloped about from one cluster of men to another," according to Grant, "and at every halt delivered a short eulogy upon the Union cause and the achievements of the command." Like the whipped men under the river bank, they thought the battle was over. This was by no means the case, as they presently discovered. Now that their own men were out of the way, the artillerists on the Columbus bluff could bring their guns to bear: particularly one big rifled Whitworth, which began to rake the captured campsite. What was more, the reinforcements arriving by boat ignored the cries, "Don't land! Go back!" and coming up during the lull, formed a line of battle, preparing to attack. Disgusted, Grant ordered the camp set afire to discourage the looters and orators, and did what he could to reassemble his command. Meanwhile other Confederate reinforcements were pouring ashore to the north, between Belmont and the transports. When an aide rode up, exclaiming, "General, we are surrounded!" — "Well," Grant said, "we must cut our way out as we cut our way in."

All this time, Grant's faulty intelligence having made the Federal plans impenetrable, Polk had refused to believe that the action across the river was anything more than a feint to distract his attention from the main effort, which he believed would come from the Kentucky side. Columbus was a prize worth bleeding for, but it made no sense, as far as he could see, for the enemy to launch a serious attack against Belmont, a place not only worthless in its own right, but obviously untenable, even if taken, under the frown of the batteries on the bluff across the river. Therefore, after sending the four regiments at the outset, he had refused to be distracted. Now, though, the attack from the east not having developed and Pillow having been flung back to the landing, Polk sent Brigadier General B. F. Cheatham with three more regiments and crossed the river himself to see how they fared. With 5000 angry, vengeful Confederates on the field, including those who had rallied after cowering under the bank, Grant's elated but disorganized 3000 were going to find it considerably harder to "cut our way out," no matter how bravely the words were spoken, than they had found it to "cut our way in."

In the end, however, that was what they did, though at the cost of abandoning most of their captured material, including four guns, as well as many of the non-walking wounded and one thousand rifles, which the defenders afterwards garnered from the field. Grant had held back no reserves to throw into the battle at critical moments, but he performed more or less as a reserve himself, riding from point to point along his line to direct and animate his troops. Except for one regiment, which was cut off in the fighting and marched upstream to be picked up later, he was the last man aboard the final transport.

The skipper had already pushed off, but looking back he recognized the general on horseback and ran a plank out for him. (Polk saw him, too, though without recognition. From the nearby skirt of timber which had screened the debarkation, the bishop, seeing the horseman, said to his staff, "There is a Yankee; you may try your marksmanship on him if you wish." But no one did.) Grant had already had one mount shot from under him today, and when he chose another he chose well. The horse — which, Grant said, "seemed to take in the situation" — put its forefeet over the lip of the bank, tucked its hind legs under its rump, and "without hesitation or urging," slid down the incline and trotted up the gangplank.

That ended the Battle of Belmont, and though the casualties were about equal — something over 600 on each side, killed, wounded, and captured — it followed in general the pattern of all the battles fought that year, the attackers achieving initial success, the defenders giving way to early panic, until suddenly the roles were reversed and the rebels were left in control of the field, crowing over Yankee cowardice. At Belmont as at Bull Run — and especially as at Ball's Bluff, which it so much resembled, the repulsed troops having narrowly missed annihilation at the end — there were indications of blundering and ineptness. "The victory is complete," Grant asserted in dispatches, but two days after the battle the Chicago *Tribune* editorialized: "The disastrous termination of the Cairo expedition to Columbus is another severe lesson on the management of this contest with the rebels. Our troops have suffered a bad defeat. . . . The rebels have been elated and emboldened while our troops have been depressed, if not discouraged." The following day, in printing the casualty lists, the editor added: "It may be said of these victims, 'They have fallen, and to what end?' "

To what end, indeed. And now began the talk of Grant the butcher. This was no victory; not a single tactical advantage had been won; he just went out and came back, losing about as many as he killed. Yet certain facts were there for whoever would see them. He had moved instead of waiting for fair weather, had kept his head when things went all against him, and had brought his soldiers back to base with some real fighting experience under their belts. They were having none of the butcher talk. They had watched him alongside them where bullets flew the thickest and had cheered him riding his trick horse up the gangplank, the last man to leave the field. What was more, they knew the expedition had been designed in the first place to save the lives of their friends in the supposedly threatened column out after Thompson, and they knew now that if ever *they* were thought to be so trapped, Grant himself would come to get them out. Best of all, they had met the rebels in a stand-up fight which proved, for one thing, that blue-bellied Yankees were not the only ones who would panic and scatter and take off for defilade, crying, "We are whipped! Go back!"

Appointed to the western command two days after the battle, Halleck, who had been a civilian as well as a soldier, could see both points of view as to Belmont and the general who fought it. However, in spite of his qualms about Grant's rashness and the chances for being embarrassed by it, he was mainly glad to have him. Experienced leaders were all too few in the West. "It is said, General," he told McClellan, "that you have as many regular officers on your personal staff as I have in this whole Department." He had, in fact, hardly an army at all, he protested, "but rather a military rabble," and upon arriving he wired Washington: "Affairs in complete chaos. Troops unpaid; without clothing or arms. Many never properly mustered into service and some utterly demoralized. Hospitals overflowing with sick."

Burdened as he was with such problems — far too little of what he wanted, far too much of what he didn't — it was no wonder that he declined to aid his rival Buell by advancing southeast up the rivers, saying quite plainly: "It seems to me madness." Nor was it any wonder that Buell, similarly laden and thus denied assistance, saw no chance of advancing in any direction, either toward Knoxville, as Lincoln and McClellan kept urging, or toward Nashville, as he himself preferred. Both generals promised results as soon as conditions permitted. Meanwhile they did what they could to improve what they had inherited from Frémont and from Sherman.

To this task they brought their skill as organizers, disciplinarians, and administrators, building a war machine for the West comparable to the one McClellan was forging in the East. Not even their worst enemies denied their considerable talents along these lines, Jefferson Davis remarking before the year's end: "The Federal forces are not hereafter, as heretofore, to be commanded by path-finders and holiday soldiers, but by men of military education and experience in war."

McClellan drew from this what solace he could, knowing it was much. Meanwhile, preparing for the great day if the great day ever came, he continued to drill and train his army, staging large and ever larger reviews, until at last, near Bailey's Crossroads, November 20, he put on the largest one of all.

Seven full divisions — 70,000 riflemen and cannoneers and troopers, equipped to the limit of the nation's purchasing and manufacturing power — swung in cadenced glitter past the reviewing stand, where ladies fluttered handkerchiefs and politicians swelled their chests with pride, covering their hearts with their hats as the colors rippled by. And yet, while the dust settled, while the troops filed off to their encampments and the civilians rode in their carriages back to Washington, there was a feeling that all this panoply, grand and enjoyable as it was, did not make up for the Quaker-gun humiliation of Munson's Hill or erase the shame of Bull Run, which still rankled. Nor, for that matter, did it reopen the Potomac or chase the rebels off the B & O. In fact, looking back on the daylong surge of armed might past the grandstand, the politicians were reinforced in their opinion that so fine an army should be used for something sterner than parading.

The soldiers did not share this let-down feeling and had no sympathy for the protests. Nor did they consider themselves inactive. Loving and trusting Little Mac, inspired by his presence when he rode his charger through their camps, they were content to leave military decisions to his superior judgment. "Marching Along," they sang on their conditioning hikes, back and forth across the "sacred soil" of their Virginia bridgehead:

> *"McClellan's our leader, he's gallant and strong;*
> *For God and our country we are marching along!"*

Prodded by the politicians, who kept pointing out that the weather was fair and the roads still firm, Lincoln hoped that the army would move southward before winter ended all chances for an advance. McClellan apparently having no such plan in mind, the President himself tried his hand at designing a frontal and flank attack on the Confederates at Manassas. This product of midnight fret and study was submitted December 1 to the young general-in-chief, who looked it over and replied ten days later that it was hardly feasible. "They could meet us in front with equal forces nearly," he objected.

Besides, he added as if by afterthought, "I have now my mind turned actively toward another plan of campaign that I do not think at all anticipated by the enemy nor by many of our own people." Thus Lincoln, who apparently was included under the general heading "our own people," received his first inkling of what came to be known as the Urbanna plan.

McClellan had never enjoyed the notion of a head-on tangle with Johnston on those plains where McDowell had gone down. Some day, given the odds, he might chance it; that was what he was building toward. But to attempt it while outnumbered, as he believed his army was, seemed to him downright folly. Then Buell's refusal to advance against and through Knoxville, which would have placed his army on Johnston's flank, in a position to coöperate with the Army of the Potomac, caused McClellan to abandon all intentions of a due south attack, present or future. Poring over headquarters maps he had evolved "another plan of campaign," one moreover enlisting the assistance of the navy, flushed with its three recent victories. He would load his soldiers aboard transports, steam down the Potomac into Chesapeake Bay, then south along the coast to the mouth of the Rappahannock, and up that river a short distance to Urbanna, a landing on the southern bank, less than fifty airline miles from Richmond, his objective. Without the loss of a man, he would have cut his marching distance in half and he would be in the rear of Johnston — who then would be forced to retreat and fight on grounds of McClellan's choosing. The more he thought about it, the better he liked it. It was not only beautifully simple. It was beautifully bloodless.

In the flush of first conception he planned to set out immediately. "I have no intention of putting the army into winter quarters," he declared. "I mean the campaign will be short, sharp, and decisive." But there were numerous details, including the assembling of transports for the 150,000 men he would take along, all of which had to be accomplished in great secrecy if Johnston was to be left holding the bag in northern Virginia. It was enough to overtax the energies of even so expert an organizer as McClellan. Presently he realized that it would probably be spring before he could get the campaign under way. Regretfully he wrote his wife, "I am doing all I can to get ready to move before winter sets in, but it now begins to look as if we were condemned to a winter of inactivity. If it is so," he added, flinching from the protest he knew must follow, "the fault will not be mine: there will be that consolation for my conscience, even if the world at large never knows it."

As if in confirmation, the rains came. The fields were turned to quagmires and the roads were axle deep in mud. At last he had a reason for not advancing which even the politicians could understand. Then, late in the month, he had an even better personal reason. He came down with a cold, which the doctors presently diagnosed as typhoid fever, and was confined to his bed for three weeks, into the new year.

His good friend Stanton, legal light of the War Department, came to his bedside, peering over his spectacles and murmuring, "They are counting on your death, and already are dividing among themselves your military goods and chattels." But when the President called — doing so for the first time since the snub McClellan had given him six weeks back — he was denied admittance. Lincoln was profoundly troubled. Not only was the general sick, but so was his chief of staff, Brigadier General R. B. Marcy, who was also his father-in-law. Subordinates might be able to administer the Army of the Potomac, which obviously was not going into action anyhow, but Lincoln wondered what was happening elsewhere, especially in the West, now that the guiding hand was paralyzed.

On the last day of the year he telegraphed Buell and Halleck, asking if they were acting by mutual arrangement. Buell replied that there were no provisions for concerted action; Halleck replied that he knew nothing of Buell's plans and that he was unable to coöperate in any case. "It is exceedingly discouraging. As everywhere else, nothing can be done," Lincoln wrote on the back of Halleck's letter, and wired for them to get in touch at once. That same day he went to the office of Quartermaster General M. C. Meigs. "General, what shall I do?" he groaned. "The people are impatient; Chase has no money, and tells me he can raise no more; the General of the Army has typhoid fever. The bottom is out of the tub. What shall I do?"

The question was rhetorical: Lincoln already knew what to do, and even how to do it. Midnight study of strategy texts, plus native common sense and conversation with professionals, had increased his understanding of the military problem. In language that was knotty and overpunctuated, showing thereby the extent to which he had labored to evolve it, he said in a letter to Buell at the time: "I state my general idea of this war to be that we have greater numbers, and the enemy has the greater facility of concentrating forces upon points of collision; that we must fail, unless we can find some way of making our advantage an over-match of his; and that this can be done by menacing him with superior forces at different points, at the same time; so that we can safely attack, one, or both, if he makes no change; and if he weakens one to strengthen the other, forbear to attack the strengthened one, but seize, and hold the weakened one, gaining so much."

However, the fact that he knew what to do, and could state it thus in one hard-breathing sentence — the awful hug of the anaconda becoming more awful still as it shifted its coils to exert more pressure where the bones would crack — only rendered more exasperating the fact that "nothing [could] be done." It was a question, Lincoln saw already, of finding the right man to do the job. Already he was looking for a general who would not only believe in his "idea of this war," but would follow it, inexorably, to the end. Meanwhile it was becoming increasingly evident that, for all his gifts, for all his soldiers' love of him, McClellan was not the man.

★   ★   ★

The bottom was not really out of the tub. That was only Lincoln's manner of speaking, designed perhaps to restore some measure of confidence when he got around to comparing the overstatement with the facts. He had known melancholy all his life, and this was one of his ways of working it off — just as sometimes, to clarify in his own mind a relationship with some individual, he would write the man a letter which he never intended to mail; Lincoln was his own psychiatrist. And yet the bottom had been almost out. Riding, or else tossed upon, the seethe and roil of popular opinion during the early weeks of what became known as The Trent Affair, public men on both sides of the ocean lost their heads, and England and the United States came closer to war than they had ever come without war following. Few doubted that it would come. Even fewer, apparently, did not welcome it in the heat of indignation, since in each case national honor seemed at stake.

Mason and Slidell had left Havana while the guns of Port Royal and Belmont were booming out accompaniments for victory and repulse. Next day, November 8, while Du Pont's sailors occupied Fort Beauregard and Grant was counting noses back at Cairo, the *Trent* and the *San Jacinto* met in the Bahama Passage, then wore apart, northward and northeastward over a glassy sea, the former having exchanged four passengers for a cargo of outrage explosive enough to blow the bottom out of any tub. In London on the 27th the captain gave the authorities the news.

Immediate and unrestrained, the reaction was in the nature of a shriek; Britannia had been touched where she was tender. "By Captain Wilkes let the Yankee breed be judged," the *Times* declared, and stigmatized both him and it: "Swagger and ferocity, built on a foundation of vulgarity and cowardice, these are his characteristics, and these are the most prominent marks by which his countrymen, generally speaking, are known all over the world." Entering a Cabinet meeting, the eighty-year-old Prime Minister, Lord Palmerston, flung his hat on the table and exploded: "You may stand for this but damned if I will!"

Accordingly, while the cry for war went up all over England, an army of 8000 boarded transports bound for Canada, where fortifications were ordered erected at strategic points along the border, and Royal Navy shipyards were thrown into a bustle of preparation beyond anything since the days when the first Napoleon was mustering all Europe for invasion. Lord John Russell was put to work drafting an ultimatum for presentation to the United States. Its terms were simple: either an abject apology, including surrender of the seized Confederate emissaries, or war.

The republic across the Atlantic had never been one to bow to ultimatums, least of all from its arch-enemy England, and especially not now, with its citizens engaged in a delirium of praise for the latest hero to twist the lion's tail. A week after taking his prisoners aboard, Captain Wilkes had put into Hampton Roads for coal, a tall, clean-shaven regular, romantic in appearance, with becoming streaks of gray in his wavy hair. From there, having informed his superiors of his action, he steamed north again, bound for Boston in accordance with instructions to deliver the rebel envoys at Fort Warren, where a congratulatory telegram awaited him from the Secretary of the Navy: "Your conduct in seizing these public enemies was marked by intelligence, ability, decision, and firmness, and has the emphatic approval of this Department." The Army Secretary was no less enthusiastic. When the news reached the War Department, that dignitary led in the giving of three cheers by a group which included the governor of Massachusetts.

From the press, from the pulpit, from the public at large came praise for the captain's forthright action. Congress rushed through a resolution thanking him for his "brave, adroit, and patriotic conduct in the arrest of the traitors," and voted a gold medal struck in his honor. He was wined and dined and paraded in Boston, and toasts to his boldness were drunk throughout the nation. For the Administration to submit to an ultimatum and apologize for the captain's action would be to disavow that action and repudiate the hero before the eyes of his adoring public. With the nation already split in half and one tremendous conflict already building toward a climax, no one could say for certain what the result would be if the people were forced to choose between their captain-hero and those who let him down.

Thus — as in 1812, with the roles reversed — the two nations were poised for a war that would surely come unless one, or both, backed down: which was plainly impossible, believing as they did the worst of each other. On one side of the water, the British assumed that the impressment had been performed under government sanction, probably in accordance with instructions. On the other, the Americans, already provoked by the granting of belligerency status to the Confederacy, saw only another instance of England's avowing her intention to further the rebellion and assist in the dismemberment of a rival in the scramble for world trade.

As if all this was not enough to make war seem inevitable, the British conception of what had fed the roots of the late outrage was reinforced by the aggressive diplomacy — the announced intention, even — of the American Secretary of State, who was known to favor war with England as a means of reuniting his divided countrymen. He had said so repeatedly, in interviews, in correspondence, and in after-dinner talk. If the North became embroiled with a foreign power, Seward believed, the South would drop its States Rights quarrel and hasten to close ranks against invasion: whereupon, with that war over, the two sections could sit down in a glow of mutual pride at having won it, and reconcile past differences without the need or desire for further bloodshed.

In this he was most likely much mistaken, for the main goal of Confederate diplomacy was to draw England into the conflict on the southern side. And yet he was not entirely wrong — at least so far as regarded human nature. Now that the hope seemed about to be fact, the reaction below the Potomac and the Ohio was not unmixed. Exultation was sobered there by the thought of Americans, under whatever flag, submitting to an old-world ultimatum. "As I read the Northern newspapers, the blood rushes to my head," one diarist wrote. "In the words of the fine fiction writers, my cheek is mantling with shame. Anyhow," she went on to predict, "down they must go to Old England, knuckle on their marrow bones, to keep her on their side — or barely neutral." Right or wrong, however, such was Seward's theory: a foreign war would still domestic strife. And now as if by the bounty of fate, without the slightest effort on his part, Captain Wilkes's action and England's reaction presented him with an all-out chance to test it.

Lincoln himself had his doubts about this theory, not only in general but in particular, as it applied to the case in point. He rather agreed with the southern diarist that there would have to be some knuckling done. "I fear the traitors will prove to be white elephants," he remarked when he received word of the seizure of Mason and Slidell. Unfamiliar with diplomacy, he was feeling his way. When a learned visitor explained to him that his blockade declaration had naturally gained for the Confederacy the rights of a belligerent in all the courts of Europe, since a nation did not blockade its own ports, Lincoln replied: "Yes, that's a fact. I see the point now, but I don't know anything about the Law of Nations and I thought it was all right. . . . I'm a good enough lawyer in a western law court, I suppose, but we don't practice the Law of Nations out there, and I supposed Seward knew all about it and I left it to him."

He left it to Seward, but he did not let him go unsupervised. It was as if Lincoln said to him, as he had said to Herndon back in Springfield, "Billy, you're too rampant." Seward was called Billy, too — Billy Bowlegs, his enemies dubbed him: a bandy-legged, untidy man with a great deal of personal charm behind the bristling eyebrows, the constant cigar, and the nose of a macaw. Mrs Lincoln detested him outright. "He draws you around his little finger like a skein of thread," she warned her husband. But when other advisers urged that he drop the New Yorker from the cabinet, Lincoln said: "Seward knows that I am his master."

Seward knew no such thing, as yet, but he was learning. Though Lincoln liked him, enjoyed his stories, and respected his political astuteness, from Sumter on he watched him and rode herd on him, toning down his overseas dispatches, which in first draft rather demonstrated his theory that a war with Europe would solve the urgent problems here at home. It was characteristic of Seward that, having styled the coming civil war an "irrepressible conflict," he met it, when it came, with various efforts to repress it. Sumter at least had taught him that Lincoln was more than a prairie bumpkin, for the Secretary informed his wife in early June: "Executive skill and vigor are rare qualities. The President is the best of us, but" — he felt obliged to add — "he needs constant and assiduous coöperation." The *Trent* affair removed this final residue of doubt, and at the same time vindicated Lincoln's decision to keep Seward at his post, despite the clamor of his enemies and the trouble he had made.

Now that the war he thought he wanted was his for the asking — or, indeed, for the not-asking — Seward discovered, perhaps to his profound surprise, that he did not want it at all. He said so, in fact, as soon as the news arrived from Hampton Roads. In the cabinet, while all around them were wild-eyed with praise for the bold captain, only Seward and Montgomery Blair perceived that in turning his quarter-deck into a prize court Wilkes had not only been rash, he had been wrong, and by his illegal action had exposed his country to embarrassment. As Lincoln put it, "We must stick to American principles concerning the rights of neutrals. We fought Great Britain [in 1812] for insisting, by theory and practice, on the right to do precisely what Wilkes has done." Seward agreed. "One war at a time," Lincoln cautioned, and Seward agreed again.

However, these three alone, Lincoln and Seward and the practical-minded Blair, could not breast the popular current running full-tilt against them; they must wait. In his December 1 message to Congress, the President left the affair unmentioned. "Mr Lincoln forgot it!" someone remarked in shocked surprise at his thus ignoring the burning question of the day. The words were passed along, laughter being added to amazement: "Mr Lincoln forgot it!" And then, perceptibly — whether because of the chilling effect of the laughter or because, as in certain diseases, the fever itself had cured the fit — the excitement ebbed.

Cooler heads took over on both sides of the Atlantic. The British began to consider that Captain Wilkes might have acted without orders from his government, and responsible Americans began to see that the Confederate envoys locked up in Fort Warren — where Slidell was being given his chance to "conspire with the mice against the cat" and Mason was abiding by his oath (though in a manner not intended) never to visit that shore again "except as an ambassador" — were accomplishing more toward the fulfillment of their diplomatic mission than they would be doing if they had continued on their way to Europe.

The first official show of reason came from England. Prince Albert, closeted with the Queen in his last illness — he would be dead before the year was out — toned down Russell's ultimatum, modifying its phraseology until the demand for an apology became, in effect, a request for an explanation; so that, instead of finding it "dictatorial or menacing," as he had feared, Seward could pronounce it "courteous and friendly." It was still an ultimatum, requiring an apology for the insult to the British flag, as well as the surrender of the envoys, but at least it opened the door for a reply in the form of something except a declaration of war. That was much. As for the apology — the one thing Seward could not give — verbal additions to the message indicated that a statement to the effect that Wilkes had acted without instructions would render it superfluous, since a nation could hardly be expected to apologize for something it had not done. Seward already had in mind the terms of his reply, but before it could be sent he would have to win

the approval of the rest of the cabinet. In the present state of public
furor, with even Lincoln feeling that surrender of the captives was "a
pretty bitter pill to swallow," nothing less than unanimous action would
suffice.

For two days Seward remained shut away in his office, composing a reply to the British demand: a reply intended not only for the
eyes of the Minister to whom it was addressed, but also for those of the
American man-in-the-street, whose sensibilities were the ones considered most in this explanation of his government's being willing to give
up the rebel envoys: so that, though in form and style the document
was brilliantly legal, showing Seward at his sparkling best — this was
one State Department dispatch Lincoln did not need to doctor — it
was not so much designed to stand up under analysis by the Admiralty
law lords, as it was to show the writer's countrymen that their leaders
were by no means trembling at the roar of the British lion. Having
complied with the basic demands of the ultimatum by 1) admitting that
Wilkes had acted without orders and 2) offering to deliver the captives
whenever and wherever they were wanted, Seward then wrote for his
countrymen's eyes, with reasoning that was somewhat specious and
language that was at times impertinent, what amounted to an indictment of the British point of view, past and present. In other words,
under cover of an apology, he gave the lion's tail a final twist.

Down on the Virginian peninsula that summer, though by the
rules of warfare he could not confiscate private property unless it was
being used against him, Ben Butler had justified the receiving of slaves
into his lines on grounds that their labor for the enemy made them
contraband of war. "I'se contraband," they would say, smiling proudly
as they crossed the freedom line, and Butler put them to work on his
fortifications. Now Seward took a page from the squint-eyed general's
book, affirming that the envoys and their secretaries were "contraband,"
liable to seizure. Wilkes therefore had done right to stop the ship and
then to board and search her. His error lay in his leniency; for he should
have brought not only the rebel envoys, but also the *Trent* and all
her cargo into port for judgment; in which case, Seward was sure, the
ship and everything aboard her, including the four Confederates, would
have become the lawful property of the United States. However —
and here was where the impertinence came in — the Secretary could
appreciate his lordship's being taken aback, for in impressing passengers
from a merchant vessel Wilkes had followed a British, not an American
line of conduct. Seward saw the present ultimatum as an admission of
past injuries inflicted by the mistress of the seas, and he congratulated
Britannia on having come round to the point of view against which she
had fought in 1812: "She could in no other way so effectually disavow
any such injury, as we think she does, by assuming now as her own the
ground upon which we then stood." Captain Wilkes had been mainly

right, but the United States wanted no advantage gained by means of an action which was even partly wrong. Seward was frank to state, however, that if his nation's safety required it he would still detain the captives; but "the effectual check and waning proportions of the existing insurrection, as well as the comparative unimportance of the captured persons themselves, when dispassionately weighed, happily forbid me from resorting to that defense.... The four persons in question are now held in military custody at Fort Warren, in the State of Massachusetts. They will be cheerfully liberated. Your lordship will please indicate a time and place for receiving them."

Doubtless Seward had enjoyed those two days he spent locked away in his office, verbally building a straw man, straw by straw, then verbally demolishing him, handful by handful. When he emerged, however, prepared to receive the applause of his fellow cabinet members, he received instead cold looks and hot objections. They could appreciate the brilliance of his performance, but it did not obscure the fact that they were being asked to yield — which most of them had sworn not to do. It took him, in fact, as long to win their indorsement of the document as he had spent composing it, and the latter two days were far more hectic than the former.

Christmas morning the ministers assembled. When they adjourned that afternoon, to spend what was left of the holiday with their families, there had been no agreement. What Lincoln called "a pretty bitter pill" was for the cabinet, one member said, "downright gall and wormwood." The war was one year old that night, the anniversary of Anderson's removal of his eighty-odd men from Moultrie to Fort Sumter. Next morning the ministers reassembled; the discussion was resumed. It went hard, being asked to go down on their marrow bones against all their oaths and boasts, with only Seward's flimsy curtain of paradox and impertinence to hide them from the public and each other. In the end, however, as one of them wrote, "all yielded to the necessity, and unanimously concurred."

Mason and Slidell were handed over on New Year's Day to continue their roundabout journey, the latter being twenty days late for the appointment he had made with his wife when he told her on parting, "My dear, we shall meet in Paris in sixty days." The public reaction to the outcome of the crisis was considerably less violent than the cabinet members had feared. Though the anti-British press continued to fulminate according to tradition, in general there was a sigh of relief at having to fight only "one war at a time." When Captain Wilkes, still wearing his laurels, was sent about his business, to be supervised more closely in the future, the public did not even feel let down. Poker was not the national game for nothing; the people understood that their leaders had bowed, not to the British, but to expediency.

Only within one group was there despondency that the rebels

had been freed. "Everybody here is satisfied with their surrender," Lincoln heard from a friend in Indiana, "except the secession sympathizers, who are wonderfully hurt at the idea that our national honor is tarnished."

★ ★ ★

On this diplomatic note, which opened shrill, then broke into falsetto, the first year of the conflict reached a close. Politically and militarily speaking, its laurels belonged to those who had established a nation within its span and defended that establishment successfully in battle, meeting and turning back attacks against both flanks of their thousand-mile frontier and staving off an advance against the center. McClellan's gains in western Virginia and the Federal navy's trident amphibious lunge did something to redress the defeats along Bull Run and Wilson's Creek, but when those checks were emphasized, east and west, by the rout at Ball's Bluff and the repulse at Belmont, there was a distinct public impression, North and South, at home and abroad, of failure by the Unionist government to deal with the Confederate bid for independence.

One side called this bid a revolution. The other insisted that it was a rebellion. Whichever it was, it was plainly a fact, and both sides saw clearly now that the contest between northern power and southern élan was not going to be the ninety-day affair they had predicted at the outset.

Realization that this was so had grown until it was unmistakable, at which point violent objections were sounded on both sides by the extremists who had been foremost in predicting that the conflict would be short and decisive. Southerners were all bluster and would not fight if their bluff was called, the abolitionists had declared, and when one fire-eater had offered to wipe up with his handkerchief all the blood that would be shed, a less squeamish colleague had backed him up by offering to drink it. Now that blood had dripped and flowed beyond their power to drink or wipe, they waxed bitterly accusative, North and South, against those who held the reins. Chagrined that the war they had done so much to bring about had been taken out of their hands when it arrived, the two groups still insisted that their prediction had turned out false only because their aims had been betrayed. It could still be rendered valid, they affirmed, provided the war was fought the way they wanted. Each favored an all-out invasion, with fire and sword and the hangman's noose, and each blamed its leader for an obvious lack of vigor in his thinking and in his actions.

"Jeff Davis is conceited, wrong-headed, wranglesome, obstinate —a traitor," Edmund Rhett declared, while back in Springfield the northern President's erstwhile law partner complained that Lincoln was attempting to "squelch out this huge rebellion by popguns filled with rose water. He ought to hang somebody and get up a name for will or decision — for character," Herndon wrote, and added scornfully: "Let him hang some child or woman if he has not the courage to hang a *man*."

Between these two extremes, while the anti-Davis and anti-Lincoln cliques were respectively consolidating their opposition and sharpening their barbs, the mass of men who would do the actual fighting, and the women who would wait for them at home, took what came with a general determination to measure up to what was expected of them. It was their good fortune, or else their misery, to belong to a generation in which every individual would be given a chance to discover and expose his worth, down to the final ounce of strength and nerve. For the most part, therefore, despite the clamor of extremists north and south of the new frontier, each side accepted its leader as a condition of the tournament, and counted itself fortunate to have the man it had and not the other. Seen from opposite banks of the Ohio and the Potomac, both seemed creatures fit for frightening children into quick obedience. On the one hand there was Davis, "ambitious as Lucifer," with his baleful eyes and bloodless mouth, cerebral and lizard-cold, plotting malevolence into the small hours of the night. On the other there was Lincoln, "the original gorilla," with his shambling walk and sooty face, an ignorant rail-splitter catapulted by long-shot politics into an office for which he had neither the experience nor the dignity required.

What they seemed to each other was another matter. Lincoln had recognized his adversary's renowned capabilities from the start, but it was not until well after Sumter — if then — that Davis, like so many of the northern President's own associates, including even his Secretary of State, began to understand that he was having to deal with an opponent not below but beyond the run of men. Their official attitude toward one another gave a certain advantage to the Southerner, since he could arraign his rival before the bar of world opinion, addressing him as a tyrant and "exposing" his duplicity; whereas Lincoln, by refusing to admit that there was any such thing as the Confederate States of America, was obliged to pretend that Davis, too, was nonexistent. However, it was a knife that cut both ways. Lincoln was not only denied the chance to answer charges, he was also relieved of the necessity for replying to a man who wasn't there. Nor was that all. Constitutionally, the Illinois lawyer-politician was better equipped for accepting vilification than the Mississippi planter-statesman was for accepting what amounted to a cut; so that, in their personal duel, the advantages of a cloak of invisibility were canceled, at least in part, by the reaction of the man who had to wear it. Davis wore it, in fact, like an involuntary hair shirt.

Followed by the admiring glances of Richmond ladies in made-over bonnets and men in last year's winter suits, he continued to take his early morning and late evening constitutionals, to and from the office where he spent long hours on administrative details rather than on executive decisions. With the bottom gone out of the slave market and gold already selling at a premium of fifty percent, the croakers were saying that he expended his energies thus to keep from facing the larger issues. But that was to overlook the fact that, rightly or wrongly, those issues had been settled back in the spring, when he committed himself and his nation to the defensive. Now he was pursuing a policy which a later southern-born President would call "watchful waiting" — watching for another northern offensive and waiting for European intervention. His task was to turn back the former and welcome the latter. In the light of Manassas, which set the battle pattern, and the *Trent* affair, which strained British-U.S. relations even further, Davis considered both of these outcomes probable, either of which would validate for all time the existing fact of his country's independence. Waiting had already brought him much, and now that it seemed likely to bring more, he continued to watch and wait, going about his duties as he saw them.

Such duties involved an occasional social function and the daily hour which he reserved for his children. Of these there now were four, Mrs Davis having borne in mid-December the child christened William Howell for her ailing father. They were Davis' chief relaxation, for much as he enjoyed the social amenities, particularly an intimate evening spent with a few close friends, he mostly denied himself that pleasure in these times. He would drop in during his wife's receptions, spend an hour exercising his remarkable memory for names and faces, then dutifully, his invariable charm and courtesy masking whatever boredom he felt, take a cup of tea before retiring to his study and the paperwork that awaited him as a result of his unwillingness to delegate authority.

The lady guests might have their reservations about his wife — she was rather too "intellectual" for their taste; "pleasant, if not wholly genial," one Richmond matron called her — but the men, coming under the sway of those attractions which had drawn her husband, seventeen years and five children ago (Samuel, the first child, died in infancy), did not feel that the breadth of her mind obscured the charm of her person. All were agreed, however, as to the attractiveness of the husband and the dignity he brought to his high office. He was showing the strain, it was true; but that only served to emphasize the wonder at how well he bore up under it, after all. Whatever their opinion as to his policy in adopting a static defensive, they all agreed that as a figurehead for the ship of state he could hardly be improved on.

Ornamentally, Lincoln served less well — though in reply to complaints about his looks his followers could repeat what had been pointed out already: "We didn't get him for ballroom purposes." Even here, however, he was trying. At White House receptions he stood in line and pumped the hands of callers, performing the duty, one witness observed, "like a wood-chopper, at so much a cord." He was learning, too. Though his big hands split through several pairs of kid gloves on such evenings, now at least the gloves were white, not black as at the opera in New York ten months before. He had most of the problems Davis had, and some that Davis did not have. Office seekers still hemmed him in and placed a constant drain on his good humor. Finding him depressed one day, a friend asked in alarm, "What is the matter? Have you bad news from the army?" "No, it isn't the army," Lincoln said with a weary smile. "It is the post office in Brownsville, Missouri."

Unlike his opponent, he had no fixed policy to refer to: not even the negative one of a static defensive, which, whatever its faults, at least had the virtue of offering a position from which to judge almost any combination of events. This lack gave him the flexibility which lay at the core of his greatness, but he had to purchase it dearly in midnight care and day-long fret. Without practical experience on which to base his decisions, he must improvise as he went along, like a doctor developing a cure in the midst of an epidemic. His advisers were competent men in the main, but they were fiercely divided in their counsels; so that, to all his other tasks, Lincoln had added the role of mediator, placing himself as a buffer between factions, to absorb what he could of the violence they directed at each other. What with generals who balked and politicians who champed at the bit, it was no wonder if he sometimes voiced the wish that he were out of it, back home in Illinois. Asked how he enjoyed his office, he told of a tarred and feathered man out West, who, as he was being ridden out of town on a rail, heard one among the crowd call to him, asking how he liked it, high up there on his uncomfortable perch. "If it wasn't for the honor of the thing," the man replied, "I'd sooner walk."

In Richmond and in Washington, one hundred miles apart — the same distance as lay between Fairview and Hodgenville, their birthplaces in Kentucky — Davis and Lincoln toiled their long hours, kept their vigils, and sought solutions to problems that were mostly the same but seemed quite different because they saw them in reverse, from opposite directions. All men were to be weighed in this time, and especially these two. At the far ends of the north-south road connecting the two capitals they strained to see and understand each other, peering as if across a darkling plain. Soon now, that hundred miles of Virginia with its glittering rivers and dusty turnpikes, its fields of grain and rolling pastures, the peace of generations soft upon it like the softness in the voices of its people, would be obscured by the swirl and bank of cannon smoke, stitched by the fitful stabs of muzzle flashes, until at last, lurid as the floor of hell itself, it would seem to have been made for war as deliberately as a chessboard was designed for chess. Even the place-names on the map, which now were merely quaint, would take on the sound of crackling flame and distant thunder, the Biblical,

Indian, Anglo-Saxon names of hamlets and creeks and crossroads, for the most part unimportant in themselves until the day when the armies came together, as often by accident as on purpose, to give the scattered names a permanence and settle what manner of life the future generations were to lead. The road ran straight, a glory road with split-rail fences like firewood ready stacked for the two armies, and many men would travel it wearing Union blue or Confederate gray. Blood had been shed along it once, and would be shed again; how many times?

Neither Lincoln nor Davis knew, but they intended to find out, and soon. The year just past had been in the nature of a prelude, whose close marked only the end of the beginning.

The Thing Gets Under Way

★ ✗ ☆

🦃 ALBERT SIDNEY JOHNSTON, THE RANKING
Confederate general in the field, was charged with maintaining the
integrity of a line that stretched westward more than five hundred
miles: from the barrens of eastern Kentucky, through the Bluegrass
region, on across the Mississippi, and beyond the kaleidoscopic swirl of
conflict in Missouri to Indian territory, where it ended, like a desert
stream, as a trickle in dry sand. To accomplish the defense of this
western-Europe-sized expanse, penetrated by rivers floating enemy
fleets and menaced along its salient points by two Federal armies, each
one larger than his own, he had a distinguished reputation, a nobility
of looks and character, a high-flown official title — General Commanding the Western Department of the Army of the Confederate States of
America — and all too little else. He was a big man, broad-shouldered
and deep-chested, over six feet tall and just under two hundred pounds
in weight. His wavy dark-brown hair touched with such gray as became his fifty-eight years, the Kentucky-born Texan gave at once an impression of strength and gentleness. No beard disguised his strong, regular features, but a heavy mustache offset somewhat the dominance of
brow and width of jaw. Commanding in presence, grave in manner, he
wore his dignity with natural charm and was not without the saving
grace of humor. It was Johnston, for example, who remarked that there
was "too much tail" to Frémont's kite.

In the thirty-five years since his graduation from West Point —
where Jefferson Davis, looking up to him from two classes below, as
at Transylvania earlier, contracted a severe and lifelong case of hero
worship — he had distinguished himself in a colorful career: frontier
officer, Texas revolutionist and Secretary of War in Sam Houston's
cabinet, gentleman farmer, Mexican War colonel, U.S. Army paymaster,
and commander of the famed 2d Cavalry, whose roster carried the

names of four future full generals, including himself and R. E. Lee, one lieutenant general, and three major generals, all Confederate, as well as two of the leading Union major generals. Zachary Taylor was reported to have said that Johnston was the finest soldier he ever commanded, and Winfield Scott had called him "a Godsend to the Army and to the country."

While the national storm was heading up, he was a brevet brigadier in command of the Pacific Coast, with headquarters at Fort Alcatraz in San Francisco Bay; but when Texas seceded he declined an offer of high rank in the Union army, tendered his resignation, and led a group of thirty pro-Confederate officers and civilians eastward on horseback across the desert toward his adopted state, dodging Apaches and Federal garrisons on the way. From Galveston he came on to New Orleans, where he was greeted as if an additional army had flocked to the Stars and Bars. His route to Richmond, through a countryside still elated over the six-weeks-old Manassas victory, was blazed with fluttering handkerchiefs and tossed hats, the news of his coming having preceded him all along the line. Davis was waiting, too, and handed him his lofty commission and the accompanying assignment to the far-flung Western Department.

"I hoped and expected that I had others who would prove generals," the southern leader afterwards declared; "but I knew I had *one*, and that was Sidney Johnston." Still later he put it even stronger, calling him "the greatest soldier, the ablest man, civil or military, Confederate or Federal, then living."

This high opinion was shared by the people of the region where the general's orders took him. From Richmond to Nashville, as from New Orleans to Richmond, the journey was one continuous ovation. Yet now that the new year had come in, with its hangover from the heady wine of Manassas and Wilson's Creek, all that seemed far away and long ago — as if it had occurred in another era, a dream world, even, divided from the present by an airtight door which slammed forever shut in mid-September when Johnston arrived and saw for himself, at unmistakable first hand, the magnitude of the task that lay before him and the paucity of the means with which he was expected to accomplish it. Politically the lines were already drawn; Kentucky and Missouri both had stars in the Confederate flag, though it was becoming increasingly clear that Lincoln had mostly won that fight, in spite of secessionist governors and Frémont. The problem now was military, and the line to be drawn lay not along the Ohio River, but along a zigzag course conforming to the mountains and rivers and railroads of Kentucky and the crazy-quilt pattern of Missouri. Such a line would be difficult to defend at best, but with the force at his disposal it was patently impossible. He had something under 50,000 men in all, scarcely amounting to more in effect than a 500-mile-long skirmish line, distributed about equally east and west of the big river that pierced his center.

In the Transmississippi the snarled military situation was aggravated by the rivalry of Price and McCulloch, whose victories had not brought them into accord. Since to elevate one would mean the probable loss of the other, along with many followers, Johnston proposed that the Richmond authorities assign to the region a field commander who would rank them both. Eventually this was done, and soon after the first of the year Major General Earl Van Dorn, West Pointer and Mississippian, a man of considerable fire and reputation, took over the job of welding the two commands into one army. Meanwhile, on his way from Richmond, Johnston stopped off at the far eastern end of his line and ordered Brigadier General Felix Zollicoffer, a former newspaper editor and Tennessee congressman, to take his little army of recruits through Cumberland Gap in order to post them where they could guard the passes giving down upon Knoxville and the Virginia-Tennessee Railroad.

Having provided thus for his flanks, Johnston looked to his center, the critical 150-mile sector extending roughly east-southeast from Columbus, Kentucky, to Nashville. Davis had empowered him to withdraw Polk from Columbus, out of consideration for the state's political sensibilities, or to sustain the occupation. It was not a difficult decision; in fact, Johnston had already made it when he sent Zollicoffer forward. But now he did more. Finding Simon Buckner waiting for him in Nashville — the former head of the Kentucky State Guard was now a private citizen, offering the South his services — Johnston commissioned him a brigadier, assigned him several regiments, and set him in motion for Bowling Green, sixty miles to the north. Far from ordering Polk's withdrawal, the new department commander swung his central sector forward, gate-like, with Columbus as the hinge. The line now extended east-northeast, and within a week of his arrival he had thrown every available armed man northward across the Kentucky border to strengthen it.

It badly needed strengthening. At the outset Johnston had fewer than 20,000 troops to man the long line from the Mississippi to the mountains — 11,000 with Polk, 4000 each with Buckner and Zollicoffer — backed up by a few scattered camps of recruits in Tennessee, some without any weapons at all. But when Johnston appealed for arms and men to the governors of Alabama and Georgia, both were prompt in refusal. "Our own coast is threatened," the former replied, while the latter, if less explanatory, was more emphatic: "It is utterly impossible for me to comply with your request." Not all were so deaf to his pleas, however. More closely threatened, Tennessee coöperated better, putting fifty regiments into the field before the end of the year, and Kentucky volunteers continued to come in, some bringing their long rifles. Four

regiments arrived from Mississippi before that state was shut off from
him by governmental notification that the area was not properly
within the limits of his command. Not that Richmond was unmindful
of the danger. It sent what it felt it could afford, including 4650
Enfield rifles brought in by blockade runners, and transferred to the
Army of Central Kentucky — so Johnston called it — several of the
Confederacy's most distinguished brigadiers.

Georgia-born William J. Hardee, forty-six — not only a West
Pointer and one-time commandant of cadets, but also the author of
Rifle and Light Infantry Tactics, formerly an Academy text and now
the official drill and tactics manual of both armies — brought his brigade
from northeast Arkansas to Bowling Green, where he took over from
Buckner and soon was promoted to major general, as befitted his wider
experience and his position as commander of the vital center. Gideon
Pillow, who had measured swords with Grant at Belmont, also was
shifted eastward to bolster the advance. He too ranked Buckner, and
for the present became second in command of the Army of the Center,
under Hardee.

Three prominent Kentuckians, all in their forties, also were
available for the defense of their state. The oldest was George B.
Crittenden, forty-nine, West Pointer and regular army man, son of the
senator whose compromise efforts had staved off war for a decade.
Commissioned a major general he was sent to the Cumberland Mountains region, with headquarters at Knoxville. Lloyd Tilghman, forty-
five, was also a West Pointer and a veteran of the Mexican War, but he
had left the army for a career in civil engineering. Johnston soon had
him busy designing and building fortifications. The youngest of the
three, forty-year-old John C. Breckinridge, was also the most distinguished. Vice President under Buchanan, he had presided over the joint
session of Congress which declared Abraham Lincoln elected President,
the office for which Breckinridge himself had been runner-up in the
electoral college. Since then, he had been elected to the Senate, where
his opposition to the Administration's war policy resulted in an order
for his arrest. When Buckner first got to Bowling Green, Breckinridge
entered his lines as a fugitive. "To defend your birthright and mine,"
he told his fellow Kentuckians, "I exchange with proud satisfaction a
term of six years in the Senate of the United States for the musket of a
soldier." Rather than a musket Johnston gave him a brigade, despite his
lack of military training.

In addition to these men of rank, all in the vigor of their prime,
the army had two cavalrymen who had already contributed exploits to
its legend. Captain John Hunt Morgan of Kentucky and Lieutenant
Colonel Nathan Bedford Forrest of Tennessee. Though the former had
fought in the Mexican War as a youth and later commanded his home-
town militia company, neither man had had a military education. The

latter, in fact, a Memphis slave dealer and a Mississippi planter, had had little formal schooling of any kind. By the end of the year, however, both had shown an aptitude for war. Morgan, who was thirty-six, took thirteen of his troopers on a reconnaissance completely around Buell's army and returned with thirty-three prisoners. In his first fight, northeast of Bowling Green, the forty-year-old Forrest improvised a double envelopment, combined it with a frontal assault — classic maneuvers which he could not identify by name and of which he had most likely never heard — and scattered the survivors of a larger enemy force. Standing in the stirrups, swinging his sword and roaring "Charge! Charge!" in a voice that rang like brass, the colonel personally accounted for three of the enemy officers, killing two and wounding one; he shot the first, sabered the second, and dislocated the shoulder of a third by knocking him off his horse. Ordinarily, infantrymen had small liking for any trooper, but these two lithe, violent six-footers caught their fancy, and soldiers of all arms predicted brilliant futures for them both — if they lived, which seemed unlikely.

Soon after New Year's the final brigadier arrived from West Virginia at the head of his command. John B. Floyd had had three months in which to recover from the rain-damped campaign under Lee in the Kanawha Valley, where he had been more successful against his Confederate rival, Henry Wise, than against the wily Rosecrans. Ranking Pillow, he now became second in command of the forces under Hardee north of Bowling Green, along the Green and Barren Rivers.

Floyd's brigade completed the order-of-battle with which Johnston was expected to fend off Halleck and Buell, whose combined armies were about twice the size of his own. In the Transmississippi, a weird collection of 20,000 regulars, militiamen, and Indian braves awaited the arrival of Van Dorn to take the offensive against a well-organized command of 30,000 Union troops. East of the river, though Johnston had managed to double the number defending Kentucky, the odds were even longer. Between Columbus and Cumberland Gap, just over 50,000 Confederates opposed just under 90,000 Federals, thus:

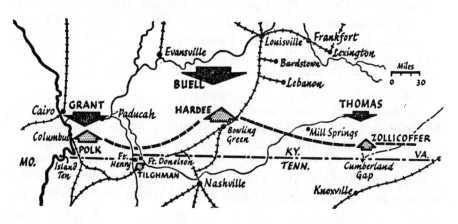

Polk on the left at Columbus had 17,000 men opposing Grant's 20,000 around Cairo; Hardee in the center at Bowling Green had 25,000 opposing Buell's 60,000 southwest of Louisville; Zollicoffer on the right had 4000 in front of Cumberland Gap, opposing 8000 under George Thomas north of Barbourville. Thus Johnston had drawn his line, badly outnumbered at the points of contact and in danger of being swamped by combinations. Fully aware of the risks he ran, he had no choice except to run them, making such use as he could of what he had and resorting to bluff whenever the danger seemed gravest, first at one point, then another. Also, a use had been found for Tilghman, who with 4500 men was stationed where geographical circumstances would give his engineering skill full scope.

The geographic factors were two rivers, the Tennessee and the Cumberland, whose existence threatened catastrophe for Johnston. Running parallel, and piercing as they did the critical center of his line, the two were like a double-barreled shotgun leveled at his heart. Despite the northern direction of their flow, they offered broad twin pathways of invasion for the steam-powered gunboats of the fleet which now controlled their mouths, twelve miles apart on the Ohio. Once into his rear, their paths diverged and they became separate threats, one deeper and the other more immediate, but both dire. Against its current, the Tennessee led down across both borders of the state whose name it bore, and then bent east and north, like a rusty hook plunged into the vitals of the South, touching northeast Mississippi on its way to Muscle Shoals in Alabama, beyond which it swung north, past Chattanooga, and finally on toward Knoxville and its source. The Cumberland, on the other hand, turned eastward soon after it crossed the northern border of Tennessee to curve back into Kentucky, across the front of Cumberland Gap and into the mountains that gave it both its waters and its name. Though the penetration was shallower, the consequences of an invasion along this line were no less stern; for during its dip into Tennessee the river ran past Clarksville and Nashville, the former being the site of the Cumberland Iron Works, second only to Richmond's Tredegar in output, and the latter, besides its importance as a manufacturing center, was the supply base for Johnston's entire army.

Those who were there before him had proposed to meet this two-pronged threat by constructing a fort to guard each river: Fort Henry, on the right bank of the Tennessee, and Fort Donelson on the left bank of the Cumberland. The first problem in each case had been location. Northward in Kentucky the rivers converged briefly to within three miles of each other, which would have allowed the forts to be mutually supporting; but since this was during the period of Bluegrass "neutrality," the chosen sites were necessarily south of the border, where the rivers were twelve miles apart — the same distance as at their mouths, fifty miles downstream — north of the two bridges over

which the railroad, running northeast out of Memphis, brought food
and munitions for the army. Work on the forts lagged badly from the
outset, with much argument among the engineers. Yet enough had been
done by the time of Johnston's arrival to cause him to leave them
where they were, rather than change their location when he swung his
long line outward, gate-like, with Bowling Green as the stop-post and
Columbus as the hinge. Consequently, the gate was badly warped,
swagged inward to include the forts commanded now by Tilghman,
whom Johnston sent to strengthen and complete them.

　　The concave swag of the Columbus-Bowling Green sector violated the military principle requiring a defending general to operate on
an interior line, so that in shifting troops from point to point, along the
chord of the arc, he would be moving them a shorter distance than his
opponent, outside the arc, would have to do. Between these salients
the case was reversed: it was Johnston who was outside the arc, with
the greater distance to travel from point to point. However, the text-
book disadvantage was offset by the presence of the railroad running
along the rear of his line, by which means he could shuttle his troops
back and forth with far greater speed than an opponent, lacking such
rapid transportation within the arc, could hope to match, despite any
difference in distance. What was more, railroad and battle line were
mutually supporting. So long as the line was held the road would
continue its fast shifting of troops, and so long as the shuttle service went
on, the line presumably could be held. The chink in the armor, Johnston knew, was where the railroad bridges spanned the rivers. Gunboats
could reduce the trestles to kindling within five minutes of opening
fire. They were only as safe as the forts downstream were strong. And
that was why he kept urging Tilghman to exert all possible effort to
get them finished.

　　Here as elsewhere, necessity being the mother of invention,
Johnston broke or rewrote the rules whenever necessity demanded.
Outnumbered severely all along his line, in each sector he improvised
defenses which, in event of attack, called for reinforcements from less
threatened points. His greatest advantage, indeed almost his only one,
was that his army was united under a single leader, whereas the enemy
forces were divided. So far, his opponents — Frémont and Anderson,
then Hunter and Sherman, and finally Halleck and Buell — had failed
to work in concert. What he would do if the latter pair mounted
coördinated or even simultaneous offensives, from end to end of the
long line or even against several points at once, he did not know and
could not know, the odds being what they were. Meanwhile, he
used the only means remaining: he used psychological warfare, including the dissemination of propaganda and misinformation. He used
it with such skill, in fact, that it kept his shaky line intact throughout

the fall and early winter and gave him time to shore it up with all the reinforcements he could find.

Throwing his troops forward he maneuvered them in a threatening manner, always as if on the verge of launching cut-and-slash attacks against the danger points. He announced to all within earshot that he had plenty of arms and plenty of men to use them; that, far from having any fears about being able to hold his ground, he was about to unleash an offensive that would roll to the Ohio, crunching the bones of whatever got in his way. The bluff had worked best against Sherman, who already had the horrors as a result of the insight which had told him just how bloody this war was likely to be. "I am convinced from many facts," he informed headquarters in a dispatch which his opponent might have dictated, "that A. Sidney Johnston is making herculean efforts to strike a great blow in Kentucky; that he designs to move from Bowling Green on Lexington, Louisville, and Cincinnati." Presently Sherman was on sick leave, restoring his Johnston-jangled nerves. If the bluff worked less dramatically on his successor, that was mainly because Buell had a less dramatic personality. At any rate, it caused him to enlarge upon the difficulties that lay between him and East Tennessee, where Lincoln so much wanted him to go. Halleck also felt its effects. They lay at the bottom of his reply that Buell's proposal for a joint advance on Nashville, up the Cumberland, "seems to me madness."

To confuse his enemies Johnston had first to mislead his friends, and this he did. Statements doubling and tripling his actual strength and hinting of an imminent offensive were printed in all the southern papers, in hopes that rival editors north of the defensive line would pick them up and spread them, which they did. Yet psychological warfare was a weapon that could boomerang, returning with a force in direct ratio to the success of its outward flight. While Halleck and Buell were counting themselves fortunate that the Confederates did not storm their lines, readers south of the border were also thoroughly taken in by Johnston, who thus compromised his reputation and risked his countrymen's morale by promising victories he knew he could never deliver with the present force at his command.

In a final effort to get more troops and supplies, on January 9, soon after the arrival of Floyd's brigade, which he had been warned would be the last, Johnston sent a personal messenger with a letter to his friend the President, reëmphasizing the gravity of the western situation. Within a week the messenger returned. He had found Davis in a "disturbed and careworn" frame of mind, but that was nothing compared to the state the Chief Executive was in by the time he had read the letter. "My God!" he cried. "Why did General Johnston send you to me for arms and reinforcements? . . . Where am I to get arms or men?"

The question was rhetorical, but the messenger, who had been primed for it, answered that they might be spared from less immediately threatened points. Davis had heard this suggestion all too often of late, along with the conflicting clamor of governors whose states had Union gunboats off their shores. Petulantly he replied that it could not be done, and remarked in closing the interview, "Tell my friend General Johnston that I can do nothing for him, that he must rely on his own resources."

The slimness of those resources was known to only a handful of men within the limits of strict confidence. Others beyond those limits thought him amply equipped and bountifully supplied, about to launch an offensive. Johnston was therefore in the position of a financier who, to stave off ruin, had overextended his credit with both friends and enemies by putting his name to a sight draft that would come due on presentation. Now that he was in too far to turn back, the President's message reached him like a notice of proceedings in bankruptcy. Kentucky was the only theater in which there had been no major clash of arms. He must have known that reverses were coming, and he must have known, too, that when they came the people would not understand.

They came soon enough. In fact, they came immediately. Coincident with the return of the messenger, Johnston's right caved in, the troops there scattering headlong, demoralized and crying like their foes the year before: "We are betrayed!"

Primarily, though, he lost that wing of his army not because of a Federal advance, as he had feared, but because of Zollicoffer's rashness and military inexperience. After occupying Cumberland Gap, the Tennessean had been ordered to move seventy miles northwest to Mill Springs, on the south bank of the Cumberland River, from which position he could parry an enemy thrust either toward the Gap, where he had posted a guard, or toward Nashville, 150 miles southwest. However, when Crittenden reached Knoxville, assuming command of the region, he learned to his amazement that Zollicoffer had not been content to remain south of the river, but had crossed and set up a camp on the opposite bank. Here at Beech Grove, with a wide unfordable river to his rear, the Tennessean was defying a Union army twice his size and attempting to stir up the doubtfully loyal citizens with proclamations which boldly inquired, "How long will Kentuckians close their eyes to the contemplated ruin of their present structure of society?"

Despite this evidence of literary skill, Crittenden now began to doubt the former editor's military judgment, and at once dispatched a courier, peremptorily ordering him to recross the river. But when he went forward on inspection in early January, to his even greater dismay he found the citizen-soldier's army still on the north bank. Zollicoffer blandly explained that Beech Grove afforded a better campsite; he had stayed where he was, in hopes that they could talk it over when Crittenden arrived. Then too, he explained — to the West Pointer's mounting horror — there were reports that the Yankees were advancing, which made falling back seem a cowardly or at any rate not a manly sort of action.

Investigation proved that the reports were all too true. Not only were the Federals advancing, they had at their head the Union-loyal Virginian George H. Thomas. Whatever his fellow Southerners might think of his "treachery" in not going with his state, they knew him to be an experienced soldier, not the least of his recommendations being that he had been a major in Johnston's 2d Cavalry. Faced with this threat, Crittenden saw that to attempt to withdraw would be to risk being hamstrung while astride the river. So he assumed command and did what he could to brace his troops in their Beech Grove camp for the shock which he believed was imminent.

What came was not the Yankees but a week of pelting rain. Despite its chill discomfort he was thankful, for if it broadened the river to his rear, it also swelled the creeks to his front and transformed into troughs of mud the roads down which the Federals were approaching. "A continuous quagmire," Thomas called them as his army slogged in double column along the opposite watersheds of Fishing Creek, which emptied into the Cumberland just above the Confederate position. Within nine miles of the rebel outposts on the 17th, he went into camp near Logan's Crossroads to rest his men, dry out their equipment, and plan the assault against Beech Grove.

The rain continued all next day, affording Thomas little respite, but presenting Crittenden with what he believed was a chance to exchange probable defeat for possible victory. In its separate camps, the enemy force was still divided by Fishing Creek, which Crittenden figured was swollen now past fording. He would move his army out that night and strike the Union left in a dawn attack. Then, having destroyed or scattered it, he would turn and deal with the other wing, beyond the flooded creek. It was a gamble, even a desperate one, but after a week spent sitting in the rain, awaiting destruction while the river ran deeper and swifter at his back, it was a gamble he was glad to take. Zollicoffer approved as soon as he heard of the plan, and at midnight the two brigades — eight regiments of infantry, plus a six-gun battery and a cavalry battalion — set out on their march through mud and rain to fight the battle variously known as Mill Springs, Fishing Creek, and Logan's Crossroads.

They soon discovered the accuracy of the description the Federal commander had given of the roads. And after a nightmare march through shin-deep mud, with rain coming hard in their faces out of a darkness relieved only by the blinding glare of lightning as they hauled at the wheels of bogged-down cannon and wagons and the heads of foundered horses, they discovered something else about George Thomas. They were launching a surprise attack against a man who could not be surprised, whose emotional make-up apparently excluded that kind of reaction to any event. Imperturbable, phlegmatic, his calm was as unruffled in a crisis as his humor was heavy-handed. Lincoln had hesitated to make the forty-five-year-old Virginian a brigadier, having doubts about his loyalty, but when he questioned Sherman and got the Ohioan's quick assurance that he personally knew Thomas to be loyal, he went ahead and signed the commission. Coming away from the interview with the President, Sherman ran into his friend on the street.

"Tom, you're a brigadier general!" he gaily announced. When Thomas showed no elation at this, Sherman began to have doubts. "Where are you going?" he asked, fearing he might be on his way to the War Department with his resignation, like so many other Virginians.

"I'm going south," Thomas replied glumly.

"My God, Tom," Sherman groaned. "You've put me in an awful position! I've just made myself responsible for your loyalty."

"Give yourself no trouble, Billy," Thomas said. "I'm going south at the head of my troops."

That was where he was going now. After a night and a day and another night spent in bivouac around Logan's Crossroads, straddling Fishing Creek, he sent a cavalry patrol out into the stormy dawn of the 19th to explore the roads leading south toward the Confederate camp. There was a spatter of musketry beyond the curtain of rain, and presently the horsemen reappeared, riding hard back up the puddled road, shouting that they had run into rebel skirmishers in advance of a heavy column. The long roll sounded. Men came stumbling big-eyed out of their tents, clutching weapons and clothes, and formed their regimental lines as if for drill, despite the rain and the fact that it was Sunday. All this while, beyond the steely glitter of the rain, an intermittent banging warned that the pickets were engaged. It sounded more like range-firing than a battle, but then the pickets came running in front of a double bank of men in muddy gray.

Crittenden kept coming. The cavalry clash had cost him the advantage of complete surprise, but he knew his troops were in better shape for an assault than for a retreat back down nine miles of churned-up road. Zollicoffer launched the attack, and at first he met with some success; the Federals recoiled from that first shock. But things went wrong in the Confederate ranks almost from the beginning. The men were cold and hungry, exhausted from their all-night march; the exhilaration of the charge burnt up what little energy they had left. Also, their flintlocks would not fire when wet, and the regiments armed with them had to be sent to the rear. Discouraged by all this, they saw the blue troops massing thick and thicker as Thomas brought up reinforcements from across the creek, whose flood stage Crittenden had mis-estimated.

The crowning blow, however, came when Zollicoffer lost his sense of direction in the rain. Conspicuous in a white rubber coat that made him an ideal target, he rode out between the lines, got turned around, and near-sightedly mistook a Federal colonel for one of his own officers. At this point his luck, which had been running strong, ran out. He was shouting an order when the colonel, a man who recognized an advantage when he saw one, leveled his revolver and put a bullet point-blank into Zollicoffer's breast.

A wail went up from the gray ranks; the Tennessean's men had loved him in spite of his rashness — if not, indeed, because of it. Their strength was mostly spent, and now this loss, occurring in plain view, cracked their spirit. They turned and made for the rear. "Betrayed!" they cried as they brushed past their officers. They ran and they kept on running, their panic infecting the other brigade, which also broke. It was Belmont in reverse, except that the Confederates had no gunboats to fall back on, or transports waiting to bear them away. Thomas replenished his ammunition and set out in pursuit, but his adversaries were well down the Beech Grove road by then. Under cover of darkness they crossed the Cumberland in relays on a rickety sternwheeler, which they burned against the southern bank. In the battle and the evacuation they lost more than 500 men, while the Federals, losing less than half as many, captured 12 guns, 1000 horses and mules, 150 wagons, and half a dozen regimental colors. By the time the pursuers could effect a crossing, there was scarcely anything left to pursue. Retreating through a region which so many of its men called home, Crittenden's army had practically ceased to exist.

Tactically complete as the Confederate defeat had been, it did not turn out to be strategically disastrous. Crossing the Cumberland, Thomas entered a region even more barren than the one he left, and though he put his men on half rations, intending to move on Knoxville, the rain continued and the roads were bottomless. He withdrew, and what was left of Crittenden's army finally called a halt at Chestnut Mound, about sixty miles from Nashville.

The respite was welcome, but it did not erase the fact that the Confederacy had suffered its first drubbing in the field. There had to be an explanation — or, failing that, a scapegoat — and Crittenden was the logical target for accusing fingers. "Betrayed!" the men had cried as they broke and fled. Investigation of what this meant turned up some strange answers, including testimony that the commanding general had been "in an almost beastly state of intoxication" throughout the battle. Remembering that his brother was a Union general, people began to suspect that his heart was not in the cause. There was even a rumor that one of his messengers had been captured bearing information to Thomas.

The South had no Joint Committee, such as the North had after the Ball's Bluff fiasco; Crittenden was spared the fate of his Federal counterpart, General Stone, languishing now in a dungeon in New York harbor. But the South had other methods. Eventually a court of inquiry found the Kentuckian innocent of treason but guilty of intoxication. He was reduced to the rank of colonel, and presently he resigned to serve as a civilian on the staff of an obscure brigadier in the Trans-mississippi, the dustbin of the Confederate army.

That was still in the future, though, and Johnston had nothing to do with it. For the present, he wired Crittenden to regroup his men and offer whatever resistance he could if Thomas came on after him. The western commander had graver worries closer to Bowling Green, where he had set up his headquarters as the best location from which to survey his long, tenuous line. For while Buell was lunging at his right, Halleck was probing his left — particularly at the point of double danger, where the incompleted forts stood guarding the parallel rivers that pierced his front.

It was here that Johnston was most touchy, and with good cause. Arriving in late November, the engineering brigadier Tilghman had reported: "I have completed a thorough examination of Henry and Donelson and do not admire the aspect of things." He wanted more troops, muskets for his unarmed men, and "more heavy guns for both places at once." The report had a gloomy, determined ending: "I feel for the first time discouraged, but will not give up."

Tilghman's gloom was warranted. Neither of the forts was in anything resembling a condition for offering stiff resistance to amphibious attacks. To make matters worse, Fort Henry was located on low ground, dominated by heights across the river and subject to flooding when the river rose. He later declared outright, "The history of military engineering records no parallel to this case."

One solution was to relocate the forts. Another was to fortify the opposite heights. Pondering which was preferable, he did neither. Johnston meanwhile sent him what he could, so that by mid-January Tilghman had 5700 troops: 3400 at Henry and 2300 at Donelson. Then came Buell's lunge and Halleck's probe. Both withdrew, Buell because of the rain and lack of rations, Halleck because he had only intended a feint; but Johnston knew they would be back soon enough. Three days after the Mill Springs rout, announcing the death of Zollicoffer and predicting a Federal strike against the forts, he made a final appeal to the Adjutant General: "The country must now be roused to make the greatest effort that it will be called upon to make during the war. No matter what the sacrifice may be, it must be made, and without loss of time. . . . All the resources of the Confederacy are now needed for the defense of Tennessee."

Now as before, Johnston did what he could with what he had.

He sent Pillow to Clarksville, sixty miles down the railroad, within supporting distance of the forts. Floyd and Buckner were sent with their brigades to Russellville, midway between Pillow and himself, within reach of both. Then, as January wore to a close, he learned to his dismay that Tilghman at Fort Henry was still pondering whether to fortify the high ground across the river. "It is most extraordinary," Johnston exclaimed. "I ordered General Polk four months ago to at once construct those works. And now, with the enemy on us, nothing of importance has been done. It is most extraordinary."

Mastering his alarm as best he could, he wired Tilghman: "Occupy and intrench the heights opposite Fort Henry. Do not lose a moment. Work all night."

★ ★ ★

Johnston was not the only commander alarmed by the success of Buell's lieutenant in East Kentucky. On the day after the battle, still not having heard the news, Henry Halleck returned to his desk after a four-day bout with the measles. During his time in bed he had reconsidered the suggested move against Nashville by means of a two-pronged advance up the Cumberland and the Tennessee. He no longer considered the operation "madness." In fact, he wrote McClellan that Monday morning, such an advance would follow "the great central line of the Western theater of war." However, he was quick to add, the movement should not be launched without a force of at least 60,000 effectives. As for Buell's proposed simultaneous advance upon the Tennessee capital, he considered it neither wise nor necessary. It was "bad strategy," he wrote, "because it requires a double force to accomplish a single object." Halleck wanted a one-man show, with Halleck as the man.

Having dispatched his letter to the General-in-Chief, the convalescent author of the *Elements of Military Art and Science* sat back and scratched his elbows. It was then that the news of Fishing Creek arrived, and the effect was as if a bomb had been exploded under his desk. What Thomas had done for Buell in eastern Kentucky was comparable to what Rosecrans had done for McClellan in western Virginia the year before. McClellan's elevation had followed swiftly after Philippi: so might Buell's after Fishing Creek — especially considering the fact that the advance had opened the way to East Tennessee, which everyone knew was Lincoln's pet concern. In the glare of that bomb-burst, Halleck saw his worst fears outlined stark before him: Buell might get the West.

That changed everything. Before he could consider what to do, however, he must somehow recover from the paralyzing shock which was his first reaction to the news. U. S. Grant returned to Cairo on the same day Halleck got up from the measles; his demonstration to immobilize Polk had not only been successful, it had given him ideas. "A fine reconnaissance," he called it, and requested permission to visit St Louis for a discussion with the commanding general. Halleck by now had the news from East Kentucky. "You have permission to visit headquarters," he replied, as if in a daze, and by Friday Grant was there. He found Halleck vague and noncommittal, still suffering from the shock of his rival's success. Consequently, the interview fell flat. "I was received with so little cordiality," Grant later declared, "that I perhaps stated the object of my visit with less clearness than I might have done, and I had not uttered many sentences before I was cut short as if my plan was preposterous." He returned to Cairo "very much crestfallen."

He was not crestfallen long. On his return he found a dispatch from Brigadier General C. F. Smith, who had demonstrated up the Tennessee while Grant had been pretending to threaten Columbus. Smith was sixty, with a ramrod stiffness, a habit of profanity, and a white walrus mustache. He had been commandant of cadets when Grant was at West Point, but now, as was often the case with old line officers who had stayed in the service, he was outranked by the volunteer commander and came under his authority. His advance had taken him down near the Tennessee line, within three miles of the fort on the east bank of the river, and in his report to Grant he stated flatly, "I think two ironclad gunboats would make short work of Fort Henry."

On his visit with Halleck in St Louis the week before, Grant had proposed a general forward movement. Now here was something specific. Returning to the charge, he promptly wired:

Cairo, January 28

Maj. Gen. H. W. Halleck
Saint Louis, Mo.:
   With permission, I will take Fort Henry on the Tennessee, and establish and hold a large camp there.

U. S. Grant
Brigadier General.

Halleck was just emerging from his state of shock. Perhaps by now he was even beginning to hear the words Grant had spoken three days ago, before he cut him short. At any rate, he saw that he must accomplish something to counterbalance the success his rival had scored at the opposite end of the line, and on second thought this looked like just the something. A week back, he had told McClellan that the advance up the rivers should not be undertaken by a force of less than 60,000 effectives. Grant had barely one-third that many men, including Smith's. However, leery as Halleck was of the wild man of Belmont, he knew that when Grant said plainly, "I will take Fort Henry," it meant an all-out effort and quick movement by field-hardened troops. There was the risk that Polk might move forward from Columbus, threatening the line of the Ohio while Grant was on his way southward up the Tennessee, but Halleck thought this unlikely, considering the success of the recent feint in that direction.

He was still pondering his decision when a telegram arrived from McClellan, reporting that a rebel deserter had just informed him that Beauregard was leaving Manassas to go to Kentucky with fifteen regiments of Confederate infantry. That resolved Halleck's final doubt. He would strike before Beauregard arrived. Next morning, Thursday the 30th, he wired Grant: "Make your preparations to take and hold Fort Henry. I will send you written instructions by mail."

Fort Henry being in Tennessee, he availed himself of the opportunity to request an enlargement of the area of his command, wiring McClellan: "I respectfully suggest that that state be added to this department." One thing remained to be done: inform Buell. With his campaign launched beyond any possibility of his rival's being able to claim a hand in its inception — but not too late to call on him for help if help was needed — Halleck telegraphed him curtly: "I have ordered an advance of our troops on Fort Henry and Dover. It will be made immediately." Now it was Buell's turn to be shocked at rival progress. "I protest against such prompt proceedings," he wrote McClellan, "as though I had nothing to do but command 'Commence firing' when he starts off."

The written instructions Halleck had promised his lieutenant were short and to the point, giving the latest intelligence on the strength of the fort, repeating McClellan's warning that Beauregard was on the way with reinforcements, and including the sentence, "You will move with the least delay possible." Knowing his man, Halleck knew that such words were as apt to produce results as a yank on the lanyard of a well-primed cannon. Grant's reply, from Paducah during the daylight hours of February 3, was the briefest yet: "Will be off up the Tennessee at 6 o'clock. Command, twenty-three regiments in all." And so it was. In the gathering dusk the transports slipped their moorings. The campaign to take Fort Henry was under way.

In the lead were four ironclad gunboats, unlike any ever seen before on this or any river. They were the invention, the product — and at this stage the property — of James B. Eads, who had built them in one hundred days on an army contract let to him in August, when they were intended, along with three others, to constitute the hard core of the column that would accomplish Frémont's lopping descent of the Mississippi. The Pathfinder was gone now, along with his plan, but the gunboats remained. Designed for river fighting, they were 175 feet long and a bit over 50 feet in the beam. Two and one-half inch overlapping plates of armor were bolted to the bows to give protection from head-on fire, and the sides were sloped at 35° to deflect shots taken broadside. For armament they mounted thirteen guns apiece, three at the bow, two at the stern, and four on each side. Despite the weight of all this metal, they were surprisingly maneuverable and drew only six feet of water: which meant, in river parlance, that they could "run on a heavy dew."

Eads, a native of Indiana and a man of industry, was one of those included in the southern sneer at the North as "a race of pasty-faced mechanics." When he arrived in St Louis to start work on his contract, the trees from which he would hew timbers were still standing in the forests. Within two weeks he had 4000 men at work around the clock, Sundays not excepted. When he ran out of money he used his own, and when that gave out he borrowed more from friends. By the end of November he had launched eight gunboats, a formidable squadron aggregating 5000 tons, with a cruising speed of nine knots an hour and an armament of 107 guns. The government was less prompt in payment, though, than Eads was in delivery. He still had not been reimbursed when the fleet set out for Henry: so that, technically, the ironclads were still his own.

The turtle-back steamers were not a navy project; the admirals left such harebrained notions to the army. For the most part, even the sailors aboard the boats were soldiers, volunteers from Grant's command who had answered a call for river- and seafaring men to transfer for gunboat service. Once the fleet was launched and manned, however, the navy saw its potential and was willing to furnish captains for its quarterdecks. Having made the offer, which was quickly accepted, the admirals did not hold back, but sent some of their most promising officers westward for service on the rivers. None among them was more distinguished, more experienced — or tougher — than the man assigned to flag command.

Commodore Andrew H. Foote was a Connecticut Yankee, a small man with burning eyes, a jutting gray chin-beard, and a long, naked upper lip. A veteran who had fought the Chinese at Canton and chased slavers in the South Atlantic, he was deeply, puritanically religious, and conducted a Bible school for his crew every Sunday, afloat or ashore. Twenty years before, he had had the first temperance ship in the U.S. Navy, and before the present year was out he would realize a lifelong ambition by seeing the alcohol ration abolished throughout the service. At fifty-six he had spent forty years as a career officer fighting the two things he hated most, slavery and whiskey. It was perhaps a quirk of fate to have placed him thus alongside Grant, who could scarcely be said to have shown an aversion for either. But if fate had juxtaposed them so, in hopes that they would strike antagonistic sparks, then fate was disappointed. Foote, like Grant, believed in combined operations, and had joined with him in bombarding Halleck with telegrams urging the undertaking of this one. Army and Navy, the commodore said, "were like blades of shears — united, invincible; separated, almost useless."

So built, so manned and led, the fleet put out in the rainy, early February darkness, southward up the swollen Tennessee: four ironclads and three wooden gunboats escorting nine transports with their cargo of blue-clad soldiers, the first of Grant's two divisions, which together totaled 15,000 men. Having landed the first, the transports would return downriver to bring the second forward; then the two would move together against the fort, the gunboats meanwhile taking it under bombardment. The initial problem was to locate a landing place as near the objective as possible and yet beyond the range of its big guns. One complication was Panther Creek, which flowed westward into the river, a little over three miles north of the fort. A landing north of the creek would mean that the troops would have to cross or go around it. That was undesirable, involving problematical delay. Yet a landing south of the creek might bring the transports under the rebel guns, with resultant havoc and probable disaster. Grant must first determine their range. He did so, characteristically, in the quickest, simplest way: by personal reconnaissance. Halting the fleet in the cold predawn darkness, eight miles short of the fort, he ordered three of the ironclads forward to draw the fire of the guns, and boarded one of them, the *Essex*, to go along and find out for himself.

He found out soon enough. The ironclads steamed past the creek mouth and opened fire within two miles of the fort. The answering shells fell short until a 6-inch rifle came into action, splashing its first shot not only beyond the gunboats, but beyond the mouth of the creek as well. Grant now had the information he wanted; no landing could be made south of the creek without bringing the transports under fire. But then the rifle's gunner made the information even more emphatic by demonstrating the kind of marksmanship the gunboats would encounter in an attack against Fort Henry. Shortening the range, he put the next shot squarely into the *Essex*. Having secured the information they sought, and more, the ironclads turned and went back down the river, the wounded *Essex* bringing up the rear with a 6-inch shell in her steerage and a wiser troop commander on her bridge.

Now that he knew how to do what must be done, Grant went back to get the movement started. The fleet proceeded southward, landing the First division north of the creek, and while the empty transports set out downriver on their hundred-mile round trip to bring the Second division forward, he completed the details of his attack plan. The key to the position, he saw — Belmont having taught him just how briefly troops could hold an objective which came under the plunging fire of enemy guns — was the high ground on the west bank, dominating the low-lying fort across the river. Reconnaissance had drawn no fire from there and Grant had been able to spot no guns through his glasses. But that was inconclusive. Intelligence had warned him that the Confederates were at work there; the batteries might be masked, under orders to hold their fire until a target worth their powder hove in view. Therefore he assigned the Second division the task of seizing the left-bank heights, planting artillery there, while the First division moved against the fort itself, angling around the head of Panther Creek to come in from the east and thus prevent the escape of the garrison in case it tried to retreat from under the fleet bombardment.

How large that garrison was he did not know. There was no way of telling how many reinforcements might have arrived overland from Donelson, twelve miles away, or by rail from Bowling Green or Memphis, since the defenders first learned of the task force moving up the Tennessee. In any case, the right-bank attack would be the main effort, and he detached one brigade from the Second division, which had three, ordering it to land on the eastern bank and support the First division, which had two. One more detachment from the Second division, a rifle company to act as sharpshooters on the warships, and Grant's attack plan was complete. If Fort Henry could be taken by 15,000 men and seven gunboats, he was going to take it.

There were other problems: the fact that the river was mined, for instance, which meant that at any minute any vessel, ironclad or transport, was apt to go sky-high in smoke and flame, the attacking force reduced to that extent by quick subtraction. Contact mines, or "torpedoes" as they were called, were a new and formidable weapon, a fiendish example of rebel ingenuity. Anchored to the river-bottom by cables that held them upright underwater, they were equipped with pronged rods extending upward to just below the surface, ready to trip the detonators on contact. The rising river had reduced their effectiveness, some being submerged by now beyond scraping distance and others floating around loose, torn from their moorings; but there was still a good deal of conjecture and concern about them.

On the afternoon of the 5th, while in conference with Foote and the two division commanders aboard the flagship, Grant got a chance to make a first-hand inspection of one of these new implements of war. A gunboat tied up alongside and her captain sent word that he had fished a torpedo out of the river. He had it there on deck, he said, in case the commodore and the generals wanted to see it. They did indeed want to see it, if only as a diversion. The conference was about finished anyhow; little remained to be done except to await the arrival of the Second division, still being brought in relays from Paducah. Crossing over to the gunboat, the commodore and his aides and the generals and their staffs clustered on the fantail and stood in a semicircle looking down at the torpedo.

It appeared to be quite as dangerous as they had feared. A metal cylinder five feet long and a foot and a half in diameter, the thing was made especially venomous-looking by the pronged rod extending from its head. Grant wanted more than a look, however. He wanted to know how it worked. So the ship's armorer came with his wrenches and chisels, and while he tinkered the interested officers watched. Suddenly, as he was loosening a nut, the device emitted an ominous hissing sound, which seemed to be mounting swiftly toward a climax. The reaction of the watchers was immediate. Some ran, exploding outward from the semicircular cluster, while others threw themselves face-downward on the deck. Rank had no precedent; it was each man for himself.

Foote sprang for the ship's ladder, and Grant, perhaps reasoning that in naval matters the commodore knew best, was right behind him. If he lacked the seaman's agility in climbing a rope ladder, he made up for it with what one witness called "commendable enthusiasm." At the top, the commodore looked back over his shoulder and found Grant closing rapidly upon him. The hissing had stopped. Whatever danger there had been was past. Foote smiled.

"General, why this haste?" he asked, and his words, though calmly spoken, were loud against the silence.

"That the navy may not get ahead of us," Grant replied.

★   ★   ★

Lloyd Tilghman was slim and dark-skinned, with a heavy, carefully barbered mustache and chin-beard, an erect, soldierly bearing, and piercing black eyes intensifying what one observer called "a resolute, intelligent expression of countenance." His resolution had not waned, but after two days of watching the Federal build-up to his front, he was beginning to realize that the fate of the fort was scarcely less predictable than that of a shoe-nail about to be driven by a very large sledge-hammer lustily swung.

His 3400 men were miserably armed with hunting rifles, shotguns, and 1812-style flintlocks, and his cannon were scarcely better. Two out of a shipment cast from what looked like pot-metal had burst in target practice, and several others had been condemned, a British observer pronouncing them less dangerous to the enemy than to the men who served them. Tilghman was threatened, in fact, by more than the gunboats and the blue-clad infantry, and weakened by more than the shortage of serviceable arms. In one week, back in mid-January when the rains came, the river had risen fourteen feet, demonstrating graphically the unwisdom of the engineers who had sited Fort Henry at this particular bend of the Tennessee. Only nine of the fifteen guns bearing riverward remained above water in early February, and now while the river continued to rise, lapping at last at the magazine, it had become a question of which would get there first, flood crest or the Yankees.

In spite of all this, the Kentucky brigadier did not despair when his lookout, peering downriver through the rainy dawn of the 4th, announced the approach of gunboats and behind them the coal-smoke plumes of the transports winding northward out of sight. Determined to fight, he wired Polk for reinforcements from Columbus, and the following day, having turned back the ironclad reconnaissance and seen that the Federals were landing in force, three miles north of the fort, he wired Johnston at Bowling Green: "If you can reinforce strongly and quickly we have a glorious chance to overwhelm the enemy." Accordingly, he sent his troops with their squirrel guns and fowling pieces to man the rifle pits blocking the landward approaches. If no help came, he would fight with what he had.

However, as the day wore on and the transports returned with further relays of northern troops, he began to realize the full length of the odds — particularly on the opposite bank, where the Union brigades were landing and preparing to move against the unfinished, unmanned works on the high ground which dominated the shipwrecked fort on this side. Without losing his resolution to give battle, he saw clearly that whoever stood on this nailhead, under the swing of that sledge, was going to be destroyed; and he saw, too, that, whatever his personal inclination, his military duty was to save what he could of a command whose doom was all but sealed.

At a council of war, called that night in the fort — the enemy build-up continued, seemingly endless, three miles downriver, on both banks — he announced his decision. While a sacrifice garrison manned whatever guns were yet above water, discouraging pursuit, the infantry would be evacuated, marching overland to join the troops at Donelson. Next morning a company of Tennessee artillery, two officers and 54 men, took their posts at the guns, awaiting the attack they knew was coming, while the foot soldiers filed out of the rifle pits and the fort, taking the road eastward.

Tilghman went a certain distance to see them on their way, and then, still resolute, turned back to join the forlorn hope. It was noon by now. As he drew near, the sound of guns came booming across water.

Two-thirds by land, one-third by water, Grant's triple-pronged upriver attack, designed as a simultaneous advance by the two divisions, one along each bank while the gunboats took the middle, was slated to get under way at 11 o'clock, by which time the final relay of troops had arrived from Paducah. Both infantry columns went forward on schedule, but Foote, on his own initiative, held back until almost noon, allowing the landsmen at least a measure of the head start they needed. The rain had stopped; the sun came through, defining the target clearly, and there was even a light breeze to clear away the battle smoke and permit the rapid and accurate fire the commodore expected of his gunners. For almost an hour the crews stood by — converted soldiers and fresh-water sailors bracing themselves for their first all-out action, with "just enough men-of-war's men," as one skipper said, "to leaven the lump with naval discipline" — until the attack pennant was hoisted and the squadron moved upstream, the ironclads steaming four abreast in the lead and the three wooden gunboats bringing up the rear.

"The flagship will, of course, open the fire," Foote had ordered, and at 1700 yards she did so. The others joined the chorus, firing as many of their 54 guns as could be brought to bear on the fort, whose nine gun-crews stood to their pieces and replied at once in kind, loosing what one of the defenders proudly called "as pretty and as simultaneous a 'broadside' as I ever saw flash from the sides of a frigate." This continued. Preceded by "one broad and leaping sheet of flame," as the same defender said, the ironclads deliberately closed the range to 600 yards while the more vulnerable wooden vessels hugged the western bank, adding the weight of their metal to the pressure on the earthworks.

Based as it was on predetermined ranges, fire from the fort was accurate and fast. For a time at least, the Tennessee artillerists seemed to be inflicting the greater damage. Aboard the warships, men were deafened by the din of solid shot pounding and breaking the iron plates and splintering heavy timbers, while shells screamed and whistled in the rigging, bursting, raining fragments. Foote's flagship, the prime target, was struck thirty-two times in the course of the action, two of her guns disabled and her stacks, boats, and after-cabin riddled. The captain of the ironclad on her left, which took thirty hits, said of one shot which he saw strike the flagship, "It had the effect, apparently, of a thunderbolt, ripping her side timbers and scattering the splinters over the vessel. She did not slacken her speed, but moved on as though nothing special had happened." Not so the luckless *Essex*. Patched up from the hurt she had received two days ago, she took another now through her boiler: an unlucky shot which left her powerless in a cloud of escaping steam, with twenty-eight scalded men aboard, some dead and others dying. Out of control, she swung broadside to the current, then careened, leaving a gap in the line of battle, and drifted downstream, out of the fight.

Encouraged by this proof that the turtle-back monsters could be hurt, the defenders cheered and redoubled their efforts. But they had done their worst — in fact, their all: for now there followed a series of accidents and mishaps which abolished whatever chance they had had for victory at the outset. Only two of their guns could really damage the ironclads, the high-velocity 6-inch rifle, which had already proved its effectiveness, and a giant columbiad which made up for its lack of range by the heft of its 128-pound projectile. The rest, low-sited as they were, with their muzzles near the water, could do no more than bounce their 32- and 42-pound shells off the armored prows of the attackers. First to go was the rifle, which burst in firing, disabling not only its own crew, but also those of the flanking pieces. Next, the big columbiad was spiked by a broken priming wire and thus put out of action, despite the efforts of a blacksmith who attempted to repair it under fire. Of the seven cannon left, which could only dent the armor and shiver the timbers of the gunboats, one had to be abandoned for lack of ammunition and two were wrecked almost at once by enemy shells. That left four guns to face the fire of the attackers, the range now being closed, almost point-blank, and even those four were served by skeleton crews, scraped together from among the survivors.

These included Tilghman. The fort commander had returned from seeing the infantry off, and was serving as a cannoneer at one of the four pieces. He had asked the artillerists to hold out for an hour, affording the garrison that much of a head start on its march to Donelson. Now that they had held out two, with the long odds growing longer all the time, the tactical considerations had been satisfied twice over, and those of honor as well. He ordered the flag struck. It was done and the firing ceased.

"That the navy may not get ahead of us," Grant had said, and it was as if he spoke from prescience. In the combined attack, as in the scramble up the ladder, Foote came out on top. The navy fired not only the first shot and the last, but also all the shots between, and suffered all the casualties as well: 12 killed and missing and 27 wounded, compared to the fort's 10 killed and missing and 11 wounded. In fact, the navy's closest rival was not the army, but the river. Another few hours would have put the remaining cannon under water. As it was, the cutter bearing the naval officers to receive the formal surrender pulled right in through the sally port.

Tilghman was waiting for them. He had already earned their respect by his bravery as an opponent, and now, by the dignity of his bearing as a prisoner, he won their sympathy as well. However, his reception of the copy-hungry northern correspondents, who were soon on hand to question him, was less congenial. As a southern gentleman he believed there were only three events in a man's life which warranted the printing of his name without permission: his birth, his marriage, and his death. So that when a Chicago reporter asked him how he spelled his name, he replied in measured terms: "Sir, I do not desire to have my name appear in this matter, in any newspaper connection whatever. If General Grant sees fit to use it in his official dispatches, I have no objection, sir; but I do not wish to have it in the newspapers."

"I merely asked it to mention as one among the prisoners captured," the correspondent said. But the Confederate either did not catch the dig or else ignored it.

"You will oblige me, sir," he repeated, as if this put an end to the matter, "by not giving my name in any newspaper connection whatever."

Grant arrived at 3 o'clock, by which time the Stars and Stripes had been flying over the fort for nearly an hour. His two divisions were still toiling through the mud on opposite banks of the river, one bogged down in the backwater sloughs of Panther Creek and the other slogging toward the empty western heights. Who won the race meant less to him, however, than the winning — and neither meant so much, apparently, as the fact that more remained to be accomplished. He had his mind on the railroad bridge fifteen miles upriver, over which Johnston could speed reinforcements from flank to flank of his line. The three wooden gunboats were dispatched at once to attend to it: which they did in fine style that same day. Nor was that all. Continuing on to Muscle Shoals, the head of navigation, they destroyed or captured six Confederate vessels, including a fast, 280-foot Mississippi steamboat being converted into an ironclad. Intended as an answer to the fleet of the invaders, she became instead a member of that fleet and saw much service.

This 150-mile gunboat thrust, all the way down past Mississippi and into Alabama, was dramatic proof of the fruits resulting from control of the Tennessee. A highway of invasion had been cleared. Yet Grant had his eye on another goal already, another fort on another river a dozen miles from the one he had just taken: as was shown by his wire to the theater commander on the day of his success. "Fort Henry is ours," the dispatch began, and ended with a forecast: "I shall take and destroy Fort Donelson on the 8th and return to Fort Henry."

Halleck passed the word along as promptly to McClellan, repeating Grant's first sentence and adding two of his own: "Fort Henry is ours. The flag of the Union is reëstablished on the soil of Tennessee. It will never be removed."

✗ 2 ✗

Grant was not alone in his belief that he could "take and destroy" the Cumberland fortress; Albert Sidney Johnston thought so, too. When word of the fall of Henry reached his headquarters at Bowling Green next day, he relayed the news to Richmond, adding that Fort Donelson was "not long tenable." In fact, such was his respect for the promptness and power with which the ironclads had reduced their first objective, he wrote that he expected the second to fall in the same manner, "without the necessity of [the Federals'] employing their land force in coöperation."

All the events he had feared most, and with good cause, had come to pass. Right, left, and center, his long defensive line was coming apart with the suddenness of a shaky split-rail fence in the path of a flood. His right at Mill Springs had been smashed, the survivors scattering deep into Tennessee while Buell inched toward Bowling Green with 40,000 effectives opposing Hardee's 14,000. The loss of Henry and its railroad bridge, with Federal gunboats making havoc up the river to his rear, had split his center from his left, outflanking Columbus and Bowling Green and rendering both untenable. When Donelson fell, as he expected in short order, the gunboats would continue up the Cumberland as they had done up the Tennessee, forcing the fall of Nashville, his main depot of supplies, and cutting off the Army of Central Kentucky from the southern bank.

This left him two choices, both unwelcome. With his communications disrupted and his lines of reinforcement snapped, he could stand and fight against the odds, opposing two converging armies, each one larger than his own. Or he could retreat and save his army while there was time, consolidating south of the river to strike back when the chance came. Whichever he did, one thing was clear: the choice must be made quickly. All those sight-drafts he had signed were coming due at once. The long winter's bluff was over. The uses of psychological warfare were exhausted. He was faced now with the actual bloody thing.

He called at once a council of war to confer with his two ranking generals. One was Hardee, commander of the center, whose prominent forehead seemed to bulge with knowledge left over from what he had packed into the *Tactics*. The other was Beauregard. The hero of Sumter and Manassas had arrived three days ago; but there were no fifteen regiments in his train, only a handful of staff officers. Davis had long since warned that he could spare no more soldiers, and he meant it. But apparently he could spare this one, whom many considered the finest soldier of them all, and by sparing him solve the double problem of removing the Creole's busy pen from the proximity of Richmond and silencing those critics who cried that the President had no thought for the western front.

Beauregard had come to Kentucky believing that Johnston was about to take the offensive with 70,000 men. When he arrived and learned the truth he reacted with a horror akin to that of Crittenden at Zollicoffer's rashness, and like Crittenden he at first proposed an immediate withdrawal. By the time of the council of war, however, he had managed to absorb the shock. His mercurial spirits had risen to such an extent, in fact, that the news of the fall of Henry only increased his belligerency. At the council, held in his hotel room on the afternoon of the 7th — the general was indisposed, down with a cold while convalescing from a throat operation he had undergone just before leaving Virginia — he proposed in a husky voice that Johnston concentrate all his troops at Donelson, defeat Grant at that place, then turn on Buell and send him reeling back to the Ohio.

Johnston shook his head. He could not see it. To give all his attention to Grant would mean abandoning Nashville to Buell, and the loss of that transportation hub, with its accumulation of supplies, would mean the loss of subsistence for his army. Even if that army emerged victorious at Donelson — which was by no means certain, since Grant might well be knocking at the gate already, his invincible ironclads out in front and his numbers doubled by reinforcements from Missouri and Illinois — it would then find Buell astride its communications, possessed of its base, twice its strength, and fresh for fighting. Johnston's army was all that stood between the Federals and the conquest of the Mississippi Valley. To risk its loss was to risk the loss of the Valley, and to lose the Valley, Johnston believed, was to lose the war in the West. It was like the poem about the horseshoe nail: Fort Henry was the nail.

Beauregard at last agreed. Along with Hardee he signed his name approving the document by which Johnston informed Richmond that, Henry having fallen and Donelson being about to fall, the army at Bowling Green would have to retreat behind the Cumberland. For the present at least, Kentucky must be given up.

Preparations for the evacuation began at once. Four days later, with Buell still inching forward, the retrograde movement began. The garrison at Donelson was expected to hold out as long as possible, keeping Grant off Hardee's flank and rear, then slip away, much as Tilghman's infantry had slipped away from Henry, to join the main body around Nashville. Beauregard was up and about by then, helping all he could, but Johnston had a special use for him. Columbus, being outflanked, must also be abandoned. Severed already from headquarters control, it required a high-ranking leader who could exercise independent command. That meant Beauregard. After a final conference with Johnston, who reached Nashville with the van of his army one week after the council of war at Bowling Green, he started for Columbus. His instructions empowered him to give up that place, if in his judgment it was necessary or advisable to do so, then fall back to Island Ten, where the Mississippi swung a lazy S along the Tennessee line, and to Fort Pillow, another sixty airline miles downriver.

Charged with the conduct of a retreat, the Creole's spirits flagged again. His heart was heavy, he wrote to a friend in Virginia; "I am taking the helm when the ship is already on the breakers, and with but few sailors to man it. How it is to be extricated from its present perilous condition, Providence alone can determine."

Southeast of Columbus, the gloom was no less heavy for being fitful. During the week since the fall of its sister fort across the way, the atmosphere at Donelson had been feverish, with a rapid succession of brigadiers hastening preparations for the attack which each believed was imminent.

First had come the fugitives from Henry, shamefaced and angry,

with lurid details of the gunboats' might and the host of Federals whose
trap they had eluded. Brigadier General Bushrod Johnson assumed command the following day, an Ohio-born West Pointer who had left the
army to teach school in Tennessee and, liking it, offered his services
when that state seceded. Two days later, on the 9th, Gideon Pillow
arrived from Clarksville. Relying on "the courage and fidelity of the
brave officers and men under his command," he exhorted them to "drive
back the ruthless invaders from our soil and again raise the Confederate
flag over Fort Henry.... Our battle cry, 'Liberty or death.' " Simon
Buckner marched in from Russellville next day. All this time, John B.
Floyd was hovering nearby with his brigade; Johnston had told him to
act on his own discretion, and he rather suspected the place of being a
trap. By now Pillow had recovered from his notion of launching an
offensive, but he wrote: "I will never surrender the position, and with
God's help I mean to maintain it." Encouraged by this show of nerve,
Floyd arrived on the 13th. Donelson's fourth commander within a week,
he got there at daybreak, in time to help repulse the first all-out land
attack. Grant's army had come up during the night.

The Federals were apt to find this fort a tougher nut than the
one they had cracked the week before. Like Henry, it commanded a
bend in the river; but there the resemblance ceased. Far from being in
danger of inundation, Donelson's highest guns, a rifled 128-pounder
and two 32-pounder carronades, were emplaced on the crown of a
hundred-foot bluff. Two-thirds of the way down, a battery mounting
a 10-inch columbiad and eight smooth-bore 32-pounders was dug into
the bluff's steep northern face. All twelve of these pieces were protected
by earthworks, the embrasures narrowed with sandbags. Landward the
position was less impregnable, but whatever natural obstacles stood in
the path of assault had been strengthened by Confederate engineers.

To the north, flowing into the river where the bluff came sheerly
down, Hickman Creek, swollen with backwater, secured the right flank
like a bridgeless moat protecting a castle rampart. The fort proper, a
rustic sort of stockade affair inclosing several acres of rude log huts, was
designed to house the garrison and protect the water batteries from incidental sorties. It could never withstand large-scale attacks such as the
one about to be launched, however, and the engineers had met this
threat by fortifying the low ridge running generally southeast, parallel
to the bend of the river a mile away. Rifle pits were dug along it, the
yellow-clay spoil thrown onto logs for breastworks, describing thus a
three-mile arc which inclosed the bluff on the north and the county-
seat hamlet of Dover on the south, the main supply base. At its weaker
and more critical points, as for instance where Indian Creek and the
road from Henry pierced its center, chevaux-de-frise were improvised
by felling trees so that they lay with their tops outward, the branches

interlaced and sharpened to impale attacking troops. All in all, the line was strong and adequately manned. With the arrival of Floyd's brigade there were 28 infantry regiments to defend it: a total of 17,500 men, including the artillery and cavalry, with six light batteries in addition to the big guns bearing riverward.

Floyd had experienced considerable trepidation on coming in, but his success in repulsing attacks against both ends of his line that morning restored his spirits and even sent them soaring. "Our field defenses are good," he wired Johnston. "I think we can sustain ourselves against the land forces." As for his chances against the ironclads, though his batteries turned back a naval reconnaissance that afternoon, he felt less secure. He wired Johnston: "After two hours' cannonade the enemy hauled off their gunboats; will commence probably again."

He was right. Steaming four abreast against his batteries next day, they did indeed commence again. When the squat black bug-shaped vessels opened fire, the cavalry commander Bedford Forrest turned to one of his staff, a former minister. "Parson, for God sake pray!" he cried. "Nothing but God Amighty can save that fort." Floyd emphatically agreed. In fact, in a telegram which he got off to Johnston while the gunboats were bearing down upon him, he defined what he believed were the limits of his resistance: "The fort cannot hold out twenty minutes."

★ ★ ★

Grant had predicted the immediate fall of Donelson to others beside Halleck. On the day the gunboats took Fort Henry he told a reporter from Greeley's *Tribune*, who stopped by headquarters to say goodbye before leaving to file his story in New York: "You had better wait a day or two.... I am going over to capture Fort Donelson tomorrow." This interested the journalist. "How strong is it?" he asked, and Grant replied: "We have not been able to ascertain exactly, but I think we can take it." The reporter would not wait. On the theory that a fort in the hand was worth two in the brush, he made the long trip by river and rail to New York, filed his story — and was back on the banks of the Cumberland before Grant's campaign reached its climax.

The initial delay was caused by a number of things: not the least of which was the fact that on the following day, the 7th, in pursuance of his intention to "take and destroy" the place on the 8th, Grant reconnoitered within a mile of the rifle pits the rebels were digging, and saw for himself the size of the task he was undertaking. To have sent his army forward at once would have meant attacking without the assistance of the gunboats, which would have to make the long trip down the Tennessee and up the Cumberland to Donelson. Besides, the river was still rising, completing the shipwreck of Henry and threatening to recapture from Grant the spoils he had captured from Tilghman, so that his troops, as he reported in explanation, were "kept busily engaged in saving what we have from the rapidly rising waters."

There was danger in delay. Fort Donelson was being reinforced; Johnston might concentrate and crush him. But Grant was never one to give much weight to such considerations, even when they occurred to him. Meanwhile, his army was growing, too. Intent on his chance for command of the West — for which he had already recommended himself in dispatches announcing the capture of Henry and the impending fall of Donelson — Halleck was sending, as he described it, "everything I can rake and scrape together from Missouri." Within a few days Grant was able to add a brigade to each of his two divisions. On second thought, with 10,000 more reinforcements on the way in transports and Foote's ironclads undergoing repairs at Cairo, he believed that he had more to gain from waiting than from haste. So he waited. All the same, in a letter written on the 9th he declared that he would "keep the ball moving as lively as possible." Hearing that Pillow, whose measure he had taken at Belmont, was now in command of the fort, he added: "I hope to give him a tug before you receive this."

By the 11th he was ready to do just that. Unit commanders received that morning a verbal message: "General Grant sends his compliments and requests to see you this afternoon on his boat." That this headquarters boat was called the *New Uncle Sam* was something of a coincidence; "Uncle Sam" had been Grant's Academy nickname, derived from his initials, which in turn were accidental. The congressional appointment had identified him as Ulysses Simpson Grant, when in fact his given name was Hiram Ulysses, but rather than try to untangle the yards of red tape that stood in the way of correction — besides the risk of being nicknamed "Hug" — he let his true name go and took the new one: U. S. Grant. There were accounts of his gallantry under fire in Mexico, and afterwards his colonel had pointed him out on the street with the remark, "There goes a man of fire." However, even for those who had been alongside him at Belmont, these things were not easy to reconcile with the soft-spoken, rather seedy-looking thirty-nine-year-old general who received his brigade and division commanders aboard the steamboat.

Almost as hard to believe, despite the whiskey lines around his eyes, were the stories of his drinking. Eight years ago this spring, the gossip ran, he had had to resign from the army to avoid dismissal for drunkenness. So broke that he had had to borrow travel money from his future Confederate opponent Simon Buckner, he had gone downhill after that. Successively trying hardscrabble farming outside St Louis and real-estate selling inside it, and failing at both, he went to Galena, Illinois, up in the northwest corner of the state, and was clerking in his father's leather goods store — a confirmed failure, with a wife out of a Missouri slave-owning family and two small children — when the war came and gave him a second chance at an army career. He was made a colonel, and then a brigadier. "Be careful, Ulyss," his father wrote when he heard the news of the fluke promotion; "you're a general now; it's a good job, don't lose it."

He was quiet, not from secretiveness (he was not really close-mouthed) but simply because that was his manner, much as another's might be loud. In an army boasting the country's ablest cursers, his strongest expletives were "doggone it" and "by lightning," and even these were sparingly employed. "In dress he was plain, even negligent," one of his officers remarked; yet it was noted — "in partial amendment," the witness added — that "his horse was always a good one and well kept." All his life he had had a way with horses, perhaps because he trusted and understood them. His one outstanding accomplishment at the Academy had been the setting of a high-jump record on a horse no other cadet would ride. There was an unbuttoned informality about him and about the way he did things; but it involved a good deal more of reticence than congeniality, as if his trust and understanding stopped at horses.

The conference aboard the *New Uncle Sam*, for instance, was as casual as the summons that convened it. What the participants mainly came away with was the knowledge that Grant had told them nothing. He had wanted to find out if they were ready to move out, and apparently he believed he could determine this better by listening than by talking or even asking. He sat and smoked his long-stem meerschaum, appearing to get considerable satisfaction from it, and that was all. The council of war ("calling it such by grace," one participant wrote) broke up and the officers dispersed to their various headquarters, where presently they received the written order. Yet even this was vague. Stating only that the march would begin "tomorrow," it gave no starting time and no exact details of attack. "The force of the enemy being so variously reported," it closed, ". . . the necessary orders will be given in the field."

Whatever qualms the troop commanders might be feeling as a result of all this vagueness, the troops themselves, being better accustomed to mystification from above, were in high spirits as the march got under way around mid-morning of Lincoln's birthday. With one quick victory to their credit — in celebration of which, they knew, the folks at home were already ringing church bells — they looked forward to another, even though it did not give promise of being quite so bloodless as the first. Besides, the sun was out and the air was cool and bracing. They were enjoying the first fine weather they had known since boarding the transports at Paducah nine days back.

The column was "light," meaning that there were no wagons for tents or baggage, but the adjective did not apply for the men in ranks, each of whom carried on his person two days' rations and forty rounds of ammunition, in addition to the normal heavy load for winter marching. Glad to be on the move, however burdened, they stepped out smartly, with the usual banter back and forth between the various candidates for the role of company clown. Once clear of the river lowlands, they entered a hilly, scrub-oak country that called for up-and-down marching, with pack straps cutting first one way, then another. Presently, as the sun rose higher and bore down harder, and perhaps as much from sheer elation at being young and on the march as from discomfort, they began to shed whatever they thought they could spare. The roads were littered in their wake with discarded blankets and overcoats and other articles not needed in fair weather.

Grant shared his men's high spirits. He now had under his command over twice as many men as General Scott had employed in the conquest of Mexico: 15,000 in the marching column, 2500 left on call at Henry, available when needed, and another 10,000 aboard the transports, making the roundabout river trip to join the overland column on arrival. Undiscouraged at being already four days past his previous forecast as to the date the fort would fall, in a telegram to Halleck announcing the launching of the movement ("We start this morning . . . in heavy force") he essayed another, but with something more of caution as well as ambiguity: "I hope to send you a dispatch from Fort Donelson tomorrow." Whether this meant from *inside* the fort or just in *front* of it, the words would make pleasant reading for the President on his birthday, in case Halleck passed them along (which he did not). But Grant, who perhaps did not even know it was Lincoln's birthday, had his mind on the problem at hand. He must get to the fort before he could take it or even figure how to take it.

He got there a little after noon, the skirmishers coming under sniper fire at the end of the brisk ten-mile hike, and threw his two divisions forward, approaching the spoil-scarred ridge along which the defenders had drawn their curving line of rifle pits. Beyond it, gunfire boomed up off the river: a welcome sound, since it indicated that the navy had arrived and was applying pressure against the Confederate rear. The Second division, led by Grant's old West Point commandant C. F. Smith, turned off to the left and took position opposite the northern half of the rebel arc, while the First, under John A. Mc-Clernand, filed off to the right and prepared to invest the southern half, where the ridge curved down past Dover.

McClernand was a special case, with a certain resemblance to the man whose birthday the investment celebrated. An Illinois lawyer-politician, Kentucky-born as well, he had practiced alongside Lincoln in Springfield and on the old Eighth Circuit. From that point on, however, the resemblance was less striking. McClernand was not tall: not much taller, in fact, than Grant: but he *looked* tall, perhaps because of the height of his aspirations. Thin-faced, crowding fifty, with sunken eyes and a long, knife-blade nose, a glistening full black beard and the genial dignity of an accomplished orator, he had exchanged a seat in Congress for the stars of a brigadier. In addition to the usual patriotic motives, he had a firm belief that the road that led to military glory while the war was on would lead as swiftly to political advancement when it ended. Lincoln had already shown how far a prairie lawyer could go in this country, and McClernand, whose eye for the main chance was about as sharp as Lincoln's own, was quite aware that wars had made Presidents before — from Zachary Taylor, through Andrew Jackson, back to Washington himself. He intended to do all he could to emerge from this, the greatest war of them all, as a continuing instance. So far as this made him zealous it was good, but it made him overzealous, too, and quick to snatch at laurels. At Belmont, for example, he was one of those who took time out for a victory speech with the battle half won: a speech which was interrupted by the guns across the river and which, as it turned out, did not celebrate a conquest, but preceded a retreat. He needed watching, and Grant knew it.

What was left of the 12th was devoted to completing the investment. The gunboat firing died away, having provoked no reply from the fort. Grant sent a message requesting the fleet to renew the attack next morning as a "diversion in our favor," and his men settled down for the night. Dawn came filtering through the woods in front of the ridge, showing once more the yellow scars where the Confederates had emplaced their guns and dug their rifle pits. They were still there. Pickets began exchanging shots, an irregular sequence of popping sounds, each emphasizing the silence before and after, while tendrils of pale, low-lying smoke began to writhe in the underbrush. Near the center, Grant listened. Then there was a sudden clatter off to the right, mounting to quick crescendo with the boom and jar of guns mixed in. McClernand had slipped the leash.

His attack, launched against a troublesome battery to his front, was impetuous and headlong. Massed and sent forward at a run, the brigade that made it was caught in a murderous crossfire of artillery and musketry and fell back, also at a run, leaving its dead and wounded to mark the path of advance and retreat. Old soldiers would have let it go at that; but there were few old soldiers on this field. Twice more the Illinois boys went forward, brave and green, and twice more were repulsed. The only result was to lengthen the casualty lists — and perhaps instruct McClernand that a battery might appear to be exposed, yet be protected. The clatter died away almost as suddenly as it had risen. Once more only the pop-popping of the skirmishers' rifles punctuated the stillness.

Presently, in response to Grant's request of the night before, gunboat firing echoed off the river beyond the ridge. To the north, Smith tried his hand at advancing a brigade. At first he was successful, but not for long. The brigade took its objective, only to find itself pinned down by such vicious and heavy sniper fire that it had to be withdrawn. The sun declined and the opposing lines stretched about the same as when it rose. All Grant had really learned from the day's fighting was that the rebels had their backs up and were strong. But he was not discouraged. It was not his way to look much at the gloomy side of things. "I feel every confidence of success," he told Halleck in his final message of the day, "and the best feeling prevails among the men."

The feeling did not prevail for long. At dusk a drizzling rain began to fall. The wind veered clockwise and blew steadily out of the north, turning the rain to sleet and granular snow and tumbling the thermometer to 20° below freezing. On the wind-swept ridge the Confederates shivered in their rifle pits, and in the hollows northern troops huddled together against the cold, cursing the so-called Sunny South and regretting the blankets and overcoats discarded on the march the day before. Some among the wounded froze to death between the lines, locked in rigid agony under the soft down-sift of snow. When dawn came through, luminous and ghostly, the men emerged from their holes to find a wonderland that seemed not made for fighting. The trees wore icy armor, branch and twig, and the countryside was blanketed with white.

Grant was not discomforted by the cold. He spent the night in a big feather bed set up in the warm kitchen of a farmhouse. But he had worries enough to cause him to toss and turn — whether he actually did so or not — without the weather adding more. The gunboat firing of the past two days had had none of the reverberating violence of last week's assault on Henry, and this was due to something beside acoustic difficulties. It was due, rather, to the fact that there was only one gunboat on hand. The others, along with the dozen transports bearing reinforcements, were still somewhere downriver. Their failure to arrive left Grant in the unorthodox position of investing a fortified camp with fewer troops than the enemy had inside it. During the night he sent word back to Henry for the 2500 men left there to be brought forward. That at least would equalize the armies, though it was still a far cry from the three-to-one advantage which the tactics books advised. They arrived at daybreak, and Grant assigned them to Smith, one of whose brigades had been used to strengthen McClernand. Doubtless Grant was glad to see them; but then even more welcome news arrived from the opposite direction. The fleet had come up in the night and was standing by while the transports unloaded reinforcements.

Presently these too arrived, glad to be stretching their legs ashore after their long, cramped tour of the rivers. Grant consolidated them into a Third division and assigned it to Lew Wallace, one of Smith's brigade commanders, who had been left in charge at Henry and had made the swift, cold march to arrive at dawn. A former Indiana lawyer, the thirty-four-year-old brigadier wore a large fierce black mustache and chin-beard to disguise his youth and his literary ambitions, though so far neither had retarded his climb up the military ladder. Grant put this division into line between the First and Second, side-stepping them right and left to make room, and thickening ranks in the process.

Along that snow-encrusted front, with its ice-clad trees like inverted cutglass chandeliers beneath which men crouched shivering in frost-stiffened garments and blew on their gloveless hands for warmth, he now had three divisions facing the Confederate two, eleven brigades investing seven, 27,500 troops in blue opposing 17,500 in gray. They were not enough, perhaps, to assure a successful all-out assault; he was still only halfway to the prescribed three-to-one advantage, and after yesterday's bloody double repulse he rather doubted the wisdom of trying to storm that fortified line. But now at last the fleet was up, the fleet which had humbled Henry in short order, and that made all the difference. Surely he had enough men to prevent the escape of the rebel garrison when the ironclads started knocking the place to pieces.

Shortly after noon — by which time he had all his soldiers in position, under orders to prevent a breakout — he sent word to the naval commander, requesting an immediate assault by the gunboats. Then he mounted his horse and rode to a point on the high west bank of the Cumberland, beyond the northern end of his line, where he would have a grandstand seat for the show.

Foote would have preferred to wait until he had had time to make a personal reconnaissance, but Grant's request was for an immediate attack and the commodore prepared to give it to him. He had done considerable waiting already, a whole week of it while the armorers were hammering his ironclads back into shape. All this time he had kept busy, supervising the work, replenishing supplies, and requisitioning seafaring men to replace thirty fresh-water sailors who skedaddled to avoid gunboat duty. Nor were spiritual matters neglected. Three days after the Henry bombardment he attended church at Cairo, where, being told that the parson was indisposed, Foote mounted to the pulpit and preached the sermon himself. "Let not your heart be troubled" was his text: "ye believe in God, believe also in me."

Next day, having thus admonished and fortified his crews, he sent one ironclad up the Cumberland — the *Carondelet*, a veteran of Henry — while he waited at Cairo to bring three more: the flagship *St Louis*, another Henry veteran, and the *Pittsburg* and the *Louisville*, replacements for the *Cincinnati*, which remained on guard at the captured fort, and the hard-luck *Essex*, which had been too vitally hurt

to share in a second attempt at quick reduction. It took the commodore
two more days to complete repairs, replace the runaway sailors, and
assemble his revamped flotilla, including two of the long-range wooden
gunboats and the twelve transports loaded with infantry reinforcements. Then on the 13th he went forward, southward up the Cumberland in the wake of the *Carondelet,* whose skipper was waiting to report
on his two-day action when Foote arrived before midnight at the bend
just north of Donelson.

The report had both its good points and its bad, though the
former were predominant. On the first day, when the *Carondelet*
steamed alone against the fort, firing to signal her presence to Grant,
who was just arriving, there was no reply from the batteries on the
bluff. The earthworks seemed deserted, their frowning guns untended.
All the same, the captain hadn't liked the looks of them; they reminded
him, he said later, "of the dismal-looking sepulchers cut into the rocky
cliffs near Jerusalem, but far more repulsive." He retired, answered
only by echoes booming the sound of his own shots back from the
hills, and anchored for the night three miles downstream. It was
strange, downright eerie. Next morning, though, in accordance with a
request from Grant, who evidently had not known there was only one
gunboat at hand, he went forward again, hearing the landward clatter
of musketry as McClernand's attack was launched and repulsed.

On this second approach, the *Carondelet* drew fire from every
battery on the heights. Under bombardment for two hours, she got off
139 rounds and received only two hits in return. This was poor gunnery
on the enemy's part, but one of those hits gave the captain — and, in
turn, the commodore — warning of what a gun on that bluff could do
to an ironclad on the river below. It was a 128-pound solid shot and it
crashed through a broadside casemate into the engine room, where it
caromed and ricocheted, ripping at steam pipes and railings, knocking
down a dozen men and bounding after the others, as one of the engineers
said, "like a wild beast pursuing its prey." Shattering beams and timbers, it filled the air with splinters fine as needles, pricking and stabbing
the sailors through their clothes, though in all the grim excitement
they were not aware of this until they felt the blood running into their
shoes. The *Carondelet* fell back to transfer her wounded and attend to
emergency repairs, but when the racket of another land assault broke
out at the near end of the line, she came forward again, firing 45 more
rounds at the batteries, and then drew off unhit as the clatter died away,
signifying that Smith's attack, like McClernand's, had not succeeded.

Aboard the flagship, Foote had the rest of the night and the
following morning in which to evaluate this information. Then came
the request for an immediate assault. As Grant designed it, the fleet
would silence the guns on the bluff, then steam on past the fort and take
position opposite Dover, blocking any attempt at retreat across the

river while it shelled the rebels out of their rifle pits along the lower ridge; whereupon the army would throw its right wing forward, so that the defenders, cut off from their main base of supplies and barred from retreat in either direction, could then be chewed up by gunfire, front and rear, or simply be outsat until they starved or saw the wisdom of surrender. The commodore would have preferred to have more time for preparation — time in which to give a final honing, as it were, to the naval blade of the amphibious shears — but, for all he knew, Grant had special reasons for haste. Besides, he admired the resolute simplicity of the plan. It was just his style of fighting. Once the water batteries were reduced, it would go like clockwork, and the example of Henry, eight days back, assured him that the hard part would be over in a hurry. He agreed to make the assault at once.

One thing he took time to do, however. Chains, lumber, and bags of coal — "all the hard materials in the vessels," as one skipper said — were laid on the ironclads' upper decks to give additional protection from such plunging shots as the one that had come bounding through the engine room of the *Carondelet.* This done, Foote gave the signal, and at 3 o'clock the fleet moved to the attack, breasting the cold dark water of the river flowing northward between the snowclad hills, where spectators from both armies were assembling for the show. One was Floyd, who took one look at the gunboats bearing down and declared that the fort was doomed. Another was Grant, who said nothing.

They came as they had come at Henry, the ironclads out in front, four abreast, while the brittle-skinned wooden gunboats *Tyler* and *Conestoga* brought up the rear, a thousand yards astern. At a mile and a half the batteries opened fire with their two big guns, churning the water ahead of the line of boats, but Foote did not reply until the range was closed to a mile. Then the flagship opened with her bow guns, echoed at once by the others, darting tongues of flame and steaming steadily forward, under orders to close the range until the batteries were silenced. Muzzles flashing and smoke boiling up as if the bluff itself were ablaze, the Confederates stood to their guns, encouraged by yesterday's success against the *Carondelet,* just as Henry's gunners had been heartened by turning back the *Essex* on the day before their battle. The resemblance did not stop there, however. After the first few long-range shots, as in the fallen fort a week ago, the big 128-pounder rifle on the crest of the bluff — the gun that had scored the only hit in two days of firing — was spiked by its own priming wire, which an excited cannoneer left in the vent while a round was being rammed. This left only the two short-range 32-pounder carronades in the upper battery and the 10-inch columbiad and eight smooth-bore 32-pounders in the lower: one fixed target opposing four in motion, each of which carried more guns between her decks than the bluff had in all, plus the long-range wooden gunboats arching their shells from beyond the smoke-wreathed line of ironclads.

Foote kept coming, firing as he came. At closer range, the *St Louis* and *Pittsburg* in the middle, the *Carondelet* and *Louisville* on the flanks, his vessels were taking hits, the metallic clang of iron on iron echoing from the surrounding hills with the din of a giant forge. But he could also see dirt and sandbags flying from the enemy embrasures as his shots struck home, and he believed he saw men running in panic from the lower battery. The Confederate fire was slackening, he afterwards reported; another fifteen minutes and the bluff would be reduced.

It may have been so, but he would never know. He was not allowed those fifteen minutes. At 500 yards the rebel fire was faster and far more effective, riddling stacks and lifeboats, sheering away flagstaffs and davits, scattering the coal and lumber and scrap iron on the decks. The sloped bulwarks caused the plunging shots to strike not at glancing angles, as had been intended, but perpendicular, and the gunboats shuddered under the blows. Head-on fire was shucking away side armor, one captain said, "as lightning tears the bark from a tree." At a quarter of a mile, just as Foote thought he saw signs of panic among the defenders, a solid shot crashed through the flagship's superstructure, carrying away the wheel, killing the pilot, and wounding the commodore and everyone else in the pilot house except an agile reporter who had come along as acting secretary.

The *St Louis* faltered, having no helm to answer, and went away with the current, out of the fight. Alongside her, the *Pittsburg* had her tiller ropes shot clean away. She too careened off, helmless, taking more hits as she swung. The *Louisville* was the next to go, struck hard between wind and water. Her compartments kept her from sinking while her crew patched up the holes, but then, like her two sister ships, she lost her steering gear and wore off downstream. Left to face the batteries alone, at 200 yards the *Carondelet* came clumsily about, her forward compartments logged with water from the holes punched in her bow, and fell back down the river, firing rapidly and wildly as she went, not so much in hopes of damaging the enemy as in an attempt to hide in the smoke from her own guns.

High on the bluff, the Confederates were elated. In the later stages of the fight they enjoyed comparative immunity, for as the gunboats closed the range they overshot the batteries. Drawing near they presented easier targets, and the cannoneers stood to their pieces, delivering hit after hit and cheering as they did so. "Now, boys," one gunner cried, "see me take a chimney!" He drew a bead, and down went a smokestack. One after another, the squat fire-breathing ironclads were disabled, wallowing helplessly as the current swept them northward, until finally the *Carondelet* made her frantic run for safety, firing indiscriminately to wreathe herself in smoke. The river was deserted; the fight was over quite as suddenly as it started. The flagship had taken 57 hits, the others about as many. Fifty-four sailors were casualties, including eleven dead. In the batteries, on the other hand, though the breastworks had been knocked to pieces, not a man or a gun was lost. The artillerists cheered and tossed their caps and kept on cheering. Fort Henry had shown what the gunboats could do: Fort Donelson had shown what they could not do.

The Confederate commander was as jubilant as his gunners. When the tide of battle turned he recovered his spirits and wired Johnston: "The fort holds out. Three gunboats have retired. Only one firing now." When that one had retired as well, his elation was complete.

It was otherwise with Grant, who saw in the rout of the ironclads a disruption of his plans. Mounting his horse, he rode back to headquarters and reported by wire to Halleck's chief of staff in Cairo: "Appearances indicate now that we will have a protracted siege here." A siege was undesirable, but the rugged terrain and the bloody double repulse already suffered in front of the fortified ridge caused him to "fear the result of an attempt to carry the place by storm with raw troops." Meanwhile, he reported, he was ordering up more ammunition and strengthening the investment for what might be a long-drawn-out affair. Disappointed but not discouraged, he assured the theater commander: "I feel great confidence . . . in ultimately reducing the place."

★ ★ ★

Glorious as the exploit had been, Floyd's elation was based on more than the repulse of the flotilla. Since the night before, he had had the satisfaction of knowing that he had successfully accomplished the first half of his primary assignment, his reason for being at Donelson in the first place: he had kept Grant's army off Hardee's flank during the retreat from Bowling Green. Johnston was in Nashville with the van, and Hardee was closing fast with the rear, secure from western molestation. Now there remained only the second half of Floyd's assignment: to extract his troops from their present trap for an overland march to join in the defense of the Tennessee capital.

This was obviously no easy task, but he had begun to plan for it at a council of war that morning, when he and his division commanders decided to try for a breakout south of Dover, where a road led south, then east toward Nashville, seventy miles away. Pillow's division would be massed for the assault, while Buckner's pulled back to cover the withdrawal. Troop dispositions had already begun when the ironclads came booming up the river. By the time they had been repulsed, the day was too far gone; Floyd sent orders canceling the attack and calling another council of war. No experienced soldier himself, he wanted more advice from those who were.

The two who were there to give it to him were about as different from each other as any two men in the Confederacy. Pillow was inclined toward the manic. Addicted to breathing fire on the verge of combat, flamboyant in address, he was ever sanguine in expectations and eager for desperate ventures, the more desperate the better. Buckner was gloomy, saturnine. Not much given to seeking out excitement, he was inclined to examine the odds on any gamble, especially when they were as long as they were now. Some of the difference perhaps was due to the fact that Pillow the Tennessean was fighting to save his native state — his country, as he called it — while Buckner the Kentuckian had just seen his abandoned. And their relationship was complicated by the fact that there was bad blood between them, dating from back in the Mexican War, when Buckner had joined not only in the censure of Pillow for laying claim to exploits not his own, but also in the laughter which followed a report that had him digging a trench on the wrong side of a parapet.

Between these two, the confident Pillow and the cautious Buckner, Floyd swung first one way, then another, approaching nervous exhaustion in the process. The indecision he had displayed in West Virginia under Lee was being magnified at Donelson, together with his tendency to grow flustered under pressure. Just now, however, with the rout of the Yankee gunboats to his credit, he was inclined to share his senior general's expectations. Adjourning the council, he announced that the breakout designed for today would be attempted at earliest dawn tomorrow. Even the gloomy Buckner admitted there was no other way to save the army, though he strongly doubted its chances for success.

All night the generals labored, shifting troops for the dawn assault. Pillow massed his division in attack-formation south of Dover, while Buckner stripped the northward ridge of men and guns to cover the withdrawal once the Union right had been rolled back to open the road toward Nashville. Another storm came up in the night, freezing the soldiers thus exposed. Yet this had its advantages; the wind howled down the shouts of command and the snowfall muffled the footsteps of the men and the clang of gunwheels on the frozen ground. No noise betrayed the movement to the Federals, huddled in pairs for warmth and sleep beyond the nearly deserted ridge. As dawn came glimmering through the icy lacework of the underbrush and trees, Pillow sent his regiments forward on schedule, Forrest's cavalry riding and slashing on the flank.

They met stiff resistance, not because the Yankees were expecting this specific attack, but because they were well-disciplined and alert. For better than three hours the issue hung in raging doubt, the points of contact clearly marked by bloodstains on the snow. Running low on ammunition, McClernand's men gave way, fought out, and as they fell back, sidling off to the left and exposing in turn the right flank

of Wallace, Pillow saw that he had achieved his objective. The Nashville road was open. He paused to send a telegram to Johnston: "On the
honor of a soldier, the day is ours!"

However, having paused he took stock, and it was as if the
telegram had used up his last ounce of energy and hope, both of which
had formerly seemed boundless. For now a strange thing happened: he
and Buckner exchanged roles. Now it was Pillow who was pessimistic,
fearing a counterattack against his flank while moving through the gap,
and Buckner who was ebullient, declaring that the success should be
exploited by ramming the column through. He had brought his soldiers
forward to hold the door ajar; he could do it, he said — and in fact he
insisted on doing it. When Pillow, standing on seniority, ordered him
back to his former position, he refused to go. It was nearing noon by
now, and all this time the road was standing open.

While the generals stood there wrangling, Floyd arrived.
Smooth-shaven, with a pendulous underlip, he stood between them,
looking from one to the other while they appealed to him to settle the
dispute. At first he agreed with Buckner and told him to stay where he
was, holding the escape hatch ajar. Then Pillow took him aside and he
reversed himself, ordering both divisions back into line on the ridge. The
morning's fight had gone for nothing, together with the bloodstains on
the snow.

Elsewhere along the curving front, practically stripped of Confederate troops for the breakthrough concentration — the sector formerly held by Buckner's whole division, for example, had been left
in charge of a single regiment with fewer than 500 men — the lines
across the way were strangely silent. To the Southerners, widely
spaced along the ridge, this seemed a special dispensation of Providence.
Actually, however, the basis for the respite, though unusual, was entirely natural.

Before daylight that morning Grant had received a note from
Flag Officer Foote, requesting an interview. The wounded commodore
was going back downriver for repairs, both to his worst-hit vessels and
to himself, and he wanted to talk with Grant before he left. Grant rode
northward to meet him aboard the flagship. Having, he said later, "no
idea that there would be any engagement on land unless I brought it
on myself," he left explicit orders that his division commanders were
not to move from their present positions. Baffled by the wintry trees
and ridges, the three-hour uproar of Pillow's assault on the opposite end
of the line reached him faintly, if at all. He rode on. Hard-pressed,
McClernand was calling for help which Grant's orders prohibited Wallace and Smith from sending, though the former, on his own responsibility, finally sent a brigade which helped to blunt the attack when his
own lines were assailed. Grant knew nothing of this until past noon,

when, riding back from the gunboat conference, he met a staff captain who informed him, white-faced with alarm, that McClernand's division had been struck and scattered into full retreat. Grant put spurs to his horse.

Speed was impossible on the icy road, however, even for so skillful a horseman as Grant. It was 1 o'clock before he reached the near end of his line, where he found reassurance in the lack of excitement among the troops of Smith's division. Even Wallace's men, already engaged in part, showed fewer signs of panic than the captain who had met him crying havoc. McClernand's, next in sight, were another matter. They had been ousted from their position, taking some rough handling in the process, and they showed it. Now that the rebels had stopped shoving, they stopped running, but as they stood around in leaderless clumps, empty cartridge boxes on display as an excuse for having yielded, they gave little evidence of wanting to regain what they had lost.

There was a report that Confederate prisoners had three days' cooked rations in their haversacks. Some took this as proof that they were prepared for three days of hard fighting, but Grant had a different interpretation. He believed it meant that they were trying to escape, and he believed, further, that they were more demoralized by having failed in a desperate venture than his own men were by a temporary setback. "The one who attacks first now will be victorious," he said to his staff, "and the enemy will have to be in a hurry if he gets ahead of me."

He told McClernand's men, "Fill your cartridge boxes, quick, and get into line. The enemy is trying to escape and he must not be permitted to do so." This worked, he said later, "like a charm. The men only wanted someone to give them a command." To the wounded Foote went a request that the gunboats "make appearance and throw a few shells at long range." He did not expect them to stage a real attack, he added, but he counted on the morale effect, both on his own troops and the enemy's, of hearing naval gunfire from the river. Reasoning also that the rebels must have stripped the ridge to mass for the attack on the south, he rode to the far end of the line and ordered Smith to charge, advising him that he would find only "a very thin line to contend with."

This was what Smith had been waiting for, and for various reasons. His bright blue eyes and oversized snowy mustache standing out in contrast to his high-colored face, he was Regular Army to the shoe-soles, the only man in the western theater, one of his fellow officers said, who "could ride along a line of volunteers in the regulation uniform of a brigadier general, plume, chapeau, epaulets and all, without exciting laughter." Like many old-army men, since that army had been predominantly southern in tone, he was suspected of disloyalty; but

Smith, who had been thrice brevetted for bravery in Mexico, was not disturbed by these suspicions. "They'll take it back after our first battle," he promised. And now, with that first battle in progress, he got his troops into line, gave them orders not to fire until the rebel abatis had been cleared, and led them forward. High on his horse, the sixty-year-old general turned from time to time in the saddle to observe the alignment and gesture with his sword, the bullets of the sharpshooters twittering round him. "I was nearly scared to death," one soldier afterwards said, "but I saw the old man's white mustache over his shoulder, and went on."

They all went on, through the fallen timber and up the ridge, where they drove back the regiment Buckner had left to man the line. All that kept them from storming the fort itself was the arrival of the rest of Buckner's division, which Floyd had ordered back. On the right, McClernand's rallied men hurried the retirement of Pillow, reoccupying the ground they had lost. Wallace took a share in this, shouting as he rode along the line of his division, "You have been wanting a fight; you have got it. Hell's before you!" Two of the battered ironclads reappeared around the bend in answer to Grant's request, lobbing long-range shells to add to the Confederate confusion.

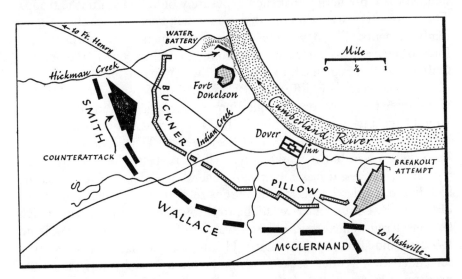

In what remained of the short winter afternoon, since saying, "The one who attacks first now will be victorious," Grant saw his army not only recover from the morning's reverses, but breach the line of rebel intrenchments as well. By daylight there would be Union artillery on the ridge where Smith had forced a lodgment. The fort, the water battery, Dover itself: the whole Confederate position would be under those guns. It was not going to be a siege, after all.

★ ★ ★

This was realized as well by the commanders inside the fort, swinging once more from elation to dejection, as it was by those outside. At the council of war, held late that night in the frame two-story Dover Inn, the prime reaction was consternation. Pillow and Buckner had reverted to their original roles. The former had thrown off his gloom, the latter his ebullience, and each accused the other of having failed to exploit the morning's gains. Pillow declared that he had halted only to send his men back after their equipment; he was ready to cut his way out in earnest, all over again. Buckner said that stopping, for whatever reason, had been fatal; the Federals had restored the line, and his men were too dispirited to make another assault. Floyd was as usual in the middle, looking from one to the other as the recriminations passed him.

This time, though, he sided more with Buckner; Smith's guns were on the ridge by now, waiting for dawn to define the targets. Forrest, who was present in his capacity as cavalry commander, reported that a riverside road was open to the south, though icy backwater stood waist-deep where it crossed a creekbed. However, the army surgeon — who had yet to learn just how tough a creature the Confederate soldier could be, despite his grousing — advised against using the flooded road, predicting that such exposure would be fatal to the troops. Then too, there was a report that Grant had received another 10,000 reinforcements. Floyd already believed his men were outnumbered four-to-one, and as far as he was concerned that settled the matter. Only one course remained: to surrender the command.

Whatever their differences at this final conference, he and Pillow were agreed at least on the question of personal surrender. Neither would have any part of it, and each had his reasons. Floyd had been indicted for malfeasance in office as Secretary of War. The charge had been nol-prossed but it might very well be reopened in a wartime atmosphere. Besides, it was a matter of general belief in the North that he had diverted federal arms and munitions to southern arsenals on the eve of secession. To surrender would be to throw himself on a mercy which he considered nonexistent. Pillow's was a different case, but he was no less determined to avoid captivity. Having sworn that he would never surrender, he intended to keep his oath. He agreed by now as to the necessity for surrender of the army, but like Floyd he refused to be included. His battle cry was "Liberty or death," and he chose liberty.

Buckner felt otherwise. He accepted the facing of possible charges of treason as one of the hazards of waging a revolution. Also, he had done the Federal commander certain personal services, including the loan of money when Grant was on his way home from California in disgrace, and this might have a happy effect when the two sat down together to arrange terms for capitulation. He would surrender the army, and himself as part of it, along with all the others who had fought here and been worsted. The necessary change of commanders was effected in order of rank:

"I turn the command over, sir," Floyd told Pillow.

"I pass it," Pillow told Buckner.

"I assume it," Buckner said. "Give me pen, ink and paper, and send for a bugler."

This colloquy omitted a fourth member of the council. Bedford Forrest rose up in his wrath. "I did not come here for the purpose of surrendering my command," he declared. Buckner agreed that the cavalryman could lead his men out if the movement began before surrender negotiations were under way.

Forrest stamped out into the night, followed by Floyd and Pillow, while Buckner composed his note to Grant: "In consideration of all the circumstances governing the present situation of affairs at this station, I propose to the commanding officer of the Federal forces the appointment of commissioners to agree upon the terms of capitulation of the forces and fort under my command, and in that view suggest an armistice until twelve o'clock today." He signed it, "Very respectfully, your obedient servant."

Buckner's men by no means shared his gloom. Except for the regiment overrun by Smith's division, they had whipped the Yankees on land and water each time they had come to grips. Rested from the previous day's exertions, they expected a renewal of the fight. Consequently, the bugler going forward to sound the parley and the messenger bearing Buckner's note and a white flag of truce had trouble getting through the lines. At last they did, however. The bugle rang out, plaintive in the frosty night, and men of the northern Second division received them and gave them escort back to the division commander. Smith read the note and set out at once through the chill predawn darkness for the farmhouse which was army headquarters.

Grant was snug in his feather bed when Smith came in saying, "There's something for you to read." During the reading the old soldier crossed to the open fire and stroked his mustache while warming his boots and backside. Grant gave a short laugh. "Well, what do you think of it?" he asked. Smith said, "I think, no terms with the traitors, by God!" Grant slipped out of bed and drew on his outer garments. Then he took a sheet of tablet paper and began to write. When he had finished he handed it to Smith, who read it by firelight and pronounced abruptly, "By God, it couldn't be better."

Once more the truce party crossed the lines, headed now in the opposite direction as they picked their way to the Dover Inn, where Buckner was waiting to learn Grant's terms. There had been considerable bustle in their absence. A steamboat had arrived in the night, bringing a final batch of 400 reinforcements who landed thus in time to be surrendered. Floyd commandeered the vessel for the evacuation of his brigade, four regiments from his native Virginia and one from Mississippi, the latter being assigned to guard the landing while the others got aboard. The first two regiments of Virginians had been deposited safely on the other shore; the boat had returned and the second pair were being loaded when word came from Buckner that surrender negotiations had been opened; all who were going must go at once. Floyd hurried aboard with his staff and gave the signal and the steamboat backed away, leaving the Mississippians howling ruefully on the bank.

Pillow had been less fortunate. The best transportation he could find was an abandoned scow, with barely room for himself and his chief of staff, and they were the only two from his command who got away in the night. Forrest, on the other hand, took not only all of his own men, but also a number of infantrymen who swung up behind the troopers, riding double across low stretches where the water was "saddle-skirt deep," as Forrest said. He believed the whole army could have escaped by this route, the venture he had urged at the council of war, only to be overruled. "Not a gun [was] fired at us," he reported. "Not an enemy [was] seen or heard."

Sitting and waiting was the harder task, and it was Buckner's. The first Confederate general to submit a request for surrender terms from an opponent, he knew what condemnation was likely to be heaped upon his head by his own people, who would see only that he had ordered his men to lay down their arms in the face of bloody fighting. Yet he took some consolation, and found much hope, in the fact that those terms would come from an old West Point comrade whom he had befriended in another time of trial, when the tide of fortune was running the other way. The truce messenger returned at last and handed him Grant's reply:

> H⁴ Qrs. Army in the Field
> Camp near Donelson, Feby 16ᵗʰ
>
> Gen. S. B. Buckner,
>   Confed. Army,
>   Sir: Yours of this date proposing Armistice, and appointment of Commissioners, to settle terms of Capitulation is just received. No terms except an unconditional and immediate surrender can be accepted.
>   I propose to move immediately upon your works.
>
> I am Sir: very respectfully
> Your obt. sevt.
> U. S. GRANT
> Brig. Gen.

This was not at all what Buckner had expected by way of return for favors past. Neither generous nor chivalrous, even aside from personal obligations, such "terms"—which were, in effect, hardly terms at all—were a far cry from those extended by Beauregard ten months ago

at Sumter, back in what already seemed a different war entirely, when
Anderson was allowed to salute his flag and march out under arms while
the victors lined the beaches and stood uncovered to watch him go. Yet
there was nothing Buckner could do about it; Floyd and Pillow had
left—which might have been considered good riddance except that the
former had taken four-fifths of his brigade, lengthening the odds—and
Forrest was gone with his hard-hitting cavalry, which otherwise might
have covered a retreat. All that remained was for Buckner to make a
formal protest and submit. This he did, informing Grant that the scattering of his own troops, "and the overwhelming forces under your
command, compel me, notwithstanding the brilliant success of the
Confederate arms yesterday, to accept the ungenerous and unchivalrous
terms which you propose."

By now it was broad open daylight. Receiving the message,
Grant rode forward, past white flags stuck at intervals along the rebel
line, into Dover where he found Lew Wallace already sharing a corn-
bread-and-coffee breakfast with the Confederates at the inn. He joined
the friendly discussion, and when Buckner remarked that if he had been
in charge during the fighting, the Federals would not have got up to
Donelson as easily as they had done, Grant replied that if such had been
the case, "I should not have tried it the way I did." Then he took over
the inn as his own headquarters. Before sending Buckner north, however,
he sought to make amends by offering his prisoner, who had done the
same for him when the degrees of fortune and misfortune were reversed,
the use of his purse. The Kentuckian declined it.

The actual surrender was accomplished without formality. One
northern correspondent observed a marked difference between rebels
from the border states and those from farther south. Moving among
them he noted that the former "were not much sorry that the result was
as it was," while "those from the Gulf states were sour, not inclined to
talk." This only applied to the enlisted men, however. Without exception, he found the officers "spiteful as hornets." By journalistic license,
another reporter deduced from what he saw that the common people of
the South cared very little which way the war ended, so long as it ended
soon.

Sullen or friendly, spiteful or morose, men who had been shooting at each other a few hours ago now mingled on the field for which
they had fought. Indeed, the occasion was so informal that some Confederates strolled unchallenged through the lines and got away. Bushrod
Johnson, who was among those who made off in this manner, later declared: "I have not learned that a single one who attempted to escape
met with any obstacle." Apparently Grant, who at this one stroke had
captured more prisoners than all the other Union generals combined, did
not particularly care. "It is a much less job to take them than to keep
them," he said laconically. As for Pillow, he need not have been in such

a hurry to escape, Grant told Buckner. "If I had captured him, I would have turned him loose. I would rather have him in command of you fellows than as a prisoner."

Throughout the North, church bells rang in earnest this Sunday morning, louder even than they had done for Fort Henry, ten days back. Men embraced on the streets and continued to celebrate into the night by the glare of bonfires. The shame of Bull Run was erased. Indeed, some believed they saw in the smashing double victory the end of armed rebellion, the New York *Times* remarking: "After this, it certainly cannot be materially postponed. The monster is already clutched and in his death struggle."

The nation had a new hero: U. S. Grant, who by an accident and a coincidence of initials now became "Unconditional Surrender" Grant. People had his message to Buckner by heart, and they read avidly of his life and looks in the papers: the features stern "as if carved from mahogany," the clear blue eyes (or gray, some said) and aquiline nose, the strong jaw "squarely set, but not sensual." One reporter saw three expressions in his face: "deep thought, extreme determination, and great simplicity and calmness." Another saw significance in the way he wore his high-crowned hat: "He neither puts it on behind his ears, nor draws it over his eyes; much less does he cock it on one side, but sets it straight and very hard on his head." People enjoyed reading of that, and also of the way he "would gaze at anyone who approached him with an inquiring air, followed by a glance of recollection and a grave nod of recognition." On horseback, they read, "he sits firmly in the saddle and looks straight ahead, as if only intent on getting to some particular point." The words "square" and "straight" and "firm" were the ones that appeared most often, and people liked them. Best of all, perhaps, they enjoyed hearing that Grant was "the concentration of all that is American. He talks bad grammar, but talks it naturally, as much as to say, 'I was so brought up, and if I try fine phrases I shall only appear silly.'"

To them the whole campaign was an absolute marvel of generalship, a superb combination of simplicity and drive, in welcome contrast to all that had gone before in the West and was continuing in the East. They did not dissect it in search of flaws, did not consider that Grant had started behind schedule, that men had frozen to death because of a lax discipline which let them throw away coats and blankets in fair weather, that individual attacks had been launched without coördination and been bloodily repulsed, nor that the commanding general had been absent from his post for better than six critical hours while one of his divisions was being mauled, the other two having been barred by his own orders from lending assistance. They saw rather, the sweep and slam-bang power of a leader who marched on Wednesday, skirmished on

Thursday, imperturbably watched his fleet's repulse on Friday, fought desperately on Saturday, and received the fort's unconditional surrender on Sunday. Undeterred by wretched weather, the advice of the tactics manuals, or the reported strength of the enemy position, he had inflicted about 2000 casualties and suffered about 3000 himself — which was as it should have been, considering his role as the attacker — and now there were something more than 12,000 rebel soldiers, the cream of Confederate volunteers, on their way to northern prison camps to await exchange for as many Union boys, who otherwise would have languished in southern prisons under the coming summer sun. People saw Grant as the author of this deliverance, the embodiment of the offensive spirit, the man who would strike and keep on striking until this war was won. Fifteen years ago, during a lull in the Mexican War, he had written home to the girl he was to marry: "If we have to fight, I would like to do it all at once and then make friends." Apparently he still felt that way about it.

★ ★ ★

Church bells were ringing that Sunday morning in Nashville, too, though not in celebration. The celebration had come the night before, following the release of telegrams from Floyd and Pillow announcing "a victory complete and glorious." Today, instead, they tolled the fall of Donelson, the loss of that whole wing of Johnston's army, and the resultant necessity for abandoning the Tennessee capital.

All morning the remnants of Hardee's 14,000, reduced to less than two-thirds of that by straggling and sickness during the icy retreat from Bowling Green, filed through the city, harrowing the populace with accounts of Buell's bloodthirsty hordes closing fast upon their rear. Thus began a week of panic. Previously the war had seemed a far-off thing, over in Virginia or across the Mississippi or a hundred miles north in Kentucky. They had been too busy, or too confident, to fortify even the river approaches. Now that it was upon them with the abruptness of a pistol shot in a theater, they reacted variously. Some wept in numb despair. Others proposed to burn the city, "that the enemy might have nothing of it but the ashes." Terrified by a rumor that Buell's army and Foote's gunboats would converge upon the city at 3 p.m. to shell it into submission, they milled about, loading their household goods onto carts and wagons. By that time a special train had left for Memphis, with Governor Harris and the state archives aboard. Later that afternoon, the Yankee soldiers and gunboats not having appeared, the mayor informed the crowd in the Public Square that Johnston had promised to make no stand in Nashville. He himself would go out to meet the Federals and surrender the city before they got there, the mayor told the frantic populace. Meanwhile they should calm their fears and stay at home. As a final mollification, he promised to distribute among them all the Confederate provisions that could not be removed by Johnston's army.

This appeal to the greed of the people, while effective, was to have its consequences. Nashville warehouses were bulging with accumulated supplies, and it was Johnston's task — though he had opposed this placing of all the army's eggs in one basket — to save what he could before the Federals got there. Next morning, when Floyd and his brigade (minus the Mississippians) arrived by steamboat, Johnston put him in charge, while he himself continued the retreat with Hardee's men. Floyd took over the railroads, commandeered what few wagons remained, and in general did what he could. The panic had lessened somewhat since the nonarrival of the Federals, but a lurid glare against the northern sky and the clang of firebells in the night caused its resurgence until the people learned that the reflection, which they had feared might be from torches carried by an army of Yankee incendiaries, was from the hulls of two unfinished Confederate gunboats ordered burned in the yards.

Next day Floyd continued his efforts to save the stores. It was unpleasant work, the citizens growing more mutinous every hour— especially after the destruction, over their protest, of their two fine bridges across the Cumberland. Floyd was greatly relieved when Forrest arrived from Donelson on Wednesday, under orders to assist him in the salvaging of government supplies: so relieved, in fact, that next morning he marched his brigade away, and left the task to Forrest and his troopers.

Instructed to stay there one more day, unless Buell arrived sooner, Forrest stayed four. His iron hand snatched order out of chaos. Rifling machinery and other ordnance equipment, rare items in the Confederacy, were sent from the gun foundry to Atlanta. A quarter-million pounds of bacon and hundreds of wagonloads of clothing, flour, and ammunition were hauled to the railroad station for shipment south. The people, seeing this new efficiency and remembering that they had been promised what was left, sought to interfere by gathering in front of the warehouses. Forrest appealed to their patriotism, and when that did not work, ordered his mounted men to lay about with the flat of their sabers, which worked better. One large mob, in front of a warehouse on the Public Square, was dispersed by the use of fire hoses squirting ice-cold muddy water from the river, and as one of the crowd remembered it later, this had "a magical effect."

All day Thursday and Friday and Saturday, Forrest and his troopers worked, on into Sunday morning, when blue pickets appeared on the north bank of the river. Mindful of his instructions to leave Nashville an open city, Forrest fell back through the suburbs, marching to join Johnston and Hardee, who by now were at Murfreesboro, forty miles southeast. The Army of Central Kentucky — or what was left of it, anyhow — would have to find a new name.

Nashville's "Great Panic," as it was called thereafter, had lasted precisely a week, though by way of anticlimax one ignominy remained. True to his promise to the people, the mayor got in a rowboat and crossed the river to deliver the city into the hands of the Yankees before they opened fire with their long-range guns. He found no guns, however, and few soldiers: only half a squad of cavalry and one Ohio captain, who, after some persuasion, agreed to receive the surrender of the city, or at any rate not to attack it. The mayor returned and announced this deliverance to the citizens, who thus were relieved of a measure of their fears — most of which had been groundless in the first place. Buell was still a long way off, toiling down the railroad and the turnpike, repairing washed-out bridges as he came. Grant remained at Donelson, receiving reinforcements. Before the end of the week he had upwards of 30,000 men in four divisions, one of which had been advanced to Clarksville. "Nashville would be an easy conquest," he wrote Halleck's chief of staff, "but I only throw this out as a suggestion . . . . I am ready for any move the general commanding may order." The general commanding ordered nothing; Grant stayed where he was.

Buell, in fact, did not reach Nashville until Wednesday, though several outfits had come on ahead. A reporter with one of the earliest wrote of what they found. All the stores and most of the better homes were closed; the State House was deserted, the legislators having fled with the governor to Memphis, which had been declared the temporary capital. The correspondent found the door of the leading hotel bolted, and when he rang there was no answer. He kept on ringing, with the persistency of a tired and hungry man within reach of food and a clean bed. At last he was rewarded. A Negro swung the door ajar and stood there smiling broadly. "Massa done gone souf," he said, still grinning.

✗ 3 ✗

Inauguration day broke cold and sullen in Richmond, with a scud of cloud that promised and then delivered rain, first a drizzle, then a steady downpour, hissing and gurgling in the gutters and thrumming against roofs and windowpanes. Davis rose early, as was his custom. Not due at the ceremonies until 11.30, he walked first to his office for an hour of the paperwork which filled so large a share of his existence, then back home. His wife, coming to warn him that the dignitaries were waiting to escort him to the Capitol, found him alone on his knees in the bedroom, praying "for the divine support I need so sorely." That too had been his custom since his first inauguration a year ago, under a cloudless Alabama sky.

The procession formed in the old Virginia Hall of Delegates, then moved out onto Capitol Square where a canopied platform had been set up alongside the equestrian statue of Washington, whose birth-day this was. Grouped about the President-elect were cabinet officers, admirals and generals, governors and congressmen, newspaper represent-atives and members of various benevolent societies. Beside him stood Vice President Stephens, undersized and sickly, huddled in layers of clothes and resembling more than ever a mummified child. Asked once to define true happiness, Stephens had replied without hesitation, "To be warm." He was not happy now, presumably, for a cold rain fell in sheets, blown under the canopy by intermittent gusts of northern wind. When the Right Reverend John Johns, Episcopal Bishop of Virginia, raised his arms to pronounce the invocation, his lawn sleeves hung limp and his heavy satin vestments were splotched with wet. Close-packed, the crowd stood and took its drenching, conscious of being present at a historic occasion. Some held strips of canvas or worn carpet over their heads, but there were enough umbrellas to give the square what one wit-ness called "the effect of an immense mushroom bed." They could hear few of the words above the impact of the rain. They saw Davis take the oath, however, and they knew they had a permanent President at last. When he bent forward to kiss the Book a shout went up. Then they quieted. The drumming of the rain was loud as he turned to address them.

He was thinner and even more austere in appearance, the cheek-bones brought into greater prominence and the eyes sunk even deeper in their sockets; "singularly imposing," one witness found him today, albeit with "a pallor painful to look upon." He wore a suit of black for the ceremonies instead of his customary gray, so that to Mrs Davis he seemed "a willing victim going to his funeral pyre." Her thoughts had been directed into such channels by an occurrence on the way. Observ-ing that the carriage moved at a snail's pace, accompanied by a quartet of black-suited Negro footmen wearing white cotton gloves, she asked the coachman, to whom she had left the arrangements, what it meant. He told her, "This, ma'am, is the way we always does in Richmond at funerals and sichlike."

A year ago there had been no talk of funerals; "joyous" was the word Davis had used to describe the atmosphere on the day of his first inaugural. It was not so now. The outlook was as different as the weather. Nor did he assume a falsely joyous manner on this second occasion of taking the oath as President of the Confederacy. After re-ferring to the birthday of the Virginian who looked out from his bronze horse nearby, he once more outlined and defended the course of events which had led to secession, characterizing the North as barbarous and expressing scorn for the "military despotism" which had "our enemies" in its grip. All this was as it had been before, but soon he passed to words that touched the present:

"A million men, it is estimated, are now standing in hostile array and waging war along a frontier of thousands of miles. Battles have been fought, sieges have been conducted, and although the contest is not ended and the tide for the moment is against us, the final result in our favor is not doubtful. We have had our trials and difficulties. That we are to escape them in the future is not to be hoped. It was to be expected when we entered upon this war that it would expose our people to sacrifices and cost them much, both of money and blood. But the picture has its lights as well as its shadows. This great strife has awakened in the people the highest emotions and qualities of the human soul. It was, perhaps, in the ordination of Providence that we were to be taught the value of our liberties by the price we pay for them. The recollection of this great contest, with all its common traditions of glory, of sacrifice and blood, will be the bond of harmony and enduring affection amongst the people, producing unity in policy, fraternity in sentiment, and just effort in war."

An invocation had opened the proceedings. Now another closed them. Davis lifted his hands and eyes to heaven as he spoke the final words. "My hope is reverently fixed on Him whose favor is ever vouchsafed to the cause which is just. With humble gratitude and adoration, acknowledging the Providence which has so visibly protected the Confederacy during its brief but eventful career, to Thee, O God, I trustingly commit myself and prayerfully invoke Thy blessing on my country and its cause."

Under the spell of that closing prayer, the people dispersed in silence and good order, "as though they had attended divine service," one remarked. Later, however, away from the magic of his voice and presence, they doubted that there was "unity in policy" or "fraternity in sentiment" or "just effort" in the prosecution of the war. Prompted by hostile editors, whose critiques of the address came out in their papers the following day — along with the news from Donelson and Nashville announcing the loss of Kentucky and most of Tennessee — they began to consider not only what he had said, but also what he had not said. He had outlined no future policy for raising the blockade, whose pinch was already being felt, or for overcoming the recent military reverses. Though his words were obviously spoken as much for foreign as for domestic ears, he had not foretold international recognition or the receiving of assistance from abroad. Except in vague and general terms, including the closing appeal to the Almighty, he had announced no single plan for coming to grips with the host of calamities they knew were included in his admission that "the tide for the moment is against us."

The fact that he refrained from explicit mention of these reverses did not mean that the people were unaware of them. They knew all too well that even a bare listing would have doubled the length of his address. Foremost among the disappointments, at least to men who took a

long view of the chance for victory, was the failure of Confederate
diplomacy. Original computations had shown that, before spring, England would have begun to suffer from the cotton famine which would
bring her to her knees. Yet the looms and jennies, spinning away at the
surplus bulging the warehouses, had not slowed. Ironically, the shortage
there was not in cotton, but in wheat, the result of a crop failure in the
British Isles. They were buying it now by the shipload from the North,
which had harvested a bumper crop with its new McCormick reapers:
another example of what it meant to fight a race of "pasty-faced mechanics."

　　Back at the outset, Southerners had predicted that the great
Northwest — meaning Michigan, Wisconsin, Minnesota, and Iowa,
along with northern Illinois and Indiana — would be pro-Confederate because of its need for an outlet to the Gulf of Mexico. Some who
lived there had thought so, too. The Detroit *Free Press* had declared at
the time: "If troops shall be raised in the North to march against the
people of the South, a fire in the rear will be opened against such troops,
which will either stop their march altogether or wonderfully accelerate
it." But events had not worked out that way at all. The men of Grant's
army were mostly from that region, and they had been accelerated, not
by any "fire in the rear," but rather by an intense concern that the
Union be preserved. Then too, instead of working an economic hardship, as the Southerners had predicted, the war had provided the farmers
of the area with a new and profitable market for their wheat. The
Northwest had not only stood by the Union; it was growing rich from
having done so.

　　To some, this one among the many was the greatest disappointment of them all. The main hope of redress was that foreign intervention
would be won by the new team of professional diplomats, Mason and
Slidell, who had made a spectacular entry into the field. Yet here, too,
there was disappointment. After serving the South so well from their
cells in Boston Harbor, they were proving far less useful now in freedom
at their posts. They stepped onto the London railway platform as if
into obscurity, unwelcomed and unnoticed save by the late friendly
Times, which announced their arrival with the following observations:
"We sincerely hope that our countrymen will not give these fellows
anything in the shape of an ovation. The civility that is due to a foe in
distress is all that they can claim. The only reason for their presence in
London is to draw us into their own quarrel. The British public has no
prejudice in favor of slavery, which these gentlemen represent. What
they and their secretaries are to do here passes our experience. They are
personally nothing to us. They must not suppose, because we have gone
to the verge of a great war to rescue them, that they are precious in our
eyes."

　　Bitter as it was for Mason to see himself and his partner referred to as unprecious "fellows," the reception he received from the Foreign Minister dampened his spirits even more. Ushered into the presence, he was about to present his credentials when his lordship checked him: "That is unnecessary, since our relations are unofficial." Icily polite, but disinclined to enter into any discussion of policy, the most Earl Russell ventured was the hope that Mason would find his visit "agreeable." In parting he did not express the hope that they might meet again. This was the treatment Yancey had broken under, and the Virginian took it scarcely better, reporting: "On the whole it was manifest enough that his personal sympathies were not with us."

Slidell, continuing his voyage across the channel, also encountered conditions which had plagued his predecessor. Unlike Mason, he had no difficulty in securing audiences. He got about as many as he wanted, and Eugénie was obviously charmed — a fact which he reported with some pride — but Napoleon would only repeat what he had said before: France could not act without England. That was the crux of the matter. The Crimean War had been a struggle between West and East, which the West had won, and now in the normal course of events, as demonstrated by history, the victors should have turned upon each other for domination of the whole. Yet it had not worked out that way. There was no such tenuous balance as had obtained at the time of the American Revolution, bringing France to the assistance of the Colonies. On the contrary, the *entente* remained strong, drawing its strength from the weakness of Napoleon, whose shaky finances and doubtful popularity would not allow him to risk bringing all of Europe down on his unprotected back. Slidell could only inform his government of these conditions. It began to seem that, economically and politically — so far at least as Europe was concerned — the South had chosen the wrong decade in which to make her bid for independence.

Like others who took the long view, seeing foreign intervention as the one quick indisputable solution to the Confederacy's being outnumbered and outgunned and outmachined, Davis received this latest news from abroad with whatever grace and patience he could muster. He could wait — though by the hardest. Meantime he had other, more immediate problems here at home, within his own official family: in evidence of which, as even the short-view men could see, the chief post in his cabinet was vacant. The Secretary of State had left in a huff that very week.

At the time when he accepted the appointment, Hunter had announced that he intended to be a responsible and independent official, not just "the clerk of Mr Davis." As Virginia's favorite-son candidate at the Democratic convention of 1860, he had his political dignity to consider. Besides, in the early days of the secession movement, when it was thought that the Old Dominion would be among the first to go, he had been slated for the presidency of the impending Confederacy. Vir-

ginia had held back and he had missed it; but there was still the future to
keep his eye on, and his dignity to be maintained. The result was a
personality clash with Davis, a build-up of bad feeling which reached a
climax during a general cabinet discussion of the military situation.
When Hunter expressed an opinion on the subject, Davis told him: "Mr
Hunter, you are Secretary of State, and when information is wished of
that department it will be time for you to speak." The Virginian's resignation was on the presidential desk next morning.

Davis of course accepted it. He made no appointment to fill the
post immediately, however. Vacant for a week at the time of the inauguration, it would remain so for three more. The man he had in mind
was too deeply embroiled in other matters, filling another cabinet position, to be considered available just yet. And this was one more item
which might have been included in any listing of reverses.

As Secretary of War, the rotund, smiling Judah P. Benjamin had
been under fire almost since the day of his appointment: not under actual
bombardment from the enemy beyond the gates, but rather from the
plain citizens and congressmen within, whose ire was aroused by his
summary treatment of the nation's military heroes, coming as they did
under the jurisdiction of his department. Benjamin had no such notion
as Hunter's concerning the duties of his post. As head of the War Department he considered himself quite literally the President's secretary
for military affairs, and it did not irk him at all to be tagged "the clerk of
Mr Davis." The field of arms was one of the few that had not previously
engaged the interest of this myriad-minded man, whereas Davis, a West
Pointer and a Mexican War hero, had been the ablest Secretary the Federal War Department ever had. Benjamin's duty, as he saw it — and here
the two men's concepts coincided — was to execute the will and, if
necessary, defend the actions of his Commander in Chief. Besides, he
saw Davis's needs, the desire for warmth behind his iciness, the ache for
understanding behind his stiff austerity. Judah Benjamin was one of the
few who perceived this, or at any rate one of the few — like Mrs Davis
— who acted on it, and in doing so he not only made himself pleasant;
in time he also made himself indispensable. That was his reward. He
gained the President's gratitude, and with it the unflinching loyalty
which Davis always gave in return for loyalty received.

Whatever he lacked in the knowledge of arms as a profession, he
brought to his job a considerable facility in the handling of administrative matters. Unlike Walker, who had fumed and stewed in tangles of
red tape and never got from under the avalanche of army paperwork,
Benjamin would clear his desk with dispatch, then sit back smiling, ready
for what came next. What came next, as often as not, was an opportunity for exercising his talent in dialectics. Here his skill was admittedly
superior — "uncanny," some called it, and they spoke resentfully; for by
the precision of his logic he could lead men where they would not go,

making them seem clumsy in the process. In taking up his superior's quarrels with the generals on the Manassas line — which seemed to him one of the duties of his post — he gave full play to his talents in this direction, undeterred by awe for the military mind. That was what had caused Beauregard to reach for his pen in such a frenzy, writing with ill-concealed irony of the pity he felt, "from the bottom of my heart," for any man who could not see "the difference between *patriotism*, the highest civic virtue, and *office-seeking*, the lowest civic occupation." It was Benjamin he meant. But in making the charge the general entered a field where his fellow Louisianian was master; and presently he went West.

Even more vulnerable in this respect, though banishment did not follow so close on the heels of contention, was Joseph E. Johnston. After Johnston's protest at being outranked, and Davis's quick slash in reply, Benjamin took up the cudgel for his chief. Johnston was a careless administrator, and whenever he lapsed in this regard, the Secretary took him to task with a letter that prickled his sensitive pride. Infuriated, the general would reply in kind, only to be brought up short by another missive which proved him even further in the wrong. A later observer wrote that Benjamin treated the Virginian as if he were "an adversary at the bar," but sometimes it was worse; he dealt with him as if he were a prisoner in the dock. Johnston's outraged protests against such treatment did him no more good than Beauregard's had done. Once when the Creole complained to Davis that the Secretary's tone was offensive and that he was being "put into the strait jackets of the law," the President replied: "I do not feel competent to instruct Mr Benjamin in the matter of style. There are few whom the public would probably believe fit for the task." As for the second objection, "You surely do not intend to inform me that your army and yourself are outside the limits of the law. It is my duty to see that the laws are faithfully executed and I cannot recognize the pretensions of anyone that their restraint is too narrow for him."

Exalted thus at the expense of those who attempted to match wits with him, Benjamin continued to maintain order at headquarters and to ride herd on recalcitrants among the military. Then, unexpectedly, he ran full tilt into a man who had no use for dialectics, who stood instead on his own ground and gave the Secretary his first check. T. J. Jackson, called "Stonewall" since Manassas, had been promoted to major general in the fall and assigned to command a division in the Shenandoah Valley, from which strategic location he had proposed that he be reinforced for an all-out invasion of the North. Having just rejected a similar proposal from Beauregard at Centerville, the Administration would send him no reinforcements, but attached to his command the three brigades of W. W. Loring, the one professional in the quartet who had tried the patience and damaged the reputation of R. E. Lee in West Virginia. Told to accomplish what he could with this total force of about 9000, Jackson launched on New Year's Day a movement designed to recover the counties flanking the western rim of the Valley theater.

The first phase of the campaign went as planned. Marching in bitter midwinter weather, Jackson's men harried the B & O Railroad, captured enemy stores, and in general created havoc among the scattered Federal camps. This done, Stonewall stationed Loring's troops at Romney, on the upper Potomac, and took the others back to Winchester, thirty-odd miles eastward, to begin the second phase. Just what that would have been remained a mystery, for Jackson was a most secretive man, agreeing absolutely with Frederick II's remark, "If I thought my coat knew my plans I would take it off and burn it." He did say, however, that he left the attached brigades on outpost duty because his own were better marchers and could move more swiftly toward any threatened point. Loring's volunteers did not subscribe to this. Rather, it was their belief that Stonewall was demented. (They saw various symptoms of this — including the fact that he never took pepper in his food, on grounds that it gave him pains in his left leg.) And so were his men, for that matter, since they had a habit of cheering him on the march. Exposed as they were to the elements and the possible swoop of Federal combinations, Loring and his officers petitioned the War Department to withdraw them from their uncomfortable position. On the next to last day of January, Jackson received the following dispatch signed by Benjamin: "Our news indicates that a movement is being made to cut off General Loring's command. Order him back to Winchester immediately."

Jackson promptly complied with the order. Acknowledging its receipt and reporting its execution, the next day he addressed the War Department: "With such interference in my command I cannot expect to be of much service in the field," wherefore he asked to be returned to his teaching job at V.M.I., or else "I respectfully request that the President will accept my resignation from the army." The letter went through channels to Johnston, who forwarded it regretfully to Richmond. He too had been by-passed, and he told Benjamin: "Let me suggest that, having broken up the dispositions of the military commander, you give whatever other orders may be necessary."

Eventually the trouble was smoothed over and Jackson's resignation returned to him, Governor Letcher and various congressmen exerting all the pressure of their influence, but not before violent recriminations had been heaped on the head of the smiling Secretary, especially by Stonewall's fellow officers. Tom Cobb of Georgia, a brigadier in the Virginia army, stated flatly: "A grander rascal than this Jew Benjamin does not exist in the Confederacy and I am not particular in concealing my opinion of him." Nor were others particular in that respect, their fury being increased when Loring was promoted in mid-

February and taken from under the stern control of Jackson, who had recommended that he be cashiered.

Benjamin kept smiling through it all, though by then the indestructibility of his smile was being tested even further. Previous recriminations had come mainly from army men, outraged at his interfering in tactical matters. Now he was being condemned by the public at large, and for a lack of similar interference.

Down on the North Carolina coast, set one above the other, Albemarle and Pamlico Sounds were divided by a low-lying marshy peninsula. At its eastern tip, where the jut of land approached the narrow sands of the breakwater guarding the coast from the gales that blew so frequently off Hatteras, lay Roanoke Island, the site of Raleigh's "Lost Colony" and birthplace of the first English child born in the Western Hemisphere. Just now, however, this boggy tract had an importance beyond the historic. Pamlico, the lower and larger sound, had fallen to Stringham's gunboats back in August; Albemarle could be taken, too, once the narrows flanking the island had been forced. Loss of the lower sound had given the Federals a year-round anchorage and access to New Bern, principal eastern depot on the vital railroad supply line to Richmond and the armies in Virginia. That was bad enough, though the invaders had not yet exploited it, but loss of the upper sound would expose Norfolk and Gosport Navy Yard to attack

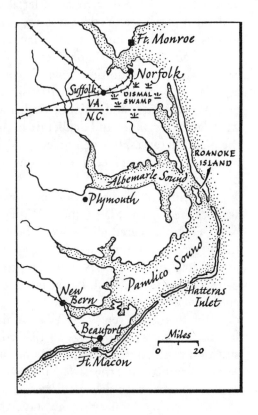

from the rear. This would be worse than bad; it would be tragic, for the Confederates had things going on in the navy yard that would not bear interruption. The focal point for its defense, as anyone could see, was Roanoke Island. Situated north of all four barrier inlets, it was like a loose-fitting cork plugging the neck of a bottle called Albemarle Sound. Nothing that went by water could get in there without going past the cork.

One who saw this clearly was Henry Wise. Still seething from his defeat in West Virginia at the hands of his fellow ex-governor Floyd, he arrived and took command of the island forces in late December. He entered upon his duties with his usual enthusiasm. By the time he was halfway through his first inspection, however, he saw that the cork was not only loose, but also apt to crumble under pressure. Little had been done to block the passes, either by driving pilings or by sinking obstructions in the channel. What was worse, the water batteries were badly sited, clustered up at the northern end of the island as if in expectation of attack from that direction after Norfolk fell, while the southern end, giving down upon Pamlico Sound — which the enemy fleet had held for four months now — was left open to amphibious assault. In the face of this threat Wise had a garrison of about 2500 men, fewer than he believed were necessary to slow, let alone halt, such an attack once the Federals got ashore. Yet he was no defeatist. He got to work, driving pilings and sinking hulks in the channel, and called on the district commander at Norfolk, Major General Benjamin Huger, for additional artillery and ammunition, pile drivers, supplies of every kind, and especially more soldiers. A fifty-six-year-old South Carolina aristocrat, West Pointer and Chief of Ordnance under Scott in Mexico, Huger was placid in manner and deliberate in judgment. He had never inspected the island defenses, but he replied to Wise's requisitions by recommending "hard work and coolness among the troops you have, instead of more men."

Being told to keep cool only lowered Wise's boiling point, which was reached when Flag Officer William F. Lynch, of the Confederate navy, commandeered all his work boats except a single tug, converting them to one-gun gunboats. A "mosquito fleet," Wise dubbed the result in derision, and left for Norfolk to protest in person. When Huger still gave him no satisfaction, he set out for Richmond, where he had influential friends bound to him during years of politics. He would appeal directly to the Secretary of War. This was contrary to Army Regulations, he knew; to go was to risk court martial. But he believed the situation justified irregularity. "Damn the execution, sir!" he had cried in West Virginia; "it's the *sound* that we want." As tactics, this could be applied to more than field artillery.

Arriving January 19 he stayed three days; but he got nowhere with the Secretary. Already Benjamin had replied to his urgent demands for cannon powder by informing him that the Confederacy's "very limited" reserve was being saved for use at more closely threatened points. "At the first indication, however, of an attack on Roanoke Island," he wrote, "a supply will be sent you." Wise replied that there *was* no more closely threatened point and that once the assault had begun it would be too late, but the Secretary had considered the matter closed. Now, face to face with Benjamin in Richmond, the Virginian fared no better in his plea for powder. Nor did he get reinforcements.

When he pointed out that Huger had 13,000 men lying idle around Norfolk, the Secretary, obviously preferring the military judgment of the professionally trained senior to that of the politically appointed subordinate, shrugged and said that he supposed the district commander knew best. He would not interfere.

Wise remained in town, complaining vociferously to his high-placed friends until the 22d, when a dispatch arrived from Commander Lynch announcing symptoms of an enemy build-up and attack: whereupon Benjamin, doubtless glad to be rid of him, issued a peremptory order for the general to go back to his island post. Bad weather and transportation difficulties delayed his return till the end of the month. On the 31st — while Stonewall Jackson was composing his resignation out in the Valley — the distraught Wise, his condition aggravated by the frustration of trying to get someone to realize the weakness of his tactical position, took to his bed with a severe attack of pleurisy.

He was still there a week later when the all-out Federal amphibious assault was launched, just as he had said it would be, against the undefended south end of the island.

In his search for someone who understood the difficulties and dangers of his assignment Wise was cut off from the one person who, next to himself, appreciated them best. The trouble was, the man wore blue and exercised his authority on the other side of the line.

Ambrose Burnside had not gone home with his Rhode Islanders when they were mustered out in early August, two weeks after crossing Bull Run as the fist of the roundhouse right McDowell had swung at Beauregard in an effort to end the war on the plains of Manassas. He had tried civilian life as a businessman a few years back and, failing, hadn't liked it. Now, at thirty-seven, an Indiana-born West Pointer and a veteran of the Mexican War, he accepted promotion to brigadier and stayed on in the service. A tall, rather stout, energetic man with large features and dark-socketed eyes, he made up for his premature baldness with a fantastic set of whiskers describing a double parabola from in front of his ears, down over his chops, and up across his mouth. This was his trademark, a half-ruff of facial hair standing out in dark-brown contrast to his shaven jowls and chin. Affecting the casual in his dress — low-slung holster, loose-fitting knee-length double-breasted jacket, and wide-brimmed bell-crowned soft felt hat — he was something of a pistol-slapper, but likable all the same for his hearty manner and open nature, his forthright, outgoing friendliness. McClellan liked him, at any rate, and called him "Dear Burn" in letters. So that when Burnside approached him in the fall with a plan for the seizure of coastal North Carolina, completing what had been begun at Hatteras Inlet and opening thereby a second front in the Confederate rear, the general-in-chief was attentive and said he would like to see it submitted in writing.

Burnside did so, expanding his original plan, and McClellan liked it even more. He indorsed it, got the Secretary of War to give it top priority, and told the Hoosier general to go ahead, the quicker the better.

The Burnside Expedition, as it was designated, was assembled and ready for action by early January, Annapolis being the staging area for its 13,000 troops and 80 vessels. Grouped into three divisions under brigadiers who had been cadets with their commander at West Point — J. G. Foster, Jesse L. Reno, John G. Park; "three of my most trusted friends," he called them — the men were mostly rock-ribbed New Englanders, "many of whom would be familiar with the coasting trade, and among whom would be found a goodly number of mechanics." The naval components of this task force, under Rear Admiral Louis M. Goldsborough, a big, slack-bodied regular of the type called "barnacles," had no such homogeneity. In addition to twenty light-draft gunboats armed with cannon salvaged from the armories of various navy yards, there was a rickety lot of sixty-odd transports and supply ships, including tugs, ferries, converted barges, and flat-bottomed river steamers: a conglomeration, in short, of whatever could be scraped together by purchasing agents combing northern rivers and harbors for vessels rejected by agents who had come and gone before them. The only characteristic they shared was that they all drew less than eight feet of water, the reported high-tide depth across the bar at Hatteras Inlet.

This was the cause of much grumbling at the outset. Seafaring men among the soldiers took one look at the shallow-draft transports and shook their heads. At the worst, they had volunteered for getting shot at, not drowned — which was what they believed would happen, once those tubs reached open water. Burnside answered the grumbling by taking the smallest, least seaworthy craft of the lot for his headquarters boat. Thus reassured, or anyhow reproached, the troops filed onto the transports, and on the morning of the 9th the flotilla steamed out of the harbor to rendezvous next day off Fort Monroe. On the 11th, clearing Hampton Roads, the skippers broke open their sealed orders and steered south.

The near-mutiny among his sea-going soldiers at the outset was only the first of Burnside's troubles. In fact, the method by which he had quelled the grumbling almost cost him his life the following night, when the fleet ran into a gale off Hatteras. The dinky little headquarters boat got into the trough of the sea and nearly foundered. As he remembered it years later, still somewhat queasy from the experience, everything not securely lashed above-decks was swept overboard, while "men, furniture, and crockery below decks were thrown about in a most promiscuous manner." Eventually, her steersman brought her head-to and she rode the storm out, staggering up and down the mast-high waves to arrive next morning off Hatteras Inlet, the entrance to Pamlico Sound, where an even worse shock awaited him.

The water through there was not eight feet deep, as he had been told, but six: which barred many of his vessels from a share in the expedition as effectively as if they had been sunk by enemy action. Here was where the "goodly number of mechanics, . . . familiar with the coasting trade," stood their commander in good stead. The tide running swift above the swash, they sent several of the larger ships full-speed-ahead to ground on the bar, and held them there with tugs and anchors while the racing current washed the sand from under their bottoms. It was a slow process, bumping them forward length by length; but it worked. By early February a broad eight-foot channel had been cut and the fleet assembled safely in the sound. On the 4th, after a conference with the flag officer, Burnside gave his brigadiers detailed instructions for the landing on Roanoke Island. Another two-day blow delayed it, but on the morning of the 7th, a fine, clear day with sunshine bright on the placid, sapphire water, the fleet steamed forward in attack formation.

Still suffering from the multiple pangs of pleurisy and frustration, Wise had been confined all this time at Nags Head, the Confederate command post on the sandy rim of Albemarle Sound, just opposite the north end of the island. He knew what was coming, and even how, though until now he had not realized the strength of the blow the Federals were aiming. Goldsborough's warships were out in front, mounting a total of 64 guns, eager to take on the seven makeshift rebel vessels, each mounting a single 32-pounder rifle. Behind the Yankee gunboats came the transports, crowded with 13,000 assault troops ready to swarm ashore and try their strength against the island's fewer than 3000 defenders. The mosquito fleet took station in front of the uncompleted line of pilings Wise had started driving across the channel, but when the Federals roared and bore down on them belching smoke and flame from 9-inch guns and 100-pounder rifles, they scurried back through the gap and out of range, leaving the water batteries to take up the defense.

There were two of these, both up toward the northern end of the island, and while the warships took them under fire the transports dropped anchor three miles astern and began unloading troops for the landing at Ashby's Harbor, midway up the island's ten-mile length. The first boats hit the beach at 4 o'clock. All this time the duel between the gunboats and the batteries continued, with more noise than damage on either side. At sundown the mosquito fleet attempted a darting attack that was repulsed about as soon as it began. By midnight all the troops were ashore. The undefended southern half of the island had been secured without the infantry firing a shot. Drenched by a chill rain, they tried to get what sleep they could before the dawn advance, knowing that tomorrow would be tougher.

Down the boggy center of the island, a little more than a mile from the opposite beaches, ran a causeway. Astride this backbone of defense the Confederates had placed a three-gun battery supported by infantry and flanked by quicksand marshes judged impenetrable. To advance along the causeway toward those guns would be like walking up a hardwood alley toward a bowler whose only worry was running out of balls before the advancer ran out of legs. Yet there was no other way, and the men of both armies knew it: Burnside as well as anyone, for he had been briefed for the landing by a twenty-year-old contraband who had run away from his island master the week before and was thoroughly familiar with the dispositions for defense. Instructing Foster to charge straight up the causeway while Reno and Park were probing the boggy flanks, Burnside put all three brigades into line and sent them forward as soon as the light was full.

Right off, the center brigade ran into murderous head-on fire. Bowled over and pinned down, they were hugging the sandy embankment and wondering what came next, when off to the right and left fronts they heard simultaneous whoops of exultation. The flank brigades had made it through the knee-deep ooze and slush of the "impenetrable" marsh. While the rebel cannoneers tried frantically to turn their guns to meet these attacks from opposite and unexpected directions, the men along the causeway jumped up, whooping too, and joined the charge. The battery was quickly overrun.

With the fall of the three-gun battery the island's defenses collapsed of a broken backbone. Burnside's infantry broke into the clear, taking the water batteries in reverse while the fleet continued its bombardment from the channel. By midafternoon the Confederates had retreated as far as they could go. Corralled on the northern tip of the island, their ammunition exhausted, they laid down their arms. Casualties had been relatively light on both sides: 264 for the attackers, 143 for the defenders. The difference came in the fruits of victory; 2675 soldiers and 32 cannon were surrendered, losses which the South could ill afford. Best of all, from the northern point of view, Burnside had won control of North Carolina's inland sea, thereby tightening the blockade one hard twist more, opening a second front in the Virginia army's rear, gaining access to the back door to Norfolk, and arousing the immediate apprehension of every rebel posted within gunshot of salt water. No beach was safe. This newly bred amphibious beast, like some monster out of mythology — half Army, half Navy: an improbable, unholy combination if ever there was one — might come splashing and roaring ashore at any point from here on down.

North and south the news went out and men reacted. In New York, Horace Greeley swung immediately to the manic, celebrating the double conquest of Roanoke Island and Fort Henry even as Grant was knocking at the gates of Donelson: "The cause of the Union now marches on in every section of the country. Every blow tells fearfully against the rebellion. The rebels themselves are panic-stricken, or despondent. It now requires no very far-reaching prophet to predict the end of this struggle."

In Richmond, as elsewhere throughout the Confederacy and among her representatives overseas, the spirits of men were correspondingly grim. As if in confirmation of Greeley's paean in the *Tribune*, letters came from Mason and Slidell. The former wrote from London that "the late reverses . . . have had an unfortunate effect upon the minds of our friends here." The latter wrote from Paris: "I need not say how unfavorable an influence these defeats, following in such quick succession, have produced in public sentiment. If not soon counterbalanced by some decisive success of our arms, we may not only bid adieu to all hopes of seasonable recognition, but must expect that the declaration of the inefficiency of the blockade, to which I had looked forward with great confidence at no distant day, will be indefinitely postponed."

These were hard lines for Davis on the eve of his inaugural, but he had other reactions to deal with, nearer and far more violent. Norfolk was in turmoil — with good cause. Lynch's mosquito fleet, attempting to make a stand against Goldsborough's gunboats at the mouth of the Pasquotank River, was wrecked in short order, six of the seven vessels being captured, rammed, blown up, or otherwise sunk. Only one made its escape up the river and through the Dismal Swamp Canal to Norfolk, barely forty miles away, bringing wild stories of the destruction it had run from and predicting that Norfolk was next on the monster's list. The consternation which followed this report was hardly calmed by the arrival of Wise, who, convalescent from pleurisy, had made his escape by marching up the breakwater from Nags Head. "Nothing! Nothing!! Nothing!!!" he proclaimed. "That was the disease which brought disaster at Roanoke Island." Thus he shook whatever confidence the citizens had managed to retain in Huger, who was charged with their defense.

The city seethed with rumors of doom, and the panic spread quickly up the James to Richmond. Davis met it as he had met the East Tennessee crisis early that winter. Five days after the inaugural in which he had excoriated Lincoln for doing the same thing, and scorned the northern populace for putting up with it, he suspended the privilege of habeas corpus in the Norfolk area, placing the city under martial law. Two days later, March 1, Richmond itself was gripped by the iron hand.

This action added fuel to the fire already raging in certain breasts. Taking their cue from Wise, who was vociferous in accusation, the people put the blame where he pointed: squarely at the Secretary of War. Benjamin took it as he took everything, blandly. "To do the Secretary justice," one observer wrote, "he bore the universal attack with admirable good nature and sang froid." More than that, "to all appearances, equally secure in his own views and indifferent to public odium, he passed from reverse to reverse with perfectly bland manner and unwearying courtesy."

The principal charge against him was that he had failed, despite repeated pleas, to supply the island defenders with powder for their cannon. He had the best possible answer to this: that there was and had been none to send. But to admit as much would have been to encourage his country's enemies and alienate the Europeans considering recognition and support. The Louisianian kept silent under attack and abuse, and Davis was given further proof of his loyalty and devotion to the cause. However, his very urbanity was more infuriating to his foes than any defense or counterattack he might have made. The Richmond *Examiner* was irked into commenting acidly, "The Administration has now an opportunity of making some reputation; for, nothing being expected of it, of course every success will be clear gain." Plainly, the ultimate sacrifice was called for. Benjamin had to go.

He had to go, but not from the cabinet entirely. That would be a loss which Davis believed the nation could not afford. At any rate *he* could not. And though, as always, he would not attempt to justify or even explain his action — would not say to the hostile editors and fuming politicians, "Let me keep this man; I need him" — he found a way to keep him: a way, however, that infuriated his critics even more.

The post of Secretary of State had been vacant since Hunter left in a huff the month before. Davis had kept it so, with this in mind. Now in mid-March the Permanent Congress, which had convened four days before his inauguration, received for confirmation the name of the man he wanted appointed to fill the vacancy: Judah P. Benjamin of Louisiana, former Attorney General and present Secretary of War. Some in that body called the move audacious. Others called it impudent. Whatever it was, Davis had the devotion of the people and the personal support of a majority of the legislators, and he was willing to risk them both, here and now, to get what he believed both he and the Confederacy needed to win the war and establish independence. And he got it. Despite the gasps of outrage and cries of indignation, Benjamin was quickly confirmed as head of the State Department and thus assured a voice in the nation's councils, a seat at the right hand of Jefferson Davis.

Having angered many congressmen by requiring them to promote the Secretary of War as a reward for what they termed his inefficiency, the President now proceeded to make them happy and proud by placing before them, for confirmation, the name of George Wythe Randolph as Benjamin's successor. Appointment of this forty-four-year-old Richmond lawyer, scion of the proud clan of Randolph, would make amends for the snub given Hunter and restore to the Old

Dominion a rightful place among those closest to the head of government. What was more, Randolph had had varied military experience as a youthful midshipman in the U.S. Navy, as a gentleman ranker in a prewar Richmond militia company, and as artillery commander under Magruder on the peninsula, where in eight months he had risen from captain to colonel, with a promotion to brigadier moving up through channels even now. All this was much, and augured well. But best of all, from the point of view of those who had the privilege of voting his confirmation, he was the grandson of Thomas Jefferson, born at the hilltop shrine of Monticello and dandled on the great Virginian's knee. Blood would tell, as all Southerners knew, and this was the finest blood of all, serving to reëmphasize the ties between the Second American Revolution and the First. The appointment was confirmed at once, enthusiastically and with considerable mutual congratulation among the senators.

Whether the highborn Randolph would bear up better than Hunter had done as a "clerk of Mr Davis" remained to be seen. For the present, at least, the Chief Executive had placated the rising anger of his friends by nominating Randolph, and had foiled his critics by tossing his personal popularity into the balance alongside the hated Benjamin, causing the opposite pan to kick the beam. How long he could continue to win by such methods, standing thus between his favorites and abuse, was another question. Certainly every such victory subtracted from the weight he would exert in any weighing match that followed. What he lost, each time, his critics gained: particularly those who railed against his static defensive policy and his failure to share with the public the grim statistics of the lengthening odds. Down in Georgia, even now, an editor was writing for all to read: "President Davis does not enjoy the confidence of the Southern people. . . . With a cold, icy, iron grasp, [he] has fettered our people, stilled their beating pulses of patriotism, cooled their fiery ardor, imprisoned them in camps and behind entrenchments. He has not told the people what he needed. As a faithful sentinel, he has not told them what of the night."

So far, the Georgian was one among a small minority; but such men were vociferous in their bitterness, and when they stung they stung to hurt. The people read or heard their complaints, printed in columns alongside the news of such reverses as Fort Donelson and Roanoke Island, and they wondered. They did not enjoy being told that they were not trusted by the man in whom their own trust was placed. A South Carolina matron, friendly to Davis and all he stood for, confided scornfully in her diary: "In Columbia I do not know a half-dozen men who would not gaily step into Jeff Davis's shoes with a firm conviction that they would do better in every respect than he does."

There was one glimmer in the military gloom — indeed, a brightness — though it was based not on accomplishment, but on continuing confidence despite the lengthening odds and the late reverses. The gleam in fact proceeded from the region where the gloom was deepest: off in the panic-stricken West, where the left wing of the Confederacy had been crippled. What his wife represented in private life, what Benjamin meant to him in helping to meet the cares of office, Albert Sidney Johnston was to Davis in military matters. He was in plain fact his notion of a hero. They had not been together since mid-September, when the tall, handsome Kentucky-born Texan came to Richmond to receive from Davis his commission and his assignment to command of the Western Department. That had been a happy time, the plaudits of the entire nation ringing in his ears. They had kept on ringing, too, until Grant called his game of bluff on the Tennessee and the Cumberland, and the whole western house of cards went crash.

At the outset the newspapers had expected "results at once brilliant, scientific, and satisfactory" (the diminution of the adjectives was prophetic) but not this: not defeat, with the loss of half his army, all of Kentucky, and a goodly portion of Tennessee including its capital. The uproar outdid anything the nation had known since the defection of Benedict Arnold. Johnston was accused of stupidity and incompetence or worse, for there were the usual post-defeat cries of treason and corruption. Those who had sung his praises loudest such a short while back were loudest now in abuse. The army was demoralized, they shrilled; Johnston must be removed or the cause would fail. New troops being sworn in made it a condition of their enlistment oath that they would not be required to serve under his command.

He took the blame as he had taken the praise. Calm at the storm center, he displayed still the nobility of mind and strength of character which had drawn men to him all his life. Urged by friends to make a public defense, he replied: "I cannot correspond with the people. What the people want is a battle and a victory. That is the best explanation I can make." Retreating again—from Murfreesboro now, all the way to Decatur, Alabama, where he would be south of the Tennessee River and on the Memphis & Charleston Railroad, in a position to coöperate with the forces under Beauregard, retreating south along the Mississippi— he wrote to Davis more explicitly of his reason for keeping his temper: "I observed silence, as it seemed to me the best way to serve the cause and the country." He offered then to yield the command, saying: "The test of merit in my profession is success. It is a hard rule, but I think it right." To concentrate and strike was his present aim, in which case "those who are now declaiming against me will be without an argument."

It was a letter to warm the heart of any superior in distress — which Davis certainly was. He replied: "My confidence in you has never wavered, and I hope the public will soon give me credit for judgment rather than continue to arraign me for obstinacy."

The public might, in time; but for the present the clamor did not die; it grew. Davis stood under an avalanche of letters, protests, and demands for his friend's dismissal. Yet all this time, as he said, he never wavered. When a delegation of Tennessee congressmen called at his office to insist en masse that Johnston be relieved — he was no general, they said scornfully — Davis stood at his desk and heard their demand with an icy silence. When they had spoken, he told them: "If Sidney Johnston is not a general, we had better give up the war, for we have no general," and bowed them out.

★   ★   ★

The other Johnston, back in Virginia, was another matter. There would never be any such letter from him, and Davis knew it: not only because it was not in Joe Johnston's nature to be selfless in a crisis — he had small belief in the efficacy of silence — but also because his problems were quite different. He had no quarrel with the public; the public, like his soldiers, now and always, showed the greatest affection for him. His difficulties were rather with his superiors, the Commander in Chief and the Secretary of War, and with the laws and regulations which Congress passed in an attempt to be what it called helpful, but which Johnston himself considered meddlesome and harmful.

A case in point was the so-called Furlough and Bounty Act, which had been passed in December in an effort to meet the crisis that would arise when the enlistments of the twelve-month volunteers expired in late winter and early spring. Obviously something would have to be done to encourage reënlistments; few men were likely to expose themselves voluntarily to a continuance of the dull life they had been leading all through the Virginia fall and winter. Under the act, all who would sign on for three years — or the duration, in case the end came first — would receive a sixty-day furlough and a fifty-dollar bounty. Further, on their return they would be allowed to transfer to whatever outfit they chose, even into another arm of service, and elect their own field- and company-grade officers once the reorganization was effected. Johnston realized the necessity for some such encouragement, but the only part of this particular act that he approved of was the bounty. The transfer and election privileges he considered ruinous, and the furloughs, if granted in numbers large enough to be effective, would expose the remainder of his army to slaughter at the hands of the Federals, already twice his strength around Manassas and likely to attack at any time. Besides, when he wrote to the War Department, asking how the act was to be applied and what numbers were to be furloughed at any one time, the Secretary replied that he was to go to the "extreme verge of prudence." Now Johnston was a very prudent man; entirely too much so, his critics said. The extreme verge of his prudence was still very prudent indeed. As a result, the act accomplished little except to vex the general charged with its application.

Another, more serious vexation was the loss of experienced officers of rank. He had lost the embittered Beauregard and he had nearly lost Stonewall Jackson as a result of Benjamin's out-of-channels interference. Kirby Smith had returned to duty, healed of his Manassas wound, only to be assigned to deal with the powder-keg East Tennessee situation. Earl Van Dorn, whose dash and brilliance promised much, had been sent to the Transmississippi. These were hard losses, and there were more, in addition to some who were so disgruntled that they threatened to resign. "The Army is crippled and its discipline greatly impaired by a want of general officers," Johnston reported plaintively to Richmond.

These were causes enough for disturbance in any commander, let alone one as irascible and gloomy as Joe Johnston; but coming as they did, at a time when the odds were what he knew them to be in northern Virginia, they filled him with forebodings of disaster. His loss of respect for McClellan's character as a man of war — in letters he now referred to him as "George" or "the redoubtable McC" or even " 'George,' " employing the pointed sarcasm of inverted commas — did not preclude a respect for McClellan's numbers or his ability to forge them into an effective striking force. And not only were the numerical odds forbidding; the situation itself was bad from the southern point of view. Operating behind the screen of the Potomac, the northern host could concentrate and strike at any point from the Blue Ridge Mountains down to Aquia Creek, and thus be on the flank or in the rear of the army around Manassas and Occoquan. All that was holding them back, so far as Johnston could see, was rainy weather and the mud that it produced. Spring was coming, the sudden vernal loveliness of blue skies, new grass, and solid roads. A week of sunshine would remove all the obstacles that stood between McClellan and success, or between Johnston and ruin.

It was at this point, aggravated further by a shortage of arms and powder, that the general was summoned to ride down to Richmond, two days before the inauguration, for a conference on the military situation. Reporting to the President at 10 o'clock that morning, he found the cabinet in session and the discussion already begun. After an exchange of greetings, in which there was no evidence of the lately strained relations, he was asked to state his views as to the disposition of his army. He replied that from its present position along Bull Run and the Potomac it could not block the multiple routes by which McClellan could march against the capital. Unequivocally, he stated that his army must fall back to a position farther south before the roads were dry. Somewhat taken aback, Davis asked to just what line the retreat would be conducted. When Johnston replied that he did not know, being unfamiliar with the country between Richmond and Manassas, Davis was even more alarmed.

As he said later, "That a general should have selected a line which he himself considered untenable, and should not have ascertained the typography of the country in his rear was inexplicable on any other theory than that he had neglected the primary duty of a commander."

For the present, however, he let this pass. If Johnston advised retreat, retreat it had to be, so long as he was in command. Davis had to content himself with trying to get assurances from the general that the army's supplies and equipment, particularly the large-caliber guns along the Potomac and the mountains of subsistence goods now stored in forward depots, would not be abandoned. He did not get it. Johnston merely said that he would do what he could to delay the retreat until the last possible moment, so that the roads would be firm enough to bear the heavy guns and the high-piled wagons. Further than that he would not go. The meeting broke up without any specific date being set for the withdrawal. All that was determined was that the army would move southward to take up a securer line whenever practicable.

Back at his hotel, it was Johnston's turn to be alarmed. He found the lobby buzzing with rumors that the Manassas intrenchments were about to be abandoned. The news had moved swiftly before him, though he had come directly from the conference: with the result that his reluctance to discuss military secrets with civilians, no matter how highly placed, was confirmed. No tactical maneuver was more difficult than a withdrawal from the presence of a superior enemy. Everything depended on secrecy; for to be caught in motion, strung out on the roads, was to invite destruction. Yet here in the lobby of a Richmond hotel, where every pillar might hide a spy, was a flurry of gossip predicting the very movement he was about to undertake. Next day, riding back to Manassas on the cars, his reluctance was reconfirmed and his anger heightened when a friend approached and asked if it was true that the Bull Run line was about to be abandoned. There could be no chance that the man had overheard the news by accident, for he was deaf. Nor did it improve the general's humor when he arrived that afternoon to find his headquarters already abuzz with talk of the impending evacuation.

Two things he determined to do in reaction: 1) to get his army out of there as quickly as he could — if possible, before McClellan had time to act on the leaked information — and 2) to confide no more in civilians, which as far as he was concerned included the Chief Executive. The first was easier said than done, however. Rain fell all the following day, drenching alike the inaugural throng on Capitol Square and the roads of northern Virginia. The army was stalled in a sea of mud, just when Johnston was most anxious to get it moving. Well-mounted cavalry, riding light, could not average two miles an hour along the roads. Four-horse teams could not haul the field artillery guns, and nothing at all could budge the heavier pieces. The general's determination to share none of his plans with the Government did not prevent his expressing his ire and apprehension in dispatches which repeated his former complaints and advanced new ones. "A division of five brigades is without generals," he wrote on the 25th, "and at least half the field officers are absent — generally sick. The accumulation of subsistence stores at Manassas is now a great evil. The Commissary General was requested more than once to suspend these supplies. A very extensive meat-packing establishment at Thoroughfare is also a great incumbrance. The great quantities of personal property in our camps is a still greater one."

He did what he could to hasten his army's departure, but with horses and wagons foundered and mired on the roads, he had to depend solely on the single-track Orange & Alexandria Railroad. Overcrowded, it quickly snarled to a standstill and pitched the general's anguished cries an octave higher. In truth, there was much to vex him, here where ruin stared him in the face. The amount of personal baggage piled along the railroad "was appalling to behold," one witness said. A "trunk had come with every volunteer," Johnston later declared, reporting now that the army, over his protest, "had accumulated a supply of baggage like that of Xerxes' myriads." All this time, while he was struggling to save what he could with so little success, there had been reports of enemy advances, each a confirmation of his fears. Soon after his return from the capital, a Union force had appeared at Harpers Ferry, from which position it could move forward and outflank him on the left. Two weeks later, March 5, he was warned of "unusual activity" on the Maryland shore opposite Dumfries, indicating preparations for attack. This was the movement he feared most, considering it not only the most dangerous, but also the most likely. An advance from there would turn his right and bring the Federals between his army and Richmond.

That did it. He did not intend to let himself get caught like that other Johnston in the West, who lost half his army through delay in pulling back when enemy pressure increased the strain beyond the breaking point. To retreat now meant the loss of much equipment. The heavy guns were still in place along the Potomac; supplies and personal baggage were still piled high along the railroad. But equipment was nothing, compared to the probable loss of men and possible loss of the war itself. Nor was terrain, not even the "sacred soil" of his native state. That same day he issued orders for all his forces east of the Blue Ridge to fall back to the line of the Rappahannock.

Davis in Richmond knew nothing of this. Ever since Johnston's departure he had been urging a delay in the retrograde movement. In fact, when Virginia officials came to him with a plan for mass recruitment to turn back the invaders, Davis took heart and urged the general to hold his ground while the army was brought up to strength for an offensive, which he now referred to as "first policy." March 10, believing that Johnston and his army still held the Manassas intrenchments, he wired: "Further assurance given to me this day that you shall be promptly and adequately reënforced, so as to enable you to maintain your position and resume first policy when the roads will permit."

Johnston was not there to receive it, nor were any of his men. The cavalry rear guard had pulled out that morning, following the southward trail of the army on its way to the Rappahannock, accompanied by its general — who was already contemplating another retreat, from there back to the Rapidan. The one in progress had not gone well. One division, in an advance position, had not been informed of the movement at all, but was left to find its way out as best it could. The heavy guns were left in their emplacements, some of them not even thrown from their carriages. Supplies and equipment, including the trunks the volunteers had brought, went up in smoke. The packing plant at Thoroughfare Gap was put to the torch, along with one million pounds of meat remaining after farmers in the neighborhood had been given all they could haul away. For twenty miles around, all down the greening slopes of Bull Run Mountain, there was a smell of burning bacon, an aroma which the natives would remember through the hungry months ahead.

✗ 4 ✗

Lincoln's efforts all this time as Commander in Chief, though on the face of it they were exerted in quite the opposite direction and for an entirely different purpose, were much like those of his southern counterpart; for while Davis had been trying to get Johnston to hold his ground, Lincoln had been doing his best to nudge McClellan forward. All through the fall and winter, as far as these two tasks were concerned, Lincoln had failed and Davis had succeeded. Both generals stayed exactly where they were. Yet in the end it was the northern leader who was successful: Johnston fell back and McClellan at last went forward. In both cases, however, on that final day, March 9, the civilian heads were shown to have urged good counsel to generals who now were exposed before the public in a cold unflattering light. Johnston fled where no man pursued, and McClellan encountered none of the bloody opposition he had predicted.

For both civil leaders the time had been long and harrowing, a season of waste and unhappiness for Lincoln no less than for Davis. The burden of action was on the North; the South had only to keep the status quo, which was exactly what she had been doing here in Virginia. If on the northern side the gloom had been relieved by victories East and West — Roanoke Island and Fort Donelson — it had no bright, original, face-to-face East-West triumph such as Manassas or Wilson's Creek to hark back to. Also, for Lincoln, the period of inaction around

Washington had been darkened by personal tragedy, including the death of one of his sons and signs that his wife was losing her mind. For him the year had opened, not with a glimmer as of dawn, but rather with gathering shadows, as of dusk. The army head was down with typhoid; the bottom was out of the tub; "What shall I do?" he groaned in his melancholy.

It was January 10; Quartermaster General M. C. Meigs replied that if the typhoid diagnosis was correct it meant a six-weeks' illness for McClellan, during which time the nation's armies would be leaderless and vulnerable. He suggested that the President call a conference of the ranking officers of the Army of the Potomac, one of whom might have to take over in a crisis. Lincoln liked the advice and called the meeting for that evening. Two generals attended, McDowell and William B. Franklin, along with several cabinet members. Lincoln told them the situation and expressed his desire for an early offensive. If McClellan did not want to use the army, he said, he would like to borrow it for a while.

McDowell replied that he would be willing to try his hand at another advance on Richmond by way of Manassas, while Franklin, who had taken part in that first debacle under McDowell and was moreover in the confidence of McClellan, favored the roundabout salt-water route, approaching the southern capital from the east. On this divided note the conference adjourned. Next night, when they met again, the generals were agreed that the overland method was best, despite the previous failure, because it would require less time for preparation. Pleased with this decision, Lincoln adjourned the second meeting, instructing the generals to go back to their headquarters, work on the plan, and return tomorrow night. They did return, having worked on it all through the day, but the third White House session was brief, since they still had much to do.

The fourth such conference, on the 13th, was the last. McClellan was there — pale and shaky, but very much there. He had gotten wind of what was going on: perhaps from Stanton, who had been visiting him and murmuring, "They are counting on your death": Stanton was adept at this kind of thing, having served in Buchanan's cabinet as an informer for the opposition. Anyhow, McClellan had learned of the meetings and had risen from his sickbed to confront these men who met behind his back. As a result, the atmosphere was strained. According to McClellan, "my unexpected appearance caused very much the effect of a shell in a powder magazine." When Lincoln asked McDowell to outline the plan he had been working on, McDowell gave it nervously and wound up with an apology for offering his opinion in the presence of his chief. "You are entitled to have any opinion you please!" McClellan said, obviously miffed.

During the discussion which followed, while Lincoln kept asking where and when an offensive could be launched, McClellan remained silent. Seward drawled that he didn't much care whether the army whipped the rebels at Manassas or in Richmond itself, so long as it whipped them *some*where. McClellan kept silent. Finally Chase questioned him directly, asking what he intended to do with the army and when he intended to do it. The general replied that he had a perfectly good plan, with a perfectly good schedule of execution, but he would not discuss it in front of civilians unless the President ordered him to do so. He would say, however, that Buell was about to move forward in Kentucky, after which he himself would move. Another awkward silence followed. Presently Lincoln asked him if he "counted upon any particular time." He was not asking him to divulge it, he added hastily; he just wanted to know if he had it in mind. McClellan said he did. "Then I will adjourn this meeting," Lincoln said.

McClellan did not go back to his sickbed. Now that he was up, he stayed up, his youth and stout constitution — he had reached thirty-five in December — permitting him to convalesce on horseback, so to speak. Once more he spent "long days in the saddle and . . . nights in the office," riding to inspect the camps and returning with a jaunty salute the worshipful cheers of his soldiers. There was something other than cheering in the air, however. For one thing, there was suspicion: which meant that the Joint Committee on the Conduct of the War was interested. Now that he was up where they could get at him, the committeemen summoned the general to appear and be examined.

Ben Wade and Zachariah Chandler — who, along with Andrew Johnson, were the members from the Senate — did most of the questioning. Chandler began it by asking why the army, after five long months of training, was not marching out to meet the enemy. McClellan began explaining that there were only two bridges across to Alexandria, which did not satisfy the requirement that a commander must safeguard his lines of retreat in event that his men were repulsed.

"General McClellan," Chandler interrupted. He spoke with the forthright tone of a man translating complicated matters into simpler terms for laymen. "If I understand you correctly, before you strike at the rebels you want to be sure of plenty of room so you can run in case they strike back."

"Or in case you get scared," Wade put in.

McClellan then went into a rather drawn-out explanation of how wars were fought. Lines of retirement were sometimes as necessary to an army's survival, he said, as lines of communication and supply. The committeemen listened scornfully. It was not this they had called him in to tell them.

"General," Wade said, "you have all the troops you have called for, and if you haven't enough, you shall have more. They are well organized and equipped, and the loyal people of this country expect that you will make a short and decisive campaign. Is it really necessary for you to have more bridges over the Potomac before you move?"

"Not that. Not that exactly," McClellan told him. "But we must bear in mind the necessity of having everything ready in case of a defeat, and keep our lines of retreat open."

After this, they let him go in disgust. When he had gone, Chandler turned to Wade and sneered. "I don't know much about war," he said, "but it seems to me that this is infernal, unmitigated cowardice."

Wade thought so, too, and as chairman he went to see Lincoln about it. McClellan must be discarded, he cried. When the President asked who should be put in his place, Wade snorted: "Anybody!"

"Wade," Lincoln replied sadly, "anybody will do for you, but I must have somebody."

Already that week he had made one replacement in a high place. For months now there had been growing reports of waste and graft in the War Department; of contracts strangely let; of shoddy cloth, tainted pork, spavined horses, and guns that would not shoot; of the Vermont jobber who boasted at Willard's, grinning, "You can sell anything to the government at almost any price you've got the guts to ask."

Simon Cameron was responsible, though there was no evidence that the Secretary had profited personally except in the use of his office to pay off his political debts and strengthen his political position. Lincoln could understand this last, having himself done likewise — in point of fact, that was how Cameron got the job — and he knew, too, that much of the waste and bungling, much of the greed and dishonesty, even, was incident to the enormous task of preparing the unprepared nation for war and increasing the army from 16,000 to better than half a million men in the process. All the same, the Pennsylvanian was unquestionably lax in his conduct of business affairs, and when Lincoln warned him of this, resisting the general outcry for his removal, Cameron made his first really serious mistake. He made it, however, not through any ordinary brand of stupidity — Cameron was a very canny man — but rather through his canniness in trying to safeguard his position in the cabinet by strengthening his position in the public eye and in the minds of the increasingly powerful radicals in Congress. He fell because he did what many men had done before and what others would do in the future, after he himself was off the scene. He underestimated Lincoln.

Despite the example of Frémont, or perhaps because he thought that the furor which had followed Frémont's dismissal would have taught Lincoln a lesson, Cameron reasoned that by ingratiating himself with the Jacobins he would insure himself against any action by the President, who would not dare to antagonize them further by molesting another man who had won their favor. Any attack on slavery was the answer. Emancipation was the issue on which Lincoln was treading softest, since it was the one that cut sharpest along the line dividing the

Administration's supporters and opponents. Accordingly, with the help of his legal adviser Stanton, Cameron drafted and included in his annual Department report a long passage advocating immediate freedom for southern slaves and their induction into the Union army, thereby adding muscle to the arm of the republic and weakening the enemy, who as "rebellious traitors" had forfeited their rights to any property at all, let alone the ownership of fellow human beings. Without consulting the President — though it was usual for such documents to be submitted for approval — the Secretary had the report printed and sent out to the postmasters of all the principal cities for distribution to the press as soon as it was being read to Congress.

So far all was well. Even when Lincoln discovered what had been done and recalled the pamphlet by telegraphic order, for reprinting without the offensive passage, things still went as Cameron had expected. Critics of the President's tread-easy policy, comparing the original with the expurgated report — some copies of course escaped destruction, so that both versions appeared in the papers — were harsh in their attacks, charging Lincoln simultaneously with dictatorship and timidity. The Jacobins reacted as expected by taking the Secretary to their bosoms and pronouncing him "one of us." Other praises came his way, less vigorous perhaps, but no less pleasant. "You have touched the national heart," a friend declared, while another, in a punning mood, wrote that he much preferred the "Simon pure" article in the *Tribune* to the "bogus" report in the *World.* From Paris a member of the consulate, hearing of the dissension in the President's official family, wrote home asking: "Are Cameron and Frémont to be canonized as martyrs?"

Cameron might be canonized, at any rate by the antislavery radicals, but it did not appear that he would be martyred by anyone, least of all by Lincoln, who seemed to have learned a dearly bought lesson in martyring Frémont. The report had been published in mid-December, and now in January he still had made no further reference to the matter. Outwardly the relationship between the two men remained cordial, though Cameron still felt some inward qualms, perhaps because he sensed that Lincoln's measure was not so easily taken. The thing had gone *too* well.

Then on January 11, a Saturday — the date of the second of the three conferences with McDowell and Franklin, none of which Cameron had been urged to attend, despite his position as Secretary of War — he learned that he had been right to feel qualms. He received a brief note in which Lincoln informed him curtly, out of the blue: "I ... propose nominating you to the Senate next Monday as Minister to Russia." Almost literally, he was being banished to Siberia for his sins.

The sins were political, and as a politician he could appreciate the justice of his punishment. He suffered anguish, though, at the manner in which it was inflicted. To be rebuked thus in a brief note, he complained, "meant personal as well as political destruction." So Lincoln, who cared little for the manner of his going, just so he went, agreed that Cameron might antedate a letter of resignation, to which he would reply with a letter of acceptance expressing his "affectionate esteem" and "undiminished confidence" in the Secretary's "ability, patriotism, and fidelity to the public trust." It was done accordingly and Cameron's name was sent to Congress for confirmation as Minister to Russia. There, however, he encountered opposition, not only from members of his own party, the Democrats, but also from some of the radical Republicans who so lately had clustered round him and proclaimed him "one of us." At last the nomination was put through; Cameron was on his way to St Petersburg, having earned not martyrdom and canonization, as some had hoped or feared, but banishment and damage to a reputation already considered shaky. One senator, a former colleague, remarked on his departure: "Ugh! ugh! Send word to the Czar to bring in his things of nights."

In this case Lincoln engaged in no fruitless search for "somebody" to replace him. The somebody was ready and very much at hand: Edwin McMasters Stanton, who as his predecessor's legal adviser had helped to charge and fuse the bomb that blew him out of the War Department and the Cabinet, while Stanton himself was sucked into the resultant vacuum and sat ensconced as successor before all the bits of wreckage had hit the ground. Whether he had proceeded with malice aforethought in this instance was not known; but it was not unthinkable. Stanton had done devious things in his time. A corporation lawyer, he delighted also in taking criminal cases when these were challenging and profitable enough. His fees were large and when one prospective client protested, Stanton asked: "Do you think I would argue the wrong side for less?" For a murder defense he once took as his fee the accused man's only possession, the house he lived in. When he had won the case and was about to convert the mortgage into cash, the man tried to persuade him to hold off, saying that he would be ruined by the foreclosure. "You deserve to be ruined," Stanton told him, "for you were guilty."

And yet there was another side to him, too, offsetting the savagery, the joy he took in fixing a frightened general or petitioner with the baleful glare of his black little near-sighted eyes behind small, thick-lensed, oval spectacles. He was a bundle of contradictions, his father a New Englander, his mother a Virginian. In private, the forty-seven-year-old lawyer sometimes put his face in his hands and wept from the strain, and if his secretary happened in at such a time he would say, "Not now, please. Not now." He was asthmatic, something of a hysteric as well, and he had more than a touch of morbidity in his nature. His bushy hair was thinning at the front, but he made up for this by letting it grow long at the back and sides. His upper lip he kept clean-shaven to expose a surprisingly sensitive mouth — a reminder that he had been considered handsome in his youth — while below his lower lip a broad streak of iron-gray ran down the center of his wide black beard. His body was thick-set, bouncy on short but energetic legs. His voice, which was deep in times of calm, rose to piercing shrillness in excitement. One petitioner, badly shaken by the experience, described a Stanton interview by saying, "He came at me like a tiger."

He came at many people like a tiger, especially at those in his Department who showed less devotion to work than he himself did. Soon after he took office he received from Harpers Ferry an urgent call for heavy guns. He ordered them sent at once. Going by the locked arsenal after hours, he learned that the guns were still there: whereupon he ordered the gates broken open, helped the watchmen drag the guns out, and saw them loaded onto a north-bound train. Next morning the arsenal officer reported that he had not found it convenient to ship the guns the day before; he would get them off this morning, he said. "The guns are now at Harpers Ferry!" Stanton barked. "And you, sir, are no longer in the service of the United States Government."

He would engage in no secret deals. Whoever came to him on business, as for instance seeking a contract, was required to make his request in the sight and hearing of all. Stanton would snap out a Yes or No, then wave him on to make way for the next petitioner. He did not care whose toes he stepped on; "Individuals are nothing," he declared. To a man who came demanding release for a friend locked up on suspicion of treason, Stanton roared: "If I tap that little bell, I can send *you* to a place where you will never hear the dogs bark. And by heaven I'll do it if you say another word!" He brought to the War Department a boundless and bounding energy. "As soon as I can get the machinery of the office working, the rats cleared out, and the rat holes stopped," he told an assistant, "we shall *move*." Lincoln himself was by no means exempt from Stanton's scorn. Asked when he took office, "What will you do?": "Do? ..." he replied. "I will make Abe Lincoln President of the United States."

The government could use such a man, despite his idiosyncrasies, his sudden judgments and hostile attitude. So could Lincoln use him in his official family, despite the abuse he knew that Stanton had been heaping on him since they first met in Cincinnati, when the big-time lawyer referred to the country one as "that long-armed creature." More recently he had been employing circus epithets; "the original gorilla," he called him, "a low, cunning clown," and "that giraffe." Lincoln knew of some of this, but he still thought he could use him — provided he could handle him. And he believed he could. Stanton's prancing and bouncing, he said, put him in mind of a Methodist preacher out West who got so wrought up in his prayers and exhortations that his congregation was obliged to put bricks in his pockets to hold him down. "We may have to serve Stanton the same way," Lincoln drawled. "But I guess we'll let him jump a while first."

The bricks were applied much sooner than anyone expected. One day the President was busy with a roomful of people and Stanton came hurrying through the doorway, clutching a sheet of paper in his hand. "Mr President," he cried, "this order cannot be signed. I refuse to sign it!" Lincoln told him calmly, "Mr Secretary, I guess that order will have to be signed." In the hush that followed, the two men's eyes met. Then Stanton turned, still with the order in his hand, and went back to his office and signed it.

Whether or not McClellan could handle him, too, was one of the things that remained to be seen. At the outset, the general had good cause to believe that the change in War Department heads would work to his advantage. For on the evening of January 13 — the one on which he rose from his sickbed to confront the men who had been conferring behind his back — Stanton came by his quarters and informed him that his nomination as Secretary of War had gone to the Senate that afternoon. Personally, he went on to say, he considered the job a hardship, but the chance of working in close harness with his friend McClellan persuaded him to undergo the sacrifice involved. If the general would approve he would accept. McClellan did approve; he urged acceptance on those grounds. Two days later the nomination was confirmed. Stanton took the post the following day. And almost immediately, from that January 16 on, McClellan found the doors of the War Department barred to him. The Secretary, suddenly hostile, became at once the Young Napoleon's most outspoken critic. McClellan had been given another lesson in the perfidy of the human animal. One more had been added, at the top, to that "set of men . . . unscrupulous and false."

What he did not know was that, all this time, Stanton had been working both sides of the street. While his name was up for approval in the Senate, Charles Sumner was saying: "Mr Stanton, within my knowledge, is one of us." Ben Wade thought so, too. And on the day the new Secretary moved into office their opinion was confirmed. After saying that he was going to "make Abe Lincoln President," Stanton added that as the next order of business, "I will force this man McClellan to fight or throw up." Later that same day he said baldly, "This army has got to fight or run away. And while men are striving nobly in the West, the champagne and oysters on the Potomac must be stopped."

Formerly he had run with the fox and hunted with the hounds. Now he was altogether with the latter. On January 20, at his own request, he appeared before the Joint Committee, and after the hearing its members were loud in his praise. "We are delighted with him," Julian of Indiana exclaimed. In the Senate, Fessenden of Maine announced: "He is just the man we want! We agree on every point: the duties of the

Secretary of War, the conduct of the war, the Negro question and everything." In the *Tribune* Horace Greeley hailed him as the man who would know how to deal with "the greatest danger now facing the country — treason in Washington, treason in the army itself, especially the treason which wears the garb of Unionism."

Treason was a much-used word these days. For Greeley to use it three times within a dependent clause was nothing rare. In fact it was indicative. The syllables had a sound that caught men's ears, overtones of enormity that went beyond such scarehead words as rape or arson or incest. Observing this, the radicals had made it their watchword, their cry in the night, expanding its definition in the process.

Many acts were treasonous now which had never been considered so before. Even a lack of action might be treason, according to these critics in long-skirted broadcloth coats. Delay, for instance: all who counseled delay were their special targets, along with those who favored something less than extermination for rebels. Obviously, the way to administer sudden death was to march out within musket range and bang away until the serpent Rebellion squirmed no more. And as a rallying cry this forthright logic was effective. Up till now the Administration's opposition had been no more than an incidental irritant. By mid-January of this second calendar year of the war, however, so many congressmen had discovered the popular value of pointing a trembling finger at "treason" in high places that their conglomerate, harping voice had grown into a force which had to be reckoned with as surely as the Confederates still intrenched around Manassas.

Lincoln the politician understood this perfectly. They were men with power, who knew how to use it ruthlessly, and as such they would have to be dealt with. McClellan the soldier could never see it at all, partly because he operated under the disadvantage of considering himself a gentleman. For him they were willful, evil men, "unscrupulous and false," and as such they should be ignored as beneath contempt, at least by him. He counted on Lincoln to keep them off his back: which Lincoln in fact had promised to do. "I intend to be careful and do as well as possible," McClellan had said. "Don't let them hurry me, is all I ask." And Lincoln had told him, "You shall have your own way in the matter, I assure you." Yet now he seemed to be breaking his promise to McClellan, just as he had broken his word to Frémont, whom he had told: "I have given you carte-blanche. You must use your own judgment, and do the best you can." Frémont had used his judgment, such as it was, and been flung aside. McClellan was discouraged.

That was something else he never understood: Lincoln himself. Some might praise him for being flexible, while others called him slippery, when in truth they were both two words for just one thing. To

argue the point was to insist on a distinction that did not exist. Lincoln
was out to win the war; and that was all he was out to do, for the present. Unfettered by any need for being or not being a gentleman, he
would keep his word to any man only so long as keeping it would help
to win the war. If keeping it meant otherwise, he broke it. He kept no
promise, anyhow, any longer than the conditions under which it was
given obtained. And if any one thing was clear in this time when
treason had become a household word, it was that the conditions of
three months ago no longer obtained. McClellan would have to go forward or go down.

On January 27, without consulting anyone — least of all Mc-
Clellan — Lincoln himself composed and issued over his signature, as
Commander in Chief of the nation's military forces, General War Order
Number 1, in which he announced that a forward movement by all
land and naval units would be launched on February 22, to celebrate
Washington's Birthday and also, presumably, to disrupt the Confederate
inaugural in Richmond. It was not a suggestion, or even a directive. It
was a peremptory order, and as such it stated that all commanders
afield or afloat would "severally be held to their strict and full responsibilities" for its "prompt execution." Lest there be any misunderstand-
ing as to whether this applied to the general-in-chief and his army
around Washington, Lincoln supplemented this with a Special Order
four days later, directing that on or before the date announced an expedition would move out from the capital, leaving whatever force would
insure the city's safety, and seize a point on the railroad "southwestward
of . . . Manassas Junction."

McClellan was aghast. He had counted on the President to keep
the hot-eyed amateurs off his back: yet here, by a sudden and seemingly
gleeful leap, Lincoln had landed there himself, joining the others in an
all-out game of pile-on. Besides, committed as he was to the Urbanna Plan for loading his army on transports, taking it down the Potomac and up the Rappahannock for a landing in Johnston's rear, the last
thing he wanted now was any movement that might alarm the enemy at
Manassas into scurrying back to safety. So he went to Lincoln and outlined for the first time in some detail the plan which would be spoiled by
any immediate "forward" movement. Lincoln did not like it. It would
endanger Washington, he said, in case the rebels tried a quick pounce
while the Federal army was making its roundabout boat-trip to Urbanna. McClellan then asked if he could submit in writing his objections
to the President's plan and his reasons for favoring his own. Lincoln
said all right, go ahead. While the general was preparing his brief he
received from Lincoln a set of questions, dated February 3: "Does not
your plan involve a larger expenditure of time and money than mine?
Wherein is a victory more certain by your plan than mine? Would it
not be less valuable in that yours would not break a great line of the

enemy's communications, while mine would? In case of disaster, would it not be more difficult to retreat by your plan than mine?"

In asking these questions Lincoln was meeting McClellan on his own ground, and McClellan answered him accordingly, professionally ticking off the flaws in Lincoln's plan and pointing up the strong points of his own. At best, he declared, the former would result in nothing more than a barren and costly victory which would leave still harder battles to be fought all the way to Richmond, each time against an enemy who would have retired to a prepared defensive position, while the Federal supply lines stretched longer and more vulnerable with every doubtful success: whereas the latter, striking at the vitals of the Confederacy, would maneuver Johnston out of his formidable Bull Run intrenchments by requiring him to turn in defense of his capital and give battle wherever McClellan chose to fight him, with control of all Virginia in the balance. Supply lines would run by water, which meant that they would be secure, and in event of the disaster which Lincoln seemed to fear, the army could retreat down the York-James peninsula, an area which afforded plenty of opportunity for maneuver because, "the soil [being] sandy," the roads were "passable at all seasons of the year." Nor was this all. Besides its other advantages, he wrote, his plan had a flexibility which the other lacked entirely. If for some reason Urbanna proved undesirable, the landing could be made at Mobjack Bay or Fortress Monroe, though admittedly this last would be "less brilliant." As for the question as to whether victory was more certain by the roundabout route, the general reminded his chief that "nothing is certain in war." However, he added, "all the chances are in favor of this project." If Lincoln would give him the go-ahead, along with a little more time to get ready, "I regard success as certain by all the chances of war."

There Lincoln had it. In submitting the questions he had said, "If you will give me satisfactory answers . . . I shall gladly yield my plan to yours." Now that the Young Napoleon had given them, Lincoln yielded; but not gladly. Though he liked McClellan's plan better now that the general had taken him into his confidence and explained it in detail, he was still worried about what Johnston's army — better than 100,000 men, according to the Pinkerton reports — might do while McClellan's was in transit. Confederates in Washington might win foreign recognition for their government, and with it independence. However, since McClellan had come out so flatly in favor of his own plan and in rejection of the other, Lincoln had no choice except to fire him or sustain him. And that in fact was no choice at all. To fire Little Mac would be to risk demoralizing the Army of the Potomac on the eve of great exertions. All the same, Lincoln did not rescind the order for an advance on the 22d. He merely agreed not to require its execution.

Whereupon the radicals returned to the charge, furious that their demands had gone unheeded. Lincoln held them off as best he could, but they were strident and insistent. "For God's sake, at least push back the defiant traitors!" Wade still cried. Lincoln saw that something had to be done to appease them — perhaps by clearing the lower Potomac of enemy batteries, or else by reopening the B & O supply line west of Harpers Ferry. Either would be at least a sop to throw the growlers. So he went again to McClellan: who explained once more that the rebels along the lower Potomac were just where he wanted them to be when he made his Urbanna landing in their rear, forcing them thus to choose between flight and capture. It would be much better to have them there, he said, than back on the Rappahannock contesting his debarkation. Lincoln was obliged to admit that as logic this had force.

As for the reopening of the B & O, McClellan remarked that he had it in mind already. What he wanted to avoid was another Ball's Bluff or anything resembling the fiasco which had resulted from making a river crossing without a way to get back in event of repulse. He was bringing up from downriver a fleet of canal boats which could be lashed together to bridge the upper Potomac. Across this newfangled but highly practical device he would throw a force for repairing and protecting the railroad, a force that would be exempt from disaster because its line of retreat would be secure. Lincoln liked the notion and was delighted that something at last was about to be done. Then came word from McClellan that the project had had to be abandoned because the boats turned out to be six inches too wide for the lift-locks at Harpers Ferry. Once more Lincoln was cast down, his expectations dashed, and Secretary Chase, a solemn, indeed a pompous man, got off his one joke of the war. The campaign had died, he said, of lockjaw.

Washington's Birthday came and went, and the Army of the Potomac remained in its training camps, still awaiting the day when its commander decided that the time had come for it to throw the round-house left designed to knock Virginia out of the war. In the West, meanwhile, Thomas had counterpunched Crittenden clean out of East Kentucky, and Grant had delivered to Sidney Johnston's solar plexus the one-two combination that sent him reeling, all the way from Bowling Green to northern Alabama. Burnside, down in North Carolina, had rabbit-punched Huger and Wise, and even now was following up with a series of successes. Everywhere, boldness had been crowned with success: everywhere, that was, except in Virginia, where boldness was unknown.

Stanton could see the moral plainly enough, and when Greeley came out with an editorial praising the new Secretary and giving him chief credit for the victories — he had been in office exactly a month on the day Fort Donelson fell — Stanton replied with a letter that was printed in the *Tribune*, declining the praise and making a quick back-thrust at McClellan in the process: "Much has been said recently of military combinations and 'organizing victory.' I hear such phrases with apprehension. They commenced in infidel France with the Italian campaign, and resulted in Waterloo. Who can organize victory? We owe our recent victories to the spirit of the Lord, that moved our soldiers to rush into battle and filled the hearts of our enemies with terror and dismay. . . . We may well rejoice at the recent victories, for they teach that battles are to be won now, and by us, in the same and only manner that they were ever won by any people, since the days of Joshua — by boldly pursuing and striking the foe. What, under the blessing of Providence, I conceive to be the true organization of victory and military combinations to win this war was declared in a few words by General Grant's message to General Buckner: 'I propose to move immediately upon your works.' "

Lincoln, too, could praise Grant and the Lord for victories in the West, but the news came at a time when there was sickness in the house and, presently, sorrow. Robert was at Harvard; "one of those rare-ripe sort," his father called him once, "that are smarter at about five than ever after." It was Willie, the middle son and his mother's favorite, who was the studious member of the family; Tad, the youngest, could still neither read nor write at the age of nine. Now Willie lay sick with what the doctor said was "bilious fever." He got better, then worse, then suddenly much worse, until one afternoon Lincoln came into the room where one of his secretaries lay half-asleep on a couch. "Well, Nicolay," he said, "my boy is gone. He is actually gone!" And then, as if having spoken the words aloud had brought their reality home to him, he broke into tears and left.

Hard as it was for Lincoln to absorb the shock in this time of strain, the blow was even harder on his wife. All her life she had been ambitious, but in her ambition she had looked forward more to the pleasures than to the trials of being First Lady — only to discover, once the place was hers, that the tribulations far outnumbered the joys. In Richmond, Varina Davis could overlook, or anyhow seem to overlook, being referred to as "a coarse Western woman," which was false. Mary Lincoln could not weather half so well being criticized for "putting on airs," which was true. A fading Kentucky belle, she clung to her gentility, already sorely tried by two decades of marriage with a man who, whatever his political attainments, liked to sit around the house in slippers and shirtsleeves. She punctuated her conversation with "sir" and spent a great deal of money on dresses and bonnets and new furnishings for the antiquated White House. Washington was not what she had expected, its former social grace having largely departed with the southern-mannered hostesses whose positions had been taken over by Republican ladies whose chief virtues were not social.

Yet these disappointments were by no means the worst she had to bear. Her loyalty was undivided, but the same could not be said of her family, which had split badly over the issues that split Kentucky and the nation. A brother and a half-sister stayed with the Union; another brother and three half-brothers went with the South, while three half-sisters were married to Confederates. This division of her family, together with her Bluegrass manner, caused critics to say that she was "two-thirds slavery and the other third secesh." The rumors were enlarged as the war continued. The President's enemies sought to make political capital with a whispering campaign, accusing Mrs Lincoln of specific acts of treason, which at last reached such proportions that the matter was taken up by a congressional investigating committee. One morning her husband came unexpectedly into one of its secret sessions to announce in a sad voice: "I, Abraham Lincoln, President of the United States, appear of my own volition before this committee of the Senate to say that I, of my own knowledge, know that it is untrue that any of my family hold treasonable communication with the enemy."

That removed her from the reach of the committee, but it did not spare her the ridicule being heaped upon her almost daily in the opposition papers, which struck at the husband through the wife. And now, with all this burden on her, to lose her favorite child was altogether more than she could bear. She wept grievously and was often in hysterics. She could neither accept nor reject her sorrow, and between the two she lost her mental balance. Lincoln had Tad, whom he took more and more for his own and even slept with. He had, too, the day-long, sometimes night-long occupation of running the country. She had nothing, not even Lincoln: who did not help matters by leading her one day to a window and pointing to the lunatic asylum as he said, "Mother, do you see that large white building on the hill yonder? Try and control your grief, or it will drive you mad and we may have to send you there."

A distracted wife was one among the many problems Lincoln faced. His main problem was still McClellan. During the weeks since the general first outlined the Urbanna plan, much of what he called its brilliance had worn off, at least for Lincoln, who still had fears that it would expose the capital to capture. Again he told McClellan his doubts, and once more McClellan sought to allay them, this time by proposing to submit the plan to his twelve division commanders for a professional decision. They assembled March 8, many of them hearing details of the plan for the first time. When the vote was taken they favored it, eight to four, and repaired in a body to the White House to announce the result to the President, whose objections thus were effectively spiked again. As he told Stanton, who shared his mistrust, "We can do nothing else than accept their plan and discard all others. . . . We can't reject it and adopt another without assuming all the responsibility in the case of the failure of the one we adopt."

One thing he could do, and did, that same day. The members of the Joint Committee had called on him the week before with a plan for reorganizing the Army of the Potomac into corps. This, they saw, would not only gain prestige for certain generals who had their favor — McDowell, for example — but would weaken McClellan's authority as general-in-chief, since, as the committeemen saw it, corps commanders would take orders directly from Stanton. Lincoln saw other merits in the plan. For one thing it would simplify the transmission of orders and lessen the burden on the Young Napoleon. Besides, he was anxious to placate Wade and the others wherever he could. When he went to Mc-Clellan, however, to urge that it be effected and to get the general's recommendations for the appointments, McClellan told him that he had already thought it over and had decided that it would be best to wait until all the division commanders had been tested in combat before making his recommendations. Once more Lincoln had been shown that he would lose in any face-to-face encounter with the general over military logic. So the following week, when he decided to act on the matter, he did so without consulting McClellan. Later that day, after having reported their vote on the Urbanna plan, the division commanders learned that four of their number had been appointed to corps command: Mc-Dowell, E. V. Sumner, S. P. Heintzelman, and E. D. Keyes. Notification came in the form of a paper headed "President's General War Order Number 2."

Whatever elation this document produced in the breasts of the men thus elevated, it came as a terrible shock to McClellan, even though the earlier General War Order's being numbered had indicated that there might well be others. The shock was mainly due to the fact that among the four who were raised to corps command — and would therefore have the principal responsibility, under McClellan himself, for executing the Urbanna plan — three had voted against it in the balloting that morning. The officers he wanted had been held back. Franklin, for instance, who had spoken in favor of the sea route at the conference held while McClellan was in bed with fever, was not appointed, nor were any of the others among his protégés; "gentlemen and Democrats," he called them, who thought of war and politics as he did. He felt himself hobbled at the outset, held in check by a high council of Republicans friendly toward the enemies who were working for his ruin.

If he had ever doubted that they were out to wreck him, any such doubts had been dispelled during the early morning hours of that same busy March 8. He learned of whispered charges, touching his honor as a soldier, and he learned of them from Lincoln himself, who had sent for him to come over to the White House after breakfast. As McClellan told it later, he found the President looking worried; there was "a very ugly matter," Lincoln said, which needed airing. Again he hesitated, and McClellan, seated opposite, suggested that perhaps it would be best to come right out with it. Well, Lincoln said, choosing his words cautiously at first, there was an ugly rumor going round, to the effect that the Urbanna plan "was conceived with the traitorous intent of removing its defenders from Washington, and thus giving over to the enemy the capital and the government, thus left defenseless." He added that the whole thing had a sound and look of treason.

The word was out, and it brought McClellan straight up out of his chair, declaring that he would "permit no one to couple the word treason with my name," and demanding an immediate retraction. No, no, Lincoln said hastily; he did not believe a word of it; he was only repeating what had been told him. Somewhat calmer, McClellan suggested "caution in the use of language," and reëmphasized that he could "permit no doubt to be thrown upon my intentions." Lincoln again apologized, and let the matter go at that. McClellan left to round up his division commanders for a vote that would prove that the proposed campaign was militarily sound, then brought them back to announce their eight-to-four support in Lincoln's presence.

As far as McClellan was concerned, that settled it. He had shown him, once and for all. But then, as soon as he turned his back, War Order 2 came dropping onto his desk, and he was upset all over again. The day had opened with charges of treason and closed with the appointment of unsympathetic officers to head the corps of the army he was about to take into battle. As he saw it, Lincoln had gone over to the scoundrels, bag and baggage; or, in McClellan's words, "the effects of the intrigues by which he had been surrounded became apparent."

He did not see, then or ever, that he had helped to bring all this trouble on himself by not taking Lincoln into his confidence sooner. And if he had seen it, the seeing would not have made the end result any easier to abide; McClellan was never one to find ease in admission of blame. Nor did he see that Lincoln had not called him to the White House merely to insult him by repeating ugly rumors, that what he was really trying to tell him was that Wade and the others were powerful and vindictive men who would hurt him all they could, and with him the cause, if they were not dealt with in some manner that would take some of the pressure off their anger: whereas the Young Napoleon, who had been before them and heard them accuse him of cowardice, was determined to yield them not a single military inch of the solid ground he stood on. Whatever they took from him they must take by force, with Lincoln's help. Already they had taken much, including his trust of Lincoln, and he could see that they were after more, with an excellent chance of getting it.

✷ ✷ ✷

Present troubles were grief enough; but as if they were not, there was added, the following morning, news of what had happened at Hampton Roads on the afternoon of that same crowded Saturday, March 8. A single Confederate ten-gun vessel, steaming out of Norfolk on what had been planned as a trial run, made obsolete the navies of the world. Between noon and sunset of that one day, the strange craft — which resembled, some said, "a terrapin with a chimney on its back" — served graphic notice that the proud tall frigates and ships of the line, with their billowing sails and high wooden sides that could flash out hundred-gun salvos, would soon be gone in all their beauty and obsolescence.

She herself had been one of them, once: the 350-ton, forty-gun U.S. steam frigate *Merrimac*, burned and scuttled in her berth when the Union forces abandoned Gosport Navy Yard the previous spring. She sank so quickly her hull and engines were saved from the fire, and Lieutenant John M. Brooke, C.S.N., went to Secretary Mallory with a plan for converting her into a seagoing ironclad, wherewith the tightening Federal blockade might be lifted. Mallory approving, she was plugged, pumped out, and raised, the salt mud swabbed out of her engines and her hull cut down to the water's edge. While some workers were attaching a four-foot iron ram-beak to her prow, others were building amidships a slope-walled structure, 130 feet long and seven feet tall, in which to house her guns, two 6- and two 7-inch rifles and six 9-inch smoothbores, the two lightest pieces being bound at the breech with iron hoops, shrunk on like the tires on wagon wheels, to strengthen them for firing extra-heavy powder charges: another Brooke innovation. Finally, they covered her all over, down to two feet below the waterline, with overlapping plates of two-inch armor rolled from railroad iron at the Tredegar Works in Richmond. She was finished. What she lacked in looks, and she was totally lacking there, she made up for in her ability to give and take a pounding.

However, she had faults more serious than her ugliness: faults which caused head-shakings and predictions that she would be "an enormous metallic burial-case" for her crew. For one, the weight of all that iron made her squat so low in the water, 22 feet, that she had to confine her movements to deep-water channels. Not that she was much at maneuvering in the first place; "unwieldy as Noah's ark," one of her officers called her. Her top speed was five knots, and what with her great length and awkward steering, it took half an hour to turn her in calm water. This was mainly because of her wheezy, antiquated engines, which had been condemned on the *Merrimac*'s last cruise and had scarcely been improved by the fire and the months of immersion. Nevertheless, Mallory and her builders expected great things of her: nothing less, in fact, than the raising of the blockade by the destruction of whatever attempted to enforce it. They renamed her the *Virginia*, recruited a large part of her 300-man crew from the army, and placed her in the charge of Commodore Franklin Buchanan, the sixty-two-year-old "Father of Annapolis," so called because, under the old flag, he had been instrumental in founding the Naval Academy and had served as its first superintendent. Some measure of Mallory's expectations of the *Virginia* was shown by the fact that he had given command of her to the ranking man in the whole Confederate navy.

When she steamed down Elizabeth River on her trial run at noon that Saturday, her inherent faults — low speed, deep draft, and sluggish handling — were immediately apparent. Her guns had not yet been fired, and workmen still swarmed over her superstructure, making last-minute adjustments. But as she came in sight of open water, Buchanan saw across the Roads five warships of the blockade squadron lying at anchor, three off Fort Monroe and two off Newport News. The three were the *Minnesota* and the *Roanoke*, sister ships of the *Merrimac*, and the fifty-gun frigate *St Lawrence*. The two were the *Congress*, another fifty-gun frigate, and the thirty-gun sloop *Cumberland*. It was more than the commodore could resist. He hove-to off Craney Island, sent the workmen ashore, cleared the *Virginia*'s decks for action, and set out north across the Roads with his crew at battle stations. The "trial run" would be just that — all-out.

On the southern shore, from Willoughby Spit to Ragged Island, gray-clad infantry and artillerymen lined the beaches. They saw his intention and tossed their caps, cheering and singing "Dixie." Across the water, from Old Point Comfort westward, men in blue observed it too, but with mixed emotions. They had heard that this strange new thing was being built, and now they saw her coming slowly toward them. To an Indiana volunteer, watching her across five miles of water, she "looked very much like a house submerged to the eaves, borne onward by a flood."

It was washday aboard the Federal warships, sailor clothes drying in the rigging. Yet there was plenty of time in which to get ready for what was coming so slowly at them. The *Congress* and the *Cumberland* cleared for action, and when the *Virginia* came within range, the former gave her a well-aimed broadside: which broke against the sloping iron with no apparent effect at all. Ports closed tight, she came on, biding her time as she closed the range, unperturbed and inexorable. Another salvo struck her, together with shots from the coastal batteries: with no more effect than before. Then her ports came open, swinging deliberately upward on their hinges to expose the muzzles of her guns. Turning, she raked the *Congress* with a starboard broadside and rammed the *Cumberland* at near right-angles just under her fore rigging, punching a hole which one of her officers said would admit "a horse and cart" — except for the iron beak which broke off in her when the Confederate swung clear. The *Cumberland* began to fill, firing as long as a gun remained above water. Called on to surrender, her captain shouted, "Never! I'll sink alongside!"

Presently he did just that, his flag still flying from the mainmast, defiant above the waves after the ship herself struck bottom. Horrified, the captain of the *Congress* slipped his cable and tried to get away before the ironclad could complete its ponderous turn, but ran aground in the attempt. The *Virginia*, held at 200-yard range by her deeper draft, raked the helpless ship from end to end until, her captain dead and her scuppers running red with blood, a lieutenant ran up the white flag of surrender.

Buchanan ceased firing and stood by to take on prisoners, but the coastal batteries redoubled their fire under command of Brigadier General Joseph K. Mansfield, West Point '22. When one of his own officers protested that the enemy had the right to take possession unmolested once the *Congress* struck her flag, the crusty old regular replied, "I know the damned ship has surrendered, but *we* haven't!" Two Confederate lieutenants were killed in this unexpected burst of artillery and musketry, and Buchanan himself was wounded. So were many of the Union sailors on the decks of the surrendered ship — including Buchanan's brother, a lieutenant who had stayed with the old flag and who presently died in the flames on the quarterdeck when the *Virginia* dropped back and retaliated by setting the *Congress* afire with red-hot cannonballs that started fires wherever they struck wood.

By now the three frigates off Old Point Comfort had started west to join the fight. Hugging the northern shore to avoid the rebel guns on Sewell's Point, however, the *Roanoke* and the *St Lawrence* ran aground, and presently the *Minnesota*, left alone to deal with the iron monster, did likewise. It was well for her that it happened so, for the *Virginia*, having finished with the *Congress*, turned to deal with her erstwhile sister ship and found that, the tide being on the ebb, she could not come within effective range. So she drew off across the Roads to unload her wounded, survey her damage, and wait for the flooding of the tide tomorrow morning, when she intended to complete this first day's work by sinking the three grounded frigates.

Her 21 killed and wounded, including Buchanan, were removed, after which the officers surveyed the effects of the fight on the ship herself. The damage, though considerable, was not vital. In spite of having been exposed to the concentrated fire of at least one hundred guns, her armor showed only dents, no cracks, and nothing inside the shell was hurt. Outside was another matter. She had lost her iron beak, and two of her guns had had their muzzles blown off; besides which, one of her crew later wrote, "one anchor, the smoke-stack, and the steam pipes were shot away. Railings, stanchions, boat-davits, everything was swept clean."

All this seemed a small enough price to pay for the victory they had won that afternoon and the one they had prepared for completion tomorrow. Officers and men stayed up on deck, too elated to sleep, and watched the *Congress* burn. She lit up the Roads from across the way and paled the second-quarter moon, which came up early. From time to time, another of her loaded guns went off with a deep reverberant boom, but the big effect did not come until 1 o'clock in the morning, when her magazine blew up. After that, the Confederate crew turned in to get some sleep. Ashore, a Georgia private, writing home of the sea battle he had watched, exulted that the *Virginia* had "invented a new way of destroying the blockade. Instead of raising it, she sinks it. Or I believe she is good at both," he added, "for the one she burned was raised to a pretty considerable height when the magazine exploded."

A telegram reached Washington from Fort Monroe within two hours of the explosion of the *Congress*, informing the War Department that the Confederates' indestructible "floating battery" had sunk two frigates and would sink three more tomorrow before moving against the fortress itself — after which there was no telling what might happen.

Lincoln had his cabinet in session by 6.30, the prevailing gloom being broken only by the Secretary of War, who put on for his colleagues a remarkable display of jangled nerves. The jaunty Seward was glum for once; Chase was petulant; the President himself seemed quite unstrung; but Stanton was unquestionably the star of the piece. According to Welles, who did not like him, he was "inexpressibly ludicrous" with his "wild, frantic talk, action, and rage" as he "sat down and jumped up . . . swung his arms, scolded and raved." The *Virginia* would "change the whole character of the war," the lawyer-statesman cried. "She will destroy, *seriatim*, every naval vessel; she will lay all the cities on the seaboard under contribution." He would recall Burnside, abandon Port Royal, and "notify the governors and municipal authorities in the North to take instant measures to protect their harbors." Then, crossing to a window which commanded a long view of the Potomac, he looked out and, trembling visibly, exclaimed: "Not unlikely, we shall have a shell or a cannonball from one of her guns in the White House before we leave this room."

Welles, who recorded with pride that his own "composure was not disturbed," replied that Stanton's fear for his personal safety was unfounded, since the heavily armored vessel would surely draw too much water to permit her passage of Kettle Bottom Shoals; he doubted, in fact, that she would venture outside the Capes. This afforded at least a measure of relief for the assembly. Besides, Welles said, the navy already had an answer to the rebel threat: a seagoing ironclad of its own. *Monitor* was her name. She had left New York on Thursday, and should have reached Hampton Roads last night. "How many guns does she carry?" Stanton asked. Two, the Naval Secretary told him, and Stanton responded with a look which, according to Welles, combined "amazement, contempt, and distress."

The gray-bearded brown-wigged Welles spoke truly. The *Monitor* had arrived the night before. She had not only arrived; she was engaged this Sunday morning, before the cabinet adjourned to pray in church for the miracle which Stanton said was all that could save the eastern seaboard. And in truth it was something like a miracle that she was there at all. Coming south she had run into a storm that broke waves over her, down her blower-pipes and stacks, flooding her hold; pumps were rigged to fight a losing battle — and the wind went down, just as the ship was about to do the same. The fact was, she had not been built to stand much weather. She was built almost exclusively for what she was about to do: engage the former *Merrimac*, rumors of which had been coming north ever since work on the rebel craft began in mid-July.

There was a New York Swede, John Ericsson, who thought he had the answer, but when he went before the naval board with his plan for "an impregnable steam-battery of light draft," the members told him that calculations of her displacement proved the proposed *Monitor* would not float. He persisted, however; "The sea shall ride over her, and she will live in it like a duck," he said; until at last they offered him a contract with a clause providing for refund of all the money if she was not as invulnerable as he claimed. Ericsson took them up on that and got to work. Her keel was laid in October, three months behind the beginning of work on her rival, and she was launched within one hundred days.

As Welles had said, she had only two guns; but they were hard-hitting 11-inch rifles, housed in a revolving turret (another Ericsson invention) which gave them the utility of many times that number, though it caused the vessel to be sneered at as "a tin can on a shingle" or "a cheese-box on a raft." Her armor was nine inches thick in critical locations, and nowhere less than five, which would give her an advantage over her thinner-skinned opponent. The factors that made her truly the David to meet Goliath, however, were her 12-foot draft and her high maneuverability, which would combine her heavy punch with light fast footwork. Her sixty-man crew, men-of-war's men all, had volunteered directly from the fleet, and "a better one no naval commander ever had the honor to command," her captain said. His name was John L. Worden, a forty-four-year-old lieutenant with twenty-eight years in the service. He had been given the assignment — admittedly no plum — after seven months in a rebel prison, the result of having been captured back in April while trying to return from delivering secret messages to the Pensacola squadron. Obviously he was a man for desperate ventures, and perhaps the Department heads believed his months in durance would make him extra-anxious to hit back at the people who had held him. If they thought so, they were right. Nine days after the *Monitor* was commissioned he took her south for Hampton Roads.

Having weathered the storm, Worden rounded Cape Henry near sundown Saturday and heard guns booming twenty miles away. He guessed the cause and cleared for battle. But when he passed the Rip Raps, just before moonrise, and proceeded up the brightly lighted roadstead — each wave-crest a-sparkle with reflections of the flame-wrapped *Congress* — all he saw of the *Virginia* was the damage she had done: one ship sunk, another burning, and three more run ingloriously aground. An account of what had happened quickly told him what to do. Believing the *Virginia* would head first for her next morning, he put the *Monitor* alongside the *Minnesota*, kept his steam up, and waited.

Dawn came and at 7.30 he saw the big rebel ironclad coming straight for his stranded charge: whereupon he lifted anchor, darted out from behind the screening bulk of the frigate, and steamed forward to the attack. The *Monitor*'s sudden appearance was as unexpected as if she had dropped from the sky or floated up from the harbor bottom, squarely between the *Virginia* and her intended prize. "I guess she took us for some kind of a water tank," one of the *Monitor* crewmen later said. "You can see surprise in a ship just as you can see it in a man, and there was surprise all over the *Merrimac*."

He was right, or almost right. Instead of a water tank, however, "We thought at first it was a raft on which one of the *Minnesota*'s boilers was being taken to shore for repairs," a *Virginia* midshipman testified, "and when suddenly a shot was fired from her turret we imagined an accidental explosion of some kind had taken place on the raft."

This mistake was not for long. Rumors of work-in-progress had been trickling south as well as north, and the *Monitor* was recognized and saluted in her own right with a salvo which broke against her turret with as little effect as the ones that had shattered against the armored flanks of the *Virginia* yesterday, when the superiority of iron over wood was first established. Now it was iron against iron. The *Monitor* promptly returned the fire, swinging her two guns to bear in rapid succession. The fight was on.

It lasted four hours, not including a half-hour midway intermission, and what it mainly showed — in addition to its reinforcement of what one of them had proved the day before: that wooden navies were obsolete — was that neither could sink the other. The *Monitor* took full advantage of her higher speed and maneuverability, of her heavier, more flexible guns, and particularly of her lighter draft, which enabled her to draw off into the shallows for a breather where the other could not pursue. The *Virginia*'s supposed advantages, so impressive to the eye, were in fact highly doubtful. Her bigness, for example — the "Colossus of Roads," one northern correspondent dubbed her —

only made her more sluggish and easier to hit, and her eight guns were limited in traverse. The effectiveness of her knockout punch, demonstrated yesterday when she rammed the *Cumberland*, was considerably reduced by the loss of her iron beak. Also, she had come out armed for the destruction of the frigates; her explosive shell shattered easily against an armored target, and she had brought only a few solid rounds to be used as hot shot. Worden's task, on the other hand, was complicated by the need for protecting the grounded *Minnesota*, which the *Virginia* would take under fire if he allowed her to get within range. Then too, his gun crews were disconcerted by whizzing screwheads that flew off the inner ends of the armor bolts and rattled about inside the turret whenever the enemy scored a direct hit.

Buchanan gone, command of the *Virginia* had passed to her executive, Lieutenant Catesby ap R. Jones. He gave the *Monitor* everything he had given the wooden warships yesterday, and more: to no avail. When he tried to ram her, she drew aside like a skillful boxer and pounded him hard as he passed. After a few such exchanges, the crews of his after-guns, deafened by the concussion of 180-pound balls against the cracking railroad iron, were bleeding from their noses and ears. Descending once to the gundeck and observing that some of the pieces were not engaged, Jones shouted: "Why are you not firing, Mr Eggleston?" The gun captain shrugged. "Why, our powder is very precious," he replied, "and after two hours' incessant firing I find that I can do her about as much damage by snapping my thumb at her every two minutes and a half."

At this point the *Monitor* hauled off into shallow water, where she spent fifteen minutes hoisting a new supply of shot and powder to her turret. Left alone, the *Virginia* made one of her drawn-out turns to come as near as possible to the grounded *Minnesota*, whose captain received her with what he called "a broadside which would have blown out of the water any timber-built ship in the world." Unwincing, the ironclad put a rifled bow-gun shell into her and was about to swing broadside, bringing all her guns to bear, when the *Monitor* came steaming out of the shallows and intervened again, Worden having refreshed himself with a stroll on the deck and a general look-round while the fresh supply of ammunition was being made handy for his guns. The two ironclads reëngaged.

Jones by now had decided that if he was going to destroy his foe, it would have to be with something other than his guns. First he tried ramming, despite the absence of his iron beak. But the *Monitor* was too spry for him. The best he could manage was a blunt-prowed, glancing blow that shivered her timbers — "a tremendous thump," one of her officers called it — but did her no real damage. The smaller ship kept circling her opponent, pounding away, one crewman said, "like a cooper with his hammer going round a cask." Doubly frustrated, Jones then determined to try an even more desperate venture, one that would bring his crew's five-to-one numerical advantage to bear. Having taken naval warfare a long stride forward yesterday, today he would take it an even longer one — back to the pistol-and-cutlass days of John Paul Jones. He would board his adversary. Equipping his men with tarpaulins for blinding the *Monitor*'s gun-slits and iron crows for jamming her turret and prying open her hatch, he had them stand by the sally ports while he maneuvered to get within grappling distance. It was a risky plan at best (far riskier than he knew; the Federal gunners were supplied with hand grenades for just such an emergency) yet it might have worked, if he could only have managed to bring the *Virginia* alongside. He could not. Nimble as a skittish horse, the smaller vessel danced away from contact every time.

For two more hours this second act of the long fight continued, and all this time the *Monitor* was pounding her opponent like an anvil, cracking and breaking her armor plate, though not enough to penetrate its two-foot oak and pitch-pine backing. Soon after noon, in a last attempt at boarding — though by now the *Virginia*'s stack was so riddled that her fires could get almost no draft and her speed, already slow, was cut in half — Jones brought his ship within ten yards of the enemy and delivered at that point-blank range a 9-inch shell which exploded against the pilot house, squarely in front of the sight-slit where Worden had taken station to direct the helm and relay fire commands. The concussion cracked the crossbeam and partly lifted the iron lid, exposing the dark interior. Worden was stunned and blinded, ears ringing, beard singed, eyes filled with burning powder; but not too stunned to feel dismay, and not so blind that he did not see the sudden glare of the noonday sky through the break in the overhead armor. "Sheer off!" he cried, and the helmsman put her hard to starboard, running for the shallows.

While the *Monitor* retired to shoal water, and remained there to assess the damage she and her captain had suffered, the *Virginia* steamed ponderously across the deep-water battle scene with the proud air of a wrestler who has just thrown his opponent out of the ring. Presently, however — the ebb tide was running, keeping her out of range of the *Minnesota*, and she had settled considerably as a result of taking water through her seams — she drew off south across the Roads for Norfolk, claiming victory. As she withdrew, the *Monitor* came forward and took her turn at dominating the scene, basing her victory counterclaim on the fact that the *Virginia* did not turn back to continue the fight. This would result in much argument all around, though privately both antagonists admitted the obvious truth: that, tactically, the fight had been a draw. In a stricter sense, the laurels went to the *Monitor* for preventing the *Virginia* from completing her mission of destruction. Yet in the

largest sense of all, and equally obvious, both had been victorious —
over the wooden navies of the world.

Stretched out on the sofa in his cabin, Worden was "a ghastly
sight," according to the executive who went to receive instructions
from him upon assuming command. When the captain could speak, lying
there with his beard singed, his face bloody, and his eyes tight shut as if
to hold the pain in, his first words were a question: "Have I saved the
Minnesota?"

"Yes," he was told, "and whipped the *Merrimac*."

"Then I don't care what happens to me," he said.

★ ★ ★

As it had a perverse tendency to do in times of crisis, the telegraph line to Washington from Fort Monroe had gone out that Sabbath morning, and it stayed dead till just past 4 that afternoon. During
all this long, exasperating time, among all the officials waiting fidgety behind the sound-proof curtain which sealed them off from news of the
fight at Hampton Roads, none awaited the outcome with a deeper concern than George McClellan. The campaign he was about to launch depended on the Federal navy's maintaining domination of the bays and
coastal rivers north of the James. It required very little imagination —
far less, at any rate, than McClellan was blessed or cursed with — to picture what would happen if enemy gunboats — even wooden ones, let
alone the frigate-killing *Merrimac-Virginia* — got among his loaded
transports on their way down Chesapeake Bay or up the Rappahannock
River.

Before news of the ironclad duel reached Washington, however,
he received outpost dispatches which shipwrecked the Urbanna plan as
completely as the sinking of the *Monitor* would have done: Joe Johnston
was gone from the Manassas line. Most of his army was already back on
the banks of the Rappahannock, intrenching itself near the very spot
McClellan had picked for a beachhead. To land at Urbanna now, he
saw, would be to land not in Johnston's rear, but with Johnston in his
own.

Despite this abrupt and, so to speak, ill-mannered joggling of the
military chessboard after all the pains he had taken to dispose the pieces
to his liking, he was none the less relieved when, immediately following
the news of Johnston's retrograde maneuver, the wire from Fort Monroe came suddenly alive with jubilant chatter of a victory by stalemate.
The rebel ironclad had gone limping back to Norfolk, neutralized. He
could breathe. What was more, he saw in this new turn of events an
opportunity to put the finishing touch to his army's rigorous eight-
month course of training: a practice march, deep into enemy territory —
under combat conditions, with full field equipment and carefully

worked-out logistics — and then another march right back again, since there was nothing there that he would not gain, automatically and bloodlessly, by going ahead with his roundabout plan for a landing down the coast. Warning orders went out that night, alerting the commanders. Next day the troops were slogging south, well-ordered dark-blue columns probing the muddy North Virginia landscape.

Excellent as this was as a graduation exercise to cap the army's basic training program, it had a bad effect on the public's opinion of Little Mac as the man to whip the rebels. Armchair strategists found in it the answer to the taunting refrain of a current popular song, "What are you waiting for, tardy George?" What he had been waiting for, apparently, was the departure of Johnston's army, which he had not ventured to risk encountering face-to-face. There was truth in this, though it omitted the balancing truth that, however frightened he might have been of Johnston, the thing he had least wanted was for Johnston to be frightened of him—frightened, that was, into pulling back and thus eluding the trap McClellan had spent all these months contriving. Lacking this restricted information, all the public could see was that Tardy George had delayed going forward until he knew there was nothing out there on the southern horizon for him to fear.

The outrage was screwed to a higher pitch when reports came back from newspapermen who had marched with the army through the supposedly impregnable fortifications along the Centerville ridge, where Quaker guns had been left in the embrasures to mock the Yankees. It was Munson's Hill all over again, the correspondents cried; "Our enemies, like the Chinese, have frightened us by the sound of gongs and the wearing of devils' masks." What was more, the smoldering wreckage of the Confederate camps showed conclusively that Johnston's army had been no more than half the size McClellan estimated. "Utterly dispirited, ashamed and humiliated," one reporter wrote, "I return from this visit to the rebel stronghold, feeling that their retreat is *our defeat*." The feeling was general. "It was a contest of inertia," another declared; "our side outsat the other."

These were nonprofessional opinions, which in general the army did not share. Civilians liked their victories bloody: the bloodier the better, so long as the casualty lists did not touch home. Soldiers — except perhaps in retrospect, when they had become civilians, too — preferred them bloodless, as in this case. The Centerville fortifications looked formidable enough to the men who would have had to assault them, peeled log guns or no. Besides, some of them — old-timers now — could contrast this march with the berry-picking jaunt which had ended so disastrously in July.

It went smoothly, with a minimum of stop-and-go. There was no need to fall out of column when everything a man could want was right there in the supply train. They were an army now, and they looked it, in their manner and their dress. There were still a few outlandish Zouave outfits to lend the column sudden garish bursts of color, like mismatched beads on a string, but for the most part they wore the uniform which had lately become standard: light-blue trousers and a tunic of dark blue, with a crisp white edge of collar showing just under the jowls of the men in regiments whose colonels, being dudes or incurable old-army martinets, preferred it so.

Whatever truth there might once have been in the Confederate claim that Southerners made better soldiers, or anyhow started from a better scratch because they came directly from life in the open and were familiar with the use of firearms, applied no longer. After six months of army drill, a factory hand was indistinguishable from a farmer. Individually, the Northerners knew, they were at least as tough as any men the South could bring against them, and probably as a whole they were better drilled — except of course the cavalry, since admittedly it took longer to learn to fork a horse in style. McClellan's men were aware of the changes he had wrought and they were proud of them; but the thing that made them proudest of all was the sight of Little Mac himself. He was up and down the column all that day, glad to be out from under the shadow of the Capitol dome and the sneers of the politicians, not answering ignorant questions or countering even more ignorant proposals, but returning the cheers of his marching men with a jaunty horseback salute.

Presently, crossing Bull Run by Blackburn's Ford, they came onto the scene of last year's smoky, flame-stabbed panorama. It was a sobering sight, for those who had been there then and those who hadn't: the corpse of a battlefield, silent and deserted except perhaps for the ghosts of the fallen. Shell-blasted, the treetops were twisted "in a hundred directions, as though struck by lightning," one correspondent wrote. Manassas Junction lay dead ahead, the embers of it anyhow, at the base of a column of bluish-yellow smoke, and off to the right were the tumbled bricks of Judith Henry's chimney, on the hill where the Stonewall Brigade had met the jubilant attackers, freezing the cheers in their throats, and flung them back; Jeb Stuart's horsemen had come with a thunder of hoofs, hacking away at the heads of the New York Fire Zouaves. All that was left now was wreckage, the charred remains of a locomotive and four freight cars, five hundred staved-in barrels of flour, and fifty-odd barrels of pork and beef "scattered around in the mud." McDowell was there, at the head of his corps, and one of his soldiers wrote that he saw him weeping over the sun-bleached bones of the light-hearted berry-picking men he had led southward under the full moon of July.

McClellan was not weeping. This field held no memories for him, sad or otherwise, except that what had happened here had prompted Lincoln to send for him to head the army he found "cowering on the banks of the Potomac" and later to replace Scott as chief of all the nation's armies. He went to bed that night, proud to have taken without loss the position McDowell had been thrown back from after spilling on it the blood of 1500 men. Next day he was happy still, riding among the bivouacs. But the day that followed was another matter. He woke to find his time had come to weep.

Once more he had turned his back on Lincoln, and once more Lincoln had struck with a War Order. This one, numbered 3, relieved McClellan as general-in-chief and left him commanding only the Department of the Potomac, one of seven in the eastern theater. The worst of it, in damage to his pride, was that he learned of the order, not through military channels, but by a telegram from friends in Washington who read it in the papers: Stanton's office had leaked the order to the press before forwarding it to McClellan in the field. Within one week of learning that his Commander in Chief had listened to charges of treason against him, of being forced to reorganize his army on the eve of committing it to action under corps commanders who had gone on record as being opposed to his military thinking, he was toppled unceremoniously from the highest rung of the professional ladder.

This was hard. Indeed, it might have been the crowning blow, except that later that same day, March 12, he was comforted by a mutual friend whom the President sent with the full text and an explanation of the order. He was relieved of the chief command "until otherwise ordered," it read: which implied that the demotion was temporary. Furthermore, the envoy explained, the order had been issued primarily to allow him to concentrate, without distractions, on the big campaign ahead. McClellan took heart at this and wrote to Lincoln at once, informing him that "I shall work just as cheerfully as before, and that no consideration of self will in any manner interfere with the discharge of my public duties."

So he said, and doubtless believed. He would have been considerably less cheerful, though, if he had known of other things that were happening behind his back, this same week in Washington; "that sink of iniquity," he called it.

Ethan Allen Hitchcock, a sixty-four-year-old Vermonter, West Point graduate and veteran of the Seminole and Mexican Wars, was surprised to receive from the War Department in mid-March a telegram summoning him to Washington. He had been retired from the army since 1855, and never would have entered it in the first place if his parents had not insisted that the grandson and namesake of the Hero of Ticonderoga was obliged to take up arms as a profession. Hitchcock's principal interests were philosophy and mysticism; he considered himself "a scholar rather than a warrior," and had written books on Swedenborg and alchemy and Jesus. His first reaction to the summons that plucked him from retirement was a violent nosebleed. He got aboard a train, however, suffering a second hemorrhage on the way and a third on arrival, each more violent than the one before. Checking into a Washington hotel, he took to the bed in a dazed, unhappy condition.

Presently the Secretary of War was at his bedside. While the old soldier lay too weak to rise and greet him, Stanton told him why he had been sent for. He and Lincoln needed him as a military adviser. The air was thick with treason! ... Before Hitchcock could recover from his alarm at this, the Secretary put a question to him: Would he consider taking McClellan's place as commander of the Army of the Potomac? Hitchcock scarcely knew what to make of this. Next thing he knew, Stanton had him out of bed and on the way to the White House, where Lincoln repeated the Secretary's request. Badly confused, Hitchcock wrote in his diary when he got back to his room that night: "I want no command. I want no department. ... I am uncomfortable." Finally he agreed to accept an appointment as head of the Army Board, made up of War Department bureau chiefs. In effect, this amounted to being the right-hand man of Stanton, who terrified him daily by alternately bullying and cajoling him. He was perhaps the unhappiest man in Washington.

Unsuspecting that the President and the Secretary of War were even now casting about for a replacement for him, McClellan completed his army's graduation exercise by marching it back to its starting point, Fairfax Courthouse, to deliver the baccalaureate address. After congratulating his soldiers on their progress, he announced that their long months of study were behind them; he was about to take them "where you all long to be — the decisive battlefield." In solicitude, he added, "I am to watch over you as a parent over his children; and you know that your general loves you from the depths of his heart. It shall be my care, as it ever has been, to gain success with the least possible loss; but I know that, if necessary, you will willingly follow me to our graves for our righteous cause. ... I shall demand of you great, heroic exertions, rapid and long marches, desperate combats, privations perhaps. We will share all these together; and when this sad war is over we will return to our homes, and feel that we can ask no higher honor than the proud consciousness that we belonged to the Army of the Potomac."

With their cheers ringing in his ears, he turned at once to perfect his plans for a landing down the coast. Urbanna was out, but Mobjack Bay and Fort Monroe were still available. In fact, though he had pronounced these alternatives "less brilliant"— by which he meant that they would not outflank the enemy, neither Johnston to the north nor Magruder to the south — now that he came to examine it intently, Fort Monroe had definite advantages Urbanna had not afforded. For one thing, the beachhead was already established, Old Point Comfort having been held throughout the secession furor despite the loss of Norfolk across the way. For another, during his advance up the York-James peninsula toward Richmond, his flanks would be protected by the navy, which could also assist in the reduction of any strongpoints he encountered within range of its big guns. The more he studied the scheme the better he liked it.

By now, however, he had learned to look back over his shoulder. Lincoln had to be considered: not only considered, but outmaneuvered. Once before, he had accomplished this by calling a conference of his generals and confronting the President with their concerted opinions as to the soundness of a military plan. In that case Lincoln had not dared to override him; nor would he now. So McClellan called his corps commanders together, there at Fairfax, and presented them with his proposal for a landing at Fort Monroe. Having heard him out, the four generals expressed unanimous approval — provided four conditions could be met. These were that the *Merrimac* could be kept out of action, that there were sufficient transportation facilities to take the army down the coast, that the navy could silence certain fortifications on York River, and that enough troops were left behind to give the capital "an entire feeling of security for its safety from menace." They were not in full agreement as to how many men would be needed to accomplish this last condition, but their estimates ran generally to 40,000.

McClellan had them put their approval in writing, that same March 13, then sent McDowell to Washington to present it to Stanton and Lincoln. As soon as McDowell had had time to get there, McClellan received a wire from Stanton. McDowell had shown up with a paper signed by the corps commanders; did McClellan intend for the plan it approved to be taken as his own? McClellan replied that it did. After another interval, allowing time for the Secretary and Lincoln to confer, a second Stanton telegram arrived. Lincoln did not exactly approve; rather, as Stanton phrased it, he "[made] no objection," so long as enough of McClellan's men were left behind to keep Washington and Manassas safe while the army was down the coast. The final paragraph, which made consent explicit, was petulant and sneering: "Move the remainder of the force down the Potomac, choosing a new base at Fortress Monroe, or anywhere between here and there, or, at all events, move such remainder of the army at once in pursuit of the enemy by some route."

Perhaps by now McClellan had learned to abide the tantrums and exasperations of his former friend and sympathizer. At any rate, having won the consent he sought, he could overlook the tone in which it was given. However, that Manassas, too, was to be afforded what the generals called "an entire feeling of security" imposed an additional manpower drain on which he had not counted. He was tempted to give Lincoln another tactics-strategy lecture, proving that the place would be in no danger, and in fact of small importance, once his landing on the Peninsula had drawn Johnston's army farther south to oppose his swoop on Richmond. But there was too much else to do just now; he had no time for arguments and lectures. The transports were being assembled at Alexandria — 113 steamers, 188 schooners, and 88 barges: by far the largest amphibious expedition the hemisphere had ever seen — to take his army down the Virginia coast, with all its equipment and supplies, guns and wagons, food and ammunition, horses and beef cattle, tents and records, all the impedimenta required to feed, clothe, and arm 146,000 men. They were to move in echelons of 10,000, on a schedule designed to complete the shuttle within three weeks. McClellan worked hard and long, giving the loading his personal attention. Within four days of receiving Lincoln's approval, or anyhow what amounted to approval, he stood on an Alexandria wharf and saw the first contingent off on its journey south.

"The worst is over," he wired Stanton. "Rely upon it that I will carry this thing through handsomely."

Such optimistic expressions by the Young Napoleon were usually precursors of disappointment or disaster. Not only was this one no exception, it had in fact a double repercussion, set off in his rear by two men who opposed McClellan as well as each other: Stonewall Jackson, who had done so much to wreck McDowell on Henry Hill, and John Charles Frémont, who had done so much — though with less success — to damage Lincoln in Missouri. The two blows landed in that order, both before the Army of the Potomac had completed its roundabout journey down Chesapeake Bay. The first echelon left Alexandria on March 17, a Monday. Before the week was up, Jackson stabbed hard at the troops McClellan had left behind (in accordance with Lincoln's concern) to block any Confederate drive on Washington through the Shenandoah Valley, that corridor pointed shotgun-like at the Union solar plexus.

When Johnston fell back to the Rappahannock he instructed Jackson to conform by retreating southward up the Valley in event of a Federal push, taking care meanwhile to protect the main army's western flank by guarding the eastern passes of the Blue Ridge. Jackson of course obeyed, but not without a plea that he be allowed at least a chance to hurt the man who pushed him. As he put it, "If we cannot be successful in defeating the enemy should he advance, a kind Providence may enable us to inflict a terrible wound and effect a safe retreat in the event of having to fall back."

Old Blue Light, his soldiers called him; they had seen the fire of battle in his eyes. He read the New Testament in his off-hours, but did his military thinking in accordance with the Old, which advised smiting the enemy, hip and thigh, and assured the assistance of Providence in the infliction of terrible wounds.

At any rate, he soon had the chance he prayed for. When Johnston fell back the Federals came forward, two divisions of them marching up the Valley in coöperation with McClellan's excursion east of the mountains. Jackson, with 4600 men, retreated watchfully before the Federal 17,000, awaiting the answer to his prayers. Then it came. As he fell back through Winchester, spies reported the enemy regiments scattered. A quick slash at the head might confuse the whole column into exposing one or two of its segments to destruction. When he called a meeting of his officers to plan the attack, however, he learned that his wagon train was already miles to the south. Without food or reserve ammunition, his hungry men would have to continue their retreat. Jackson was furious, somehow placing the blame on the assembly of officers. "That is the last council of war I will ever hold!" he vowed. And it was.

The retreat continued through Kernstown, four miles to the south, then another forty miles up the Valley pike, past the slopes of the Massanuttons. All through the retreat Jackson watched and prayed, but for ten days Providence did not smile on him again. Then suddenly it did. On Friday the 21st his cavalry commander reported the enemy pulling back; one division had turned off eastward toward Manassas, and the other was retiring north toward Winchester. Next morning Jackson had his infantry on the road. Twenty-five miles they marched that day and fifteen the next, retracing their steps to reach Kernstown at 2 p.m. Sunday and find the horse artillery already skirmishing with what the cavalry commander said was the Federal rear guard, four regiments left to protect the tail of the column slogging north for Harpers Ferry. Jackson's blue eyes lighted. Here was the chance to inflict that terrible wound.

Certain considerations urged postponement. He had made no detailed personal reconnaissance. His ranks were thinned by 1500 stragglers he had left along the pike in the past two days. Last but not least, this was the Lord's day; Jackson would not even write a letter on a Sunday, or post one that would be in transit then, fearing that Providence might punish the profanation. These were all set aside, however, when weighed against the chances for success. There must be no delay; the sun was already down the sky. Without taking time to brief his commanders, he put his men into attack formation, the Stonewall Brigade in the center, and threw them forward. This was his first full-scale battle on his own, and he intended to make the victory sudden and complete.

It was sudden enough, but it was so far from complete that it was not even a victory. It was a repulse, and a bloody one at that. When the men in gray went forward, the Federals absorbed the shock and held their ground, returning the fire. Quickly it swelled to crescendo as Jackson sent in his reserves. Presently, to his amazement, men began to stumble out of the roar and flash of battle, making for the rear. He rode forward to block the way. "Where are you going, man?" he shouted at one retreater. The soldier explained that he had fired all his cartridges. "Then go back and give them the bayonet!" Jackson cried. But the man ran on, unheeding, one among many. Even the Stonewall Brigade, with its hard core of veterans who had stood fast on Henry Hill, was wavering. Just as it was about to break, its commander Brigadier General Richard Garnett gave the order to retreat. Amazed at what appeared to be his army's disintegration, Jackson seized a drummer boy by the shoulder and dragged him onto a knoll, shouting as he held him: "Beat the rally!" The roll of the drum did nothing to slow the rout; Jackson fell back in the demoralized wake of his soldiers. Fortunately for him, the Federals did not pursue. The Battle of Kernstown, such as it was, was over.

Suffering 700 casualties to the enemy's 590, Jackson's men had done a better job than Jackson himself when it came to estimating Federal strength. That was no mere rear guard they had charged, but a whole 9000-man division. When he learned that he had thus unknowingly reversed the dictum that the attacker must outnumber the defender three-to-one, Jackson did not allow it to temper the sternness of his discipline. Garnett had retreated without orders; peremptorily Jackson relieved him of command and put him in arrest to await court martial for neglect of duty. It did not matter that he had graduated from West Point the year before Jackson came there as a plebe, that he was a member of the proud Tidewater family which had given the Confederacy the first general officer lost in battle, or that his men loved him and resented the harshness that took him from them. It did not even matter that his brigade might have been cut to pieces if he had held it there, outnumbered, outflanked, and out of ammunition, while he went fumbling along the chain of command in search of permission to withdraw. What mattered was that the next officer who found himself in a tight spot would stay there, awaiting higher sanction, before ordering a retreat.

As for accepting any personal blame for this loss of nearly one-fourth of his little army because of ragged marching, faulty reconnaissance, poor intelligence, ill-prepared assault, or disorganized retreat, Jackson could not see it. In fact, he did not seem to understand that he had been defeated. "The Yankees don't seem willing to quit Winchester, General," a young cavalryman said in bivouac that night. Jackson replied, "Winchester is a very pleasant place to stay in, sir." The trooper attempted a further pleasantry: "It was reported that they were retreating, but I guess they were retreating after us." Jackson, who had a limited sense of humor, kept looking into the campfire. "I think I may say I am satisfied, sir," he said.

How far he saw into the future as he said this would remain a question to be pondered down the years, but most likely Old Blue Light would have been still more "satisfied" if he had known the reaction his repulse was producing that night in the enemy camp, even as he warmed his hands at the bivouac fire and refused to admit that what he had suffered was a defeat. His adversary, while congratulating himself on a hard-fought victory, could not believe that Jackson would have dared to attack without expecting reinforcements. Orders went out, recalling to the Valley the division that had left for Manassas two days ago: which meant, in effect, a loss of 8000 men for McClellan, who was charged with leaving a covering force to protect the Junction when the balance of his army sailed. Equally important, if not more so, was the effect on Lincoln, who quarter-faced at the news of the battle, victory or no, and found himself looking once more down the muzzle of the Shenandoah shotgun. The Kernstown explosion seemed to prove that it was loaded.

Whatever it was for Lincoln, news of the battle, coupled with the recall of the division headed eastward, was a thorn in McClellan's side — a hurt which in time might fester and hurt worse. As such, however, it was no sharper than the thorn that stuck him one week later, on the eve of his own departure for Fort Monroe. He had in his army, in Sumner's corps, a division commanded by Louis Blenker, a man of considerable flamboyance. Blenker was a soldier of fortune, a German, and his men were known as Germans, too, this being the current generic term for immigrants of all origins except Ireland. But the fact was, they were almost everything: Algerians, Cossacks, Sepoys, Turks, Croats, Swiss, French Foreign Legionnaires, and a Garibaldi regiment with a Hungarian colonel, one d'Utassy, who had begun his career as a circus rider and was to end it as an inmate of Sing Sing. Blenker affected a red-lined cape and a headquarters tent made of "double folds of bluish material, restful to the eye," where the shout, *"Ordinans numero eins!"* was the signal for the serving of champagne. His soldiers got lager beer and there was a prevailing aroma of sauerkraut around the company messes. All this — the glitter of fire-gilt buttons, the babble of polyglot commands, and the smell of German cooking — was reminiscent of one of Frémont's old Transmississippi outfits. And the fact was, Frémont was doing all he could to get hold of the division even now.

The Pathfinder was back on the road to glory, though it led now, not through Missouri or down the winding course of the Mississippi, but along the western border of Virginia and across the rolling peaks of the Alleghenies. Under pressure from the Jacobins, who had never stopped protesting their favorite's dismissal and urging that he be returned to duty, Lincoln, in the same War Order which removed McClellan from over-all command, plucked Frémont out of retirement and gave him what was called the Mountain Department, specially created for this purpose, along with 25,000 men. Having learned that the former explorer was a poor administrator, he now presented him with this chance to prove himself a fighter. Frémont at once came up with a plan he knew would delight the President. Give him 10,000 additional soldiers, he said, and he would capture Knoxville. What was more, he had a particular 10,000 in mind: Blenker's Germans.

Lincoln pricked up his ears at this offer to accomplish one of his pet war aims, then went down to Alexandria to see if McClellan was willing to give up the division. Far from willing, McClellan urged the Commander in Chief not to weaken the Army of the Potomac at the moment when it was half-embarked on its trip to the gates of Richmond. Lincoln agreed on second thought that it would not do, and returned to Washington. Once more he had gotten nowhere with McClellan face-to-face. Within the week, however, on the final day of March, the general received a presidential note: "This morning I felt constrained to order Blenker's division to Frémont; and I write this to assure you that I did so with great pain, understanding that you would wish it otherwise. If you could know the full pressure of the case I am confident that you would justify it, even beyond a mere acknowledgment that the Commander in Chief may order what he pleases. Yours very truly, A. Lincoln."

The closing phrase had a Stantonian ring, administering a back-hand cut that stung; but what alarmed McClellan most was the undeniable evidence that, under political pressure, the nation's leader would swerve into paths which he knew were militarily unwise. How much grief this might hold for the army remained to be seen. For the present, McClellan could only repeat what he had written to his wife three weeks ago, when he learned of War Order 3: "The rascals are after me again. I had been foolish enough to hope that when I went into the field they would give me some rest, but it seems otherwise. Perhaps I should have expected it. If I can get out of this scrape you will never catch me in the power of such a set again."

Now as then, however, he was too busy to protest. Just before embarking next afternoon — All Fools' Day — he sent Lincoln a roster of the troops he was leaving for the protection of the capital. His generals had advised a covering force of 40,000. McClellan listed 77,456, thus: 10,859 at Manassas, 7780 at Warrenton, 35,476 in the Shenandoah Valley, 1350 along the lower Potomac, and 22,000 around Washington proper. This done, he went aboard a steamer, worked in his cabin on last-minute paperwork details till after midnight, then set out for Fort Monroe. McDowell's corps and what was left of Sumner's were to come along behind within the week. Looking back on the journey after landing at Old Point Comfort, he informed his wife, "I did not feel safe until I could see Alexandria behind us."

What was called for now, he saw, was action. He kept busy all that day and the next. "The great battle," he wrote his wife, "will be

(I think) near Richmond, as I have always hoped and thought. I see my way very clearly, and, with my trains once ready, will move rapidly." The following morning, April 4, he put two columns in motion for Yorktown, where the Confederate left was anchored on York River, behind fortifications whose reduction his corps commanders had said would depend on naval coöperation. All went well on the approach march. The day was clear, the sky bright blue, the trees new-green and shiny. Near sundown, exultant, he wired Stanton: "I expect to fight tomorrow."

His spirits were much improved at the prospect, and also perhaps from having observed what he called "a wonderfully cool performance" by three of his soldiers that afternoon. The trio of foragers had chased a sheep within range of the rebel intrenchments, where, ignoring the fire of sharpshooters — but not the fact that they were being watched by McClellan and their comrades while they demonstrated their contempt for the enemy's marksmanship — they calmly killed and skinned the animal before heading back for their own lines. The Confederates then brought a 12-pounder to bear, scoring a near miss. Undaunted, the soldiers halted, picked up the shot, and lugged it along, still warm, for presentation to Little Mac.

"I never saw so cool and gallant a set of men," he declared, seeing in this bright cameo of action a reflection of the spirit of his whole army. "They did not seem to know what fear is."

This gap in their education was about to be filled, however.

☆ II ☆

War Means Fighting . . .

★ ✗ ☆

🔊 EARL VAN DORN CAME WEST WITH GREAT
expectations. He knew what opportunities awaited a bold commander
there, and his professional boldness had been tested and applauded.
Approaching his prime at forty-one, he was dark-skinned and thin-
faced, with a shaggy mustache, an imperial, and a quick, decisive manner; "Buck," his fellow Confederates called him. Except for his size (he
was five feet five: two inches taller than Napoleon) he was in fact the
very beau sabreur of Southern fable, the Bayard-Lochinvar of maiden
dreams. Not that his distinction was based solely on his looks. He was a
man of action, too — one who knew how to grasp the nettle, danger,
and had done so many times. Appointed to West Point by his great-
uncle Andrew Jackson, he had gone on to collect two brevets and five
wounds as a lieutenant in the Mexican War and in skirmishes with Co-
manches on the warpath. In the end, he had been rewarded with a cap-
taincy in Sidney Johnston's 2d Cavalry, adding his own particular glitter
to that spangled company.

He was a Mississippian, which simplified his decision when the
South seceded; for him there was little or none of the "agony" of the
border state professionals. Furthermore, as it did for others blessed or
cursed with an ache for adventure, the conflict promised deferment of
middle age and boredom. He came home and was made a brigadier,
second only to Jefferson Davis in command of Mississippi troops, and
then received the command itself, with the rank of major general, when
Davis left for Montgomery. This was much, but not enough. Wanting
action even more than rank, and what he called "immortal renown"
more than either, Van Dorn resigned to accept a colonel's commission
in the Confederate army and assignment to service in Texas. Here he
found at least a part of what he was seeking. At Galveston he assembled
a scratch brigade of volunteers and captured three Federal steamships in

the harbor — including the famous *Star of the West*, which had been fired on, back in January, for attempting relief of Sumter — then marched on Indianola, where he forced the surrender of the only body of U.S. regulars in the state.

For these exploits, characterized by incisiveness and daring, he was tendered a banquet and ball in San Antonio and had his praises sung in all the southern papers, though perhaps the finest compliment paid him was by a northern editor who put a price of $5000 on his head, this being nearly twice the standing offer for the head of Beauregard. In acknowledgment of his services and fame, the government gave him a double promotion and summoned him to Richmond; he was a major general again, this time in command of all the cavalry in Virginia. Even this did not seem commensurate with his abilities, however. Presently, when Davis was in need of a commander for what was to be called Transmississippi Department Number 2, he had to look no farther than his fellow-Mississippian Earl Van Dorn, right there at hand. It was another case, apparently, of History attending to her own.

Within nine days of his mid-January assignment to the West, despite the fact that he was convalescing from a bad fall suffered while attempting a risky ditch jump — he was an excellent horseman; his aide, required by custom to try it too, was injured even worse — Van Dorn established headquarters at Pocahontas, Arkansas, and began a first-hand estimate of the situation. This in itself was quite a task, since the command included all of Missouri and Arkansas, Indian Territory, and Louisiana down to the Red River. But one thing he had determined at the outset: he would go forward, north along the line of the Mississippi, taking cities and whipping Yankee armies as he went. In short, as Van Dorn saw it, the campaign was to be a sort of grand reversal of Frémont's proposed descent of the big river. On the day of his appointment, already packing for the long ride west from Richmond, he had written his wife: "I must have St Louis — then huzza!"

So much he intended; but first, he knew, he must concentrate his scattered troops for striking. Ben McCulloch's army of 8000 was camped in the Boston Mountains south of Fayetteville, the position it had taken after the victory over Lyon at Wilson's Creek. Off in the Territory, moving to join him, was a band of about 2000 pro-Confederate Indians, Creeks and Seminoles, Cherokees, Chickasaws and Choctaws, won over by the persuasions of the lawyer-poet, scholar-duelist, orator-soldier Albert Pike, who led them. Sterling Price's 7000 Missourians, under pressure from a superior Federal army after their late fall and early winter successes in their home state, had fallen back to a position near the scene of their August triumph. Combined, these three totaled something under half the striking force the new commander had envisioned; but 17,000 should be enough to crush the Federals threatening Springfield — after which would come St Louis, "then huzza!" Van

Dorn planned to unite at Ironton, fight, and then swing north, augmented by the enthusiasts a victory would bring trooping to the colors.
Deep in the bleak western woods, he hailed his army with Napoleonic
phrases: "Soldiers! Behold your leader! He comes to show you the way
to glory and immortal renown. . . . Awake, young men of Arkansas, and
arm! Beautiful maidens of Louisiana, smile not on the craven youth who
may linger by your hearth when the rude blast of war is sounding in
your ears! Texas chivalry, to arms!"

    This might have brought in volunteers, a host bristling with
bayonets much as the address itself bristled with exclamation points,
though as events turned out there was no time for knowing. By now
it was late February, and the pressure of the 12,000-man northern
army against Springfield was too great. Price gave way, retreating while
his rear guard skirmished to delay the Federals: first across the Arkansas
line, then down through Fayetteville, until presently he was with McCulloch in the Boston Mountains, the southernmost reach of the Ozarks. By
that time, Pike had come up too; Van Dorn's command was concentrated — not where he had wanted it, however, and not so much by his
own efforts as by the enemy's. Then too, except in the actual heat of
battle, Price and McCulloch had never really got along, and they did no
better now. Both appealed to their leader at Pocahontas to come
and resolve their differences in person.

    Van Dorn was more than willing. In four days, after sending
word for them to stand firm and prepare to attack, he rode two hundred
horseback miles through the wintry wilds of Arkansas. Arriving March
3, he was given a salute of forty guns, as befitted his rank, and that
night orders went out for the men to prepare three days' cooked rations
and gird themselves for a forced march, with combat at its end. The
Federals, widely separated in pursuit of Price, were about to be destroyed in detail.

    Early next morning the Southerners set out, 17,000 men and
sixty guns moving north to retake what had been lost by retrograde:
as conglomerate, as motley an army as the sun ever shone on, East or
West — though as a matter of fact the sun was not shining now. Snow
fell out of an overcast sky and the wind whipped the underbrush
and keened in the branches of the winter trees. Price's Missourians led
the way, marching homeward again, proud of the campaign they had
staged and proud, too, of their 290-pound ex-governor commander,
who could be at once so genial and majestic. McCulloch, the dead-shot
former Ranger, wearing a dove-gray corduroy jacket, sky-blue trousers,
Wellington boots, and a highly polished Maynard rifle slung across one
shoulder, rode among his Texans and Arkansans; "Texicans" and "Rack-
ansackers," they were called — hard-bitten men accustomed to life in
the open, who boasted that they would storm hell itself if McCulloch
gave the order. Off on the flank, in a long thin file, the Five Nations

Indians followed their leader Albert Pike, a big man bearded like Santa Claus except that the beard was not white but a vigorous gray. He rode in a carriage and was dressed in Sioux regalia, buckskin shirt, fringed leggins, and beaded moccasins, while his braves, harking back to their warpath days, wore feathers stuck in their hats and scalping knives in their waistbands, some marching with a musket in one hand and a tomahawk in the other. The knives were for more than show; they intended to use them, having promised their squaws the accustomed trophies of battle.

Van Dorn also rode horse-drawn. He rode, in fact, supine in an ambulance, still feeling the effects of the ditch-jump back in Virginia and down as well with chills and fever as a result of swimming his mare across an icy river two days ago in his haste to join the army and get it moving. The mare was hitched alongside now, available in emergencies, and Price rode alongside too, identifying passing units and ready to re-lay orders when the time came. The new commander was nothing if not a man of action, bold and forward, sick or well, and the troops he led had caught something of his spirit. Trudging up the road down which they had retreated just the week before, they were in a high good humor despite the norther blowing wet snow in their faces.

The previous afternoon, some dozen miles away on a grassy knoll near Cross Hollows, Arkansas, where his headquarters tent was pitched, the commander of the army that had just cleared southwest Missouri of organized Confederates sat writing a letter home. At fifty-seven, having put on weight, he found that long hours in the saddle wearied him now a good deal more than they had done fifteen years be-fore, when he had abandoned army life for civil engineering. A dish-faced man with a tall forehead and thinning, wavy hair, hazel eyes and a wide, slack-lipped mouth, he drew solace from such periods of re-laxation as this, sitting in full uniform, polished boots, epaulets and spurs, enjoying the sounds of camp life in the background and the singing of the birds, while he inscribed to the wife of his bosom letters which he signed, rather ponderously, "yours Saml R. Curtis." A West Pointer like the opponent he did not yet know he was facing, he had com-manded an Ohio regiment in the Mexican War, had been chief engineer for the city of St Louis, and had served for the past three years as Re-publican congressman from Iowa. Of all his accomplishments, however, he was proudest of the current one, performed as a brigadier general of volunteers. Chasing the rebels out of Missouri might not sound like much, compared to Grant's recent unconditional capture of two forts and one whole army in Tennessee, but Curtis felt that it was a substan-tial achievement. He was saying so in the letter when his writing was interrupted by the sudden far-off rumble of cannon. It came from the south, and he counted forty well-spaced booms: the salute for a major general.

This gave him pause, and with the pause came doubts. His four divisions were rather scattered, two of them twelve miles in his rear and two thrown forward under Franz Sigel, the immigrant mathematics instructor who had shown a talent for retreat at Wilson's Creek. Curtis was a cautious or at any rate a highly methodical person; he liked to allow for contingencies, an engineer's margin for stress and strain, and he could never feel comfortable until he knew he had done so. Back in the fall, inspecting Frémont's pinwheel dispositions, he had reported that the Pathfinder "lacked the intelligence, the experience, and the sagacity necessary to his command." Placing as he did the highest value on all three of these qualities — especially the last, which he himself personified — that was about the worst he could say of a man. Accordingly, when Frémont was removed and Curtis was given the task of driving the rebels out of Missouri — which Frémont had considered more or less incidental to the grand design — he went about it differently. He gave it his full attention, and it went well: too well, in fact, or anyhow too easy. Price fell back and the Federals followed through a deserted region, cabins empty though food was still bubbling in pots on ranges, laundry soaking in lukewarm sudsy water, clocks ticking ominously on mantels, and now this: forty booms from across the wintry landscape, signifying for all to hear that an over-all enemy chieftain had arrived. Curtis thought perhaps he had better consolidate to meet developments that threatened stress and strain.

Next day his fears were reinforced, and indeed confirmed, when scouts — including young Wild Bill Hickok, addicted to gaudy shirts and a mustache whose ends could be knotted behind his head — came riding in with reports that the Confederates were marching north in strength. Convinced and alarmed, Curtis sent word for Sigel to exercise his talent by falling back on Sugar Creek, up near the Missouri line, where he himself would be waiting with the other two divisions. There they would combine and, in turn, await the enemy. It was a good defensive position, with a boggy stream across the front and a high ridge to protect the rear, as both men knew from having come through it the week before, in pursuit of Price. Also, if they hurried, there would be time to fortify. Curtis fell back, as planned, and presently received word that Sigel was coming, skirmishing as he came. Near sundown, March 6, he got there with the grayback cavalry close behind him, hacking at his rear. He strode into the commander's tent, a small, quick-gestured, red-haired man in gold-frame spectacles, each lens scarcely bigger around than a quarter, and announced in broken English that he was hungry. He had lost two regiments, pinched off in the chase as had been feared; otherwise he was whole and hearty, eager for more fighting. Just now, though, he was hungry.

Curtis hardly knew what to make of such a man, but he fed him and took him out for an inspection of the lines. Sigel's two divisions were on the right, the other two having side-stepped to make room for them on the two-mile-long shelf of land overlooking the hollow of Sugar Creek. A mile to their rear was the hamlet of Leetown, a dozen cabins clustered around a store and blacksmith shop, which in turn lay about halfway between the line of battle and the sudden rise of Pea Ridge, rearing abruptly against the northern sky like a backdrop for a theatrical production. Outcropped with granite and feathered with trees along its crest, the ridge extended eastward for two miles, then gave down upon a narrow north-south valley. Through this defile ran the Springfield-Fayetteville road, known locally as the wire road because the telegraph had its southern terminus here in a two-story frame building where the telegrapher lived and took in lodgers overnight; Elkhorn Tavern, it was called, acquiring its name from the giant skull and antlers nailed to the rooftree. The tavern lay to the left rear of the position Curtis had chosen, and the road led down past it, through the intrenchments his troops had been digging all that day, and on across the creek to where the rebel army, filing in, was settling down and kindling campfires in the dusk.

They had brought their weather with them. It was snowing, and their fires twinkled in the gathering moonless darkness, more and more of them as more soldiers filed in from the south to extend the line. Down to 10,500 as a result of Sigel's losses, the Federals were outnumbered and they knew it, watching the long, strung-out necklace of enemy campfires growing longer every hour. Still, they felt reasonably secure behind their new-turned mounds of dirt and logs, white-blanketed under the sift of snow falling softly out of the darkness. They built their own fires higher against the cold, then bedded down for a good night's sleep before the dawn which they believed would light the way for an all-out Confederate lunge across the creek and against their works.

March 7 came in bleak and gray, overcast but somewhat warmer. The snow had stopped; the wind had fallen in the night. As Curtis' men turned out of their bedrolls, peering south through the fog that rose out of the hollow, they saw something they had not expected to see. The plain was empty over there. Last night's rebel campfires were cold ashes, and the men who had kindled and fed them were nowhere in sight.

In the past three days the Confederates had marched better than fifty miles, the wind driving wet snow in their faces all the way. Their rations were gone, consumed on the march, and they were tired and hungry. There had to be a battle now, if only for the sake of capturing enemy supplies.

However, Van Dorn had no intention of sending his weary men against breastworks prepared for their reception. Impetuous though he was, that was not his way. Conferring with his generals, who knew the country well, he decided to send half his troops on a night march, clean around the north side of Pea Ridge, then down the road past Elkhorn Tavern for a dawn attack on the Union left rear. Once this was launched, the other half of his army, having made a coincidental, shorter march to the west end of the ridge, would come down through Leetown to strike the enemy right rear, which by then should be in motion to support the hard-pressed left. In short, it was to be a double envelopment much like the one Nathaniel Lyon had attempted at Wilson's Creek, except that this time the attackers would outnumber the defenders, 17,000 men with sixty guns opposing 10,500 with fifty.

Price's Missourians drew the longer march, beyond the screening ridge. McCulloch and Pike, with their Texans, Arkansans, Louisianians, and Indians, would make the secondary attack. Van Dorn himself, still in his ambulance — the three-day ride through wind and snow had not reduced his fever — would go with the roundabout column, to be on hand for the charge that would open the conflict. Soon after dark the army filed off to the left, leaving its long line of campfires burning to deceive the Federals, and moved northward in column beyond the enemy right flank. In this hare-and-tortoise contest — the youthful, impetuous cavalryman Earl Van Dorn against the aging, methodical engineer Sam Curtis — the hare was off and running.

Puzzled by the disappearance of the rebels from across the creek next morning, Curtis was in the worse-than-tortoise position of not even knowing that a race was being run, let alone that the goal was his own rear. Through the early morning hours, while the sun climbed higher up the sky to melt away the fog and fallen snow, he was left wondering where and why Van Dorn had gone. Then suddenly he knew. Just as they had confirmed his fears about the forty-gun salute he had heard on Monday, so now on Friday his scouts came riding in to solve the mystery of the rebels' disappearance. They were behind Pea Ridge, about to enter the north-south valley that gave down upon his unprotected rear. They had been delayed by obstructions along the road, the scouts reported, but they were coming fast now and in strength. Curtis would have to do one of two things. He could wheel about and meet them here, fighting with his back to his own intrenchments, or he could try to make a run for it. In the latter case, the choice lay between possible and probable destruction. If he tried to get away northward, up the wire road through the defile, the Confederate spearhead would be plunged into the flank of his moving column. If on the other hand he ran southward, through enemy country — retreating *forward*, so to speak — Van Dorn would be across his lines of supply and communication; the rebels would have him bottled in a wintry vacuum.

He chose to meet them. His four divisions were in line, facing south: Sigel's two on the right, led by Peter Osterhaus and Alexander Asboth, the former a German, the latter a Hungarian: then his own two, under Eugene Carr, a vigorous, hard-mannered regular, and an Indiana-born colonel with the improbable name of Jefferson Davis. Curtis ordered them to about-face, the rear thus becoming the front, the left the right, the right the left. Carr was sent at once to meet the threat beyond Elkhorn Tavern. Osterhaus moved up past Leetown to protect

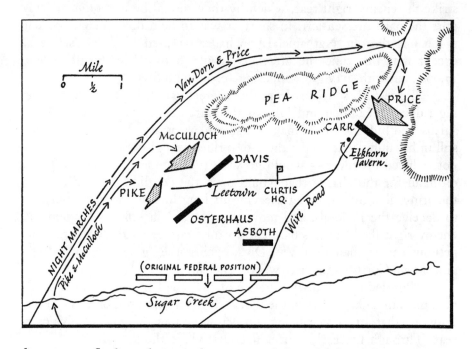

the western flank, and presently on second thought Curtis sent Davis to support him, while Asboth remained under Sigel, in reserve. Curtis had confidence in his commanders. Colonels Osterhaus, Carr, and Davis had had considerable combat experience, the first two at Wilson's Creek and the third from as far back as Fort Sumter, where he had been an artillery lieutenant; Asboth, a brigadier, had been Frémont's chief of staff and a fighter under Kossuth back in Europe. How far beyond the claims of past performance they deserved their leader's confidence was about to be determined. And this was especially true of Carr, who stood where the first blow was about to fall.

At 10.30 it fell, and it fell hard. Tired and hungry after their stumbling all-night march, but keyed up by the order to charge at last, Price's men came crashing through the brush along both sides of the wire road, guns barking aggressively on the flanks and from the rear. Carr had prepared a defense in depth, batteries staggered along the road and a strong line of infantry posted to support the foremost while the other three fired over their heads. Presently, though, they had nothing to support. A well-directed salvo knocked out three of the four guns and blew up two caissons, killing all the cannoneers. Unnerved, the infantry fell back on the second battery, just north of the tavern, where they managed to repulse the first attack, then the second, both of which were piecemeal. Bearded like a Cossack, Carr rode among his soldiers, shouting encouragement. Out front, the brush was boiling with butternut veterans forming for a third assault. This one would come in strength, he knew, and he doubted if his thin line could resist it. He sent a courier galloping back to Curtis with an urgent request for reinforcements.

Curtis had his headquarters on a little knoll just south of a farm road leading from Elkhorn Tavern to Leetown; here the courier found him surrounded by his staff, mounted and resplendent, wearing their best clothes for battle. They were looking toward the left front, their attention drawn by a sudden rattle of musketry and a caterwaul of unearthly, high-pitched yelling. Carr's message had scarcely been delivered when a horseman came riding fast from that direction. Osterhaus had been swamped by a horde of befeathered, screaming men who bore down on him brandishing scalping knives and hatchets. Taken aback — they had bargained for nothing in all the world like this — his troops had broken, abandoning guns and equipment. Davis had moved up; he was holding as best he could, but he needed reinforcements. Appealed to thus by the commanders of both wings at once, Curtis chose to wait before committing his reserve. He sent word for both to hold with what they had. At this point the battle racket swelled to new and separate climaxes, right and left.

In contrast to the gloom that had descended on him — first as a result of his failure to gobble up the scattered Federal units on the march, and then because of the delay of his flanking column as it moved around Pea Ridge in the night, which had thrown him three hours behind schedule and cost him the rich fruits of full surprise — Van Dorn was exultant. Price's men were surging ahead, knocking back whatever stood in their way, and off to the west the rolling crackle of McCulloch's attack told him of success in that quarter as well. The fighting still raged furiously at the near end of the ridge; Carr's second line was thrown back by the all-out third assault, so that presently the Missourians were whooping around the tavern itself and drinking from the horse trough in the yard.

All this took time, however. As the sun slid down the sky, Van Dorn's exultation began to be tempered by concern. His men had had no sleep all night and nothing to eat since the day before, whereas the Federals had had a good night's rest and a hot breakfast. The Confederates still fought grimly, battering now at Carr's third line, drawn south and west of the tavern, but weariness and hunger were sapping their strength; much of the steam had gone out of their attacks. Worse still, there was no longer any sound of serious fighting on the far side of the field, where McCulloch's earlier gains had been announced by the clatter moving south and east to mark his progress. Van Dorn was left wondering until near sundown, when a messenger arrived to explain the silence across the way.

There, as here, the battle had opened on a note of victory. Pike's Indians, delighted at having frightened Osterhaus into hurried retreat, pranced around the cannon the white men had abandoned; "wagon guns," they called them, and took the horse collars from the slaughtered animals to wear about their own necks; "me big Injun, big as horse!" they chanted, dancing so that the trace-chains jingled against the frozen ground. It was a different matter, though, when Pike tried to get them back into line to help McCulloch, who had run into stiffer resistance on the left. They had had enough of that. They wanted to fight from behind rocks or up in trees, not lined up like tenpins, white-man-style, to be struck by the iron bowling balls the wagon guns threw with a terrifying boom and a sudden, choking cloud of smoke. Some stood firm — a dismounted cavalry battalion of mixbloods, for example, under Colonel Stand Watie, a Georgia-born Cherokee — but, in the main, whatever was to be accomplished from now on would have to be done without the help of anything more than a scattering of red men.

Not that McCulloch particularly minded. He was not given to calling on others for help, either back in his Texas Ranger days or now. When his advance was held up by an Illinois outfit which had rallied behind a snake-rail fence at the far end of a field, he brought up an Arkansas regiment, shook out a skirmish line, and took them forward, sunlight glinting on the sharpshooter's rifle he carried for emergencies and sport. The Illinois troops delivered a volley that sent the butternuts scampering back across the field. They re-formed and charged again. Sixty yards short of the tree-lined fence, they came upon a body in sky-blue trousers and a dove-gray corduroy jacket, sprawled in the grass: McCulloch. His rifle was gone, along with a gold pocket watch he had prized, but he still wore the expensive boots he had died in when the bullet found his heart.

Quickly then word spread among the men who had sworn that they would storm hell itself at his command: "McCulloch's dead. They killed McCulloch!" Their reaction to the news was much the same, in effect, as the Indians' reaction to artillery. Whatever they had sworn they would do with McCulloch to lead them, it soon became clear that they would do little without him. To complete the confusion, his successor was killed within the hour, and the third commander was captured while attempting to rally some soldiers who, as it turned out, were Federals. By the time Pike was found and notified — he had been trying vainly, all the while, to reorganize his frightened or jubilant Indians —

the sun was near the landline and there were considerably fewer troops for him to head. Dazed with grief for their lost leader, many had simply wandered off the field, following him in death as they had in life; Osterhaus and Davis, having themselves had enough fighting for one day, had been content to watch them go, unmolested. At sundown Pike assembled what men he could find and set out on a march around the north side of Pea Ridge to join Van Dorn and Price, whose battle still raged near Elkhorn Tavern.

News of his right wing's disintegration reached Van Dorn as one more in a series of disappointments and vexations. Repeated checks and delays, here on the left where Price's men were being held up by less than half their number, had brought him to the verge of desperation. There was another problem, no less grave and quite as vexing. Having left his wagon train on the far side of the battleground, the diminutive commander had discovered an unwelcome military axiom: namely, that when you gain the enemy's rear you also place him in your own, unless you bring it with you. Consequently, in addition to a numbing lack of sleep and food, just as he was doing all he could to launch a final charge that would crush Carr at last and sweep the field before nightfall ended the fighting and gave the Federals a chance to realign their now superior forces, his men were experiencing an ammunition shortage. Desperately he ordered them forward, putting all he had into what he knew would use up the last of daylight, as well as the last of their strength and ammunition. Price was there to help him. Nicked by a bullet, but refusing to retire for medical treatment, he wore his wounded arm in a sling as he rode from point to point to bolster his men's spirits for an all-out climax to the night-long march and day-long battle. At last, between the two of them, they got the Missourians into assault formation and sent them forward, streaming around the tavern and down both sides of the wire road, across which Carr had drawn his third stubborn line of resistance.

The red ball of the sun had come to rest on the horizon; Carr's men could see it over their left shoulders — the direction in which they had been watching all these hours for reinforcements that did not come. Now as before, their batteries were distributed in depth along the road, and now as then the Confederates wrecked them, gun by gun, with a preliminary bombardment. After an ominous lull they saw the rebels coming, yelling and firing as they came, hundreds of them bearing down to complete the wreckage their artillery had begun. As the Federals fell back from their shattered pieces an Iowa cannoneer paused to toss a smoldering quilt across a caisson, then ran hard to catch up with his friends. Still running, he heard a tremendous explosion and looked back in time to see a column of fire and smoke standing tall above the place where he had fuzed the vanished caisson. Stark against the twilight sky, it silhouetted the lazy-seeming rise and fall of blown-off arms and legs and heads and mangled trunks of men who just now had been whooping victoriously around the captured battery position.

Over on his headquarters knoll, Curtis heard and saw it too, and finally — as if that violent column of smoke and flame standing lurid against the twilight on the right, followed after an interval by the boom and rumble as the sound of the explosion echoed off the ridge to the north, had at last brought home to him, like the ultimate shout of despair from a drowning man, at least some measure of the desperation Carr had been trying to communicate ever since Price first struck him, eight hours back — responded. By then the sporadic firing on the left had died away; Osterhaus and Davis reported the rebels gone or going. Van Dorn was tricky, but Curtis felt the danger from that direction had been removed; he could look to the right, where by now the column of fire had turned into a mushrooming pillar of smoke. Asboth, who had remained all this time in reserve to meet disaster in either direction, was sent up the wire road in relief of Carr.

Arriving at 7 he found the firing reduced to a sputter here as well. Torn and weary, Carr's regiments moved back from their fourth position of the day, retiring through the ranks of the division that relieved them. Forward of there, extending right and left of the tavern, half a mile each way, the Confederates were bedding down for the rest they sorely needed, their campfires in the tavern yard illuminating the building up to the bleached skull and antlers on the rooftree. The long day's fight was over.

Curtis rode out for a night inspection of his lines, which at some points were so near the enemy's that the opposing soldiers could overhear each other's groans and laughter. Despite their bone-deep weariness, the men were still too keyed up for sleep. They amused themselves by taunting the rebs across the way, hooting at the replies provoked, and recounting, for mutual admiration, exploits they had performed on the field today. Several could even substantiate their claims. One, for example — an Illinois private, Peter Pelican by name — displayed a gold watch he had taken as a trophy off a rebel he had shot: an officer, he said, in "sky-blue britches" and a dove-colored jacket. Some other quick-thinking scavenger had got the Maynard rifle, much to Pelican's regret, and the Johnnies had come swarming back too soon for him to have time to strip the dead man of his fancy boots.

The Federal commander might have heard this as he made the rounds, along with much else like it; but the truth was, he took little pleasure in small talk, and especially not now. He had too much on his mind. For one thing, he was irked at Sigel, who he considered had undertaken considerably less than his share of the work today, sparing Osterhaus and Asboth while Davis and Carr were doing most of the bleeding. Consequently, when he discovered that the German planned a temporary withdrawal to feed his troops, his temper snapped. "Let Sigel's men hold their lines. Send supper out, not the men in," he said gruffly. And having thus relieved his spleen he returned to his headquarters tent. It was time to decide what to do about tomorrow. Still fully dressed, he lay down on some blankets spread on a pile of straw and sent for his division commanders to join him for a council of war.

It was midnight when they assembled. Sigel spoke first, and he spoke from desperation, proposing his specialty: slashing retreat. The army, he said, must select an escape route and cut its way out in the morning. Osterhaus agreed, and so did Carr, whose command had been fought to a frazzle. He was nursing a wound, as was Asboth, who had been winged by a stray bullet in the dark and also saw no answer but retreat. Davis was silent, but that was his manner — a gloomy man with a long nose and lonesome-looking eyes. Reclined on the blanketed pile of straw, Curtis weighed their counsel. No less deliberate in conference than he had been in combat, he was not going to be stampeded by his own commanders, any more than he had been stampeded by Van Dorn. In his opinion the Confederates had most likely shot their bolt. The threat to his left having been abolished, he could reinforce his right. Thus bolstered, the army could hold its own, he believed, and even perhaps go forward. On this note the council adjourned, and its members, their advice declined, went out into the darkness to consolidate their commands and await the dawn.

The night was cold and windless, so that when dawn came through at last, smoke from yesterday's battle still hung in long folds and tendrils about the fields, draping the hillsides and filling the hollows level-full. The sun rose red, then shone wanly through the haze, like tarnished brass; Van Dorn's dispositions were at once apparent across the way. South and west of Elkhorn Tavern, between the Federals and the sunrise, Price's Missourians held the ground they had won when nightfall closed the fighting. Pike having arrived in the night with his and McCulloch's remnants, the Confederate commander had stationed the Indians along the crest of Pea Ridge, supporting several batteries — stark up there against the sky they looked like stick-men guarding toy guns — while the Texans and Arkansans occupied the fields along its base.

It was a long, concave line, obviously drawn with defense in mind: Curtis had been right. Also right, as it turned out, were the dispositions he had made to meet what dawn revealed. Davis was posted opposite the tavern, with Carr's division in support, still binding up its wounds. The left belonged to Sigel, who had strung out Osterhaus and Asboth to overlap the enemy in the shadow of the ridge. After a drawn-out silence, during which the Unionists enjoyed a hot breakfast and the rebels ate what they could find in the knapsacks of the fallen, Van Dorn opened with his batteries, stirring the smoke that wreathed the Federal line.

The cannonade was perfunctory and had no real aggressive drive behind it. Low as he was on ammunition — his unprotected train had gone off southward, fearing capture — Van Dorn fired his guns, not as a prelude to attack, nor even to signify his readiness to receive one, but merely to see what the Yankees would do. In fact, that was why he had remained in position overnight. It had seemed wrong to retreat after the gains he had made, and for all he knew the dawn might show the Federals gone or ready to surrender. Dawn had shown no such thing. It showed them, rather, in what seemed greater strength than ever: a long, compact line, with batteries glinting dangerously through the coppery haze. Hungry, weary, down to their last rounds of ammunition, Van Dorn's men had done their worst and he knew it. Yet, for all he knew, after yesterday's hard knocks Curtis too might be reduced to his last ounce of powder and resistance, needing no more than a prod to send him scampering. At any rate the Mississippian thought it worth a try.

It soon became apparent that the Federals could take a good deal more prodding than the Southerners could exert. Sensing the weakness behind the cannonade, Curtis sent word to Sigel on the left. Yesterday the German had held back: now let him seize the initiative and go forward if he could. Sigel could and did. With a precision befitting a mathematician, he ordered his infantry to lie down in the muddy fields while he advanced his batteries 250 yards out front and opened fire. He rode among the roaring guns, erect as on parade except when he dismounted to sight an occasional piece himself, then patted the breech and stepped back, as if for applause, to observe the effects of his gunnery. It was accurate. Battery after Confederate battery was shattered along the ridge and on the flat, and when others came up to take their places, they were shattered, too. Sigel's soldiers, many of them German like himself, cheered him wildly as they watched the rebel cannoneers fan backward from the wreckage of their guns. Over on the right, the men of Carr and Davis, watching too, began to understand the pride that lay behind the boast: "I fights mit Sigel."

Van Dorn's artillerymen were not the only ones disconcerted by the deadliness of the Yankee gunnery. His infantry showed signs of wavering, too. Sigel rode back to where his cheering soldiers lay obedient in the mud. Gesturing with his saber, he ordered them to stand up and go forward. They did so, still cheering, in a long, undulating line, like a huge snake moving sideways, the head coiling over the lower slope of the ridge, the center thrusting forward with a lunging, sidewinder motion, the tail following in turn. On it moved, with a series of curious sidewise thrusts, preceded by a scattering of graybacks as it slithered over whatever stood in its broad path. The reserve Union regiments, waiting in ranks, tossed their hats and contorted their faces with screams of pride and pleasure at the sight. Exhilarated, Sigel stood in his stirrups, saber lifted, eyes aglow. "Oh — dot was lofely!" he exclaimed.

Over near the tavern, watching the great snake glide sideways up the ridge, the men with Davis began shouting for a charge on this front too, lest Sigel's troops get all the loot and glory. Curtis was with them. Indeed, he was everywhere this morning; already two of his orderlies had been killed riding with him as he galloped amid shellbursts to inspect his line and strengthen weak spots. All the same, active as he was, he had not put aside his meticulous insistence on precision. Sending for reinforcements, he remained to check their prompt arrival by the second hand on his watch, then was off again through the smoke and whistling fragments of exploding shells. When the men in front of the tavern began yelling for a chance to match the tableau Sigel was staging on the left, Curtis nodded quick assent and rode forward onto a low knoll — he had a fondness for such little elevations, in battle or bivouac — to watch as they advanced.

Close-ranked and determined, they surged past him, cheering. Abruptly then, beyond their charging front, he saw the Confederates give way, retreating before contact, and heard his soldiers whooping as they swarmed around and past Elkhorn Tavern, where the telegrapher's family huddled in the cellar and rebel dead were stacked like cordwood on the porch. The Union right and left wings came together with a shout, driving the gray confusion of scampering men, careening guns, and wild-eyed horses pell-mell up the wire road through the defile, past the position Carr's men had abandoned under pressure from the opening guns, twenty-four hours back.

As quickly as that, almost too sudden for realization, the battle was over — won. Curtis rode down off the knoll, then cantered back and forth along his lines. His aging engineer's brown eyes were shining; all his former stiff restraint was gone. Boyishly he swung his hat and shouted, performing a little horseback dance of triumph as he rode up and down the lines of cheering men. "Victory!" he cried. He kept swinging his hat and shouting. "Victory! Victory!" he cried.

Thus Curtis. But Van Dorn was somewhat in the predicament of having prodded a shot bear, thinking it dead, only to have the creature rear up and come charging at him, snarling. Consequently, his main and in fact his exclusive concern, in the face of this sudden show of teeth and claws, was how to get away unmangled. Horrendous as it was, however, the problem was not with him long. His soldiers solved it for him. Emerging from the north end of the defile, they scattered in every direction except due south, where the prodded bear still roared. All through what was left of the day and into the night (while, a thousand miles to the east, the *Merrimac-Virginia* steamed back from her first sortie, leaving the burning *Congress* to light the scene of wreckage

she had left in Hampton Roads) various fragments of his army retreated north and east and west, swinging wide to avoid their late opponents when they turned back south to reach the Boston Mountains.
Though unpursued, they took a week to reassemble near Van Buren.

Back at his starting point in the foothills of the Ozarks, Van
Dorn counted noses and reported his losses as 1000 killed and wounded,
300 captured. He was by no means willing to admit that the battle had
been anything more than a temporary setback. Least of all could it be
considered a defeat; "I was not defeated, but only foiled in my intentions," he told Richmond. Still with his main goal in mind, he was ready
to try again, this time by marching "boldly and rapidly toward St
Louis, between Ironton and the enemy's grand depot at Rolla."

Within another week, March 23, he was heading north with
16,000 effectives when he received a peremptory order to turn east,
crossing the river by "the best and most expeditious route," and join
the concentration being effected in North Mississippi by Johnston and
Beauregard after their long retreat from Kentucky. "Your order received," Van Dorn replied, pleased no doubt at the prospect of exchanging the wilds of Arkansas for the comparative comforts of his native
state.

Unlike his opponent, who was as dashing, or as slapdash, on a
retreat as in an advance, Curtis had not been satisfied to report his casualties in round figures. That would have been neither respectful to the
dead nor indicative of sound administration. Consolidating subordinate
reports, which showed that Carr's division had suffered more than
the other three combined, he prepared a careful table — killed, 203;
wounded, 980; captured or otherwise missing, 201; total, 1384 — and
forwarded it to Halleck, declaring that he had "completely routed the
whole rebel force, which retired in great confusion, but rather safely,
through the deep, impassable defiles."

He did not speculate, as others would surely have done in his
place — especially Van Dorn — on what the future might reveal as to
the importance of the victory he had won at Elkhorn Tavern, in the
shadow of Pea Ridge. That was not his way. Besides, he had no means
of knowing that Van Dorn would be called east, beyond the Mississippi,
and would not be coming back. He did not claim, as in truth he could
have done, that he had secured Missouri to the Union for all time; that
guerilla bands might rip and tear her, that raider columns of various
strengths might cut swaths of destruction up and down her, but that her
star in the Confederate flag, placed there like Kentucky's by a fleeing
secessionist legislature, represented nothing more from now on than the
exiles who bore arms beneath that banner.

Though he did not deal in military imponderables, other imponderables were another matter: those of nature, for example. Spring

had come to upland Arkansas at last, and it put him in mind of the ones he had known in his Ohio boyhood. The day after the battle a warm rain fell, washing away the bloodstains, but as the burial squads went about their work the air was tainted with decay. Curtis moved his headquarters off a ways, once more to enjoy the singing birds as he sat at a camp table, writing home. "Silent and sad" were words he used to describe the present scene of recent conflict. "The vulture and the wolf have now communion, and the dead, friends and foes, sleep in the same lonely grave." So he wrote, this highly practical and methodical engineer. Looking up at the tree-fledged ridge with its gray outcroppings of granite, he added that he hoped it would serve hereafter as a monument to perpetuate the memory of those who had fallen at its base.

★ ★ ★

South and west of Pea Ridge lay Texas, where Van Dorn had first shown dash and won success. North and west of Texas — twice the size of that vast Lone Star expanse — the Territories of Utah and New Mexico stretched on beyond the sunset to the California gold fields and the shores of the Pacific. In the minds of most, this sun-baked half-million-square-mile wasteland with its brackish lakes and its few, thirsty rivers was of less than doubtful value, fit only as a breeding ground of lizards and Apaches. Others knew better: Jefferson Davis, for one. Believing in his Union days that the nation's destiny pointed south and west, he had engineered the Gadsden Purchase and even imported camels in an attempt to solve the sandy transportation problem.

Now in his Confederate days, the nebulous future being translated into terms of the urgent present, his belief was reinforced. Out there beyond the sunset lay the gold fields and the ocean. Control of the former would establish sound financial credit on which the South could draw for securing war supplies abroad, while the opening of Confederate ports along the Pacific Coast would insure their delivery by stretching the tenuous Federal blockade past the snapping point. Satisfying as all this was as a solution to present problems, an even more dazzling prospect still remained. Having forged its independence in the crucible of war, the new nation could then return to the old southern nationalist dream of expansion, acquiring by purchase or conquest the adjoining Mexican states of Chihuahua, Sonora, and Baja California. After these would come others, less near but no less valuable: Cuba, for instance, then Central America, and all that lay between. Van Dorn seizing St Louis as a base for a march through Illinois to subdue the Middle West, Beauregard dictating peace terms in the White House after the Battle of Cleveland or Lake Erie — glorious as these scenes were to contemplate in the mind's eye, they were pale indeed in contrast to the glittering light of victory by way of California.

None of this could be accomplished, however, until safe passage west had been assured at the start by clearing Federal troops from the Territory of New Mexico. The answer to this, as Davis knew, lay in control of the Rio Grande. It was therefore with considerable pleasure, two months after Sumter, that he welcomed to Richmond a forty-four-year-old Louisiana-born West Pointer, Henry H. Sibley, lately Major, U.S. Army. Indeed, from Davis' point of view the caller might have tumbled straight out of heaven into the arms of the Confederacy. He had come to offer his services — preferably for duty in the region where he had been stationed for years, commanding various forts throughout the Southwest and along the Rio Grande. An enterprising officer, he had invented a conical tent modeled after the wigwams of the Sioux, and he had kept busy in other ways out there. What was more, he had a plan. And as he told it — a stocky, wind-burnt man with a big-featured face and a heavy mustache that grew down past the corners of his mouth so that his aggressive chin looked naked as a heel — Davis might have been listening to the echo of his own thoughts on the dazzling possibilities of victory by way of California. Granted the authority, Sibley said, he would raise a force in Texas and set out northward from El Paso, capturing forts along the river all the way to Santa Fe. This done, he would consolidate and turn west, his ranks swollen with volunteers whose watchword would be "On to San Francisco."

Davis liked the sound of it and was more than willing to grant him the authority he asked. Unfortunately, however, that was all he had to offer. The government could spare no arms or munitions; in fact it could spare no equipment at all. The ex-major would have to scrape together what he could find in Texas on his own, then make up the balance out of enemy stores from the forts he took as he marched upriver. No matter how fruitful the project promised to be, it would have to be self-sustaining: Davis made that quite clear at the outset, before granting the authority.

In early July, two weeks before Manassas, Sibley was made a brigadier and assigned to command the Department of New Mexico. Like much of his equipment, the department itself was still in Union hands; but that would be corrected, too, when he had accomplished the first stage of the plan he had outlined in the President's office. Davis wished him Godspeed, and Sibley returned at once to Texas, where he recruited a brigade of three mounted regiments by the end of the year and set out for El Paso, the jump-off point for his campaign to control the Rio Grande.

Two men, David E. Twiggs and John R. Baylor, had accomplished much for him already, before and since his trip to Richmond. Twiggs, a Federal brigadier in command of the Texas Department during the secession furor, had repeatedly asked Washington for instructions through that stormy time. Receiving none, he acted in accordance with a statement he had made: "If an old woman with a broomstick should come with full authority from the state of Texas to demand the public property, I would give it to her." He did just that, surrendering all the troops, forts, and equipment in his charge, not to an old woman, but to a posse of citizens who styled themselves a "committee for public safety." Northern howls of "treason to the flag" went up, and Twiggs, being summarily dismissed from the U.S. army, repaired forthwith to New Orleans, where he was solaced and rewarded with a commission as a Confederate major general.

In time, a portion of this surrendered equipment was inherited by Sibley, who needed it badly. Meanwhile Baylor, his other helper, had kept as busy as the first. Issuing a blanket invitation to whoever would join him on what he announced as a 1000-man "buffalo hunt" in Old Mexico, he showed his commission as a Confederate lieutenant colonel to the 350 volunteers who turned up, swore them in, organized them into a regiment called the Texas Mounted Rifles, and marched them to El Paso in time to receive the surrender of Fort Bliss, across the river from the Mexican hamlet.

Upstream the Rio Grande was divided like the nation, north and south, and Baylor saw in this a chance to accomplish a great deal more. For some time now there had been a movement among New Mexicans to split the territory along the 34th parallel and detach the southern portion as Arizona. Since in general the people of this lower region favored the Confederacy, he decided to go up there and help them, adding thereby a future new state to his new nation. There was one problem. Forty miles upriver from El Paso, just this side of the village of Mesilla, Fort Fillmore blocked the way, its garrison of 700 U.S. regulars commanded by Major Isaac Lynde, a veteran of thirty-four years in the infantry. Undeterred at being thus outnumbered two to one, Baylor spent no time musing on the odds. In mid-July — while Sibley was on the final leg of his round-trip journey to Richmond — the Texan led his Mounted Rifles north.

On the night of the 24th, though the Federals had been warned that he was coming, he camped unmolested within 600 yards of the fort on the opposite bank of the river, then next morning splashed across and occupied Mesilla. When Lynde at last marched out to challenge the invaders, the townspeople, who had greeted Baylor with vivas and hurrahs, climbed a nearby hill to watch the contest. After demanding an immediate surrender, and receiving an immediate refusal, the graybearded major sent one squadron forward in a tentative, head-on charge that was repulsed with four men killed and seven wounded. As a battle it wasn't much; but it was quite enough for Lynde. Abandoning any notion of holding the fort, he fired a few short-falling rounds in the direction of the hill where the ungrateful — and unarmed — men, women, and children were cheering the secessionists, then ordered a retreat northeast to Fort Stanton, 150 sandy miles beyond the Organ Mountains.

Next day, displaying what one of his officers called "a sublimity of majestic indifference," he was taking lunch at San Augustín Springs when he discovered that the empty fort had been no more than a tub to Baylor's whale. The Texan wanted the soldiers, too, and was there at hand, demanding their surrender or a fight. Lynde decided the former would be best. After paroling the 492 officers and men taken here — the other 200-odd had already been picked up as stragglers — Baylor returned to Mesilla and on August 1 issued a proclamation establishing the Confederate Territory of Arizona, with the 34th parallel as its northern boundary and himself as its military governor. Richmond quickly sustained his action, and Congress welcomed the delegate who soon arrived to represent the new far-western territory.

Such, then, was the situation Sibley found awaiting him when he reached Fort Bliss in mid-December with his newly recruited brigade. Between them, in their different ways, Twiggs and Baylor had accomplished much of his project for him already, supplying his men with surrendered equipment and clearing the Rio Grande well beyond the Texas border. Fort Stanton's garrison had withdrawn to Albuquerque, while the Unionists at Fort Thorn, fifty miles above Mesilla, had retreated eighty miles upriver to Fort Craig, which now remained the only prepared defensive position in Federal hands below the boundary parallel. Once it fell, the others to the north should fall like toppled blocks: Albuquerque, Santa Fe, and Fort Union, eastward beyond the foothills of the Sangre de Cristo mountains. At Fort Craig, he knew, 4000 troops were preparing to move against him, with perhaps as many more in support beyond the parallel. He himself had 3700, including Baylor's.

Yet he was no more discouraged by these odds than Baylor had been by longer ones. Three days after New Year's he marched northward, four regiments in a long, mounted column, and within the week he occupied Fort Thorn. The rest of the month was spent developing the situation. Then on February 7 he set out for Fort Craig, where the Federals were massing. His purpose was offensive; he did not intend to surrender the initiative. On the 19th, after a series of probing actions by his scouts, the main body came up and made camp on an open plain across the river from the fort on the west bank. The stage was set for the first major clash to determine who would control the Rio Grande.

That night, when the wind was from the east, Confederate voices could be heard across the water by the troops inside the fort. Colonel Edward R. S. Canby was in command, not only of the fort but also of the whole department, and this was only the latest of his trials since the advent of secession. He had taken over by appointment upon the departure into enemy ranks of the previous commander, W. W. Loring, the one professional in the quartet of prima donnas who brought grief to R. E. Lee in West Virginia. Indiana-born, tall, clean-shaven and soldierly-looking, with mild manners and a big nose that dominated his otherwise sur-prisingly delicate features, Canby was a year younger than Sibley and had finished at West Point a year behind him. Thrust into command at the outbreak of hostilities, he had about 1000 territorial militia, poorly armed and even more poorly trained, to supplement the scattering of peacetime regulars stationed at the vari-ous posts and forts in his de-partment. Supplies were as scarce as distances were vast. Consequently, while Baylor took Fort Bliss and then Fort Fillmore, Canby could do nothing but work with what he had in an attempt to strengthen his defenses, mean-while sending out repeated calls for volunteers. All this time, Sibley was raising soldiers down in Texas: for what pur-

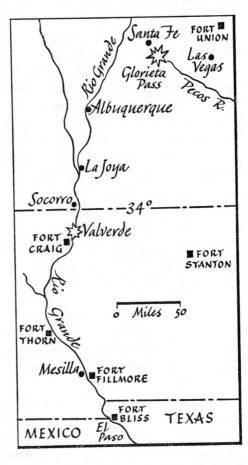

pose his opponent knew all too well for his mind's ease. By the end of the year Canby had five regiments, recruited by prominent New Mexicans — Kit Carson was one — and sent them out to bolster such remaining scattered strongpoints as had not been abandoned or sur-rendered during the build-up.

All through January he continued his preparations to move southward from Fort Craig. Perhaps he might even have done so, in time, if Sibley had not spared him the risk and trouble by moving north against him, arriving February 19 and making camp within earshot of the fort on the opposite bank of the Rio Grande. In expectation of a siege, Canby spent the night making his strong position even stronger, preparing to repulse the attack which he believed would come at dawn. It did not come. Instead, as the light grew, he looked across the river and saw, between him and the rising sun, enemy wagons rolling

north: Sibley was bypassing the fort, leaving it — and the Federals inside it — to wither on the vine, while he moved northward into the
unprotected region on beyond the parallel, the region whose protection
was Canby's primary assignment. What he had seen, out there between
him and the rising sun, left the Union commander no choice. He himself would have to attack, to fight without the defensive advantage of
the adobe walls he had been strengthening all this time. Accordingly, he
sent a regiment up the western bank, under orders to cross the river
five miles upstream and charge the rebels, who he believed were
moving north across the mesa of Valverde in march column.

In this he was mistaken. Sibley had not intended to go north
without at least an attempt to cripple any enemy force he left behind.
He was maneuvering for a crossing and an assault against the fort. But
now that Canby had obliged him by coming out for a fight in the open,
Sibley was appreciative and ready. Crashing through the rust-colored
reeds on the eastern bank, then charging up the slope onto the mesa,
the Federals found the Texans waiting with double-shotted guns. Cannon and rifle fire broke up the attack in short order, the blue troopers
scattering for what little cover they could find. They clung there,
under sniper fire through what was left of daylight, and withdrew after
dark to report to their commander that the rebels were still there:
very much so, in fact. The two-day Battle of Valverde was half over.

For Canby, that first day had begun in error and ended in repulse. Now at least, as dawn of the second came glimmering through,
there would be no error in estimating the enemy situation. Sibley was
there, outnumbered, and he would attack him. He sent three more regiments up to join the first, with orders to force the crossing in strength
and whip the rebels, still drawn up on the mesa within musket range
of the river. He had not wanted this kind of fighting; these 4000 men
were all he had to protect the whole Southwest. But now that it could
no longer be avoided, he was determined to make the work as short
and decisive as possible, no matter how bloody.

It was far from short work, but it turned out bloody enough.
After losing a good many men at the crossing — they came under a
galling fire and the bodies of men and horses floated slowly downstream, bumping along in the shallow water — they managed to get
their guns across and with them knock the enemy back into the sandy
ridges at the far edge of the mesa. From there, the Texans tried cavalry
charges against the flanks and dismounted charges against the center,
the sand-polished rowels of their spurs as big and bright as silver
dollars. Past midday the charges continued; all were repulsed. Then at
2.45 Canby himself came up from the fort, bringing the remaining
regiment. He assumed command just as Colonel Tom Green, on the
other side, took over from Sibley, who had become indisposed — from
the heat, some said, while others said from whiskey. Whichever it was,

it was a Confederate advantage: Green was an all-out fighter. He put
his cavalry out front, massing behind them all the dismounted men
he could lay hands on, and sent them charging all together against a
six-gun battery at the north end of the Federal line. For eight minutes,
one participant said, the fighting was "terrific beyond description." By
then Green's men were among the guns; the battery officers and cannoneers were dead. When the Texans turned the captured pieces against
the line they had so lately been a part of, it broke badly, one Confederate declaring that the Northerners, in their haste to reach the west
bank of the river, became "more like a herd of frightened mustangs than
men." Once again there was slaughter at the crossing and more bodies
floating sluggishly downstream in the blood-stained water.

Green was reassembling his elated troopers, preparing to use
what was left of the short hot winter day to butcher or capture what
was left of the rattled Federal army before it could reach the fort five
miles downstream. He got his men together and was about to charge
the enemy drawn up shakily on the opposite bank, when a truce party
came forward under a white flag: Canby requested an armistice, time
to care for the wounded and bury the dead. His chivalry thus appealed
to, Green agreed to the cease fire, and while the defeated New Mexicans
retreated under its protection to the adobe fastness of Fort Craig the
victorious Texans rifled the knapsacks of the fallen, bolting "Yankee
light-bread and other most delicious eatables," washed down with
whiskey found in the canteens of the Union dead. Darkness fell; the
battle was over. The men poured the sand from their boots and took
their rest.

Recovered from his indisposition next morning, Sibley found
that Green had left it to him to decide whether to go after the survivors
in the fort, bagging the lot, or turn his back on them and continue the
march northward. Federal casualties had been 263, Confederate 187, but
the victory had been even more decisive as to proof of who would fight
and who would panic under pressure. The opening phase of the campaign to seize the Southwest as a base for operations farther west had
been accomplished; ahead lay the chief cities of the region, Albuquerque
and Santa Fe. As Sibley saw it, such poor soldiers as Canby's were not
worth the time that would be spent in completing their destruction. He
gave his Texans a full day's rest as a reward for their exertions, then
pressed on north without delay.

Within a week, having paused to establish a hospital for his
wounded at Socorro, just beyond the boundary parallel, he had covered the hundred-odd miles to Albuquerque. He had good reason for
haste. This was desert country, where loss of a canteen or a last handful of crackers could be as fatal as a bullet through the heart, and he had
left Valverde with only five days' rations in his train. Fortunately, he
had encountered no enemy soldiers on the way; apparently they had

heard what had happened to their friends the week before and were falling back from contact. Then, as he came within sight of Albuquerque, he saw something that affected him worse than if he had seen a whole new Federal army drawn up for battle on the outskirts. Three great columns of smoke stood tall and black above the town. Anticipating his arrival, and his hunger, the Union garrison had set fire to their rich depot of supplies when they fell back on Santa Fe that morning.

He moved in unopposed and took the place, scraping together what few provisions he could buy or commandeer in order to continue the movement north. Four days later, March 5, he occupied the capital. Here too he was unopposed; the garrison pulled out on the eve of his arrival. All Sibley and his Texans got of the Santa Fe depot was its ashes.

The burnings had been done under orders from Canby. When he fell back on Fort Craig under cover of the flag of truce on the night of his defeat, he sent couriers to the northward posts with instructions that all public properties, "and particularly provisions," were to be destroyed as soon as the invaders seemed about to come within reach. He knew this country and what it could do to an army without supplies. Having tried stand-up fighting at Valverde, and having lost, he adopted now a "scorched earth" policy, one not difficult to apply in a region where the earth was already scorched enough to burn the sole off a boot in a morning's walk.

Sibley's men were already feeling the pinch. Nor were the discomforts of short rations, threadbare clothes, and sand-leaking boots relieved by any considerable sympathy from the people of Albuquerque or Santa Fe. Expecting cheers and volunteers at the end of their long victory march, the Texans instead had found the atmosphere definitely unfriendly ever since they crossed the parallel. The southern commander's prediction that troops of sympathizers would come marching in to join him, miners and trappers from Utah Territory and beyond, had by no means been fulfilled; in fact, there were rumors that groups there were organizing to join the other side. Sibley was finding that all he won with victory was miles and miles of sand. Still, he had done nearly all of what he set out to do in preparing a base for the conquest of the Far West. Those miles and miles included the Rio Grande and the territorial capital. Except for the stunned remnant of Canby's army, still cowering inside the adobe protection of Fort Craig, all that remained was Fort Union, sixty miles east of Santa Fe, beyond the foothills of the Sangre de Cristo Mountains, so called because their slopes were the color of blood each day at sunset.

Fort Union had been the rallying point for all the garrisons Sibley had flushed from their accustomed posts. By now, he knew, it was held in strength, and he figured he would have to fight to take it.

Preparing to do so, he advanced a picket of 600 men from Santa Fe twenty miles southeast to the mouth of Apache Canyon, which led on to Las Vegas, the new capital, and Fort Union. They were to hold the canyon mouth, preventing any Federal advance, while the rest of the Confederates were being assembled to join them; then they would all go forward together to wipe out the final enemy stronghold. Preparations continued through most of March. Then, on the 26th, the picket got word that a small force — "200 [New] Mexicans and about 200 regulars" — was coming through the canyon for an attack on Santa Fe. It sounded too good to be true, but the Texans were not missing any chance to give the Yankees another drubbing. They mounted up and rode forward, taking two guns along for good measure.

Four miles up the canyon they caught sight of what they had been told to expect: a column of 400 Union troopers riding foolhardily within gun range of a body of seasoned Confederates who had them outnumbered three-to-two. There in the rocky trough of the pass the Texans formed their line for slaughter. Slaughter it was, but not as had been intended. Suddenly, one wrote his wife, Federal infantry "were upon the hills on both sides of us, shooting us down like sheep." They had been sucked into an ambush. As they fell back, startled, they could see up on the overhead ledges enemy sharpshooters "jumping from rock to rock like so many mountain sheep." Losing men at every attempt to take up a new position, they were near panic, not only because of the bullets, but also from sheer astonishment. New Mexicans — "Mexicans," they called them, with all the contempt a Texan could put into the word — had never fought like this. Then they discovered something else, which startled them even more. "Instead of Mexicans and regulars, they were regular demons . . . in the form of Pike's Peakers, from the Denver City gold mines."

That was what they were, all right, recruits from frontier mining towns; 1st Colorado, they called themselves, 1342 volunteers, with one battery of field guns and another of mountain howitzers. They had made a long cold wet march to reach Fort Union on the same day Sibley pulled into Santa Fe at the end of his long hot dry one. After two weeks of sandy drill in the vicinity of the fort, they felt ready and came looking for a fight. Now they had it, here in Apache Canyon. The Texans had finally rallied and were making a last-ditch stand near the mouth of the canyon. Drawn up in a strong position behind the moat of a dry streambed, they felt ready at last for whatever came. What came was the Federal cavalry. Released from decoy duty, they came riding fast, leaped the arroyo, and landed among the defenders, hacking and shooting. The Texans broke and fled, all but 71 who surrendered, bringing their casualties to 146 in all. The Coloradans had lost a total of 19.

While the Federals withdrew to meet reinforcements from Fort

Union, the Confederate survivors sent out news of the disaster, which brought two regiments hurrying next day to their support. By dawn of the third day, March 28, the main bodies of both armies were moving through the canyon from opposite directions. An hour before noon they met at Glorieta Pass: "a terrible place for an engagement," a northern lieutenant afterward remembered, "a deep gorge, with a narrow wagon-track running along the bottom, the ground rising precipitously on each side, with huge bowlders and clumps of stunted cedars interspersed." Maneuver was impossible. All the two forces could do was scramble for cover and start banging away, the tearing rattle of pistol and rifle fire punctuated cacophonously by the deeper booms of cannon. Neither could advance, yet both knew that to fall back would be even more fatal than to stay there. For five hours the fighting continued in a boiling cloud of rock dust. Then an armistice was called to permit care for the wounded and burial of the dead.

The Texas commander had proposed it, and during the lull he received word of a calamity in his rear. A party of 300 Coloradans, led by a former preacher, had circled around behind the hills and come down upon the Confederate supply train, capturing the guard, burning the 85 provision-laden wagons, and bayoneting the nearly 600 horses and mules. In addition to Yankees, the Texans now would be fighting thirst and starvation. Against those odds they pulled back under cover of the truce and got away, out of the canyon and up the road to Santa Fe. The Federals, who had inflicted 123 casualties at a cost of 86, were all for going after them, up to the gates of the capital itself. But word had come from Canby at Fort Craig. He feared an attack on Fort Union by some roundabout route, perhaps across the eastern plains from the Texas panhandle. They were to hold that final stronghold "at all hazards, and to leave nothing to chance." Grudgingly the Coloradans obeyed, retracing their steps back through the canyon where they had fought and won two battles.

Four days later, April 1 — the day McClellan took ship at Alexandria for his overnight voyage to the Peninsula — Canby left Fort Craig at last, marching north on Sibley's five-weeks-old trail. He was a brigadier general now, promoted as of the day before. On the 8th he arrived before Albuquerque. Sibley was ready for him, having been there all the while with half his army. The two exchanged artillery salvos, and Canby retired beyond the nearby Sandía Mountains, calling for the Fort Union garrison to come out and reinforce him. Sibley likewise sent word for the Glorieta survivors, licking their wounds in Santa Fe, to join him there on the banks of the Rio Grande. Both armies thus were concentrating within one day's march of each other. The great winner-take-all battle of the Southwest, to which all that had gone before would have served as prologue, seemed about to be fought near Albuquerque.

It was never fought, either there or elsewhere, and for several reasons — mostly Sibley's. The countryside was too poor to support an invading army without the help of the people living there or supply lines leading back to greener regions, and he had neither. Rather, the inhabitants were unexpectedly hostile, more inclined to cache their scant provisions than to exchange them for Confederate money, which they considered worthless. Sibley's artillery ammunition was nearly exhausted and his wagon train had been destroyed. The recruits he expected had not appeared, or if they had — the Pike's Peakers, for example — they came against him wearing blue, so that the numerical odds were even longer now than they had been at the outset. Perceiving all this, he saw his dream dissolve in the encroaching gloom. There was but one thing left for him to do with his ragged, ill-fed, weary army: get it out of there and back to Texas. He was by no means certain that he could manage this, however, depending as it did on whether he would have the coöperation of his opponent.

He got it in full. Canby, having fought once at Valverde, wanted no more fighting he could possibly avoid. Sibley began his retreat on April 12, crossing the river with his main body to make camp that night, twenty miles south, on the west bank at Los Lunas. Next day, having stayed behind to bury their brass field pieces, for which they had neither shells nor powder, the remainder followed down the east bank to Peralta, nearly opposite. Canby marched in pursuit, his reinforcements having arrived that day from Fort Union. He was not trying to cut the rebels off and then destroy them. The last thing he wanted, in fact, was for them to turn and fight or even stop to catch their breath. What he wanted was for them to leave, the sooner the better; he wanted them out of the territory for whose protection he was responsible. At Peralta, coming upon the smaller Confederate segment, he gave it a nudge. "As we galloped across the bottom toward them they fluttered like birds in a snare," a Coloradan wrote. But that was all. When they scurried across the river, then turned south with the main body to continue the retreat, Canby turned south, too, but he remained on the eastern bank. For two days the retreat continued in this fashion, the two armies marching in plain view of each other, often within cannon range, on opposite banks of the fordable Rio Grande. Canby's men were outraged, shouting for him to send them across the river to slaughter the tatterdemalions who had been so arrogant two months before, when they were headed in the opposite direction. The northern commander was deaf alike to protests and appeals, however passionate. If there was to be any killing done, he would rather let the desert do it for him.

Beginning with the third day, the desert got its chance. When the Federals woke to reveille that morning near La Joya, they could see campfires burning brightly across the river. Dawn showed no signs of life in the camp, however, and after waiting a long while for the

Texans to begin their march Canby sent some scouts across, who returned with news that the camp was abandoned; the rebels had left in
the night. Sibley, it appeared, had wanted a battle even less than Canby
did. Approaching Socorro, with Fort Craig only a day's march beyond,
he had left under cover of darkness in an attempt to shake his pursuers
and swung westward on a hundred-mile detour to avoid a clash with whatever troops the fort's commander might have left to garrison it. Canby
did not pursue. He knew the country Sibley was taking his men through,
out there beyond the narrow valley benches. It was all desert, and he
was having no part of it. He marched his troopers leisurely on to the
safety and comfort of Fort Craig, arriving April 22. By that time Sibley's Texans were at the midpoint of their detour. Canby was content
to leave their disposal to the desert.

It was one of the great marches of all time, and one of the great
nightmares ever after for the men who survived it. They had no guide,
no road, not even a trail through that barren waste, and they began the
ten-day trek with five days' poor rations, including water. What few
guns they had brought along were dragged and lowered up- and
downhill by the men, who fashioned long rope harnesses for the purpose. For miles the brush and undergrowth were so dense that they had
to cut and hack their way through with bowie knives and axes. Skirting the western slopes of the Madelenas, they crossed the Sierra de San
Mateo, then staggered down the dry bed of the Palomas River until
they reached the Rio Grande again, within sight of which the Texans
sent up a shout like the "Thalassa!" of Xenophon's ten thousand. From
start to finish, since heading north at the opening of the year, they had
suffered a total of 1700 casualties. Something under 500 of these fell
or were captured in battle, and of the remaining 1200 who did not get
back to Texas, a good part crumpled along the wayside during this
last one hundred miles. They reached the river with nothing but their
guns and what they carried on their persons. A northern lieutenant, following their trail a year later, reported that he "not infrequently found
a piece of a gun-carriage, or part of a harness, or some piece of camp or
garrison equipage, with occasionally a white, dry skeleton of a man. At
some points it seemed impossible for men to have made their way."

Sibley reached Fort Bliss in early May, with what was left of
his command strung out for fifty miles behind him. Here he made his
report to the Richmond government, a disillusioned man. He did not
mention the California gold fields or the advantages of controlling
the Pacific Coast. He confined his observations to the field of his late
endeavor, and even these were limited to abuse: "Except for its geographical position, the Territory of New Mexico is not worth a quarter of the blood and treasure expended in its conquest. As a field for
military operations it possesses not a single element, except in the multiplicity of its defensible positions. The indispensable element, food, can-

not be relied on." Nor did he express any intention of giving the thing another try. The grapes had soured in the desert heat, setting his teeth on edge. "I cannot speak encouragingly 'or the future," he concluded, "my troops having manifested a dogged, irreconcilable detestation of the country and the people."

The report was dated May 4. Ten days later he assembled the 2000 survivors on the parade ground, all that were left of the 3700 Texans he had taken north from there four months ago. After thanking them for their devotion and self-sacrifice during what he called "this more than difficult campaign," he continued the retreat to San Antonio, where he took leave of them and they disbanded. It was finished. All his high hopes and golden dreams had come to nothing, like the newly founded Territory of Arizona, which had gone out of existence with his departure. Any trouble the Unionists might encounter in the upper Rio Grande Valley from now on would have to come from rattlers and Apaches; the Confederates were out of there for good. As far as New Mexico and the Far West were concerned, the Civil War was over.

★ ★ ★

All this time, while Sibley and Van Dorn were undergoing their defeats and suffering frustration of their plans, Beauregard kept busy doing what he could to shore up the western flank of the long line stretching eastward from the Mississippi River. Loss of Henry and Donelson, along with the troops who were charged with their defense, had irreparably smashed its center, throwing left and right out of concert and endangering the rear. "You must now act as seems best to you," Johnston had told him. "The separation of our armies is for the present complete." He was alone.

Gloomily the Creole left Nashville on February 15. Two days later — the day after Donelson fell — he passed through Corinth, the northeast Mississippi railroad nexus, on his way to inspect Polk's dispositions at Columbus, but his sore throat got sorer from anxiety and exposure, forcing him off the train at Jackson, Tennessee. From a hotel bed he summoned the bishop-general to join him for a conference. Waiting, he was downcast. Now indeed, as he had said, the ship of state was "on the breakers." When Polk arrived Beauregard informed him that Columbus must be abandoned.

The bishop protested. He had spent the past five months strengthening "the Gibraltar of the West" for just such an emergency, he said. But his fellow Louisianian explained that the manpower expense was too great. The 17,000-man garrison must fall back to New Madrid, forty miles downriver near the Tennessee line, where the swampy terrain would require less than half as large a defensive force, freeing the balance to assist in restoring the shattered center. In desperation

Polk then offered to hold Columbus with 5000 men. Beauregard shook his head. It would not do. They would be by-passed and captured at leisure, cut off from assisting in the defense of Memphis, which seemed next on the Federal list of major downriver objectives, or from coöperating with Johnston, who was retreating southwest with Hardee's troops for a possible conjunction. Polk returned to his fortified bluff, as heavy-hearted now as his commander, and set about dismounting his heavy guns and packing his wagons. Orders were orders; he would retreat — but not without every ounce of equipment charged against his name.

Beauregard's new line, covering Memphis and the railroads running spokelike from that hub, extended generally north-northwest along the roadbed of the Mobile & Ohio, from Corinth on the right, through Jackson and Humboldt, Tennessee, to the vicinity of New Madrid on the left. To defend this 150-mile airline stretch he had only such men as would be available from Polk's command when they pulled out of Columbus. As he examined the maps in his sickroom he saw that, despite the renewed advantage of a railroad shuttle from flank to flank of his line, he was worse off, even, than Johnston had been in Kentucky. However, his spirits rose as his health improved, until presently he had recovered his accustomed Napoleonic outlook. Back in Nashville he had seen the problem: "We must defeat the enemy *somewhere*, to give confidence to our friends. . . . We must give up some minor points, and concentrate our forces, to save the most important ones, or we will lose all of them in succession." To relieve what he called his "profound anxiety," he addressed on the 21st a confidential circular to the governors of Louisiana, Alabama, Mississippi, and Tennessee, unfolding for them a plan that would transmute disaster into glorious success by turning the tables on the Yankees. If the governors would send him reinforcements to bring his strength to 40,000 he would take the offensive forthwith. He would march on Paducah, then on Cairo, and having taken those two points he would lay St Louis itself under siege. This last would involve Van Dorn, across the river. Describing the project and invoking his assistance, the Creole general inquired of the Mississippian: "What say you to this brilliant programme?"

Van Dorn's reply came two weeks later, in the form of a dispatch giving news of his defeat at Elkhorn Tavern. This ruled out any chance of his coöperating in an advance against St Louis, even if the governors east of the river had been able to send the troops requested; which they had not. But Beauregard did not relapse into his former depression. He kept busy, issuing rhetorical addresses to his soldiers and rallying the populace to "resist the cruel invader." In an attempt to repair his shortage of artillery, for example, he broadcast an appeal to the planters of the Mississippi Valley for brass and iron bells to provide metal for casting cannon: "I, your general, intrusted with the command of the army embodied of your sons, your kinsmen, and your neighbors, do now call on you to send your plantation bells to the nearest railroad depot, subject to my order, to be melted into cannon for the defense of your plantations. Who will not cheerfully and promptly send me his bells under such circumstances? Be of good cheer; but time is precious." This produced more poetry in southern periodicals than bells in Confederate foundries, but the general refused to let his spirits be dampened, even by such taunts as the one his appeal provoked in the pro-Union Louisville *Courier:* "The rebels can afford to give up all their church bells, cow bells and dinner bells to Beauregard, for they never go to church now, their cows have all been taken by foraging parties, and they have no dinner to be summoned to."

Polk meanwhile was completing his preparations to evacuate Columbus, working mainly at night to hide his intentions from prying enemy eyes. This was no easy task, involving as it did the repulse of a gunboat reconnaissance on the 23d and the removal of 140 emplaced guns and camp equipment for 17,000 men, but he accomplished it without loss or detection. By March 2, the heaviest guns and 7000 of his soldiers having been sent downriver to New Madrid, he was on his way south with the remainder. Within the week he reached Humboldt, the crossing of the Mobile & Ohio and the Memphis & Louisville Railroads, where he stopped. From here, his 10,000 troops could be hurried to meet whatever developed in any direction, either up where they had just come from, or down at Corinth, or back in Memphis. Little as he approved of retreat in general, the militant churchman had shown a talent for it under necessity.

The detached 7000 saw less cause for gladness on occupying the post assigned them around New Madrid. Rather, it seemed to them on arrival that they had been sent to the swampy back-end of nowhere. After they had been there a while, however, they began to appreciate that the difficulty of the terrain was what made the position especially suitable for defense. Both banks of the river were boggy swamps, impenetrable to marching men; besides which, the Mississippi itself collaborated with the defenders to render its placid-looking, chocolate surface something less than convenient as a highway for invaders. As it approached the Kentucky-Tennessee line, several miles upstream, the river began one of its compass-boxing double twists, like a snake in convulsions, describing an S drawn backwards and tipped on its face, so that two narrow peninsulas lay side by side, the one to the west pointing north, the other south. Off the tip of the former, across the river in Missouri, lay the town of New Madrid, whose three forts, mounting seven guns each, commanded the second bend. At the tip of the other peninsula, nearer the Tennessee bank, was Island Ten — so called because it was the tenth such in the forty winding miles below the mouth

of the Ohio — whose 39 guns, including a 16-gun floating battery tied
up off the foot of the island, commanded the straight stretch of river
leading into the first bend. Beauregard placed much reliance on those
60 guns; they constituted the twin-fluked, left-flank anchor of his
tenuous line. The next defensible position was Fort Pillow, another
hundred miles downriver. Engineers had been ordered there to con-
strict the fortifications so that they could be held by 3000 troops instead
of the 10,000 for which they had been designed in the palmier days just
past. That would take time, however. For the present, as Beauregard
saw it, the fall of the batteries at New Madrid and Island Ten "must
necessarily be followed immediately by the loss of the whole Mississippi
Valley to the mouth of the Mississippi River." His instructions were
that they were to be "held at all costs," which in soldier language meant
that those guns were worth their weight in blood and must be served
accordingly.

Polk thought so too. Forwarding heavy guns and reinforcements,
he expressed his hopes and confidence to a colonel whose regiment
had been stationed in the area all along: "Your position is a strong one,
which you have well studied, and I have no doubt of the vigor and
efficiency of your defense. Keep me informed."

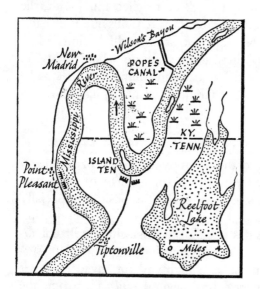

Another who agreed
was Commodore Andrew
Foote. He agreed, in fact,
with both of them: with Beauregard in stressing the importance to the Confederates of
their river-line defense, and
with Polk in expecting that it
would be conducted with vigor
and efficiency, taking full account of all the advantages in
their favor. The Federal flag
officer had had time to think
the problem over. After the
sudden victory at Henry and
the abrupt repulse at Donel-
son, he had returned to Cairo for badly needed repairs, both to his
battered gunboats and to himself. The fall of the forts having delivered
the whole Tennessee-Cumberland water system into Union hands, he
could now give full attention to the western navy's primary assignment:
the clearing of the Father of Waters, all the way to the Gulf.

This would be a much harder job than what had gone before,
and the commodore knew it. For one thing, there was the distance.
From the mouth of the Ohio to the mouth of the Mississippi was about

500 crow-flight miles, but it was well over twice that far by the twisting course his boats would have to take. A tawny vastness lay before him, winding south beyond the enemy horizon, with various obstacles in and on and around it, natural and man-made. For another, there was the difference in the rivers themselves. The Mississippi ran swifter — and it ran the other way. This meant that he would have to fight down-stream, in which case even a slight mishap, such as a fouled rudder or a sudden loss of steam, could lead to destruction or capture. Highly vulnerable except from dead ahead, his ironclads carried little armor back from the prow and none at all at the stern. What was more, ex-periments conducted on the Mississippi during the refitting showed that they could not maintain station under reverse power, even with the help of anchors, which could get no firm purchase on the river's slimy bottom. If one of them went out of control in a downstream fight, through breakdown or damage to her engine or her steering apparatus, she would not drift rearward to safety — as three out of four had done in the upstream fight just past — but forward, under enemy guns and into enemy hands. Consideration brought doubts. When his brother, a judge in Ohio, reminded him that the public expected "dash and close fighting, something sharp and decisive," Foote replied: "Don't you know that my gunboats are the only protection you have upon your rivers . . . that without my flotilla everything in your rivers, your cities and your towns would be at the mercy of the enemy? My first duty then is to care for my boats, if I am to protect you." He had not spoken thus before the point-blank assault on Donelson. But now, with the wound in his ankle not yet healed and the sound of breaking armor still loud in his memory of that repulse, the commodore took counsel of his fears.

Despite his qualms, Foote set off downriver before daylight, March 4, prepared to assault the Columbus bluff with all seven of his ironclads. Arriving he found the fortress strangely silent, no stir of life on the ramparts and no metal frowning down from the embrasures. Two officers and thirty men, covered by all the guns of the fleet, made a dash for shore in a tug — and presently returned, more sheepish than exultant, with word that the Union flag had been flying there since yesterday. Out on a scout, four companies of Illinois cavalry had found the place deserted, then trooper-like had settled down and made themselves at home, rooting into the conglomerate litter Polk's men had left behind. Foote went ashore for a look at the fortifications, wrote a formal report on their capture, supervised further repairs to his gun-boats — necessary because the armor above the Texas decks was so badly cracked and buckled that the civilian pilots refused to continue downriver until it had been replaced — then finally, on the 17th, set off again for his next objective: Island Ten.

Arriving that day, he moored his flotilla against the Missouri

bank, three miles above the head of the fortified island, and began lobbing shells across the low-lying southern tip of the first peninsula. His
fire was not very effective at that range, but neither was the enemy's,
which was the commodore's main concern in his present frame of mind.
In fact he had come prepared for this style of fighting. His seven ironclads were supplemented by eleven strange vessels, compressed hexa-
gons 60 feet long and 25 feet wide, each with a single 13-inch mortar
bolted to its deck. Originally there had been doubts as to whether they
would stand the recoil, but three of the gunboat captains had settled
that by firing the first shot: in spite of which they were still suspected
of being about as dangerous at one end of the trajectory as the other.
When the piece was loaded, the crew slipped through a door cut in one
end of the surrounding seven-foot armored bulwark and stood on tiptoe
on the outer deck, hands over ears, mouths agape, knees flexed against
the concussion, until it was fired; then they would hurry back inside
for the reloading. Foote at least was happy with them, despite the
doubts and drawbacks. As soon as he got within range of the island he
had them towed to the head of the column and started them firing in
the direction of the nearest Confederate batteries, two airline miles
away.

    Army men, who had been on the scene for two weeks now, an-
ticipating the arrival of the gunboats with their Sunday punch, were
much less happy about these new-style naval tactics, so different from
what had gone before. At Henry the navy had taken the lead, leaving the
landsmen with little to do, and now that the case was more or less reversed, the army howled with resentment. As time went by, the commodore refusing to budge from his upstream station, the howls took on
a note of shrill derision. One exasperated colonel, when asked just
what the flotilla was accomplishing, replied contemptuously, "Oh, it is
still bombarding the state of Tennessee at long range."

    None among the soldiers was more critical of the navy than
their commander, Brigadier General John Pope. In protesting against
caution he stood on solid ground. His notion of the way to fight a war
was to locate the enemy and then go after him, preferably point-blank.
These tactics were especially valid when operating, as Pope was here,
with the advantage of three-to-one numerical odds, and he had proceeded to put them into practice. A forty-year-old West Pointer with
a robust physique to match his positive manner, he had brought his four
divisions overland down the right bank of the river, arriving March 3,
and moved without delay against New Madrid and Point Pleasant, eleven
miles below. Within ten days — four days before the navy's tardy arrival — he had captured both places, along with 25 heavy guns and
quantities of equipment and supplies, when the defenders retreated to the
security of the east bank and the fastness of Island Ten. He would have
taken that place, too — he knew exactly how to go about it — except

that he could not effect a crossing without protection for his transports. Confederate batteries commanded the river from the opposite bank, and even worse there was a motley collection of makeshift rebel gunboats on patrol. Neither of these deterrents would be much of a problem for even a single ironclad, Pope declared, if Foote would only send it. But this the naval commander would not do. Any attempt to run the gauntlet of the island batteries, he replied, "would result in the sacrifice of the boat, her officers and men, which sacrifice I would not be justified in making."

Pope was more vexed than discouraged. A week after his capture of New Madrid, in recognition of his hard-hitting competence, he had been made a major general. He would keep up the pressure, hoping in time to stiffen the navy's backbone. Meanwhile he had the rebels in a cul-de-sac, backed up against the swamps that lay between Reelfoot Lake and the river. There was no way out for them, and no way in for supplies, except along the road leading south through Tiptonville. Once the Federals were astride the river, the road would be cut; he could bag the lot by quick assault or, at the worst, by siege. All he wanted was a chance to ferry his men across with a fair degree of safety. Suspecting that the navy would never get up nerve enough to run past Island Ten, he began to construct a navy of his own: high-sided barges armored with boiler plate, designed to accommodate field guns. He kept busy in other ways as well, manning the captured heavy guns to strengthen his domination of Madrid Bend and bringing down supplies and reinforcements from upriver. This last took ingenuity, for the right-bank swamps blocked the direct route, but the general had that too. He had his engineers cut a channel (a canal, it was called, 50 feet wide, 9 miles long, and 4½ feet deep — this being the depth at which the flooded trees were sawed off under water) connecting the river, five miles north of the gunboat station, with Wilson's Bayou, which gave down upon New Madrid, thus by-passing the bend commanded by the guns on Island Ten. Shallow-draft transports got through with another whole division, bringing Pope's total strength to 23,000, but not the gunboats, whose bottoms would have been torn out by the stumps. Their only way led down past the cannon-bristled island, which Foote believed would sink in short order whatever came within range.

All but one of the gunboat captains agreed with the flag officer's estimate as to the outcome of a downstream fight or a try at running the batteries. That one was Commander Henry Walke, skipper of the *Carondelet*. For two weeks now the diurnal mortar bombardment had continued, and except for a single boat expedition, which spiked some guns in an abandoned battery on All Fools' Night, all that had been accomplished by the navy was a heavy expenditure of ammunition. A fifty-four-year-old Virginia-born Ohioan and a veteran of all the river engagements from Belmont on, Walke was touched in his pride, and had been so ever since Donelson, when, as last boat out of the fight, he had retreated firing blindly in an attempt to hide in the gunsmoke. It was his belief that the run could be made with a good chance of success, provided it was made in silence and by the dark of the moon. If the rebels did not know he was there, they would not shoot; or if they knew he was there, but could not see him, they would not be likely to hit him. At any rate he was willing to give it a try, and he said so at a conference on the flagship in late March. Foote was pleased to hear that someone thought the run could be made, though he himself was doubtful. The army gibes had begun to sting, and there were reports that the Confederates were building a fleet of giant ironclads at Memphis: he might soon have a downstream fight on his hands, against much longer odds, whether he wanted it or not. He asked Walke if he would be willing to back up his opinion by trying the run in the *Carondelet.* Walke said he would, emphatically. Foote said all right, go ahead. He would not order a man to try what he himself had already said was too risky, but he would approve it on a volunteer basis. Walke began his preparations at once.

The moon would be new and early-down on the night of April 4, which left him just under a week for getting ready. During this time he piled his decks with planks from a wrecked barge to give protection from plunging shot, coiled surplus chain in vulnerable spots, and wound an 11-inch hawser round and round the pilothouse as high up as the windows. Cordwood barriers were built to inclose the boilers, and a coal barge loaded with bales of hay was lashed to the port side, which caused an observer to remark that the gunboat resembled "a farmer's wagon prepared for market." The only light she carried would be a lantern in the engine room, invisible from outside, and to insure silence the engines were muffled by piping the escape steam through the paddle-wheel housing instead of through the stacks as usual. The one thing Walke was to avoid beyond all others was being captured; fighting upstream in rebel hands, the *Carondelet* might be a match for all her sister ships combined. To guard against this, the crew was armed with cutlasses, pistols, and hand grenades; two dozen volunteer sharpshooters were taken aboard; hot-water hoses were connected to the boilers for the purpose of scalding boarders; and if all else failed, Walke's orders were that she was to be sunk beneath their feet. Through the early evening of April 4 the sickle moon shone brightly, if intermittently, over and under a scud of black clouds racing past. Then came moonset, 10 o'clock; Walke passed the word, "All ready," and the gunboat slipped her moorings. The muffled engines merely throbbed; the gathering clouds had masked the stars. So absolute were the darkness and the silence as the *Carondelet* stood out for New Madrid, the officers on deck asked through the speaking pipes if the engineer was going ahead on her.

It was not so for long. Just as she cleared the line of mortai rafts at the head of the moored column, the storm broke with tropical fury. Vast and vivid streaks of lightning split the sky, so that to one who watched it was as if the gates of hell "were opened and shut every instant, suffering the whole fierce reflection of the infernal lake to flash across the sky." Thunder crashed and rumbled and the rain came down in gulfs. The river ahead was an illuminated highway, with Island Ten looming in ominous silhouette, its drowsy lookouts no doubt startled into wide-eyed action at seeing the Yankee gunboat bearing down on them like something on a brightly lighted stage. Yet apparently not: Walke held his course past the first battery without being fired on — when suddenly, of her own accord, the *Carondelet* signaled her presence to her enemies ashore. Dry soot in her chimneys, normally kept wet by the escape steam, took fire and shot five-foot torches from their crowns, bathing with a yellow glare the upper deck and everything around. That did it. Ashore, there were cries of alarm and an officer shouting, "Elevate! Elevate!" and then the crash of gunfire through the thunder.

Carondelet went with the current, a leadsman knee-deep in muddy foam on her bow to sing out the soundings. The coal barge lashed alongside impeded her speed, but was no less welcome for that, coming as it did between the batteries and their target. Shells shrieked overhead or were heard plunging into the water as the island guns were echoed by others along the Tennessee bank. Wallowing in the wind-whipped waves, still under the crash and flash of thunder and lightning, the little ironclad held her course and took no hits. Clear of the island, she still had the floating battery to pass, but the final six shots from there were misses, like the rest. She had made it. Pulling up to the New Madrid landing, where army cannoneers were giving the navy its due at last by tossing their caps and cheering, Walke proudly took up a speaking trumpet and announced his arrival to those on bank, then turned to his bosun's mate and authorized the sounding of "grog, oh." Against regulations, the main brace then was spliced.

Pope at last had what he had been saying was all he needed, a gunboat south of Island Ten; and presently he had two. Learning of the *Carondelet*'s successful run — she had taken two hits after all, it turned out: one in the coal barge, one in a bale of hay — Foote sent the *Pittsburg* down to repeat the performance on the night of the 6th, which was also dark and stormy. The makeshift rebel flotilla scattered, awed, and the ironclads knocked out the batteries opposite Point Pleasant. Pope put his men on transports and had the gunboats herd them over. The Tiptonville road was cut within an hour of the unopposed landing. All he had to do then was put his hand out; the 7000 Confederates were in it, along with more than a hundred pieces of light and heavy artillery, 7000 small arms, horses and mules by droves, mounds of equipment including tents for 12,000 men, and several boatloads of provisions.

It was all over before the dawn of April 8, accomplished without the loss of a single man in combat. The North had another hero: bluff John Pope. A forthright combination of ingenuity and drive — large-bodied, with stolid eyes and a full beard that spread down over his upper chest, his broad, flat face framed by dark brown hair brushed straight back from the bulging expanse of forehead and falling long at the sides — he commanded confidence by his very presence. Once he saw what he wanted, he went after it on his own, unflinchingly. The military worth of such a man was clear for all to see, including his commander. Halleck wired, exuberant: "I congratulate you and your command on your splendid achievement. It excels in boldness and brilliancy all other operations of the war. It will be memorable in military history and will be admired by future generations. You deserve well of your country."

Thus Halleck rejoiced and Pope basked in well-earned laudation, while their opponent Beauregard experienced quite opposite emotions. Once more on the eve of scoring what he had hoped would be "a beautiful *ten strike*," he was suddenly faced instead with the imminent testing of his prediction that the fall of New Madrid and Island Ten would mean the immediate loss of the whole Mississippi Valley. For him this meant the loss of the war, and he was correspondingly cast down. Midway of the campaign, which was stretching his nerves to the breaking point — one fluke of his left-flank anchor had snapped, and the other seemed about to snap as well — he wrote to a friend in Congress, inquiring distractedly: "Will not heaven open the eyes and senses of our rulers? Where in the world are we going to, if not to destruction?"

✗ 2 ✗

Good news was doubly welcome in St. Louis, where Halleck had sat desk-bound all this time, scratching his elbows and addressing his goggle-eyed stare in the general direction of the back-area correspondents who came clamoring for information he could not give because he did not have it. The month between the mid-February capture of Fort Donelson and the mid-March fall of New Madrid had been for him a time of strain, one in which he saw his probable advancement placed in precarious balance opposite his probable stagnation. He had come out top man in the end, but the events leading up to that happy termination — as if, perversely, the fates had established a sort of inverse ratio between the success of Federal arms and the rise of Henry Halleck — had contained, for him, far more of anguish than of joy. There was small consolation in realizing later that the fates had been with him all along, that the cause for all that anguish had existed only in his own mind, as a product of fear and suspicion.

His first reaction, the day after the fall of the Cumberland fortress, was to request promotions for Buell, Grant, and C. F. Smith — and advancement for himself. "Give me command of the West," he wired McClellan. "I ask this in return for Forts Henry and Donelson." His second reaction, following hard on the heels of the first, was fear that Grant's victory might sting the Confederates into desperation. Even now perhaps they were massing for a sudden all-or-nothing lunge, northward around Grant's flank. Beauregard's plan for an attack on Paducah and Cairo had not gone beyond the dream stage, but Halleck feared it quite literally, and called urgently for Buell to come help him. Buell replied in effect that he had troubles of his own, and Halleck was even more firmly convinced of the necessity for authority to bend him to his will. "I must have command of the armies of the West," he told McClellan in a second wire, sent three days after the first, which had gone unanswered. "Hesitation and delay are losing us the golden opportunity. Lay this before the President and the Secretary of War. May I assume command? Answer quickly." This time McClellan did answer quickly, but not as his fretful subordinate had hoped. Replying that he believed Buell could handle his own army better from Bowling Green than Halleck could do from St Louis, he declined to lay Old Brains' self-recommendation on the presidential desk.

Perhaps it was what Halleck had expected. At any rate he had already put a second string to his bow, forwarding for Stanton's out-of-channels approval a plan for reorganizing the western department under his command. February 21, the day after McClellan's refusal, Stanton replied that he liked the plan, "but on account of the domestic affliction of the President" — Willie Lincoln had died the day before and was lying in state in the White House — "I have not yet been able to submit it to him." Halleck's hopes took a bound at this. Determined to strike while the iron was hot, he wired back that same day, urging the won-over Secretary to break in on the President's family trouble, whatever it was. "One whole week has been lost already by hesitation and delay," he complained. "There was, and I think there still is, a golden opportunity to strike a fatal blow, but I can't do it unless I can control Buell's army. . . . There is not a moment to be lost. Give me the authority, and I will be responsible for results." Stanton's reply came the following day, and Halleck's hopes hit bottom with a thud. The Secretary had gotten to Lincoln, but "after full consideration of the subject," he telegraphed, "[the President] does not think any change in the organization of the army or the military departments at present advisable."

Halleck's bow was completely unstrung; there was no one left to appeal to, either in or out of channels. After two days spent absorbing the shock, he replied with what grace he could muster: "If it is thought that the present arrangement is best for the public service, I have nothing to say. I have done my duty in making the suggestions, and I leave it to my superiors to adopt or reject them." For others closer at hand, however, he either had less grace to spare or else it was exhausted. Encountering signs of paperwork confusion down at Cairo that same day, he testily informed his chief of staff: "There is a screw loose in that command. It had better be fixed pretty soon, or the command will hear from me."

That was still his irascible, sore-pawed frame of mind the following week, when his worst fears in regard to Grant appeared to have been realized. At a time when Halleck was most concerned about a possible rebel counterattack, launched with all the fury of desperation, Grant and his 30,000 soldiers — the combat-hardened core of any defense the department commander might have to make — lost touch with headquarters, apparently neglecting to file reports because he was off on a double celebration of victory and promotion. The former alcoholic captain was now a major general, tenth-ranking man in the whole U.S. Army; Lincoln had signed the recommendation on the night of the day the Donelson news reached Washington, and the Senate had promptly confirmed it as of the Unconditional Surrender date. Halleck himself had urged the promotion, but not as warmly as he had urged several others, and he had yet to congratulate Grant personally for the capture of the forts. Other promotions were in the mill, soon to be acted on — Buell and Pope were to be major generals within a week, along with others, including Smith — but Grant would outrank them, which was not at all what Halleck had intended or expected. The fact was, absorbed as he had been in his rivalry with Buell, he was beginning to see that he had raised an even more formidable hero-opponent right there in his own front yard. Donelson having caught the public fancy, the public in its short-sighted way was giving all the credit to the general on the scene, rather than to the commander who had masterminded the campaign from St Louis. Irked by this, he then was confronted with what he considered the crowning instance of Grant's instability. Having won his promotion, the new hero apparently thought himself above the necessity for filing reports as to his whereabouts or condition. Where he was now, Halleck did not know for sure; but there were rumors.

On March 3 McClellan received a dispatch indicating that Halleck's sorely tried patience at last had snapped: "I have had no communication with General Grant for more than a week. He left his command without my authority and went to Nashville. His army seems to be as much demoralized by the victory of Fort Donelson as was that of the Potomac by the defeat of Bull Run. It is hard to censure a successful general immediately after a victory, but I think he richly deserves it. I can get no returns, no reports, no information of any kind from him. Satisfied with his victory, he sits down and enjoys it without any regard to the future. I'm worn-out and tired with this neglect and inefficiency." McClellan, whose eye for a possible rival was quite as sharp as Halleck's own, was sudden in reply: "Generals must observe discipline as well as private soldiers. Do not hesitate to arrest him at once if the good of the service requires it. . . . You are at liberty to regard this as a positive order if it will smooth your way."

Halleck did not hesitate. The order went by wire to Grant at once: "You will place [Brig.] Gen. C. F. Smith in command of expedition, and remain yourself at Fort Henry. Why do you not obey my orders to report strength and positions of your command?" The question was largely rhetorical; Halleck believed he already knew the answer, and he gave it in a telegram informing McClellan of his action in the matter: "A rumor has just reached me that since the taking of Fort Donelson, General Grant has resumed his former bad habits. If so, it will account for his neglect of my often-repeated orders." To anyone with an ear for army gossip, and McClellan's was highly tuned in that respect, this meant that Grant was off on a bender. "I do not deem it advisable to arrest him at present," Halleck continued, "but have placed General Smith in command of the expedition up the Tennessee. I think Smith will restore order and discipline."

Grant had been guilty of none of these things, and he said so in a telegram to Halleck as soon as he had complied with the instructions to turn over his command: "I am not aware of ever having disobeyed any order from headquarters — certainly never intended such a thing." The communications hiatus was explained by the defection of a telegraph operator who took Grant's dispatches with him, unsent, when he deserted. It was true, Grant said, that he had been to Nashville, but that was because Halleck had told him nothing; he had gone there to meet Buell and work out a plan for coöperation. When Halleck still showed resentment at having been left in the dark, Grant observed that there must be enemies between them, and asked to be relieved from further duty in the department. Halleck refused to agree to this, but continued to bolster his case by forwarding an anonymous letter charging that the property captured at Fort Henry had been questionably handled. His dander really up now, Grant replied: "There is such a disposition to find fault with me that I again ask to be relieved from further duty until I can be placed right in the estimation of those higher in authority."

Suddenly, incredibly, all was sweetness and light at Halleck's end of the wire. "You cannot be relieved from your command," he answered. "There is no good reason for it. . . . Instead of relieving you, I wish you as soon as your new army is in the field to assume command and lead it on to new victories."

There were a number of reasons behind this sudden change in attitude and disposition, all of which had occurred between the leveling and the withdrawing of the charges against Grant. First, the evacuation of Columbus had relieved Halleck's fears that the Confederates were about to unleash an attack on Cairo or Paducah, and while Curtis was stopping Van Dorn at Elkhorn Tavern, Pope was applying a bear hug on New Madrid. Then, just as he was congratulating himself on these improvements in the tactical situation, a stiff letter came from the Adjutant General, demanding specifications for the vague charges he had been making against his new major general. Trial-by-rumor would not do, the army's head lawyer informed him. "By direction of the President, the Secretary of War desires you to ascertain and report whether General Grant left his command at any time without proper authority, and, if so, for how long; whether he has made to you proper reports and returns of his force; whether he has committed any acts which are unauthorized or not in accordance with military subordination or propriety, and, if so, what." To reply as directed would be to give Grant what he had been seeking, a chance to "be placed right in the estimation of those higher in authority." Besides, Halleck had no specifications to report, only rumors. Instead, he replied that he was "satisfied" Grant had "acted from a praiseworthy although mistaken zeal. . . . I respectfully recommend that no further notice be taken of it. . . . All these irregularities have now been remedied."

However, there was something more behind this sudden volte-face, this willingness to bury the hatchet he had been flourishing lately. March 11 — the day after the Adjutant General's call for specifics, and two days before he blandly informed Grant that there was "no good reason" for relieving him — the fond hope for which he had labored in and out of channels all these months was realized. He got the West. His command, which was called the Department of the Mississippi and extended for better than 500 miles eastward, from Kansas to a north-south line through Knoxville, was awarded him by Lincoln in the same War Order that deposed McClellan as general-in-chief and recalled Frémont to active duty. Receiving it that way, out of the blue, after two solid weeks of despair, Halleck was in no mood to quarrel with anyone, not even Grant: in fact, especially not Grant. Beauregard was reported to be intrenching around Corinth, reinforced to a strength of 20,000 men. "If so, he will make a Manassas of it," Halleck said. That meant hard fighting: in which case he wanted his hardest-fighting general in command: and that meant Grant, whatever his instability in other respects. "The power is in your hands," Halleck told him. "Use it, and you will be sustained by all above you."

So Grant got aboard a steamboat at Fort Henry and went up the Tennessee to rejoin his army.

★ ★ ★

Beauregard was at Corinth, and he had been reinforced: Halleck's information was true, as far as it went. But the Creole was not planning a Manassas. He was planning a Cannae, or at least an Austerlitz, and for once (though he did not neglect the accustomed flourish at the outset: "Soldiers: I assume this day the command of the Army of the Mississippi, for the defense of our homes and liberties, and to resist the subjugation, spoliation, and dishonor of our people. Our mothers and wives, our sisters and children, expect us to do our duty even to the sacrifice of our lives. ... Our cause is as just and sacred as ever animated men to take up arms, and if we are true to it and to ourselves, with the continued protection of the Almighty, we must and shall triumph") his dream was built on something more than rhetoric and hope.

Recent and looming disasters at last had jarred the Richmond government into action. The fall of Henry and Donelson, followed at once by the loss of Kentucky and Middle Tennessee, now threatened the railroad leading eastward from Memphis, through Corinth and Tuscumbia, to Chattanooga, where it branched south, through Atlanta, to Charleston and Savannah, and north, through Knoxville, to Lynchburg and Richmond. "The vertebrae of the Confederacy," former War Secretary L. P. Walker called it, and rightly; for once this only east-west all-weather supply line was cut, the upper South would be divided — as prone for conquest as a man with a broken backbone. Now when Beauregard cried wolf, as he had done unheeded so often before, the authorities listened. Without Major General Braxton Bragg and the 10,000 soldiers he commanded at Mobile and Pensacola, the southern coast would be wide open to amphibious attack, but under the press of necessity the dispersed defensive was out, no matter the risk; Bragg and his men were ordered north to Corinth. So were Brigadier General Daniel Ruggles and his 5000 from New Orleans, though their departure left the South's chief city without infantry to defend it. By early March they were with Beauregard, absorbed into the Army of the Mississippi. Combined with Polk's 10,000 — so that in point of fact it was they who did the absorbing — they brought the expansive Creole's total strength to 25,000 men.

His spirits were lifted toward elation by this considerable transfusion of troops from his native shore — including one elite New Orleans outfit which carried his name on its roster as an honorary private; "Pierre Gustave Toutant Beauregard!" rang out daily at roll call, like the sudden unfurling of a silken banner; "Absent on duty!" the color-sergeant proudly answered for him. He looked forward to combinations and maneuvers that would be nothing less than Napoleonic in concept and execution. Johnston by now was across the Tennessee, marching westward from Decatur with the remnant of what had been the Army of Kentucky. Floyd's brigade had been sent to

Chattanooga, but Forrest's troopers had caught up with the column, bringing Hardee's total to 15,000. When they arrived there would be 40,000 soldiers around Corinth, exactly the number the impatiently waiting general had said would allow a strike at Cairo and Paducah. Nor was that all. Van Dorn's 15,000, licking their Elkhorn Tavern wounds in Arkansas, had been alerted for an eastward march that would bring them across the Mississippi at Memphis, where they would find boxcars waiting to bring them rapidly down the vital railroad line to Corinth. The total then would soar to 55,000. Any twinge of regret for the 20,000 lost at Donelson and penned up now on Island Ten was quickly assuaged by the thought that, even without them, the Army of the Mississippi would not only be the largest any Confederate had ever commanded, but in fact would be almost twice as large as the combined force that had covered itself and its generals — particularly Beauregard — with glory at Manassas. As he waited now for Johnston he rehearsed in his mind the recommendations he would make for the utilization of this strength.

Scouts had been bringing him full reports of the enemy situation all this time. Grant's army was twenty-odd miles to the north, in camp on the left bank of the Tennessee, awaiting the arrival of Buell's army, which was moving west from Nashville. Even with the addition of Van Dorn and Johnston, the southern army would not be as large as the two northern armies combined, but it would be larger than either on its own. The answer, then — provided the gray-clad reinforcements won the race, which seemed likely, since the Yankees marching overland from Nashville were encountering various obstacles such as burned bridges — was a slashing attack. If Van Dorn and Johnston reached Corinth before Buell reached the Tennessee, the superior Confederate army would pounce on Grant and accomplish his destruction, then fall in turn on Buell and treat him likewise, after which the way to Louisville and St Louis would lie open. Beauregard saw and rehearsed it thus in his mind, complete no doubt with the final surrender ceremonies at the point of deepest penetration, wherever that might be. When Johnston arrived on the 24th at the head of the column which now reached the end of its long retreat from Bowling Green, he considered the race half won.

The tall, handsome Texan, who had set out seven months ago, buoyed up by the confident hopes of the South that he would drive the blue invaders from the soil of his native Kentucky, now came back to Mississippi oppressed by the seething resentment of those who had cheered him loudest then. He took it calmly, the flared mustache and deep-set eyes masking whatever hurt the barbs of criticism gave him. "What the people want is a victory," he had said, and he welcomed Beauregard's proposal — the more so since it coincided with plans he had made on the march — as a chance to give them one. In fact, as a sign of appreciation for all the Louisiana general had done in the trying past few weeks, Johnston made the gesture of offering him command of the army for the coming battle; he himself would act as department commander, he said, with headquarters at Memphis or at nearby Holly Springs. Beauregard's heart gave a leap at this, touching his fiery ambition as it did, but he recognized a gesture when he saw one, and declined. Then the two got down to preparing the army for combat, prescribing rigid training schedules for the soldiers, who being raw needed all the instruction they could possibly absorb, and reorganizing them into four corps: 10,000 under Polk, 16,000 under Bragg, 7000 under Hardee, and 7000 under Breckinridge. (The last was designated as Crittenden's at first, but he was presently removed to suffer demotion for the Fishing Creek debacle.) The 15,000 under Van Dorn would add a substantial fifth corps when they got there, but even without them the army was about as large as the one Grant had in camp on the near bank of the Tennessee, twenty-two miles to the north.

The reinstated Federal commander had been with his army a week by the time Johnston joined Beauregard at Corinth. After the hundred-mile boat ride Grant came ashore at Savannah, a hamlet on the east bank, where C. F. Smith, an old soldier who never neglected the creature comforts, had established headquarters in a fine private mansion overlooking a bend of the Tennessee. One division was at Crump's Landing, three miles upstream on the opposite bank, and as Grant arrived the other five were debarking at Pittsburg Landing, six miles farther south and also on the west side of the river. The site had been recommended by the commander of one of the new divisions; a "magnificent plain for camping and drilling," he called it, "and a military point of great strength."

This was Tecumseh Sherman. He too had been reinstated, Halleck having decided that he was not really insane after all, just highstrung and talkative; besides, he had a brother in the Senate. Grant, for one, thought highly of him. During the Donelson campaign Sherman had worked hard, forwarding reinforcements and supplies and offering to waive his then superior rank for a chance to come up and join the fighting. But the men assigned to him were not so sure, not at the outset anyhow. Red-headed and gaunt, with sunken temples and a grizzled, short-cropped ginger beard, he had a wild expression around his eyes and a hungry look that seemed to have been with him always. "I never saw him but I thought of Lazarus," one declared. His shoulders twitched and his hands were never still, always picking at something, twirling a button or fiddling with his whiskers. They had not fancied getting their first taste of combat under a man who had been sent home such a short while back under suspicion of insanity. Three days before Grant's arrival, though at first their fears were intensified, they learned

better. Smith sent them south for a try at breaking the vital Memphis &
Charleston Railroad, down across the Mississippi line.

They came off the transports at midnight in a blinding rain. By
daylight they were far inland, and still the rain came pouring. Bridges
were washed out, so that the cavalry, scouting ahead, lost men and
horses, drowned while trying to ford the swollen creeks. Behind them,
the Tennessee was rising fast, threatening to cut them off by flooding
the bottom they had marched across. At this point, just when things
were at their worst, Sherman ordered them back to the transports. It
had been a nightmare operation, and probably they had done no earthly
good; they were wet, tired, hungry, cold; for the most part they had
been thoroughly frightened. But curiously enough, when they were
back aboard the transports, drinking hot coffee and snuggling into
blankets, they felt fine about the whole thing. They had been down
into enemy country, the actual Deep South — a division on its own,
looking for trouble: that gave them the feeling of being veterans —
and they had seen their commander leading them. Sherman was not the
same man at all. He was not nervous; his shoulders did not twitch; he
was calm and confident, and when he saw the thing was impossible he
did not hesitate to give it up. Whatever else he might be, he certainly
was not crazy. They knew that now, and they were willing to follow wherever he led them.

Grant too had changed, the veterans saw when he came up to
Pittsburg to inspect them. Mostly it was the aura of fame that had been
gathering around him in the month since the news from Donelson first
set the church bells ringing. He was Unconditional S. Grant now, and
his picture was on the cover of *Harper's Weekly*. There was a hunger
for particulars about him, for instance how he "generally stood or
walked with his left hand in his trousers pocket, and had in his mouth
an unlighted cigar, the end of which he chewed restlessly." The cigar
was an example of the change that stemmed from fame. Learning that
he had kept one clamped in his teeth that critical afternoon at Donelson,
whenever he was not using it like a marshal's baton to point the direction
for attack, readers had sent him boxes of them to express their admiration, and since Grant had never been one to waste things, least of
all good tobacco, the long-stemmed meerschaum that had given him so
much satisfaction in the past was put away while he concentrated on
smoking up those crates of gift cigars. One other change he had made
on his own. His beard, which formerly had reached down past the
second button on his coat, had been clipped short. It seemed to the
soldiers, observing him now, a gesture not unlike that of a man rolling
up his sleeves in preparation for hard work.

For him, work meant fighting; that was his trade, the only one
he had ever been any good at or able to earn a living by, and he wanted
to be at it right away. Restrained by Halleck, however — "We must

strike no blow until we are strong enough to admit no doubt of the result," the department commander warned — all Grant could do now was prepare for the attack he would launch when Buell got there. Meanwhile the position appeared to him to be about as good as Sherman had reported. A hundred-foot yellow-clay bluff rose abruptly from the narrow shelf of the landing, where steamboats had unloaded peace-time cargoes for Corinth, to a plateau eroded by gullies and covered with second-growth timber except for scattered clearings cut by farm-ers for orchards and grain fields. It was not quite a "magnificent plain," but it did have points of military strength, the flanks being protected by Lick and Snake Creeks, which emptied into the Tennessee above and below the landing. The area between them, a quadrilateral vary-ing roughly from three to five miles on a side, gave plenty of room for drilling the five divisions camped there and was conveniently cross-hatched by a network of wagon trails leading inland and connecting the small farms. But Grant's primary interest was on the main road leading southwest to Corinth, one hard day's march away. That was the one he would take when the time came: meaning Buell. Halleck reported him nearing Waynesboro, forty miles away, but cautioned Grant: "Don't let the enemy draw you into an engagement now. Wait till you are properly fortified and receive orders."

This raised another question; for the position had not been fortified at all. Smith had already expressed an opinion on that. The crusty general had been put to bed with an infected leg, having skinned his shin on the sharp edge of a rowboat seat, but he was quite un-daunted. "By God," he said, "I ask nothing better than to have the rebels come out and attack us! We can whip them to hell. Our men suppose we have come here to fight, and if we begin to spade it will make them think we fear the enemy." Grant agreed and left things as they were, despite the warning. The war was on its last legs, he told Halleck, and the enemy too demoralized to constitute a danger: "The temper of the rebel troops is such that there is but little doubt but that Corinth will fall much more easily than Donelson did when we do move. All accounts agree in saying that the great mass of the rank and file are heartily tired."

One man at least did not agree at first, and that was Sherman. Privately he was telling newsmen, "We are in great danger here." But when asked why he did not protest to those in charge, he shrugged; "Oh, they'd call me crazy again." As time went by, however, and no attack developed, he became as complacent as the rest. Before the end of March he wrote gaily to an army friend in Cairo: "I hope we may meet in Memphis. Here we are on its latitude, and you have its longi-tude. Draw our parallels, and we breakfast at the Gayoso, whither let us God speed, and then rejoice once more at the progress of our cause."

Already there had been cause for rejoicing by some of his

fellow generals, promotions having come through on the 21st for the three who commanded divisions at Donelson. Smith received his in bed — his leg was getting worse instead of better — but McClernand took his step-up with the continuing belief that other advancements were in store, and Lew Wallace was now the youngest major general in the army. Smith's division was placed in charge of W. H. L. Wallace, an Ohio lawyer who had won his stars at Donelson. Two of the three divisions added since were led by brigadiers who had moved to Illinois from the South and stood by the Union when trouble came: Benjamin M. Prentiss, a Virginia-born merchant, and Stephen A. Hurlbut, a lawyer originally from Charleston, South Carolina. Sherman, commanding the remaining green division, had had less combat experience than any of them — none at all, in fact, since that grievous July afternoon on the banks of Bull Run in far-away Virginia, where McClellan, now that April was at hand, was boarding a steamer to go down the coast and join his army for an advance up the James peninsula — but he was the only one of the six who was regular army, and Grant left the tactical arrangements in general to him, commuting daily by steamboat from the Savannah mansion, nine miles away.

Between them, these six commanded eighteen brigades: 74 regiments containing 42,682 soldiers, some raw, some hardened by combat. Green or seasoned, however, they approved to a man of their commander's intention to march down to Corinth, as soon as Buell arrived with 30,000 more, and administer another dose of the medicine they had forced down rebel throats the month before.

Johnston had sixteen brigades, 71 regiments with a total strength of 40,335. But even apart from the day-to-day danger of Buell's reaching Pittsburg Landing with three fourths that many more, the present near-equality in numbers was considerably offset by a contrasting lack of combat experience. Two thirds of Grant's men had been in battle — in fact had been victorious in battle — whereas in Johnston's army, except for Forrest's troopers and the handful Polk had sent to Pillow's aid five months ago at Belmont, few had heard a shot fired in anger, and only Hardee's men had even done much real marching. Bragg referred to the forces around Corinth as "this mob we have, miscalled soldiers," and complained that a good part of them had never done a day's work in their lives. Johnston of course was aware of these shortcomings, but his scouts having kept him well informed he counted much on the element of surprise. He knew what he would find up there: an army camped with its back to a deep river, unfortified, hemmed in by boggy creeks, disposed for comfort, and scattered the peacetime way. Meanwhile, drill and instruction were repairing the Confederate flaws Bragg had pointed out so harshly. He would strike as soon as he felt it possible. The question was, how long would he have before Buell got there or Grant saw the danger and corrected his dispositions or, worse, moved out and beat him to the punch?

Late at night, April 2, a telegram from Bethel, twenty miles north on the M & O, seemed to Beauregard to confirm the last and worst of these fears: Lew Wallace was maneuvering in that direction. Taking this for the beginning of a full-scale attack on Memphis, he forwarded the message to Johnston after writing on the bottom: "Now is the moment to advance, and strike the enemy at Pittsburg Landing." Johnston read it, then crossed the street to confer with Bragg, who had been made chief of staff in addition to his other duties under last week's reorganization. Johnston wanted more time for drilling his army and awaiting the arrival of Van Dorn, but Bragg was insistent in support of Beauregard's indorsement. Whatever this latest development meant, Buell was drawing closer every day. It had to be now or never, he said, and Johnston at last agreed. Ready or unready, Van Dorn or no Van Dorn, they would go up to Pittsburg and attack the Federal army in its camp. Within an hour of the telegram's midnight arrival, orders went out for the four corps commanders to "hold their commands in hand, ready to advance upon the enemy in the morning by 6 a.m. with three days' cooked rations in haversacks, 100 rounds of ammunition for small arms, and 200 rounds for field-pieces."

Early next morning Beauregard's chief of staff got to work, preparing the march instructions from notes the general had made on scraps of paper during the night. As he worked he had at his elbow Napoleon's Waterloo order, using it as a model despite the way that battle had turned out for the one who planned it. Since this would require considerable time — first the writing, then the copying and the distribution — Beauregard called Hardee and Bragg to his room to explain the march routes verbally; their corps would lead the way, and the written instructions could be delivered after they got started. As he spoke he drew a crude map on the top of a camp table, indicating distances and directions.

Two roads ran from Corinth up to Pittsburg. On the map they resembled a strung bow leaned sideways, curved side up, with the two armies at the top and bottom tips. The lower route, through Monterey, was the string; the upper route, through Mickey's, was the bow. Bragg and Breckinridge were to travel the string, Hardee and Polk the bow, in that order. Hardee was to reach Mickey's that night, bivouac, then at 3 a.m. pass on and form for battle in the fields beyond. Polk was to wait while Bragg marched up the road from Monterey and cleared the junction at Mickey's, then follow him into position, clearing the way for Breckinridge in turn. They were to regulate their columns so as not to delay each other, keeping their files well closed and the various elements properly spaced. So much for the march order; the battle order followed.

Beyond Mickey's, within charging distance of the enemy out-posts, they were to form for battle in successive lines, Hardee across the front with one brigade from Bragg, who was to form a second line five hundred yards in rear. Polk and Breckinridge were to mass their corps to the left and right, a half-mile behind Bragg, so that when he went forward, following Hardee, Polk could spread out wide in his

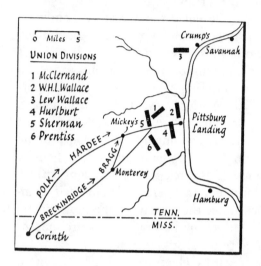

support, leaving Breckinridge in column as the general re-serve. The flanks of the army, with the three lead corps ex-tending individually across the entire front, rested on the creeks that hemmed Grant in. As they advanced, each line would thus support the one in front, and the reserve corps would feed troops from the rear toward those points where resistance turned out stiffest. The attack on the right was in-tended to move fastest, bear-ing generally left in a long curve, first along the watershed of Lick Creek and then down the west bank of the Tennessee, so as to sweep the Federals clear of the landing and drive them back against the boggy northward loop of Snake Creek, where they could be destroyed.

Today was Thursday, April 3. According to schedule, the troops would complete the twenty-mile approach march and be de-ployed for battle no later than midmorning tomorrow. But when the council broke up at 10 o'clock, already four hours past the starting time, and the generals dispersed to get their columns on the road, troops and wagons quickly snarled to a standstill, blocking the streets of Corinth. Polk at last got clear of the jam, but had to wait while Hardee doubled his column and took the lead. By then it was late afternoon, and Polk was held up till after sunset. When he stopped for the night he had covered a scant nine miles. Down on the lower road, Bragg's unwieldy column did no better. Manifestly, the schedule would have to be revised. Beauregard set it forward a whole day, intending now to be deployed in time to strike the Federals early Saturday morning.

But if Thursday had been like a bad dream, Friday was a night-mare. The march, which had seemed so easy to regulate on the flat, un-cluttered table-top, turned out to be something quite different on the ground, which was neither flat nor uncluttered — nor, as it turned out, dry. The abrupt, thunderous showers of a Mississippi April broke over the winding column, and soon the wagon and artillery wheels had

churned the roads into shin-deep mud. There were halts and unaccountable delays, times when the men had to trot to keep up, and times
when they stood endlessly in the rain, waiting for the file ahead to
stumble into motion. In their wake, the roadsides were littered with
discarded equipment, overcoats and playing cards, bowie knives and
Bibles. A more welcome delay was the rest halt given each regiment
while its colonel read the commanding general's address, written in
Corinth while they were assembling for the march.

> Soldiers of the Army of the Mississippi:
> I have put you in motion to offer battle to the invaders of your
> country. With the resolution and disciplined valor becoming men
> fighting, as you are, for all worth living or dying for, you can but
> march to a decisive victory over the agrarian mercenaries sent to
> subjugate and despoil you of your liberties, property, and honor.
> Remember the precious stake involved; remember the dependence of
> your mothers, your wives, your sisters, and your children on the
> result; remember the fair, broad, abounding land, the happy homes
> and the ties that would be desolated by your defeat.
> The eyes and hopes of eight millions of people rest upon you. You
> are expected to show yourselves worthy of your race and lineage;
> worthy of the women of the South, whose noble devotion in this
> war has never been exceeded in any time. With such incentives to
> brave deeds, and with the trust that God is with us, your generals
> will lead you confidently to the combat, assured of success.
> A. S. JOHNSTON, General

It was delivered in various styles, ranging from the oratorical, with
flourishes, to the matter-of-fact, depending on the previous civil occupation of the reader. The troops cheered wildly or perfunctorily,
depending on their degree of weariness and in part on how the address
was read, then fell back into column on the muddy roads for more of the
stop-and-go marching.

But the one who had it worst that day was Bragg. He too had
made a late start out of Corinth, and the head of his oversized column
did not reach Monterey, where it should have bivouacked the night
before, until near midday. One of his divisions was lost somewhere in
the rear, perhaps sidetracked, and he had had no word from Breckinridge at all. As a result, though Hardee and Polk were marching hard
to make up for yesterday's wasted time, the latter was held up short of
Mickey's, waiting for Bragg to clear the junction, and the former had
no sooner got past it than he received a message asking him to call a
halt so that Bragg's dragging column could close the expanding gap.
Bragg was a tall, gangling man, a West Pointer and a Mexican War
hero — "A little more grape, Captain Bragg," Zachary Taylor was
supposed to have told him at Buena Vista, as every schoolboy knew
(though what he really said was, "Captain, give 'em hell") — a native

North Carolinian, lately a Louisiana sugar planter, in his middle forties but looking ten years older because of chronic stomach trouble and a coarse gray-black beard which emphasized his heaviness of jaw and sternness of aspect; not that the latter needed emphasis, already having been rendered downright ferocious by the thick bushy eyebrows which grew in a continuous line across the bottom of his forehead. It galled him to have to send that message to Hardee, amounting as it did to an admission of being to blame for the delay; for he was a strict disciplinarian, and like most such he was quick to lose his temper when things went wrong.

Still jammed on the roads leading into and out of Mickey's, when they should have been moving into the final position where they would deploy for the attack tomorrow morning, the weary and bedraggled troops were caught that night in the same thunderstorm that attended the *Carondelet* on her run past Island Ten, just over a hundred miles away. All semblance of order dissolved under torrents of rain. When Johnston and Beauregard rode into Mickey's soon after sunrise, expecting to find the army arrayed for combat — they had left Corinth the day before and spent the night at Monterey — the rain had stopped and the sun was shining bright on the flooded fields, but the army was far from arrayed. In fact, most of it had not even arrived. Hardee was approximately in position, but he was waiting for the brigade from Bragg that would complete his line. By the time it got there, the sun was already high in the sky and Beauregard was fuming. He had cause. As they marched forward to file into line, the men began to worry about the dampness of the powder in their rifles; but instead of drawing the charges and reloading, they tested them by snapping the triggers; with the result that, within earshot of the Federal outposts, there was an intermittent banging up and down the columns, as rackety as a sizeable picket clash. Nor was that all. The returning sun having raised their spirits, the men began to tune up their rebel yells and practice marksmanship on birds and rabbits.

For two hours then, with Johnston and Beauregard standing by, Bragg continued to deploy the remainder of his corps — all but the rear division, which still had not arrived. When Johnston asked where it was, the harassed Bragg replied that it was somewhere back there; he was trying to locate it. Johnston waited, his impatience mounting, then took out his watch: 12.30. "This is perfectly puerile! This is not war!" he exclaimed, and set off down the road himself to look for the missing division. He found it wedged behind some of Polk's troops, who had not been willing to yield the right of way. The daylight hours were going fast. By the time Johnston got the road cleared and the last of Bragg's men passed to the front, his watch showed 2 o'clock. Polk's deployment used up another two hours, and Breckinridge, who had come up at last, was still to be brought forward. The shadows were get-

ting longer every minute. It was not until about 4.30, however, that
Johnston received the worst shock of all.

Riding forward he came upon a roadside conference between
Beauregard and Polk and Bragg. The Creole's big sad bloodhound eyes
were rimmed with angry red and his hands were fluttering as he spoke.
He was upset: which was understandable, for it was already ten hours
past the time when he expected to launch the attack. He favored canceling the whole movement and returning at once to Corinth. In his mind,
surprise was everything, and what with the delay piled on the previous
postponement, the constant tramping back and forth and the racket the
men had been making, all chance for surprise had been forfeited. He
knew this, he said, because at one point that afternoon he had heard a
drum rolling, but when he sent to have it silenced, the messenger came
back and reported that it could not be done; the drum was in the
Union camp. Beauregard reasoned that if he could hear enemy drum-
taps, there was small doubt that the Federals had heard the random
firing and whooping in the Confederate columns. Besides, ten southern
troopers had been captured in a cavalry clash the night before; surely
by now they had been questioned, and one at least had talked.

"There is no chance for surprise," he ended angrily. "Now they
will be intrenched to the eyes."

Johnston heard him out, then turned to Polk, his West Point
roommate. The bishop disagreed. His troops were eager for battle;
they had left Corinth on the way to a fight, he said in that deep, pulpit
voice of his, and if they did not find one they would be as demoralized
as if they had been whipped. Bragg said he felt the same way about it.
While he was speaking Breckinridge rode up. Surprised that withdrawal
was even being considered, he sided with Polk and Bragg, declaring
that he would as soon be defeated as retire without a fight. Hardee was
the only corps commander not present, but there was no doubt which
side he would favor; he was already formed for battle, anxious to go
forward. The vote was in, and Johnston made it official. There would
be another delay, another postponement, but there would be no turning back.

"Gentlemen, we shall attack at daylight tomorrow," he said.

He told the corps commanders to complete the deployment and
have the troops sleep on their arms in line of battle. Beauregard was
protesting that Buell most likely had come up by now, bringing the
Federal total to 70,000. But that made no difference either: not to
Johnston, who had reached what he believed would be his hour of
vindication after his long retreat. As he walked off he spoke to one of his
staff. "I would fight them if they were a million," he said. "They can
present no greater front between those two creeks than we can, and
the more men they crowd in there, the worse we can make it for them."

While the army completed its deployment, the troops bedding

down so that when they woke in darkness they would already be in line for the dawn assault, the sun set clear and red beyond the tasseling oaks. There was a great stillness in the blue dusk, and then the stars came out, dimming the pale sickle moon already risen in the daylight sky. Mostly the men slept, for they were weary; but some stayed awake, huddled around fires built in holes in the ground to hide them. In part they stayed awake because of hunger, for it was a Confederate belief that rations carried lighter in the stomach than in a haversack, and they had consumed their three days' rations at the outset. The nearest of them could hear Yankee bugles, faint and far like foxhorns three fields off, sounding out of the dark woods where tomorrow's battle would be fought. "The elephant," veterans called combat, telling recruits the time had come to meet the elephant.

Strictly speaking, Beauregard was right, at least in part. Buell had arrived — that is, he slept that night on the outskirts of Savannah, intending to confer with Grant next morning — but with only one of his divisions, the others being scattered along twenty miles of the road back toward Nashville. They would arrive tomorrow and the next day. Grant, being informed of this, could go to bed that night rejoicing that things had worked out so well at last. He intended to send Buell's men upstream to Hamburg. The road from there to Corinth was a mile shorter than the one leading down from Pittsburg, and the two converged eight miles this side of the objective. Conditions thus were ideal for his intention, which was to attack as soon as Buell's army could be transferred to the west bank for coöperation with his own. Irksome as the delay had been, it had given him time to study the terrain and whip his reinforcements into shape, including even some seasoning clashes with rebel cavalry who ventured up to probe the rim of his camp at Pittsburg Landing.

The men themselves were feeling good by now, too, though at the outset they had had their doubts and discomforts. They had spent a rough first week clearing campsites, a week full of snow and sleet and a damp cold that went through flesh to bone. "The sunny South!" they jeered. All night, down the rows of tents, there was coughing, a racking uproar. Diarrhea was another evil, but they made jokes about that too; "the Tennessee quickstep," they called it, laughing ruefully on sick call when the surgeons advised them to try the application of red-hot pokers. Then suddenly the weather faired, and this was the sunny South indeed; even the rain was warm. By the end of March Grant was reporting, "The health of the troops is materially improving under the influence of a genial sun which has blessed us for a few days past."

He knew because he had been among them, making his daily commuter trip by steamboat from Savannah. Mostly, though, he kept his mind on the future, the offensive he would launch when Buell got

there. He left the present — the defensive — largely to Sherman, who
had kept busy all this time confirming his commander's high opinion of
him. The red-haired Ohioan's green division was the largest in the army,
and he had awarded it the position of honor, farthest from the landing.
Three miles out, on the Corinth road, his headquarters tent was
pitched alongside a rude log Methodist meeting-house called Shiloh
Chapel. Two of his brigades were in line to the west of there, extending over toward Owl Creek, which flowed into Snake Creek where it
turned northwest, a mile from the river, leaving Owl Creek to protect
the army's right flank south of the junction. His third brigade was east
of the chapel, and his fourth was on the far side of the position, beyond
Prentiss's two brigades, whose camp was in line with his own. The
others were three-brigade divisions: McClernand's just in rear of Sherman's, Hurlbut's and W. H. L. Wallace's well back toward the landing,
and Lew Wallace's five miles north, beyond Snake Creek. It was not so
much a tactical arrangement, designed for mutual support, as it was
an arrangement for comfort and convenience, the various positions being selected because of the availability of water or open fields for drilling. In Sherman's mind, as in Grant's, the main concern was getting
ready to move out for Corinth as soon as Buell arrived. He had long
since got over his original concern, privately admitted, that the army
was "in great danger here."

The same could not be said for all his officers. One in particular,
the colonel of the 53d Ohio, had sounded the alarm so often that his
soldiers were jeered at for belonging to what was called the Long Roll
regiment. High-strung and jumpy — like Sherman himself in the old
days — he was given to imagining that the whole rebel army was just
outside his tent flap. During the past few days his condition had
grown worse. Friday, April 4, he lost a picket guard of seven men,
gobbled up by grayback cavalry, and when he advanced a company
to develop the situation they ran into scattered firing and came back.
All day Saturday he was on tenterhooks, communicating his alarm to
Sherman. That afternoon he piled on the last straw by sending word to
headquarters that a large force of the enemy was moving on the
camp. Sherman mounted and rode out to confront him. While the
colonel told excitedly of the hordes of rebels out there in the brush,
Sherman sat with his mouth clamped down, looking into the empty
woods. At last the man stopped talking. Sherman sat glaring down at
him, then jerked the reins to turn his horse toward camp. "Take your
damned regiment back to Ohio," he said, snapping the words. "Beauregard is not such a fool as to leave his base of operations and attack
us in ours. There is no enemy nearer than Corinth."

So he said, adding the final remark to sharpen the sting of the
rebuke, though actually he knew better. This was but one of several
such clashes, including one the previous evening in which ten rebel

prisoners were taken, and just this morning he had notified Grant: "The enemy has cavalry in our front, and I think there are two regiments of infantry and one battery of artillery about 2 miles out. I will send you 10 prisoners of war and a report of last night's affair in a few minutes."

There was a need for frequent reports, for Grant would not be coming up to visit the camps today. He had sprained his ankle during the violent thunderstorm the night before, when his horse slipped and fell on his leg. The soft ground had saved him from serious injury, but his boot had had to be cut off because of the swelling and he was limping painfully on crutches. The first dispatch from Sherman had opened, "All is quiet along my lines," and presently there was another, apparently sent after he got back from administering the stinging rebuke to the Ohio colonel: "I have no doubt that nothing will occur today more than some picket firing. The enemy is saucy, but got the worst of it yesterday, and will not press our pickets far. . . . I do not apprehend anything like an attack on our position."

The prisoners, if sent, went unquestioned. What could they possibly have to say that would interest a man who had already made up his mind that if he was to have a battle he would have to march his soldiers down to Corinth and provoke it? Sustained in his opinion by reports such as these two from Sherman, Grant refused to be disconcerted by incidentals. Besides, the staff officer who was best at conducting interrogations was at Hamburg, inspecting the campsite selected for Buell's army. No time was to be lost now, for the lead division had arrived at noon, along with a note from Buell: "I shall be in Savannah tomorrow with one, perhaps two, divisions. Can I meet you there?" The note was dated yesterday; "tomorrow" meant today. But Grant either did not observe the heading (another incidental) or else he was in no hurry. "Your dispatch received," he replied. "I will be there to meet you tomorrow" — meaning Sunday.

Ever since his run-in with Halleck, regarding the alleged infrequency of his reports, he had kept the St Louis wire humming. Before he went to bed tonight in the fine big house on the bluff at Savannah, with nothing to fret him but the pain in his swollen ankle, he wrote a letter informing his chief that Buell's lead division had arrived; the other two were close on its heels and would get there tomorrow and the next day. He told him also of yesterday's picket clash. "I immediately went up," he said, "but found all quiet." Then he added: "I have scarcely the faintest idea of an attack (general one) being made upon us, but will be prepared should such a thing take place."

Next morning at breakfast he heard a distant thunder from the south. The guns of Shiloh were jarring the earth.

★　★　★

Until then, Beauregard had not given up urging a withdrawal. Between dawn and sunup, wearing for luck the jaunty red flat-topped cap he had worn at Manassas, he came to Johnston's overnight camp for a last-minute plea that the attack plan be abandoned. He looked fresh and rested after a sound sleep in his ambulance — his personal tent had been misplaced on the march — but he had lost none of yesterday's conviction that the assault could not succeed. In fact he was more than ever convinced that all chance for surprise was gone. He had heard Federal bands playing marches in the night and there had been bursts of cheering from the direction of the landing. This meant only one thing, he said: Buell had come up, urged forward by the alerted Grant, and now there were 70,000 men in the Union camp, intrenched and expectant, waiting for the Confederates to walk into the trap.

The reply came not from Johnston, who stood with a cup of coffee in his hands, sipping from it as he heard him out, but from the army itself. The Creole was caught in midsentence by a rattle of musketry from dead ahead, a curious ripping sound like tearing canvas. Staff officers looked in that direction, then back at Johnston, who was handing the half-empty cup to an orderly. "The battle has opened, gentlemen," he said. "It is too late to change our dispositions." Beauregard mounted and rode away; the argument was no longer a matter for words. Johnston swung onto his horse and sat there for a long moment, his face quite grave. Then he twitched the reins, and as the big bay thoroughbred began to walk toward the sound of firing, swelling now across the front, the general turned in the saddle and spoke to his staff: "Tonight we will water our horses in the Tennessee River."

The opening shots had been fired ahead of schedule because one of Prentiss's brigade commanders, sleepless and uneasy in the hours before dawn, had sent a three-company reconnaissance out to explore the woods to his front. Encountering a portion of Hardee's skirmish line, which had not yet gone forward, they mistook it for a scouting party and attacked with spirit, driving the skirmishers back on the main body. Repulsed in turn by heavy volleys, they fell back to give the alarm that the enemy was moving in strength against the Federal position. Prentiss thus was warned of what was coming before it got there, and turned his green division out to meet the shock.

Sherman too was warned, but took no heed because the alarm was sounded by the same colonel he had rebuked for crying wolf the day before. A man had stumbled out of a thicket into the Ohio camp, holding a wound and crying, "Get in line! The rebels are coming!" A captain who went to investigate quickly returned shouting, "The rebs are out there thicker than fleas on a dog's back!" But when the colonel sent a courier to inform Sherman, word came back: "You must be badly scared over there."

Presently, though, riding forward with an orderly to where the colonel was shakily getting his men into line, he saw for himself the Confederates advancing across a large field in front, the skirmishers holding their rifles slantwise like quail hunters and the main body massed heavily behind them. The sun, which had risen fast in a cloudless sky — "the sun of Austerlitz," Southerners called it, seeing in this a Napoleonic omen — flashed on their bayonets as they brought their rifles up to fire. "My God, we're attacked!" Sherman cried, convinced at last as the volley crashed and his orderly fell dead beside him. "Hold your position; I'll support you!" he shouted, and spurred away to send up reinforcements. But: "This is no place for us," the colonel wailed, seeing his general head for the rear, and went over and lay face-down behind a fallen tree. His men were wavering, firing erratically at the attackers. When the next enemy volley crashed, the colonel jumped up from behind the tree; "Retreat! Save yourselves!" he cried, and set the example by taking off rearward at a run.

Most of his men went with him, believing they knew a sensible order when they heard one, but enough stayed to give Sherman time to warn the brigades on his other flank to drop their Sunday breakfast preparations and brace themselves for the assault. They formed in haste along the ridge where their tents were pitched, looking out over a valley choked with vines and brambles, and began to fire into the wave of gray that was surging out of the woods on the far side. Green as they were, they held their ground against four successive charges, firing steadily until the fifth swept up the slope, then gave way in tolerable good order to take up a second position farther back. The 6th Mississippi, for one, could testify to the accuracy of their fire; for it started across that valley with 425 men and reached the tented ridge with just over 100; the rest lay dead or wounded among the brambles. So thick they lay, the dead of this and the other four regiments in those charges, that one observer remarked that he could have walked across that valley without touching his feet to the ground; "a pavement of dead men," he called it.

Prentiss was fighting as doggedly on the left, and McClernand had marched to the sound of guns, filling the gap between the two divisions, so that the three were more or less in line, resisting stubbornly. All three were leaking men to the rear, the faint-hearted who sought safety back at the landing under the bluff, but the ones who stayed were determined to yield nothing except under pressure that proved itself irresistible. By the time Sherman's soldiers got settled in their second position, waiting for what came next, they had the feel of being veterans. Whatever came next could not possibly be worse than what had gone before, and having their commander move among them added to their confidence. He had been hit twice already, but gave no sign of even considering leaving the field. The first time was in the hand; he wrapped it in a handkerchief and thrust it into his breast, never taking his eyes off the enemy. The other bullet clipped a shoulder strap, nicking the skin, but that did not seem to bother him much either. When a headquarters aide came riding up to ask how things were going, he found Sherman leaning against a tree, propped on his uninjured hand, watching the skirmishers. "Tell Grant if he has any men to spare I can use them," he said, still narrow-eyed. "If not, I will do the best I can. We are holding them pretty well just now. Pretty well; but it's hot as hell."

By midmorning Grant himself was at his lieutenant's elbow, amid the bursting shells and whistling bullets. Brought to his feet by the rumble of guns from the south, he had left the breakfast table and gone aboard his steamer at the wharf below the mansion, pausing only long enough to send two notes. One was to Buell, canceling their meeting in Savannah, and the other was to Brigadier General William Nelson, whose division had arrived the day before, directing him to "move your entire command to the river opposite Pittsburg." On the way upstream — it was now about 8.30 — he found Lew Wallace waiting for him on the jetty at Crump's. The firing sounded louder; Pittsburg was definitely under attack, but Grant still did not know but what a second attack might be aimed in this direction. Without stopping the boat he called out to Wallace as he went by, "General, get your troops under arms and have them ready to move at a moment's notice." Wallace shouted back that he had already done so. Grant nodded and went on.

When he docked and rode his horse up the bluff from the landing, a crutch strapped to the saddle like a carbine, the tearing rattle of musketry and the steady booming of cannon told him the whole trouble was right here in the three-sided box where his main camp had been established. Wounded men and skulkers were stumbling rearward, seeking defilade, and beyond them the hysterical quaver of the rebel yell came through the crash of gunfire and the deeper-throated shouts of his own soldiers. Grant's first act was to establish a straggler line, including a battery with its guns trained on the road leading out of the uproar. Then he went forward to where W. H. L. Wallace and Hurlbut had formed ranks and by now were sending reinforcements to the hard-pressed divisions on the far edge of the fight. The situation was critical, but Grant kept as calm as he had done at Donelson in a similar predicament. This time, though, he had reserves, and he sent for them at once. A summons went to Lew Wallace, five miles away, instructing him to join the embattled army. Another went to Nelson, presumably already toiling across the boggy stretch of land between Savannah and the river bank opposite Pittsburg, urging him to "hurry up your command as fast as possible."

By 10 o'clock he was up front with Sherman. One of the Ohioan's brigades had disintegrated under fire, but the other two were resisting heavy pressure against their second position, half a mile back from the ridge where their tents were pitched. He said his biggest worry was that his men would run out of ammunition, but Grant assured him that this had been provided for; more was on the way. Satisfied that Sherman could look out for himself, the army commander then visited Mc-Clernand, fighting as hard in rear of Shiloh Chapel, and finally Prentiss, whose division had been repulsed by the fury of the initial onslaught, but in falling back across the open field had come upon an eroded wagon trail which wound along the edge of some heavy woods on the far side. They had got down into the shallow natural trench of this sunken road to make a stand, and that was what they were doing when Grant arrived. In fact they were doing a thorough job of it, dropping the Confederates in windrows as they charged across the fields. Approving of this execution, Grant told Prentiss to "maintain that position at all hazards." Prentiss said he would try.

He not only tried, he did maintain that position against repeated headlong charges delivered without apparent concern for loss. Elsewhere, however, conditions were much worse. At noon, when Grant returned to his headquarters near the rim of the bluff, he found the fugitives streaming rearward thicker than ever, through and past the straggler line, white-faced and unmindful of the officers who tried to rally them. Bad news awaited him: Sherman and McClernand had been forced back still farther. Both were retiring sullenly, fighting as they did so, but if either division broke into a rout, the rebels would come whooping down on the landing and the battle would be over. W. H. L. Wallace and Hurlbut had committed all their troops, and nothing had been heard from Lew Wallace, who should have completed his five-mile march before now, nor from Nelson across the river. There was no reserve at hand to block a breakthrough. In desperation Grant sent two staff officers beyond Snake Creek to hurry Wallace along and a third across the Tennessee with a note for Nelson, worded to show the urgent need for haste: "If you will get upon the field, leaving all your baggage on the east bank of the river, it will be a move to our advantage, and possibly save the day to us. The rebel force is estimated at over 100,000 men."

Beauregard had taken over the log church called Shiloh, and from this headquarters he performed for the army commander the service the other Johnston had performed for him at Manassas, exercising control of the rear area and forwarding reinforcements to those points where additional strength was needed. Thus Johnston was left free to move up and down the line of battle, encouraging the troops, and this he did. Some he sought to steady by speaking calmly. "Look along your guns, and fire low," he told them. Others he sought to inspirit with fiercer words: "Men of Arkansas, they say you boast of your prowess with the bowie knife. Today you wield a nobler weapon: the bayonet. Employ it well!" Whichever he did, or whether he did neither, but merely rode among them, tall and handsome on his tall, handsome horse, the men cheered at the sight of their commander exposing himself to the dangers he was requiring them to face. This was indeed his hour of vindication.

His men swept forward, overrunning the enemy's front-line camps and whooping with elation as they took potshots at the backs of fleeing Yankees. Where resistance stiffened, as along the ridge where Sherman's tents were pitched, they matched valor against determination and paid in blood for the resultant gain. Not that there were no instances of flinching at the cost. An Arkansas major reported angrily that a Tennessee regiment in front of his own "broke and ran back, hallooing 'Retreat, retreat,' which being mistaken by our own men for orders of their commander, a retreat was made by them and some confusion ensued." No sooner was this corrected than the same thing happened again, only this time the major had an even more shameful occurrence to report: "They were in such great haste to get behind us that they ran over and trampled in the mud our brave color-bearer." There were other, worse confusions. The Orleans Guard battalion, the elite organization with Beauregard's name on its muster roll, came into battle wearing dress-blue uniforms, which drew the fire of the Confederates they were marching to support. Promptly they returned the volley, and when a horrified staff officer came galloping up to tell them they were shooting at their friends: "I know it," the Creole colonel replied. "But dammit, sir, we fire on everybody who fires on us!"

Such mishaps and mistakes could be corrected or even overlooked by the high command. More serious were the evils resulting from straggling, caused mainly by hunger and curiosity. When some Northerners later denied that they had been surprised at Shiloh, a Texan who had scalded his arm in snatching a joint of meat from a bubbling pot as he charged through one of the Federal camps replied that if Grant's army had not been surprised it certainly had "the most devoted mess crews in the history of warfare." Sunday breakfasts, spread out on tables or still cooking over campfires, were more than the hungry Confederates could resist. Many sat down, then and there, to gorge themselves on white bread and sweet coffee. Others explored the Yankee tents, foraging among the departed soldiers' belongings, including their letters, which they read with interest to find out what northern girls were like. Hundreds, perhaps thousands, were lost thus to their comrades forging ahead, and this also served to blunt the impetus of the attack which in its early stages had rolled headlong over whatever got in its way.

Most serious of all, though, were the flaws that developed when the attack plan was exposed to prolonged strain. Neatly efficient as the thing had looked on paper, it was turning out quite otherwise on the rugged plateau with its underbrush and gullies and its clusters of stubborn blue defenders. Attacking as directed — three corps in line from creek to creek, one behind another, each line feeding its components piecemeal into the line ahead — brigades and regiments and even companies had become so intermingled that unit commanders lost touch with their men and found themselves in charge of strangers who never before had heard the sound of their voices. Coördination was lost. By noon, when the final reserves had been committed, the army was no longer a clockwork aggregation of corps and divisions; it was a frantic mass of keyed-up men crowded into an approximate battle formation to fight a hundred furious skirmishes strung out in a crooked line. Confusing as all this was to those who fought thus to the booming accompaniment of two hundred guns, it was perhaps even more confusing to those who were trying to direct them. And indeed how should they have understood this thing they had been plunged into as if into a cauldron of pure hell? For this was the first great modern battle. It was Wilson's Creek and Manassas rolled together, quadrupled, and compressed into an area smaller than either. From the inside it resembled Armageddon.

Attempting to regain control, the corps commanders divided the front into four sectors, Hardee and Polk on the left, Bragg and Breckinridge on the right. Coördination was lacking, however, and all the attacks were frontal. Besides, compliance with Johnston's original instructions — "Every effort will be made to turn the left flank of the enemy, so as to cut off his line of retreat to the Tennessee River and throw him back on [Snake] Creek, where he will be forced to surrender" — was being frustrated by Prentiss, who stood fast along the sunken road. "It's a hornets' nest in there!" the gray-clad soldiers cried, recoiling from charge after charge against the place. When Sherman and McClernand gave way, taking up successive rearward positions, the Confederate left outstripped the right, which was stalled in front of the Hornets Nest, and thus presented Johnston with the reverse of what he wanted. He rode toward the far right to correct this, carrying in his right hand a small tin cup which he had picked up in a captured camp. Seeing a lieutenant run out of one of the tents with an armload of Yankee souvenirs, Johnston told him sternly: "None of that, sir. We are not here for plunder." Then, observing that he had hurt the young man's feelings, which after all was a poor reward for the gallantry shown in the capture, by way of apology he leaned down without dismounting and took the tin cup off a table. "Let this be my share of the spoils today," he said, and from then on he had used it instead of a sword to direct the battle. He used it so now, his index finger hooked through the loop of the handle, as he rode toward the right where his advance had stalled.

At this end of the battle line, on the far flank of the Hornets Nest, there was a ten-acre peach orchard in full bloom. Hurlbut had a heavy line of infantry posted among the trees, supported by guns whose smoke lazed and swirled up through the branches sheathed in pink, and a bright rain of petals fell fluttering like confetti in the sunlight as bullets clipped the blossoms overhead. Arriving just after one of Breckinridge's brigades had recoiled from a charge against the orchard, Johnston saw that the officers were having trouble getting the troops in line to go forward again. "Men! they are stubborn; we must use the bayonet," he told them. To emphasize his meaning he rode among them and touched the points of their bayonets with the tin cup. "These must do the work," he said. When the line had formed, the soldiers were still hesitant to reënter the smoky uproar. So Johnston did what he had been doing all that morning, all along the line of battle. Riding front and center, he stood in the stirrups, removed his hat, and called back over his shoulder: "I will lead you!" As he touched his spurs to the flanks of his horse, the men surged forward, charging with him into the sheet of flame which blazed to meet them there among the blossoms letting fall their bright pink rain.

This time the charge was not repulsed; Hurlbut's troops gave way, abandoning the orchard to the cheering men in gray. Johnston came riding back, a smile on his lips, his teeth flashing white beneath his mustache. There were rips and tears in his uniform and one bootsole had been cut nearly in half by a minie bullet. He shook his foot so the dangling leather flapped. "They didn't trip me up that time," he said, laughing. His battle blood was up; his eyes were shining. Presently, however, as the general sat watching his soldiers celebrate their capture of the orchard and its guns, Governor Isham Harris of Tennessee, who had volunteered to serve as his aide during the battle, saw him reel in the saddle.

"General — are you hurt?" he cried.

"Yes, and I fear seriously," Johnston said.

None of the rest of his staff was there, the general having sent them off on various missions. Riding with one arm across Johnston's shoulders to prevent his falling, Harris guided the bay into a nearby ravine, where he eased the pale commander to the ground and began unfastening his clothes in an attempt to find the wound. He had no luck until he noticed the right boot full of blood, and then he found it: a neat hole drilled just above the hollow of the knee, marking where the femoral artery had been severed. This called for a knowledge of tourniquets, but the governor knew nothing of such things. The man who knew most about them, Johnston's staff physician, had been ordered by the general to attend to a group of Federal wounded he encountered on his way to the far right. When the doctor protested, Johnston cut him off: "These men were our enemies a moment ago. They are our prisoners now. Take care of them." So Harris alone was left to do what he could to staunch the bright red flow of blood.

He could do little. Brandy might help, he thought, but when he poured some into the hurt man's mouth it ran back out again. Presently a colonel, Johnston's chief of staff, came hurrying into the ravine. But he could do nothing either. He knelt down facing the general. "Johnston, do you know me? Johnston, do you know me?" he kept asking, over and over, nudging the general's shoulder as he spoke.

But Johnston did not know him. Johnston was dead.

It was now about 2.30. When the command passed to Beauregard — who in point of fact had been exercising it all along, in a general way, from his headquarters at Shiloh Chapel — his first order was that news of Johnston's death was to be kept from the men, lest they become disheartened before completing the destruction of the northern army. There would be no let-up; the attack was to continue all along the line, particularly against the Hornets Nest, whose outer flank was threatened now by the Confederates who had flung Hurlbut's men gunless out of the orchard and taken their place. After a lull, which allowed for the shifting of troops to strengthen the blow, the line was ready to go forward. A dozen separate full-scale assaults had been launched against the sunken road, each one over a thickening carpet of dead and wounded. All twelve had failed; but this one would not fail. Pressure alone not having been enough, now pressure was to be combined with blasting. At point-blank range, with Beauregard's approval, Dan Ruggles had massed 62 guns to rake the place with canister and grape.

When those guns opened, clump by clump, then all together, blending their separate crashes into one continuous roar, it was as if the Hornets Nest exploded, inclosing its defenders in a smoky, flame-cracked din of flying clods, splintered trees, uprooted brush, and whirring metal. Elsewhere on the field that morning a wounded soldier, sent to the rear by his company commander, had soon returned, shouting to be heard above the racket: "Captain, give me a gun! This durn fight aint got any rear!" Presently this was quite literally true for Prentiss, who held fast along the sunken road. On the flanks, the men of Hurlbut and W. H. L. Wallace scrambled backward to get from under the crash. The line was bent into a horseshoe. Then Wallace fell, cut down as he tried to rally his men, and they gave way entirely, running headlong. Hurlbut's followed suit. Only Prentiss's troops remained steadfast along the sunken road, flanked and then surrounded. The horseshoe became an iron hoop as the Confederates, pursuing Hurlbut and the remnants of Wallace around both flanks of Prentiss, met in his rear and sealed him off.

He could hear them yelling back there, triumphant, but he fought on, obedient to his strict instructions to "maintain that position at all hazards." The dead lay thick. Every minute they lay thicker. Still he fought. By 5.30 — two long hours after Ruggles' guns began their furious cannonade — further resistance became futile, and Prentiss knew it. He had the cease-fire sounded and surrendered his 2200 survivors, well under half the number he had started with that morning. Sherman and McClernand on the right, and Hurlbut to a lesser degree on the left, had saved their divisions by falling back each time the pressure reached a certain intensity. Prentiss had lost his by standing fast: lost men, guns, colors, and finally the position itself: lost all, in fact, but honor. Yet he had saved far more in saving that. Sherman and Mc-Clernand had saved their divisions by retreating, but Prentiss had saved Grant by standing fast.

Beauregard saw it otherwise. During twelve hours of fighting, in addition to much other booty found in the captured camps, his army had taken 23 cannon, exclusive of those surrendered by Prentiss, and flushed the Northerners from every position they had chosen to try for a stand. The Hornets Nest, if the toughest of these, was merely one more in a series of continuing successes. Now that the sunken road lay in rear of the advance, the shortened line could be strengthened for the final go-for-broke assault that would shove what was left of Grant's army over the bluff and into the Tennessee. So he thought, at any rate; until he tried it. On the left, Hardee and Polk were pecking away at Sherman and McClernand, but the attacks were not delivered with spirit or conviction. Too many of their men had died or straggled, and those who stayed were near exhaustion. On the right, where more could be expected in the wake of the recent collapse, Bragg and Breckinridge fared even worse. Their casualties had been about as high and the number of stragglers was even higher; hundreds stayed behind to gawk at the captured thousands, including one real live Yankee general, who came marching out of the Hornets Nest under guard. Two of Bragg's brigades — or the remnants — tried an assault on the left flank of the Federals, who were crowded into a semi-circular position along the road that led from the landing to the bridge that spanned Snake Creek. However, it was delivered across a ravine knee-deep in backwater, and when the weary troops emerged on the far side they were met by massed volleys almost as heavy as those that had shattered Prentiss. They ran back, scrambling for cover, and the long day's fight was over.

The sun was down. Beauregard merely made the halt official when he sent couriers riding through the gathering twilight with orders for the attacks to be suspended and the men brought back to rest for the completion of their work tomorrow morning. Much of the Yankee army might escape under cover of darkness, but it could not be helped. The lesson of Manassas was repeated. For green troops, victory could be as destructive of effective organization as defeat, and even more exhausting. As the men withdrew, a patter of rain began to sound. The rumble of heavy guns, fired intermittently from beyond the bluff, was

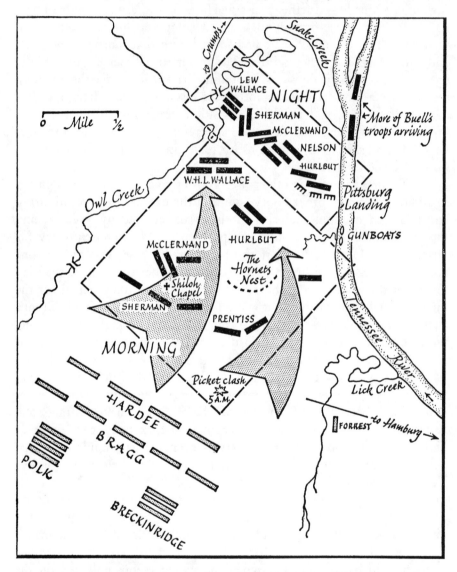

mixed with peals of thunder. Lightning flashed; the rain fell harder. A hundred miles northwest, the *Pittsburg*'s crew was thankful for the storm as they prepared to make their run past Island Ten; the *Carondelet* was waiting. Here on the battlefield which took its name from the log church called Shiloh — interpreted by Bible scholars to mean "the place of peace" — those who could found shelter in the Federal camps and had their dreams invaded by the drum of rain on canvas. Others slept in the open, where the rain fell alike on the upturned faces of the dead and of those who slept among them, inured by having seen so much of death that day already, or else just made indifferent by exhaustion.

★ ★ ★

Confidence south of the battle line, that when the attack was renewed tomorrow the Federals would be driven into the river, was matched by confidence north of it, at least on the part of the northern commander, that the reverse would rather be the case. Surrounded by his staff Grant sat on horseback just in rear of the guns whose massed volleys had shattered the final rebel assault. His army had been driven two miles backward; one division had surrendered en masse; another had been decimated, its commander killed, and the other three were badly shaken, bled to half their strength. So that when one of the staff officers asked if the prospect did not appear "gloomy," it must have seemed an understatement to the rest; but not to Grant. "Not at all," he said. "They can't force our lines around these batteries tonight. It is too late. Delay counts everything with us. Tomorrow we shall attack them with fresh troops and drive them, of course."

Fresh troops were the answer, and he had them; Buell's men were arriving as he spoke. By morning, 20,000 of them would have climbed the bluff in the wake of Nelson's lead brigade, which had been ferried across from the opposite bank in time to assist in repulsing the attack against the fifty guns assembled on the left. The navy, too, was in support and had a share in wrecking the last assault. Though all the ironclads were at Island Ten, two wooden gunboats were at Pittsburg, anchored where a creek ran out of the last-ditch ravine into the river, and thus were able to throw their shells into the ranks of the Confederates as they charged. Nor was that all. As twilight deepened into dusk, Lew Wallace at last came marching across Snake Creek bridge to station his division on the right flank of the army. He had marched toward what he thought was such a junction as soon as he received Grant's first order, but then had had to countermarch for the river road when he learned that the flank had been thrown back near the landing. Five hours behind schedule, he got jaundiced looks on arrival, but his 6000 soldiers, mostly Donelson veterans, were no less welcome for being late. Combined with Buell's troops and the survivors of the all-day fight, they meant that Grant would go into battle on the second day with more men than he had had at dawn of the first. Then too, well over half of them would be unworn by fighting: whereas the Confederates would not only have been lessened by their casualties, but would most likely not have recovered from the weariness that dropped so many of them in their tracks as soon as the firing stopped.

Grant had another sizeable reserve — 6000 to 12,000 men, depending on various estimates — but he did not include them in his calculations. These were the skulkers, fugitives who took shelter along the river bank while the battle raged on the plateau overhead. Every man on the field had come up this way, debarking from the transports, so that when the going got too rough they remembered that high bluff, reared up one hundred feet tall between the landing and the fighting, and made for it as soon as their minds were more on safety than on honor. Some were trying to cadge rides on the ferries plying back and forth; others, more enterprising, paddled logs and jerry-built rafts in an attempt to reach the safety of the eastern bank. Still others were content to remain where they were, calling out to Buell's men as they came ashore: "We are whipped! Cut to pieces! You'll catch it! *You*'ll see!" Nelson, a six-foot five-inch three-hundred-pound former navy lieutenant, lost his temper at the sight. "They were insensible to shame and sarcasm," he later declared, "for I tried both; and, indignant of such poltroonery, I asked permission to fire on the knaves." However, the colonel who commanded the fuming general's lead brigade was more sickened than angered by the display. "Such looks of terror, such confusion, I never saw before, and do not wish to see again," he recorded in his diary.

Perhaps like the colonel Grant preferred to leave them where they were, out of contact with the men who had stood and fought today or were expected to stand and fight tomorrow. Fear was a highly contagious emotion, and even if threats or cajolery could have herded them back up the bluff, they would most likely run again as soon as the minies began whizzing. Perhaps, too, he saw them as a reproach, a sign that his army had been surprised and routed, at least to this extent, because its commander had left it unintrenched, green men to the front, and had taken so few precautions against an enemy who, according to him, was "heartily tired" of fighting. At any rate he allotted the skulkers no share in his plans for tomorrow. Nor did he return to the fine big house nine miles downriver, or even seek shelter in one of the steamboat cabins. After inspecting his battle line — his four divisions would take the right, Buell's three the left — he wrapped himself in a poncho and lay down under a large oak to get some sleep. The rain had already begun, however, and presently it fell in torrents, dripping through the branches to add to the discomfort of his aching ankle. Unable to sleep, he wandered off to take refuge in a cabin on the bluff. But that would not do either. The surgeons had set up a field hospital there and were hard at work, bloody past the elbows. Driven out by the screams of the wounded and the singing of the bone-saws, Grant returned to his oak and got to sleep at last, despite the rain and whatever twinges he was feeling in his ankle and his conscience.

He had an insomniac counterpart beyond the line of battle. But
Bedford Forrest's ankle and conscience were intact; his sleeplessness
proceeded from entirely different causes. His regiment had been assigned
to guard the Lick Creek fords, but after some hours of hearing the guns
he had crossed over on his own initiative and claimed a share in the
fighting. It stopped soon after sundown, but not Forrest. Out on a scout,
he reached the lip of the bluff, south of the landing, and saw Buell's reinforcements coming ashore. For Forrest this meant just one thing: the
Confederates must either stage a night attack or else get off that table-
land before the Federals charged them in the morning. Unable to locate
Beauregard, he went from camp to camp, telling of what he had seen
and urging an attack, but few of the brigadiers even knew where their
men were sleeping, and those who did were unwilling to take the responsibility of issuing such an order. At last he found Hardee, who informed him that the instructions already given could not be changed;
the cavalryman was to return to his troops and "keep up a strong and
vigilant picket line." Forrest stomped off, swearing. "If the enemy
comes on us in the morning, we'll be whipped like hell," he said.

Unlocated and uninformed — he slept that night in Sherman's
bed, near Shiloh Chapel — Beauregard not only did not suspect that
Buell had arrived, he had good reason for thinking that he would not
be there at all, having received from a colonel in North Alabama — it
was Ben Hardin Helm, one of Lincoln's Confederate brothers-in-law —
a telegram informing him that Buell had changed his line of march and
now was moving toward Decatur. The Creole went to bed content
with what had been done today and confident that Grant's destruction
would be completed tomorrow. Before turning in, he sent a wire to
Richmond announcing that the army had scored "a complete victory,
driving the enemy from every position."

His chief of staff, sharing an improvised bed in the adjoining
headquarters tent with the captured Prentiss, was even more ebullient,
predicting that the northern army would surrender as soon as the battle
was resumed. The distinguished captive, accepting his predicament
with such grace as became a former Virginian, did not agree with his
host's prognostication; nor was he reticent in protest. "You gentlemen
have had your way today," he said, "but it will be very different tomorrow. You'll see. Buell will effect a junction with Grant tonight and
we'll turn the tables on you in the morning." No such thing, the Confederate declared, and showed him the telegram from Helm. Prentiss
was unimpressed. "You'll see," he said.

Outside in the rain, those who had been too weary to look for
shelter, along with those who had looked without success, got what
sleep they could, in spite of the 11-inch shells fired two every fifteen
minutes by the gunboats. Their fuzes describing red parabolas across

the starless velvet of the night, they came down steeply, screaming, to explode among the sleepers and the wounded of both sides; "wash pots" and "lampposts," the awed soldiers called the big projectiles. All night the things continued to fall on schedule. Dawn grayed the east, and presently from the direction of the sunrise came the renewed clatter of musketry, the crack and boom of field artillery. As it swelled quickly to a roar, Prentiss sat bolt upright on the pallet of captured blankets inside Sherman's headquarters tent, grinning at his Confederate bedmate. "There is Buell!" he cried. "Didn't I tell you so?"

★ ★ ★

It was Buell, just as Prentiss said. His other two divisions, under Brigadier Generals Alexander D. McCook and Thomas L. Crittenden — the latter being the brother of the Confederate corps commander who had been relieved on the eve of battle — had come up in the night; he was attacking. Grant's four divisions — one hale and whole, if somewhat shamefaced over its roundabout march the day before, the others variously battered and depleted, but quite willing — took up the fire on the right, and at 7 o'clock the general sent a message to the gunboats. They were to cease their heavy caliber bombardment; the army was going forward.

Grant's orders, sent as soon as he rose at dawn from his sleep beneath the dripping oak, directed his generals to "advance and re-capture our original camps." At first it was easy enough. The rebels. having broken contact the night before, were caught off balance and gave ground rapidly, surprised to find the tables turned by unexpected pressure. Wallace, Sherman, and McClernand, with Hurlbut's remnants in reserve, pushed forward to the vicinity of McClernand's camp before they ran into heavy artillery fire and halted, as Sherman said, "patiently waiting for the sound of General Buell's advance." They had not long to wait: Buell's men were taking their baptism of fire in stride. One Indiana colonel, dissatisfied with signs of shakiness when his men encountered resistance — Sherman, who was looking on, referred to it as "the severest musketry fire I ever heard" (which would make it severe indeed, after all he had been through yesterday) — halted them, then and there, and put them briskly through the manual of arms, "which they executed," he later reported, "as if on the parade ground." Considerably steadied, the Hoosiers resumed their advance. By noon, Buell's men had cleared the peach orchard on the left and Grant's were approaching Shiloh Chapel on the right. There the resistance stiffened.

After the initial shock of finding Buell on the field after all, Beauregard recovered a measure of his aplomb and went about the task of preparing his men to receive instead of deliver an attack. This was by no means easy, not only because of the gallant rivalry which urged the two armies of Westerners forward against him, but also because his own troops had scattered badly about the blasted field in their search for food and shelter the night before. Polk, in fact, had misunderstood the retirement order and marched his survivors all the way back to their pre-battle camp on the Corinth road. Improvising as best he could, the Creole assigned Hardee the right, Breckinridge the center, and Bragg the left. When Polk returned, belatedly, he put him in between the last two. It was touch and go, however. Like Johnston, he found it necessary to set a spirited example for his men. Twice he seized the colors of wavering regiments and led them forward. Reproved for rashness by a friend who doubtless recalled what had happened to Johnston yesterday, Beauregard replied: "The order now must be 'Follow,' not 'Go'!"

At one point that afternoon he received a shock that was followed in quick succession by a hopeful surge of elation and a corresponding droop of disappointment. He noticed in some woods along his front a body of troops dressed in what appeared to be shiny white silk uniforms. At first he thought they were Federals who had breached his line, but when he saw that they were firing north, it occurred to him — though he had long since given up the notion that they could possibly arrive on time — that they might be the vanguard of Van Dorn's 15,000 reinforcements, hurried east by rail from Memphis. Certainly there were no such uniforms in the Army of the Mississippi, while there was no telling what outlandish garb the Elkhorn Tavern veterans might wear. Presently, however, a staff officer, sent to investigate, returned with the explanation. They were the general's own Orleans Guard battalion, who had turned their dress blue jackets wrong side out to put an end to being fired on by their friends. Yesterday they had startled the defenders of the Hornets Nest by charging thus with the white silk linings of their coats exposed; "graveyard clothes," the Federals had called them.

The Confederates had their backs up and were holding well along the ridge where Sherman's tents were pitched; today as yesterday Shiloh Chapel was army headquarters. But the men were bone-weary. Clearly they had no chance of defeating the reinforced Federals now applying pressure all along the line, the breaking of a single link of which might prove disastrous to the whole. Not only were they weary: their spirits had flagged at the sudden frown of fortune, the abrupt removal of victory just as it seemed within their grasp. Governor Harris, still a volunteer aide, sensed this feeling of futility in the soldiers. Shortly after 2 o'clock, he expressed his fear of a collapse to the chief of staff, who agreed and went to Beauregard with the question: "General, do you not think our troops are very much in the condition of a lump of sugar thoroughly soaked in water — preserving its original shape, though ready to dissolve? Would it not be judicious to get away with what we

have?" Beauregard nodded, looking out over the field of battle. "I
intend to withdraw in a few moments," he said calmly.

Couriers soon rode out with orders for the corps commanders
to begin the retreat. Breckinridge was posted along the high ground
just south of Shiloh Chapel, his line studded with guns which kept up a
steady booming as the other corps retired. Executed smoothly and
without disorder, the retrograde maneuver had been completed by
4 o'clock, with time allowed for captured goods to be gleaned from
the field and loaded into wagons, including five stands of regimental
colors and twenty-one flags of the United States. Hardee, Bragg, and
Polk marched their men a mile beyond and camped for the night where
they had slept on their arms two nights before, in line of battle for
Sunday's dawn assault. Breckinridge stayed where he was, prepared to
discourage pursuit. But there was none to discourage: Grant's men
were content with the recovery of their pillaged camps.

All day there had been intermittent showers, brief but thunderous downpours that drenched the men and then gave way to steamy
sunshine. That night, however, the rain came down in earnest. Privates
crowded into headquarters tents and stood close-packed as bullets in
a cartridge box, having lost their awe of great men. When Breckinridge
moved out next morning to join the long Confederate column grinding
its way toward Corinth, the roads were quagmires. The wind veered,
whistling out of the north along the boughs of roadside trees, and
froze the rain to sleet; the countryside was blanketed with white. Hailstones fell as large as partridge eggs, plopping into the mud and rattling
into the wagon beds to add to the suffering of the wounded, who, as
one of them said, had been "piled in like bags of grain." Beauregard
doubled the column all day to encourage and comfort the men, speaking to them much as he would do on a visit to one of their camps a
week later, when, seeing a young soldier with a bandaged head, he rode
up to him, extended his hand, and said: "My brave friend, were you
wounded? Never mind; I trust you will soon be well. Before long we
will make the Yankees pay up, interest and all. The day of our glory
is near." Cheered by the bystanders, he gave them a bow as he rode
away, and that night the boy wrote home: "It is strange Pa how we
love that little black Frenchman."

For the present, though, the cheers were mostly perfunctory
along that column of jolted, sleet-chilled men. They had had enough
of glory for a while. It was not that they felt they had been defeated.
They had not. But they had failed in what they had set out to do,
and the man who had led them out of Corinth to accomplish the destruction of "agrarian mercenaries" was laid out dead now in a cottage
there. All the same, they took much consolation in the thought that
they had held their lines until they were ready to leave, and then had
done so in good order, unpursued.

They were not entirely unpursued. In the Federal camp the burial details were at work and the surgeons moved about the field, summoned by the anguished cries of mangled soldiers from both armies; but Sherman was not there. Prompted by Grant, he had moved out that morning with one brigade to make a show of pursuit, or at any rate to see that the Confederates did not linger. A show was all it was, however, for when he reached a point on the Corinth road, four miles beyond his camps, he was given a lesson hunters sometimes learned from closing in too quickly on a wounded animal.

The place was called the Fallen Timbers, a half-mile-wide boggy swale where a prewar logging project had been abandoned. The road dipped down, then crested a ridge on the far side, where he could see enemy horsemen grouped in silhouette against the sky. Not knowing their strength or what might lie beyond the ridge, he shook out a regiment of skirmishers, posted cavalry to back them up and guard their flanks, then sent them forward, following with the rest of the brigade in attack formation at an interval of about two hundred yards. The thing was done in strict professional style, according to the book. But the man he was advancing against had never read the book, though he was presently to rewrite it by improvising tactics that would conform to his own notion of what war was all about. "War means fighting," he said. "And fighting means killing." It was Forrest. Breckinridge had assigned him a scratch collection of about 350 Tennessee, Kentucky, Mississippi, and Texas cavalrymen, turning over to him the task of protecting the rear of the retreating column.

As he prepared to defend the ridge, outnumbered five-to-one by the advancing blue brigade, he saw something that caused him to change his mind and his tactics. For as the skirmishers entered the vine-tangled hollow, picking their way around felled trees and stumbling through the brambles, they lost their neat alignment. In fact, they could hardly have been more disorganized if artillery had opened on them there in the swale. Forrest saw his chance. "Charge!" he shouted, and led his horsemen pounding down the slope. Most of the skirmishers had begun to run before he struck them, but those who stood were knocked sprawling by a blast from shotguns and revolvers. Beyond them, the Federal cavalry had panicked, firing their carbines wildly in the air. When they broke too, Forrest kept on after them, still brandishing his saber and crying, "Charge! Charge!" as he plowed into the solid ranks of the brigade drawn up beyond. The trouble was, he was charging by himself; the others, seeing the steady brigade front, had turned back and were already busy gathering up their 43 prisoners. Forrest was one gray uniform, high above a sea of blue. "Kill him! *Kill* the goddam rebel! Knock him off his horse!" It was no easy thing to do; the horse was kicking and plunging and Forrest was hacking and slashing; but one of the soldiers did his best. Reaching far out, he shoved the muzzle of his rifle into the colonel's side and pulled the trigger. The force of the explosion lifted Forrest clear of the saddle, but he regained his seat and sawed the horse around. As he came out of the mass of dark blue uniforms and furious white faces, clearing a path with his saber, he reached down and grabbed one of the soldiers by the collar, swung him onto the crupper of the horse, and galloped back to safety, using the Federal as a shield against the bullets fired after him. Once he was out of range, he flung the hapless fellow off and rode on up the ridge where his men were waiting in open-mouthed amazement.

Sherman was amazed, too, but mostly he was disgusted. As soon as he had gathered up his wounded and buried his dead, he turned back toward Pittsburg Landing. Snug once more in his tent near Shiloh Chapel, he wrote his report of the affair. It concluded: "The check sustained by us at the fallen timbers delayed our advance.... Our troops being fagged out by three days' hard fighting, exposure and privation, I ordered them back to camp, where all now are."

★   ★   ★

The ball now lodged alongside Forrest's spine as he followed the column grinding its way toward Corinth was the last of many to draw blood in the Battle of Shiloh. Union losses were 1754 killed, 8408 wounded, 2885 captured: total, 13,047 — about 2000 of them Buell's. Confederate losses were 1723 killed, 8012 wounded, 959 missing: total, 10,694. Of the 100,000 soldiers engaged in this first great bloody conflict of the war, approximately one out of every four who had gone into battle had been killed, wounded, or captured. Casualties were 24 percent, the same as Waterloo's. Yet Waterloo had settled something, while this one apparently had settled nothing. When it was over the two armies were back where they started, with other Waterloos ahead. In another sense, however, it had settled a great deal. The American volunteer, whichever side he was on in this war, and however green, would fight as fiercely and stand as firmly as the vaunted veterans of Europe.

Now that this last had been proved beyond dispute, the leaders on both sides persuaded themselves that they had known it all along, despite the doubts engendered by Manassas and Wilson's Creek, which dwindled now by contrast to comparatively minor engagements. Looking instead at the butcher's bill — the first of many such, it seemed — they reacted, as always, according to their natures. Beauregard, for example, recovered his high spirits in short order. Two days after the battle he wired Van Dorn, still marking time in Arkansas: "Hurry your forces as rapidly as possible. I believe we can whip them again." He believed what he told the wounded soldier, "The day of our glory is near," and saw no occasion for retracting the announcement of "complete victory" sent to Richmond on the night of the first day. In fact, the further he got from the battle in time, the greater it seemed to him as a continuing demonstration of the superiority of southern arms. Nor did Davis retract the exultant message he sent to Congress in passing the telegram along. He was saddened, however, by other news it contained: namely, the loss of Albert Sidney Johnston. "When he fell," Davis wrote long afterward, "I realized that our strongest pillar had been broken."

Reactions on the other side were also characteristic. Once more Halleck saw his worst fears enlarged before his eyes, and got aboard a St Louis steamboat, bound for Pittsburg Landing, to take charge of the army himself before Grant destroyed it entirely. "Your army is not now in condition to resist an attack," he wired ahead. "It must be made so without delay." Grant tightened his security regulations, as instructed, but he did not seem greatly perturbed by the criticism. Now as always, he was a good deal more concerned with what he would do to the enemy than he was with what the enemy might try to do to him, and in any case he had grown accustomed by now to such reactions from above. The battle losses were another matter, providing some grim arithmetic for study. Total American casualties in all three of the nation's previous wars — the Revolution, the War of 1812, and the Mexican War: $10,623+6765+5885$ — were $23,273$. Shiloh's totaled $23,741$, and most of them were Grant's.

Perhaps this had something to do with his change of mind as to the fighting qualities of his opponents. At any rate, far from thinking them "heartily tired" and ready to chuck the war, he later said quite frankly that, from Shiloh on, "I gave up all idea of saving the Union except by complete conquest."

✷ 3 ✷

While the ironclad gunboats of the western navy were pounding out their victories on the Tennessee, the Cumberland, and the mile-wide Mississippi — past Island Ten, they now were bearing down on undermanned Fort Pillow; Memphis, unbraced for the shock, was next on the list — the wooden ships of the blue-water navy were not idle in the east. Along the coasts of the Atlantic and the Gulf, where the thickened blockade squadrons hugged the remaining harbors and river outlets, the fall and winter amphibious gains had been continued and extended. Three times the *Monitor* had declined the *Merrimac-Virginia*'s challenge to single combat in Hampton Roads; if the rebel vessel wanted trouble, let her make it by trying to interfere with the *Monitor*'s task of protecting the rest of the fleet off Old Point Comfort. This she could not or would not do, and the *Monitor* maintained station in shoal water, content with a stalemate, while elsewhere other Federal warships were stepping up the tempo of Confederate disasters.

By mid-March the month-old Roanoke Island victory had been extended to New Bern and other important points around the North Carolina sounds, including control of the railroad which had carried men and supplies to the armies in Virginia. Simultaneously, down on the Florida coast, Fernandina was seized, followed before the end of the month by the uncontested occupation of Jacksonville and St Augustine. Charleston and Savannah had been threatened all this time by the army-navy build-up at Port Royal. In April, while preparations were under way for a siege of the South Carolina city, an attack was mounted against Fort Pulaski, a stout brick pentagon on Cockspur Island, guarding the mouth of the Savannah River. Heavy guns and mortars knocked it to pieces, breaching the casemates and probing for the powder magazine. After thirty-odd hours of bombardment, the white flag went up and the blue-clad artillerists moved in to accept the surrender. Mostly they were New Englanders, and when a Georgian made the inevitable allusion to wooden nutmegs, a Connecticut man, pointing to a 10-inch solid shot that had pierced the wall, told him: "We don't make them of wood any longer."

Savannah itself was not taken, and indeed there was no need to take it. Sealed off as it was by the guns of Fort Pulaski, it was no more important now, at least from the naval point of view, than any other inland Confederate city which had lost its principal reason for existence. Wilmington, North Carolina, a much tougher proposition, with stronger and less accessible defenses, was presently the only major Atlantic port not captured or besieged by Union soldiers. Here the sleek low ghost-gray blockade-runners made their entrances and exits, usually by the dark of the moon, burning smokeless coal and equipped with telescopic funnels and feathered paddles to hide them from the noses, eyes, and ears of their pursuers. Martial and flippant names they had, the *Let Her Be* and *Let Her Rip*, the *Fox, Leopard, Lynx* and *Dream*, the *Banshee, Secret, Kate* and *Hattie*, the *Beauregard*, the *Stonewall Jackson*, the *Stag* and *Lady Davis*. The risks were great (one out of ten had been caught the year before; this year the odds were one-to-eight) but the profits were even greater. Two trips would pay the purchase price; the third and all that followed were pure gravy, as well as a substantial aid to the southern problem of supply. Last fall, one of the slim speedy vessels had steamed into Savannah with 10,000 Enfield rifles, a million cartridges, two million percussion caps, 400 barrels of powder, and a quantity of cutlasses, revolvers, and other badly needed materials of war. For all their reduction of the number of ports to be guarded, the blockade squadrons had their hands full.

Meanwhile, down along the Gulf, another Federal fleet was

scoring corresponding successes to maintain the victory tempo set by
its Atlantic rivals. At the mouth of the Florida river whose name it
bore, Apalachicola fell in early April, followed in quick succession by
the seizure of Pass Christian and Biloxi, on the Mississippi coast.
These were bloodless conquests, the defenders having left to fight at
Shiloh alongside the main body summoned north from Pensacola,
which in turn was taken early the following month. Like Wilmington,
Mobile remained — a much tougher proposition; but even before the
capture of Pensacola, the Federals had made substantial lodgments on
the coast of every southern state except Texas and Alabama.

Satisfying as all these salt-water victories were to the over-all
command, the fact remained that, unlike the western navy on its way
down the Mississippi, they had merely nibbled at the rim of the rebellion. Except for simplifying the blockade difficulties — which was much
— they had accomplished very little, really, even as diversions. The
problem, seen fairly clearly now by everyone, from Secretary Welles
down to the youngest powder monkey, was conquest: *divide et impera*,
pierce and strangle: which had been the occupation of the river gunboats all these months while the blue-water ships were pounding at the
beaches. It was time for them, too, to try their hand at conquest by division instead of subtraction.

If the Mississippi could be descended, perhaps it could be ascended as well, so that when the salt- and fresh-water sailors met
somewhere upstream like upper and nether millstones, having ground
any fugitive elements of the enemy fleet between them, the Confederacy — and the task of its subjugation — would be riven. Much effort
and much risk would be involved; the problems were multitudinous,
including the fact that the thing would have to be done by wooden
ships. But surely it was worth any effort, and almost any risk, considering the prize that awaited success at the very start: New Orleans.

The Crescent City was not only the largest in the South, it was
larger by population than any other four combined, and in the peacetime volume of its export trade, as a funnel for the produce of the
Mississippi Valley, it ranked among the foremost cities of the world. Its
loss would not only depress the South, and correspondingly elate the
North; it would indicate plainly to Europe — especially France, where
so many of its people had connections of blood and commerce — the
inability of the rebels to retain what they had claimed by rebellion. In
short, its capture would be a feather, indeed a plume, in the cap of any
man who could conceive and execute the plan that would prise this chief
jewel from the crown of King Cotton.

One man already had such a plan, along with an absolute ache
for such a feather. Commodore David Porter had made naval history
as captain of the *Essex* in the War of 1812, and his son David Dixon

Porter, forty-eight years old and recently promoted to commander, was determined to have at least an equal share of glory in this one. What was more, in the case of New Orleans he knew whereof he spoke. Thirty trips in and out of the Passes during a peacetime hitch in the merchant marine had familiarized him with the terrain, and months of blockade duty off the river's four main mouths had given him a chance to talk with oystermen and pilots about recent developments in the city's defenses. He knew the obstacles, natural and man-made, and he believed he knew how to get around or through them. Nor was he one to wait for fame to find him. In late '61 he turned up in Washington to unfold his plan for the approval of the Navy Secretary.

New Orleans itself was a hundred miles upriver, but its principal defense against attack from below was a pair of star-shaped masonry works, Forts Jackson and St Philip, built facing each other on opposite banks of the river, just above a swift-currented bend three fourths of the way down. Formerly part of the U.S. system of permanent defenses, they had been taken over and strengthened by the Confederates. Fort Jackson, on the right bank, was the larger, mounting 74 guns; Fort St Philip, slightly upstream on the east bank, mounted 52. Between them, with a combined garrison of 1100 men and an armament of 126 guns, they dominated a treacherous stretch where approaching ships would have to slow to make the turn. Originally there had been doubt that all this strength would be needed, rivermen having assured the defenders that no deep draft vessel could ever get over the bars that blocked the outlets. However, this had been disproved in early October when the commander of the Gulf Blockade Squadron, finding the task of patrolling the multi-mouthed river well-nigh impossible from outside, sent three heavy warships across the southwest bar and stationed them fifteen miles above, at the juncture called Head of the Passes, a deep-water anchorage two miles long and half as wide, where the river branched to create its lower delta. As long as those sloops and their frowning guns remained there, nothing could get in or out of the Passes; New Orleans would languish worse than ever, her trade being limited to what could be sneaked out by the roundabout route through Lake Pontchartrain and past the vigilant Federals on Ship Island, which had been seized the month before.

Clearly this was intolerable, and the city's defenders prepared to correct it at once. They had a makeshift fleet of four flat-bottomed towboats mounting two guns each, a seven-gun revenue cutter seized from Mexico before the war, under highly improbable charges of piracy, and a Boston-built seagoing tug covered over with boiler plate and equipped with an iron beak and a single 32-pounder trained unmovably dead ahead. Perhaps to offset her ugliness — all that metal caused her to ride so low in the water, she rather resembled a floating eggplant — the authorities had given the ram the proud name *Manassas*.

On the dark night of October 11, moving swiftly with the help of the four-knot current, she led the way downriver for an attack on the three big warships patrolling the Head of the Passes. Surprise was to be the principal advantage; the six-boat flotilla moved with muffled engines and no lights. To help offset the armament odds — 16 guns, of moderate size or smaller, would be opposed by 51, over half of which were 8-inch or larger — tugs brought along three "fire-rafts," long flatboats loaded with highly combustible pine knots and rosin, which would be ignited and sent careening with the current when the time came. The plan was for the *Manassas* to make a ram attack in darkness, then fire a rocket as the signal for the fire rafts to be lit and loosed and the gunboats to come down and join the melee.

The Federals had no lookout stationed, only the normal anchor watches they would have carried in any harbor. The first they knew of an attack was at 3.40 a.m. when a midshipman burst into his captain's cabin crying, "Captain, there's a steamer alongside of us!" On deck, the skipper barely had time to see "an indescribable object" emit a puff of smoke even darker than the night. As Beat-to-Quarters sounded there was a crash; the *Manassas* had struck the 1900-ton flagship *Richmond*, which now began firing indiscriminate broadsides, like bellows of pain, and hoisted three light-signals in rapid succession: ENEMY PRESENT. GET UNDER WAY. ACT AT DISCRETION. All three of the sloops were firing frantically, though none of them could see anything to aim at. The *Manassas* was groping blindly, filled with coal smoke. She had struck a barge lashed alongside the Federal flagship; the force of the blow had knocked her engines loose and a hawser had carried her stacks away, flush with the deck. In time she got the rocket off, how-ever, and presently three distant sparks appeared upriver, growing in size as the rafts flamed higher and drew closer.

Aboard the sloops, delay had only served to increase the panic. PROCEED DOWN SOUTHWEST PASS. CROSS THE BAR, the flagship signaled, and all three went with the current, the sluggish *Richmond* swinging broadside to it, helpless. One got over; the next lodged fast on the bar, stern upriver; then the *Richmond* struck and stuck, still broadside. The fire-rafts had run harmless against bank, but the Confederate gunboats, which up to now had not engaged, took the grounded sloops under fire with their small-caliber long-range Whitworths. Presently the Union flag-officer, Captain John Pope — called "Honest John" to distinguish him from the general who would win fame at Island Ten — was amazed to see the skipper of the other stranded vessel appear on the flagship's quarterdeck, wrapped in a large American flag. He had aban-doned ship, bringing his colors with him, after laying and lighting a slow fuze to the powder magazine, intending thus to keep her from falling into the hands of the rebels.

After a long wait for the explosion — which would bring what

an observer called "a shower of 1½-ton guns through the decks and
bottom of almost any near-by ship" — it finally became evident that
the sloop was not going to blow after all. Pope sent the flag-draped
captain back to defend her and, if possible, get her afloat; which he
subsequently managed to do by heaving most of her guns and ammunition over the side. (It later developed that the seaman charged with
lighting the fuze had obeyed orders, but then, not being in sympathy
with them, had cut off the sputtering end and tossed it overboard.) By
now it was broad open daylight; the Confederates withdrew upstream,
satisfied with their morning's work of clearing the Head of the
Passes, and Pope made a tour of inspection to assess damages. Except
for a small hole punched in the flagship when the *Manassas* struck the
coal barge, there were none. Not a man had been hurt, not a hit had
been scored; or so he thought until next morning, when he found a
6-pound Whitworth solid lodged in his bureau drawer. Explaining his
performance, Honest John reported: "The whole affair came upon
me so suddenly that no time was left for reflection." His request that
he be relieved of command "on account of ill health" was quickly
granted. "I truly feel ashamed for our side," one executive said when
the smoke had cleared away.

Porter, on blockade duty outside the Southwest Pass at the time,
expressed a stronger opinion. It was, he said, "the most ridiculous affair
that ever took place in the American Navy." All the same, it helped in
the formulation of his plan by showing what manner of resistance
could be expected below New Orleans. In addition to the problem of
getting across the bar and past the heavily gunned forts, he knew that
the small Confederate flotilla would attempt to make up, in daring and
ingenuity, for what it lacked in size. Besides, it might not be so small
in time. There were reports of two monster ironclads, larger and
faster than any the Federal navy had ever dreamed of, already under
construction in the city's shipyards. Then too, there were land batteries at Chalmette, where Andrew Jackson's volunteers had stood behind a barricade of cotton bales and mowed down British regulars
fifty years ago. The bars, the forts, the rebel boats, the batteries — these
four, plus unknown others: but the greatest of these, as things now
stood, was the problem of passing the forts. It was as a solution of this
that Porter conceived and submitted his plan for the capture of New
Orleans. The rest could be left to a flag-officer who, having done his
reflecting beforehand, would not panic in a crisis.

The naval expedition, as Porter saw it, would have at its core a
flotilla of twenty mortar vessels, each mounting a ponderous 13-inch
mortar supplied with a thousand shells. Screened by intervening trees,
they would tie up to bank, just short of the bend, and blanket the forts
with high-angle fire while the seagoing sloops and frigates made a run
past in the darkness and confusion. The fleet was to mount no fewer

than 200 heavy guns, exclusive of the mortars, which would assure it more firepower than the enemy had in his forts and boats combined, with the Chalmette batteries thrown in for good measure. Once past the forts, it could wreck the rebel vessels and batteries by the sheer weight of thrown metal: New Orleans, under the frown of Federal warships, would have to choose between destruction and surrender. Army troops, brought along for the purpose — otherwise the show would be purely Navy — would go ashore to guard against internal revolt and outside attempts at recapture, thus freeing the fleet for other upriver objectives: Baton Rouge, Natchez, Vicksburg, and conjunction with Foote's ironclads steaming south. The Mississippi would be Federal, from Minnesota all the way to the Gulf.

By mid-November Porter was in Washington, submitting his proposal to the Secretary. Welles had small use for the commander personally — he had too much gasconade for the New Englander's taste, and before the war he had associated overmuch with Southerners — but the plan itself, coinciding as it did with some thinking Welles had been doing along this line, won his immediate approval. He took him to see the President, who liked it too. "This should have been done sooner," Lincoln said, and arranged a conference with McClellan, whose coöperation would be needed. McClellan saw merit in the plan, but raised some characteristic objections. In his opinion the expedition would entail a siege by 50,000 troops, for the heavy guns inside the forts would crush the wooden ships like eggshells. Bristling, Welles replied that the navy would do the worrying about the risk to its ships; all he wanted from the army was 10,000 men, to be added to the 5000 which Benjamin Butler, flushed by the recent amphibious victory at Hatteras Inlet, was raising now in Massachusetts for service down on the Gulf. When McClellan replied that he could spare that many — Butler in particular could be spared, along with his known talent for cabal — the conference at once got down to specifics.

Secrecy, a prime element of the plan, would be extremely difficult to maintain because of the necessarily large-scale preparations. However, if the expedition's existence could hardly be hidden, perhaps its destination could. With this in mind, a new blockade squadron would be set up in the West Gulf, coincident with some loose talk about Pensacola, Mobile, Galveston — any place, in fact, except New Orleans. Next a roster of ships was drawn up, with an armament of about 250 guns. The choice of a fleet commander was left to Assistant Secretary G. V. Fox, himself a retired Annapolis man, who conferred with Porter on the matter, combing the list of captains. One after another they were rejected, either for being otherwise employed or else for being too much of the Honest John type. At last they came to David Glasgow Farragut, thirty-seventh on the list. Of Spanish extraction, sixty years old and sitting now as a member of a retirement board at Brooklyn Navy Yard, Farragut was a veteran of more than fifty years' active service, having begun as a nine-year-old acting midshipman aboard the *Essex*, whose captain, Porter's father, had informally adopted him and supervised his baptism of fire in the War of 1812. Here was a possibility. He was known to be stout-hearted and energetic; every year on his birthday he turned a handspring, explaining that he would know he was beginning to age when he found the exercise difficult. The trouble was he was southern born, a native of Knoxville, and southern married — twice in fact, both times to ladies from Norfolk — which raised doubts as to his loyalty and accounted for his present inactive assignment. Porter, on his way to New York to arrange for the purchase and assembly of the mortar flotilla, was instructed to call on his foster brother and sound him out.

The retirement board member was waiting for him, a smooth-shaven, square-built, hale-looking man with hazel eyes and heavy eyebrows, wearing his long side hair brushed across the top of his head to hide his baldness. Porter began by asking what he thought of his former associates now gone South. "Those damned fellows will catch it yet," Farragut replied. Asked if he would accept a command to go and fight "those fellows," he said he would. Porter then badgered him by pretending that the objective would be Norfolk, his wife's birthplace. Farragut jumped up crying, "I will take the command: only don't you trifle with me!"

Summoned to Washington, still without suspecting the purpose, he was questioned next by Fox, who asked — as if for a purely theoretical opinion — if he thought New Orleans could be taken from below. "Yes, emphatically," Farragut told him. "The forts are well down the river; ships could easily run them, and New Orleans itself is undefended. It would depend somewhat on the fleet, however."

"Well," Fox said, "— with such a fleet as, say, two steam frigates, five screw sloops of the cities class, a dozen gunboats, and some mortar vessels to shell the forts from high angle?"

"Why, I would engage to run those batteries with two thirds of such a force...."

"What would you say if appointed to head such an expedition?"

"What would I say?" Farragut cried. He leaped to his feet and began to prowl about the room. Now he understood. The goal was to be New Orleans, which he knew well from years of living in it, and he was to have the flag. "What would I say?" he cried, and broke into exclamations of delight.

So it was settled. He received his orders during the last week of the year and began at once to fit out the eighteen warships assigned to his fleet, including two steam frigates, seven screw sloops, and nine gunboats, all of wood and mounting 243 guns, most heavy. Porter meanwhile had been assembling his mortar flotilla of twenty schooners; the weapons themselves were cast in Pittsburgh, along with 30,000 bomb-shells, while the beds were manufactured in New York. In late January Farragut dropped down to Hampton Roads, Porter coming along behind, and by mid-February reached Key West, where final orders from Welles were broken open: "This most important operation of the war is confined to yourself and your brave associates. . . . If successful, you open the way to the sea for the great West, never again to be closed. The rebellion will be riven in the center, and the flag to which you have been so faithful will recover its supremacy in every State."

Convinced by inspection that the way to stop the small-time blockade runners working in and out of the coastal lakes and bayous was to intercept them with vessels adapted to the task, Farragut wrote to the Navy Department asking for some light ships of five-foot draft or less. Since he neglected to say what use would be made of them, Fox thought they were wanted for the upriver attack, which would have meant an unconscionable delay. Dismayed, the Assistant Secretary began to suspect that he had erred in his choice of a fleet commander. Instead of writing to Farragut, however, he wrote to Porter: "I trust that we have made no mistake in our man, but his dispatches are very discouraging. It is not too late to rectify our mistake. You must frankly give me your views. . . . I shall have no peace until I hear from you." Porter replied that it was too late for a change, but that he would do what he could to bolster the old man's shaky judgment. "Men of his age in a seafaring life are not fit for important enterprises, they lack the vigor of youth. He talks very much at random at times and rather underrates the difficulties before him without fairly comprehending them. I know what they are, and as he is impressible hope to make him appreciate them also." He added by way of consolation, "I have great hopes of the mortars if all else fails."

Happily unaware of the distrust of his superiors or the condescension of his adoptive brother, Farragut proceeded to Ship Island for refueling and refitting. By mid-March he was off the mouths of the Mississippi, maneuvering for an entrance, which was finally effected by sending Porter's mortars and the gunboats through Pass à l'Outre and taking the heavier frigates and sloops around to Southwest Pass. After much sweat and inch-by-inch careening — back-breaking labor that tried even Farragut's sunny disposition — all got over the bar except the largest, a 50-gun frigate, twenty of whose guns were distributed among the other vessels of the fleet now assembled at Head of the Passes. There the schooners discharged their seagoing spars and made ready for the work they had been built to do.

By mid-April the preparations were complete. Butler's soldiers were at hand: 18,000 of them, so persuasively had the former politician done his recruiting job in New England. The fleet was at anchor two miles below the bend where the mortar schooners had tied up to both banks, the tips of their masts disguised with foliage lest they show above the trees that screened the vessels from the forts. Ranges were quickly established: 2850 yards to Fort Jackson, 3680 to Fort St Philip. Farragut was somewhat doubtful as to the efficacy of the snub-nosed weapons, but Porter declared confidently that two days of mortar bombardment would reduce both forts to rubble. April 18 — Good Friday — he opened fire.

★ ★ ★

Holy Week was gloomy in New Orleans, the more so because of the contrast between the present frame of mind, with danger looming stark in both directions, and the elation felt six months ago at the comic repulse of the sloops from the Head of the Passes, which had seemed to give point to the popular conviction that "Nothing afloat could pass the forts. Nothing that walked could get through our swamps." Since then a great deal had happened, and all of it bad.

For one thing, the blockade had tightened. Roustabouts no longer swarmed on the levee, for there were no cargoes to unload; the wharves lay idle, and warehouses formerly bulging with cotton and sugar and grain yawned hollow; trade having come to a standstill, ready money was so scarce that there was a current joke that an olive-oil label would pass for cash "because it was greasy, smelt bad, and bore an autograph." For another, Foote's gunboats and Pope's soldiers were smashing obstacles so rapidly upriver that the danger seemed even greater from that direction, with neither forts nor swamps to slow them down. In the midst of these discouragements and fears, troops assigned to the city's defense were called north to fight at Shiloh, and all that returned from that repulse were the members of the honor guard with Sidney Johnston's body, following the muffled drums and the empty-saddled warhorse out St Charles Street to fire the prescribed three volleys across his crypt. Now there was this: Yankee ships once more across the bar, but in such strength that no small-scale attack, however ingenious and daring, could hope to budge them. For New Orleans, as for the South at large, the prospect was grim in this season of death and resurrection.

No one responsible for the city's defense was more aware of the danger than the man who was most responsible of all: Mansfield Lovell, a thirty-nine-year-old Maryland-born West Pointer who had resigned as New York Deputy Street Commissioner to join the Confederacy in September. Impressed with the Chapultepec-brevetted artilleryman's record as an administrator, Davis made him a major general and sent him to replace the over-aged Twiggs in New Orleans; which would not only give the city an energetic and efficient commander, but would also call widespread attention to the fact that willingness to fight for the South's ideals was by no means restricted to men of southern background, Lovell having spent most of his civilian years as a New Jersey ironworks executive. The new major general arrived in early October, and was appalled at the unpreparedness. There was plenty of Gallic enthusiasm, but it found release at champagne parties rather than at work. He wrote to Richmond, protesting that the city was "greatly drained of arms, ammunition, clothing, and supplies for other points." Presently it was drained of fighting men as well, leaving him with what he called a "heterogeneous militia" of 3000 short-term volunteers, "armed mostly with shotguns against 9- and 11-inch Dahlgrens."

The Creoles did not resent his criticisms. They found his intensity amusing and his presence ornamental. "A very attractive figure," one pronounced him, "giving the eye, at first glance, a promise of much activity." His horsemanship was especially admirable; they enjoyed watching him ride dragoon-style "with so long a stirrup-leather that he simply stood astride the saddle, as straight as a spear." To add to the effect, he wore a facial ruff of hair much like Burnside's, except that it was light brown and somewhat less flamboyant.

Despite his activity, no one was more surprised when the Union fleet showed its true intention. Not that he had not known it was assembling. Agents had kept him informed of its strength and location; but they had also relayed the loose talk about Mobile and Pensacola, and Lovell believed them — perhaps because he wanted to. What misled him most, though, was the presence of Ben Butler, who at the Democratic convention of 1860 had voted fifty-seven consecutive times for the nomination of Jefferson Davis before switching over to Breckinridge with the majority. "I regard Butler's Ship Island expedition as a harmless menace so far as New Orleans is concerned," Lovell had told Richmond in late February. "A black Republican dynasty will never give an old Breckinridge Democrat like Butler command of any expedition which they had any idea would result in such a glorious success as the capture of New Orleans." Now he knew better; the warships were across the bar, above the Head of the Passes. But the knowledge came too late. He had been looking upriver all this time, where the Foote-Grant Foote-Pope amphibious teams were wrecking whatever stood in their way, ashore or afloat.

Hastening to meet the threat from above — his intelligence reports were quite good from that direction: too good, as it turned out — he had commandeered fourteen paddle-wheel steamers and converted them into one-gun gunboats, plating their outer bulwarks with inch-thick railroad iron to give them mass and rigidity for use as rams. Launched one by one between January and April, they made up the River Defense Fleet under J. E. Montgomery, a river captain, and were independent of Commander J. K. Mitchell, whose miniature flotilla had thrown such a scare into Honest John Pope six months before. Lovell did not like the command arrangement, which left him no real control over either. Besides, the new gunboats were put in the hands of a notoriously independent breed of men; "fourteen Mississippi river captains and pilots will never agree about anything once they get under way," he predicted. As fast as they came off the ways, eight of the boats were sent upriver to challenge the descending Union fleet at Memphis or Fort Pillow, though Lovell managed to hold onto six of them for the immediate protection of New Orleans. They would not amount to much in the way of a deterrent once the heavy-gunned armada below the forts broke into the clear, but anything that would delay or distract the Federal fleet, however briefly — even to the extent of making it pause to brush them aside — might be of enormous value because of something else that was going on inside the city. He had an ace in the hole; two, in fact. The question was whether he would have time to bring them out and play them.

Porter had heard aright in his talks with the pilots and oystermen; the Confederates were at work on two giant ironclads in the city's shipyards, each of them more formidable than the *Merrimac-Virginia,* which had just completed her work of destruction in Hampton Roads against vessels as stout as any in Farragut's fleet. The first, the *Louisiana,* mounting sixteen heavy rifles, had been launched and cased in a double row of T-shaped rails for armor, the inner rails bolted vertically to the bulwarks, the outer ones reversed and driven down the gaps. There had been various delays, including strikes — one lasted three full weeks — because the workers were unwilling to take Confederate bonds for pay, but the main trouble now was her power plant, which had been transferred from a steamboat. While Farragut was crossing the bar, mechanics were trying without success to coax the *Louisiana*'s engines into motion.

The other ironclad, the *Mississippi,* was an even more novel and formidable proposition, at least in prospect. Over 4000 tons in weight, 270 feet long and 58 feet in the beam, drawing only 14 feet and mounting 20 guns, she was a true dreadnought, designed to wear three-inch armor, have an iron snout set over a casing three feet thick, and be propelled by three engines at a speed of 14 knots; all of which would make her the most powerful and fastest warship ever built. The plan for her use was quite in scale with her proportions. She was to clear the Mississippi of enemy vessels, then the Gulf and the Atlantic, after which she would lay the northern coastal cities under levy. Improbable as this program sounded, it was by no means impossible; certainly nothing afloat or under construction could stand in her way. But first she would have to be finished, and she was still a considerable way from that. She had been launched, her timberwork completed, but so far she was armored only below the gun deck, and her vital

50-foot central drive shaft was too big a casting job for any southern rolling mill except the Tredegar in Richmond, which began work on the order in February. It would be weeks, or months, before delivery and installation of the shaft would permit her to move under her own power.

Time, then, was golden. Lovell bought what he could and tried to buy more by calling for the eight departed gunboats to be returned from upriver. This the government would not do, considering them more needed there to stem the rout at Island Ten and make a shield for Memphis; New Orleans would have to resist with what she had. Primarily then — with the Federal fleet already approaching the bend they guarded — that put the burden on Forts Jackson and St Philip, whose strength or vulnerability had become a subject of disagreement among the river men who had been so confident such a short time back. A chain boom, held afloat by cypress logs, spanned the Mississippi just below the forts, so that when the Yankees ran afoul of it or stopped to try and break it, plunging fire from the parapets would blow them out of the water like sitting ducks. So the river men had reckoned; but the March floods — the highest in anyone's memory — brought such a press of uprooted trees and brush against it that the boom gave way, depriving the gunners of their hope for stationary targets. Quickly the break was mended and the obstacle strengthened by adding a line of hulks to buoy it up. Now that it had broken once, however, there was considerable doubt that it would hold against the pressure, which was building up again.

In desperation Lovell ordered the *Louisiana* towed downstream, to be tied up to the east bank just above Fort St Philip. No less than fifty mechanics continued to tinker with her engines, but even if they never got them going she could serve as a floating battery, adding the weight of her bow and starboard guns to those of the forts. Work continued aboard the *Mississippi*, too, on the outside chance that her drive shaft would arrive before the Federals did. It was Holy Week; Ash Wednesday, then Good Friday, and a message arrived from downriver; both forts were under heavy bombardment, receiving two 200-pound mortar shells a minute. Lovell rode down to see for himself how bad it was.

★ ★ ★

It was bad enough, or anyhow it seemed so. At the end of the first day's firing, the citadel and barracks of Fort Jackson were ablaze, rubble and sandbags thrown about and the protective levee cut, letting backwater into the place. "I was obliged to confine the men most rigidly to the casemates," the commandant reported, "or else we should have lost the best part of the garrison." They huddled there, white-faced with alarm, while the world outside seemed turned to flame and thunder. And yet it was by no means as bad as it seemed, being a good deal more spectacular than effective. Casualties were extremely low in both forts, and nothing really vital was hit in either. In fact, when Porter slowed the rate of fire at nightfall to give his weary crews some rest, his own men were rather more shaken up than those at the opposite ends of the looping trajectories. Soon after noon the lead east-bank schooner had taken a solid through her deck and bottom and had to be shifted down the line. What was more, the work itself was heavy, each piece being required to deliver a round every ten minutes, and the strain of absorbing the ear-pounding, bone-jarring concussions was severe. It was as if the bombardiers had spent those hours inside a tolling bell.

Porter had them back at their rapid-fire work by dawn. He had said he would silence the forts by sunset of the second day, and he intended to do it. All day the firing continued, but with less apparent effect than yesterday, the bursting shells having done all the superficial damage there was to do. At dusk the rebel casemate guns were still in action. Porter did not slacken fire. All night it continued; all Easter Day, all Easter night, all Monday; still the guns replied. In 96 hours — twice Porter's original estimate as to the time it would take to reduce them — the forts had absorbed over 13,000 shells, at a cost of only four men killed, fourteen wounded, and seven guns disabled. Porter's crews were near exhaustion, but he would not slacken fire. All Monday night, all Tuesday, Tuesday night, and Wednesday morning it continued; 16,800 shells had been pumped into the forts, which still replied. Then Farragut intervened. He had never placed much reliance on the mortars anyhow.

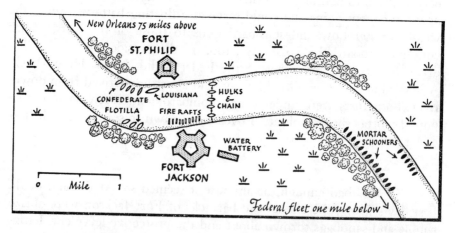

"Look here, David," he said. "We'll demonstrate the practical value of mortar work." He turned to his clerk. "Mr Osbon, get two small flags, a white one and a red one, and go to the mizzen topmasthead and watch the shells fall. If inside the fort, wave the red flag. If outside, wave the white one." In the beginning the fire had been accurate, but the gunners had been numbed into indifference by now; the white flag waved from the masthead far more often than the red. Farragut said calmly, "There's the score. I guess we'll go up the river tonight."

Porter protested, heart and soul. Even if the fleet got past the forts, it would leave them alive in its rear; how would the infantry manage the run in unarmed and unarmored transports? Besides, with the Federal warships gone upriver, what would prevent the surviving enemy gunboats from attacking the mortar flotilla? Farragut replied casually that Butler's men could make a roundabout trip, coming in through the Gulf bayous. As for the threat of rebel survivors, he didn't intend for there to be any; but if there were, then Porter would just have to look out for himself. He called his gig and made the rounds of all his ships, confirming the orders already issued for the run to be made that night. He would "abide by the result," he told them: "conquer or be conquered."

His two biggest worries — how to get across or through the boom and how to deal with fire-rafts — had already been lessened or disposed of. Sunday night two gunboats had gone forward under heavy fire and opened a gap by releasing the chain from one of the hulks. When the defenders responded by sending a fire-raft through the breach, flames leaping a hundred feet in the air, considerable frenzy had ensued, including a collision between two ships whose captains panicked at the threat of being roasted. However, by the time the current had carried the burning mass of pitch and pine harmlessly into the east bank, they knew better how to deal with or avoid them. Farragut had been for running the forts the following night, but a strong north wind had risen to slow him down. It blew through Tuesday; then Wednesday it died and he was ready, having spent the interim preparing his wooden ships for the ordeal. Chains were looped down over the sides to protect the engines and magazines; Jacob's ladders were hung all round, so the carpenters could descend quickly and patch from the outside any holes shot in the hulls. Tubs of water were spotted about, and each ship had a well-drilled fire brigade equipped with grapnels for handling fire-rafts. The outer bulwarks were smeared with mud to hide the ships from the spotters in the forts, but the decks and the breeches of the guns were given a coat of whitewash to provide reflected light for nightwork. As a final touch — one that never failed to provoke a sensation at the pit of every sailor's stomach, no matter how often he had seen it done before — the area around each gun was strewn with sand and ashes, so that when the fight grew hot the guncrews would not slip in their own blood. That was all. Now there was only the waiting, which a gunner aboard the flagship thought the hardest job of all. "One has nothing to do to occupy the mind," he complained. "The mind runs on the great uncertainty about to take place, until it is a relief when the battle opens."

At 2 a.m. — it was Thursday now, the 24th — the hour being, as Farragut said, "propitious" — he had just received a signal that the gateway through the boom was still ajar — two red lanterns appeared at the *Hartford*'s mizzen peak, and the lead division began to move upstream. His original plan had been to lead the attack himself, aboard the flagship, but the senior captains, agreeing that the losses would be heavy, persuaded him that to risk losing the fleet commander at the outset would be to court disaster through confusion. So Farragut had arranged his seventeen warships in three divisions of eight, three, and six vessels, himself at the head of the second. It was a powerful aggregation, heavily gunned, and backed by the fire of the mortars. If the weight of thrown metal was to decide the issue, there could be but one result, for an entire round of projectiles from all the Federal guns would weigh more than ten tons, while one from all the Confederate guns, afloat and ashore, would weigh just three and a half. Farragut and his captains were not aware of these figures, however, or at any rate not the latter. All they knew was what they had been taught: that one gun ashore was worth four afloat. They knew, too, that the forts were built of brick and mortar, while the ships were built of wood. Farragut was confident, even cheerful, but when his clerk declared that he did not expect the fleet to lose beyond a hundred men, the Tennessee-born captain shook his head in doubt. "I wish I could think so," he said.

There were delays as the various sloops and gunboats jockeyed for position, each division moving in line ahead, breasting the broad dark current. Then at 3.40 the rebel lookouts spotted the lead division just as it reached the boom and started through the gap. Now delay was on the other side; the first eight ships were clear of the chain before the forts reacted. But when they did, according to an army man who had come up to watch the show, the effect was tremendous: "Imagine all the earthquakes in the world, and all the thunder and lightnings together in a space of two miles, all going off at once. That would be like it." Flaming brush-piles along the banks and fire-rafts on the river cast an eerie refulgence, pocked with rolling clouds of gunsmoke and the sudden scarlet of exploding shells. At this point the *Hartford*, leading the second division through the gap, made her entrance as if upon a brightly lighted stage.

It seemed to Farragut, high in the mizzen rigging, his feet on the ratlines and his back against the shrouds, "as if the artillery of heaven were playing on earth," but one of his gunners drew a comparison from the opposite direction: "My youthful imagination of hell did not equal the scene about us at this moment." Presently, however, there could be little doubt as to which description was more fitting. Attempting to dodge a fire-raft, the flagship's helmsman ran her into shallow water, directly under the guns of Fort St Philip. Farragut, who had descended to the quarterdeck just before a shellburst cut away most of the rigging where he had been standing, saw a mud flat dead ahead. "Hard a-port!" he shouted. Too late; she ran aground. Fortunately, the casemate gunners, expecting a landing party when they saw the *Hartford*'s bowsprit looming over their heads, deserted their pieces. But the fire-raft, pushed by a tug, changed course and rammed the flank of the grounded sloop, flames curling over the bulwarks and shooting up the rigging.

When Farragut saw his ship afire, his men giving back from the press of heat as the tug held the mass of burning pine firmly against her quarter, he threw up his hands and clasped them over his head in an anguished gesture. "My God, is it to end this way?" he cried. But he soon recovered his composure. Down on the gundeck, his clerk had conceived the notion of rolling some 20-pound shells onto the flaming raft, where they would explode and sink it. As he knelt to unscrew the fuze-caps Farragut saw him and mistook his attitude. "Come, sir, this is no time for prayer," he told him sternly, and called down also to the gunners, still holding back from the licking tongues of flame: "Don't flinch from that fire, boys. There's a hotter fire than that waiting for those who don't do their duty. Give that rascally little tug a shot!"

Then suddenly the worst was over. Catching the old man's spirit, despite the heat, the port crews returned to their guns and gave the tug two shots that hulled and sank her. The clerk got three of the shells uncapped and dropped them onto the blazing raft, which was torn apart by the explosion and went down in a hissing cloud of steam. While the fire brigade got busy with hoses and buckets, extinguishing the flames, the helmsman called for full power astern, and the ship careened off the mud flat, free to continue her course upriver and join in the destruction of the rebel flotilla.

Very little of it was left by now. When the skippers of the dozen Confederate vessels saw the northern warships clear the boom, run the gauntlet of fire from the forts, and head directly for them, apparently unscathed, big guns booming, they reacted with dismay — as well they might; all twelve of them together, with the immobilized *Louisiana* thrown in for good measure though only six of her 16 guns could be brought to bear, could not throw as much metal as a single Federal sloop. They scattered headlong, some for bank, where their crews set them afire and took to the swamps, while others tried for a getaway upriver. Three stayed to accept the challenge, upholding naval tradition by a form of naval suicide.

Two of the three were from the Confederate flotilla: the 7-gun former Mexican revenue cutter, which was reduced to kindling by the converging fire of three Union men-of-war as soon as she came within their range, and the low-riding armored ram *Manassas*, which headed downriver as soon as the guns began to roar and gave one of the heavy sloops an ineffectual glancing bump, firing her Cyclops cannon as she struck. (Aboard the sloop the cry went up, "The ram, the ram!" and the captain saw a rebel officer come out of the iron hatch and run forward along the port gunnel to inspect the damage, if any. Suddenly he whirled with an odd, disjointed motion and tumbled into the water. Hardly able to believe his eyes, the captain called to the leadsman in the chains, asking if he had seen him fall. "Why, yes sir," he said: "I saw him fall overboard. In fact, I helped him; for I hit him alongside the head with my hand-lead.") The *Manassas* backed off and continued downriver, intending to do better with the next one, but took a terrific pounding from the guns of both forts, whose cannoneers mistook her for a disabled Federal vessel. She came about, staggering back upstream, her armor pierced, her engines smashed, and was pounded again by four of the enemy warships. Avoiding a fifth, which charged to run her down, she veered into bank and stuck there, smoke curling from her hatch and punctures. What was left of her crew jumped ashore and scurried to safety while the Union gunboats flailed the brush with canister and grape.

Third to accept the challenge was the unarmored sidewheel steamboat *Governor Moore*, one of two vessels sent by the state of Louisiana to make up a third division of the fleet defending New Orleans. When the firing began she moved upriver, adding rosin to her fires to get up steam before turning to join the fight. As she moved through the darkness she saw the 1300-ton screw steamer *Varuna*, the fastest ship in the Federal fleet, coming hard upstream in pursuit of the fugitive gunboats. The *Moore* carried two guns, one forward and one aft; the *Varuna* carried ten, eight of them 8-inchers; but the former, undetected against a dark backdrop of trees along the bank, had the advantage of surprise. She opened fire at a hundred yards — and missed. Startled, the Federal replied, strewing the steamboat's decks with dead and wounded. The *Moore* was now too close to bring her forward gun to bear, her bow being in the way, but the captain ordered the piece depressed and fired it through his own deck. The first shot was deflected by a hawse pipe, but the second, fired through the hole in the deck and bow, burst against the *Varuna*'s pivot gun, inflicting heavy casualties. The third came as the *Moore* rammed her opponent hard amidships, receiving a broadside in return. She backed off, then fired and rammed again. That did it. The *Varuna* limped toward bank; whereupon one of the fleeing Confederate gunboats, seeing her distress, turned and gave her another bump before she made it. She went down quickly then, leaving her topgallant forecastle above water, crowded with survivors.

The *Moore*'s captain, having his blood up, ordered a downriver course, intending to take on the whole Yankee fleet with one broken-nosed steamboat. The crew seemed willing, what there was left — well over half were dead or dying — but the wounded first lieutenant at the helm had had enough. "Why do this?" he protested. "We have no men left. I'll be damned if I stand here to be murdered." And with that he slapped the wheel hard to starboard, making a run for the west bank. Five Union ships, within range by now, cut loose at her with all their guns; she seemed almost to explode. All told, her crew of 93, mostly infantry detachments and longshoremen, lost 57 killed and 17 wounded. The rest were captured or escaped through the swamps when she struck bank, already ablaze, her colors burning at the peak.

Dawn glimmered and spread through the latter stages of the fighting. When the sun came up at 5 o'clock the Federal ships broke out their flags to greet it and salute their victory. All being safely past the forts except the sunken *Varuna* and three of the lighter gunboats — one had taken a shot in her boiler, losing her head of steam; another had got tangled in the barricade; a third had turned back, badly cut up by the crossfire — Farragut ordered them to anchor, wash down, and take count. Casualties were 37 dead and 149 wounded, nearly twice the clerk's hopeful estimate and more than three times the losses in the forts: 12 dead and 40 wounded. On the other hand, the Confederate flotilla was utterly destroyed, including the fleeing gunboat which had given the *Varuna* a final butt; her skipper burned her at the levee in New Orleans.

Below the boom, Porter's anxiety was relieved as he watched the charred remnants of the rebel fleet come floating down the river. When his demand for immediate surrender of the forts was declined, he put his mortar crews back to work, firing up the remainder of their shells.

New Orleans was in a frenzy of rage and disappointment at the news from downriver. Other cities might accept defeat and endure the aftermath in sullen silence; but not this one. All afternoon and most of the night, while crowds milled in the streets, brandishing knives and pistols and howling for resistance to the end, drays rattled over the cobbles, hauling cotton from the presses for burning on the quays, where crates of rice and hogsheads of molasses were broken open and thrown into the river. This at least won the people's approval; "The damned Yankees shall not have it!" they cried, and the night was hazed with acrid smoke that hid the stars.

They were no less violent next morning when they heard the guns of the enemy fleet make short work of the Chalmette batteries, then come slowly into view around Slaughterhouse Bend as a drizzle of rain began to fall; "silent, grim, and terrible," one among the watchers called the warships, "black with men, heavy with deadly por-

tent." Their great hope had been the ironclads, built and launched in
their own yards. One had already gone downriver, powerless, and been
by-passed. Now here came the other, the unfinished *Mississippi*, drifting
helpless, set afire to keep her from falling into Federal hands. The
crowd howled louder than ever at the sight, shouting "Betrayed! Betrayed!" and screaming curses at the Yankee sailors who watched from
the decks and yardarms. Aboard the *Hartford*, one old tar grinned
broadly back at them as he stood beside a 9-inch Dahlgren, holding the
lanyard in one hand and patting the big black bottle-shaped breech
with the other. The rain came down harder.

Despite the threats and invective from the quay, Farragut's
strength was so obvious that he didn't have to use it. Two officers went
ashore and walked unescorted through the hysterical mob to City Hall,
where the mayor was waiting for them. Lovell had retreated, leaving
New Orleans an open city. However, if the citizens were willing to
undergo naval bombardment, he offered to "return with my troops
and not leave as long as one brick remained upon another." The offer
was declined: as was the navy's demand for an immediate surrender.
"This satisfaction you cannot obtain at our hands," the mayor told the
two officers. He would not resist, but neither would he yield; if they
wanted the city, let them come and take it.

Farragut wanted no pointless violence; he had had enough violence the day before, when, as he told a friend, "I seemed to be breathing
flame." Saturday, while negotiations continued, he ordered his captains
to assemble their crews at 11 o'clock the following morning and "return thanks to Almighty God for his great goodness and mercy for
permitting us to pass through the events of the past two days with so
little loss of life and blood. At that hour the Church pennant will be
hoisted on every vessel of the fleet, and their crews assembled will, in
humiliation and prayer, make their acknowledgments thereof to the
Great Disposer of all human events." That would be ceremony enough
for him, with or without a formal surrender by the municipal authorities.

The occupation problem still remained, but not for long. Monday the garrisons of Forts Jackson and St Philip — they were "mostly
foreign enlistments," the commandant said; "A reaction set in among
them," he explained — mutinied, spiked the guns, and forced their
officers to surrender. Still powerless, the *Louisiana* was blown up to
forestall capture. Butler's 18,000 men ascended the river unopposed and
marched into the city on the last day of the month. "In family councils,"
a resident wrote, "a new domestic art began to be studied — the art
of hiding valuables" from looters under the general known thereafter
as "Spoons" Butler. One cache he uncovered with particular satisfaction:
418 bronze plantation bells collected there in answer to Beauregard's
impassioned pleas for metal. Sent to Boston, they sold for $30,000

to mock the rebels from New England towers and steeples. Other aspects of the occupation were less pleasant for the visitors. Not only was southern hospitality lacking, the people seemed utterly unwilling to accept the consequences of defeat: particularly the women, who responded to northern overtures with downright abuse. Butler knew how to handle that, however. "I propose to make some brilliant examples," he wrote Stanton.

Farragut now was free to continue his trip upriver, and in early May he did so. Baton Rouge fell as easily as New Orleans, once the guns of the fleet were trained on its streets and houses; the state government had fled the week before to Opelousas, which was safely away from the river. Natchez was next, and it too fell without resistance. Then in mid-May came Vicksburg, whose reply to a demand for surrender was something different from the others: "Mississippians don't know, and refuse to learn, how to surrender to an enemy. If Commodore Farragut or Brigadier General Butler can teach them, let them come and try." The ranks were wrong; Butler was a major general, Farragut a captain; but the writer seemed to mean what he was saying. The guns frowned down from the tall bluff — "so elevated that our fire will not be felt by them," Farragut said — and there were reports of 20,000 reinforcements on the way from Jackson. Deciding to label this first attempt a mere reconnaissance, he left garrisons at Baton Rouge and Natchez, and was back in New Orleans before the end of May. Vicksburg was a problem that could wait. In time he intended to "teach them," but just now it needed study.

Welles was angry, hotly demanding to know why the attack against Vicksburg's bluff had not been pressed, but the feeling in the fleet was that enough had been done in one short spring by one upriver thrust. New Orleans was now in northern hands and a second southern capital had fallen — both delivered as outright gifts to the army from the navy. Southerners agreed that it was quite enough, though some found bitter solace in protesting that the thing had been done by mechanical contrivance, with small risk and no gallantry at all. The glory was departing. "This is a most cowardly struggle," a Louisiana woman told her diary. "These people can do nothing without gunboats. . . . These passive instruments do their fighting for them. It is at best a dastardly way to fight." Then she added, rather wistfully: "We should have had gunboats if the Government had been efficient, wise or earnest."

✵ 4 ✵

The North had found a new set of western heroes — Farragut, Curtis, Canby, Pope, Ben Butler: all their stars were in ascendance — but some of the former heroes now had tarnished reputations: Grant, for instance. If the news from Donelson had sent him soaring like a rocket in the public's estimation, the news from Shiloh dropped him sparkless like the stick. Cashiered officers, such as the Ohio colonel who cried "Retreat! Save yourselves!" at first sight of the rebels, were spreading tales back home at his expense. He was incompetent; he was lazy; he was a drunk. Correspondents, who had come up late and gathered their information in the rear — "not the best place from which to judge correctly what is going on in front," Grant remarked — were soon in print with stories which not only seemed to verify the rumors of "complete surprise," but also included the casualty lists. Shocking as these were to the whole country, they struck hardest in the Northwest, where most of the dead boys were being mourned.

Hardest hit of all was Ohio, which not only had furnished a large proportion of the corpses, but also was smarting under the charge that several Buckeye regiments had scattered for the rear before firing a shot. Governor David Tod was quick to announce that these men were not cowards; they had been caught off guard as a result of the "criminal negligence" of the high command. By way of securing proof he sent the lieutenant governor down to talk with the soldiers in their camps. They agreed with the governor's view, and the envoy returned to publish in mid-April a blast against "the blundering stupidity and negligence of the general in command." He found, he said, "a general feeling among the most intelligent men that Grant and Prentiss ought to be court-martialed or shot." Grant himself was an Ohioan, but they disclaimed him; he had moved to Illinois.

Nor was Ohio alone in her resentment. Harlan of Iowa rose in Congress to announce that he discerned a pattern of behavior: Grant had blundered at Belmont until he was rescued by Foote's navy, had lost at Donelson until C. F. Smith redeemed him, and had been surprised at Shiloh and saved by Buell. "With such a record," Harlan declared, "those who continue General Grant in active command will in my opinion carry on their skirts the blood of thousands of their slaughtered countrymen."

Eventually the problem landed where the big ones always did: on the shoulders of Abraham Lincoln. Late one night at the White House a Pennsylvania spokesman made a summary of the charges. Grant had been surprised because of his invariable lack of vigilance and because he disregarded Halleck's order to intrench. In addition, he was reported drunk: which might or might not have been true, but in any case he had lost the public's confidence to such an extent that any future blood on his hands would be charged against the officials who sustained him. He had better be dismissed. Lincoln sat there thinking it over, profoundly alone with himself, then said earnestly: "I can't spare this man. He fights."

He was not fighting now, nor was he likely to be fighting any time in the near future. Halleck had seen to that by taking the field himself. As soon as he reached Pittsburg Landing, four days after the battle, he began reorganizing his forces by consolidating Grant's Army of the Tennessee and Buell's Army of the Ohio with Pope's Army of the Mississippi, summoned from Island Ten. When George Thomas, now a major general as a reward for Fishing Creek, arrived with Buell's fifth division — the other four, or parts of them, had come up in time for a share in the fighting — Halleck assigned it to Grant's army and gave Thomas the command in place of Grant, who was appointed assistant commander of the whole, directly under Halleck. That way he could watch him, perhaps use him in an advisory capacity, and above all keep him out of contact with the troops. Having thus disposed of one wild man, he attended to another. McClernand, with his and Lew Wallace's divisions, plus a third from Buell, was given command of the reserve. So organized, Halleck told his reshuffled generals, "we can march forward to new fields of honor and glory, till this wicked rebellion is completely crushed out and peace restored to our country." He was confident, and with good cause. His fifteen divisions included 120,172 men and more than 200 guns.

Thomas and Pope were pleased with the arrangement; but not Buell and McClernand. Buell, whose command was thus reduced to three green divisions while his former lieutenant Thomas had five, all veteran, protested: "You must excuse me for saying that, as it seems to me, you have saved the feelings of others very much to my injury." McClernand, too, was bitter. He saw little chance for "honor and glory," as Halleck put it, let alone advancement, when his army — if it could be called such; actually it was a pool on which the rest would call for reinforcements — did not even have a name. But the saddest of all was Grant. He had no troops at all, or even duties, so far as he could see. When he complained about being kicked upstairs into a supernumerary position, Halleck snapped at him with charges of ingratitude: "For the past three months I have done everything in my power to ward off the attacks which were made upon you. If you believe me your friend you will not require explanations; if not, explanations on my part would be of little avail."

C. F. Smith, who at Donelson had proved himself perhaps the hardest fighter of them all, was not included in the reshuffling because he was still confined to his sickbed in Savannah. After Shiloh, the infected shin got worse; blood poisoning set in. Or perhaps it was simply a violent reaction of the old man's entire organism, outraged at being kept flat on his back within earshot of one of the world's great battles. At any rate, he sickened and was dead before the month was out. Halleck ordered a salute fired for him at every post and aboard every warship in the department. The army would miss him, particularly the volunteers who had followed where he led, alternately cursed and cajoled, but always encouraged by his example. Grant would miss him most of all.

April 28, having completed the reorganization and briefed the four commanders, Halleck sent his Grand Army forward against Beauregard, who was intrenched at Corinth with a force which Halleck estimated at 70,000 men. Buell had the center, Thomas the right, and Pope the left; McClernand brought up the rear. Halleck intended to follow along, though for the present he kept his command post at Pittsburg. The great day had come, but he did not seem happy about it according to a reporter who saw him May Day: "He walks by the hour in front of his quarters, his thumbs in the armpits of his vest, casting quick looks, now to the right, now to the left, evidently not for the purpose of seeing anything or anybody, but staring into vacancy the while." Part of what was fretting him was the thing that had fretted Grant the year before, when he marched for the first time against the enemy and felt his heart "getting higher and higher" until it seemed to be in his throat. What Halleck felt was the presence of the enemy. "The evidences are that Beauregard will fight at Corinth," he wired Washington this same day.

Certain comparisons were unavoidable for a man accustomed to weighing all the odds. In the fight to come it would be Beauregard, who had co-directed the two great battles of the war, versus Halleck, the former lieutenant of engineers, who had never been in combat. True, he had written or translated learned works on tactics; but so had Hardee, waiting for him now beyond the woods. Bragg was there, grim-faced and wrathful, alongside Polk, the transfer from the Army of the Lord, and Breckinridge, an amateur and therefore unpredictable. So was Van Dorn, who had crossed the Mississippi with 17,000 veterans of Pea Ridge, where the diminutive commander had thrown them at Curtis in a savage double envelopment. It had failed because Curtis had kept his head while the guns were roaring. Could Halleck keep his? He wondered. Besides, Van Dorn might have learned enough from that experience to make certain it did not fail a second time.... For Halleck, the woods were filled with more than shadows.

Nevertheless, he put on a brave face when he wired Washington two days later: "I leave here tomorrow morning, and our army will be before Corinth tomorrow night."

Pope was off and running, in accordance with the reputation earned at New Madrid. Advancing seven miles from Hamburg on the 4th, he did not stop until he reached a stream appropriately called Seven Mile Creek, and from there he leapfrogged forward again to another creekline within two miles of Farmington, which in turn was only four miles from Corinth. He reported his position a good one, protected by the stream in front and a bog on his left, but he was worried about his other flank; "I hope Buell's forces will keep pace on our right," he told headquarters. It turned out he was right to worry. Buell was not there. Lagging back, he was warning Halleck: "We have now reached that proximity to the enemy that our movements should be conducted with the greatest caution and combined methods." The last phrase meant siege tactics, and the army commander took his cue from that. "Don't advance your main body at present," he told Pope. "We must wait till Buell gets up."

Buell was back near Monterey, with Thomas conforming on his right. Presently Pope was back there, too: Beauregard made a stab at his front, and he had to withdraw to avoid an attempt to envelop the flank protected by the bog. In fact the whole countryside was fast becoming boggy. Assistant Secretary Thomas Scott, an observer down from the War Department, wired Stanton: "Heavy rains for the past twenty hours. Roads bad. Movement progressing slowly." Gloomily Halleck confirmed the report: "This country is almost a wilderness and very difficult to operate in." Scott attended a high-level conference and passed the word along: Halleck would continue the advance, and "in a few days invest Corinth, then be governed by circumstances." He made no conjecture as to what those circumstances might be, but Stanton could see one thing clearly. Last week's "tomorrow" had stretched to "a few days."

It was more than a few. Every evening the troops dug in: four hours' digging, six hours' sleep, then up at dawn to repel attack. The attack didn't come, not in force at least, but Halleck had every reason to expect one. Rebel deserters were coming in with eye-witness accounts of the arrival of reinforcements for the 70,000 already behind the formidable intrenchments. He took thought of the host available to Beauregard by rail from Fort Pillow, Memphis, Mobile, and intermediary points. No less than 60,000 could be sped there practically overnight, he computed, which would give the defenders a larger army than his own. Taking thought, he grew cautious; he grew apprehensive. "Don't let Pope get too far ahead," he warned, acutely aware by now that he had another wild man on his hands. "It is dangerous and effects no good."

He had cause for caution, especially since the accounts of deserters were confirmed by observers of his own. In mid-May the officer in charge of pickets reported that he had heard trains pulling into Corinth during the night. "Such trains were greeted with immense cheering on arrival," he declared. "The enemy are concentrating a powerful army." Next night it was repeated. A scouting party, working near town, heard more trains arriving "and, after they stopped, marching music from the depot in the direction of the front lines." Intelligence could hardly be more definite, and Halleck found his apprehension shared. Indiana's Governor O. P. Morton, down to see how well his Hoosiers had recovered from the bloody shock of Shiloh, wired Stanton on May 22: "The enemy are in great force at Corinth, and have recently received reinforcements. They evidently intend to make a desperate struggle at that point, and from all I can learn their leaders have utmost confidence in the result. . . . It is fearful to contemplate the consequences of a defeat at Corinth." Halleck thought it fearful, too: the more so after McClernand capped the climax with a report he had from a doctor friend, captured at Belmont and recently exchanged. The Illinois general, fretting in his back-seat position, was finding "the amount of duty . . . very great, indeed exhausting, if not oppressive." Now he crowded into the frame of the big picture by passing along what he heard from the doctor, who had left Memphis on May 15. While there, he had spoken with some former classmates now in the rebel army, who "informed him that on that date the enemy's force at Corinth numbered 146,000." Other details were given, the doctor said, "prospectively increasing their number to 200,000." To palliate the shock of this, he added that "a considerable portion of the force . . . consists of new levies, being in large part boys and old men."

Two hundred thousand of anything, even rabbits, could make a considerable impression, however, if they were launched at a man who was unprepared: which was the one thing Halleck was determined not to be. Orders went out for the troops to dig harder and deeper, not only on the flanks, but across the center. They cursed and dug — the rains were over; summer was almost in — sweating in wool uniforms under the Mississippi sun. Only the Shiloh veterans, looking back, saw any sense in all that labor. Apparently all but four of the ranking generals shared their commander's apprehension: Pope, who chafed at restraint, bristling offensively on the left: Thomas, who did not have it in his nature to be quite apprehensive about anything: Sherman, who, happy over a pending promotion, called the movement "a magnificent drill": and Grant. Not even Shiloh had taught him caution to this extent. He suggested once to Halleck that he shift Pope's army from the left to the right, out of the swamps and onto the ridge beyond the opposite flank, then send it bowling directly along the high ground into the heart of Corinth. Halleck gave him a fish-eye stare of unbelief. "I was silenced so quickly," Grant said later, "that I felt that possibly I had suggested an unmilitary movement." He drew back and kept his own counsel. This was not his kind of war.

It was Halleck's kind, and he kept at it, burrowing as he went. An energetic inchworm could have made better time — half a mile a day now, sometimes less — but not without the danger of being swooped on by a hawk: whereas, by Halleck's method, the risk was small, the casualties low, and the progress sure. The soldiers, digging and cursing under the summer sun, might agree with the disgruntled McClernand's definition of the campaign as "the present unhappy drama," but they would be there for roll call when the time came for the bloody work ahead. Besides, nothing could last forever; not even this. By the morning of May 28 — a solid month from the jump-off — all three component armies were within cannon range of Beauregard's intrenchments. After four weeks of marching and digging, Halleck had his troops where he had said they would be "tomorrow." He had reached the second stage, the one in which he had said he would "be governed by circumstances."

★ ★ ★

East and far northeast of Corinth, Halleck had two more divisions, both left behind by Buell when he marched for Pittsburg Landing. The latter, commanded by Brigadier General George W. Morgan, was maneuvering in front of Cumberland Gap, prepared to move in if the Confederates evacuated or weakened the already small defensive force. Morgan had further plans, intending not only to seize the gap, but to penetrate the Knoxville region — a project dear, as everyone knew, to the heart of Abraham Lincoln. However, the place was a natural fortress; Morgan reported it "washed into deep chasms or belly-deep in mud." So long as the rebels stayed there he could do nothing but hover and maneuver. The more substantial threat would have to come from the opposite direction, beyond the gap, and that was where Buell's other division, under Brigadier General Ormsby M. Mitchel, came in.

He was already in North Alabama, deeper into enemy country than any other Federal commander, having occupied Huntsville the day Halleck got to Pittsburg. From there he pushed on and took Bridgeport just as Halleck's army started south. A bright prospect lay before him. Once he had taken Chattanooga, thirty miles away, he would continue his march along the railroad and threaten Knoxville from the rear. This would cause the evacuation of Cumberland Gap, and when Morgan came through, hard on the heels of the defenders, Mitchel would join forces with him and make Lincoln's fondest hope a fact by chasing the scattered rebels clean out of East Tennessee. That was his plan at the outset, and it tied in well with another he had already put in motion, which resulted in what was known thereafter as the Great Locomotive Chase.

James J. Andrews, a Kentucky spy who had gained the trust of Confederates by running quinine through the lines, volunteered to lead a group of 21 Ohio soldiers, dressed like himself in civilian clothes, down into Georgia to burn bridges and blow up tunnels along the Western & Atlantic, the only rail connection between Atlanta and Chattanooga. Andrews and his men infiltrated south and assembled at Marietta, Georgia, where — on April 12, the day after Mitchel took Huntsville — they boarded a northbound train as passengers. During the breakfast halt at

Big Shanty they made off with the locomotive and three boxcars, heading north. The conductor, W. A. Fuller, took the theft as a personal affront and started after them on foot. Commandeering first a handcar, then a switch engine, and finally a regular freight locomotive, along with whatever armed volunteers he encountered along the way, he pressed the would-be saboteurs so closely that they had no time for the destruction they had intended. Overtaken just at the Tennessee line, where they ran out of fuel and water, they took to the woods, but were captured. Eight were hanged as spies, including Andrews; eight escaped while awaiting execution, and the remaining six were exchanged. All received the Congressional Medal of Honor in recognition of their valor "above and beyond the call of duty." Fuller and his associates received a vote of thanks from the Georgia legislature, but no medals. The Confederacy never had any, then or later.

Andrews' failure meant that the rebels could reinforce Chattanooga rapidly by rail. Advancing toward it, Mitchel found other drawbacks to his plan, chief among them being a shortage of supplies. Except for the fact that he could bring food and other necessities along the railroad, he told Washington, "it would be madness to attempt to hold my position a single day." Presently gray raiders were loose in his rear, capturing men and disrupting communications. "As there is no [hope] of an immediate advance upon Chattanooga," he wired Stanton, "I will now contract my line." He remained in North Alabama, doing what he could — mainly destroying railroad bridges which later Union commanders would have to replace — but on the day that Halleck halted within range of the Corinth intrenchments, Mitchel requested a transfer to another theater. "My advance beyond the Tennessee River seems impossible," he said.

Chattanooga was untaken, and though Morgan still hovered north of Cumberland Gap, Knoxville was spared pressure from either direction. Halleck could expect no important strategic diversion on his left as he entered the final stage of his campaign against Corinth.

It turned out, simultaneously, that he could expect none on his right flank either. Farragut turned back from frowning Vicksburg, abandoning for the present his planned ascent of the Mississippi, and the descending fleet of ironclads, steaming south after the fall of Island Ten, received a jolt which gave the Confederates not only a sense of security on the river, but also a heady feeling of elation, long unfamiliar, and a renewal of their confidence in the valor of southern arms.

Midway between New Madrid and Memphis, Fort Pillow was next on the navy's list of downriver objectives, and Foote did not delay. With a burst of his old-time energy, he had the place under mortar bombardment within a week of the fall of Island Ten. The plan was for him to apply pressure from the river, while Pope moved in from the land side, a repetition of his tactics in Missouri. However, when Halleck took the field in person he summoned Pope to Pittsburg Landing, leaving only two regiments to coöperate with the navy. Foote felt let down and depressed. Fort Pillow was a mean-looking place, with the balance of the guns from Columbus dug into its bluff, and he did not think the navy could do the job alone. Downstream there was a Confederate flotilla of unknown strength, perhaps made stronger than his own by the addition of giant ironclads reportedly under construction in the Memphis yards. The commodore was feverish — "much enfeebled," one of his captains wrote — still on crutches from his Donelson wound, which would not heal in this climate, and distressed, as only a brave man could be, by his loss of nerve. In this frame of mind he applied to Welles for shore duty in the North; which was granted with regret.

May 9 he said farewell on the deck of the flagship, crowded with sailors come for a last look at him. He took off his cap and addressed them, saying that he regretted not being able to stay till the war was over; he would remember all they had shared, he said, "with mingled feelings of sorrow and of pride." Supported by two officers, he went down the gangway and onto a transport, where he was placed in a chair on the guards. When the crew of the flagship cheered him he covered his face with a palm-leaf fan to hide the tears which ran down into his beard. As the transport pulled away, they cheered again and tossed their caps in salute. Greatly agitated, Foote rose from the chair and cried in a broken voice across the widening gap of muddy water: "God bless you all, my brave companions! . . . I can never forget you. Never, never. You are as gallant and noble men as ever fought in a glorious cause, and I shall remember your merits to my dying day." It was one year off, that dying day, and when the doctors told him it had come he took the news without regret. "Well," he said quietly, "I am glad to be done with guns and war."

His successor, Commodore Charles Henry Davis, a fifty-five-year-old Bostonian with a flowing brown mustache and gray rim whiskers, had been a salt-water sailor up to now, a member of the planning board and chief of staff to Du Pont at Port Royal, but before he had spent a full day in his new command he got a taste of what could happen on the river. His first impression had been one of dullness. Agreeing with Foote that the fleet alone could never take Fort Pillow — though in time, if ordered to do so, he would be willing to try running past it — he kept all but one of the gunboats anchored at Plum Run Bend, five miles above the fort. That one was stationed three miles below the others, protecting the single mortar-boat assigned to keep up a harassing fire by dropping its 13-inch shells at regular intervals into the rebel fortifications. "Every half-hour during the day," a seaman later wrote, "one of these little pills would climb a mile or two into the air, look around a bit at the scenery, and finally descend and disintegrate around the fort, to the great interest and excitement of the occupants." There was little interest and still less excitement at the near end of the trajectory. This had been going on for some weeks now, and as duty it was dull. The seven ironclads took the guard-mount times about, one day a week for each.

While Foote was telling his crew goodbye, J. E. Montgomery, the river captain who had brought the eight River Defense Fleet gunboats up from New Orleans, was holding a council of war at Memphis. The bitter details of what Farragut's blue-water ships had done to the Confederate flotilla above Forts Jackson and St Philip had reached Memphis by now, along with the warning that Farragut himself might not be far behind; he was on his way, and in fact had captured Baton Rouge the day before. Montgomery's captains believed they could do better when the time came, but in any case there was no point in waiting to fight both Federal fleets at once. They voted to go upriver that night and try a surprise attack on the ironclads next morning, May 10.

It was Saturday. The ironclad *Cincinnati* had the duty below, standing guard while *Mortar 10* threw its 200-pound projectiles, one every half-hour as usual, across the wooded neck of land hugged by the final bend above Fort Pillow. The gunboat was not taking the assignment very seriously, however. Steam down, she lay tied to some trees alongside bank, and her crew was busy holystoning the decks for weekly inspection. About 7 o'clock one of the workers gave a startled yell. The others looked and saw eight rebel steamboats rounding the bend, just over a mile away — eight minutes, one of the sailors translated — bearing down, full steam ahead, on the tethered *Cincinnati*. Things moved fast then. While the deck crew slipped her cables, the engineers were throwing oil and anything else inflammable into her furnaces for quick steam. They were too late. The lead vessel, the *General Bragg*, came on, twenty feet tall, her great walking-beam engine driving so hard she had built up a ten-foot billow in front of her bow. The *Cincinnati* delivered a broadside at fifty yards, then managed to swing her bow around and avoid right-angle contact. The blow, though glancing, tore a piece out of her midships six feet deep and twelve feet long, letting a flood into her magazine.

Three miles upstream, around Plum Run Bend, the rest of the fleet knew nothing of the sudden attack until they heard the guns. They too were lazing alongside bank, steam down. By the time they got up pressure enough to maneuver — which they did as soon as possible, the *Mound City* leading the way — they were too late to be of any help to their sister ship below. When the *General Bragg* sheered off, the second ram-gunboat, *Sumter*, struck the *Cincinnati* in the fantail, wrecking her steering gear and punching another hole that let the river in. Next came the *Colonel Lovell*, whose iron prow crashed into the port quarter. Taking water from three directions, the proud *Cincinnati*, the fleet's first flagship and leader of the crushing assault on Henry, rolled first to one side, now the other, then gave a convulsive shudder and went down in water shallow enough to leave her pilot-house above the surface for survivors to cling to, including her captain, who had taken a sharp-shooter's bullet through the mouth. It appeared that one of the ironclad monsters could be sunk after all. And having proved it, the attacking flotilla proceeded to re-prove it.

The *Mound City* arrived too late for the *Cincinnati*'s good, and too early for her own. A fourth ram-gunboat, the *General Van Dorn*, met her almost head-on, and punched such a hole in her forward starboard quarter that the *Mound City* barely managed to limp toward bank in time to sink with her nose out of water. Two down and five to go: but when the rest of the ironclads came on the scene, their 9-inch Dahlgrens booming, the river captains decided enough had been done for one day. They drew off downstream, unpursued, to the protection of Fort Pillow's batteries. Montgomery brought up the rear in his jaunty flagship *Little Rebel*.

After a full year of war, afloat and ashore, a contradictory pattern was emerging. In naval actions — with the exception of Fort Donelson — whoever attacked was the winner; while in land actions of any size — again with the same notable exception — it was the other way around. Montgomery was satisfied, however, with the simpler fact that an ironclad could be sent to the bottom. He knew because he had done it twice in a single morning. Returning to a cheering reception at Memphis he informed Beauregard that if the Federal fleet remained at its present strength, "they will never penetrate farther down the Mississippi."

★ ★ ★

The Creole had need of all the assurance and encouragement he could get. With Halleck knocking at its gate, Corinth was one vast groaning camp of sick and injured. Hotels and private residences, stables and churches, stores and even the railroad station were jammed, not only with the wounded back from Shiloh — eight out of ten amputees died, victims of erysipelas, tetanus, and shock — but also with a far greater number incapacitated by a variety of ailments. For lack of sanitary precautions, unknown or at any rate unpracticed, the inadequate water supply was soon contaminated. While dysentery claimed its toll, measles and typhoid fever both reached epidemic proportions. By mid-May, with the arrival of Van Dorn, Beauregard had 18,000 soldiers on the sick list, which left him 51,690 present for duty: well under half the number Halleck was bringing so cautiously against him.

He had done what he could to increase that caution at every opportunity. Many of the "deserters," for example, who had given the Union commander such alarming information as to the strength and intentions of the invaders, had been sent out by Beauregard himself, after intensive coaching on what to say when questioned. Valid prisoners were almost as misleading, for Beauregard had a report spread through the ranks that immediate advances were intended, and interrogated captives passed it on. Nor did the inventive general neglect to organize diversions which he hoped would cause detachments from the army in his front. Two regiments of cavalry were ordered to assemble at Trenton, Tennessee, then dash across western Kentucky for an attack on lightly held Paducah, meanwhile spreading the rumor that they were riding point for Van Dorn's army, which was on its way to seize the mouth of the Tennessee River and thus cut off Halleck's retreat when Beauregard struck him in front with superior numbers. A second, less ambitious cavalry project was intrusted to Captain John H. Morgan, who had shown promise on outpost duty the year before. He was promoted to colonel, given a war bag of $15,000, and sent to Kentucky to raise a regiment for disrupting the Federal rear. Though the former scheme was a failure — Beauregard blamed "the notorious incapacity of the officer in command" — the latter was carried out brilliantly from the outset. These were the gray raiders who caused Ormsby Mitchel to "contract" his line in North Alabama. However, it worked less well on the Corinth front. When Andrew Johnson protested that troops were needed to restrain Tennessee "disloyalists," the War Department referred the matter to Halleck, who refused to be disconcerted. "We are now at the enemy's throat," he replied, "and cannot release our great grasp to pare his toenails."

If Old Brains was to be stopped it would have to be done right here in front of Corinth, and Beauregard did what he could with what he had. His army took position along a ridge in rear of a protective creek, three to six miles out of town, thus occupying a quadrant which extended from the Mobile & Ohio on the north to the Memphis & Charleston Railroad on the east. Polk had the left, Bragg the center, and Hardee the right; Breckinridge and Van Dorn supported the flanks, being posted just in rear of the intersections of the railroads and the ridge. All through what was left of April and most of May, the defenders intrenched as furiously as the attackers, but with the advantage that while their opponents were honeycombing the landscape practically all the way from Monterey, their own digging was done in the same place from day to day. Even before Halleck started forward, the natural strength of the lines along the Corinth ridge had been greatly increased, and as he drew nearer they became quite formidable — especially in appearance. This was what Beauregard wanted: not only to give his men the added protection of solid-packed red earth, but also to free a portion of them for operations beyond the fortified perimeter, in case some segment of the advancing host grew careless and exposed itself, unsupported, to a sudden crippling slash by the gray veterans who had practiced such tactics at Elkhorn Tavern and Shiloh.

Pope was the likeliest to expose himself to such treatment, bristly as he was, and he had not been long in doing so. When he rushed forward in early May and took up an isolated position at Farmington, calling for the other commanders to hurry and catch up, Beauregard planned to destroy him by throwing Bragg at his front and Van Dorn on his flank. "Soldiers, can the result be doubtful?" he asked. "Shall we not drive back into the Tennessee the presumptuous mercenaries collected for our subjugation?" However, the result was worse than doubtful. Bragg hit Pope as planned, and hit him hard, but Van Dorn found the flank terrain quite different from the description in the attack order; Pope scurried back to safety before his flank was even threatened. In late May, when he returned to his old position — this time by more gradual approaches, allowing his fellow commanders to keep pace — Beauregard ordered the same trap sprung. Once more his hopes were high. "I feel like a wolf and will fight Pope like one," Van Dorn declared as he set out. But the results were the same as before, except that this time the Federals did not fall back, neither Pope nor the others alongside him.

The failure of this second attempt to repulse the Union host before it got a close-up hug on his intrenchments confirmed what Beauregard had suspected since mid-May. Outnumbered as he was, he would never be able to hold onto Corinth once the contest became a siege. In fact, if it came to that, he might not be able to hold onto his army. In addition to the water shortage and the lengthening sick-list, there was now a scarcity of food. The arrival of a herd of cattle, driven overland from Texas, had already saved the defenders from starvation, but the herd was dwindling fast. Even if the Yankees failed, disease and hunger would force him out in time. So on May 25 he called a conference of his generals: Bragg, Van Dorn, Polk, Hardee, Breckinridge, and Price. Hardee, as became a student, had prepared a statement of primer-like simplicity: "The situation . . . requires that we should attack the enemy at once, or await his attack, or evacuate the place." To attack such numbers, intrenched to their front, "would probably inflict on us and the Confederacy a fatal blow." The only answer, as Hardee saw it, was to fall back down the line of the M & O while there was still a chance to do so unmolested, no matter how slim that chance appeared to be.

Beauregard and the others could do nothing but agree: the more so two days later, when Halleck got his whole Grand Army up within range of the fortified ridge and next morning — May 28 — opened a dawn-to-dusk cannonade, which paused from time to time to allow the infantry to probe for weak spots in the Confederate defenses. Fortunately, none developed; the wily Creole was left free to continue his plans for a withdrawal so secret that few of his officers suspected that one was intended. While the wounded and sick, along with the heavy baggage and camp equipment, were being evacuated by rail, the able-bodied men in the intrenchments were issued three days' cooked rations and told that they were about to launch an all-out attack: with the result that a timorous few — who indeed had cause to be frightened, being conscious of the odds — went over to the enemy with the news. Meanwhile the march details were formulated and rehearsed, the generals being assembled at army headquarters and required to repeat their instructions by rote until all had mastered their parts. No smallest detail was neglected, down to the final arrangements for bewildering the Federal pursuit by removing all the finger boards and mileposts south of Corinth.

Next afternoon, of necessity, the front-line troops were told of the planned deception in time to prepare for it that evening. They responded with enthusiasm, glad to have a share in what promised to be the greatest hoax of the war, and some proved almost as resourceful and inventive as their commander. When they stole out of the intrenchments after nightfall, they left dummy guns in the embrasures and dummy cannoneers to serve them, fashioned by stuffing ragged uniforms with straw. A single band moved up and down the deserted works, pausing at scattered points to play retreat, tattoo, and taps. Campfires were left burning, with a supply of wood alongside each for the drummer boys who stayed behind to stoke them and beat reveille next morning. All night a train of empty cars rattled back and forth along the tracks through Corinth, stopping at frequent intervals to blow its whistle, the signal for a special detail of leather-lunged soldiers to cheer with all their might. The hope was that this would not only cover the incidental sounds of the withdrawal, but would also lead the Federals to believe that the town's defenders were being heavily reinforced.

It worked to perfection. Beauregard would have been delighted if he had had access to the messages flying back and forth in reaction behind the northern lines. At 1.20 in the morning Pope telegraphed Halleck: "The enemy is reinforcing heavily, by trains, in my front and on my left. The cars are running constantly, and the cheering is immense every time they unload in front of me. I have no doubt, from all appearances, that I shall be attacked in heavy force at daylight." He turned his men out and did what he could to brace them for the shock, while Halleck alerted the other commanders. At 4 o'clock, mysteriously, the rattling and the cheering stopped, giving way to a profound silence which was broken at dawn by "a succession of loud explosions." Daylight showed "dense black smoke in clouds," but no sign of the enemy Pope expected to find massed in his front. Picking his way forward he came upon dummy guns and dummy cannoneers, some with broad grins painted on. Otherwise the works were deserted. So, apparently, was the town beyond. He sent back word of the evacuation, adding: "The whole country here seems to be fortified."

Halleck came out to see for himself. He had wanted a victory as bloodless as digging and maneuvering could make it; but not this bloodless, and above all not this empty. Even rebel civilians were scarce, all but two of the local families having departed with Beauregard's army. Seven full weeks of planning and strain, in command of the largest army ever assembled under one field general in the Western Hemisphere, had earned him one badly smashed-up North Mississippi railroad intersection.

In hope that more could yet be done, the order went out: "General Pope, with his reinforcements from the right wing, will proceed to feel the enemy on the left." Happy at being unleashed at last, Pope was hot on the trail with 50,000 men. At first there was little for him to "feel," but he reported joyfully: "The roads for miles are full of stragglers from the enemy, who are coming in in squads. Not less than 10,000 men are thus scattered about, who will come in within a day or two." This was mainly hearsay — like the information from a farmer that Beauregard, in a panic, had told his men to take to the woods and "save themselves as best they could" — but Halleck, anxious for a substantial achievement to put on the wire to Washington, was glad to hear it. Two days later, when Pope reported continuing success — a cavalry dash had destroyed an ammunition train and captured about 200 Confederate wounded — Halleck misunderstood him to mean that his former prediction had been fulfilled, and passed the news along to the War Department that 10,000 prisoners and 15,000 stand of arms had been seized because of the boldness of Pope's pursuit. Duly elated, Stanton replied: "Your glorious dispatch has just been received, and I have sent it into every State. The whole land will soon ring with applause at the achievement of your gallant army and its able and victorious commander."

Adjectivally, this was rather in line with Halleck's own opinion. The day after Corinth fell he informed his troops that they had scored "a victory as brilliant and important as any recorded in history," one that was "more humiliating to [the leaders of the rebellion] and to their cause than if we had entered the place over the dead and mangled bodies of their soldiers." However, this was a good deal more than any of his generals would say: except possibly John Pope. McClernand still considered the campaign an "unhappy drama," and not even Sherman, glad as he was to be out in the open, wearing his new major general's stars, praised it for being anything more than a "drill." Harsher words were left to the newspaper correspondents, who had never admired the elbow-scratching commander anyhow. "General Halleck . . . has achieved one of the most barren triumphs of the war," the Chicago *Tribune* asserted. "In fact, it is tantamount to a defeat." The Cincinnati *Commer-*

cial extended this into a flat statement that, by means of his sly withdrawal, "Beauregard [has] achieved another triumph."

These verdicts, these *ex post facto* condemnations, were delivered before all the testimony was in. Hoax or no, the Confederate retrograde movement was, after all, a retreat; and as such it had its consequences. Fort Pillow, being completely outflanked, was evacuated June 4, along with the supplementary Fort Randolph, fifteen miles below. Now all that stood between the Federal ironclads and Memphis was the eight-boat flotilla which had been resting on its laurels since the affair at Plum Run Bend. Captain Montgomery had said then that the Yankees would "never penetrate farther down" unless their fleet was reinforced; but two days after Pillow and Randolph were abandoned he discovered, in the most shocking way, that it had indeed been reinforced.

Back in March — after years of failing to interest the navy in his theory — an elderly civil engineer named Charles Ellet, Jr., wrote and sent to the War Department a pamphlet applying the formula $f = mv^2$ to demonstrate the superiority of the ram as a naval weapon, particularly in river engagements, which allowed scant room for dodging. Stanton read it and reacted. He sent for the author, made him a colonel, and told him to build as many of the rams as he thought would be needed to knock the rebels off the Mississippi. Ellet got to work at once, purchasing and converting suitable steamers, and joined the ironclad fleet above Fort Pillow on May 25 with nine of the strange-looking craft. They carried neither guns nor armor, since neither had any place in the mass-velocity formula; nor did they have sharp dogtooth prows, which Ellet said would plug a hole as quickly as they punched one. All his dependence was on the two formula-components. Velocity was assured by installing engines designed to yield a top speed of fifteen knots, which would make them the fastest things on the river, and "mass" was attained by packing the bows with lumber and running three solid bulkheads, a foot or more in thickness, down the length of each vessel, so that the impact of the whole rigid unit would be delivered at a single stroke. Engines and boilers were braced for the shock of ramming, and the crews were river men whose courage Ellet tested in various ways, getting rid of many in the process. Perhaps his greatest caution, however, was shown in the selection of his captains. All were Pennsylvanians, like himself, and all were named Ellet. Seven were brothers and nephews of the designer-commander, and the eighth was his nineteen-year-old son.

Anxious to put $f = mv^2$ to work, the thin-faced lank-haired colonel was for going down and pitching into the rebel flotilla as soon as he joined up, but Flag Officer Davis had learned caution at Plum Run Bend. In spite of the fact that both sunken ironclads had been raised from their shallow graves and put back into service, the fleet was still under strength, three of its seven units having returned to Cairo for repairs. No matter, Ellet said; he and his kinsmen were still for immediate action, with or without the ironclads. But Davis continued to refuse the "concurrence" Stanton had told the colonel he would have to have in working with the navy.

The Confederates in Memphis, knowing nothing of all this, had assumed from reports that the new arrivers were some kind of transport. They relied on the guns of Forts Pillow and Randolph; or if the batteries failed to stop the Yankees, there was still the eight-boat flotilla which had given them such a drubbing three weeks back. Moreover, as at New Orleans, the keels of two monster ironclads, the *Arkansas* and the *Tennessee*, had been laid in the city's yards. The former, having been launched and armored up to her maindeck, was floated down to Vicksburg, then towed up the Yazoo River for completion in safety after the fall of Island Ten; but the latter was still on the stocks, awaiting the arrival of her armor. Like the city itself, she would have to take her chances that the enemy would be stopped.

Those chances were considerably thinned by the evacuation of Corinth and the two forts upriver. It now became a question of which would get there first, a sizeable portion of Halleck's Grand Army or the Federal fleet. The citizens hoped it would be the latter, for they had the gunboat flotilla to stand in its way, while there was absolutely nothing at all to stand in the way of the former. They got their wish. At dawn of June 6, two days after Fort Pillow was abandoned, the ironclads showed up, coming round the bend called Paddy's Hen and Chickens, four of them in line abreast just above the city, offering battle to the eight Confederate gunboats. The people turned out in tens of thousands, lining the bluffs for a grandstand seat at what they hoped would be a reënactment of the affair at Plum Run Bend. The first shot was fired at sunup, and they cheered and waved their handkerchiefs as at a tableau when the southern gunboats, mounting 28 light cannon, moved out to meet their squat black bug-shaped northern opponents, mounting 68, mostly heavy.

Ellet had his rams in rear of the ironclad line of battle. When the first shot was fired, he took off his hat and waved it to attract the attention of his brother commanding the ram alongside his own. "Round out and follow me! Now is our chance!" he cried. Both boats sprang forward under full heads of steam and knifed between the ironclads, whose crews gave them a cheer as they went by. Ellet made straight for the *Colonel Lovell*, leader of the Confederate line, and when she swerved at the last minute to avoid a head-on collision, struck her broadside and cut her almost in two. She sank within a few minutes: brief, conclusive proof of the relation between force and mv^2. Meanwhile his brother had accomplished something different. Striking for the *General Price*, which held her course while the *General Beauregard* moved to aid her by converging on the ram, he darted between the two — which then collided in his wake. The *General Price* lost one of her sidewheels, sheared off in the crash, and while she limped toward bank, out of the fight, the ram came about in a long swift curve and rammed the *Beauregard* at the moment the rebel's steam drum was punctured by a shell from one of the ironclads. She struck her colors.

Four of the remaining five did not last much longer, and none ever managed to come to grips with an adversary. Montgomery's *Little Rebel,* the only screw steamer of the lot, took a shell in her machinery, then went staggering into the Arkansas bank, where her crew made off through the woods. The *Jeff Thompson* was set afire by a Federal broadside; the *Sumter* and the *Bragg,* like the flagship, were knocked into bank by the Dahlgrens. The whole engagement lasted no longer than the one at Plum Run Bend, which it avenged. One Confederate was sunk beyond raising; two were burned; four were captured, and in time became part of the fleet they had fought. *Van Dorn,* the only survivor, managed to get enough of a head start in the confusion to make a getaway downriver. Two of the rams gave chase for a while, but then turned back to join the celebration.

The cheering was all on the river, where the rams and ironclads anchored unopposed, not on the bluffs, where the cheers had turned to groans. Smoke had blanketed the water; all the spectators could see was the flash of Union guns and the tall paired stacks of Confederate steamboats riding above the murk. Pair by pair, in rapid order, the crown-top chimneys disappeared. "The deep sympathizing wail which followed each disaster," one who heard it wrote, "went up like a funeral dirge from the assembled multitude, and had an overwhelming pathos." When the sun-dazzled smoke finally cleared away they saw that their flotilla had been not only defeated but abolished, and they turned sadly away to await the occupation which the Corinth retreat had made inevitable anyhow. There still was time to burn the *Tennessee,* sitting armorless on the stocks, and this they did, taking considerable satisfaction in at least making sure that she would never be part of the fleet whose destruction had been the aim of her designers. It was bitter, however, to surrender as they did to a nineteen-year-old medical cadet, Colonel Ellet's son, who landed in a rowboat with three seamen and a folded flag, the stars and stripes, which presently he was hoisting over the post office. Later that day the two regiments Pope had left behind marched in for the formal occupation. Thus was Memphis returned to her old allegiance.

Colonel Ellet himself did not come ashore. The only Federal casualty of the engagement, he had been pinked in the knee by a pistol ball while waving his hat on the hurricane deck of his flagship, directing the ram attack. The wound, though painful, was not considered dangerous; prone on the deck, he continued in command throughout the fight; but infection set in, and he died of it two weeks later, while being taken north aboard one of the rams. Before his death, however, he had the satisfaction of proving his theory in action and of knowing that his genius — in conjunction with the no doubt larger genius of that other civil engineer, James Eads — had cleared the Mississippi down to Vicksburg, whose batteries now would be grist for Davis' and Farragut's upper and nether millstones.

★　★　★

At Tupelo, where he called a halt fifty-two miles south of Corinth, Beauregard was infuriated by Halleck's widely circulated dispatch which glorified Pope at the Creole's expense by claiming a large bag of demoralized prisoners and abandoned equipment. He hotly replied, through the columns of newspapers guilty of spreading this libel, that the report "contained as many lies as lines." Far from being a rout, he said, or even a reverse, "the retreat was conducted with great order and precision, doing much credit to the officers and men under my orders, and must be looked upon, in every respect, by the country as equivalent to a brilliant victory."

Not all of his own countrymen agreed with him, any more than Halleck's had agreed with Halleck; but in the Southerner's case the dissenters included the Chief Executive. While the army was falling back, exposing his home state and the river down its western flank to deeper penetration, Davis told his wife: "If Mississippi troops lying in camp, when not retreating under Beauregard, were at home, they would probably keep a section of the river free for our use and closed against Yankee transports." The general had been sent west to help recover territory, not surrender more, and when it became evident after Shiloh that this was not to be accomplished, an intimate of the Davis circle wrote prophetically in her diary in reference to the hero of Sumter and Manassas: "Cock robin is as dead as he ever will be now. What matters it who killed him?"

As if in confirmation, soon after the loss of Memphis and its covering flotilla opened the river south to Vicksburg, the Tupelo commander received from the Adjutant General in Richmond a telegraphic warning that trouble was brewing for him there: "The President has been expecting a communication explaining your last movement. It has not yet arrived." Beauregard replied: "Have had no time to write report. Busy organizing and preparing for battle if pursued. . . . Retreat was a most brilliant and successful one," he added, maneuvering for solid ground on which to meet objections now that he had begun to see that the hoax might seem less fruitful and amusing from a distance. Next day, June 13, he forwarded a complete report, inclosing a clipping from the Chicago *Tribune* which showed that the enemy, at least, admired his generalship. He ended with a prediction that Halleck would find Corinth "a barren locality, which he must abandon as wholly worthless for his purposes."

If the document lacked his usual verve, there were more reasons than the melancholia resulting from lack of appreciation from above. Though the army's health was improving rapidly in the more salubrious Tupelo surroundings, the general's own was not. He had never entirely recovered from the throat operation he had undergone in Virginia, and the strain of long-odds campaigning had lowered his resistance even more. For months his doctors had been urging him to take a rest. Always he had replied that the military crisis would not permit it. But now that his army was out of contact with the enemy, he thought he might safely go to Bladon Springs, a resort north of Mobile, for a week or ten days of rest and relaxation before returning to take up the reins again. Bragg, the next ranking general, could hold them in his absence; Beauregard considered him fully qualified, having recommended him for the position just after Shiloh. Armed with a certificate of disability from his medical director, he was packing to leave on the 14th when he learned that Bragg had received, clean over his commander's head, a War Department order instructing him to assume command of the Vicksburg defenses.

Angry at having been by-passed, Beauregard wired that Bragg could not be spared. He himself was taking a short sick leave, he said, and was leaving the North Carolinian in charge of the army during his absence. Then, as if suddenly aware that this was the first he had told the authorities of his intended departure, he wrote a letter describing his run-down physical condition, quoting his doctors' insistence that he take a rest, and giving his travel schedule. He did not ask permission to go; he simply told the government he was going. Nor did he send the information by wire. He sent it by regular mail, and was on his way to Bladon Springs before the letter got to Richmond.

Bragg considered his position awkward, knowing the trouble that was brewing, and with Regular Army prudence wired Richmond for instructions as soon as his chief was gone. The reaction was immediate, perhaps because the wire arrived on the same day as news of another consequence of the retreat, the fall of Cumberland Gap. As far as Davis was concerned, the situation at Tupelo spoke for itself: Beauregard was AWOL. Accordingly, a telegram went to Bragg at once, assigning him to permanent command. The Creole first learned of the action from a telegram Bragg sent to intercept him in Mobile. "I envy you, and am almost in despair," Bragg said. Beauregard replied: "I cannot congratulate you, but am happy for the change."

He was not happy; he just said that to cover his anger and disappointment. Four months ago he had come west full of resentment at having been shunted away from the main field of endeavor into a vaster but relatively much less important theater. Since then, he had learned better. The war was to be won or lost as readily here as in the East. What was more, he had come to respect and love the western army, just as it loved and respected him, and he was bitter against the man who had taken it from him as abruptly as if by a pull on the trigger of a pistol already leveled at his head. Replying to a letter of sympathy sent by a friend, he wrote: "If the country be satisfied to have me laid on the shelf by a man who is either demented or a traitor to his high trust — well, let it be so. I require rest and will endeavor meanwhile by study and reflection to fit myself for the darkest hours of our trial, which I foresee are yet to come." Part at least of the study and reflection was devoted to composing other phrases which he considered descriptive of the enemy who had wronged him. "That living specimen of gall and hatred," he called Davis now; " 'that Individual.' "

CHAPTER

☟ **5** ☟

Fighting Means Killing

★ ☟ ☆

☟ DISASTER CAME IN VARIOUS FORMS THIS
spring, and it moved to various tempos. In the West it came like fire-
works, looming after a noisy rush and casting a lurid glow. Whole states,
whole armies fell at once or had large segments broken off by the tread
of the invader. Kentucky and Missouri, most of Tennessee, much of
Arkansas, North Alabama and North Mississippi were lost in rapid succession, along with 30,000 fighting men, dead or in northern prison
camps, and finally New Orleans, Memphis, and the fleets that had been
built — or, worse, were being built — to hold the river that ran between
them. That was how it reached the West. In the East it came otherwise:
not with a gaudy series of eruptions and collapses and attendant pillars
of fire, but with a sort of inexorable hover, an inching-forward through
mist and gloom, as if it were conserving energy for an even more spectacular climax: the collapse of the national capital, the destruction of
the head and front of Government itself. On damp evenings, such as
the one that fell on May Day, the grumble of McClellan's guns at
Yorktown, faintly audible from Richmond's hills, reached listeners
through what seemed to them the twilight of the gods.

Nowhere, east or west, had there been a victory to celebrate
since Ball's Bluff in October seven months ago. Foreign intervention, the
cure-all formerly assured by early spring because that was when England's cotton reserves were supposed to be exhausted, now seemed
further away than ever. "There are symptoms that the Civil War cannot very long be protracted," the once friendly London *Times* was
saying. "Let its last embers burn down to the last spark without being
trodden out by our feet." Confederates could tell themselves they had
known all along that the English had never made a habit of retrieving
other people's chestnuts; but additional, less deniable disappointments
loomed much nearer. Although the near-exhaustion of the nation's war

supplies, especially powder, was kept secret, other effects of the naval blockade were all too well known. After a disastrous attempt at price control was abandoned, the regulated items having simply disappeared from grocery shelves, prices went up with a leap. Meat was 50¢ a pound, butter 75¢, coffee $1.50, and tea $10: all in contrast to cotton, which had fallen to 5¢. Salt — "Lot's wife" in the slang of the day — was scarce after the loss of the Kanawha works, and sugar went completely out of sight with the news of the fall of New Orleans. What was more, all this took place in an atmosphere not only of discouragement, but also of suspicion. Treasonable slogans were being chalked on fences and walls: "Union men to the rescue!" "Now is the time to rally round the Old Flag!" "God bless the Stars and Stripes!" There were whispers of secret and mysterious Union meetings, and one morning a black coffin was found suggestively near the Executive Mansion, a noosed rope coiled on its lid.

Few citizens approved of the coffin threat, but many approved of its implication as to where the blame for their present troubles lay, and so did a number of their elected representatives. The permanent Congress was different from the one that had come to Richmond from Montgomery — not so much in composition, however, as in outlook. Though for the most part they were the same men, reëlected, they served under different circumstances, the bright dawn having given way to clouds. A member who had resigned to enter the army, but who kept in touch with his former colleagues, told his wife, "It seems that things are coming to this pass; to be a patriot you must hate Davis." They took their cue from R. B. Rhett, whose Charleston *Mercury* was saying, "Jefferson Davis now treats all men as if they were idiotic insects." One among them who felt that way was Yancey. Back from his fruitless European mission, he was angrily demanding to know why Virginia had twenty-nine generals and Alabama only four. Another was Tom Cobb, who wrote home that he and his fellows were secretly debating the deposition of Davis. "He would be deposed," Cobb declared, "if the Congress had any more confidence in Stephens than in him."

If they could not get rid of him, they could at least try the next best thing by limiting his powers: especially in the conduct of military affairs. This had been the basis for the virulent attack on Benjamin, who administered the War Department under the close supervision of his chief. Reasoning that a professional soldier would be less pliant, they attempted to oust Benjamin by recommending R. E. Lee for the position. When Davis refused to make the change, on grounds that the law required a civilian at the post, Congress retaliated with an act calling for the appointment of a commanding general who would have full authority to take charge of any army in the field whenever he thought best. Davis vetoed the measure as a violation of his rights as Commander in Chief, but at the same time — it was early March by then — ordered Lee "to duty at the seat of government," where he would be charged with the conduct of military operations "under the direction of the President." Thus Davis frustrated his enemies in Congress. He gained a military secretary — "an orderly sergeant," one newspaper sneered — without sacrificing one jot of his constitutional prerogative. Lee saw well enough what it came to. Returning to Richmond from his work on the South Atlantic coastal defenses, he observed: "I cannot see either advantage or pleasure in my duties. But I will not complain, but do the best I can."

His best was better than might have been expected, considering the limitations of his authority and his early failures in the field. Mainly what he accomplished was done through tactful handling of the President, whose admission that "events have cast on our arms and hopes the gloomiest shadows" Lee now saw at first hand was the mildest possible statement of conditions. Not only was there a crippling shortage of weapons, it now appeared probable that there soon would be a lack of men to shoulder the few they had. The so-called "bounty and furlough law" having proved a failure, except as a disruptive influence, few of the volunteers whose Sumter-inspired one-year enlistments would expire in April seemed willing to forego at least a vacation at home before signing up again, and many were saying quite openly that they were through with army life for good. In the heat of their conviction that they had earned a rest, the already badly outnumbered southern armies seemed likely to melt away just as the northern juggernaut was scheduled to gather speed in the East as in the West. Virginia had already met the problem by providing for a general enrollment in the state militia of all citizens between the ages of eighteen and forty-five, to be used as replacements for the men whose army enlistments expired. Under the influence of Lee, Davis proposed more stringent measures on a larger scale. In a late-March message to Congress he recommended outright conscription, within the same age bracket, throughout the Confederacy — to make sure, he said, that the burden of fighting did not fall "exclusively on the most ardent and patriotic."

Congress debated hotly, then on April 16, after lowering the upper age limit to thirty-five, passed the first national conscription law in American history. They passed it because they knew it was necessary, but they blamed Davis for having made it necessary by adopting the "dispersed defensive," which they said had dampened national enthusiasm. His reply — that "without military stores, without the workshops to create them, without the power to import them, necessity not choice has compelled us to occupy strong positions and everywhere to confront the enemy without reserves" — did nothing to assuage the anger of the States Righters, who saw in conscription a repudiation of the principles for which the war was being fought. Georgia's governor

Joseph E. Brown flatly declared that no "act of the Government of the United States prior to the secession of Georgia struck a blow at constitutional liberty so fell as has been struck by the conscription act." The fire-eaters, already furious at having been denied high offices, renewed their attacks on Davis as a despot. He replied in a letter to a friend, "When everything is at stake and the united power of the South alone can save us, it is sad to know that men can deal in such paltry complaints and tax their ingenuity to slander because they are offended in not getting office. . . . If we can achieve our independence, the office seekers are welcome to the one I hold."

However, the critics were in full bay now and were not to be turned aside by scorn or reason. Ominously, they pointed out that Napoleon's rise to absolute power had been accomplished by just such an act of conscription. Nothing Davis said or did was above suspicion. Even his turning to the solace of religion — up till now he had never been a formal member of any church — was seen as a possibly sinister action. "The President is thin and haggard," a War Department clerk observed in mid-April, "and it has been whispered that he will immediately be baptised and confirmed. I hope so, because it may place a great gulf between him and the descendant of those who crucified the Saviour. Nevertheless, some of his enemies allege that professions of Christianity have sometimes been the premeditated accompaniments of usurpation. It was so with Cromwell and Richard III."

The descendant referred to, of course, was the clerk's former department chief, Benjamin, now head of the State Department. He was as skillful an administrator as ever, but the problems here were not the kind that could be solved by rapid pigeon-holing. Europe was reacting to the news of Union successes along the line of the Mississippi, and that reaction worked strongly against Confederate recognition. Slidell was beginning to weary of the French emperor's slippery courtesies, which led to nothing above-board or official, and Mason was suffering from the same feeling of affront that had vanquished Yancey. He wrote that he intended to present his next proposal for recognition "as a demand of *right;* and if refused — as I have little doubt it would be — to follow the refusal by a note, that I did not consider it compatible with the dignity of my government, and perhaps with my own self-respect, to remain longer in England." Benjamin's smile faded, for once, as he replied, imploring Mason not to act rashly. His mere presence in London was of enormous value; he must await eventualities.

Fortunately, the Virginian had not acted on his impulse, but his patience was wearing thin, and this was one more worry that had to be passed along to Davis. He had tried to steel his harrowed nerves against the criticisms flung at him from all sides, telling his wife: "I wish I could learn just to let people alone who snap at me — in forbearance and charity to turn away as well from the cats as the snakes."

But it was too much for him. He could approach his work with humility, but not his critics. When they snapped he snapped back. Nor was he highly skilled as an arbitrator; he had too much admiration and sympathy for those who would not yield, whatever their cause, to be effective at reconciling opponents. In fact, this applied to a situation practically in his own back yard. The White House stood on a tall hill, surrounded by other mansions. On the plain below were the houses of the poor, whose sons had formed a gang called the Butcher Cats, sworn to eternal hatred of the Hill Cats, the children of the gentry on the hill. The two gangs had rock fights and occasional gouging matches. After one particularly severe battle, in which his oldest son was involved, Davis walked down the hill to try his hand at arbitration. He made them a speech, referring to the Butcher Cats as future leaders of the nation. One of them replied: "President, we like you. We don't want to hurt any of your boys. But we aint *never* going to be friends with them Hill Cats."

Davis came back up the hill.

Everywhere Lee had been in this war he had arrived to find disaster looming ready-made, and this was no exception. Militarily as well as politically, the mid-March outlook in Virginia was bleak indeed. Federal combinations totaling well over 200,000 men were threatening less than 70,000 Confederates strung out along an arc whose chord extended northwest-southeast through Richmond. At the lower end, Huger held Norfolk with 13,000, threatened from below by Burnside with the same number. Down near the tip of the York-James peninsula, Major General John B. Magruder's 12,000 were intrenched in front of Fort Monroe and its garrison of the same number. Northward, after retreating to their new position at Fredericksburg and along the near bank of the Rapidan, Johnston's 37,000 had been followed as far as Manassas by McClellan, who had 175,000 effectives in and out of the Washington defenses. Both main armies — the Army of Northern Virginia, as Lee now began to style it, and the Army of the Potomac — had detachments in the Shenandoah Valley, where Jackson with 5000 was falling back before Major General Nathaniel P. Banks with twice as many. Finally, at the upper or western end of this long arc, beyond Staunton, a little force of 2800 under Brigadier General Edward Johnson prepared to do what it could to block Frémont's proposed descent of the Alleghenies with McClellan's old army of 12,500, which in time would be doubled, despite McClellan's protests, by accretions from his new one.

Much of this was unknown to Lee — especially enemy strengths, which in general were overestimated; the Confederate spy system was yielding very little information these days — but one thing was quite clear. After leaving a sizeable garrison to hold the Washington intrenchments, McClellan's large main body could slide anywhere along that arc, or rather under cover just beyond it, then bull straight through for Richmond, outnumbering three-to-one — or for that matter ten-to-one, depending on where it struck — any force that stood in its path. Just now its actions were suspicious. After following Johnston's army as far as Manassas, it turned mysteriously back and reëntered the cordon of forts around the northern capital. This seemed to indicate that it was about to start its slide, but before Lee could even begin to try to second-guess its destination, news arrived from the south that upset his already inadequate dispositions: Burnside had taken New Bern. This was a challenge that had to be met, for he was now within sixty miles of Richmond's only direct rail connection with the South Atlantic states. Lee met it in the only way he could: by weakening what was far too weak already. Detaching several regiments from Huger at Norfolk and two brigades from Johnston's right wing at Fredericksburg, he sent them south into North Carolina under Major General Theophilus Holmes, a native of the threatened area.

The following week, March 23, Stonewall Jackson turned on Banks at Kernstown, intending to "inflict a terrible wound" on what he thought was a small segment, but soon retreated, badly cut up himself, when the segment turned out to be a full division. One more defeat was added to the growing list, though the news was less discouraging than it might have been, arriving as it did on the heels of more disturbing information. Just as Lee returned to giving the main danger — McClellan — his main attention, Huger reported by tele-

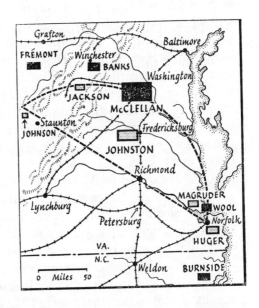

graph that more than twenty transports had come down Chesapeake Bay the night before and were disembarking troops at Old Point Comfort, across the way. Soon afterward, this alarming news was confirmed by a wire from Magruder calling urgently for reinforcements. The force confronting him, he said, had risen to 35,000 overnight. Neither general identified the enemy units, but Lee considered their arrival a probable sign that McClellan had started his slide along the arc.

However, even if Lee had been certain of this, he still could not be certain of their goal. They might be on their way to Burnside for operations in North Carolina. They might be mounting an offensive against Norfolk. They might be intended as a diversion to hold Magruder in position while the main body jumped on Johnston. Or they might be the advance of McClellan's whole army, arriving for an all-out drive up the Peninsula. Until he knew which of these possibilities was (or were) at least probable, he would be taking an enormous risk in strengthening the arc at any point by weakening it at another. To lose Norfolk, for example, would be to lose the *Virginia*, which was all that was keeping the Federal gunboats from wrecking Magruder's right flank on their way up the James to bombard Richmond. Or to weaken Johnston's army, already reduced by more than ten percent as a result of detaching the two brigades for Holmes, might be to expose that mainstay of the Confederate defense to utter destruction.

While awaiting further indications, Lee warned Huger and Magruder to be ready for mutual assistance, one to reinforce the other as soon as events showed which was the Federal objective, Norfolk or Yorktown. Meanwhile, the water batteries along the James were strengthened, particularly the ones at Drewry's Bluff, eight miles below Richmond, and the city's scant reserves — two regiments of infantry and some odd squadrons of cavalry — were dispatched to Magruder, who was told to put on as brave a show as possible in the face of the build-up at Fort Monroe. If it became necessary to give ground, he was told to yield it stubbornly, fighting all the way to the gates of the city, sixty miles in his rear. Magruder answered excitedly that a council of war, held the night before, had voted to evacuate Yorktown unless 10,000 reinforcements were sent to him at once. Lee replied that councils of war were always timid in such situations, then repeated his instructions: keep up a bold front and yield nothing except to absolute pressure. He would send him what he could.

Whatever he sent him would have to come from Johnston, who had already expressed his unwillingness to furnish any more troops for other commanders. He would bring his whole army down, if ordered, but he was opposed to piecemeal reinforcement as a violation of sound principles. Concentration, not dispersal, was the answer, he declared. He could spare two more brigades — another ten percent of his original force — but that was all. Lee took them, duly thankful for small favors; sent one to Magruder, salving his anxiety a bit, and one to Holmes, hoping thus to keep Burnside out of the squeeze play; and then proceeded to exercise on the touchy Johnston the same tact and delicacy he was using simultaneously in his dealings with Davis, who was quite as touchy. Lighthorse Harry Lee and Peter Johnston had soldiered together in the First Revolution; now their sons worked together in the Second. During the ten days between March 24, when the arrival of the transports was reported, and April 4, Lee managed by gradual detachment to transfer three of Johnston's six divisions from the Rapidan to the James. By the latter date, the Army of Northern

Virginia — exclusive of Jackson, out in the Valley — had been reduced to 23,000, while Magruder had 31,500 troops either with him
or on the way.

They were in capable hands and well employed. If Magruder
was high-strung and overimaginative by ordinary standards, it presently
developed that these qualities, so doubtful in a military leader, could
be positive advantages in an extraordinary situation, such as the one that
involved him now. A fifty-two-year-old Virginian, tall and flamboy-
antly handsome, with a great shock of dark hair, bushy sideburns, and a
large but carefully barbered mustache — "Prince John," he had been
called in the old army — he spoke with a lisp except when he sang in a
clear tenor, as he often did, songs of his own composition. That had
been his greatest spare-time pleasure: staging concerts and amateur
theatricals, in which he took a leading role, to relieve the tedium of
peacetime garrison duty. Now he had a chance to exercise his talents
on a larger scale and for a more deadly purpose. Exploiting to the full
Lee's admonition to show a brave front to the heavily reinforced enemy,
he staged an extravaganza with a cast of thousands, playing as it were
to a packed house. He bristled aggressively whenever he imagined a
Yankee spyglass trained in his direction, shifting his artillery from point
to point along his line and firing noisily at anything in sight. No
wheeze was too old for Magruder to employ it. One morning he sent
a column along a road that was heavily wooded except for a single gap
in plain view of the enemy outposts. All day the gray files swept past
in seemingly endless array, an army gathering in thousands among the
pines for an offensive. They were no such thing, of course. Like a
low-budgeted theatrical director producing the effect with an army of
supernumeraries, Magruder was marching a single battalion round and
around, past the gap, then around under cover, and past the gap again.

He had the men working as well as parading; the buskin was
supplementary to the spade. Utilizing the old British earthworks around
Yorktown, moldering since the days of the Revolution, they dug
furiously down to the Warwick River, which was dammed near its
mouth and at several points upstream to create an intermittent moat in
front of the high ground leading southward to the James. This was the
first peninsular line, fourteen miles in length: a great deal too long for
the number of men available to defend it. Its principal drawback, however, was that the flanks were open to naval bombardment if the Union
warships decided to brave the *Virginia* on the right or the additional
water battery on the left, across the York at Gloucester Point. Ten
miles in his rear, just east of Williamsburg, Magruder was constructing
a second defensive line, though in fact it was not so much a line as it was
a sort of rally-point in case the first gave way. Here he had two
streams to protect his flanks from infantry assault, one flowing north,
the other south. On the high ground in the center, just in front of the

old colonial capital, he was improvising a bastioned earthwork which he or his officers, after the Thespian custom of sometimes naming a theater for a star, christened Fort Magruder. This second peninsular line had all the drawbacks of the first, plus certain intrinsic weaknesses all its own. Magruder was not a skilled engineer; he admitted it, and even complained about it. But he tried to make up in energy for what he lacked in skill. A dozen small redoubts were scattered about for the fort's protection; fields of fire were cleared by felling trees; additional rifle pits were dug, extending the line behind the tidal creeks. Magruder was doing the best he could.

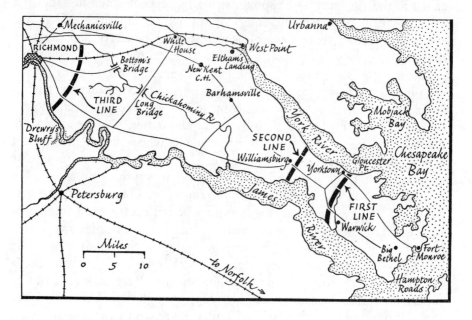

In case that best was not enough — which seemed likely, considering the odds and limitations — Lee had a third line under construction, forty miles behind the second and within ten miles of Richmond. Its right was anchored on the James and its left on the Chickahominy, a boggy stream which also covered a portion of the front with a tributary known as White Oak Swamp. This was the strongest of the three peninsular lines, being immune from naval attack, but Lee did not want to use it until he had to. Resistance below would give him time to bring up whatever troops he could spare from other points and to complete the reorganization now in progress while Congress debated conscription. That was why he was sending all the men he could lay hands on, including half of Johnston's army, down to Yorktown.

For a time he feared that he had guessed wrong. The Federals were strangely inactive at Fort Monroe. Then on April 4 he received word from Jeb Stuart, on outpost duty north of the Rappahannock, that another relay of transports was on its way down the Potomac. Simultaneously, Magruder reported heavy blue columns moving in his direction. These two pieces of evidence were strong, but Lee was still not sure that this was McClellan's main effort. Then five days later, on the heels of the depressing news that Albert Sidney Johnston had fallen at Shiloh, a minister who had escaped from Alexandria gave a detailed account of Unionist activities at that port of embarkation, adding that he personally had seen McClellan himself board one of the steamers for the journey down the coast. For Lee, this was conclusive. He went to Davis with the evidence, and that same day — April 9 — the President ordered Johnston to report at once to Richmond, bringing his two strongest divisions along for duty on the Peninsula.

He arrived on the 12th. Two of his divisions, under Major Generals G. W. Smith and Longstreet, were in his wake; the third, under Major General Ewell, stayed where it was, with instructions to co-operate with Jackson if the necessity arose. Informed that his command now included the Peninsula and Norfolk, Johnston left Richmond that same day for an inspection of the Yorktown and Williamsburg lines. Two mornings later, April 14, he was back again, waiting in the presidential office when Davis arrived for work. The bleakness of his outlook matched the brevity of his absence. Both of Magruder's defensive lines were utterly untenable, he told Davis. Not only were they improperly sited and too long; vulnerable as they were to artillery in front and amphibious landings in the rear, they would most likely prove a trap for any army that tried to hold them. In short, he favored an immediate withdrawal to the third line of defense. Davis, somewhat taken aback at this suggestion that the war be brought forthwith to the gates of Richmond, asked the general to return at 11 a.m. and present his views to Lee and Secretary Randolph. This being the case, Johnston asked that Smith and Longstreet also be invited, thus to preserve the balance. Davis agreed.

When the six men assembled at the specified hour it was evident that the general had chosen his supporters wisely. Longstreet had won considerable renown as a poker player, but had given it up three months ago, on the eve of his forty-first birthday, when his three children died of scarlet fever, all within a week. Grief had given him a stolid and ponderous dignity, augmented by a slight deafness which he could sit behind, when he chose, as behind a wall of sound-proof glass. He chose to sit so now. A large, square-built, hairy man, a native of the Deep South — born in South Carolina, raised in Georgia, and appointed to West Point from Alabama — he left the talking to Smith, who was a year younger but had been trained for disputation as Street Commissioner of New York City. Like Mansfield Lovell, his New York deputy, Smith had joined the Confederacy late, after waiting to see what his native Kentucky would do. Two months after Manassas he made his choice, which Davis applauded by making him a major general and giving him a division under Johnston, who admired him; the two were "Joe" and "G.W." to each other. A big-framed man with a large nose and firm-set lips, a West Pointer and a Mexico veteran, a former assistant professor of engineering at the Academy, Smith had been a civilian for the past eight years and was quite accustomed to attending such high-level councils as this. With Davis' and Johnston's permission, he said, he would like to submit a memorandum he had prepared. Johnston looked it over, then passed it to Davis, who read it aloud.

It was as if the ghost of Beauregard had been transported eastward 700 airline miles from Mississippi. What Smith proposed, in essence, was a withdrawal from Norfolk and the lower Peninsula, a concentration of all available troops, and then a sudden strike, either against McClellan as he came up, or against the northern heartland beyond the Potomac. Smith was convinced that the fast-marching southern army could occupy Philadelphia or New York before McClellan could take Richmond. Johnston, questioned by Randolph, said he agreed — up to a point. He was not anxious to march on New York but he did want to cripple McClellan, and this was the way to do it; Norfolk and Yorktown were untenable anyhow. Randolph, a former navy man, protested that the loss of Gosport Navy Yard would mean the loss of the *Virginia*, which could neither put to sea nor ascend the James, unseaworthy and deep-drafted as she was, as well as the loss of all hope of ever building a real Confederate fleet. Johnston replied that it could not be helped. To attempt to hold positions that could readily be flanked would be to invite the destruction not only of the future navy but also of the present army.

All day the discussion continued, Randolph and Lee against Johnston and Smith, with Longstreet saying little and Davis acting as moderator. At suppertime they recessed for an hour, then reassembled at the Executive Mansion, where the argument continued into the night, apparently without affecting the convictions of any of the six. Then at 1 a.m. Davis adjourned the meeting with the decision to hold both Norfolk and Yorktown by uniting Johnston's and Magruder's armies on the lower Peninsula, under instructions to resist all Federal attempts to advance. Johnston thus was being sent to defend a position which he had declared untenable. He would have been removed, Davis later wrote, except that "he did not ask to be . . . and I had no wish to separate him from troops with whom he was so intimately acquainted." Johnston had his reasons, though he did not give them then. "The belief that events on the Peninsula would soon compel the Confederate government to adopt my method of opposing the Federal army," he wrote later, "reconciled me somewhat to the necessity of obeying the President's order."

As the general returned to Yorktown, convinced that things would work out his way in the end, Longstreet's men were marching through Richmond to join him. "The Walking Division," they called themselves, and one of them grumbled: "I suppose that if it was intended to reinforce Savannah, Mobile, or New Orleans with our division, we would be compelled to foot it all the way." But now that they were nearing the end of the march their spirits rose. It was the anniversary of Virginia's secession and the whole city had turned out to greet them with cheers and armloads of early spring flowers. Jonquils, hyacinths, narcissuses, and violets were tossed and caught, looped into wreaths or stuck into rifle muzzles. The drab mud-stained column seemed to burst into bloom as it swung down Main Street, a riot of colors dominated by the bright nodding yellow of the jonquils. Bands played "Dixie" and "The Bonnie Blue Flag," and the men returned the cheers of the crowd along the way. At one window they saw a lady and a pale young man waving handkerchiefs, and one of the bearded veterans shouted: "Come right along, sonny. The lady'll spare ye. Here's a little musket for ye!" The answer came back: "All right, boys. Have you got a leg for me, too?" As he spoke he placed on the window sill the stump of the leg he had lost at Manassas. The battalion made an effective apology. Wheeling spontaneously into line, it halted, presented arms, and rattled the windows of the block with cheering.

Johnston found a quite different spirit around Yorktown, fifty miles below. Magruder and his men were worn out by the strain of the long bluff. Their food was poor and their uniforms in rags. What was more, the enemy had begun to probe the Warwick River line with field artillery. There were night alarms and occasional stampedes, one including a work party of several hundred slaves, who broke for the rear and in their flight swept away part of the infantry support. Whatever his vaunted gallantry in the open field, the southern volunteer did not relish this kind of warfare, huddling under bombardments and waiting to be overrun. One detachment gave way completely under the tension, a member of the relief party reporting that he had found "some of these poor lads . . . sobbing in their broken sleep, like a crying child just before it sinks to rest. It was really pathetic. The men actually had to be supported to the ambulances sent down to bring them away."

They had the sympathy of their new commander, who was convinced that they should not have stayed there in the first place. To the War Department the last ten days of April brought word of the fall of New Orleans and the opening of Halleck's campaign against Corinth, as well as a trickle of I-told-you-so dispatches from the lower Peninsula. Johnston declared that Magruder's lines were even more defective than he had supposed when he made his first inspection. "No one but McClellan could have hesitated to attack," he reported on the 22d, and urged that some bridges across the Chickahominy, twenty-odd miles in his rear, should be repaired at once. Two days later he was suggesting that supplies be sent to meet the army on its way to the gates of the city "in the event of our being compelled to fall back from this point." On the 27th he instructed Huger to prepare to evacuate Norfolk. Two days later he wrote to Lee in the plainest language he had yet employed: "The fight for Yorktown, as I said in Richmond, must be one of artillery, in which we cannot win. The result is certain; the time only doubtful. . . . We must abandon the Peninsula at once."

There they had it; he had been right all along. May Day was a time of gloom in the southern capital. Ball's Bluff seemed far away and long ago.

★ ★ ★

One source of consolation existed, but it was unknown in Richmond, being hidden in the fog of war, far down the James and beyond the enemy lines. Johnston's worries were balanced — more than balanced, at least in number — by the woes of his opponent, which differed as much in quality as they did in multiplicity. The southern commander's fretfulness was based almost exclusively on strictly tactical considerations: the weakness of the Yorktown defenses and the shortage of troops to man them. But McClellan's was the product of a variety of pressures, roughly divisible under three main headings: 1) downright bad luck, 2) Lincoln, and — as always — 3) his own ripe imagination.

The first of a rapid succession of blows, like the preliminary tap of a farrier taking aim, landed the moment he stepped off the steamer at Old Point Comfort. Flag Officer Goldsborough, up from the North Carolina sounds to provide naval support for the movement up the narrow tongue of land, met him with word that the fleet would not be able to assist in reducing the enemy batteries on the York or the James. The navy already had its hands full, he said, patrolling Hampton Roads to neutralize the *Merrimac-Virginia*. One of the primary conditions of success, as stated by the corps commanders on the eve of departure, thus was removed before the campaign had even begun. Fortunately, McClellan had a full day in which to absorb the shock of this. But after that brief respite the blows began to land with trip-hammer rapidity.

On the second day, April 4, as he started his army forward — much gratified by the "wonderfully cool performance" of the trio of foragers who brought him the still-warm 12-pound shot — he made two dreadful discoveries. The first was that his handsome Coastal Survey maps were woefully inaccurate. The roads all ran the wrong way, he complained, and the Warwick River, shown on the maps as an insignificant creek flowing parallel to the James, was in fact a considerable barrier, cutting squarely across his line of march. To add to its effectiveness as an obstacle, the Confederates had dammed it in five places, creating five unwadable lakes and training their heavy artillery on the boggy intervals. McClellan was amazed at the river's location and condition; "[It] grows worse the more you look at it," he wailed.

As he stood gazing forlornly at this waste of wetness in his path, another unexpected development overtook him, also involving water. It began to rain. And from this there grew an even worse disclosure. Those fine sandy roads, recommended as being "passable at all seasons on the year," turned out to be no such thing. What they were was gumbo — and they were apparently bottomless. Guns and wagons bogged past the axles, then sat there, immovably stuck. One officer later testified that he saw a mule go completely out of sight in one of the chunk-holes, "all but the tips of its ears," but added, in the tall-tale tradition, that the mule was a rather small one.

No navy, no fit maps, no transportation: McClellan might well have thought the fates had dealt him all the weal they intended. Writing to his wife of his unenviable position — "the rebels on one side, and the abolitionists and other scoundrels on the other" — he said, "Don't worry about the wretches; they have done nearly their worst, and can't do much more." He was wrong, and before the day was over he would discover just how wrong he was. The people he referred to could do a great deal more. If McClellan did not realize this, Lincoln's two young secretaries knew it quite well already. "Gen McC is in danger," one was telling the other. "Not in front, but in rear."

Returning to army headquarters at the close of that same busy day — his first in bristling proximity to the enemy since the campaign in West Virginia, almost nine months ago — McClellan found the atmosphere of the lantern-hung interior as glum as the twilit landscape of rain-soaked fields and dripping woods through which he had just ridden. Sorrow and anger, despair and incredulity were strangely combined on the faces of his staff. Soon the Young Napoleon was sharing these mixed emotions; for the answer, or answers, lay in a batch of orders and directives just off the wire from Washington. The first was dated yesterday, April 3: Fort Monroe and its garrison of 12,000, placed under McClellan two weeks ago as a staging area and a pool from which to draw replacements, were removed forthwith from his control. Before he could recover from the shock of learning that he had lost not only that number of troops, but also command of his present base of operations, he was handed a second order, more drastic than the first. McDowell's corps of 38,000, still awaiting sailing orders at Alexandria — McClellan intended to bring it down in mass as soon as he decided where to land it, whether on the south bank of the York, for operations against Yorktown, or on the north bank, against Gloucester Point — was detached and withheld as part of the force assigned to provide close-in protection for the capital. This action was given emphasis by a supplementary order creating what was called the Department of the Rappahannock, under McDowell, as well as another new one, called the Department of the Shenandoah, under Banks, whose corps was also declared no longer a part of the Army of the Potomac. McClellan was floored. Even without the loss of Banks, which made no actual change in dispositions, the combined detachments of Blenker, McDowell, and the Fort Monroe garrison — an approximate total of 60,000 fighting men — reduced by well over one third the 156,000 he had said at the outset would be necessary for the success of his Peninsula campaign.

Nor was this all. As he took to his troubled bed that night he had something else to think about: something that seemed to him and his staff conclusive proof that the Administration, disapproving of the campaign in the first place, was determined to assure its failure before the opening shot was fired. A final order, dated yesterday and signed by the Adjutant General for distribution to the governors of all the loyal states, put an end to the recruiting of volunteers throughout the Union. All recruiting offices were closed, the equipment put up for sale to the highest bidders, and all recruiting personnel were reassigned to other duties. In some ways this was the hardest blow of all, or anyhow the most incredible. At a time when the Confederate authorities, sixty miles away in Richmond, were doing all they could to push through the first conscription law in American history — a law which could be expected to swell the ranks of the army facing him — it seemed to McClellan that his Washington superiors, twice that distance in his rear, had not only taken a full one third of his soldiers from him, but then had proceeded to make certain that they could never be replaced. The fact was, on the eve of bloody fighting, Lincoln and Stanton had seen to it that he would not even be able to replace his casualties. So it seemed to McClellan. At any rate, as he went to bed that night he could say, "They have done nearly their worst," and be a good deal closer to the truth.

Next morning, if somewhat daunted by all the knocks he had had to absorb in one short night, he was back at the front, probing the enemy defenses with his three remaining corps. Heintzelman and Keyes, on the right and left, had two divisions each, with a third on the way down Chesapeake Bay for both. Sumner, in the center, had only one; his second was en route, and his third had been Blenker. All three of these brigadiers were hard-shell regulars — Sumner had put in seven of his forty-three years of army service before McClellan was born, and both of the others were thirty-year men or better — but after coming under heavy fire from long-range guns and bogging down in the flooded approaches, all agreed with the Chief Engineer's report that the rebel line was "certainly one of the most extensive known to modern times." If the navy had been there to wreck the batteries on the flanks, or if the weight of McDowell's corps, the largest of the original four, could be added to the pressure the army could exert, things might be different. As it was, however, all felt obliged to agree with Keyes, who later reported bluntly: "No part of [the Yorktown-Warwick River] line, so far discovered, can be taken by assault without an enormous waste of life."

If the Confederate defenses could not be broken by flanking operations, if assault was too doubtful and expensive, only one method remained: a siege. McClellan would do it that way if he had to; he had studied siege tactics at Sebastopol. But he much preferred his original plan, which he now saw was impractical without his original army. As he rode back to headquarters this second night he decided to make a final appeal to Lincoln. Under the heading "Near Yorktown, 7.30 p.m." he outlined for the President the situation as he saw it, neglecting none of the drawbacks, and begged him to "reconsider" the order detaching McDowell. "In my deliberate judgment," he wrote, "the success of our cause will be imperiled by so greatly reducing my force when it is actually under the fire of the enemy and active operations have commenced.... I am now of the opinion that I shall have to fight all the available forces of the rebels not far from here. Do not force me to do so with diminished numbers."

Lincoln's reply, the following day, was a brief warning that delay on the Peninsula would benefit the Confederate defenders more than it would the Federal attackers: "You now have over 100,000 troops with you.... I think you better break the enemy's line from Yorktown to Warwick River at once." McClellan's first reaction, he told his wife, was "to reply that he had better come and do it himself." Instead, he wired on the 7th that, after the three recent detachments, his "entire force for duty" amounted to about 85,000 men, more than a third of whom were still en route from Alexandria. Lincoln took a day to study this, then replied on the 9th at considerable length. He was puzzled, he said, by "a curious mystery." The general's own report showed a total strength of 108,000; "How can the discrepancy of 23,000 be accounted for?"

Beyond this, however, the President's main purpose was to point out to McClellan that more factors were involved in this war than those which might occur to a man with an exclusively military turn of mind. In other words, this was a Civil war. The general was aware of certain pressures in his rear, but Lincoln suggested in a final paragraph that he would gain more from studying those pressures, and maybe finding ways to relieve them, than he would from merely complaining of their presence. It was a highly personal communication, and in it he gave McClellan some highly personal advice:

"Once more let me tell you that it is indispensable to *you* that you strike a blow. *I* am powerless to help this. You will do me the justice to remember I always insisted that going down the bay in search of a field, instead of fighting at or near Manassas, was only shifting and not sur-

mounting a difficulty; that we would find the same enemy and the same
or equal intrenchments in either place. The country will not fail to note
— is now noting — that the present hesitation to move upon an intrenched enemy is but the story of Manassas repeated. I beg to assure you
that I have never written you or spoken to you in greater kindness of
feeling than now, nor with a fuller purpose to sustain you, so far as, in
my most anxious judgment, I consistently can. But you must act."

That "most anxious judgment" had been under considerable
strain ever since McClellan's leading elements started down the coast in
transports. Ben Wade and Zachariah Chandler were bombarding Lincoln with protests that the general's treasonable intent was plain at
last for any eye to see: The whole campaign had been designed to side-
track the main Union army by bogging it down in the slews southeast of
Richmond, thus clearing the path for a direct rebel sweep on Washington, with little to stand in its way. Stanton not only encouraged the
presentation and acceptance of this view, but also enlarged it by
assigning additional motives to account for his former intimate's
treachery: McClellan was politically ambitious, "more interested in re-
constructing the Democratic party than the Army of the Potomac."
Lincoln wondered. He did not believe McClellan was a traitor,
but in suggesting that the capital was in danger the Jacobins had
touched him where he was tender. "This is a question which the country
will not allow me to evade," he said. He could not afford the slightest
risk in that direction; too much hung in the balance — including war
with England and France as a result of the recognition both would almost certainly give the Confederacy once its army had occupied Washington. Then, as he pondered, an alarm was sounded which seemed to
give substance to his fears.
On the day McClellan landed at Old Point Comfort, Brigadier
General James Wadsworth, the elderly commander of the Washington
defenses and one of the founders of the Republican Party, came to
Stanton complaining that his force was inadequate for its task, both in
numbers and in training. The Secretary sent his military assistant, the
hapless Hitchcock, and Adjutant General Lorenzo Thomas to investigate, and when they confirmed Wadsworth's report that the capital
was in danger, Stanton took him triumphantly to Lincoln. McClellan's
note of the day before, claiming that he had left 77,456 men behind to
give Washington the stipulated "entire feeling of security," was checked
for accuracy. Certain discrepancies showed at once, and the harder the
three men looked the more they saw. In the first place, by an arithmeti-
cal error, the troops at Warrenton had been counted twice. Proposed
reinforcements from Maryland, Pennsylvania, and New York had not
arrived, though they were listed. Blenker's division, on the way to
Frémont, had also been included, on grounds that Banks could interrupt

its march if it was needed. All these had to be subtracted. And so for that matter did the two divisions already with Banks in the Valley; Patterson's army, out there in July, had done nothing to protect the capital after the debacle at Bull Run. In fact, by actual count as Lincoln saw it, once McClellan's whole army had gone down the coast, there would be fewer than 29,000 men in all to stand in the way of a direct Confederate drive on Washington: 11,000 less than the general's own corps commanders had said were necessary.

The way to keep this from happening was to stop one corps from going to join McClellan, and that was what Lincoln did, creating in the process the Departments of the Rappahannock and the Shenandoah to give McDowell and Banks their independence. The former would make his headquarters at Falmouth, opposite Fredericksburg, and in time — conditions permitting — march overland to join his former chief in front of Richmond. That way, he would always be in a position to strike the front or flank of any rebel force that tried a direct lunge at Washington, and yet he would still be in on the kill when the time came. Lincoln did not want to hurt McClellan any more than he had to. In fact, on the day after telling him, "You must act," he released Mc-Dowell's lead division, under Franklin — a great favorite of Mc-Clellan's, who asked in a final desperate plea that this, at least, not be withheld — to proceed by the water route as originally planned. Exuberantly grateful, McClellan wired on April 13: "We shall soon be at them, and I am sure of the result."

Lincoln had heard him say such things before; they were part of what made the Young Napoleon at once so likeable and exasperating. The President knew by now not to put much stock in such expressions, which after all only meant that McClellan was feeling good again. Lincoln himself was not. The past week had been a strain, in some ways harder than the strain which had followed defeat on the plains of Manassas. His sadness had deepened, along with the lines in his face, though he still kept his wry sense of humor. A country editor called at the White House, claiming to have been the first to suggest Lincoln's nomination for President. Lincoln was busy, but when he tried to escape by saying he had to go over to the War Department on business, the editor offered to accompany him. "Come along," Lincoln said. When they got there he told his visitor, "I shall have to see Mr Stanton alone, and you must excuse me." He turned to enter, but then, perhaps considering this too abrupt, turned back and took the editor by the hand. "Goodbye," he said. "I hope you will feel perfectly easy about having nominated me. Don't be troubled about it. I forgive you."

As April wore on and the rains continued, so did the siege preparations; McClellan was hard at work. He had not wanted this kind of campaign, but now that he had it he was enjoying it immensely.

Back in the West Virginia days he had said, "I will not throw these raw men of mine into the teeth of artillery and intrenchments if it is possible to avoid it." He still felt that way about it. "I am to watch over you as a parent over his children," he had told his army the month before, and that was what he was doing. If it was to be a siege, let it be one in the grand manner, with fascines and gabions, zigzag approaches, and much digging and shifting of earth, preparatory to blasting the rebel fortifications clean out of existence. "Do not misunderstand the apparent inaction here," he wired Lincoln on the 23d, concerned lest a civilian fail to appreciate all this labor. "Not a day, not an hour has been lost. Works have been constructed that may almost be called gigantic."

Gigantic was particularly the word for the fifteen ten-gun batteries of 13-inch siege mortars being installed within two miles of Yorktown; on completion, they would be capable of throwing 400 tons of metal daily into the rebel defenses. Six were installed and ready before the end of the month, but McClellan held his fire, preferring to open with all of them at once. Meanwhile he neglected nothing which he thought would add to the final effect. On the 28th he wired Stanton: "Would be glad to have the 30-pounder Parrotts in the works around Washington. Am short of that excellent gun." When Lincoln saw the request, his thin-stretched patience snapped. "Your call for Parrott guns . . . alarms me," he answered on May Day, "chiefly because it argues indefinite procrastination. Is anything to be done?" McClellan replied that the Parrotts would hasten, not delay, the breaking of the enemy lines; "All is being done that human labor can accomplish." The build-up continued. Then suddenly, May 4, it paid off. The noonday Sabbath quiet of the War Department telegraph office was broken by the brief, jubilant clatter of a message from the Peninsula: "Yorktown is in our possession. Geo. B. McClellan."

That there was more to it than that, in fact a great deal more, became apparent from the messages which followed. McClellan had not "taken" Yorktown; he had received it by default. Joe Johnston had been observing all those large-scale preparations, then had pulled back on the eve of what was to have been the day of his destruction. It was Centerville-Manassas all over again, except this time the guns he left behind were real ones: 56 heavy siege pieces, many with their ammunition still neatly stacked and only three of them damaged. However, he had saved all of his field artillery and given his army a head start toward whatever defensive line he intended to occupy next. McClellan did not mean for him to do so unmolested. He sent the cavalry in pursuit at once, despite a thunderstorm that approached cloudburst proportions, and followed it with the whole army, under Sumner, while he himself remained at Yorktown to launch an amphibious end run up the York, attempting to cut off Johnston's retreat by landing Franklin's division in his rear. The result was a bloody rear-guard action next day in front of

Williamsburg, anticipated and reviewed in two telegrams he sent, the first at 9 a.m. and the last at 9.40 p.m. The former was to Stanton, an announcement of intention: "I shall push the enemy to the wall." The latter was to Franklin, who was coming up by water while McClellan himself hurried overland to where Sumner's guns were growling: "We have now a tangent hit. I arrived in time."

Johnston, whose men were plodding along the single miry road behind their slow-grinding wagon train, had not planned a halt until he crossed the Chickahominy, but the Union infantry was closing fast, unimpeded by wagons, and the cavalry was taking potshots at his rear guard before sundown. So he instructed Longstreet's division to delay the pursuit by holding Fort Magruder long enough to give the rest of the army time to draw off. When Sumner's men came slogging up they were met by a spatter of musketry that stopped them for the night. The fight next day — dignified by time into the Battle of Williamsburg — was confusion from start to finish, with lunges and counterlunges and a great deal of slipping and sliding in the mud. Cannonfire had a metallic ring in the saturated air, and generals on both sides lost their sense of direction in the rain. Sumner kept pushing and probing; Longstreet had to call for help, and Major General D. H. Hill countermarched his whole division and joined the melee. In the end, the Confederates managed to hang on until nightfall, when they fell back and the Federals took possession of Fort Magruder. Both claimed a victory: the latter because they had gained the field, the former because they had delayed the pursuit. The only apparent losers were the casualties: 1703 for the South, 2239 for the North.

Whatever else it amounted to, and that seemed very little, the day-long battle had given the troops of both sides two clear gains at least. The first was that, as soldiers, they were tangibly worth their salt. Despite the confusion and the milling about, which gave the action a superficial resemblance to Bull Run, the men had fought as members of military units, not as panicky individuals. This in itself was a substantial gain, one they knew was beyond value. Training had paid off. But the second was even more appealing. This was a new confidence in their respective commanding generals, in spite of the fact that neither had been present for the fighting.

Johnston was toiling westward through the mud with his main body. Coming upon a deeply mired 12-pound brass Napoleon which a battery lieutenant was about to abandon in obedience to orders that nothing was to be allowed to impede the march, Johnston said: "Let me see what I can do." He dismounted, waded into the bog — high-polished boots, gold braid, and all — and took hold of a muddy spoke. "Now, boys: all together!" he cried, and the gun bounded clear of the chunk-hole. After that, one cannoneer said, "our battery used to swear by Old Joe."

McClellan's performance was no less endearing. Arriving just at the close of the battle, mud-stained from hard riding, his staff strung out behind him trying desperately to keep up, he went from regiment to regiment, congratulating his men for their victory and acknowledging their cheers. Often he paused for a question-and-answer exchange, strophe and antistrophe:

"How do you feel, boys?"

"We feel bully, General!" they cried.

"Do you think anything can stop you from going to Richmond?"

"No! No!" they shouted, all together.

Little Mac would give them his jaunty salute, made even flashier today by the glazed waterproof cover he was wearing on his cap, and be off down the line at a gallop, to halt again in front of another regiment:

"How do you feel, boys?"

"We feel bully, General!"

"Do you think anything can stop you from going to Richmond?"

"No! No!"

Rain-soaked and hungry, but glad to be out of the trenches, the Confederates continued their march toward the Chickahominy. Smith, in the lead, was instructed to halt at Barhamsville, eighteen miles beyond Williamsburg, and guard against a flank attack from the direction of York River while the other three divisions were catching up. He got there on the afternoon of the 6th, just as Franklin's men were coming ashore at Eltham Landing, six miles away, to execute the movement Johnston feared. Informed of this, Johnston ordered Magruder, Longstreet, and Hill to hurry forward. While they were doing so, Smith moved toward Eltham to attack. Deciding that it would be better not to try to stop the Yankees within range of their gunboats, he waited until next morning when they were a couple of miles from the landing, then hit them with Hampton's Legion and a brigade of Texans and Georgians under a 30-year-old West Pointer named John Bell Hood, a prewar junior lieutenant in Sidney Johnston's 2d Cavalry. Franklin's men, deep in unfamiliar country and not knowing how many graybacks might be coming at them, gave ground rapidly until they regained the covering fire of the gunboats.

They had been hit harder than Johnston intended, anxious as he was to avoid the delay another general engagement would have entailed. Later he admonished the blond-bearded six-foot-two-inch Kentucky brigadier: "General Hood, have you given an illustration of the Texas idea of feeling an enemy gently and falling back? What would your Texans have done, sir, if I had ordered them to charge and drive back the enemy?" Hood's blue eyes were somber. He said gravely, "I suppose, General, they would have driven them into the river, and tried to swim out and capture the gunboats."

At any rate Smith was satisfied; Franklin was disposed of, and the wagon train was well along the road. He led his and Magruder's divisions on through New Kent Courthouse and made camp the following night beside the road, nineteen miles from Barhamsville and within easy reach of Bottom's Bridge across the Chickahominy. Five miles downstream, at Long Bridge, the divisions of Hill and Longstreet tried to sleep in a torrent of rain which finally sent them sloshing off in search of higher ground. Whatever their discomfort, Johnston's reaction was primarily a feeling of relief that his 54,000 soldiers had escaped a trap laid by twice their number. Not that he was through retreating. Already he had notified Lee in Richmond: "The want of provision and of any mode of obtaining it here, still more the dearth of forage, makes it impossible to wait to attack [the enemy] while landing. The sight of the ironclad boats makes me apprehensive for Richmond, too, so I move on. . . ."

The Federals were after him, moving slowly, however, along the cut-up roads. Sumner at Williamsburg and Franklin at Eltham Landing had failed to bag the retreating enemy, but McClellan was not discouraged. His men had shown all the dash a commander could ask for, and the rebels were dribbling casualties and equipment as they fled. "My troops are in motion and in magnificent spirits," he informed the War Department. "They have all the air and feelings of veterans. It will do your heart good to see them." The frontal attack, up the middle of the Peninsula, had left the foe no time to get set for another prolonged resistance, and the long end run, despite the savage repulse next day, had "fully served its purpose in clearing our front to the banks of the Chickahominy." In accordance with plans made months ago, when Urbanna was the intended place of debarkation, he set up his base at West Point, the terminus of the 35-mile-long Richmond & York River Railroad. Here the Mattapony and the Pamunkey converged to form the York, which afforded a deep-draft supply line all the way back to Chesapeake Bay. Regiment after regiment, division after division of reinforcements could be landed here, fresh for combat, and McClellan was quick to suggest that this be done. May 8 he wired Stanton: "The time has arrived to bring all the troops in Eastern Virginia into perfect coöperation. I expect to fight another and very severe battle before reaching Richmond and with all the troops the Confederates can bring together. . . . All the troops on the Rappahannock, and if possible those on the Shenandoah, should take part in the approaching battle. We ought immediately to concentrate everything."

The wire did not have to go all the way to Washington; the Secretary was at Fort Monroe. He had arrived two days ago with Lincoln and Chase, primarily for relaxation and a look-see, but as it turned out was lending a hand in the direction of one of the strangest small-scale campaigns in American military history.

Amazed to find that McClellan had made no provision for the capture of Norfolk, outflanked by the drive up the opposite bank of the James, the President decided to undertake the operation himself, employing the fortress garrison under Major General John E. Wool. Wool was 78, two years older than Winfield Scott, and though he was more active physically than his fellow veteran of the War of 1812 — he could still mount a horse, for instance — he had other infirmities all his own. After twenty-five years as Inspector General, his hands trembled; he repeated things he had said a short while back, and he had to ask his aide if he had put his hat on straight. However, there was no deficiency of the courage he had shown under Anthony Wayne. He said he would gladly undertake the movement his Commander in Chief proposed.

The first trouble came with the navy: Goldsborough thought it would be dangerous to ferry the men across the Roads with the *Merrimac* still on the loose. But Lincoln not only overruled him, he and Chase got in separate tugs and reconnoitered the opposite shore for a suitable landing place. When they returned, however, they found that Wool had already chosen one from the chart and was embarking with the troops who were to seize it. Chase went along, but Lincoln and Stanton stayed behind to maintain a command post at the fort and question various colonels and generals who, the President thought, were to follow in support.

"Where is your command?" he asked one, and got the answer: "I am awaiting orders." To another he said, "Why are you here? Why not on the other side?" and was told: "I am ordered to the fort." Experiencing for the first time some of the vexations likely to plague a field commander, Lincoln lost his temper. He took off his tall hat and slammed it on the floor. "Send me someone who can write," he said, exasperated. When the someone came forward — a colonel on Wool's staff — the President dictated an order for the advance to be pushed and supported.

As things turned out, no push or support was needed. The Confederates had evacuated Norfolk the day before, leaving only a handful of men behind to complete the wrecking of Gosport Navy Yard. Chase and Wool were met just short of the city limits by a municipal delegation, including the mayor, who carried a large bunch of rusty keys and a sheaf of documents which he insisted on reading, down to the final line, before making the final formal gesture of handing over the keys. Unknown to Wool and the Secretary, while the mayor droned on, the rebel demolition crew was completing its work and setting out for Richmond. Then Chase and the general moved in with their troops and took charge, sending word back to Lincoln that his first field campaign had been a complete success, despite vexations.

★   ★   ★

One demolition job remained, and it was done that night. No nation ever owed more to a single ship than the Confederacy owed the *Merrimac-Virginia;* yet, with Norfolk gone, she had not only lost her home, she had lost her occupation. Josiah Tattnall, who had dipped his colors in salute to his old friend Du Pont at Port Royal and had been in command of the ironclad since late March, saw two choices: either to steer her out into the Roads for a suicidal finish, taking as many of the enemy with her as possible when she sank, or else to try and lighten her enough to ascend the James. In point of fact, however, there was really no choice. No matter how fitting the former seemed as a death for a gallant vessel, it obviously would not benefit the country; whereas the latter course would preserve her for future service, a second career. She now drew twenty-three feet as a result of recent additions to her armor, but the pilots assured the commodore that if she could be lightened to eighteen feet before daylight they would take her up to Harrison's Landing or City Point, where she could be put in fighting trim again. Tattnall assembled the crew and told them what had to be done. They gave three cheers and got to work, heaving everything movable over the side except her powder and shot. She had been lightened three feet by midnight — when the pilots announced that a strong west wind had reduced the tide so much that she could not be taken up at all.

The first choice was gone with the second, for the work had exposed two feet of her hull below the shield, and to let in water ballast to settle her again would be to flood her fires and magazines. Now that she could neither run nor fight, a third choice, unconsidered at the outset, was all that remained: to destroy her. Tattnall gave the necessary orders. The *Virginia* was run ashore near Craney Island and set afire. By the light of her burning, the crew set out on their march to Suffolk, where they took the cars for Richmond. There they were ordered to Drewry's Bluff, whose batteries now were all that stood between the Confederate capital and the Federal fleet, including their old adversary the *Monitor.*

Those batteries were of primary concern to Lee, who also had lost a good part of his occupation when Johnston came down and took command on the Peninsula. All through late April and early May, while Johnston was warning that he was about to bring the war to the outskirts of Richmond, Lee had been supervising work on the close-in defenses, of which the installations at Drewry's were a part, and now that Johnston was falling back with all the speed the mud allowed, Lee continued to do what he could to protect his ancestral capital from assault. Called on at a cabinet meeting to say where the next stand could be made if the city had to be abandoned, he made an unaccustomed show of his emotions. It would have to be along the Staunton River, he said calmly, a hundred miles southwest. Then suddenly his eyes brimmed with tears. "But Richmond must not be given up; it shall not be given up!" he exclaimed.

Davis felt much the same way about it. Twice he had ridden down to Drewry's with Lee to inspect the work in progress there, the hulks being sunk alongside pilings driven across the channel and the heavy naval cannon being emplaced on the high bluff. But in spite of hearing that Butler's men, with Farragut on his way up the Mississippi, were sacking and looting Briarfield, he kept an even closer rein on his emotions than did the Virginian who had been nicknamed "The Marble Monument" while they were at the Academy together. Many interpreted this calmness to mean a lack of concern by the Chief Executive, and when he was baptized and confirmed at St Paul's on the 9th, the *Examiner* took him to task for finding time for such ministrations on the day of Norfolk's evacuation. Faced with imminent assault by land and water, the people wanted assurance from Davis that Richmond would be defended, block by block and house by house. A committee called at his office on the morning of May 15, inquiring whether the government shared their determination, but their spokesman was interrupted by a messenger who came to inform the President that the masts of Federal warships had been sighted on the James from the hills of the city. "This manifestly concludes the matter," Davis said, dismissing the committee.

Soon the guns began to roar, clangorous on the hilltops and reverberant in the hollows. They kept it up for three full hours and twenty minutes, rattling Richmond windows from a distance of eight miles. It was deafening; people trembled at the sound. Then suddenly it stopped, and that was worse. With the abrupt descent of silence, they took their hands down from their ears and looked at one another, not knowing which to expect: a messenger announcing that the assault had been repulsed, or the gunboats celebrating a victory by lobbing 11-inch shells into the city. Presently they had the answer.

The attack had been led by two ironclads, the *Monitor* and the *Galena*, supported by two wooden vessels. The latter kept their distance, but the armored ships began the bombardment at a range of 800 yards. The *Monitor* soon retired, unable to elevate her guns enough to reach the batteries on the bluff. The *Galena* stayed and took twenty-eight hits, including eighteen perforations which cost her 13 killed and 11 wounded, before she dropped back down the river with the others, winding lamely out of sight around the bend. The Confederate gunners leaped on the unfinished parapets, cheering and tossing their caps: especially the sailors off the *Virginia*, who at last had scored the triumph that had been beyond their reach at water level.

Richmond had been delivered, at least for a day. But Johnston was still retreating. That same morning he abandoned the middle and lower stretches of the Chickahominy, taking up an intermediary position which he abandoned in turn, two days later, because he found it tactically weak and inadequately supplied with drinking water. What he would do next he would not say, not even to the President. A South Carolinian recalled that before the war Wade Hampton had brought Johnston down there on a bird hunt, but Johnston had not fired a shot all day. "The bird flew too high or too low; the dogs were too far or too near. Things never did suit exactly." It seemed to be that way with him now, but one thing at least was clear. The next withdrawal would have to be beyond the capital. His present left was at Fairfield Race Course, just outside the northeast city limits, and his right was on the near bank of the James, across from Drewry's Bluff. Richmond was beleaguered. At nightfall people saw from her hills the semicircular twinkle of the campfires of the Army of Northern Virginia. Beyond them, a greater refulgence along the eastern and northeastern sky reflected the glow of campfires kindled by McClellan's hundred thousand.

In preparation for what he believed might be the last great battle of the war, the Federal commander had reorganized his army while it was still on the march toward the Chickahominy crossings. Shuffling and reconsolidating while in motion, he created two new corps, one under Fitz-John Porter, the other under Franklin — both of them original pro-McClellan brigadiers — which gave him five corps in all, each with two three-brigade divisions. The order of battle, as reported in mid-May:

SUMNER	HEINTZELMAN	KEYES	PORTER	FRANKLIN
Richardson	Hooker	Couch	Morell	Slocum
Sedgwick	Kearny	Casey	Sykes	Smith

gave him a tightly knit yet highly flexible fighting force of 102,236 front-line soldiers and 300 guns. Another 5000 extra-duty men, including cooks and teamsters, laborers and suchlike, were with the advance, while 21,000 more had been left at various points along the road from Fort Monroe, sick or absent without leave or on garrison duty, to give him an over-all total of 128,864.

McClellan did not consider this a man too many. In fact he was convinced it was not enough. Pinkerton was at work again, questioning prisoners and contrabands and totting up figures he received from his operatives beyond the enemy lines. A month ago, in front of Yorktown, he had said that the Confederates were issuing 119,000 daily rations. Presently this grew to 180,000, reported along with a warning that the figure was probably low, since 200 separate regiments of southern infantry had already been identified on the Peninsula, plus assorted battalions of artillery, cavalry, and combat engineers. One corps commander wrote in his journal that 240,000 rebels were concentrated in front of the northern army. McClellan never believed the figure was quite that high, but he clearly believed it might be. Complaining to the War Department on May 10 that he himself could put barely 70,000 on the firing line, he continued to plead for more: "If I am not reinforced, it is probable that I will be obliged to fight nearly double my numbers, strongly intrenched."

Whatever their strength, the Confederates kept falling back and McClellan continued to follow. By May 15 he had advanced his base another fifteen miles along the railroad, from West Point to the head of navigation on the Pamunkey, which gave him both water and rail facilities for bringing supplies forward. Here was a large southern mansion called the White House, where the nation's first President had courted the Widow Custis, and there was a note attached to the front door. "Northern soldiers who profess to reverence Washington," it read, "forbear to desecrate the home of his first married life, the property of his wife, now owned by her descendants. A Grand-daughter of Mrs Washington." The author of the note was Mrs R. E. Lee. She had already lost one home in the path of war — Arlington, near Alexandria — and McClellan respected her wishes in regard to this one. He pitched his headquarters tents in the yard and set up a permanent supply dump at the landing, but he stationed guards around the house itself to keep out prowlers and souvenir-hunters, and provided an escort with a flag of truce to see the lady through the lines to join her husband.

Glad of this chance to show that the practice of chivalry was not restricted to soldiers dressed in gray, he then enjoyed a brief sojourn among the relics. Even though the house itself was a reconstruction, the sensation of being on the site where Washington had slept and eaten and taken his ease gave the youthful commander a feeling of being borne up and on by the stream of history; he hoped, he said, "that I might serve my country as well as he did." Riding toward the front on May 16, he came to old St Peter's Church, where Washington was married. Here too he stopped, dismounted, and went in. That night he wrote his wife: "As I happened to be there alone for a few minutes, I could not help kneeling at the chancel and praying."

What followed next day was enough to convince an agnostic of the efficacy of prayer. Officially and out of the blue, he heard from Stanton that McDowell was being reinforced by a division already on its way from Banks in the Shenandoah Valley. As soon as it got there, McClellan was told, McDowell would move south to join him in front of Richmond with an additional 40,000 men.

This was the one calamity beyond all others Lee had been seeking for means to avoid. McClellan was a hovering threat — his frontline troops could hear the clocks of Richmond strike the hours — but at least Johnston stood in his path; whereas at present there was nothing between McDowell and Richmond that he could not brush aside with an almost careless gesture, and if Johnston sidled to block him too, the capital's defenses would be stretched beyond the snapping point. The fall of the city would follow as surely as nightfall followed sunset of the day McDowell got there.

For possible deliverance, Lee looked north. Numerically the odds were even longer in Northern Virginia than they were on the Peninsula — three-to-two against Johnston, three-to-one against the troops he had left behind — but Johnston was wedged tight in coffin corner, while northward there was still room for maneuver. If anything, there was too much room. A brigade of 2500 under Brigadier General Charles Field — another of Sidney Johnston's ubiquitous former U.S. Cavalry lieutenants — had been left on the Rappahannock to watch McDowell. Jackson's command, grown by now to about 6000, opposed Banks in the Valley. Ewell's 8500 were posted at Gordonsville, equidistant from both, instructed to be ready to march in support of whichever needed him worse. Beyond Jackson, Edward Johnson with 2800 was observing Frémont's Allegheny preparations. McDowell, with Franklin detached, had 30,000; Banks had 21,000; Frémont had 17,000 and more on the way. Numerically, then — with 68,000 Federals distributed along a perimeter guarded by just under 20,000 Confederates — the outlook was as gloomy there as elsewhere, even gloomier. But Lee saw possibilities through the gloom. If the two largest southern commands, under Jackson and Ewell, could be combined, they might be able to hit one of the three opposing forces hard enough to alarm the Union high command into delaying the advance of all the rest: including McDowell. That is, Lee would stop McDowell not by striking him — he was too strong — but by striking Banks or Frémont, who would call on him for help.

Daring as the conception was, a great deal more than daring would be needed before it could be translated into action. Field, for instance, would have to be reinforced. To leave him where he was, without support from Ewell, would be to invite McDowell to smother him. But when Lee appealed to Johnston to spare the men from the Yorktown intrenchments, Johnston would not hear of it. "To detach troops from this position would be ruin to those left," he said. Once more Lee had to improvise, robbing Peter to pay Paul, and this he did. Burnside's aggressiveness having subsided, he took three brigades from North and South Carolina, 10,000 men in all, and sent them up to Fredericksburg under Brigadier General J. R. Anderson, who combined them with Field's brigade and assumed command by seniority. Ewell could now slide westward toward the Blue Ridge and conjunction with Jackson.

They were a strange pair: so strange, indeed, that perhaps the most daring thing about Lee's plan was that he was willing to trust it to these two to carry out. Dick Ewell was an eccentric, a queer-looking forty-five-year-old bachelor who spoke with a sort of twittering lisp and subsisted on a diet of cracked wheat to palliate the tortures of dyspepsia. With his sharp nose and bald-domed head, which he frequently let droop far toward one shoulder, he reminded many people of a bird — an eagle, some said; others said a woodcock. He was a West Pointer, but a generation of frontier duty, he declared, had taught him all about handling fifty dragoons and driven all other knowledge from his mind. So far, his only appreciable service in the war had been at the Battle of Manassas, where he crossed and recrossed Bull Run, far on the right, and never came to grips with the enemy at all. He had a habit of interjecting odd remarks into everyday conversations: as for instance, "Now why do you suppose President Davis made me a major general anyway?"

Stonewall seemed about as bad. The fame he had won along with his nickname at Manassas had been tarnished by last winter's fruitless Romney expedition, which resulted in much friction with the War Department, as well as by the bloody repulse he had blundered into recently at Kernstown. His abrupt cashiering of Garnett after that fight had caused his officers to think of him distastefully, and quite accurately, as a man who would be quick to throw the book at a subordinate who stepped or wandered out of line. Like Ewell, who was three months his junior in rank and seven years his senior in age, he had adopted a peculiar diet to ease the pains of dyspepsia: raspberries and plain bread and milk, supplemented by lemons — many lemons — though he would take no seasoning in his food: pepper made his left leg ache, he said. Nor was his appearance reassuring. His uniform was a single-breasted threadbare coat he had worn in the Mexican War, a rusty V.M.I. cadet cap, which he wore with the broken visor pulled well down over his weary-looking eyes, and an outsized pair of flop-top cavalry boots. A religious fanatic, he sometimes interrupted his soldiers at their poker and chuck-aluck games by strolling through camp to hand out Sunday School pamphlets. They did not object to this so much, however, as they did to the possible truth of rumors that he imagined himself a southern Joshua and in combat got so carried away by the notion that he lost his mental balance. They feared it might be so with him, for they had seen his pale blue eyes take on a wild unearthly glitter in the gunsmoke; Old Blue Light, they called him. And there was substance for their fears. Just now he was writing his wife that he hoped to make his Valley command "an army of the living God as well as of its country."

Such as they were, they were all Lee had — and strictly speaking he did not even have them. Both were still a part of Johnston's army, subject to Johnston's orders, and Johnston was extremely touchy about out-of-channels interference. Whatever was to be done in Northern Virginia would have to be done with his coöperation, or anyhow his acquiescence, which he seemed likely to withhold in the case of a proposal that violated, as this one did, his cherished principles of "concentration." On the other hand, Lee had Davis to sustain him. Unlike Lincoln, who did not count a soldier as part of the Washington defenses unless he could ride out and touch him in the course of an afternoon's round-trip carriage drive from the White House, Davis could see that a man a hundred miles away might do more to relieve the pressure, or stave off a threat, than if he stood on the capital ramparts. With the President's approval, Lee went ahead, trusting that he and Johnston would not issue conflicting orders — or, in Lee's case, suggestions — to the generals out in the Valley.

April 21 he wrote to Jackson, outlining the situation at Richmond and emphasizing the need for holding McDowell on the Rappahannock line. The key force, as he saw it, was Ewell's, which could be used in one of three ways: either by leaving it where it was, or by reinforcing Field — Anderson was still on the way — or by reinforcing Jackson. Lee preferred the latter, and he was writing to find out whether Stonewall thought it practicable: "If you can use General Ewell's division in an attack on General Banks, and to drive him back, it will prove a great relief to the pressure on Fredericksburg." A letter went to Ewell the same day, stressing the necessity for "a speedy blow." Four days later this emphasis on the necessity for speed was added in another note to Jackson: "The blow, wherever struck, must, to be successful, be sudden and heavy. The troops used must be efficient and light."

Jackson replied that he did indeed think an attack was practicable, either against Banks, who had advanced to Harrisonburg, or against Frémont's lead division, which was threatening Edward Johnson near the village of McDowell, west of Staunton. In fact, now that Ewell was at hand, Jackson had formulated three alternate plans of attack: 1) to reinforce Johnson for a sudden lunge at Frémont, leaving Ewell to watch Banks; 2) to combine with Ewell for a frontal assault on Banks; or 3) to march far down the Valley and strike Banks's rear by swinging around the north end of Massanutton Mountain. For the present, he wrote, he preferred the first; "for, if successful, I would afterward only have Banks to contend with, and in doing this would be reinforced by General Edward Johnson."

That was the last Lee heard from Stonewall for a while, though on May Day Ewell informed him, in a postscript to a report: "He moves toward Staunton and I take his position." Plan One was in the course of execution. Ten days later the silence was broken by a wire from Jackson himself. Routed through Staunton, it was dated the 9th: "God blessed our arms with victory at McDowell yesterday."

In normal times the dispatch would have been received with an exultation to match the sender's, but this was the day the Federals took Norfolk, forcing the *Virginia*'s destruction, and Pensacola toppled, down on the Gulf. From Mississippi came news that Farragut had followed his occupation of New Orleans by forcing the upriver surrender of Baton Rouge and Natchez, while Halleck's ponderous southward advance inched closer and closer to Corinth. Worse still, from Richmond's point of view, Johnston's army was crossing the Chickahominy, near the end of its muddy retreat up the Peninsula. The government archives were being loaded onto canal boats for shipment to Lynchburg, in anticipation of the fall of the capital; the Treasury's gold reserve was packed aboard a special train with a full head of steam kept in its boiler, ready to whisk it out of the city ahead of the Yankees. President Davis had sent his wife and children to North Carolina, and there was talk that he and the cabinet were soon to follow. The soldiers seemed disheartened by their long retreat, and their general had submitted his resignation in a fit of pique because men under his command on the south side of the James had been ordered about by Lee. "My authority does not extend beyond the troops immediately around me," Johnston wrote. "I request therefore to be relieved of a merely nominal geographical command."

Lee managed to calm Johnston down — "suage him" was the term he generally employed in such cases — but the flare-up seemed likely to occur again whenever the general thought he detected signs of circumvention; which he well might do if he looked out toward the Valley. It was a testy business at best. By now, too, details of Jackson's "victory at McDowell" had shown it to be less spectacular than the brief dispatch had indicated. As at Kernstown, more Confederates than Federals had fallen. In fact, except that the outnumbered enemy had retreated, it hardly seemed a victory at all. Meanwhile, alarming news had come from Ewell: Banks was moving northward down the Valley toward the Manassas Gap Railroad, which could speed his army eastward to reinforce McDowell or McClellan. Apparently Jackson's strategy had soured. His attack on Frémont's van seemed to have had an effect quite opposite from the one he had intended.

Lee did not despair. On May 16, the day after the repulse of the Union gunboats on the James — perhaps as McClellan knelt in prayer at the chancel of St Peter's — he wrote to Stonewall, urging an immediate attack: "Whatever may be Banks' intention, it is very desirable to prevent him from going either to Fredericksburg or the Peninsula. . . . A successful blow struck at him would delay, if it does not prevent, his moving to either place." A closing sentence opened vistas; Banks was not the only high-ranking Federal the Valley blow was aimed at. "Whatever movement you make against Banks do it speedily, and if successful drive him back toward the Potomac, and create the impression, as far as practicable, that you design threatening that line."

✗ 2 ✗

McDowell, the sharp but limited engagement fought twenty-five miles beyond Staunton on May 8, was in the nature of a prologue to the drama about to be performed in the Shenandoah Valley. Jackson at any rate thought of it as such, and though, like a good actor, he gave it his best effort, all through it he was looking forward to the larger action whose cast and properties — Ewell and Banks, with their two armies, and the mountains and rivers with their gaps and bridges — were already in position, awaiting the entrance of the star who would give them their cues and put them to use. In the wings there were supernumeraries, some of whom did not yet know that they were to be called on stage: McDowell, for example, who by coincidence shared his surname with the furious little battle that served as prologue and signaled the raising of the curtain.

As such it held the seeds of much that followed, and this was especially true of the manner in which Stonewall put his army in motion to reinforce Edward Johnson for the attack on Frémont's van. Staunton lay to the southwest, with Johnson west of there; but Jackson marched southeast, toward Richmond, so that his men, along with whatever Federal scouts and spies might be observing, thought they were on the way to help Joe Johnston stop McClellan. Leaving his cavalry with Ewell, who moved in through Swift Run Gap to take over the job of watching Banks while he was gone, the Valley commander took his 5000 infantry through Brown's Gap, then — apparently in rehearsal for the boggy work awaiting them on the Peninsula — exposed them to a three-day nightmare of floundering through eighteen miles of ankle-deep mud before they struck the Virginia Central Railroad, ten miles short of Charlottesville, and boarded a long string of boxcars, double-headed for speed with two locomotives. When the train jerked into motion the men cheered; for it headed not east, toward Richmond, but west toward Staunton. Sunday, May 4, they got there — to the delight of the townspeople, who had thought they were being left at the mercy of Frémont, whose 3500-man advance under Brigadier General Robert Milroy was already pressing Johnson back. In compensation for the violated Sabbath, Jackson gave his men two days' rest, acquired a new uniform — it was homespun and ill-fitting, but at least it was regulation gray — then marched westward to combine with Johnson for a surprise attack that would outnumber the enemy better than two to one.

Numerically it did not work out that way; nor was it a surprise. Despite Stonewall's roundabout approach and careful picketing of the roads, Federal scouts and spies had informed Milroy of the odds he faced. He fell back to the village of McDowell — a sort of miniature Harpers Ferry, surrounded by heights — and called for help from his

fellow brigadier, Robert Schenck, thirty-four miles away at Franklin.
Schenck got started before midday of May 7, made a driving all-night
march with 1500 men, and arrived next morning, just as Jackson was
assembling his 8000 for a downhill charge against Milroy, who was in
position on the outskirts of McDowell, firing gamely with the trails of
his guns set in trenches to elevate the tubes. Reinforced to 5000, he
decided to attack before the Confederates got their artillery on the
heights. It was done with spirit, catching Jackson off balance and
rocking him on his heels. But Milroy fell back on the town, lacking the
strength for anything more than one hard punch, and retreated toward
Franklin under cover of darkness, having inflicted 498 casualties at a
cost of 256.

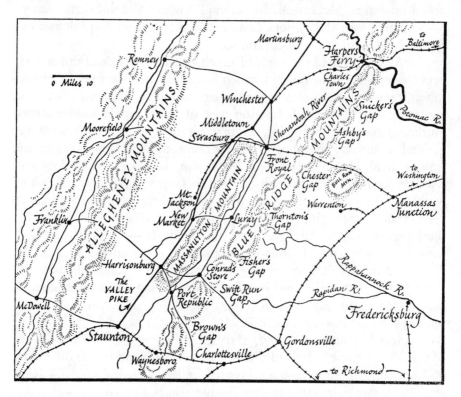

    Jackson took up the pursuit next morning and continued it for
three days, including another violated Sabbath, but gained nothing from
it except some abandoned wagons. Milroy was not only too quick for
him; to make matters worse, he set the woods afire along the road,
causing the rebels to dance on embers as they groped their way through
eye-stinging clouds of smoke. With regretful admiration, Stonewall
called a halt near Franklin and issued a congratulatory order, urging
his men "to unite with me, this morning, in thanksgiving to Almighty
God, for having thus crowned your arms with success." Having done
what he came west to do — knock Frémont back from Staunton — he

now was ready, as he later reported, to "return to the open country
of the Shenandoah Valley, hoping, through the blessing of Providence,
to defeat Banks before he should receive reinforcements."

It was open only by comparison, but it had opened itself to him.
Long and painful hours spent committing its geography to memory with
the assistance of mileage charts, listing the distance between any two
points in the region, had enabled him to quote from the map as readily
as he could quote from Scripture, sight unseen. From Staunton to
Winchester, eighty miles, the Valley Turnpike led northeast, cradled
by the Blue Ridge and the Alleghenies. Whoever controlled the macadamized pike could move the fastest, particularly in rainy weather; but
there were possibilities for maneuver. East of the pike, from Harrisonburg to Strasburg, lay a smoke-colored ridge forty miles long, called
Massanutton Mountain, and an alternate road led through the narrow
valley just beyond it, connected to the turnpike by roads leading
westward from Conrad's Store and Front Royal, around the upper and
lower ends of the mountain. Embraced by the twin forks of the Shenandoah, which combined at Front Royal and flowed northward into
the Potomac, the ridge could be crossed at only one point, about midway, by a road connecting New Market and Luray. Here was where
Jackson fixed his eye, and the harder he looked the more he saw in the
way of opportunities. The road net thus inclosing Massanutton resembled an elongated italicized capital *H:*

Strasburg	Front Royal
New Market	Luray
Harrisonburg	Conrad's Store.

The crossbar was the key. Whoever held it could move up or down
either shank of the H, not only with his own flank protected, but also
with an excellent chance of striking the flank of an enemy in motion on
the opposite side. Then too, the narrow eastern valley afforded an ideal
covered approach for gaining the rear of an army coming southward up
the pike, as Banks had done. Afterwards, if necessary, the attacker
could make a quick escape by retracing his steps and swinging eastward through the passes of the Blue Ridge while the enemy was trying
to get at him by marching around either end of the forty-mile-long
mountain.

Ripe as were the opportunities awaiting him back in the Valley,
they would never be available to an army that straggled as badly as his
had done on the march to Kernstown. Since then, the marching had
improved; but not enough. Mindful of Lee's suggestion that the troops
must be "efficient and light," Jackson issued on May 13, while his men
were clearing their lungs of the smoke they had breathed in pursuit of

Milroy, an order requiring strict discipline on the march. The troops were to fall in at attention, step off in cadence, hold it for two or three hundred yards before shifting to route step, and maintain prescribed intervals thereafter. No one was to leave the column for any reason whatever, except by express permission from an officer. Fifty minutes of each hour they were to march. The other ten were for rest, which preferably was to be taken prone. "A man rests all over when he lies down," Jackson said. He had little patience with frailty; a broken-down man and a straggler were two of a kind to him. As one of his officers remarked, "He classed all who were weak and weary, who fainted by the wayside, as men wanting in patriotism. If a man's face was as white as cotton and his pulse so low you could scarcely feel it, he looked upon him merely as an inefficient soldier and rode off impatiently." The men grumbled, seeing in the order further evidence of their general's crackbrained meticulosity; but, having no choice, they obeyed. In time they even saw sense in it, especially after compliance had transformed them into such rapid marchers that they became known as "foot cavalry."

Having prescribed the exact manner in which it was to be conducted, Stonewall was ready that same day to begin his march back to Staunton and beyond. Whatever its shortcomings as a tactical victory, the Battle of McDowell had earned him certain definite advantages. Despite his losses, he would be returning to the Valley with about 2500 more soldiers than he had had when he left, two weeks ago. Johnson himself would not be coming — he had suffered a bad leg wound in the fight — but his men would, in spite of the fact that it meant leaving Frémont's advance down the Alleghenies unopposed. As far as Jackson was concerned, there was no longer much danger from that direction. He could turn his back on Frémont and walk off, as if dismissing him absolutely from his mind. In bullfight terms — or, for that matter, in veterinary jargon — he had "fixed" him.

For Ewell, back at Conrad's Store, the past two weeks had been "the most unhappy I ever remember. . . . I never suffered as much with dyspepsia in my life." He had cause. Recently he had learned that one of Banks' two divisions was preparing to march east to join McDowell. According to Johnston's orders, this would require him to follow, but Jackson had left strict instructions for him to stay where he was until the rest of the Valley command returned. Ewell hardly knew what to do; "I have been keeping one eye on Banks, one on Jackson, all the time jogged up from Richmond, until I am sick and worn down." Stonewall — "that enthusiastic fanatic," Ewell called him — was keeping his intentions to himself, limiting his communications mostly to announcements of things past: as for instance a dispatch informing his lieutenant that, with the aid of divine Providence, he had captured much of

Milroy's wagon train. Ewell could find little comfort in this, nor could he fathom the connection. "What has Providence to do with Milroy's wagon train?" he asked, distracted and outdone.

On May 17 the crisis became acute with the arrival of definite information that one of Banks' divisions, under Major General James H. Shields, had already crossed the Blue Ridge, on its way to Fredericksburg. Though Johnston's orders left him no choice except to follow, Ewell saw that to do so would be to give up a rare chance to annihilate Banks, who was pulling his remaining division back down the pike toward Strasburg. Deciding to delay his departure at least long enough for a talk with Jackson, next morning Ewell rode west, beyond Harrisonburg, and met the Valley commander approaching that place at the head of his marching men. Stonewall's eyes flashed at the news of Banks' depletion, but then were clouded with regret that Johnston's orders denied him the chance to take advantage of it. Infected by his enthusiasm, Ewell offered to stay and lend a hand if Jackson would cover him with a letter of instructions. Quickly this was done, and Ewell returned to Conrad's Store, much happier than when he left that morning. Jackson had given him orders to prepare to march, as well as a dazzling glimpse into the secret corners of his mind.

Banks now had 9000 men occupying the three points of a triangle which rested against the northern face of Massanutton Mountain: 1500 at Winchester, his main base of supplies, 1000 at Front Royal, where the vital Manassas Gap Railroad crossed the Shenandoah River, and 6500 at Strasburg, intrenched to block an attack down the Valley pike. As protection against guerilla raids, these dispositions were judicious, but they were something less than that against anything more substantial. Banks was quite aware of this, and as a result had been feeling apprehensive ever since he learned of Ewell's arrival at Conrad's Store. In point of fact, however, he had brought this predicament on himself. A self-made man at forty-six, he had risen rapidly in politics and business. Three times governor of Massachusetts, speaker of the Federal House of Representatives, and president of the Illinois Central Railroad, he was determined to do as well in his new career, which might bring him the largest rewards of all.

On April 28 he had wired the War Department that he was "entirely secure" at Harrisonburg. "The enemy is in no condition for offensive movements," he declared. Two days later, while Jackson was setting out on his roundabout march to Staunton, Banks reported him "bound for Richmond. This is the fact, I have no doubt.... There is nothing to be done in this Valley." There was the rub. He wanted to be where guns were booming and reputations could be gained, not off in an inactive theater, watching the war go by. That night he wired again, suggesting that his corps be sent to join McDowell or McClellan. Satisfied that this would be "the most safe and effective disposition possible," he added: "I pray your favorable consideration. Such order will electrify our force."

Stanton took him at his word — but not to the extent he had intended. After conferring with Lincoln, the Secretary instructed Banks to send (not bring) one (not both) of his divisions beyond the Blue Ridge to McDowell, who would move south to join McClellan's assault on Richmond as soon as the Valley troops arrived to reinforce him. Here, then, was the natural explanation for the seemingly miraculous response to McClellan's prayers at the chancel of St Peter's. As for Banks, his plan for gaining a share of the glory available on the Peninsula had resulted in nothing, so far, but the loss of half his force — and the better half at that, for it was Shields who had whipped Jackson at Kernstown, back in March. Meanwhile, Ewell had come onto the scene, replacing the vanished Stonewall, who was presently making havoc west of Staunton. Banks, growing cautious, drew back to Strasburg and dug in, preparing to fight whatever came at him down the pike.

The electrification he had sought was closer than he knew, and it would not come from Washington. After sending Ewell back to Conrad's Store with instructions to advance two of his three brigades to Luray, Jackson continued his march through Harrisonburg, preceded by a screen of cavalry, and made camp just south of New Market on May 20. Later that day, Ewell's third brigade joined him after a trek around the south end of the mountain. Jackson sat on a rail fence, sucking thoughtfully at a lemon as he watched the troops arrive. Bayonets glinting steely in sunlight, 3000 neat gray uniforms glided past in strict alignment above the cadenced flash of white gaiters. They were Louisianians: Creoles and Irishmen, plus a battalion of New Orleans wharf rats under Roberdeau Wheat, who had put his case on record at Manassas. When they reached their assigned bivouac areas, the commands to halt were given in French — gobble-talk, the Valley soldiers called it, and hooted at the sound. Presently they had more to hoot about. The bands switched to polkas; the men broke ranks, clasped each other about the waist, and began to dance. Stonewall sat and watched in silence, the lemon gleaming yellow in his beard. "Thoughtless fellows for serious work," he said.

Another command crisis was threatening to cost him their services even now. Some hours before, a courier from Ewell had crossed the mountain with a dispatch just received from Johnston, vetoing the proposed attack and ordering him to follow Shields across the Blue Ridge while Jackson stayed behind to observe Banks. This meant that the plan to "drive him back toward the Potomac" would have to be abandoned: Ewell had no choice except to obey, unless the peremptory order was countermanded by higher authority: meaning Davis himself. Jackson moved swiftly, wiring an appeal to Lee in Richmond — "Please answer by telegraph at once," it ended — and instructing Ewell to stay where he was, pending the outcome of the plea for intercession. Now there was the strain of waiting. None of it showed, however, as Stonewall sat on the rail fence pulling thoughtfully at the lemon. When the commander of the Louisianians, Brigadier General Richard Taylor, requested instructions for tomorrow's march, Jackson merely informed him that it would begin at earliest dawn and the newly arrived brigade would head the column. When Taylor asked — not unreasonably, it seemed to him — in which direction they would move, Jackson replied that he would be with him by then to point the way.

He was there before daylight glimmered, and if there was extreme pleasure in his face this morning he had reason: Lee had conferred with Davis and wired back, countermanding Johnston's orders. The march would be north, Jackson told Taylor, and sat his horse beside the pike to watch the gaitered dandies set off down it. His mount was a close-coupled thick-necked ox-eyed creature, taken from the enemy a year ago this month; Little Sorrel was its name, but the men called it "Fancy" in derision. They made a strange pair, the undersized, rather muscle-bound horse and the tall, angular rider with his ill-fitting clothes and his taciturnity. A certain aura was gathering around him, a magnetism definite but impersonal. "No one could love the man for himself," one of his officers wrote home. "He seems to be cut off from his fellow men and to commune with his own spirit only, or with spirits of which we know not." Another put it more briefly, calling him "a one-idea-ed man." Two things he believed in absolutely, "the vigorous use of the bayonet and the blessings of Providence," and he would not be distracted in his efforts to employ them. Lately he had inquired sharply about a missing courier and was told that the boy had just been killed while delivering a message under fire. "Very commendable. Very commendable," Jackson muttered, and went back to the matter at hand.

A mile beyond New Market, just as Taylor's men settled down for the twenty-five-mile march he thought would end with an assault on Banks' main body in its Strasburg intrenchments, the Louisiana brigadier got orders to swing right and take the road across Massanutton — back into the narrow valley he had left the day before. He scarcely knew what to make of this, but presently, hiking through the lofty gap that gave simultaneous breath-taking views of the Blue Ridge and the Alleghenies, he decided that Stonewall was "an unconscious poet" who "desired to give strangers an opportunity to admire the beauties of his Valley." Though his father and his brother-in-law, Zachary Taylor and Jefferson Davis, had been professional soldiers, Taylor himself had attended Yale and Harvard, not West Point. He could not yet see that his arrival had thickened the column which, by now, Banks' scouts would have reported advancing northward on the pike: an illusion that was being continued by the cavalry, which had been left on the west side of the mountain, under orders to keep up the threatening movement, letting no one through or past with information that the infantry had turned off.

It was a hard, leg-throbbing march, steeply uphill, then steeply down, but at its end the two wings of the Army of the Valley were united at Luray. When the cavalry crossed the ridge tomorrow morning Jackson would have 17,000 soldiers concentrated for a strike at Banks' dispersed 9000. Rewarded at last for sticking by a man he swore was crazy, Ewell had absorbed his commander's spirit to such an extent that he spoke with his very accent. "We can get along without anything but food and ammunition," he warned his subordinates; "The road to glory cannot be followed with much baggage." Not only Ewell but a good part of the men in the ranks could appreciate now what Stonewall had wrought, usually to their bewilderment and over their muttered objections. Twenty miles ahead lay Front Royal. Once its 1000-man garrison had been scattered or wiped out, Jackson would be on Banks' flank and astride the Manassas Gap Railroad, blocking his path of retreat across the Blue Ridge. If he stayed to fight, outnumbered worse than two to one, with his back to his Strasburg intrenchments, he would be overwhelmed. Or if he fled northward down the pike toward the Potomac, he might be caught in motion and destroyed. Jackson had the answer to his prayers. Meanwhile — as always — his principal concern was secrecy, and for this he had the covered approach of the Luray Valley, leading directly to Front Royal.

Next day, May 22, while the cavalry was fading back from Strasburg to rejoin the main body, the infantry marched to within ten miles of Front Royal — near enough to get there early the following afternoon, with plenty of daylight left for fighting, yet far enough back to keep from alarming the unsuspecting garrison — then halted for a good night's sleep before the day of battle. Up and on the way by dawn, with Ewell in the lead, Jackson sent his troopers ahead to circle east and west of the town, tearing up sections of railroad track and clipping telegraph wires to prevent the arrival of reinforcements from Strasburg or Manassas and the spreading of alarm in either direction. The odds being what they were, seventeen-to-one, the fight could have only one outcome. But Stonewall wanted more than a lopsided victory that would yield him nothing more than control of an isolated outpost. He wanted to kill or capture every bluecoat in the place.

That was about what it came to, in the end, though for a time the thing was touch and go. Learning that the garrison was the Federal 1st Maryland, Ewell halted his column long enough to pass the Confederate 1st Maryland to the front. They came at a trot, anxious to have at the "homemade Yankees," as they called them. About 2 o'clock they struck the advance picket, drove it back through the streets of Front

Royal, and came upon the main body, drawn up north of town, preparing to resist what its colonel thought was a guerilla raid. He soon found out better, but he continued fighting, determined to hold his ground, whatever the odds. Both forks of the Shenandoah were at his back, crossable only by three narrow bridges, two over the South Fork and one over the North; so that when he saw a body of grayback cavalry riding hard to cut him off, he knew it was no use. Falling back, he won the race for the North Fork bridge, crossed it, and held off the troopers with his two rifled guns while his rear guard set the wooden span afire.

Jackson looked down from the heights south of town and saw the Federals escaping, a compact blue column hurrying north beyond the spiral of smoke from the burning bridge whose flames kept the Confederates from pursuit. "Oh, what an opportunity for artillery! Oh that my guns were here!" he cried, and turning to his staff he shouted, "Order up every rifled gun and every brigade in the army!" It was easier said than done; the guns were far back, and only three of the forty-eight were rifled. But Stonewall did not wait for their arrival. He rode down the hill and beyond the town, where a glad sight awaited him. The skirmishers had beaten out the flames, preserving enough of the damaged span to permit a crossing by horsemen. The general sent about 250 cavalry in pursuit of the Federals, who had disappeared over a ridge. They soon caught up, forcing a stand, and charged. The blue-coats broke, tried another stand, were charged again, and scattered. By now the infantry had caught up. Gleefully the rebel Marylanders beat the bushes, rounding up their late compatriots and neighbors. Out of 1063, the Federals lost 904 killed or captured. Jackson had fewer than 50 casualties, all told. Mostly they were cavalry, shot from their saddles in the two headlong charges that made his victory complete.

When first reports of the disaster reached Strasburg that same Friday, Banks informed Washington that the attack had been made by a rebel force of 5000, which "had been gathering in the mountains, it is said, since Wednesday. Reinforcements should be sent us if possible." Troops would be sent, he was told in reply; "Do not give up the ship before succor can arrive." He had no intention of giving up the ship, but by the following morning his estimate of the enemy strength had risen to "not less than 6000 to 10,000. It is probably Ewell's force, passing through the Shenandoah valley. Jackson is still in our front." He added: "We shall stand firm."

Presently the ugly truth came home. Jackson was not "in our front," nor was Ewell merely "passing through." They were not only united, they were united on Banks' flank: moving, he heard, toward Middletown, which was six miles in his rear, one third of the way to Winchester, his main supply base. Still, Banks was determined not to budge. "I must develop the force of the enemy," he kept saying. When one of his brigade commanders, Colonel G. H. Gordon, who had attended West Point with Jackson, came to reason with him, urging that the proper action would be to fall back in an attempt to save his men and supplies, the former governor said he would not hear of it; he intended to stand firm.

"It is not a retreat," Gordon explained, "but a true military movement to escape from being cut off — to prevent stores and sick from falling into the hands of the enemy."

"By God, sir!" Banks cried hotly, "I will not retreat. We have more to fear from the opinions of our friends than the bayonets of our enemies!"

Gordon now saw what the trouble was: Banks was afraid of being accused of being afraid. The colonel rose. "This, sir, is not a military reason for occupying a false position," he said. He returned to his camp, saw to the packing of his stores and baggage, got the wagons headed for Winchester, and alerted his men for the order he knew was inevitable. At last it came. The army would fall back, Banks informed him.

Jackson spent a good part of the night staring thoughtfully into a campfire, exploring a problem in geometry. At Strasburg and Front Royal, opposite ends of the base of the triangle resting against the northern face of Massanutton, he and Banks were equidistant from the apex at Winchester. By marching fast he could get there first and capture or destroy the Federal supply dump. But Stonewall wanted more than Banks' supplies; he wanted his army, too. There was the nub of the problem. If he set out north in a race for Winchester, Banks might move eastward, across his wake, and get away eastward beyond the Blue Ridge. Or if he marched west, against Strasburg, Banks might flee northward, down the pike, and save both his army and his stores. Morning came before the problem had been solved, but at least it had been explored. The latter being the graver risk, Jackson decided to take the former. With luck — or, as he preferred to express it, "with the assistance of an ever kind Providence" — he might still accomplish both his goals.

Luck or Providence seemed at first to be against him. The weather had turned blustery overnight, and the wind was whipping rain in the men's faces. Slow to fall in, they were even slower in getting started. Before long, the rain turned to hail, plopping into the mud and pelting the marchers. "Press on, men; press on," Jackson urged them, riding alongside. His impatience increased when he received a cavalry report that Banks was blowing up his Strasburg ammunition dump, preparing to evacuate. In hopes of catching the Federals in motion on the pike, he sent a section of artillery, supported by Wheat's Tigers, on a road that branched west to Middletown, seven miles away, while the rest of the army continued slogging north, straining to outstrip the head of the Federal column somewhere short of Winchester, where their paths converged.

Almost nothing went right for the Southerners today, and to lengthen the odds — in spite of his original reluctance, which had given him an even later start than his opponent — Banks was showing a real talent for retreat. His rested men hiked fast on the macadamized pike, while Stonewall's plodded wearily through mud. Twice the Union column was cut, at Middletown and five miles beyond, with resultant slaughter and confusion, but both were basically rear-guard actions, marred by the fact that the hungry Confederates could not be kept from plundering abandoned wagons instead of forging ahead after more, and the cavalry practically disbanded as the troopers set out for their nearby homes with captured horses. Jackson was furious, but neither he nor Taylor, who brought his brigade across country to join the pursuit along the turnpike, could deal with more than a handful at a time, and even these returned to their looting as soon as the generals' backs were turned. They would fight when they had to — as for instance in repulsing a 2000-man cavalry charge, which they did in style, emptying hundreds of saddles — but otherwise they were concerned with nothing they could not stuff in their mouths or pockets.

For all their slackness, the pursuers were gleaning a rich harvest of prisoners and equipment. Too badly outnumbered to turn and fight until he gained a strong defensive position, Banks was sacrificing companies in rear-guard ambuscades and dribbling wagons in his wake like tubs to Jackson's whale. With them he was buying time and distance so successfully that by sunset it was obvious that his main body was winning the race for Winchester, where just such a strong position awaited him. Even Stonewall was obliged to admit it. But he had no intention of allowing his quarry any more time than he could possibly avoid. He pushed his weary brigades through the gathering twilight. "Press on. Press on, men," he kept saying. Impatiently he rode with the handful of cavalry in advance, when suddenly the darkness ahead was stitched with muzzle flashes. The troopers drew rein. "Charge them! Charge them!" Jackson shouted. A second volley crashed ahead; bullets whistled past; the horsemen scattered, leaving the general alone in the middle of the road. "Shameful!" he cried after them in his shrill, womanish voice. "Did you see anybody struck, sir? Did you see anybody struck?" He sat there among the twittering bullets, still complaining. "Surely they need not have run, at least until they were hurt."

Sheepishly the troopers returned, and Jackson sent them forward, following with the infantry. Kernstown lay dead ahead, the scene of blundering in March. Tonight — it was Sunday again by now, as then — there was only a brief skirmish in the darkness. Winchester lay four miles beyond, and he did not intend to allow Banks time to add to the natural strength of the double line of hills south of town. When one officer remarked that his men were "falling by the roadside from fatigue and loss of sleep. Unless they are rested," he complained, "I shall be able to present but a thin line tomorrow," Jackson replied: "Colonel, I yield to no man in sympathy for the gallant men under my command, but I am obliged to sweat them tonight that I may save their blood tomorrow." He pressed on through Kernstown, but eventually saw that the colonel was right. If he kept on at this rate he would arrive with almost no army at all. He called a halt and the men crumpled in their tracks, asleep as soon as their heads touched the ground.

Jackson did not share their rest. He was thinking of the double line of hills ahead, outlining a plan of battle. At 4 o'clock, unable to wait any longer, he had the sleepy men aroused and herded back onto the road. Before the stars had paled he was approaching the high ground south of Winchester. To his relief he saw that Banks had chosen to make his stand on the second ridge, leaving only a few troops on the first. Quickly Stonewall threw out skirmishers, drove the pickets off, and brought up guns to support the assault he would launch as soon as his army filed into position. Banks had his cannon zeroed in, blasting away at the rebel guns while the infantry formed their lines. Jackson saw that the work would be hot, despite his advantage of numbers. Riding back to bring up Taylor, whose Louisianians he planned to use as shock troops, he passed some Virginia regiments coming forward. They had been ordered not to cheer, lest they give away their position, but as Jackson rode by they took off their hats in salute to the man who had driven them, stumbling with fatigue, to where the guns were growling. He removed his battered cap, riding in silence past the uncovered Virginians, and came upon Taylor, whom he greeted with a question:

"General, can your brigade charge a battery?"

"It can try."

"Very good; it must do it then. Move it forward."

Taylor did so. Passing along the ridge the Louisianians came under fire from the Union guns. Shells screamed at them, tearing gaps in their ranks, and the men began to bob and weave. "What the hell are you dodging for?" Taylor yelled. "If there is any more of it, you will be halted under this fire for an hour!" As they snapped back to attention, he felt a hand on his shoulder. He looked around.

"I am afraid you are a wicked fellow," Jackson said, and rode away.

What followed was brief but decisive. Taylor's charge, on the left, was a page out of picture-book war: a long line of men in gray sweeping forward after their commander, who gestured on horseback, pointing the way through shellbursts with his sword. On the opposite flank, Ewell had come into position up the Front Royal road in time to share in the assault. In the center, the Stonewall Brigade surged forward, down the first slope and up the second, where 7000 Federals were breaking for the rear at the sight of 16,000 Confederates bearing down on them — or, strictly speaking, up at them — from three different directions. The attackers swept over the second ridge and charged through Winchester, firing after the bluecoats as they ran. Jackson rode among his soldiers, his eyes aglow at the sight.

"Order forward the whole line! The battle's won!" he shouted. All around him, men were kneeling to fire after the scampering Yankees. He snatched off his cap and waved it over his head in exultation. "Very good!" he cried. "Now let's holler!" The men took it up, and the Valley army's first concerted rebel yell rang out so loud it seemed to rock the houses. Stonewall cheered as wildly as the rest. When a staff officer tried to remonstrate with him for thus exposing himself, he paid him no mind except to shout full in his face: "Go back and tell the whole army to press forward to the Potomac!"

The Potomac was thirty-six miles ahead, but distance meant nothing to Jackson so long as an opportunity like the present was spread before his eyes. North of Winchester, all the way to the horizon, Banks' army was scattered in headlong flight, as ripe for the saber this fine May morning as grain for the scythe in July. At Front Royal his artillery had failed him; today it was his cavalry. As he watched the blue fugitives scurry out of musket range, the Valley commander clenched his fists and groaned: "Never was there such a chance for cavalry! Oh that my cavalry were in place!" Attempting to improvise a horseback pursuit, he brought up the nearest batteries, had the teams uncoupled, and mounted the cannoneers. But he soon saw it would not do; the horses were worn out, wobbly from fatigue, and so were the men. The best he could manage was to follow at a snail's pace through the waning Sunday afternoon, picking up what the fleeing enemy dropped.

Added to what had already been gleaned in three days of marching and fighting, the harvest was considerable, entirely aside from the Federal dead, the uncaptured wounded, and the tons of goods that had gone up in smoke. At a cost of 400 casualties — 68 killed, 329 wounded, and 3 missing — Jackson had taken 3030 prisoners, 9300 small arms, two rifled cannon, and such a wealth of quartermaster stores of all descriptions that his opponent was known thereafter as "Commissary" Banks.

Those were only the immediate and material fruits of the opening phase of the campaign. A larger gain — as Lee had foreseen, or at any rate had aimed at — was in its effect on Lincoln, who once more swung round to find the Shenandoah shotgun loaded and leveled at his head. Banks put on a brave face as soon as he got what was left of his army beyond the Potomac. "It is seldom that a river crossing of such magnitude is achieved with greater success," he reported. Though he admitted that "there were never more grateful hearts in the same number of men than when at midday of the 26th we stood on the opposite shore," he denied that his command had "suffered an attack and rout, but had accomplished a premeditated march of nearly 60 miles in the face of the enemy, defeating his plans and giving him battle wherever he was found."

Lincoln was not deceived. Anxious though he was for reassurance, he saw clearly that Banks was in no condition to repulse the rebels if they continued their advance beyond the Potomac. In fact, he had already reacted exactly as Lee had hoped and intended. Shields had reached McDowell, and they had set out to join McClellan in front of Richmond; but on Saturday, as soon as news reached Washington of the disaster at Front Royal, they were halted six miles south of the Rappahannock and ordered to countermarch for operations against Jackson. McDowell replied with "a heavy heart" that he would attempt what the President commanded, though he did not believe the movement would succeed. "I am entirely beyond helping distance of General Banks," he told Lincoln; "no celerity or vigor will avail so far as he is concerned." Nor did he have a high opinion of Lincoln's scheme to use him to recover control of the Valley. "I shall gain nothing for you there, and shall lose much for you here. . . . I feel that it throws us all back, and from Richmond north we shall have our large masses paralyzed." The Commander in Chief thanked him for his promptness, but rejected his advice. "For you it is a question of legs," he urged as soon as McDowell's men were on the march for the Valley. "Put in all the speed you can."

Lincoln had something more in mind than the relief of pressure on Banks or even the salvation of Washington. He wanted to capture Jackson, bag and baggage. Poring over maps of Northern Virginia, he had evolved a plan whereby he would block the rebel general's retreat and crush him with overwhelming numbers. McDowell's command, advancing on the Valley from the east, was one jaw of the crusher; Frémont's was the other. Concentrated at Franklin, the Pathfinder was thirty miles from Harrisonburg, which was eighty miles in Stonewall's rear. Lincoln wired instructions for him "to move against Jackson at Harrisonburg, and operate against the enemy in such a way as to relieve Banks." He added: "This movement must be made immediately. You will acknowledge the receipt of this order and specify the hour it is received by you." Frémont replied within the hour that he would march at once. "Put the utmost speed into it. Do not lose a minute," Lincoln admonished. And having ordered the combination of two large forces in the presence of the enemy — the movement Napoleon characterized as the most difficult in the art of war — he sat back, like a long-distance chess player, to await results.

Not that he was not kept busy with other matters growing out of this one. The North was in turmoil. "Intelligence from various quarters leaves no doubt that the enemy in great force are advancing on Washington," Stanton wired the governors of thirteen states, asking them to send him whatever militia they could lay hands on. Three others were told, "Send all the troops forward that you can immediately. Banks is completely routed. The enemy in large force are advancing upon Harpers Ferry." Recruiting offices were reopened. The railroads were taken over to provide speedy transportation for reinforcements before the capital was beleaguered. Rumors spread fast on Monday, so quickly had Sunday's bolt come tumbling. The New York *Herald*, whose morning edition had carried an editorial captioned "Fall of Richmond," replaced it with a report that the whole rebel army was on the march for the Potomac. Harried by congressmen and distraught citizens, Lincoln hoped that his opponent in the Confederate seat of government could be given a hard time, too. To McClellan in front of Richmond went a wire: "Can you get near enough to throw shells into the city?"

The Young Napoleon was scarcely in a mood to throw anything at anybody: except possibly at Lincoln. When he first got the news that McDowell would not be joining him just yet, after all, his first reaction was, "Heaven save a country governed by such counsels!" On second thought, however, he could see at least one benefit proceeding from the panic in the capital: "A scare will do them good, and may bring them to their senses." But the President wired on Sunday that the enemy movement was "general and concerted," not merely a bluff or an act of desperation — "I think the time is near," he wrote, "when you must either attack Richmond or else give up the job and come to the defense of Washington" — McClellan reacted fast. The last thing he wanted in this world was to return to "that sink," within reach of "those hounds." Replying that "the time is very near when I shall attack," he added that he disagreed with Lincoln's appraisal of Confederate strategy: "The object of the movement is probably to prevent reinforcements being sent to me. All the information from balloons, deserters, prisoners, and contrabands agrees in the statement that the mass of the rebel troops are still in the immediate vicinity of Richmond, ready to defend it."

Lincoln knew how to translate "very near" and also how to assess McClellan's estimates as to the strength of an enemy intrenched to his front; he had encountered both before. Just now, though, his attention was distracted. On Tuesday, May 27, he received from Frémont a message that alarmed him: not because of what it said, but because of the heading, which showed that the Pathfinder had moved north instead of east. "I see that you are at Moorefield," Lincoln wired. "You were expressly ordered to march to Harrisonburg. What does this mean?" Frémont replied that it meant the road leading east from

Franklin was "impossible," that he had swung north to pick up food for his men, who otherwise would have starved, and that he was obeying instructions to "relieve Banks" in the best way he saw fit: by marching on Strasburg. "In executing any order received," he declared, "I take it for granted that I am to exercise discretion concerning its literal execution, according to circumstances. If I am to understand that literal obedience to orders is required, please say so."

The reply threw Lincoln into much the same state as when he flung his hat on the floor at Fort Monroe, three weeks ago. Frémont now had seventy miles to march instead of thirty. However, McDowell was closing in fast from the east, and Jackson was still reported near Harpers Ferry. There was plenty of time to cut him off, if the troops marched on schedule. On May 30 Lincoln sent two wires, one to Frémont: "You must be up in the time you promised," the other to McDowell: "The game is before you." Three days later he had Stanton give them both a final warning: "Do not let the enemy escape you."

For once, Jackson — "the game," as Lincoln styled him — was exactly where the Federal high command had him spotted: at Charles Town, with his infantry thrown forward to demonstrate against Harpers Ferry, seven miles away. Though he had known for two days now of the forces moving east and west toward a convergence that would put 35,000 soldiers in his rear, nothing in his manner showed that the information bothered him at all. After setting Monday aside for rest and prayer, in compensation for another violated Sabbath, he had come on by easy marches, driving the enemy not merely "toward the Potomac," as Lee had suggested, but to and beyond it. While the reassembled cavalry was pressing northward down the Valley pike, through Martinsburg and on to the Williamsport crossing, the infantry took the fork that branched northeast to Harpers Ferry. It was all rather anticlimactic, though, even lackadaisical, compared to what had gone before, and on the 28th — the day he was warned of the movement that threatened to cut off his retreat — he ordered his troops to resume the prescribed four hours of daily drill. Howls went up from the ranks at this, but the howls availed the outraged soldiers no more than did the complaints of the staff that the present delay would result in utter ruin. If Jackson was oblivious to the danger in his rear, they certainly were not. Once more they called him crack-brained, and one young officer muttered darkly: "*quem Deus vult perdere, prius dementat.*"

There was no middle ground for confidence where Stonewall was concerned; you either trusted him blindly, or you judged him absolutely mad. That was the obverse of his method, never better illustrated than now. It was true that he had already wrung every possible psychological advantage from his present exposed position, which he knew was growing more perilous by the hour, but there were other considerations. He had 2300 unparoled prisoners on his hands, each of whom could be exchanged for a southern soldier now in a northern prison camp, and near Winchester his chief of transportation was assembling a double line of wagons eight miles long, loaded with a wealth of captured goods, including 9000 badly needed rifles, mostly new, and invaluable medical equipment shut off from the Confederacy by blockade. All this took time, but Jackson was determined to give the grinding column of spoils and captives a head start up the Valley turnpike before he attempted to bring his army out of the two-jawed trap about to snap shut in its rear.

On May 30, when the long train started rolling south, there were even more urgent reasons for the army to follow in its wake at once. Intelligence reports placed the advance of McDowell's column within a day's march of Front Royal and Frémont's about the same distance from Strasburg, both of which places were more than forty miles in Jackson's rear. Banks had been reinforced at Williamsport and presumably was about ready to take the field again, tamping the Confederates into the grinder that would be created when Frémont and McDowell met in the shadow of the northern face of Massanutton Mountain. Nothing in Stonewall's manner expressed concern, however, when he emerged from his tent this Friday morning. After receiving a delegation of Charles Town ladies who called to pay their respects, he rode toward Harpers Ferry and watched some desultory skirmishing. When a shower of rain came up, he stretched out under a tree for shelter and presently fell asleep.

He woke to find A. R. Boteler, a Valley congressman who had volunteered for duty on his staff, making a sketch of him. Jackson studied it, then remarked: "Colonel, I have some harder work than this for you to do, and if you'll sit down here now I'll tell you what it is. . . . I want you to go to Richmond for me; I must have reinforcements. You can explain to them down there what the situation is here." Boteler replied that he would be glad to go, but that he was not sure he understood the situation: whereupon Jackson outlined it for him. "McDowell and Frémont are probably aiming to effect a junction at Strasburg, so as to cut us off from the upper Valley, and are both nearer to it now than we are. Consequently, no time is to be lost. You can say to them in Richmond that I'll send on the prisoners, secure most if not all of the captured property, and with God's blessing will be able to baffle the enemy's plans here with my present force, but that it will have to be increased as soon thereafter as possible." If Boteler thought the general wanted to use those reinforcements merely to help stand off the various columns now converging on him, he was much mistaken — as he discovered from what Stonewall said in closing: "You may tell them, too, that if my command can be gotten up to 40,000 men a movement may be made . . . which will soon raise the siege of Richmond and transfer this campaign from the banks of the Potomac to those of the Susquehanna."

★　★　★

Riding south with all the speed he could manage — by rail to Winchester, by horseback to Staunton, by rail again to Richmond — the congressman-colonel arrived to find that the eastern theater's first major engagement since Manassas, eighty miles away and ten full months ago, had been fought at the city's gates while he was traveling. With his back to the wall and the choice narrowed to resistance or evacuation, Johnston at last had found conditions suitable for attack.

In point of fact, despite his fondness for keeping the tactical situation fluid—in hopes that his opponent would commit some error or be guilty of some oversight and thereby expose a portion of the blue host to destruction—Johnston really had no choice. With McDowell poised for a southward advance, a junction that would give the Federals nearly a three-to-one advantage over the 53,688 Confederates drawn up east of Richmond, not even evacuation would assure the salvation of Johnston's army, which now as always was his main concern: McClellan would still be after him, and with overwhelming numbers. The only thing to do, he saw, was to strike one Mac before the other got there. Besides, the error he had been hoping for seemed already to have been committed. McClellan's five corps were unequally divided, three north and two south of the Chickahominy. Normally a sluggish stream, not even too broad for leaping in the dry months, the river was greatly swollen as a result of the continual spring rains, and thus might serve to isolate the Union wings, preventing their mutual support and giving the Confederates a chance to slash at one or the other with equal or perhaps superior numbers. Johnston would have preferred to attack the weaker south-bank wing, keeping Richmond covered as he did so; but this would not only leave McDowell's line of advance unblocked, it would probably also hasten the junction by provoking a rapid march from Fredericksburg when McClellan yelled for help. By elimination, then, Johnston determined to strike down the north bank, risking uncovering Richmond for the sake of wrecking McClellan's right wing and blocking McDowell's advance at the same time.

He had his plan, a product of necessity; but as usual he took his time, and kept his counsel as he took it. Least of all did he confer with the President, afterwards explaining: "I could not consult him without adopting the course he might advise, so that to ask his advice would have been, in my opinion, to ask him to command for me." The result, with the Federals a rapid two-hour march away, was a terrible strain on Davis. Unable to get the general's assurance that an all-out defense of the city would be attempted, he never knew from day to day which flag might be flying over the Capitol tomorrow. May 22, riding out the

Mechanicsville turnpike with Lee, he found few troops, no fortifications, indeed no preparations of any kind, as he wrote Johnston, for blocking a sudden Union drive "toward if not to Richmond." Two days later Johnston came to town for a conference, but he told his superior nothing except that he intended to be governed by circumstances. To make matters worse, while he was there the Federals seized Mechanicsville, five miles north, just as Davis had predicted. Not only was this an excellent location for a hook-up when McDowell made his three- or four-day march from Fredericksburg, but now there was nothing at all to stand in the way of such an advance, Johnston having instructed Anderson to fall back from the line of the Rappahannock.

Two days later, May 26, while he was reviewing the situation with Lee, the President's anxiety over Johnston's undivulged intentions was so obviously painful that Lee proposed, "Let me go and see him, and defer this discussion until I return." When he was gone a dispatch arrived from Jackson, who broke his silence with an outright shout of joy. "During the past three days," it began, "God has blessed our arms with brilliant success." Banks had been routed and Stonewall was in pursuit, "capturing the fugitives." Whether this would have the intended effect of frightening the Union high command into holding back Mc-Dowell remained to be seen, but the news was a tonic for Davis, arriving as it did at the very crisis of his concern. Presently Lee returned, to be heartened by this early yield from the seeds of strategy he had sown in the Valley and to deliver tidings that bore directly on the subject of the President's anxiety. Johnston at last had announced his decision to attack. Intended to crumple McClellan's right wing, which brushed the purlieus of the city, the strike would be made on the 29th.

That was Thursday; today was Monday. Davis braced himself for the three-day wait.

McClellan was quite aware of the danger of straddling what he called "the confounded Chickahominy," but his instructions left him no choice. In the dispatch of the 17th, rewarding his prayers with the announcement that McDowell would be moving south as soon as Shields arrived, Stanton had told McClellan: "He is ordered — keeping himself always in position to save the capital from all possible attack — so to operate as to place his left wing in communication with your right wing, and you are instructed to coöperate, so as to establish this communication as soon as possible, by extending your right wing to the north of Richmond."

That was that, and there was nothing he could do to change it, though he tried. Next day, as if he knew how little an appeal to Stanton would avail him, he wired Secretary Seward: "Indications that the enemy intend fighting at Richmond. Policy seems to be to concentrate everything there. They hold central position, and will seek to meet us

while divided. I think we are committing a great military error in having so many independent columns. The great battle should be fought by
our troops in mass; then divide if necessary." Three days later, when
this had brought no change in his instructions, he wrote to his friend
Burnside: "The Government have deliberately placed me in this position. If I win, the greater the glory. If I lose, they will be damned forever, both by God and men."

Consoled by this prediction as to the verdict that would be recorded in history as in heaven, and reassured the following day by a
message from Fredericksburg — "Shields will join me today," McDowell wrote, and announced that he would be ready to march on the 24th
with 38,000 men and 11,000 animals — McClellan took heart and labored to make the dangerous waiting period as brief as possible. On the
scheduled date he sent his cavalry to drive the rebels out of Mechanicsville, thus extending his grasp north of Richmond in accordance with
Stanton's instructions. Before the day was over, however, he received a
telegram from the President which informed him that he was clutching
at emptiness: "In consequence of General Banks' position, I have been
compelled to suspend McDowell's movements." Next day, with Banks
"broken up into a total rout," Lincoln explained his action by combining a justification with an appeal: "Apprehensions of something like
this, and no unwillingness to sustain you, have always been my reason
for withholding McDowell from you. Please understand this, and do the
best you can with the force you have."

That was what McClellan did. Though he found the order "perfectly sickening," he took comfort at least in the fact that McDowell's
southward movement had been "suspended," not revoked, and he
worked hard to strengthen his army's position astride the river and to
pave the way for the eventual junction on the right as soon as the Fredericksburg command got back from what McDowell himself considered
a wild-goose chase. Eleven new bridges, "all long and difficult, with extensive log-way approaches," were erected across the swollen Chickahominy between Mechanicsville and Bottom's Bridge, twelve miles
apart. It was an arduous and unending task, for the spans not only had to
be constructed, they often had to be replaced; the river, still rising
though it was already higher than it had been in twenty years, swept
them away about as fast as they were built. While thus providing as best
he could for mutual support by the two wings in event that either was
attacked, he saw to the improvement of the tactical position of each.
Keyes, supported by Heintzelman on the south bank, pushed forward
along the Williamsburg road on the 25th and, a mile and a half beyond
Seven Pines, constructed a redoubt within five miles of the heart of the
enemy capital. Though McClellan could not comply with Lincoln's request next day that he "throw some shells into the city," he could see
Richmond's tallest steeples from both extremities of his line, north and

south of the river, and hear the public clocks as they struck the quiet hours after midnight.

On the north bank, Porter was farthest out; behind him were Franklin, in close support, and Sumner, who occupied what was called the center of the position, eight miles downstream from Mechanicsville. The latter's corps was theoretically on call as a reserve for either wing, though the rising flood was steadily increasing its pressure on the two bridges he had built for crossing the river in event of an attack on Keyes or Heintzelman. To protect his rear on the north bank, and to shorten McDowell's march from Fredericksburg, McClellan on the 27th had Porter take a reinforced division twelve miles north to Hanover Court-house, where a Confederate brigade had halted on its fifty-mile retreat from Gordonsville. Porter encountered the rebels about noon, and after a short but sharp engagement drove them headlong, capturing a gun and two regimental supply trains. At a cost of 397 casualties, he inflicted more than 1000, including 730 prisoners, and added greatly to the morale of his corps.

It was handsomely done; McClellan was delighted. The sizeable haul of men and equipment indicated a decline of the enemy's fighting spirit. Lying quiescent all this time in the Richmond intrenchments, despite his reported advantage in numbers, Joe Johnston seemed to lack the nerve for a strike at the divided Federal army. At this rate, the contest would soon degenerate into a siege — a type of warfare at which his young friend George was an expert. "We are getting on splendidly," McClellan wrote his wife before he went to bed that night. "I am quietly clearing out everything that could threaten my rear and communications, providing against the contingency of disaster, and so arranging as to make my whole force available in the approaching battle. The only fear is that Joe's heart may fail him."

That seemed to be about what had happened Thursday morning when, after hurrying through some office work, Davis rode out to observe the scheduled attack, but found the troops lounging at ease in the woods and heard no sound of gunfire anywhere along the line. Johnston had told him nothing of canceling or postponing the battle; Davis was left to wonder and fret until late in the day, when investigation uncovered what had happened.

At a council of war held the previous night for issuing final instructions, something in the nature of a miracle had been announced. Only the day before, Johnston had been given definite information that McDowell was on the march; already six miles south of Fredericksburg, his advance was within thirty miles of Hanover Courthouse, where Porter had been waiting since his midday repulse of the Confederate brigade. But now, at the council held on Wednesday evening, a dispatch from Jeb Stuart announced that McDowell, with nothing at all between

him and a junction with McClellan, had halted his men and was countermarching them back toward the Rappahannock. It seemed entirely too
good to be true; yet there it was. Johnston breathed a sigh of relief and
canceled tomorrow's attack. That was why Davis heard no gunfire
when he rode out next morning, expecting to find the battle in full
swing.

Johnston did not abandon his intention to wreck one wing of
McClellan's divided army, but he was doubly thankful for the delay.
For one thing, it gave him additional time, and no matter how he
squandered that commodity while backing up, time was something he
prized highly whenever he considered moving forward. For another,
with McDowell no longer a hovering threat, he could shift the attack to
the south bank of the Chickahominy, where the Federals were less numerous and reportedly more open to assault. With this in mind he drew
up a plan of battle utilizing three roads that led eastward out of the capital so patly that they might have been surveyed for just this purpose. In
the center was the Williamsburg road, paralleling the York River Railroad to the Chickahominy crossing, twelve miles out. On the left was the
Nine Mile road, which turned southeast to intersect the railroad at
Fair Oaks Station and the Williamsburg road at Seven Pines, halfway to
Bottom's Bridge. On the right, branching south from the Williamsburg
road about two miles out, was the Charles City road, which reached a
junction six miles southeast leading north to Seven Pines and Fair Oaks.
Thus all three roads converged upon the objective, where the advance
elements of the Federal left wing were intrenched. The attack could
be launched with all the confidence of a bowler rolling three balls at
once, each one down a groove that had been cut to yield a strike.

A third advantage of the delay was that it brought in reinforcements. R. H. Anderson's command, at the end of its long withdrawal
from the line of the Rappahannock, was combined with the brigade that
had been thrown out of Hanover Courthouse, thus creating a new division for A. P. Hill, a thirty-seven-year-old Virginia West Pointer just
promoted to major general. Another division was on the way from
Petersburg under Huger, who had stopped there after evacuating Norfolk. These additions would bring Johnston's total strength to nearly
75,000 men, giving him the largest army yet assembled under the Stars
and Bars. What was more, the six divisions were ideally located to fit the
plan of battle. A. P. Hill and Magruder, north of Richmond, could
maintain their present positions, guarding the upper Chickahominy crossings. Smith and Longstreet were camped in the vicinity of Fairfield
Race Course, where the Nine Mile road began; Longstreet would move
all the way down it to strike the Union right near Fair Oaks, while
Smith halted in reserve, facing left as he did so, to guard the lower
river crossings. D. H. Hill was east of the city, well out the Williams-

burg road; he would advance and deliver a frontal attack on signal from
Huger, who had the longest march, coming up from the south on the
Charles City road. The object was to maul Keyes, then maul Heintzel-
man in turn as he came up, leaving McClellan a single wing to fly on.

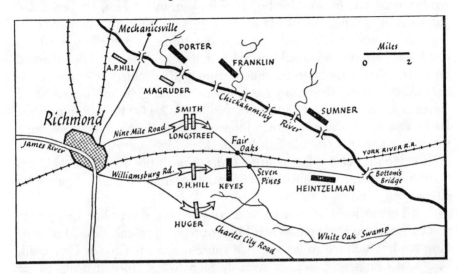

It was a simple matter, as such things went, to direct the attacking
divisions to their separate, unobstructed routes. On the evening of May
30, as Johnston did so, a pelting rainstorm broke, mounting quickly to
unprecedented violence and continuing far into the night. This would no
doubt slow tomorrow's marches on the heavy roads and add to the difficulty of deploying in the sodden fields, but it would also swell the
Chickahominy still farther and increase the likelihood that the Federal
right wing would be floodbound on the northern bank, cut off from
rendering any help to the assailed left wing across the river. Johnston
was glad to see the rain come down, and glad to see it continue; this was
"Confederate weather" at its best. Some of the instructions to his six
division commanders were sent in writing. Others were given orally,
in person. In either case, he stipulated that the attack, designed to throw
twenty-three of the twenty-seven southern brigades against a single
northern corps, was to be launched "early in the morning — as early as
practicable," he added, hearing the drumming of the rain.

The most remarkable thing about the ensuing action was that a
plan as sound as Johnston's appeared at the outset — so simple and forthright, indeed, as to be practically fool-proof, even for green troops under green commanders — could produce such an utter brouhaha, such a
Donnybrook of a battle. Seven Pines, or Fair Oaks as some called it, was
unquestionably the worst-conducted large-scale conflict in a war that
afforded many rivals for that distinction. What it came to, finally, was a

military nightmare: not so much because of the suffering and bloodshed, though there was plenty of both before it was over, but rather because of the confusion, compounded by delay.

Longstreet began it. Since his assigned route, out the Nine Mile road, would put him under Smith, who outranked him, he persuaded Johnston to give him command of the forces on the right. As next-ranking man he was entitled to it, he said, and Johnston genially agreed, on condition that control would revert to him when the troops converged on Seven Pines. Longstreet, thus encouraged, decided to transfer his division to the Williamsburg road, which would give him unhampered freedom from Smith and add to the weight of D. H. Hill's assault on the Union center. He did not inform Johnston of this decision, however, and that was where the trouble first began. Marching south on the outskirts of Richmond, across the mouth of the Nine Mile Road, he held up Smith's lead elements while his six brigades of infantry trudged past with all their guns and wagons.

This in itself amounted to a considerable delay, but Longstreet was by no means through. When Huger prepared to enter the Williamsburg road, which led to his assigned route down the Charles City road, he found Longstreet's 14,000-man division to his front, passing single file over an improvised bridge across a swollen creek. Nor would the officers in charge of the column yield the right of way; first come first served, they said. When Huger protested, Longstreet informed him that he ranked him. They stood there in the morning sunlight, the South Carolina aristocrat and the broad, hairy Georgian, and that was the making of one career and the wrecking of another. Huger accepted the claim as true, though it was not, and bided his time while Longstreet took the lead.

The morning sun climbed up the sky, and now it was Johnston's turn to listen, as Davis had done two days ago, for the boom of guns that remained silent. As he waited with Smith, whose five brigades were in position two miles short of Fair Oaks Station, his anxiety was increased by the fact that he had lost one of his divisions as completely as if it had marched unobserved into quicksand. Nobody at headquarters knew where Longstreet was, nor any of his men, and when a staff officer galloped down the Nine Mile road to find him, he stumbled into the enemy lines and was captured. When at last Longstreet and his troops were found — they were halted beside the Williamsburg road, two miles out of Richmond, while Huger's division filed past to enter the Charles City road — Johnston could only presume that Longstreet had misinterpreted last night's verbal orders. The delay could be ruinous. Everything depended on the action being completed before nightfall; if it went past that, McClellan would bring up reinforcements under cover of darkness and counterattack with superior numbers in the morning. As the sun went past the overhead, Johnston remarked that he wished his army was back in its suburban camps and the thing had never begun.

He could no more stop it, however, than he could get it started. All he could do was wait; and the waiting continued. Lee rode out from Richmond, determined not to spend another day like the office-bound day of Manassas. Johnston greeted him courteously, but spared him the details of the mix-up. Presently there came from the southeast an intermittent far-sounding rumble of cannon. It grew until just after 3 o'clock, with ten of the fifteen hours of daylight gone, the rumble was vaguely intensified by a sound that Lee believed was musketry. No, no, Johnston told him; it was only an artillery duel. Lee did not insist, although it seemed to him that the subdued accompaniment was rising in volume. Then at 4 o'clock a note came from Longstreet, informing the army commander that he was heavily engaged in front of Seven Pines and wanted support on his left.

That was the signal Johnston had been awaiting. Ordering Smith's lead division to continue down the Nine Mile road until it struck the Federal right, he spurred ahead to study the situation at first hand. As he rode off, the President rode up; so that some observers later said that the general had left in haste to avoid an irksome meeting.

Davis asked Lee what the musketry meant.

Had he heard it, too? Lee asked.

Unmistakably, Davis said. What was it?

Mostly it was D. H. Hill. He had been in position for six hours, awaiting the signal from Huger as instructed, when at 2 o'clock he ran out of patience and surged forward on his own. (It was just as well; otherwise the wait would have been interminable. Cutting cross-country to take his assigned position on Hill's right, Huger had become involved in the upper reaches of White Oak Swamp. He would remain so all through what was left of this unhappy Saturday, as removed from the battle — except that the guns were roaring within earshot — as if he had been with Jackson out in the Shenandoah Valley.) Hill's attack was no less furious for being unsupported on the flanks. A forty-year-old North Carolinian, a West Point professional turned schoolmaster as a result of ill health, he was a caustic hater of all things northern and an avid critic of whatever displeased him anywhere at all. Dyspeptic as Stonewall Jackson, his brother-in-law, he suffered also from a spinal ailment, which gave him an unmilitary bearing whether mounted or afoot. His friends called him Harvey; that was his middle name. A hungry-looking man with haunted eyes and a close-cropped scraggly beard, he took a fierce delight in combat — especially when it was hand to hand, as now. His assault swept over the advance Federal redoubt, taking eight guns and a brigade camp with all its equipment and supplies. Scarcely pausing to reform his line, he went after the rest of Keyes' corps, which was drawn up to receive him just west of Seven Pines.

Here too the fight was furious, the Federals having the advantage of an abatis previously constructed along the edge of a line of woods, while the Confederates, emerging from a flooded swamp, had to charge unsupported across an open space to reach them. Longstreet's complaint, made presently when he appealed to Johnston for help on the left, that green troops were "as sensitive about the flanks as a virgin," did not apply to Hill's men today. Especially it did not apply to the lead brigade, four regiments from Alabama and one from Mississippi, under Brigadier General Robert E. Rodes. Inexperienced as they were, their only concern was the tactics manual definition of the mission of the infantry in attack: "to close with the enemy and destroy him." Advancing through the swamp, thigh-deep in mud and stagnant water, they propped their wounded against the trunks of trees to keep them from drowning, and came on, yelling as they came. They reached the abatis, pierced it, and drove the bluecoats back again.

It was gallantly done, but at a dreadful cost: Rodes' 2000-man command, for instance, lost 1094 killed, wounded, or drowned. And there were no replacements near at hand. Out of thirteen brigades available to Longstreet here on the right — his six, Hill's four, and Huger's three — less than half went into action. Three of his six he had sent to follow Huger into the ooze of White Oak Swamp, and a fourth he had posted on the left to guard against a surprise attack, in spite of the fact that there was nothing in that direction except the other half of the Confederate army. However, the Federals were forming a new line farther back, perhaps with a counterattack in mind, and he was not so sure. Huger was lost on the right; so might Smith be lost on the left. At any rate, that was when he sent the note to Johnston, appealing for the protection of his virginal left flank.

Smith's division, reinforced by four brigades from Magruder and A. P. Hill, followed the army commander down the Nine Mile road toward Fair Oaks, where the leading elements were formed under his direction for a charge that was intended to strike the exposed right flank of Keyes, whose center was at Seven Pines, less than a mile away. Late as the hour was, Johnston's juggernaut attack plan seemed at last to be rolling toward a repetition of his triumph at Manassas. But not for long. Aimed at Keyes, it struck instead a substantial body of men in muddy blue, who stood and delivered massed volleys that broke up the attack before it could gather speed.

They were strangers to this ground; the mudstains on their uniforms were from the Chickahominy bottoms. It was Sumner's corps, arrived from across the river. Commander of the 1st U.S. Cavalry while Albert Sidney Johnston commanded the 2d — Joe Johnston was his lieutenant-colonel, McClellan one of his captains — Sumner was an old army man with an old army notion that orders were received to be obeyed, not questioned, no matter what obstacles stood in the way of execution. "Bull" Sumner, he was called — in full, "the Bull of the Woods" — because of the loudness of his voice; he had a peacetime custom of removing his false teeth to give commands that carried from end to end of the regiment, above the thunder of hoofs. Alerted soon after midday (Johnston's aide, who had ridden into the Union lines in search of Longstreet, had told his captors nothing; but his presence was suspicious, and the build-up in the woods and swamps out front had been growing more obvious every hour) Sumner assembled his corps on the north bank, near the two bridges he had built for this emergency. Foaming water had buckled them; torn from their pilings, awash knee-deep in the center, they seemed about to go with the flood. When the order to support Keyes arrived and the tall white-haired old man started his soldiers across, an engineer officer protested that the condition of the bridges made a crossing not only unsafe, but impossible. "Impossible?" Sumner roared. "Sir, I tell you I *can* cross! I am ordered!"

Marching toward the sound of firing, he got his men over the swaying bridges and across the muddy bottoms, on to Fair Oaks and the meeting engagement which produced on both sides, in about equal parts, feelings of elation and frustration. If Sumner had kept going he would have struck the flank of Longstreet; if Smith had kept going he would have struck the flank of Keyes. As it was, they struck each other, and the result was a stalemate. Smith could make no headway against Sumner, who was content to hold his ground. Hill, to the south, had shot his bolt, and Keyes was thankful that the issue was not pressed beyond the third line he had drawn while waiting for Heintzelman, who had sent one division forward to help him but did not bring the other up till dusk.

By then the battle was practically over. Seven Pines, the Southerners called it, since that was where they scored their gains; to the Northerners it was Fair Oaks, for much the same reason. The attackers had the advantage in spoils — 10 guns, 6000 rifles, 347 prisoners, and a good deal of miscellaneous equipment from the captured camp — but the price was excessive. 6134 Confederates were dead or wounded: well over a thousand more than the 5031 Federals who had fallen.

These were the end figures, not known or attained until later, but they included one casualty whose fall apparently tipped the balance considerably further in favor of the Yankees. Near Fair Oaks, Johnston watched as the uproar swelled to a climax; then, as it diminished, he rode closer to the battle line, and perceiving that nothing more could be accomplished — the flame-stabbed dusk was merging into twilight — sent couriers to instruct the various commanders to have their men cease firing, sleep on their arms in line of battle, and prepare to renew the contest in the morning. Just then he was hit in the right shoulder by a bullet. As he reeled in the saddle, a shell fragment struck him in the chest and unhorsed him. Two aides carried the unconscious general to a less exposed position and were lifting him onto a stretcher when the President and Lee came riding up. As they dismounted and approached, Johnston opened his eyes and smiled. Davis knelt and took his hand, beginning to express his regret that the general had been hit. This affecting scene was interrupted, however, by Johnston's shock at discovering that he had lost his sword and pistols: the "unblemished" sword of which he had written in protest at being oversloughed by the man who now held his hand and murmured condolences. "I would not lose it for $10,000," he said earnestly. "Will not someone please go back and get it and the pistols for me?" They waited then while a courier went back under fire, found the arms where they had fallen, and returned them to Johnston, who rewarded him by giving him one of the pistols. This done, the stretcher-bearers took up their burden and set off.

Davis and Lee went looking for Smith, who as the next-ranking field commander would now take charge of the uncompleted battle. Presently they found him. But the man they found bore little resemblance to the stern-lipped, confident "G.W." who the month before had urged an all-or-nothing assault on Philadelphia and New York. He had learned of Johnston's misfortune and he counted it as his own. It made him tremble. He looked sick. In fact he *was* sick: not from fear, or anyhow not from any ordinary fear (he was brave as the next man in battle, if not braver) but from the strain of responsibility suddenly loaded on his shoulders. The effect was paralyzing — quite literally — for within two days he would leave the army, suffering from an affliction of the central nervous system. Just now, when Davis asked what his plans were, he replied that he had none. First he would have to discover Longstreet's situation on the right, of which he knew nothing. He might have to withdraw; on the other hand, he might be able to hold his ground. . . . Davis suggested that he take the latter course. The Federals might fall back in the night; if the Confederates stayed they would gain the moral effect of a victory. Smith said he would if he could.

The best that could be hoped for under present circumstances was that the army would be able to disengage itself tomorrow, without further excessive losses, for a future effort under a new commander. As Davis and Lee rode together up the Nine Mile road, clogged like all the others tonight with wounded and disheartened men who had stumbled and hobbled out of the day-long nightmare of bungled marches and mismanaged fire-fights, one thing at least was clear. The new commander would not be Smith, who had had retreat in the front of his mind before he even knew the situation. The two men rode in silence under a sickle moon: Davis was making his choice. If he hesitated, there was little wonder. His companion was the obvious candidate; but he could easily be by-passed. Davis, knowing better than anyone how well Lee had served in his present advisory capacity, could as logically keep him there as he kept Samuel Cooper at the Adjutant General's post. "Evacuating Lee," the press had called the fifty-five-year-old graybeard, and with cause. Disappointing lofty expectations, he had shown a woeful incapacity to deal with high-strung subordinates in the field — and Johnston's army had perhaps the greatest number of high-strung troop commanders, per square yard, of any army ever assembled. Besides, in the more than thirteen months of war, Lee had never taken part in a general engagement. Today in fact, riding about the field as an observer, he had been under close-up rifle fire for the first time since Chapultepec, nearly fifteen years ago.

Nevertheless, by the time the lights of beleaguered Richmond came in sight Davis had made his decision. In a few words lost to history, but large with fate for the two riders and their country, he informed Lee that he would be given command of the army known thereafter as the Army of Northern Virginia.

★ ★ ★

In a telegram to McClellan, written while the guns were roaring around Seven Pines and Sumner was assembling his corps for its march across the Chickahominy, Lincoln described the geometrical dilemma he had created for the Confederates in the Shenandoah Valley: "A circle whose circumference shall pass through Harpers Ferry, Front Royal, and Strasburg, and whose center shall be a little northeast of Winchester, almost certainly has within it this morning the forces of Jackson, Ewell, and Edward Johnson. Quite certainly they were within it two days ago. Some part of their forces attacked Harpers Ferry at dark last evening and are still in sight this morning. Shields, with McDowell's advance, re-took Front Royal at 11 a.m. yesterday ... and saved the bridge. Fré-mont, from the direction of Moorefield, promises to be at or near Strasburg at 5 p.m. today. Banks, at Williamsport with his old force, and his new force at Harpers Ferry, is directed to coöperate." He added, by way of showing that the picture was brightening all over: "Corinth is certainly in the hands of General Halleck."

The circle was not quite complete, however. There was still the Front Royal-Strasburg gap, and Jackson — who knew as well as Lincoln that for him, as for the blue columns attempting a convergence, the question was one of "legs" — was making for it with all the speed he could coax from his gray marchers. Leaving the Stonewall Brigade to continue the demonstration against Harpers Ferry, he had boarded the train yesterday at Charles Town for a fast ride to Winchester, where the rest of the army was being assembled for the race up the Valley turnpike. Time was running out now and he knew it. Still, nothing in his manner showed distress. Folding his arms on the back of the seat ahead, he rested his face on them and went to sleep. He was wakened by a mounted courier, who flagged the train to a stop and handed him a message through the window. Jackson read it without comment, then tore it up and dropped the pieces on the floor. "Go on, sir, if you please," he told the conductor. He put his head on his arms again, and soon was rocked to sleep by the vibration of the train.

At Winchester, when the other passengers learned the contents of the dispatch that had been delivered en route, they wondered that Stonewall had not blenched. Shields had turned the tables on him. Marching fast from the east through Manassas Gap, the leader of McDowell's advance had surprised the Front Royal garrison, a regiment of Georgians whose colonel fled at the first alarm, leaving his men and $300,000-worth of captured goods to be scooped up by the Yankees. Jackson interviewed the runaway colonel that night — "How many men did you have killed?" "None"; "How many wounded?" "None, sir"; "Do you call that much of a fight?" — and put him in arrest. Fortunately, the senior captain had taken command, burned the supplies, and brought the troops out. But the damage was done, and the implications were ominous. Shields stood squarely across the entrance to the narrow eastern valley with its many avenues of escape through the passes of the Blue Ridge. Stonewall's only remaining line of retreat was up the Valley pike, through Strasburg. At Front Royal, Shields was only eleven miles from there: Jackson, at Winchester with his wagon train and prisoners and the main body of his army, was seventeen. Worst of all, the Stonewall Brigade, still menacing Harpers Ferry, had forty-four miles to go before it reached that mid-point in the narrowing gap where Shields and Frémont would converge. Jackson sent a staff officer to bring up the brigade with all possible speed. "I will stay in Winchester until you get here if I can," he told him, "but if I cannot, and the enemy gets here first, you must bring it around through the mountains."

The army was moving by dawn, May 31: first the wagon train, a double column eight miles long, loaded with captured goods that were literally priceless; then the prisoners, a brigade-sized throng of men in blue, who, having missed the pell-mell northward retreat from here to the Potomac the week before, would march faster under Jackson than they had ever done before: and finally the main body, the "foot cavalry," already looking a little larger than life because of the fame they were beginning to share with their strange captain. By early afternoon they had cleared the town, all but a couple of cavalry regiments left to wait for the Stonewall Brigade. Winchester's seven days of liberation were about over. Ahead lay Strasburg, which they might or might not clear before Lincoln's steel circumference was closed. They did not worry about that, however. They left such worries to Jackson, who knew best how to handle them. The worst it could mean was fighting, and they had fought before. Nor did they worry about the rain, a slow drizzle that gave promise of harder showers to come. In fact, they welcomed it. They had the macadamized pike to march on, while their opponents slogged through mud. "Press on; press on, men," Stonewall urged them.

They pressed on, halting for ten minutes out of every hour, as prescribed, and joking among themselves that Jackson would never allow the train to be captured; he had his reserve supply of lemons in one of the wagons. Presently, sure enough, good news was passed back down the line. The head of the column had entered Strasburg — and found the gap unclosed. To the east and west, the cavalry was skirmishing within earshot, but the infantry saw no sign of bluecoats as they swung into sight of the little town and made camp for the night. Eighteen miles they had marched today, despite the long wait for the wagons and the prisoners to clear the road ahead, and now they had reached the rim of the map-drawn circle. They were into the clear.

Good news came from the rear as well. By midnight the Stonewall Brigade was four miles south of Winchester, the men dropping dog-tired in their tracks after a record-breaking march of thirty-five miles. Next morning they were off again on wobbly legs, cursing their old commander for having left them far in the rear to fight the whole compounded Yankee army. Always he gave them the dirty end of the stick, lest he be accused of favoritism — and now they were to be sacrificed for the sake of this glory-hunter's mad gyrations. So they complained. Approaching Strasburg, however, they heard a spatter of musketry from the west, mixed in with the boom of guns. It was Jackson, fighting to hold the gap ajar for the men of his old brigade. Their hearts were lifted. Once more they sang his praises. "Old Jack knows what he's about! He'll take care of us, you bet!"

It was a strange day, this June 1 Sunday: particularly for Ewell. Except for a feint by one brigade, repulsed the afternoon before, Shields seemed to be resting content with the retaking of Front Royal; but Frémont was hovering dangerously close in the opposite direction, as if he were tensing his muscles for a leap at the west flank of the long column. Ewell was given the task of holding him back while the Stonewall Brigade caught up with the main body, plodding southward up the pike behind the train and the leg-weary captives. He was warned not to bring on a general engagement; all Jackson wanted was a demonstration that would encourage the Pathfinder to hesitate long enough for the Stonewall Brigade to pass through Strasburg. The warning seemed superfluous, however. Contact was established early, but nothing would provoke Frémont into close-up fighting. He stopped as soon as his skirmishers came under fire.

If Frémont was not provoked, Ewell was. "I can't make out what those people are about," he said. "They won't advance, but stay out there in the woods, making a great fuss with their guns." Taylor suggested that he place his brigade on the Federal flank and then see what developed. "Do so," Old Baldy told him; "that may stir them up, and I am sick of this fiddling about." Taylor gained the position he wanted, then walked down Frémont's line of battle until he came under fire from Ewell's other brigades; there he stopped and they came up alongside him. Frémont gave ground, refusing to be provoked into what he evidently thought was rashness. After all that marching, seventy miles in seven days, lashed by rain and pelted by hail as he picked his way over mountain roads, the Pathfinder seemed to want no part of what he had been marching toward. It was strange.

At last, about midafternoon, the Stonewall Brigade passed Strasburg. Ewell broke off the fight, if it could be called that, and followed the main body up the turnpike. Frémont again became aggressive, slashing so savagely at the rear of the moving column that Taylor's men and the cavalry had all they could do to hold them off. Up front, Jackson was having his troubles, too. Twelve miles beyond Strasburg, a portion of the train fell into confusion and presently was overtaken by the lead brigade. The result was turmoil, a seemingly inextricable mix-up of wagons and men and horses. Stonewall came riding up and rebuked the infantry commander:

"Colonel, why do you not get your brigade together, keep it together, and move on?"

"It's impossible, General. I can't do it."

"Don't say it's impossible! Turn your command over to the next officer. If he can't do it, I'll find someone who can, if I have to take him from the ranks."

He got the tangle straightened out and pressed on southward under a scud of angry-looking clouds and jagged streaks of lightning. Soon after sunset the tempest broke. Rain came down in torrents. (Near Strasburg, Frémont called a halt for the night, wiring Lincoln: "Terrible storm of thunder and hail now passing over. Hailstones as large as hens' eggs.") Jackson kept moving, having just received word that he was now involved in another race. McDowell had joined Shields at Front Royal, and had sent him south up the Luray valley to parallel Jackson's advance on the opposite side of Massanutton Mountain. If Shields marched fast he would intercept the rebels as they came around the south end of the ridge; or he might cross it, marching from Luray to New Market, and thus strike the flank of the gray column moving along the turnpike. Either way, Jackson would have to stop and deploy, and Frémont could then catch up and attack his rear, supported perhaps by Banks, who had reëntered Winchester, urged by Lincoln to lend a hand in accomplishing Jackson's destruction.

Once more it was "a question of legs," and Stonewall was duly thankful for the downpour. Even though it bruised his men with phenomenal hailstones, it would deepen the mud in the eastern valley and swell the South Fork of the Shenandoah, which lay between Shields and the mountain. To make certain he did not cross it, Jackson sent a detail to burn the bridges west of Luray. That way, he would have only Frémont to deal with, at least until he passed Harrisonburg. When he finally stopped for the night, the Sabbath was over; he could write a letter to his wife. "[The Federals] endeavored to get in my rear by moving on both flanks of my gallant army," he told her, "but our God has been my guide and saved me from their grasp." And he added, with a tenderness that would have shocked the men he had been driving southward through rain and hail, under sudden forks of lightning: "You must not expect long letters from me in such busy times as these, but always believe your husband never forgets his little darling."

All next day the rain poured down; "our God," as Stonewall called Him, continued to smile on the efforts of the men in gray. Jackson, never one to neglect an advantage, continued to press the march of his reunited army along the all-weather pike. There was an off chance that Shields, within earshot of Frémont's guns as he slogged through the mud in the opposite valley, might somehow have managed to rebuild the Luray bridges and thereby have gained access to the road across the mountain. A staff officer, sent to check on the work of destruction, returned and reported it well done, but Jackson did not rest easy until he entered New Market with the advance and found the mountain road empty.

Meanwhile, far back down the pike, the rear guard was having its hands full. Shields had sent his troopers around through Strasburg to coöperate with Frémont, and they were doing their work with dash and spirit. Several times that day they charged the Confederate rear guard, throwing it into confusion. Late in the afternoon they made their most effective attempt, breaking through the scattered ranks and riding hard up the pike until they struck a Virginia regiment, which had halted to receive them with massed volleys. The result was as if they had ridden into a trip wire. Saddles were emptied and horses went down screaming; all except one of the attackers were killed or captured. That night, reporting the incident to Jackson, the Virginia colonel expressed his regret at having had to deal so harshly with such gallantry. The general heard him out, then asked: "Colonel, why did you say you saw those Federal soldiers fall with regret?" Surprised at Stonewall's inability to appreciate chivalrous instincts, the colonel said that it was because he admired their valor; he hated to have to slaughter such brave men. "No," Jackson said dryly. "Shoot them all. I do not wish them to be brave."

He had in mind the expectation that he would soon be facing them in battle: not a series of piecemeal rear-guard actions, fought to gain time for retreating, but a full-scale conflict into which he would throw every soldier in his army. Having employed defensive tactics to escape the first and second traps at Strasburg and New Market, he now was thinking of ways to assume the offensive in dealing with the third, which he would encounter somewhere beyond Harrisonburg when he rounded the south end of Massanutton. At that point he might be able to turn on one or another of the Federal columns and give it a mauling before the other could come to its relief. He would await developments; meanwhile that was what he had in mind.

Before it could be attempted, however, he would have to give his men a chance to rest. Next day — June 3 — they got it. The North Fork of the Shenandoah intersected the Valley turnpike just above the railroad terminus at Mount Jackson, and as Frémont's advance approached that place, the last gray cavalrymen crossed the bridge and set it afire, leaving their pursuers stranded on the northern bank. Stonewall took advantage of this to give his men a full day's badly needed rest and the wagon train and prisoners a substantial head start toward the Virginia Central, where they could be loaded for shipment by rail to warehouses and prisons down near Richmond. If there seemed to be a considerable risk in this delay, he felt he could afford it. Beyond the mountain, Shields was toiling through the mud; he would be at least a day behind and badly worn by the time he reached Conrad's Store, where he would reënter the tactical picture. On this side, there was the danger that Frémont might bridge the swollen river — he had brought a pontoon train across the Alleghenies for just such an emergency — but Jackson doubted if this could be successful, considering all the water that was trickling down the slopes of all the mountains. It was not. Frémont got his pontoon bridge across, all right, but before he could make much use of it, the North Fork rose twelve feet in four hours. He had to cut it loose from the southern bank to keep it from being swept away and lost in the raging water.

While his men were taking their ease beyond New Market, and leg-weary stragglers were catching up to share in the first hot meals the army had had since leaving Winchester four days ago, Jackson took out his Valley map and resumed his study of geography. As always, the harder he looked the more he saw. Resting against the southern face of Massanutton there was a road-net triangle much like the one at the opposite end, which he had used to discomfort Banks; and as Stonewall pored over the map he began to see possibilities for using this upper triangle in an even more ambitious venture against Shields and Frémont. Its base ran from Harrisonburg to Conrad's Store; its apex was at Port Republic, which lay at the tip of a tongue of land where North and South Rivers joined to form the South Fork of the Shenandoah. A bridge spanned North River, connecting the town with Harrisonburg, nine miles away, but all the other crossings were badly swollen fords. Once the South Fork bridge at Conrad's Store was destroyed, this upper bridge at Port Republic would be Shields' only way of joining Frémont. If Jackson's army got there first, he would be between the two, and therefore able to deal with them one at a time. Defensively, too, the position was a sound one. If Frémont attempted an advance on Staunton, Jackson would be on his flank; or if Shields somehow managed to cross the South Fork and marched toward a junction at Harrisonburg, he could then be served in the same fashion. Or if everything went wrong and disaster loomed, Jackson could make a quick getaway by moving southeast through Brown's Gap, as he had done the month before on his roundabout march to fight the Battle of McDowell. All this was much, but mainly he prized the offensive advantages of the position, which would put his army between Frémont and Shields, with a chance to strike at one or the other; or both.

Resuming the march that afternoon, he dispatched two mounted details to perform two separate but allied tasks: one to burn the bridge at Conrad's Store, the other to establish a signal station on the southernmost peak of Massanutton Mountain. The first would frustrate Shields when he attempted to turn west. The second would observe his reaction. Meanwhile, fed and rested, each man carrying two days' cooked rations and a fresh supply of ammunition on his person, the main body made good time up the turnpike. The rain had slacked to a drizzle, which meant that Frémont would soon be able to recommission his pontoon bridge, but for the present the Valley soldiers enjoyed an unmolested march. After stopping for the night just short of Harrisonburg, they entered that place next morning, June 5, and turned southeast toward Port Republic and the execution of Stonewall's design.

As soon as they left the turnpike they encountered what Shields had had to cope with all along: Napoleon's "fifth element," mud. Presently it became obvious that they were not much better at coping with the stuff than they had been on the nightmare march near here five weeks ago. By nightfall the head of the column was approaching North River, but the tail was no more than a mile from Harrisonburg, while the rest of the army was strung out along the six or seven intervening miles of boggy road. Jackson's wrath was mollified, however, by the return of the detail he had sent to Conrad's Store. They had won the race and done their job. From the signal station, high on Massanutton, came a message that Shields had halted two miles north of the burned bridge, which placed him fourteen muddy miles from Port Republic. Frémont was a good deal farther back. He had crossed North Fork above Mount Jackson, but the cavalry was hacking away at the head of his column, impeding his progress up the pike. Reassured, though still regretful, Stonewall called a halt. The rain had slacked to a mizzle by now; perhaps tomorrow the road would be firmer.

It was. Saturday, after an early start, Ewell's division stopped just beyond the hamlet of Cross Keys, six miles from Harrisonburg, to stand in Frémont's path when he came up. Jackson's plodded another three miles and went into position on the heights above the confluence of the rivers at Port Republic, overlooking the low-lying opposite bank of the South Fork, where the road wound southwest from Conrad's Store; this would be Shields' line of advance, and the guns on the heights would enfilade his column at close range. Neither of the Union forces was yet in sight, however, so the Valley soldiers had time for reading their mail, which had just been forwarded along with the latest newspapers. Elated by their victories, the editors had broken

out their blackest type. The Charleston *Mercury* called Stonewall "a true general" and predicted that he would soon be "leading his unconquerable battalions through Maryland into Pennsylvania." By way of contrast, gloomy reports from the northern press were reprinted in adjoining columns, and the Richmond *Whig* combined a mock protest with a backhand swipe at the Administration: "This man Jackson must be suppressed, or else he will change the humane and Christian policy of the war, and demoralize the Government." The men, of course, enjoyed this flood of praise. Jackson, too, had an ache for fame — "an ambition boundless as Cromwell's," Taylor called it, "and as merciless" — but he considered this a spiritual infirmity, unbecoming in a Christian and a deacon of the Presbyterian Church. Also, he was pained that the glory was not ascribed to its true source: God Almighty. Members of his staff observed that from this time on he gave up reading the papers — perhaps for the same reason he had given up drinking whiskey: "Why, sir, because I like the taste of [it], and when I discovered that to be the case I made up my mind to do without [it] altogether."

Included in the packet of mail was a congratulatory letter in the handwriting of the President. Congressman Boteler had delivered Jackson's request for more troops; Davis regretted that none were available. "Were it practicable to send you reinforcements it should be done, and your past success shows how surely you would, with an adequate force, destroy the wicked designs of the invader of our homes and assailer of our political rights." For the present, however, the Chief Executive added, "it is on your skill and daring that reliance is to be placed. The army under your command encourages us to hope for all which men can achieve."

Welcome though the praise was, the letter itself was disappointing. Without substantial reinforcements Jackson knew he could not hope to drive Shields and Frémont from the Valley as he had driven Banks. In fact, unless they came against him in his present strong position — which seemed unlikely, considering their caution; neither was yet in sight — he could scarcely even hope to give them a prod. So he began thinking of alternatives, including the possibility of taking his little army down to the Peninsula for a knockout combination against his old academy classmate, McClellan. Replying that same day (not to Davis, but to Johnston, who he thought was still in charge despite his wound) Stonewall wrote: "Should my command be required at Richmond I can be at Mechum's River Depot, on the Central Railroad, the second day's march, and part of the command can reach there the first day, as the distance is 25 miles. At present," he added, unhappy in the middle of what seemed to be a stalemate, "I do not see that I can do much more than rest my command and devote its time to drilling."

In this he was much mistaken. He could, and indeed would have to, do a great deal more — as he found out next morning in a most emphatic manner. Shields was a politician, having represented both Illinois and Minnesota in the U.S. Senate, but he was also a veteran of the Black Hawk War and a Mexico brigadier. A fifty-six-year-old native of Tyrone County, Ireland, he had proved his fighting ability by whipping Jackson at Kernstown back in March, and now that his opponent's fame had risen he was anxious to prove it again in the same way. From Conrad's Store, where he had paused to let his division catch its breath near the end of its wearing march up the narrow valley, he sent two brigades forward along the right bank of the South Fork to explore the situation at Port Republic. Stonewall was there already and might launch a sudden attack across the river, so Shields sent a message requesting cooperation from Frémont, whose guns he had been hearing intermittently for a week: "If he attempts to force a passage, as my force is not large there yet, I hope you will thunder down on his rear. . . . I think Jackson is caught this time."

He very nearly was: quite literally. The Valley chieftain had spent the night at Port Republic, saddened by the death of his cavalry commander, Brigadier General Turner Ashby, who had fallen that afternoon in a skirmish just this side of Harrisonburg. Ashby had had his faults, the main one being an inability to keep his troopers on the job when there was loot or applejack within reach, but he had established a reputation for personal bravery that was never outdone by any man in either army. In death the legend was complete; "Charge, men! For God's sake, charge!" he cried as he took the bullet that killed him; now only the glory remained. "As a partisan officer I never knew his superior," Jackson declared. Next morning, June 8, when the chief of staff — a theologian who, conditions permitting, did double duty by preaching Sunday sermons in the camps — inquired if there would be any military operations today, Stonewall told him there would not; "You know I always try to keep the Sabbath if the enemy will let me."

The men put no stock in this at all. Convinced by now that Jackson thought he enjoyed an advantage when fighting on the Lord's day, they believed that he did so every time he got the chance. Statistics seemed to bear them out, and presently this statistical trend was strengthened. As the minister-major went back into the house to compose his sermon and the rest of the staff prepared to ride out for an inspection of the camp on the northward ridge, a rattle of musketry shattered the Sunday-morning stillness and a cavalryman came galloping with alarming news. The Federals had forded South River, scattering the pickets, and were entering the town! "Go back and fight them," Jackson snapped. He mounted and rode hard for the North River bridge, clattering across the long wooden structure just in time. A colonel and a lieutenant who brought up the rear were cut off and captured.

Gaining the heights, which overlooked the town, Jackson ordered his batteries to open fire on the bluecoats in the streets below, and sent two brigades of infantry to clear them out at the point of the bayonet. It was smartly done; the Federals fell back in haste, abandoning a fieldpiece and the prisoners they had taken. Stonewall, peering down from the ridge as his men advanced across the bridge and through the smoke that hung about the houses, dropped the reins on his horse's neck and lifted both hands above his head, palms outward. When the men looked up and saw him stark against the sky, invoking the blessing of the God of battle, they cheered with all their might. The roar of it reached him there on the heights, and the cannoneers swelled the chorus.

As the cheering subsided, the men on the ridge became aware of a new sound: the rumble and boom of cannon, swelling from the direction of Cross Keys. It was Frémont, responding to Shields' request that he "thunder down." Going forward, however, he struck not Jackson's rear but Ewell's front. The first contact, after a preliminary bombardment, was on the Confederate right, where Ewell had posted a Virginia brigade along a low ridge overlooking some fields of early grain. Frémont came on with unaccustomed vigor, a regiment of New Yorkers in the lead, their boots crunching the young stalks of buckwheat. As they started up the slope there was a sudden crash of gunfire from the crest and the air was full of bullets. A second volley thinned the ranks of the survivors as they tried to re-form their shattered line. They fell back, what was left of them. Frémont, reverting to the form he had shown at Strasburg, settled down to long-range fighting with his artillery, which was skillfully handled. Out in the buckwheat the wounded New Yorkers lay under this fire, crying for water. Their cries decreased as the day wore on and Frémont continued his cannonade.

In essence that was all there was to the Battle of Cross Keys.

Ewell, fretting because he could not get the Pathfinder to make another attack, at last pushed forward for more than a mile until he occupied the ground from which the Federals had advanced that morning. There he stopped, having been warned not to put too much space between the two wings of the army. Frémont, with 10,500 infantry effectives, faded back before Ewell's 5000. It was finished. The North had lost 684 men, nearly half of them lying dead of their wounds in the grainfields; the South had lost 288, only 41 of them killed. Jackson's trust in Old Bald Head was confirmed. Except for a quick ride out, to see how things were going, he had let Ewell fight his own battle while he himself remained on the heights above Port Republic. Asked if he did not think there was some danger that Shields would advance to help Frémont, whose guns were within earshot, Stonewall gestured toward his batteries and said grimly: "No, sir; no; he cannot do it! I should tear him to pieces." As he stood there, listening to the sound of Ewell's battle, intoxicated as if by music, he remarked to his ministerial chief of staff: "Major, wouldn't it be a blessed thing if God would give us a glorious victory today?" One who overheard him said that as he spoke he wore the expression "of a child hoping to receive some favor."

But, childlike, having received it, he was by no means satisfied. He wanted more. That night he issued orders for Ewell to leave a reinforced brigade in front of Frémont and march the rest of his division through Port Republic to join the other wing for a combined assault on the Union troops beyond the river. Once Shields was properly broken up, they could both return and fall on Frémont, completing the destruction Ewell had begun today.

The march began at earliest dawn of what was to be a lovely sun-drenched day. Jackson's division came down off the heights, crossed the North River bridge, filed through the town, and forded South River. The Stonewall Brigade was in the lead, under thirty-three-year-old Brigadier General Charles S. Winder, a tall, wavy-haired Maryland West Pointer who, by strict discipline and a resolute bearing under fire, had gained the respect of his men, despite their resentment at losing Garnett. For an hour the advance up the right bank of the South Fork continued. Then at 7 o'clock word came back that Federal pickets had been encountered. Jackson studied the situation briefly, then told Winder to go ahead and drive them. He did not know the enemy strength, but he believed more would be gained by a sudden assault than by a detailed reconnaissance of the position. Besides, Ewell would soon be coming up, and Stonewall wanted to get the thing over with quickly, so as to return and deal with Frémont before the Pathfinder, discovering the weakness of the force to his front, pushed it back into Port Republic and burned the bridge.

Winder went forward, driving hard, but entered a maelstrom of bullets and shells that stopped the charge in its tracks. Once more, as at Kernstown against these same men, Jackson's old brigade had to pay in blood for his rashness. What was worse, by way of indignity — though he did not know it — there were only two small brigades before him, fewer than 3000 soldiers. But they made up in fury and grit for what they lacked in numbers. Their commander, Brigadier General E. B. Tyler, had placed six of his sixteen guns in a lofty charcoal clearing on his left. While the blue infantry held in front, these guns delivered a rapid and accurate fire, enfilading the stalled ranks of the attackers. Winder sent two regiments to flank and charge the battery, but they were met by volleys of grape and flung back with heavy losses. All this time the Stonewall Brigade was being decimated, its ranks plowed by shells from the guns in the coaling.

Jackson was dismayed, seeing his hopes dissolve in the boil and swirl of gunsmoke. Frémont by now must have attacked in response to the uproar, and Ewell was nowhere in sight. It seemed likely that McDowell might be coming up with the rest of his 20,000 troops: in which case there was nothing to do but concentrate everything against him for a decisive battle right here, or else retreat and put a sorry ending to the month-long Valley campaign. Stonewall chose the former course, sending couriers to hasten Ewell's march and inform the holding force at Cross Keys to fall back through Port Republic, burning the North River bridge behind them so that Frémont, at least, would be kept out of the action. Meanwhile, Winder must hang on. His men were wavering, almost out of ammunition, but he held them there, perhaps remembering what had happened to his predecessor after falling back from a similar predicament.

Presently the unaccustomed frown of fortune changed suddenly to a smile. Taylor appeared, riding at the head of his Louisianians; he had marched toward the sound of firing. Jackson greeted him with suppressed emotion, saying calmly: "Delightful excitement." Taylor looked at the hard-pressed front, then off to the right, where smoke was boiling up from the hilltop clearing. If those guns were not silenced soon, he said, the army "might have an indigestion of such fun." Stonewall agreed, and gave him the job.

While Taylor was setting out to perform it, the Valley commander joined Winder, whose men were dropping fast along the front. From his horseback perch Jackson saw enemy skirmishers beginning to creep forward. Quickly he ordered a charge, hoping to shock them into caution until Taylor reached their flank. The Stonewall Brigade gave him what he asked for. Winder's troops advanced, the skirmishers recoiling before them, and took up a new position behind a snake-rail fence. Here they were even worse exposed to the shells that tore along their line. Wavering, they began to leak men to the rear. A gap appeared. Rapidly it widened. Soon the brigade was in full retreat — past

Winder, past Jackson, past whatever tried to stand in their way or slow them down. It was a rout worse than Kernstown.

But fortune's smile was steady. The men of Ewell's brigade, arriving on the left soon after Taylor's men filed off to the right, replaced Winder's and blocked a Federal advance. As they did so, a terrific clatter erupted at the far end of the line. It was Taylor; he had come up through a tangle of laurel and rhododendron. Three charges he made against double-shotted guns, and the third charge took them, though the cannoneers fought hard to the last, swinging rammer-staffs against bayoneted rifles. Then, as the Union commander attempted a left wheel, intending to bring his whole force against Taylor, Ewell's third brigade arrived in time to go forward with the second. Outnumbered three to one, fighting now with both flanks in the air and their strongest battery turned against them, the Federals fell back, firing erratically as they went. For the Confederates it was as if all the pieces of a gigantic jigsaw puzzle had fallen suddenly into place of their own accord. Eyes aglow, Stonewall touched Ewell's arm and pointed: "He who does not see the hand of God in this is *blind*, sir. Blind!"

It was now 11 o'clock; a good eight hours of daylight remained for pursuit. Pursue was easier said than done, however. Tyler's men withdrew in good order, covering the retreat with their ten remaining guns. Jackson had to content himself with gleaning 800 muskets from the field while the cavalry pressed the retreating column, picking up prisoners as they went. Soon the ambulances were at work. When all the wounded Confederates had been gathered, the aid men gave their attention to the Federals. However, this show of mercy was interrupted by Frémont. Free at last to maneuver, he put his guns in position on the heights across the river and, now that the battle was over, began to shell the field. Jackson, much incensed, ordered the ambulances back. Federal casualties for the day were 1018, most of them inflicted during the retreat, including 558 prisoners; Stonewall's were in excess of 800, the heaviest he had suffered.

The battle was over, and with it the campaign. Jackson put his army in motion for Brown's Gap before sundown, following the prisoners and the train, which had been sent ahead that morning. By daylight he was astride the gap, high up the Blue Ridge, well protected against attack from either direction and within a day's march of the railroad leading down to Richmond, which the past month's fighting in the Valley had done so much to save. He intended to observe Shields and Frémont from here, but that turned out to be impossible: Lincoln ordered them withdrawn that same day. Frémont was glad to go — he had "expended [his troops'] last effort in reaching Port Republic," he reported — but not Shields, who said flatly: "I never obeyed an order with such reluctance." Jackson came down off the mountain, sent his cavalry ahead to pick up 200 sick and 200 rifles Frémont abandoned at

Harrisonburg, and recrossed South River, making camp between that stream and Middle River. There was time now for rest, as well as for looking back on what had been accomplished.

"God has been our shield, and to His name be all the glory," he wrote his wife. Not that he had not coöperated. To one of his officers he confided that there were two rules to be applied in securing the fruits which the Lord's favor made available: "Always mystify, mislead, and surprise the enemy, if possible. And when you strike and overcome him, never let up in the pursuit so long as your men have strength to follow; for an army routed, if hotly pursued, becomes panic-stricken, and can then be destroyed by half their number. The other rule is, never fight against heavy odds if by any possible maneuvering you can hurl your own force on only a part, and that the weakest part, of your enemy and crush it. Such tactics will win every time, and a small army may thus destroy a large one in detail, and repeated victory will make it invincible."

Application of these strategic principles, plus of course the blessing of Providence — particularly in the form of such meteorological phenomena as cloudbursts and hailstones large as hen-eggs — had enabled Stonewall, with 17,000 troops, to frustrate the plans of 60,000 Federals whose generals were assigned the exclusive task of accomplishing his destruction. Four pitched battles he had fought, six formal skirmishes, and any number of minor actions. All had been victories, and in all but one of the battles he had outnumbered the enemy in the field, anywhere from two- to seventeen-to-one. The exception was Cross Keys, where his opponent showed so little fight that there was afterwards debate as to whether it should be called a battle or a skirmish. Mostly this had been done by rapid marching. Since March 22, the eve of Kernstown, his troops had covered 646 miles of road in forty-eight marching days. The rewards had been enormous: 3500 prisoners, 10,000 badly needed muskets, nine rifled guns, and quartermaster stores of incalculable value. All these were things he could hold and look at, so to speak. An even larger reward was the knowledge that he had played on the hopes and fears of Lincoln with such effect that 38,000 men — doubtless a first relay, soon to have been followed by others — were kept from joining McClellan in front of Richmond. Instead, the greater part of them were shunted out to the Valley, where, fulfilling their commander's prediction, they "gained nothing" and "lost much."

Beyond these tangibles and intangibles lay a further gain, difficult to assess, which in time might prove to be the most valuable of all. This was the campaign's effect on morale, North and South. Federals and Confederates were about equally fagged when the fighting was over, but there was more to the story than that. There was such a thing as a tradition of victory. There was also such a thing as a tradition of defeat. One provoked an inner elation, *esprit de corps,* the other an inner weariness. Banks, Frémont, and Shields had all three had their commands broken up in varying degrees, and the effect in some cases was long-lasting. The troops Stonewall had defeated at McDowell were known thereafter, by friend and foe, as "Milroy's weary boys," and he had planted in the breasts of Blenker's Germans the seeds of a later disaster. Conversely, "repeated victory" — as Jackson phrased it — had begun to give his own men the feeling of invincibility. Coming as it did, after a long period of discouragement and retreat, it gave a fierceness to their pride in themselves and in their general. He marched their legs off, drove them to and past exhaustion, and showed nothing but contempt for the man who staggered. When they reached the field of battle, spitting cotton and stumbling with fatigue, he flung them into the uproar without pausing to count his losses until he had used up every chance for gain. When it was over and they had won, he gave the credit to God. All they got in return for their sweat and blood was victory. It was enough. Their affection for him, based mainly on amusement at his milder eccentricities, ripened quickly into something that very closely resembled love. Wherever he rode now he was cheered. "Let's make him take his hat off," they would say when they saw him coming. Hungry as they often were, dependent on whatever game they could catch to supplement their rations, they always had the time and energy to cheer him. Hearing a hullabaloo on the far side of camp, they laughed and said to one another: "It's Old Jack, or a rabbit."

✕ 3 ✕

Confederate authorities at the seat of government did what they could to keep the news of Johnston's wound and the subsequent change of commanders out of the papers. Enterprising newsboys sometimes wandered out beyond the fortifications, profitably hawking their journals in the Union camps, and the authorities feared that the enemy might find comfort and encouragement in the news. They were right. "I prefer Lee to Johnston," McClellan declared when he heard of the shift — meaning that he preferred him as an opponent. "The former is too cautious and weak under grave responsibility. Personally brave and energetic to a fault, he yet is wanting in moral firmness when pressed by heavy responsibility, and is likely to be timid and irresolute in action."

He wrote this under the influence of a new surge of confidence and elation. At the time of Fair Oaks, in addition to the depression he felt at hearing that McDowell was being withheld, he had been confined to bed with neuralgia and a recurrent attack of malaria, contracted long ago in Mexico; but he was feeling much better now. Pride in the reports of his army's conduct in that battle — so fierce that eight out of the nine general officers in Keyes' corps had been wounded or had had their horses shot from under them — restored his health and sent his spirits soaring: as was shown in the congratulatory address he issued a few days later. "Soldiers of the Army of the Potomac!" it began. "I have fulfilled at least a part of my promise to you. You are now face to face with the rebels, who are held at bay in front of their capital. The final and decisive battle is at hand. Unless you belie your past history, the result cannot be for a moment doubtful. . . . Soldiers!" it ended. "I will be with you in this battle and share its dangers with you. Our confidence in each other is now founded on the past. Let us strike a blow which is to restore peace and union to this distracted land. Upon your valor, discipline and mutual confidence the result depends."

The men enjoyed the sound of this, the reference to their valor and the notion that the war was being fought for peace. Some of them had wondered; now they knew. It was being fought to get back home. That knowledge was a gain, and there were others. Having done well in one big battle, they felt they would do better in the next one. They could laugh now at things that had seemed by no means humorous at the time: for instance, the boy going up to the firing line with the fixed stare of a sleepwalker, pale as moonlight, moaning "Oh Lord, dear good Lord," over and over as he went. They had a familiarity with the mechanics of death in battle. Coming up the Peninsula they had passed a rebel graveyard with a sign tacked over the gate: "Come along, Yank. There's room outside to bury you." Since then, many of them had served on burial details, fulfilling the implication, and undertakers were doing a rush business with both the quick and the dead, embalming the latter and accepting advance payments from the former, in return for a guarantee of salvation from a nameless grave in this slough they called the Chicken Hominy. The going price was $20 for a private and up to $100 for an officer, depending on his rank.

Their main consolation was McClellan. He gave the whole thing meaning and lent a glitter to the drabness of their camps. They cheered him as he rode among them; they took their note of confidence from him. Presently, after fretful news from the Shenandoah Valley, they saw his confidence increase. He had just been informed that Lincoln had called off the goose-chase after Jackson and was bringing McDowell back to Fredericksburg, with orders to resume the advance on Richmond as soon as his men recovered from their exertions. Best of all, as a cause for immediate rejoicing, the 9500-man division of Brigadier General George A. McCall — left on the Rappahannock while the rest of the First Corps was crossing the Blue Ridge — had been ordered to join McClellan at once, moving by water to assure the greatest speed. Their transports began to arrive at White House June 11, five days after the march order was issued. As these reinforcements came ashore a dispatch arrived from Stanton: "Be assured, General, that there has never been a moment when my desire has been otherwise than to aid you with my whole heart, mind and strength since the hour we first met. . . . You have never had and never can have anyone more truly your friend or more anxious to support you."

Next day army headquarters moved to the south bank of the Chickahominy, where three of the five corps now were: Keyes on the left at White Oak Swamp, Heintzelman covering the Williamsburg road in the center, and Sumner on the right, astride the railroad. Porter and Franklin were still on the north bank, the former advanced to Mechanicsville, the latter in support. When McCall arrived he would be assigned to Porter, whose strength would be 27,500 men, and Franklin would join the main body, taking position between Sumner and the river. The army then would present an unbroken front, anchored firmly on the left and extending a strong right arm to meet McDowell, who had wired on June 8: "McCall goes in advance by water. I will be with you in ten days with the remainder by land from Fredericksburg."

McClellan had plenty to do while he waited. The rains had returned with a vengeance, taking the bridges out again, flooding the bottoms, and sweeping away the corduroy approaches. "The whole face of the country is a perfect bog," he informed Washington. "The men are working night and day, up to their waists in water." Lincoln and Stanton kept wanting to know when he would be ready to attack, and he kept stalling them off with a series of loop-holed replies. A week after Fair Oaks he told them: "I shall be in perfect readiness to move forward and take Richmond the moment McCall reaches here and the ground will admit the passage of artillery." Six days later, with McCall on hand and four corps consolidated south of the Chickahominy, he declared: "I shall attack as soon as the weather and the ground will permit." June 18 the rain slacked and he wired: "After tomorrow we shall fight the rebel army as soon as Providence will permit."

It was a tantalizing progression of near-commitments and evasions: first McCall, then the weather, and finally Providence itself: Lincoln and Stanton scarcely knew what to think. McClellan knew, though. He had read rumors that the powers in Washington were engaged in a frenzy of backbiting over the recent fiasco in the Valley. "Alas! poor country that should have such leaders," he groaned, adding: "When I see such insane folly behind me I feel that the final salvation of the country demands the utmost prudence on my part, and that I must not run the slightest risk of disaster, for if anything happened to this army our cause would be lost." He saw his way to victory. According to the Pinkertons, the rebels had the advantage of numbers, but he had the advantage of superior training and equipment. Therefore he would make the contest a siege. Employing "the utmost prudence" to avoid "the slightest risk," he had evolved a formula for victory, ponderous but sure. He kept it from Lincoln and Stanton, who would neither approve nor understand, but he told it gladly to his wife, who would do both: "I will push them in upon Richmond and behind their works. Then I will bring up my heavy guns, shell the city, and carry it by assault."

Whether Lee was "cautious . . . weak . . . wanting in moral firmness . . . timid and irresolute" remained to be seen, but part at least of McClellan's judgment of his opponent had already been confirmed. He was "energetic" — and southern soldiers agreed with the northern commander that it was "to a fault." Reverting to his former role as King of Spades, he had them digging as they had never dug before. Their reaction was the one he had encountered in the Carolinas: that intrenchments were cowardly affairs, and that shoveling dirt wasn't fit work for a white man. Lee's reply was that hard work was "the very means by which McClellan has [been] and is advancing. Why should we leave to him the whole advantage of labor? . . . There is nothing so military as labor, and nothing so important to an army as to save the lives of its soldiers." A third complaint, that digging would never drive the Yankees away from the gates of Richmond, he left for time to answer. Meanwhile there were those who, remembering his earnest statement back in May — "Richmond must not be given up; it shall not be given up!" — considered that he might be saving his soldiers' lives for a quite different purpose, entirely aside from the sheer humanity of the thing.

He saw the problem posed for him by his fellow engineer: "McClellan will make this a battle of posts. He will take position from position under cover of his heavy guns and we cannot get at him." What Lee needed in the face of this was time, and he got it. The first ten days of June were solid rain. "You have seen nothing like the roads on the Chicky bottom," he reported thankfully. McClellan's big guns were immobilized unless he brought them forward on the York River Railroad, and Lee moved quickly to block this route by mounting a long-range 32-pounder on a railway truck and running it eastward to outrange the swamp-bound Federal ordnance. This was the birth of the railroad gun, fathered by necessity and Lee.

The men could appreciate this kind of thing, its benefit being immediately apparent. They could appreciate, too, the new administrative efficiency which brought them better rations and an equitable distribution of the clothes and shoes it prised from quartermaster warehouses. There was a rapid improvement of their appearance and, in consequence, their tone. Lee himself was frequently among them, riding the lines to inspect the progress of their work on the intrenchments. Tall, handsome, robust, much younger-looking up close than from a distance, he had a cheerful dignity and could praise them without seeming to court their favor. They began to look forward to his visits, and even take pride in the shovel work they had performed so unwillingly up to now. The change for the better was there for every-one to see, including their old commander, convalescent in Richmond. "No, sir," Johnston said manfully when a friend remarked that his wound was a calamity for the South. "The shot that struck me down is the very best that has been fired for the southern cause yet. For I possess in no degree the confidence of our government, and now they have in my place one who does possess it, and who can accomplish what I never could have done: the concentration of our armies for the defense of the capital of the Confederacy."

This in fact was a main key to Lee's success in the course of his first weeks as head of the army in Virginia. He knew how to get along with Davis. Unlike Johnston, who had kept his intentions from the President as assiduously as if the two had been engaged as opponents in high-stakes poker, Lee sought his advice and kept him informed from day to day, even from hour to hour. One of the first letters he sent from the field was to Davis, describing certain administrative difficulties in one of the commands. "I thought you ought to know it," he wrote. "Our position requires that you should know everything and you must excuse my troubling you." Davis fairly basked in the unfamiliar warmth — and gave, as always, loyalty for loyalty received. Knowing him well, Lee knew that this support would never be revoked. Whatever lay be-fore him, down the months and years, he knew that he would never have to look back over his shoulder as he went. Nor would he, like his opponent, have to step cautiously in anticipation of a fall from having the rug jerked from under him by wires leading back to his capital.

What lay before him now was McClellan, whose "battle of posts" would begin as soon as the weather turned Union and dried the roads. Such a battle could have only one outcome, the odds being what they were. As Lee saw it, he had but two choices: to retreat, abandoning Richmond, or to strike before his opponent got rolling. The former course had possibilities. He could fall back to the mountains, he said, "and if my soldiers will stand by me I will fight those people for years to come." However, it was the latter course he chose. At first he con-sidered a repetition of Johnston's tactics, an attack on the Federal left, but he soon rejected the notion of making a frontal assault against an intrenched and superior enemy who, even if defeated, could retreat in safety down the Peninsula, much as Johnston had retreated up it. The flank beyond the Chickahominy was weaker and more exposed to attack, and once it was crushed or brushed aside, the way would be open for seizure of McClellan's base at White House. Cut off from his food and munitions, the Union commander would be obliged to come out of his intrenchments and fight the Confederates on ground of their choice, astride his lines of supply and communication.

When Lee submitted the plan for presidential approval, **Davis** raised a question. If McClellan behaved like an engineer, giving all his concern to his line of supply, the thing might work; but what if he assaulted the weakened line in front of Richmond while Lee was mounting the flank attack with troops stripped from the capital defenses? Would that not mean the fall of the city? Lee bridled at the reference to engineers, his own branch of the service as well as McClellan's, but said that he did not believe his opponent would attempt such a desperate venture. Besides, that was why he had put the men to digging: to enable a thin line to withstand an assault by superior numbers. It would not have to be for long. "If you will hold as long as you can at the intrenchments, and then fall back on the detached works around the city, I will be on the enemy's heels before he gets here." So he said, and Davis, after consideration, agreed that the long odds required long chances. He approved the plan of attack.

The first problem, once the plan had been approved, was the securing of reinforcements. No matter how ingenious the tactics, 61,000 Confederates could not hope to drive more than 100,000 Federals from a position they had been strengthening ever since their repulse of the full-scale assault two weeks before. As a problem it was thorny. South Carolina could spare no men at all, Charleston being menaced by an amphibious force assembling at Hilton Head; but Burnside seemed to be resting on his New Bern laurels, so that the rest of Holmes' division could be brought from North Carolina, adding 6500 bayonets to the ranks. Georgia could furnish a single brigade; Lee sent it to Jackson. "We must aid a gallant man if we perish," he said, having already weakened his army for this purpose. Besides, it was in the nature of a loan. Stonewall was to use the troops offensively if the opportunity arose, discouraging the Washington authorities from sending reinforcements to the Peninsula from the Valley or the line of the Rappahannock. Then, when everything was ready for the leap at McClellan, he was to leave his cavalry and his least effective infantry units in their present location, and take the cars for Richmond, adding 18,500 veterans to the column of assault.

This would bring Lee's total strength to 86,000: still about 20,-000 short of McClellan's. Total strengths were not as important, however, as critical strengths at the point of vital contact — and that was where Lee proposed to secure the advantage. He would hold the Richmond intrenchments with the combined commands of Magruder, Huger, and Holmes, while those of Longstreet, the two Hills, and Jackson struck the isolated enemy corps on the north bank of the Chickahominy. In round figures, 30,000 men would be facing 75,000 to the east, while 55,000 assaulted 30,000 to the north; or, more roughly speaking, one third of Lee's army would resist three fourths of McClellan's, while the remaining two thirds attacked the remaining one fourth. The risk was great, as Davis said, but not so great as the possibilities for gain. As the

Federal main body, its right wing crushed, fell back to recover or protect its seized or threatened base, the Confederates would catch it in motion and destroy it, flank and rear. Richmond would be delivered.

No matter how devoutly this consummation was to be wished, a great deal remained to be done before it could begin to be accomplished. Jackson's approach march from the railroad would be along the ridge between the Chickahominy River and Totopotomoy Creek, an affluent of the Pamunkey. Lee knew that McClellan had withdrawn Porter's troops from Hanover Courthouse soon after the junction with McDowell was suspended, but he did not know the present location of Porter's right or the condition of the roads in that direction. Both of these necessary pieces of information could be gathered, along with possibly much else, by a reconnaissance in force. That meant cavalry, and cavalry meant Jeb Stuart. Accordingly, on June 10, Lee sent for him and told him what he wanted.

Stuart was delighted. A brigadier at twenty-nine, square-built, of average height, with china-blue eyes, a bushy cinnamon beard, and flamboyant clothes — thigh-high boots, yellow sash, elbow-length gauntlets, red-lined cape, soft hat with the brim pinned up on one side by a gold star supporting a foot-long ostrich plume — he had had no chance for individual distinction since the charge that scattered the Fire Zouaves at Manassas. He had a thirst for such exploits, both for his own sake and his troopers', whose training he was conducting in accordance with a credo: "If we oppose force to force we cannot win, for their resources are greater than ours. We must substitute *esprit* for numbers. Therefore I strive to inculcate in my men the spirit of the chase." That partly explained the gaudy fox-hunt clothes, and it also explained what he proposed as soon as Lee had finished speaking. Once he was in McClellan's rear, he said, it might be practicable to ride all the way around him.

Lee might have expected something of the sort, for Stuart had been an industrious collector of demerits as an adventurous cadet at the Point while his fellow Virginian was superintendent. At any rate, in the written instructions sent next day while Jeb was happily selecting and assembling 1200 troopers for the ride, the army commander warned him explicitly against rashness: "You will return as soon as the object of your expedition is accomplished, and you must bear constantly in mind, while endeavoring to execute the general purpose of your mission, not to hazard unnecessarily your command or to attempt what your judgment may not approve; but be content to accomplish all the good you can, without feeling it necessary to obtain all that might be desired." These were sobering words, but Stuart was pleased to note that the general called the proposed affair an "expedition," not merely a scout or a raid.

At 2 a.m. on the 12th he passed the word to his unit commanders standing by: "Gentlemen, in ten minutes every man must be in the saddle." Within that time they set out, riding north out of Richmond as if bound for the Shenandoah Valley. Only Stuart, who rode at the head of the column, knew their true destination. His high spirits were heightened by the knowledge that his opposite number, commanding McClellan's cavalry, was Brigadier General Philip St George Cooke, his wife's father, an old-line soldier who, to his son-in-law's discomfort and chagrin, had stayed with the old flag. "He will regret it but once," Jeb said, "and that will be continuously."

The three-day wait, following Stuart's disappearance into the darkness, was a time of strain for Lee and the Army of Northern Virginia. For one thing, the weather turned Union; the roads were drying fast under the influence of a hot spell. For another, there was information that McClellan was receiving reinforcements; McCall's division had come up the York in transports, adding its strength to the preponderance of numbers already enjoyed by the blue army in front of Richmond. Taken together, these two factors indicated that the "battle of posts" was about to begin before Lee could put his own plan into execution. The strain was not considerably relieved by the arrival of a courier, late on the 14th, with the first news from Stuart since he left. Far in the Federal rear, after wrecking a wagon train and capturing more than 300 men and horses, he had decided that it would be safer to continue on his way instead of turning back to cut a path through the disrupted forces gathering in his rear. Accordingly, he had pushed on eastward, then veered south to complete his circuit of the enemy army. But when he reached the Chickahominy, thirty-odd miles below the capital, he found the bridges out and the water too swift and deep for fording. That had been his plight when the courier left him: a swollen river to his front and swarms of hornet-mad Federal horsemen converging on his rear. However, he was confident he would get out all right, he said, if Lee would only make a diversion on the Charles City road to distract the bluecoats while he continued his search for an escape route.

Lee was not given to swearing, or else he would have done so now. At any rate, the day was too far gone for the diversion Stuart requested, and next morning, before the order could be issued, Jeb himself came jingling up to headquarters. His fine clothes were bedraggled and the face above the cinnamon beard showed the effects of two nights in the saddle without sleep, but he was jubilant over his exploit, which he knew was about to be hailed and bewailed in southern and northern papers. Improvising a bridge, he had crossed the Chickahominy with his entire command, guns and all, then ridden up the north bank of the James to report to Lee in person. At a cost of one man, lost in a skirmish two days back, he had brought out 170 prisoners, along with 300 horses and mules, and added considerably to whatever regret his father-in-law had been feeling up to now. Beyond all this, he had also brought out the information Lee had sent him after. McClellan's base was still at White House, and there was no indication that he intended to change it. The roads behind the Federal lines, which the enemy would have to use in bringing his big guns forward, were in even worse shape than those in the Confederate front. And, finally, Porter's right did not extend to the ridge between the Chickahominy and Totopotomoy Creek. In fact, that whole flank was practically "in the air," open to Jackson's turning movement along the ridge.

The moment was at hand. After feeling out the enemy lines that afternoon to determine whether Stuart's ride around McClellan had alarmed the northern commander into weakening his front in order to reinforce his flank beyond the river — it had not — Lee wrote to Jackson next morning, June 16. Five days ago, congratulating Stonewall for the crowning double victory at Cross Keys and Port Republic, he had sent him a warning order, alerting him for the march toward Richmond. Now the instructions to move were made explicit, though in language that was courteous to the point of being deferential: "The present ... seems to be favorable for a junction of your army with this. If you agree with me, the sooner you can make arrangements to do so the better. In moving your troops you can let it be understood that it was to pursue the enemy in your front. Dispose those to hold the Valley so as to deceive the enemy, keeping your cavalry well in their front, and at the proper time suddenly descending upon the Pamunkey.... I should like to have the advantage of your views and to be able to confer with you. Will meet you at some point on your approach to the Chickahominy."

With the date of the attack dependent on Jackson's rate of march, there was little for the southern commander to do now except wait, perfecting the details of the north-bank convergence, and hope that his opponent would remain astride the river with his right flank in the air. The strain of waiting was relieved by good news of a battle fought in South Carolina on the day Lee summoned Stonewall from the Valley. The Federals had mounted their offensive against Charleston, landing 6500 troops on James Island, but were met and repulsed at Secessionville by Shanks Evans with less than half as many men. Inflicting 683 casualties at a cost of 204, Evans increased the reputation he had won above the stone bridge at Manassas and on the wooded plateau above Ball's Bluff and was proclaimed the savior of Charleston. Though this minor action scarcely balanced the recent loss of Fort Pillow and Memphis, or the evacuation of Cumberland Gap two days later, it made a welcome addition to the little string of victories won along the twin forks of the Shenandoah River. Lee was encouraged to hope that the tide was turning, at least in the East, and that the blue host in front of Richmond might soon be caught in the undertow and swept away or drowned. "Our enemy is quietly working within his lines, and collecting additional forces to drive us from our capital," he wrote in a private letter June 22, three weeks after taking command. "I hope we shall be able yet to disappoint him, and drive him back to his own country."

Next afternoon the possibility of such a deliverance was considerably enhanced by the arrival of a dusty horseman who came riding out the Nine Mile road to army headquarters. It was Jackson. Stiff from fourteen hours in the saddle, having covered fifty-two miles of road on relays of commandeered horses, he presently was closeted with Lee and the other three division commanders who would share with him the work of destruction across the river. Lee spread a crude map and explained the plan as he had worked it out.

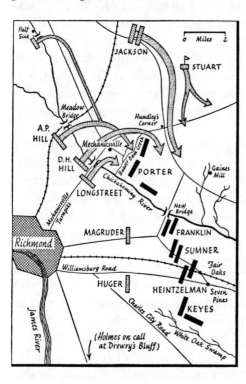

Stonewall, coming down from the north with Stuart's troopers guarding his left, was to clear the head of Beaver Dam Creek, outflanking Porter and forcing him to evacuate his main line of resistance, dug in along the east bank of the stream. That way, there would be no fighting until after the enemy had been flushed from his intrenchments, and by then the other three attack divisions would be on hand, having crossed the Chickahominy as soon as they learned that Jackson was within range. The crossing was to be accomplished in sequence. A. P. Hill would post a brigade at Half Sink, four miles upstream from his position at Meadow Bridge.

Informed of Jackson's approach, this brigade would cross to the left bank and move down it, driving Porter's outposts eastward until they uncovered Meadow Bridge, which Hill would cross to advance on Mechanicsville. This in turn would uncover the turnpike bridge, permitting a crossing by D. H. Hill and Longstreet at that point and in that order. The former would move past his namesake's rear and swing wide around Beaver Dam Creek in support of Jackson. The latter would form on A. P. Hill's right for the advance through Porter's abandoned intrenchments. All four commands would then be in line — in echelon, from left to right: Jackson, D. H. Hill, A. P. Hill, and Longstreet — for the sweep down the left bank of the Chickahominy. Once they cleared New

Bridge, four miles below Mechanicsville, they would be in touch with
Magruder and Huger, who would have been maneuvering Prince-John-
style all this time to discourage an attack on their thin line by the Federal
main body in their front. With contact reëstablished between the two
Confederate wings, the danger of such an attack would have passed; as
Lee said, they would "be on the enemy's heels" in case he tried it. The
advance beyond the river would continue, slashing McClellan's communications and coming between him and his base of supplies at White
House.

There were objections. Harvey Hill had expressed the opinion
that an attack on the Federal left would be more rewarding; McClellan
might respond to the assault on his right by changing his base to the
James, beyond reach of the attackers. Lee had pointed out, however,
that this would involve the army in the bogs of White Oak Swamp and
rob it of the mobility which was its principal asset. Besides, Stuart's
reconnaissance had shown that the Union base was still at White House,
and Lee did not believe the Federals would attempt to make the shift
while under attack. Longstreet, too, had indicated what he thought were
disadvantages, the main one being the great natural strength of Porter's
position along Beaver Dam Creek. However, this objection would be
nullified by Jackson, whose approach would maneuver Porter out of his
intrenchments by menacing his rear, and if he fell back to another creek-
bank stronghold — there were several such in his rear, at more or less
regular intervals along the north bank of the Chickahominy — the same
tactics could be applied, with the same result. Thus were Hill and Longstreet answered. Stonewall made no comment, being a stranger to the
scene, and A. P. Hill, the junior officer present, held his tongue. After
the brief discussion, Lee retired to give the quartet of generals a chance
to talk his plan over among themselves.

They were young men, all four of them, though they disguised
the fact with beards. Longstreet was the oldest, forty-one, A. P. Hill
the youngest, thirty-seven; D. H. Hill was forty, Jackson thirty-
eight; they had been at West Point together, twenty years ago. Longstreet spoke first, asking Jackson to set the date for the attack, since his
was the only command not on the scene. The 25th, Jackson replied without hesitation. Longstreet demurred, advising him to take an extra day
to allow for poor roads and possible enemy interference. All right, Jackson said, the 26th. Presently Lee returned and approved their decision.
Today was Monday; the attack would be made on Thursday, at the
earliest possible hour. He would send them written orders tomorrow.

The council broke up about nightfall. Jackson had spent most of
the previous night in the saddle, but he would take no rest until he rejoined his men on the march. Mounting, he rode through the darkness,
accompanied as before by a single aide, whom he had instructed to call
him Colonel as a precaution against being recognized before he got his

army into position to come booming down along McClellan's flank.

While Stonewall clattered north along unfamiliar roads to rejoin the Valley soldiers moving to meet him, McClellan sat alone in his tent, winding up a long day's work by writing to his wife. For various reasons, some definite, some vague, but all disturbing, he felt uneasy. Intelligence reports showed that his army was badly outnumbered, and Stuart's circumferential raid had not only afforded hostile journalists much amusement at the Young Napoleon's expense, it had also emphasized the danger to his extended flank and to his main supply base, both of which lay on the far side of what he still called "the confounded Chickahominy." He had protested, for McDowell's sake as well as his own, against the instructions requiring that general's overland advance and "an extension of my right wing to meet him." Such dispositions, he warned Stanton, "may involve serious hazard to my flank and line of communications and may not suffice to rescue [him] from any peril in which a strong movement of the enemy may involve him."

Nothing having come of this, he was obliged to keep Porter where he was. The danger to his base was another matter, one in which he could act on his own, and that was what he did. On the day Stuart returned to his lines and reported to Lee, McClellan ordered a reconnaissance toward James River, intending to look into the possibility of establishing a new base in that direction. Three days later, June 18, he began sending transports loaded with food and ammunition from White House down the Pamunkey and the York, up the James to Harrison's Landing. Gunboats, stationed there to protect them, would also protect his army in case it was thrown back as a result of an overwhelming asault on its present all-too-vulnerable position astride the Chickahominy. Meanwhile he continued to reconnoiter southward, sending cavalry and topographical engineers beyond White Oak Swamp to study the largely unknown country through which the army would have to pass in order to reach the James.

He had the satisfaction of knowing that he was doing what he could to meet such threats as he could see. However, there were others, vague but real, invisible but felt, against which he could take no action, since all he could feel was their presence, not their shape. He felt them tonight, writing the last lines of the bedtime letter to his wife: "I have a kind of presentiment that tomorrow will bring forth *something —what*, I do not know. We will see when the time arrives."

What tomorrow brought was a rebel deserter who gave his captors information confirming McClellan's presentiment of possible disaster. Picked up by Federal scouts near Hanover Courthouse, the man identified himself as one of Jackson's Valley soldiers; Stonewall now had three divisons, he said, and was moving rapidly south and east for an all-out attack on the Union flank and rear. It would come, he added, on

June 28: four days away. McClellan alerted Porter and passed the news along to the War Department, asking for "the most exact information you have as to the position and movements of Jackson." Stanton replied next day, June 25, that Jackson's army, with an estimated strength of 40,000, was variously reported at Gordonsville, at Port Republic, at Harrisonburg, and at Luray. He might be moving to join Lee in front of Richmond; other reports had him marching on Washington or Baltimore. Any one of them might be true. All of them might be false. At any rate, the Secretary concluded, the deserter's information "could not safely be disregarded."

McClellan scarcely knew what to believe, though as always he was ready to believe the worst: in which case only the stump of a fuze remained before the explosion. He opened at once with all his artillery, north and south of the river, and sent Heintzelman's corps out the Williamsburg road to readjust its picket lines and test the enemy strength in that direction. The result was a confused and savage fight, the first in a sequence to be known as the Seven Days. He lost 626 men and inflicted 541 casualties on Huger, whose troops finally halted the advance and convinced the attackers that the front had not been weakened in that direction. McClellan's spirits rose with the sound of firing — he shucked off his coat and climbed a tree for a better view of the fighting — but declined again as the firing died away. Though his line south of the river was now within four miles of the enemy capital, he could not clear his mind of the picture of imminent ruin on the opposite flank, drawn by the deserter the day before.

Returning to headquarters at sundown he wired Stanton: "I incline to think that Jackson will attack my right and rear. The rebel force is stated at 200,000. . . . I regret my great inferiority in numbers, but feel that I am in no way responsible for it, as I have not failed to represent repeatedly the necessity of reinforcements; that this was the decisive point, and that all the available means of the Government should be concentrated here. I will do all that a general can do with the splendid army I have the honor to command, and if it is destroyed by overwhelming numbers, can at least die with it and share its fate. But if the result of the action which will probably occur tomorrow, or within a short time, is a disaster, the responsibility cannot be thrown on my shoulders; it must rest where it belongs."

Riding toward the sound of heaviest firing, Lee had arrived in time to see Huger's men stop Heintzelman's assault before it reached their main line of resistance. The attack had been savage, however, and it had the look of at least the beginning of a major push. A fine rain was falling, the first in a week, but not hard enough to affect the roads, which had dried out considerably during the hot spell: McClellan might be starting his "battle of posts," advancing his infantry to cover the arrival of his siege guns. Or he might have attacked to beat Lee to the punch, having learned somehow that the line to his front had been weakened to mount the offensive against his flank. In either case, the safest thing for the Confederates to do was call off the north-bank assault and concentrate here for a last-ditch defense of the capital.

These things were in Lee's mind as he rode back through the camps where the men of Longstreet and D. H. Hill were cooking three days' rations in preparation for their march to get in position under cover of darkness for the attack across the Chickahominy next morning. He weighed the odds and made his decision, confirming the opinion one of his officers had given lately in answer to doubts expressed by another as to the new commander's capacity for boldness: "His name might be Audacity. He will take more desperate chances, and take them quicker, than any other general in this country, North or South. And you will live to see it, too." The plan would stand; the Richmond lines would be stripped; McClellan's flank would be assaulted, whatever the risk. And as Lee rode to his headquarters, people drawn to the capital hills by the rumble of guns looked out and saw what they took to be an omen. The sun broke through the mist and smoke and a rainbow arched across the vault, broad and clear above the camps of their defenders.

It held and then it faded; they went home. Presently, for those in the northeast suburbs unable to sleep despite the assurance of the spectral omen, there came a muffled sound, as if something enormous was moving on padded feet in the predawn darkness. Hill and Longstreet were in motion, leaving their campfires burning brightly behind them as they marched up the Mechanicsville turnpike and filed into masked positions, where they crouched for the leap across the river as soon as the other Hill's advance uncovered the bridges to their front. By sunup Lee himself had occupied an observation post on the crest of the low ridge overlooking the Chickahominy. The day was clear and pleasant, giving a promise of heat and a good view of the Federal outposts on the opposite bank. The bluecoats took their ease on the porches and in the yards of the houses that made up the crossroads hamlet. Others lolled about their newly dug gun emplacements and under the trees that dotted the landscape. They seemed unworried; but Lee was not. He had received unwelcome news from Jackson, whose foot cavalry was three hours behind schedule as a result of encountering poor roads and hostile opposition.

This last increased the cumulative evidence that McClellan suspected the combination Lee had designed for his destruction. At any moment the uproar of the Union assault feared by Davis might break out along the four-mile line where Magruder, his men spread thin, was attempting to repeat the theatrical performance he had staged with such success at Yorktown, back in April. By 8 o'clock all the units were in position along the near bank of the river, awaiting the sound of Stonewall's guns or a courier informing them that he too was in position. But there was only silence from that direction. A. P. Hill sent a message to the brigade posted upstream at Half Sink: "Wait for Jackson's notification before you move unless I send you other orders." Time wore on. 9 o'clock: 10 o'clock. The three-hour margin was used up, and still the only word from Jackson was a note written an hour ago, informing the commander of Hill's detached brigade that the head of his column was crossing the Virginia Central — six hours behind schedule.

President Davis came riding out and joined the commanding general at his post of observation. Their staffs sat talking, comparing watches. 11 o'clock: Lee might have remembered Cheat Mountain, nine months ago in West Virginia, where he had attempted a similar complex convergence once before, with similar results. High noon. The six-hour margin was used up, and still no sound of gunfire from the north. 1 o'clock: 2 o'clock: 3 o'clock. Where was Jackson?

McClellan knew the answer to that. His scouts had confirmed his suspicions and kept him informed of Stonewall's whereabouts. But he had another question: Why didn't he come on?

After the dramatic and bad-tempered telegram sent at sundown of the day before, he had ridden across the river to check on Porter's dispositions, and finding them judicious — one division posted behind Beaver Dam Creek, the other two thrown forward — had returned in better spirits, despite a touch of neuralgia. "Every possible precaution is being taken," he informed the authorities in Washington before turning in for the night. "If I had another good division I could laugh at Jackson.... Nothing but overwhelming forces can defeat us." This morning he had returned for another look, and once more he had come back reassured. Now, however, as the long hours wore away in silence and the sun climbed up the sky, apprehension began to alternate with hope. At noon he wired Stanton: "All things very quiet on this bank of the Chickahominy. I would prefer more noise."

✗ 4 ✗

If noise was what he wanted, he was about to get it — in full measure — from a man who had plenty of reasons, personal as well as temperamental, for wanting to give it to him. Before the war, A. P. Hill had sued for the hand of Ellen Marcy. The girl was willing, apparently, but her father, a regular army career officer, disapproved; Hill's assets were $10,000, a Virginia background, and a commission as a Coast Survey lieutenant, and Colonel Marcy aimed a good deal higher for his daughter than that. Ellen obeyed her father, whose judgment was rewarded shortly thereafter when George McClellan, already a railroad president at thirty-three, with an annual income amounting to more than the rejected lieutenant's total holdings, made a similar suit and was accepted, thereby assuring the daughter's freedom from possible future want and the father's position, within a year, as chief of staff to the commander of the Army of the Potomac. Hill meanwhile had gone his way and married the beautiful sister of John Hunt Morgan of Kentucky, red-haired like himself and so devoted to her husband that it sometimes required a direct order from the commander of the Army of Northern Virginia to remove her from the lines when a battle was impending. Hill, then, had in fact more cause to feel gratitude than resentment toward the enemy chief of staff and commander for rejecting and supplanting him. However, he was a hard fighter, with a high-strung intensity and a great fondness for the offensive; so that in time McClellan's soldiers, familiar with the history of the tandem courtships, became convinced that the Virginian's combativeness was a highly personal matter, provoked by a burning determination to square a grudge. Once at least, as Hill's graybacks came swarming over the landscape at them, giving that high-throated fiendish yell, one of McClellan's veterans, who had been through this sort of thing before, shook his head fervently and groaned in disgust: "God's sake, Nelly — why didn't you marry him?"

A narrow-chested man of average height, thin-faced and pale, with flowing hair, a chiseled nose, and cheekbones jutting high above the auburn bush of beard, Hill had a quick, impulsive manner and a taste that ran to the picturesque in clothes. Today, for instance — as always, when fighting was scheduled — he wore a red wool deer-hunter's shirt; his battle shirt, he called it, and his men, knowing the sign, would pass the word, "Little Powell's got on his battle shirt!" More and more, however, as the long hours wore away in front of Meadow Bridge, they began to think he had put it on for nothing. The detached brigade had crossed at Half Sink soon after 10 o'clock, when Jackson sent word that he had reached the railroad. Since then, nothing had been heard from that direction; five hours had passed, and barely that many still remained of daylight. Hill chafed and fretted until he could take no more. At 3 o'clock, "rather than hazard the failure of the whole plan by longer deferring it," as he subsequently reported, "I determined to cross at once."

From his post on the heights overlooking the river Lee heard a sudden popping of musketry from upstream. As it swelled to a clatter he saw bluecoats trickling eastward from a screen of woods to the northwest, followed presently by the gray line of skirmishers who had flushed them. Then came the main body in heavy columns, their bayonets and regimental colors glinting and gleaming silver and scarlet in the sunlight. The Yankees were falling back on Mechanicsville, where tiny figures on horseback gestured theatrically with sabers, forming a line of battle. East of the village, the darker foliage along Beaver Dam Creek began to leak smoke as the Union artillery took up the challenge. Far to the north, directly on Jackson's expected line of advance, another smoke cloud rose in answer; Stonewall's guns were booming. As Little Powell's men swept eastward, the troops of D. H. Hill and Longstreet advanced from their masked positions along the turnpike and prepared to cross the Chickahominy in support. Late as it was — past 4 now, with the sun already halfway down the sky — the plan was working. All the jigsaw pieces were being jockeyed into their assigned positions to form Lee's pattern of destruction for the invaders of Virginia.

As usual, there were delays. The turnpike bridge had to be repaired before Harvey Hill and Longstreet could go to the assistance of A. P. Hill, who was fighting alone on the north bank, prodding the makeshift Yankee line back through Mechanicsville. Lee sent him word not to press too close to the guns massed along Beaver Dam Creek until support arrived and Jackson had had time to outflank the fortified position. While the repairmen were still at work on the bridge, a cavalcade of civilians, mostly congressmen and cabinet members, clattered across in the wake of President Davis, who was riding as always toward the sound of firing. D. H. Hill and Longstreet followed, and at 5 o'clock Lee came down off the heights and crossed with them.

The plain ahead was dotted with bursting shells and the disjointed rag-doll shapes of fallen men. A. P. Hill had taken the village, and by now there were no armed Federals west of Beaver Dam Creek. But there were plenty of them along it, supporting the guns creating havoc on the plain. Unable to remain out in the open, in clear view of the Union gunners, Hill's men had pushed eastward, against Lee's orders, to find cover along the near bank of the creek. Here they came under infantry fire as well, taking additional losses, but fortunately the artillery was firing a little too high; otherwise they would have been slaughtered. Several attempts to storm the ridge beyond the creek had been bloodily repulsed. The position was far too strong and Porter had too many men up there — almost as many, in fact, as Longstreet and both Hills combined. Everything depended on Jackson, who should have been rounding their flank by now, forcing them to withdraw in order to cover their rear. However, there was no sign of this; the Federals stood firm on the ridge, apparently unconcerned about anything except killing the Confederates to their front. The question still obtained: Where was Stonewall? And now Lee learned for the first time that Little Powell had crossed the Chickahominy with no more knowledge of Jackson's whereabouts than Lee himself had, which was none at all.

To add to his worries, there on the plain where Union shells were knocking men and horses about and wrecking what few guns A. P. Hill had been able to bring within range, Lee saw Davis and his cavalcade, including the Secretaries of State and War, sitting their horses among the shellbursts as they watched the progress of the battle. A single burst might topple them like tenpins any minute. Lee rode over and gave Davis a cold salute. "Mr President, who is all this army and what is it doing here?" Unaccustomed to being addressed in this style, especially by the gentle-mannered Lee, Davis was taken aback. "It is not my army, General," he replied evasively. Lee said icily, "It is certainly not *my* army, Mr President, and this is no place for it." Davis shifted his weight uneasily in the saddle. "Well, General," he replied, "if I withdraw, perhaps they will follow." He lifted his wide-brim planter's hat and rode away, trailing a kite-tail of crestfallen politicians. Once he was out of sight, however, he turned back toward the battle, though he took a path that would not bring him within range of Lee. He did not mind the shells, but he wanted no more encounters such as the one he had just experienced.

This minor problem attended to, Lee returned to the major one at hand: the unequal battle raging along Beaver Dam Creek, where he had not expected to have to fight at all. Jackson's delay seemed to indicate that McClellan, having learned in advance of the attempt to envelop his flank, had intercepted Stonewall's march along the Totopotomoy ridge. Still worse, he might be mounting an overwhelming assault on the thinly held intrenchments in front of Richmond before Lee could get in position to "be on his heels." Immediately, the southern commander sent messages ordering Magruder to hold his lines at all costs and instructing Huger to test McClellan's left with a cavalry demonstration. Daylight was going fast. Until Lee reached New Bridge, two miles beyond the contested ridge, both wings of his army would be fighting in isolation: McClellan well might do to him what he had planned to do to McClellan. If the Federals were not dislodged from Beaver Dam today, they might take the offensive in the morning with reinforcements brought up during the night. In desperation, Lee decided to attempt what he had been opposed to until now. He would storm the ridge beyond the creek.

All of A. P. Hill's men had been committed, but Harvey Hill's were just arriving. Lee ordered the lead brigade to charge on the right, near the river, and flank the Federals off the ridge. They went in with a yell, surging down the slope to the creek, but the high ground across the way exploded in their faces as the Union guns took up the challenge. Shattered, the graycoats fell back over their dead and wounded, losing more men as they went. The sun went down at 7.15 and the small-arms fire continued to pop and sputter along the dusky front. By 9 o'clock it had stopped. The enemy artillery fired blind for another hour, as if in mockery of the attackers. Then it too died away, and the cries of the wounded were heard along the creek bank. The Army of Northern Virginia's first battle was over.

It was over and it was lost, primarily because of the absence of the 18,500 troops whose arrival had been intended to unhinge the Federal line along the ridge. The persistent daylong question, Where was Jackson? still obtained. In a way, that was just as well; for in this case, disturbing as the question was, the answer was even more so. Finding his advance expected and contested by enemy cavalry, Stonewall had moved cautiously after crossing the Central Railroad six hours late. At 4.30 that afternoon, after a southward march of seven miles in seven hours — he was now ten hours behind schedule — he reached his objective, Hundley's Corner. From there he could hear the roar of guns along Beaver Dam, three airline miles away. However, with better than three hours of daylight still remaining, he neither marched toward the sound of firing nor sent a courier to inform Lee of his arrival. Instead, he went into bivouac, apparently satisfied that he had reached his assigned position, however late. His men were much fatigued, being unaccustomed to the sandy roads and dripping heat of the lowlands, and so was their commander, who had had a total of ten hours' sleep in the past four nights. If Lee wanted him to fight the Yankees, let him drive them across his front as had been arranged.

While Stonewall's veterans took their rest, A. P. Hill's green troops were fighting and losing their first battle. Lee's ambitious plan for a sweep down the north bank of the river, cutting the enemy off from his base and forcing him to choose between flight and destruction, had begun with a total and bloody repulse that left McClellan a choice of two opportunities, both golden. He could reinforce his right and take the offensive here tomorrow, or he could hold the river crossings and bull straight through for Richmond on the south, depending on which he wanted first, Virginia's army or Virginia's capital. Such was the result of Lee's first battle. Hill's impetuosity and Jackson's lethargy were to blame, but the final responsibility was the army commander's; he had planned the battle and he had been present to direct it. Comparatively speaking, though there was little time for assessment, it had been fought in such a disjointed fashion as to make even Seven Pines seem a masterpiece of precision. Of the 56,000 men supposedly available on this bank of the Chickahominy, Lee had got barely one fourth into action, and even these 14,000 went in piecemeal. Mercifully, the casualty figures were hidden in the darkness and confusion, but time would disclose that the Confederates had lost 1350 soldiers, the Federals 361. In short, it was the worst fiasco either army had staged since Ball's Bluff, back in October, when the figures were approximately reversed.

McClellan was elated. Though he left all the tactical dispositions to Porter, he had recrossed the river in time to watch the battle from start to finish. At 9 o'clock, with the guns still intermittently booming defiance, he wired Stanton: "The firing has nearly ceased.... Victory of today complete and against great odds. I almost begin to think we are invincible."

However, he was by no means ready to take advantage of either of the golden opportunities afforded by Lee's repulse. Believing himself as heavily outnumbered on the left as on the right, he did not consider a shift to the offensive on either bank of the Chickahominy. He was proud in fact to be holding his own, and he restrained his elation somewhere short of rashness. Nor did he consider reinforcing the embattled Porter with troops from Sumner, Heintzelman, Keyes, or Franklin, who reported the rebels unusually active on their front. Convinced as he was that Lee had at least 180,000 men, McClellan saw all sorts of possible combinations being designed for his destruction. The attack on Mechanicsville, for example, might be a feint, intended to distract his attention while troops were massed for overrunning the four-mile line that covered Seven Pines and Fair Oaks. Such considerations weighed him down. In point of fact, his elation and his talk of being invincible were purely tactical, so to speak. Strategically, he was already preparing to retreat.

Ever since the beginning of the action he had been shifting Porter's wagons and heavy equipment to the south bank — "impediments," he called them — in preparation for a withdrawal as soon as the pressure grew too great. Jackson's late-afternoon arrival within striking distance of Porter's flank and rear, though his attitude when he got there was anything but menacing, had the effect Lee had intended. As soon as the Beaver Dam fight was broken off, McClellan instructed Porter to fall back down the Chickahominy, out of reach of Stonewall, who had brought not only his Valley army, but also his Valley reputation with him. After crossing Powhite Creek, three miles in his rear, Porter was to dig in along the east bank of Boatswain Swamp, a stream inclosing a horseshoe-shaped position of great natural strength, just opposite the northern end of the four-mile line beyond the river.

At daybreak Porter carried out the movement with such skill that McClellan, who had already crossed, wired Stanton in delight: "This change of position was beautifully executed under a sharp fire, with but little loss. The troops on the other side are now well in hand, and the whole army so concentrated that it can take advantage of the first mistake made by the enemy."

★ ★ ★

Lee's safest course, after yesterday's repulse, would have been to recross the Chickahominy at Mechanicsville Bridge and concentrate for a defense of his capital by occupying, in all possible strength, the

line of intrenchments now thinly held by Huger and Magruder. But he
no more considered turning back, apparently, than McClellan had considered moving forward. After sending a staff officer to locate Jackson
and instruct him to continue his march eastward beyond the Union
flank, Lee ordered a renewal of the assault on the ridge overlooking
Beaver Dam, which the bluecoats seemed to be holding as strongly as
ever. He intended to force its evacuation by a double turning movement, right and left; but before it could be organized, the Federals
pulled back. They were only a rear guard, after all. Lee sent A. P. Hill
and Longstreet in direct pursuit, with instructions to attack the enemy
wherever they found him, while Harvey Hill swung wide around the
left to reinforce Jackson in accordance with the original plan. Though
the element of surprise was lost and there were no guarantees against
breakdowns such as the one that had occurred the day before, the
machine was back in gear at last.

    About 9.30 Lee rode forward, doubling Longstreet's column,
and mounted the ridge beyond the creek, where burning stores and
abandoned equipment showed the haste with which the enemy had departed. Two miles eastward he came upon Jackson and A. P. Hill standing together in a country churchyard. Hill soon left, but Lee dismounted
and sat on a cedar stump to confer with Stonewall. The two were a
study in contrast, the immaculate Lee and the dusty Jackson, and so
were their staffs, who stood behind them, looking each other over. Any
advantage the former group had in grooming was more than offset by
the knowledge that the latter had worn out their clothes in fighting.
Now that D. H. Hill had joined him, Stonewall had fourteen brigades
under his command: two more than Longstreet and the other Hill
combined. Lee expected the enemy to make a stand at Powhite Creek,
just over a mile ahead, and his instructions were for Jackson to continue
his march to Cold Harbor, three and a half miles east. There he would
be well in rear of the Federals and could cut them off or tear their flank
as they came past him, driven by A. P. Hill and Longstreet. Jackson
nodded approval, then mounted and rode away.

    Lee overtook the head of A. P. Hill's column as it approached
Powhite Creek. It was now about noon, and the gravest danger of the
original plan was past. Hill's advance had uncovered New Bridge; the
two wings of the army were again in contact; Magruder could be reinforced from across the Chickahominy if McClellan lunged for Richmond on that side. Ahead, as Lee had expected, enemy riflemen held the
high ground beyond the creek. Determined to force a crossing without
delay, Little Powell sent his lead brigade forward unsupported. After a
short fire-fight, centered around a brick and timber structure known as
Gaines Mill — there was a dam there with a spillway and a sizeable
pond above it, placid, shaded by oaks; a cool, unwarlike place of refuge

on a hot day in any June but this — the Federals withdrew. Hill's men followed, crossing the creek and occupying the high ground without further opposition. Unlike yesterday, rashness had paid off.

It had been easy: too easy, Lee thought as he mounted the slope and reached the seized position. Then he found out why. Ahead there was a sudden, tearing clatter of musketry, and the men of Hill's lead brigade came stumbling wild-eyed out of the wooded valley into which they had pursued the fleeing bluecoats. "Gentleman, we must rally those men," Lee told his staff, riding forward. Now he knew. Not here along the Powhite as he had expected, but somewhere down in that swale, or just beyond it, the enemy was at bay. While the panicked troops were being rallied — a good many more of them had gone in than had come back out — Hill brought up three additional brigades, and at 2.30, with Longstreet just arriving on the right, sent them forward. Again that sudden clatter erupted, now with the boom of guns mixed in, and again the men came stumbling back, as wild-eyed as before.

Penetrating deeper into the swampy woods, they had come face to face with the death-producing thing itself: three separate lines of Federal infantry, dug one above another into the face of a long, convex hill crowned with guns. McClellan, with his engineer's skill, had chosen a position of enormous strength, moated along its front by a boggy stream called Boatswain Swamp. Rising below Cold Harbor, two miles east of Gaines Mill, it flowed southwest, then turned back east and south around the face of Turkey Hill, affording a clear field of fire for Porter's three successive lines and the batteries massed on the dominant plateau. None of this was shown on the crude map Lee was using, not even Boatswain Swamp; Hill had had to find it for him, groping blind and paying in blood for discouraging information. Now he knew the worst. Yesterday's Union position, overlooking Beaver Dam, had been strong enough to shatter everything he had been able to throw against it; but today's was infinitely stronger. McClellan had found himself a fortress, ready-made.

Lee's hope was that Jackson, threatening the Federal right from the direction of Cold Harbor, would cause Porter to weaken his left by shifting troops to meet him. Until that happened, to continue the assault would be suicidal. In fact, the shaken condition of Hill's men made it doubtful whether they would be able to hold their ground if the enemy counterattacked. Sending word for Longstreet to discourage this with a demonstration on the right, Lee set out for the left to find the answer to yesterday's question, which applied again today: Where was Jackson? On the way, he met Ewell and found out. Harvey Hill had reached Cold Harbor, but Stonewall had been delayed by taking a wrong road. Riding ahead, he had found Hill deploying for attack — precisely what Lee, across the way, was hoping for — and had stopped him; Lee's instructions were for him to strike the Federals after they had been dislodged, not before. To stave off disaster while he digested this bad news, Lee told Ewell to go in on A. P. Hill's left, supporting him, while he himself rode on to talk with Jackson.

Ewell's veterans started forward with a shout. "You need not go in!" Little Powell's troops called out when they saw them coming. "We are whipped; you can't do anything!" The Valley men did not falter. "Get out of our way," they growled as they went by. "We'll show you how to do it." Yelling, they went in on the double. Again there was that uproarious clatter, as if a switch had been tripped, and that triple line of fire ripping back and forth across the face of Turkey Hill, and the roar of guns from the crest. Still on the double, the Valley soldiers came back out again. It was more than they had bargained for, despite the warning, and they were considerably fewer now than when they started forward. Roberdeau Wheat was lying dead in there, along with hundreds of others who had been through Kernstown, Winchester, Cross Keys, and Port Republic. Dick Taylor was not; he had been confined to an ambulance with a mysterious ailment that paralyzed his legs. Missing his firm grip, the gaitered Louisianians broke within sight of the fuming hill and had to be withdrawn. The rest of Ewell's survivors hung on, deep in the swampy woods alongside Hill's, while concentrations of shell and canister flailed the brush around them. Their aim distracted by a constant shower of broken twigs and branches, they kept up a blind long-range fire across Boatswain Swamp.

Riding toward the left, Lee heard a welcome sound from that direction: the popping of muskets and the quaver of the rebel yell. Jackson at last had realized the changed situation and had unleashed Harvey Hill against the Union right, meanwhile sending word to his other division commanders: "This affair must hang in suspense no longer. Sweep the field with the bayonet!" He sounded like himself again, and presently Lee saw him approaching, horse and rider covered with dust, the dingy cadet cap pulled so far down over his face that the bill almost touched the lemon he was sucking.

"Ah, General," Lee said as he rode up, "I am very glad to see you. I had hoped to be with you before." Stonewall jerked his head at the implied rebuke and muttered something indistinguishable in the din. Ewell's attack was reaching its climax; Jackson's division, under Winder, would go in on Ewell's right, filling a widening gap between him and A. P. Hill. "That fire is very heavy," Lee said. "Do you think your men can stand it?" Jackson listened, then replied, raising his voice to be heard above the racket: "They can stand almost anything! They can stand that."

It was now past 5 o'clock, but Lee at last had all of his troops within reach or in position. Far on the right, Longstreet had examined the enemy line with deliberate care and found it too strong to be affected by a feint; only an all-out attack would serve, he said, and he was preparing to deliver one. Lee approved, having reached the same conclusion everywhere along the front. The sun was near the landline; time was running out. At this late hour, no matter what it cost in blood, nothing less than a general assault, all down the line — D. H. Hill and Ewell on the left, Jackson in the center, A. P. Hill and Longstreet on the right — could possibly convert defeat into victory by sweeping the Federals off the face of Turkey Hill and back across the plateau where their massed guns boomed defiance.

Fitz-John Porter was holding his own, and he intended to go on holding it, whatever the rebels brought against him. His three divisions had been reinforced by a fourth from Franklin, sent him by McClellan along with a message expressing his pride in the fighting qualities of the men on the north bank: "Send word to all your troops that their general thanks them for their heroism, and says to them that he is now sure that nothing can resist them. Their conduct and your own have been magnificent, and another name is added to their banners.... I look upon today as decisive of the war. Try to drive the rascals and take some prisoners and guns."

Much of the credit was due to the division on the right. Its members were U.S. regulars to a man, all 6000 of them, and they fought with the same steady determination they had shown at Bull Run, where they had been fewer than 1000. Their commander, now as then, was George Sykes, then a major but now a major general. He was from Delaware, forty years old, and he held his lines today with a special doggedness, knowing the attacks were launched by Harvey Hill, who had been his roommate at West Point. Porter left the defense of that flank to Sykes and gave his main attention to the left and center of his convex line, supporting his two divisions in that direction with the fourth, which came up soon after 4 o'clock. His 35,000 soldiers were outnumbered three to two, but they gained confidence from every repulse they administered to the screaming graybacks who came charging through the swamp just under their rifles. It was shooting-gallery work, with an excitement out of proportion to the danger involved. Meanwhile they were improving their hillside position, piling dirt and logs, stacking rocks and even knapsacks to thicken and raise the breastworks along their triple line. Dead rebels lay in windrows at the base of the slope, but the defenders had suffered comparatively little. Wherever Porter checked — a handsome man with a neatly barbered, lustrous dark-brown beard, clean linen, and a calm, unruffled manner that matched his clothes — he found his men in excellent spirits, elated over their success and ready to continue it as long as he required.

It would not be much longer now; McClellan had made it clear from the start that this was primarily a holding action. The sun was already red beyond the trees along the Chickahominy when a follow-up message arrived from the army commander, setting a definite limit to their stay: "I am ordering up more troops. Do your best to hold your own . . . until dark."

But the blow was about to fall. Except for two brigades that were coming up now in rear of A. P. Hill, Lee had all his men in position along a nearly semicircular three-mile arc. He planned to use these late arrivers for a breakthrough at the point where Little Powell had tried and failed. One of the two was the Texas Brigade, under John B. Hood, which had shown an aptitude for this kind of work at Eltham Landing. Lee rode back, met Hood at the head of the column, and — omitting none of the difficulties the previous attackers had encountered — told him what he wanted.

"This must be done," he said. "Can you break his line?" Hood did not know whether he could or not; but he said he was willing to try. That was enough for Lee. As he turned to ride away he raised his hat. "May God be with you," he said.

Hood formed along the line of departure, a Georgia regiment on the right, Hampton's Legion on the left, and three Texas regiments in the center. Beyond the Legion, the other brigade commander, Colonel E. M. Law, aligned his four regiments, two from Mississippi and one each from Alabama and North Carolina. Longstreet and Jackson had already gone into action on the right and left when these men from the Deep South started forward. The sun was down behind the ridge, twilight gathering in the valley, as Hood and Law passed through the shattered ranks of A. P. Hill and beyond into a clearing, in full view of the blue tiers on the hillside and the batteries massed on the crest, which went into a rapid-fire frenzy at the sight, stabbing the dusk with spits of flame as fast as men could pull triggers and lanyards, then load and pull again. Still the gray-clad attackers came on, through the tempest of iron and lead, not pausing to fire, not even yelling, but moving with long strides down the slope, their rifles at right shoulder lift, closing ranks as they took their losses, which were heavy. If they had looked back they would have seen the ground behind them strewn with their dead and wounded; nearly a thousand had fallen before they reached the near bank of Boatswain Swamp, where they paused to fix bayonets and dress their line. But they did not look back; they looked forward, moving now at the double, across the creek and up the slope on the enemy side, yelling as they came on. Not a shot had been fired by the charging men, but their rifles were now at a carry, the bayonets glinting: twenty yards from the Union line, then ten . . . and the bluecoats scattered in unison, scrabbling uphill and swamping the second line, which joined them in flight, overrunning the third. In the lead, the Texans fired their first volley at a range where every bullet lodged in flesh, then surged over the crest and onto the plateau, where they fired again into a heaving mass of horses and men as the cannoneers tried to limber for a withdrawal. Too late: Hood was out front, tall and blond, gesturing with his sword. Fourteen guns were taken here, while two full regiments from Pennsylvania and New Jersey threw down their arms in surrender, along with other large detachments. Lee now had the breakthrough he had asked for.

Longstreet and Jackson widened the breach in both directions, pumping additional volleys into the wreckage and turning back a desperate cavalry charge, delivered Balaklava-style, which accomplished nothing except the addition of pain-crazed, riderless horses to the turmoil. Ewell, moving forward beyond Jackson, outflanked Sykes and forced him to fall back under pressure from D. H. Hill. Eight more guns were taken and several hundred more prisoners were rounded up in the gathering dusk. However, there was too much confusion and too little daylight for the final concerted push that might have swept the Federals off the sloped plateau and into the boggy flats of the Chickahominy. Besides, in retreat as in resistance, the signs were clear that McClellan's

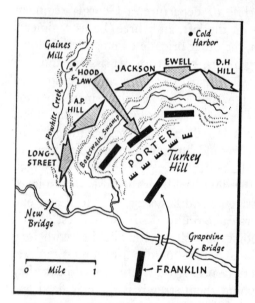

was a very different army from the one that had broken and scattered in the twilight at Manassas; whereas the Confederates, now as then, were too disrupted for pursuit. Not only did Sykes' regulars maintain their reputation by retiring in good order, but as the frightened survivors of the other three divisions broke for the bridges leading south to safety, they met two brigades coming up from Sumner, reinforcements ordered north by McClellan while the battle racket was swelling toward its climax. The fugitives cheered and rallied. Porter saved his reserve artillery and got his soldiers across the river in the darkness, using these fresh troops and the unshaken regulars to cover the withdrawal.

"Profoundly grateful to Almighty God," Lee sent a dispatch informing Davis that the Army of Northern Virginia had won its first victory. Twenty-two guns and more than 2000 prisoners had been taken, together with a great deal of excellent equipment and a clear road leading eastward to the Union base at White House. But it had been accomplished at a fearful price. Lee had lost 8500 fighting men, the bravest and best the South could ever give him; Porter had lost 6837. Numerically, here at the critical point of contact, the odds were growing longer every day. Its right wing drawn in, shaken but uncrushed, McClellan's army was now assembled as a unit for the struggle that lay ahead, while the southern army was still divided.

"We sleep on the field," Lee closed his dispatch to the President, "and shall renew the contest in the morning."

★ ★ ★

McClellan met that night with his corps commanders at Savage Station, a point on the York River Railroad about midway between Fair Oaks and the Chickahominy crossing. They were not there to help him arrive at a decision, but rather to receive instructions for carrying out a decision already reached. Early that afternoon, before Porter had completed his occupation of the position overlooking Boatswain Swamp, McClellan notified Flag Officer Goldsborough of his desire "that you will forthwith instruct the gunboats in the James River to cover the left flank of this army.... I am obliged to fall back." And at 8 o'clock — as the uproar died away beyond the Chickahominy, but before he knew the results of the fighting there — he wired Stanton from his south-bank headquarters: "Have had a terrible contest. Attacked by greatly superior numbers in all directions on this side.... The odds have been immense. We hold our own very nearly."

The decision to retreat — or, as McClellan preferred to express it, the decision to "change his base" — was supported by dispatches he had been receiving all day from troop commanders along the four-mile line that ran from Grapevine Bridge down into the near fringe of White Oak Swamp. Here Prince John Magruder had repeated his Yorktown performance with such remarkable success, marching and countermarching his men, demonstrating noisily and retiring stealthily to threaten or seem to threaten other points along the front, thundering aggressively all the while with his guns — "They have it in mind to advance," Joseph Hooker of Heintzelman's corps reported; "I can be whipped before the reserve will get up" — that all four of the south-bank corps commanders were apprehensive that they were about to be swamped, individually and collectively, by overwhelming numbers. Late in the day, when McClellan asked what additional troops they could spare to help Porter, they replied that they needed all they had in order to hold their ground. In fact, they said, if any more reinforcing was being considered, it had better be done in their direction.

By nightfall, having combined these tactical reports with information received from Pinkerton, McClellan was convinced that Lee was jabbing with his left in preparation for throwing a knockout right. The thing to do, if time permitted, was to step back before it landed; or if not back, then sideways. Porter's withdrawal across the Chickahominy had given the Confederates access to the York River supply line and a clear shot at the left flank of McClellan's moving column if he attempted a retreat back down the Peninsula. The only way to go was south to the James, where his foresight had provided a sanctuary under the guns of the fleet and a landing place for the reinforcements Lincoln would be obliged to send, now that a near-disaster had proved the need for them.

Accordingly, at the Savage Station conference he issued instructions for a withdrawal in that direction. Keyes, being farthest south, would cross White Oak Swamp in the morning, followed by Porter as soon as he completed the retirement now in progress. Together they would guard the flank against an attack below the swamp, while Franklin, Sumner, and Heintzelman held the present lines above it and the Chickahominy crossings to the north, covering the passage of the army train with its 25,000 tons of food, ammunition, and medical supplies. Once the train was across the swamp with its 3600 wagons, 700 ambulances, and a herd of 2500 beeves, the remaining corps would follow, guarding the rear on the way to Harrison's Landing.

It was well conceived, well thought out: McClellan took pride in the foresight and coolness which had enabled him to improvise the details under pressure. He did not consider the movement a retreat. It was a readjustment, a change of base required by a change in conditions. However, once the conference was over and the corps commanders had gone out into the night with their instructions for tomorrow, he began to consider the adverse reaction that might follow: not among his soldiers — they would understand — but among the members of the body politic, the public at large, and especially among the molders of popular opinion: the editors, and later the historians. The record would speak for itself in time. He was confident that it would show how Lincoln and Stanton had thwarted him, diverting his troops when his back was turned and ignoring his pleas for reinforcements, in spite of documentary evidence that he was facing an army twice the size of his own. Meanwhile, though, he was not only in danger of being condemned and ridiculed; about to undertake one of the most difficult maneuvers in the art of war, the transfer of an army from one base to another across a fighting front, he was in danger of being physically destroyed. In that event, the record would indeed have to speak for itself, since he would not be there to supplement it before the bar of judgment. Therefore it had better be supplemented in advance, bolstered so as to present the strongest possible case in the strongest possible language. Shortly after midnight, before retiring to sleep for what he knew would be a grinding day tomorrow, he got off a wire to Stanton.

"I now know the full history of the day," it began. After saying flatly, "I have lost this battle because my force was too small," he got down to cases: "I again repeat that I am not responsible for this, and I say it with the earnestness of a general who feels in his heart the loss of every brave man who has been needlessly sacrificed today.... If, at this instant, I could dispose of 10,000 fresh men, I could gain a victory tomorrow. I know that a few thousand more men would have changed this battle from a defeat to a victory. As it is, the Government must not and cannot hold me responsible for the result." The clincher came at the end: "I feel too earnestly tonight. I have seen too many dead and wounded comrades to feel otherwise than that the Government has not sustained this army. If you do not do so now the game is lost. If I save this army now, I tell you plainly that I owe no thanks to you or to any other persons in Washington. You have done your best to sacrifice this army."

Having thus unburdened his troubled mind, and bolstered the record in the process, he took to his bed. "Of course they will never forgive me for that," he subsequently told his wife. "I knew it when I wrote it; but as I thought it possible that it might be the last I ever wrote, it seemed better to have it exactly true."

Saturday's dawn, June 28, showed Confederate ambulances moving about the field where thousands of wounded soldiers from both armies had suffered through the night. Lee was there before sunrise. Presently couriers began to arrive from Longstreet and Jackson, informing him that Porter had pulled out. They had pushed down toward the Chickahominy without encountering any live Federals except the injured and stragglers, including one of McCall's brigade commanders, Brigadier General John F. Reynolds, who had slept too long in the woods and was captured. The bridges had been burned, they said, and guns were massed on the ridge beyond to challenge any attempt to rebuild them.

Lee did not mind the watchful guns or the wrecked bridges; he had no intention of crossing the river here. However, the original plan for marching in force down the left bank to get astride McClellan's communications could not be followed until he knew for certain in which direction the Federals were retreating — toward White House, toward Williamsburg, or, conceivably, toward the James — or whether, indeed, they might not be massing on the right bank for a drive on Richmond, slicing between the divided wings of the Confederate army to get there. A move in the wrong direction would throw Lee out of position for interfering with either of McClellan's remaining alternatives. Until he knew, he was stymied. For the present all he could do was order Stuart to press on down the left bank, supported by Ewell's division, and cut the railroad at or near Dispatch Station, the advance Union supply base just east of the river. McClellan's reaction to that would tell him much. Meanwhile, there was little to do but attend the wounded, bury the dead, and take such rest as fretfulness would permit.

A sort of wanderlust came over the army in its idleness. Too much had happened too fast these past two days, apparently, for the troops to sit still now. As the sun climbed up the sky, giving promise of much heat, they began to roam the field, singly or in groups, mingling with the burial squads in their search for missing friends and relatives. Even Stonewall was infected. Examining the terrain where Hood and Law had made their breakthrough, the dead still lying thick to mark the path of their assault, he shook his head and exclaimed in admiration: "The men who carried this position were soldiers indeed." Lee too took time to ride in search of his youngest son Robert, an eighteen-year-old cannoneer in a Virginia battery. At first the boy could not be found, but a comrade finally spotted him sleeping under a caisson, unresponsive to the shouts. Prodded with a sponge staff, he came out into the sunlight, grimy and blinking. Lee spoke to him and rode on, and nobody seemed to think it strange that the son of the army commander should be serving in the ranks.

Information began to trickle in. Shortly before midday one of Ewell's brigadiers reported that a man he had sent up a tree with a spyglass had seen the Federals moving south in heavy columns. As if in confirmation, a widening cloud of dust began to darken the sky beyond the river, rising over the treetops. Then came flashes, followed by the crump and rumble of distant explosions and pillars of smoke standing tall along the horizon. Magazines were being fired; McClellan was unquestionably on the march. But where to? Lee did not know, though presently he learned at least that it was not toward White House. A courier arrived from Stuart. He had cut the railroad at Dispatch Station, encountering only token resistance, and the Federal horsemen, falling back, had burned the Chickahominy trestle. Definitely, then, McClellan was abandoning his base on the Pamunkey.

Three alternatives were left to him: a retreat down the Peninsula, a change of base to the James, or a lunge at Richmond. Without anything resembling definite evidence — any one of the three, for instance, might be preceeded by a movement south — Lee now began to consider the second of these choices the most likely. This belief was arrived at by a process of elimination, rejecting those movements which did not seem to him to be in keeping with the character of his opponent. He did not think McClellan had the boldness to adopt the latter course, nor did he think he would willingly risk the damage to his prestige that would result from adopting the former. If this logic was correct, then he was making for the James: in which case there was a need for haste if Lee was to cut him off before he reached the shelter of his gunboats. But the stakes were too great and the odds too long for a gamble based on logic. Confederate guns, shelling the wooded ridge beyond the Chickahominy, were receiving return fire. The Federals were still there, and as long as that was so, Lee could not afford to risk throwing three fourths of his army out of position by sending it off on what might turn out to be an empty chase. Sunset came, then nightfall. The long day was over, and all Lee knew for certain was that McClellan was not reacting as he had expected him to do.

Early Sunday morning two of Longstreet's engineers made a reconnaissance across the river, and soon after sunrise Lee received a message from them which added considerable weight to yesterday's logic. The extensive fortifications covering the key Federal position opposite the mouth of Powhite Creek had been abandoned.

This meant that McClellan had no intention of making a lunge at Richmond. He was retreating, and almost certainly he was retreating in the direction of the James, since neither Stuart nor Ewell had reported any movement toward the lower crossings of the Chickahominy. It was not conclusive evidence; the Federals' nonarrival at Bottom's Bridge or Long Bridge, another five miles downstream, might have been caused by a bungled march or a late start; but it shortened the odds at least enough for Lee to risk a gamble. His original plan had been designed to force the enemy to fall back from in front of Richmond or else come out from behind his intrenchments, where he could be hit. McClellan had obliged by doing both. In doing so, however, he had moved in an unexpected direction and had gained a full day's head start in the process. Lee's problem now was to devise a new plan: one that would take advantage of the opportunities created by the old one, now outmoded, and at the same time overcome the advantage his opponent had made for himself. In brief, Lee wanted a plan by which he could overtake McClellan and destroy him.

Before he could be overtaken, however, he would have to be impeded, and Lee's principal asset in this regard was White Oak Swamp. A sort of miniature Chickahominy, it rose southwest of Seven Pines, in the angle between the Williamsburg and Charles City roads, and flowed in a slow crescent across the Federal line of march, emptying into the parent river midway between Bottom's Bridge and Long Bridge. Scantily spanned and badly swollen, impenetrable along most of its length, the stream disguised its quicksand deadliness behind a mazy screen of vines and creepers, luring the northern commander toward an excellent possibility of destruction. If this army could be caught with its head south and its tail north of this boggy stretch, it might be slaughtered like a hamstrung ox, more or less with impunity. McClellan might or might not be aware of this; Lee was. Before the sun was mid-morning high, he had begun to compose and issue orders which, if carried out, would place his troops in position to begin the butchery.

Magruder, moving east along the railroad and the Williamsburg road, was to attack the tail, supported on the left by Jackson, who was to repair and cross Grapevine Bridge with his own and D. H. Hill's divisions. Huger, moving southeast along the Charles City road, was to attack the head, supported on the right by Longstreet, who was to cross New Bridge with his own and A. P. Hill's divisions, marching across Huger's rear to get in position south of the swamp. Meanwhile, on the off chance that McClellan might veer east and try for a getaway down the Peninsula, Ewell was to hold his present position at Bottom's Bridge, supported by Stuart farther down. The assault on the head, below the swamp, could not be made today; Longstreet and Little Powell had fifteen dusty miles to go before they would be in position; their attack would have to be launched on Monday. However, the assault on McClellan's hindquarters could and should be made without delay, since it would impede him further by causing him to have to turn in mid-career and fight a rear-guard action north of White Oak Swamp.

Once more then, with his orders issued, Lee had to wait for the execution of another ambitious convergence. If this one worked, McClellan's oxhide would hang dripping on the Confederacy's barn door before tomorrow's sun went down. Now as before, however, the first move was up to Stonewall — and Magruder.

★ ★ ★

Prince John had been having his troubles all along. In fact, so wholly had he flung himself into the part he was playing — his "method" presaged that of Stanislavsky, who would not be born till the following year, five thousand miles away — his theatrical exertions had been as hard on his own nervous system as on those of the blue-coated spectators out front. This intensity had infected his supporting players, too. Yesterday, for example, one of his brigadiers — fiery, slack-mouthed Robert Toombs, Georgia statesman turned Georgia troop commander — had got so carried away that he converted a demonstration into a full-scale assault on the heavily manned Federal intrenchments. The result, of course, was a bloody repulse and, Magruder believed, a decided increase in the likelihood that the enemy would discover the true weakness behind the ferocious mask. Ever since then, like an actor with the illusion lost and the audience turned irate, he had been expecting to be booed and overrun.

This morning, after dosing himself with medicine in an attempt to ease the pangs of indigestion, he decided to stage an attack. The enemy guns had slacked their fire and then had fallen silent in the fortifications to his immediate left front. Mindful of his instructions to keep pressure on the Union lines, he was determined to develop the situation in strength. However, when he sent word to Lee of his intention, the army commander replied facetiously that a forward movement was indeed in order, but that in storming the works he was to exercise care not to injure Longstreet's two engineers, who had already occupied them. Chagrined, Magruder advanced and was relieved to find it true. Not that there was any lessening of the general tension. Whatever victories had been scored on the far side of the Chickahominy, the peril here on the south bank, now that all five of the Federal corps were united in his front, seemed to him even greater today than yesterday or the day before. Presently, with the arrival of Lee's orders for overhauling and destroying McClellan, Prince John's alarm increased at once to the point of horror and unbelief. Except for the doubtful assistance of that unpredictable eccentric, Stonewall Jackson — who had yet to arrive anywhere on time — it seemed to Magruder that he was being required to assault the whole 100,000-man Yankee army with his one frazzled 13,000-man division.

Lee rode over before midday and explained in person just what it was he wanted. Magruder was to push eastward along the railroad, making contact with Jackson south of Grapevine Bridge, and together they would assail the Union rear. Magruder listened and nodded distractedly; Lee rode on, convinced that his orders were understood. However, Prince John's misgivings were by no means allayed. He got his men into assault formation, straddling the tracks so that Lee's big railway gun protected his center, and started forward. At Fair Oaks, surrounded by piles of smoldering equipment abandoned by the Federals in haste, he came under long-range artillery fire; whereupon he halted and called for help from Huger, who was advancing down the Charles City road. Huger countermarched with two brigades, stayed with him briefly, then went his way, unable to see that he was needed. Magruder went forward again, but with mounting misgivings.

Sure enough, just short of Savage Station, two miles down the track, he came under heavy close-up fire and saw bluecoats clustered thickly in his front, supported by batteries massed in their rear. It was 5 o'clock; Magruder was where Lee wanted him, due south of Grapevine Bridge, in position to press the Federals when Jackson came slamming down on their flank. But now it was his turn to ask the question others had been asking for the past two days: Where was Jackson? There was no sign of him off to the left, no sound of his guns, not even any dust in that direction. Nettled, Prince John went on without him; or anyhow he tried, probing tentatively at the Union line and banging away with the "Land Merrimac."

None of it did any good at all. The Federals repulsed every advance and concentrated so much counterbattery fire on the railway gun that it was forced to backtrack and take shelter in a cut. Night came on, and the cannon kept up their long-range quarrel. Then at 9 o'clock a thunderstorm broke and ended the Battle of Savage Station, in which about 500 men had fallen on each side. Magruder had advanced five miles in the course of the day, but the Federals had not yielded a single unwilling inch. Fighting stubbornly, they had preserved the integrity of their line wherever challenged. More important, they had covered the retreat of the slow-grinding wagon train, which wound southward unmolested. In effect, McClellan had gained another day in his race against time and Lee.

The one person most responsible for this success was not the Union commander or any of his lieutenants, however stubbornly they had fought. Nor was it Magruder, who had fumbled his way forward and then had fought without conviction. It was Jackson, who had not fought at all. Thursday and Friday he had had reasons for failing to strike or threaten the Federal flank on schedule: not good ones, but anyhow reasons. He had been delayed on the march. He had gotten lost. Today, as the sound of Magruder's guns rolled up from the south, he replied to a request for help by saying that he had "other important duties to perform." Presumably this was the repairing of Grapevine Bridge, so listlessly attempted that it turned out to be an all-day job. At any rate, he had kept his men on the north bank of the Chickahominy while Magruder's were fighting and dying at Savage Station.

Consequently, there were some who recalled an early rumor as to how he won his battle name on the field of Manassas. According to this version, Bee had called him Stonewall, not in admiration of his staunchness, but in anger at his refusal to come to his assistance there on the forward slope of Henry Hill. What the South Carolinian had really said, men whispered now about the camps, was: "There stands Jackson — like a damned stone wall!"

Lee now knew the results of the day, and mostly they were worse than disappointing. North of the swamp, where Magruder had faltered and Jackson had stood stock still, the limited attack had probably done more to assist than to impede McClellan's withdrawal. Southward, the situation was not much better. Delayed by a countermarch which had served no purpose, Huger had moved a scant half-dozen miles down the Charles City road and had gone into camp without making contact with the enemy. But even this poor showing put him well in advance of Longstreet and A. P. Hill, who had been stopped by darkness and the thunderstorm, six miles short of tomorrow's objective. Such encouragement as there was came from Stuart, and it was more of a negative than of a positive nature: McClellan had destroyed his base at White House and severed all connections with the Pamunkey and the York.

Thus assured that there was now not even an outside chance that his opponent had it in mind to veer off down the Peninsula, Lee could withdraw Ewell's division from its post at Bottom's Bridge and add its weight to the attempted strike at McClellan's flank and rear. Also, he learned from Richmond, Holmes' division had crossed from Drewry's Bluff, so that it too would be available when — and if — the retreating Federal host was brought to bay.

To effect this end, while thunder pealed and lightning described

its garish zigzag patterns against the outer darkness where the men of
his scattered divisions took such rest as they could manage in the rain-
lashed woods and fields, Lee gave his attention to the map, once more
studying ways and means to correct a plan that had gone awry. For all
its sorry showing today, the army was approximately in position for
the destructive work he had assigned it for tomorrow. Three roads led
southeast below White Oak Swamp, roughly parallel to each other and
perpendicular to the Federal line of retreat: the Charles City road, the
Darbytown road, and the New Market road. Huger was on the former,
nearest the swamp; Holmes was on the latter, nearest the James; Longstreet and A. P. Hill were in the center. Advancing, all three columns
would enter the Long Bridge road, which led east-northeast to the
Chickahominy crossing that gave it its name, and encounter McClellan's

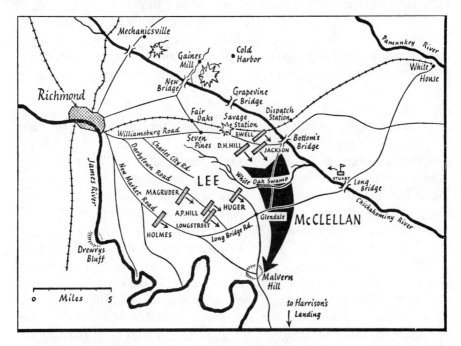

southbound column in the vicinity of Glendale, a crossroads hamlet
located at the intersection of the Charles City and the Long Bridge
roads. These four divisions, reinforced by Magruder — who would
countermarch on the Williamsburg road, then swing south and take
position as a general reserve well down the Darbytown road — would
constitute the striking force. Its mission was to intercept and assail the
head and flank of the enemy column, while Jackson and Harvey Hill,
rejoined by Ewell, would continue (or rather, begin) to press the Federal rear, to and beyond White Oak Swamp. Caught in the resultant
squeeze, with 45,000 graybacks on his flank and another 25,000 in his
rear — so that, observed from above, his predicament somewhat resembled that of a thick-bodied snake pursued by hornets — McClellan

would be forced to stop and fight, strung out in the open as he was, thereby affording Lee the best chance so far to destroy him.

His orders written and given to couriers who rode out into the slackening storm, Lee could sleep at last for what he hoped would be a happier tomorrow. Seeking to avoid delay — the main cause of disappointment up to now — he had instructed his troop commanders to move at dawn. Huger, being nearest the enemy, was to signal the opening of the battle by firing his guns as soon as he made contact, whereupon the others were to close in for the destruction according to plan. Unless today's ragged performance was improved, however, that goal would never be attained. Lee knew this, of course, and the knowledge made him edgy: so much so, in fact, that in his concern he rebuked not Jackson — the principal offender — but Magruder, the only one of his generals who had struck a blow in the past two days.

"I regret very much that you have made so little progress today in the pursuit of the enemy," he informed him by courier. "In order to reap the fruits of our victory the pursuit should be most vigorous. . . . We must lose no more time, or he will escape us entirely."

★　　★　　★

Always, up to now, when McClellan spoke to them of tests and hardships — Yorktown, Williamsburg, Fair Oaks: the victory hill got steeper with every step — the men had cheered him and kept climbing, reinforcing their belief in their commander, Little Mac, with an increasing belief in themselves. Now there was this sterner downhill test.

In some ways, the past four days had been harder on the Federals south of the Chickahominy than on those who were fighting for their lives on the opposite bank. Thursday and Friday there had been a boiling cloud of smoke obscuring the northern sky, and conflicting reports of battles won or lost as the boom and rumble of guns swelled or sank in that direction. Saturday the smoke and noise subsided, then rose again in the afternoon, farther east and of a different intensity, more deliberate than frantic: supply and ammunition dumps were burning and exploding. Also, there was a constant movement of men and wagons across the rear: Porter's troops were over the river, slogging south in the wake of Keyes', who had pulled out on the left. The men of Franklin and Sumner and Heintzelman, left behind, looked at one another and passed the word along: "It's a big skedaddle."

Sunday they themselves had backtracked, fighting a series of rear-guard skirmishes as they moved eastward down the railroad. Then at Savage Station they called a halt and rocked the pursuers back on their heels, "Land Merrimac" and all. It was a victory, and they felt considerably better: especially Sumner, whose battle blood was up. The old man could scarcely believe his ears when he got orders to continue the retrograde movement. "I never leave a victorious field," he sputtered. "Why, if I had 20,000 more men I would crush this rebellion!" When someone finally found a candle, struck a light, and showed him the written order, he still protested. "General McClellan did not know the circumstances when he wrote that note. He did not know that we would fight a battle and gain a victory." Finally, though, he acquiesced; orders were orders. Heintzelman had already left, and Franklin and Sumner followed, crossing White Oak Swamp in the darkness. By 10 o'clock next morning the last man was safely across and the bridge had been burned to discourage pursuit.

It had not been accomplished without losses. A hospital camp of 2500 sick and wounded was abandoned at Savage Station, together with an ample supply of medicines and surgeons who volunteered to stay behind with their charges. At the Chickahominy railroad crossing, loaded ammunition trains were set afire and run full tilt off the wrecked bridge, with spectacular results. Sunday's landscape was smudged with the acrid smoke of burning cloth and leather, relieved from time to time by the more pleasant aroma of coffee and bacon given to the flames instead of to the rebels. The price, in fact, had been heavy; but so was the gain. Whatever else might be in store, McClellan's army was not going to be caught astride the only natural obstacle that lay athwart its line of march to the James.

Monday was Lee's last, best chance for the Cannae he had been seeking all along, and as usual he was early on the scene. The main blow, as he designed it, would be delivered by Longstreet and A. P. Hill just south of Glendale. If successful, this would sever the Union column, interrupt its retreat, and expose its disjointed segments to destruction in detail. But much depended also on the commanders of the various other columns of attack: on Huger, who would open the action on the left: on Jackson, who would force a crossing of White Oak Swamp and press the Federal rear: on Magruder, who would come up in support of the center: and on Holmes, who would advance on the right so as to bring the disorganized bluecoat survivors under his guns as they fled past him, reeling from the effect of the multiple blows.

Since Magruder had the longest march, Lee rode over to Savage Station before sunrise to make certain he understood the orders and started promptly. The first commander he encountered there was not Prince John, however, but Jackson, who had finally repaired Grapevine Bridge and started his men across it before dawn. Both generals dismounted and advanced for a handshake, Lee removing his gauntlet as he came forward. According to a young artillery officer who observed the meeting, Stonewall "appeared worn down to the lowest point of flesh consistent with active service. His hair, skin, eyes and clothes were all one neutral dust tint, and his badges of rank so dulled and tarnished as to be scarcely perceptible." Yesterday's strange lethargy had left him, along with his accustomed reticence. He "began talking in a jerky, impetuous way, meanwhile drawing a diagram on the ground with the toe of his right boot. He traced two sides of a triangle with promptness and decision; then, starting at the end of the second line, began to draw a third projected toward the first. This third line he traced slowly and with hesitation, alternately looking up at Lee's face and down at the diagram, meanwhile talking earnestly." Suddenly, as the third line intersected the first, he stamped his foot, apparently indicating the point at which McClellan would be wrecked beyond repair. "We've got him," he said decisively, and signaled for his horse.

Lee watched him go, that strange man in another of his strange guises, then mounted too and continued his search for Magruder. Presently he found him. After making certain that Prince John understood today's orders as well as Stonewall did, Lee hurried down the Darbytown road to establish army headquarters in rear of the proposed center of the impending battle.

As events turned out, however, there was no need for haste: at any rate, not on his part. Longstreet's men were going forward, supported by Hill's, but it was noon by the time they formed their line near the junction with the Long Bridge road, facing eastward to await the already overdue boom of Huger's guns signaling contact on the left. What came instead was a message: the South Carolinian's progress was "obstructed" — whatever that meant. Lee was left wondering. Southward, Holmes was silent too; nor was there any indication that Jackson was pressing down from the north against the enemy rear. Somewhere out beyond the screening pines and oaks, east of where Lee stood waiting for his lost columns to converge, the Federals were hurrying southward past the point where he had intended to stage his Cannae. He might still stage it — seven hours of daylight still remained — if he could find the answer to certain questions: What had delayed Huger? What had happened to Holmes? And again, as so often before: Where was Jackson?

Huger had the shortest march of all, and what was more he had made an early start. But he went slowly, fearing ambush, for which the terrain was particularly suited. This had been tobacco country in the old days, checkerboard-neat for the most part, but in time the soil had leached out; neglected, it had gone back to second-growth scrub timber, broken here and there by clearings where men still tried to scratch a living from it. The general's natural caution was further increased by the presence of White Oak Swamp, which afforded a covered approach to his left flank. Presently, to make matters worse, word came back that the road ahead was obstructed, the Yankees having chopped down trees that fell across it as they retreated. Instead of leaving his artillery behind or trying to clear the fallen timber from his path, Huger ordered a new road cut through the woods, parallel to the old one. Progress was slowed to even more of a snail's pace than before. And while he chopped, Longstreet and Hill, having formed for battle, waited. At 2.30, detecting signs of the enemy ahead, Huger brought up a couple of light fieldpieces and shelled the brush.

Holmes too was involved in a nightmare this day — a far bloodier and noisier one than Huger's contest of axes, though in point of fact the noise was not a very disturbing element for the fifty-seven-year-old North Carolinian, who was deaf. After waiting most of the afternoon at the junction of the New Market and Long Bridge roads, he received word that the bluecoats were streaming in thousands across Malvern Hill, a tall ridge three miles ahead, in the final stage of deliverance from the unsprung trap Lee had contrived for their destruction around Glendale. His 6000 men were too few for a successful infantry attack on the heavy column of Federals, but Holmes decided to do what he could with his artillery to frustrate their escape. Accordingly he rode forward, found a position well within range of the hill, then brought up six rifled pieces, supported by a regiment of infantry, and prepared to open fire.

While the guns were being laid he stepped into a house by the side of the road. Just then a single large-caliber projectile broke with a clap like sudden blue-sky thunder over the heads of his startled men, followed promptly by what one of them called "a perfect shower of shells of tremendous proportion and hideous sound." The result was instantaneous pandemonium. Infantry and artillery alike, the green troops clustered and scattered and milled aimlessly about in search of cover, which was scarce. Some in their greenness took shelter from the ten-inch shells by crouching behind two-inch saplings; others simply knelt in their tracks and clasped their hands, palms down, on the tops of their heads. Placid in the midst of all this uproar — bursting projectiles, screaming men and horses, hoarse and futile shouts of command by rattled captains — Holmes emerged from the roadside house, suspiciously cupping one ear. "I thought I heard firing," he said.

The big shells, called "lamp posts," came from gunboats on James River, which looped northward within half a mile of the Confederate position. Soon Malvern Hill was wreathed in smoke as siege guns on its crest added canister to the weight of metal already falling on Holmes' demoralized soldiers. He pulled them back out of range. It was nearly sunset, and like Huger — whose daylong two-mile march left him a full mile short of contact with the Federal main body hastening south across his front — Holmes had taken no appreciable part in the day's fighting. Nor had Magruder, who came up in rear of Longstreet just as the uproar exploded on the far right, near the James, and was sent in that direction to help stem what sounded like a full-scale counterattack up the River road. Nor had Jackson, with better than one third of the whole army under his command.

After the early morning Savage Station conference with Lee, Stonewall had pushed on down toward White Oak Swamp, gleaning in the woods and fields a bumper harvest of abandoned U.S. equipment and prisoners as he went. This was always a pleasant task for the "wagon hunter," and today it gave him particular satisfaction, affording as it did an outlet for his apparent superabundance of nervous energy. When a companion protested that the captives would be of considerable expense to the government, Jackson shook his head. "It is cheaper to feed them than to fight them," he said. He pressed on, encountering no opposition. There was time, even, to stop and write the usual Monday letter to his wife. "An ever-kind Providence has greatly blessed our efforts," it began. About noon, approaching the sodden jungle of the swamp, he found that the Federals had already crossed it, burning the bridge behind them, and had emplaced their artillery on a commanding southside ridge, supported by heavy columns of infantry. Promptly he brought up his own guns under cover, opened suddenly on the enemy batteries, and saw them displace in frantic haste, abandoning three pieces in their confusion. Delighted, Jackson ordered his cavalry to ford the stream at once, intending for them to harry the fleeing bluecoats, and — in accordance with Lee's instructions — put a crew to work without delay, rebuilding the bridge in order to take up the pursuit with his infantry.

So far it had gone well: Stonewall seemed to have recovered his identity. But now, quite abruptly, it stopped cold. The cavalry, having crossed, was repulsed by the Federal batteries, which had not fled, as had been thought, but had simply moved to a new position, where they outgunned their smooth-bore rivals north of the swamp. Worse still, the ring of the sharpshooter's rifle, accompanied from time to time by the sickening thwack of a bullet striking flesh, drove the bridgebuilders from their work almost as soon as they got started. Worst of all, however, was Jackson's reaction, which was rather as if the mainspring of some tightly wound-up mechanism had suddenly lost its resilience or run down. Formerly alert and energetic, he grew taciturn and drowsy, even sullen. Recalling his troops from exposure to danger, he lay down under a tree and went to sleep.

That was about 3 o'clock. When he woke an hour later — or half-woke, rather, sitting slump-shouldered on a log, the bill of his dingy cadet cap pulled down over his sleep-puffed eyes — he heard sounds of heavy firing from the south. It made little impression on him, though. Nor did the suggestions of his lieutenants, who had been reconnoitering for a way around the impasse while he slept. A cavalry colonel sent word that he had located a useable ford nearby, but Jackson ignored the message. Wade Hampton, commanding an infantry brigade, went off on his own and presently returned to report in person that he had found an excellent downstream crossing that would bring his men in position to strike the unsuspecting Federal flank. Jackson stirred. Could Hampton build a bridge there? Yes, the South Carolinian said, but the noise might alert the enemy. Build the bridge, Jackson told him. Hampton left. Soon he was back, reporting that the work had been done without alarming the Union troops. Stonewall gave no sign that he had heard him. For a long time he sat there on the log, silent, collapsed like a jointed doll whose spinal string had snapped. Then abruptly he rose, still without replying, and walked away.

Hampton's bridge went unused — as did Jackson's third of Lee's army, which remained north of White Oak Swamp, out of touch with the enemy all day. At supper, soon after dark, Stonewall went to sleep with a piece of unchewed biscuit between his teeth. Jarred awake by his own nodding, he looked blankly about, then got up from the table. "Now, gentlemen," he told his staff, "let us at once to bed ... and see if tomorrow we cannot do something."

Of all the days in the eventful month since that last night in May when the President tendered him command of the leaderless army as they rode back from the confused and gloomy field of Seven Pines, this final day of June had been for Lee the longest and the saddest. None had promised more at the outset, or yielded less in the end, than this in which better than two thirds of his soldiers were withheld from contact with the fleeing enemy by the inabilities and eccentricities of the commanders of three out of his four intended columns of attack.

Davis was with him, now as then. At 2.30, mistaking the boom of Huger's guns, shelling the brush on the Charles City road, for the prearranged signal that the battle had opened on the left, Lee hurried north on the Long Bridge road in search of Longstreet and found him talking with the President in a little clearing of stunted pines and broomstraw. As Lee rode up, Davis greeted him with a question designed to forestall a repetition of the repulse he had suffered at the Virginian's hands four days ago at Mechanicsville: "Why, General, what are you doing here? You are in too dangerous a position for the commander of the army."

"I'm trying to find out something about the movements and plans of those people," Lee replied. (For him, the Federals were invariably "those people.") Then, attempting to recover the initiative, he added: "But you must excuse me, Mr President, for asking what *you* are doing here, and for suggesting that this is no place for the Commander in Chief of all our armies."

"Oh," Davis told him with a smile, airy but determined, "I am here on the same mission that you are."

Lee had to let it go at that, though presently the danger was considerably heightened. When Longstreet rode away and had some nearby batteries open fire in acknowledgment of what he thought was Huger's signal, the reply came not from the Confederates to the north, but from the Federals to the east. Suddenly the clearing was dotted with bursting shells. Concerned with the peril to Davis and Lee, A. P. Hill came dashing up and addressed them sternly: "This is no place for either of you, and as commander of this part of the field I order you both to the rear!" The two moved off — "We will obey your orders," Davis said — but when they drew rein, still within the zone of fire, red-bearded Little Powell overtook them and spoke with the same mock harshness as before: "Did I not tell you to go away from here, and did you not promise to obey my orders? Why, one shot from that battery over yonder may presently deprive the Confederacy of its President and the Army of Northern Virginia of its commander." Abashed, the two withdrew beyond range of the exploding shells and the explosive Hill.

It was then that Lee received unwelcome news that McClellan was closer to safety than he had supposed. A cavalry commander, patrolling ahead of Holmes on the River road, informed him by courier that the enemy, undamaged and unhindered, was crossing Malvern Hill within gunshot of the James. Lee at once rode down and saw for himself the truth of the report. The bulk of the Union supply train, accompanied by heavy columns of infantry, was making its escape. If the Confederate attack was delayed much longer, it would strike not the enemy flank, but the enemy rear: which meant that the chance for a Cannae would be gone. In fact, it might be gone already. Having approved Holmes' intention to disrupt the retreat as much as possible with his guns, Lee turned back toward Glendale. He still had heard nothing from Jackson, and nothing from Huger except that his route was "obstructed." But time was running out. Concentrated or not, he would throw what he had at the Federal flank before the tail of the blue column cleared the junction near which Hill and Longstreet had been waiting all this time.

Encountering Davis, who reproached him again for rashly exposing himself, Lee replied quite truly — it was, in fact, the crux of the problem, what with the inadequate communications and the lack of an adequate staff — that all he could learn of the situation was what he saw with his own eyes. As he rode northward, the uproar of the naval bombardment exploded behind him. What it meant he did not know, but when he returned to the broomstraw clearing, still under fire from the batteries ahead, he found that Magruder, arriving at last, had been ordered south by Longstreet, who interpreted the heavy-caliber uproar as a counterattack by the Federals near the James. For all Lee knew, that was what it was. Besides, there was no time for recalling Magruder.

If the assault was to be delivered before the bluecoats cleared the junction, it would have to be launched at once by the troops at hand; that is, by the divisions of Longstreet and A. P. Hill. He told them to go forward — which they did. The result was the Battle of Glendale; or Frayser's Farm, it was sometimes called, since much of the hottest fighting occurred on this two-hundred-acre property south of the junction.

Not that it wasn't hot enough all over. In sending two divisions against an enemy force of undetermined strength, Lee's hope was that they would find the Federals strung out on the roads and unprepared. As it turned out, however, he was hoping for a good deal more of an advantage than his opponent was willing to grant. McClellan had disposed his eleven divisions with several eventualities in mind, and in fact was readier for this than for any other. Keyes' two divisions, along with two of Porter's, were already in position on Malvern Hill; two more — one from Sumner and one from Franklin — were on rear-guard duty, observing the quiescent Jackson across White Oak Swamp; Franklin's other division was astride the Charles City road, blocking Huger. The remaining four — Heintzelman's two and one each from Sumner and Porter — were in front of Glendale, ready for whatever came their way. The result was a savage, stand-up fight, beginning two hours before sundown and continuing through twilight into darkness.

Longstreet went in, driving hard and capturing guns in the rush, but presently, encountering stiffer resistance as the blue mass absorbed the blow, called for help. Hill's men charged with a yell on the left and right, their backs to the setting sun. Again the Federals yielded; again they rallied. The fighting now was hand to hand. Bayonets crossed and musket butts cracked skulls. More guns were taken, lost, and retaken as the lines surged back and forth in the dusk,

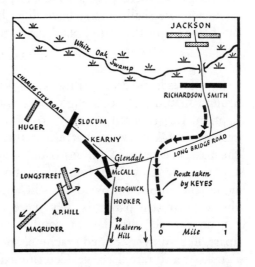

across clearings and through woods. Longstreet remained calm, feeding men into the holocaust and matching his skill against the odds. When a group of jubilant Virginians brought him a captured brigadier, he recognized an old army comrade, George McCall, commander of Porter's third division. About to extend his hand in greeting, he saw that the prisoner was in no mood for the amenities, however, and directed instead that he be taken at once to Richmond as a trophy.

Gradually the battle racket died away in the darkness: the Confederates held the field. Having paid for it with the blood of 3300 men, they received by way of dividend eighteen Yankee guns and one Yankee general. But these were the only substantial results. The real objective — McClellan's supply train and reserve artillery, for which he would have had to turn and fight without the alternative of an orderly retreat — was not obtained, and in fact had been unobtainable since midday, five hours before the battle started. Under cover of night, the Federals continued their withdrawal toward the James.

McClellan himself was there already, having gone aboard the ironclad *Galena* to confer with the gunboat commander and arrange for support while Keyes and Porter were filing into position on Malvern Hill. A telegram from Lincoln, sent two days ago and rerouted through Fortress Monroe, showed something of the official reaction up to the time the White House line was cut. "Save your army at all events," the President urged him. "Will send reinforcements as fast as we can. . . . If you have had a drawn battle or a repulse it is the price we pay for the enemy not being in Washington. . . . It is the nature of the case, and neither you nor the Government are to blame."

Though he agreed with no more than half of the final sentence, McClellan was too worn down by exertion and anxiety to press the point just yet. At sundown, proud but gloomy, he replied: "My army has behaved superbly, and have done all that men can do. If none of us escape, we shall at least have done honor to the country. I shall do my best to save the army. Send more gunboats."

★ ★ ★

Tuesday's dawn, July 1, showed the Union lines abandoned around Glendale, and though there was no longer a chance for interception, Lee ordered his army to concentrate for pursuit. He had no real way of knowing what effect the past six days of fighting — and the past five days of falling back — might have had on the Federals. Up to now they had fought stubbornly and hard; but last night's fierce encounter, followed by still another retreat, might have tipped the scale toward panic. If they were in fact demoralized, the slightest tap on this seventh day of combat might cause the blue host to fly apart, like an overstrained machine, and thus expose it to destruction in detail. At any rate, Lee was determined to take advantage of any opening McClellan might afford him for striking a crippling blow.

Magruder was already on hand, having countermarched in the night to relieve the battle-weary men of Hill and Longstreet. The southern commander joined these three while awaiting the arrival of Jackson and Huger, whose advance was unopposed. He bore himself calmly, but it was obviously with considerable effort. The cumulative strain of watching his combinations fail and his plans go awry because of fumbling had upset his digestion and shortened his temper. Longstreet, on the other hand, seemed as confident as ever, if not more so. When a Union surgeon came to request protection and supplies for the wounded he had stayed behind to tend, Longstreet asked him what division he belonged to. McCall's, the doctor said. "Well, McCall is safe in Richmond," Longstreet told him, adding that if it had not been for the Pennsylvanian's stubborn resistance along this road the day before, "we would have captured your whole army. Never mind," he said. "We will do it yet."

Lee said nothing. But Harvey Hill, whom they presently encountered, did not agree with the burly, eupeptic Georgian. One of Hill's chaplains, a native of the region, had given him a description of the terrain ahead. It was well adapted for defense, he said: particularly Malvern Hill, which the bluecoats were reported to have occupied already. "If General McClellan is there in strength, we had better let him alone," the saturnine Hill declared.

"Don't get scared, now that we have got him whipped," Longstreet broke in with a laugh.

Hill made no reply to this. Nor did Lee, who apparently had all he could do to maintain his composure. In this he was not entirely successful, however. When a newly arrived brigadier came up to the group and expressed concern lest McClellan escape, the gray-bearded commander's patience snapped. "Yes, he will get away," Lee said bitterly, "because I cannot have my orders carried out!"

Events coming hard on the heels of this uncharacteristic outburst did not improve the general's disposition. Malvern Hill was less than three miles away, no more than a normal one-hour march, but with seven divisions crowding a single southward road, the result was confusion and delay. (A parallel road, half a mile to the east, which Keyes had taken with his whole corps the previous night, went unused because it was not shown on Lee's crude map.) On top of all this, a mix-up in Magruder's orders sent his division swinging off on a tangent; time was lost before he was missed, and still more before he could be found and put back on the track. It soon developed that today, as on every other of what was to be known as the Seven Days — one gigantic twenty-mile-long conflict, with bewildering intermissions, not for resting, but for groping spastically in the general direction of an enemy who fought so savagely when cornered that the whole thing had been rather like playing blindman's buff with a buzz saw — Lee's army would not be within striking distance of the day's objective until well past noon. In fact, it was 1.30 before six of the eight Confederate divisions — Magruder was still off on his tangent, and Holmes was still licking yesterday's wounds, down on the River road — had filed into position facing the 150-foot height, which bristled with guns parked hub-to-hub to the front and rear of long blue stalwart-looking lines of Federal infantry.

Bad as it looked at first glance from the attacker's point of view, closer inspection of the position McClellan had chosen produced even stronger confirmation of D. H. Hill's long-range opinion that "we had better let him alone." Porter, who was in tactical command, was obviously ready for anything Lee might throw at him there on the undulating plateau, a mile and a half long and half as wide. He and Keyes, with two divisions each, held a line about midway up the slope; Heintzelman was in immediate reserve with two more, while Sumner and

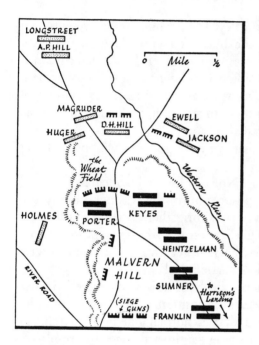

Franklin remained on call, in case their four were needed; which seemed unlikely, considering the narrow front, the apparently unassailable flanks, and the direct support of more than one hundred guns. These last were what made the position especially forbidding, and it was on them that Porter seemingly placed his chief reliance. First, in advance of the heavy ranks of infantry on the left and center, fieldpieces were massed in a long crescent so as to sweep the open ground across which the graybacks would have to charge if they were to come within musket range of the defenders. Other batteries were in support, all the way back to the brow of the hill, where siege guns were emplaced. Still farther back, on the James itself, naval gunners stood to their pieces, ready to arch their heavy-caliber shells into the ranks of the attackers.

In full view of all those cannon frowning down, attack seemed outright suicide. But this was Lee's last chance to destroy McClellan before he reached the safety of the river, rested and refitted his army under cover of the gunboats, then launched another drive on Richmond, giving the Confederates the bloody task of driving him back again. This first repulse had been hard enough to manage; a second, with the Federal host enlarged by reinforcements and based securely on the James, might be impossible. With this in mind — and also the thought that the stalwart look of the Union troops, near the end of their long retreat, might be no more than a veneer that covered profound despair — Lee ordered his men to take up assault positions while he searched for a way to get at "those people" and administer the rap which he hoped would cause them to come apart at the seams. Huger was on the right, D. H. Hill in the center; Magruder would form between them when he arrived. Jackson and Ewell were on the left. Longstreet and A. P. Hill, still weary from yesterday's fight, were in reserve; Holmes, around on the River road, would coöperate as developments permitted. This arrangement left much to be desired, but it would have to do until a better could be evolved. What that would be Lee did not know until he was on his way to reconnoiter Jackson's front, which seemed to offer the best chance for success.

As he set out, a message came from Longstreet, who reported that he had found a good artillery position on the right, a terraced knoll with a direct line of fire to the Union batteries. From there, he added, he could see on the Confederate left an open field which also afforded an excellent position. If guns were massed at these two points, Longstreet said — forty on the right, say, and twice that many on the left — a converging fire would throw the northern batteries into confusion and open the way for an attack by the southern infantry. Lee saw in this the opportunity he was seeking: a charge in the style of the one across Boatswain's Swamp four days ago, with even greater rewards to follow success. Accordingly, he ordered the guns to occupy the two positions and notified his front-line commanders of the plan. One of Huger's brigades, posted closest to the enemy, would be able to judge best the effect of the bombardment. If it was successful, the brigade would go forward with a yell, which in turn would be the signal for an end-to-end assault by the whole gray line, the object being to close with the blue army and destroy it there on the rolling slopes of Malvern Hill.

It was not going to be easy; it might even be impossible; but as a last chance Lee thought it worth a try. In any case, if the bombardment failed in its purpose, the infantry need not advance. Already they were taking punishment from the siege guns on the brow of the hill as they filed through the wooded and swampy lowlands to get in position for the jump-off. The heavy-caliber fire was deliberate and deadly: as Harvey Hill could testify. While his troops were forming under a rain of metal and splintered branches, the North Carolinian sat at a camp table on the exposed side of a large tree, drafting orders for the attack. When one of his officers urged him at least to put the trunk between him and the roaring guns: "Don't worry about me," Hill said. "Look after the men. I am not going to be killed until my time comes." With that, a shell crashed into the earth alongside him, the concussion lifting the predestinarian from his chair and rolling him over and over on the ground. Hill got up, shook the dirt from his coat, the breast of which had been torn by a splinter of iron, and resumed his seat — on the far side of the tree. This and what followed were perhaps the basis for his later statement that, with Confederate infantry and Yankee artillery, he believed he could whip any army in the world.

What followed was a frustrating demonstration that southern gunners were no match for their northern counterparts: not here and now, at any rate. On the right and left, batteries came up piecemeal, no more than twenty guns in all — less than a fifth the number Longstreet had recommended — and piecemeal they were bludgeoned by counter-battery fire. Nowhere in this war would Federal artillerists have a greater advantage, and they did not neglect it. Sometimes concentrating as many as fifty guns on a single rebel battery, they pounded it to pulp and wreckage before changing deflection to repeat the treatment on the next one down the line. Half an hour was all they needed. By 2.30, with the whole Union position still billowing smoke and coughing flame — one six-gun battery near the center, for example, fired 1300 rounds in the course of the afternoon — not a single Confederate piece with a direct line of fire remained in action. What had been intended as a preliminary bombardment, paving the way for the infantry, had been reduced to a bloody farce. If Lee's soldiers were to come to grips with the bluecoats on that gun-jarred slope, they would have to do it some other way than this.

The southern commander resumed his reconnaissance on the left, hoping to find an opening for an attack that would flank the Federals off the hill. Far on the right, Huger's lead brigade was working its way forward. In its front was a large field of wheat, lately gleaned, with sharpshooters lurking behind the gathered sheaves of grain. Little would be gained by taking the wheatfield — on its far side, just beyond musket range, the crescent of guns standing hub to hub could clip the stubble as close as the scythe had lately done — but Huger's men, bitterly con-scious that theirs was the only division which had done no real fight-ing since the opening attack six days ago, were determined to have a share in the bloody work of driving the invaders. Taking their losses, they surged ahead and finally took cover in a gully at the near edge of the wheatfield, well in advance of the rest of the army, while the sharp-shooters fell back on their guns. Magruder, arriving about 4 o'clock to assume command of the right, notified Lee that he was on hand at last and that Huger's men had driven the enemy and made a substantial lodgment.

Lee meanwhile had found what he thought might be an opening on the left, and had sent word for the men of Longstreet and A. P. Hill to come forward and exploit it. Weary though they were, they were all he had. Just then, however, as Lee rode back toward the center, the message arrived from Magruder, together with one from the left re-porting signs of a Federal withdrawal. That changed everything. This first advantage, if followed up, might throw McClellan's army into panic and open the way for an all-out flank-to-flank assault. Quickly he gave verbal orders, which the messenger took down for delivery to Magruder: "General Lee expects you to advance rapidly. He says it is reported the enemy is getting off. Press forward your whole command."

By now Prince John had had a chance to look into the situation a bit more carefully on the right, and as a result he was feeling considerably less sanguine. However, Lee's three-hour-old order, calling for a general advance if the preliminary bombardment was successful, reached him soon after he arrived. Since it bore no time of dispatch, Magruder assumed that it was current: an assumption presently strengthened by the prompt arrival of the message directing him to "press forward your whole command." That was what he did, and he did it without delay, despite the unpromising aspect which a hasty examination had revealed on this shell-torn quarter of the field. Quickly he formed his men and sent them forward on the right of Huger's lead brigade, which cheered at the sight of this unexpected support, leaped eagerly out of the gully, and joined the charge across the wheatfield. On the far side of the cropped plain, the long crescent of guns began to buck and jump with redoubled fury, licking the stubble with tongues of flame.

After the failure of the preliminary bombardment and the encounter with the shell that had seemed to have his name written on it, D. H. Hill had decided that no large-scale attack would be delivered. All the same, since Lee had never countermanded the tentative order for an advance if Huger's troops raised a yell, he kept his brigade commanders with him, ready to give them time-saving verbal instructions in case the unexpected signal came. Near sundown, just as he was advising them to return to their men and prepare to bed them down for the night, the firing rose suddenly to crescendo on the smoky hill and the sound of cheering broke out on the right. "That must be the general advance!" Hill exclaimed. "Bring up your brigades as soon as possible and join it." Quickly they rejoined their commands and led them forward through the woods. By the time they came out into the open, however, a fair proportion of the troops who had attacked on the right were lying dead or dying in the wheatfield, and the rest were either hugging what little defilade they could find or else were running pell-mell toward the rear. The flaming crescent of Union guns shifted east in time to catch the new arrivers at the start of their advance up the long slope. "It was not war, it was murder," Hill said later.

That was what it was, all right: mass murder. Hill and Magruder and Huger gave it all they had, despite the hurricane of shells, only to see charge after charge break in blood and flow back from the defiant line of guns. Dusk put an end to the fighting — none of it had been hand to hand, and much of it had been done beyond musket range — though the cannon sustained the one-sided argument past dark. By that time, 5590 Confederates had fallen, as compared with less that a third that many Federals, and all for nothing. The Seven Days were over; Lee had failed in his final effort to keep McClellan from reaching the James.

Now that he had examined the ground over which the useless attack had been launched, he saw that it had clearly been foredoomed, and he could not understand how any commander, there on the scene, with all those guns staring down his throat, could not have known better than to undertake it in the first place. So he went looking for Magruder. At Savage Station, two days ago, he had reproached him by messenger; this time he intended to do it in person, or at any rate demand an explanation. At last he found him. "General Magruder, why did you attack?" he said. Prince John had remained silent under the previous rebuke; but this time he had an answer, and he gave it. "In obedience to your orders, twice repeated," he told Lee.

Jackson's men, at the far end of the line of battle, had spent another non-fighting day — their sixth out of the seven. Only the artillery had been engaged on the left. The infantry, moving forward through the swampy underbrush, had not been able to come up in time to take part in the assault, though as Stonewall rode through the gathering dusk he found one of Ewell's brigadiers forming his troops under cover of the woods, their faces reflecting the eerie red flicker of muzzle-flashes out on the slope ahead. Jackson drew rein.

"What are you going to do?" he asked.

"I am going to charge those batteries, sir!"

"I guess you had better not try it," Stonewall told him. "General D. H. Hill has just tried it with his whole division and been repulsed; I guess you had better not try it, sir."

Presently the firing died to a rumble. About 10 o'clock it stopped, and out of the moonless darkness came the agonized cries of the wounded, beyond reach on the uptilted, blood-soaked plain. Jackson lay down on a blanket and went to sleep. Three hours later he was wakened by Ewell and Harvey Hill, who believed that McClellan was preparing to launch a dawn attack and had come to ask if Stonewall wanted them to make any special dispositions to meet it. One sleepy officer, seeing the three men squatting in a circle, thought they resembled a triumvirate of frogs. "No," Jackson said quietly, "I believe he will clear out in the morning."

★ ★ ★

He was right; McClellan did clear out, but not without having to override the protests of several high-ranking subordinates. Even Porter, who was his friend and generally favored all his actions, opposed this one, saying that he believed a determined advance from Malvern Hill would throw Lee into retreat through the streets of his capital. Phil Kearny, the hardest fighter among the brigade commanders — a spike-bearded New Jersey professional whose thirst for combat had not been slaked by the loss of an arm while leading a cavalry charge in Mexico — was the most vociferous of all. When the retirement order reached him at the close of the battle, he rose in the presence of his staff and cried out in anger: "I, Philip Kearny, an old soldier, enter my solemn protest against this order for retreat. We ought instead of retreating to follow up the enemy and take Richmond. And in full view of the responsibility of such a declaration, I say to you all, such an order can only be prompted by cowardice or treason."

McClellan either ignored this protest, or else he never heard it. In any case, his reply to Kearny would have been the same as the one he had made three days ago, when a cavalry colonel suggested a dash on the southern capital while Lee still had most of his men on the north bank of the Chickahominy: "If an army can save this country it will be the Army of the Potomac, and it must be saved for that purpose." He was taking no chances. If Lee would let him alone for the present, he was more than willing to return the favor.

And so it was that the same cavalry colonel found himself and his regiment alone on the hilltop next morning at dawn, with only a skirmish line of infantry left for show, while the rest of the army followed the road to Harrison's Landing. A mizzling rain had fallen before daylight, and mist blotted the lower slope from view. He could see nothing down there, but out of the mist came a babble of cries and wails and groans from the wounded who had managed to live through the night. After a while the sun came out, and when it burned the mist away he saw a thing he would never forget, and never remember except with a shudder. Down there on the lower slope, the bodies of five thousand gray-clad soldiers were woven into a carpet of cold or agonized flesh. "A third of them were dead or dying," he later wrote, "but enough of them were alive and moving to give the field a singular crawling effect."

Disposing his troops in a pretense of strength, the colonel presently agreed with feigned reluctance to an informal truce, and while rebel ambulance details came out of the woods and moved among the sufferers on the hillside, he withdrew under cover of a drenching rain and joined the rear of the retreating column, the van of which was led by the army commander. "My men are completely exhausted," McClellan wired Washington, "and I dread the result if we are attacked today by fresh troops. . . . I now pray for time. My men have proved themselves the equals of any troops in the world, but they are worn-out. . . . We have failed to win only because overpowered by superior numbers."

He had not lost: he had "failed to win." Nor had he been outfought: he had been "overpowered." So he said. And if his words were unrealistic, it might be added in extenuation that all the events of the past week had occurred in an atmosphere of unreality. Watching the week-long twenty-mile-wide conflict had been something like watching a small man beat a large one, not by nimble footwork or artful dodging or even boxing skill, but rather by brute force, driving headlong, never relinquishing the offensive, and taking a good deal more punishment than he inflicted. This last was confirmed by the casualty lists, which were beginning to be compiled now that the two armies were out of contact.

Three months ago the news of Shiloh had arrived from the West with a dreadful shock; 23,741 American fighting men had been killed, wounded, or captured in that battle. Now the East's turn had come. The best, and the worst, that could be said of the battle known as the Seven Days was that this grim western figure had been exceeded by more than half; 36,463 was the total. And though in the earlier conflict most of the casualties had been Union, here it was the other way around; 15,849 Federals and 20,614 Confederates were on the list. In killed and wounded, moreover, the advantage increased from almost three to four to better than one to two. Nearly 10,000 Federals had fallen, 1734 killed and 8062 wounded, as opposed to nearly 20,000 Confederates, 3478 and 16,261. However, this preponderance was considerably reduced by the 6053 Federals missing in action; only 875 Confederates were in that category. In the end, since approximately half of the uncaptured wounded would return in time to the ranks of their respective armies, this made the actual loss of fighting men somewhat lower for the Confederates, 8000 of whom would be returning, whereas half of the Federal wounded had been captured, leaving only half of the remainder to return — about 2000 — so that the actual loss in combat strength, after recuperation of the injured, would be 14,000 Federals and 12,500 Confederates.

Knowing as he did that the South could not afford a swapping game on anything like a man-for-man basis of exchange, Lee found little solace in such figures. When Jackson and Longstreet came by headquarters, seeking refuge from the storm while the aid men and the burial squads worked among the wounded and the dead on the rain-swept hillside, he asked Longstreet for his impression of the fighting. "I think you hurt them about as much as they hurt you," the forthright Georgian told him. Lee winced at this, for he knew how badly his army had suffered, and there was a touch of irony in his reply: "Then I am glad we punished them well, at any rate."

Longstreet left. Soon afterward, unexpectedly, President Davis walked in, taking Lee so much by surprise that he omitted the Mister from his salutation. "President," he said, "I am delighted to see you." They shook hands. Across the room, Jackson had risen and was standing at attention beside his chair. Lee saw Davis looking at him. "Why, President, don't you know General Jackson? This is our Stonewall Jackson." They were acquainted, of course, but the relationship had been strained by the Romney controversy, in which the Mississippian had supported

Benjamin and the Virginian had submitted his resignation. The result, in this first meeting since then, was a curious exchange. Observing the Valley general's bristling manner, Davis did not offer his hand. Instead he bowed, and Jackson replied with a rigid salute. Neither of them said anything to the other.

Their last encounter had been under similar circumstances, after the victory at Manassas, and here again the question was how or whether to pursue a driven foe. Stonewall felt the same way about it as he had felt a year ago, but Lee and Davis agreed that the disorganized condition of the southern army precluded any chance to overcome the Federals' substantial head start down the muddy road, which would be under gunboat fire at several points. Asked for his opinion, Jackson said dourly: "They have not all got away if we go immediately after them." Lee shook his head. For the present at least, pursuit would have to be left to the cavalry, which had arrived the night before. The rest of the army would spend what was left of the day attending the wounded, burying the dead, and preparing to resume the chase tomorrow.

For today, then — as well as for a good part of tomorrow, since Harrison's Landing was eight muddy miles from Malvern Hill — Jeb Stuart had McClellan to himself. And the truth was, he preferred it so. Except for an encounter with a gunboat on the Pamunkey, three days ago — he reported with pride that he had repulsed it with a single howitzer, forcing the monster to close its ports and slink off, full-speed-astern; "What do you think of that?" he wrote his wife — outpost duty along the lower Chickahominy had kept his troopers out of the main channel of events during the past momentous week, affording them little chance for a share in the glory of driving the Yankees away from the gates of Richmond. All that was behind them at last, however, and now that they were back in the limelight — stage center, so to speak — their plumed commander intended to make the most of whatever opportunities came his way. Today there were few, the pursuit being mainly a matter of gathering up the stragglers and equipment which the blue host dribbled in its wake on the River road. Night fell before he found what he was seeking.

Next morning, though — July 3; the rain had slacked and stopped in the night; the day was bright and sunny — he came within sight of the answer to his prayers. The northern army had gone into camp beside the James, and Stuart, mounting a low ridge called Evelington Heights, looked down and saw the quarry spread out before him, close-packed and apparently ripe for destruction. McClellan had chosen the position with care. The creeks on his flanks, one of which curved along his front as well, and the gunboats anchored in his rear, their big guns trained across the meadows, gave him excellent protection from attack by infantry. But in failing to occupy Evelington Heights he had left his soldiers open to terrible punishment from the plunging fire of any guns the Confederates might bring up. Stuart saw this at once, and quickly got off a message informing Lee of the opportunity. Unwilling to wait, however, and with no regard for the long odds or concern for the consequences of alerting the Federals to the danger of leaving the dominant ridge unoccupied, he brought up the little howitzer that had peppered a gunboat into retreat four days ago, and at 9 o'clock opened fire on the bluecoats huddled on the mudflats down below.

The effect was instantaneous and spectacular, a moil of startled men and rearing horses thrown abruptly into milling consternation. Stuart was delighted. Informed by Lee that Longstreet, Jackson, and A. P. Hill were on the march to join him, he kept the little fieldpiece barking terrier-like to sustain the confusion until they arrived to compound it. But it was a case of too little too soon. Spotting the trouble at last, the Federals moved to get rid of it by advancing a six-gun battery and a regiment of infantry. Stuart held his position until he was down to his last two rounds, still hoping for the arrival of support. At 2 o'clock, with hostile guns approaching his front and infantry probing around his flanks, he fired his two last shells and pulled back off the ridge. He had done no appreciable damage, but he was pleased that he had found this chance to give McClellan one last prod. Moreover, he wrote home next day, "If the army had been up with me we would have finished his business."

As it was, however, the lead elements of Longstreet's division, moving in front of the other two, did not arrive until sunset, too late to undertake an attack even if the heights had still been naked of guns, which they were not; McClellan had been shown his mistake and had moved to rectify it. Next morning the ridge was crowned with batteries, supported by heavy columns of infantry. Hill and Jackson had come up by then, and Longstreet, who assumed command by seniority, put them in line for an all-out assault, holding his own division in reserve. Lee arrived to find Jackson protesting that his men were too weary and the heights too strong for the attack to be anything but a fiasco. After looking the situation over, Lee was obliged to agree regretfully with Stonewall; the assault was canceled, and the troops went into camp. The campaign was over.

Certain regiments were left on picket duty to observe the enemy, and one among them was stationed in a clump of woods overlooking an open field, beyond which there was another clump of woods where a Federal regiment was posted. All in all, the situation indicated a sudden renewal of bloodshed. This was the Fourth of July, however, and what was more the field was full of ripe blackberries; "so," as one rebel private later remembered, "our boys and the Yanks made a bargain not to fire at each other, and went out in the field, leaving one man on each post with the arms, and gathered berries together and talked over the fight, traded tobacco and coffee and exchanged newspapers as peacefully and kindly as if they had not been engaged for the last seven days in butchering one another."

The Sun Shines South

★ ⚔ ☆

NAPOLEON WAS TAKING THE WATERS AT
Vichy when news of the Seven Days reached him in mid-July. Hard
on its heels came John Slidell, with an offer of one hundred thousand
bales of cotton if France would denounce the Federal blockade. Unable to act alone in the matter, however eager he might be to feed his
country's looms, the Emperor — called "Napoleon the Little" to distinguish him from his illustrious uncle — promptly telegraphed his
Foreign Minister: "Demandez au gouvernement anglais s'il ne croit pas
le moment venu de reconnaître le Sud."

Across the channel the mills were hungry, too, and though
Mason was somewhat handicapped by the impracticality of offering an
Englishman anything so indelicate as a bribe, the time was propitious
from the Confederate point of view. "There is an all but unanimous
belief that you *cannot* subject the South to the Union," an influential
partisan of Northern interests was informing a friend across the ocean.
"I feel quite convinced that unless cotton comes in considerable quantities before the end of the year, the governments of Europe will be
knocking at your door." Moreover, even as he wrote, a pro-Confederate
member was introducing a motion before Parliament for British-
French mediation in the American Civil War, which in effect amounted
to recognition of the infant nation as a reward for throwing the blue
invader off its doorstep. Fortunately, however — from the Federal
point of view — the long vacation was under way, and before the issue
could be forced the Cabinet was scattered from Scotland to Germany,
in pursuit of grouse and relaxation. Action was deferred.

Distracting as these transatlantic dangers were, or might have
been, the truth was Lincoln had more than enough material for full-
time worry here at home. Hedged in by cares, blamed alike by critics

right and left of the hostile center, he later said of the period under question: "I was as nearly inconsolable as I could be and live." In contrast to the adulation heaped on Davis, whose critics had been muzzled by the apparent vindication of his policies and whose countrymen now hailed him as a second Hezekiah, the northern leader heard himself likened unto Sennacherib, the author and director of a ponderous fiasco. Henry Ward Beecher was saying of him from a pulpit in Brooklyn, "Not a spark of genius has he; not an element for leadership. Not one particle of heroic enthusiasm." Wendell Phillips thought him something worse, and said so from a Boston lecture platform: "He may be honest — nobody cares whether the tortoise is honest or not. He has neither insight, nor prevision, nor decision. . . . As long as you keep the present turtle at the head of the government, you make a pit with one hand and fill it with the other."

The politicians were in full bay, particularly those of his own party who had been urging, without success, his support of antislavery legislation which he feared would lose him the border states, held to the Union so far by his promise that no such laws would be passed. It also seemed to these Republicans that entirely too many Democrats were seated in high places, specifically in the cabinet and the army; and now their anger was increased by apprehension. About to open their campaigns for reëlection in November, they had counted on battlefield victories to increase their prospects for victory at the polls. Instead, the main eastern army, under the Democrat McClellan — "McNapoleon," they called him — had held back, as if on purpose, and then retreated to the James, complaining within hearing of the voters that the Administration was to blame. Privately, many of the Jacobins agreed with the charge, though for different reasons, the main one being that Lincoln, irresolute by nature, had surrounded himself with weak-spined members of the opposition party. Fessenden of Maine put it plainest: "The simple truth is, there was never such a shambling half-and-half set of incapables collected in one government since the world began."

The people themselves were disconsolate. "Give me a victory and I will give you a poem," James Russell Lowell wrote his publisher; "but I am now clear down in the bottom of the well, where I see the Truth too near to make verses of." Apparently the people shared his gloom. Their present reaction was nothing like the short-lived panic they had staged five weeks ago, when Stonewall Jackson broke through to the line of the Potomac. Nor was it characterized by aroused determination, as in the period following Bull Run the year before. It was in fact strangely apathetic and difficult to measure, even for a man who had spent a lifetime with one hand on the public pulse, matching the tempo of his actions to its beat. Lincoln watched and wondered. One indication was the stock market, which broke badly under the impact of the news from the Peninsula; another was the premium on the gold in the Union dollar, which had stood at three and one-half percent a month ago, but since then had risen to seventeen. He watched and wondered, unable to catch the beat.

In response to McClellan's call for reinforcements on the day of Malvern Hill — "I need 50,000 more men, and with them I will retrieve our fortunes" — Lincoln told him: "Maintain your ground if you can, but save the army at all events, even if you fall back to Fort Monroe. We still have strength enough in the country, and will bring it out." Well, McClellan had "saved the army," and the "strength enough" was there; but Lincoln was uncertain as to how to "bring it out." The present apathy might be a lull before the storm that would be brought on by another call for troops. As he phrased it, "I would publicly appeal to the country for this new force were it not that I fear a general panic and stampede would follow, so hard is it to have a thing understood as it really is."

As usual, he found a way. To call for troops was one thing; to receive them was another. Seward was sent to New York to confer with men of political and financial power, explain the situation, and arrange for the northern governors to "urge" the President to issue a call for volunteers to follow up "the recent successes of the Federal arms." Lest there be any doubt as to whether the Administration intended to fight this war through to a finish, Seward took with him a letter: "I expect to maintain this contest until successful, or till I die, or am conquered, or my term expires, or Congress or the country forsake me.... Yours, very truly, A. Lincoln."

Seventeen governors, plus the president of the Military Board of Kentucky, responded promptly by affixing their signatures to a communication written by Seward, addressed to the Chief Executive, and saying in part: "We respectfully request, if it meets with your entire approval, that you at once call upon the several States for such number of men as may be required ... to garrison and hold all of the numerous cities and military positions that have been captured by our armies, and to speedily crush the rebellion that still exists in several of the Southern States, thus practically restoring to the civilized world our great and good Government." Being thus urged, Lincoln took his cue and in early July — "fully concurring in the wisdom of the views expressed to me in so patriotic a manner" — issued a call for 300,000 volunteers. In fact, so entirely did the request meet with his approval, he followed this first call with another, one month later, for 300,000 more.

Lowell, "clear down in the bottom of the well," had said he could produce no poem unless he received a victory as payment in advance; but lesser talents apparently required a lesser fee. J. S. Gibbons found in this second call a subject fit for his muse, and Stephen Foster set the result to music:

If you look up all our valleys where the growing harvests shine
You may see our sturdy farmer boys fast forming into line,
And children from their mothers' knees are pulling at the weeds
And learning how to reap and sow against their country's needs,
And a farewell group stands weeping at every cottage door:
We are coming, Father Abraham, three hundred thousand more!

Reinforcements would be welcome all along the line; there was scarcely a mile of it that did not have some general calling plaintively or angrily for more soldiers. But more soldiers, even half a million of them, would not solve the basic problem, which was one of high command. For four months now, ever since the abrupt relief of McClellan back in March, the overall conduct of the war had been directed by Lincoln and Stanton — a sort of two-headed, four-thumbed amateur — with results just short of disastrous in the theater which had received their main attention. Stonewall Jackson, for example, had frightened Stanton and decoyed Lincoln into breaking up the combinations McClellan had designed for taking Richmond: so that Davis and Lee, professionals both, had been able to turn the tables on the Army of the Potomac, effecting countercombinations that drove it headlong to the James. Part of the fault could be assigned to flaws that developed in subordinate commanders — on the one hand, Frémont's ineptness; on the other, McClellan's lack of aggressive instincts — but most of it lay with the overall direction, which had permitted the enemy to bring pressure on those flaws.

Lincoln could see this now in retrospect, much of it at any rate, and in fact he had begun to suspect it soon after the failure of his chessboard combinations in the Valley. In his distress, before the blow fell on the Peninsula, his mind turned back to Winfield Scott, the one general who had shown thus far that he really knew what war was all about. The old man was in retirement up the Hudson at West Point, too infirm for travel. So on June 23 — a Monday; the first of the Seven Days was two days off — Lincoln boarded a special train and rode north to see him. What they talked about was a secret, and it remained so. But when McClellan wired the War Department on June 27, while Porter was under attack on Turkey Hill: "I will beg that you put some one general in command of the Shenandoah and of all troops in front of Washington for the sake of the country. Secure unity of action and bring the best men forward," Lincoln, who had returned two days before, had already done what he suggested, even before his visit up the Hudson. That is, he had united the troops under one commander. Whether he had brought the best man forward remained to be seen.

John Pope was the man: Halleck had praised him so highly he had lost him. Indeed, for months now the news from that direction had seemed to indicate that the formula for victory, so elusive here on the seaboard, had been discovered by the generals in the West — in which case, as Lincoln and Stanton saw it, the thing to do was bring one of them East and give him a chance to apply it. Grant's record having been tarnished by Shiloh and the subsequent rumors of negligence and whiskey, Pope was the more or less obvious choice, not only because of Island Ten and Halleck's praise of his aggressiveness during the campaign against Corinth, but also because Lincoln, as a prairie lawyer pleading cases in Pope's father's district court, had known him back in Illinois. There were objections. Montgomery Blair, for instance, warned that old Judge Pope "was a flatterer, a deceiver, a liar and a trickster; all the Popes are so." But the President could not see that these were necessarily drawback characteristics in a military man. While admitting the general's "infirmity" when it came to walking the chalk-line of truth, he protested that "a liar might be brave and have skill as an officer." Also, perhaps as a result of a belief in the Westerner's ability to combine effectively the several family traits Blair had warned of, he credited him with "great cunning," a quality Lincoln had learned to prize highly as a result of his brush with Stonewall Jackson in the Valley. So Pope was sent for.

Arriving while Lincoln was up the country seeing Scott, he made at once an excellent impression on Stanton and the members of the Committee on the Conduct of the War, who saw in him the antithesis of McClellan. For one thing, there was nothing of caution about him; he was a talker, and his favorite words were "I" and "forward." (If he had been placed in charge of the West in the early spring, he said, nothing could have stopped his march on New Orleans; by now he would have split the South in two and gone to work on the crippled halves.) For another, he was sound on the slavery question, assuring the committee that he and it saw eye to eye on the matter. Wade and the others were delighted, not only with his opinions, civil as well as military, but also with his appearance, which they found as reassuring as his beliefs. He had shaved his cheeks and his upper lip, retaining a spade-shaped chin beard that bobbed and wagged decisively as he spoke, lending weight and point to his utterances and increasing the overall impression of forcefulness and vigor. Lincoln, when he returned from the visit with Scott, was pleased to see the confidence Pope had managed to invite within so brief a span, and gave him at once his orders and his assignment to the command of an army expressly created for his use.

The Army of Virginia, it was called. Its strength was 56,000 men and its mission was to move in general down the line of the Orange & Alexandria Railroad, just east of the Blue Ridge Mountains, so as to close in on the Confederate capital from the west and north, while McClellan's Army of the Potomac applied pressure from the east; thus Richmond would be crushed in a giant nutcracker, with Pope as the upper jaw. His army was created by consolidating the commands of McDowell, Banks, and Frémont. All three of these generals outranked him — an unusual arrangement, to say the least — but only one of them took official umbrage. This was Frémont: which solved another problem. His protest resignation was accepted, and Lincoln replaced him with Franz Sigel, whose appointment, though it involved a thousand-mile transfer, was considered especially felicitous since so many of the troops involved were of German extraction.

Pope's instructions, issued June 26 as part of the order creating his army, required him to operate so as to protect Washington from "danger or insult" and to "render the most effective aid to relieve General McClellan and capture Richmond." It was a large order, but Pope only laid down one condition: McClellan must be given peremptory orders to attack the minute he heard that Pope was engaged. This was necessary, Pope said, because of the known timidity and irresolution of his partner in the squeeze play.

For the present, however — as he learned all too soon — the stipulation was unnecessary. On the day the Army of Virginia came officially into being, McClellan no longer had any choice in the matter; the Seven Days had opened, and the Army of the Potomac found itself engaged in a tremendous struggle for survival, trying first to fend off Lee's assault down the north bank of the Chickahominy and then to reach the gunboat sanctuary of the James. When news of the attack reached Washington, Pope showed that there were elements of caution in his make-up after all. He advised Lincoln not to let McClellan fall back southward, since this would unhinge the jaws of the nutcracker, but to order him to retire in the direction of the York. That way, Pope said, he could eventually go to his assistance — and vice versa, in case the Army of Virginia ran into similar trouble moving south. But there was nothing Lincoln could do about it, even if he had wanted to; the wires were cut and the Army of the Potomac was already in motion for the James. Pope began to see the handwriting on the wall. It warned him plainly that there was an excellent chance that he would be entirely on his own as he moved down the road that led to Richmond.

Discouraging as this prospect was to the newly arrived commander, a look into the backgrounds of the three groups he was expected to weld into an effective striking force proved equally discouraging, if not more so. Two of the three (Banks' and Sigel's) had traditions of defeat, and the third (McDowell's) had slogged all over northern Virginia, seemingly without profit to anyone, least of all to itself. Unquestionably, even in their own eyes — "Milroy's weary boys" were a case in point — this was the second team, restricted to an occasional scrimmage which served primarily to emphasize its lack of style, while the first team got the cheers and glory on the Peninsula. For all his bluster, Pope saw one thing clearly. However second-rate his material might be in some respects, he had here the makings of a first-class disaster, unless he could somehow restore or establish confidence in the breasts of his downhearted charges. Accordingly, as a first step before he took the field, he issued an address "To the Officers and Soldiers of the Army of Virginia," giving them, along with much else in the way of advice, a chance to see what manner of man was about to lead them against the rebel force that had just finished mauling the first team and flinging it back from the goal-post gates of Richmond.

"Let us understand each other," he told them. "I have come to you from the West, where we have always seen the backs of our enemies; from an army whose business it has been to seek the adversary and to beat him when he was found; whose policy has been attack and not defense.... I presume that I have been called here to pursue the same system and to lead you against the enemy. It is my purpose to do so, and that speedily." He supposed they longed for distinction in the jar and shock of battle, and he was prepared to show them how to win it. In any event, he said, "I desire you to dismiss from your minds certain phrases, which I am sorry to find so much in vogue amongst you. I hear constantly of 'taking strong positions and holding them,' of 'lines of retreat,' and of 'bases of supplies.' Let us discard such ideas. The strongest position a soldier should desire to occupy is one from which he can most easily advance against the enemy. Let us study the probable lines of retreat of our opponents, and leave our own to take care of themselves. Let us look before us, and not behind. Success and glory are in the advance, disaster and shame lurk in the rear."

The words had a Stantonian ring, which Pope explained long afterwards by identifying the Secretary himself as their author. At any rate, whoever wrote them, the effect was something other than the one that had been intended: particularly among the men the undersigned general addressed. They found the comparison odious, and they resented the boasting tone in which it was made. "Five Cent Pope," they dubbed their new commander, while old-time regulars recalled a parody that had made the army rounds some years ago, when he issued oversanguine reports of success in boring for artesian water on the bone-dry plains of Texas:

> *Pope told a flattering tale*
> *Which proved to be bravado*
> *About the streams which spout like ale*
> *On the Llano Estacado.*

McClellan's supporters of course resented him, too: Fitz-John Porter for example, who declared that Pope had "written himself down [as] what the military world has long known, an ass.... If the theory he proclaims is practiced you may look for disaster."

Beyond the lines, where the address enjoyed wide circulation, the Confederate reaction combined contempt and amusement. Reports that this new spread-eagle opponent was heading his dispatches "Headquarters in the Saddle" prompted a revival of the old army jibe that he had his headquarters where his hindquarters ought to be.

By the time Pope's flamboyant address was issued in mid-July, Lincoln had been down to the Peninsula and back. Between the two boat-rides, going and coming, he not only made a personal inspection of the Army of the Potomac and questioned its chief and subordinate generals, but he also made up his mind about a matter he had been pondering ever since his visit to Winfield Scott three weeks ago — a command decision, involving this and all the other armies of the Union.

Within two days of his July 1 plea for 50,000 men, with which to "retrieve our fortunes" after the blood-letting of the Seven Days, McClellan doubled the ante; 100,000 would now be needed, he declared. Lincoln replied on the 4th that any such figure "within a month, or even six weeks, is impossible. . . . Under these circumstances the defensive for the present must be your only care. Save the army — first, where you are, if you can; secondly, by removal, if you must." He added, perhaps ironically: "P.S. If at any time you feel able to take the offensive, you are not restrained from doing so." Once more he was losing patience fast. Sending troops to McClellan, he said, was like trying to shovel fleas across a barnlot; so few seemed to get there. Also, there were alarming rumors as to the condition of the men the general already had. Lincoln decided to see for himself. Boarding a steamer on the night of July 7, he reached Harrison's Landing late the following afternoon and rode out at once with the army commander for a sundown inspection of the camps.

Apparently to his surprise he found the men in good condition and high spirits — though the latter could be accounted for, at least in part, as a reaction to seeing the President on horseback. For one thing, an observer wrote home, there was the imminent danger that his long legs "would become entangled with those of the horse . . . and both come down together." Occupied as he was in the attempt to control his mount, which seemed equally nervous, he had trouble tipping his tall hat in response to cheers that were redoubled when the difficulty was seen. "That arm with which he drew the rein, in its angles and position resembled the hind leg of a grasshopper — the hand before, the elbow away back over the horse's tail. . . . But the boys liked him," the soldier-observer added. "In fact his popularity with the army is and has been universal. Most of our rulers and leaders fall into odium, but all have faith in Lincoln. 'When he finds out,' they say, 'it will be stopped.' . . . God bless the man and give answer to the prayers for guidance I am sure he offers."

If guidance was what he was seeking he could find it right there alongside him, astride Dan Webster. Less than three weeks ago Mc-Clellan had requested permission to present his views on the state of military affairs throughout the country; Lincoln had replied that he would be glad to have them — preferably in a letter, he said — if their presentation would not divert too much of the general's time and attention from his immediate duties. So tonight, when they returned to headquarters, McClellan handed the President a letter "covering the whole ground of our national trouble" and setting forth the conditions under which he believed the struggle could be won.

The rebellion, he said, had now "assumed the character of a war," and "as such . . . it should be conducted upon the highest principles known to Christian civilization. It should not be a war looking to the subjugation of the people of any State in any event. It should not be at all a war upon population, but against armed forces and political organizations. Neither confiscation of property, political executions of persons, territorial organization of States, or forcible abolition of slavery should be contemplated for a moment." This last was a point he emphasized, since "a declaration of radical views" in this direction would "rapidly disintegrate our present armies." More strictly within the military province, he advised concentration as the guiding rule. "The national force should not be dispersed in expeditions, posts of occupation, and numerous armies, but should be mainly collected into masses, and brought to bear upon the armies of the Confederate States. Those armies thoroughly defeated, the political structure which they support would soon cease to exist," and the southern people, unembittered by depredations, would turn against the willful men who had misled them out of the Union and sue at once for peace and reëntry. So he saw it. However, no matter what "system of policy" was adopted, he strongly urged the appointment of a general-in-chief, "one who possesses your confidence, understands your views, and who is competent to execute your orders." He did not ask that post for himself, he said; but he made it clear that he would not decline the reappointment, since he was "willing to serve you in such position as you may assign me," including this one. In closing he added a final explanation and disclaimer: "I may be on the brink of eternity, and as I hope forgiveness from my Maker I have written this letter with sincerity toward you and from love for my country."

Lincoln took it and read it through, with McClellan standing by. "All right," he said, and put it in his pocket. That was all. Apparently he had not come down here in search of guidance.

What he had come for, it developed, was a look at the present condition of the army and some specific answers to a specific question which he put the following day to the five corps commanders: "If it were desired to get the army away from here, could it be safely effected?" Keyes and Franklin replied that it could and should be done. The other three thought otherwise. "It would be ruinous to the country," Heintzelman said; "We give up the cause if we do it," Sumner said;

"Move the army and ruin the country," Porter said. Once the questioning was over, Lincoln and the generals took a glass of wine together and the President got ready to go back to Washington.

McClellan was upset: particularly by the evidence that the Administration might order him to evacuate the Peninsula. After seeing Lincoln off next morning, he wrote his wife that he feared the President had some "paltry trick" up his sleeve; his manner, he said, "seemed that of a man about to do something of which he was ashamed." For a week the general brooded and delivered himself of judgments. Lincoln was "an old stick, and of pretty poor timber at that," while Stanton was "the most unmitigated scoundrel I ever knew, heard, or read of." He believed he saw which way the wind was blowing: "Their game seems to be to withhold reinforcements, and then to relieve me for not advancing, well knowing that I have not the means to do so." Accordingly, in mid-July he wrote to his friend William H. Aspinwall, asking the New York transportation tycoon to be on the lookout for a job for him.

Lincoln meanwhile had made up his mind to act on the command decision which he had been considering for weeks. All through the previous autumn, old General Scott had held out in Washington for as long as he could, putting up with McClellan's snubs and digs for the sake of Halleck, who was on his way from California. It was Scott's hope that Old Brains would be there to take his place when he retired as general-in-chief. But the way was long and the digs were sharp; the old man gave up before Halleck got there, and McClellan got the job. Since then, the contrast in accomplishments East and West seemed to reinforce Scott's original opinion, which he repeated when the President came to West Point on the eve of the Seven Days. Lincoln saw merit in the recommendation, but he thought he would have a talk with Halleck before he acted on it. Back in Washington in time for the outbreak of the Seven Days, he wired the western commander: "Please tell me, could you make me a flying visit for a consultation without endangering the service in your department?"

Halleck did not want to come, and said so. Even if he did, he added, "I could advise but one thing: to place all the [eastern] forces ... under one head, and hold that head responsible."

Refusal was always provocative for Lincoln; in the course of the war, several men were to learn that the surest way to get something from him was to pretend they did not want it. He almost made up his mind, then and there. Down on the Peninsula, however, the matter was more or less cinched by McClellan himself. His Harrison's Landing letter, an exegesis of the conservative position, was the strongest possible proof that its author was not the kind of man to fight the kind of war Lincoln was rapidly coming to believe the country was going to have to fight if it was going to win. Returning to Washington on the night of July 10, he had Stanton send a wire to Corinth next morning, which left the recipient no choice in the matter: "*Ordered, that Maj. Gen. Henry W. Halleck be assigned to command the whole land forces of the United States as General-in-Chief, and that he repair to this capital as soon as he can with safety to the positions and operations within the department under his charge.*"

There were delays; Halleck did not arrive for nearly two weeks, being occupied with the incidentals of transferring his command. The delay was hard on Lincoln; "I am very anxious — almost impatient — to have you here," he wired. Down on the Peninsula, McClellan was spared for nine days the shock of hearing that his old post had gone to a rival. Then he read of it in a newspaper. "In all these things," he wrote his wife, "the President and those around him have acted so as to make the matter as offensive as possible. He has not shown the slightest gentlemanly or friendly feeling, and I cannot regard him as in any respect my friend. I am confident that he would relieve me tomorrow if he dared to do so. His cowardice alone prevents it. I can never regard him with other feelings than those of contempt."

★ ★ ★

This was going to be a harder war from here on out, and Lincoln knew it. He knew it because he was going to make it so. In fact, he was going to make it just as hard as he had to, and he said as much quite frankly to anyone who asked him. Most particularly, despite conflicting advice from McClellan and men like him, it was going to be harder on civilians. Of the four actions which the general had said "should [not] be contemplated for a moment" — 1) confiscation of property, 2) political execution of persons, 3) territorial organization of states, and 4) forcible abolition of slavery — the first and second had already been carried out with governmental sanction, the third was in the legislative works, and the fourth was under urgent consideration.

The second of these was the most obviously harsh, and for that reason should be the most obviously effective in securing obedience to occupation rule. So Benjamin Butler reasoned, at any rate, when he reached New Orleans and found that the national ensign, prematurely raised over the Mint, had been ripped from its staff by the mob. "They have insulted our flag — torn it down with indignity," he notified the War Department. "This outrage will be punished in such manner as in my judgment will caution both the perpetrators and abettors of the act, so that they shall fear the stripes if they do not reverence the stars in our banner." As good as his word, Butler found a man still wearing a tatter of the outraged bunting in his buttonhole, brought him before a drumhead court, and carried out the resultant sentence by hanging him in public from a window of the building where the crime had been committed.

It worked about as well as he had expected. The sight of one
man dangling by his neck from the eaves of the Mint sobered the
others considerably. Fear, not reverence, was what Butler had wanted,
and he got it — at least from the men. The women were another
matter. In them he saw no signs of fear, and certainly none of reverence.
In fact, they missed no chance to show their contempt for the blue-
clad invaders. Passing them on the street, they drew their skirts aside
to escape contamination, or else they walked straight ahead, taking their
half of the sidewalk out of the middle, and forced oncoming Yankees
to step off into the mud. The climax came when one of them, taking
careful aim from an upstairs window, emptied a slopjar onto the
head of Farragut himself. Butler retaliated with a general order, directing
"that hereafter when any female shall, by word, gesture or movement,
insult or show contempt for any officer or soldier of the United States,
she shall be regarded and held liable to be treated as a woman of the
town plying her avocation."

At home and abroad, the reaction was uproarious. Beauregard
made Butler's order the subject of one of his own: "Men of the South!
shall our mothers, our wives, our daughters and our sisters be thus outraged by the ruffianly soldiers of the North, to whom is given the right
to treat, at their pleasure, the ladies of the South as common harlots?
Arouse, friends, and drive back from our soil those infamous invaders
of our homes and disturbers of our family ties!" Overseas, Lord Palmerston remarked: "Any Englishman must blush to think that such an act
has been committed by one belonging to the Anglo-Saxon race." In
Richmond, before the year was out, Davis branded Butler a felon, an
outlaw, an enemy of mankind, and ordered that in the event of his
capture "the officer in command of the capturing force do cause him to
be immediately executed by hanging."

Southerners and their blushful friends abroad were not the only
ones offended by the cock-eyed general's zeal. Pro-Union men of the
region he controlled found that they too came under his strictures,
particularly in economic matters such as the seizure of cotton and the
freezing of foreign funds, and they were equally vociferous in protest.
But Lincoln had little use or sympathy for them. If these riders on the
ship of state thought they were "to touch neither a sail nor a pump,
but to be merely passengers — deadheads at that — to be carried snug
and dry throughout the storm, and safely landed right side up," they
were mistaken. He gave them a midsummer warning that the voyage
was about to get rougher.

"The true remedy," he said, switching metaphors, "does not
lie in rounding the rough angles of the war, but in removing the
necessity for war." This they could accomplish, he replied to one
protestant, by bringing Louisiana back into the Union. Otherwise, "it
is for them to consider whether it is probable I will surrender the

government to save them from losing all. If they decline what I suggest, you scarcely need to ask what I will do. What would you do in my position? Would you drop the war where it is? Or would you prosecute it in future with elder-stalk squirts charged with rosewater? Would you deal lighter blows rather than heavier ones? Would you give up the contest, leaving any available means unapplied?" The questions were rhetorical, and he closed by answering them: "I am in no boastful mood. I shall do no more than I can, and I shall do all I can, to save the government, which is my sworn duty as well as my personal inclination. I shall do nothing in malice. What I deal with is too vast for malicious dealing."

Already he had sent an official observer, a Maryland senator, down to New Orleans to look into the situation. But when the senator reported that there was indeed much harshness and irregularity (Butler's brother was getting rich on confiscated cotton, and the general himself had been given the nickname "Spoons," implying considerable deftness in the execution of his duties) as well as much disturbance of the master-slave relationship by the enlistment of Negroes in labor battalions, Lincoln was even more forthright in his statement of conditions and intentions: "The people of Louisiana — all intelligent people everywhere — know full well that I never had a wish to touch the foundations of their society or any right of theirs. With perfect knowledge of this they forced a necessity upon me to send armies among them, and it is their own fault, not mine, that they are annoyed." Here again the remedy was reëntry into the Union. "And might it not be well for them to consider whether they have not already had time enough to do this? If they can conceive of anything worse ... within my power, would they not better be looking out for it? ... I am a patient man, always willing to forgive on the Christian terms of repentance. Still, I must save this Government if possible. What I cannot do, of course, I will not do; but it may as well be understood, once for all, that I shall not surrender this game leaving any available card unplayed."

The unplayed card was emancipation. Mindful, so far, of his inaugural statement: "I have no purpose, directly or indirectly, to interfere with the institution of slavery in the states where it exists. I believe I have no lawful right to do so, and I have no inclination to do so," Lincoln had resisted all efforts to persuade him to repudiate his words. He resisted mainly on practical grounds, considering the probable reaction in the border states; "We should lose more than we should gain," he told one Jacobin delegation. Not only had he refused to issue such a proclamation as they were urging on him, he had revoked three separate pronouncements or proclamations issued by subordinates: one by Frémont, one by Cameron, and recently a third by Hunter in South Carolina. In the instance of the latter revocation, however, he had shown which way his mind was turning in mid-May: "Whether it be competent for me, as Commander in Chief of the army and navy, to declare the slaves of any state or states free, and whether, at any time, in any case, it shall have become a necessity indispensable to the maintenance of the government to exercise such supposed power, are questions which, under my responsibility, I reserve to myself."

This was putting a new face on the matter. What a President had no right or inclination to do in peacetime, Lincoln was saying, might become an indispensable necessity for a wartime Commander in Chief. Besides, he had done some ciphering back in March, and had come up with a simple dollars-and-cents solution to the problem. Figuring the cost of the war at two million dollars a day, and the cost of slaves at four hundred dollars a head, he had found the value of Delaware's 1798 slaves to be less than the cost of half a day of fighting. Extending his computations on this basis, he found that the total value of the 432,622 slaves in the District of Columbia and the four border states — Delaware, Maryland, Kentucky, Missouri — amounted to less than the cost of three months of warfare. Accordingly, he laid these figures before Congress in support of a resolution proposing compensated emancipation. In early April it was adopted, despite the objections of abolitionists who considered it highly immoral to traffic thus in souls; but nothing practical came of it, because the slave-state legislatures would not avail themselves of the offer. Lincoln was saddened by this failure, and on revoking Hunter's proclamation the following month addressed a special plea to the people of the border region: "I do not argue — I beseech you to make arguments for yourselves. You cannot, if you would, be blind to the signs of the times. I beg of you a calm and enlarged consideration of them, ranging, if it may be, far above personal and partisan politics. This proposal makes common cause for a common object, casting no reproaches upon any. It acts not the Pharisee. The change it contemplates would come gently as the dews of heaven, not rending or wrecking anything. Will you not embrace it? So much good has not been done, by one effort, in all past time, as in the providence of God it is now your high privilege to do. May the vast future not have to lament that you have neglected it."

The signs of the times were indeed plain to read; they had in fact the glistening clarity of wet paint, most of them having been posted about the legislative landscape during the current session of Congress. In March, subscribing to the opinion that the Dred Scott decision did not constitute law, the members fulfilled a Republican campaign promise by passing an act prohibiting slavery in all present or future national territories. The following month, the "peculiar institution" was abolished in the District of Columbia, with compensation for the owners and provisions for colonization of the freedmen, which Lincoln considered the best practical solution to the problem. "There has never been in my mind any question upon the subject," he declared as he signed the bill, "except the one of expediency, arising in view of all the circumstances." In May, the United States and Britain agreed by treaty to coöperate in suppressing the slave trade: a diplomatic move that gave much pleasure to the Jacobins, whom Lincoln had been at pains to please whenever he could. For their sake he had proposed that the country give formal recognition to the Negro republics of Haiti and Liberia, which Congress gladly did, and back in February — despite the known leniency of his nature in such matters — he sustained the sentence of execution brought against Nathaniel Gordon of Portland, Maine, the first and only slave trader ever hanged in accordance with Federal law.

Gratifying as all this was, including the hanging, the Jacobins were by no means satisfied. They wanted more, much more, and they never stopped letting Lincoln know it. "The pressure in this direction is still upon me and increasing," he said on July 12 when he called twenty border-state congressmen into his office for a final appeal before next week's adjournment sent them scattering for their homes. He spoke of the continuing attempts by the seceded states to persuade their sister slave communities farther north to join them in revolt — attempts which, incidentally, if successful would deprive these representatives of their jobs. The pull was strong, Lincoln admitted, and he wanted these men to help him weaken it. "You and I know what the lever of their power is. Break that lever before their faces and they can shake you no more forever." Besides, he said, slavery was failing fast already. "If the war continues long . . . the institution in your states will be extinguished by mere friction and abrasion. . . . How much better for you and for your people to take the step which at once shortens the war and secures substantial compensation for that which is sure to be wholly lost in any other event."

They heard him out, and then they shook their heads. The adopted resolution not only seemed to them a violation of State Rights, but they also questioned the constitutional power of Congress to appropriate funds for such a purpose. What was more, they doubted the sincerity of their fellow congressmen; the offer, one of the callers said, "was but the enunciation of a sentiment which could not or was not likely to be reduced to an actual tangible proposition." If Congress really meant it, let the money be put in the President's hands, and then they would consider acceptance. Then too — though this objection went unspoken — the plan entailed payment in government bonds, and though slave property was admittedly precarious and declining fast in value, the national credit was declining even faster. In short, they wanted no part of the offer as things now stood. Respectfully they bowed and took their leave, and Lincoln was left saddened and alone.

Left alone, he would act alone. He knew well enough the arguments against what McClellan, four days before, had called "a declaration of radical views" on the slavery issue: possible loss of the border states, possible loss of large segments of the army through desertion, possible loss of the fall elections. He knew, too, of currents that ran deeper — of Archbishop John Hughes of New York, for example, who had warned in a widely reprinted official declaration: "We, Catholics, and a vast majority of our brave troops in the field, have not the slightest idea of carrying on a war that costs so much blood and treasure just to gratify a clique of Abolitionists in the North." A Westerner, Lincoln knew the rabid division on the subject in the West, where candidates were tagged "charcoal" and "snowflake" in anger and derision, regardless of party. Such considerations, the concrete along with the nebulous, had weight. But he also knew the arguments in favor of positive action. First, it would allay the danger of foreign intervention by engaging the sympathy and arousing the enthusiasm of the rank and file of Europe, against which not even the most avid of the pro-Confederate rulers and ministers would dare to act. Second, whatever it did to the Democrats here at home, it would heal the split in his own party, which was rapidly getting out of hand.

Beyond if not above all these, and entirely aside from his promises to those who claimed to have removed themselves from his authority, there was the question of personal ethics, of whether the considered step was consonant with honor. He had called the nation to arms in support of a single issue, the preservation of the Union; could he now adopt a second — superimpose it, so to speak — without being guilty of chicanery or worse? He believed he could, and he based his persuasion on necessity. "Things had gone on from bad to worse," he later explained, "until I felt that we had reached the end of our rope on the plan of operations we had been pursuing; that we had about played our last card, and must change our tactics or lose the game." The truth was, the war had already outlasted the heady burst of enthusiasm that had flared up after Sumter. What was needed was a new cause, not to supplant, but to supplement the old; and this was it. Having appealed at the outset to reason, he now would appeal to conscience. He would translate the conflict into the terms of a holy war — a crusade — for which Julia Ward Howe had already composed the anthem:

> *In the beauty of the lilies Christ was born across the sea …*
> *As he died to make men holy, let us die to make men free,*
> *While God is marching on.*

Before the night was over, though the details were still to be worked out, he had completed his decision. He would do it. And next afternoon — much to their surprise, since always before, as one of them said, "he had been prompt and emphatic in denouncing any interference by the general government with the subject" — he spoke of it to two members of his cabinet.

The occasion was a funeral; the Stantons had lost a new-born child, and Lincoln rode to the burial in a carriage with Welles and Seward. According to Welles, the President "dwelt earnestly on the gravity, importance, and delicacy" of the slavery question and the advisability of issuing an emancipation proclamation "in case the rebels did not cease to persist in their war on the government ... of which he saw no evidence." He said he "had about come to the conclusion that it was a military necessity absolutely essential for the salvation of the Union, that we must free the slaves or be ourselves subdued." Asked for their opinions on the matter, both men were at first too taken aback by what Welles called "this new departure" to say anything at all. Seward, recovering first, replied that "his present opinion inclined to the measure as justifiable," but he would rather think the matter through before giving a final answer. Welles said he felt the same way about it. Lincoln let it go at that, though he made it clear that he was "earnest in the conviction that something must be done."

Four days later, July 17, Congress came very close to stealing his thunder. In August of the previous year, this body had passed a Confiscation Act endorsing Butler's contention that the slaves of disloyal masters were "contraband," liable to seizure and eligible for freedom on entering Union lines. Now, in the final hours before adjournment of the current session, a second such Act was passed. Considerably sharper-toothed than the one that had gone before, it provided "That every person who shall hereafter commit the crime of treason against the United States, and shall be adjudged guilty thereof, shall suffer death, and all his slaves, if any, shall be declared and made free." Discretion was left to the courts as to whether a prison term and/or a fine should be substituted in lieu of the death penalty, but no leeway was allowed as to the disposition of a traitor's slaves, who were automatically freed upon his conviction. At first glance, with nearly the whole slave region in rebellion, this appeared to be the very proclamation Lincoln was considering. However, closer reading showed it to be no such thing. No slave was to be freed by it until his master had been convicted of treason in a federal court. There was the rub. Secession — or rebellion, as the Jacobins preferred to call it — might be treason, but no court had ever said so (or ever would say so) no matter what opinion the radicals had on the matter. All the Acts really did was provide a sanctuary for such slaves as crossed the Federal lines: with the result that the U.S. government became, in effect, the greatest slaveholder the world had ever known, not excepting the Pharaohs of Egypt.

Lincoln doubted the legality of the Act; "It is startling to say that Congress can free a slave within a State," he declared in a veto message which he had prepared against its passage. All the same, he signed it as soon as it reached his desk; but in doing so he forwarded the proposed veto message in order to make his objections part of the record when the legislation was tested in the courts. Read in both houses as a prelude to adjournment, the message was greeted with sneers and laughter by the radicals, who took it as an admission that when the chips were down he did not dare to oppose them with anything but words.

In this they were much mistaken, though words were very much a part of what he had in mind. On July 22, to the surprise of all but Welles and Seward, who had been prepared for something of the sort by his remarks in the funeral carriage nine days back, he read to the assembled cabinet an emancipation proclamation which he proposed to issue without delay. Unlike the Confiscation Act, which required that individuals be convicted of treason before their slaves were freed, Lincoln's edict left no burden of proof upon the government. He intended it as a military pronouncement, designed to help win the war, and that was all. He was not concerned with "legality," as such, since he did not deal with individuals as such; all he required was that they live within an area where the authorities, after a specified date, continued to defy the federal government. The object of the war, he repeated, was the preservation of the Union; "And as a fit and necessary military measure for effecting this object, I, as Commander in Chief of the Army and Navy of the United States, do order and declare that on the first day of January, in the year of our Lord one thousand eight hundred and sixty-three, all persons held as slaves within any State or States wherein the constituted authority of the United States shall not then be practically recognized, submitted to, and maintained, shall then, thenceforward, and forever be free."

Reactions varied. Chase and Stanton approved, but wanted it stronger; Bates wanted it as it was; Welles wanted it weaker; Blair and Smith did not want it at all, or at least not before the fall elections. Then Seward spoke, having turned the matter over in his mind. "Mr President," he said, "I approve of the proclamation, but I question the expediency of its issue at this juncture. The depression of the public mind, consequent upon our repeated reverses, is so great that I fear the effect of so important a step. It may be viewed as the last measure of an exhausted government, a cry for help; the government stretching forth its hands to Ethiopia, instead of Ethiopia stretching forth her hands to the government. It will be considered our last *shriek* on the retreat. Now, while I approve the measure, I suggest, sir, that you postpone its issue until you can give it to the country supported by military success, instead of issuing it, as would be the case now, upon the greatest disasters of the war."

Lincoln had not considered this aspect of the question, but now that he did so, he perceived its wisdom and acted in accord with Seward's view. "I put the draft of the proclamation aside," he later told an artist friend, "as you do your sketch for a picture, waiting for a victory." Halleck, the man he counted on to give him one, was on the way at last: would arrive, in fact, tomorrow. Meanwhile, this thunderbolt would keep.

✗ 2 ✗

There was gloom in the West as in the East, but it was of a different nature, proceeding from different causes. Here too the advance had stalled; yet it was precisely in this apparent similarity that the difference obtained. McClellan had been stopped by Lee, but Halleck stopped himself. Curiously enough, or perhaps not curiously at all, the men on the Peninsula who had fought and fallen back, fighting as they went, had developed a fierce pride that burned brighter at the end of their retreat than it had ever burned before; they had fought well and they knew it; whereas Halleck's soldiers felt less elation at the end of their burrowing advance than at the start, not having fought at all. That was the source of a different kind of gloom.

Sherman did not share it, still being happy with the new stars on his shoulders and the sense of having "found" himself in the ordeal of Shiloh. But when he called by army headquarters not long after the fall of Corinth, he heard something that caused him to suspect that his friend Grant was in lower spirits than ever. Halleck happened to remark that Grant had applied for a thirty-day leave; he was going away next morning. Halleck said he did not know why, but Sherman took it to mean that Grant, "chafing under the slights," intended this as a first step in submitting his resignation. Determined to stop him if he could, Sherman rode over and found him sitting in his tent, sorting some letters and tying them into bundles with red tape. Grant said it was true that he was leaving, and when the red-headed general asked him why, he replied: "Sherman, you know. You know I am in the way here. I have stood it as long as I can, and can endure it no longer."

Where was he going? "St Louis," Grant said. Did he have any business there? "Not a bit," Grant said. So Sherman, being then in what he called "high feather," began to argue with him, illustrating Grant's case with his own. Look at him, he said. They had called him crazy as a loon, but he had hung on through Shiloh, and "that single battle had given me new life." Besides, if Grant went away, "events would go right along, and he would be left out; whereas, if he remained, some happy accident might restore him to favor and his true place." This had its effect; Grant promised to wait, or at any rate not to leave without seeing Sherman again or sending him word. Satisfied, Sherman left, and before the week was out received a note from Grant. He had reconsidered; he would stay. Sherman replied that he was glad to hear it; "for you could not be quiet at home for a week when armies were moving."

Armies were moving now, though not in the direction of the Confederates who had fallen back before them. Like a man riding an oversized mettlesome horse, which he feared might take the bit in its teeth and bolt off with him any minute, Halleck kept as close a rein as possible on his 120,000-man army. Even so, the advance had already covered more ground than he had intended. Once he had accomplished what he set out for — in particular, control of a sizeable stretch of the Memphis & Charleston Railroad — he was more than ready to call a halt and consolidate his gains. Four days after the occupation of Corinth, he warned the commander of the pursuit against goading the rebels into rashness. All he wanted, he said, was for them to fall back far enough to be beyond reach of the railroad. And he added: "There is no object in bringing on a battle if this object can be obtained without one. I think by showing a bold front for a day or two the enemy will continue his retreat, which is all that I desire."

Having withheld his army from pursuit, he now proceeded to dismember it. Eastward, westward, even northward he dispersed it: every way, in fact, but southward. On June 9 he instructed Pope — who presently was on his way to Washington, superseded by Rosecrans — to draw back closer to Corinth and take up outpost positions to defend it. And that same day the scattering began: a scattering that divided the Grand Army into four main parts, rather as if the aforementioned timid rider had decided not only to get rid of his mettlesome horse, but to do so by having it drawn and quartered. Buell was ordered east with four divisions to make connection with Ormsby Mitchel, who had encountered so much difficulty in North Alabama; his goal was Chattanooga, which would put him within possible reach of Knoxville or Atlanta. Sherman was sent west; he would garrison Memphis with two divisions, repairing the railroad on the way and doing what he could to restore the wrecked economy by "assur[ing] all country people that they will be permitted to take their cotton freely to market and that the ordinary channels of trade will be immediately reopened." McClernand, with a similar force, was given a similar mission, except that his destination lay fifty miles north at Jackson, Tennessee; he too was to repair the lines of supply and give the "country people" whatever assurance was needed to make them happy. Halleck himself would remain with the force at Corinth, coördinating the efforts of the other three.

His main concern in ordering the dispersal, he told Stanton, was the "sanitary condition" of the men. At present it was good, he said, but the question arose: "Can it be kept so during the summer?" He thought it could, provided he steered clear of a southward advance; for "if we follow the enemy into the swamps of Mississippi there can be no doubt that the army will be disabled by disease." (At least one of the general's wool-clad soldiers agreed with him. After being exposed to what Halleck was now avoiding, an Indiana veteran declared: "You load a man down with a sixty-pound knapsack, his gun and forty rounds of ammunition, a haversack full of hardtack and sow belly, and a three-pint canteen full of water, then start him along this narrow roadway with the mercury up to 100 and the dust so thick you could taste it, and you have done the next thing to killing this man outright.") "And yet," Halleck wrote, "to lie still, doing nothing, will not be satisfactory to the country nor conducive to the health of the army." He had therefore "deemed it best" to do as he had done. There was one drawback, one calculated risk: "This plan is based on the supposition that the enemy will not attempt an active campaign during the summer months. Should he do so . . . the present dispositions must be varied to suit the change of circumstances."

One immediate result the shake-up had. George Thomas returned to his old division, which was stationed under Halleck's eye at Corinth, and Grant was restored to the command of his old Army of the Tennessee, which included the divisions under Sherman and McClernand. Receiving permission to establish headquarters at Memphis, he set out on June 21 with a dozen troopers as escort, and after narrowly escaping capture on the way — Confederate horsemen, tipped off that he was coming, missed intercepting him by less than an hour — arrived three days later to find affairs "in rather bad order, secessionists governing much in their own way." He reported that there was even a plot to burn the city, which he thought might "prove partially successful," though he believed that such an action would "operate more against the rebels than ourselves." The main thing he needed, he told Halleck, was more troops.

Old Brains was in no mood just now to give him anything but trouble. By the end of June they had renewed their old-time wrangle. Halleck began it, wiring: "You say 30,000 men are at Shelbyville to attack La Grange. Where is Shelbyville? I can't find it on any map. Don't believe a word about an attack in large force on La Grange or Memphis. Why not send out a strong reconnaissance and ascertain the *facts*? It looks very much like a mere stampede. Floating rumors must never be received as facts. . . . I mean to make somebody responsible for so gross a negligence." Grant replied: "I did not say 30,000 troops at Shelbyville, but at Abbeville, which is south of Holly Springs, on the road to Grenada." Then he too got his back up. "I heed as little of floating rumors about this city as anyone," he protested. He had asked for more troops, he said, "that I might do effectively what you now ask. Stampeding is not my weakness. On the contrary, I will always execute any order to the best of my ability with the means at hand."

Halleck drew in his horns at this, replying four days later: "I made no insinuation that there had been the slightest neglect on your part.... Nor did I suppose for a moment that you were stampeded; for I know that is not in your nature." Then — as if he had leaned down to stroke Old Rover, only to have Old Rover snap at his hand — he added: "I must confess that I was very much surprised at the tone of your dispatch and the ill-feeling manifested in it, so contrary to your usual style, and especially toward one who has so often befriended you when you were attacked by others."

This was more or less the note on which the other hassle had ended, four months back; Grant was willing to let it go at that. But five days later, July 8, Halleck was at him again: "The Cincinnati *Gazette* contains the substance of your demanding reinforcements and my refusing them. You either have a newspaper correspondent on your staff or your staff is very leaky." Three days later, the Memphis telegraph receiver clacked off a blunt one dozen words from Corinth: "You will immediately repair to this place and report to these headquarters."

Just what have I done now? Grant must have thought. It was not his way to worry, but he apparently had cause. For the past two weeks — and, indeed, before — Halleck had shown all the earmarks of a commander engaged in the old army game of needling an unwanted subordinate enough to keep him edgy and fatten the record against him, but of holding back from the big pounce until something downright ruinous turned up to head the list of charges and specifications. Whether his sin was one of omission or commission, Grant did not know, though he had three full days for wondering while his horse retraced the steps taken three weeks ago with its head in the opposite direction. At last, July 15, the worried general reached Corinth and was face to face with his tormentor. What he was confronted with, however, was not the climax to a series of well-organized reproaches, but rather the accomplishment of the "happy accident" Sherman had persuaded him to wait for. Halleck was ordered to Washington to take over the direction of all the armies, East and West, and Grant was to receive, by seniority, the lion's share of what he left behind. Specifically, this included command of two armies — his own, now under McClernand and Sherman, and Pope's, now under Rosecrans — and of the department embracing North Mississippi, West Tennessee, and Kentucky west of the Cumberland River.

He had what he wanted, but not as he preferred it. The fact was, he disapproved of nearly all that had been done since Halleck's arrival from St Louis, later saying: "For myself I am satisfied Corinth could have been captured in a two days' campaign commenced promptly on the arrival of reinforcements after the battle of Shiloh." Most of all he disapproved of what had been done, or left undone, since Beauregard's sly evacuation of Corinth. With the Mississippi in Union hands, northward above Baton Rouge and southward below Memphis, "the Confederates at the west were narrowed down for all communication with Richmond to the single line of road running east from Vicksburg." That was the true goal now: that city, that stretch of river, that railroad. "To dispossess them of this . . . would be equal to the amputation of a limb in its weakening effects." As he saw it, "after the capture of Corinth a moveable force of 80,000 men, besides enough to hold all the territory acquired, could have been set in motion for the accomplishment of [this] great campaign for the suppression of the rebellion." Thus Grant, by hindsight. But Halleck could not see it, or else he feared to undertake it, and "the work of depletion commenced."

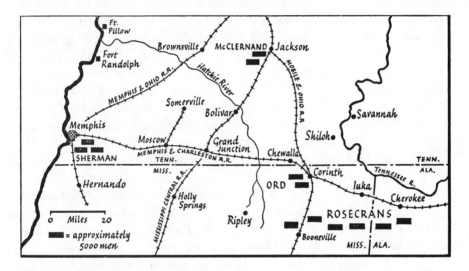

Even so, when he wound up his paperwork and departed for Washington two days later, he left his successor in immediate command of more than the 80,000 troops which Grant afterwards said would have been enough for the taking of Vicksburg that summer. The trouble was, they were far from "moveable," except when they were needed as reinforcements in adjoining departments. Before he had been at his post a week he was ordered to send a division to strengthen Samuel Curtis, who had marched from Northwest Arkansas to Helena, where the St Francis River flowed into the Mississippi, fifty airline miles below Memphis. Still, this left Grant with well over 75,000 effectives. Sherman had 16,000 at Memphis, and McClernand had 10,000 around Jackson. Another 7500 were stationed at Columbus, Cairo, and Paducah, while the rest of the Army of the Tennessee, 12,000 men under Major General E. O. C. Ord — a West Point classmate of Halleck's, just arrived from Virginia — were at Corinth. Rosecrans' Army of the Mississippi, 32,000 strong, was spread along a thirty-five-mile front that extended from south of Corinth to Cherokee, Alabama.

It was a sizeable force, but deep in enemy country as he was, charged with the consolidation of all that had been gained since Donelson and Shiloh, Grant found that its very size increased his major immediate problem: which was how to keep it fed and equipped. Just as the foregoing spring had set records for rainfall, so now the summer was breaking records for drouth, and as a result the Tennessee River was all but worthless as a supply line. So was the Memphis & Charleston Railroad, for the rebels had torn up the track between Chewalla and Grand Junction, and west of there the line had had to be abandoned for lack of rolling stock. All that was left him — except in Memphis, which of course could be supplied by river; the Mississippi never got really thirsty — was the slender thread of the Mobile & Ohio, stretching back to Columbus across more than a hundred miles of guerilla-infested West Tennessee, vulnerable throughout its length to attack by bands of regular and irregular cavalry, equally skilled at burning bridges and wrecking culverts, of which there were many. Tactically, too, the problems were not simple. Principal among them was the presence in North Mississippi of a highly mobile Confederate force, reckoned at 35,000 men, under the command of the resourceful and diabolical Earl Van Dorn, who sooner or later was probably going to succeed in one of his hair-trigger schemes. Its strength was less than half Grant's own, but its advantages were large. Van Dorn, for example, did not have to post a single man on guard in his rear, and best of all — or worst — he could choose the point of attack. He could strike the unconnected extremities, Corinth at one end, Memphis at the other, or he could pierce the lightly held center and knife straight through for Bolivar, Jackson, or Brownsville. What was more, he could choose the time.

Grant did not look forward to the coming months. Committed as he was to the defensive — much as he had been while biding his time before Shiloh — this was still not his kind of war. It was true, he had learned from what had happened then; from now on, he would keep in close touch with his field commanders and see to it that they had their men intrench. But he still did not like it, and he declared long afterwards that these midsummer months had been for him "the most anxious period of the war."

★ ★ ★

Discontent was general — amphibious, so to speak. For the navy, too, the successes of late spring and early summer, up and down the falling river, north and south of Vicksburg, were followed by a hot-weather season of doubts and tribulations. Every victory was accompanied by a setback, and the fruits thereof were bitter, their savor turning to ashes in the mouth. For Flag Officers Farragut and Davis, as for Grant, the midsummer word was *anxious*.

Davis ran into trouble first. As if Plum Run Bend had not been proof enough that his ironclads were vulnerable, it was presently re-

proved in backwoods Arkansas, and on one of the resurrected victims
of that earlier disaster. In the course of his eastward march from Pea
Ridge to Helena, Curtis had to cross White River: a task that was complicated by the presence of a Confederate fort at St Charles, sixty miles
from the mouth. Given orders to reduce it immediately after his Memphis triumph, Davis assigned the mission to four gunboats and an Indiana
regiment which went along in transports. Raised, pumped out, and
patched, the *Mound City* had the flag; this was her first outing since
her encounter with the *Van Dorn*, back in May. When the flotilla came
within sight of the fort, June 17, the Hoosier colonel requested permission to assault by land — there were only just over a hundred rebels
in the place — but the naval commander refused to yield or even share
the honors. Closing with the flagship, he opened fire at point-blank
range: whereupon the fort replied with a 42-pound solid that pierced
the *Mound City*'s casemate and went right through her steam drum,
scalding to death or drowning 125 out of her crew of 175 men, injuring
25 more, and leaving only 25 unhurt. (It was freakish in more ways
than one, including arithmetically; for the round-looking casualty figures were exact.) Helpless, the ironclad went with the current and the
other gunboats withdrew, leaving the proposed reduction to the Indian-
ians, who encircled the fort and took it without the loss of a man. Davis
had himself another victory, though he had it at far from a bargain price
and the credit went to the army.

Farragut's troubles, downriver, were at once less bloody and
more personal, and having a slopjar emptied onto his head from a French
Quarter window was only the least of them. Five days after congratulating him for his "magnificent execution" and "unparalleled achievements" at New Orleans, Assistant Secretary Fox heard that the Tennessee sailor had abandoned the attempt against Vicksburg. "Impossible!" Fox cried. "Sending the fleet up to meet Commodore Davis was
the most important part of the whole expedition. The instructions
were positive." Quickly he reiterated them in triplicate, dispatching the
original and two copies in three different ships to make certain of delivery: "It is of paramount importance that you go up and clear the
river with utmost expedition. Mobile, Pensacola, and, in fact, the whole
coast sinks into insignificance compared with this." Two days later he
repeated the admonition in a second dispatch, invoking the support of
higher authority: "The President requires you to use your utmost exertions (without a moment's delay, and before any other naval operation
shall be permitted to interfere) to open the Mississippi and effect a
junction with Flag Officer Davis."

On his previous trip upriver, Farragut had explained to Butler
why he did not think a limited expedition against Vicksburg should be
undertaken: "As they have so large a force of soldiers here, several
thousand in and about the town, and the facility of bringing in 20,000

in an hour by railroad from Jackson, altogether, [I] think it would be useless to bombard it, as we could not hold it if we take it." He still felt that way about it; but the orders from Fox, which presently arrived, left him no choice. He put the fleet in order for the 400-mile ascent, taking part of Porter's mortar flotilla with him this time, as well as 3000 men from Butler, and came within sight of Vicksburg's red clay bluff on the same day the *Mound City* took the solid through her boiler. He was back again, and though he still did not like the task before him, he wrote home that he was putting his trust in the Lord: "If it is His pleasure to take me, may He protect my wife and boy from the rigors of a wicked world."

He spent ten days reëxamining the problem and giving the mortars time to establish ranges. Then on the night of June 27 he made his run. Eleven warships were in the 117-gun column: three heavy sloops, two light sloops, and six gunboats. Skippers of the eight smaller vessels were instructed to hug the western bank while the large ones took the middle, the *Richmond* leading because her chase guns were situated best for high-angle fire, then the flagship *Hartford*, and finally the *Brooklyn*, lending a heavy sting to the tail. Two hours after midnight the attack signal was hoisted, and for the next three hours it was New Orleans all over again — except that this time the rebel gunners, high on their 200-foot bluff, were taking little punishment in return. Down on the river, by contrast, everything was smoke and uproar; the *Brooklyn* and two of the gunboats were knocked back, and all of the others were hit repeatedly. Total casualties were 15 killed and 30 wounded. But when daylight came, eight of the ships were beyond the hairpin turn, and Farragut was farther from salt water than he had been since he first left Tennessee to join the navy, more than fifty years before.

Two days later, July 1, Davis brought his gunboats down from Memphis and the two fleets were joined. There was much visiting back and forth, much splicing of the main brace — and with cause. Upper and nether millstones had come together at last, and now there was not even grist between them.

There, precisely, was the trouble; for now that Farragut was up here, there was nothing left for him to do. The day before the blue-water ships steamed past the batteries, Colonel A.W. Ellet, his brother's successor, took two of his rams up the Yazoo River, which emptied into the Mississippi a dozen miles above Vicksburg, to investigate a report that the rebels had three gunboats lurking there. It turned out to be true, one of them being the *Van Dorn*, only survivor of the Memphis rout; but all three were set afire as soon as the rams hove into view, and Ellet came back out again to report that he had destroyed the fag end of Confederate resistance on the western rivers. Then the Gulf squadron made its run and the two fleets rode at anchor, midway between Vicksburg and the mouth of the Yazoo. As far as Farragut could see, however, all the exploit had really yielded was more proof that he could take his ships past fortifications: a fact he had never doubted in the first place. "We have done it," he informed the Department, "and can do it again as often as may be required of us." Just now, though, what he mainly wanted was a breath of salt air in his lungs. Requesting permission from Washington to go back downriver again, he emphasized the point that there were now two fleets biding their time in an area where there was not even work enough for one.

While awaiting an answer he did what he could to keep his sailors busy, including having them fire a high-noon 21-gun salute in celebration of the Fourth. The 3000 soldiers were no problem in this respect. With an ingenuity worthy of Butler himself, their commander Brigadier General Thomas Williams had them digging a canal across the narrow tongue of land dividing the shanks of the hairpin bend in front of Vicksburg. When the river rose, the general said, it would widen the ditch and sluice out a passage for the fleet, beyond the range of the batteries on the bluff. But there was the rub. The river was not rising; it was falling. It was falling so fast, in fact, that Farragut had begun to fear that his deep-draft sea-going fleet would be stranded up here all summer. On July 13 he sent a wire which he hoped would jog the Department into action on his request: "In ten days the river will be too low for the ships to go down. Shall they go down, or remain up the rest of the year?"

One problem more there was, though he did not consider it a matter for real concern, never having had much of an ear for rumor. In addition to the three gunboats whose destruction Ellet had effected when he appeared up the Yazoo, there were whispers that the Confederates were building themselves an ironclad up there. Farragut did not give the rumor much credence. Even if it were true, he said, there was small chance that the rebels would ever be able to use such a craft, bottled up as she was, with two powerful Federal fleets standing guard in the Mississippi, just below the only point of exit. "I do not think she will ever come forth," he reported.

Davis was not so sure. Unlike Farragut, he had Plum Run Bend in his memory, which had taught him what havoc a surprise attack could bring. Determined not to suffer such a reverse again, he ordered three warships up the Yazoo to investigate and take up lookout stations. They left immediately after early breakfast, July 15: the ironclad *Carondelet*, the wooden gunboat *Tyler*, and the steam ram *Queen of the West*.

The rumors were all too true, as Farragut was about to discover. The mystery ship was the *Arkansas*, floated unfinished down the Mississippi and towed up the Yazoo to Greenwood after the fall of Island Ten exposed her to capture in Memphis. Naval Lieutenant Isaac Newton Brown, a forty-five-year-old Kentuckian who had held the same rank as a Vera Cruz veteran in the old navy, which he had entered from

Mississippi nearly thirty years ago, was given command of her in late May, together with orders to "finish and equip that vessel without regard to expenditure of men or money."

He did not realize what a large order this was until he got to Greenwood and saw her. Unfinished was not the word; she was scarcely even begun.

"The vessel was a mere hull, without armor. The engines were apart. Guns without carriages were lying about the deck. A portion of the railroad iron intended as armor was at the bottom of the river, and the other and far greater part was to be sought for in the interior of the country." So he later reported; but now he got to work. After a day spent fishing up the sunken iron, he towed the skeleton *Arkansas* 150 miles downriver to Yazoo City, where the facilities were better, though not much. Scouring the plantations roundabout, he set up fourteen forges on the river bank and kept them going around the clock, rural blacksmiths pounding at the wagonloads of scrap iron brought in from all points of the compass. Two hundred carpenters added to the din, hammering, sawing, swarming over the shield and hull. Perhaps the biggest problem was the construction of carriages for the guns; nothing of the sort had ever been built in Mississippi; but this too was met by letting the contract to "two gentlemen of Jackson," who supplied them from their Canton wagon factory. Other deficiencies could not be overcome, and were let go. Since there was no apparatus for bending the iron around the curve of the vessel's quarter or stern, for example, boiler plate was tacked over these parts — "for appearance' sake," Brown explained. Also, the paint was bad. She was intended to be chocolate brown, the color of the river, but no matter how many coats were applied she kept her original hue, rusty red. Despite all this, the work in the improvised yard went on. Within five weeks, according to one of her lieutenants, "we had a man-of-war (such as she was) from almost nothing."

By July 12 she was as finished as she would ever be. Brown sent the mechanics ashore and dropped down to Sartartia Bar, where, as he later said, "I now gave the executive officer a day to organize and exercise his men." In the crew of about 175, two thirds were from the recently burned gunboats; the rest were infantry volunteers, distributed among the ten guncrews serving weapons of various calibers, three in each broadside, two forward, and two aft. July 14, the descent resumed. Fifteen miles below, at the mouth of the Sunflower River — the guns of the two Union fleets, engaged in target practice out on the Mississippi, were plainly audible from here — it was discovered that steam from the engines and boiler had penetrated the forward magazine. Brown tied up alongside a sawmill clearing, landed the wet powder, and spread it on tarpaulins to dry in the sun. "By constant shaking and turning," he reported, "we got it back to the point of ignition before the sun sank below the trees." Packing what they could of it into the after magazine, the guncrews came back aboard and the *Arkansas* continued on her way, "guns cast loose and men at quarters, expecting every moment to meet the enemy."

At midnight her commander called a rest-halt near Haines Bluff; then at 3 a.m. — July 15 — continued down the river. Information received from Vicksburg put the number of enemy warships at thirty-seven, and Brown intended to be among them by daylight, with every possible advantage of surprise. It was not to be. The twin-screw vessel's engines had a habit of stopping on dead center, one at a time, which would throw her abruptly into bank, despite the rudder, and this was what happened now in the predawn darkness. While the rest of the crew was engaged in getting her off again, a lieutenant went ashore in search of information. He came to a plantation house, but found that the residents had fled at the first sound of a steamer on the river. All that was left was one old Negro woman, and she would tell him nothing, not even the whereabouts of her people. In fact, she would not admit that they had been there in the first place.

"They have but just left," the lieutenant insisted. "The beds are yet warm."

"Don't know 'bout that. And if I did, I wouldn't tell you."

"Do you take me for a Yankee? Don't you see I wear a gray coat?"

"Certain you's a Yankee," the woman said. "Our folks aint got none them gumboats."

It took an hour to get the unwieldy *Arkansas* underweigh again; the lieutenant returned from his profitless excursion with time to spare. Attempting to get back on schedule, Brown called for all the speed the engineers could give him, but it was by no means enough. When daylight filtered through, the ironclad was still in the Yazoo. The sun came up fiery as she entered Old River, a ten-mile lake formed by a cutoff from the Mississippi, and the lookout spotted three Union warships dead ahead, steaming upstream in line abreast, the *Carondelet* in the center, flanked by the *Tyler* and the *Queen of the West*. Brown made a brief speech, ending: "Go to your guns!" Stripped to the waist in the early morning heat, with handkerchiefs bound about their heads to keep the sweat from trickling into their eyes, the guncrews stood to their pieces. The officers, too, had removed their coats, and paced the sanded deck in their undershirts — all but Brown, who remained in full uniform, his short, tawny beard catching the breeze as he stood on the shield, directly over the bow guns, which he ordered not to fire until the action was fully joined, "lest by doing so we should diminish our speed." He and the *Carondelet's* captain, Henry Walke, had been friends in the old navy, messmates on a voyage around the world, and he wanted nothing to delay this first meeting since they had gone their separate ways.

The Federal skippers reacted variously to their first glimpse of the rust-red vessel bearing down on them out of nowhere. The *Queen of the West*, unarmed and with her speed advantage canceled by the current, turned at once and frankly ran. The *Carondelet* and *Tyler* stayed on course, intending to fire their bow guns, then swing round and make a downstream fight with their stern pieces, hoping the noise would bring help from the rest of the fleet. Both fired and missed. By the time they had turned to run for safety, the *Arkansas* was upon them.

She chose the *Carondelet*, the slower of the two, pumping shells into her lightly armored stern, which ate at her vitals and slowed her even more. The return shots glanced off the *Arkansas'* prow, doing no considerable damage except to one seaman who, more curious than prudent, stuck his head out of a gunport for a better view and had it taken off by a bolt from an 8-inch rifle. The headless body fell back on the deck, and a lieutenant, fearing the sight would demoralize the rest of the guncrew, called upon the nearest man to heave it overboard. "Oh, I can't do it, sir! It's my brother," he replied.

Other casualties followed, one among them being Brown himself. Most of the shots from dead ahead struck the inclined shield and were deflected back and upwards, ricocheting, but presently one did not carom high enough and Brown received what he later called "a severe contusion on the head." He thought he was done for until he drew a handful of clotted blood from the wound and failed to find any particles of brain mixed in. He stayed at his post, continuing to direct both the gunnery and the navigation. Just then, however, the *Tyler* dropped back to help the crippled *Carondelet*, her riflemen firing volleys at Brown, the only live target outside the shield. A minie struck him over the left temple, tumbling him down a hatchway and onto the forward guns. When he regained consciousness, the aid men were laying him among the dead and wounded below deck. He promptly got up and returned to his place on the shield.

The *Carondelet* was much closer now, he saw, and so was the mouth of the river. Just as she reached it, and just as he was about to ram her stern, she veered into bank, leaking steam and frantic survivors from all her ports. Brown did not stay to complete her destruction or force her surrender. Instead, he took up pursuit of the *Tyler*, which by now had entered the Mississippi and was doing all she could to overtake the *Queen*. Aboard the fleet, the sailors had heard the firing, but had assumed that the boats were shelling snipers in the woods. Now they saw better, though they still did not understand what they saw. Observing the gunboat returning with a strange red vessel close on her heels, one officer remarked: "There comes the *Tyler* with a prize."

They soon learned better. Within range of the fleet — "a forest of masts and smokestacks," Brown called it; "In every direction, except astern, our eyes rested on enemies" — noting that the army rams were anchored behind the bigger ships, in position to dart out through the intervals, the Confederate skipper told his pilot: "Brady, shave that line of men-of-war as close as you can, so that the rams will not have room to gather headway in coming out to strike us." Brady gave him what he asked for, and the second battle opened.

At its beginning, steam down, guns unloaded, not a single Federal vessel was prepared for action; but this was presently so thoroughly corrected that Brown could later say, "I had the most lively realization of having steamed into a real volcano." Guns were flashing, and as he advanced "the line of fire seemed to grow into a circle constantly closing." Even so, he saw one definite advantage to fighting solo from an interior position, and the *Arkansas* was not neglectful of it, "firing rapidly to every point of the circumference, without the fear of hitting a friend or missing an enemy."

Now, though, she was taking about as much punishment as she gave. The big ocean-going sloops had run their guns out, and the Davis ironclads were firing for all they were worth. The *Arkansas* took hits from all directions. An 11-inch solid broke through her casemate armor and laid a sixteen-man guncrew dead and dying on her deck. A rifle bolt laid out eleven more. Shrapnel quickly gave her stack the look of a nutmeg grater, so that for lack of draft the pressure dropped from 120 pounds to 20, barely enough to turn the engines. The temperature in the fire-room soared to 130°, and the engineers worked fifteen-minute shifts, by the end of which they had to be hauled up, half-roasted, and relieved by men from the guns. Sixty dead and wounded men were in her; her cast-iron snout was broken off; one whole section of plating was ripped from her flank; her boats were shot away and dragging. However, she still was giving as good as she got, or better. Out on the shield, where he had had his spyglass shot from his hands, her captain had never stopped calling orders to the pilot house and guns. A ram broke into the clear at last, driving hard in a final effort to block the way; "Go through him, Brady!" Brown shouted. But one of the bow guns averted the need for a collision by putting a shell through the Federal's boiler. Steam went up like a geyser and the bluejacket crew went overboard.

That was the final round. The *Arkansas* was into the clear, past the outer rim of the volcano. Limping badly, but unpursued, she held her course for Vicksburg, where a crowd had assembled on the bluff to greet her. Soldiers and townspeople alike, they tossed their hats in joy and admiration, but the cheers froze in their throats when they looked down and saw the carnage on her gundeck.

Farragut was infuriated. He had been sleeping late that morning, and when the cannonade erupted he appeared on the *Hartford*'s deck in his nightshirt. However, the flagship's engines were under repair; there was nothing he could do but watch and fire at the strange vessel **as it** went by. When the action was over he surveyed the wreckage — which was not only considerable, but was largely self-inflicted by cross fire — then returned to his cabin, muttering as he went: "Damnable neglect, or worse, somewhere!"

The more he thought about it, the madder he got. By the time he came back on deck again, fully dressed, he had made up his mind to steam down to Vicksburg with all his ships and attack the *Arkansas* in broad open daylight, hillside batteries and all. His staff managed to dissuade him from this — at least give the fleet captains time to wash the blood from their scuppers, they said — but, even so, the old man would not be put off any longer than nightfall: Porter's mortar schooners, together with the *Brooklyn* and the two laggard gunboats, were still below the city, where the apparently unsinkable rebel ironclad might engage them any minute. He ordered all guns loaded with solid and suspended his heaviest anchor from the tip of the *Hartford*'s port mainyardarm, intending to drop it through the *Arkansas*' deck and bottom when he got alongside her. The Davis gunboats and the Porter mortars would give covering fire, above and below, while he went in and dragged the upstart monster from its lair. Just before sunset he hoisted the familiar pennant for attack, and the fleet moved downriver.

It did not work out at all the way he intended. For one thing, in the ruddy murk between sunset and dusk, the rust-red boat was almost invisible under the red clay bank. The first each skipper saw of her as the ships came past in single file, taking in turn a pounding from the batteries overhead, was the flash of her guns as he crossed her line of fire. By then it was too late to attempt to check up and grapple; all there was time for was one quick broadside in reply, before the current swept him out of range. Aboard the *Arkansas*, dismay at having to fight the day's third battle, tied to bank and with less than half her crew still functional, gave way to elation as the action progressed. One by one, the ships glided past with their towering spars in silhouette against the glow of the western cloudbank, and one by one they took them under fire, as if in a gigantic shooting gallery. But when the *Hartford* stood in close, groping blindly with the anchor swaying pendulous from her yardarm, and they loosed a broadside at her, she thundered back with a tremendous salvo. An 11-inch solid pierced the side of the *Arkansas* just above the waterline, crashed through the engine room, killing and mangling as it went, and lodged in the opposite casemate armor, making what one of her officers called "a bulging protuberance outside." She kept firing until the river stopped sending her targets. Then once more there was silence.

Farragut was where he wanted to be, south of the infernal bluff, and he had made the downstream run with fewer casualties than before — 5 killed, 16 wounded: only a handful more than his adversary had suffered — but he was far from satisfied. He wanted that ram, and he intended to have her, whatever the cost. At daylight he sent an urgent message to Davis, proposing that both fleets go in together at high noon and fight the rebel to a finish. Davis declined the invitation, counseling prudence and self-control. "I have watched eight rams for a month," he replied, "and now find it no hard task to watch one."

He continued to resist the pressure which Farragut kept applying. Five days later, July 21 — the *Arkansas* having ventured out meanwhile on a sortie that was aborted by another engine failure — he agreed to make an attempt next morning with the ironclad *Essex* and the *Queen of the West*. The plan was for the gunboat to shove the rebel vessel hard against bank and hold her there, sitting-duck fashion, so that the ram could butt a hole in her side and send her to the bottom. But this did not work either. Brown had the *Arkansas* moored with her head upstream, and when he saw the *Essex* coming at him he slacked his bow-line and presented his sharp armored prow to the blunt-nosed gunboat, which swerved at the last minute to avoid being sliced in two, taking and giving punishment as she passed. The *Queen*, following close behind, anxious to redeem her performance up the Yazoo the week before, could manage no more than a glancing blow. She worked her way back upstream, rejoining Davis, but the *Essex* went with the current, her engines badly shot up in the melee, and joined the fleet below.

Farragut threw up his hands at this. Fuel was low, and what with the need for keeping up steam in case the *Arkansas* staged another sudden appearance, was getting considerably lower every day. Sanitation was also a problem, as Halleck had foreseen. The swampy Mississippi heat had nearly half of Farragut's sailors on the sick list, along with three quarters of the canal-digging soldiers. The falling river seemed about to make good its threat to strand him up here, out of circulation for the rest of the year. Besides, a message from Welles — sent before the Secretary learned of the rebel ram's emergence — had just arrived: "Go down the river at discretion." That was what Farragut did, and he did it without delay. Starting south on July 26, he dropped the orphaned *Essex* and two of the smaller wooden gunboats off at Baton Rouge, along with Williams' shovel-weary soldiers, and put into New Orleans for repairs that would fit the rest of his salt-water ships for more agreeable blockade duty along the Gulf. Back in his native element at last, able to breathe all the way to the depths of his lungs, he said goodbye to the Mississippi — forever, he hoped.

Davis pulled out northward that same day, transferring his base to Helena, two hundred miles upstream. Vicksburg was delivered, along with a great stretch of the river between Napoleon and Natchez.

Welles was extremely angry when he heard the news. He told Farragut, "It is an absolute necessity that the neglect or apparent neglect of the squadron should be wiped out by the destruction of the *Arkansas*." Nothing came of this as far as Farragut was concerned; he was downstream and he stayed there. But it was an event that rankled in the Secretary's memory ever after — worse than Donelson, worse than Hampton Roads; worse, even, than Head of the Passes or Plum Run Bend. Bitter and chagrined, Welles later wrote: "The most disreputable naval affair of the war was the descent of the steam ram *Arkansas* through both squadrons, until she hauled into the batteries of Vicksburg, and there the two Flag Officers abandoned the place and the ironclad ram, Farragut and his force going down to New Orleans, and Davis proceeding with his flotilla up the river."

On Vicksburg's bluff, conversely, there was rejoicing and there was pride, not only because the naval siege had been raised, but also because of the manner in which the feat had been accomplished. The combined might of two victorious Union fleets had been challenged, sundered, and repulsed by a single homemade ten-gun ironclad, backed by the industry and daring of her builder and commander. Coming as it did, after a season of reverses, this exploit gave the people of the Lower Mississippi Valley a new sense of confidence and elation. They were glad to be alive in a time when such things could happen, and they asked themselves how a nation could ever be conquered when its destiny rested with men like those who served aboard the *Arkansas* under Isaac Newton Brown.

★ ★ ★

In the Transmississippi, too, there was the discomfort of indigestion, proceeding from a difficulty in assimilating all that had been gained.

Sam Curtis was glad to have the Davis rams and gunboats with him: almost as glad as he had been to receive the division from Grant, which reached Helena the week before and brought his total strength to 18,000. This was the largest force he had yet commanded, half again larger than the army with which he had won the Battle of Pea Ridge; but, as he saw it, he had need of every man and gun he could get, ashore or afloat. Looking back on that savage conflict, which involved the repulse of a slashing double envelopment by Price and McCulloch, with Van Dorn hovering wild-eyed in the background and swarms of painted Indians on his flank, he perceived a hundred things that might have spelled defeat if they had gone against instead of for him. It seemed to him now in late July that events were building up to another such encounter, in which the scales — balanced against him, he believed, as they had been in early March — might tip the other way.

For a time it had been otherwise. Through April and May he had occupied a vacuum, so to speak; Van Dorn and Price had crossed the Mississippi and left Arkansas to him. On the final day of May, however, this leisure season ended with the Confederate appointment of Major General Thomas C. Hindman, a Helena lawyer and congressman who had led a division at Shiloh, to command the area including Missouri, Arkansas, Louisiana south to the Red, and Indian Territory. A dapper little man just over five feet tall, addicted to ruffled shirts and patent-leather boots, Hindman — like his predecessor, Earl Van Dorn — made up in activity for what he lacked in size. He had need of all his energy now. The situation on his arrival was about as bad as it could be, the scarcity of volunteers lending support to the postwar tall tale that the entire state of Montana was afterwards populated by rebel fugitives from Elkhorn Tavern; but he went immediately to work, issuing fiery proclamations and enforcing the new conscription law in his native state with troops brought from Texas. Lacking arms and munitions, he set up factories and chemical works to turn them out, operated lead mines and tanyards, and even organized the women of his department into sewing circles to furnish uniforms for all the able-bodied men he could lay hands on. Word of his activity soon spread, and recruits began to trickle in from Missouri, some of whom he sent back home with orders to raise guerilla bands to harass the invader's rear. Before long, Curtis was receiving intelligence reports that put the Confederate strength in midland Arkansas at 25,000 men.

His plan had been to march on Little Rock as soon as his army had recovered from its exertions, thus adding to the southern list of fallen capitals, but the presence of Hindman's newborn army in that direction changed his mind. Instead, after much conferring back and forth with Washington, he moved toward Helena for a possible share in the amphibious descent of the Mississippi. Even that was hard enough. All through June, bridge-burners and irregular cavalrymen, instructed by Hindman to bushwhack Union pickets, destroy all food, and pollute the water "by killing cattle, ripping the carcasses open and throwing them in," harassed his line of march and kept him in almost constant expectation of being swamped by overwhelming numbers. At last he reached the big river — only to find that the descent had been called off; Halleck was busy consolidating his gains. It was just as well, as far as Curtis was concerned. He began to fortify his Helena position, not knowing what all-out mischief Hindman might be plotting in the brush.

Even after the arrival of the division from Memphis and the ironclads from Vicksburg, together with siege guns brought down-river from Birds Point, Columbus, and Fort Pillow, he felt far from easy about his situation. Not only was there danger in front; he now learned of a new danger in his rear. The Missourians who had gone back home with instructions for making trouble were showing a good deal of talent for such work. Brigadier General John M. Schofield, the Federal commander there, reported that he had discovered "a well-devised scheme" for a monster guerilla outbreak involving thirty to fifty thousand men who were assembling now at designated places to await the appointed signal "and, by a sudden *coup de main*, seize the important points in the state, surprise and capture our small detachments guarding railroads, &c., thus securing arms and ammunition, and coöperate with an invading army from Arkansas." He called on Curtis to deal with this invasion force, which had moved into the vacated area around Pea Ridge, while he did his best to deal with the guerillas. "You are aware, General, that I have no force sufficient to drive them back without your assistance," he implored. "Let me ask you to act as quickly as possible."

Curtis could not help him. If it came to the worst, he wasn't even sure he could help himself. He had all sorts of troubles. As a result of trying to encourage trade in cotton, he said, his camp was "infested with Jews, secessionists, and spies." Then too, his health was failing; or, as he put it, "I am not exactly well." At any rate, whatever rebel hosts were gathering in Northwest Arkansas, the last thing he intended was a re-tracing of his steps on the harried march he had just completed. All he could do was hold what he had, probing occasionally at the country roundabout as the long hot summer wore on toward a close.

Schofield's fears for Missouri were soon fulfilled, though in a less concerted fashion than he had predicted. No less than eighty skirmishes were fought there during July and August, including one that resulted in the capture of Independence by guerillas under Charles Quantrill, who presently was commissioned a Confederate captain as a reward for this exploit. Kansas too was threatened. Jim Lane, the grim Jayhawk chieftain, was raising Negro troops; "Zouaves d'Afrique," they were called, for they drilled in baggy scarlet pantaloons Stanton had pur-chased, in the emergency, from France. North of there, in the absence of soldiers transferred south and east, the Minnesota Sioux went on the warpath, massacring settlers by the hundreds.

Everywhere Curtis looked he saw trouble, though most of it was fortunately well beyond his reach at Helena. Remaining in the fine big house on a hill overlooking the river — it was Hindman's, or it had been; Curtis had taken it for his headquarters — he improved his fortifica-tions, put his trust in the Mississippi as a supply line, and shook his head disapprovingly at the chaos all around him. "Society is terribly muti-lated," he reported.

★ ★ ★

At the opposite end of the western line, Buell was moving east-ward; or he had been, anyhow, until he encountered troubles he would gladly have swapped for those of Curtis and Grant combined, with Scho-field's thrown in for good measure. As it turned out, he not only had supply and guerilla problems as acute as theirs; presently it became obvi-ous, too, that his was the column that was to receive the main attention of the main Confederate army in the West — beginning with the twin thunderbolts, Morgan and Forrest, who were thrown at him soon after he got started.

In giving him instructions for the eastward move, ten days after the fall of Corinth, Halleck was heeding the repeated suggestion of

Ormsby Mitchel, who for a month had been signaling frantically that he could see the end of the war from where he stood in Northeast Alabama. If he were reinforced, he said, he could march straight into Chattanooga, then turn south and take Atlanta. From there, he added, the way lay open to Richmond's back door, through a region that was "completely unprotected and very much alarmed." Old Brains could see merit in this — and he also saw a possible variation. Knoxville, too, lay beyond that mountain gateway: an objective he knew was dear to the heart of Lincoln, who was anxious to disenthrall the pro-Union citizens of East Tennessee and gain control of the railroad connecting Virginia and North Georgia. Accordingly, Halleck gave Buell his instructions on June 9 for a lateral offensive, the only one of any kind that he intended to launch in the West this summer, simultaneously notifying Washington of the intended movement, and two days later received the expected reply: Lincoln was " greatly delighted."

The extent of the President's delight was shown before the month was out. Alarmed by Lee's assault on McClellan, who was crying for reinforcements as he fell back, the War Department called on the western commander for 25,000 troops to be shifted to the East; but when Halleck replied that to send them would mean that the Chattanooga expedition would have to "be abandoned or at least be diminished," the reaction was immediate and negative, and it came in the form of a telegram from Lincoln himself. This must not be done on any account, he said. "To take and hold the railroad at or east of Cleveland, in East Tennessee, I think fully as important as the taking and holding of Richmond."

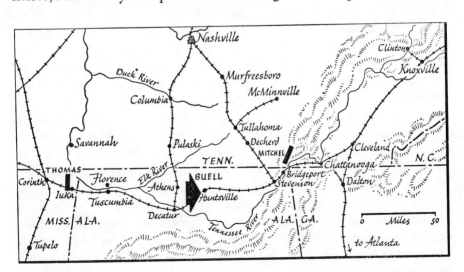

By that time Buell was well on his way. He had by no means reached Cleveland — a junction thirty miles beyond his immediate objective, where the railroad, coming down from Knoxville, branched west to Chattanooga and south to Atlanta — but he had advanced his four divisions to Huntsville, having ferried the Tennessee River at Florence, and had repaired the Memphis & Charleston line as far east as Decatur. He had about 35,000 men in his present column, including cavalry and engineers, and Mitchel was waiting up ahead with 11,000 more. Off to the north, ready to coöperate as soon as Knoxville became the goal, George Morgan occupied Cumberland Gap with a division of 9000, which was also a component of Buell's Army of the Ohio. In addition to these 55,000 troops, Thomas was at Iuka, awaiting orders to march east with his own division of 8000, plus two from Grant, which had been promised in case they were required. Just now, however, Buell did not want them. He was having trouble enough feeding the men he had, and the problem got progressively worse as he moved eastward, lengthening his supply line.

The 300 tons of food and forage needed daily — 3¼ pounds for a man, 26 for a horse, 23 for a mule — were more than the guerilla-harried railroads could supply. Besides a shortage of rolling stock, destruction of the Elk River bridge on the Nashville-Decatur line necessitated a forty-mile wagon haul around the break, and sniper fire was so frequent and effective that ironclad boxcars had to be provided for the protection of the train crews. Buell put his men and animals on half rations, much to the discomfort of both. "We are living from day to day on short supplies and our operations are completely crippled," he complained to the Louisville quartermaster. Ahead, he knew, lay additional problems: the river crossing at Bridgeport, for example. Retiring from in front of Chattanooga the month before, Mitchel had burned the mile-long span, and Buell had no material with which to build another. In an attempt to fill the shortage and make amends, Mitchel ordered all the sawmills between Huntsville and Stevenson put to work supplying lumber for pontoons and a bridge floor, but this too was an occasion for guerilla interference, causing the workers to run away for fear of being murdered on the job or in their beds.

All in all, the prospect was grim. Buell's chief solace was the knowledge that he was doing the best he could with what he had, and his chief hope was that his industry was appreciated by those above him. The latter was dispelled by an alarming and discouraging message from Halleck, July 8. The alarm came first: Bragg's army was reported to be in motion, either against Grant at Memphis or Corinth, or against Buell at Tuscumbia or Chattanooga. "A few days more may reduce these doubts to a certainty, when our troops will operate accordingly," Halleck reported, unruffled. Then came the discouragement: "The President telegraphs that your progress is not satisfactory and that you should move more rapidly. The long time taken by you to reach Chattanooga will enable the enemy to anticipate you by concentrating a large force to meet you. I communicate his views, hoping that your movements hereafter may be so rapid as to remove all cause of complaint, whether well founded or not."

Buell later declared, "I was so astonished at the message that I made no reply until three days afterward." What jogged him then was a six-word dispatch: "I want to hear from you. H. W. Halleck." In reply, Buell reviewed his difficulties, remarking as he did so: "I regret that it is necessary to explain the circumstances which must make my progress seem so slow." As he saw it, the object was not only to reach his goal quickly, but also to be in condition to fight when he got there. "The advance on Chattanooga must be made with the means of acting in force; otherwise it will either fail" — as Mitchel's had done — or else the city would "prove a profitless and transient prize." His arrangements, made in accordance with this, were "being pushed forward as rapidly as possible," and though he quite understood that "these are matters of fact that cannot be gratifying," he added: "The dissatisfaction of the President pains me exceedingly."

Next day Halleck responded with assurances of personal good will. He could see both sides of the question, and he urged Buell to be more tolerant of the amateurs above them. "I can well understand the difficulties you have to encounter and also the impatience at Washington. In the first place they have no conception of the length of our lines of defense and of operations. In the second place the disasters before Richmond have worked them up to boiling heat." At any rate, he assured him, "I will see that your movements are properly explained to the President."

This was helpful in relieving the pain — lately added to by John Morgan, who had led his gray raiders up through Middle Tennessee and was capturing railroad guards, burning bridges, and smashing culverts in Kentucky — but still more comforting to Buell was the fact that his advance was now past Stevenson, where the Nashville & Chattanooga, coming down through Murfreesboro and Tullahoma, joined the Memphis & Charleston, thus affording him an additional rail supply line. Anticipating this, he had work gangs all along the road, repairing the damage done by retreating Confederates, and to make certain that it was not wrecked again, either by raiders or guerillas, he had stationed a brigade at Murfreesboro — two regiments of infantry, a cavalry detachment, and a four-gun battery — ready to move out in either direction at the first sign of trouble. On June 12, the date of Halleck's sympathetic message, Buell was informed that the repairs had been completed. The first trainload of supplies would leave Nashville tomorrow or the next day; he would be able to take his soldiers off half rations and replace their worn-out shoes as soon as it got there.

What got there tomorrow, however, was not a trainload of supplies, but rather an announcement of disaster. In the gray dawn light, Bed-

ford Forrest struck Murfreesboro with three regiments of cavalry, wrecking the railroad at that point and capturing the Federal commander,
Brigadier General T. T. Crittenden, together with all his men, guns,
and equipment. Stung, Buell reacted fast by hurrying William Nelson's
whole division to the scene; but when it got there, the hard-riding Confederate and his captives had disappeared eastward, in the direction of the
mountains. Nor was that all. The work gangs had barely completed their
repairs when, eight days later, Forrest struck again — this time up near
Nashville, where he celebrated the anniversary of Manassas by firing his
captured guns within sight of the capitol tower and wrecking the three
bridges across Mill Creek. When Nelson's division marched from Murfreesboro to intercept him, he took a side road, camped for the night
within earshot of the bluecoats tramping northward on the pike, then
once more made his escape into the mountains beyond McMinnville.

Nettled but not disheartened, Buell put his repair gangs back to
work. Within a week, practice having increased their skill, they had the
line in operation. July 29, the first train pulled into Stevenson from Nashville with 210,000 rations, followed next day by another with a comparable amount. The troops went back on full allowances of food, and
Nelson's infantry replaced the shoes they had worn out chasing Forrest's
cavalry. This was a help and was duly appreciated; but something more
than footgear had been damaged in the process, and there were pains in
other regions than the stomach. Morale and pride were involved here,
too. Buell's men began to consider that, with the doubtful exception of
Shiloh — which was not really their fight, since they only arrived on the
second day and even then were only engaged in part — the Army of the
Ohio was the only major Federal command that had never fought a
pitched battle on its own. The blame for this, as they saw it, rested with
Buell, whose military policy was referred to by one of his colonels as
that of a dancing master: "By your leave, my dear sir, we will have a
fight; that is, if you are sufficiently fortified. No hurry; take your time."

Distasteful as this was to the men, there was something else
about their commander that irked them even more. When Ormsby
Mitchel's division came through this region, back in May, one soldier
wrote happily in his diary: "Our boys find Alabama hams better than
Uncle Sam's side meat, and fresh bread better than hard crackers." Buell,
on the other hand, not only put them on half rations, but issued and enforced stern orders against foraging, which he believed would discourage
southern civilians from returning to their old allegiance. However true
this was or wasn't, it seemed to the men that he was less concerned
with their hunger pangs than he was with the comfort and welfare of the
rebels, who after all were to blame for their being down here in the first
place. Also, he was denying them the fun and profit enjoyed by comrades
who had come this way before them. For example, in reprisal for guerilla
activities, one of Mitchel's brigade commanders, Colonel John Basil

Turchin — formerly Ivan Vasilevich Turchininov, of the Imperial Rus·
sian Army — had turned the town of Athens over to his three regiments,
saying, "I shut mine eyes for one hour": whereupon the Illinois, Ohio,
and Indiana boys took it completely apart, Cossack-style, raping Negro
servant girls and stuffing their pockets and haversacks with $50,000
worth of watches, plate, and jewelry. Grudgingly, Buell's men complained that he would never turn them loose like that, despite the fact
that, officially, it would apparently do his career far more good than
harm. Turchin was court-martialed and dismissed for the Athens de-
bauch, but before the summer was over he was reinstated and promoted
to brigadier. Likewise Mitchel, though he was called to Washington in
early July to explain illegal cotton transactions made in his department,
was promoted to major general and transferred to the mild, sea-scented
atmosphere of coastal South Carolina, where unfortunately he died of
yellow fever in October.

Actually, though, the trouble with Buell lay deeper. It was not so
much what he did as what he was. Other generals shared his views on the
subject of foraging, and enforced them quite as sternly: notably Mc-
Clellan and, at the present stage of the conflict, Sherman. "This demoralizing and disgraceful practice of pillage must cease," the West Tennessee commander admonished his troops in a general order, "else the
country will rise on us and justly shoot us down like dogs or wild beasts."
In fact, on the face of it, both were harder on offenders than Buell ever
was or tried to be. In Sherman's command, for example, the punishment
for molesting civilians or stealing was confinement on bread and water,
and he sent out patrols with instructions to shoot if foragers tried to
escape arrest. But they gave their men something instead. Better situated,
they fed better, and they moved among their soldiers in a way that made
the individual feel that, outside battle, his comfort and well-being were
his general's main concern. Above all, in their different ways, they had a
flair for the dramatic. McClellan's men would turn from their first hot
meal in days for a chance to cheer him riding past, and Sherman could
make a soldier proud for weeks by asking him for a light for his cigar.
It was personal, a matter of personality.

Buell was seldom "personal," and never at all in public. In private,
he had a parlor trick which he sometimes performed to amaze his guests
with the strength of his rather stubby arms and his stocky, close-knit
torso. Grasping his hundred-and-forty-pound wife by the waist, he
would lift her straight out before him, hold her there with her feet
dangling clear of the carpet, then perch her deftly on the mantelpiece. It
was a good trick, and it won him the admiration of those who watched
him do it. But the soldiers never saw this side of his nature. He was a
headquarters general, anyhow. They saw him only briefly as he made his
hurried, sour-mouthed inspections, peering at them with his beady eyes
and poking his hawk-beak nose into unexpected corners. The good he

took for granted; it was the less-good he was looking for, and he seldom failed to find it. As a result, there was an absence of warmth — and an absence, too, of incidents in which men let their food grow cold while they took time out to cheer him riding by or fished in their pockets for a light for his cigar. They were well drilled, beyond question. Three months ago, their professional tone had been such that when Grant's skulkers saw them march ashore at Shiloh they had cried, "Here come the regulars!" Under fire next day, their confident demeanor as they rolled the rebels back had sustained the basic accuracy of this mistake. Since then, however, a great deal had happened, and all of it bad. The inchworm advance on Corinth, with empty earthworks at the end, had been followed by these two belt-tightening months in North Alabama, where they observed with disgust — as if, by a process of unnatural reversion, a butterfly were to have its wings refolded and be stuffed unceremoniously back into its cocoon — their transformation from happy-go-lucky soldiers into ill-fed railroad workers. Out of this had come a loss of former gladness, and a suspicion that they had lost their fighting edge.

This might or might not be the case, but at any rate the signs had been increasing that a test was about to come. Bragg was not only on the move: both Grant and Rosecrans reported him moving eastward, in the direction of Chattanooga. Before Halleck left for Washington in mid-July he released Thomas to Buell's control, bringing his total strength to 46,000, exclusive of the force at Cumberland Gap. Of these, however, 15,000 were needed for guarding Nashville and the railroads, which left him no more than 31,000 for a forward move. For two weeks the advance had been stalled by the lack of a bridge across the Tennessee at Bridgeport; lumber for the pontoons had been cut by now, but there was still a shortage of nails, oakum, and pitch. While waiting for them, Buell was doing his best to build up a forward supply depot from which to feed and equip his men when they crossed the river to close in on the city. He was still at it on the last day of July, when a message reached his Huntsville headquarters from the commander of his advance division, reporting that Bragg himself had arrived in Chattanooga two days ago — apparently in advance of his whole army. "On the same evening two trains came in with soldiers. Railroad agent says he has orders to furnish cars for 30,000 as fast as he can."

Informed of this, Halleck replied that Grant would furnish reinforcements "if you should find the enemy too strong." Six days later, learning that Bragg's troops had not yet come up, he prodded Buell again: "There is great dissatisfaction here [in Washington] at the slow movement of your army toward Chattanooga. It is feared that the enemy will have time to concentrate his entire army against you." Buell wired back: "It is difficult to satisfy impatience, and when it proceeds from anxiety, as I know it does in this case, I am not disposed to complain of it.

My advance has not been rapid, but it could not be more rapid under the circumstances. I know I have not been idle nor indifferent." Next day, August 7, he got down to specifics. The Confederate force in East Tennessee was estimated at 60,000 men, he said; "yet I am prepared to find the reports much more exaggerated than I have supposed, and shall march upon Chattanooga at the earliest possible day, unless I ascertain certainly that the enemy's strength renders it imprudent. If, on the other hand, he should cross the river I shall attack him, and I do not doubt that we shall defeat him." Encouraged, Halleck replied that Grant had been ordered to transfer two divisions to the Army of the Ohio if they were needed; but he cautioned Buell, "Do not ask for them if you can avoid it with safety."

With that, the roof fell in: quite literally. John Morgan had left Kentucky in late July, but now he suddenly reappeared in Middle Tennesee. On August 12 he captured the guard at Gallatin, above Nashville, and wrecked the L & N Railroad by pushing blazing boxcars into the 800-foot tunnel, seven miles north of there, so that the timbers burned and let the dirt cave in. Unplugging it would be a long-term if not an impossible job, and with the Cumberland River too low for shipping, Buell was cut off from his main supply base at Louisville: which meant that his army would have to eat up the rations collected at Stevenson for the intended drive on Chattanooga. Learning next that a Confederate force estimated at 15,000 men had left Knoxville, bound for Nashville and other points in his rear, he called for the two divisions from Grant and on the 16th detached William Nelson to go to Kentucky with a cadre of experienced officers "to organize such troops as could be got together there to reëstablish our communications and operate against Morgan's incursions." Nor was that all; for the pressure came from various directions, including Washington. Two days later, when Halleck threatened to fire him if he did not speed up his operations — "So great is the dissatisfaction here at the apparent want of energy and activity in your district, that I was this morning notified to have you removed. I got the matter delayed till we could hear further of your movements" — Buell replied forthrightly: "I beg that you will not interpose on my behalf. On the contrary, if the dissatisfaction cannot cease on grounds which I think might be supposed if not apparent, I respectfully request that I may be relieved. My position is far too important to be occupied by any officer on sufferance. I have no desire to stand in the way of what may be deemed necessary for the public good."

Either he was past caring or else he recognized a bluff when he saw one. At any rate, whatever satisfaction this gave him, he had only a short time to enjoy it. Next morning, August 19, he learned that Bragg's army was crossing the river in force at Chattanooga. This was the eventuality in which he had said, "I shall attack him"; but now that he was faced with the actual thing, it began to seem to him that his first responsibility was the protection of Nashville, lying exposed in his rear. Accordingly, he shifted his headquarters to Decherd, forty miles northeast on the railroad leading back to the capital. Four days later — by which time Bragg was reported to have crossed the Tennessee with fifty regiments, "well armed and [with] good artillery" — he had made up his mind. Orders went to the commanders of the two divisions on their way from Grant; they were to change direction and "move by forced marches on Nashville." Simultaneously, the officer in charge of the advance depot at Stevenson was told to "expedite the shipment of stores . . . in every possible way, and be ready to evacuate the place at a moment's notice." The work of nailing and caulking the floats for the 1400-yard-long span at Bridgeport had been completed two weeks before, and this too was remembered: "Let engineers quietly prepare the pontoons for burning, and when you leave destroy everything that cannot be brought away."

Presently, like the campaign itself, the unused bridge went up in smoke. "Don Carlos won't do; he won't do," one division commander muttered when he received the order to retire. Others protested likewise, but to no avail. Before the end of August the withdrawal was complete, and the Decherd provost marshal, describing himself as "weak, discouraged, and worn out," recorded in his diary: "The whole army is concentrated here, or near here; but nobody knows anything, except that the water is bad, whiskey scarce, dust abundant, and the air loaded with the scent and melody of a thousand mules."

✕ 3 ✕

Having accomplished Buell's repulse without the firing of a shot on either side — except in his rear, when Forrest and Morgan were on the rampage — Bragg now turned his mind to larger prospects, involving nothing less than the upset and reversal of the entire military situation in the enormous theater lying between the Appalachians and the Mississippi, the Ohio and the Gulf of Mexico.

The actual movement which placed him in a position to accomplish this design had been undertaken as the result of a decision reached on the spur of a moment in late July: specifically, the anniversary of Manassas. Before that, he had spent a month reorganizing and refitting the army he inherited when Beauregard left Tupelo for what he thought would be a ten-day convalescence. It had been no easy job. After the long retreat, the troops were badly in need of almost everything, including rest. What they needed most, however, was discipline; or so Bragg told "the brave men of Shiloh and of Elkhorn" in an address issued on June 27, the date of his official appointment to command the Army of the Mississippi.

"I enter hopefully on my duties," he declared. "But, soldiers, to secure the legitimate results of all your heavy sacrifices which have brought this army together, to infuse that unity and cohesion essential for a resolute resistance to the wicked invasion of our country, and to give to serried ranks force, impetus, and direction for driving the invader beyond our borders, be assured discipline at all times and obedience to the orders of your officers on all points, as a sacred duty, an act of patriotism, is an absolute necessity." Great events were impending. "A few more days of needful preparation and organization and I shall give your banners to the breeze ... with the confident trust that you will gain additional honors to those you have already won on other fields." After much that was turgid, he ended grimly: "But be prepared to undergo privation and labor with cheerfulness and alacrity."

Cheerfulness was by no means a primary characteristic of this sixth among the Confederacy's full generals; dyspepsia and migraine had made him short-tempered and disputatious all his life. In the old army there was a story that in his younger days, as a lieutenant commanding one of several companies at a post where he was also serving as quartermaster, he had submitted a requisition for supplies, then as quartermaster had declined by indorsement to fill it. As company commander he resubmitted the requisition, giving additional reasons for his needs, but as quartermaster he persisted in denial. Having reached this impasse, he referred the matter to the post commandant, who took one look at the correspondence and threw up his hands: "My God, Mr Bragg, you have quarreled with every officer in the army, and now you are quarreling with yourself!" Other stories were less humorous: as for instance that one of his soldiers had attempted to assassinate him not long after the Mexican War by exploding a 12-pound shell under his cot. When the smoke cleared away, the cot was reduced to tatters and kindling, but Bragg himself emerged without a scratch.

He had left the army in 1856 for a civilian career, not in his native North Carolina but as a sugar planter and commissioner of swamp lands in Louisiana. With the coming of the present war — which he believed had been brought on by such ill-advised political measures as the extension of "universal suffrage" — he had sustained his former reputation as a disciplinarian and a fighter by whipping his Gulf Coast command rapidly into a state of efficiency and leading it aggressively at Shiloh. There, he said in his report immediately afterwards, the army had been given "a valuable lesson, by which we should profit — never on a battlefield to lose a moment's time, but leaving the killed, wounded, and spoils to those whose special business it is to care for them, to press on with every available man, giving a panic-stricken and retreating foe no time to rally, and reaping all the benefits of success never complete until every enemy is killed, wounded, or captured."

He was now in a position, with the approval of the authorities in

Richmond, to give this precept large-scale application. After informing him on June 29 that his department had been "extended so as to embrace that part of Louisiana east of the Mississippi, the entire states of
Mississippi and Alabama, and the portion of Georgia and Florida west of
the Chattahoochee and Apalachicola Rivers," Secretary Randolph not
only authorized an offensive, but urged him to "Strike the moment an
opportunity offers." That was what Bragg had already told his soldiers
he intended to do, as soon as he had completed the reorganization-in-
progress. However, this was attended by many difficulties. One problem,
beyond the need for restoring (or, Bragg would say, injecting) discipline, was the army's health. The troops had brought their Corinth ailments with them; including the men from the Transmississippi, the July 1
"aggregate present" of 61,561 was reduced to 45,393 by deduction of
those who were sick or in arrest or on extra duty. Healthier conditions
at Tupelo, plus the absence of strain — the nearest bluecoat was two
days off — would restore a good part of these 16,000 soldiers to the
ranks. More serious, as Bragg saw it, was the shortage of competent
high-ranking officers. Van Dorn was gone, transferred to Vicksburg
in mid-June when Davis and Farragut threatened the city from above
and below; Breckinridge went with him, taking 6000 troops to oppose a
landing by the men from Butler, and Hindman was detached at the same
time to raise an army in Arkansas. Polk having been relieved of his corps
and named second in command of the whole, Hardee and Price were the
only experienced major generals left in direct charge of troops. The rest,
Bragg told Richmond, including most of the brigadiers in the sweeping
indictment, were "in my judgment unsuited for their responsible positions"; were, in fact, "only incumbrances, and would be better out of
the way."

Despite these shortcomings — and despite the fact that the War
Department increased his difficulties by not allowing him to consolidate
under-strength regiments bled white at Shiloh, then further reduced to
skeletons by pestilence at Corinth — he kept his army hard at work,
convinced that this was the sovereign remedy for injured health as
well as for injured discipline. In compensation for long hours of drill he
issued new uniforms and better rations, both of which had an additional
salutary effect. New problems were dealt with as they arose, including
an upsurge of desertion. He met it harshly. "Almost every day we would
hear a discharge of musketry, and knew that some poor trembling
wretch had bid farewell to mortal things here below," one soldier afterwards recalled. The effectiveness of such executions was increased, Bragg
believed, by lining up the condemned man's former comrades to watch
him pay for his crime. It worked; desertion decreased; but at a price.
"We were crushed," the same observer added bitterly. "Bragg, so the
soldiers thought, was the machine that did it. . . . He loved to crush the
spirit of his men. The more of a hangdog look they had about them

the better was General Bragg pleased. Not a single soldier in the whole army ever loved or respected him."

True or false, all this was rather beside the point as far as Bragg was concerned. He was not out after love or respect; he was after results, and he got them. On July 12 he informed the Adjutant General that the time since his last report, forwarded to Richmond when he assumed official command two weeks before, "has been diligently applied to organization, discipline, and instruction, with a very marked improvement. The health and general tone of the troops, too, exhibits results no less gratifying. Our condition for service is good and has reached a culminating point under the defective skeleton organization."

He was ready to strike. The question was, where? In what direction? Grant's army, considerably larger than his own and occupying strong positions under Sherman and Rosecrans at Memphis and Corinth, seemed practically unassailable; besides which, Bragg told Richmond, "A long and disastrous drouth, threatening destruction to the grain crop, continues here and renders any move [into North Mississippi] impracticable for want of water." As for Buell, his lateral advance had been so slow and apparently so uncertain that for a long time the Confederates had found it impossible to determine his objective. It might be Chattanooga — in that case, Bragg had already sent a 3000-man brigade of infantry to reinforce the troops in East Tennessee — or it might be Atlanta, depending on what direction he took after crossing the river at Bridgeport. Whichever it was, Bragg decided in mid-July to give him all the trouble he could by sending two brigades of cavalry, under Colonel Joseph Wheeler and Brigadier General Frank Armstrong, to harass his lines of supply and communication in West Tennessee and North Alabama.

They had excellent models for their work, commanders who had already given cavalry operations — and, indeed the war itself — a new dimension, based on their proof that sizeable bodies of hard-riding men could not only strike and create havoc deep in the enemy's rear, Jeb Stuart-style, but could stay there to strike again and again, spreading the havoc over hundreds of miles and wearing out their would-be pursuers by causing them to converge repeatedly on thin air. By now the whole Confederate West was ringing with praise for Morgan and Forrest: particularly the former, whose exploits had surrounded him with the aura of a legend. A tall, white-faced, handsome, cold-eyed man, soft-spoken and always neatly dressed in conservative but obviously expensive clothes — fine gray broadcloth, fire-gilt buttons, richly polished boots, and spotless linen — he knew the effectiveness of reticence, yet he could be flamboyant on occasion. "Kentuckians!" he exhorted in a broadside struck off at Glasgow and distributed on his sweep through the Bluegrass, "I have come to liberate you from the hands of your oppressors." Calling for volunteer recruits, "fifty thousand of Kentucky's bravest sons," and implying thereby that he would take only the bravest, he broke into verse:

> *"Strike — for your altars and your fires;*
> *Strike for the green graves of your sires,*
> *God, and your native land!"*

He was seldom flamboyant, however, except for a purpose. For example, he carried with him a telegrapher, a wire-tap expert who, though he would sometimes chat waggishly with enemy operators — once he even went so far as to complain directly to Washington, in Morgan's name, about the inferior grade of mules being furnished Buell's army — not only intercepted messages that kept his chief informed of the Federal efforts to surround him, but also sent out false instructions that turned the converging blue columns off his trail. Such devices yielded profits. Leaving Knoxville on July 4 with fewer than 900 men, he made a thousand-mile swing through Middle Tennessee and Kentucky, in the course of which he captured seventeen towns, together with tons of Union supplies, paroled nearly 1200 regular army prisoners, and dispersed about 1500 home-guarders, all at a cost of less than 90 casualties, and returned before the end of the month with an additional 300 volunteers picked up along the way. Two weeks later he was back again. Lest it be thought that he was merely a hit-and-run sort of soldier, after wrecking the Gallatin tunnel he turned on his pursuer — Brigadier General R. W. Johnson, a West Pointer and fellow-Kentuckian, whom Buell had assigned the task of intercepting the raiders with an equal force — and whipped him soundly, breaking up his command and capturing the general and his staff.

Forrest was a different sort of man; different in method, that is, if not in results. Recuperating in Memphis from his Fallen Timbers wound — the ball had lodged against his spine and was removed in the field a week later, without the benefit of an anesthetic — he put a recruiting notice in the local paper, calling for "able-bodied men ... with good horse and gun. I wish none but those who desire to be actively engaged. . . . Come on, boys, if you want a heap of fun and to kill some Yankees." When he returned to Corinth, shortly before the evacuation, Beauregard sent him to Chattanooga with orders to weld the scattered East Tennessee cavalry units into a brigade. He arrived in late June, assembled his men, and, believing active duty the best possible training for a green command, crossed the Tennessee River on July 9 to camp the following night atop Cumberland Mountain, deep in enemy territory. At dawn Sunday, three mornings later and ninety roundabout miles away, civilian hostages held in the Murfreesboro jail — several were under sentence of death, in retaliation for the bushwhacking of Union soldiers on or near their farms — heard what one of them later called "a strange noise like the roar of an approaching storm." It was hoofbeats: Forrest's 1400 troopers were pounding up the turnpike. Two regiments of infantry, one from Michigan, one from Minnesota, each with a section of artillery and cavalry support — their combined strength was about the same as Forrest's, except that he had no guns — were camped on opposite sides of town, with detachments guarding the jail and the courthouse, in which the brigade supplies were stored. Quickly the town was taken, along with the Federal commanding general, and fire-fights broke out on the outskirts, where the blue infantry prepared to defend its camps. Once the hostages had been freed and the captured goods packed for removal along with the prisoners already taken, some of the raiders, believing the alarm had spread to other Union garrisons by now, suggested withdrawal. But Forrest would have none of that. "I didn't come here to make half a job of it," he said, influenced perhaps by the fact that today was his forty-first birthday; "I'm going to have them all."

He got them, too — though he hastened matters somewhat by sending notes to the two commanders in their barricaded camps, demanding "unconditional surrender . . . or I will have every man put to the sword." He added, by way of extenuation and persuasion: "This demand is made to prevent the effusion of blood," and though like Morgan he was still a colonel, in his signature he promoted himself to "Brigadier General of Cavalry, C.S. Army," doubtless to lend additional weight to the threat. It worked. The two blue colonels surrendered in sequence, and Forrest marched his 1200 prisoners back eastward to McMinnville, where he paroled them and forwarded the captured arms and supplies to Chattanooga — all but the guns; he kept them for use around Nashville the following week, where he gave Nelson the slip after re-wrecking Buell's vital railroad supply line.

"I am happy to see that my two lieutenants, Morgan and Forrest, are doing such good service in Kentucky and Tennessee," Beauregard wrote from Bladon Springs, where he was still in exile. "When I appointed them I thought they would leave their mark wherever they passed." This was said in reply to a letter from Bragg, in which the present army commander told his former chief, "Our cavalry is paving the way for me in Middle Tennessee and Kentucky." The letter was dated July 22. By that time Bragg had decided not only on Buell's intentions, but also on his own. After a forty-day Federal head start, it was to be a race for Chattanooga: with further possibilities as the prize.

Kirby Smith, commanding in East Tennessee, had never had much doubt about Buell's intentions from the outset. Promoted to major general after recovering from being shot through the neck at Manassas, Smith had been given the thorny job of restoring order in the area around Knoxville, and in this he had succeeded remarkably well, considering the extent to which the region was torn by conflicting loyalties and ambitions. But since the fall of Corinth the military situation had grown increasingly ominous; George Morgan occupied Cumberland Gap, an immediate threat to Knoxville itself, and Buell began his eastward advance in the direction of Chattanooga, while Smith himself had less than 15,000 of all arms with which to resist the two-pronged menace. The arrival of the 3000-man brigade from Bragg afforded some relief, but not for long. Learning from northern papers in mid-July that several of Grant's divisions had been released to Buell, he protested to Davis in Richmond: "This brings an overwhelming force that cannot be resisted except by Bragg's coöperation." Four days later, July 19, he reported to the Adjutant General that "Buell with his whole force" had reached Stevenson, thirty miles from Chattanooga, which he was "daily expected to attack." Fortunately, Smith added, Forrest had broken the Union supply line at Murfreesboro. "This may delay General Buell's movement and give General Bragg time to move on Middle Tennessee. The safety of Chattanooga depends upon his coöperation." Next day, not knowing of his opponent's difficulties in procuring pitch and oakum, he made a telegraphic appeal to Bragg himself: "Buell has completed his preparations, is prepared to cross near Bridgeport, and his passage there may be hourly expected. General Morgan's command moving on Knoxville from Cumberland Gap. Your coöperation is much needed. It is your time to strike at Middle Tennessee."

Bragg's reply, sent from Tupelo that same day, was not encouraging. "Confronted here by a largely superior force strongly intrenched" and threatened on the left by Curtis, who would "now be enabled to unite against us," he found it "impossible . . . to do more than menace and harass the enemy from this quarter." The land was parched; both armies, Grant's and his own, were living out of wells; so that whichever ventured far from its base in search of the other would die of thirst. "The fact is we are fearfully outnumbered in this department, the enemy having at least two to our one in the field, with a comparatively short line upon which he may concentrate." After this recital of obstacles and woes, he made it clear that Smith would have to shift for himself in East Tennessee, without the hope of further reinforcements.

Then overnight he changed his mind. Next day was the anniversary of Manassas, and he saluted it with a telegram as abruptly brief as the discharge of a starting-gun in the race which it announced:

Tupelo, Miss., July 21

President Jefferson Davis,
          Richmond, Va.:
     Will move immediately to Chattanooga in force and advance from there. Forward movement from here in force is not practicable. Will leave this line well defended.

BRAXTON BRAGG

Next day, in the midst of large-scale preparations for the shift — he was not waiting for specific governmental approval; "Strike the moment an opportunity offers," he had been told three weeks ago — he expanded this somewhat in a second wire to Davis, who he knew must have been startled at being told, without preamble, that the army which was the mainstay of his native Mississippi was being removed forthwith: "Obstacles in front connected with danger to Chattanooga induce a change of base. Fully impressed with great importance of that line, am moving to East Tennessee. Produce rapid offensive from there following the consternation now being produced by our cavalry. Leave this State amply protected by Van Dorn at Vicksburg and Price here."

In a letter to Beauregard that same day — the one in which he wrote, "Our cavalry is paving the way" — he gave a fuller explanation. "As I am changing entirely, under altered circumstances, the plan of operations here," he told his former chief, "I submit to you what I propose and beg your candid criticism, and in view of the cordial and sincere relations we have ever maintained, I trust to your compliance." With Smith "so weak as to give me great uneasiness for the safety of his line," Bragg had had to choose between four alternatives: 1) to remain idle at Tupelo, 2) to attack Grant, 3) to move into Middle Tennessee by crossing the river in Buell's rear and thus disrupt his and Grant's supply lines, or 4) to attack Buell. Of these, the first was unthinkable; the second was impracticable, considering the drouth in North Mississippi and the strength of the fortifications at Memphis and Corinth; the third was unwise and overrisky, since it would invite both Grant and Buell to assault him simultaneously from opposite directions. Therefore he had chosen the fourth, which would not only provide for a combination with Smith, but would also afford possibilities for maneuver and mystification. "By throwing my cavalry forward toward Grand Junction and Tuscumbia" — this referred to Wheeler and Armstrong, who had left three days ago — "the impression is created that I am advancing on both places and [the Federals] are drawing in to meet me. The Memphis & Charleston road has been kept cut, so they have no use of it and have at length given it up. Before they can know my movement I shall be in front of Buell at Chattanooga, and by cutting off his transportation may have him in a tight place. . . . Thus you have my plan."

As might have been expected — for, though it lacked the language, it had nearly the grandeur of one of the Creole's own — Beauregard gave the plan his fervent approval. "Action, action, and action is what we require," he replied, paraphrasing Danton's "De l'audace, encore l'audace, et toujours de l'audace," and added with a paternalistic glow: "I have no doubt that with anything like equal numbers you will meet with success." By the time these encouraging words reached him, however, Bragg was far from Tupelo. He left on July 24, after notifying the Adjutant General: "Major General Van Dorn, with about 16,000 effectives, will hold the line of the Mississippi. Major General Price, with a similar force, will face the enemy on this frontier, and a sufficient garrison will be left for Mobile and the Gulf. With the balance of the forces, some 35,000 effectives, I hope, in conjunction with Major General Smith, to strike an effective blow through Middle Tennessee, gaining the enemy's rear, cutting off his supplies and dividing his forces, so as to encounter him in detail. In any event much will be accomplished in simply preserving our line and preventing a descent into Georgia, than which no greater disaster could befall us."

His confidence that he would win the race, despite the handicap of a six-week lag — not to mention the sobering example of the hare-and-tortoise fable — was based on an appreciation of railroads as a strategic factor in this war. (For one thing, by bringing Joe Johnston's men down from the Valley, through Manassas Gap, to unload within earshot of the Union guns, they had won the battle whose anniversary had now come round.) Ever since his assumption of command Bragg had kept busy, doing not only all he could to wreck Buell's rail facilities, but also all he could to improve his own, especially in urging the completion of a line connecting Meridian and Selma. In the former effort, by grace of Morgan and Forrest, he had been successful, but in the latter he had failed; the Confederacy, it appeared, could afford neither the effort nor the iron. Consequently, with the Memphis & Charleston wrecked and in Federal hands, the only rail connection between Tupelo and Chattanooga was a roundabout, far-south route through Mobile and Atlanta, involving a journey of 776 miles over no less than half a dozen separate railroads, with through trains prohibited by the water gap across Mobile Bay and the narrow gauge of the Montgomery & West Point road. Nevertheless, the sending of the 3000-man brigade to Smith in late June, as a trial run over this route, had opened Bragg's eyes to the possibilities it afforded for a rapid, large-scale movement. The troops had left Tupelo on June 27, and despite congestion all along the line — conflicting orders from Richmond had put other units simultaneously on the rails — reached Chattanooga on July 3, within a week of the day the movement order had been issued.

Now he was out to repeat or better the performance with ten times as many soldiers, the "effective total" of his four divisions being 31,638 of all arms. Horse-drawn elements, including engineers and wagon trains, as well as cavalry and artillery, would move overland — due east to Rome, then north — but the bulk of the command would go by rail, dispatched from Tupelo a division at a time. For this, though they were made on quite short notice, the preparations were extensive, with the emphasis on discipline, as was always the case when Bragg was in charge. Each man was to be handed seven days' cooked rations as he stepped aboard, thus forestalling any excuse for foraging en route, and unit commanders were cautioned to be especially vigilant at junction points to prevent the more adventurous from disrupting the schedule by stealing away for a visit to the fleshpots. The first division left on July 23, the second and third immediately thereafter, and the fourth on July 29: by which time the units forwarded from Mobile and other scattered points to clear the line had been in Chattanooga for two full days. They were followed by a week-long procession of jam-packed cars whose engines came puffing around Missionary Ridge and into the city.

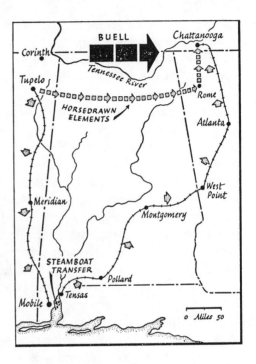

In all the bustle and hurry of preparation and departure, and in spite of the number of wires and letters flying back and forth, Bragg had neglected to mention his sudden volte-face to the one person most immediately concerned: Kirby Smith. While changing trains in Montgomery, however, he was handed an intercepted letter the East Tennessee commander had sent from Knoxville on the 24th — the day Bragg left Tupelo — proposing, with what amounted to clairvoyance if not downright telepathy, the very movement now in progress: "Buell's movements and preparations indicate a speedy attack. . . . Can you not leave a portion of your forces in observation in Mississippi, and, shifting the main body to this department, take command in person? There is yet time for a brilliant summer campaign; you will have a good and secure base, abundant supplies, the Tennessee can be crossed at any point by the aid of steam and ferry boats, and the campaign opened with every prospect of regaining possession of Middle Tennessee and possibly Kentucky." He added: "I will not only coöperate with you, but will cheerfully place my command under you subject to your orders."

With this in his pocket, a happy omen as well as an affirmation of his strategic judgment, Bragg continued his journey and reached Chattanooga early on the morning of July 30. Informed of his arrival, Smith came down from Knoxville the following day to confer with him on what Bragg called "measures for material support and effective coöperation." Smith had two divisions, one in front of Cumberland Gap, observing the Federals who occupied that point, the other at Chattanooga; their strength was about 9,000 men each, including the brigade that had arrived four weeks ago to thicken the ranks of the slim force confronting Buell. Bragg was reorganizing his still-arriving army into two "wings," one under Polk, the other under Hardee, each with two infantry divisions and a cavalry brigade; their combined strength was 34,000, including the units forwarded in driblets from points along the railroad. His problem was how best to employ these 52,000 men — his and Smith's — against the larger but badly scattered Federal forces to his front and on his flank.

The solution, as communicated to the Adjutant General on August 1, was for Smith to "move at once against General Morgan in front of Cumberland Gap," while Bragg was collecting supplies and awaiting the arrival of his artillery and trains for an advance from Chattanooga. This would require ten days or two weeks, he said. At the end of that time, if Smith had been successful against Morgan, both armies would then combine for a march "into Middle Tennessee with the fairest prospect of cutting off General Buell, should that commander continue in his present position. Should he be reinforced from the west side of the Tennessee River, so as to cope with us, then Van Dorn and Price can strike and clear West Tennessee of any force that can be left to hold it." Furthermore, once Grant and Buell had been disposed of, either by destruction or by being maneuvered into retreat, he considered the time propitious for an invasion of the region to the north. "The feeling in Middle Tennessee and Kentucky is represented by Forrest and Morgan to have become intensely hostile to the enemy, and nothing is wanted but arms and support to bring the people into our ranks, for they have found that neutrality has afforded them no protection."

Returning to Knoxville much encouraged by these developments, Smith informed his wife that he had found his new partner "a grim old fellow" (he himself was thirty-eight; Bragg was forty-five) "but a true soldier." Presently he was further gladdened by the arrival of two brigades detached by Bragg to reinforce him for the offensive, one from Polk and one from Hardee, and being thus strengthened on the eve of his advance he began to see larger prospects looming out beyond the horizon — prospects based in part on a dispatch from John Morgan, who had reported from northern Kentucky in mid-July: "I am here with a force sufficient to hold all the country outside of Lexington and Frankfort. These places are garrisoned chiefly with Home Guards. The bridges between Cincinnati and Lexington have been destroyed. The whole country can be secured, and 25,000 or 30,000 men will join you at once. I have taken eleven cities and towns with very heavy army stores." If one small brigade of cavalry could accomplish all this, Smith reasoned, what might a whole army do? Accordingly, on August 9 he wrote to Bragg that he "understood" the Federals intrenched at Cumberland Gap had "nearly a month's supply of provisions. If this be true the reduction of the place would be a matter of more time than I presume you are willing I should take. As my move direct to Lexington, Ky. would effectually invest [the Gap] and would be attended with other most brilliant results in my judgment, I suggest my being allowed to take that course, if I find the speedy reduction of the Gap an impractical thing."

Bragg too was nurturing hopes in that direction, though not without reservations. He replied next day: "It will be a week yet before I can commence crossing the river, and information I hope to receive will determine which route I shall take, to Nashville or Lexington. My inclination is now for the latter." All the same, Smith's plan to by-pass Cumberland Gap and head straight for North Central Kentucky was more than his partner had bargained for, even though Smith reinforced his proposal by inclosing a letter from John Morgan's lieutenant-colonel, stressing the opinion that flocks of eager volunteers were waiting to double the size of his army as soon as it reached the Bluegrass. Strategically, Bragg approved, but tactically he urged caution: "It would be unadvisable, I think, for you to move far into Kentucky, leaving [George] Morgan in your rear, until I am able to fully engage Buell and his forces on your left. But I do not credit the amount of Morgan's supplies [at Cumberland Gap] and have confidence in his timidity. When once well on the way to his rear you might safely leave but 5000 to his front, and by a flank movement draw the rest to your assistance. He will never advance to escape."

Smith's ebullience was contagious: as was shown in the final sentence of Bragg's letter. "Van Dorn and Price will advance simultaneously with us from Mississippi on West Tennessee, and I trust we may all unite in Ohio."

★ ★ ★

Just now, however, Van Dorn was looking south, not north; he had New Orleans on his mind, not Ohio. The grim determination he had brought to embattled Vicksburg in late June — "Let it be borne in mind by all that the army here is defending the place against occupation. This will be done at all hazards, even though this beautiful and devoted city should be laid in ruin and ashes" — gave way to elation in mid-July when the *Arkansas* made her run through the Yankee sloops and gunboats. "Glorious for the navy, and glorious for her heroic commander, officers, and men," he wired Davis. The iron ram changed everything. "Smokestack riddled; otherwise not materially damaged," he exulted. "Soon be repaired and then, Ho! for New Orleans." Both enemy fleets were still on hand, and across the way the bluecoats were still digging their canal; but Van Dorn no longer saw them as much of a threat. A week later, after two all-out attempts to sink the *Arkansas* under the tall red bluff, he pronounced "the failure so complete that it was almost ridiculous." The same went for the engineering project. "Nothing can be accomplished by the enemy," he told Richmond, "unless they bring overwhelming number of troops. This must be anticipated."

His favorite method of anticipation, now as always, was to seize the offensive; to snatch the ball from his opponent and start running. That was what he had done, or tried to do, in Arkansas back in the early spring, and that was what he decided to do now in his native Mississippi in midsummer. When Davis and Farragut gave up the game, turned their backs on each other and went their separate ways — the former to Helena, the latter to New Orleans after dropping the infantry off at Baton Rouge — Van Dorn ordered Breckinridge to pursue southward with 4000 men and knock the bluecoats off balance in the Louisiana capital before they could get set for a return. If possible, he was to take the city: after which, as Van Dorn saw it, would come much else. Five months ago the byword had been "St Louis, then huzza!" Now it was "Ho! for New Orleans."

Breckinridge wasted no time in getting started. On July 27, the day after the Yankee fleets took off in opposite directions, he put his troops aboard railroad cars and proceeded by way of Jackson to Ponchatoula, Louisiana, where they detrained the following afternoon to prepare for the overland advance on Baton Rouge, sixty miles to the west. On the 30th the march began, but was halted the following morning when reports came in "that the effective force of the enemy was not less than 5000 and that the ground was commanded by three gunboats lying in the river." Down to 3400 men as a result of sickness, Breckinridge wired Van Dorn that he would nonetheless "undertake to capture the garrison if the *Arkansas* could be sent down to clear the river or divert the fire of the gunboats." Promptly the reply came back: The ram would be in front of Baton Rouge at dawn, August 5. Breckinridge made his plans accordingly.

Isaac Brown was not in Vicksburg at the time, having left his shipmates "to sustain without me the lassitude of inaction" while he took a four-day leave in Grenada. If rest and relaxation were what he was after (which was probable; he had had precious little of either in the past two months) he was disappointed in more ways than one. For one thing, he had no sooner arrived than he was taken violently ill and put to bed. For another, while he was in this condition, supposedly unable to lift his head off the pillow, he received a wire from his first lieutenant, informing him that the *Arkansas* was under orders to proceed at once to Baton Rouge, despite the fact that her engines were under major repair and much of her rusty plating had still not been refastened to her battered sides. Brown replied with "a positive order to remain at Vicksburg until I could join him," and had himself carried to the depot, where he boarded the first southbound train. Collapsed on some mail bags, too weak to sit up or even change his position, he rode the 130 miles to

Jackson, where he applied for a special train to take him the rest of the way, only to learn that the *Arkansas* had already gone downriver.

She cast off Sunday evening, August 3, barely thirty hours before she was due at her Tuesday-morning rendezvous with Breckinridge, 300 winding miles below. This called for her best speed: with the result that there were stoppages from overstrain all along the way, each requiring additional make-up speed thereafter, which produced more frequent breakdowns. Caught up in this vicious cycle, her engines had become so cranky by the time she reached the mouth of the Red, 200 miles out of Vicksburg, that her substitute skipper, Lieutenant Henry Stevens, called a council of war to decide whether to continue or turn back. The decision was to press on. At daybreak, August 5, approaching the final bend above Baton Rouge, the crew heard the boom of guns, which told that the land attack was under way. The *Arkansas* herself appeared to sense this; or, as one of her officers put it, "Like a war horse she seemed to scent the battle from afar, and in point of speed outdid anything we had ever before witnessed." Then, just before rounding the bend, they heard a familiar sound: the crack and jar of naval guns mixed in with the bark of field artillery. The ironclad *Essex* and the two Farragut gunboats were adding the weight of their metal to the attempt to fling back the Confederate attackers. Urged on by the knowledge "that our iron sides should be receiving those missiles which now were mowing down our ranks of infantry," Stevens decided to make an immediate ram attack on the *Essex*, sinking her where she lay, then steam below the city to cut off the retreat of the two wooden gunboats, reducing them to kindling at his leisure. Such was his intention: whereupon the starboard engine suddenly quit, and before the helmsman could port her wheel, the ram ran hard aground. The engineers got to work at once with files and chisels, trying to coax the balky engine into motion, but it would obviously be some hours before they could succeed. Meanwhile, the land attack continued. "There lay the enemy in plain view," one of the *Arkansas* lieutenants afterwards wrote, still mortified years later, "and we as helpless as a shear-hulk."

Breckinridge had marched to within ten miles of the place the night before in order to launch his assault on schedule, although by now he was down to 2600 effectives as a result of sickness brought on by the heat and an irregular diet, the rail movement having been made in such haste that commissary supplies and cooking utensils were left behind. "The day before the battle we had nothing to eat but roasting ears," one Kentucky infantryman afterwards recalled, "and these we ate raw because we had not time to stop long enough to roast them. Our command, with the horses, consumed forty acres of green corn one evening; for we stopped only long enough to gather the corn and feed the horses, [and] we then moved forward to take position to make the attack at daylight." His brigade, which had left Vicksburg with 1800 men, was reduced to 580 within two weeks. "Such were the ravages of sickness, exposure, and battle," he declared.

Of these, the last were the least as the thing turned out, in spite of the fact that they found the enemy waiting to receive them. The Federal commander, Thomas Williams, had formed his line closer to the town than some of his regimental camps, contracting it thus because he was down to about the same effective strength as the attackers: not because of exposure or bad food, but because so many of his men had still not recovered from lowland ailments encountered while plying their shovels opposite Vicksburg. However, he had the advantage in artillery, eighteen pieces to eleven, besides the tremendous added power of the gunboats, plowing the ranks of the charging rebels by arching their big projectiles over the capital, where a naval observer directed their fire by signals from the tower of the statehouse. In the face of this, Breckinridge scored considerable early success, forcing the bluecoats back through the suburbs on the right and capturing two guns; but the warships, unopposed by the missing *Arkansas*, more than tipped the balance. By 10 o'clock, having lost the commanders of one of his two divisions and three of his four brigades, he halted to adjust his line. Williams, observing this, ordered a charge to recover what had been yielded, but then was killed by a bullet through his chest — the first Union general to fall in battle since Nathaniel Lyon died much the same way at Wilson's Creek, a year ago next week. Breckinridge held his ground until late afternoon, hoping to renew the attack as soon as the *Arkansas* arrived. When he learned that the ram was lying helpless four miles above town, he left a small force in observation and pulled the main body back to the Comite River, from which he had marched the night before. The Federals did not follow.

Aboard the grounded ram, the engineers were still at work with their files and chisels. Stevens got her afloat by throwing off some railroad iron lying loose on her deck, and by dusk the black gang had her engines back in operation. She started down the four-mile reach, where the Union boats were standing guard, but had gone no more than a hundred yards when the crankpin in the rocking shaft of the starboard engine snapped. A forge was set up on the gundeck, and one of the engineers, a former blacksmith, hammered out a new one. By the time it was finished, dawn was glimmering through and the lookout spotted the *Essex* coming upstream, making a scant two knots against the current. Hurriedly, the new pin was installed; the rust-red *Arkansas* stood out for battle. Stevens intended to make a short run upstream, then turn and launch a ram attack with the added momentum. Before he could start back, however, the port engine suddenly quit and spun the vessel once more into bank. The *Essex* was coming slowly on, firing as she came, and the *Arkansas* was hard aground, able to bring only one of her guns to bear. The situation spoke for itself. Stevens ordered the crew ashore and fired the vessel, tears streaming down his face as he did so. When the flames reached the gundeck, the loaded guns began to explode: so that the *Arkansas* not only kept the *Essex* at a respectful distance during her death throes, but administered her own *coup de grâce* and fired her own salute as she went down. Thus she made a fitting end to her twenty-three-day career.

Brown almost got there in time to see it. Cured of his fever by the news that his ram had gone downriver without him, he got back onto the southbound train and rode to Ponchatoula, where he transferred to horseback and struck out westward for the river, in hope that he could hail the *Arkansas* from bank and somehow manage to board her or at any rate be near enough to watch and cheer her as she fought. What he saw instead were exultant Union gunboats steaming back and forth across the muddy water where she had exploded and sunk with her colors flying. Sadly — though he was proud, he later wrote, that her deck "had never been pressed by the foot of an enemy" — he rode back the way he had come and returned to Vicksburg.

Breckinridge shared the pride, but not the sadness, at the outcome of the brief campaign. This reaction was based not on the casualty lists — both sides had lost 84 killed, though the Confederate total of wounded and captured was the larger: 372 to 299 — but on his view of the fighting qualities shown. "In one respect the contrast between the opposing forces was very striking," he declared. "The enemy were well clothed, and their encampments showed the presence of every comfort and even luxury. Our men had little transportation, indifferent food, and no shelter. Half of them had no coats, and hundreds were without either shoes or socks; yet no troops ever behaved with greater gallantry and even reckless audacity. What can make this difference unless it be the sublime courage inspired by a just cause?"

Whether right made might, or might made right — or, indeed, whether either was on the former Vice President's side in this case — was a question open to much debate, then and thereafter. Butler, for one, did not agree with his assessment. According to him, the rebels "took advantage of [the garrison's] sickness from the malaria of the marshes of Vicksburg to make a cowardly attack," which was bloodily repulsed with "more than a thousand killed and wounded." But the Southerner's claim to physical as well as moral victory was considerably strengthened two weeks later when Butler, after congratulating his soldiers for their staunchness — "The Spanish conqueror of Mexico won imperishable renown by landing in that country and burning his transport ships, to cut off all hope of retreat. You, more wise and economical, but with equal providence against retreat, sent yours home" — ordered Baton Rouge abandoned, and dispatched those same transports upriver to bring the endangered troops back to New Orleans.

The flow of what Horace Greeley, back in May, had been calling "A Deluge of Victories" was seemingly reversed, and there was corresponding elation in the South. Next to the capture of a northern capital, what could be better than the recovery of a southern one? More important, tactically speaking, the Federal grip on the Mississippi — so close to strangulation a month ago — had been loosened even further, and to make sure that it was not reapplied Breckinridge had already sent most of his troops to occupy and fortify Port Hudson, a left-bank position of great natural strength. Potentially another Vicksburg, its bluff commanded a sharp bend of the river about midway between Baton Rouge and the mouth of the Red, thus assuring a continuation of commerce with the Transmississippi, including the grainlands of Northwest Louisiana and the cattle-rich plains of Texas.

That was but part of the brightening overall picture. In Virginia, McClellan had been repulsed. Grant was stalled in North Mississippi. Buell had lost the race for Chattanooga. And in all these widespread regions Confederate armies were poised to take the offensive: particularly in East Tennessee, as Breckinridge learned from a letter Bragg sent him immediately after the fight at Baton Rouge. Extending an invitation to the former Bluegrass politician, the terrible-tempered North Carolinian was in a strangely rollicking mood: "My army has promised to make me military governor of Ohio in ninety days (Seward's time for crushing the rebellion), and as they cannot do that without passing your home, I have thought you would like to have an escort to visit your family." He added, in a more serious vein, "Your influence in Kentucky would be equal to an extra division in my army.... If you desire it, and General Van Dorn will consent, you shall come at once. A command is ready for you, and I shall hope to see your eyes beam again at the command 'Forward,' as they did at Shiloh, in the midst of our greatest success."

This was seconded by Hardee, who telegraphed on August 23, five days before the Chattanooga jump-off: "Come here, if possible. I have a splendid division for you to lead into Kentucky."

Breckinridge wired back: "Reserve the division for me."

One prominent Kentuckian already commanded a division under Hardee: Simon Buckner. Exchanged at last, after five months in prison at Fort Warren, he reported in late July to Richmond, where he was promoted to major general and assigned to duty with the army then on its way to Chattanooga. The army commander was glad to have him, not only because of his proved fighting qualities, but also as a recruiting attraction in his native state; spare muskets were being taken along in wagons, ready for transfer to the shoulders of Kentucky volunteers. Bragg was glad, too, to have the approval of the President for the campaign he was about to undertake, though Davis warned him at the outset with a two-edged compliment predicting future strife, off as well as on the field of battle: "You have the misfortune of being regarded as my personal friend, and are pursued, therefore, with malignant censure by men regardless of truth, and whose want of principle to guide their conduct renders them incapable of conceiving that you are trusted because of your known fitness for command and not because of friendly regard. Revolutions develop the high qualities of the good and the great, but they cannot change the nature of the vicious and the selfish."

Kirby Smith — described in the same letter as "one of our ablest and purest officers ... [whose] promotions, like your own, have come unsought" — left Knoxville on August 14 to move against his West Point classmate George Morgan at Cumberland Gap. The two brigades received from Bragg had raised his striking force to 21,000 men, well over twice the number holding the gap; but finding, as he had predicted, that Morgan was better prepared to resist a siege than he himself was prepared to maintain one, he left a 9000-man division in front of the mountain stronghold, as Bragg had advised, and with the rest of his army crossed the Cumberlands thirty miles to the southwest at Big Creek Gap. This was no raid, he told Richmond. "My advance is made in the hope of permanently occupying Kentucky. It is a bold move, offering brilliant results, but will be accomplished only with hard fighting, and must be sustained by constant reinforcements." He marched fast, swinging north for Barbourville, which he occupied on August 18. The "constant reinforcements," of course, would have to be in the form of local volunteers; but none were forthcoming here. Six days later, while preparing to resume the march, he notified Bragg: "Thus far the people are universally hostile to our cause. This sentiment extends through the mountain region of Eastern Kentucky. In the bluegrass region I have better expectations and shall soon test their loyalty."

Bragg's own estimate was rosier and a good deal more specific. "Everything is ripe for success," he informed his co-commander. "The country is aroused and expecting us. Buell's forces are much scattered, and from all accounts much demoralized. By rapid movements and vigorous blows we may beat him in detail, or by gaining his rear very much increase his demoralization and break him up." On August 27, the day before the jump-off, he sent word to Sterling Price, holding the line in North Mississippi: "We move from here immediately, later by some days than expected, but in time we hope for a successful campaign. Buell has certainly fallen back from the Memphis & Charleston Railroad and will probably not make a stand this side of Nashville, if there. He is now fortifying that place. General Smith, reinforced by two brigades from this army, has turned Cumberland Gap, and is now marching on Lexington, Ky. ... We shall thus have Buell pretty well disposed of. Sherman and Rosecrans we leave to you and Van Dorn, satisfied that you can dispose of them, and we shall confidently expect to meet you on the Ohio and there open the way to Missouri."

Unquestionably — even without the inclusion of Missouri, which was scarcely more than a closing flourish for the benefit of Price — this was an ambitious project. But Bragg was not only ready and willing to undertake its execution; he had already selected a guide, a model. Beauregard and McClellan, along with a cluster of lesser lights, might take Napoleon. Not Bragg. His chosen prototype was a contemporary, a man who in fact was seven years his junior. Back in Tupelo, on the occasion of promising his soldiers to "give your banners to the breeze," he also told them: "Others of your countrymen, under the lead of Jackson and Ewell in the Valley of Virginia, have recently shed imperishable renown on our arms, and shown what a small, obedient, disciplined volunteer army can do." What he intended now, as he stood poised for the jump-off, was a Valley Campaign on a much larger scale, with Smith as Ewell and himself as Stonewall. Like him, he could expect to be badly outnumbered strategically (he had fewer than 30,000 of all arms); yet like him, too, he would translate this disadvantage into "imperishable renown" by means of "rapid movements and vigorous blows." So far, it was true, the only attributes original and copy had in common were dyspepsia and a readiness to stand deserters before a firing squad. However, it was Bragg's intention to extend these similarities into other fields of reaction and endeavor during the trial that lay ahead.

Some measure of this intention, complete with Old Testament overtones, was communicated to his troops in a general order read to them before they left their camps around Chattanooga:

> The enemy is before us, devastating our fair country, imprisoning our old and venerated men (even the ministers of God), insulting our women, and desecrating our altars. It is our proud lot to be assigned the duty of punishing and driving forth these deluded men, led by desperate adventurers and goaded on by Abolition demagogues and demons. Let us but deserve success and an offended Deity will certainly assure it. Should we be opposed, we must fight at any odds and conquer at any sacrifice. Should the foe retire, we must follow him rapidly to his own territory and make him taste the bitters of invasion.
>
> Soldiers, the enemy is before you and your banners are free. It is for you to decide whether our brothers and sisters of Tennessee and Kentucky shall remain bondmen and bondwomen of the Abolition tyrant or be restored to the freedom inherited from their fathers.

Having heard him out, the long files shouldered their muskets and headed north.

✗ 4 ✗

In Virginia, though the basis for it was obviously a good deal less substantial — westward, the blue glacier had not only ground to a halt, it had even reversed direction, whereas here in the East no more than a pause, a hesitation of the mass, had seemingly been effected; McClellan, after all, was scarcely a dozen miles farther from Richmond than he had been on the eve of the Seven Days, besides being more securely based on the James than he had been while crouched astride the treacherous Chickahominy, and Pope was hovering northward, a considerably graver threat, both in numbers and position, than McDowell had ever been — the elation mounted higher. One reason was that the result, however far it fell short of expectation, had been obtained by actual fighting, not by maneuver or mere Federal acquiescence. Another was the return of confidence in the government: especially in the President, whose vindication now appeared complete.

Less than a week before the launching of the assault that flung the bluecoats back from the capital gates, Tom Cobb had been declaring that he saw in Davis "the embodiment and concentration of cowardly littleness [which] he garnishes over with pharisaical hypocrisy. How can God smile upon us while we have such a man [to] lead us?" Few were asking that question now: God *had* smiled upon them, and a large part of the credit went to the man who by deed as well as title filled the position of Commander in Chief and triumphed over the adversary who occupied that post in the country to the north. The Hezekiah-Sennacherib analogy still held.

As far as the soldiers themselves were concerned, however, the credit went to the general who had been placed at their head in their darkest hour and in one short month, despite their initial resentment, had welded their four disparate components — Johnston's Manassas army and Magruder's frazzled Yorktown brigades, Jackson's Valley command and Huger's unblooded Norfolk division — into a single striking force, the Army of Northern Virginia, which he hurled with cunning and fury at the blue invaders, massed in their thousands within sight and hearing of Richmond's steeples and public clocks, and sent them reeling backwards or sidling crablike to their present mud-flat sanctuary under the muzzles of their gunboats. Granny Lee, Evacuating Lee, the King of Spades, had become for his troops what he would remain: Mars Robert. They watched him as he rode among them, the high-colored face above and behind the iron-gray beard, the active, dark-brown eyes, the broad forehead whose upper half showed unexpectedly dazzling white when he removed his wide-brimmed hat to acknowledge their cheers. Distrust had yielded to enthusiasm, which in turn was giving way to awe.

On horseback, deep-chested and long-waisted, with his big, leonine head set thick-necked on massive shoulders, he looked gigantic. Partly that was the aura. It must have been; for when he dismounted, as he often did, to rest his horse — he had a tender concern for the welfare of all animals, even combat infantrymen, aside from those times when he flung them into the crackling uproar of battle like chaff into a furnace — you saw the slight legs, the narrow hips, and realized, with something of a shock, that he was no larger than many of the men around him, and not as large as some. The same contrast, above and below, was apparent in his extremities; the hands were oversized and muscular, the feet tiny as a woman's. He was in fact just under six feet tall and weighed less than 170 pounds. Quickly, though, you got over the shock (which after all was only the result of comparing flesh and perfection. However he *was* was how you preferred him) and when you saw him thus in the field your inclination was to remove your hat — not to wave it: just to hold it — and stand there looking at him: Mars Robert.

Not everyone offered such adulation, either in or out of the army. Robert Toombs, for one, who had commanded a brigade under Magruder throughout the Peninsula campaign, considered Lee "far below the occasion." The Charleston *Mercury* for another, while it praised the strategy — "projected, as we hear, by General Johnston" — agreed with Toombs as to the tactics: "The blundering manner in which [McClellan] has been allowed to get away, the desultory manner in which he has been pursued by divisions instead of our whole force, enabling him to repulse our attacks, to carry off his artillery, and, finally, to make a fresh stand with an army reinforced are facts, we fear, not very flattering to the generalship of General Lee."

Lee was rather inclined to agree with the former Georgia statesman, as well as with the South Carolina editor, not only because of his inherent modesty, but also because he knew that what they said was largely true. "His great victory did not elate him, so far as one could see," his cannoneer son later recalled. This was not for lack of material success. The booty had been ample: 52 fine Union guns (by coincidence, one for every battery in the Army of the Potomac), 31,000 rifles (which gave some measure of the Federal panic, since half were either dropped by casualties or handed over by captives, while the other half were abandoned by men who preferred to travel light) and 10,000 prisoners, most of them unwounded. All this was duly appreciated, especially the rifled guns and the badly needed small arms, but Lee's essential agreement with Toombs and the *Mercury* was based on a consideration of what had been left undone, as well as of what had been done — on the contrast, in fact, between conception and execution. "Under ordinary circumstances," he said in his report to the Adjutant General, "the Federal army should have been destroyed."

Sound strategy had largely counterbalanced woeful tactics to produce, within limits, a successful campaign. After all, Richmond was no longer even semi-beleaguered. But for the failure, so far as it was a failure beyond those limits, there were three main reasons: 1) poor maps and intelligence, which left the Confederates groping blind, or half blind, all the way from Mechanicsville to Harrison's Landing, inclusively; 2) poor staff work, especially in the transmission of orders, which was the basis for much of the lack of coördination; and 3) the Army of the Potomac, the hard-core staunchness of its infantry and the skill with which its superior artillery was employed. Of these, the last — referred to by one of Lee's own aides as "the character and personality of the men behind the Federal guns" — was clearly the most decisive in preventing the wreckage intended, but it was the first which caused what Harvey Hill summed up in one acid sentence: "Throughout this campaign we attacked just when and where the enemy wished us to attack."

Time and effort, self-application on Lee's part, might correct the first two of these drawbacks; the third would be with him from here on out. Yet there was still another problem — one he would always face with reluctance, though it too would remain. This was the task of assessing the character and performance of his lieutenants. Longstreet and the two Hills, whatever their personal eccentricities, whether headstrong or impetuous or caustic, had emerged from the test of combat with brighter laurels than before. The same could not be said of another trio: Magruder, Holmes, and Huger. Their reasons for failure were varied — overexcitability, deafness, chronic bad luck — but now that Lee had faced the problem, no matter with what reluctance, he was quick to act. He got rid of them. In Magruder's case it was simple; for he had been offered, and had accepted, command of a department in the Transmississippi. Lee wished him Godspeed along with Holmes, who went out there too, being placed in charge of the whole far-western theater. That left Huger; but not for long. He was kicked upstairs to the War Department, as chief inspector of artillery and ordnance.

In the course of replacing these departed leaders and redistributing their twelve brigades — which meant, in effect, a drastic reorganization for the work that lay ahead — Lee dealt with another problem of command: the question of what to do about Jackson, whose poor showing throughout the Seven Days was now the subject of much talk. He was reported to have said that he did not intend for his men to do all the fighting, and when he overheard some of his staff discussing his strange delay above White Oak Swamp while Longstreet was struggling desperately at Glendale, he remarked coldly: "If General Lee had wanted me, he could have sent for me." Lee of course did not join the chorus of critics, nor did he consider shunting Stonewall off to the Transmississippi; but in his regrouping of the army's nine divisions into two "wings" under its two ranking generals, Longstreet and Jackson, the former was assigned twenty-eight brigades, the latter seven. Stonewall thus had only half as many as had been under him during the late campaign, while Old Pete had nearly five times as many as the half dozen with which he had crossed the Chickahominy.

All through this period of refitting and reorganization, of distributing the captured arms and replacing his veterans' flop-soled shoes and tattered jackets, Lee had also kept busy trying to determine the enemy's intentions. It was a complicated problem, involving no less than four Federal armies of various strengths, all unknown. First there was the main force, under McClellan at Harrison's Landing. Then there was Pope's newly consolidated Army of Virginia, assumed to be in the vicinity of Manassas. Either or both might take the offensive at any time. The third was at Fredericksburg, threatening Richmond from the north, much as McDowell had done for months. The fourth was Burnside's, brought up from North Carolina in the emergency, but still kept aboard its transports, anchored mysteriously off Fort Monroe. Both of these last two forces were in positions from which they could move rapidly to combine and join either of the other two: Pope, for an advance against the vital Virginia Central Railroad: or McClellan, for a renewal of his drive on the capital itself. For the present, though both of course were possible, Lee could find out nothing that would indicate which was probable. All he knew for certain was that delay was not to the advantage of the South. Northern determination had stiffened after this defeat, just as it had done the year before, and Lincoln's call for 300,000 volunteers had gone out on the day of Malvern Hill.

In chess terms, Lee's immediate problem was whether to keep his pieces where they were, concentrated to checkmate the king — McClellan — or to disperse them in order to meet an advance by the knights and bishops, off on another quarter of the board. While awaiting developments he withdrew his infantry from the malarial swamps and left the observation of Harrison's Landing to the cavalry, newly gathered into a two-brigade division under Stuart, who was promoted to major general. Simultaneously, by way of discouraging an attack from that direction, he put his engineers to work constructing permanent fortifications. Anchored to the James at Drewry's Bluff and extending north along an arc shielding Richmond, these installations would also permit his present lines to be more thinly held if alternate pressure required dispersion. Once they were completed he would be much better prepared for whatever came.

What came, on July 12, was startling news from the north: Pope had occupied Culpeper that morning. What made this startling was that Culpeper was on the Orange & Alexandria, less than thirty miles above Gordonsville. And Gordonsville was on the Virginia Central, at the northern apex of an exposed bend known as "the Gordonsville loop," which led on westward to Charlottesville and Staunton. This was alternate pressure indeed; for if Pope took Gordonsville he would cut the

Confederate supply line connecting Richmond and the Shenandoah Valley, where a bumper crop of corn and wheat was ripening for the harvest. Lee was obliged to meet this threat, and he did so the following day by sending Jackson with his own and Ewell's divisions — the old Army of the Valley — by rail to Louisa Courthouse, fifteen miles this side of Gordonsville, which he was instructed to occupy if Pope had not already got there in too great strength to be dislodged. The movement was made rapidly by way of Hanover Junction, using eighteen trains of fifteen cars each to transport Stonewall's 10,000 infantry and artillery, while his cavalry and wagons moved by road.

Strategically, this riposte was as sound as it was necessary, but Lee had other compelling reasons for ordering the movement: one being that he had developed a scathing contempt for the leader of the force at which it was aimed. After issuing the bombastic address to his soldiers ("Let us understand each other. . . . Disaster and shame lurk in the rear") Pope had joined them in the field and had proceeded at once, in a series of formal orders, to give his attention to the civilians in his prospective theater of operations. One directed his army to live off the country and to reimburse only those persons who could prove devotion to the flag he represented. Another prescribed stern measures to be taken in retaliation for guerilla activities. A third provided for the arrest of all male noncombatants within his lines, the expulsion of those who refused to take a loyalty oath, and their prosecution as spies if they returned. Furthermore, any man or woman who remained would be liable to the death penalty for attempting to communicate with the enemy — presumably including a mother who wrote to a son in the southern army. These mandates were not in accordance with Lee's notion of civilized warfare; he was downright contemptuous of the man who ordered their adoption. "The miscreant Pope," he called him, and he said of him: "He ought to be suppressed if possible."

Just now it was not possible, Jackson reported. He had beaten Pope to Gordonsville, arriving there from Louisa on July 19, but the bluecoats around Culpeper were too numerous to be attacked at present. Reinforce him, Stonewall added, and he would gladly undertake all the suppression Lee could ask for. That was what Lee was considering, though the risk was admittedly great. Left with just under 70,000 men — including Holmes' former command, shifted south of the James to cover Petersburg and placed under D. H. Hill with an eye toward possible future operations in his native North Carolina — he knew he was badly outnumbered by McClellan, who moreover was beginning to show signs of activity. Besides, there were those other two armies, at Fredericksburg and off Fort Monroe: Lee still did not know in which direction they might move. Much as he wanted Pope whipped and driven back across the Rappahannock, the odds were long against weakening the capital defenses for that purpose. Nevertheless he decided to take the gamble. On July 27 he ordered A. P. Hill to Gordonsville, where the Light Division would join the Valley Army for a strike at Pope.

His hope was that this combined force would deliver its blow quickly, disposing of Pope with a knockout punch, then return to Richmond in time to help block any assault McClellan might attempt when he learned of its detachment. This would call for rapid, well-coördinated movements and a style of fighting characterized by a minimum of confusion and hesitation: quite the opposite, in fact, of the style Jackson had demonstrated throughout the Seven Days. One reason for his poor showing on the Peninsula, Lee suspected, was his known reluctance to take subordinate commanders into his military confidence. Also, in consideration of Little Powell's sensitive and highly volatile nature — he had already clashed with Longstreet over what he considered a slight to his division in the distribution of honors, and Longstreet had promptly put him in arrest, from which Lee had released him for the present expedition — there was the danger of an explosion when he came into contact with the stern and taciturn Stonewall. Accordingly, Lee wrote Jackson a letter in which he alluded tactfully to the problem. After repeating the injunction, "I want Pope to be suppressed," he concluded: "A. P. Hill you will, I think, find a good officer, with whom you can consult, and by advising with your division commanders as to your movements much trouble will be saved you in arranging details, as they can act more intelligently. . . . Cache your troops as much as possible till you can strike your blow, and be prepared to return to me when done, if necessary. I will endeavor to keep General McClellan quiet till it is over, if rapidly executed."

Keeping McClellan quiet might well turn out to be a good deal easier said than done. With one third of his army off after Pope, Lee was down to 56,000 men, including two brigades that arrived next day from South Carolina: whereas McClellan was not only half again larger now, he would have twice as many troops as Lee if he were reinforced by Burnside and the brigades at Fredericksburg, which Lee could do absolutely nothing to prevent. Besides, the Young Napoleon had considerable freedom of action. He could stay where he was, a hovering threat; he could steam back up the Potomac to join Pope and the others; he could advance from his present camp against the southern capital, less than twenty airline miles away. In the latter case, two routes were available to him. He could move up the left bank of the James, more or less as before, except that he would be securely based; or he could cross the river, under cover of his gunboats, capture Petersburg, and swarm into Richmond by the back door. All were possibilities to fret the mind of Lee, who so far had been able to find no clew as to which course his adversary favored. "In the prospect before me," he wrote his wife, "I cannot see a single ray of pleasure during this war."

One way to keep McClellan quiet, Lee reasoned paradoxically, or at any rate make him hug his camp while the southern army was divided, might be to stir him up; that is, make him think he was about to be attacked. An infantry feint being impractical, Lee decided on an artillery demonstration. Under cover of darkness, forty-three guns of various calibers were concentrated on the south side of the James at Coggin's Point, opposite Harrison's Landing, and on the last night of July they opened fire on the Federal camp. The result, as in the case of Stuart's popgun bombardment four weeks back, was more spectacular than effective. After some original confusion, the Union artillerists and sailors brought their heavier guns to bear and smothered the Confederate batteries. On August 3, threatened with capture by an amphibious countermovement, they had to be withdrawn. Except for the effect it might have had on McClellan himself, enlarging his natural caution, the demonstration was a failure.

Two days later, by way of recompense, Lee got his first real hint as to the Federal overall strategy. A young Confederate cavalry officer, Captain John S. Mosby, had been captured two weeks before while on his way upstate to find recruits for a partisan command, and had been taken to Fort Monroe to await exchange. As soon as he was released he came to Lee with information he had picked up while imprisoned: Burnside was under orders to take his transports up the Potomac, debark his troops at Aquia Creek, and march them overland to Fredericksburg. If true, this meant considerable danger to Jackson, who was already badly outnumbered by the enemy north of Gordonsville, as well as to the Virginia Central, which led westward to the Valley granary. What was more, it was a strong indication that the enemy's next major effort would be in northern Virginia, where Lee was weakest, not here on the James. He would have moved at least a portion of his force to meet this threat at once, except that on the same day his cavalry reported a heavy force advancing from Harrison's, up the left bank of the river, against Richmond. Apparently it was not McClellan's caution which had been enlarged by the abortive Coggin's Point demonstration, but rather his self-confidence.

Lee marched three divisions out to meet him the following day, August 6, and approaching Malvern Hill near sundown found the Federals drawn up menacingly on the crest. Intending no repetition of last month's headlong, blind attack up the rolling slope, he extended his left, skirmished briskly on the right, and braced his troops for the downhill assault. At nightfall there was every indication that the armies would be locked in battle tomorrow. Instead — as had been more or less the case five weeks ago — dawn showed the hill empty of all but a handful of blue vedettes, who at the first sign of a Confederate advance scampered down the reverse slope to join the main body, already well on its way back to its camp on the James.

This was strange indeed: passing strange. Lee decided that the only explanation for McClellan's sudden advance-and-retreat was that it was intended to cover the movement Mosby had discerned at Fort Monroe. If this was so, and Burnside was headed for Fredericksburg, there still remained the question of what he would do when he got there. He could join Pope directly; he could operate against Richmond from the north; or he could attempt to cut the Virginia Central in Jackson's rear, between Gordonsville and Hanover Junction. The best way to forestall this last — the most immediately dangerous of the three — would be for Jackson to strike Pope, who would then be likely to call on Burnside for support. Until Lee knew whether McClellan intended to renew his advance on Richmond, however, he did not feel that he could further weaken the capital defenses in order to reinforce Jackson; nor did he feel that he should give him peremptory orders to attack, unsupported, without himself knowing the tactical situation at first hand. Accordingly, before the day was over, he did the next best thing. He sat down and wrote Stonewall a long letter in which he made it clear that he relied on his discretion.

After warning him not to count on reinforcements — "If I can send them I will; if I cannot, and you think it proper and advantageous, act without them" — he outlined the dilemma as he saw it and suggested what he believed was the best solution, an immediate thrust at Pope, though he cautioned against rashness: "I would rather you should have easy fighting and heavy victories." It was a warning addressed more to the erstwhile hard-driving hero of the Valley, who smote the enemy hip and thigh, wherever found, than to the sluggard of the Seven Days, who dawdled and withheld his hand from bloodshed. Apparently Lee had put the latter out of his mind. "I must now leave the matter to your reflection and good judgment," he concluded. "Make up your mind what is best to be done under all the circumstances which surround us, and let me hear the result at which you arrive. I will inform you if any change takes place here that bears on the subject."

Mosby was right: Burnside had been ordered to Fredericksburg a week ago, on August 1, nine days after Halleck's arrival in Washington from the West. Having scattered the armies there for an assimilation of what had been won, Old Brains now proposed to unite those of the East for a new beginning. In both cases, however — since the concentration was not to be on the Peninsula, where defeat was recent, but in northern Virginia, where defeat was a full year old — the effect was the same: to shift the Union juggernaut into reverse. McClellan, too, was about to be withdrawn.

Nothing less than a new beginning would put the derailed engine back on the track; or so it seemed to the newly appointed general-in-chief, who had reached the capital in a time of gloom. Flags drooped at half-mast under the press of heat and crape festooned the public buildings in observance of the death of Martin Van Buren, a used-up man. No such honors had marked the passing of the Virginian John Tyler the month before; but that was in a sunnier time, and even in the present instance the crape seemed more an expression of the general mood than grief for a particular man, ex-President or not; Van Buren was already part of ancient history. Halleck, at any rate, wasted little time in speculation on such matters. Instead, after spending a day in Washington, he got aboard a steamer and went straight to what he believed was the source of discontent: the Army of the Potomac, camped now on the mud flats of the James.

In spite of the pride he took in having executed the movement under pressure, and in spite of the fact that Lincoln had been congratulatory and Stanton even fawning, McClellan had been expecting trouble ever since his change of base. The President had wired him "a thousand thanks" after Malvern Hill. "Be assured," he added, "the heroism and skill of yourself and officers and men is, and forever will be, appreciated. If you can hold your present position [at Harrison's] we shall hive the enemy yet." Stanton put it stronger, or anyhow longer. "Be assured," he wrote, "that you shall have the support of this Department as cordially and faithfully as was ever rendered by man to man, and if we should ever live to see each other face to face you will be satisfied that you have never had from me anything but the most confiding integrity." That was larding it pretty thick, but he larded it even thicker in conversation with McClellan's father-in-law, who went to Washington to see him. "General Marcy," he told the chief of staff, with a sudden rush of feeling, "I have from the commencement of our acquaintance up to the present moment been General McClellan's warmest friend. I feel so kind toward him that I would get down on my knees to him if that would serve him. Yes sir," he continued, warming as he spoke. "If it would do him any service I would be willing to lay down naked in the gutter and allow him to stand upon my body for hours."

Stanton lying naked in the gutter was a prospect McClellan could contemplate with pleasure, but he was not deluded into thinking such a scene would ever be staged — except in his mind's eye. He knew well enough that Stanton was working against him, tooth and nail. Nor did Lincoln's assurances carry their former weight: especially after the arrival of John Pope and the Administration's tacit approval of the mandates he issued regarding noncombatants in his theater of operations. That was what really tore it, McClellan wrote his wife. "When you contrast the policy I urged in my letter to the President with that of Congress and of Mr Pope, you can readily agree with me that there can be little natural confidence between the government and myself. We are the antipodes of each other; and it is more than probable that they will take the earliest opportunity to relieve me from command and get me out of sight."

Now here came Halleck, slack-fleshed and goggle-eyed, formerly his subordinate, now his chief, holding the office he himself had lost. It was bitter. Presently, however, after a hasty review of the troops, Halleck calmed McClellan's apprehensions by informing him that he had not come to undermine him or relieve him of command, but to find out what he required in the way of additional men in order to renew the drive on the rebel capital. McClellan brightened and unfolded a map on which he began to indicate, with pride and enthusiasm, a new plan of attack. He would cross the James and capture Petersburg, outflanking the enemy fortifications and severing the southside supply lines, then swing north and enter Richmond by the back door. Halleck shook his head. Too risky, he said, and vetoed the proposal then and there. Mc-Clellan, his enthusiasm dampened, proceeded to an estimate of the situation. His effective strength, he said, was 88,665; Lee's was 200,000. Nevertheless, if the government would give him 30,000 reinforcements he would assault the northside intrenchments with "a good chance of success." Halleck frowned. No more than 20,000 were available, and if these would not suffice, he said, the army would have to be withdrawn from the Peninsula to unite with Pope in the vicinity of Washington. Horrified at the notion, McClellan excused himself in order to confer with his corps commanders. Next morning he reported, somewhat gloomily, that he was "willing to try it" with that number. Halleck nodded and got back aboard the steamboat to return to Washington. McClellan's genial spirits rose again. "I think that Halleck will support me and give me the means to take Richmond," he wrote his wife.

Whatever Halleck intended when he left, his final decision was considerably affected by a telegram he found waiting for him when he docked. It was from McClellan; apparently it had been sent almost as soon as Halleck's steamer passed from sight. Confederate reinforcements, he said, were "pouring into Richmond from the South." To meet this new development, and to enable him to deliver "a rapid and heavy blow," he wanted more troops than the 20,000 just agreed on. "Can you not possibly draw 15,000 or 20,000 men from the West to reinforce me temporarily?" he pleaded. "They can return the moment we gain Richmond. Please give weight to this suggestion; I am sure it merits it."

Halleck was amazed, and went to Lincoln with the problem. Lincoln was not amazed at all. In fact, he found the telegram very much in character. If by some magic he could reinforce McClellan with 100,000 troops today, he said, Little Mac would be delighted and would promise to capture Richmond tomorrow; but when tomorrow came he would report the enemy strength at 400,000 and announce that he could not advance until he got another 100,000 reinforcements. Halleck turned this over in his mind, together with another consideration. If Lee was as strong as McClellan said he was — stronger than Pope and Mc-Clellan combined — it was folly to keep the Federal armies exposed to destruction in detail. It was in fact imperative to unite them without delay. At last he made his decision, agreeing with Lincoln that McClellan's army would have to be withdrawn. On July 29 he ordered every available steamer in Baltimore harbor to proceed at once to the James, and next day he instructed McClellan to prepare to evacuate his sick and wounded. He did not tell him why; he merely remarked ambiguously that this was being done "in order to enable you to move in any direction." Two days later, Burnside was told to take his transports up the Potomac to Aquia Creek, where the troops would debark for a twelve-mile march to Fredericksburg. McClellan's own orders were sent on August 3: "It is determined to withdraw your army from the Peninsula to Aquia Creek. You will take immediate measures to effect this, covering the movement as best you can."

McClellan was thunderstruck. The order for the removal of his sick had aroused his suspicions five days ago, despite — or perhaps because of — the disclaimer that it would leave him free "to move in any direction," and he had been prompt to register his protest: "Our true policy is to reinforce [this] army by every available means and throw it again upon Richmond. Should it be determined to withdraw it, I shall look upon our cause as lost." Perhaps he thought the weight of this opinion would forestall any such calamity. If so, he now saw how useless it had been. Yet he did not abandon hope; or anyhow he did not stop trying to ward off the blow. At noon on August 4 he knelt figuratively at the feet of Halleck and made a final anguished plea. "Your telegram of last evening is received. I must confess that it has caused me the greatest pain I ever experienced, for I am convinced that the order to withdraw this army to Aquia Creek will prove disastrous to our cause." First he pointed out that it was tactical folly to make "a march of 145 miles to reach a point now only 25 miles distant, and to deprive ourselves entirely of the powerful aid of the gunboats and water transportation. Add to this the certain demoralization of this army which would ensue, and these appear to me sufficient reasons to make it my imperative duty to urge in the strongest terms afforded by our language that this order may be rescinded." Then came the impassioned words to which the rest had served as prologue: "Here, directly in front of this army, is the heart of the rebellion. It is here that all our resources should be collected to strike the blow which will determine the fate of the nation.... It matters not what partial reverses we may meet with elsewhere. Here is the true defense of Washington. It is here, on the banks of the James, that the fate of the Union should be decided."

Halleck replied by wire and by mail. "I must take things as I find them," he said in the letter. "I find the forces divided, and I wish to unite them. Only one feasible plan has been presented for doing this. If you or anyone else had presented a better plan I certainly should have adopted it. But all of your plans require reinforcements, which it is impossible to give you. It is very easy to ask for reinforcements, but it is not so easy to give them when you have no disposable troops at your command." The telegram, being briefer, was more to the point. After saying, "You cannot regret the order of withdrawal more than I did the necessity of giving it," Halleck put an end to the discussion: "It will not be rescinded and you will be expected to execute it with all possible promptness." Next day, August 7 — the date of Lee's letter urging Jackson to consider a strike at Pope — the need for haste was emphasized in a second wire received by the harassed commander at Harrison's Landing. "I must beg of you, General, to hurry along this movement," Halleck told him. "Your reputation as well as mine may be involved in its rapid execution."

Left with neither voice nor choice in the matter, McClellan worked hard to speed the evacuation. But he wrote his wife: "They are committing a fatal error in withdrawing me from here, and the future will show it. I think the result of their machination will be that Pope will be badly thrashed within ten days, and that they will be very glad to turn over the redemption of their affairs to me."

The danger, the crying need for haste as Halleck saw it, was that Lee might take advantage of his interior lines and attack one or the other of the two main Federal forces before the northward shift began, or, worse still, while the movement was in progress. Of the two — Pope on the Rappahannock and McClellan on the James — Old Brains was most concerned about the former. As he put it to McClellan, who was struggling to extract his troops from the malarial Peninsula bottoms, "This delay might not only be fatal to the health of your army, but in the meantime General Pope's forces would be exposed to the heavy blows of the enemy without the slightest hope of assistance from you."

Pope was worried too, although he did not let it show in his manner. Privately he was complaining to Halleck about "the supineness of the Army of the Potomac," which he said "renders it easy for the enemy to reinforce Jackson heavily," and he urged: "Please make McClellan do something." Publicly, however, he showed no symptoms of doubt or trepidation. On August 8, when he transferred his headquarters southward to Culpeper, Halleck wired him uneasily: "Do not advance, so as to expose yourself to any disaster, unless you can better your line of defense, until we can get more troops upon the Rappahannock. . . . You must be very cautious." Pope seemed unalarmed; he appeared, in fact, not to have a single cautious bone in his whole body. He intended to hold where he was, despite the risk involved in the knowl-

edge that Stonewall Jackson was before him with a force he estimated
at 30,000 men.

Numerically, as of early August, his confidence was well
founded. Exclusive of Burnside, whose 12,000 had debarked at Aquia
and were now at Falmouth, he had 77,779 soldiers in the Army of Virginia. Even after deducting the troops in the Washington fortifications,
along with those in the Shenandoah Valley and beyond, he was left
with just over 56,000 in the
eight divisions of infantry and
two brigades of cavalry comprising the three corps under
McDowell, Banks, and Sigel.
This was the field force proper,
and it seemed ample for the
execution of the project he had
conceived at the outset. His intention had been to operate
southward down the Orange
& Alexandria to Gordonsville
and beyond, thereby menacing
the Virginia Central so that
Lee would weaken the Richmond defenses to the point
where McClellan could make

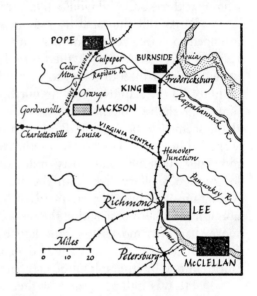

a successful assault. McClellan's pending withdrawal would alter at
least a part of this, of course, but Pope still thought the plan a good
one: not the least of its advantages being that it had the approval
and support of the Administration, since it simultaneously covered
Washington. What was more, his assignment — formerly minor, or anyhow secondary — now became major. Instead of setting Richmond up
for capture by McClellan, he would take the place himself · and be
known thereafter as the man who broke the back of the rebellion. That
was a thought to warm the heart. He would consolidate his gains, then
proceed with his advance, reinforced by such numbers as reached him
from the Army of the Potomac.

At present, it was true, his striking force was rather scattered.
More than a third of McDowell's corps — 11,000 infantry, with 30
guns and about 500 cavalry — was still at Fredericksburg, under Brigadier General Rufus King, blocking the direct approach to Washington.
Now that Burnside had arrived, Pope might have summoned King to
join him, but just now he preferred to keep him where he was, menacing Jackson's supply line and playing on Lee's fears for the safety of his
capital. Besides, he felt strong enough without him. Banks and Sigel had
come eastward through the passes of the Blue Ridge, and though their

five divisions had not been consolidated, either with each other or with
McDowell's two, Pope still had better than 44,000 troops with which to
oppose the estimated 30,000 rebels in his immediate front. The situation
was not without its dangers: Halleck kept saying so, at any rate, and old
General Wool, transferred from Fort Monroe to Maryland, had warned
him at the outset: "Jackson is an enterprising officer. Delays are dangerous." But Pope was not alarmed. If the highly touted Stonewall wanted
a fight, at those odds, he would gladly accommodate him.

    Banks felt the same way about it, only more so; for while Pope
intended to earn a reputation here in the East, Banks was determined to
retrieve one. On August 8, therefore, he was pleased to receive at Culpeper an order directing him to march his two divisions south: Jackson
had crossed the Rapidan, moving north, and Pope wanted Banks to delay
him while the rest of the army was being assembled to give him the battle he seemed to be seeking. Banks did not hesitate. McDowell and Sigel
were behind him; King was on the way from Fredericksburg. Next
morning, eight hot and dusty miles out of Culpeper, he came under
long-range artillery fire from the slopes of a lone peak called Cedar
Mountain, and pressing on found rebel infantry disposed in strength
about its northern base and in the woods and fields off to the right. After
more than two months of brooding over the shocks of May, he was
face to face with the old Valley adversary whose soldiers had added insult to injury by giving him the nickname "Commissary" Banks.

    He was itching to attack, then and there, but in the face of the
known odds — he was down to about 8000 men as a result of multiple
detachments, while Jackson was reported to have at least three times
that many — he did not feel free to do so on his own responsibility.
Then a courier arrived from Culpeper, a staff colonel sent by Pope with
a verbal message which seemed to authorize an immediate all-out attack.
(The officer's name was Louis Marshall, a Union-loyal Virginian and a
nephew of R. E. Lee, who had said of him: "I could forgive [his] fighting against us, but not his joining Pope.") Welcome as the message was,
Banks could scarcely believe his ears. In fact, he had it written down and
then read back for verification:

> General Banks will move to the front immediately, assume com-
> mand of all the forces in the front, deploy his skirmishers if the
> enemy approaches, and attack him immediately as soon as he
> approaches, and be reinforced from here.

This ambiguous farrago, dictated by Lee's nephew in the name
of Pope, was open to conflicting interpretations. It might mean that the
attack was to be made with skirmishers only, holding the main body on
the defensive until McDowell arrived to even the odds and Sigel came
up to stretch them in favor of the Union. On the other hand, it might
mean what it said in the words that were quickest to catch the eye: "At-

tack him immediately as soon as he approaches." That sounded like the army commander who three weeks ago had admonished his generals "to seek the adversary and to beat him when he was found." At any rate, whatever the odds, Banks took him at his word. He put his men in attack formation and sent them forward, on the left and on the right.

Lee's letter of August 7, recommending a swipe at Pope, had not been needed; for while he was writing it Jackson was already putting his 25,000 soldiers in motion to carry out the strategy it suggested. His cavalry having reported the superior enemy forces badly scattered beyond the Rapidan, he hoped to make a rapid march across that stream, pounce on one of the isolated segments, and withdraw Valley-style before Pope could concentrate against him. So far, it had not worked at all that way, however — primarily because another letter of Lee's, while needed, had not been heeded. A. P. Hill was kept as much in the dark as to his chief's intentions as Winder and Ewell had ever been. "I pledge you my word, Doctor," the latter told an inquiring chaplain before the movement got under way, "I do not know whether we march north, south, east or west, or whether we will march at all. General Jackson has simply ordered me to have the division ready to move at dawn. I have been ready ever since, and have no further indication of his plans. That is almost all I ever know of his designs."

Stonewall was still Stonewall, especially when secrecy was involved, and no one — not even Robert E. Lee, of whom he said: "I am willing to follow him blindfolded" — was going to change him. The result, as Lee had feared, was mutual resentment and mistrust. Not only did Jackson not "consult" with his red-haired lieutenant, whose so-called Light Division was as large as the other two combined; he rode him unmercifully for every slight infraction of the rules long since established for the Army of the Valley. Consequently, glad as he had been to get away from Longstreet, Hill began to suspect that he had leaped from the frying pan into the fire. Resentment bred confusion, and confusion mounted quickly toward a climax in the course of the march northward against Pope. Having reached Orange in good order the first day, August 7, Jackson issued instructions for the advance across the Rapidan tomorrow, which would place his army in position for a strike at Culpeper the following day. The order of march would be Ewell, Hill, Winder; so he said; but during the night he changed his mind and told Ewell to take an alternate road. Uninformed of the change, Hill had his men lined up next morning on the outskirts of town, waiting for Ewell to take the lead. That was where Jackson found him. Angry at the delay, he rebuked him and passed Winder to the front. The result was further delay and a miserable showing, complicated by Federal cavalry probing at his wagon train. Ewell made barely eight miles before sundown, Winder about half that, and Hill was less than two miles out of Orange when the army halted for the night. Jackson was furious. So was Hill. Ewell fretted. Winder was down with fever, riding in an ambulance despite his doctor's orders that he leave the field entirely. Several men had died of sunstroke, and the rest took their cue from their commanders, grumbling at the way they had been shuffled about in the dust and heat.

Overnight, Jackson's wrath turned to gloom. The fast-stepping Army of the Valley, formerly such a close-stitched organization, seemed to be coming apart at the seams. Rising next morning to resume the march, he informed Lee: "I am not making much progress. ... Today I do not expect much more than to close up [the column] and clear the country around the train of the enemy's cavalry. I fear that the expedition will, in consequence of my tardy movements, be productive of but little good."

Ewell had the lead; Winder was in close support; Hill was marching hard to close the gap. The morning wore on, hot as yesterday. Noon came and went. Presently, up ahead, there was the boom of guns, and word came back to Jackson that the Federals were making a stand, apparently with horse artillery. He rode forward and made a brief reconnaissance. This was piedmont country, rolling, heavily wooded except for scattered fields of grain. The bluecoats did not appear to be present in strength, but there was no real telling: Jackson decided to wait for Hill before advancing. Off to the right was Cedar Mountain, obviously the key to the position. Ewell was told to put his batteries there and his infantry below them, along the northern base; Winder would take position on the left in order to overlap the Yankee line when the signal was given to go forward. There was no hurry. It was now past 2 o'clock and Culpeper was eight miles away: too far, in any event, for an attack to be made on it today. Jackson went onto the porch of a nearby farmhouse and lay down to take a nap.

Meanwhile the artillery duel continued, the Union guns firing accurately and fast. This was clearly something more than a mere delaying action staged by cavalry; there was infantry out there beyond the woods, though in what strength could not be told. Manifestly weak, pale as his shirt — he was in fact in his shirt sleeves — Winder had left his ambulance, ignoring the doctor's protests, put his troops in line, extending the left as instructed, and then had joined his batteries, observing their fire with binoculars and calling out corrections for the gunners. It was now about 4 o'clock. An officer went down alongside him, clipped on the head by a fragment of shell; another was eviscerated by a jagged splinter; a third was struck in the rump by an unexploded ricochet and hurled ten feet, though he suffered only bruises as a result. Then came Winder's turn. Tall and wavy-haired, he kept his post, and as he continued to direct the counterbattery fire, calm and cool-looking in his shirt sleeves, with the binoculars held to his eyes, a shell came screaming at him, crashing through his left arm and tearing off most of the ribs on that side of his chest. He fell straight back and lay full length on the ground, quivering spasmodically.

"General, do you know me?" a staff lieutenant asked, bending over the sufferer in order to be heard above the thunder of the guns.

"Oh yes," Winder said vaguely, and his mind began to wander. The guns were bucking and banging all around him, but he was back at home again in Maryland. In shock, he spoke disconnectedly of his wife and children until a chaplain came and knelt beside him, seeking to turn his thoughts from worldly things.

"General, lift up your head to God."

"I do," Winder said calmly. "I do lift it up to him."

Carried to the rear, he died just at sundown, asking after the welfare of his men, and those who were with him were hard put for a comforting answer. By then the fury of the Union assault had crashed against his lines, which had broken in several places. Jackson's plan for outflanking the enemy on the left had miscarried; it was he who was outflanked in that direction. The sudden crash of musketry, following close on the news that Winder had been mangled by a shell, brought him off the farmhouse porch and into the saddle. He rode hard toward the left, entering a moil of fugitives who had given way in panic when the bluecoats emerged roaring from the cover of the woods. Drawing his sword — a thing no one had ever seen him do before in battle — he brandished it above his head and called out hoarsely: "Rally, brave men, and press forward! Your general will lead you; Jackson will lead you! Follow me!"

This had an immediate effect, for the sight was as startling in its way as the unexpected appearance of the Federals had been. The men halted in their tracks, staring open-mouthed, and then began to rally in response to the cries of their officers, echoing Stonewall, who was finally persuaded to retire out of range of the bullets twittering round him. "Good, good," he said as he turned back, Winder's successor having assured him that the Yankees would be stopped. Whether this promise could have been kept in the face of another assault was another matter, but fortunately by now the battle was moving in the opposite direction: A. P. Hill had arrived with the Light Division. Opening ranks to let the fugitives through, Little Powell's veterans swamped the blue attackers, flung them back on their reserves, and pursued them northward through the gathering twilight. So quickly, after the manner of light fiction, had victory been snatched from the flames of defeat, if not disaster.

Thankful as Jackson was for this deliverance, he was by no means satisfied. Banks had escaped him once before; he did not intend to let him get away again. A full moon was rising, and he ordered the chase continued by its light. Whenever resistance was encountered he passed his guns to the front, shelled the woods, and then resumed the pursuit, gathering shell-dazed prisoners as he went. Four hundred blue-coats were captured in all, bringing the total Federal losses to 2381; Jackson himself had lost 1276. At last, however, receiving word from his cavalry that the enemy had been heavily reinforced, he called a halt within half a dozen miles of Culpeper and passed the word for his men to sleep on their arms in line of battle. He himself rode back toward Cedar Mountain, seeking shelter at roadside houses along the way. At each he was told that he was welcome but that the wounded filled the rooms. Finally he drew rein beside a grassy plot, dismounted stiffly, and lay face down on the turf, wrapped in a borrowed cloak. When a staff officer asked if he wanted something to eat: "No," he groaned, "I want rest: nothing but rest," and was soon asleep.

Sunday, August 10, dawned hot and humid, the quiet broken only by the moans and shrieks of the injured, blue and gray, presently augmented by their piteous cries for water as the sun rose burning, stiffening their wounds. Surgeons and aid men passed among them, and burial details came along behind. The scavengers were active, too, gleaning the field of arms and equipment; as usual, Old Blue Light wanted all he could lay hands on. Thus the morning wore away, and not a shot was fired. Aware that Sigel and McDowell had arrived to give Pope two whole corps and half of a third — King was still on the way from Fredericksburg, where Burnside was on call — Jackson would not deliver a Sabbath attack; but he was prepared to receive one, whatever the odds, so long as there were wounded men to be cared for and spoils to be loaded into his wagons. That afternoon, as always seemed to be the case on the morrow of a battle, the weather broke. There were long peals of thunder, followed by rain. Jackson held his ground, and the various details continued their work into the night.

Next morning a deputation of Federal horsemen came forward under a flag of truce, proposing an armistice for the removal of the wounded. Jackson gladly agreed; for King's arrival that night would give Pope better than twice as many troops as he himself had, and this would afford him additional time in which to prepare for the withdrawal he now knew was necessary. While the soldiers of both armies mingled on the field where they had fought, he finished packing his wagons and got off a message to Lee: "God blessed our arms with another victory." When darkness came he lighted campfires all along his front, stole away southward under cover of their burning, and re-crossed the Rapidan, unmolested, unpursued.

Another victory, he called it: not without justification. He had inflicted a thousand more casualties than he suffered, and for two days after the battle he had remained in control of the field. Yet there were other aspects he ignored. Banks had done to him what he had tried to do to Shields at Kernstown, and what was more had done it with considerably greater success, even apart from the initial rout; for in the end it was Stonewall who retreated. But now that the roles were reversed he applied a different set of standards. Privately, according to his chief of staff, he went so far as to refer to Cedar Mountain as "the most successful of his exploits." Few would agree with him in this, however, even among the men in his own army. They had been mishandled and they knew it. Outnumbering the enemy three to one on the field of fight, he had been careless in reconnaissance, allowing his troops to be outflanked while he drowsed on a farmhouse veranda, and had swung into vigorous action only after his left wing had been shattered. Following as it did his sorry performance throughout the Seven Days, the recrossing of the Rapidan gave point to a question now being asked: Had Stonewall lost his touch? "Arrogant" was the word applied by some. Others remarked that his former triumphs had been scored against secondraters out in the Valley, "but when pitted against the best of the Federal commanders he did not appear so well." Then too, there had always been those who considered him crazy — crazy and, so far, lucky. Give him "a month uncontrolled," one correspondent declared, "and he would destroy himself and all under him."

Time perhaps would show who was right, the general or his critics, but for the present at least two other men derived particular satisfaction from the battle and its outcome, despite the fact that they viewed it from opposite directions. One of the two was A. P. Hill. Still fuming because of the undeserved rebuke he had received on the outskirts of Orange the day before, he had marched toward the sound of firing and reached the field to find his tormentor face to face with disaster. After opening his ranks to let the fugitives through — including hundreds from the Stonewall Brigade itself — he had launched the counterattack that saved the day and provided whatever factual basis there was for Jackson's claim to "another victory." Revenge was seldom sweeter; Hill enjoyed it to the full.

The other satisfied observer was John Pope, who celebrated his eastern debut as a fighting man by publishing, for the encouragement of his army, Halleck's personal congratulations "on your hard earned but brilliant success against vastly superior numbers. Your troops have covered themselves with glory." Pope thought so too, now, although at first he had experienced definite twinges of anxiety and doubt. Alarmed by what had happened to Banks as a result of misinterpreting the verbal message garbled by Lee's nephew, he had hastened to assemble his eight divisions (including King's, which arrived Monday evening to give him well over 50,000 men) for a renewal of the contest on the morning after the armistice expired. While Jackson was stealing away in the darkness behind a curtain of blazing campfires, Pope was wiring Halleck: "The enemy has been receiving reinforcements all day.... I think it almost certain that we shall be attacked in the morning, and we shall make the best fight we can." This did not sound much like the belligerent commander who had urged his subordinates to "discard such ideas" as the one of " 'taking strong positions and holding them.' " However, when he found Stonewall gone with the dawn he recovered his former tone and notified Halleck: "The enemy has retreated under cover of the night. . . . Our cavalry and artillery are in pursuit. I shall follow with the infantry as far as the Rapidan." Now it was Halleck's turn to be alarmed. "Beware of a snare," he quickly replied. "Feigned retreats are secesh tactics."

But he need not have worried; not just yet. Pope was content to follow at a distance, and when he reached the near bank of the Rapidan he stopped as he had said he would do. Presently he fell back toward Culpeper, pausing along the way to publish Halleck's congratulations. He was "delighted and astonished," he told his soldiers, at their "gallant and intrepid conduct." Whatever their reaction to this astonishment might be, he went on to venture a prophecy: "Success and glory are sure to accompany such conduct, and it is safe to predict that Cedar Mountain is only the first in a series of victories which shall make the Army of Virginia famous in the land."

★ ★ ★

Lee saw it otherwise. Pleased with Jackson's repulse of Banks, he congratulated him "most heartily on the victory which God has granted you over our enemies" and expressed the hope that it was "but the precursor of others over our foe in that quarter, which will entirely break up and scatter his army." However, the withdrawal to Gordonsville on August 12, despite Stonewall's subsequent double-barreled explanation that it was done "in order to avoid being attacked by the vastly superior force in front of me, and with the hope that by thus falling back General Pope would be induced to follow me until I should be reinforced," not only ended the prospect that his lieutenant would be able to "suppress" Pope and return to Richmond in time to help deal with McClellan; it also re-exposed the Virginia Central. This was as intolerable now as it had been a month ago, and Lee moved promptly to meet the threat the following day by ordering Longstreet to Gordonsville with ten brigades, which reduced by half the army remnant protecting the capital from assault on the east and south. Simultaneously he sent Hood, who now commanded a demi-division composed of his own and Law's brigades, to Hanover Junction in order to block an advance from Fredericksburg; or if Burnside moved westward to join Pope, Hood could parallel his march and join Jackson. Something of a balance was thus maintained in every direction except McClellan's, potentially the most dangerous of them all.

Still, potential was a long way from kinetic: especially where McClellan was concerned. A week ago, when the bluecoats marched up

Malvern Hill and then back down again, Lee had said of him: "I have no
idea that he will advance on Richmond now." He took the risk, not
thinking it great, and presently found it even smaller than he had supposed. On this same August 13, while Longstreet's men were boarding
the cars for their journey out to the piedmont, an English deserter came
into the southern lines with a story that part of McClellan's army was
being loaded onto transports. Next day this was confirmed by D. H. Hill,
whose scouts on the south side of the James reported Fitz-John Porter's
corps already gone. That was enough for Lee. Convinced that Pope was
about to be reinforced from the Peninsula — though he did not know to
what extent — he decided to turn his back on Little Mac and give his
undivided close-up personal attention to "the miscreant" on the Rapidan.
The time was short. Before he went to bed that night he notified Davis:
"Unless I hear from you to the contrary I shall leave for G[ordonsville]
at 4 a.m. tomorrow. The troops are accumulating there and I must see
that arrangements are made for the field." Tactfully — for he expected
to be busy and he understood the man with whom he dealt — he added:
"When you do not hear from me, you may feel sure that I do not think it
necessary to trouble you. I shall feel obliged to you for any directions
you may think proper to give."

In this sequence of events, Halleck's worst fears moved toward
realization. The Federal dilemma, as he saw it, was that the rebels might
concentrate northward and jump Pope before McClellan completed his
roundabout transfer from the James to the Rappahannock. The southern commander had already proved himself an opponent not to be
trusted with the initiative; yet that was precisely what he would have so
long as the Army of the Potomac was in transit. The contest was in the
nature of a race, with the Army of Virginia as the prize to be claimed by
whichever of the two superior armies moved the fastest.

Lee was not long in seeing it that way, too, and once he had seen
it he acted. In fact — necessity, in this case, being not only the mother of
invention, but also first cousin to prescience — he acted before he saw
it: first, by detaching Jackson: then by reinforcing him with Hill: finally,
by sending Longstreet up to reinforce them both: so that, in a sense, he
was already running before he heard the starting gun. And now that he
heard it he ran faster. As a result he not only got there first, he got there
before McClellan had done much more than lift his knees off the cin-
ders. Yet that was all: Fortune's smile changed abruptly to a frown. Having reached the finish line, Lee found himself unable to break the ribbon
he was breasting.

The ribbon was the Rapidan, and Pope was disposed behind it.
However, it was not the Union commander who forestalled the
intended destruction, but rather a recurrence of the malady which had
plagued the Confederates throughout the Seven Days: lack of coördination. Detraining at Gordonsville on August 15, Lee conferred at once

with Longstreet and Jackson, who showed him on the map how rare an opportunity lay before him. Nine miles this side of Fredericksburg, the Rapidan and the Rappahannock converged to form the apex of a V laid on its side with the open end to the west. Pope's attitude within the V, and consequently the attitude of the fifty-odd thousand soldiers he had wedged in there between the constricting rivers, was not unlike that of a browsing ram with his attendant flock. Unaware that the butcher was closing in, he had backed himself into a fence corner, apparently in the belief that he and they were safer so.

In this he was considerably mistaken, as Lee was now preparing to demonstrate. Across the open end of the V, at an average distance of twenty miles from the apex, ran the Orange & Alexandria Railroad, leading back to Manassas Junction, the Army of Virginia's main supply base. While the infantry of the Army of Northern Virginia was being concentrated behind Clark's Mountain, masked from observation from across the Rapidan, the cavalry would swing upstream, cross in the darkness, and strike for Rappahannock Station. Destruction of the railroad bridge at that point, severing Pope's supply line and removing his only chance for a dry-shod crossing of the river in his rear, would be the signal for the infantry to emerge from hiding and surge across the fords to its front. Pope's army, caught off balance, would be tamped into the cul-de-sac and mangled.

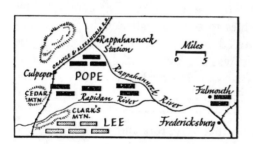

Both wing commanders approved of the plan. Jackson, in fact, was so enthusiastic that he proposed to launch the assault tomorrow. But Longstreet, as on the eve of the Seven Days, and no doubt recalling the Valley general's faulty logistics on that occasion, suggested a one-day wait. Moreover, though he approved of the basic strategy proposed, he thought better results would be obtained by moving around the enemy right, where the army could take up a strong defensive position in the foothills of the Blue Ridge, forcing Pope to attack until, bled white, too fagged to flee, he could be counterattacked and smothered. Lee agreed to the delay — which was necessary anyhow, the cavalry not having arrived — but preferred to assault the enemy left, so as to come between Pope and whatever reinforcements might try to join him, by way of Fredericksburg, either from Washington or the Peninsula. Next day it was so ordered. The army would take up masked positions near the Rapidan on Sunday, August 17, and be prepared to cross at dawn of the following day, on receiving word that the bridge was out at Rappahannock Station.

That was when things started going wrong: particularly in the cavalry. Stuart had two brigades, one under Wade Hampton, left in front of Richmond, the other under Fitzhugh Lee, the army commander's nephew, stationed at Hanover Junction. The latter was to be used in the strike at Rappahannock Station; he was expected Sunday night, and Stuart rode out to meet him east of Clark's Mountain, in rear of Raccoon Ford. Midnight came; there was no sign of him; Jeb and his staff decided to get some sleep on the porch of a roadside house. Just before dawn, hearing hoofbeats in the distance, two officers rode forward to meet what they thought was Lee, but met instead a spatter of carbine fire and came back shouting, "Yankees!" Stuart and the others barely had time to jump for their horses and get away in a hail of bullets, leaving the general's plumed hat, silk-lined cape, and haversack for the blue troopers, who presently withdrew across the river, whooping with delight as they passed the captured finery around. Subsequently it developed that the ford had been left unguarded by Robert Toombs, who, feeling mellow on his return from a small-hours celebration with some friends, had excused the pickets. Placed in arrest for his neglect, he defied regulations by buckling on his sword and making an impassioned speech to his brigade: whereupon he was relieved of command and ordered back to Gordonsville, much to the discomfort of his troops. This did little to ease Stuart's injured pride and nothing at all to recover his lost plumage. Skilled as he was at surprising others, the laughing cavalier was not accustomed to being surprised himself. Nor were matters improved by the infantrymen who greeted him for several days thereafter with the question, "Where's your hat?"

Fitz Lee's nonarrival, which required a one-day postponement of the attack — it was as well; not all the infantry brigades were in position anyhow — was explained by the fact that, his orders having stressed no need for haste, he had marched by way of Louisa to draw rations and ammunition. When this was discovered it caused another one-day postponement, the attack now being set for August 20. Even this second delay seemed just as well: Pope appeared oblivious and docile, and in the interim Lee would have time to bring another division up from Richmond. Before nightfall on the 18th, however, word came to headquarters that the Federals were breaking camp and retiring toward Culpeper. Next morning Lee climbed to a signal station on Clark's Mountain and saw for himself that the report was all too true. The sea of tents had disappeared. Long lines of dark-clothed men and white-topped wagons, toylike in the distance, were winding away from the bivouac areas, trailing serpentine clouds of dust in the direction of the Rappahannock. After watching for a time this final evidence of Pope's escape from the destruction planned for him there between the rivers, Lee put away his binoculars, took a deep breath, and said regretfully to Longstreet, who stood beside him on the mountain top: "General, we little thought that the enemy would turn his back upon us thus early in the campaign."

If there could be no envelopment, at least there could be a pursuit. Lee crossed the Rapidan the following day: only to find himself breasting another ribbon he could not break. This time, too, the ribbon was a river — the Rappahannock — but the failure to cross this second stream was not so much due to a lack of efficiency in his own army as it was to the high efficiency of his opponent's. Pope knew well enough now what dangers had been hanging over his head, for he had captured along with Stuart's plume certain dispatches showing Lee's plan for his destruction, and in spite of his early disparagement of defensive tactics he was displaying a real talent for such work. After pulling out of the suicidal V, he skillfully took position behind its northern arm, and for two full days, four times around the clock, wherever Lee probed for a crossing there were solid ranks of Federals, well supported by artillery, drawn up to receive him on the high left bank of the Rappahannock.

Notified of the situation, Halleck wired: "Stand firm on that line until I can help you. Fight hard, and aid will soon come." Pope replied: "You may rely upon our making a very hard fight in case the enemy advances." Halleck, preferring firmer language, repeated his instructions: "Dispute every inch of ground, and fight like the devil till we can reinforce you. Forty-eight hours more and we can make you strong enough." Encouraged by this pep talk, as well as by his so-far success in preventing a crossing of the river to his front, Pope reassured the wrought-up Washington commander: "There need be no apprehension, as I think no impression can be made on me for some days."

Once more Lee was in disagreement. He not only intended to make what his opponent called an "impression," he knew he had to make one soon or else give up the game. Information from Richmond, added to what he gleaned from northern papers, had convinced him by now that the whole of the Army of the Potomac was on its way to the Rappahannock. Burnside's troops, under Major General Jesse L. Reno, had already joined Pope, bringing his total strength to 70,000 according to Lee's computations, and this figure would in turn be more than doubled when McClellan's men arrived. To oppose this imminent combination, Lee himself had 55,000 of all arms, plus 17,000 still at Richmond. Manifestly, with the odds getting longer every day, whatever was to be done must be done quickly. At any rate, the present stalemate was intolerable. Perhaps one way to break it, Lee reasoned, would be to startle Pope and make him jump by sending Stuart to probe at his rear, particularly the Orange & Alexandria Railroad, which stretched like an exposed nerve back to his base at Manassas. Stuart thought so, too. Ever since the loss of his plume, five days ago near Raccoon Ford, he had been chafing under the jibes and begging Lee to turn him loose. "I intend to make the Yankees pay for that hat," he had written his wife.

He took off on the morning of August 22, crossing the Rappahannock at Waterloo Bridge with 1500 troopers and two guns. His goal was Catlett's Station on the O & A, specifically the bridge over Cedar Run just south of there, and he intended to reach it by passing around the rear of Pope's army, which was drawn up along the east bank of the river north of Rappahannock Station to contest a crossing by Lee's infantry. During a midday halt at Warrenton a young woman informed him that she had wagered a bottle of wine against a Union quartermaster's boast that he would be in Richmond within thirty days. "Take his name and look out for him," Stuart told one of his staff. The column pushed on toward Auburn Mills, rounding the headwaters of Cedar Run, and then proceeded southeastward down the opposite watershed. At sunset a violent storm broke over the troopers' heads. Night came early; "the darkest night I ever knew," Stuart called it; but he pressed on, undetected in the rain and blackness, and within striking distance of Catlett's was rewarded with a piece of luck in the form of a captured orderly, a contraband who, professing his joy at being once more among his "own people," offered to guide them to the private quarters of General Pope himself. Stuart took him up on that. Surrounding the brightly lighted camp, he had the bugler sound the charge, and a thousand yelling horsemen emerged from the outer darkness, swinging sabers and firing revolvers. The startled bluecoats scattered, and the troopers pursued them, spotting targets by the sudden glare of lightning. It was strange. A lightning flash would show the road filled with running men; then the next would show it empty, the runners vanished.

Despite the effectiveness of evasive tactics which appeared to enlist the aid of the supernatural, more than 200 prisoners and about as many horses were rounded up, including a number of staff officers and blooded animals, along with a good deal of miscellaneous loot. From Pope's tent — though the general himself, fortunately or unfortu-

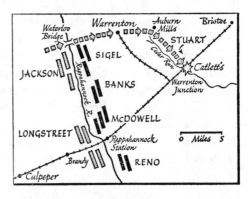

nately, was away on a tour of inspection — the raiders appropriated his personal baggage, a payroll chest stuffed with $350,000 in greenbacks, and a dispatch book containing headquarters copies of all messages sent or received during the past week. The railroad bridge over Cedar Run, however — the prime objective of the raid — resisted all attempts at demolition. Too wet to burn, too tough to chop, it had to be left intact when Stuart pulled out before dawn, returning the way he had come.

By daylight, one bedraggled trooper remarked, "guns, horses, and men look[ed] as if the whole business had passed through a shower of yellow mud last night." But Stuart's spirits were undampened. At Warrenton he called a halt in front of the young woman's house and had the captured quartermaster brought forward to collect the wagered bottle of wine for drinking in Libby Prison. Fitz Lee was in equally high spirits. Safely back across Waterloo Bridge that afternoon, he hailed an infantry brigadier and said he had something to show him. Stepping behind a large oak, he presently emerged wearing the cockaded hat and blue dress coat of a Federal major general. The infantryman roared with laughter, for the coat was so much too long for the bandy-legged Lee that the hem of it nearly covered his spurs. Stuart laughed hardest of all, and when he saw the name John Pope on the label inside the collar, he extended the joke by composing a dispatch addressed to the former owner: "You have my hat and plume. I have your best coat. I have the honor to propose a cartel for a fair exchange of the prisoners." Although nothing came of this — the coat was sent instead to Richmond, where it was put on display in the State Library — Stuart was quite satisfied. "I have had my revenge out of Pope," he told his wife.

Pope's coat was a prize R. E. Lee could appreciate as well as the next man, not excepting his charade-staging nephew; but more important to him, by far, was the captured dispatch book which reached his headquarters the following morning, August 24. In it he found laid before him, as if he were reading over his adversary's shoulder, a sequent and detailed account of the Federal build-up beyond the Rappahannock. In addition to Reno, whose two divisions had already joined, Pope had other forces close at hand, including one on its way from western Virginia by rail and canal boat. Most urgent, though, was the news that Porter, whose corps was the advance unit of McClellan's army, had debarked at Aquia Creek three days ago and marched next day to Falmouth, which placed him within twenty miles of Pope's left at Kelly's Ford, five miles downstream from Rappahannock Station. He might have joined today — or yesterday, for that matter — along with Heintzelman, whose corps was reported steaming northward close behind him. "Forty-eight hours more and we can make you strong enough," Halleck had wired Pope, and Pope had replied: "There need be no apprehension." That, too, was three days ago, while Porter's men were filing off their transports. The race was considerably nearer its finish than Lee had supposed.

In point of fact, it was over. Pope was already too strong and too securely based for Lee to engage him in a pitched battle with anything like certainty of the outcome. Unless he could maneuver him out of his present position, and by so doing gain the chance to fall on some exposed detachment, Pope would go unscathed. And unless Lee could do this quickly, he could not do it at all; for once McClellan's whole army was on the scene, or even the greater part of it, the odds would be hopeless. Lee, then, had two choices, neither of which included standing still. He could retreat, or he could advance. To retreat would be to give up the piedmont and probably the Shenandoah Valley; the siege of Richmond, lately raised, would be renewed under conditions worse than those which had followed Joe Johnston's retreat. That would not do at all. And yet to advance might also worsen matters, since Pope might retire on Fredericksburg and thereby hasten the concentration Lee was seeking to delay.

The gray-bearded general studied his map, and there he found what he thought might be the answer. Pope's supply line, the Orange & Alexandria Railroad, extended northeastward in his rear, so that to maneuver him in that direction would be to make him increase the distance between his present force and the troops coming ashore at Aquia Creek. Twice already Lee had tried to cut that artery: once with a blow aimed at Rappahannock Station, which had failed because Pope pulled back before it landed, and once more with another aimed at Catlett's, which had failed because the rain soaked the bridge too wet for burning. Now he would try again, still farther up the line. If successful, this would not only provoke a longer retreat by threatening Pope's main base of supplies, miles in his rear, but would also repeat the months-old Valley ruse of seeming to threaten Washington, which had yielded such rich dividends before. In reasoning thus, Lee was not discouraged by his two previous failures; rather, he resolved to profit by them. This time he would swing a heavier blow. Instead of using cavalry, he would use infantry. And he would use it in strength.

Infantry in this case meant Stonewall: not only because his three divisions were on the flank from which the march around Pope's right would most conveniently begin, but also because he knew the country he would be traversing and his men had won their "foot cavalry" fame for long, fast marches such as the one now proposed. Conversely, Longstreet too would be assigned the kind of work he preferred and did best: holding, with his four divisions, the line of the Rappahannock against possible assault by Pope's ten divisions across the way. This was risky in the extreme, both for Jackson and Old Pete. Pope was not only stronger now than both of them combined; he was apt to be heavily reinforced at any time, if indeed he had not been already. Furthermore, in dividing his army Lee was inviting disaster by reversing the basic military principle of concentration in the presence of a superior enemy. Yet he did not plan this out of contempt for Pope (Pope the blusterer, Pope the "miscreant" had handled his army with considerable skill throughout the five days since his escape from the constricting V); he planned it out of necessity. Unable on the one hand to stand still, or on the other to retire — either of which would do no more than postpone ruin and make it all the more ruinous when it inevitably came — Lee perceived that the only way to deal with an opponent he did not feel strong enough to fight was to maneuver him into retreat, and to do that he would have to divide his army. Thus the argument, pro and con, came full circle to one end: He would do it because there was nothing else to do. The very thing which made such a division seem overrash — Pope's numerical superiority — was also its strongest recommendation, according to Lee, who later remarked: "The disparity . . . between the contending forces rendered the risks unavoidable."

Today was Sunday. Shortly after noon, having made his decision, he rode to left-wing headquarters at Jeffersonton to give Stonewall his assignment. Jeffersonton was two miles back from the river, where a noisy artillery duel was in progress from opposite banks; Lee spoke above the rumble of the guns. The march would begin tomorrow, he said. Moving upstream for a crossing well above Pope's right, Jackson would then swing northward behind the screen of the Bull Run Mountains, beyond which he would turn southeast through Thoroughfare Gap — the route he had followed thirteen months ago, coming down from the Valley to reach the field where he had won his nickname — for a strike at Pope's supply line, far in his rear. No precise objective was assigned. Anywhere back there along the railroad would do, Lee said, just so Pope was properly alarmed for the safety of his communications, the welfare of his supply base, and perhaps for the security of Washington itself. Lee explained that he did not want a general engagement; he wanted Pope drawn away from the reinforcements being assembled on the lower Rappahannock. Once that was done, the two wings would reunite in the vicinity of Manassas and take advantage of any opening Pope afforded, either through negligence or panic.

Jackson began his preparations at once. After sending a topographical engineer ahead to select the best route around the Bull Run Mountains, he set his camps astir. The march would begin at earliest dawn, "with the utmost promptitude, without knapsacks" — without everything, in fact, except weapons, the ordnance train, and ambulances. Beef on the hoof would serve for food, supplemented by green corn pulled from fields along the way. Ewell would lead, followed by A. P. Hill; Winder's division, now under Brigadier General W. B. Taliaferro, would bring up the rear, with orders to tread on the heels of Hill's men if they lagged. During the night, Longstreet's guns replaced Jackson's along the Rappahannock south of Waterloo Bridge, and Lee, who would be left with 32,000 troops — including Stuart's cavalry, which would join the flanking column the second day — prepared to stage whatever demonstrations would be needed to conceal from Pope the departure of Jackson's 23,000.

What with the moving guns, the messengers coming and going, the night-long activity in the camps, Stonewall himself got little sleep before the dawn of August 25. He rose early, ate a light breakfast, and took a moment, now that the Sabbath was over, to write a brief note to his wife. In it he said nothing of the march that lay ahead; merely that "I have only time to tell you how much I love my little pet dove." Presently he was in the saddle, doubling the column. The men looked up and sideways at him as he passed, the bill of his mangy cadet cap pulled down over his pale eyes. As usual, they did not know where they were going, only that there would most likely be fighting when they got there. Meanwhile, they did the marching and left the thinking to Old Jack. "Close up, men. Close up," he said.

Ten days ago, still down on the Peninsula, preparing for the withdrawal he had unsuccessfully protested, McClellan had warned Halleck: "I don't like Jackson's movements. He will suddenly appear where least expected."

This was not exactly news to Halleck, coming as it did on the heels of Banks' repulse at Cedar Mountain. Besides, Old Brains had other problems on his mind: not the least of which was the situation in the West, where his carefully worked-out tactical dispositions seemed about to come unglued. Kirby Smith left Knoxville that same week, bound for Kentucky, and Bragg had his whole army at Chattanooga, apparently poised for a leap in the same direction. Lincoln was distressed, and so was Halleck. So, presently, was McClellan. Earlier, to encourage haste in the evacuation, Halleck had assured him: "It is my intention that you shall command all the troops in Virginia as soon as we can get them together." McClellan's spirits rose at the prospect. To Burnside, who arrived with further assurances of Halleck's good will, he said as they stood beside the road down which his army was withdrawing to Fort Monroe: "Look at them, Burn. Did you ever see finer men? Oh, I want to see those men beside of Pope's." But there were subsequent delays, chiefly the result of a shortage of transports, and Halleck's cries for haste once more grew strident: so much so, in fact, that McClellan felt obliged to take official exception to what he called his "tone." Privately he protested to his wife that Halleck "did not even behave with common politeness; he is a *bien mauvais sujet* — he is not a gentleman. . . . I fear that I am very mad."

All the same, he made what haste he could. Porter left for Aquia Creek on August 20, and Heintzelman left next day for Alexandria. Both were to join Pope at once, the former by moving up the left bank of the Rappahannock, the latter by moving down the Orange & Alexandria Railroad. But Lee was across the Rapidan by now. "The forces of Burnside and Pope are hard-pressed," Halleck wired, "and require aid as quickly as you can send it. Come yourself as soon as you can." The bitter satisfaction McClellan found in this appeal was expressed in a letter to his wife: "Now they are in trouble they seem to want the 'Quaker,' the 'procrastinator,' the 'coward,' and the 'traitor.' *Bien.*" Two days later, Franklin followed Heintzelman to Alexandria, and Sumner embarked the following day to follow Porter to Aquia Creek. Four of the five corps were gone, leaving Keyes to man the Yorktown defenses: McClellan had answered Halleck's cries for haste. But he no longer put any stock in any promises made him, either by the general in chief or by any other representative of the Administration. In fact, he told his wife as he left Old Point Comfort, August 23, "I take it for granted that my orders will be as disagreeable as it is possible to make them — unless Pope is beaten," he added, "in which case they will want me to save Washington again. Nothing but their fears will induce them to give me any command of importance or to treat me otherwise than with discourtesy."

Sure enough, when he got to Aquia next morning — Sunday — he found that Porter and Heintzelman had already been released to Pope, and when he wired for instructions Halleck replied: "You can either remain at Aquia or come to Alexandria, as you may deem best, so as to direct the landing of your troops." In other words, it didn't matter; the Young Napoleon was merely to serve as an expediter, dispatching the rest of his men to Pope as fast as they came ashore at those two points. He chose Alexandria, presumably to be close at hand for the call he believed would follow the calamity he expected. Monday and Tuesday were doubtful days; Pope's scouts had spotted a column of "well-closed infantry" moving northward, up the far bank of the Rappahannock, and Pope reported Lee's whole army bound for the Shenandoah Valley "by way of Luray and Front Royal." Then Tuesday night the line went dead. All was silent beyond Manassas Junction, where there had been some sort of explosion. . . .

The next five days were smoke and flame; McClellan ran the gamut of emotions. With Porter and Heintzelman committed, he sent Franklin to join them, saying: "Go, and whatever may happen, don't allow it to be said that the Army of the Potomac failed to do its utmost for the country." Sumner followed. "You now have every man . . . within my reach," McClellan told Halleck, requesting that "I may be permitted to go to the scene of battle with my staff, merely to be with my own men, if nothing more. They will fight none the worse for my being with them." Halleck replied, "I cannot answer without seeing the President, as General Pope is in command, by his orders, of the department." When McClellan asked where this left him, the answer came from the War Department: "General McClellan commands that portion of the Army of the Potomac that has not been sent forward to General Pope's command." In all, this amounted to nothing more than his staff and the handful of convalescents at Alexandria. Instead of being removed from command, as he had feared at the outset, he now perceived that his command had been removed from him.

He was left, he told his wife, "flat on my back without any command whatever. . . . I feel too blue and disgusted to write any more now, so I will smoke a cigar and try to get into a better humor." It did no good. Far off, beyond Fairfax, he could hear the rumble of guns from a field where his soldiers were fighting under a man he despised and considered professionally incompetent. Unable to go, yet unable to sit still, doing nothing, he took up his pen. "They have taken all my troops from me! I have even sent off my personal escort and camp guard, and am here with a few orderlies and the aides. I have been listening to the sound of a great battle in the distance. My men engaged in it and I away! I never felt worse in my life."

★ ★ ★

"Let us look before us," Pope had said, "and not behind." In taking advantage of this policy, obligingly announced for all to hear, Jackson not only fulfilled McClellan's prediction that he would "suddenly appear where least expected," but he did so — in accordance with Lee's instructions — by landing squarely and emphatically astride those lines of retreat which Pope had said could be left "to take care of themselves."

In point of fact, however sudden his appearance was to Pope, to his own men it was something else again, coming as it did at the end of two of the longest and hardest days of marching any 23,000 soldiers ever did. At the outset the two views coincided. Like Pope, whose lookouts promptly reported the upstream movement, when they first marched into Monday's dawn they thought they were headed for another bloody game of hide-and-seek out in the Valley. That was fine with them. Rations had been scarce of late, and they recalled the largess of Commissary Banks. They swung on through the dust and heat, a long column of striding men whose uniforms, as one of their number later said, were "of that nondescript hue which time and all weathers give to ruins": Jeffersonton to Amissville, then northward across the river to Orlean, halfway through the first day's march, which would end just short of Salem, a station on the Manassas Gap Railroad. Where they would go from there they did not know. Nor did they seem to care. Approaching that place, with twenty-five leg-aching miles behind them, they forgot their weariness when they saw Jackson standing upon a large stone by the roadside, cap off, watching the sun turn red as it went down beyond the Blue Ridge. But when they cheered him, as was their custom, he made a startled gesture of protest and sent an officer to explain that the noise might give away their presence to the Yankees. So they raised their hats in mute salute as they swung past him, smiling, proud-eyed, silent except for the shuffle of feet in the dust. Flushed with pleasure, for their silence was more eloquent than cheers, Stonewall turned to his staff. "Who could not conquer with such troops as these?" he asked.

Wherever it was they were going, they knew next morning it was not to be the Valley; for at Salem they turned east toward White Plains, then southeast, following the railroad into the sunrise, blood red at first, then fiery in the broad notch of Thoroughfare Gap. That was the critical point. If it was held, there would be fighting and the loss of a large portion of the element of surprise. They quickened the step. Then word came down the column, Ewell to Hill to Taliaferro: the gap was empty, not a Federal in sight. They pressed on, eastward to Hay Market, then south-southeast to Gainesville, where they struck the Warrenton Turnpike, which led east-northeast from Pope's position on the Rappahannock, traversing the scene of last year's triumph on the plains of Manassas, across Bull Run at Stone Bridge, then on to Centerville and Alexandria. Tactically — so far, at least, as it had been kept from the marchers themselves — the secret was more or less out. "Disaster and shame lurk in the rear," Pope had said. Now Jackson lurked there, too.

It became obvious at once, though, that he intended to do a good deal more than simply lurk there. Stuart having arrived with all the cavalry — Lee had released him late the night before; he had ridden hard to catch up by midafternoon, when the head of the infantry column got to Gainesville — Jackson fanned the troopers out to the right, protecting the flank in the direction of the Rappahannock, and pushed on southward across the turnpike. Six miles ahead was Bristoe Station, where the Orange & Alexandria crossed Broad Run; destruction of the bridge there would sever Pope's supply line for days. "Push on, men. Push on," he told the marchers. But this was easier said than done. They were showing the effects of strain, and there was much less talk and horseplay up and down the column. Nearing Bristoe they had covered more than fifty miles, most of it in blazing heat and on secondary roads, with little to eat but green corn and apples along the way. Still, now that the goal was nearly in sight, according to one admiring cavalryman, "the feeling seemed to be a dread with each one that he would give out and not be there to see the fun." Many did give out, especially during this last half-dozen miles. As usual, however, though the column dribbled blown and blistered stragglers in its wake, Stonewall showed no pity for either the fainting or the stalwart, whatever their rank. Just short of Bristoe he dismounted and went onto the porch of a roadside cabin to wait for the column to close. He sat in a split-bottom chair, tilted back against the wall, and fell asleep. Presently a staff officer arrived and shouted him awake: "General Blank failed to put a picket at the crossroads! and the following brigade took the wrong road!" The eyelids lifted; two pale blue chinks appeared in the thin-lipped mask. "Put him under arrest and prefer charges," Jackson snapped. The eyelids dropped and he was back asleep at once.

The lead brigade hit Bristoe just at sunset. Coming forward on the run, the whooping graybacks overpowered the startled guards and were taking charge when they heard the approaching rumble of a northbound train. Hurriedly they threw crossties on the track and began a frantic attempt to unbolt a rail. Too late: the engine was upon them, scattering ties and men, then clattering out of sight in the gathering dusk — doubt-less to give warning up the line. Their disappointment was relieved, however, by news that this was the hour when empty supply trains made their run, one after another from Pope's advance depots around Warren-ton, back to Manassas and Alexandria. When the next prize came along the raiders were ready. Riflemen lining one flank of the right-of-way gave the locomotive a volley as it thundered past, struck an open switch, and plunged with half its cars down the embankment, where it struck with a gaudy eruption of red coals and hissing steam. Delighted with this effect, the Confederates gathered round and were pointing with elation at a bullet-pocked portrait of Lincoln on the steam dome — the engine was called *The President* — when the whistle of a third train was heard. It rammed into the cars left on the track, creating another rackety tableau of splintered wood and twisted iron: whereupon still a fourth whistle sounded. But while the watchers were getting set to enjoy an-other eruption of sparks and steam, they heard instead a screech of brakes as the locomotive stopped, then backed rapidly away and out of sight. The raiders cursed the engineer for his vigilance. Now the alarm would be sounded below as well as above the captured station; the fire-works fun was at an end.

Though he had enjoyed all this as much as anyone, now that it was over Jackson wasted no time on regret that it could not have lasted longer. Instead, he put his troops to work at once on the job for which he had brought them here in the first place: destruction of the Broad Run railroad bridge. While this was being done he stood beside a fire, hastily kindled for light, and began to interrogate one of the captured engineers. Across the way, a Federal civilian was laid out on the ground; a middle-aged man — probably a politician, for he had come down from Washington on a visit to Pope's army — he had suffered a broken leg in one of the train wrecks. Hearing who his captors were, and that their commander was just on the opposite side of the campfire, he asked to be lifted, despite the pain, for a look at the famed rebel. When the soldiers obliged, he saw beyond the dancing flames a stoop-shouldered figure in outsized boots and road-colored clothes slouched with a crumpled cadet cap pulled far down over his nose. For half a minute the civilian stared at the plain-looking man his captors assured him was the gallant Stonewall, scourge of the Yankee nation. Then, anticipation having given way to incredulity, which in turn gave way to disillusionment, he said with a groan of profound disgust: "O my God! Lay me down."

Jackson himself knew nothing of this: which was why he never understood the basic implication of the expression used by his soldiers in almost every conceivable situation from now on, whether confronted with an issue of meager rations or a charging Union line: "O my God! Lay me down!" In any case, even if he had heard it, he had no time for laughter. Interrogation of the engineer, along with other captives, had divulged that Pope's main base of supplies, four miles up the line at Manassas, was lightly guarded and wide open to attack. How long it would remain so, now that the alarm had been sounded in both directions, was another matter. Jackson decided to take no chance on being shut off from this richest of all prizes. Leg-weary though the men were, some of them would have to push on through the darkness to Manassas, block the arrival of reinforcements sent by rail from Alexandria, and hold the place until their comrades joined them in the morning. Two of Ewell's regiments drew the duty; or, more strictly speaking, were volunteered for it by their commander, Brigadier General Isaac Trimble. It was Trimble, a sixty-year-old Virginia-born Kentucky-raised Marylander, who had wanted to make a twilight charge up the blasted slope of Malvern Hill the month before; Stonewall had restrained him then, but he remained undaunted; "Before this war is over," he declared as the army started northward, "I intend to be a major general or a corpse." He set off into the night, riding out of Bristoe at the head of his two foot-sore regiments, a burly white-haired West Pointer with a drooping black mustache. On second thought, Jackson sent Stuart and his troopers along to support him. Then the rest of the command bedded down, too weary to worry overmuch about the fact that they were sleeping between an army of 75,000 bluecoats and the capital whose safety was supposedly that army's first concern.

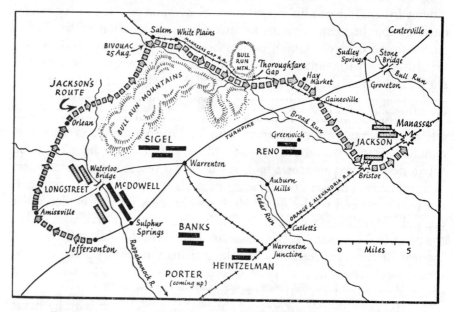

Early next morning, August 27, leaving the rest of Ewell's division to guard the Broad Run crossing in his rear, Jackson moved on Manassas with the troops of Hill and Taliaferro. The sight that awaited them there was past the imagining of Stonewall's famished tatterdemalions. Acres — a square mile, in fact — of supplies of every description were stacked in overwhelming abundance, collected here against the day when the armies of Pope and McClellan combined for another advance on Richmond. Newly constructed warehouses overflowed with rations, quartermaster goods, and ordnance stores. Two spur tracks, half a mile long each, were jammed with more than a hundred brand-new boxcars, similarly freighted. Best of all, from the point of view of the luxury-starved raiders, sutler wagons parked hub-to-hub were packed with every delicacy their vanished owners had thought might tempt a payday soldier's jaded palate. There it all was, spread out before the butternut horde as if the mythical horn of plenty had been upended here, its contents theirs for the taking. So they supposed; but when they broke ranks, surging forward, they found that Jackson, frugal as always, had foreseen their reaction and had moved to forestall it by placing Trimble's men on guard to hold them back. For once, though, he had underrated their aggressive instincts. Veterans of harder fights, with infinitely smaller rewards at the end, they broke through the cordon and fell on the feast of good things. Canteens were filled with molasses, haversacks with coffee; pockets bulged with cigars, jackknives, writing paper, handkerchiefs, and such. However, the chief object of search, amid the embarrassment of riches, was whiskey. This too their commander had foreseen, and by his orders the guards staved in the barrels and shattered the demijohns; whereupon the looters dropped to their hands and knees, scooping and sipping at the pools and rivulets before the liquor soaked into the earth or drained away. Some, more abstemious, were satisfied with loaves of unfamiliar light-bread, which they ate like cake. Others, preferring a still richer diet, found pickled oysters and canned lobster more to their taste, spooning it up with grimy fingers and washing it down with bottles of Rhine wine.

Off to the east, a troublesome Federal battery had been banging away in protest all this while. Jackson sent one of his own to attend to it, but presently word came back that enemy infantry was crossing the Bull Run railroad bridge and forming for attack. Most of Hill's division was moved out quickly to meet the threat, which turned out to be a brigade of four New Jersey regiments sent down by rail from Alexandria under a zealous and badly informed commander, Brigadier General George W. Taylor. His orders were to save the bridge, but he decided to press on to the junction itself and drive away the raiders, whom he mistook for cavalry. The Jerseymen came on in style, green and eager, not knowing that they were up against the largest and probably the hardest-fighting division in Lee's whole army. Jackson opened on them with his guns — prematurely it seemed to Little Powell's men, waiting with cocked rifles for the interrupters of their feast to come within butchering distance. But the bluecoats took their long-range losses and kept coming, bayonets fixed and fire in their eyes.

Then Stonewall did an unfamiliar thing. Admiring their valor, which he knew was based on ignorance — the charge, he said later, "was made with great spirit and determination and under a leader worthy of a better cause" — he called a cease-fire and rode out in front of the guns, waving a handkerchief and shouting for the Federals to surrender and be spared extermination. By way of reply, one attacker took deliberate aim and sent a bullet whistling past him. Cured of his lapse into leniency, Jackson rode back and ordered the fire resumed. By now the Jerseymen were nearer, and this time it was as if they struck a trip-wire. Suddenly demoralized, they turned and scampered, devil-take-the-hindmost. Their losses were surprisingly light, considering the danger to which their rashness had exposed them: 200 captured and 135 killed or wounded, including their commander, who, as he was being carried dying to the rear, appealed to his men to rally "and for God's sake . . . prevent another Bull Run."

They paid him no mind; nor did Jackson. Already burdened with more spoils than he could handle — victim, as it were, of the law of diminishing utility — for once he was unconcerned about pursuit. The whole comic-opera affair was over before noon. After burning the railroad bridge to insure against further interruption from that direction, he brought Hill's men back to the junction, where some measure of order had been restored in their absence. It was maintained, at least for a while. While the plunderers were held at bay, the ambulances and ordnance wagons — all the rolling stock he had — were filled with such Federal stores as were most needed, principally medical supplies. Once this was done, the rest were thrown open to the troops, who fell upon them whooping, their appetites whetted by the previous unauthorized foray. Painful as it was to Stonewall, watching the improvident manner in which his scarecrow raiders snatched up one luxurious armload only to cast it aside for another, he was reconciled to the waste by the knowledge that what was rejected would have to be given to the flames. Word had come from Ewell that he was under attack at Bristoe from the opposite direction; Jackson knew the time had come to abandon his exposed position for one in which he could await, with some degree of security, the arrival of Longstreet and reconsolidation of the army under Lee.

By now, of course, Pope had learned the nature of the explosion in his rear. Instead of heading for the Shenandoah Valley, as had been supposed when the signal station reported a well-closed gray column moving north two days ago, Lee had divided his army and sent half of it swinging around the Bull Run Mountains for a strike at Manassas; that half of it was there now, under Jackson. But Pope was not dismayed. Far from it; he was exultant, and with cause. He had forty brigades of infantry on hand, including a dozen of McClellan's, with others on the way. It seemed to him that Lee, who had less than thirty brigades — fourteen in one direction, fifteen in another, more than twenty airline miles apart, with 75,000 Federals on the alert between the two segments — had committed tactical suicide. Hurrying to Bristoe, where Hooker's division of Heintzelman's corps was skirmishing with the enemy, Pope arrived as night was falling and found that the rebels, soundly thrashed according to Hooker, had retreated across Broad Run. Encouraged by today's success, he decided to bring up six more divisions and with them crush Jackson's three before the sun went down tomorrow. A depot of supplies, however vast, seemed a small price to pay for bait when it brought such a catch within his reach.

To Phil Kearny, commanding Heintzelman's other division at Warrenton Junction, went a wire: "At the very earliest blush of dawn push forward ... with all speed to this place.... Jackson, A. P. Hill, and Ewell are in front of us. ... I want you here at day-dawn, if possible, and we shall bag the whole crowd. Be prompt and expeditious, and never mind wagon trains or roads till this affair is over." To Reno, at Greenwich with Burnside's two divisions, went another: "March at the earliest dawn of day ... on Manassas Junction. Jackson, Ewell, and A. P. Hill are between Gainesville and that place, and if you are prompt and expeditious we shall bag the whole crowd. ... As you value success be off at the earliest blush of dawn." A third wire went to McDowell, whose three divisions were helping to hold the line of the Rappahannock: "Jackson, Ewell, and A. P. Hill are between Gainesville and Manassas Junction. We had a severe fight with them today, driving them back several miles along the railroad. If you will march promptly and rapidly at the earliest dawn of day upon Manassas Junction we shall bag the whole crowd. ... Be expeditious, and the day is our own."

Northeastward, exploding ammunition dumps imitated the din of a great battle and the night sky was lurid with the reflection of a square mile of flames: Jackson's graybacks were evidently staging a high revel, oblivious to the destruction being plotted by their adversary, five short miles away. But next morning, after fording Broad Run unopposed and marching past the wreckage at Bristoe Station, when Pope reached Manassas all he found was the charred evidence of what one of his staff colonels called "the recent rebel carnival." The scene was one of waste and desolation. "On the railroad tracks and sidings stood the hot and smoking remains of what had recently been trains of cars laden with ordnance and commissary stores intended for our army. As far as the eye could reach, the plain was covered with boxes, barrels, cans, cooking utensils, saddles, sabers, muskets, and military equipments generally; hard bread and corn pones, meat, salt, and fresh beans, blankets, clothes, shoes, and hats, from brand-new articles, just from the original packages, to the scarcely recognizable exuviae of the rebels, who had made use of the opportunity to renew their toilets." Of the revelers themselves there was no sign. Nor was there agreement among the returning guards and sutlers as to the direction in which they had disappeared. Some said one way, some another. As far as Pope could tell, the earth had swallowed them up.

As things now stood, last night's orders would result in nothing more than a convergence on a vacuum. Presently, however, reports began to come in, pinpointing the gray column first in one place, then another, most of them quite irreconcilable. Pope sifted the conflicting evidence, rejecting this, accepting that, and arrived at the conviction that Stonewall was concentrating his three divisions at Centerville. Revised orders went out accordingly, canceling the convergence on Manassas; Centerville was now the place. If they would still be expeditious, the day would still be Pope's.

His exuberance and zest were undiminished; he kept his mind, if not his eye, on the prize within his reach. But for others under him — particularly the dust-eating soldiers in the ranks, left hungry by the destruction of their commissary stores — the chase, if it could be called such, had already begun to pall. Marched and countermarched since the "earliest blush of dawn" in pursuit of phantoms, they were being mishandled and they knew it. The very terrain was of evil memory. It seemed to them that they were heading for a repetition of last year's debacle on these same rolling plains, under some of these same commanders. McDowell, for example; "I'd rather shoot McDowell than Jackson," men were saying. Now as then, they turned on him, muttering imprecations. Nothing about him escaped suspicion, even his hat, a bamboo-and-canvas affair he had invented to keep his scalp cool in the Virginia heat. They suspected that it was a signaling device, to be used for communicating with the rebels or as an identification to keep him from being shot by mistake. "That basket," they called it, contemptuous not only of the helmet, but also of the general it shaded. "Pope has his headquarters in the saddle, and McDowell his head in a basket."

All through the long hot afternoon of August 28 Pope kept groping, like the "it" in a game of blindman's buff, arms outstretched, fingers spread, combing the landscape for the ubiquitous, elusive rebel force: to no avail. Riding into Centerville at sunset, in advance of most of the twelve divisions he had slogging the dusty roads — all, that is, but the two with Banks, which, being still unrecovered from the shock of Cedar Mountain, had been left behind to guard the army trains — he found that he had ordered another convergence on another vacuum. The graybacks had been there, all right, but they were there no longer. They had vanished. Once more it was as if the earth had swallowed them, except that this time he would have to look for them in darkness, with troops worn down by fourteen hours of fruitless marching. Pope felt the first twinges of dismay. Not because of fear; he was afraid of nothing, not even Stonewall; but because the time allotted for the destruction of Lee's army, wing by isolated wing, was running out. Such fear as he felt was that Jackson would make his escape and rejoin Longstreet, who by now would be moving to meet him.

Pope's dismay was short-lived, however. After nightfall, two dispatches reached him that changed everything and sent his spirits soaring higher than ever. The first informed him that Longstreet's column, after penetrating Thoroughfare Gap, had been driven back to the west side of Bull Run Mountain. This afforded considerable relief, allowing as it did additional time in which to catch the rebel host divided. But the best news of all came just before 10 o'clock. Late that afternoon, marching as ordered toward Centerville, one of McDowell's divisions had found Jackson lurking in the woods beside the Warrenton Turnpike, two miles short of Stone Bridge, and had flushed him. There on the field of last year's battle, Pope wired Halleck, "a severe fight took place, which was terminated by darkness. The enemy was driven back at all points, and thus the affair rests."

Determined not to let it rest there long, he sent peremptory orders to the commanders of his five converging corps for the execution of a plan he improvised, then and there, for the absolute destruction of his just-found adversary. McDowell and Sigel, with 30,000 men, would attack at dawn from the south and west, blocking any possible withdrawal by way of Thoroughfare Gap, while Heintzelman, Porter, and Reno, with another 30,000, would attack from the east: twin hammers whose concerted blows would pound to a pulp the 23,000 butternut marauders, pinned to the anvil by their own commander. Pope's instructions were explicit: "Assault him vigorously at daylight in the morning." Exultant — and with cause; Jackson's 14 gray brigades were about to be mauled simultaneously by 34 in blue, 17 from one direction, 17 from another — he added: "I see no possibility of his escape."

Stoutly conceived though the plan was, and stoutly though he strove to put it into execution, Pope was again the victim of several misconceptions. For one thing, Jackson was not trapped; nor was he trying to "escape." He very much wanted to be where he was, and he very much hoped that Pope could be persuaded to attack him, whatever the odds. In fact, if he could have been at Federal headquarters, with control over the messages coming and going, he scarcely would have changed a line in a single one of them. His luck was in and he knew it — the old Valley luck, by which even his worst errors worked to his advantage. The night march out of Manassas, for example:

When Ewell came up from Bristoe about sunset, having disengaged from the skirmish with Hooker's division across Broad Run, Stonewall gave these late arrivers a chance at the fag end of the feast — "What we got was...not of a kind to invigorate," one cannoneer grumbled, "consisting as it did of hard-tack, pickled oysters, and canned stuff generally" — then put all three divisions in motion while the rear guard set fire to the picked-over wreckage left behind. What followed, as the troops slogged more or less northward in three columns, looking back over their shoulders at the spreading glow of flames, was one of the worst executed marches in the history of his command. Heavy-stomached, with bulging haversacks and pockets, the men fell by the way-side or crawled under bushes to sleep off their excesses of food and drink. The result was confusion and a great deal of lost time as the file-closers probed the countryside, rounding them up and persuading them to fall back into column. Taliaferro did best, moving almost due north up the Sudley Springs road to Groveton, the designated point of concentration, where that road intersected the Warrenton Turnpike. Hill did worst; he went all the way to Centerville, then swung west. Ewell, following Hill for a time, crossed Bull Run at Blackburn's Ford, then re-crossed it at Stone Bridge, Hill coming along somewhere behind. Morning found the three divisions badly scattered and dangerously exposed; it was midday before they were reunited at Groveton. For this there were various causes — Jackson's sketchy instructions, inefficient guides, the droves of stragglers — but even this blundering performance worked to Stonewall's advantage, providing as it did the basis for the conflicting Federal reports of his whereabouts, which led Pope off on a tangential pursuit.

Whatever blame he deserved for the confusion in all three columns along the way, Jackson had chosen their destination with care and daring. A rapid withdrawal to rejoin Lee beyond the mountains was in order, but it was not Stonewall's way to turn his back on a situation, no matter how risky, so long as possible benefits remained within his reach. Tomorrow or the next day, Longstreet would be coming down through Thoroughfare Gap or up the Warrenton Turnpike. At Groveton, Jackson knew from last year's extended stay in the area, there was an excellent covered position in which to await Old Pete's arrival by either route, and if the pressure grew too great his line of retreat would be reasonably secure. Meanwhile, the Federals — or, as he preferred to express it, "a kind Providence" — might afford him a chance at the infliction of another "terrible wound." About midday, when he finally got his scattered divisions back together, he put the men in position just north of the turnpike, behind a low ridge and under cover of some woods. One soldier later remembered that they were "packed [in there] like herring in a barrel." They stacked arms and lounged about, all 23,000 of them (minus stragglers) snoozing, playing cards, and munching at more of the good things they had in their haversacks by courtesy of Commissary Pope. The bands were silent; the troops were instructed not to shout; but as that same soldier remembered it, there were "no restrictions as to laughing and talking . . . and the woods sounded like the hum of a beehive in the warm sunshine."

Jackson himself remained on the ridge, which afforded a clear view of the pike in both directions. When a report arrived that a strong Union column was advancing from Gainesville, he moved Taliaferro and Ewell two miles west and posted them in the woods adjacent to the pike for a surprise attack on the flank of the passing bluecoats. Nothing came of this; the column turned off south toward Manassas before it came abreast. Stonewall was cross and restless, reminding one observer of "an explosive missile, an unlucky spark applied to which would blow you sky high." Lee had told him to avoid a general engagement, but he did not like to see the Federals escape the ambush he had laid. Besides, he knew now that reinforcements from the Peninsula were at Alexandria — better than 30,000 of them, in addition to the two corps already joined. If Pope withdrew in that direction, the combined might of his and McClellan's forces would be too great for a strike at them, even after Lee arrived with Longstreet. So Jackson continued to patrol the ridge, trotting back and forth on his horse, peering up and down the pike. His staff and several brigade and regimental commanders sat their mounts at a respectful distance, not wanting to come near him in his present frame of mind or take a chance on interrupting his prayers that Providence would send another blue column into the trap the first had avoided.

Along toward sunset, his prayers were answered after the flesh. A well-closed Federal column was approaching, trudging hard up the turnpike in the direction of Stone Bridge, flankers out. Jackson rode down off the ridge for a closer look and trotted back and forth, within easy musket range of the bluecoats, who gave him no more attention than a casual rebel cavalryman deserved. Back on the ridge, the officers watched in horror and fascination. "We could almost tell his thoughts by his movements," one declared. "Sometimes he would halt, then trot on briskly, halt again, wheel his horse, and pass again along the [flank] of the marching column." They thought they knew what he would do, and presently he did it. When the head of the blue column drew abreast, he whirled and galloped back toward the group on the ridge. "Here he comes, by God," one shouted. Jackson pulled up, touched his cap, and said calmly: "Bring your men up, gentlemen." At this, they turned and rode fast toward the woods where the infantry was waiting. "The men had been watching their officers with much interest," the same observer remarked, "and when they wheeled and dashed toward them they knew what it meant, and from the woods arose a hoarse roar like that from cages of wild animals at the scent of blood."

The artillery led off. Three batteries emerged from the woods, went into position in the open, and began to slam away at the compact column on the pike. As the cannonade got under way, Taliaferro's men swarmed down the slope, yelling as they came, the battle flags of the Stonewall Brigade gleaming blood-red in the fading light. The result should have been panic, for the bluecoats taken thus unawares were from Rufus King's division — specifically, John Gibbon's brigade of four regiments, three from Wisconsin and one from Indiana — one of the largest but also one of the greenest in Pope's conglomerate command. However, instead of panicking at this abrupt baptism of fire, the Westerners wheeled to meet the attackers and stopped them in their tracks with massed volleys. Gibbon was regular army, loyal to the Union despite the fact that three of his North Carolina brothers went with the Stars and Bars. Supported by two regiments sent forward from Abner Doubleday's brigade, he handled his troops skillfully, holding off Taliaferro, who presently was reinforced by two brigades from Ewell. What ensued, first by the red glare of sunset, then on through dusk and twilight into darkness, with 2800 Federals facing nearly twice as many Confederates, was one of the hardest close-quarter fights of the whole war.

Jackson did not attempt to maneuver. Contrary to his usual practice once the advance had stalled, he was content to let the weight of numbers settle the issue. In point of fact, however, neither the pressure nor the savagery of his veterans settled anything at all. If the Wisconsin and Indiana farm boys were in a hopeless predicament, outnumbered nearly two to one by fighters whose fame was the highest in either army, they did not seem to recognize the odds. Experience had afforded them nothing by way of comparison; for all they knew, combat was supposed to be like this. The opposing lines stood face to face, parade-style, and slugged it out for two solid hours. Gibbon, who at thirty-five had a long career ahead of him, said afterwards that this was the heaviest infantry fire he ever heard, and Taliaferro referred to the engagement as "one of the most terrific conflicts that can be conceived of."

Finally the firing slacked; by 9 o'clock it died away, by mutual consent. The Federals withdrew across the turnpike, unpursued. More than a thousand of them had fallen, well over a third of the number engaged; the 2d Wisconsin, which had gone into the fight 500 strong, came out with 202, having begun tonight to establish the record it would set, before the war was over, by having more of its members killed in combat than any other regiment in the U.S. Army. Gibbon and Doubleday wondered what to do. Their latest orders called for a march on Centerville, but if the two-hour fight proved nothing else, it certainly had proved that the way was blocked in that direction. King was sick in an ambulance; no one knew where McDowell was. (He was in fact lost in the woods, having strayed from the pike in the darkness, and would not himself know where he was till morning.) So Gibbon and Doubleday, conferring with the ailing King, decided that the best thing to do would be to swing on down to Manassas, the original objective, taking such of their wounded along as could be recovered from the field. Grass-green three hours ago, the western soldiers fell back in and set off down the road as veterans. They were known as the Black Hat Brigade, Gibbon having seen to it that they were equipped with nonregulation black felt hats. In time, the rebels too would know them by that name; "Here come them damn black hat fellers!" the gray pickets would yell. But presently they changed it. Within a month they were calling themselves the Iron Brigade.

Few men anywhere were inclined to question their right to call themselves by any name they fancied — least of all Taliaferro's and Ewell's, who had suffered about as heavily as the troops they sought to ambush. The Stonewall Brigade took 635 soldiers into the twilight conflict and came out with 425, a ghost of the proud 3,000-man command that won its *nom de guerre* on nearby Henry Hill the year before and then passed through the glory of the Valley Campaign and the carnage of the Seven Days. Some of its most famous regiments were reduced to the size of a small company; the 27th Virginia, for example, was down to a scant two dozen men by the time the firing stopped. Murderous as these figures were, they told but part of the story, for they included a high percentage of officers of all ranks. The 2d Virginia had only one captain and one lieutenant left with the colors, and others were stripped almost as bare of leaders. Nor were the losses restricted to those of field and company grade. This fight brought down generals, too, including two of the three ranking just under Jackson himself. Taliaferro, who had succeeded Winder less than three weeks ago, was thrice wounded. He kept on his feet till the melee ended, but then, bled white, was carried off the field. His successor, Brigadier General William E. Starke — a former New Orleans cotton man, professionally untrained in arms — had been promoted on the eve of Cedar Mountain and had led a brigade in action for the first time tonight. Now suddenly he found himself in command of the most famous of all Confederate divisions.

The other high-ranking casualty was Ewell. Unable to resist the lure of close-up combat, he had gone forward to direct a charge by the 21st Georgia. As he knelt, squinting under the smoke for a glimpse of the enemy line, several of the Georgians called out proudly: "Here's General Ewell, boys!": whereupon the Federals, hearing the cheering, cut loose with heavy volleys in that direction. The regiment scattered, taking such losses here and elsewhere that it emerged from the battle with only 69 of its 242 men unhurt. Old Bald Head himself was found on the field when the fight was over, unconscious from loss of blood, one knee badly shattered by a minie. The surgeons assessed the damage and pronounced the verdict: amputation. Apparently he was out of the war for good. His successor was Alexander R. Lawton, who had held the rank of brigadier for sixteen months — longer than any other general in the army — apparently because Jackson, who had by-passed him in favor of Winder, did not consider him competent for divisional command. Now, as a result of attrition, his seniority could no longer be denied.

Any fight that cost the Confederacy the services of the profane and eccentric Ewell, along with those of the fast-developing Taliaferro and nearly a thousand other veterans of all ranks, could scarcely be called an unclouded victory, no matter who held the field when the smoke cleared. Moreover, Jackson himself had displayed symptoms of a relapse into tactical lethargy once the thing was under way. Yet if he felt either dismay or dissatisfaction at being thus deprived of two of his three chief lieutenants — all, in fact, but the one he trusted least, the thin-skinned and erratic A. P. Hill — he showed no signs of it, any more than he showed signs of apprehension for what Pope would surely try to do to him tomorrow. He seemed in fact, according to one of his soldiers, "calm as a May morning." What was left of the night he devoted to sleep. Purposely, as if with a shout of Boo! in the game of blindman's buff he was playing, he had attracted Pope's attention, hoping to hold him there by absorbing his attacks until Lee arrived with Longstreet and made possible a shift to the offensive he preferred.

★　★　★

Longstreet was nearer than Jackson knew: near enough, even, to have heard the tearing rattle of musketry in the twilight west of Groveton, six miles off, and to wonder at the silence that ensued. For Lee, who was with the approaching column, this was one more enigma to be added to the many that had fretted him since Stonewall marched away, four days ago. The first day had been spent continuing the artillery demonstration along the Rappahannock. That night, after wiring Davis to ask if more troops could be spared from the Richmond defenses, he sent Stuart off with all the cavalry. Next morning, August 26, he continued the cannonade, hoping to keep Pope's attention fixed on his front while Jackson moved around his flank to strike his rear. By midday, however, there were signs that the Federals were beginning to pull back: which might or might not mean that the ruse had been detected. Lee sent for Longstreet. The time had come to reunite the two wings of the army, he said, and he left to him the choice of routes, either up the Warrenton Pike or roundabout through Salem. Old Pete chose the latter. Leaving Major General R. H. Anderson's division, formerly Huger's, to hold the fords and mask the movement, he set out that afternoon with his other three divisions — Hood's, reinforced by Shanks Evans, whose brigade had come up from South Carolina; Brigadier General D. R. Jones', formerly half of Magruder's; and Longstreet's own, now split in two, under Brigadier Generals Cadmus Wilcox and James Kemper. This gave him, in effect, five divisions, each with three brigades; 32,000 men in all.

He made eleven miles before bivouacking near Orlean after nightfall, and by noon of the following day the head of the column had passed through Salem, matching the performance of Stonewall's fabled marchers over these same roads, thirty-six hours ago. That was gratifying indeed. Even more so, however, were two dispatches Lee received before going into bivouac on the outskirts of White Plains. The first was from Jackson, informing him that he had taken Bristoe and Manassas the night before. He was concentrating now at the latter place, he added, squarely in Pope's rear, and saw no evidence, so far, that the Federals were massing against him. The second welcome dispatch, brought by a courier from the opposite direction, was from Davis, replying to Lee's request for reinforcements. They were on the way, the President told him: Wade Hampton's cavalry brigade and two divisions of infantry under Harvey Hill and Major General Lafayette McLaws, the latter having been assigned the other half of Magruder's old command. Howls of protest might ordinarily be expected when his critics learned that the seat of government was being stripped of defenders, Davis said, but "confidence in you overcomes the view which would otherwise be taken of the exposed condition of Richmond, and the troops retained for the defense of the capital are surrendered to you on a new request."

Lee's anxiety, both for the present and the future, was considerably relieved. In addition to the badly needed brigade of cavalry — he had none at all for the screening of Longstreet's column; riding point that morning near Salem, he and his staff had barely avoided capture by a roving Federal squadron — the arrival of the promised ten brigades of infantry would add 17,000 veteran bayonets to his army. That would by no means even the odds Pope and Burnside and McClellan could bring to bear, combined, but it would at any rate reduce them to the vicinity of two to one: 150,000 vs 72,000. If the present odds were less heartening — McClellan, after all, might be with Pope already — in other respects the situation appeared quite promising. Reinforcements on the way, Jackson astride the railroad in Pope's rear, the main Union supply base up in flames: all this was much, besides which it held out interesting possibilities for maneuver. Manassas being just twenty-two miles from White Plains, Longstreet's present bivouac, Lee could reasonably expect to have the two wings of his army reunited by tomorrow night, prepared to undertake the completion of the "suppression" already begun. Before dawn, more good news arrived. Jackson informed him by courier that he was withdrawing from his exposed position at Manassas and would concentrate at Groveton, thus reducing by three full miles the interval between himself and Longstreet.

Refreshed by sleep, Old Pete's veterans swung off into a rising sun that seemed destined to shine today on a reunited Army of Northern Virginia. Only one natural obstacle lay in their path: Thoroughfare Gap. If the Yankees held it in strength there would be the delay of an uphill fight or a roundabout march, either of which would throw the schedule out of kilter. This seemed unlikely, though, since Jackson's couriers had been coming through unhindered, and presently another arrived, bringing further assurance that the pass was open and that his chief had reached Groveton, unmolested and unobserved, and was concentrating his troops in the woods overlooking the turnpike at that place. At 3 o'clock, topping the final rise that brought the gap into view, Longstreet's lead division pushed rapidly forward. Back with the main body, Lee presently heard from up ahead the reverberant clatter of musketry in the gorge. "Its echoes were wonderful," one staff officer later recalled. "A gun fired in its depths gave forth roars fit to bring down the skies."

Lee's reaction was less esthetic, for this of all sounds was the one he least wanted to hear. Then came the message that confirmed his fears: The Federals not only held the pass itself, they also had a reserve line posted on a dominant ridge beyond. John Pope had turned the tables, it seemed. Instead of panicking when he found Stonewall interposed between himself and Washington, the Union commander apparently had seized the initiative and posted his superior force between the two Confederate wings, preparing to crush them in sequence.

This was the darkest possible view. But Longstreet — "that undismayed warrior," his chief of staff afterwards called him, adding that he was "like a rock in steadiness when sometimes in battle the world seemed flying to pieces" — put his troops at once in motion to test the validity of such gloom. While Jones, supported by Kemper, kept up the pressure dead ahead, Hood probed for an opening near at hand and Wilcox set out for Hopewell Gap, three miles north. These dispositions took time. Near sunset, during lulls in the firing here at the pass, Lee heard from the direction of Groveton the mutter of distant musketry, mixed in with the grumble of guns. This was presently blotted out, however, by the stepped-up firing close at hand: Hood's men had found a cleft in the ridge and were on the Federal flank. Promptly the bluecoats retreated, unplugging the gap and withdrawing from the ridge beyond. (They were only a single division, after all, sent by McDowell on his own initiative, shortly before he wandered off and got himself lost in the woods.) Jones and Kemper marched through unopposed, joining Hood on the eastern slope, and the three divisions settled down to await the arrival of Wilcox, who had likewise penetrated Hopewell Gap.

Now that their own guns were silent, they heard again the growl and rumble of those near Groveton, half a dozen miles away. The uproar swelled to climax. Then it sank. At 9 o'clock it stopped. This might mean almost anything; all that was certain was that Jackson had been engaged. Whether he had won or lost — whether, indeed, that wing of the army still existed — they would know tomorrow. Whichever it was, it was over now. After sending a courier to inform Stonewall that the main body was safely through the pass, Lee told Longstreet to bed his men down for a good night's sleep in preparation for a fast march at sunup.

Friday, August 29, Hood's troops took the lead, marching so fast that their commander later reported proudly, "General Longstreet sent me orders, two or three times, to halt, since the army was unable to keep within supporting distance of my forces." There was need for haste. Ahead, the guns were booming again and a great white bank of smoke was piling up against the hot, bright blue, windless sky. Comforting though this was as proof that Jackson's men were still alive and kicking, it also demonstrated Pope's determination to destroy them before reinforcements got there. The Texans pushed on through Hay Market, raising a red cloud of dust with their feet, then down to Gainesville, where they struck the Warrenton Turnpike and swung left, advancing another three miles toward the ground-jarring thunder of guns, until they came upon Stonewall's right flank, above Groveton. It was now about 10 o'clock: Lee's army was reunited. Hood went into position north of the pike, establishing contact, and the other divisions filed into position on his right, extending the line generally southward, across the pike and down toward the Manassas Gap Railroad. From left to right, Longstreet's order of battle was Hood, Kemper, Jones, Wilcox. Anderson, who had masked the withdrawal from the Rappahannock line, was due to arrive by nightfall.

Moving from the scene of last night's bloody encounter, Jackson had placed his three divisions along the grade of an unfinished railroad. Part cut, part fill, it furnished an excellent defensive position, practically a ready-made system of intrenchments, roughly parallel to the turnpike across which Longstreet's line was drawn. When the Valley soldiers heard that their comrades had completed the march from Thoroughfare Gap and were filing into position on the right — "covered with dust so thick," one cavalryman observed, "that all looked as if they had been painted one color" — they rose and cheered them, despite the cannonade, which had scarcely slacked since sunup. Presently, though, they had more to worry about than bursting shells. The blue infantry was swarming to the attack.

The Federal chieftain's plans for a simultaneous double blow at both of Stonewall's flanks had gone astray, Porter having been delayed by darkness and two of the missing McDowell's three divisions having fallen back on Manassas after their twilight fights at Groveton and the Gap. "God damn McDowell, he's never where I want him," Pope was saying, angry but undaunted. He sent staff officers to locate them and hurry them along. Meanwhile, Sigel, Reno, and Heintzelman were at hand, and he flung them forward, still convinced that Jackson was trying to escape. One after another, they surged across the open fields, breaking in waves against the embankment where Stonewall's bayonets glittered. The closest they came to success was on the rebel left, where some woods afforded a covered approach. This was on Little Powell's front, the extreme flank of which was held by Brigadier General Maxcy Gregg's South Carolinians. Kearny's division struck hard here, effecting a lodgment astride the ramp and pressing down on the end of the line as if to roll it up. On a rocky knoll, here on the far-east margin of the conflict, Rebs and Yanks fought hand to hand. Bayonets crossed; rifle butts cracked skulls. A bachelor lawyer, somewhat deaf, Gregg strode up and down, brandishing an old Revolutionary scimitar and calling for a rally. "Let us die here, my men. Let us die here," he said. Many did die, something over 600 in all, but the knoll was held. The Federals withdrew.

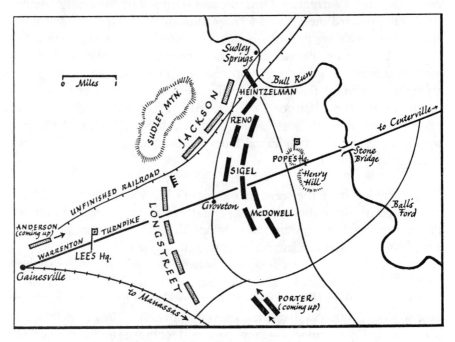

Hill did not think it would be for long. He sent word to Jackson that he would do his best, but that he doubted whether his men could withstand another such assault. Jackson sent the courier back with a sharp message: "Tell him if they attack him again he must beat them!" Riding toward the left to see for himself, he met the red-haired Hill coming to speak to him in person. "General, your men have done nobly," Jackson told him. "If you are attacked again, you will beat the enemy back." At this, the clatter broke out again in the woods on the left. "Here it comes," Hill said. As he turned his horse and rode back into the uproar, Jackson called after him: "I'll expect you to beat them!" The clatter rose to climax, then subsided. A messenger came galloping out of the smoke and pulled up alongside Jackson: "General Hill presents his respects and says the attack of the enemy was repulsed." Jackson smiled. "Tell him I knew he would do it," he said.

That was how it went, touch and go, all along his line all afternoon. Pope paid no mind to Longstreet, being unaware that he was even on the field: which, indeed, might practically as well have been the case, so far as relief of the pressure on Jackson was concerned, except for some batteries in brisk action on a ridge to Hood's left where the lines were hinged, like widespread jaws gaping east-southeast. Lee was quick to suggest that Old Pete swing the lower jaw forward and upward in order to engage the bluecoats and absorb some of the single-minded pressure they were applying to the weary men along the unfinished railroad. But Longstreet demurred. He never liked to go piecemeal into battle unprepared; Anderson was not yet up, and he had not had time enough for a thorough study of the ground. Besides, Stuart reported a force of undetermined strength gathering on the right; this, too, would have to be investigated. Regretfully Lee agreed to a delay. Longstreet left on a personal reconnaissance, then presently returned. He did not like the look of things. More Federals were coming up from the south, he said, in position to stab at his flank if he moved east. If they would venture squarely into the jaws, he would gladly clamp and chew them with gusto; but for the present he saw little profit, and much risk, in advancing.

Jackson rode up, dusty and worn. The two generals greeted him, and in reply to his statement that his line was hard pressed Lee turned to Longstreet. "Hadn't we better move our line forward?" he suggested.

"I think not," Longstreet said. "We had better wait until we hear more from Stuart about the force he has reported moving against us from Manassas."

A step-up in the firing toward the east caused Jackson to ride off in that direction. Federal dead and wounded were heaped along the forward slope where the Confederates, drawing their beads under cover of the cuts and fills, had dropped them. Charge after charge was repulsed all down the line, but this was accomplished at a high cost to the badly outnumbered defenders: especially when the fighting was conducted at close quarters, as it often was today. In Starke's division, on the right, not a single brigade was under a general officer, and one was led by a major. In Lawton's, when bull-voiced old Ike Trimble was hit and carried from the field, command of his brigade passed for a time to a captain. For the survivors, fighting their battle unrelieved and unsupported, this was the longest of all days. One remembered, years afterward, how he spent the infrequent lulls "praying that the great red sun, blazing and motionless overhead, would go down." He added, looking back: "For the first time in my life I understood what was meant by 'Joshua's sun standing still on Gibeon,' for it would not go down."

At last, however, as it approached the landline, Lee suggested for the third time that Longstreet attack. But Longstreet still demurred.

Stuart had identified the hovering bluecoats as Porter's corps, two veteran divisions. Besides, Old Pete had a new objection: There was too little daylight left. The best thing to do, he said, would be to make a forced reconnaissance at dusk; then, if an opening was discovered, the whole army could exploit it at dawn tomorrow. Once more Lee deferred to Longstreet, who assigned the task to Hood.

The Texans moved out at sunset, advancing up the Warrenton Turnpike, "the light of battle in our eyes — I reckon," one recalled — "and fear of it in our hearts — I know." They collided in the dusk with King's division, returning from Manassas, in a fight so confused that one Union major was captured when he tried to rally a regiment that turned out to be the 2d Mississippi. Hood held his ground, driving the weary Federals back, but when he reported to Lee and Longstreet after dark, he recommended that his troops be withdrawn to their original position. Nor did he think that an attack next morning would succeed in that direction; the enemy position was too strong, he said. Thus Longstreet's daylong judgment was apparently confirmed. Lee gave Hood permission to withdraw, which he did, encountering in the darkness the men of Anderson's division, just arrived from Thoroughfare Gap, and thus prevented them from stumbling blindly into the Union lines.

The long day's fight was over. Out across the night-shrouded fields and in the woods behind the corpse-strewn embankment, the groans of the wounded were incessant. "Water! For God's sake, water!" men were crying. Jackson's medical director, reporting the heavy casualties to his chief, said proudly: "General, this day has been won by nothing but stark and stern fighting." Stonewall shook his head. "No," he said. "It has been won by nothing but the blessing and protection of Providence."

Dawn found Pope in excellent spirits. His headquarters were on a little knoll in the northeast quadrant formed by the intersection of the Manassas-Sudley road with the Warrenton Turnpike, and as he stood there in the growing light, burly and expansive, smoking a cigar and chatting informally with his staff and those commanders who found time to ride over for a visit, the gruffness which was habitual — one of his aides referred to it as "infusing some of his western energy into the caravan" — seemed merely a form of bantering this morning, pleased as he was with the overall success of his efforts to keep Stonewall from escaping. He had cast his net and the foe was entangled; now all that remained, apparently, was the agreeable task of hauling him in, hand over hand.

By no means had all gone to suit him yesterday. The attacks, though pressed with vigor, had been delivered somewhat piecemeal. Most irksome of all, Fitz-John Porter had declined to advance against

Jackson's right flank, claiming that Longstreet barred the way with something like three times as many men as he himself had. Pope did not believe this for an instant. At 4.30 he repeated his orders for Porter to "press forward into action at once on the enemy's flank, and, if possible, on his rear." Porter balked, still insisting that he had more than half of the rebel army to his front, and darkness fell before Pope could budge him. Disappointed, the Federal commander moved the sluggish Porter around to the main line, paralleling the turnpike, and prepared for an all-out assault at dawn, when he wired Halleck a summary of his achievements: "We fought a terrific battle here yesterday ... which lasted with continuous fury from daybreak until dark, by which time the enemy was driven from the field, which we now occupy. Our troops are too much exhausted yet to push matters, but I shall do so in the course of the morning. . . . The enemy is still in our front, but badly used up. We have lost not less than 8000 men killed and wounded, but from the appearance of the field the enemy lost at least two to one. He stood strictly on the defensive, and every assault was made by ourselves. Our troops behaved splendidly. The battle was fought on the identical battlefield of Bull Run, which greatly increased the enthusiasm of our men." In midparagraph he added, "The news just reaches me from the front that the enemy is retreating toward the mountains. I go forward at once to see."

He did go forward, onto the knoll at any rate, and what he saw encouraged him still more. Where bayonets had glittered yesterday along the bed of the unfinished railroad, the goal of so many charges that had broken in blood along its base, today there was stillness and apparent vacancy. Only a few gray riflemen contested the sniping from Federal outposts. Combined with the knowledge of Hood's withdrawal down the turnpike after midnight, this intelligence led Pope to believe that Jackson had pulled out, leaving only a skeleton force to discourage the blue pursuit. Still, anxious though he was to garner the utmost fruits of victory, Pope curbed his tendency toward rashness. In the end, he knew, more would be gained if the chase was conducted in a well-coördinated fashion than if he took off half-cocked and overeager. While he stood there on the headquarters knoll, wreathed in cigar smoke as he chatted with his staff, orders went out prescribing the dispositions for pursuit. McDowell would be in general charge of the two-pronged advance. Porter's corps and two divisions from McDowell's would move directly down the pike; Heintzelman's corps, supported by McDowell's other division, would move up the Hay Market road. With Stonewall's getaway thus contested in both directions, troop commanders were expressly instructed to "press him vigorously during the whole day."

All this took time, but Pope felt he could afford it now that he had a full-scale victory under his belt. Careful preparations, with strict attention to details, would pay dividends in the long run, when the rebels were brought to bay and the mopping-up began. Noon came and went. A heavy silence lay over the heat-shimmered field, broken from time to time by sputters of fire exchanged by the men on outpost. At 2 o'clock, informed that all was in order at last, Pope gave the signal and the pursuit got under way.

　　Deliberate though these preparations were, the pursuit itself — or anyhow what Pope conceived as such — was probably the briefest of the war. Jackson was by no means retreating; he had merely withdrawn his troops for some unmolested and hard-earned rest in the woods along the base of Sudley Mountain just in his rear, leaving a thin line to man the works and give the alarm in case the Yankees showed signs of advancing. He doubted that they would do so, after their failures yesterday, but he was perfectly willing to meet them if they tried it. Longstreet — who was very much on hand with all five of his divisions, no matter what evidence Pope had received (or deduced) in denial of the fact — was more than willing; he was downright eager. In fact, now that Porter's corps had been shifted from its threatening position off his flank, he desired nothing in all the world quite so much as that the Federals would launch a full-scale attack across his front, though he too doubted that Fortune's smile could ever be that broad.

　　Lee, who doubted it most of all, began to be concerned that Pope would get away unsuppressed, having suffered only such punishment as Jackson had managed to inflict while receiving his headlong charges the day before. As the long morning wore away, marked by nothing more eventful than the occasional growl of a battery or the isolated sputter of an argument between pickets, Lee took the opportunity to catch up on his correspondence. "My desire," he wrote the President, "has been to avoid a general engagement, being the weaker force, and by maneuvering to relieve the portion of the country referred to." By this he meant the region along the Rappahannock, whose relief had been accomplished by forcing Pope's retreat on Manassas. Now his mind turned to the possibilities at hand. If Pope would not attack, then he would have to be "maneuvered." About noon, while Lee was working on a plan for moving again around his opponent's right, crossing Bull Run above Sudley Springs in order to threaten his rear, Stuart came to headquarters with an interesting report. He had sent a man up a large walnut tree, Jeb said, and the man had spotted the bluecoats massing in three heavy lines along Jackson's front. Quickly Lee sent couriers to warn of the danger. Jackson alerted his troops but kept them in the woods. He had been observing the Federal activity for some time, but, concluding that nothing would come of it, had remarked to the colonel commanding the Stonewall Brigade: "Well, it looks as if there will be no fight today. . . ."

Shortly before 3 o'clock he found out just how wrong he was. Suddenly, without even the warning preamble of an artillery bombardment, the blue infantry came roaring at him in three separate waves, stretching left and right as far as the eye could see. Buglers along the unfinished railroad gobbled staccato warnings, and the startled troops came running out of the woods to man the line. This was far worse than yesterday. Not only were the attacking forces much heavier; they seemed much more determined, individually and in mass, not to be denied a lodgment. Immediately Jackson began to receive urgent requests for reinforcements all along the front. One officer rode up to report that his brigade commander had been shot down and the survivors were badly shaken. They needed help.

"What brigade, sir?" Jackson asked, not having caught the name.

"The Stonewall Brigade."

"Go back," Jackson told him. "Give my compliments to them, and tell the Stonewall Brigade to maintain her reputation."

For the present, reduced though it was to a ghost of its former self, the brigade managed to do as its old commander asked; but how long it would be able to continue to do so, under the strain, was another question. Rifle barrels grew too hot to handle, and at several points the defenders exhausted their ammunition. At one such critical location, the enemy having penetrated to within ten yards of the embankment, the graybacks beat them back with rocks. All along the two-mile front, the situation was desperate; no sooner was the pressure relieved in one spot than it increased again in another. Broken, then restored, Hill's line wavered like a shaken rope. He was down to his last ounce of strength, he reported, and still the bluecoats came against him, too thick and fast for killing to do more than slow them down. Whereupon Jackson, who had no reserves to send in response to Hill's plea for reinforcements, did something he had never done before. Outnumbered three to one by the attackers, whose bullets he was opposing with flung stones, he appealed to Lee to send him help from Longstreet.

In the Federal ranks there was also a measure of consternation, especially at the brevity of what they had been assured was a "pursuit." Recovering from the shock of this discovery, however, the men fought with redoubled fury, as if glad of a chance to take their resentment of Pope out on the rebels. As usual, McDowell came in for his share of their bitterness — as witness the following exchange between a gray-haired officer and a wounded noncom limping rearward out of the fight:

"Sergeant, how does the battle go?"

"We're holding our own; but McDowell has charge of the left."

"Then God save the left!"

For the better part of an hour they came on, running hunched as if into a high wind, charging shoulder to shoulder across fields where long tendrils and sheets of gunsmoke writhed and billowed, sulphurous and "tinged with a hot coppery hue by the rays of the declining sun." One among them was to remember it so, along with the accompanying distraction of rebel shells "continually screeching over our heads or plowing the gravelly surface with an ugly rasping whirr that makes one's flesh creep." Still they came on. Time after time, they faltered within reach of the flame-stitched crest of the embankment, then time after time came on again, stumbling over the huddled blue forms that marked the limits of their previous advances. They battered thus at Jackson's line as if at a locked gate, beyond which they could see the cool green fields of peace. Determined to swing it ajar or knock it flat, they struck it again and again, flesh against metal, and feeling it tremble and crack at the hinges and hasp, they battered harder.

Longstreet stood on the ridge where his and Jackson's lines were hinged. This not only gave him a panoramic view of the action, it also afforded an excellent position for massing the eighteen guns of a reserve artillery battalion which had arrived at dawn. The batteries were sighted so that they commanded, up to a distance of about 2000 yards to the east and northeast, the open ground across which the Federals were advancing. For the better part of an hour the cannoneers had watched hungrily while the blue waves were breaking against Stonewall's right and center, perpendicular to and well within range of their guns. This was the answer to an artillerist's prayer, but Old Pete was in no hurry. He was saving this for a Sunday punch, to be delivered when the time was right and the final Union reserves had been committed. Then it came: Jackson's appeal for assistance, forwarded by Lee with the recommendation that a division of troops be sent. "Certainly," Longstreet said. He spoke calmly, suppressing the excitement he and all around him felt as they gazed along the troughs and crests of the blue waves rolling northward under the muzzles of his guns. "But before the division can reach him, the attack will be broken by artillery."

So it was. When Longstreet turned at last and gave the signal that unleashed them, the gunners leaped to their pieces and let fly, bowling their shots along the serried rows of Federals who up to now had been unaware of the danger to their flank. The effect was instantaneous. Torn and blasted by this fire, the second and third lines milled aimlessly, bewildered, then retreated in disorder: whereupon the first-line soldiers, looking back over their shoulders to find their supports in flight, also began to waver and give ground. This was that trembling instant when the battle scales of Fortune signal change, one balance pan beginning to rise as the other sinks.

Down on the flat, just after remarking calmly to one of his staff as he watched a line of wagons pass to the front, "I observe that some of those mules are without shoes: I wish you would see to it that all of the animals are shod at once," Lee heard the uproar and divined its meaning. Without a change of expression, he sent word to Longstreet that if he saw any better way to relieve the pressure on Jackson than by sending troops, he should adopt it. Headquarters wigwagged a signal station on the left: "Do you still want reinforcements?" When the answer came back, "No. The enemy are giving way," Lee knew the time had come to accomplish Pope's suppression by launching an all-out counterstroke to compound the blue confusion. An order went at once to Longstreet, directing him to go forward with every man in his command. It was not needed; Old Pete was already in motion, bearing down on the moil of Federals out on the plain. A similar order went to Jackson, together with a warning: "General Longstreet is advancing. Look out for and protect his left flank." But this also was unnecessary. When Stonewall's men saw the bluecoats waver on their front, they too started forward. Right and left, as the widespread jaws began to close, the weird halloo of the rebel yell rang out.

Porter's corps was on the exposed flank, under the general direction of McDowell, and Porter, who had been expressing dark forebodings all along — "I hope Mac is at work, and we will soon get ordered out of this," he had written Burnside the night before — had taken the precaution of stationing two New York regiments, the only volunteer outfits in Sykes' division of regulars, on his left as a shield against disaster. Facing west along the base of a little knoll on which a six-gun battery was posted, these New Yorkers caught the brunt of Longstreet's assault, led by Hood. One regiment, thrown forward as a skirmish line, was quickly overrun. The other — Zouaves, nattily dressed in white spats, tasseled fezzes, short blue jackets, and baggy scarlet trousers — stood on the slope itself, holding firm while the battery flailed the attackers, then finally limbered and got away, permitting the New Yorkers to retire. They did this at a terrible cost, however. Out of 490 present when the assault began, 124 were dead and 223 had been wounded by the time it was over: which amounted to the largest percentage of men killed in any Federal regiment in any single battle of the war. Next morning, one of Hood's men became strangely homesick at the sight of the dead Zouaves strewn about in their gaudy clothes. According to him, they gave the western slope of the little knoll "the appearance of a Texas hillside when carpeted in the spring by wild flowers of many hues and tints."

The respite bought with their blood, however brief, had given Pope time to bring up reinforcements from the right, and they too offered what resistance they could to the long gray line surging eastward along both sides of the pike. This was undulating country, with easy ridges at right angles to the advance, so that to one defender it seemed that the Confederates, silhouetted against the great red ball of the setting sun, "came on like demons emerging from the earth." There was delay as Longstreet's left became exposed to enfilading fire from some batteries on Jackson's right, but when these were silenced the advance swept on, tilted battle flags gleaming in the sunset. On Henry Hill, where Stonewall had won his nickname thirteen months ago, Sykes' regulars stood alongside the Pennsylvanians of Reynolds' division — he had been exchanged since his capture near Gaines Mill — and hurled back the disjointed rebel attacks that continued on through twilight into darkness.

There was panic, but it was not of the kind that had characterized the retreat from this same field the year before. The regulars were staunch, now as then, but there was by no means the same difference, in that respect, between them and the volunteers. Sigel's Germans and the men with Reno also managed to form knots of resistance, while the rest withdrew across Stone Bridge in a drizzle of rain. McDowell, seeing the Iron Brigade hold firm along a critical ridge, put Gibbon in charge of the rear guard and gave him instructions to blow up the bridge when his Westerners had crossed over.

After McDowell left, Phil Kearny rode up, empty sleeve flapping, spike whiskers bristling with anger at the sudden reverse the army had suffered. "I suppose you appreciate the condition of affairs here, sir," he cried. "It's another Bull Run, sir. It's another Bull Run!" When Gibbon said he hoped it was not as bad as that, Kearny snapped: "Perhaps not. Reno is keeping up the fight. He is not stampeded; I am not stampeded; you are not stampeded. That is about all, sir. My God, that's about all!"

Two miles west of there, near Groveton, Lee was composing a dispatch to be telegraphed to Richmond for release by the President:

> This army today achieved on the plains of Manassas a signal victory over combined forces of Generals McClellan and Pope. . . . We mourn the loss of our gallant dead in every conflict, yet our gratitude to Almighty God for his mercies rises higher and higher each day. To Him and to the valor of our troops a nation's gratitude is due.

His losses were 1481 killed, 7627 wounded, 89 missing; Pope's were 1724 killed, 8372 wounded, 5958 missing. Lee reported the capture of 7000 prisoners, exclusive of 2000 wounded left by Pope on the field, along with 30 guns and 20,000 small arms, numerous colors, and a vast amount of stores in addition to those consumed or destroyed by Jackson at Manassas Junction two days back.

Nor was that all. A larger triumph was reflected in the contrast between the present overall military situation, here in the East, and that which had existed when Lee assumed command three months ago. McClellan had stood within sight of the spires of Richmond; Jackson had been in flight up the Shenandoah Valley, pursued by superior enemy combinations; West Virginia had been completely in Federal hands, as well as most of coastal North Carolina, with invasion strongly threatened from both directions. Now Richmond had not only been delivered, but the Union host was in full retreat on Washington, with the dome of the Capitol practically in view and government clerks being mustered for a last-ditch defense of the city; the Valley was rapidly being scoured of the blue remnants left behind when Pope assembled his army to cross the Rappahannock; West Virginia was almost cleared of Federals, and the North Carolina coast was safe. Except for the garrisons at Fort Monroe and Norfolk, the only bluecoats within a hundred miles of the southern capital were prisoners of war and men now busy setting fire to U.S. stores and equipment at Aquia Creek, just north of Fredericksburg, preparing for a hasty evacuation.

Nor was that all, either. Beyond all this, there was the transformation effected within the ranks of the Army of Northern Virginia itself: a lifting of morale, based on a knowledge of the growth of its fighting skill. Gone were the clumsy combinations of the Seven Days, the piecemeal attacks launched headlong against positions of the enemy's own choice. Here in the gallant rivalry of Manassas, where Longstreet's soldiers vied with Jackson's for the "suppression" of an opponent they despised, the victory formula had apparently been found; Lee's orders had been carried out instinctively, in some cases even before they were delivered. Tonight at army headquarters, which had been set up in an open field with a campfire of boards to read dispatches by, there was rejoicing and an air of mutual congratulation as officer after officer arrived to report new incidents of triumph. Lee — who had told his wife a month ago, "In the prospect before me I cannot see a single ray of pleasure during this war" — stood in the firelight, gray and handsome, impeccably uniformed, welcoming subordinates with the accustomed grace of a Virginia host.

"General, here is someone who wants to speak to you," a staff captain said.

Lee turned and saw a smoke-grimed cannoneer standing before him, still with a sponge staff in one hand. "Well, my man, what can I do for you?"

"Why, General, don't you know me?" Robert wailed.

There was laughter at this, a further lifting of spirits as troop commanders continued to report of the day's successes. Hood rode up, weary but still elated over what he called "the most beautiful battle scene I have ever beheld." When Lee, adopting the bantering tone he often used in addressing the blond young man, asked what had become of the enemy, Hood replied that his Texans had driven them "almost at a double-quick" across Bull Run. He added that it had been a wonderful sight to see the Confederate battle flags "dancing after the Federals as they ran in full retreat." Lee dropped his jesting manner and said gravely, "God forbid I should ever live to see our colors moving in the opposite direction."

While Lee was at Groveton, composing the dispatch to Davis, Pope was at Centerville, composing one to Halleck. All things being considered, the two were by no means as different as might have been expected.

> We have had a terrific battle again today.... Under all the circumstances, both horses and men having been two days without food, and the enemy greatly outnumbering us, I thought it best to draw back to this place at dark. The movement has been made in perfect order and without loss. The troops are in good heart, and marched off the field without the least hurry or confusion.... Do not be uneasy. We will hold our own here.... P.S. We have lost nothing; neither guns nor wagons.

Of the several inaccuracies here involved (one being the comparison of forces; Lee had had 50,000 men engaged, while Pope had had 60,000 — exclusive of Banks, who was guarding his trains) the greatest, perhaps, was the one in which he declared that his troops were "in good heart." It was true that, after the first wild scramble for an exit, they had steadied and retired in column, under cover of the rear-guard action on Henry Hill; but their spirits were in fact so far from being high that they could scarcely have been lower. If Pope did not know the extent of his defeat, his men did. They agreed with the verdict later handed down by one of their corps historians, that Pope "had been kicked, cuffed, hustled about, knocked down, run over, and trodden upon as rarely happens in the history of war. His communications had been cut; his headquarters pillaged; a corps had marched into his rear, and had encamped at its ease upon the railroad by which he received his supplies; he had been beaten or foiled in every attempt he had made to 'bag' those defiant intruders; and, in the end, he was glad to find a refuge in the intrenchments of Washington, whence he had sallied forth, six weeks before, breathing out threatenings and slaughter."

They agreed with this in all its harshness, but just now what they mainly were was sullen. They had fought well and they knew it. Defeat had come, not because they were outfought, but because they were outgeneraled — or misgeneraled. As one of their number put it, "All knew and felt that as soldiers we had not had a fair chance." The fault, they believed, was Pope's; he had "acted like a dunderpate." And McDowell's; he had revived their suspicions by repeating his past performance on this field. "General McDowell was viewed as a traitor by a large majority of the officers and men," one diarist wrote, adding: "Thousands of soldiers firmly believed that their lives would be purposely wasted if they obeyed his orders in the time of the conflict." The story was told that one of his regiments had stepped gingerly up to the firing line, loosed a random volley, then turned and made for the rear, the men shouting over their shoulders as they ran: "You can't play it on us!" Slogging tonight through the drizzle of rain, they saw him sitting his horse beside the pike, identifiable in the murk because of the outlandish silhouette of his canvas helmet. One Massachusetts private nudged another, pointing, and said darkly: "How guilty he looks, with that basket on his head!"

Pope, too, came in for his share of abuse. "Open sneering at General Pope was heard on all sides," one veteran observed. Another, passing the luckless commander by the roadside, hailed him with a quote from Horace Greeley: "Go west, young man! Go west!" Perhaps this had something to do with changing his mind as to the state of his men's hearts. At any rate, when morning came — Sunday, August 31 — he wired Halleck: "Our troops are ... much used-up and worn-out," and he spoke of giving the enemy "as desperate a fight as I can force our men to stand up to." Franklin's corps had come up the night before, in time to establish a straggler line in front of Centerville; Sumner too was at hand, giving Pope 20,000 fresh troops with which to oppose the rebels. But his confidence was ebbing. He told Halleck, "I should like to know whether you feel secure about Washington should this army be destroyed. I shall fight it as long as a man will stand up to the work. You must judge what is to be done, having in view the safety of the capital."

No sooner had he sent this, however, than a reply to last night's rosy message bucked him up again. "My Dear General: You have done nobly," Halleck wired. "Don't yield another inch if you can avoid it." Pope thanked him for this "considerate commendation" and passed along the encouraging news that "Ewell is killed. Jackson is badly wounded. ... The plan of the enemy will undoubtedly be to turn my flank. If he does so he will have his hands full." Meanwhile, Franklin's soldiers mocked and taunted the bedraggled Army of Virginia, jeering along the straggler line at its "new route" to Richmond. Overnight, Pope's confidence took another sickening drop. Three hours after sunrise, September 1, he got off another long dispatch to Halleck. After a bold beginning — "All was quiet yesterday and so far this morning. My men are resting; they need it much. ... I shall attack again tomorrow if I can; the next day certainly" — he passed at once to darker matters: "I think it my duty to call your attention to the unsoldierly and dangerous conduct of many brigade and some division commanders of the forces sent here from the Peninsula. Every word and act and intention is discouraging, and calculated to break down the spirits of the men and produce disaster." In the light of this, he closed with a recommendation that ran counter to the intention expressed at the outset: "My advice to you — I give it with freedom, as I know you will not misunderstand it — is that, in view of any satisfactory results, you draw back this army to the intrenchments in front of Washington, and set to work in that secure place to reorganize and rearrange it. You may avoid great disaster by doing so."

While waiting to see what would come of this, he found that Jackson (who was no more wounded than Ewell was dead) was in the act of fulfilling his prediction that Lee would try to turn his flank. Stonewall's men had crossed Bull Run at Sudley Springs, then moved north to the Little River Turnpike, which led southeast to Fairfax Courthouse, eight miles in the Union rear. Pope pulled the troops of Phil Kearny and Brigadier General I. I. Stevens, who commanded Burnside's other division under Reno, out of their muddy camps and sent them slogging northward to intercept the rebel column. They did so, late that afternoon. There beside the pike, around a mansion called Chantilly, a wild fight took place during a thunderstorm so violent that it drowned the roar of cannon. Jackson's march had been slow; consequently he was in a grim and savage humor. In the rain-lashed confusion, when one of his colonels requested that his men be withdrawn because their cartridges were too wet to ignite, the reply came back: "My compliments to Colonel Blank, and tell him the enemy's ammunition is just as wet as his."

This spirit was matched on the Federal side by Kearny, who dashed from point to point, his empty sleeve flapping as he rode with the reins clamped in his teeth in order to have his one arm free to gesture with his saber, hoicking his troops up to the firing line and holding them there by showing no more concern for bullets than he did for raindrops. His prescription for success in leading men in battle was a simple one; "You must never be afraid of anything," he had told a young lieutenant two days ago. Stevens followed his example, and between them they made Stonewall call a halt. The firing continued into early darkness, when on A. P. Hill's front the men were surprised to see a Union general come riding full-tilt toward them, suddenly illuminated by a flash of lightning. They called on him to surrender, but he whirled his mount, leaning forward onto its withers with his arm around its neck, and tried to gallop away in the confusion. They fired a volley that unhorsed him, and when they went out to pick him up they found that he was dead, lying one-armed in the mud, the back of his coat and the seat of his trousers torn by bullets. They brought his body into their lines. "Poor Kearny," Hill said, looking down at him. "He deserved a better death than that."

Stevens too was dead by now, shot while leading a charge, and the Federals fell back down the pike and through the woods. They did so more from being disheartened by the loss of their leaders, however, than from being pressed; Jackson did not pursue. Thus ended the Battle of Chantilly, a rain-swept drama with off-stage thunder, vivid flashes of lightning, and an epilogue supplied next morning by Lee, who sent Kearny's body forward under a flag of truce, "thinking that the possession of his remains may be a consolation to his family."

Pope by then was back at Fairfax, within twenty miles of Washington, having received from Halleck the instructions he had sought: "You will bring your forces as best you can within or near the line of fortification." As the army retreated — "by squads, companies, and broken parts of regiments and brigades," according to one enlisted diarist — its commander lost the final vestige of his former boldness. "The straggling is awful in the regiments from the Peninsula," he complained to Halleck. "Unless something can be done to restore tone to this army it will melt away before you know it." This was a new and different Pope, a Pope not unlike a sawdust doll with most of its stuffing leaked away. A surgeon who looked through a headquarters window the previous evening saw him so: "He sat with his chair tipped back against the wall, his hands clasped behind his head, which bent forward, his chin touching his breast — seeming to pay no attention to the generals as they arrived, but to be wholly wrapped in his own gloomy reflections." The doctor wrote long afterward, and being a kind-hearted man, who had dealt with much misery in his life, he added: "I pitied him then. I pity him now."

It was perhaps the only pity felt for him by anyone in the whole long weary column slogging its way eastward. Last night's thunderstorm had deepened the mud along the pike, and overhead a scud of clouds obscured the sun, which shed an eerie yellow light upon the sodden fields. In a way, though, the weather was fitting, matching as it did the mood of the retreat. "Everyone you met had an unwashed, sleepy, downcast aspect," one officer observed, "and looked as if he would like to hide his head somewhere from all the world." Now that the immediate danger was past, a still worse reaction of sullenness had set in among the troops, whose mistrust of Pope quite balanced his expressed mistrust of them. As one colonel put it, "No salutary fear kept them in the ranks, and many gave way to the temptation to take a rest. ... There was everywhere along the road the greatest confusion. Infantry and cavalry, artillery and wagons, all hurried on pell mell, in the midst of rallying cries of officers and calls and oaths of the men."

Banks had come up from Bristoe Station, bringing the army's wagons with him though he had been obliged to put the torch to all the locomotives and freight cars loaded with stores and munitions from Warrenton and other points below the wreckage of Broad Run bridge. His corps, having seen no fighting since Cedar Mountain, was assigned the rear guard duty, which consisted mainly of prodding frazzled stragglers back into motion and gathering up abandoned equipment littered along the roadside. At the head of the column — miles away, for the various units were badly strung out, clotted in places and gapped in others as a result of accordion action — rode Pope and McDowell, attended by their staffs and followed closely by the lead division, formerly King's but now under Brigadier General John P. Hatch, who had succeeded the ailing King. That afternoon the sun came out, but it did little to revive the downcast marchers: least of all Hatch, who had more cause for gloom than most. He had commanded a cavalry brigade, that being the arm of service he preferred, until Pope relieved him for inefficiency and transferred him to the infantry. So Hatch had this to brood over, in addition to the events of the past few days. Then suddenly, up ahead, he saw something that made him forget his and the army's troubles.

Off to one side loomed Munson's Hill, which Joe Johnston had held with a dummy gun last winter. From its crown, Hatch knew, you could see the dome of the Capitol. But what engaged his attention just now was a small group of horsemen coming down the road toward Pope and McDowell: particularly the man in front, who rode a large black horse and wore a vivid yellow sash about his waist. Hatch thought there was something familiar about the trim and dapper way he sat his charger. Then, as the man reined to a halt in front of the two generals, returning their salutes with one of his own which "seemed to carry a little of personal good fellowship to even the humblest private soldier," Hatch knew the unbelievable was true; it was Little Mac. He spurred ahead in time to hear McClellan tell Pope and McDowell he had been authorized to take command of the army. Off to the left rear just then there was a sudden thumping of artillery, dim in the distance. What was that? McClellan asked. Pope said it was probably an attack on Sumner, whose corps was guarding the flank in that direction. Then he inquired if there would be any objection if he and McDowell rode on toward Washington. None at all, McClellan replied; but as for himself, he was riding toward the sound of gunfire.

Before the two could resume their journey, Hatch took advantage of the chance to revenge the wrong he believed had been done when his cavalry brigade was taken from him the month before. Trotting back to the head of his infantry column, within easy hearing distance of Pope and McDowell, he shouted: "Boys, McClellan is in command of the army again! Three cheers!" The result, after an instant of shock while the words sank in, was pandemonium. Caps and knapsacks went sailing high in the air, and men who a moment ago had been too weary and dispirited to do anything more than plant one leaden foot in front of the other were cheering themselves hoarse, capering about, and slapping each other joyfully on the back. "From an extreme sadness," one Massachusetts volunteer recalled, "we passed in a twinkling to a delirium of delight. A deliverer had come." This was the reaction all down the column as the news traveled back along its length, pausing at the gaps between units, then being taken up again, moving westward like a spark along a ten-mile train of powder.

Such demonstrations were not restricted to green troops, volunteers likely to leap at every rumor. Sykes' regulars, for example, were far back toward the rear and did not learn of the change till after nightfall. They were taking a rest-halt, boiling coffee in a roadside field, when an officer on picket duty saw by starlight the familiar figure astride Dan Webster coming down the pike. "Colonel! Colonel!" he hollered, loud enough to be heard all over the area, "General McClellan is here!" Within seconds every man was on his feet and cheering, raising what one of them called "such a hurrah as the Army of the Potomac had never heard before. Shout upon shout went out into the stillness of the night; and as it was taken up along the road and repeated by regiment, brigade, division and corps, we could hear the roar dying away in the distance. The effect of this man's presence upon the Army of the Potomac — in sunshine or rain, in darkness or in daylight, in victory or defeat — was electrical." Hard put for words to account for the delirium thus provoked, he could only add that it was "too wonderful to make it worth while attempting to give a reason for it."

Nor was the enthusiasm limited to veterans of Little Mac's own army, men who had fought under him before. When Gibbon announced the new commander's arrival to the survivors of the Iron Brigade, they too reacted with unrestrained delight, tossing their hats and breaking ranks to jig and whoop, just as the Peninsula boys were doing. Later that night, Gibbon remembered afterward, "the weary, fagged men went into camp cheerful and happy, to talk over their rough experience of the past three weeks and speculate as to what was ahead."

It was Lincoln's doing, his alone, and he had done it against the will of a majority of his advisers. Chase believed that the time had come, beyond all doubt, when "either the government or McClellan must go down," and Stanton had prepared and was soliciting cabinet signatures for an ultimatum demanding "the immediate removal of George B. McClellan from any command in the armies of the United States." When Welles protested that such a document showed little consideration for their chief, the War Secretary bristled and said coldly: "I know of no particular obligation I am under to the President. He called me to a difficult position and imposed on me labors and responsibilities which no man could carry." Already he had secured four signatures — his own, Chase's, Bates', and Smith's — and was working hard for more (Welles and Blair were obdurate, and Seward was still out of town) when, on the morning of this same September 2, he came fuming into the room where his colleagues were waiting for Lincoln to arrive and open the meeting. It was a time of strain. Reports of Pope's defeat had caused Stanton to call out the government clerks, order the contents of the arsenal shipped to New York, and forbid the retail sale of spirituous liquors in the city. Now came the climactic blow as he announced, in a choked voice, the rumor that McClellan had been appointed to conduct the defense of Washington.

The effect was stunning: a sort of reversal of what would happen later that day along the blue column plodding east from Fairfax. Just as Chase was declaring that, if true, this would "prove a national calamity," Lincoln came in and confirmed the rumor. That was why he was late for the meeting, he explained. He and Halleck had just come from seeing McClellan and ordering him to assume command of the armies roundabout the capital. Stanton broke in, trembling as he spoke: "No order to that effect has been issued from the War Department." Lincoln turned and faced him. "The order is mine," he said, "and I will be responsible for it to the country."

Four nights ago he had gone to bed confident that the army had won a great victory on the plains of Manassas: a triumph which, according to Pope, would be enlarged when he took up the pursuit of Jackson's fleeing remnant. Overnight, however, word arrived that it was Pope who was in retreat, not Stonewall, and Lincoln came into his secretary's room next morning, long-faced and discouraged. "Well, John, we are whipped again, I am afraid," he said. All day the news got worse as details of the fiasco trickled through the screen of confusion. Halleck was a weak prop to lean on; Lincoln by now had observed that his general in chief was "little more than . . . a first-rate clerk." What was worse, he was apt to break down under pressure; which was presently what happened. Before the night was over, Old Brains appealed to McClellan at Alexandria: "I beg of you to assist me in this crisis with your ability and experience. I am utterly tired out."

Lincoln's mind was also turning in Little Mac's direction, although not without reluctance. Unquestionably, it appeared to him, McClellan had acted badly in regard to Pope. One of his subordinates had even been quoted as saying publicly, "I don't care for John Pope a pinch of owl dung." It seemed to Lincoln that they had wanted Pope to fail, no matter what it cost in the blood of northern soldiers. McClellan, when appealed to for counsel, had advised the President to concentrate all the reserves in the capital intrenchments and "leave Pope to get out of his scrape" as best he could. To Lincoln this seemed particularly callous, if not crazy; his mistrust of the Young Napoleon was increased. But early Tuesday morning, when Pope warned that "unless something can be done to restore tone to this army it will melt away before you know it," he did what he knew he had to do. "We must use what tools we have," he told his secretary. "There is no man in the army who can man these fortifications and lick these troops of ours into shape half as well as [McClellan]. . . . If he can't fight himself, he excels in making others ready to fight."

So he went to him and told him to return to the army whose wounded were already beginning to pour into the city. And that afternoon, despite the howls of the cabinet — Stanton was squelched, but Chase was sputtering, "I cannot but feel that giving command to McClellan is equivalent to giving Washington to the rebels" — Lincoln had Halleck issue the formal order: "Major General McClellan will have command of the fortifications of Washington and of all the troops for the defense of the capital." This left Pope to be disposed of, which was done three days later. "The Armies of the Potomac and Virginia being consolidated," he was told by dispatch, "you will report for orders to the Secretary of War." Reporting as ordered, he found himself assigned to duty against the Sioux, who had lately risen in Minnesota. From his headquarters in St Paul, where he was settled before the month was out, Pope protested vehemently against the injustice of being "banished to a remote and unimportant command." But there he stayed, for the duration.

Two Advances; Two Retreats

★ ✗ ☆

🔫 ON THE DAY LEE WRECKED POPE ON THE plains of Manassas, driving him headlong across Bull Run to begin his scamper for the Washington intrenchments, Kirby Smith accomplished in Kentucky the nearest thing to a Cannae ever scored by any general, North or South, in the course of the whole war. This slashing blow, the first struck in the two-pronged offensive Bragg had designed to recover for the Confederacy all that had been lost by his predecessors, was delivered in accordance with Smith's precept, announced at the outset, that "brilliant results . . . will be accomplished only with hard fighting."

Accordingly, on August 25, after a week's rest at Barbourville, he had resumed his northward march. There were 21,000 men in his four divisions, but the largest of these — 9000-strong; the others had about 4000 each — remained in front of Cumberland Gap, observing the 9000 Federals who held it, while the rest continued their advance toward the Bluegrass. Meanwhile this was still the barrens, which meant that water was scarce, the going rough, and people in general unfriendly. This last might well have been based on fear, however, for the appearance of the marchers, whether they came as "liberators" or "invaders," struck at least one citizen as anything but prepossessing: "[They were] ragged, greasy, and dirty, and some barefoot, and looked more like the bipeds of pandemonium than beings of this earth. . . . They surrounded our wells like the locusts of Egypt and struggled with each other for the water as if perishing with thirst, and they thronged our kitchen doors and windows, begging for bread like hungry wolves. . . . They tore the loaves and pies into fragments and devoured them. Some even threatened to shoot others if they did not divide with them." ("Notwithstanding such a motley crew," the alarmed observer added with relief, "they abstained from any violence or depredation and appeared exceedingly grateful.") As a supplement to what could be cadged in this manner, they gathered apples and roasting ears from roadside orchards and fields, eating them raw on the march with liberal sprinklings of salt, a large supply of which had been procured at Barbourville. Spirits were high and there was much joking, up and down the column. CSA, they said, stood for "Corn, Salt, and Apples."

No matter how much horseplay went on within the column itself, passing through London on the 27th the men continued to obey their commander's insistence upon "the most perfect decorum of conduct toward the citizens and their property." Two days later, by way of reward for good behavior, they climbed Big Hill, the northern rim of the barrens, and saw spread out before them, like the promised land of old, the lush and lovely region called the Bluegrass. Years afterward, Smith would remember it as it was today, "a long rolling landscape, mellowing under the early autumn rays," and would add that when it "burst upon our sight we were astonished and enchanted." However, there was little time for undisturbed enjoyment of the Pisgah view. Up ahead, near the hamlet of Rogersville, seven miles short of Richmond, the principal settlement this side of the Kentucky River, the cavalry encountered resistance and was driven back upon the infantry. This was a sundown affair, soon ended by darkness. Although he did not know the enemy strength, Smith was not displeased at this development; for it indicated that the Federals would make a stand here in the open, rather than along the natural line of defense afforded by the bluffs of the river eight miles beyond Richmond. Earlier that week he had written Bragg that he would "fight everything that presents itself," and now, having issued instructions for his men to sleep on their arms in line of battle, he prepared to do just that at dawn. After more than a hundred miles of marching, they were about to be required to prove their right to be where they were and — if they won — to penetrate farther into what Smith would call the "long rolling landscape."

The bluecoats slept in line of battle, too, and there were about 7000 of them. They were under William Nelson, whom Buell had sent north two weeks ago, a month after his promotion to major general, to take charge of the defense of his native Kentucky. "The credit of the selection will be mine," Buell had told him. "The honor of success will be yours." Nelson was of a sanguine nature — "ardent, loud-mouthed, and violent," a fellow officer called him — but by now, having completed a tour of inspection of what he had to work with, he was not so sure that either credit or success, let alone honor, was very likely to come his way as a result of the contest he saw looming. Kirby Smith was closing on him with an army of 12,000 hardened veterans, while his own, hastily organized into two small divisions under two ex-civilian brigadiers, was composed almost entirely of green recruits hurried forward by the governors of Ohio and Indiana in response to an urgent call from Washington. Their periods of service ranged in general from three weeks to three days, and for all his arrogant manner, his six feet five inches of height and his three hundred pounds of weight, Nelson was considerably worried as to what they would do when they heard the first shot fired in their direction.

He was not long in finding out. At 2.30 in the morning, August 30, a courier knocked at his bedroom door in Lexington and informed him that the Confederates had come over Big Hill the previous afternoon, approaching Richmond, but that his two brigadiers — Mahlon Manson and Charles Cruft — were on the alert and had intercepted the gray column before it reached the town. This was not at all what Nelson wanted to hear, for he was doubtful that his green men could be maneuvered in open combat, and had intended for them to be pulled back to a better defensive position. Apprehensive, he got dressed and rode forward to see for himself, hearing gunfire as soon as he crossed the Kentucky River. It was well past noon by the time he got to Richmond, however, since he was obliged to travel the byroads to avoid being picked up by rebel horsemen. Arriving at last he found the troops, as he later declared, "in a disorganized retreat or rather rout." With the assistance of Manson and Cruft he got what was left of his army into line on the edge of town, partly under cover of the rock walls and tombstones of a cemetery. Once the rallied men were in position, he walked up and down the firing line, exposing his huge bulk to enemy marksmen and talking all the while to encourage his nervous recruits. "If they can't hit me they can't hit anything!" he roared as he strode back and forth amid the twittering bullets.

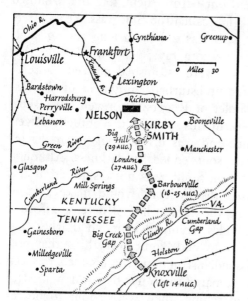

In this he was mistaken, as he presently found out. They hit him twice, in fact, both flesh wounds, no less painful for being superficial. But what hurt him worst, apparently, was the conduct of his men, who refused to be encouraged by his example. "Our troops stood about three rounds," he afterwards reported, "when, struck by a panic, they fled in utter disorder. I was left with my staff almost alone." He made his escape, considerably hampered by a bullet in his thigh. So did Cruft; but not Manson, who was pinned under his fallen horse and captured.

Nelson listed his casualties as 206 killed, 844 wounded, 4303 captured or missing.

Smith's were 78 killed, 372 wounded, 1 missing out of the approximately 7000 he too had had engaged. After the initial decision to give battle he had left the tactical details to the commander of his lead division, Brigadier General Patrick R. Cleburne, who had charge of the two brigades sent by Bragg from Chattanooga. Cleburne was Irish — about as Irish in fact as possible, having been born in County Cork on St Patrick's Day, thirty-four years ago. As a youth he had done a hitch in the British army, rising to the rank of corporal, then had emigrated to Helena, Arkansas, where he studied and practiced law with the same diligence he applied to his other two prime absorptions, pistol marksmanship and chess. When the war broke out he was elected captain of the local volunteer company, the Yell Rifles. By the time of Shiloh he had attained his present rank and led his brigade of Tennesseans, Mississippians, and Arkansans with conspicuous skill and gallantry through that fight. Today in Kentucky he did likewise, keeping up a slow fire with his guns until the situation was developed, then launching an attack which broke the first of the three lines the bluecoats managed to form between then and sundown. Cleburne himself was not on hand for the breaking of the others, nor for the rounding up of the fugitives in the twilight. While speaking to a wounded colonel, he was struck in the left cheek by a bullet that knocked his teeth out on that side before emerging from his mouth — "which," as one who was with him said, "fortunately happened to be open" — and forced his retirement, speechless, from the field. But the continued application of his tactics against the subsequent two rallies produced the same results, together with the capture of about 4000 prisoners, the entire Union wagon train, substantial army stores, 10,000 small arms, and 9 guns.

"Tomorrow being Sunday," Smith announced in his congratulatory order, "the general desires that the troops shall assemble and, under their several chaplains, shall return thanks to Almighty God, to whose mercy and goodness these victories are due." The day was also spent attending the wounded, burying the dead, and paroling the host of prisoners, after which preparations were made for continuing the advance. September 1, unopposed — three fourths of Nelson's army had been shot or captured; the rest were fugitives, hiding out in the woods and cornfields — the gray marchers crossed the Kentucky River and made camp on the northern bank. Next day they entered Lexington, where large numbers of townspeople turned out to greet them with smiles and cheers, including a delegation of ladies who presented Smith with a flag they had embroidered in his honor. September 3 his troopers rode into Frankfort, to find the governor and the legislature fled to Louisville. Having no suitable Confederate ensign with them, the graybacks raised the colors of the 1st Louisiana Cavalry over the state house. Another southern capital had returned to what the victors called its true allegiance.

Lexington had been the goal announced by Smith when he left Knoxville, and there he made his headquarters throughout September, in virtual control of Central Kentucky, while waiting for Bragg to join or send for him. Back at Cumberland Gap, after holding out through a month of siege, the Federals under George Morgan blew up their magazine, set fire to a warehouse containing 6000 small arms, and made their escape across the barrens, via Manchester and Booneville, to Greenup on the Ohio River, eluding pursuers all two hundred miles of the way. This was a disappointment to Smith, who had counted on capturing his West Point classmate, but at least it permitted his other division to join him at Lexington. Meanwhile he had not been idle. In addition to occupying Frankfort, Cynthiana, Georgetown, and Paris, he sent sizeable detachments of cavalry and infantry to demonstrate against Louisville and Cincinnati, both of which were thrown into turmoil. Summoned to command the defense of the latter city, Lew Wallace decreed martial law, ordered all business activities suspended, and impressed citizens to resume work on the fortifications begun the year before at Covington and Newport, on the opposite bank of the Ohio. "To arms!" the Cincinnati *Gazette* urged its readers. "The time for playing war has passed. The enemy is now approaching our doors!"

Smith was not so much concerned with the reaction of the people of Ohio, however, as he was with the reaction of the people of Kentucky. So far, this had been most gratifying, he informed the Adjutant General on September 6. "It would be impossible for me to exaggerate the enthusiasm of the people here on the entry of our troops. They evidently regarded us as deliverers from oppression and have continued in every way to prove to us that the heart of Kentucky is with the South in this struggle. . . . If Bragg occupies Buell we can have nothing to oppose us but raw levies, and by the blessing of God will always dispose of them as we did on the memorable August 30."

His purpose in seeming to threaten Cincinnati, he added, was "in order to give the people of Kentucky time to organize," and by way of encouragement he broadcast assurances to the citizens in the form of proclamations:

> Let no one make you believe we come as invaders, to coerce your will or to exercise control over your soil. Far from it. . . . We come to test the truth of what we believe to be a foul aspersion, that Kentuckians willingly join the attempt to subjugate us and to deprive us of our prosperity, our liberty, and our dearest rights. . . . Are we deceived? Can you treat us as enemies? Our hearts answer, "No!"

★ ★ ★

Bragg too was in Kentucky by now, and he too was issuing proclamations assuring the people that he had come, not to bind them, but
to assist them in striking off their chains:

> Kentuckians, I have entered your State with the Confederate Army
> of the West, and offer you an opportunity to free yourselves from
> the tyranny of a despotic ruler. We come not as conquerors or as
> despoilers, but to restore to you the liberties of which you have been
> deprived by a cruel and relentless foe. We come to guarantee to all
> the sanctity of their homes and altars, to punish with a rod of iron
> the despoilers of your peace, and to avenge the cowardly insults to
> your women. . . . Will you remain indifferent to our call, or will you
> rather vindicate the fair fame of your once free and envied State? We
> believe that you will, and that the memory of your gallant dead who
> fell at Shiloh, their faces turned homeward, will rouse you to a manly
> effort for yourselves and posterity.
>
> Kentuckians, we have come with joyous hopes. Let us not depart
> in sorrow, as we shall if we find you wedded in your choice to your
> present lot. If you prefer Federal rule, show it by your frowns and
> we shall return whence we came. If you choose rather to come within
> the folds of our brotherhood, then cheer us with the smiles of your
> women and lend your willing hands to secure you in your heritage
> of liberty.

Dated September 14 at Glasgow, which he had reached the day before,
the proclamation was issued during a two-day rest halt, the first he had
made in the course of the more than one hundred and fifty miles his
army had covered since leaving Chattanooga, seventeen days ago. Despite their exertions, the men were in excellent spirits. Marching over
Walden's Ridge, then up the lovely Sequatchie Valley to Pikeville,
where they swung east across the Cumberland Plateau — thus passing
around Buell's left wing at Decherd — they enjoyed the scenery, the
bracing air of the uplands, and the friendly offerings of buttermilk and
fried chicken by country people all along the way.

Bragg was happy, too, and with cause. Strategically, as events
disclosed, the movement had been as sound as it was rapid. He had predicted that Buell would "recede to Nashville before giving us battle,"
and now his scouts reported that this was just what Buell was doing,
as fast as he could: which meant that North Alabama and Chattanooga,
along with much of Middle Tennessee, had already been relieved without the firing of a shot. To cap the climax, when he drew near Sparta
on September 5, halfway across Tennessee, he received a dispatch from
Kirby Smith reporting the destruction of Nelson's army and urging him
"to move into Kentucky and, effecting a junction with my command
and holding Buell's communications, to give battle to him with superior
forces and with certainty of success." Then and there, by way of cele-

bration, Bragg issued a congratulatory address to his soldiers, informing them of Smith's lopsided victory and Buell's hasty withdrawal:
"Comrades, our campaign opens most auspiciously and promises complete success. . . . The enemy is in full retreat, with consternation and
demoralization devastating his ranks. To secure the full fruits of this
condition we must press on vigorously and unceasingly."

Press on they did, and vigorously, for Bragg had now decided
on his goal. Finally abandoning any intention to launch an assault on
Nashville, where Buell was concentrating his forces and improving the
fortifications, he marched hard for Glasgow. Eight days later he arrived
and, calling a halt, issued the proclamation announcing his "joyous
hopes" that the people of Kentucky would assist him in "punish[ing]
with a rod of iron the despoilers of your peace." He was exactly where
he wanted to be: squarely between Buell and Kirby Smith, whom he
could summon to join him. Or if he chose, he could move on to the
Bluegrass and the Ohio, combining there with Smith to capture Louisville or Cincinnati, both of which were nearer to him now than they
were to Buell.

On the day Bragg issued his proclamation at Glasgow, where his
four divisions were taking a hard-earned rest, Buell entered Bowling
Green, thirty-five miles to the west. He had five divisions with him
and three more back at Nashville under Thomas, who was serving as
his second-in-command through the present crisis. His total strength,
including a division just arrived from Grant, was 56,000: exactly twice
Bragg's, though Buell did not know this, having lately estimated it at
60,000, not including the troops with Kirby Smith.

The past two weeks had been for him in the nature of a nightmare. So much had happened so fast, and nearly all of it unpleasant.
Having transferred his headquarters in rapid succession from Stevenson
to Decherd to McMinnville, he shifted them once again to Murfreesboro on the day Bragg set out north from Chattanooga. He did this,
he told Thomas, by way of preparation for the offensive: "Once concentrated, we may move against the enemy wherever he puts himself if
we are strong enough." This sentence, as a later observer remarked,
had "an escape clause at both ends," and Buell was not long in giving
more weight to them than to the words that lay between. Two days
later, while Bragg was passing around his left and Smith was wrecking
Nelson up at Richmond, he notified Andrew Johnson, the military
governor of Tennessee: "These facts make it plain that I should fall
back on Nashville, and I am preparing to do so. I have resisted the reasons which lead to the necessity until it would be criminal to delay any
longer."

He arrived September 2 to find the capitol barricaded with cotton bales and bristling with cannon. Inside, Governor Johnson defied the rebels, declaring heatedly that he would defend the citadel with his heart's blood and never be taken alive. Encouraged by this, as well as by the arrival of 10,000 men from Grant, Buell wired Halleck: "I believe Nashville can be held and Kentucky rescued. What I have will be sufficient here with the defenses that are being prepared, and I propose to move with the remainder of the army against the enemy in Kentucky." Two nights ago, swamped by troubles resulting from Nelson's and Pope's simultaneous defeats, Old Brains had thrown up his hands and complained to McClellan that he was "utterly tired out." By now, though, he had recovered enough to send a one-sentence reply to Buell's wire. "Go where you please," he told him, "provided you will find the enemy and fight him."

Buell went nowhere un-
til September 7. Warned then
that Bragg was headed for
Bowling Green, where a large
supply of provisions had been
stored for the campaign which
had already gone up in smoke,
he set out for that point with
five of his eight divisions, leaving Thomas to hold Nashville
with the others in case the gray
invaders doubled back. A week
later he got there, only to find
that Bragg was at Glasgow,
which not only placed him
nearer Louisville than the Federals were, but also enabled him
to call on Smith for reinforcements. In danger of being attacked (as he thought) by
superior numbers, Buell wired

for Thomas to hurry north with two divisions, explaining the grounds on which he thus was willing to risk the Tennessee capital: "If Bragg's army is defeated Nashville is safe; if not, it is lost." Another wire went to Halleck. He was "not insensible to the difficulty and embarrassment of the position," Buell declared, and he further assured the harassed general in chief: "I arrived here today ... and shall commence to move against Bragg's force on the 16th."

The day before the one on which Buell had said he would "commence to move," Bragg himself was in motion with his whole army. He moved, however, not toward Buell's main body at Bowling Green, but toward the Green River, twenty miles north, where a 4000-man Federal detachment held a fort on the south bank, opposite Munfordville, guarding the L & N railroad crossing at that point. His original intention had been to hold his ground at Glasgow, receiving attack if Buell turned east, or to lunge forward and strike his flank if he pushed on toward Louisville. What changed his mind was what he later called an "unauthorized and injudicious" action, precipitated two days before by Brigadier General James R. Chalmers.

Chalmers, whose infantry brigade was on outpost and reconnaissance duty at Cave City, ten miles northwest of Glasgow, had made contact on the 13th with one of Kirby Smith's far-ranging cavalry regiments, the colonel of which had sent him word of what he called a rare opportunity. His troopers had cut the railroad north of Munfordville, isolating the south-bank garrison, but his request for its capitulation had been sharply refused. Would Chalmers move up and add the weight of his brigade to the demand? Chalmers would indeed. A youthful and ardent Mississippian, one of the authentic Shiloh heroes, he put his troops in motion at once, without bothering to notify Bragg at Glasgow. Arriving at daylight next morning, he launched an attack on the fort, then drew back and sent a note complimenting the bluecoats on their "gallant defense," pointing out the hopelessness of their position, with Bragg's whole army "a short distance in my rear," and demanding an unconditional surrender "to avoid further bloodshed." The reply, signed by Colonel J. T. Wilder, 17th Indiana Volunteers, was brief and to the point: "Thank you for your compliments. If you wish to avoid further bloodshed keep out of the range of my guns."

Concluding from this that the Hoosier colonel had better be left alone, Chalmers gathered up his dead and wounded — which amounted to exactly four times as many as Wilder's: 288, as compared to 72 — and withdrew. Back at Cave City next morning he reported the affair to Bragg, expressing "fear that I may have incurred censure at headquarters by my action in this matter." He was right. Bragg was furious that this first show of combat should be a blot on the record of a campaign which had already yielded such rich fruits without the firing of a shot. Accordingly, being as he said "unwilling to allow the impression of a disaster to rest on the minds of my men," he prepared at once to erase it. All four divisions started that same day for Munfordville.

He was taking no chances. Hardee's wing moved through Cave City that evening, making the direct approach, while Polk's crossed the river a few miles above and circled around to the rear, occupying positions on the bluffs overlooking the fort on the opposite bank. By mid-afternoon, September 16, the investment was complete. After firing a few rounds to establish ranges, Bragg sent a note informing the Federal commander that he was surrounded by an overwhelming force and repeating the two-day-old demand for an unconditional surrender to avoid "the terrible consequences of an assault." When Wilder asked for proof that such a host was really at hand, Bragg replied: "The only evidence I can give you of my ability to make good my assertion of the presence of a sufficient force to compel your surrender, beyond the statement that it now exceeds 20,000, will be the use of it.... You are allowed one hour in which to make known your decision."

Wilder was in something of a quandary. A former Indiana industrialist, he had been thirteen months in service, but nothing so far in his experience had taught him how much credence to give the claims that accompanied such demands for capitulation. Finally he arrived at an unorthodox solution. Knowing that Simon Buckner commanded a division on this side of the river, and knowing moreover that Buckner was a man of honor, he went to him under a flag of truce and asked his advice — as one gentleman to another. If resistance was hopeless, he said, he did not want to sacrifice his men; but neither did he want to be stampeded into surrendering because of his lack of experience in such matters. What should he do? Buckner, taken aback, declined to advise him. Wars were not fought that way, he said. He offered, however, to conduct him on a tour of the position and let him see for himself the odds against him. The colonel took him up on that, despite the fact that it was now past midnight and the truce had expired two hours ago. After counting 46 guns in position on the south bank alone, Wilder was convinced. "I believe I'll surrender," he said sadly.

It was arranged without further delay; Bragg subsequently listed the capture of 4267 prisoners, 10 guns, 5000 rifles, "and a proportionate quantity of ammunition, horses, mules, and military stores." While the bluecoats were being paroled — officers retaining their side arms and the men marching out, as Wilder proudly reported, "with all the honors of war, drums beating and colors flying" — Bragg wired the Adjutant General: "My junction with Kirby Smith is complete. Buell still at Bowling Green."

He had cause for elation. Already astride the Green River, halfway across Kentucky, the western prong of his two-pronged offensive had scored a victory as rich in spoils as the one the eastern prong had scored against Nelson, eighteen days ago at Richmond. In an order issued at Munfordville that same morning, he congratulated his soldiers "on the crowning success of their extraordinary campaign which this day has witnessed," and he told the Adjutant General: "My admiration of and love for my army cannot be expressed. To its patient toil and admirable discipline am I indebted for all the success which has attended this perilous undertaking."

This last sounded more like McClellan than it did like Bragg, and less like Jackson than it did like either: the Jackson of the Valley, that is, whom Bragg had announced as his prototype. And now that he had begun to sound like Little Mac, the terrible-tempered Bragg began to imitate his manner. After telling his men, "A powerful foe is assembling in our front and we must prepare to strike him a sudden and decisive blow," when Buell moved forward to Cave City, still waiting for Thomas to join him, Bragg left Polk's wing north of the Green and maneuvered Buckner's division across Buell's front, attempting to provoke him into attacking the south-bank intrenchments much as Chalmers had done, to his sorrow, five days back. But when Buell refused to be provoked, Bragg pulled Hardee's troops across the river and resumed his northward march, leaving Buell in his rear.

He had his reasons, and gave them later in his report: "With my effective force present, reduced . . . to half that of the enemy, I could not prudently afford to attack him there in his selected position. Should I pursue him farther toward Bowling Green he might fall back to that place and behind his fortifications. Reduced at the end of four days to three days' rations, and in a hostile country, utterly destitute of supplies, a serious engagement brought on anywhere in that direction could not fail (whatever its results) to materially cripple me. The loss of a battle would be eminently disastrous. . . . We were therefore compelled to give up the object and seek for subsistence."

So he said. But it seemed to others in his army that there was more to it than this; that the trouble, in fact, was personal; that it lay not within the situation which involved a shortage of rations and a surplus of bluecoats, but somewhere down deep inside Bragg himself. For all the audacity of his conception, for all his boldness through the preliminaries, once the critical instant was at hand he simply could not screw his nerves up to the sticking point. It was strange, this sudden abandonment of Stonewall as his model. It was as if a lesser poet should set out to imitate Shakespeare or Milton. With luck and skill, he might ape the manner, the superficial arrangement of words and even sentences; but the Shakespearian or Miltonic essence would be missing. And so it was with Bragg. He lacked the essence. Earlier he had said that the enemy was to be broken up and beaten in detail, Jackson-style, "by rapid movements and vigorous blows." Now this precept was revised. As he left Munfordville he told a colonel on his staff: "This campaign must be won by marching, not fighting."

When Thomas came up on the 20th, Buell pushed forward and found the rebels gone. Convinced that they were headed for Louisville, he followed at a respectful distance, fearing an ambush but hoping to strike their rear while they were engaged with the troops William Nelson was assembling for the defense of the city. To his surprise, however, less than twenty miles beyond the river Bragg swung east through Hodgenville, over Muldraugh's Hill and across the Rolling Fork to Bardstown, leaving his opponent a clear path to Louisville. Gratefully Buell took it.

He was not the only one who was grateful. Nelson, his flesh wounds healing rapidly since the removal of the bullet from his thigh, had been preparing feverishly, and with a good deal of apprehension based on previous experience, to resist the assault he expected Bragg to launch at his second collection of recruits. When he learned that the gray column had turned off through Lincoln's birthplace he drew his first easy breath since the early-morning knocking at his bedroom door, almost four weeks ago, first warned him that

Kirby Smith's invaders had come over Big Hill and were nearing Richmond. The arrival, September 24, of Buell's advance division — 12,000 veterans and half a dozen batteries of artillery — produced a surge of confidence within his shaggy breast. He wired department headquarters, Cincinnati: "Louisville is now safe. We can destroy Bragg with whatever force he may bring against us. God and liberty."

✗ 2 ✗

As Pope's frazzled army faded eastward up the pike toward Washington, and as Lee's — no less frazzled, but considerably lighter-hearted — poked among the wreckage in search of hardtack, the problem for them both was: What next? For the former, the battered and misused conglomeration of troops now under McClellan, who had ridden out to meet them, the question was answered by necessity. They would defend their capital. But for the victors, confronted as usual with a variety of choices, the problem was more complex. Lee's solution, reached before his men's clothes were dry from the rain-lashed skirmish at Chantilly, resulted — two weeks later, and by coincidence on the same date as Wilder's surrender to Bragg at Munfordville — in the bloodiest single day of the whole war.

The solution, arrived at by a narrowing of choices, was invasion.

He could not attack the Washington defenses, manned as they were by McClellan's army, already superior in numbers to his own and about to be strengthened, as he heard, by 60,000 replacements newly arrived in response to Lincoln's July call for "300,000 more." Nor could he keep his hungry soldiers in position where they were. The northern counties had been stripped of grain as if by locusts, and his wagon train was inadequate to import enough to feed the horses, let alone the troops. A third alternative would be to fall back into the Valley or south of the Rappahannock. But this not only would be to give up much that had been gained; it would permit a renewal of pressure on the Virginia Central — and eventually on Richmond. By elimination, then, the march would be northward, across the Potomac.

Not that there were no practical arguments against taking such a step. After much strenuous marching on meager rations, the men were bone-weary and Lee knew it. What was more, he wrote Davis on September 3, "The army is not properly equipped for an invasion of an enemy's territory. It lacks much of the material of war, is feeble in transportation, the animals being much reduced, and the men are poorly provided with clothes, and in thousands of instances are destitute of shoes. . . . What occasions me the most concern is the fear of getting out of ammunition." Nevertheless, in Lee's mind the advantages far outweighed the drawbacks. Two successful campaigns within two months, on Virginia soil and against superior numbers, had won for the Confederacy the admiration of the world. A third, launched beyond the Potomac in conjunction with Bragg's two-pronged advance beyond the Cumberland, might win for her the foreign recognition which Davis had known from the start was the one best assurance that this second Revolution, like the first, would be successful. Besides, Maryland was a sister state, not enemy territory. Thousands of her sons were in the Virginia army, and it was believed that thousands more would join the colors once they were planted on her soil. In any event, invasion would draw off the northern armies and permit the Old Dominion farmers, now that the harvest was at hand, to gather their crops unmolested. The one thing Lee could not do was nothing; or as he put it, "We cannot afford to be idle, and though weaker than our opponents in men and military equipments, must endeavor to harass them if we cannot destroy them." Next day, having convinced himself — and hoping, by the usual kid-gloves treatment, to have convinced the President — he wired Davis that he was "fully persuaded of the benefit that will result from an expedition into Maryland, and I shall proceed to make the movement at once, unless you should signify your disapprobation."

Without waiting for a reply — indeed, without allowing time for one — he put the army in motion that same day for White's Ferry, twenty miles south of Frederick, the immediate objective. Approaching the ford on September 6 and 7, the men removed their shoes, those who had them, rolled up their trouser legs, and splashed across the shallows into Maryland. One cavalryman considered it "a magnificent sight as the long column . . . stretched across this beautiful Potomac. The evening sun slanted upon its clear placid waters and burnished them with gold, while the arms of the soldiers glittered and blazed in its radiance." There were for him, in the course of the war, "few moments . . . of excitement more intense, or exhilaration more delightful, than when we ascended the opposite bank to the familiar but now strangely thrilling music of *Maryland, My Maryland.*"

Not everyone was so impressed, however, with the beauty of the occasion. A boy who stood on that opposite bank and watched the vermin-infested scarecrows come thronging past him, hairy and sunbaked, with nothing bright about them but their weapons and their teeth, was impressed by them in much the same way as the Kentucky civilian, this same week, had been impressed by their western counterparts. They made him think of wolves. "They were the dirtiest men I ever saw," he afterwards recalled, "a most ragged, lean, and hungry set of wolves." Accustomed to the Federals he had seen marching in compact formations and neat blue uniforms, he added: "Yet there was a dash about them that the northern men lacked. They rode like circus riders. Many of them were from the far South and spoke a dialect I could scarcely understand. They were profane beyond belief and talked incessantly."

Their individuality, which produced the cackling laughter, the endless chatter, and the circus-rider gyrations, was part of what made them "terrible in battle," as the phrase went. But in the present instance it also produced hampering effects: one being that Lee had considerably fewer men in Maryland than he had counted on when he made his decision to move north. Hampton's cavalry brigade, the reserve artillery, and three divisions of infantry under D. H. Hill, Major General Lafayette McLaws, and Brigadier General John G. Walker — 20,000 troops in all — had been forwarded from Richmond and had joined the army on its march to the Potomac. After the deduction of his Manassas casualties, this should have given Lee a total strength of 66,000. The truth was, he had barely more than 50,000 men in Maryland; which meant that close to 15,000 were absent without leave. Some few held back because of conscientious objections to invasion, but most were stragglers, laggards broken down in body or skulkers broken down in spirit. They would be missed along the thin gray line of battle, invalids and cowards alike, though their defection gave the survivors an added sense of pride and resolution. "None but heroes are left," one wrote home.

Hard-core veterans though they were, they were subject to various ills. Diarrhea was one, the result of subsisting on green corn; "the Confederate disease," it was coming to be called, and the sufferers, trotting white-faced to catch up with the column, joked ruefully about it, offering to bet that they "could hit a dime at seven yards." Another was sore feet; a fourth of the army limped shoeless on the stony Maryland roads. In addition to these ailments, mostly but by no means entirely confined to the ranks, a series of accidents had crippled the army's three ranking generals, beginning with Lee himself. Clad in rubber overalls and a poncho, he had been standing beside his horse on the rainy last day of August when a sudden cry, "Yankee cavalry!" startled the animal. Lee reached for the bridle, tripped in his clumsy clothes, and caught himself on his hands as he fell forward, with the result that a small bone was broken in one and the other was badly sprained. Both were put in splints, and Lee, unable to handle a mount, entered Maryland riding in an ambulance. Longstreet too was somewhat incapacitated by a raw blister on his heel; he crossed the river wearing a carpet slipper on his injured foot. Marylanders thus were robbed of the chance to see these two at their robust and energetic best. The third high-ranking casualty was Jackson. Ox-eyed Little Sorrel having been missing for two weeks, the gift of a sinewy gray mare from a group of Confederate sympathizers was welcome on the day he crossed the Potomac. Next morning, however, when he mounted and gave her the reins she did not move. He touched her with his spur: whereupon she reared, lost her balance, and toppled backward. Stunned, Jackson lay in the dust for half an hour, fussed over by surgeons who feared for a spinal injury, then was transferred, like Lee, to an ambulance.

These were partial incapacitations. Two others involving men of rank were unfortunately total, at least for the time being. The charges against Bob Toombs had been dropped in time for him to share in the final hour of victory at Manassas, but no sooner was the battle won than his place in arrest was taken by a general whose services the army could less afford to lose. When Shanks Evans laid claim to some ambulances Hood's Texans had captured, Hood, although outranked, refused to give them up. Evans referred the matter to the wing commander, who ruled in his favor, and when Hood still declined to yield, Longstreet ordered him back to Culpeper to await trial for insubordination. Lee intervened to the extent of allowing Hood to remain with his division, though not to exercise command.

By then the trouble between A. P. Hill and Jackson had come to a head, with the result that another of the army's hardest fighters was in arrest. On the march to the Potomac, Little Powell's division straggled badly. As far as Stonewall could see, Hill was doing little to correct this. What was more, he broke regulations by not calling rest-halts at the specified times. Finally Jackson himself halted one brigade: whereupon the red-bearded general came storming back down the column, asking by whose orders the troops were being delayed. The brigadier indicated Stonewall, who sat his horse beside the road. Hill unbuckled his sword and held it out to Jackson. "If you are going to give the orders, you have no need of me," he declared, trembling with rage. Stonewall did not take it. "Consider yourself under arrest for neglect of duty," he said coldly. "You're not fit to be a general," Hill snapped, and turned away.

With his army thus short of equipment and presenting its worst appearance, himself and his two chief lieutenants distracted by injuries, and two of his best division commanders in arrest, Lee busied himself and his staff with the composition, in accordance with instructions received from Davis, of a proclamation addressed "To the People of Maryland":

> The people of the Confederate States ... have seen with profound indignation their sister State deprived of every right and reduced to the condition of a conquered province. ... [We] have long wished to aid you in throwing off this foreign yoke, to enable you again to enjoy the inalienable rights of freemen. ... We know no enemies among you, and will protect all, of every opinion. It is for you to decide your destiny freely and without constraint ... and while the Southern people will rejoice to welcome you to your natural position among them, they will only welcome you when you come of your own free will.

Having thus complied with the President's recommendations, he made some of his own concerning another matter. The time had come, it seemed to him, in view of the present military situation, for the Confederacy to make a peace proposal to the North, based of course on permanent separation. "Such a proposition, coming from us at this time, could in no way be regarded as suing for peace," he wrote Davis; "but, being made when it is in our power to inflict injury upon our adversary, would show conclusively to the world that our sole object is the establishment of our independence and the attainment of an honorable peace. The rejection of this offer would prove to the country that the responsibility of the continuance of the war does not rest upon us, but that the party in power in the United States elect to prosecute it for reasons of their own." This he thought might have an effect upon the pending congressional elections in the North, enabling the voters "to determine ... whether they will support those who favor a prolongation of the war, or those who wish to bring it to a termination, which can but be productive of good to both parties without affecting the honor of either."

This was perhaps more opportune than he suspected, especially with regard to the effect it might have on foreign opinion, if Davis would act on the advice and Lee could give him time in which to do so. Napoleon III had been friendly all along; but now, stimulated by the offer of one hundred thousand bales of badly needed cotton, as well as by concern for the success of certain machinations already in progress south of the Texas border, he was downright eager. Across the English Channel, meanwhile, the news of Pope's defeat and Lee's entry into Maryland caused Lord Palmerston to write Earl Russell: "The Federals ... got a very complete smashing. ... Even Washington or Baltimore may fall into the hands of the Confederates. If this should happen, would it not be time for us to consider whether in such a state of things England and France might not address the contending parties and recommend an arrangement on the basis of separation?" The Foreign Minister replied: "I agree with you that the time is come for offering mediation to the United States Government, with a view to recognition of the independence of the Confederates. I agree further that, in case of failure, we ought ourselves to recognize the Southern States as an independent State." Presently the Prime Minister wrote again: "It is evident that a great conflict is taking place to the northwest of Washington, and its issue may have a great effect on the state of affairs. If the Federals sustain a grave defeat, they may be at once ready for mediation, and the iron should be struck while it is hot. If, on the other hand, they should have the best of it, we may wait a while and see what may follow."

What followed was in a large part up to Lee and his tatterdemalion army, and having given his attention to the question of peace, he turned his mind once more to thoughts of war — in particular to the problem of securing his lines of communication and supply. Once he moved westward, beyond the Catoctins and the trans-Potomac prolongation of the Blue Ridge, these would extend southward up the Shenandoah Valley, through Martinsburg and Winchester. He had expected the Federals to evacuate those places when they found him in their rear, and in the latter case they had done so; but the former still was occupied in strength, as was Harpers Ferry, sixteen miles away. Lee felt obliged to detach part of his army to reduce them before continuing his advance. When he broached this to Longstreet, however, Old Pete argued forcefully against such a division of strength in the enemy's own back yard. Jackson, on the other hand — recovered by now from his fall the day before — was delighted at the prospect, remarking somewhat wistfully that of late he had been entirely too neglectful of his friends in the Valley. Lee thought so, too. Dividing the army had worked wonders against Pope; now he would attempt it against McClellan, whose return to command had been announced in the northern papers. Despite Longstreet's objections, Lee began to work out a plan, not only for removing the threat to his supply line, but also for capturing the bluecoats who made it.

The result was Special Orders 191, which called for another of those ambitious simultaneous convergences by widely separated columns upon an assigned objective; in short, a maneuver not unlike the one that had failed, a year ago this week, against Cheat Mountain. In this case, however, since the capture of the Federals could be effected only by cutting off all their avenues of escape, the complication was unavoidable. The basis for it was geography. Low-lying Harpers Ferry, more trap than fortress, was dominated by heights that frowned down from three directions: Bolivar Heights to the west, Maryland Heights across the Potomac, and Loudoun Heights across the Shenandoah. With this in mind, Lee designed a convergence that would occupy all three. Jackson, who had been in command of the Ferry the year before and therefore knew it well, would be in general charge of the operation in its final stage. He would move with his three divisions through Boonsboro to the vicinity of Williamsport, where he would cross the Potomac and descend on Martinsburg, capturing the garrison there or driving it eastward to Harpers Ferry, where he would occupy Bolivar Heights. McLaws, with his own and Anderson's divisions, would move southwest and take position on Maryland Heights. Walker would move south with his two-brigade division, cross the Potomac below Point of Rocks, and occupy Loudoun Heights. The result, with all those guns

bearing down on the compact mass of bluecoats, should be something like shooting fish in a rain barrel. Longstreet meanwhile would move westward, beyond the mountains, and occupy Boonsboro with his other four divisions, supported by D. H. Hill. The order was dated September 9; all movements would begin the following morning, with the convergence scheduled for the 12th.

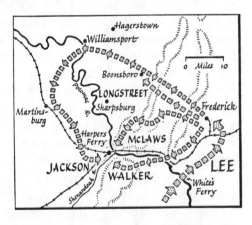

After the capitulation, which was expected to be accomplished that same day, or the next day at the latest, Jackson, McLaws, and Walker would rejoin the main body at Boonsboro for a continuation of the campaign through Maryland and into Pennsylvania.

Distribution of the order, which was quite full and gave in detail the disposition of Lee's whole army for the next four days, was to the commanders of the various columns as well as to the commanders of those divisions whose normal assignments were affected. Longstreet

took one look at it and, realizing the danger if it should fall into unfriendly hands, committed it to memory; after which he tore it up and
chewed the pieces into pulp. Jackson, too, hugged it close. Observing,
however, that Harvey Hill, who had been attached to his wing for the
river crossing, was now assigned to Longstreet, he decided that the best
way to let his brother-in-law know that he was aware of the transfer
would be to send him a copy of the order. With his usual regard for
secrecy, Stonewall himself made the transcript in his spidery handwriting and dispatched it under seal. Hill studied it, then put it carefully
away. When the copy arrived from Lee's adjutant, one of Hill's staff
officers decided to keep it for a souvenir, but meanwhile used it as a
wrapper for three cigars which he carried in his pocket.

Lee knew nothing of this duplication, nor of the menial use to
which an important army order was being put. He was doing all he
could, however, to make certain that nothing went astray in the intended convergence, as unfortunately had happened every time such
a maneuver had been attempted in the past. One precaution he took was
to have a personal interview with each of the generals in charge: with
Longstreet, who would guard the trains while the others were gone, and
with Jackson, McLaws, and Walker, who would be on their own
throughout the expedition. In the latter's case this was particularly apt;
for Walker, a forty-year-old regular army Missourian, had just come up
from the James with his small division — formerly a part of Holmes',
in which he had commanded a brigade during the Seven Days — and
was therefore unfamiliar with what had since become the army's operational procedure. Lee went over the plan with him, indicating details
on the map with his crippled hands. When this was done, he spoke of
what he intended to do once his forces were reunited north of the
Potomac. If Walker, with his "Show Me" background, had been inclined
to suspect that much of the recent praise for the Virginian's audacity
was overdone, that doubt was ended now. The sweep and daring of
the prospect Lee exposed, speaking quietly here in the fly-buzzed stillness of his tent, widened Walker's eyes and fairly took his breath away.

Sixty airline miles beyond Hagerstown lay Harrisburg, Pennsylvania, where the Pennsylvania Railroad crossed the Susquehanna River.
"That is the objective point of the campaign," Lee explained. Destruction of the bridge there, supplementing the previous seizure of the
B & O crossing at Harpers Ferry and the wrecking of the Monocacy
aqueduct of the Chesapeake & Ohio Canal — this last would be done
by Walker, in accordance with instructions already given him, on the
way to Point of Rocks — would isolate the Federal East from the
Federal West, preventing the arrival of reinforcements for McClellan
except by the slow and circuitous Great Lakes route. "After that,"
Lee concluded, "I can turn my attention to Philadelphia, Baltimore,

or Washington, as may seem best for our interests." The war would be over — won.

Observing Walker's astonishment, Lee said: "You doubtless regard it hazardous to leave McClellan practically on my line of communication, and to march into the heart of the enemy's country?" When the Missourian said he did indeed, Lee asked him: "Are you acquainted with General McClellan?" Walker replied that he had seen little of him since the Mexican War. "He is an able general," Lee said, "but a very cautious one. His enemies among his own people think him too much so. His army is in a very demoralized and chaotic condition, and will not be prepared for offensive operations (or he will not think it so) for three or four weeks. Before that time I hope to be on the Susquehanna."

★ ★ ★

This judgment contained several errors of degree as to the Federal potential, but in none of them was Lee more mistaken than in his estimate of the present condition of the Army of the Potomac, which in fact was less "chaotic" than his own, at least so far as its physical well-being was concerned. Nor was it "demoralized." McClellan was back, along with regular rations, a sense of direction, and a general sweeping up of croakers such as had followed the previous Bull Run fiasco which had brought him on the scene the year before. All this had been the source of much rejoicing, but there were others, no less heartening for being negative. Pope and McDowell, whom the men considered the authors of their woe, were gone — the former to pack his bags for the long ride to Minnesota, the latter to await the outcome of a formal hearing he had demanded in order to clear himself of all the charges brought by rumor — and so was Banks, a sort of junior-grade villain in their eyes, to assume command of the Washington defenses after McClellan marched the field force out the National Road to challenge the invaders up in Maryland.

That too was heartening. After four solid weeks of retreating, some from the malarial bottoms of the Peninsula, some from the blasted fields that bordered the dusty rivers of northern Virginia, and some from both — followed always by eyes that watched from roadside windows, hostile and mocking — not only were they moving forward, against the enemy, but they were doing it through a region that was friendly. "Fine marching weather; a land flowing with milk and honey; a general tone of Union sentiment among the people, who, being little cursed by slavery, had not lost their loyalty; scenery, not grand but picturesque," one young abolition-minded captain wrote, "all contributed to make the march delightful." A Maine veteran recorded that, "like the Israelites of old, we looked upon the land and it was good."

Best of all was Frederick, which they entered after the rebels had withdrawn beyond the Catoctins. "Hundreds of Union banners floated from the roofs and windows," one bluecoat recalled, "and in many a threshold stood the ladies and children of the family, offering food and water to the passing troops, or with tiny flags waving a welcome to their deliverers." Army rations went uneaten, "so sumptuous was the fare of cakes, pies, fruits, milk, dainty biscuit and loaves." A Wisconsin diarist apparently spoke for the whole army in conferring the accolade: "Of all the memories of the war, none are more pleasant than those of our sojourn in the goodly city of Frederick."

Presently it developed that there was more here for soldiers than an abundance of smiles and tasty food. For two of them, at any rate — three, in fact, if Private B. W. Mitchell and Sergeant J. M. Bloss, Company E, 27th Indiana, decided to share the third with a friend — there were cigars. Or so it seemed at the outset. Saturday morning, September 13, the Hoosier regiment was crossing an open field, a recent Confederate camp site near Frederick, when the men got orders to stack arms and take a break. Soon afterwards Mitchell and Bloss were lounging on the grass, taking it easy, when the former noticed a long thick envelope lying nearby. He picked it up and found the three cigars inside, wrapped in a sheet of official-looking paper. While Bloss was hunting for a match, Mitchell examined the document. "Headquarters, Army of Northern Virginia, Special Orders 191," it was headed. At the bottom was written, "By command of General R. E. Lee: R. H. Chilton, Assistant Adjutant-General." In between, eight paragraphs bristled with names and place-names: Jackson, Martinsburg, Harpers Ferry; Longstreet, Boonsboro; McLaws, Maryland Heights; Walker, Loudoun Heights. Mitchell showed it to Bloss, and together they took it to the company commander, who conducted them to regimental headquarters, where the colonel examined the handwritten sheet, along with the three cigars — as if they too might have some hidden significance — and left at once for division headquarters, taking all the evidence with him. Mitchell and Bloss returned to their company area and lay down again on the grass, perhaps by now regretting that they had not smoked the lost cigars before taking the rebel paper to the captain. As it turned out, they had sacrificed most of their rest-halt, too; for, according to Bloss, "In about three-quarters of an hour we noticed orderlies and staff officers flying in all directions."

McClellan's first considered reaction, after the leap his heart took at his first sight of the document which dispelled in a flash the fog of war and pinpointed the several components of Lee's scattered army, was that it must be spurious, a rebel trick. It was just too good to be true. But a staff officer who had known Chilton before the war identified the writing as unquestionably his. This meant that the order was valid beyond doubt: which in turn meant that McClellan's army, once it crossed the unoccupied Catoctins just ahead, would be closer to the two halves of Lee's army than those halves were to each other. What was more, one of those halves was itself divided into unequal thirds, the segments disposed on naked hilltops on the opposite banks of unfordable rivers. The thing to do, quite obviously, was to descend at once on Boonsboro, where the nearest half was concentrated, overwhelm it, and then turn on the other, destroying it segment by segment. The war would be over—won. At any rate that was how McClellan saw it. Standing there with the documentary thunderbolt in his hand, he said to one of his brigadiers: "Here is a paper with which if I cannot whip Bobby Lee I will be willing to go home."

Partly his elation was a manic reaction to the depression he had been feeling throughout most of the eleven days since Halleck's order, issued in confirmation of Lincoln's verbal instructions, gave him "command of the fortifications of Washington and of all the troops for [its] defense." This had not been supplemented or broadened since. What he did beyond its limitations he did on his own — including the march into Maryland to interpose his army between Lee's and the capital whose defense was his responsibility. Consequently, as he said later, he felt that he was functioning "with a halter around my neck. . . . If the Army of the Potomac had been defeated and I had survived I would, no doubt, have been tried for assuming authority without orders." What the Jacobins wanted, he knew, was his dismissal in disgrace, and he had long since given up the notion that the President would support him in every eventuality. In fact, knowing nothing of Lincoln's defiance of a majority of the cabinet for his sake, he no longer trusted the President to stand for long between him and the political clamor for his removal; and he was right. Back at the White House, after telling Hay, "McClellan is working like a beaver. He seems to be aroused to doing something after the snubbing he got last week," Lincoln added thoughtfully: "I am of the opinion that this public feeling against him will make it expedient to take important command from him . . . but he is too useful just now to sacrifice."

All this while, moreover, Halleck had been giving distractive twitches to the telegraphic lines attached to the halter. Though Banks had three whole corps with which to man the capital fortifications — Heintzelman's, Sigel's, and Porter's, which, together with the regular garrison, gave him a total defensive force of 72,500 men — the general in chief swung first one way, then another, alternately tugging or nudging, urging caution or headlong haste. Four days ago he had wired: "It may be the enemy's object to draw off the mass of our forces, and then attempt to attack us from the Virginia side of the Potomac. Think of this." Two days later he was calmer: "I think the main force

of the enemy is in your front. More troops can be spared from here."
Today, however, his fears were back, full strength: "Until you know
more certainly the enemy forces south of the Potomac you are wrong
in thus uncovering the capital." McClellan, his natural caution thus enlarged and played on—he estimated Lee's army at 120,000 men, half
again larger than his own — pushed gingerly northwestward up the National Road, which led from Washington to Frederick, forty miles,
then on through Hagerstown and Wheeling, out to Ohio.

He averaged about six miles a day, despite the fact that he had
reorganized his army into two-corps "wings" in order to march by
parallel roads rather than in a single column, which would have left
the tail near Washington while the head was approaching Frederick.
The right wing, assigned to Burnside, included his own corps, still
under Reno, and McDowell's, now under Hooker, who had already
won the nickname "Fighting Joe." The center wing was Sumner's and
included his own and Banks' old corps, now under the senior division
commander, Brigadier General Alpheus Williams. The left wing, Franklin's, included his own corps and the one division so far arrived from
Keyes', still down at Yorktown. Porter's corps, which was released to
McClellan on the 12th, the day his advance units reached Frederick,
was the reserve. Including the troops arrived from West Virginia and
thirty-five new regiments distributed throughout the army since its retreat from Manassas, McClellan had seventeen veteran divisions, with
an average of eight brigades in each of his seven corps; or 88,000 men
in all. Yet he believed himself outnumbered, and he could not forget
that the army he faced — that scarecrow multitude of lean, vociferous,
hairy men who reminded even noncombatants of wolves — had two
great recent victories to its credit, while his own had just emerged
from the confusion and shame of one of the worst drubbings any American army had ever suffered. Nor could he dismiss from his mind the
thought of what another defeat would mean, both to himself and to his
country. Despised by the leaders of the party in power, mistrusted by
Lincoln, badgered by Halleck, he advanced with something of the manner of a man walking on slippery ice through a darkness filled with
wolves.

It was at Frederick, that "goodly city," that the gloom began to
lift. "I can't describe to you for want of time the enthusiastic reception
we met with yesterday in Frederick," he wrote his wife next morning.
"I was nearly overwhelmed and pulled to pieces. I enclose with this a
little flag that some enthusiastic lady thrust into or upon Dan's bridle.
As to flowers — they came in crowds! In truth, I was seldom more affected. . . . Men, women, and children crowded around us, weeping,
shouting, and praying." Then, near midday, his fears were abolished
and his hopes were crowned. "Now I know what to do," he exclaimed
when he read Special Orders 191, and one of the first things he did

was share his joy with Lincoln in a wire sent at noon. In his elation he had the sound of a man who could not stop talking:

"I have the whole rebel force in front of me, but am confident, and no time shall be lost. I have a difficult task to perform, but with God's blessing will accomplish it. I think Lee has made a gross mistake, and that he will be severely punished for it. The army is in motion as rapidly as possible. I hope for a great success if the plans of the rebels remain unchanged. We have possession of Catoctin. I have all the plans of the rebels, and will catch them in their own trap if my men are equal to the emergency. I now feel that I can count on them as of old. . . . My respects to Mrs. Lincoln. Received most enthusiastically by the ladies. Will send you trophies."

He said he would lose no time, and five days ago he had told Halleck, "As soon as I find out where to strike, I will be after them without an hour's delay." But that did not mean he would be precipitate. In fact, now that the once-in-a-lifetime opportunity was at hand, its very magnitude made him determined not to muff it as a result of careless haste. Besides, despite its fullness in regard to the location of the Confederate detachments, the order gave him no information as to their various strengths. For all he knew, Longstreet and Hill had almost any conceivable number of men at Boonsboro, and the nature of the terrain between there and Frederick afforded them excellent positions from which to fight a delaying action while the other half of their army shook itself together and rejoined them — or, worse still, moved northward against his flank. He already had the Catoctins, as he said, but beyond them reared South Mountain, the lofty extension of the Blue Ridge. The National Road crossed this range at Turner's Gap, with Boonsboro just beyond, while six miles south lay Crampton's Gap, pierced by a road leading down to Harpers Ferry from Buckeystown, where Franklin's left wing was posted, six miles south of Frederick. These roads and gaps gave McClellan the answer to his problem. He would force Turner's Gap and descend on Boonsboro with his right and center wings, smashing Longstreet and Hill, while Franklin marched through Crampton's Gap and down to Maryland Heights, where he would strike the rear of Anderson and McLaws, capturing or brushing their men off the mountaintop and thereby opening the back door for the escape of the 12,000 Federals cooped up in Harpers Ferry. That way, too, the flank of the main body would be protected against an attack from the south, in case resistance delayed the forcing of the upper gap.

By late afternoon his plans were complete, and at 6.20 he sent Franklin his instructions. After explaining the situation at some length, he told him: "You will move at daybreak in the morning. . . . Having gained the pass"— Crampton's Gap — "your duty will be first to cut off, destroy, or capture McLaws' command and relieve [Harpers

Ferry]." After saying, "My general idea is to cut the enemy in two and beat him in detail," he concluded: "I ask of you, at this important moment, all your intellect and the utmost activity that a general can exercise." Intellect and activity were desirable; haste, apparently, was not. Just as he did not ask it of himself, so he did not ask it of Franklin. Lee's disjointed army lay before him, and the best way to pick up the pieces — as he saw it — was deliberately, without fumbling. The army would get a good night's sleep, then start out fresh and rested "at daybreak in the morning."

And so it was. At sunrise, Franklin's 18,000 — who should indeed have been rested; they had seen no combat since the Seven Days, and not a great deal of it then except for the division that reinforced Porter at Gaines Mill — pushed westward out of Buckeystown, heading for the lower gap, a dozen miles away. The other two wings, 70,000 men under Sumner and Burnside, with Porter bringing up the rear, moved down the western slope of the Catoctins, then across the seven-mile-wide valley toward Turner's Gap, a 400-foot notch in the 1300-foot wall of the mountain, where a fire fight was in progress. They moved in three heavy columns, along and on both sides of the National Road, and to one of the marchers, down in the valley, each of these columns resembled "a monstrous, crawling, blue-black snake, miles long, quilled with the silver slant of muskets at a 'shoulder,' its sluggish tail writhing slowly up over the distant eastern ridge, its bruised head weltering in the roar and smoke upon the crest above, where was being fought the battle of South Mountain."

McClellan was there beside the pike, astride Dan Webster, the central figure in the vast tableau being staged in this natural amphitheater, and the men cheered themselves hoarse at the sight of him. It seemed to one Massachusetts veteran that "an intermission had been declared in order that a reception might be tendered to the general in chief. A great crowd continually surrounded him, and the most extravagant demonstrations were indulged in. Hundreds even hugged the horse's legs and caressed his head and mane." This was perhaps the Young Napoleon's finest hour, aware as he was of all those thousands of pairs of worshipful eyes looking at him, watching for a gesture, and the New England soldier was pleased to note that McClellan did not fail to supply it: "While the troops were thus surging by, the general continually pointed with his finger to the gap in the mountain through which our path lay."

★ ★ ★

Harvey Hill was watching him, too, or anyhow he was looking in that direction. Seeing from the notch of Turner's Gap, which he had been ordered to hold with his five-brigade division, the serpentine approach of those four Union corps across the valley — twelve divisions with a total of thirty-two infantry brigades, not including one corps which was still beyond the Catoctins — he said later that "the Hebrew poet whose idea of the awe-inspiring is expressed by the phrase, 'terrible as an army with banners,' [doubtless] had his view from the top of a mountain." He experienced mixed emotions at the sight. Although it was, as he observed, "a grand and glorious spectacle, and it was impossible to look at it without admiration," he added that he had never "experienced a feeling of greater *loneliness*. It seemed as though we were deserted by 'all the world and the rest of mankind.' "

Despite the odds, all too apparent to anyone here on the mountaintop, he had one real advantage in addition to the highly defensible nature of the terrain, and this was that he could see the Federals but they could not see him. Consequently, McClellan knew little of Hill's strength, or lack of it, and nothing at all of his loneliness. He thought that Longstreet, in accordance with Special Orders 191, was there too; whereas he was in fact at Hagerstown, a dozen miles away. Lee had sent him there from Boonsboro, three days ago, to head off a blue column erroneously reported to be advancing from Pennsylvania. After protesting against this further division of force — "General," he said in a bantering tone which only partly covered his real concern, "I wish we could stand still and let the damned Yankees come to us" — Longstreet marched his three divisions northward through the heat and dust. As a result, while McClellan back in Frederick was saying that he intended "to cut the enemy in two," Lee had already obliged him by cutting himself in five:

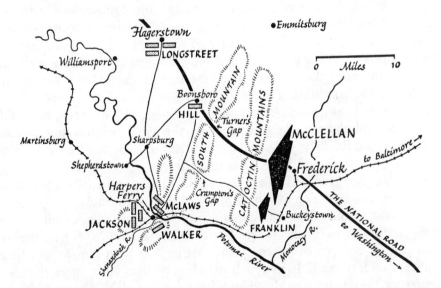

It was puzzling, this manifest lack of caution on McClellan's part, until late that night a message from Stuart explained the Young Napoleon's apparent change of character. A Maryland citizen of southern sympathies had happened to be at Federal headquarters when the lost order arrived, and he had ridden west at once, beyond the Union outposts, to give the news to Stuart, who passed it promptly on to Lee. So now Lee knew McClellan knew his precarious situation, and now that he knew he knew he moved to counteract the disadvantage as best he could. He sent for Longstreet and told him to march at day-break in support of Hill, whose defense of Turner's Gap would keep the Federal main body from circling around South Mountain to relieve the Harpers Ferry garrison by descending on McLaws. Longstreet protested. The march would have his men so blown that they would be in no shape for fighting when they got there, he said, and he urged instead that he and Hill unite at Sharpsburg, twelve miles south of Hagerstown and half that far from Boonsboro; there, near the Potomac, they could organize a position for defense while awaiting the arrival of the rest of the army, or else cross in safety to Virginia in case the troops from Harpers Ferry could not join them in time to meet McClellan's attack. Lee overruled him, however, and Longstreet left to get some sleep. After sending word to McLaws of the danger to his rear and stressing "the necessity of expediting your operations as much as possible," Lee received a note from Longstreet repeating his argument against opposing the Federals at South Mountain. Later the Georgian explained that he had not thought the note would alter Lee's decision, but that the sending of it "relieved my mind and gave me some rest." What effect it had on Lee's rest he did not say. At any rate, he received no reply, and the march for Turner's Gap began at dawn.

As usual, once he got them into motion, Longstreet's veterans marched hard and fast, trailing a long dust cloud in the heat. Shortly after noon they came within earshot of the battle Hill was waging on the mountain. The pace quickened on the upgrade. About 3 o'clock, nearing the crest, Lee pulled off to the side of the road to watch the troops swing past him. Though his hands were still in splints, which made for awkward management of the reins, he was mounted; he could abide the ambulance no longer. Presently the Texas brigade approached. "Hood! Hood!" they yelled when they saw Lee by the roadside. For two weeks Hood had been in arrest, but now that they were going into battle they wanted him at their head. "Give us Hood!" they yelled. Lee raised his hat. "You shall have him, gentlemen," he said.

When the tail of the column came abreast he beckoned to the tall young man with the tawny beard and told him: "General, here I am just on the eve of entering into battle, and with one of my best officers under arrest. If you will merely say that you regret this occurrence"— referring to the clash with Evans over the captured ambulances — "I will release you and restore you to the command of your division." Hood shook his head regretfully and replied that he "could not consistently do so." Lee urged him again, but Hood again declined. "Well," Lee said at last, "I will suspend your arrest till the impending battle is decided." Beaming, Hood saluted and rode off. Presently, from up ahead, loud shouts and cheers told Lee that the Texans had their commander back again.

It was well that they did, for they had need of every man they could muster, whatever his rank. Hill had been fighting his Thermopylae since early morning, and events had shown that the gap was by no means as defensible as it had seemed at first glance. High ridges dominated the notch from both sides, and there were other passes north and south, so that he had had to spread his small force thin in order to meet attacks against them all. Coming up just as Hill was about to be overwhelmed — one brigade had broken badly when its commander Brigadier General Samuel Garland was killed, and others were reduced to fighting Indian-style, scattered among the rocks and trees — Longstreet counterattacked on the left and right and managed to stabilize the situation until darkness ended the battle. McClellan had had about 30,000 men engaged, Lee about half that many. Losses were approximately 1800 killed and wounded on each side, with an additional 800 Confederates taken captive. Among the dead was Jesse Reno, shot from his saddle just after sundown while making a horseback inspection of his corps. Lieutenant Colonel Rutherford B. Hayes of the 23d Ohio, fifteen years away from the Presidency, was wounded. Sergeant William McKinley, another future President from that regiment, was unhurt; the bullet that would get him was almost forty years away.

For Lee it was a night of anxiety. He had saved his trains and perhaps delayed a showdown by holding McClellan east of the mountain, but he had done this at a cost of nearly 3000 of his hard-core veterans. What was more, he knew he could do it no longer: Hill and Longstreet both reported that the gap could not be held past daylight, and defeat here on the mountain would mean annihilation. The only thing to do, Lee saw, was to adopt the plan Old Pete had favored so argumentatively the night before. Gone were his hopes for an invasion of Pennsylvania, the destruction of the Susquehanna bridge, the descent on Philadelphia, Baltimore, or the Union capital. Gone too was his hope of relieving Maryland of what he called her foreign yoke. Outnumbered worse than four to one, this half of the army — which in fact was barely more than a third: fourteen brigades out of the total forty — would have to retreat across the Potomac, and the other half would have to abandon its delayed convergence on Harpers Ferry. For Jackson and Walker this would not be difficult, but McLaws was already in the gravest danger. Soon after nightfall Lee sent him a message admitting defeat: "The day has gone against us and this army will go by Sharpsburg and cross the river. It is necessary for you to abandon your position tonight." McLaws of course would not be able to do this over the Ferry bridge, which was held by the Federal garrison; he would have to cross the Potomac farther upstream. Lee urged him, however, to do this somewhere short of Shepherdstown, which was just in rear of Sharpsburg. He wanted that ford clear for his own command, which would be retreating with McClellan's victorious army hard on its heels.

The evacuation began with Hill, followed by Longstreet; the cavalry brought up the rear. Obliged to abandon his dead and many of his wounded there on the mountain where they had fallen, Lee did not announce that he intended to withdraw across the Potomac, nor did he tell the others that he had instructed McLaws to abandon Maryland Heights. But news that arrived while the retreat was just getting under way confirmed the wisdom, indeed the necessity, of his decision. Crampton's Gap, six miles south, had been lost by the troopers sent to defend it: which not only meant that the Federals were pouring through, directly in rear of McLaws, but also that they were closer to Sharpsburg than Hill and Longstreet were. Unable to count any longer on McClellan's accustomed caution and hesitation, Lee saw that the march would have to be hard and fast, encumbered though he was with all his trains, if he was to get there first. Whereupon, with the situation thus at its worst and his army in graver danger of piecemeal annihilation than ever, Lee displayed for the first time a side to his nature that would become more evident down the years. He was not only no less audacious in retreat than in advance, but he was also considerably more pugnacious, like an old gray wolf wanting nothing more than half a chance to turn on whoever or whatever tried to crowd him as he fell back. And presently he got it.

It came in the form of a message from Jackson, to whom Lee had been sending couriers with information of the latest developments. "Through God's blessing," Stonewall had written at 8.15 p.m. from Bolivar Heights, "the advance, which commenced this evening, has been successful thus far, and I look to Him for complete success tomorrow. . . . Your dispatch respecting the movements of the enemy and the importance of concentration has been received." To Lee this represented a chance to retrieve the situation. By the shortest route, Harpers Ferry was only a dozen miles from Sharpsburg. If the place fell tomorrow, that would mean that a part at least of the besieging force could join him north of the Potomac tomorrow night; for when Jackson said that instructions had been "received," he meant that they would be obeyed. McLaws, too, might give the Federals the slip and march northwest without crossing the river. Accordingly, while Hill and Longstreet pushed on westward unpursued, Lee sent couriers galloping southward through the darkness. Unless the Army of the Potomac got into position for an all-out attack on Sharpsburg tomorrow — which seemed doubtful, despite McClellan's recent transformation; for one thing, there would be no more lost orders — the Army of Northern Virginia would not return to native ground without the shedding of a good deal more blood, Union and Confederate, than had been shed on South Mountain.

McLaws was a methodical man, not given to indulging what little imagination he had, and in this case — his present dangers being what they were, with McClellan's left wing coming down on his rear through Crampton's Gap — that was preferable. A forty-one-year-old Georgian, rather burly, with a bushy head of hair and a beard to match, he had been four months a major general, yet except for commanding two brigades under Magruder during the Seven Days had seen no previous service with Lee's army. Now he had ten brigades, his own four and Anderson's six, and he had been given the most critical assignment in the convergence on Harpers Ferry. Maryland Heights was the dominant one of the three. If the place was to be made untenable, it would be his guns that would do most to make it so.

His march from Frederick had been deliberate: so much so that he was a day late in approaching his objective, after which he spent another day brushing Federal detachments off the hilltop and a night cutting a road in order to manhandle his guns up the side of the mountain. At last, two days late, he got them into position on the morning of September 14 and opened wigwag communications with Jackson and Walker, across the way. Northward, up the long ridge of South Mountain, D. H. Hill's daylong battle rumbled and muttered; but McLaws, having posted three brigades in that direction to protect his rear, kept his mind on the business of getting his high-perched guns laid in time to open a plunging fire on the Ferry whenever Stonewall, who was a day late and still completing his dispositions, gave the signal. During the afternoon a much nearer racket broke out northward, but whatever qualms McLaws felt at the evidence that his rear guard was under attack were eased by Stuart, who had ridden down from Turner's Gap. The bluecoats in front of Crampton's Gap did not amount to more than a brigade, he said, and McLaws turned back to his guns. Presently, though, as the noise swelled louder, he rode in that direction to see for himself — and arrived to find that he had a first-class panic on his hands. Right, left, and center, his troops had given way and were fleeing in disorder. That was no blue brigade pouring through the abandoned gap, they told him. It was McClellan's entire left wing, a reinforced corps.

Fortunately they had given a good account of themselves before they broke: good enough, at any rate, to instill a measure of caution in their pursuers. McLaws had time to rally the fugitives and bring three more brigades down off the heights, forming a line across the valley less than two miles south of the lost gap. The day was far gone by then, the valley filled with shadows, and Franklin did not press the issue. McClellan had told him to "cut off, destroy, or capture Mc-Laws' command," and apparently he figured that the seizure of Crampton's Gap had fulfilled the first of these alternatives. Also, now that he was in McLaws' rear, he had the worry of knowing that the Confederate main body was in *his*. Anyhow he decided not to be hasty; he had his men bed down for the night in line of battle.

Next morning, as he was about to proceed with his advance, the rebels just ahead began to cheer. One curious bluecoat sprang up on a stone wall and called across to them:

"What the hell are you fellows cheering for?"

"Because Harpers Ferry is gone up, God damn you!"

"I thought that was it," the Federal said, and he jumped back down again.

McLaws had stood fast and Jackson had kept the promise sent by courier to Lee twelve hours before. One hour of plunging fire from the surrounding heights smothered the batteries below. Soon afterwards the white flag went up. Except for two regiments of cavalry that had escaped under cover of darkness — across the Potomac, then northward up the same road old John Brown had come south on, three years ago next month — the whole garrison surrendered, including the men who had marched in from Martinsburg. "Our Heavenly Father blesses us exceedingly," Jackson wrote his wife, enumerating his gains: 12,520 prisoners, 13,000 small arms, 73 cannon, and a goodly haul of quartermaster stores.

According to a northern reporter's O-my-God lay-me-down reaction to his first sight of Stonewall and his men, they had great need of the latter — especially the general himself. "He was dressed in the coarsest kind of homespun, seedy and dirty at that; wore an old hat which any northern beggar would consider an insult to have offered him, and in general appearance was in no respect to be distinguished from the mongrel, bare-footed crew who follow his fortunes. I had heard much of the decayed appearance of the rebel soldiers, but such a looking crowd! Ireland in her worst straits could present no parallel, and yet they glory in their shame." The captive Federals (except perhaps the Irish among them) could scarcely argue with this, but they drew a different conclusion. "Boys, he isn't much for looks," one declared, inspecting Jackson, "but if we'd had him we wouldn't have been caught in this trap."

Pleased as he was, the Valley commander took little time for gloating. "Ah," he said to a jubilant companion as they stood looking at the booty, "this is all very well, Major, but we have yet much hard work before us." Though he was unaware of the lost order — "I thought I knew McClellan," he remarked, "but this movement of his puzzles me" — he was aware that Lee was being pressed, and he was eager to move to his support. Five of the six divisions started for Sharpsburg that afternoon and night. The sixth was A. P. Hill's. Like Hood, once combat was at hand, he had burned to pass from the rear to the front of his division on the march to Harpers Ferry, but like Hood he would not compromise his honor with an expression of regret. He simply requested, through a member of the staff, to be released from arrest for the duration of the fighting, after which he would report himself in arrest again. Jackson not only assented; he gave him a prominent part in the operation, and afterwards left him in charge of the place while he himself rode off in the wake of a message he had sent Lee that morning soon after he saw the white flag go up:

> Through God's blessing, Harpers Ferry and its garrison are to be surrendered. As Hill's troops have borne the heaviest part of the engagement, he will be left in command until the prisoners and public property shall be disposed of, unless you direct otherwise. The other forces can move off this evening so soon as they get their rations.

"That is indeed good news," Lee said when it reached him at Sharpsburg about noon. "Let it be announced to the troops."

★ ★ ★

McClellan's soldiers were feeling good, and so was their commander. For the first time since Williamsburg, back in early May, they were following up a battle with an advance, and as they went forward, past clumps of fallen rebels, they began to observe that their opponents were by no means the supermen they had seemed at times; were in fact, as one New York volunteer recorded, "undersized men mostly ... with sallow, hatchet faces, and clad in 'butternut,' a color running all the way from a deep, coffee brown up to the whitish brown of ordinary dust." He even found himself feeling sorry for them. "As I looked down on the poor, pinched faces, worn with marching and scant fare, all enmity died out. There was no 'secession' in those rigid forms, nor in those fixed eyes staring blankly at the sky."

They left them where they lay and pushed on down the western slope, following McClellan, whose enthusiasm not even the fall of Harpers Ferry could dampen. Though this deprived him of 12,000 reinforcements which he thought he needed badly, it also vindicated the judgment he had shown in vainly urging the general in chief to order the post evacuated before Jackson rimmed the heights with guns. Moreover, though Old Brains could take no credit for it, his blunder had resulted in the dispersion of Lee's army, and this in turn had made possible yesterday's victory at South Mountain, as well as the larger triumph which now seemed to be within McClellan's grasp. Elated, he passed on this morning to Halleck "perfectly reliable [information] that the enemy is making for Shepherdstown in a perfect panic," and that "Lee last night stated publicly that he must admit they had been shockingly whipped." To old General Scott, in retirement at West Point, went a telegram announcing "a signal victory" and informing him that his fellow Virginian and former protégé had been soundly trounced: "R. E. Lee in command. The rebels routed, and retreating in disorder." Both reactions were encouraging. "Bravo, my dear general! Twice more and it's done," Scott answered, while Lincoln himself replied to the earlier wire: "God bless you and all with you. Destroy the rebel army if possible."

That was precisely what McClellan intended to do, if possible, and that afternoon, five miles southeast of Boonsboro — the scene of another triumphal entry and departure — he came upon a line of hills overlooking a shallow, mile-wide valley through which a rust-brown creek meandered south from its source in Pennsylvania; Antietam Creek, it was called. Beyond it, somewhat lower than the ridge on which he stood with his staff while his army filed in and spread out north and south along the line of hills outcropped with limestone, rose another ridge that masked the town of Sharpsburg, all but its spires and rooftops, and the Potomac, which followed a tortuous southward course, dividing Maryland and Virginia, another mile or so away. What interested him just now, though, was the ridge itself. There were Confederates on it, and Confederate guns, and one reason that they interested him was that they took him under fire. He sent his staff back out of range, dissolving the gaudy clot of horsemen who had drawn the fire in the first place, and went on with his study of the terrain.

A mile to the right of the point where the cluster of spires and gables showed above the ridge, and facing the road that led northward along it to Hagerstown, a squat, whitewashed building was set at the forward edge of a grove of trees wearing their full late-summer foliage; the autumnal equinox was still a week away. The sunlit brick structure, dazzling white against its leafy backdrop, was a church, but it was a Dunker church and therefore had no steeple; the Dunkers believed that steeples represented vanity, and they were as much opposed to vanity as they were to war, including the one that was about to move into their churchyard. On the near side of the road, somewhat farther to the right, was another grove of trees, parklike on the crown of the ridge, and between the two was a forty-acre field of dark green corn, man-tall and ripening for the harvest.

McClellan put his glasses back in their case and retired to do some thinking. Lee had chosen his army's position with care, disposing it along the high ground overlooking the shallow valley so that its flanks were anchored at opposite ends of the four-mile bend of the Potomac. That was his strength; but McClellan thought it might also be his weakness. Once Lee was dislodged from that ridge, with only a single ford in his rear, he might be caught in the coils of the river and cut to pieces. The problem was how to dislodge him, strong as he was. McClellan estimated yesterday's rebel casualties at 15,000 men, but that still left Lee with more than 100,000 according to McClellan, whose total strength — including Franklin, still hovering north of Harpers Ferry — was 87,164. Fortunately, however, there was no hurry; not just yet. The army was still filing in, hot and dusty from its march, and anyhow the day was already too far gone for an attack to succeed before darkness provided cover for a rebel getaway. He decided to work the thing out overnight. Meanwhile the troops could get a hot meal and a good night's rest by way of preparation for whatever bloody work he designed for them to do tomorrow.

Tomorrow came, September 16, but such bloody work as it brought was done by long-range shells from batteries on those ridges east and west of the mile-wide valley with its lazy little copper-colored creek. Wanting another good look at the terrain before completing his attack plan, McClellan rose early and went to the observation post where his staff had set up headquarters. Off to the right of the Boonsboro road and half a mile north of the center of the position, it was an excellent location, just beyond reach of the rebel guns, and there was plenty of equipment there for studying the enemy dispositions, including high-power telescopes strapped to the heads of stakes driven solidly into the ground. Unfortunately, however, these could not penetrate the thick mist that overhung the field until midmorning. By then the sun had burned enough of it away for McClellan to see that the Confederates had made some changes, shifting guns at various points along their line. The time consumed in noting these was well spent, he felt, for he wanted to eliminate snags and thus leave as little to chance as he possibly could. When the blow fell he wanted it to be heavy. Noon came and went, and on both sides men lay drowsing under the press of heat while the cannoneers continued their intermittent argument, jarring the ground and disrupting an occasional card game. By 2 o'clock McClellan had his attack plan: not for today — today, like yesterday, was too far gone — but for tomorrow.

It was based essentially on the presence of three stone bridges that spanned the creek on the left, center, and right. The one on the left was closest to Sharpsburg and the enemy line; in fact it was barely more than its own length away from the latter, since the western ridge came down sharply here, overlooking the bridge and whoever tried to use it. The center bridge, crossed by the Boonsboro road a mile above the first, had some of the same drawbacks, being under observation from the ridge beyond, as well as some of its own growing out of the fact that it debouched onto an uphill plain that was swept by guns clustered thickly along the rebel center. The upper bridge, a mile and a half above the second, had none of these disadvantages, being well out of range of the batteries across the way. What was more, an upstream crossing would permit an unmolested march to a position astride the Hagerstown road, well north of Lee's left flank, and a southward attack from that direction, if successful, would accomplish exactly what McClellan most desired. It would bowl the Confederates off their ridge and — in conjunction with attacks across the other two bridges, launched when the first was under way with all its attendant confusion — expose them to utter destruction.

In essence that was McClellan's plan, the outgrowth of much poring over the landscape and the map, and now that it had been formulated, all that remained — short, that is, of the execution itself — was for him to assign the various corps their various tasks in the over-all scheme for accomplishing Lee's downfall. Scrapping the previous organization into "wings," he decided that Fighting Joe Hooker was the man to lead the attack down the Hagerstown road, supported by Brigadier General J. K. F. Mansfield, who had arrived from Washington the day before to take over Banks' corps from Williams. Sumner, too, would come down from that direction, bringing a total of three corps, half of the whole army, to bear on Lee's left flank. If that did not break him, Franklin too could be thrown in there — he had been summoned from Maryland Heights and was expected to arrive tomorrow morning — raising the preponderance to two thirds. Burnside, back in command of his own corps after the death of Reno, was given the job of forcing the lower bridge and launching the direct assault on Sharpsburg, after which he would seize the Shepherdstown ford and thus prevent the escape of even a remnant of the shattered rebel force. Porter, astride the Boonsboro road, in rear of the center bridge, would serve a double function. As the army reserve, his corps could be used to repulse any counterattack Lee might launch in desperation, or it could be committed to give added impetus at whatever point seemed most critical, once success was fully in sight. Or else he could force the middle bridge for an uphill charge that would pierce Lee's center and chop him in two; whereupon Porter could wheel left or right to assist either Burnside or Hooker in wiping out whichever half of the rebel army survived the amputation.

The battle would open at daylight tomorrow, but McClellan — after taking his staff on a fast two-mile ride along his outpost line, drawing fire all the way from the guns across the creek, which permitted his own superior batteries, emplaced along the eastern ridge, to spot and pound them heavily — decided to use what was left of today in getting his men into position to launch the opening attack. Accordingly, about 4 o'clock that afternoon, Hooker's corps began its upstream crossing, the general leading the way on a high-stepping big white charger. The crossing itself was well beyond range of the rebel guns, but the line of march led near the grove of trees northeast of the Dunker Church, with the result that as the flank of the column went past that point it struck sparks, like a file being raked across a grindstone. Hooker drew off; he wanted those woods, but not just yet; and made camp for the night in line of battle astride the Hagerstown road, less than a mile beyond the Confederate left-flank outposts. Poised to strike as soon as there was light enough for him to aim the blow, he was exactly where McClellan wanted him.

So were the others, or anyhow they soon would be. Mansfield was crossing now in the darkness, to be followed by Sumner; Franklin was on the way. Porter was bivouacked in an open field, protected by defilade, just across the Boonsboro road from army headquarters. Farthest south, Burnside had massed his troops in rear of the triple-arched stone bridge which after tomorrow would bear his name. The night was gloomy, with a slow drizzle of rain and occasional sputters of musketry when the outpost men got nervous. For security reasons, the high command had forbidden fires. This was not so bad in itself — for all its dampness, the night was fairly warm — except that it kept the soldiers from boiling water. All along that dark, four-mile arc of blue-clad men, many of whom were going to die tomorrow, those who could not sleep chewed unhappily on dry handfuls of ground coffee.

The sun had burned the mist away that morning, but it could not disperse the mental fog which hid from McClellan, whose eye was glued to a telescope even then across the way, the fact that Lee at the time had less than one fifth as many troops as his opponent gave him credit for. He had in fact, along and behind the Sharpsburg ridge, barely 18,000 soldiers under D. H. Hill and Longstreet — fewer than were in Sumner's corps alone — until Jackson arrived at noon with three thin divisions, his own and Ewell's, under Brigadier General J. R. Jones and Lawton, and Walker's, which had crossed the Shenandoah to join him on the march from Harpers Ferry the night before. This brought the total to 26,000 and lowered the odds to three to one. McLaws and Anderson, still on the march, would not arrive before nightfall, and A. P. Hill was still at the Ferry; he might well not arrive at all. Even if he did, so heavy had the straggling been, together with the losses at South Mountain, Lee would not be able to count on putting more than 40,000 men into his line of battle, including the cavalry and artillery, and would still face odds worse than two to one.

Aware of this, Walker expected to find Lee anxious and careworn when he joined him on the outskirts of Sharpsburg, just after noon on the 16th. "Anxious enough, no doubt, he was," Walker observed; "but there was nothing in his look or manner to indicate it. On the contrary, he was calm, dignified, and even cheerful. If he had had a well-equipped army of a hundred thousand veterans at his back, he could not have appeared more composed and confident."

His confidence was doubly based: first, on the troops themselves, the hard-core men who had proved their battle prowess at Manassas and their hardiness by surviving the stony Maryland marches; and, second, on the advantages of the position he had established here on the ridge behind Antietam Creek. "We will make our stand on those hills," he had said as he came within sight of them at dawn of the day before. Unwilling to end his ambitious invasion campaign with the repulse just suffered at South Mountain, he crossed the shallow valley and spread his army north and south along the low western ridge. Longstreet took the right, blocking the near approach, from Sharpsburg down to the heights overlooking the lower bridge; Hill the center, posting his men along a sunken lane that crooked across the northeast quadrant formed by the intersection of the Boonsboro and Hagerstown roads; and Hood the left, occupying the woods beyond the Dunker Church. Next day, when Jackson and Walker came up, Lee sent the former to take charge of the left, joining Hood with his two divisions, while Walker extended Longstreet's right in order to guard the lower fords of the Antietam.

The long odds were somewhat offset by the fact that he would have the interior line, with a good road well below the crest for shifting troops to threatened points along the ridge. In addition, he had the advantage of knowing that McClellan could not swing around his flanks, securely anchored as they were near the Potomac in both directions. This last, however, was also the source of some concern. Just as the river afforded the enemy no room for maneuver in his rear, so too it would afford him none in case his army was flung back off the ridge, and what was more there was only a single ford, a mile below the former site of the Shepherdstown bridge, which had been destroyed. He did not expect to be dislodged, but he did take the precaution of covering the ford, from the Virginia side, with such guns as could be spared from the reserve under Brigadier General W. N. Pendleton, his chief of artillery. That completed his preparations. Until McLaws and Anderson came up, Jackson's, Hill's, and Longstreet's 26,000 were all the troops he would have for opposing the blue host whose officers were examining his dispositions from the higher ground across the valley and whose superior guns had already begun the pounding that would make this field "artillery hell" for Confederate cannoneers. "Put them all in, every gun you have, long range and short range," Longstreet said to his battery commanders, but Lee had already cautioned them not to waste their limited ammunition in duels with the heavier Federal pieces. Save it for the infantry, he told them.

Hooker's upstream crossing, and the resultant brush with the Texans in the woods beyond the Dunker Church, gave Lee fair warning that tomorrow's first blow would be aimed at Jackson and Hood. This was not without its comforting aspect, for the men who stood in its path not only were the ones who had held the unfinished railroad against repeated assaults by Pope, but were also the ones who had led the charge that wrecked him; perhaps they would serve Hooker the same way. However, the odds were even longer now, and as night came down Lee's apprehension increased. He had heard nothing from McLaws and Anderson, without whom he had no reserves with which to plug a break in his line or follow up a Federal repulse. Improvising as best he could, he ordered Stuart out beyond the left, hoping that he would find a position there from which to harass the flank of the attacking column or possibly launch a distracting counterstroke. He also sent a courier to A. P. Hill, seventeen miles away at Harpers Ferry, urging him to join the army with all possible speed. Whether this would get him there in time for a share in tomorrow's battle was highly doubtful, but at least Lee knew that Hill would make the effort.

As Lee was about to retire for the night, conscious that he had drawn his final card in the high-stakes game of showdown he was about to play with McClellan, Hood came to report that his men were near exhaustion, having received only half a ration of beef in the past three days. He requested that they be withdrawn from the line to get some rest and fry some dough and bacon. Distressed though Lee was to hear that his shock brigades were enfeebled, he was obliged to admit that he had no others to put in their place. He told him to see Jackson, and while Lee turned in, the rain murmurous on the canvas, Hood left to do just that.

He found him asleep under a large tree whose exposed roots made a pillow for his head. Hood nudged him awake, and when Stonewall sat up, blinking, told him what he wanted. Jackson had already rearranged his line, shifting troops around to the north and west to meet the attack he knew would come at dawn against those two stretches of woodland and the cornfield in between, but he agreed to spread them thinner in order to give Hood's hungry soldiers a chance to cook their rations, provided they were kept close at hand, ready to come running when he called. Hood agreed, and about midnight his two brigades filed southward to kindle their cookfires in the Dunker churchyard.

Presently a great stillness settled down, broken from time to time by picket firing, the individual shots coming sharp as handclaps through the mist and drizzle. All along the Sharpsburg ridge, while their opposite numbers munched ground coffee in the encircling darkness, men who could not sleep took out their pipes and smoked and thought about tomorrow.

★ ★ ★

It came in gray, with a pearly mist that shrouded the fields and woodlands, and it came with a crash of musketry, backed by the deeper roar of cannonfire that mounted in volume and intensity until it was continuous, jarring the earth beneath the feet of the attackers and defenders. Hooker bore down, his three divisions in line abreast, driving the rebel pickets southward onto the high ground where the road, flanked by what now was called the East Wood and the West Wood, ran past the squat white block of the Dunker Church. That was his immediate objective, barely a thousand yards away, though he was already taking heavy losses. Noting the glint of bayonets and the boil of smoke from the forty-acre cornfield, he called a halt while six of his batteries came up and began to flail the standing grain with shell and canister, their three dozen fieldpieces joined presently by heavier long-range guns pouring in a crossfire from the ridge beyond the creek. Haversacks and splintered muskets began to leap up through the dust and smoke, along with the broad-leafed stalks of corn and the dismembered heads and limbs of men. Hooker said later that "every stalk in the northern and greater part of the field was cut as closely as could have been done with a knife."

Yet when he got his batteries quieted and started his soldiers forward again, the fire seemed no less heavy. Entering the woods on the left and right, and approaching the shattered cornfield in the center, they ran into blinding sheets of flame and the air was quivering with bullets. "Men, I cannot say fell; they were knocked out of ranks by the dozen," one survivor wrote. Still they came on, their battle flags swooping and fluttering, falling and then caught up again. The red flags of the Confederates staggered backward, and still the bluecoats came on, driving them through the blasted corn and through the early morning woods, until at last they broke and fled, their ranks too thin to rally. The Dunker Church lay dead ahead. But just as the Federals saw it within their reach, a butternut column emerged from the woods beyond it and bore down on them, yelling. At point-blank range, the rebels pulled up short, delivered a volley which one receiver said "was like a scythe running through our line," and then came on again, the sunlight glinting and snapping on their bayonets.

It was Hood; Jackson had called for him while his men were preparing their first hot meal in days, and perhaps that had something to do with the violence of their assault. Leaving the half-cooked food in their skillets, they formed ranks and charged the bluecoats who were responsible. Their attack was necessarily unsupported, for Jackson's and

Ewell's divisions were shattered. J. R. Jones had been stunned by a shell that exploded directly above his head, and Starke, who resumed command, received three wounds, all mortal, within minutes; command of the Stonewall Division passed to a colonel. Lawton was down, badly wounded, and in his three brigades only two of the fifteen regimental commanders were still on their feet. But Hood took no account of this,

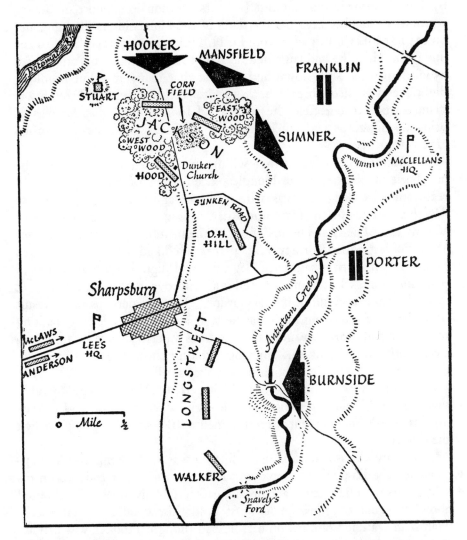

nor did his men. Intent on vengeance, they struck the Federals north of the Dunker Church and drove them back through the cornfield, whooping and jeering, calling for them to stand and fight. They did so at the far edge of the field, forming behind their guns, and there the two lines engaged. With only 2400 men in his two brigades, Hood knew that he would not be able to hold on long in the face of those guns, but he was determined to do what he could. When a staff officer arrived to inquire after the situation, Hood said grimly: "Tell General Jackson unless I get reinforcements I must be forced back, but I am going on while I can."

His chances of going on just now were better than he knew; for though the uproar had not slacked perceptibly, Hooker had already shot his bolt. Assailed in front by the demoniacal Texans, on the right by Early's brigade moving east from its position in support of Stuart, whose guns had been tearing the flank of the blue column all along, and on the left by two brigades from D. H. Hill, he was forced back to the line from which he had launched his dawn assault, two hours ago. With 2500 of his men shot down and at least that many more in headlong flight, he was through and he knew it. As he retreated through the shambles of the cornfield, he sent word to Mansfield that he was to bring up his corps and try his hand at completing the destruction so expensively begun.

Mansfield was altogether willing. So far in the war, though he had been in charge of the bloodless occupation of Suffolk, the only real action he had seen was with the coastal batteries that took the *Merrimac* under fire at Hampton Roads. Now he had two divisions of Valley and Manassas veterans, most of them unborn at the time of his West Point graduation forty years before. He liked them and they liked him, even on short aquaintance. "A calm and dignified old gentleman," one called him, while another noted with approval that he had "a proud, martial air and was full of military ardor." This last perhaps was a result of his habit of removing his hat as he rode among them, letting his long white hair and beard stream in the wind. As a performance it was effective, and he did it again this morning, evoking cheers from his troops as they moved forward in response to Hooker's call.

"That's right, boys — cheer!" he cried. "We're going to whip them today!" Doubling the column, he kept waving his hat and repeating his words to regiment after regiment: "Boys, we're going to lick them today!"

They almost did, but not while he was with them. As they approached the East Wood, deploying for action, Hooker rode up on his white horse. "The enemy are breaking through my lines!" he shouted above the roar of guns. "You must hold this wood!" Taken aback, Mansfield watched him gallop off; he had thought Hooker was driving the graybacks handsomely and that his own corps had been summoned to complete the victory. By now his lead regiments had reached a rail fence at the near edge of a field just short of the woods, and he saw to his horror that they had spread along it and were shooting at figures that moved in the shadows of the trees. "You are firing at our own men!" he cried. As soon as he got them stopped he leaped his horse over the fence, intending to ride ahead and see for himself. "Those are rebels,

General!" a soldier yelled. Mansfield pulled up, leaning forward to peer into the shadows. "Yes — you're right," he said, and as he spoke his words were confirmed by a volley that came crashing out of the woods, crippling his horse. He dismounted and walked back to the fence, but as he tried to climb over it, moving with the terrific deliberation of an old man among young ones, a bullet struck him in the stomach. He went down, groaning. Three veterans, who saw in the wounded general a one-way ticket out of chaos, took him up and lugged him back to an aid station, where a flustered surgeon half-strangled him with a jolt of whiskey, and presently he died.

Williams resumed command of the corps and sent both divisions forward, swinging one to the right so that its advance swept through the cornfield. Hood's survivors were knocked back, yielding ground and losing a stand of colors for the first time in their brief, furious history. On the bluecoats came, a Massachusetts colonel waving the captured Texas flag. They followed the route Hooker's men had taken an hour ago — and, like them, were stopped within reach of the Dunker Church by a two-brigade counterstroke. Jackson had called for reinforcements at the height of the first attack, and Lee had sent Walker's division from the right flank to the left, taking a chance that the Federals would not storm the lower Antietam crossings. These two North Carolina brigades arrived too late to contest the first penetration, but they got there in time to meet the second at its climax. Like Hooker's, Mansfield's men were stopped. However, they did not fall back. They stayed where they were, and Williams sent word to headquarters that if he could be reinforced he would have the battle won.

Reinforcements were already on the way — three divisions of them under Sumner, whose corps was the largest in the army — but they came by a different route: not down the Hagerstown road or parallel to it, but in at an angle through the lower fringes of the East Wood, which had been cleared of all but dead or dying rebels. So far, the close-up fighting had been left to troops formerly under Pope; now McClellan's own were coming in, led by the man who had saved the day at Fair Oaks. Dragoon-style, Sumner rode at the head of his lead division, leaving the others to come along behind. As he emerged from the woods he saw to his right the wreckage of the cornfield and up ahead the Dunker Church, dazzling white through rifts in the smoke boiling up from the line which Mansfield's men were struggling to hold against Walker's counterstroke. As Sumner saw it, the thing to do was get there fast, before that line gave way. With what his corps historian later called "ill-regulated ardor," he kept the lead division in march formation, three brigades close-packed in as many files, moving southwest across the open stretch of ground between the East Wood and the church. It was then that he was struck, two thirds of the way back down the column and squarely on the flank, with results that were sudden and altogether murderous. Too tightly wedged to maneuver as a unit, or even dodge as individuals, men fell in windrows, the long files writhing like wounded snakes. More than two thousand of them were shot down within a quarter of an hour. "My God, we must get out of this!" Sumner cried. His soldiers thought so, too, scrambling frantically for the rear as the graybacks charged.

It was McLaws. When his and Anderson's divisions finally reached Sharpsburg about 7 o'clock that morning — incredibly, they had been delayed at the outset because the paroled Federals, impatient to get home from Harpers Ferry, had clogged the bridge leading northward across the Potomac to the foot of Maryland Heights — more time was lost in a search for Lee, who was away from headquarters inspecting his right and center while Hooker was hammering at his left. When they found him, nearly an hour later, he sent Anderson to reinforce Hill, and McLaws to reinforce Jackson, who by then was receiving the full force of Mansfield's attack. This too had been stopped by the time McLaws got there, but just as he came over the ridge he saw Sumner's lead division emerge from the East Wood, driving straight for the Dunker Church with its flank exposed. He struck it, wrecked it, and took up the pursuit with his four brigades, joined on the left by Walker and Early, who threw Williams into retreat as well. Hooker by now was one of the nearly 7000 casualties the Federals had suffered at this end of the field; he rode northward out of the fight, dripping blood from a wounded foot, and his men followed, along with Mansfield's and Sumner's, to reform beyond the line of guns from which they had taken off at dawn. In rapid sequence, two whole corps and part of a third — six divisions containing 31,000 men — had been shattered and repulsed.

Jackson's losses had been comparable — probably in excess of 5000, which represented a larger percentage of casualties than he had inflicted — but he was strangely elated. Looking out over the shambles of the cornfield, which had just changed hands for the fourth time that morning and which by now was so thickly carpeted with dead men that one witness claimed you could walk in any direction across it and never touch the ground, his pale blue eyes had a fervent light to them. "God has been very kind to us this day," he said. For the first time since daylight glimmered across the eastern ridge his lines were free of pressure, and so was he himself. Sitting his horse in the yard of the Dunker Church, he ate a peach while his medical director submitted a preliminary casualty report. Stonewall made no comment, except to remark between bites that it was heavy, but when the surgeon expressed the fear that the survivors were too badly shaken to withstand another assault he shook his head, apparently unconcerned, and pointed in the direction of the bluecoats, huddled behind their line of guns a mile to the north. "Dr McGuire, they have done their worst," he said.

He was right, so far as concerned the left; the Federals there had done their worst and best. But Sharpsburg was, in effect, three battles piled one on top of another, and just as the first had ended with the repulse of Sumner's lead division, so did the second open with the repulse of the other two. Recovering his balance in the midst of disaster, the old man rode back through the woods in search of the rest of his corps, which was missing. One division he found had failed to cross the creek on schedule, while the other had lost contact and veered south, coming upon an eroded country lane from which a zigzag line of graybacks loosed a close-up volley that shattered the lead brigade and sent the others scrambling back. The third division, coming up at last, received the same reception and gave ground, but presently rallied and formed a line on which the second rallied, too. And thus, no sooner was Jackson's battle over, than Hill's got under way.

Here along the center the Confederates occupied what amounted to an intrenched position, the only one on the field. For the lane was not only worn below the level of the ground, affording them a considerable measure of protection, but it also ran between snake-rail fences, and they had dismantled the outer fence to make a substantial breastworks of the rails. What was more, the crest of the ridge was just over a hundred yards forward and uphill, so that the bluecoats could not see what they had to face until they were practically upon it, within easy musket range and outlined target-sharp against the eastern sky. This was unnerving, to say the least, and to make matters worse — psychologically, at any rate — the rebels jeered and hooted at the dark-clothed attackers coming over the rise, silhouetted against the glare of sunlight. "Go away, you black devils! Go home!" they yelled as they loosed their volleys. They felt confident and secure, and so did Hill: for a time at least. But as the Federals continued to press their attack with increasing persistency and numbers — Sumner had more than 12,000 men in his remaining two divisions, while Hill himself had less than 7,000, even after Anderson's arrival — the issue began to grow doubtful. Then presently, as a result of two unforeseen mishaps, it grew worse than doubtful. It grew impossible.

The first of these was that Anderson was severely wounded and carried from the field, command of his division passing to the senior brigadier, long-haired Roger Pryor, who by now had proved that his reluctance to fire the first shot at Fort Sumter had not proceeded from a lack of nerve, but whose talents were still primarily oratorical. From that time on, the division no longer functioned as a unit, and in fact went out of existence except as a loose collection of regiments and companies, each one fighting on its own as it saw fit. Which perhaps was just as well, in the end; for that was what happened to Hill's division, too, though its commander emerged unscathed from the experience of having three horses shot from under him in rapid succession.

This second disintegration was a result of the second mishap, which occurred when the brigade on the left, receiving the order to "refuse" its threatened flank, misunderstood the command and pulled out altogether; whereupon the opposing Federals hurried forward, occupied the abandoned portion of the line, and began to lay down an enfilading fire which gave the sunken road the name it bore thereafter: Bloody Lane. What had been a sheltered position, one from which to hoot at charging Yankees and shoot them down when they were so unmissably close that their faces filled the gunsight, became a trap. Quite suddenly, as if they had tumbled headlong by the hundreds out of the sky, dead men filled whole stretches of the road to overflowing. Horrified, unit by unit from left to right, the survivors broke for the rear, and now it was the Yankees doing the hooting and the shooting.

Faced with the abrupt disintegration of the isolated center, the exploitation of which would mean the end of Lee's army, Hill did what he could to rally the fugitives streaming back across the ridge, and though few of them had a mind for anything but their present dash for safety, he managed to scrape together a straggler line along the outskirts of Sharpsburg. While these men were delivering a sporadic fire against the bluecoats, who were massing along the sunken road, apparently preparing to continue their advance, Hill sent an urgent call for guns and reinforcements. There were none of the latter to send him; the right had been stripped and the left had been fought to exhaustion. But Longstreet had seen the trouble and was already sending every cannon he could lay hands on. He had not wanted to fight this battle in the first place — or for that matter, the odds being what they were, any battle in which there was so little to gain and so very much to lose — but now that it was unavoidably under way, he gave it everything he had. Limping about in carpet slippers and gesturing with an unlighted cigar, he ordered gun crew after gun crew to put their pieces in action along the ridge where Hill was forming his thin new line. As fast as these guns came into the open, the powerful Union batteries took them under fire from across the way, exploding caissons and mangling cannoneers. Observing one section of guns whose fire was weak because there were too few survivors to serve them properly, Old Pete dismounted his staff and improvised two high-ranking gun crews, himself holding their horses and correcting the ranges while they fired.

Hill meanwhile had been watching the bluecoats down in the sunken road. He believed they were about to attack him. Such an attack would surely be successful, weak as he was, and the only way he knew to delay it was to attack them first. However, when he called along his line for volunteers, there was no answer until presently one man said he would go if Hill would lead. Quickly taking him up on that, Hill seized a rifle and started forward with a shout, joined by about two hundred others who were persuaded by his example. The attack was brief; in fact, it was repulsed almost as soon as it began; but Hill believed it served its purpose. Here opposite the denuded Confederate center, the Federals stayed where they were for the rest of the day. According to Hill, this was either because he had frightened them into immobility or else it was an outright miracle.

It was neither, unless it was something of both. What it really was was Sumner — and McClellan. Franklin had come up by now, and though he had left one division on Maryland Heights, he still brought more than 8000 soldiers onto the field. One brigade had shared in the fight on the right, and now he wanted to use the other five in an assault on the gray line beyond the sunken road. But Sumner stopped him. The old man's corps had lost 5100 men today, more than Hooker's and Mansfield's combined; apparently he had seen enough of killing north of the Dunker Church and here in front of Bloody Lane. The thirty-nine-year-old Franklin tried to argue, but Sumner, who not only outranked him but was also nearly twice his age, kept insisting that the army was on the verge of disintegration and that another repulse would mean catastrophe. Presently a courier arrived from McClellan, bringing a suggestion that the attack be pressed by both commands if possible. Sumner — to whom, except for his long, pointed nose, old age had given the glaring look of a death's head — turned on him and cried hotly: "Go back, young man, and tell General McClellan I have no command! Tell him my command, Banks' command, and Hooker's command are all cut up and demoralized. Tell him General Franklin has the only organized command on this part of the field!"

When McClellan received this message he came down off the hill and crossed the creek to see for himself the situation in the center. Sumner and Franklin presented their arguments, and now that he had a close-up view of the carnage, McClellan sided with the senior. He told them both to hold what had been won; then he rode back across the creek. It was now about 2 o'clock, and the second battle, which like the first had lasted about four hours, was over. The third was about to begin.

In a broader sense, it had already been going on for as long as the other two combined. That is, the opponents had been exchanging shots across the lower reaches of the creek since dawn. But, so far, all that had come of this was the maiming of a few hundred soldiers, most of them in blue. Despite McClellan's repeated orders — including one sent at 9 o'clock, directing that the crossing be effected "at all hazards" — not a man out of the nearly 14,000 enrolled in Burnside's four divisions had reached the west bank of the Antietam by the time the sun swung past the overhead. "McClellan appears to think I am not trying my best to carry this bridge," the ruff-whiskered general said testily to a staff colonel his friend the army commander sent to prod him. "You are the third or fourth one who has been to me this morning with similar orders."

As he spoke he sat his horse beside a battery on a hilltop, looking down at the narrow, triple-arched stone span below. He watched it with a fascination amounting to downright prescience, as if he knew already that it was to bear his name and be in fact his chief monument, no matter what ornate shafts of marble or bronze a grateful nation might raise elsewhere in his honor. So complete was his absorption by the bridge itself, he apparently never considered testing the depth of the water that flowed sluggishly beneath it. If he had, he would have discovered that the little copper-colored stream, less than fifty feet in width, could have been waded at almost any point without wetting the armpits of the shortest man in his corps. However, except for sending one division downstream in search of a local guide to point out a ford that was rumored to exist in that direction, he remained intent on effecting a dry-shod crossing.

Admittedly this was no easy matter. The road came up from the southeast, paralleling the creek for a couple of hundred yards, and then turned sharply west across the bridge, where it swung north again to curve around the heights on the opposite bank. Just now those heights were occupied by rebels — many of them highly skilled as marksmen, though at that range skill was practically superfluous — which meant that whoever exposed himself along that road, in the shadow of those heights, was likely to catch a faceful of bullets. Nevertheless, this was the only route Burnside could see, and he kept sending men along it, regiment by regiment, intermittently all morning, with predictable results.

Observing from across the way the ease with which this lower threat was being contested, Lee all this time had been stripping his right of troops in order to strengthen his hard-pressed left and center. By noon he was down to an irreducible skeleton force; so that presently, when he learned that Hill had lost the sunken road and was calling in desperation for reinforcements, he had none to send him. Like Hill in this extremity, knowing that he probably could not withstand an assault, he decided that his only recourse was to deliver one — preferably on the left, which had been free of heavy pressure for two hours. Accordingly, he sent word for Jackson to attack the Federal right, if possible, swinging it back against the river. Stonewall was delighted at the prospect, and set out at once to reconnoiter the ground in that direction. "We'll drive McClellan into the Potomac," he said fervently. Back at Sharpsburg, meanwhile, Lee was doing what little he could to make this possible. When the captain of a shattered Virginia battery reported with his few surviving men, he instructed him to join Jackson for the proposed diversion. One of the smoke-grimed cannoneers spoke up: "General, are you going to send us in again?" Lee saw then that it was Robert. "Yes, my son," he told him. "You all must do what you can to help drive these people back." The battery left, heading northward; but no such attack was delivered. Reconnoitering, Stonewall found the Union flank securely anchored to the east bank of the river and well protected by massed artillery. He had to abandon his hopes for a counterstroke. "It is a great pity," he said regretfully. "We should have driven McClellan into the Potomac."

By the time Lee learned that the proposed attack could not be delivered, that no diversion to relieve the pressure against the sagging center would be made, the urgent need for it had passed. Hill's thin line — along which, in accordance with his instructions now that his feeble two-hundred-man charge had been repulsed, the colorbearers flourished their tattered battle flags, hiding his weakness behind gestures of defiance — went unchallenged by the bluecoats massed along the sunken road. But Lee was not allowed even a breathing space in which to enjoy the relaxation of tension. Catastrophe, it seemed, was still with him; had in fact merely withdrawn in order to loom up elsewhere. Immediately on the heels of the news that the Federal advance had stalled in front of the center, word came from the right that the contingency most feared had come to pass. Burnside was across the bridge at last.

Robert Toombs was in command there, holding the heights with three slim Georgia regiments against four Federal divisions. Lately, just as previously he had wearied of his cabinet post, he had been feeling disenchanted with the military life. Exasperated, now as then, by the obtuseness of those around him, he had decided to resign his commission, but not before he had distinguished himself in some great battle. "The day after such an event," he wrote his wife, "I will retire if I live through it." Such an event was now at hand, and he had been in his glory all that morning, successfully challenging with 550 men the advance of more than twenty times their number. At 1 o'clock, after seven hours of fitful and ineffectual probing, Burnside at last sent two regiments pounding straight downhill for the bridge, avoiding the suicidal two-hundred-yard gauntlet-run along the creek bank. They got across in a rush, joined presently by others, until the west-bank strength had increased to a full division at that point. Meanwhile the downstream division had finally located the ford and splashed across it, the men scarcely wetting their legs above the knees. About to be swamped from the front and flank, Toombs reported the double crossing and received permission to avoid capture by withdrawing from the heights. He did so in good order, proud of himself and his weary handful of fellow Georgians, whom he put in line along the rearward ridge. There on the outskirts of Sharps-

burg with the rest of Longstreet's troops — not over 2500 in all, so
ruthlessly had Lee thinned their ranks in his need for reinforcements on
the left and center — they prepared to resist the advance of Burnside's
four divisions.

What came just then, however, was a lull. After forming ranks
for a forward push, the commander of the lead blue division found that
his men had burnt up most of their ammunition banging away all morning at the snipers on the heights. Informed of this, Burnside decided to
replace them with another division instead of taking time to bring up
cartridges. This too took time though. It was nearly 3 o'clock before
the new division started forward. Off to the left, after crossing the ford
and floundering in the bottoms, the other division at last recovered its
sense of direction and joined the attack. Few though the rebels seemed
to be, they were laying down a mass of fire out of all proportion to their
numbers. A New York soldier, whose regiment was pinned down by
what he termed "the hiss of bullets and the hurtle of grapeshot," later
recalled that "there burst forth from it the most vehement, terrible
swearing I have ever heard." When the order came to rise and charge,
he observed another phenomenon: "The mental strain was so great that
I saw at that moment the singular effect mentioned, I think, in the life
of Goethe on a similar occasion — the whole landscape for an instant
turned slightly red."

Across this reddened landscape they came charging, presenting a
two-division front that overlapped the Confederate flank and piled up
against the center. Down at his headquarters, beyond the town (the lull
had been welcome, but he could only use it to rest his men, not to bring
up others; he had no others, and would have none until — and if —
A. P. Hill arrived from Harpers Ferry) Lee heard the uproar drawing
nearer across the eastern hills, and presently the evidences of Federal
success were visual as well. The Sharpsburg streets were crowded with
fugitives, their demoralization increased by shells that burst against the
walls and roofs of houses, startling flocks of pigeons into bewildered
flight, round and round in the smoke. Blue flags began to appear at
various points along the ridge above. The men who bore them had advanced almost a mile beyond the bridge; another mile would put them
astride the Shepherdstown road, which led west to the only crossing of
the Potomac.

Observing a column moving up from the southeast along the
ridge line, Lee called to an artillery lieutenant on the way to the front
with a section of guns: "What troops are those?" The lieutenant offered
him his telescope. "Can't use it," Lee said, holding up a bandaged hand.
The lieutenant trained and focused the telescope. "They are flying
the United States flag," he reported. Lee pointed to the right, where
another distant column was approaching from the southwest, nearly

perpendicular to the first, and repeated the question. The lieutenant swung the glass in that direction, peered intently, and announced: "They are flying the Virginia and Confederate flags." Lee suppressed his elation, although the words fulfilled his one hope for deliverance from defeat. "It is A. P. Hill from Harpers Ferry," he said calmly.

It was indeed. Receiving Lee's summons at 6.30 that morning, Little Powell had left one brigade to complete the work at the Ferry, and put the other five on the road within the hour. Seventeen rounda- bout miles away, the crash and rumble of gunfire spurred him on — particularly when he drew near enough for the sound to be intensified by the clatter of musketry. Forgotten were Stonewall's march regula- tions, which called for periodic rest-halts; Hill's main concern was to get to Sharpsburg fast, however bedraggled, not to get there after sundown with a column that arrived well-closed and too late for a share in the fighting. Jacket off because of the heat, he rode in his bright red battle shirt alongside the panting troops, prodding laggards with the point of his saber. Beyond this, he had no dealings with strag- glers, but left them winded by the roadside, depending on them to catch up in time if they could. Not many could, apparently; for he began the march with about 5000 men, and ended it with barely 3000. But with these, as was his custom, he struck hard.

In his path, here on the Federal left, was an outsized Connecticut regiment, 900-strong. That was a good many more soldiers than Hill had in any one of his brigades, but they were grass green, three weeks in service, and already considerably shaken by what they had seen of their first battle. To add to their confusion, a large proportion of the rebels bearing down on them wore new blue uniforms captured at Harpers Ferry. The first thing they received by way of positive identification was a close-up volley that dropped about four hundred of them and broke and scattered the rest. A Rhode Island outfit, coming up just then, was likewise confused, as were two Ohio regiments which arrived to find bluecoats fleeing from bluecoats and held their fire until they too were knocked sprawling. With that, the Union left gave way in a backward surge, pursued by Hill, whose men came after it, screaming their rebel yell. The panic spread northward to the outskirts of Sharps- burg, where several blue companies, meeting little resistance, had al- ready entered the eastern streets of the town; Burnside's whole line came unpinned, and presently the retreat was general. Toombs' Geor- gians, along with the rest of Longstreet's men, took up the pursuit and chased the Northerners back onto the heights they had spent the morn- ing trying to seize.

And now in the sunset, here on the right, as previously on the left and along the center, the conflict ended; except that this time it was for good. Twilight came down and the landscape was dotted with burn-

ing haystacks, set afire by bursting shells. For a time the cries of
wounded men of both armies came from these; they had crawled up
into the hay for shelter, but now, bled too weak to crawl back out
again, were roasted. Lee's line was intact along the Sharpsburg ridge.
McClellan had failed to break it; or, breaking it, had failed in all three
cases, left and center and right, to supply the extra push that would keep
it broken.

★ ★ ★

There were those in the Federal ranks who had been urging him
to do just that all afternoon. Nor did he lack the means. The greater part
of four divisions — two under Franklin, two under Porter: no less than
20,000 men, a solid fourth of his effective force — had stood idle while
the battle raged through climax after climax, each of which offered
McClellan the chance to wreck his adversary. But he could not dismiss
the notion that somewhere behind that opposite ridge, or off beyond the
flanks, Lee was massing enormous reserves for a knockout blow. The
very thinness of the gray line, which was advanced as an argument for
assaulting it, seemed to him to prove that the balance of those more than
100,000 rebels were being withheld for some such purpose, and when it
came he wanted to have something with which to meet it.

"At this critical juncture," he afterwards reported, "I should
have had a narrow view of the condition of the country had I been willing to hazard another battle with less than an absolute assurance of success. At that moment — Virginia lost, Washington menaced, Maryland invaded — the national cause could afford no risks of defeat. Lee's
army might then have marched as it pleased on Washington, Baltimore, Philadelphia, or New York . . . and nowhere east of the Alleghenies was there another organized force able to arrest its march."

It never occurred to him, apparently, to look at the reverse of
the coin: to consider that Lee's army, like his own, was the only organized force that blocked the path to its capital. But it did occur to Sykes,
who appealed to him, late in the day and in the presence of Porter, to
be allowed to strike at the rebel center with his regulars. Part of one of
his brigades had been up close to the western ridge, serving as a link
between Sumner's left and Burnside's right, and its officers had seen
that D. H. Hill was about to buckle — indeed, had buckled already, if
someone would only take advantage of the fact. Let him launch an
attack against that point, Sykes said, supported by Porter's other division and one from Franklin, and he would cut Lee's line in two, thereby
exposing the severed halves to destruction.

At first McClellan seemed about to approve; but in the moment
of hesitation he looked at Porter, and Porter slowly shook his head.
"Remember, General," one witness later quoted him as saying, "I command the last reserve of the last army of the republic." That cinched it.

The attack was not made. Porter and Franklin, who between them lost only 548 of today's more than 12,000 casualties, remained in reserve.

As night came down, the two armies disengaged, and when the torches of the haystack pyres went out, darkness filled the valley of the Antietam, broken only by the lanterns of the medics combing the woods and cornfields for the injured who were near enough to be brought within the lines. Lee remained at his headquarters, west of Sharpsburg, greeting his generals as they rode up. Jackson, the two Hills, McLaws and Walker, Hood and Early, all had heavy losses to report. The gray commander spoke with each, but he seemed unshaken by the fact that more than a fourth of his army lay dead or wounded on the field. Nor did he mention the word that was in all their minds: retreat. "Where is Longstreet?" he asked, after he had talked with all the others. Presently Old Pete arrived, still limping in carpet slippers and still chewing on the unlighted cigar; he had stopped in the town to help some ladies whose house was on fire. Lee stepped forward to greet him. "Ah," he said, placing his crippled hands on the burly Georgian's shoulders. "Here is Longstreet. Here is my old warhorse."

This last report was as gloomy as the others. The army was bled white and near exhaustion, with all its divisions on the firing line. Aside from a trickle of stragglers coming in, Lee's only reserve, and in fact the only reserve in all northern Virginia, was the one brigade A. P. Hill had left to complete the salvage work at Harpers Ferry. All the generals here informally assembled were agreed that another day like today would drive the surviving remnant headlong into the Potomac. All, that is, but Lee. When he had heard his lieutenants out, he told them to return to their men, make such tactical readjustments as would strengthen their defenses, and see that rations were cooked and distributed along the present line of battle. If McClellan wanted another fight, he would give him one tomorrow.

McClellan, it seemed, wanted no such thing. Despite an early morning telegram to Halleck: "The battle will probably be renewed today. Send all the troops you can by the most expeditious route," and a letter in which he told his wife: "[Yesterday's battle] was a success, but whether a decided victory depends on what occurs today," he soon took stock and found the portents far from favorable. Reno and Mansfield were dead, along with eight other general officers; Hooker was out of action, wounded; Sumner was despondent; Burnside was even doubtful whether his troops could hold the little they had gained the day before. After what he called "a careful and anxious survey of the condition of my command, and my knowledge of the enemy's force and position," McClellan decided to wait for reinforcements, including two divisions on the way from Maryland Heights and Frederick. As a result, the armies lay face to face all day, like sated lions, and between them, there on the slopes of Sharpsburg ridge and in the valley of the Antietam, the dead began to fester in the heat and the cries of the wounded faded to a mewling.

There were a great many of both, the effluvium of this bloodiest day of the war. Nearly 11,000 Confederates and more than 12,000 Federals had fallen along that ridge and in that valley, including a total on both sides of about 5000 dead. Losses at South Mountain raised these doleful numbers to 13,609 and 14,756 respectively, the latter being increased to 27,276 by the surrender of the Harpers Ferry garrison. Lee had suffered only half as many casualties as he had inflicted in the course of the campaign; but even this was more than he could afford. "Where is your division?" someone asked Hood at the close of the battle, and Hood replied, "Dead on the field." After entering the fight with 854 men, the Texas brigade came out with less than three hundred, and these figures were approximated in other veteran units, particularly in Jackson's command. The troops Lee lost were the best he had — the best he could ever hope to have in the long war that lay ahead, now that his try for an early ending by invasion had been turned back.

Orders for the retirement were issued that afternoon, and at nightfall, in accordance with those orders, fires were kindled along the ridge to curtain the retreat across the Potomac. Longstreet went first, forming in support of Pendleton's guns on the opposite bank. Two brigades of cavalry followed, then moved upstream, prepared to recross and harry the enemy flank in case the withdrawal was contested. Walker's division was the last to cross. At sunup, as Walker followed the tail of his column into the waist-deep water of the ford, he saw Lee sitting his gray horse in midstream. Apparently he had been there all night. When Walker reported all of his troops safely across the river except some wagonloads of wounded and a battery of artillery, which were close at hand, Lee showed for the first time the strain he had been under. "Thank God," he said.

That was in fact the general reaction, though in most cases it was expressed with considerably less reverence. Crossing northward two weeks ago, the bands had played "My Maryland" and the men had gaily swelled the chorus; but now, as one of the round-trip marchers remarked, "all was quiet on that point. Occasionally some fellow would strike up that tune, and you would then hear the echo, 'Damn my Maryland.'" Another recorded his belief that "the confounded Yankees" could shoot straighter on their home ground. Nor was this aversion restricted to the ranks. "I have heard but one feeling expressed about [Maryland]," one brigadier informed his wife, "and that is a regret at our having gone there." A youthful major on Lee's own staff wrote home to his sister: "Don't let any of your friends sing 'My Maryland' — not 'My Western Maryland' anyhow."

Presently there was apparent cause for greater regret than ever.

Leaving Pendleton with forty-four guns and two slim brigades of infantry to discourage pursuit by holding the Shepherdstown ford, Lee moved the rest of his army into bivouac on the hills back from the river, then lay down under an apple tree to get some badly needed sleep himself. Not long after midnight he woke to find Pendleton bending over him. The former Episcopal rector was shaken and bewildered, and as he spoke Lee found out why. McClellan had brought up his heavy guns for counterbattery work, Pendleton explained, and then at the height of the bombardment had suddenly thrown Porter's corps across the Potomac, driving off the six hundred rear-guard infantry and the startled cannoneers. All the guns of the Confederate reserve artillery had been captured.

"*All?*" Lee said, brought upright.

"Yes, General, I fear all."

Unwilling to attempt a counterattack in the dark with his weary troops, Lee decided to wait for daylight. But when Jackson heard the news he was too upset to wait for anything. He had A. P. Hill's men turn out at once and put them in motion for the ford, arriving soon after sunrise to find that things were by no means as bad as the artillery chief had reported. A subordinate had brought off all but four of the guns, and only a portion of Porter's two divisions had crossed the river. "With the blessing of Providence," Stonewall informed Lee, "they will soon be driven back." They were. Hill launched another of his savage attacks: one of those in which, as he reported, "each man felt that the fate of the army was centered in himself." Something over 250 Federals were shot or drowned in their rush to regain the Maryland bank, and when it was over, all who remained in Virginia were captives. Hill drew back to rejoin the main body, unpursued.

What at first had been taken for a disaster turned out in the end to be a tonic — a sort of upbeat coda, after the crash and thunder of what had gone before. The army moved on to Martinsburg, where by September 22 enough stragglers had returned to bring its infantry strength to 36,418. A week later, with all ten divisions — or at any rate what was left of them — resting between Mill Creek and Lick River, Lee wrote Davis: "History records but few examples of a greater amount of labor and fighting than has been done by this army during the present campaign. . . . There is nothing to report, but I desire to keep you always advised of the condition of the army, its proceedings, and prospects."

He had occupied his present position near Winchester, he told the President, "in order to be prepared for any flank movement the enemy might attempt." It soon developed, however, that he had no grounds for worry on that score. McClellan was not contemplating a flank movement. In point of fact, despite renewed pressure from Washington, McClellan was not contemplating any immediate movement at all.

After completing the grisly and unaccustomed work of cleaning up the battlefield, he reoccupied Harpers Ferry with Sumner's corps and spread the others along the north bank of the Potomac, guarding the fords. The main problem just now, as he saw it, was the old one he had always been so good at: reorganizing, drilling, and resupplying his 93,149 effectives. Lee's strength — precisely tabulated at 97,445 — forbade an advance, even if the Federal army had been in any condition to make one, which McClellan did not believe to be the case.

As he went about the familiar task of preparing his men for what lay ahead, he looked back with increasing pride on what had gone before. Originally he had been guarded in his pronouncements as to the outcome of the battle on the 17th. "The general result was in our favor," he wrote his wife next morning; "that is to say, we gained a great deal of ground and held it." But now that he had had time to consider the overall picture, he said, "I feel that I have done all that can be asked in twice saving the country." He felt, too, "that this last short campaign is a sufficient legacy for our child, so far as honor is concerned." And he added, rather wistfully: "Those in whose judgment I rely tell me that I fought the battle splendidly and that it is a masterpiece of art."

✗ 3 ✗

For Lincoln it was something less, and also something more. The battle had been fought on a Wednesday. At noon Monday, September 22, he assembled at the White House all the members of his cabinet, and after reading them an excerpt from a collection of humorous sketches by Artemus Ward, got down to the business at hand. "When the rebel army was at Frederick," he told them, "I determined, as soon as it should be driven out of Maryland, to issue a proclamation of emancipation, such as I thought most likely to be useful. I said nothing to anyone; but I made the promise to myself and" — hesitating slightly — "to my Maker. The rebel army is now driven out, and I am going to fulfill that promise." And with that he began to read from a manuscript which was the second draft of the document he had laid aside, two months ago today, on Seward's advice that to have issued it then would have been to give it the sound of "our last *shriek* on the retreat" down the Peninsula. Second Bull Run had been even worse, particularly from this point of view. But now had come Antietam, and though it was scarcely a "masterpiece," or even a clear-cut victory, Lincoln thought it would serve as the occasion for his purpose.

It was highly characteristic, and even fitting, that he opened this solemn conclave with a reading of the slapstick monologue, "High Handed Outrage at Utica," not only because he himself enjoyed it, along with most of his ministers — all except Stanton, who sat glumly through the dialect performance, and Chase, who maintained his reputation for never laughing at anything at all — but also because it was in line with the delaying tactics and the attitude he had adopted toward the question during these past two months. With the first draft of the proclamation tucked away in his desk, only awaiting a favorable turn of military events to launch it upon an unsuspecting world, he had seemed to talk against such a measure to the very people who came urging its promulgation. Presumably he did this in order to judge their reaction, as well as to prevent a diminution of the thunderclap effect which he foresaw. At any rate, he had not even hesitated to use sarcasm, particularly against the most earnest of these callers.

One day, for example, a Quaker woman came to request an audience, and Lincoln said curtly: "I will hear the Friend." She told him she had been sent by the Lord to inform him that he was the minister appointed to do the work of abolishing slavery. Then she fell silent. "Has the Friend finished?" Lincoln asked. She said she had, and he replied: "I have neither the time nor disposition to enter into discussion with the Friend, and end this occasion by suggesting for her consideration the question whether, if it be true that the Lord has appointed me to do the work she has indicated, it is not probable he would have communicated knowledge of the fact to me as well as to her?"

Similarly, on the day before the Battle of South Mountain, when a delegation of Chicago ministers called to urge presidential action on the matter, he inquired: "What good would a proclamation of emancipation from me do, especially as we are now situated? I do not want to issue a document that the whole world will see must necessarily be inoperative, like the Pope's bull against the comet. Would my word free the slaves, when I cannot even enforce the Constitution in the rebel states? Is there a single court or magistrate or individual that would be influenced by it there? . . . I will mention another thing, though it meet only your scorn and contempt. There are fifty thousand bayonets in the Union armies from the border slave states. It would be a serious matter if, in consequence of a proclamation such as you desire, they should go over to the rebels." In parting, however, he dropped a hint. "Do not misunderstand me because I have mentioned these objections. They indicate the difficulties that have thus far prevented action in some such way as you desire. I have not decided against a proclamation of liberty to the slaves, but hold the matter under advisement. . . . I can assure you that the subject is on my mind, by day and night, more than any other. Whatever shall appear to be God's will, I will do."

Sadly the Illinois ministers filed out; but one, encouraged by the closing words, remained behind to register a plea in that direction. "What you have said to us, Mr President, compels me to say to you in reply, that it is a message to you from our Divine Master, through me, commanding you, sir, to open the doors of bondage that the slaves may go free." Lincoln gave him a long look, not unlike the one he had given the Quaker woman. "That may be, sir," he admitted, "for I have studied this question by night and by day, for weeks and for months. But if it is, as you say, a message from your Divine Master, is it not odd that the only channel he could send it by was the roundabout route by way of that awful wicked city of Chicago?"

These remarks were in any case supplementary to those he had made already in reply to Horace Greeley, who published in the August 20 *Tribune* an open letter to the President, titled "The Prayer of Twenty Millions," in which he charged at some length that Lincoln had been "strangely and disastrously remiss in the discharge of your official and imperative duty." The first such duty, as Greeley saw it, was to announce to the army, the nation, and the world that this war was primarily a struggle to put an end to slavery. Lincoln, having heard that the New Yorker was preparing to attack him, had asked a mutual friend, "What is he wrathy about? Why does he not come down here and have a talk with me?" The friend replied that Greeley had said he would not allow the President of the United States to act as advisory editor of the *Tribune*. "I have no such desire," Lincoln said. "I certainly have enough on my hands to satisfy any man's ambition." But now that the journalist had aired his grievance publicly, Lincoln answered two days later with a public letter of his own, headed "Executive Mansion" and addressed to Greeley:

> As to the policy I "seem to be pursuing," as you say, I have not meant to leave anyone in doubt.
>
> I would save the Union. I would save it the shortest way under the Constitution. The sooner the national authority can be restored, the nearer the Union will be "the Union as it was." If there be those who would not save the Union unless they could at the same time save slavery, I do not agree with them. If there be those who would not save the Union unless they could at the same time destroy slavery, I do not agree with them. My paramount object in this struggle is to save the Union, and is not either to save or destroy slavery. If I could save the Union without freeing any slave, I would do it; and if I could save it by freeing all the slaves, I would do it; and if I could save it by freeing some and leaving others alone, I would also do that. What I do about slavery and the colored race, I do because I believe it helps to save the Union; and what I forbear, I forbear because I do not believe it would help to save the Union. I shall do less whenever I shall believe what I am doing hurts the cause, and I shall do more whenever I shall believe doing more will help the cause. I shall try to correct errors when shown to be errors, and I shall adopt new views so fast as they shall appear to be true views.
>
> I have here stated my purpose according to my view of official duty; and I intend no modification of my oft-expressed personal wish that all men everywhere could be free.

And having thus to some extent forestalled his anticipated critics — particularly the conservatives, whose arguments he advanced as his own while pointing out the expediency of acting counter to them — he read to the cabinet this latest draft of what he called a Preliminary Emancipation Proclamation. Two opening paragraphs emphasized that the paper was being issued by him as Commander in Chief, upon military necessity; that reunion, not abolition, was still the primary object of the war; that compensated emancipation was still his goal for loyal owners, and that voluntary colonization of freedmen, "upon this continent or elsewhere," would still be encouraged. In the third paragraph he got down to the core of the edict, declaring "That on the first day of January, in the year of our Lord one thousand eight hundred and sixty-three, all persons held as slaves within any State or designated part of a State the people whereof shall then be in rebellion against the United States, shall be then, thenceforward, and forever free." He closed, after quoting from congressional measures prohibiting the return of fugitive slaves to disloyal masters, with the promise that, on restoration of the Union, he would recommend that loyal citizens of all areas "be compensated for all losses by acts of the United States, including the loss of slaves."

In this form, after adopting some minor emendations suggested by Seward and Chase, Lincoln gave the document to the world next morning. *Return to the Union within one hundred days,* he was telling the rebels, *and you can keep your slaves — or anyhow be compensated for them, when and if (as I propose) the law takes them away. Otherwise, if you lose the war, you lose your human property as well.* It was in essence counterrevolutionary, a military edict prompted by expediency. Whoever attacked him for it, whatever the point of contention, would have to attack him on his own ground.

This the South was quick to do. Recalling his inaugural statement, "I have no purpose, directly or indirectly, to interfere with the institution of slavery in the states where it exists. I believe I have no lawful right to do so, and I have no inclination to do so," southern spokesmen cried that Lincoln at last had dropped the mask. They quoted with outright horror a passage from the very core of the proclamation which seemed to them to incite the slaves to riot and massacre: "The Executive Government of the United States, including the military and naval authority thereof . . . will do no act or acts to repress such persons, or any of them, in any efforts they may make for their actual freedom." What was this, they asked, if not an invitation to the Negroes to murder them in their beds? Bestial, they called Lincoln, for here he had touched the quick of their deepest fear, and the Richmond *Examiner* charged that the proclamation was "an act of malice towards the master, rather than one of mercy to the slave." Abroad, the London *Spectator* reinforced this view of the author's cynicism: "The principle is not that a human being cannot justly own another, but that he cannot own him unless he is loyal to the United States." Jefferson Davis, while he deplored that such a paper could be issued by the head of a government of which he himself had once been part, declared that it would inspire the South to new determination; for "a restitution of the Union has been rendered forever impossible by the adoption of a measure which . . . neither admits of retraction nor can coexist with union."

In the North, too, there were critics, some of whom protested that the proclamation went too far, while others claimed that it did not go far enough. Some, in fact, maintained that it went nowhere, since it proclaimed freedom only for those unfortunates now firmly under Confederate control. One such critic was the New York *World*, whose editor pointed out that "the President has purposely made the proclamation inoperative in all places where we have gained a military footing which makes the slaves accessible. He has proclaimed emancipation only where he has notoriously no power to execute it." Not only were the loyal or semiloyal slave states of Delaware and Maryland, Kentucky and Missouri omitted from the terms to be applied, but so was the whole rebel state of Tennessee, as well as those parts of Virginia and Louisiana under Federal occupation. This was a matter of considerable alarm to the abolitionists. For if emancipation was not to be extended to those regions a hundred days from now, they asked, when would it ever be extended to them? What manner of document was this anyhow?

Yet these objections were raised only by those who read it critically. Most people did not read it so. They took it for more than it was, or anyhow for more than it said; the container was greater than the thing contained, and Lincoln became at once what he would remain for them, "the man who freed the slaves." He would go down to posterity, not primarily as the Preserver of the Republic — which he was — but as the Great Emancipator, which he was not. "A poor *document*, but a mighty *act*," the governor of Massachusetts privately called the proclamation, and Lincoln himself said of it in a letter to Vice-President Hamlin, six days later: "The time for its effect southward has not come; but northward the effect should be instantaneous." Whatever truth there was in Davis' claim that it would further unite the South in opposition, Lincoln knew that it had already done much to heal the split in his own party; which was not the least of his reasons for having released it.

Seward understood such things. Asked by a friend why the cabinet had done "so useless and mischievous a thing as to issue the proclamation," he told a story. Up in New York State, he said, when the news came that the Revolutionary War had been won and American independence at last established, an old patriot could not rest until he had put up a liberty pole. When his neighbors asked him why he had gone to so much trouble — wasn't he just as free without it? — the patriot replied, "What is liberty without a pole?" So it was with the present case, Seward remarked between puffs on his cigar: "What is war without a proclamation?"

Something more it had done, or was doing, which was also included in Lincoln's calculations. Abroad, as at home, a bedrock impact had been felt. In London, like the pro-Confederate *Spectator*, the *Times* might call the proclamation "A very sad document," which the South would "answer with a hiss of scorn"; a distinguished Member of Parliament might refer to it as "a hideous outburst of weak yet demoniacal spite" and "the most unparalleled last card ever played by a reckless gambler"; Earl Russell himself might point out to his colleagues that it was "of a very strange nature" and contained "no declaration of a principle adverse to slavery." Yet behind these organs of opinion, below these men of influence, stood the people. In their minds, now that Lincoln had spoken out — regardless of what he actually said or left unsaid — support for the South was support for slavery, and they would not have it so. From this point on, the editors might favor and the heads of state might ponder ways and means of extending recognition to the Confederacy, but to do this they would have to run counter to the feelings and demands of the mass of their subscribers and electors. Not even the nearly half-million textile workers already idle as a result of the first pinch of the cotton famine were willing to have the blockade broken on such terms. And the same was true in France. With this one blow — though few could see it yet: least of all the leader most concerned — Lincoln had shattered the main pillar of what had been the southern President's chief hope from the start. Europe would not be coming into this war.

Another change the document had wrought, though this one was uncalculated, occurring within the man himself. Sixteen years ago, back in Illinois, when an election opponent charged that he was an infidel, Lincoln refuted it with an open letter to the voters; but this was mainly a denial that he was a "scoffer," and not even then did he make any claim to being truly religious. Herndon, who saw him almost daily through that period, as well as before and after, later declared that he had never heard his partner mention the name of Jesus "but to confute the idea that he was the Christ." The fact remains that in a time when even professional soldiers called upon God in their battle reports, Lincoln seemed not to be a praying man and he never joined a church. Concerned as he had always been with logic, he had not yet reached a stage of being able to believe in what he could not comprehend. But now, in this second autumn of the war, a change began to show. In late September, when an elderly Quaker woman came to the White House to thank him for having issued the Emancipation Proclamation, Lincoln replied in a tone quite different from the one with which he had addressed her fellow Quaker the month before.

"I am glad of this interview," he told her, "and glad to know that I have your sympathy and prayers. We are indeed going through a great trial — a fiery trial. In the very responsible position in which I happen to be placed, being a humble instrument in the hands of our Heavenly Father, as I am, and as we all are, to work out his great purposes, I have desired that all my works and acts may be according to his will; and that it might be so, I have sought his aid. But if, after endeavoring to do my best in the light which he affords me, I find my efforts fail, I must believe that for some purpose unknown to me, he wills it otherwise. If I had had my way, this war would never have been commenced. If I had been allowed my way, this war would have been ended before this. But we find it still continues, and we must believe that he permits it for some wise purpose of his own, mysterious and unknown to us; and though with our limited understandings we may not be able to comprehend it, yet we cannot but believe that he who made the world still governs it."

This was a theme that would bear developing. In the proclamation itself he had omitted any reference to the Deity, and it was at the suggestion of Chase that he invoked, in the body of a later draft, "the gracious favor of Almighty God." But now, out of the midnight trials of his spirit, out of his concern for a race in bondage, out of his knowledge of the death of men in battle, something new had come to birth in Lincoln, and through him into the war. After this, as Davis said, there could be no turning back; Lincoln had sounded forth a trumpet that would never call retreat. And having sounded it, he turned in these final days of September to the inscrutable theme he had touched when he thanked the second Quaker woman for her prayers. His secretary found on the presidential desk a sheet of paper containing a single paragraph, a "Meditation on the Divine Will," which Lincoln had written with no thought of publication. Hay copied and preserved it:

The will of God prevails. In great contests each party claims to act in accordance with the will of God. Both may be, and one must be, wrong. God cannot be for and against the same thing at the same time. In the present civil war it is quite possible that God's purpose is something different from the purpose of either party; and yet the human instrumentalities, working just as they do, are of the best adaptation to effect his purpose. I am almost ready to say that this is probably true; that God wills this contest, and wills that it shall not end yet. By his mere great power on the minds of the now contestants, he could have either saved or destroyed the Union without a human contest. Yet the contest began. And, having begun, he could give the final victory to either side any day. Yet the contest proceeds.

✖ 4 ✖

Whatever else it was or might become, whatever reactions it produced within the minds and hearts of men — including Lincoln's — the proclamation was first of all a military measure; which meant that, so far, its force was merely potential. Its application dependent on the armies of the Union, its effect would be in direct ratio to their success, 1) in driving back the Confederate invaders, and 2) in resuming the southward movement whose flow had been reversed, east west, by the advances of Lee and Bragg into Maryland and Kentucky. The nearer of these two penetrating spearheads had been encysted and repelled by McClellan, and for this Lincoln was grateful, though he would have preferred something more in the way of pursuit than an ineffectual bloodying of the waters at Shepherdstown ford. Even this, however, was better than what he saw when he looked westward in the direction of his native state. The other spearhead was not only still deeply embedded in the vitals of Kentucky, but to Lincoln's acute distress it seemed likely to remain so. After winning by default the race for Louisville, Buell appeared to be concerned only with taking time to catch his breath; with the result that, near the end of September, Lincoln's thin-stretched patience snapped. He ordered Buell's removal from command.

His distress no doubt would have been less acute if he had known that, with or without pressure from Buell, Bragg was already considering a withdrawal. At the outset the North Carolinian had announced that he would make the "Abolition demagogues and demons . . . taste the bitters of invasion," but now he found his own teeth set on edge. From Bardstown, which he had reached three days before, he reported to Richmond on September 25 that his troops were resting from "the long, arduous, and exhausting march" over Muldraugh's Hill. "It is a source of deep regret that this move was necessary," he declared, "as it has enabled Buell to reach Louisville, where a very large force is now concentrated." Then he got down to the bedrock cause of his discontent: "I regret to say we are sadly disappointed at the want of action by our friends in Kentucky. We have so far received no accession to this army. General Smith has secured about a brigade — not half our losses by casualties of different kinds. We have 15,000 stand of arms and no one to use them. Unless a change occurs soon we must abandon the garden spot of Kentucky to its cupidity. The love of ease and fear of pecuniary loss are the fruitful sources of this evil."

In saying this he took his cue from Smith, who — though privately he admitted, "I can understand their fears and hesitancy; they have so much to lose" — had written him from Lexington the week before: "The Kentuckians are slow and backward in rallying to our standard. Their hearts are evidently with us, but their blue-grass and fat cattle are against us." The day after Bragg reached Bardstown — with Buell still moving northward, more or less across his flank and rear — Smith told him that he regarded "the defeat of Buell before he effects a junction with the force at Louisville as a military necessity, for Buell's army has always been the great bugbear to these people, and until [it is] defeated we cannot hope for much addition to our ranks." In other words, before the citizens would risk their lives and property in open support of the Confederates, they wanted to be assured that they would *stay* there. But to Bragg it seemed that this was putting the cart before the horse. He later explained his reluctance in a letter to his wife: "Why should I stay with my handful of brave Southern men to fight for cowards who skulked about in the dark to say to us, 'We are with you. Only whip these fellows out of our country and let us see you can protect us, and we will join you'?"

And so for a time the two Confederate commanders, both flushed with recent victories, remained precisely where they were, Smith at Lexington and Bragg at Bardstown, fifty airline miles apart, gathering supplies and issuing recruiting appeals which largely went unanswered. The former kept urging the latter to pounce on Buell, claiming that he could whip him unassisted, while he himself continued to load his wagons and round up herds of cattle. Bragg was unwilling to move on Louisville alone, and yet he was also unwilling to ask Smith to abandon the heart of the Bluegrass region by moving westward to join him. Between the two, they had arrived at a sort of impasse of indecision, behind which both were intent on the fruitful harvest they were gleaning against the day when they would retrace their steps across the barrens. What had been announced as a full-scale offensive, designed to establish and maintain the northern boundary of the Confederacy along the Ohio River, had degenerated into a giant raid.

This did not mean that Bragg abandoned all his hopes. Unwilling though he was to risk a pitched battle while Buell hugged the Louisville intrenchments, he thought there still might be a bloodless way to encourage prospective bluegrass volunteers by replacing the Unionist state government, which had fled its capital, with one that was friendly to the South. Moreover, he had the means at hand. In November of the previous year, an irregular convention had met at Russellville to declare the independence of Kentucky, establish a provisional government, and petition the Confederacy for admission. All this it did, and was accepted; Kentucky had representatives in the Confederate Congress and a star in the Confederate flag. Presently, however, when Albert Sidney Johnston's long line came unhinged at Donelson, the men who followed that star were in exile — including Provisional Governor George W. Johnson, who fell at Shiloh and was succeeded by the lieutenant governor, Richard Hawes. Hawes was now on his way north from Chattanooga, and it was Bragg's intention to inaugurate him at Frankfort. With a pro-Confederate occupying the governor's chair in the capitol, sup-

ported by a *de facto* government of Confederate sympathies, the entire
political outlook would be changed; or so Bragg thought. At any rate, he
considered it so thoroughly worth the effort that he decided to see it
done himself, lending his personal dignity to the occasion.

Accordingly, leaving Polk in charge of the army around Bardstown, he set out for Lexington on September 28 to confer with Smith
before proceeding to Frankfort. Joined by Hawes and his party two
days later at Danville, he wrote Polk: "The country and the people
grow better as we get into the one and arouse the other." October
1, he reached Lexington, where he arranged for Smith to move his
whole army up to Frankfort for the inaugural ceremonies, two or three
days later. By now, however, though he still expected much from the
current political maneuver, his reaction to what he had seen during his
ride through the Bluegrass was mixed. "Enthusiasm is unbounded, but
recruiting at a discount," he wired Polk. "Even the women are giving
reasons why individuals cannot go."

Bragg was not the only army commander displaying symptoms
of discouragement at this stage of the far-flung campaign. A Cincinnati
journalist, watching Buell ride north through Elizabethtown at the head
of his retrograding column on September 24, was unfavorably impressed: "His dress was that of a brigadier instead of a major general. He
wore a shabby straw hat, dusty coat, and had neither belt, sash or
sword about him. . . . Though accompanied by his staff, he was not engaged in conversation with any of them, but rode silently and slowly
along, noticing nothing that transpired around him. . . . Buell is, certainly, the most reserved, distant and unsociable of all the generals in
the army. He never has a word of cheer for his men or his officers, and
in turn his subordinates care little for him save to obey his orders, as
machinery works in response to the bidding of the mechanic." The reporter believed that this lack of cheer and sociability on the part of the
commander was the cause of the army's present gloom. McClellan, for
example, had "an unaccountable something, that keeps this machinery
constantly oiled and easy-running; but Buell's unsympathetic nature
makes it 'squeak' like the drag wheels of a wagon."

More than the past was fretting Buell; more, even, than the
present. After the lost opportunities down along the Tennessee River,
after the long hot weary trudge back north to the Ohio, he was confronted with the prospect of having to fight two opponents who, inured
by and rested from their recent victories, could now combine to move
against him. Nor was this all. Near the end of his 250-mile withdrawal
— aware that his superiors were hostile, ready to let fall the Damoclean
sword of dismissal, and that his subordinates were edgy, ready to leap at
his own and each other's throats — he was also suffering forebodings:
forebodings which were presently borne out all too abruptly. Passing

through Elizabethtown, he reached Louisville next day. Within another three days he had his whole army there. On the day after that, September 29, in the midst of a general reorganization, he was struck two knee-buckling blows, both of which fell before he had even had time to digest his breakfast.

The first was that, in a time when aggressiveness was at a considerable premium, he lost William Nelson, the most aggressive of his several major generals. He lost him because the Indiana brigadier Jefferson Davis, home from the Transmississippi on a sick leave, had come down to Louisville to assist Nelson in preparing to hold the city against Smith. Nelson was overbearing, Davis touchy; the result was a personality clash, at the climax of which the former ordered the latter out of his department. Davis went, but presently he returned, bringing the governor of Indiana with him. This was Oliver P. Morton, who also had a bone to pick with Nelson over his alleged mishandling of Hoosier volunteers during the fiasco staged at Richmond a month ago tomorrow. They accosted him in the lobby of the Galt House, Buell's Louisville headquarters, just after early breakfast. In the flare-up that ensued, Davis demanded satisfaction for last week's rudeness, and when Nelson called him an "insolent puppy," flipped a wadded calling-card in his face; whereupon Nelson laid the back of a ham-sized hand across his jaw. Davis fell back, and the burly Kentuckian turned on Morton, asking if he too had come there to insult him. Morton said he had not. Nelson started up the staircase, heading for Buell's room on the second floor. "Did you hear that damned insolent scoundrel insult me, sir?" he demanded of an acquaintance coming down. "I suppose he don't know me, sir. I'll teach him a lesson, sir." He went on up the stairs, then down the hall, and just as he reached the door of Buell's room he heard someone behind him call his name. Turning, he saw Davis standing at the head of the stairs with a pistol in his hand.

Davis had not come armed to the encounter, but after staggering back from the slap he had gone around the lobby asking bystanders for a weapon. At last he came to a certain Captain Gibson. "I always carry the article," Gibson said, producing a pistol from under his coat. Davis took it, and as he started up the stairs Gibson called after him, "It's a tranter trigger. Work light." So when Nelson turned from Buell's door and started toward him, Davis knew what to do. "Not another step farther!" he cried; and then, at a range of about eight feet, shot the big man in the chest. Nelson stopped, turned back toward Buell's door, but fell before he got there. "Send for a clergyman; I wish to be baptized," he told the men who came running at the sound of the shot. Gathering around him, they managed to lift the 300-pound giant onto a bed in a nearby room. "I have been basely murdered," he said. Half an hour later he was dead.

Buell had Davis placed in arrest, intending to try him for mur-

der, but before he could appoint a court or even prepare to conduct
an investigation — indeed, before Nelson's blood had time to dry on the
rug outside his door — he found that he no longer had any authority
in the matter. The second blow had landed. Halleck's order for Buell's
removal, issued at Lincoln's insistence, was delivered by special courier
that morning. The courier, a colonel aide of Halleck's, acting under instructions similar to the ones given in Frémont's case the year before —
that is, the order was not to be delivered if Buell had fought or was
about to fight a battle — had left Washington on the 24th, before Lincoln or Halleck knew the outcome of the race for Louisville. Three days
later, learning that Buell had reached the Ohio ahead of Bragg, Halleck
wired the colonel: "Await further orders before acting." But it was too
late. At noon of the 29th the reply came back: "The dispatches are
delivered. I think it is fortunate that I obeyed instructions. Much dissatisfaction with General Buell." On its heels came a wire from Buell
himself: "I have received your orders ... and in further obedience ... I
shall repair to Indianapolis."

The government thus was put in the position of having sacked
the man who, in some quarters at least, was being hailed as the savior of
Louisville and his home state of Ohio. The reaction was prompt. Three
congressmen and a senator from the region wired that the double catastrophe of Nelson's death and Buell's supersession had produced "great
regret and something of dismay.... In our judgment the removal of
General Buell will do great injury to the service in Kentucky." However, the courier had carried not one message, but three: a brief note
informing Buell that he was relieved, a War Department order appointing George Thomas to succeed him, and a letter warning the new commander that the general-in-chief expected "energetic operations." Thomas
answered without delay: "General Buell's preparations have been completed to move against the enemy, and I therefore respectfully ask that
he may be retained in command. My position is very embarrassing."
Halleck replied: "You may consider the order as suspended until I can
lay your dispatch before the Government and get instructions." This was
a way out, and Lincoln took it; the order changing commanders was
suspended, "by order of the President." Whatever doubt there was that
Buell would be willing to turn the other cheek and expose himself to
another buffeting was removed by the acknowledgment he sent the
following day: "Out of sense of public duty I shall continue to discharge the duties of my command to the best of my ability until otherwise ordered."

That was the last day of September. By then he had completed
the reorganization, incorporating the green men with the seasoned men
— seasoned, that is, by marching, if not by fighting; his army still had
never fought a battle on its own — for a total of better than 75,000
effectives. This was half again more than were with Bragg and Smith,

he knew, but he was also aware that, except for the few recruits they had managed to attract in the Bluegrass, their troops were veterans to a man, whereas no less than a third of his own had barely progressed beyond the manual of arms. Whatever qualms proceeded from this, on the first day of October he moved out. Too busy to concern himself with Nelson's slayer or spare the officers for a court to try him, he recommended that Halleck appoint a commission to look into the case. But nothing came of this, not even the filing of charges. Later that month a Louisville grand jury indicted Davis for manslaughter, but nothing came of this either; he was admitted to bail and released. Presently he was back on duty, having acquired a reputation as a man whom it was advisable not to provoke.

Buell had ten divisions, nine of them distributed equally among three corps led by major generals, with Thomas as second in command of the whole. The march was southeast, out of Louisville toward Bardstown, and the army made it in three columns, a corps in each, commanded (left to right) by Alexander McCook, T. L. Crittenden, and Charles Gilbert. Bragg was in that direction, Smith at Frankfort. Buell figured his chances were good if he could keep them divided and thus encounter them one at a time; less good — in fact, not good at all — if he had to face them both at once. So he feinted toward the latter place with a division detached from McCook, supported by the large 15,000-man tenth division, composed almost entirely of recruits under Brigadier General Ebenezer Dumont. That way, Buell would not only cover Louisville; but also, by confusing his opponents as to his true objective, he might keep them from combining against him in the battle he was seeking at last. After four months of building and repairing roads and railroads, tediously advancing and hastily backtracking, enduring constant prodding from above, he was about to fight.

★ ★ ★

Down in Mississippi all this while, Van Dorn and Price had been pursuing separate courses, neither of which had produced anything substantial even in the way of a diversion. Not only were they independent of each other; Van Dorn was also independent of Bragg, and now that he (and Isaac Brown) had accomplished the salvation of Vicksburg, the diminutive Mississippian had larger things in mind than keeping Grant amused along the lower Tennessee border while Bragg got all the glory in Kentucky. After the loss of the *Arkansas* and Breckinridge's repulse at Baton Rouge, Van Dorn had abandoned his "Ho! for New Orleans" notion and shifted his gaze upriver, reverting to his earlier slogan: "St Louis, then huzza!" His plan was to swing through West Tennessee, skirting Memphis to pounce on Paducah, from which point he would move "wherever circumstances might dictate." So when Price, mindful of Bragg's instructions to harry the Federals in

North Mississippi, called on his former chief for aid, Van Dorn replied that he would rather have Price join *him*. Price declined. Nettled, Van Dorn invoked his seniority and appealed directly to the Secretary of War: "I ought to have command of the movements of Price, that there may be concert of action. . . . Bragg is out of reach; I refer to you." Davis himself wired back: "Your rank makes you the commander, and such I supposed were the instructions of General Bragg."

Van Dorn had what he wanted. But Price had already moved on his own, striking for Iuka, twenty-odd miles down the Memphis & Charleston Railroad from Corinth, the fortified eastern anchor of Grant's contracted line. September 14, as Price's nearly 15,000 troops approached, the badly outnumbered Union garrison retreated in haste, leaving a quantity of confiscated cotton and army stores behind. Price burned the one and appropriated the other. It was now his intention to march on Middle Tennessee, to which Bragg informed him the Federals were retiring; but finding that this was not entirely the case — that Grant, though he had sent three of his five left-flank divisions to Buell, still had the other two near Iuka under Rosecrans — he hesitated to leave such a substantial force in his rear. While he was pondering this dilemma and distributing the captured stores, the problem was solved by the arrival of a courier from Van Dorn's headquarters at Holly Springs, sixty miles west of Corinth, informing Price that the President had authorized his fellow Mississippian to order a junction of the two armies, under his command, for whatever "concert of action" he had in mind.

The Missourian's intention was to stay in Iuka until he heard from Van Dorn just what it was he wanted him to do; then he would move out, more or less at his leisure, in whatever direction Van Dorn advised in order to combine the two commands for a resumption of the offensive. However, this was overlooking Grant's plans in the matter — and Grant intended not only to interrupt Price's leisure, but also to destroy him. In fact, he said later, "It looked to me that, if Price would remain in Iuka until we could get there, his annihilation was inevitable."

By "we" he meant himself and Rosecrans, whose two divisions contained about 9000 effectives, and he also meant Ord, who would advance from Corinth with another two divisions, leaving a strong garrison to man the fortifications in case Van Dorn pushed east from Holly Springs for an assault while he was gone. Price had 15,000 men; Rosecrans and Ord had 17,000 between them. This in itself was by no means enough of a preponderance to assure the annihilation Grant expected, but he had designed a tactical convergence to accomplish that result. Ord would swing north and descend on Iuka from that direction, while Rosecrans came up from the south. Once Price had his attention thoroughly fixed on the former, the latter would fall on his rear; so that the rebels, demoralized and cut off from all avenues of escape, would have to choose between death and capitulation. Advised of the plan, both of Grant's subordinate commanders were as optimistic as their chief, though Rosecrans warned: "Price is an old woodpecker," meaning that he would be hard to take by surprise.

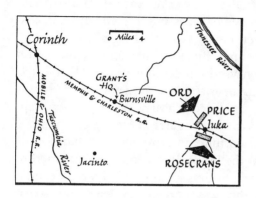

Accordingly, on September 17 (while Lee, with his back to the Potomac, was defending Sharpsburg against McClellan, and Wilder, with his back to the Green, was surrendering Munfordville to Bragg) Ord moved twelve miles down the Memphis & Charleston to Burnsville, where Grant established headquarters, having instructed Rosecrans to concentrate at Jacinto, eight miles south. From these two points, the four divisions were to push on to within striking distance of Iuka the following day in order to deliver their sequential north-south attacks soon after dawn of the 19th. But that was not to be. Rosecrans reported that one of his divisions had been so badly delayed that he could not be in position before midafternoon of the appointed day. Ord moved up on schedule, however, establishing contact with the Confederate cavalry outposts, and Grant used the waiting time to engage in a bit of psychological warfare.

Last night he had received from the telegraph superintendent at Cairo a dispatch concerning the Battle of Antietam. According to this gentleman, the news was very good indeed: "Both sides engaged until 4 p.m. at which time Hooker gained position, flanked rebels, and threw them into disorder. Longstreet and his entire division prisoners. General Hill killed. Entire rebel army of Virginia destroyed, Burnside having reoccupied Harpers Ferry and cut off retreat. . . . Latest advices say entire rebel army must be captured or killed, as Potomac is rising and our forces pressing the enemy continually." Grant sent the message forward to Ord, who passed it on to the Confederates this morning under a flag of truce. "I think this battle decides the war finally," he explained in a covering note, "and that upon being satisfied of its truth General Price or whoever commands here will avoid useless bloodshed and lay down his arms. There is not the slightest doubt of the truth of the dispatch in my hand." The reply was prompt. Formally employing the third person, Price said flatly that he did not believe the report was true, but "that if the facts were as stated in those dispatches they would only move him and his soldiers to greater exertions in behalf of their country, and that neither he nor they will ever lay down their arms — as humanely suggested by General Ord — until the independence of the Confederate States shall have been acknowledged by the United States."

Psychological warfare having failed to produce the desired result, Grant told Ord to go ahead with the opening phase, diverting Price's attention northward, though he warned: "[Rosecrans] is behind where we expected. Do not be too rapid in your advance . . . unless it should be found that the enemy are evacuating." Ord moved forward, encountering light resistance, but since there still was no word that the southward escape route was blocked, Grant told him to halt within four miles of the town "and there await sounds of an engagement between Rosecrans and the enemy before engaging the latter." Ord did so, and the afternoon wore on. About 6 o'clock he received a message written two hours before by the commander of his lead division: "For the last twenty minutes there has been a dense smoke arising from the direction of Iuka. I conclude that the enemy are evacuating and destroying the stores." Ord pushed forward tentatively, but still hearing no sound of conflict from the south, halted his troops in line of battle, and there they remained through twilight into darkness, a northwest wind blowing hard against their backs. His total loss for the day, in both divisions, was 1 man wounded.

The smoke had been beyond, not in the town, and it came from Price's guns, not his stores. Just as Grant had intended, the "old woodpecker" had concentrated northward against Ord; but about 2 o'clock, learning that another Union column was approaching from the south, he shifted one brigade in that direction and presently followed it with another. Soon afterwards, since Ord seemed disinclined to press the issue, he called for a third. Before it got there, the fight with Rosecrans had begun. Seeing the lead blue division waver, Price ordered a charge that drove the Federals back on their supports and captured nine of their guns. Upwind, Ord heard nothing. Grant, in fact, did not suspect that his other column was at hand until next morning, when he received a note Rosecrans had written the night before. Headed "Two miles south of Iuka," it reported that he had "met the enemy in force just above this point. . . . The ground is horrid, unknown to us, and no room for development. . . . Push on into them until we can have time to do something." The convergence, though delayed, had worked exactly as Grant planned it; but instead of producing a victory, as expected, had resulted in a repulse which, though it cost him nine guns and nearly 800 soldiers, gained him nothing.

An ill wind had blown no good, but now at least he knew he had both of his columns in position north and south of the town, ready to put the squeeze on Price, who was boxed in. Or so Grant thought when he told Ord at 8.35 that morning, "Get your troops up and attack as soon as possible." Ord did so, banging away with his guns as he advanced, and so did Rosecrans: only to find that they were converging on emptiness. Price — whose wagons had been packed for the move before the Federals appeared — had evacuated Iuka during the night, taking a southeast road which Rosecrans left unguarded. At Grant's insistence, the latter took up the pursuit, hoping at least to recapture the stores being hauled away, but abandoned it when he ran into an ambush eight miles out. All Grant's strategic pains had netted him was an empty town and the task of burying the dead of both armies. Rosecrans had lost 790 men, Price 535, and the latter had gotten away with all his spoils.

Ord meanwhile was hurrying back west by rail, in case Van Dorn had left Holly Springs and crossed the Hatchie River for a leap at Corinth. The prospect of this held no dismay for Rosecrans. In fact, he welcomed it. Whatever blunders he had committed against Price, he looked forward to a contest with Van Dorn. They had been classmates, West Point '56; he had finished fourth from the top, the Southerner fourth from the bottom, and Rosecrans was eager to extend this proof of his superiority beyond the academic. Back at Jacinto that night, he wired Grant: "If you can let me know that there is a good opportunity to cross the railroad and march on Holly Springs to cut off the forces of Buck Van Dorn I will be in readiness to take everything. If we could get them across the Hatchie they would be clean up the spout."

He was about to be accommodated in his desire for a bloody reunion east of the Hatchie, although not in the manner he imagined, since it would involve a change of roles. Instead of the hunter, he would be the hunted.

Van Dorn had set aside the elaborate scheme for a march on Paducah, which would expose both of his flanks to attack by superior numbers, and had decided to precede it with a much simpler, though in its way no less daring, operation. He was planning a direct assault on Corinth. That place, he saw now, was the linchpin of the Federal defenses in North Mississippi. Once it was cracked and unseated, he could move at will on Memphis or he could revert to his earlier plan for a march on St Louis, gobbling up blue detachments as he went. "We may take them in detail if they are not wary," he explained in a dispatch that reached Price the day before the Battle of Iuka; "but once combined we will make a successful campaign, clear out West Tennessee, and then ——"

His new plan, outlined in this and other messages written after Price's hairbreadth escape from Iuka with the aid of a friendly wind, was for their two commands to unite at Ripley, just west of the Hatchie, then move north, up that bank of the river, as if against Bolivar. However, this would only be a feint, serving to immobilize Grant's reserve force under Hurlbut at that point. When they reached the Memphis &

Charleston at Pocahontas, they would turn sharp right and drive for Corinth, twenty miles away, blocking the path of reinforcements from the northwest and striking before Rosecrans had time to bring in troops from the east for its defense. Combined, Van Dorn and Price had 22,000 men, while in Corinth, the former explained, there were no more than 15,000, the rest — about 8000 — being posted out toward Burnsville and Jacinto, guarding against attack from that direction. These odds, he said, gave him "a reasonable hope of success" in driving the defenders from their guns and intrenchments and capturing the lot, together with the supplies being collected for an advance.

Price, who had been associated with the Mississippian in a similar venture against Curtis seven months before in the wilds of Arkansas — with results barely short of disastrous — was not so sure; but at any rate, after eight weeks of being hamstrung by conflicting orders and exposed to ridicule, he was glad to be doing *some*thing. Back in his home state, the

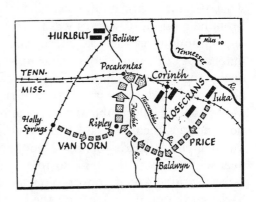

290-pound Missourian had been nicknamed "Old Skedad" by Unionist editors, one of whom remarked that "as a racer he has seen few equals for his weight." To cap the climax, rumors had been spread that he was a West Pointer. After these and other such vexations (although the educational slander was promptly refuted by a friendly correspondent who assured the public that Price "owes his success to practical good sense and hard fighting. He never attended a military school in his life") he was glad of a chance to move against the enemy, even though Van Dorn himself, sanguine as he was by nature, characterized their "hope of success" as no more than "reasonable."

Accordingly, both commands reached Ripley on September 28: Van Dorn's one division under Mansfield Lovell — who, like his chief, was out to redeem misfortune, New Orleans bulking even larger in this respect than Elkhorn Tavern — and Price's two under Brigadier Generals Dabney Maury and Louis Hébert. Lovell began the northward march that afternoon, followed by Maury and Hébert the next morning. They had fifty miles to go, thirty up to Pocahontas, then twenty down to Corinth, all along a single narrow road through densely wooded country, bone-dry after the summer-long drouth. The final lap would be the hardest, not only because it called for speed and accurate timing to achieve concerted action and surprise, but also because, after they crossed the Hatchie, there would be no water until they reached Corinth, where they would have to fight for it and win or else go thirsty. Nevertheless, according to Van Dorn, "the troops were in fine spirits, and the whole Army of West Tennessee" — so he called it, anticipating the movement which would follow victory — "seemed eager to emulate the armies of the Potomac and of Kentucky." Like their leaders, the soldiers were out to undo past reverses. Van Dorn himself reported: "No army ever marched to battle with prouder steps, more hopeful countenances, or with more courage."

October 1 the van approached Pocahontas and, ending the feint at Bolivar, swung east. Encountering cavalry here and infantry the following day at Chewalla, ten miles short of Corinth, Van Dorn knew that whatever the element of secrecy could accomplish was behind him. From here on in, Rosecrans was forewarned. The Confederates pressed on, skirmishing as they advanced, and next morning, October 3, two miles short of their objective, came upon a heavy line of Federal infantry occupying the intrenchments Beauregard — and, incidentally, Van Dorn himself — had dug along the crescent ridge to hold off Halleck, back in May. Unlike Halleck, the Mississippian put his troops into assault formation and sent them forward without delay: Lovell on the right, astride the Memphis & Charleston, and Maury and Hébert beyond him, reaching over to the Mobile & Ohio, so that as they moved east and south the three divisions would converge on the crossing. Whooping, the graybacks started up the ridge after the bluecoats firing down at them from the crest, and that was the beginning of what turned out to be a two-day battle which was one of the most violent of the war.

The reason it stretched to two days, despite its having been designed as a slashing attack that would crumple in a matter of hours whatever stood in its path, was that Rosecrans was not only braced for the shock but actually outnumbered his assailants. For the wrong reasons, he had done the right things; and what was more he had done them mostly on his own. Grant, following the post-Donelson pattern — the Shiloh pattern, too, for that matter — had gone off to St Louis to confer with Curtis about the possibility of bringing reinforcements across the river from Helena, and, failing in this, had not returned to his headquarters at Jackson, Tennessee, until Van Dorn and Price had already begun their northward march out of Ripley. Supposing — as Van Dorn intended for him to suppose — that the rebels were moving against Hurlbut at Bolivar, Rosecrans reacted in a fashion which his opponent had not foreseen. That is, he called in his troops from Burnsville and Jacinto, two full divisions of them, and prepared to go to Hurlbut's assistance; so that when the Confederates swung east at Pocahontas, ending their feint and driving hard in his direction, the Corinth commander was ready for them. Instead of catching 15,000 Federals unaware, Van Dorn and his 22,000 were moving against an army which had not only been consolidated, but also in fact outnumbered his own by more than a thousand men.

As if this was not advantage enough, Rosecrans had his four divisions posted behind a formidable double line of intrenchments. Three were thrust forward along the northward ridge, where Beauregard had done their digging for them, and one was held in reserve to man the works recently constructed along the northern and western perimeter of the town itself. Van Dorn and Price struck hard. Advancing with thirsty desperation, the Confederates threw the defenders off the outer ridge soon after midday, taking several pieces of artillery in the process. But the Federals were stubborn. Yielding each to only the heaviest pressure, they took up four separate positions between the two fortified lines. The sun was near the land line and the attackers were near exhaustion by the time they came within musket range of the gun-bristled outskirts of Corinth. Regretfully, while his men dispersed to draw water from the captured Union wells, Van Dorn deferred the coup de grâce — or anyhow what he conceived as such — till morning.

Losses on both sides had been heavy. Rosecrans (though he was later to claim, like Van Dorn, that another hour of daylight would have meant victory on the first day of battle) was thankful for the respite. That morning, with the graybacks bearing down on him, he had complained to Grant at Jackson: "Our men did not act or fight well." Now, though, he felt better. "If they fight us tomorrow," he wired Grant half an hour before midnight, "I think we shall whip them." Then, bethinking himself of the unpredictable nature of his classmate Buck Van Dorn, he added: "If they go to attack you we shall advance upon them."

Van Dorn, however, was through with trickery, double envelopments and the like — at least for the present. His blood was up; it was Rosecrans he was after, and he was after him in the harshest, most straightforward way imaginable. Today he would depend not on deception to complete the destruction begun the day before, but on the rapid point-blank fire of his guns and the naked valor of his infantry. Before dawn, October 4, his artillery opened on the Federal inner line, which was prompt in reply. "It was grand," one Union brigadier declared. "The different calibers, metals, shapes, and distances of the guns caused the sounds to resemble the chimes of old Rome when all her bells rang out." This continued until after sunrise, when a long lull succeeded the uproar, punctuated by sharpshooters banging away at whatever showed a head. Rosecrans was curious but cautious, wondering what was afoot out there beyond the screen of trees. "Feel them," he told one regimental commander, "but don't get into their fingers." "I'll feel them!" the colonel said, and led a sally. Entering the woods, the regiment was received with a crash of musketry and fell back, badly cut up, its colonel having been shot through the neck and captured. All that Rosecrans learned from this was that Van Dorn was still there, in strength.

Shortly after 10 o'clock he received even more emphatic proof that this was the case; for at that hour Van Dorn launched his all-or-

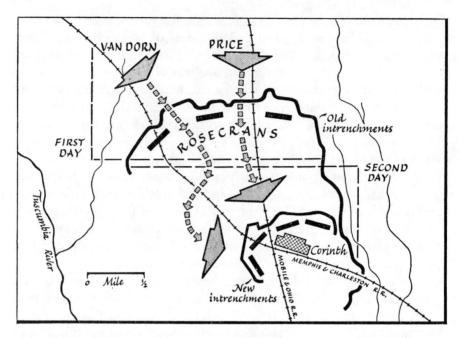

nothing assault. Price's two divisions began it, surging forward in echelon, to be met with a blast of cannonfire. The left elements suffered a sudden and bloody repulse, but three regiments in the center achieved a breakthrough when the Union cannoneers fell back from their guns in a panic that spread to the supporting infantry. Yelling men in butternut burst into the streets of Corinth, driving snipers out of houses by firing through the windows, swept past Rosecrans' deserted headquarters and on to the depot beyond the railroad crossing. At that point, however, finding their advance unsupported and the Federals standing firm, they turned and fought their way back out again. On the far right, pinned down by heavy fire from a ridge to its immediate front, Lovell's division gained no ground at all. The day was hot, 94° in the shade; panting and thirsty, the attackers hugged what cover they could find. From time to time they would rise and charge, urged on by their officers, but after the original short-lived penetration they had no luck at all. The bluecoats stood firm. "Our lines melted under their fire like snow in thaw," one Confederate afterwards recalled. Perhaps the hardest fighting of the day occurred in front of Battery Robinette, just north of the Memphis & Charleston Railroad, a three-gun redan protected by a five-foot ditch which overflowed with dead and dying Texans and Arkansans within two hours. By then it was noon and Van Dorn knew his long-shot gamble had failed. "Exhausted from loss of sleep, wearied from hard marching and fighting, companies and regiments without officers," he later reported, "our troops — let no one censure them — gave way. The day was lost."

How lost it was he would not know until he counted the casualties he had suffered, and weighed them against the number he had inflicted: 4233 Confederates, as compared to 2520 Federals, with well over one third of the former listed as "missing." Price wept as he watched his thinned ranks withdraw, the men's faces sullen with the knowledge that hard fighting had won them nothing more than the right to stitch the name of another defeat on their battle flags. By 1 o'clock they were in full retreat — unpursued. Instead of pressing their rear, Rosecrans was riding along his battered line to deny in person a rumor that he had been slain. "Old Rosy," his men called him, a red-faced man in his middle forties, with the profile of a Roman orator. At Battery Robinette he drew rein, dismounted, bared his head, and told his soldiers, most of whom were Ohioans like himself: "I stand in the presence of brave men, and I take my hat off to you." Van Dorn meanwhile had stopped for the night at Chewalla, from which he had launched his first attack the day before. Next morning, finding the Hatchie crossing blocked by 8000 fresh troops sent down from Bolivar, he fought a holding action in which about 600 men fell on each side, then turned back south and crossed by a road leading west out of Corinth, which Rosecrans — as at Iuka — had left open. Stung into vigor, Old Rosy at last took up the pursuit, complaining bitterly when Grant called him off. Van Dorn returned to Holly Springs by way of Ripley, accompanied by Price.

The brief, vicious campaign was over. What had been intended as a third prong in the South's late-summer early-fall offensive had snapped off short as soon as it was launched. Including the holding action on the Hatchie, it had gained the Confederacy nothing except the infliction of just over 3000 casualties on the Federals in North Mississippi, and for this Van Dorn had paid with nearly 5000 of his own. A cry went up that the nation could no longer afford to pay in blood for the failure of his thick-skulled fights and harebrained maneuvers. Nor were the protests limited in reference to his military judgment. The man himself was under fire. "He is regarded as the source of all our woes," a senator from his native state complained, "and disaster, it is prophesied, will attend us so long as he is connected with this army. The atmosphere is dense with horrid narratives of his negligence, whoring, and drunkenness, for the truth of which I cannot vouch; but it is so fastened in the public belief that an acquittal by a court-martial of angels would not relieve him of the charge." These and other allegations — specifically, that he had been drunk on duty at Corinth, that he had neglected his wounded on the retreat, and that he had failed to provide himself with a map of the country — resulted in a court of inquiry, called for by the accused himself. The court, by a unanimous decision, cleared him of all blame, adding that the charges "are not only not proved, but they are disproved."

Thus were Van Dorn's critics officially answered and rebuked. However, the best answer, although unofficial, had already been made for him on the field of battle itself, shortly after his departure. Near Battery Robinette, having bared his head "in the presence of brave men," Rosecrans came upon an Arkansas lieutenant, shot through the foot and propped against a tree. He offered him a drink of water. "Thank you, General; one of your men just gave me some," the Confederate replied. When the Federal commander, glancing around at the heaped and scattered corpses in their butternut rags, remarked that there had been "pretty hot fighting here," the rebel Westerner agreed. "Yes, General, you licked us good," he said. "But we gave you the best we had in the ranch."

★ ★ ★

The best they had was not enough; but even if it had served the Mississippi general's purpose, it would have been of small help to Bragg, three hundred airline miles northeastward in Kentucky. At the same hour of the same day that Van Dorn broke off the fight at Corinth and retreated — 1 p.m. October 4 — the boom of Union guns lobbing shells into the outskirts of Frankfort disrupted the inaugural ceremonies and ended in midsentence the address being delivered by Confederate Governor Hawes, who had been sworn in at high noon and whose *de facto* tenure of office thus was brief.

Despite a shortage of cavalry for outpost work and scouting — Forrest had been sent back to Middle Tennessee to raise another new brigade, and John Morgan was off chasing his Federal namesake across the barrens — Bragg was not entirely surprised at this development. Nor was he in any sense dismayed. In fact, having been forewarned, he had expressed the hope that Buell would attempt just such a maneuver. Informed two days before, October 2, that a blue column was moving east from Louisville toward Shelbyville and Frankfort, he passed the word along to Polk, whom he had left in command of the four divisions around Bardstown while he himself joined Kirby Smith to attend the inauguration at the capital. "It may be a reconnaissance," he added, "but should it be a real attack we have them. . . . With Smith in front and our gallant army on the flank I see no hope for Buell if he is rash enough to come out. I only fear it is not true. . . . Hold yourself informed by scouts toward Shelbyville, and if you discover a heavy force that has moved on Frankfort strike without further orders." A few hours later, more positive evidence was at hand, and Bragg followed this first message with a second: "The enemy is certainly advancing on Frankfort. Put your whole available force in motion . . . and strike him in flank and rear. If we can combine our movements he is certainly lost."

Couriers taking these messages to Bardstown — Pennsylvania's Stephen Foster's Old Kentucky Home — passed en route a courier bringing a dispatch Polk had written that same morning. He too was being advanced on, he declared: not by a single Federal column, but by three, all moving southeast out of Louisville on as many different roads.

His original instructions, in the event that he was menaced by a superior force, had been to fall back eastward. Accordingly, he told Bragg, "I shall keep the enemy well under observation, and my action shall be governed by the circumstances which shall be developed. If an opportunity presents itself I will strike. If it shall be clearly inexpedient to do that I will, according to your suggestion, fall back on Harrodsburg and Danville on the roads indicated by you, with a view to a concentration [of both armies]." Pointedly, he observed in closing: "It seems to me we are too much scattered."

Next morning, October 3, having received Bragg's two messages of the day before, instructing him to strike the flank and rear of the column moving against Frankfort, he replied: "The last twenty-four hours have developed a condition of things on my front and left flank which I shadowed forth in my last note to you, which makes compliance with this order not only eminently inexpedient but impractical. I have called a conference of wing and division commanders to whom I have submitted the matter, and find that they unanimously indorse my views of what is demanded. I shall therefore pursue a different course, assured that when facts are submitted to you you will justify my decision." Reverting to his original instructions to fall back eastward, he added: "The head of my column will move this evening."

Bragg concurred: at least for the time being. Receiving Polk's dispatch at Frankfort during the early hours of inauguration day, he replied: "Concentrate your force in front of Harrodsburg.... Smith's whole force is concentrating here and we will strike the enemy just as soon as we can concentrate." Mindful of the effect the retrograde movement might have on the troops, he admonished the bishop-general: "Keep the men in heart by assuring them it is not a retreat, but a concentration for a fight. We can and must defeat them." Near midday he followed this with further assurance: "We shall put our governor in power soon and then I propose to seek the enemy." Just then, however, the ceremony was interrupted by the boom of guns. The enemy, it appeared, had sought *him*. So Bragg tacked a postscript on the message: "1.30 p.m. Enemy in heavy force advancing on us; only 12 miles out. Shall destroy bridges and retire on Harrodsburg for concentration and then strike. Reach that point as soon as possible."

Throughout the greater part of this exchange, despite the sudden and apparently unpremeditated changes of decision and direction — which came full circle and brought him back to the start before the finish — Bragg had given an effective imitation of a man who not only knew where he was going, but also knew what he was going to do when he got there; "concentrate" and "strike" were the predominant verbs, especially the former. But the truth was, he was badly confused, whether he knew it or not. Buell's feint toward Frankfort, led by Brigadier General Joshua Sill's division and supported by the oversized division of green

men under Dumont, succeeded admirably: Bragg, being directly confronted, considered this the major Federal effort and, discounting Polk's
specific warning to the contrary, underrated the strength of the three-
corps column moving down toward Bardstown.

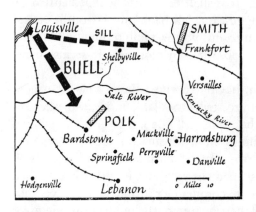

Not that Buell himself
had no problems. Though his
army was large — 55,000 soldiers in one column, 22,000 in
the other; the former alone was
larger than Bragg's and Smith's,
even if they had been combined, which they had not —
size also had its drawbacks, particularly on the march, as he
was rapidly finding out. Besides, at least one third of this
77,000-man collection were re-
cruits, so-called Squirrel Hunters, rallied to the call of startled governors who had suddenly found the war approaching their Ohio River
doorsteps. A gloomy-minded general, and Buell was certainly that,
would be inclined to suppose that such troops had established their all-
time pattern of behavior at the Battle of Richmond, five short weeks
ago: in which case, panic being highly contagious in combat, they were
likely to prove more of a liability than an asset. Nor was this inexperience limited to the ranks. The corps commanders themselves, raised
to their present positions during the hasty reorganization at Louisville
the week before, were doubtful quantities at best, untested by the
pressure of command responsibility in battle. Crittenden had dignity,
but according to a correspondent who knew and respected him, his
talents were mainly those of a country lawyer. In his favor was a fervid
devotion to the Union, no doubt intensified by the fact that his
brother had chosen the opposite side. McCook, on the other hand, was
"an overgrown schoolboy" according to the same reporter. Barely
thirty-one, he had a rollicking manner and was something of a wag,
and as such he irritated more often than he cheered. By all odds, however, the strangest of the three, at least in the method by which he
had arrived at his present eminence, was Gilbert. A regular army
captain of infantry, he had happened to be in Louisville when Bragg
started north, and the department commander at Cincinnati, alarmed
and badly in need of professional help, issued the order: "Captain C. C.
Gilbert, First Infantry, U.S. Army, is hereby appointed a major general
of volunteers, subject to the approval of the President of the United
States." Lincoln in time appointed him a brigadier, subject to confirmation by Congress — which decided after some debate that he was
only a captain after all. For the present, though, he was apparently a

bona fide major general, and as such he received the corps command to which his rank entitled him.

These, then, were the troops with which Buell was expected to fling Bragg's and Smith's veterans out of Kentucky, and these were the ranking officers on whom he depended for execution of his orders. In partial compensation, there was Thomas; but Old Pap, as he was coming to be called, had never been one to offer unsolicited advice. Officially designated as second in command of the whole army, for the present he was riding with Crittenden's column as a sort of super corps commander. This arrangement not only placed Buell's most competent subordinate in a superfluous position and beyond his immediate reach, but what was more it led in time to trouble.

The Confederates having evacuated Bardstown on the 4th, the Federals entered or by-passed the place that evening and slogged on down the dusty roads toward Mackville, Springfield, and Lebanon, encountering only rebel horsemen who faded back whenever contact was established. This was satisfactory, but there was a disturbing lack of coördination between the three columns with which Buell was groping for Bragg as if with widespread fingers. On the left, McCook wrote Thomas, who was with Crittenden on the right, twenty miles away: "Please keep me advised of your movements, so that I can coöperate. I am in blissful ignorance." Another lack was more immediately painful, at least to the marchers themselves. One Illinois volunteer later recalled that after the summer-long drouth, which had stretched into fall, creeks and even rivers were "either totally dry or shrunken into little, heated, tired-looking threads of water, brackish and disagreeable to taste and smell." Brackish or not, water was much on the men's minds, as well as on the minds of their commanders. Pushing on through Springfield, Buell ordered a concentration near Perryville on the 7th. There was water there — in Doctor's Creek, a tributary of Chaplin River, which in turn was a tributary of the Salt. There were also rebels there, or so he heard, in strength. After four hard months of marching hundreds of miles, sneered and sniped at by the authorities much of the time, the Army of the Ohio was about to come to grips with the gray-clad authors of its woes.

They did come to grips that evening, or nearly to grips — part of them at any rate. McCook, coming down through Mackville, was delayed by a bad road and went into camp eight miles short of his objective. Crittenden, coming up from Lebanon, was delayed by a detour Thomas authorized him to make in search of water; he too had to stop for the night, ten miles short of the designated point of concentration. Only Gilbert's central column, trudging east from Springfield by the direct route, reached the field on schedule. His troops marched in near sundown, tired and thirsty, but found Doctor's Creek defended by snipers on a ridge across the way. Sorely in need of the water standing in pools along the creek bed, the bluecoats launched a vigorous downhill attack. Repulsed, they fell back toward the sunset, re-formed, and tried again, this time by the light of a full moon rising beyond the ridge where enemy riflemen lay concealed to catch them in their sights. Again they were repulsed. Exhausted by these added exertions, and thirstier than ever, they made a dry camp in the woods, tantalized by the thought of water gleaming silver in the moonlight just ahead.

It was an inauspicious beginning. What was more, Buell himself was indisposed, having been lamed and badly shaken up as a result of being thrown by a fractious horse that afternoon. But he was not discouraged. He had suffered and sweltered too much and too long, all through the long summer into fall, to be anything but relieved by the thought that he had Bragg's whole army at last within reach of the widespread fingers now being clenched into a fist. The feint at Frankfort having served its purpose, Sill was on the way south to rejoin McCook, who himself had only a short way left to come. Off to the southwest, Crittenden too was within easy marching distance. To make certain that his army was concentrated without further delay, Buell had his chief of staff send a message to Thomas, urging him to be on the road by 3 a.m. Bragg had been brought to bay at Perryville, he told him, adding: "We expect to attack and carry the place tomorrow."

Buell's estimate of the enemy situation, particularly in regard to the strength of the force which had denied his men a drink from Doctor's Creek, was considerably mistaken. Bragg's whole army was not there on the opposite ridge; only a part of it was — so far only half, in fact — which in turn was the result of a mistake in the opposite direction. Still confused by the feint at Frankfort, Bragg assumed that only a part of Buell's army was approaching Perryville. And thus was achieved a curious balance of error: Buell thought he was facing Bragg's whole army, whereas it was only a part, and Bragg thought he was facing only a part of Buell's army, whereas it was (or soon would be) the whole. This compound misconception not only accounted for much of the confusion that ensued, but it was also the result of much confusion in the immediate past.

At Harrodsburg that morning Bragg had issued a confidential circular, calling for a concentration of both armies near Versailles, south of Frankfort, west of Lexington, and east of the Kentucky River. Polk was to move his two divisions there at once, joining Kirby Smith, while Hardee followed, delaying the enemy column as he fell back. It was all quite carefully worked out; each commander was told just what to do. But no sooner was it completed than Bragg received a dispatch Polk had written late the night before, reporting that he had told Hardee "to ascertain, if possible, the strength of the enemy which may be covered by his advance. I cannot think it large." Polk meant by this that he did not think the Federal covering force, or advance guard, was large; but Bragg took him to mean the main body. Accordingly, he decided to have Hardee give the enemy column a rap that would slow it down and afford him the leisure he needed to cross the Salt and Kentucky Rivers and effect the concentration. Polk was instructed to have one of his divisions continue its march to join Smith beyond the river, but to return to Perryville with the other in order to reinforce Hardee for this purpose. "Give the enemy battle immediately," Bragg wrote. "Rout him, and then move to our support at Versailles."

This was written at sundown, just as the Federals began their fight for the water west of Perryville. A copy of it reached Hardee, together with the confidential circular, just after the second repulse. The *Tactics* author read them both, and while he approved of the circular, finding it militarily sound, he was horrified by the instructions given Polk to divide his wing and precipitate a battle in which Bragg would employ only three of the four divisions of one of the armies moving toward a proper concentration. So horrified was Hardee, in fact, by this violation of the principles he had outlined in his book on infantry tactics, that he retired at once to his tent and wrote the commanding general a personal letter of advice:

> Permit me, from the friendly relations so long existing between us, to write you plainly. Do not scatter your forces. There is one rule in our profession which should never be forgotten; it is to throw the masses of your troops on the fractions of the enemy. The movement last proposed will divide your army and each may be defeated, whereas by keeping them united success is certain. If it be your policy to strike the enemy at Versailles, take your whole force with you and make the blow effective; if, on the contrary, you should decide to strike the army in front of me, first let that be done with a force which will make success certain. Strike with your whole strength first to the right then to the left. I could not sleep quietly tonight without giving expression to these views. Whatever you decide to do will meet my hearty co-operation.

He signed it, "Your sincere friend," then added a postscript: "If you wish my opinion, it is that in view of the position of your depots you ought to strike this force first," and gave it to an officer courier for immediate delivery.

Three hours would suffice to bring an answer, but there was none: except that Polk arrived in the night with one division, which in itself was a sort of negative answer, and assumed command by virtue of his rank. The Confederate over-all strength was 16,000 men. What the Federal strength was, neither Polk nor Hardee knew, though they suspected that it was considerably larger than their own. At earliest dawn, while they were discussing whether to attack as Bragg had ordered, Buell solved the problem for them by attacking first.

Once more it was a dash for water, and this time it succeeded. Where other units had failed the night before, Brigadier General Philip H. Sheridan, commanding a division under Gilbert, went forward with one of his brigades in the gray twilight before sunrise, October 8, and seized not only a stretch of the creek itself, with several of its precious pools of water, but also the dominant heights beyond, throwing the rebel snipers back and posting his own men along the ridge to prevent their return. A thirty-one-year-old bandy-legged Ohioan with heavy, crescent-shaped eyebrows, cropped hair, and a head as round as a pot, he looked more like a Mongolian than like the Irishman he was. Less than ten years out of West Point, he had received his star two weeks ago and had been a division commander just nine days, previous to which time he had been a commissary captain under Halleck for six months until by a fluke he secured a promotion to colonel and command of a Michigan cavalry regiment which he led with such dash, in pursuit of Beauregard after the Corinth evacuation, that in late July five of his superiors, including Rosecrans, recommended his promotion with the indorsement: "He is worth his weight in gold."

Now in Kentucky, having received his star, he was out to prove the validity of their claim, as well as his right to further advancement. Other inducements there were, too. The son of immigrant parents — born in County Cavan, some said, or en route in mid-Atlantic, according to others, though Sheridan himself denied this: not only because he was strenuously American and preferred to think of himself as having sprung from native soil, but also because he learned in time that no person who drew his first breath outside its limits could ever become President of the United States — he had an intense dislike of Southerners, particularly those with aristocratic pretensions, and had suffered a year's suspension from the Academy for threatening with a bayonet a Virginia upperclassman whose tone he found offensive on the drill field. He was a man in a hurry. In addition to other provocations, real or imaginary, he felt that the South owed him repayment, preferably in blood, for the year he had lost; and this morning he began to collect in earnest. However, the fury of his attack across Doctor's Creek was apparently about as alarming to his own corps commander as it had been to the Confederates. Gilbert kept wigwagging messages forward, imploring the young enthusiast not to bring on a general engagement contrary to Buell's wishes. Sheridan, who was up where he could see what was going on, later wrote that he "replied to each message that I was not bringing on an engagement, but that the enemy evidently intended to do so, and that I believed I should shortly be attacked."

Attacked as he predicted, he brought up his other brigades and held his ground; after which a long lull ensued. Gilbert, taking heart at this, sent the other two divisions forward to take position along the ridge

and astride the Springfield road, which crossed it on the way to Perryville, just under two miles ahead. This done, he went to report his success to army headquarters, three miles back down the road. He got there
about 12.30 to find that McCook had just arrived. Much to Buell's relief, his two divisions were filing in on the Mackville road to take position on Gilbert's left, separated from it by a quarter-mile-wide valley
cradling a bend of Doctor's Creek. Within another half hour, more good
news was received: Crittenden too was at hand, entering by the Lebanon
road and preparing to move northward up the ridge beyond the creek,
taking position on Gilbert's right and thus extending the line of battle.

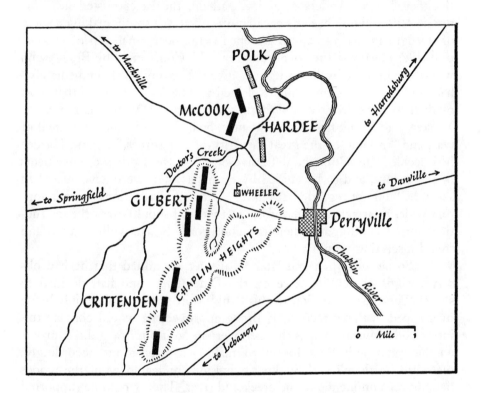

During these early afternoon hours everything was falling into
place, as if the pieces of an enormous jigsaw puzzle had suddenly inter-
locked of their own accord: a common enough phenomenon, but one
that never failed to exhilarate and amaze. Except for Sill's division, which
was on the way from Frankfort, and the green division under Dumont,
which was continuing the feint, Buell at last had all his troops collected.
Eight divisions, with an over-all strength of 55,000 men, were posted
along a six-mile front. His latest information was that Hardee was
definitely at Perryville with two divisions. What else might be there he
did not know, but for the present all was suspiciously quiet in that direction. At any rate, the Federal fist was clenched and ready to strike.

This time, though, it was Buell's turn to be beaten to the punch — with results a good deal more costly than the loss of a few spare pools of brackish water. What would be lost now was blood.

Bragg had waited at Harrodsburg through the early morning hours, cocking an ear to catch the steady roar of guns ten miles southwest, which would signify that the attack he had ordered was under way; but, hearing nothing, had ridden down to Perryville to see for himself the reason for delay. Arriving about 10 o'clock, he found Polk reconnoitering the high ground near the confluence of Doctor's Creek and Chaplin River. The three divisions were in line: from right to left, Buckner, Patton Anderson, and Cheatham, the latter posted near the town itself, while Wheeler's cavalry was off to the south, making a show of strength in that direction. Except for the occasional pop of an outpost rifle, a heavy silence overhung the field. Confronted by Bragg, who wanted to know why his orders to "give the enemy battle immediately" had not been carried out, Polk explained that he was convinced that most of Buell's entire army was gathering in his front. What was more, the Yankees had struck first. Consequently, he had called another council of war, and "in view of the great disparity of our forces," he and Hardee had decided "to adopt the defensive-offensive, to await the movements of the enemy, and to be guided by events as they were developed." In short, he "did not regard [last night's] letter of instructions as a peremptory order to attack at all hazards, but that . . . I should carry the instructions into execution as judiciously and promptly as a willing mind and sound discretion would allow."

So he said, then and later. However, he added that he had observed signs of activity here on the Federal left and had decided to switch Cheatham's division to this flank in order to guard against being overlapped in this direction. If Bragg approved, he would convert this into an offensive as soon as the men were in position. Bragg did approve, emphatically, and Polk began to make his dispositions accordingly, massing Cheatham's and Buckner's divisions under cover of the woods beyond the confluence of the creek and river. They would be supported by two brigades from Anderson, whose remaining two brigades would make a simultaneous holding attack to the south and west, thereby discouraging any weakening of the enemy right to bolster the left when it was assailed. By 1 o'clock, apparently without Federal detection of what was going on behind the screen of trees, the butternut troops were in assault formation, supported rank on rank by heavy concentrations of artillery. Soon afterward, Polk passed the word for both divisions to move forward.

The attack could scarcely have come at a more propitious time: propitious for the Confederates, that is. The bluecoats Polk had spotted late that morning on the Federal left were members of McCook's advance elements, reconnoitering for occupation of the position by his two

divisions shortly after noon. While they were filing in, McCook himself rode back to report to Buell at army headquarters, having explained
to the commander of his lead division, Brigadier General J. S. Jackson,
that he was to form a line of battle along the near bank of Chaplin River.
Jackson was glad to hear this, for his men were thirsty after their dusty
march. So was his senior brigade commander, Brigadier General William Terrill, whom he told to advance his skirmishers to the river bank
as soon as he had his troops in attack formation. "I'll do it, and that's
my water," Terrill said. He was a Union-loyal Virginian. In fact, he
was the former cadet Sheridan had lunged at with a bayonet, ten years
ago at the Academy. Since then, they had shaken hands and agreed to
forget their grievance. Sheridan was thankful ever afterwards that they
had staged this reconciliation; for Terrill was dead within an hour of his
arrival on the field.

Cheatham and Buckner struck with tremendous force and all the
added impact of surprise, emerging suddenly from the drowsy-looking
woods in a roaring charge. Terrill's men were mostly green, and being
taken thus while they were advancing toward their baptism of fire, they
heard in the rebel yell the fulfillment of their dry-mouthed apprehensions. Jackson, who was with them when the blow fell, was killed by one
of the first volleys. They wavered, then broke completely when a
bullet cut down Terrill. Behind them, the other deploying brigades were
also taken unawares. Some of the men fled at once under the shock.
Others stood and fought, sometimes hand to hand. Steadily, though, they
were thrown back, the massed Confederate batteries knocking down the
stone walls and fences behind which the retreating Federals had sought
refuge. A mile or more they were driven, losing fifteen guns in the
process. By the time McCook returned from the rear he found his two
divisions near demoralization and utter ruin staring him in the face. In
this extremity he called across the way for help from Gilbert.

That general also had his hands full, however. Or anyhow he
thought so. He had repulsed Anderson's attack down the south bank
of the creek, but he did not know how soon another would be launched
or in what strength. Sheridan, from his advanced position on the left,
could look across the intervening valley and see the graybacks sweeping
westward, driving McCook's troops before them. All he could do for
the present was turn his guns in that direction, heaving shells into the
flank of the gray columns as they crossed his line of fire. This threw
them into considerable confusion and encouraged Gilbert to
detach first one brigade, then another, to go to McCook's assistance.
When they had left, he counterattacked with his right-flank brigade
and drove Anderson back on Perryville, capturing a fifteen-wagon ammunition train. But this was late in the day. Having advanced so far, the
brigade commander put his batteries in position west of the town and,
firing his shells across the rooftops, engaged some rebel guns on the op-

posite side until darkness put an end to the duel and relieved the terror
of the civilians, who had crouched in their cellars and heard the projectiles arching overhead with a flutter as of wings.

Such was Gilbert's contribution, and such was the contribution
of his 20,000 men, who faced barely 2500 Confederates while McCook
and his 12,500 were being mauled by nearly equal numbers, just beyond easy musket range on the left. Crittenden, on the right with
22,500 men, contributed even less; in fact he contributed nothing
at all, being bluffed into immobility by Joe Wheeler's 1200 horsemen
and two guns. Thus it was that 16,000 rebels could successfully challenge 55,000 bluecoats, not more than half of whom were seriously engaged. In partial extenuation, because of unusual atmospheric and topographical factors reminiscent of Grant's experience with the ill wind at
Iuka, the clatter of musketry did not carry far today; so that in this respect the six-mile-long scene of action (or nonaction) was compart-
mented, each sector being sealed off from the others as if by soundproof
walls. One Union staff officer, riding the field, later made the incredible
statement that "at one bound my horse carried me from stillness into the
uproar of battle." Partially, too, this explained the lack of over-all control which should have remedied the drawback of temporary deafness.
Buell, nursing yesterday's bruises back at headquarters, not only did not
know what had hit him today; it was after 4 o'clock before he even knew
he had been struck.

By that time the battle was more than two hours old, and the
Confederates too had been thrown into considerable confusion. This
was accomplished partly by Sheridan's gunners, bowling shells across the
narrow valley to crush the flank of the advancing files, toppling men
like tenpins — including Pat Cleburne, who had recovered from the face
wound he had suffered at Richmond in time to receive a leg wound
here when his horse was shot from under him by one of the fast-firing
guns across the way — and partly by the disorganization incident to the
rapid advance itself. Units had intermingled, not only gray and gray, but
also blue and gray, as some stood fast and others retreated. On both sides
there was much anguished crying of "Friends! You are firing into
friends!" However, this too was not without its advantages to the attackers: particularly in one instance. When the commander of one of the
brigades Gilbert had sent to reinforce McCook approached an imposing-
looking officer to ask for instructions as to the posting of his troops —
"I have come to your assistance with my brigade!" the Federal shouted
above the uproar — the gentleman calmly sitting his horse in the midst of
carnage turned out to be Polk, who was wearing a dark-gray uniform.
Polk asked the designation of the newly arrived command, and upon
being told raised his eyebrows in surprise. For all his churchly faith in
miracles, he could scarcely believe his ears. "There must be some mistake about this," he said. "You are my prisoner."

Fighting without its commander, the brigade gave an excellent account of itself. Joined presently by the other brigade sent over from the center, it did much to stiffen the resistance being offered by the remnants of McCook's two divisions. Sundown came before the rebels could complete the rout begun four hours ago, and now in the dusk it was Polk's turn to play a befuddled role in another comic incident of confused identity. He saw in the fading light a body of men whom he took to be Confederates firing obliquely into the flank of one of his engaged brigades. "Dear me," he said to himself. "This is very sad and must be stopped." None of his staff being with him at the time, he rode over to attend to the matter in person. When he came up to the erring commander and demanded in angry tones what he meant by shooting his own friends, the colonel replied with surprise:

"I don't think there can be any mistake about it. I am sure they are the enemy."

"Enemy!" Polk exclaimed, taken aback by this apparent insubordination. "Why, I have only just left them myself. Cease firing, sir! What is your name, sir?"

"Colonel Shryock, of the 87th Indiana," the Federal said. "And pray, sir, who are you?"

The bishop-general, learning thus for the first time that the man was a Yankee and that he was in rear of a whole regiment of Yankees, determined to brazen out the situation by taking further advantage of the fact that his dark-gray blouse looked blue-black in the twilight. He rode closer and shook his fist in the colonel's face, shouting angrily: "I'll soon show you who I am, sir! Cease firing, sir, at once!" Then he turned his horse and, calling in an authoritative manner for the blue-coats to cease firing, slowly rode back toward his own lines. He was afraid to ride fast, he later explained, because haste might give his identity away; yet "at the same time I experienced a disagreeable sensation, like screwing up my back, and calculated how many bullets would be between my shoulders every moment."

Screened at last by a small copse, he put the spurs to his horse and galloped back to the proper side of the irregular firing line. But the fighting was practically over by now. Two of his brigades had been withdrawn to meet Gilbert's threat to the left rear, ending all chance for a farther advance, even if Bragg had been willing to risk a night engagement. Presently even the guns east and west of Perryville ceased their high-angle quarrel across the rooftops. . . . Buell had fought his first battle, and fought it badly, having been assaulted and outdone by an army less than a third the size of his own. More than 7600 men had fallen. 4211 Federals, 3396 Confederates. The former had had 845 killed, 2851 wounded, and 515 captured or missing, while the latter had lost 510, 2635, and 251 in those same categories. Buell consoled himself for this disparity by predicting that the conflict would "stand conspicuous for its severity in the history of the rebellion." Bragg agreed, later reporting that "for the time engaged, it was the severest and most desperately contested engagement within my knowledge."

The moon being only just past the full, the night was nearly as bright as day, and there were those in the Union army who were in favor of launching an immediate full-scale counterattack. Buell himself had tried to get such a movement under way on the right as soon as he discovered he had a battle on his hands; but the messenger, who set out at 4.15 with a verbal order for Thomas to have Crittenden move forward, got lost in the tricky bottoms of Doctor's Creek and did not find him till past sunset. Thomas, who was convinced that the rebels were in heavy strength to his front, sent back word that it was too late for an attack today, but that he would "advance in the morning with the first sound of action on the left." Dissatisfied with this dependence on his shattered left, which he knew was in no condition for more fighting, Buell replied that Thomas was to tell Crittenden "to press his command forward as much as possible [tonight] and be prepared to attack at daylight in the morning." The Virginian then rode back to army headquarters, where Buell repeated these instructions after midnight. Thomas passed them along to Crittenden at 1.30: "Have your different divisions ready to attack at daylight. Issue orders at once." Crittenden replied: "I am all ready. My post will be to the rear of the center of the line."

Morning came, October 9, but with it there came to headquarters no sound of conflict on the right. Buell waited, then waited some more. At 8 o'clock, three hours past dawn, he had his chief of staff send Crittenden the message: "Have you commenced the advance? What delays your attack?" Crittenden replied that he had received no orders to attack; he had been told, rather, to have his troops "ready to attack," and that was precisely what he had done. If they wanted him to go forward, let them say so. Exasperated, Buell told him to get moving, and he did. But Bragg was gone.

★   ★   ★

The Confederates had pulled out after midnight. Convinced at last that he had most of Buell's army to his front, and moreover having accomplished what he had intended when he told Polk to "rout him" and thus gain time for a concentration to the east, Bragg ordered a prompt junction with Kirby Smith, whom he instructed to move forward from Versailles to Harrodsburg for that purpose. Two miles short of the latter place, having crossed the Salt and burned the bridges behind him, Polk halted and formed a line of battle in the rain, the long drouth apparently having been broken by the booming of heavy guns the day before. Receiving word from Wheeler, who had charge of the rear-guard cavalry, that the Federals had not ventured beyond Perryville today, Polk rode with Chaplain C. T. Quintard — afterwards a bishop like himself — to an Episcopal church in Harrodsburg, where the Tennessee chaplain donned his surplice and stole and entered the sanc-tuary. While Polk knelt at the altar, Quintard read the litany and pro-nounced the benediction, accompanied by the murmur of rain against the stained-glass windows. Overcome by emotion as he contrasted the peace of the present interlude with what he had seen yesterday in one of the great battles of that fratricidal war, the gray-clad bishop bowed his head and wept.

Kirby Smith arrived next morning, several hours before Buell at last came up. Bragg now had all his available troops consolidated, and that night the two armies lay face to face outside the town, each wait-ing to see what the other was going to do. "Fifty thousand effectives" was Buell's estimate of the Confederate strength, and though he himself had sixty thousand — including Sill, who had promised to join him *"without fail* tomorrow, I think" — he could not forget that Bragg, with less than a third his present number of men, had wrecked one wing of the Federal army when it had been nearly as large as it was now. So Buell did nothing, waiting for Bragg to show his hand. And Bragg did nothing either.

"For God's sake, General," Smith exclaimed, "let us fight Buell here."

"I will do it, sir," Bragg replied.

But he did not. Whatever it was that had come over him three weeks ago at Munfordville, when he stood aside while Buell passed around his flank and on to Louisville, came over him again. What was more, disheartening news from North Mississippi informed him that Van Dorn and Price had failed at Corinth, just as Lee had failed in Mary-land; Bragg's was the only one of the three intended invasion barbs still stuck in the enemy's hide. Besides, unable to see that he had much to gain from a victory — whereas a defeat might cost him not only the bountiful supply of goods and foodstuffs he had collected, but also his army — he had already decided to withdraw. As he put it in the letter to his wife, "With the whole southwest thus in the enemy's possession, my crime would have been unpardonable had I kept my noble little army to be ice-bound in a northern clime, without tents or shoes, and obliged to forage daily for bread, etc."

Evincing what one observer called "a perplexity and vacillation which had now become simply appalling to Smith, to Hardee, and to Polk," Bragg ordered a retreat toward Bryantsville that night. At dawn, when Buell found the southern army gone again, he could scarcely be-lieve that it was not maneuvering for a better position in which to fight the battle which he, and indeed practically everyone else in both armies except Bragg, believed was about to be fought. He followed warily through Harrodsburg, waiting for Bragg to make a stand or else come flailing back at him, guns booming. Beyond Dick's (or Dix) River, the

Confederates again formed line of battle near Camp Dick Robinson, but Buell once more found the position too strong for him to risk attacking it. For a full day Bragg stayed there; then on the following day, October 13, when Buell sidled around toward the south, threatening his line of retreat, he got under way in earnest for Cumberland Gap. As long ago as September 29, anticipating withdrawal from Kentucky ten days before the Battle of Perryville, he had ordered 100,000 rations collected there, as well as another 200,000 at London, half way between the present position of his army and the gap.

The retreat — though Bragg did not call it that; he called it a withdrawal, the successful completion of a giant raid — was in two columns, Polk and Hardee marching by way of Lancaster and Crab Orchard, Kirby Smith by way of Big Hill, accompanying the heavy-laden trains. It was, as a later observer remarked, "a dismal but picturesque affair." Cavalry fanned out front and rear and flankwards to protect the enormous droves of hogs, sheep, and beef cattle, herded by cowboys recruited from Texas regiments. Conspicuous among the motley aggregation of vehicles in the creaking train, which included carriages, omnibuses, and stagecoaches pressed into service to remove the mountain of supplies, were the 400 bright new wagons, each with "US" stenciled on its canvas, which had been captured nearby from Nelson in late August. Approaching Big Hill from the opposite direction, Smith was feeling none of the elation he had experienced then, with victory still before him, not behind. "My command from loss of sleep for five nights, is completely exhausted," he reported during the early morning hours of October 14. "The straggling has been unusually great. The rear of the column will not reach here before daybreak. I have no hope of saving the whole of my train, as I shall be obliged to double teams in going up Big Hill, and will necessarily be delayed there two or three days."

His near-despair was based on an overrating of Buell, who he thought would press him hard, and an underrating of his own troops, particularly those in the rear guard under Wheeler. These horsemen fought no less than twenty-six separate engagements during the first five days and nights of the march — one for each year of their youthful colonel's life — beating off Federal attempts to hack at the long, slow-moving line of wagons. By dawn of the second day, however, Smith's gloom had deepened. Still at Big Hill, he notified Bragg: "I have little hope of saving any of the train, and fear much of the artillery will be lost." But here again he was unduly pessimistic. While Stevenson's division held a line beyond range of the hill, Heth's men lined the difficult slope from foot to summit and, as one of them later wrote, when "starved and tired mules faltered and fell, seized the wagons and lifted them by sheer force over the worst places." All day, all night, until noon of the following day, October 16, "the trains, in one unbroken stream, continued to pour over Big Hill, and then the troops followed." Smith felt considerably better now, having broken into the clear. Even the fact that this was hostile country had its advantages, since it encouraged stragglers to keep up. Beyond Mount Vernon next day at Big Rockcastle River, he appealed to Polk, who had already crossed: "Cannot we unite and end this disastrous retreat by a glorious victory?"

But even if Bragg had been willing — which he was not — it was too late. Hearing from Nashville this same day that a Confederate force was "rapidly concentrating" against that place, Buell broke contact just beyond London, abandoned the pursuit, and turned west. "I have no apprehension," the Nashville commander had assured him; but Buell more than made up for this lack. He was apprehensive not only for the safety of the Tennessee capital but also for the safety of his army, which by now had entered the barrens. He wired Halleck: "The enemy has been driven into the heart of this desert and must go on, for he cannot exist in it. For the same reason we cannot pursue in it with any hope of overtaking him, for while he is moving back on his supplies and as he goes consuming what the country affords we must bring ours forward. . . . I deem it useless and inexpedient to continue the pursuit, but propose to direct the main force under my command rapidly upon Nashville, which General Negley reported to me as already being invested by a considerable force and toward which I have no doubt Bragg will move the main part of his army."

In thus abandoning the pursuit, which in the end might have taken him into East Tennessee — the one region Lincoln most wanted "delivered" — Buell knew that he was fanning the wrath of his superiors, who had removed him from command once already and had restored him only under political pressure after his successor had declined the post. Anticipating what would follow, he told Halleck: "While I shall proceed with these dispositions, deeming them to be proper for the public interest, it is but meet that I should say that the present time is perhaps as convenient as any for making any change that may be thought proper in the command of this army." And having thus invited his dismissal, he said of the army he had led: "It has not accomplished all that I had hoped or all that faction might demand; yet, composed as it is, one half of perfectly new troops, it has defeated a powerful and thoroughly disciplined army in one battle and has driven it away baffled and dispirited at least, and as much demoralized as an army can be under such discipline as Bragg maintains over all troops that he commands."

Bragg would have appreciated the closing compliment, dealing as it did with the quality on which he placed the strongest emphasis, but just now he was satisfied with being allowed to continue his withdrawal unmolested. He pressed on through Barbourville, leaving Kirby Smith to bring up the rear. That general, much disgusted, formally resumed command of the Department of East Tennessee on October 20, as soon as he reached Flat Lick, Kentucky. Approaching Cumberland Gap two days later, he was astounded and enraged to receive from Bragg, already in Knoxville, orders for him to leave 3000 men at that strategic point and prepare the remainder for another joint incursion — this time into Middle Tennessee. His troops were "worn down," he replied, "much in want of shoes, clothing, and blankets," and reduced by straggling to about 6000 effectives. "Having resumed the command of my department," he added pointedly, "I am directly responsible to the Government for the condition and safety of my army." It was in effect a bill of divorcement. He wanted no more joint campaigns, not with Bragg at any rate, and doubtless he was relieved to find the North Carolinian gone from Knoxville when he himself arrived October 24, so weary and discouraged that he slipped into town under cover of darkness in order to avoid a public reception planned in his honor. The main thing he wanted now was rest, which he hoped would enable him to forget the final lap of his seventy-day round-trip journey through Central Kentucky.

No such rousing welcome had been planned for Bragg, whose problem on his return was the avoidance, not of praise, but of blame amounting to downright condemnation. Though he had never courted or apparently even desired popularity, much preferring to be respected for the sternness of his discipline rather than admired for the warmth of his nature — of which, in truth, he had little — this opprobrium, heaped on the shoulders of the man who had conceived and led the most successful offensive so far launched by a Confederate commander outside the strict national limits, seemed to him as unfair as it was unrealistic. Where Lee had failed, for example, he (Bragg) had succeeded, not only with a smaller army against longer odds, but with far fewer casualties and far greater material results; yet Lee was praised and he was blamed. In his final report of the campaign, submitted some months later, though he avoided comparisons, he attempted to refute his critics point by point. Whatever there was of failure, or shortcoming, he assigned to the backwardness of the expected Kentucky volunteers, who by their lack of native patriotism — so he called or thought of it — had forced him to travel the long road back to Tennessee with 20,000 unused muskets in his wagons. Nor was he reticent in summing up his gains:

> Though compelled to yield to largely superior numbers and fortuitous circumstances a portion of the valuable territory from which we had driven the enemy, the fruits of the campaign were very large and have had a most important bearing upon our subsequent military operations here and elsewhere. With a force enabling us at no time to put more than 40,000 men of all arms and in all places in battle, we had redeemed North Alabama and Middle Tennessee and recovered possession of Cumberland Gap, the gateway to the heart of the Confederacy. We had killed, wounded, and captured

no less than 25,000 of the enemy; taken over 30 pieces of artillery, 17,000 small-arms, some 2,000,000 cartridges for the same; destroyed some hundreds of wagons and brought off several hundreds more with their teams and harness complete; replaced our jaded horses by a fine mount; lived two months upon supplies wrested from the enemy's possession; secured material to clothe the army, and finally secured subsistence from the redeemed country to support not only the army but also a large force of the Confederacy to the present time.

Though some of this was actually understated, it made no real impression on his critics. They were not so much concerned with what he had done, which admittedly was considerable, as they were with what he had not done. In fact, their complaints in this respect were so immediately vociferous that on October 23, the day after he reached Knoxville, Bragg was summoned to Richmond by a wire from the Adjutant General, who informed him: "The President desires . . . that you will lose no time in coming here." Amid rumors that he was about to be relieved, he caught an eastbound train the following morning, thus avoiding a meeting with Kirby Smith, who arrived that night.

Whatever weight Davis and Cooper might attach to Bragg's claims in determining whether to sustain or fire him, Lincoln and Halleck apparently were inclined not only to accept them at face value, but also to deduct them from what little credit his opponent had left in their direction. Receiving Buell's dispatch of October 17, wherein he announced that he was abandoning the pursuit to return to Nashville, the general-in-chief replied next morning: "The great object to be attained is to drive the enemy from Kentucky and East Tennessee. If we cannot do it now we need never to hope for it." This was followed by another wire, in which Halleck brought Lincoln's logic to bear by indirect quotation, reinforcing the protest he had made the day before: "The capture of East Tennessee should be the main object of your campaign. You say it is the heart of the enemy's resources; make it the heart of yours. Your army can live there if the enemy's can. . . . I am directed by the President to say to you that your army must enter East Tennessee this fall, and that it ought to move there while the roads are passable. . . . He does not understand why we cannot march as the enemy marches, live as he lives, and fight as he fights, unless we admit the inferiority of our troops and of our generals."

Logic was a knife that could cut both ways, however, and prewar service in the Adjutant General's office had made Buell familiar with its use. He replied October 20 with a long, closely reasoned exegesis on the difficulties of what was being required of him. But that was not what Lincoln and Halleck wanted to hear. Besides, as an indication of his progress, the sequential headings on his telegrams — Mount Vernon,

Crab Orchard, Danville — spoke a clearer language than their contents. Despite his former suggestion that "the present time is perhaps as convenient as any for making any change that may be thought proper," Buell's military life line was running out much faster than he thought. Previously, after being relieved, he had been restored to command partly as a result of political pressure in his favor; but such pressure as was being exerted now was in the opposite direction. His old enemy Governor Morton, for example, was wiring Lincoln: "The butchery of our troops at Perryville was terrible. . . . Nothing but success, speedy and decided, will save our cause from utter destruction. In the Northwest distrust and despair are seizing upon the hearts of the people." Armed with this, and presently reinforced by similar expressons of displeasure from Yates of Illinois and Tod of Ohio, Halleck told Buell on October 22: "It is the wish of the Government that your army proceed to and occupy East Tennessee with all possible dispatch. It leaves to you the selection of the roads upon which to move to that object. . . . Neither the Government nor the country can endure these repeated delays. Both require a prompt and immediate movement toward the accomplishment of the great object in view — the holding of East Tennessee."

Buell now had his orders, the first specific ones he had received. But before he could put them into execution (and on the same day Bragg left Knoxville, bound for Richmond) the following was delivered:

Washington, October 24

Maj. Gen. D. C. Buell, *Commanding, &c.:*

General: The President directs that on the presentation of this order you will turn over your command to Maj. Gen. W. S. Rosecrans, and repair to Indianapolis, Ind., reporting from that place to the Adjutant General of the Army for further orders.

Very respectfully, your obedient servant,

H. W. Halleck
General-in-Chief.

CHAPTER

8

Last, Best Hope of Earth

★ ✗ ☆

🔫 BUELL WAS NOT THE FIRST NOR WAS HE
the last of the blue-clad puppets whose strings had been cut, or would be
cut, in what turned out to be a season of dismissals. Others had been or
were about to be packed away in their boxes, mute, their occupations
gone like Othello's and themselves removed, like him, from "the big
wars, That make ambition virtue." Halleck, from his position near the
vital center, had forecast the political weather at the outset, back in
August, when he told a friend: "I can hardly describe to you the feeling
of disappointment here in the want of activity," and added: "The Government seems determined to apply the guillotine to all unsuccessful generals. It seems rather hard to do this where the general is not in fault,
but perhaps with us now, as in the French Revolution, some harsh
measures are required."

The ax was descending. Pope's head rolled before Buell's; Mc-
Dowell, too — though admittedly he was more sinned against than
sinning — was gone, complaining wistfully as he went: "I did not ask
to be relieved. I only asked for a court." Even the navy, barnacle-
encrusted during the nearly fifty peacetime years since the War of 1812,
had stretched some necks beneath the blade. Down on the Gulf, glad to
be breathing salt air after the Vicksburg-*Arkansas* fiasco, Farragut
gave his late-summer and early-fall attention to the Texas coast, where
the blockaders worked without the advantage of a lodgment on the
mainland. With this in mind, he sent out three expeditions in as many
months. The first attacked Corpus Christi in mid-August but, having
no occupation troops, withdrew after giving the place a pounding. Next
month the second expedition went up Sabine Pass, wrecked the railroad
bridge and the fort at Sabine City, captured a pair of rebel steamers, and retired again to the bay. The third was more ambitious, being
aimed at Galveston. It was also more successful. Two regular gunboats

and two converted ferries hit the port on October 5, drove the Confederates out with a few well-aimed salvos, then landed a token force of
260 men commanded by a colonel; after which, by a tacit understanding,
the warships patrolling the bay refrained from further shelling on
condition that the rebels would not move artillery into Galveston over
the two-mile-long bridge connecting the island town with the mainland.
Alabama was now the only southern state with an unoccupied coast,
and Farragut had redeemed, at least in part, his midsummer performance
up the Mississippi.

　　Gratifying as this redemption was to Secretary Welles — whom
Lincoln dubbed "Father Neptune" and sometimes "Noah" — it also
called attention to the contrast between the Tennessee sailor's make-up
and that of his former upriver partner, the Boston Brahmin Charles H.
Davis, who had run into little but trouble since he replaced Foote as
flotilla commander on the upper Mississippi, back in May. He was, as
one of his officers said, "a most charming and lovable man," author of
two esoteric books, and a member of the commission which had planned
the strikes at Hatteras and Port Royal, but it was becoming increasingly
apparent that he lacked what Farragut had and what Foote had had
before him: a hard-driving, bulldog, cut-and-slash aggressiveness, a
preference for action at close quarters, and a burning sense of personal
insult at the slightest advantage gained by an opponent at his expense.
Since it was this quality, or combination of qualities, which would be
needed for the work that lay ahead on the big river, Welles decided
Captain Davis had to go. In mid-October he acted. Davis was eased
upstairs to the Bureau of Navigation, where he would find work better
suited to his intellectual capacities.

　　There was little that was surprising in this removal. What was
surprising was the Secretary's choice of a successor: David Dixon Porter.
Porter was only a junior commander, so that to give him the job Welles
had to disappoint and outrage more than eighty senior officers. Besides,
there were personal drawbacks. Like his brother Dirty Bill, Porter was
not above claiming other men's glory as his own; he would stretch or
varnish the truth to serve his purpose; he would undermine a superior;
he would promise a good deal more than he could deliver — all of
which he had done at New Orleans, and then had gone on to do them
again at Vicksburg. Yet he had virtues, too, of the sort which Othello
said proceeded from ambition in "the big wars." Like Lincoln in his pre-
Manassas judgment of John Pope, Welles apparently believed that "a
liar might [yet] be brave and have skill as an officer." Weighing the
virtues against the vices, the gray-bearded brown-wigged naval head
confided in his diary: "Porter is but a Commander. He has, however,
stirring and positive qualities, is fertile in resources, has great energy,
excessive and sometimes not overscrupulous ambition; is impressed with
and boastful of his own powers, given to exaggeration in relation to him-

self — a Porter infirmity — is not generous to older and superior living officers, whom he is too ready to traduce, but is kind and patronizing to favorites who are juniors; is given to cliquism, but is brave and daring like all his family. He has not the conscientious and high moral qualities of Foote to organize the flotilla, and is not considered by some of our best naval men a fortunate officer. His selection will be unsatisfactory to many, but his field of operations is peculiar, and a young and active officer is required for the duty to which he is assigned."

Having decided that the credits overbalanced the debits, in weight if not in number, Welles called Porter into his office and informed him that he was being sent as an acting rear admiral to take charge of the navy on the western waters. The order was dated October 9; Porter, who had come north on leave, hoping to cure a touch of fever he had contracted in the region to which his chief was now returning him, accepted both the assignment and the promotion as no more than his due. Six days later he was in Cairo, where he assumed command of the 125 vessels comprising the Mississippi Squadron, together with 1300 officers, only twenty-five of whom had been in the old navy, and approximately 10,000 sailors. What he would do with these boats and officers and men — and whether Welles would be sustained by circumstance in his choice of a man whose character he doubted — remained to be seen.

At any rate, Buell and Davis had been brought down. And now as October wore toward a close, giving occasion in the East for a mocking revival of "All Quiet Along the Potomac," Lincoln was after larger game. In fact he was after the top-ranking man in the whole U.S. Army: George B. McClellan. The other two had been wing shots — targets of opportunity, so to speak — but this one he was stalking with care, intending to catch him on the sit.

According to some observers this should not be difficult, since that was the Young Napoleon's accustomed attitude. The managing editor of the New York *Tribune*, for example, had written privately in late September, a week after the Battle of Antietam, that one of his reporters had just returned from the army, "and his notion is that it is to be quiet along the Potomac for some time to come. George, whom Providence helps according to his nature, has got himself on one side of a ditch, which Providence had already made for him, with the enemy on the other, and has no idea of moving. Wooden-head at Washington will never think of sending a force through the mountains to attack Lee in the rear, so the two armies will watch each other for nobody knows how many weeks, and we shall have the poetry of war with pickets drinking from the same stream, holding friendly converse and sending newspapers across by various ingenious contrivances." In other words, this Indian summer, with its firm roads and its fair skies tinged with woodsmoke, was to be wasted, militarily, like the last one, in getting ready for a movement which bad weather would postpone. Whether the country would stand for another such winter of apparent inactivity Lincoln did not know. But he himself could not; nor did he intend to.

On the first day of October, without sending word that he was coming, he boarded a train and rode out to Western Maryland to see the general and his army. McClellan, however, got word that he was on the way and met him at Harpers Ferry. Pleased to find that the President had brought no politicians with him, "merely some western officers," McClellan wrote his wife: "His ostensible purpose is to see the troops and the battlefield; I incline to think that the real purpose of his visit is to push me into a premature advance into Virginia. I may be mistaken, but think not."

He was not mistaken. That was precisely why Lincoln had come; "I went up to the field to try to get [McClellan] to move," he said later. But as usual when he was face to face with Little Mac, discussing military matters, he got nowhere. Apparently he did not really try very hard; the primary inertia was too great. When he urged an advance, McClellan went into an explanation of shortages and drawbacks, and Lincoln dropped the subject. According to the general, "He more than once assured me that he was fully satisfied with my whole course from the beginning; that the only fault he could possibly find was that I was perhaps too prone to be sure that everything was ready before acting, but that my actions were all right when I started." Later they sat on a hillside, Lincoln with his long legs drawn up so that his knees were almost under his chin, and McClellan afterwards wrote that Lincoln told him: "General, you have saved the country. You must remain in command and carry us through to the end." When McClellan said that this would be impossible — "The influences at Washington will be too strong for you, Mr President. I will not be allowed the required time for preparation" — Lincoln replied: "General, I pledge myself to stand between you and harm."

It was a three-day visit, and much of the time was spent reviewing the troops. The President "looked pale," according to one veteran who saw him, while another remarked that as he "rode around every battalion [he] seemed much worn and distressed and to be looking for those who were gone." Doubtless he was thinking of the fallen, but he was also thinking of the men he saw — and of what they represented. A Union surgeon noted that Lincoln was "well received" by the soldiers, "but by no means so enthusiastically as General McClellan." Lincoln did not mind this much. What he minded was the thought that this gave rise to. "The Army of the Potomac is my army as much as any army ever belonged to the man that created it," McClellan told a member of his staff about this time. "We have grown together and fought together. We are wedded and should not be separated." The army felt that way, too, and Lincoln knew it. He also knew that if the soldiers felt it strongly enough, mutiny would follow any order for the general's removal from command. This was much on his mind during the visit, and resulted in a curious scene. Just before dawn of the second morning, he woke O. M. Hatch, an Illinois friend. "Come, Hatch," he said, "I want you to take a walk with me." Together they climbed to a hilltop overlooking the camps, and as sunrise lighted the valley where the troops lay waiting for reveille, Lincoln made an abstracted gesture, indicating the tented plain below. "Hatch, Hatch," he said in a husky voice, barely above a whisper. "What is all this?" His companion was confused. "Why, Mr Lincoln, this is the Army of the Potomac," he replied. Lincoln shook his head. "No, Hatch, no. This is General McClellan's body-guard."

He returned to Washington, October 4. Two days later Halleck astonished McClellan with a telegraphic dispatch: "The President directs that you cross the Potomac and give battle to the enemy or drive him south. Your army must move now while the roads are good. ... I am directed to add that the Secretary of War and the General-in-Chief concur with the President in these instructions." McClellan replied that he was "pushing everything as rapidly as possible in order to get ready for the advance." Beyond this bare acknowledgment, however, the only sign he gave that he had received the directive was a step-up in the submission of requisitions for more supplies of every description. He wanted shoes, hospital tents, and horses: especially horses, the need for which was presently emphasized by Jeb Stuart, who once more covered himself with glory at the Young Napoleon's expense.

Under instructions from Lee to scout the Federal dispositions — and, if possible, destroy the railroad bridge over the Conococheague near Chambersburg, which would limit McClellan's rail supply facilities to the B & O — Stuart crossed the Potomac above Martinsburg at early dawn, October 10. He had with him 1800 horsemen and four guns. By noon he was across the Pennsylvania line, approaching Mercersburg. Soon after dark, the lights of Chambersburg were in view. Demanding and receiving the surrender of the place, he appointed Wade Hampton "Military Governor," quite as if he intended to stay there all fall, and bivouacked that night in the streets of the town. There were two disappointments. A bank official had escaped with all the cash in the vault, and the Conococheague bridge, being built of iron, proved indestructible. However, there were material compensations, including the capture and parole of 280 bluecoats, the opportunity to spend Confederate money in well-stocked Pennsylvania stores, and the impressment of more than a thousand excellent horses. Many of these last were draft animals of Norman and Belgian stock, and it was fortunate that they were seized in harness, since no southern quartermaster could furnish collars large enough for the big-necked creatures soon to be hauling rebel guns and wagons. Their former owners, never having seen an actual secessionist, were under the impression that Stuart's troopers were Federal soldiers, sent to harass farmers suspected of disloyalty, and many of them protested indignantly as the raiders led their heavy-footed animals away: "I'm just as good a Union man as any of you!"

Jeb's men had come nearly forty miles to reach their assigned objective, stirring up a hive of enemy cavalry in the process, and now the problem was how to get them back. Stuart met it as he had done before. When the column formed outside Chambersburg next morning, he led it, not southwest in the direction he had come from, but due east. Though he would have to ride more than twice as far to reach the Potomac by this route, it gave him the advantage of being unexpected along the way. The gray-jackets whooped at this evidence that they were about to repeat their Peninsula performance by staging another "Ride Around McClellan." Eastward they rode, beyond the Blue Ridge, on through Cashtown, where they stopped to feed the horses, then turned south, avoiding the college town of Gettysburg, eight miles off. Late that afternoon they recrossed the Pennsylvania line and entered Emmitsburg; beyond which, riding in darkness now and frequently changing to captured horses to spare their own, they forded the Monocacy. Some fought sleep by dismounting to walk a mile or so from time to time. Others slumped in their saddles and frankly slept, their snores droning loud above the hoofclops.

Word of the raid had spread to Washington by now. "Not a man should be permitted to return to Virginia," Halleck wired McClellan, who replied: "I have given every order necessary to insure the capture or destruction of those forces, and I hope we may be able to teach them a lesson they will not soon forget." But that was not to be. Sunday morning, October 12, near the mouth of the Monocacy — where Lee had crossed with his whole army, marching north the month before — Stuart broke through a weak link in the cordon, splashed across the Potomac, and regained the safety of the Confederate lines. He had two men missing, victims most likely of commandeered Yankee whiskey, and a handful slightly wounded. That seemed to him a small price to pay for the nearly three hundred bluecoats paroled at Chambersburg and the thirty-odd public officials brought back as hostages to secure the release or considerate treatment of Southerners now in Union hands. More than a quarter of a million dollars in public and railroad property had been destroyed, and in exchange for about sixty lame or worn-out animals abandoned along the way, the gray troopers had brought 1200 horses back from Pennsylvania for service under the Stars and Bars. Most satisfactory of all — at least to Stuart, who thus once more had justified his plume — was the knowledge that all this had been accomplished in the immediate presence of more than 100,000 enemy soldiers whose commander, midway through the raid, had announced his intention to "teach [the rebels] a lesson" by effecting their capture or destruction.

Instead it was McClellan who had been taught a lesson, though whether he would profit from it was doubtful; apparently he had failed to absorb much from the same lesson when it was first administered, four months ago on the Peninsula. Now as then, he was the object of much derision, North and South — only this time Lincoln himself led the chorus. He was aboard a steamer, returning from a troop review at Alexandria, when someone asked him: "Mr President, what about McClellan?" Without looking up, Lincoln drew a circle on the deck with the ferrule of his umbrella. "When I was a boy we used to play a game," he said, " 'Three Times Round, and Out.' Stuart has been round him twice. If he goes around him once more, gentlemen, McClellan will be out."

A new and biting note of mockery was coming into the President's references to the commander of the Army of the Potomac. Formerly this had been restricted mainly to comments on Little Mac's political suggestions — as when the governor of Massachusetts asked what Lincoln was going to reply to some advice McClellan had offered on a civil matter; "Nothing," Lincoln said. "But it made me think of the man whose horse kicked up and stuck his foot through the stirrup. He said to the horse, 'If you are going to get on I'll get off.' " Thus he had dealt with McClellan the would-be statesman, reserving his respect for McClellan the soldier. Now this too was fading. On the day after Stuart got back from his raid, Lincoln sent the circumnavigated Young Napoleon a long letter full of advice, in effect a lecture on strategy and tactics. "You remember my speaking to you of what I called your over-cautiousness. Are you not over-cautious when you assume that you cannot do what the enemy is constantly doing? Should you not claim to be at least his equal in prowess, and act upon the claim? ... Exclusive of the water-line, you are now nearer Richmond than the enemy is by the route you can and he must take. Why can you not reach there before him, unless you admit that he is more than your equal on the march? ... I would press closely to him, fight him if a favorable opportunity should present, and at least try to beat him to Richmond on the inside track. I say 'try'; if we never try, we shall never succeed." That was the main thing, as Lincoln saw it: Beat him. A stalemate would not serve. Even a repulse was not enough. "We should not so operate as to merely drive him away. As we must beat him somewhere or fail finally, we can do it, if at all, easier near to us than far away. If we cannot beat the enemy where he now is, we never can, he being again within the intrenchments of Richmond. ... It is all easy if our troops march as well as the enemy, and it is unmanly to say they cannot do it." He added: "This letter is in no sense an order."

Thus Lincoln. But McClellan apparently had as little respect for Lincoln the would-be strategist as Lincoln had for McClellan the would-be statesman. October's perfect weather went sliding by, and the army hugged its camps while its commander, despite his own chief quartermaster's protest that "no army was ever more perfectly supplied than this one has been as a general rule," continued to call for more and more supplies. He also wanted more soldiers, believing himself outnumbered, though his strength report of October 20 listed 133,433 men "present for duty," with an "aggregate present" of 159,860. Next day Halleck wired him: "Telegraph when you will move, and on what lines you propose to march." McClellan replied that he was nearly ready, but when he followed this with an urgent request for more horses, claiming that the ones he had were broken down by arduous service and weakened by foot-and-mouth disease, Lincoln lost his temper. "I have just read your dispatch about sore-tongued and fatigued horses," he wired on October 25. "Will you pardon me for asking what the horses of your army have done since the battle of Antietam that fatigues anything?"

McClellan was upset. "It was one of those little flings that I can't get used to when they are not merited," he wrote his wife, and he protested at some length to Lincoln the following day, defending his troopers and announcing that the long-awaited movement of his army across the Potomac had begun. Mollified, the President replied that he had "intended no injustice to any, and if I have done any I deeply regret it. To be told, after more than five weeks' total inaction of the army . . . that the cavalry horses were too much fatigued to move, presents a cheerless, almost hopeless, prospect for the future, and it may have forced something of impatience in my dispatch." McClellan had an apology, such as it was, yet his gloom was unrelieved. Through it he saw plainly what was coming. When one of his corps commanders indicated a spot on the map where he thought the next great battle would be fought, he nodded agreement but added sadly: "I may not have command of the army much longer. Lincoln is down on me."

Lincoln was indeed down on him. Though he wired that he was "glad to believe you are crossing," privately he was saying that he was tired of trying to "bore with an auger too dull to take hold." However, he had a final secret test in mind. Lee's army, drawn up around Winchester, was farther from Richmond than McClellan's, which was crossing the Potomac below Harpers Ferry; "His route is the arc of a circle, while yours is the chord," Lincoln had said in the tactics lecture, two weeks before. If, in spite of this disadvantage, the Confederate commander managed to interpose his troops between the advancing Federals and his capital, McClellan would be out. So Lincoln decided, and kept his decision to himself, watching and waiting. He waited long. It took the blue host nine days to cross the river and begin its southward creep, east of the Blue Ridge, toward a concentration around Warrenton. By that time, Lee — unmolested — had shifted half his army to Culpeper, squarely across the Federal line of march. McClellan had failed the test, and Lincoln's mind was made up. He would remove him.

Fearing that this was about to happen, old Francis Blair pled against it with all the persuasion learned in a lifetime spent advising Presidents. McClellan was the Union's one best hope for preservation, he declared. Lincoln disagreed. "I said I would remove him if he let Lee's army get away from him, and I must do so. He has got the slows, Mr Blair."

He would remove him: but not just yet. November 4 was the first Tuesday in the month, which meant that it was election day in most of the northern states, and therefore not a propitious time for disturbing voters who were disturbed enough already. Even Chase, who vied with Stanton in the intensity of his desire to see McClellan ousted, admitted privately that it was inexpedient to fire the general on the eve of the congressional elections, lest the Administration's motives be misconstrued as a sop to the radicals. There was a widespread conviction among conservatives that the Preliminary Emancipation Proclamation had been sop enough in that direction. Political unrest found its basis there, together with objection to arbitrary arrests and the general lack of satisfaction with the prosecution of the war itself, which seemed to have stalled on every front. Nor was this dissatisfaction limited to moderates and conservatives. Iowa Senator J. W. Grimes, a loyal Republican whose constituents had voted heavily for Lincoln in 1860, was saying flatly: "We are going to destruction as fast as imbecility, corruption, and the wheels of time can carry us." Lyman Trumbull of Lincoln's home state was complaining bitterly of a "lack of affirmative, positive action and business talent in the cabinet," while to Governor Andrew of Massachusetts it seemed that "the President has never yet seemed quite sure that we [are] in a war at all."

Such remarks were straws in the wind, down which Democrats sniffed victory in November. And in many instances they got it. New York, Pennsylvania, Ohio, Indiana — all of which had gone solidly Republican in the election held two years ago — sent Democratic delegations to the House of Representatives. So did Illinois, where Lincoln's good friend Leonard Swett went down in defeat to John T. Stuart, the President's former law partner, who thus made one among the nine Democrats elected as opposed to five Republicans. New Jersey, which had split its vote before, now went solidly Democratic; Wisconsin, on the other hand, now split her six-man delegation down the middle. Although the number of Democratic congressmen increased from 44 to 75 as a result of this election, the Republicans would remain the majority party because they managed to carry three widely scattered regions:

New England, the Border States, and the Far West. Such comfort as
Lincoln found in this was considerably soured, however, by the fact that
most observers saw in the individual defeats a rebuke of the party leader
and a rejection of his policies on the conduct of the war. The friendly
New York *Times* ran the election story under the heading, "Vote of
Want of Confidence," and in Lincoln's own home state the Salem *Ad-
vocate* declared: "We saw the President of the United States stretching
forth his hand and seizing the reins of government with almost absolute power, and yet the people submitted. On the 4th day of November,
1862, the people arose in their might, they uttered their voice, like the
sound of many waters, and tyranny, corruption and maladministration
trembled."

Lincoln took it philosophically, though he found it hard to
do so, remarking that he felt like the boy who stubbed his toe on the
way to see his girl; he was too big to cry, he said, and it hurt too much
to laugh. One thing it did, at any rate, however it came out. It cleared
the way for action on McClellan. November 5, before the election
tabulations were complete, Lincoln had the orders for his removal
drawn up. The following evening they were given to Brigadier General
C. P. Buckingham, the so-called "confidential assistant adjutant-general
to the Secretary of War," who left with them next morning, November 7, aboard a special train bound for McClellan's headquarters at
Rectortown, near Manassas Gap. The first snowfall of winter was whit-
ening the North Virginia landscape and the car in which he rode was
drafty; but Buckingham did not wonder that an officer with so much
rank as his was being exposed to such discomfort and employed as a
sort of overdressed messenger boy, Stanton having explained that Mc-
Clellan might refuse to relinquish command of his army if the order
was presented to him by a man with anything less than stars on his
shoulders. Even with them, the Secretary had added darkly, there
was a strong possibility of some such mutinous action on the part
of the commander of the Army of the Potomac. He advised the brigadier to make his arrival unannounced, thus gaining the military advantage of a surprise attack.

It was still snowing at 11 o'clock that night. McClellan sat alone
in his tent, ending the day as usual with a letter to his wife, who was
busy getting settled in their new home at Trenton, New Jersey. Nothing in his manner showed that the proposed surprise had failed; but it had.
He knew that Buckingham had arrived early that evening, and he knew
what his arrival probably meant. Whatever there was of real surprise
lay in the fact that, instead of coming directly from the depot to army
headquarters here at Rectortown, the War Department emissary had
ridden down to Salem, five miles south, where Burnside's corps was
posted. Presently, however, this too was explained. A knock came at
the tent pole, and when McClellan looked up from his letter, calling

for whoever it was to enter, the canvas flap lifted and there stood Buckingham and Burnside, snow collected on the crowns and brims of their hats and sifted into the folds of their greatcoats. Behind his facial ruff of dark brown whiskers — also lightly powdered with snow, so that it resembled a badly printed trademark — "Dear Burn" looked both embarrassed and distressed.

McClellan knew what that meant, too, but for the present he gave no sign of this. He invited the visitors in, quite as if for an informal midnight chat, and for a time he and Buckingham exchanged pleasantries, Burnside sitting glumly by, looking rather as if he had been struck a hard blow on the head. Finally, though, the staff brigadier remarked that he had come to deliver some papers; and with that he passed them over. There were two of them, both dated November 5. Lincoln having authorized Halleck, "in [his] discretion, to issue an order [removing McClellan] forthwith, or so soon as he may deem proper," the general-in-chief had deemed it proper to act without delay:

> Major General McClellan, *Commanding, &c.:*
> General: On receipt of the order of the President, sent herewith, you will immediately turn over your command to Major General Burnside, and repair to Trenton, N.J., reporting, on your arrival at that place, by telegraph, for further orders.
> Very respectfully, your obedient servant.

The second was from the Adjutant General's office, and was a direct quotation of the first sentence of Lincoln's message to Halleck:

> By direction of the President of the United States, it is ordered that Major General McClellan be relieved from the command of the Army of the Potomac, and that Major General Burnside take the command of that army.
> By order of the Secretary of War.

Neither of the orders being really any stronger than the other, it appeared that the Young Napoleon's superiors considered two blows likelier to floor him than just one. However that might have been, he kept his balance under the double impact. He read both sheets, then said with a smile and in the same pleasant tone as before: "Well, Burnside, I turn the command over to you." Close to tears, the Indiana-born Rhode Islander implored McClellan to stay with him for a day or two while he began to get accustomed to handling the reins. He had not wanted this job; had, in fact, refused it twice already, pleading incompetence, and once again this evening when Buckingham first came to Salem — that was why they had arrived so late; he had spent two hours arguing against his appointment — but Buckingham had reminded him that this was no request, it was a double-barreled order; he had no choice. Besides, the staff brigadier had added, if Burnside declined the command it would go to Hooker. That decided it; he had accepted, and all he asked now was that Little Mac stay with him for a couple of days to help him get settled in the driver's seat. McClellan agreed, and the two generals went back out into the snowy night.

Alone again, the deposed commander took up his pen and returned to his letter: "Another interruption — this time more important. It was in the shape of Burnside, accompanied by Gen. Buckingham.... Alas for my poor country! I know in my inmost heart she never had a truer servant." He did not say, as he had said before, that this was a temporary step-down, that he would be recalled when things went as wrong for Burnside as they had gone for Pope. He was through and he knew it. But he added: "Do not be at all worried — I am not. I have done the best I could for my country; to the last I have done my duty as I understand it. That I must have made many mistakes I cannot deny. I do not see any great blunders; but no one can judge of himself. Our consolation must be that we have tried to do what was right."

All that really remained to be done was say goodbye to the army whose affection for him was, in the end, his most enduring monument. Next day, when the order for his removal was published, the reaction combined disbelief and horror, both of which gave way to rage, which in turn was tempered by sadness. The various corps, drawn up for a farewell exchange of salutes, broke ranks as they had done before at his approach. Now as before, they crowded around him, touched his boots, and stroked the flanks of his horse, only this time the tears were produced by sorrow, not by jubilation. Nor had all the anger been drained off. "Send him back! Send him back!" they cried in his wake, as if their shouts could be heard in the capital, fifty miles away. The Irish brigade cast its colors in the dust for him to ride over; "but, of course," one observer wrote, "he made them take them up again." The same man heard a general say he "wished to God that McClellan would put himself at the head of the army and throw the infernal scoundrels at Washington into the Potomac." Another yelled: "Lead us to Washington, General — we'll follow you!" Burnside shared the prevailing gloom, still so badly choked up that when one division commander, having voiced his regrets to McClellan, turned to him and offered congratulations, the new army head could hardly speak. "Couch, don't say a word about it," he implored.

McClellan accepted this adulation with as much satisfaction as ever, possibly more, but he remained strangely calm in the midst of it and did nothing to encourage the various expressions of resentment. "The officers and men feel terribly about the change," he wrote his wife on the second night after receiving the order for his removal. "I learn today that the men are very sullen and have lost their good spirits entirely." This was putting it mildly indeed; but the truth was, he had lost much of his former flamboyance. Even his written farewell to his soldiers was comparatively restrained. "In you I have never found doubt or coldness," he told them, and he added: "We shall ever be comrades in supporting the Constitution of our country and the nationality of its people."

That was all; or almost all. November 11 he took his final leave of them, riding down to Warrenton Junction, where a train was waiting to carry him away. After receiving the salute of a 2000-man detachment stationed here, he boarded the train and took his seat. But before the engineer could obey the highball, the troops broke ranks, surrounded the car, then uncoupled it and ran it back, yelling threats against the Administration and insisting that McClellan should not leave. "One word, one look of encouragement, the lifting of a finger," one witness later declared, "would have been a signal for a revolt against lawful authority, the consequences of which no man can measure." Instead, McClellan stepped onto the front platform and delivered a short address to the men, who had fallen silent as soon as he appeared. "Stand by General Burnside as you have stood by me, and all will be well," he said. Calmed, the soldiers recoupled the car and the train pulled out, followed by "one long and mournful huzza [as the men] bade farewell to their late commander." His route led through the capital, but he had already told his wife: "I shall not stop in Washington longer than for the next train, and will not go to see anybody."

In their tears, in their passionate demonstrations of affection for this man who moved them in a way no other general ever had or ever would, it was as if the soldiers had sensed a larger meaning in the impending separation; it was as if they knew they were saying goodbye to something more than just one stocky brown-haired man astride a tall black horse. It was, indeed, as if they were saying goodbye to their youth — which, in a sense, they were. Or it might also have been prescience, intimations of mortality, intimations of suffering down the years. There had been Pope, and now it appeared that there would be others more or less like him. Knowing what that meant, they might well have been weeping for their own lot, as well as for McClellan's. "My army," he had called them from the start, and it was true. He had made them into what they were, and whatever they accomplished he would accomplish too, in part, even though he would no longer be at their head.

That was no doubt his greatest satisfaction; but there were others, no less welcome for being delayed. Five years after the guns had cooled and were parked in town squares and on courthouse lawns, with sparrows building nests in their muzzles, he received what was perhaps his finest professional compliment, and received it from the man who had occupied the best of all possible positions from which to formulate a judgment. Asked then who was the ablest Federal general he had opposed throughout the war, Robert E. Lee replied without hesitation: "McClellan, by all odds."

★ ★ ★

McClellan was gone, and others were gone with him: Fitz-John Porter, for example, who was relieved from command by authority of the same message Lincoln had sent Halleck on November 5, relieving Little Mac. His corps went to Hooker, whose own had been severely cut up at Antietam, and Porter himself was brought back to Washington to face charges for having failed to obey Pope's order for an attack on the Confederate right "at or near Manassas, in the State of Virginia, on or about the 29th day of August, 1862." The court having convicted him, Lincoln ordered that he be "cashiered and dismissed from the service . . . and forever disqualified from holding any office of trust or profit under the Government of the United States." Winged thus by a stray pellet from the blast that felled his chief, Porter had to wait long for vindication. It came at last, officially, nearly a quarter of a century later, when Congress in 1886 commissioned him a regular-army colonel, to rank from 1861, and permitted him to retire immediately thereafter, without back pay but with honor.

One other major figure was to go, though not entirely: Benjamin Butler was too useful a man, and too powerful a politician, to be assigned to limbo alongside Buell and McClellan. Like them he was a Democrat, but he was blatantly so — with the result that what had been for them a disadvantage was for him a downright blessing. So long as he occupied a high position in the army, the Administration could not be accused of conducting a strictly Republican war, whereas his dismissal would have exactly the reverse effect. Butler of course was aware of this advantage, and operated accordingly. What was more, he was efficient, particularly as an administrator. Yet for all his ingenuity in dealing with the problems attending the occupation of New Orleans (he had not only succeeded in making the Creoles "fear the stripes" in his flag, he had also brought them some of the sanitary benefits of Lowell, Massachusetts, including an intensive flushing-out of their sewers and an equally intensive regulation of their morals) the squint-eyed general had not fulfilled his early promise as a terror to the rebels in the field. Of late, in fact, he had entirely neglected that side of military life, even having gone so far as to pull his troops out of Baton Rouge in order to avoid a return engagement with the Confederates who had attacked the place in early August. Obviously he would not do for the bloody work Lincoln now saw would have to be done if the war was ever to end. However, the disposition of Butler was no large problem. His talents were so manifold that he would be about as useful in one place as another. He could be shifted.

Fortunately for Lincoln's purpose he had a replacement there at hand, in the form of the commander of the Washington defenses. Banks, like Butler, was a Massachusetts politician, so that to exchange them, one for another, would not upset the voters of their region. Besides, Banks was resourceful, energetic, and pugnacious: a combination of qualities all too rare of late, in more places than New Orleans. In short, he was just the kind of man Lincoln thought he wanted for the job he had in mind. It was true that wherever he had fought he had been whipped, sometimes rather spectacularly, but this had not been the result of any unwillingness to fight; quite the reverse — and generally it had been against Stonewall Jackson, whom he would be unlikely to encounter down in Louisiana or up the Mississippi. That was where Lincoln intended to send him. On November 8, the day after Buckingham left for Rectortown with the orders placing Burnside in command of the Army of the Potomac, Lincoln had the Adjutant General issue an order assigning Banks "to the command of the Department of the Gulf, including the State of Texas," and the following day he had Halleck write the new commander a letter of instructions, explaining the purpose — or, more strictly speaking, purposes — for which he was being transferred so far south.

Vicksburg and Mobile were to be his primary objectives, and he was to have the coöperation of the navy in effecting their reduction. "The President regards the opening of the Mississippi River as the first and most important of all our military and naval operations," he was told, "and it is hoped that you will not lose a moment in accomplishing it." Following this, Halleck continued — quite as if the thing had been done already with a flourish of the pen — Banks was to move eastward from Vicksburg to Jackson, "and thus cut off all connection by rail between Northern Mississippi . . . and Atlanta . . . the chief military depot of the rebel armies in the West." This done, he would return approximately to his starting point in order to "ascend with a naval and military force the Red River as far as it is navigable, and thus open an outlet for the sugar and cotton of Northern Louisiana." Not even then did Halleck allow him time for a breather. "It is also suggested that, having Red River in our possession, it would form the best base for operations in Texas." There at last he closed with the assurance, "These instructions are not intended to tie your hands or to hamper your operations in the slightest degree . . . and I need not assure you, general, that the Government has unlimited confidence not only in your judgment and discretion, but also in your energy and military promptness."

Although this was clearly one of the largest tasks ever assigned a commander in all the history of warfare — and unquestionably the most difficult ever assigned a nonprofessional who, after eighteen months in the field and a major share in three campaigns, lacked so much as a single tactical victory to his credit — Banks shared Halleck's "unlimited confidence" that the thing could be done and that he was the man to do it. Summoned to Washington and informed that he would be given 20,000 reinforcements to accompany him on the coastal voyage to New Orleans — one expeditionary force would sail from New York, the other from Hampton Roads — the New Englander was delighted. "Eve-

rything is favorable for my purpose," he had replied to an earlier warning order. "I shall obtain troops at once, and be ready for movement
as early as you wish. . . . Requisitions will be made and forwarded by
mail. No material delay will occur, unless for want of transports."
Now, having conferred in person with Lincoln and Halleck as to the
details of the multi-faceted project, he was more enthusiastic than ever.
There was "much to do," he said as he departed for New York, but he
would "lose no time."

  Lincoln was delighted, too: not only by the prospect of seeing
so much accomplished, but also by the unfamiliar experience of having
sat face to face with a commander who recognized the worth of time
and the military fruits that haste could gather. Moreover, it augured
well for larger matters. For all the vastness of the project thus assigned
to Banks, the main value of his operations would be diversionary, serving
1) to drain off rebel front-line troops by threatening their rear, and 2)
to distract the enemy high command from concentrating against the
Federal main effort, about to be exerted against their front. After a
hundred thousand casualties and a year and a half of successes, near-
successes, and sickening failures — the last, as Lincoln saw them, being
mainly due to the vacillation and nonaggressiveness of generals like
Buell and McClellan, who, desiring combat less than they feared defeat,
believed in preparation more than they believed in movement — a victory pattern had emerged. Three southern cities were the three main
northern objectives. Richmond, Chattanooga, and Vicksburg were the
brain, heart, and bowels of the rebellion. A successful blow struck any
one of the three might well prove fatal, in time, to the corpus as a
whole; but *three* successful blows, struck simultaneously, would produce immediate results. Whatever movement followed then, on the part
of the creature named Rebellion, would be no more than death throes
and the setting in of rigor mortis.

  Immediate results being what he was after, Lincoln had assigned
these three main objectives to the commanders of the three main armies
of the Union: Burnside, Rosecrans, and Grant. He himself had chosen
the first and second, and he had sustained the third against strident demands for his dismissal, saying of him: "I can't spare this man. He fights."
He believed he could say it of the other two as well. Whatever shortcomings they might develop under pressure (Grant's, for instance, was
said to be whiskey; hearing which, the President was supposed to have
asked what brand he drank, intending to send a barrel each to all his
other generals) it seemed unlikely that a distaste for combat was going
to be the flaw in any case. All three had fought, and fought hard: Burnside at Roanoke Island and Antietam, Rosecrans in West Virginia and at
Corinth, Grant at Belmont, Donelson, and Shiloh — which was practically to call the roll of all the victories the army could lay claim to,
east of the Mississippi, even by stretching the point in an instance or

two or three. So had Banks fought hard, and though admittedly it had been with less success, Lincoln believed that the war had reached a stage where hard fighting, sustained by the superior resources of the nation, would create its own success. At any rate, that was what he was asking for now: hard fighting. And with this in mind, as Commander in Chief, he had placed his major armies under leaders he considered most likely to give it to him without delay.

So he thought, this melancholy man with his incurable optimism: only to find that what his high hopes mainly afforded him — once more, alas — was another occasion for exploring the gap that yawned between conception and execution. One by one, two by two, and finally all four together, his hand-picked generals failed his expectations as to haste. And, paradoxically, he discovered that the reason for delay, in all four cases, was just those superior resources which he had thought assured them victory.

Banks was first, the most enthusiastic of the lot. He had scarcely been gone from the capital a week before the President saw a monster requisition the Massachusetts general submitted, calling for mountains of supplies and thousands of horses to haul them through the jungles of the Lower South. Horses were a sore subject with Lincoln just now, anyhow, and when he was assured by the chief quartermaster that the requisition could not "be filled and got off within an hour short of two months," he wrote Banks a letter in which anger vied with sorrow for predominance. "I have just been overwhelmed and confounded," he declared, and continued: "My dear general, this expanding and piling up of impedimenta has been so far almost our ruin, and will be our final ruin if it is not abandoned.... When you parted with me you had no such ideas in your mind. I know you had not, or you could not have expected to be off so soon as you said. You must get back to something like the plan you had then or your expedition is a failure before you start. You must be off before Congress meets. You would be better off anywhere, and especially where you are going, for not having a thousand wagons doing nothing but hauling forage to feed the animals that draw them, and taking at least 2000 men to care for the wagons and animals, who otherwise might be 2000 good soldiers." In closing he added a further admonition: "Now, dear general, do not think this is an ill-natured letter; it is the very reverse. The simple publication of this requisition would ruin you."

As usual in cases where the offense presaged delay, Banks had what he considered a reasonable explanation. Two days later, November 24, he replied that the request for supplies "was drawn up by an officer who did not fully comprehend my instructions, and inadvertently approved by me without sufficient examination." In other words, he had signed without looking. "My purpose has not been changed since I left Washington," he assured Lincoln, "and I have waited [for] nothing not absolutely necessary." Apparently, though, a great many items fell in that category; for the waiting continued. Banks kept saying he would be off any day now, but the disillusioned President had doubts. And his doubts were valid. Banks' purpose might not have changed, but his schedule had. November went out; December came in; Banks remained at his New York starting point. Finally, on December 4, he sailed for Fort Monroe. How long he would stay there before continuing on to New Orleans, Lincoln did not know.

Anyhow, he had a good deal more on his mind by then. Troubles of a similar nature, involving delay, but derived from a different and even more unexpected source, were looming in the West: specifically in Grant's department, and even more specifically in U. S. Grant himself. After the ill-wind fiasco at Iuka and the bloody repulse of the rebels at Corinth, which he had missed, Grant had been sounding oddly unlike himself. When Halleck, after the latter fight, asked why he did not press the defeated and retreating foe — "Why order a return of our troops? Why not . . . pursue the enemy into Mississippi, supporting your army on the country?" — Grant replied that an army could not "subsist itself on the country except in forage. . . . Disaster would follow in the end." This did not sound like the Grant of old, who never spoke of disaster except with the intention of inflicting it, and presently he was sounding even less so, calling urgently for reinforcements in expectation of having to fight another battle. This fall, in fact, his aggressive instincts mostly seemed reserved for the Jews in his department. "Refuse all permits to come south of Jackson for the present," he wired Hurlbut at that place, adding: "The Israelites especially should be kept out." He instructed his railroad superintendent to "give orders to all conductors on the road that no Jews are to be permitted to travel on the railroad southward from any point. They may go north and be encouraged in it; but they are such an intolerable nuisance that the department must be purged of them."

Lincoln would not have admired this talk of purges, not only because it ran counter to his personal belief in the equality of men before the law (whether the law was military or civil) but also because it could be applied to a father or mother on the way to visit a soldier son; for there were, of course, Jewish soldiers in all the nation's armies — even Grant's. In time this would be called to his attention, but for the present Lincoln was disturbed enough at the general's tone in regard to the pursuit of a beaten foe. One explanation was given by Rosecrans in a private letter to Halleck, written on the day before he was ordered north to replace Buell. He complained of "the spirit of mischief among the mousing politicians on Grant's staff," spoke of Grant becoming "sour and reticent," and asked to be "relieved from duty here." When a fighter Lincoln respected as much as he did Rosecrans asked for a

transfer, apparently all was not well in the area he wished himself away
from. Also — as always — there was talk that Grant had reverted
to his old fondness for the bottle. Doubtless, too, Lincoln heard gossip
similar to what a Chicago reporter heard from his fellow passengers as he
rode south about this time on a train bound for Memphis. Officers and
men returning from leaves and furloughs declared that Grant "never
did amount to anything, and never would. He had been kicked out of
the United States Army once, and would be again. He was nothing but
a drunken, wooden-headed tanner, that would not trouble the country
very long. &c. &c."

Whatever his past successes, Vicksburg was too important a prize
for its capture to hinge entirely on the problematic advance of a man
who was the subject of so many ugly rumors and whose character,
even aside from the truth or falseness of such talk, seemed to have
undergone a discouraging reversal. At any rate, Lincoln in this case had
provided not one but two extra strings for the bow that was to be
bent in that direction. While Banks was moving upriver against the
place, supported by warships from Farragut's fleet, and Grant was
marching overland down the Mississippi Central from Grand Junction,
a third force was to descend the river from southern Illinois, its mission
being to coöperate with Porter's ironclad flotilla for an attack on the
stronghold which Jefferson Davis had called "the Gibraltar of the
West." This third force was irregular and highly secret in nature, its
purpose known only to three men: Lincoln, Stanton, and its commander,
John McClernand. They had created it — out of the whole cloth, so to
speak. McClernand had come north on leave in late September, saying
privately that he was "tired of furnishing brains" for Grant's army, and
had appealed to his friend the President to "let one volunteer officer try
his abilities." In accordance with the plan he submitted, Stanton gave
him on October 21 a confidential order authorizing him "to proceed
to the States of Indiana, Illinois, and Iowa, and to organize the troops
remaining in those States and to be raised by volunteering or draft
... to the end that, when a sufficient force not required by the operations of General Grant's command shall be raised, an expedition may be
organized under General McClernand's command against Vicksburg ...
to clear the Mississippi River and open navigation to New Orleans."
A presidential indorsement further authorized him to show this confidential document "to Governors, and even others, when in his discretion
he believes so doing to be indispensable to the progress of the expedition."

Armed with this order, which he saw as placing his star in the
ascendant — his ambition had not been lessened by the singeing he took
at Donelson while seeking the bubble reputation at the cannon's mouth
— McClernand left for his home state in late October, there to begin
assembling the force which he believed would put him not only in

Vicksburg but also in the White House. Even the first of these steps would take time, however; and time, he knew, was the foe of secrecy. Sure enough, by early November Grant began hearing what he called "mysterious rumors of McClernand's command." Glad as he had been to get rid of his fellow Illinoisan, he did not want him back in his department at the head of a rival army. When Halleck — whom the three lawyers had also not let in on their secret — informed him that Memphis would "be made the depot of a joint military and naval expedition on Vicksburg," Grant took alarm and wired back: "Am I to understand that I lie still here while an expedition is fitted out from Memphis, or do you want me to push as far south as possible? Am I to have Sherman move subject to my orders, or is he and his forces reserved for some special service?" Halleck replied blandly: "You have command of all troops sent to your department, and have permission to fight the enemy where you please."

That was enough for Grant. Receiving Halleck's go-ahead message near Grand Junction on November 11, he had cavalry in Holly Springs two days later. He followed at once with the infantry, established a supply base there, and continued his advance down the Mississippi Central. By December 1 his cavalry was across the Hatchie, the rebels fading back. Still Grant followed. Within another week he had occupied Oxford, fifty miles beyond his starting point, setting up a command post in the courthouse and repairing the railroad in his rear.... Whatever else McClernand's behind-the-scenes maneuver might accomplish in the end, it had effected at least one thing before it even got beyond the plans-and-training stage: Grant's mind had emerged from the tunnel it had entered after Shiloh. He was himself again, or anyhow he appeared to be, and this in itself was encouraging to Lincoln. However, he could also see that in North Mississippi, as elsewhere along the thousand-mile front, the fine autumn weather had mostly gone to waste, so far as offensive operations were concerned. Grant was still 150 airline miles from Vicksburg, and neither Banks nor McClernand had even begun to move.

Here in the East, delay was especially discouraging for being close at hand; Lincoln's torture, as a result, was not unlike that of Tantalus, who saw the surface of the pool recede each time he bent to drink. In this case, too, he was soon obliged to suspect that he had made an error in personal judgment, no matter how well founded that judgment had seemed at the time he acted on it. In addition to native combativeness, demonstrated on independent service, Burnside had other qualities which had caused Lincoln to overrule his twice-repeated protest that he was not competent to command the Army of the Potomac, despite the fact that his rank entitled him to the post. Less than three years older than McClellan, he had been his friend before and during the war and had taken no part in the bickering that surrounded him.

It was Lincoln's hope that this would ease the blow and soften the reaction when "McClellan's bodyguard" got the news that its hero had been replaced. Also, Burnside had no political opinions: a lack that might have been expected to spare him the mistrust and enmity of the Jacobins who had hounded his predecessor. Both calculations, one regarding the army, the other Congress, appeared to have been valid at the outset. For a time, they even worked; or else they seemed to. But the President was not long in finding out that both had been something less than inclusive. According to one general in a group who came to congratulate Burnside on his promotion, he thanked them "and then, with that transparent sincerity which made everyone believe what he said, he added that he knew he was not fit for so big a command, but he would do his best." The witness remarked: "One could not help feeling a certain tenderness for the man. But when a moment later the generals talked among themselves, it was no wonder that several shook their heads and asked how we could have confidence in the fitness of our leader if he had no such confidence in himself?" Such in part was the reaction in the army he was about to lead into battle. As for the radicals in Congress, it soon became apparent that an absence of politics was by no means a recommendation in their eyes. They had no objection to politics, per se; they merely insisted that the politics be Republican. All they really knew of Burnside was that he was the acknowledged friend of the man whose ruin they were proud to have helped accomplish, and they were prepared to do as much for him in turn, if on closer acquaintance it appeared that he deserved it.

Such objections were mainly personal, however, and Lincoln did not share them, or if he did he thought them incidental. His main concern was with Burnside as a strategist, a seeker after battle: which was where his doubts came in. Aware that the President wanted immediate action, and had in fact removed his predecessor for not giving it to him, the new commander immediately prepared a plan which he submitted for approval. Not liking the army's present location — which seemed to him uncomfortably similar to the one John Pope had occupied before he came to grief — Burnside had the notion of converting the advance just east of the Blue Ridge into a feint, under cover of which he would "accumulate a four or five days' supply for the men and animals; then make a rapid move of the whole force to Fredericksburg, with a view to a movement upon Richmond from that point." This was the so-called "covering approach" which Lincoln had always favored, since it protected Washington. But in this case he thought the plan defective, in that it made the southern capital the primary Federal objective, not Lee's army, which in fact it seemed that Burnside was attempting to avoid. Halleck felt that way about it, too, and on November 12 went down to Warrenton for a talk with the lush-whiskered general, who argued forcefully in favor of the change of base.

Still doubtful, Halleck returned to Washington and reported the discussion to the President. Lincoln too was unconvinced, but he was so pleased at the prospect of early action — here in the East, if nowhere else — that he agreed to let Burnside go ahead — or, more strictly speaking, sideways, then ahead — provided he moved fast. Halleck passed the word to Warrenton on the 14th: "The President has just assented to your plan. He thinks that it will succeed, if you move very rapidly; otherwise not."

Burnside did move rapidly, "very rapidly." Despite the tremendous supply problems which went with having an "aggregate present" of approximately 250,000 officers and men for whose welfare he was responsible — 150,441 in the field force proper, 98,738 in the capital defenses — the fact was, he had turned out to be an excellent administrator. On the day he received Lincoln's qualified assent to an eastward shift, he regrouped his seven corps into Right, Left, and Center "Grand Divisions" of two corps each, respectively under Sumner, Franklin, and Hooker, leaving the seventh in "independent reserve" under Sigel. With his army thus reorganized for deft handling, he took up the march for Falmouth the following day, November 15. Sumner went first, followed on subsequent days by Franklin, Hooker, and the cavalry. Moving down the north bank of the Rappahannock, which thus covered the exposed flank of the column, the Right Grand Division arrived on the 17th and the others came along behind on schedule. Burnside himself reached Falmouth on the 19th, just in advance of the rear-guard elements. Proudly he wired Washington: "Sumner's two corps now occupy all the commanding positions opposite Fredericksburg. . . . The enemy do not seem to be in force." So far, indeed, except for an occasional gray cavalry vedette across the way, the only sign of resistance had come from a single rebel battery on the heights beyond the historic south-bank town, and it had been smothered promptly by counterbattery fire. Lincoln had asked for speed, and Burnside had given it to him. He seemed about to give him all else he had asked for, too — hard fighting — for he added: "As soon as the pontoon trains arrive, the bridge will be built and the command moved over."

But there was the rub. Burnside had left the sending of the pontoons to Halleck, who in turn had left it to a subordinate, and somewhere along the chain of command the word "rush" had been dropped from the requisition. The army waited a week, during which a three-day rain swelled the fords and turned the roads into troughs of mud. Still the pontoons did not come. On the eighth day they got there; but so by then had something else; something not nearly so welcome. "Had the pontoon bridge arrived even on the 19th or 20th, the army could have crossed with trifling opposition," Burnside notified Halleck on the 22d. "But now the opposite side of the river is occupied by a large rebel force under General Longstreet, with batteries ready to be placed in position to operate against the working parties building the bridge and the troops in crossing." Vexed that his forty-mile change of base, executed with such efficiency and speed that it had given him the jump on his wily opponent, had gained him nothing by way of surprise in the end, he said flatly: "I deem it my duty to lay these facts before you, and to say that I cannot make the promise of probable success with the faith that I did when I supposed that all the parts of the plan would be carried out. . . . The President said that the movement, in order to be successful, must be made quickly, and I thought the same."

Lincoln was distressed: not only because of the delay, which he had predicted would be fatal to the success of the campaign, but also because the new commander, in the face of all those guns across the river, seemed to believe it was part of his duty to expose his army to annihilation by way of payment for other men's mistakes. November 25, the day the first relay of pontoons reached Falmouth, the President wired: "If I should be in a boat off Aquia Creek at dark tomorrow (Wednesday) evening, could you, without inconvenience, meet me and pass an hour or two with me?" He made the trip, saw Burnside and the situation — which he characterized by understatement as "somewhat risky" — then returned to Washington, worked out a supplementary plan of his own, and sent for the general to come up and discuss it with him and Halleck. As he saw it, the enemy should be confused by diversionary attacks, one upstream from Fredericksburg, the other on the lower Pamunkey, each to be delivered by a force of about 25,000 men and the latter to be supported by the fleet. Both generals rejected the plan, however, on grounds that it would require too much time for preparation. So Lincoln, with his argument stressing haste thus turned against him, had to content himself with telling Burnside to go back to his army and use his own judgment as to when and where he would launch an assault across the Rappahannock.

Burnside returned to Falmouth on the next to last day of November. His notion was to strike where Lee would least expect it, and the more he thought about the problem, the more it seemed to him that this would be at Fredericksburg itself, where Lee was strongest. Accordingly, he began to mass his 113,000 effectives — Sigel having been posted near Manassas — along and behind the north-bank heights, overlooking the streets of the Rappahannock town whose citizens had already been given notice to evacuate their homes. November was gone by then, however. In the East as in the West, to Lincoln's sorrow, there had been no fall offensive, only a seemingly endless preparation for one which had not come off.

Between these two East-West extremes, the trouble in Middle Tennessee, while similar to the trouble in Virginia and North Mississippi, was in its way even more exasperating. Burnside and Grant at least regretted the delay and expressed a willingness to end it, but

Rosecrans not only would not say that he regretted it, he declared flatly that he would not obey a direct order to end it until he personally was convinced that his hard-marched army was ready for action, down to the final shoenail in the final pair of shoes. This came as a shock to Lincoln, who had expected Old Rosy's positivism to take a different form. He would have been less surprised, no doubt, if he had known Grant's reaction when that general learned in late October that his then subordinate was leaving. "I was delighted," he later wrote, adding: "I found that I could not make him do as I wished, and had determined to relieve him from duty that very day."

Whatever reasons lay behind Rosecrans' reluctance to move forward, they could not have proceeded from any vagueness in his instructions, which were covered in a letter Halleck sent him along with his appointment as Buell's successor: "The great objects to be kept in view in your operations in the field are: First, to drive the enemy from Kentucky and Middle Tennessee; second, to take and hold East Tennessee, cutting the line of railroad at Chattanooga, Cleveland, or Athens, so as to destroy the connection of the valley of Virginia with Georgia and the other Southern States. It is hoped that by prompt and rapid movements a considerable part of this may be accomplished before the roads become impassable from the winter rains." After emphasizing "the importance of moving light and rapidly, and also the necessity of procuring as many of your supplies as possible in the country passed over," the general-in-chief concluded on an even sterner note: "I need not urge upon you the necessity of giving active employment to your forces. Neither the country nor the Government will much longer put up with the inactivity of some of our armies and generals."

There he had it, schedule and all; even the name of the army was changed, so that what had been called the Army of the Ohio was now the Army of the Cumberland, signifying the progress made, as well as the progress looked forward to. He knew well enough that Buell had been relieved because the authorities in Washington lacked confidence in his inclination or ability to get these missions accomplished in a hurry. That, too — in addition to the reluctance shown in declining the same appointment a month before — was why Thomas had been passed over in order to give the job to Rosecrans, whom they apparently considered the man to get it done. As a sign of this confidence, Halleck at once agreed to let him do what he had been unwilling to grant Buell. That is, he allowed him to return to Nashville with the army, agreeing at last with Buell's old contention that this was the best starting point for an advance on Chattanooga. Having won this concession, Rosecrans moved into the fortified Tennessee capital, and while butternut cavalry under Morgan and Forrest tore up tracks in his rear and slashed at his front, he set about reorganizing his command, more or less in the manner of Burnside, into Right, Left, and Center "Wings" of four divisions each.

Gilbert having faded back into the obscurity he came out of, these went respectively to McCook, Crittenden, and Thomas. The mid-November effective strength of the army was 74,555 men — as large or larger, it was thought, than the enemy force at Murfreesboro, thirty-odd miles southeast — but Rosecrans still had not advanced beyond the outskirts of Nashville. He was hoping, he said, for a sudden rise of the Tennessee River to cut off the rebels' retreat; in which case, as he put it, "I shall throw myself on their right flank and endeavor to make an end of them." For the present, however, he confided, "I am trying to lull them into security, that I do not intend soon to move, until I can get the [rail]road fully opened and throw in a couple of millions of rations here."

The Confederates might be lulled by his apparent inactivity, but his own superiors were not. Alarmed by this casual reference to "a couple of millions of rations" — followed as it was by urgent requisitions for "revolving rifles," back pay, "an iron pontoon train long enough to cross the Tennessee," and much else — Halleck told him sternly on November 27: "I must warn you against this piling up of impediments. Take a lesson from the enemy. Move light." The Tennessee commander protested that he was asking for nothing that was not "indispensable to an effectual and steady advance, which is the only one that will avail us anything worth the cost." By now it was December, and Rosecrans had begun to sound more like Buell than Buell himself had done. Halleck lost his temper, wiring curtly: "The President is very impatient.... Twice have I been asked to designate someone else to command your army. If you remain one more week in Nashville, I cannot prevent your removal." Rosecrans, unintimidated, bristled back at him: "Your dispatch received. I reply in few but earnest words. I have lost no time. Everything I have done was necessary, absolutely so; and has been done as rapidly as possible.... If the Government which ordered me here confides in my judgment, it may rely on my continuing to do what I have been trying to do — that is, my whole duty. If my superiors have lost confidence in me, they had better at once put someone in my place and let the future test the propriety of the change. I have but one word to add, which is, that I need no other stimulus to make me do my duty than the knowledge of what it is. To threats of removal or the like I must be permitted to say that I am insensible."

Now Lincoln knew the worst. With autumn gone and winter at hand, not a single one of the three major blows he had hoped for and designed had been struck. Right, left, and center, for all he knew — and he had observed signs of this with his own eyes, down on the Rappahannock — all that had been accomplished in each of these three critical theaters was a fair-weather setting of the stage for a foul-weather disaster. Halleck was saying of him during this first week in December: "You can hardly conceive his great anxiety," and Lincoln himself had told a friend the week before: "I certainly have been dissatisfied with the slowness of Buell and McClellan; but before I relieved them I had great fears I should not find successors to them who would do better; and I am sorry to add that I have seen little since to relieve those fears."

★ ★ ★

These words were written in a letter to Carl Schurz, a young German emigrant whom the Republican central committee had sent to Illinois four years ago to speak in Lincoln's behalf during the senatorial race against Douglas. Grateful for this and later, more successful work, Lincoln appointed him Minister to Spain in 1861, and when Schurz resigned to come home and fight, the President made him a brigadier under Frémont in the Alleghenies. After the fall election returns were in, he wrote Lincoln his belief that they were "a most serious reproof to the Administration" for placing the nation's armies in "the hands of its enemies," meaning Democrats. "What Republican has ever had a fair chance in this war?" Schurz asked, apparently leaving his own case out of account, and urged: "Let us be commanded by generals whose heart is in the war." Lincoln thought this over and replied: "I have just received and read your letter of [November] 20th. The purport of it is that we lost the late elections and the Administration is failing because the war is unsuccessful, and that I must not flatter myself that I am not justly to blame for it. I certainly know that if the war fails, the Administration fails, and that I will be blamed for it, whether I deserve it or not. And I ought to be blamed if I could do better. You think I could do better; therefore you blame me already. I think I could not do better; therefore I blame you for blaming me." Having thus disposed of the matter of blame, he passed on to the matter of hearts. "I understand you now to be willing to accept the help of men who are not Republicans, provided they have 'heart in it.' Agreed. I want no others. But who is to be the judge of hearts, or of 'heart in it'? If I must discard my own judgment and take yours, I must also take that of others; and by the time I should reject all I should be advised to reject, I should have none left, Republicans or others — not even yourself. For be assured, my dear sir, there are men who have 'heart in it' that think you are performing your part as poorly as you think I am performing mine. . . . I wish to disparage no one, certainly not those who sympathize with me; but I must say I need success more than I need sympathy, and that I have not seen the so much greater evidence of getting success from my sympathizers than from those who are denounced as the contrary."

He closed with a suggestion that the citizen soldier come to see him soon at the White House: which Schurz did, arriving early one morning, and was taken at once to an upstairs room where he found the President sitting before an open fire, his feet in large Morocco slippers.

Told to pull up a chair, he did so: whereupon Lincoln brought his hand down with a slap on Schurz's knee. "Now tell me, young man, whether you really think that I am as poor a fellow as you have made me out in your letter." He was smiling, but Schurz could not keep from stammering as he tried to apologize. This made the tall man laugh aloud, and again he slapped his visitor's knee. "Didn't I give it to you hard in my letter? Didn't I? But it didn't hurt, did it? I did not mean to, and therefore I wanted you to come so quickly." Still laughing, he added: "Well, I guess we understand one another now, and it's all right." They talked for the better part of an hour, and as Schurz rose to leave he asked whether he should keep on writing letters to the President. "Why, certainly," Lincoln told him. "Write me whenever the spirit moves you."

It was Schurz's belief that the visit had done Lincoln good, and unquestionably it had. Busy as he was with the details of office, not all of which were directly connected with the war, he had all too few occasions for relaxation, let alone laughter, the elixir he had always used against his natural melancholia. Out in Minnesota, for example, John Pope had been more successful against the marauding Sioux than he had against Lee and Jackson. He had defeated Chief Little Crow in battle and brought the surviving braves before a military court which sentenced 303 of them to be hanged. Reviewing the list, Lincoln reduced to thirty-eight the number slated for immediate execution and ordered the rest held, "taking care that they neither escape nor are subjected to any unlawful violence." This was of course only one distraction among many, the most troublesome being the host of importunate callers, all of whom wanted some special favor from him. Sometimes he lost patience, as when he told a soldier who came seeking his intervention in a routine army matter: "Now, my man, go away. I cannot attend to all these details. I could as easily bail out the Potomac with a spoon!" But mostly he was patient and receptive. He put them at ease, heard their complaints, and did what he could to help them. When a friend remarked, "You will wear yourself out," he shook his head and replied with a sad smile: "They don't want much; they get but little, and I must see them."

One place of refuge he had, the war telegraph office, and one companion whose demands on his time apparently brought him nothing but pleasure, Tad. Often he would combine the two, taking his son there with him during the off-hours, when the place was quiet, with only a single operator on duty. He would sit at a desk, reading the accumulated flimsies, while the nine-year-old went to sleep on his lap or rummaged around in search of mischief, which he seldom failed to find. John Hay once remarked that Tad "had a very bad opinion of books, and no opinion of discipline." The former was mainly his father's fault. "Let him run," Lincoln said. "There's time enough yet for him to learn his letters and get poky." So was the latter; for since the death of Willie, eight months before, this youngest child had been overindulged by way of double compensation. "I want to give him all the toys I did not have," Lincoln explained, "and all the toys I would have given the boy who went away." Nor would he allow his son to be corrected. Once when they were at the telegraph office Tad wandered into the adjoining room, where he found the combination of black ink and white marble-topped tables quite irresistible. Presently the operator, whose name was Madison Buell, saw what was being done. Indignant at the ruin, he seized the dabbler by the collar and marched him out to his father, pointing through the open door at the irreparable outrage. Lincoln reacted promptly. Rising, he took the boy in his arms, unmindful of the hands still dripping ink. "Come, Tad," he said; "Buell is abusing you," and left.

In these and other ways he sought relaxation during this season which had opened with reverses and closed before the big machine could overcome the primary inertia which had gripped it when it stalled. Such large-scale battles as had been fought — Antietam, Corinth, Perryville — had been set down as Union victories; but they had been near things at best — particularly the first and the last, which the rebels also claimed — and what was more, all three had been intrinsically defensive; which would not do. It would do for the insurgents, whose task was merely to defend their region against what they called aggression, but not for the loyalists, whose goal could be nothing short of conquest. Besides, the defensive encouraged the fulfillment of Lincoln's two worst fears: utter war-weariness at home, and recognition for the Confederacy abroad. Other developments might prolong the war, but these two could lose it, and he had taken their avoidance as his personal responsibility. During the period just past, he had sought to prevent the first by appealing directly to the people for confidence in his Administration, and to forestall the second by issuing the Preliminary Emancipation Proclamation. How well he had done in both cases he did not know; it was perhaps too soon to tell, though here too the signs were not encouraging. Some said the fall elections were a rejection of the former, while the latter had been greeted in some quarters — including England, so far as could be judged from the public prints — with derision.

He would wait and see, improvising to meet what might arise. Meanwhile, the armies were getting into position at last for another major effort — and, incidentally, fulfilling the *Tribune* reporter's prediction about "the poetry of war." Down on the Rappahannock, for example, another of Greeley's men overheard the following exchange between two pickets on opposite banks:

"Hallo, Secesh!"

"Hallo, Yank."

"What was the matter with your battery Tuesday night?"

"You made it too hot. Your shots drove the cannoneers away, and they haven't stopped running yet. We infantry men had to come out and withdraw the guns."

"You infantry men will run, too, one of these fine mornings."

The Confederate picket let this pass, as if to say it might be so, and responded instead with a question:

"When are you coming over, bluecoat?"

"When we get ready, butternut."

"What do you want?"

"Want Fredericksburg."

"Don't you wish you may get it!"

x 2 x

As if in accordance with the respective limitations of their available re- sources — which of course applied to men as well as to the food they ate, the powder they burned, and the shoes and clothes and horses they wore out — while Lincoln was getting rid of experienced commanders, Davis was making use of those he had. Yet this difference in outlook and action was not merely the result of any established ratio between profligacy and frugality, affordable on the one hand and strictly nec- essary on the other; it was, rather, an outgrowth of the inherent difference in their natures. Lincoln, as he said, was more in need of success than he was in need of sympathy. And while this was also true of Davis, he placed such value on the latter quality — apparently for its own sake — that its demands for reciprocal loyalty, whatever short- comings there might be in regard to the former, were for him too strong to be denied.

Braxton Bragg and R. E. Lee were cases in point. Ever since the western general began his retreat from Harrodsburg, Davis had been receiving complaints of dissension in the ranks of the Army of Ken- tucky, along with insistent demands that its commander be removed: in spite of which (if not, indeed, because of them; for such agitations often seemed to strengthen instead of weaken Davis' will) the summons Bragg found waiting for him in Knoxville had not been sent with any notion of effecting his dismissal, but rather with the intention of giving him the chance to present in person his side of the reported controversy. When he got to Richmond, October 25, the President received him with a smile and a congratulatory handshake. On the face of it, both were certainly deserved: the first because it was not Davis' way to dissolve a friendship or condemn any man on the basis of hearsay evidence, and the second because, of the three offensives designed to push Confederate arms beyond the acknowledged borders of secession, only Bragg's had been even moderately successful. In fact, "moderately" was putting it all too mildly. Whatever else had been left undone, a campaign which relieved the pressure on Chattanooga and recovered for the Confederacy all of northwest Alabama, as well as eastern and south-central Tennessee, including Cumberland Gap — not to mention the fact that its two columns had inflicted just under 14,000 battle casualties while suffering just over 4000, and had returned with an enormous train of badly needed supplies and captured matériel, including more than thirty Union guns — could scarcely be called anything less than substantial in its results. What was more, Bragg had conceived and, in conjunction with Kirby Smith, executed the whole thing, not only without prodding from above, but also without the government's advance permission or even knowledge. Initiative such as that was all too rare. Davis heard him out, and though he did not enjoy hearing his old friend and classmate Bishop Polk accused of bumbling and disloyalty, sustained him. Bragg was told to rejoin his army, which meanwhile was moving rapidly by rail, via Stevenson, Alabama, from Knoxville to Tullahoma and Murfreesboro, where it would threaten Nashville and block a Federal advance from that direction.

Polk was summoned to the capital as soon as Bragg had left it. Invited to present his side of the controversy, the bishop came armed with documents — messages from Bragg to him, messages from him to Bragg, and affidavits provided by fellow subordinates, similarly disaffected — which he believed would protect his reputation and destroy his adversary's, or at any rate neutralize the poison lately poured into the presidential ear. "If you choose to rip up the Kentucky campaign you can tear Bragg into tatters," Hardee told him. However, Davis urged him to put them away, appealing to his patriotism as well as his churchman's capacity for forgiveness, and the bishop agreed to go back and do his Christian best along those lines. By way of compensation, the President handed him his promotion to lieutenant general, a new rank lately authorized by Congress at the same time it legalized the previously informal division of the armies into "wings" and corps. That was gratifying. Equally so was the news that his friend Hardee's name appeared immediately below his own on the seven-man list of generals so honored.

Above them both — next to the very top, in fact — was Kirby Smith, who thus was rewarded for his independent accomplishments in Kentucky, even though he had written to the War Department soon after his return, complaining acidly of Bragg's direction of the campaign during its later stages and requesting transfer to Mobile or elsewhere, anywhere, if staying where he was would require further coöperation with that general. Davis himself replied to this on October 29. He agreed that the campaign had been "a bitter disappointment" in some respects, but he also felt that events should not be judged by "knowledge acquired after they transpired." Besides, having talked at length with Bragg that week, he could assure Smith that "he spoke of you in the most complimentary terms, and does not seem to imagine your dissatisfaction." Davis admitted some other commanders might "excite more enthusiasm" than the dyspeptic North Carolinian, but he doubted that they would be "equally useful" to the country. In motion now for Middle Tennessee, Bragg would need reinforcements in order to parry the Federal counterthrust from Nashville. Where were they to be procured if not from Smith? He asked that, and then concluded: "When you wrote your wounds were fresh, your lame and exhausted troops were before you. I hope time may have mollified your pain and that future operations may restore the confidence essential to cheerfulness and security in campaign."

That was enough for Smith, whose admiration for Davis was such that, if the President requested it, he would not only coöperate with Bragg, he would even serve under him if it was absolutely necessary. Grateful, Davis sent for him to come to Richmond in early November. Smith went and, like Polk, gave the President his personal assurance that his rancor had been laid by — as indeed it had. A week later he sent Bragg his strongest division, Stevenson's, and neither Smith nor any member of his staff permitted himself a public word of criticism of the leader of the Kentucky campaign for the balance of the war. Returning to Knoxville by way of Lynchburg (where he had convalesced from his Manassas wound and married the young lady who had nursed him) he had an unexpected encounter during a change of trains. "I saw Gen. Bragg," he wrote his wife; "everyone prognosticated a stormy meeting. I told him what I had written to Mr. Davis, but he spoke kindly to me & in the highest terms of praise and admiration of 'my personal character and soldierly qualities.' I was astonished but believe he is honest & means well."

Breckinridge was already with Bragg: in fact, had preceded the army to its present location. Following the repulse at Baton Rouge, after wiring Hardee to "reserve the division for me," he had reached Knoxville in early October with about 2500 men. Reinforced by an equal number of exchanged prisoners, he had been about to start northward in order to share in the "liberation" of his native Bluegrass, when he received word that Bragg was on the way back and wanted him to proceed instead to Murfreesboro, where he was to dispose his troops "for the defense of Middle Tennessee or an attack on Nashville." He got there October 28, joining Forrest, who had been deviling the Federals by way of breaking in his newly recruited "critter companies." Bragg's 30,000 veterans arrived under Polk and Hardee ten days later, and when Stevenson's 9000-man division marched in from Knoxville shortly afterward, the army totaled 44,-000 infantry and artillery effectives, plus about 4000 organic cavalry under Wheeler. This was by no means as large a force as Rosecrans was assembling within the Nashville intrenchments, but Bragg did not despair of whipping him when he emerged. Returning from Richmond with assurances of the President's confidence, he set about the familiar task of drilling his troops and stiffening the discipline which Buell had admired. Meanwhile, he turned Forrest and Morgan loose on Rosecrans, front and rear. "Harass him in every conceivable way in your power," he told them. And they did, thus fulfilling the anticipation announced in general orders, November 20: "Much is expected by the army and its commander from the operations of these active and ever-successful leaders."

Nor were the infantry neglected in their commander's announcement of his hopes. Having posted Stevenson's division in front of Manchester, Hardee's corps at Shelbyville, and Polk's at Murfreesboro — the latter now including Breckinridge, so that Polk had three and Hardee two divisions — Bragg announced in the same general order that the army had a new name: "The foregoing dispositions are in anticipation of the great struggle which must soon settle the question of supremacy in Middle Tennessee. The enemy in heavy force is before us, with a determination, no doubt, to redeem the fruitful country we have wrested from him. With the remembrance of Richmond, Munfordville, and Perryville so fresh in our minds, let us make a name for the now Army of Tennessee as enviable as those enjoyed by the armies of Kentucky and the Mississippi."

Presumably this was the best that could be done in that direction: Davis had sustained the army commander and persuaded his irate subordinates to lay aside their personal and official differences in order to concentrate on the defense of the vital center in Tennessee. South and west of there, however, the problem was not one of persuading delicate gears to mesh, but rather one of filling the near vacuum created by the bloody repulse Van Dorn and Price had suffered in front of Corinth. Vicksburg was obviously about to become the target for a renewed endeavor by Federal combinations. What these would be, Davis did not know, but whatever they were, they posed a problem that would have to be met before they got there. He met it obliquely, so to speak, by turning initially to a second problem, seven hundred miles away, whose solution automatically provided him with a solution to the first.

This was the problem of Charleston, where the trouble was also an outgrowth of dissension. John Pemberton, in command there, had been a classmate of Bragg's and had several of that general's less fortunate characteristics, including an abruptness of manner which, taken in conjunction with his northern birth, had earned him a personal unpopularity rivaling the North Carolinian's. Indeed, not being restricted to the army, it surpassed it. He was "wanting in polish," according to one Confederate observer, "and was too positive and domineering ... to suit the sensitive and polite people among whom he had been thrown." As a result, he had not been long in incurring the displeasure of Governor Pickens and the enmity of the Rhetts, along with that of other Charlestonians of influence, who by now were clamoring for his removal. They wanted their first hero back: meaning Beauregard. It was a more or less familiar cry to Davis, for others were also calling for the Creole, still restoring his "shattered health" at Bladon Springs. In mid-September two Louisiana congressmen brought to the President's office a petition signed by themselves and fifty-seven fellow members, requesting the general's return to command of the army that had been taken from him. Davis read the document aloud, including the signatures, then sent for the official correspondence relating to Beauregard's removal for being absent without leave. This too he read aloud, as proof of justice in his action on the case, and closed the interview by saying: "If the whole world were to ask me to restore General Beauregard to the command which I have already given to General Bragg, I would refuse it."

In any case, he had decided by then to use him in the opposite direction: meaning Charleston. Orders had been drawn up in late August, appointing Beauregard to command the Department of South Carolina and Georgia, with headquarters in Charleston. Whether he would accept the back-area appointment, which amounted in effect to a demotion, was not known. Yet there should have been little doubt; for the choice, after all, lay between limited action and *in*action. "*Nil desperandum* is my motto," he had declared, chafing in idleness earlier that month, "and I feel confident that ere long the glorious sun of Southern liberty will appear more radiant than ever from the clouds which obscure its brilliant disk." He wanted a share in scouring those clouds away. Receiving the orders in early September, he told a friend: "If the country is willing I should be put on the shelf thro' interested motives, I will submit until our future reverses will compel the Govt to put me on duty. I scorn its motives and present action." He wired acceptance, took the cars at Mobile on September 11, and received a tumultuous welcome on the 15th when he returned to the city whose harbor had been the scene of his first glory.

This not only freed the embittered Charlestonians of Pemberton; it also freed Pemberton for the larger duty Davis had in mind for him, along with a promotion as seventh man on the seven-man list of new lieutenant generals. Slender and sharp-faced, the forty-eight-year-old Pennsylvanian had been pro-Southern all his adult life, choosing southern cadets as his West Point friends and later marrying a girl from Old Point Comfort. He was, indeed, an out-and-out States Righter, and it was generally known in army circles that in making his choice of sides in the present conflict, despite the fact that two of his brothers had joined a Philadelphia cavalry troop, he had declined a Federal colonelcy in order to accept a commission as a Confederate lieutenant colonel and assignment to Norfolk, where he had been charged with organizing

Virginia's cavalry and artillery. Efficiency at that assignment had won
him a brigadier's stars and transfer to Charleston, where his ability as an
administrator — whatever his shortcomings when it came to social converse — had won him another promotion and eventually still another,
along with another transfer, in connection with the larger duty Davis
had in mind. This was for Pemberton to take charge of a department
created October 1, consisting of the whole state of Mississippi and that
part of Louisiana east of the Mississippi River. Instructed to "consider
the successful defense of those States" — one already invaded from the
north, the other already invaded from the south — "as the first and
chief object of your command," he was told to proceed at once to his
new post: which he did. Arriving October 14, he established department
headquarters at Jackson, Mississippi.

There were, as usual, objections. Mainly these came from men
over whose heads he had been advanced in his rush up the ladder of
rank, including Van Dorn and Lovell, here in his own department, as
well as others back in the theater he had come from; "officers who," as
one of them protested, "had already distinguished themselves and given
unquestioned evidence of capacity, efficiency, and other soldierly qualities." By this last, the disgruntled observer meant combat — for Pemberton had seen none since the Mexican War. Also, it was felt that he
lacked the flexibility of mind necessary to independent command of a
region under pressure from various directions. But the fact was, Davis
had already taken this into consideration. Pemberton's main job would
be to keep a bulldog grip on Vicksburg and Port Hudson, denying
free use of the Mississippi to the Federals and keeping the stretch of
river between those two bastions open as a Confederate supply line connecting its opposite banks. Inflexibility in the performance of such a
job — even tactical and strategic near-sightedness, of which the new
commander was also accused by those who had known him in the East
— might turn out to be a positive virtue when he was confronted, as
surely he would be, by combinations which well might cause a more
"flexible" man to fly to pieces. So Davis reasoned, at any rate, when
he assigned the Northerner to defend his home state. And at least one
Vicksburg editor agreed, declaring that Pemberton's arrival at last
demonstrated that the far-off Richmond government had not "failed
to appreciate the vast importance of preserving this important region"
and that Mississippians were no longer "to be put off and imposed upon
with one-horse generals."

Whatever their resentment of his rapid rise, his northern birth,
his lack of exposure to gunfire, and his uncongenial manner, Pemberton's by-passed fellow officers — even Van Dorn, whose ruffled feathers
Davis smoothed by explaining that the appointment had been made, not
to overslough him, but to unburden him of paperwork and other back-
area concerns, in order to free him for the offensive action which he

so much preferred — would doubtless have been less envious if they had been able to compare the magnitude of the new commander's "first and chief object" with the means which he had inherited for effecting it. He had fewer than 50,000 troops of all arms in his entire department: 24,000 under Van Dorn and Price — disaffected Transmississippians for the most part, anxious to get back across the river for the close-up protection of their homes — and another 24,000 mainly comprising the permanent garrisons of Vicksburg and Port Hudson. Even without knowledge of the three-pronged Federal build-up now in progress north and south of these two critical points (a combined force of more than 100,000 men, supported by the guns of two fleets) it was obvious that the difficulties of the assignment would be exceeded only by the clamor which would follow if he failed, whatever the odds.

Here too, however, Davis had done what he could and as he thought best. Having sustained Bragg, installed Pemberton, and incidentally disposed of Beauregard, he found it in a way a relief to give his attention to the army closest to the capital: for its troubles, although manifold, were at least of a different nature. Though Lee's invasion had been less profitable than Bragg's, and his repulse far bloodier, no one could accuse him of unwillingness to exploit any opening the enemy afforded, regardless of the numerical odds or the tactical risks of annihilation. As a result, such disaffection as arose was not directed against him, either by his army or by the public it protected, but against Congress, which bridled at passing certain measures Lee suggested for the recruitment of new men, the establishment of proper supply facilities for the benefit of the men he had — including the more than 10,000 who now were marching barefoot in the snow — and the authority to tighten discipline.

The President supported Lee in the controversy and wrote him of the scorn he felt for their opponents, who were reacting simultaneously to rumors that the enemy was about to advance on Richmond from Suffolk: "The feverish anxiety to invade the North has been relieved by the counter-irritant of apprehension for the safety of the capital in the absence of the army, so long criticised for a 'want of dash,' and the class who so vociferously urged a forward movement, in which they were not personally involved, would now be most pleased to welcome the return of that army. I hope their fears are as poor counselors as was their presumption." He assured the Virginian, "I am alike happy in the confidence felt in your ability, and your superiority to outside clamor, when the uninformed assume to direct the movements of armies in the field." Lee replied characteristically: "I wish I felt that I deserved the confidence you express in me. I am only conscious of an earnest desire to advance the interests of the country and of my inability to accomplish my wishes."

Davis left the field work to Lee, while he himself took up the fight with Congress throughout its stormy second session, which extended from mid-August to mid-October. Two of the general's recommendations resulted in much violent debate: 1) that a permanent court martial be appointed, with authority to inflict the death penalty in an attempt to reduce straggling and desertion, and 2) that the Conscription Act be extended to include all able-bodied men between the ages of eighteen and forty-five. The first of these suggestions was not only not acceptable to the law-makers, it led to vigorous inquiries as to whether such powers had not been overexercised already. But it was the second which provoked the greatest furor, especially after Davis gave it presidential support. Yancey was particularly vitriolic, shouting that if he had to have a dictator, he wanted it to be Lincoln, "not a Confederate." Joe Brown of Georgia thought so, too, declaring that the people had "much more to apprehend from military despotism than from subjection by the enemy." A Texas senator added point to the assertion, as here applied, by recalling that it had been conscription which "enabled [Napoleon] to put a diadem on his head." Davis met these charges with a bitterness matching that of the men who made them; and in the end he won the fight. Conscription was extended, but not without the estrangement of former loyal friends whose loss he could ill afford. As always, he was willing to pay the price, though it was becoming increasingly steep in obedience to the law of diminishing utility.

At any rate the measure helped secure for Lee the men he badly needed, and while Davis engaged these wranglers in the army's rear, the bluecoats to its front were obligingly idle, affording time for rest, recruitment, and reorganization of its shattered ranks. The need for these was obvious at a glance. Recrossing the Potomac, only fourteen of the forty brigades had been led by brigadiers, and many of them had dwindled until they were smaller than a standard regiment. Yet the return of stragglers and convalescents, along with the influx of conscripts, more than repaired the shortage in the course of the five-week respite the Federals allowed. By October 10, Lee's strength had risen to 64,273 of all arms, and within another ten days — on which date McClellan reported 133,433 present for duty in the Army of the Potomac — he had 68,033, or better than half as many as his opponent. High spirits, too, were restored. Pride in their great defensive fight at Sharpsburg, when the odds had been even longer, and presently their jubilation over Stuart's second "Ride Around McClellan," solidified into a conviction that the Army of Northern Virginia was more than a match for whatever came against it, even if the Yankees continued to fight as well as they had fought in Maryland. Shortages of equipment there still were, especially of shoes and clothes, but these were accepted as rather the norm and relatively unimportant. A British army observer, visiting Lee at the time, expressed surprise at the condition of the trousers of the men in Hood's division, the rents and tatters being especially apparent after the first files had passed in review. "Never mind the raggedness, Colonel," Lee said quietly. "The enemy never sees the backs of my Texans."

He spoke, the colonel observed, "as a man proud of his country and confident of ultimate success." However, this was for the southern commander a time of personal sorrow. Soon after October 20 he heard from his wife of the death on that date of the second of his three daughters. She was twenty-three years old and had been named for his mother, born Ann Carter. He turned to some official correspondence, seeking thus to hide his grief, but presently an aide came into the tent and found him weeping. "I cannot express the anguish I feel at the death of my sweet Annie," he wrote home.

Work was still the best remedy, he believed, and fortunately there was plenty to occupy him. The previously informal corps arrangement was made official in early November with the promotion of Longstreet and Jackson, respectively first and fifth on the list of lieutenant generals. By that time, moreover, the Federals had crossed the river which gave their army its name, and Lee had divided his own in order to cover their alternate routes of approach, shifting Old Pete down to Culpeper while Stonewall remained in the lower Valley, eager to pounce through one of the Blue Ridge gaps and onto the enemy flank. But this was not Pope; this was McClellan. He maneuvered skillfully, keeping the gaps well plugged as he advanced against the divided Confederates. Then suddenly, inexplicably, he stopped. For two days Lee was left wondering: until November 10, that is, when he learned that Little Mac had been relieved. The southern reaction was not unmixed. Some believed that the Federals would be demoralized by McClellan's removal, while others found assurance in the conviction that his successor would be more likely to commit some blunder which would expose the blue host to destruction. Lee, however, expressed regret at the departure of a familiar and respected adversary. "We always understood each other so well," he said wryly. "I fear they may continue to make these changes till they find someone whom I don't understand."

When Burnside shifted east in mid-November, Lee's first plan was to occupy the line of the North Anna, twenty-five miles south of the Rappahannock. From there he would draw the bluecoats into the intervening wintry swamps and woodlands, then move forward and outflank them in order to slash at them from astride their line of retreat. If successful, this would have been to stage a Sedan eight years ahead of the historical schedule; Jackson, for one, was very much in favor of it. If on the other hand the Confederates contested the Rappahannock crossing, where the position afforded little depth for maneuver and was dominated by the north-bank heights, it was Stonewall's opinion that they would "whip the enemy, but gain no fruits of victory." However, Lee did not want to give up the previously unmolested territory and expose the vital railroad to destruction; so while Burnside balked at Falmouth, awaiting the delayed pontoons, the southern commander moved Longstreet onto the heights in rear of Fredericksburg. This suited Old Pete fine; for the position offered all the defensive advantages he most admired, if only "the damned Yankees" could be persuaded to "come to us."

Apparently they were coming, here or somewhere near here, but they were taking their time about it. ("When are you coming over, bluecoat?" "When we get ready, butternut.") For ten days Lee left the vigil to Longstreet, withholding Jackson for a flank attack if Burnside crossed upstream. Then, as the indications grew that a crossing would be attempted here, he sent for Stonewall, whose troops began to file into position alongside Longstreet's on the first day of December. By that time the army had grown to 70,000 infantry and artillery, plus 7000 cavalry, and its spirit was higher than ever, despite the fact that one man in every six was barefoot. They now bore with patience, one officer remarked, "what they once would have regarded as beyond human endurance." Even a four-inch snowfall on the night of December 5, followed by bitter cold weather, failed to lower their morale. Rather, they organized brigade-sized snowball battles, during which their colonels put them through the evolutions of the line, and thus kept in practice while waiting for the Yankees to cross the river flowing slate gray between its cake-icing banks.

Lee shared their hardships and their confidence. Sometimes, though, alone in his tent, he was oppressed by sorrow for the daughter who had died six weeks ago. "In the quiet hours of the night, when there is nothing to lighten the full weight of my grief," he wrote home, "I feel as if I should be overwhelmed. I have always counted, if God should spare me a few days after this Civil War has ended, that I should have her with me, but year after year my hopes go out, and I must be resigned." Mainly his consolation was his army. Though he told his wife, "I tremble for my country when I hear of confidence expressed in me. I know too well my weakness, and that our only hope is in God," his admiration for the men he led was almost without bounds. "I am glad you derive satisfaction from the operations of the army," he replied to a congratulatory letter from his brother. "I acknowledge nothing can surpass the valor and endurance of our troops, yet while so much remains to be done, I feel as if nothing had been accomplished. But we must endure to the end, and if our people are true to themselves and our soldiers continue to discard all thoughts of self and to press nobly forward in defense alone of their country and their rights, I have no fear of the result. We may be annihilated, but we cannot be conquered. No sooner is one [Federal] army scattered than another rises up. This snatches from us the fruits of victory and covers the battlefield with our dead. Yet what have we to live for if not victorious?"

It was this spirit which made Lee's army "terrible in battle," and it was in this spirit that he and his men awaited Burnside's crossing of the Rappahannock.

★ ★ ★

Off in the Transmississippi, the sixth of the new lieutenant generals, Theophilus Holmes, had established headquarters at Little Rock and from there was surveying a situation which was perhaps as confusing for him as the one near Malvern Hill, where he had cupped a deaf ear in the midst of a heavy bombardment and declared that he thought he "heard firing." If he was similarly bewildered it was no wonder, considering the contrast between the geographical vastness of his command and the slimness of his resources. In addition to Texas and Missouri, the two largest states of the old Union, he was theoretically responsible for holding or reclaiming Arkansas, Indian Territory, West Louisiana, and New Mexico, in all of which combined he had fewer than 50,000 men, including guerillas. These last were sometimes as much trouble to him as they were to the enemy, especially as an administrative concern, and even the so-called "regulars" were generally well beyond his reach, being loosely connected with headquarters, if at all, by lines of supply and communication which could only be characterized as primitive, telegraph wire being quite as rare as railroad iron. By late October, after three months of pondering the odds, he had begun to consider not only the probability of total defeat, but also the line of conduct he and his men would follow in the wake of that disaster. In this he showed that, whatever his physical shortcomings and infirmities, his spirit was undamaged. "We hate you with a cordial hatred," he told an Indiana colonel who came to Little Rock bearing messages under a flag of truce. "You may conquer us and parcel out our lands among your soldiers, but you must remember that one incident of history: to wit, that of all the Russians who settled in Poland not one died a natural death."

Moreover, his three department commanders — John Magruder, Richard Taylor, and Thomas Hindman, respectively in charge of Texas, West Louisiana, and Arkansas — shared his resolution, but not his gloom. All three were working, even now, on plans for the recovery of all that had been lost. Prince John for example, as flamboyant in the Lone Star State as ever he had been in the Old Dominion, was improvising behind the scenes a two-boat cotton-clad navy with which he intended to steam down Buffalo Bayou and retake Galveston, the only Federal-held point in his department. Taylor's ambition was longer-ranged — as well it had to be; New Orleans was occupied by something more than ten times as many soldiers and sailors as he had in his whole command —

but he had hopes for the eventual recapture of the South's first city, along with the lower reaches of the Father of Waters itself. Meanwhile, having recovered from the mysterious paralysis which had gripped his legs on the eve of the Seven Days, thus preventing any addition to the reputation he had won under Jackson in the Valley, he was working hard with what little he had in the way of men and guns, seeking first to establish dispersed strong-points with which to forestall a further penetration by the gunboats and the probing Union columns, after which he intended to swing over to the offensive and reclaim what had been lost to amphibious combinations heretofore considered too powerful to resist with any substantial hope of success.

Of the three, so far, it was Hindman who had accomplished most, however, and against the longest odds. Operating in a region which had been stripped of troops when Van Dorn crossed the Mississippi back in April, he yet had managed to raise and equip an army of 16,000 men, and with them he had already begun to launch an offensive against Schofield, who had about the same number for the protection of the Missouri border. By late August, Hindman was across it; or anyhow a third of his soldiers were, and he was preparing to join them with the rest. Skirting Helena, where 15,000 Federals were intrenched — they now were under Brigadier General Frederick Steele, Curtis having moved on to St Louis and command of the department, belatedly rewarded for his Pea Ridge victory — the Confederate advance occupied Newtonia, beyond Neosho and southwest of Springfield. All through September they stayed there, 2500 Missouri cavalry under Colonel J. O. Shelby and about 3000 Indians and guerillas, called in to assist in holding the place until Hindman arrived with the other two thirds of his hastily improvised army. Shelby was a graduate of the prewar Kansas border conflict, a stocky, heavily bearded man approaching his thirty-second birthday. Called "Jo" for his initials, just as Stuart was called "Jeb," and wearing like him an ostrich plume attached to the upturned brim of a soft felt hat, he was a veteran of nearby Wilson's Creek and of Elkhorn Tavern, forty miles to the south. With him out front, and the stone walls of the town to fight behind, the garrison was more than a match for a 4000-man column Schofield sent to retake Newtonia on the last day of September. The Confederates broke the point of the counterthrust and drove the bluecoats north. However, learning three days later (October 3: Van Dorn and Price were moving against Corinth) that the Federals had been reinforced to thrice their former strength, they fell back next day in the direction of the Boston Mountains, Shelby skillfully covering the retreat with a succession of slashing attacks and quick withdrawals.

Hindman was not discouraged by this turn of events. In fact, he saw in it certain advantages. Schofield should be easier to whip if he advanced into Arkansas, lengthening his lines of supply — and lengthening, too, the distance he would have to backtrack through the wintry woods in order to regain the comparative security of Missouri. Under such disadvantages, a simple repulse might be transformed into a disaster. At any rate, Hindman intended to do all he could to bring about that result. But as he prepared to move forward in early November, consolidating the segments of his army, he received news that was discouraging indeed. It came from Holmes, who had just received in Little Rock a dispatch from Richmond, dated October 27 and signed by the Secretary of War: "Coöperation between General Pemberton and yourself is indispensable to the preservation of our connection with your department. We regard this as an object of first importance, and when necessary you can cross the Mississippi with such part of your forces as you may select, and by virtue of your rank direct the combined operations on the eastern bank."

This meant, in effect, that Hindman's offensive would have to be abandoned. And when it was followed in mid-November by a specific request from the Adjutant General ("Vicksburg is threatened and requires to be reinforced. Can you send troops from your command — say 10,000 — to operate either opposite to Vicksburg or to cross the river?") Holmes perceived that it meant the abandonment, not only of his hopes for regaining Missouri, but also of his hopes for hanging onto Arkansas. "I could not get to Vicksburg in less than two weeks," he protested. "There is nothing to subsist on between here and there, and [Steele's] army at Helena would come to Little Rock before I reached Vicksburg."

However, he need not have worried. He was not going anywhere. Nor was Hindman's offensive to be interrupted: at any rate not by anyone in Richmond, and least of all by Thomas Jefferson's grandson George Randolph. Presently it became fairly clear that the original dispatch sent by that official, though couched in the form of a military directive, was in effect an act of political suicide, whereby the Confederacy lost the third of its several Secretaries of War.

Joe Johnston was one of the first to get inside news of the impending disruption in the President's official family, and what was more he got it at first hand. His Seven Pines wound had proved troublous, resulting in what the doctors called "an obstinate adhesion of the lungs to the side, and a constant tendency to pleurisy," for which the prescribed treatments were "bleedings, blisterings, and depletions of the system." All three were stringently applied: in spite of which, having sufficiently recovered by early November to begin taking horseback exercise — "My other occupation," he told a friend, "is blistering myself, to which habit hasn't yet reconciled me" — the general called at the War Department on the 12th of that month to report himself fit for duty. Closeted with the Secretary, he learned that the government intended to send him West, where his assignment would be to coördinate the efforts of Bragg and Pemberton for the defense of Tennessee and Mississippi. Perceiving that each was not only too weak to reinforce the other, but also most likely too weak to handle what was coming at him — particularly the latter, since the Federals were certain to make Vicksburg their prime objective in the offensive they were clearly about to launch — Johnston at once suggested that the best solution would be to bring additional troops from the Transmississippi to assist in the eastbank defense of the big river.

Randolph replied that he had reached the same decision, more than two weeks ago, and read to his fellow Virginian the dispatch he had sent Holmes. When he had finished, he smiled rather strangely and took up another document, which he also read aloud. It was dated today and signed by Jefferson Davis: "I regret to notice that in your letter to General Holmes of October 27, a copy of which is before me, you suggest the propriety of his crossing the Mississippi and assuming command on the east side of the river. His presence on the west side is not less necessary now than heretofore, and will probably soon be more so. The coöperation designed by me was in co-intelligent action on both sides of the river of such detachment of troops as circumstances might require and warrant. The withdrawal of the commander from the Trans-Mississippi Department for temporary duty elsewhere would have a disastrous effect, and was not contemplated by me."

Johnston recognized the tone, having received such directives himself. He knew, too, what response this son of Thomas Jefferson's oldest daughter was likely to make to such a letter. The question was, what had made him so deliberately provoke it? Yet Johnston knew the answer here as well. Eight months of service as "the clerk of Mr Davis," sometimes learning of vital military decisions only after they had been made and acted on, had brought home to Randolph the truth of one observer's remark "that the real war lord of the South resided in the executive mansion." The message to Holmes, sent without previous consultation with the Commander in Chief, was in the nature of a gesture of self-assertion, desperate but necessary to the preservation of his self-respect. And now he accepted the consequences. Two days later, having added an indorsement to the offending document sent by Davis — "Inclose a copy of this letter to General Holmes, and inform the President that it has been done, and that [Holmes] has been directed to consider it as part of his instructions" — he submitted his formal resignation.

This had been neither intended nor expected by Davis, who up to now had been highly pleased with Randolph as a member of his cabinet. Except for two particulars, he had not even disapproved of the Secretary's decision to bring troops across the river to assist in the defense of Vicksburg. In fact, he himself ordered this done that same week, when he had the Adjutant General send Holmes the request for 10,000 men to be used for this very purpose. What he objected to, most strenuously, were the two particulars: 1) that Holmes himself was advised to cross, which would leave his department headless, and 2) that the thing had been done behind his back, without his knowledge. It was this last which disturbed him most. As Commander in Chief he saw himself as chief engineer of the whole vast machine; if adjustments were made without his knowledge, a wreck was almost certain. In this case, however, receiving the tart letter of resignation, he sought to prevent a break by suggesting a personal interview at which he and the Virginian could discuss their differences. Randolph declined, and Davis would bend no further. "As you thus without notice and in terms excluding inquiry retired," he replied, "nothing remains but to give you this formal notice of the acceptance of your resignation."

G. W. Smith, recovered from the collapse he had suffered when Johnston's fall left him in charge of the confused and confusing field of Seven Pines, had been serving as commander of the Richmond defenses ever since Lee and his army departed to deal with Pope, back in August. Now Davis found a further use for the former New York Street Commissioner by assigning him to serve as head of the War Department during the three-day interim, which he himself spent in search of a permanent — if the word could be used properly in reference to a position which, so far, had been so impermanent — replacement for Randolph, who retired at once to private life and subsequently "refugeed" in Europe with his family.

Once more the Old Dominion had been left without a representative among the President's chief advisers, and once more Davis solved the problem, this time by appointing James A. Seddon to be Secretary of War. A Richmond lawyer who had served two terms as U.S. Congressman from the district, a former occupant of the present Confederate White House, and a descendant of James River grandees, Seddon ranked about as high in the complicated Virginia caste system as even Randolph did, with the result that his selection was a source of considerable satisfaction to those who had become accustomed to looking down their noses at what they called "the middle-class atmosphere" of official Richmond. Moreover, he had a reputation as a scholar and a philosopher, though what service this would be to him in his new position was unknown; he had had no previous military experience whatever. Nor was his appearance reassuring. "Gaunt and emaciated," one observer called him, "with long straggling hair, mingled gray and black." He was forty-seven, but looked much older, perhaps because of chronic neuralgia, which racked him nearly as badly as it racked Davis. He looked, in fact, according to the same diarist, "like a dead man galvanized into muscular animation. His eyes are sunken and his features have the hue of a man who has been in his grave a full month."

At any rate, whatever his lack of the kind of training which would have cautioned him to guard his flanks and rear, it soon became apparent that he did not intend to expose himself to attack from above, as his predecessor had done. Johnston went to him on November 22, the new Secretary's first full day in office, and renewed his suggestion that troops be ordered east from the Transmississippi. Seddon listened sympathetically. But when Johnston received his orders two days later, assigning him to the region lying between the Blue Ridge Mountains and the Mississippi River, he was surprised to find that they contained no reference to troops not already within those limits. "The suggestion was not adopted or noticed," he afterwards recorded dryly.

Davis had a higher opinion of Johnston's abilities at this stage than the Virginian probably suspected. "I wish he were able to take the field," the President had told Mrs Davis during the general's convalescence. "Despite the critics, who know military affairs by instinct, he is a good soldier, never brags of what he did do, and could at this time render most valuable service." In no way, indeed, could the Commander in Chief have demonstrated this confidence more fully than by assigning him, as soon as he was fairly up and about, to what was called "plenary command" of the heartland of the Confederacy, an area embracing all of Tennessee, Mississippi, and Alabama, together with parts of North Carolina, Florida, and Georgia, including the main regional supply base at Atlanta. Moreover, he placed on him no restrictions within that geographical expanse, either as to his movements or the location of his headquarters, which he was instructed to establish "at Chattanooga, or such other place as in his judgment will best secure facilities for ready communication with the troops within the limits of his command, and will repair in person to any part of said command wherever his presence may, for the time, be necessary or desirable."

These instructions embodied a new concept of the function of departmental command, which in turn had been prompted by the example of R. E. Lee in his conduct of the defense of his native state. Lee's achievements here in Virginia, before as well as after he had been given field command, were in a large part the result of a successful coördination of the efforts of separate forces, either through simultaneous actions at divergent points — as when Jackson took the offensive in the Valley, threatening Washington to play on Lincoln's fears, while Johnston delayed McClellan's advance up the Peninsula — or through rapid concentration against a common point, as when all available forces were brought together for the attack which opened the Seven Days and accomplished the deliverance of Richmond. Subsequent repetition of this strategy, with a similar coördination of effort, had brought about the "suppression" of Pope and opened the way for invasion of the North, removing the war to that extent beyond the Confederate border.

Now it was Davis' hope that such methods, which had won for southern arms the admiration of the world and for Lee a place among history's great captains, would result in similar achievements in the West and give to the commander there a seat alongside Lee in Valhalla.

Choice of Johnston for the post was prompted by more than the fact that he was entitled to it by rank. Not only did Davis consider him a "good soldier" who could "render most valuable service," but the Virginian had also been asked for already by two of the three generals who would be his chief subordinates. During their recent visits to the capital, Bragg and Kirby Smith had both expressed an eagerness to have him over them, and doubtless Pemberton would be equally delighted to have the benefit of his advice, along with whatever reinforcements would become available in times of crisis as a result of the shuttle service the new theater commander was expected to establish between his several departments. How well he would do — whether he was potentially another Lee, and whether Bragg and Pemberton would serve him as well as Longstreet and Jackson had served the eastern commander — remained to be seen. So far, however, the resemblance had been anything but striking. His first reaction, expressed in a letter sent to the Adjutant General on the day he received the appointment, was a protest that his forces were "greatly inferior in number to those of the enemy opposed to them, while in the Trans-Mississippi Department our army is very much larger than that of the United States." He also complained of the presence of the Tennessee River, "a formidable obstacle" which divided his two main armies, and found it highly irregular that his department commanders — by an arrangement which Davis had designed "to avoid delay" — would be in direct correspondence with the War Department. This combination of drawbacks and irregularities, discerned by him before he even left Richmond, had already led him to suspect what he later stated flatly: "that my command was a nominal one merely, and useless."

Depressed by these several misgivings, he began at once to make arrangements for his journey west, and five days later he was off, accompanied by his wife and a new staff. In the interim, however, he found time to attend a farewell breakfast given in his honor and also in the hope that it would effect a reconciliation between two of his political friends, Senators Foote and Yancey, who had quarreled despite the common bond of their detestation of Davis. Under the healing influence of their admiration for Johnston, along with that of a bountiful meal accompanied by champagne, the two statesmen forgot their differences. Presently Yancey called for fresh glasses and proposed a toast. "Gentlemen, let us drink to the only man who can save the Confederacy. General Joseph E. Johnston!" All applauded, drank their wine, and took their seats: whereupon the guest of honor rose, glass in hand, and responded. "Mr Yancey," he said firmly, "the man you describe is now in the field — in the person of General Robert E. Lee. I will drink to his health." Not to be outdone, the silver-tongued Yancey rose and countered: "I can only reply to you, sir, as the Speaker of the House of Burgesses did to General Washington: 'Your modesty is only equaled by your valor.'" Again the celebrants applauded and drank the balding general's health. But he remained taciturn and preoccupied, as if his mind was already engaged by the frets he knew awaited him in the West.

In the course of the five-day trip to Chattanooga, delayed by no less than three railroad accidents, Johnston was much wearied, despite the ministrations of his wife and the cheers from station platforms along the way. Early on the morning of December 4 he got there. After resting briefly, he issued an order formally accepting his new responsibilities, although his gloom was unrelieved. "Nobody ever assumed a command under more unfavorable circumstances," he wrote to a friend in Richmond that same day.

★ ★ ★

Johnston's gloom, though it was not shared by the people in general, East or West — nor, for that matter, by those who cheered him from station platforms as he traveled from one to the other — was nonetheless reflected in the value of their dollar. After holding at 1.5 through August, it fell in October to 2, in November to 2.9, and by December it had dropped to 3. Statistics were dreary at best, however, except perhaps for those who dealt in money as a commodity. It was in terms of what the stuff would buy, shoved coin by coin across a counter or laid down bill by badly printed bill, that the meaning of such quotations really struck home. Now with winter hard upon the upper South, coal was $9 a handcartload and wood $16 a cord. Bacon was 75¢ a pound, sugar five cents higher. Butter was $1.25 and coffee twice that. To the despair of Richmond housewives, laundry soap was 75¢ a cake, flour $16 a barrel, and potatoes $6 a bushel.

For those of an analytical turn of mind, accustomed to looking behind effects for causes, it was more or less clear that the cause behind this particular close-to-home effect was the failure of the Confederacy's one concerted effort at invasion, East and West. Yet even here their reaction contained a good deal more of pride than of regret. "It was to be expected," Davis had told them, back at the outset, "... that [this war] would expose our people to sacrifices and cost them much, both of money and blood. .... It was, perhaps, in the ordination of Providence that we were to be taught the value of our liberties by the price we pay for them." In the light of this, Bragg's thousand-mile hegira through Kentucky and Lee's bloody defense of the Sharpsburg ridge became for their countrymen, not occasions for despair, but instances for the promotion of the growth of national pride and the evocation of applause from those who watched from afar. "Whatever may be the fate of the new nationality," the London *Times* was saying, "in its subsequent claims to the respect of mankind it will assuredly begin its career with a reputation for genius and valour which the most famous nations might envy."

Such public praise was welcome, as were certain private remarks from that same quarter. Thomas Carlyle, for example — though he pleased neither side with a reference to the American war as the burning out of a dirty chimney, a conflagration which could be regarded only with satisfaction by neighbors too long plagued by soot — amused and gladdened Southerners by subsequently professing his impatience with people who were "cutting each other's throats, because one half of them prefer hiring their servants for life, and the other by the hour." Most gratifying of all, however, were the observations colorfully expressed in the course of a banquet speech made at Newcastle, October 7, by Chancellor of the Exchequer William E. Gladstone. Professing the kindliest feeling toward the people of the North — "They are our kin. They were ... our customers, and we hope they will be our customers again" — he denied that the British government had "any interest in the disruption of the Union." But he also declared, with particular emphasis: "There is no doubt that Jefferson Davis and other leaders of the South have made an army. They are making, it appears, a navy. And they have made what is more than either; they have made a nation." This was greeted with applause and cheers. "Hear, hear!" the diners cried. When they subsided, Gladstone added: "We may anticipate with certainty the success of the Southern States so far as regards their separation from the North."

Coming as it did from the third-ranking member of the Cabinet, the statement was assumed to reflect the views of the Government: which it did, except that Palmerston and Russell considered it precipitate and unpropitious: which it was, the Prime Minister having recently advised the Foreign Secretary that he thought it best to "wait awhile and see what may follow" Lee's retreat from Maryland. What had followed was the Preliminary Emancipation Proclamation, and though this document was greeted with sneers on the one hand and confusion on the other, it too provided an occasion for more waiting. Gladstone's outburst caused an immediate drop in the price of cotton, which apparently would soon be plentiful as a result of the lifting of the blockade, as well as an increase of activity by Members of Parliament sympathetic to the North. On October 22, two weeks after the Newcastle speech, Palmerston wrote Russell: "We must continue to be mere lookers-on till the war shall have taken a more decided turn."

On that same day, the French Emperor granted Slidell an audience at St Cloud during which he let the Confederate minister understand that he considered the time ripe for joint mediation by France,

England, and Russia. "My own preference is for a proposition of an armistice of six months," he said. "This would put a stop to the effusion of blood, and hostilities would probably never be resumed. We can urge it on the high grounds of humanity and the interest of the whole civilized world. If it be refused by the North, it will afford good reason for recognition, and perhaps for more active intervention." Eight days later, as good as his word — and with his eye still fixed on the promised hundred thousand bales of cotton — he addressed, through his Minister of Foreign Affairs, a dispatch to his ambassadors at St Petersburg and London, proposing that the three governments "exert their influence at Washington, as well as with the Confederates, to obtain an armistice." Russia's answer was emphatic: "In our opinion, what ought specially to be avoided [is] the appearance of any pressure whatsoever of a nature to wound public opinion in the United States and to excite susceptibilities very easily aroused at the bare idea of foreign intervention." England's was scarcely less so, Russell declining for the reason "that there is no ground at the present moment to hope that the Federal government would accept the proposal suggested, and a refusal from Washington at the present time would prevent any speedy renewal of the offer."

Napoleon, then, was as far as ever from those hundred thousand bales, and so was the Confederacy from recognition by the powers of Europe. England was to blame; for France could act without Russia, but not without England; England swung the balance. And yet, admittedly, Southerners already had much to be thankful for, if not from the British government, then at least from British individuals: particularly the owners of and workers in shipyards up the Mersey. Gladstone's remark that the Confederates "are making, it appears, a navy" was based on solid ground — ground which, indeed, was of his own countrymen's making. In late July, a powerful new screw steamer known mysteriously as the *290* had steamed down from Liverpool, supposedly on a trial run, but headed instead for the open sea and a rendezvous off the Azores, where she took on provisions, coal, and guns, struck her English colors in favor of the Stars and Bars, swore in a crew, and exchanged her numerical designation for a name: the *Alabama*. She was the second to follow this course. Four months before, another such vessel, called the *Oreto*, had accomplished this same metamorphosis from merchantman to raider, and already she was at work as the Confederate cruiser *Florida*, her mission being the high-seas destruction of Federal commerce. Commanded by Captain J. N. Maffit, she was to take thirty-four prizes before her career ended two years later; but it was the *Alabama* which did most in this direction, provoking a rise of more than 900 percent in U.S. marine insurance and the transfer of over seven hundred Union merchant ships to British registry. Also, she gave the South another hero in the person of her skipper, Captain Raphael Semmes, a fifty-three-year-old Maryland-born Alabamian, known to his crew — mostly foreigners off the docks of Liverpool, whom he referred to as "a precious set of rascals" — as "Old Beeswax" because of the care he gave his long black needle-sharp mustachios.

He had had considerable experience at this kind of work as captain of the *Sumter*, the first of the rebel raiders. A commander in the old navy, ensconced in comfort as head of the Lighthouse Board in Washington, he had gone south in February of the year before and offered his services to the new government in Montgomery. Secretary Mallory sent him back north on a purchasing expedition, and when he returned informed him that the Confederacy had acquired a small propeller steamer of 500 tons. She was tied up to a New Orleans wharf, he added, awaiting a chance to slip past the Federal blockaders in order to undertake disruption of the sea lanes. "Mr Secretary, give me that ship," Semmes said. "I think I can make her answer the purpose." Mallory gave him what he asked for, along with general instructions: "On reaching the high seas you are to do the enemy's commerce the greatest injury in the shortest time. Choose your own cruising grounds. Burn, sink, and destroy, and be guided always by the laws of the nations and of humanity." That was in mid-April; Semmes made his escape from the mouth of the Mississippi on the last day of June, and took his first prize four days later. In the course of the next seven months he took seventeen more barks, brigantines, and schooners, which he captured, burned, or ransomed in the Gulf and the Atlantic. Bottled up in Gibraltar from January to April, he sold the *Sumter*, discharged her crew, and took passage for Southampton. Late in May he left for Nassau, intending to board a blockade runner there and get back home. If the navy had another ship for him, he would take it; if not, he planned to transfer to the army. What awaited him at Nassau, however, were instructions for him to return to England and assume secret command of the *290-Alabama*.

He took over, officially, off the island of Terceira on August 24, when the cruiser was formally commissioned. Having named the *Florida* for his native state, Mallory had named this second English-built warship for the state in which the Confederacy itself was born. Bark-rigged, with handsome, rakish lines, she was 235 feet in length, 32 feet in the beam, and displaced a thousand tons. Her armament was eight guns, three 32-pounders on each broadside and two pivot guns on the center line, one a 7-inch rifle and the other an 8-inch smoothbore. Two 300-horsepower engines gave her a speed of ten knots on steam alone, but with the help of her sails and a friendly wind she could make nearly fifteen, which approached top speed for sea-going ships of the time. When traveling under sail alone — as she often would, to conserve fuel; the 275 tons of coal in her bunkers were barely enough for eighteen days of steaming at moderate speed — her two-bladed screw could be triced up into a propeller well, clear of the water, and thus afford no drag. To her crew of 24 gray-clad officers and 120 men, she was a beautiful thing on her commissioning day. Her brass was bright; her decks were clean and fragrant; her taunt-hauled rigging gleamed with newness. To Semmes himself she seemed "a bride with the orange wreath about her brows, ready to be led to the altar."

Led instead on her shakedown cruise, she took her first prize twelve days later, the whaling schooner *Ocmulgee* of Edgartown, Massachusetts, caught with her sails furled, a dead whale moored alongside, and her crew busy stripping blubber. Brimming with sperm oil, she was valued at $50,000 and made a spectacular conflagration. Semmes took her crew aboard the *Alabama*, released them next day within sight of land, their whaleboats loaded to the gunnels with all they had managed to salvage before their ship was burned, and continued his search for other prizes. Before September was over he had taken ten. In October he took eleven. By early December he had raised the total to twenty-six, removing from each its chronometer, which he added to the others in his collection, including the eighteen transferred from the *Sumter*, and wound them regularly by way of counting tally.

By now his fame, or infamy, was established. To Northerners, despite the invariable courtesy and consideration he showed his temporary captives, he was a bloodthirsty pirate, an "Algerine corsair." To his crew, often vexed that he allowed no individual pillage, he seemed no such thing. In time, despite the strangeness of his manner, including the fact that he seldom spoke to anyone, and the tightness of his discipline — "Democracies may do very well for the land," he once explained, "but monarchies, and pretty absolute monarchies at that, are the only successful governments for the sea" — the officers and men of the *Alabama* paid him not only his due of absolute obedience, but also the homage of genuine affection. It was not a question of patriotism. Few of the officers and none of the men were even Americans, let alone Southerners; they were mostly English, Welsh, and Irish, with a scattering of French, Italian, Spanish, and Russian sailors among them. Their allegiance was to him and the *Alabama*. They liked to watch his gray eyes glint blue when he sighted a prize off on the bulge of the horizon, and they approved of his Catholic devoutness, knowing that he began and ended each day on his knees before the little shrine in his cabin.

Blurred by distance, to his countrymen he was something less — and also something more. He was, in fact, a member of that growing band of heroes who, as the *Alabama* began her career with the burning of the *Ocmulgee*, seemed about to make good the impossible claims and threats with which the fire-eaters had prefaced the reality of war. Lee was crossing the Potomac, Bragg was on the march for Kentucky, and Kirby Smith was in Lexington; Semmes was therefore proof that the South could take the offensive at sea as well as on land. Moreover, though those others had been turned back, he kept on, taking prizes which he burned or sank or, if it was impractical to remove their crews and passengers to safety, released on "ransom bond." This last, sometimes resorted to when the cruiser was crowded to capacity with captives, was an agreement between Semmes and the master of the vessel, whereby the latter pledged the owner to pay a stipulated amount "unto the President of the Confederate States of America ... within thirty days after the conclusion of the present war." It was, in effect, a bet that the South would win, and as such it did much to increase the pride of Southerners in their lawyer-raider, who thus expressed before the eyes of the world their confidence in the outcome of their struggle for independence.

Another cause for pride in southern arms derived from an older source: in fact, from the oldest source of all. Though Lee and Bragg and Kirby Smith had returned from their expeditions, disappointing the hopes that had gone with them, Beauregard — the original hero, back on the scene of his original triumph — had not been long in justifying the cheers with which Charlestonians had greeted his return. October 22, five weeks after his arrival, a Federal attempt to cut the Charleston & Savannah Railroad at Pocotaligo, midway between those two coastal cities, was foiled when 4500 bluecoats under Ormsby Mitchel — within eight days of sudden death from yellow fever — were thrown back to their landing boats by half as many rebels. Casualties were 340 and 163, respectively. "Railroad uninjured," Beauregard wired Richmond. "Abolitionists left dead and wounded on the field. Our cavalry in hot pursuit." Old Bory was himself again.

★ ★ ★

Slight though they were — by comparison, that is, with the resounding double failure, East and West, of the Confederacy's first concerted attempt at all-out invasion — these late fall and early winter successes, afloat and ashore, did much to sustain or restore the confidence of the southern people. Besides, they could tell themselves, the strategic offensive was for extra: a device to be employed from time to time, not so much with the intention of keeping the graybacks north of the Potomac or the Cumberland, but rather of establishing an interlude for harvesting the crops in forward areas and thereby gaining a breathing spell in which the natives could enjoy at least a temporary freedom from the oppressive presence of the bluecoats. It was the strategic defensive that counted; it was this they had been pledged to by their President when he told the world, "All we ask is to be let alone." And in this — considering the odds — they had been singularly successful: especially in the East, where three full-scale attempts at invasion had been smashed and a fourth halted dead in its tracks when its commander was retired for the second time. In the West, too, there was occasion for rejoicing and self-congratulation. After a long season of reverses, a series of collapses under inexorable pressure, the front of the principal sector had been advanced a hundred and fifty miles, from North Mississippi to Middle Tennessee; on the Mississippi itself, the upper and lower Union fleets, conjoined triumphantly above Vicksburg, had been sundered and sent their separate ways by a single homemade ironclad; while across the river, in Arkansas, an army created seemingly out of thin air was on the march for Missouri.

All this was much, enough indeed to satisfy the hungriest of seekers after glory, and the thought of such accomplishments went far toward offsetting the pain of earlier reverses. However, to ease the ache was not to cure the ailment; the effect of the worst of the early reverses still remained. Norfolk was lost, and with it the one hope for the home construction of a Confederate deep-sea navy. So — continuing clockwise, down and around the coast — were the North Carolina sounds, Port Royal and Fort Pulaski, Brunswick and Fernandina, Jacksonville and St Augustine, Apalachicola and Pensacola, Biloxi and Pass Christian, Ship Island and Galveston. All these were tangent hits, mainly painful to southern pride (and to southern pocketbooks, augmenting as they did the effectiveness of the Federal blockade) but there were others that hurt worse, being vital. Nashville was gone, and so were New Orleans and Memphis. At the time of their loss, people had told themselves that these cities would be recovered, along with the outlying points around the littoral, once the pressure in front had been relieved. Apparently, though, that had been mere whistling in the dark. Four times now the pressure had eased up: after First Manassas, Wilson's Creek, the evacuation of Corinth, and Second Manassas: yet in all four instances the southern commanders who tried to take advantage of the respite gained were either repulsed when they moved forward or else they fell back eventually of their own accord. In fact, of the four advances which had followed these events — Johnston's into northern Virginia, Price's into northern Missouri, Bragg's into Kentucky, and Lee's into Maryland — all but Bragg's had wound up south of the point from which they had been launched. It was small wonder then, at this stage, that Southerners discounted the advantages of the offensive, considering how little had been gained from three of these four attempts and how much had been lost by two others, Shiloh and Baton Rouge, even though both were generally referred to as tactical victories and were prime sources of the glory, which, so far, had been the South's chief gain from twenty months of war.

Yet glory was a flimsy diet at best, containing far more of what Southerners called "suption" than of substance. No one realized this better than Davis, who had had an overplus of glory down the years and who, familiar with it as he was, knew how little real sustenance it afforded. Moreover, as a professional soldier, in touch with every department of the army he commanded, he not only recognized the odds his country

faced in its struggle for independence; he saw that they were lengthening with every passing month as the North's tremendous potential was
converted into actuality. In that sense, not only was time against him;
even success was against him, for each northern reverse brought on a
quickening of the tempo of conversion. And yet, paradoxically, it was
time for which he was fighting. Time alone could bring into being, in
the North, the discouragement — the sheer boredom, even — which
was the South's chief hope for victory if foreign intervention failed to
materialize, as now seemed likely.

Meanwhile, there were the odds to face, and Davis faced them.
He did not know what future combinations were being designed for
the Confederacy's destruction, but he knew they would be heavy when
they came. Here in the East, Lee could be trusted to cope with whatever forces the Union high command might conceive to be his match.
Likewise in the Transmississippi, though the outlook was far from bright,
Hindman's improvisations, Magruder's theatrical ingenuity, and Taylor's hard-working common sense gave promise of achieving at least a
balance. It was in the West — that region between the Blue Ridge and
the Mississippi, where Federal troops had scored their most substantial
gains — that the Commander in Chief perceived the gravest danger.
Whether Johnston would prove himself another Lee, coördinating the

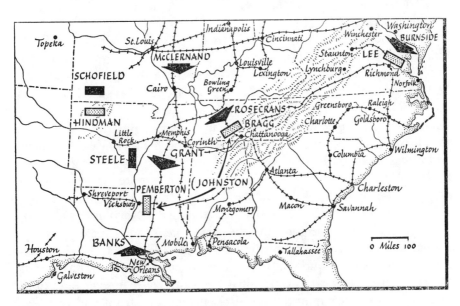

efforts of his separate armies in order to frustrate those of his opponents, remained to be seen. So far, though, the signs had not been
promising. A gloom had descended on the gamecock general, who
seemed more intent on acquiring troops from outside his department
than on setting up a system for the mutual support of those within it.
Also, there were continuing rumors of dissension in Bragg's army. All

this seemed to indicate a need for intervention, or at any rate a personal inspection, by the man who had designed the new command arrangement in the first place. Davis had not been more than a day's trip from Richmond since his arrival in late May of the year before, but now in early December he packed his bags for the long ride to Chattanooga and Vicksburg. Thus he would not only see at first hand the nature of the problems in the region which was his home; he would also provide an answer to those critics who complained that the authorities in the capital had no concern for what went on outside the eastern theater.

One drawback this had, and for Davis it was of the kind that could never be taken lightly. The trip would mean another separation from the family he had missed so much while they were in North Carolina for the summer. "I go into the nursery as a bird may go to the robbed nest," he had written his wife in June, and he added: "My ease, my health, my property, my life I can give to the cause of my country. The heroism which could lay my wife and children on any sacrificial altar is not mine." For all the busyness and anxiety of those days and nights when McClellan's campfires rimmed the east, the White House had seemed to him an empty thing without the laughter of his sons and the companionship of the woman who was his only confidante. "I have no attraction to draw me from my office now," he wrote, "and home is no longer a locality."

In September they returned, to his great joy. Mrs Davis found him thinner, the failing eye gone blinder and the lines grooved deeper in his face. "I have no political wish beyond the success of our cause," he had written her, "no personal desire but to be relieved from further connection with office. Opposition in any form can only disturb me inasmuch as it may endanger the public welfare." But the critics were in full bay again as the fall wore on, including his own Vice President, and it was clear to his wife that he was indeed disturbed. At the outset, back in Montgomery, he had spoken of "a people united in heart, where one purpose of high resolve animates and actuates the whole." Lately this evaluation had been considerably modified. "Revolutions develop the high qualities of the good and the great," he wrote, "but they cannot change the nature of the vicious and the selfish." He had this to live with now, this change of outlook, this reassessment of his fellow man: with the result that he was more troubled by neuralgia than ever, and more in need of his wife's ministrations. Present dangers, front and rear, had given even pretended dangers an increased reality and had added to his sympathy for all sufferers everywhere, including those in the world of light fiction. One day, for example, when he was confined to bed with a cloth over his eyes and forehead, she tried to relieve the monotony by reading to him from a current melodramatic novel. He was so quiet she thought he was asleep, but she did not stop for fear of waking him.

As she approached the climax of the story, wherein the bad man had the heroine in his power and was advancing on her for some evil purpose, Mrs Davis heard a voice exclaim: "The infernal villain!" and looking around saw her husband sitting bolt upright in bed, with both fists clenched.

Whether this was the result of too much imagination, or too little, was a question which would linger down the years. But some there were, already, who believed that nothing except short-sightedness could hide the eventual outcome of the long-odds struggle from anyone willing to examine the facts disclosed in the course of this opening half of the second year of conflict. Senator Herschel V. Johnson of Georgia, Stephen Douglas's running-mate in the 1860 election and now a prominent member of the Confederate Congress, replied to a question from a friend in late October: "You ask me if I have confidence in the success of the Southern Confederacy? I pray for success but I do not expect success. . . . The enemy in due time will penetrate the heart of the Confederacy . . . & the hearts of our people will quake & their spirits will yield to the force of overpowering numbers." He saw the outcome clearly, and he found it unavoidable. "The enemy is superior to us in everything but courage, & therefore it is quite certain, if the war is to go on until exhaustion overtake the one side or the other side, that we shall be the first to be exhausted."

Whether or not this would be the case — whether the South, fighting for such anachronisms as slavery and self-government, could sustain the conflict past the breaking point of northern determination — Davis did not know. Much of what his dead friend Albert Sidney Johnston had called "the fair, broad, abounding land" had already fallen to the invaders. How much more would fall, or whether the rising blue tide could be stemmed, was dependent on the gray-clad men in the southern ranks and the spirit with which they followed their star-crossed battle flags. Just now that spirit was at its height. "We may be annihilated," the first soldier of them all had said, "but we cannot be conquered." Davis thought so, too, though he offered no easy solutions in support of his belief. Now in December, as he prepared to leave on his journey to the troubled western theater, he could only repeat what he had told his wife in May: "I cultivate hope and patience, and trust to the blunders of our enemy and the gallantry of our troops for ultimate success."

�֍ 3 �֍

"Our cause, we love to think, is specially God's," the Connecticut theologian Horace Bushnell told his Hartford congregation. "Every drum-beat is a hymn; the cannon thunder God; the electric silence, darting victory along the wires, is the inaudible greeting of God's favor-

ing word." His belief that the evil was all on the other side was based
on a conviction that war had come because willful men beyond the
Potomac had laid rude hands on the tabernacle of the law. "Law ...
is grounded in right, [and] right is a moral idea, at whose summit stands
God, as the everlasting vindicator." Thus the logic came full circle:
"We associate God and religion with all we are fighting for, and we are
not satisfied with any mere human atheistic way of speaking as to means,
or measures, or battles, or victories, or the great deeds to win them."

The assertion that this was a holy war — in fact, a crusade — was
by no means restricted to those who made it from a pulpit. "Vindicating
the majesty of an insulted Government, by extirpating all *rebels*, and
fumigating their nests with the brimstone of unmitigated Hell, I conceive
to be the holy purpose of our further efforts," a Massachusetts colonel
wrote home to his governor from Beaufort, South Carolina, and being
within fifty airline miles of the very birthplace of rebellion, he added:
"I hope I shall ... do something ... in 'The Great Fumigation,' before the sulphur gives out." Just what it was that he proposed to do,
with regard to those he called "our Southern brethren," he had announced while waiting at Annapolis for the ship that brought him down
the coast. "Do we fight them to avenge ... insult? No! The thing we
seek is *permanent* dominion. And what instance is there of permanent
dominion without changing, revolutionizing, absorbing, the institutions,
life, and manners of the conquered peoples? ... They think we mean
to take their *Slaves*. Bah! We must take their *ports*, their *mines*, their
water power, the very *soil* they plough, and develop them by the hands
of our *artisan* armies. ... We are to be a regenerating, colonizing
power, or we are to be whipped. Schoolmasters, with howitzers, must
instruct our Southern brethren that they are a set of d----d fools in
everything that relates to ... modern civilization. ... *This army must
not come back*. Settlement, migration must put the seal on battle, or we
gain nothing."

Tecumseh Sherman, biding his time in Memphis — where sharp-
eyed men with itchy palms had followed in the wake of advancing armies,
much as refuse along the right-of-way was sucked into the rearward
vacuum of a speeding locomotive — threw the blame in another direction. "The cause of the war is not alone in the nigger," he told his wife,
"but in the mercenary spirit of our countrymen. ... Cincinnati fur-
nishes more contraband goods than Charleston, and has done more to
prolong the war than the State of South Carolina. Not a merchant there
but would sell salt, bacon, powder and lead, if they can make money by
it." So the volatile red-haired general wrote, finding his former nerve-
jangled opinion reinforced by the difficulties since encountered all along
the fighting front. "If the North design to conquer the South, we must
begin at Kentucky and reconquer the country from there as we did
from the Indians. It was this conviction then as plainly as now that made

men think I was insane. A good many flatterers now want to make me a prophet."

Prophet or not, he could speak like one in an early October letter to his senator brother: "I rather think you now agree with me that this is no common war.... You must now see that I was right in not seeking prominence at the outstart. I knew and know yet that the northern people have to unlearn all their experience of the past thirty years and be born again before they will see the truth." None of it had been easy thus far, nor was it going to be any easier in the future. The prow of the ship might pierce the wave, yet once it was clear of the vessel's stern the wave was whole again: "Though our armies pass across and through the land, the war closes in behind and leaves the same enemy behind. ...I don't see the end," he concluded, "or the beginning of the end, but suppose we must prevail and persist or perish." He saw only one solution, an outgrowth of the statement to his wife that the Federal armies would have to "reconquer the country...as we did from the Indians." What was required from here on was harshness. "We cannot change the hearts of the people of the South," he told his friend and superior Grant: "but we can make war so terrible that they will realize the fact that however brave and gallant and devoted to their country, still they are mortal and should exhaust all peaceful remedies before they fly to war."

For Lincoln, too, it was a question of "prevail and persist or perish." For him, moreover, there was the added problem of coördinating the efforts — and, if possible, reconciling the views — of these three random extremists, together with those of more than twenty million other individuals along and behind the firing line. The best way to accomplish this, he knew, was to unite them under a leader whose competence they believed in and whose views they would adopt as their own, even when those views came into conflict with their preconceptions. In facing this task, he started not from scratch, but from somewhere well behind it. "The President is an honest, plain, shrewd magistrate," *Harper's Weekly* had told its readers a year ago this December. "He is not a brilliant orator; he is not a great leader. He views his office as strictly an executive one, and wishes to cast responsibility, as much as possible, upon Congress." This tallied with the view of Attorney General Edward Bates, who wrote in his diary after attending a cabinet meeting held at about the same time, "The President is an excellent man, and in the main wise, but he lacks will and purpose, and I greatly fear he has not the power to command."

Since then, a good many high-placed men — including Bates, who had seen Cameron banished and the bricks applied to Stanton — had had occasion to learn better: though not all. The poet Whittier, for example, saw victory only through a haze of *ifs*. "The worst of the *ifs* is the one concerning Lincoln," he privately declared. "I am much afraid that a domestic cat will not answer when one wants a Bengal tiger." His fellow poet William Cullen Bryant agreed. "The people after their gigantic preparation and sacrifice have looked for an adequate return, and looked in vain," he editorialized in the New York *Evening Post*. "They have seen armies unused in the field perish in pestilential swamps. They have seen their money wasted in long winter encampments, or frittered away on fruitless expeditions along the coast. They have seen a huge debt roll up, yet no prospect of greater military results." Wendell Phillips, bitter as ever, continued to aim an indignant finger at the White House. "The North has poured out its blood and money like water; it has leveled every fence of constitutional privilege," he declaimed, "and Abraham Lincoln sits today a more unlimited despot than the world knows this side of China. What does he render for this unbounded confidence? Show us something," he cried in the direction he was pointing, "or I tell you that within two years the indignant reaction of the people will hurl the Cabinet in contempt from their seats."

Confronted with such judgments handed down by public men, who thus came between him and his purpose of unification, Lincoln kept his temper and his poise. If he failed in his attempts to win these critics over by means of personal discussion, face to face in his office — "What is he wrathy about? Why does he not come down here and have a talk with me?" — he went beyond them to the people. Sometimes he did so in cold print, as in the case of his answer to Greeley's "Prayer of Twenty Millions," but generally he proceeded in a manner that was strangely intimate in its effect, acting on a larger stage the role he had played in Illinois. In Washington, as in Springfield, he received all comers, and for the most part he received them with a sympathy which, by their own admission, equaled or exceeded their deserving. He shook their hands at frequent public receptions held in the White House, which was his home and yet belonged to them; he attended the theater, a form of relaxation which kept him still within their view; he drove or rode, almost daily, through the spokelike streets of the hive-dense city, returning the looks and salutes of men and women and children along the way. Thousands touched him, heard him, saw him at close range, and scarcely one in all those thousands ever forgot the sight of that tall figure, made still taller by the stovepipe hat, and the homely drape of the shawl across the shoulders. Never forgotten, because it was unforgettable, the impression remained, incredible and enduring, imperishable in its singularity — and, finally, dear.

Millions who did not see him saw his picture, and this too was a part of the effect. Widely broadcast as it was — the result of recent developments in photography and the process of reproduction — his had become, within two crowded years, the most familiar face in American history. At first sight this might appear to be a liability. The Paris

correspondent of the *New York Times*, for example, sent home a paragraph titled "Lincoln's Phiz in Europe," in which he suggested the
wisdom of declaring an embargo on portraits of the President, at least
so far as France was concerned: "The person represented in these pic-
tures looks so much like a man condemned to the gallows, that large
numbers of them have been imposed on the people here by the shop-
keepers as Dumollard, the famous murderer of servant girls, lately
guillotined near Lyons. Such a face is enough to ruin the best of causes.
... People read the name inscribed under it with astonishment, or
rather bewilderment, for the thing appears more like a hoax than a
reality." Yet here, too, something worked in his favor. It was as if,
having so far overshot the mark of ugliness, the face was not to be
judged by ordinary standards. You saw it not so much for what it was,
as for what it held. Suffering was in it; so were understanding, kindli-
ness, and determination. "None of us to our dying day can forget that
countenance," an infantryman wrote on the occasion of a presidential
visit to the army. "Concentrated in that one great, strong, yet tender
face, the agony of the life and death struggle of the hour was revealed
as we had never seen it before. With a new understanding, we knew
why we were soldiers."

Herein lay the explanation for much that otherwise could not be
understood — by Jefferson Davis, for one, who had expressed "contemptuous astonishment" at seeing his late compatriots submit to what
he called "the mere edict of a despot." They did not see their submission
in that light. "I know very well that many others might ... do better
than I can," Lincoln had told the cabinet in September, "and if I were
satisfied that the public confidence was more fully possessed by any one
of them than by me, and knew of any constitutional way he could be
put in my place, he should have it. I would gladly yield it to him. But
... I do not know that, all things considered, any other person has
more [of the confidence of the people]; and, however this may be,
there is no way in which I can have any other man put where I am. I
am here. I must do the best I can, and bear the responsibility of taking
the course which I feel I ought to take." Though these words were
spoken in private, their import carried over: with the result that such
power as he seized — and it was much, far more in fact than any President had ever had before, in peace or war — was surrendered by the
people in confidence that the power was not being seized for its own
sake, or even for Lincoln's sake, but rather for the sake of preserving the
Union. They gave him the power, along with the responsibility, glad to
have a strong hand on the reins.

This fear of weakness had been the source of their gravest doubt
through the opening year of conflict, as well as the subject of the
editors' most frequent complaint — Lincoln was lacking in "will and
purpose." Now they knew that their fears had been misplaced. A Ken-

tucky visitor, turning to leave the White House, asked the President what cheering news he could take home to friends. By way of reply, Lincoln told him a story about a chess expert who had never met his match until he tried his hand against a machine called the Automaton Chess Player, and was beaten three times running. Astonished, the defeated expert got up from his chair and walked slowly around and around the machine, examining it minutely as he went. At last he stopped and leveled an accusing finger in its direction. "There's a man in there!" he cried. Lincoln paused, then made his point: "Tell my friends there is a man in here."

Something else he was, as well — a literary craftsman — though so far this had gone unrecognized, unnoticed, and for the most part would remain so until critics across the Atlantic, unembarrassed by proximity, called attention to the fact. Indeed, complaints had been registered that he wrote "like a half-educated lawyer" with little or no appreciation for the cadenced beauties latent in the English language, awaiting the summons of the artist who knew how to call them up. That there was such a thing as the American language, available for literary purposes, had scarcely begun to be suspected by the more genteel, except as it had been employed by writers of low dialog bits, which mainly served to emphasize its limitations. Lincoln's jogtrot prose, compacted of words and phrases still with the bark on, had no music their ears were attuned to; it crept by them. However, an ambiguity had been sensed. Remarking "the two-fold working of the two-fold nature of the man," one caller at least had observed the contrast between "Lincoln the Westerner, slightly humorous but thoroughly practical and sagacious," and "Lincoln the President and statesman . . . seen in those abstract and serious eyes, which seemed withdrawn to an inner sanctuary of thought, sitting in judgment on the scene and feeling its far reach into the future."

Here was a clew; but it went uninvestigated. Apparently it was miracle enough that a prairie lawyer had become President, without pressing matters further to see that he had also become a stylist. In fact, so natural and unlabored had his utterance seemed, that when people were told they had an artist in the White House, their reaction was akin to that of the man in Molière who discovered that all his life he had been speaking prose. "I am here. I must do the best I can," Lincoln had said, and that best included this. Natural perhaps it was; unlabored it was not. Long nights he toiled in his workshop, the "inner sanctuary" from which he reached out to the future, and here indeed was the best clew of all. For he worked with the dedication of the true artist, who, whatever his sense of superiority in other relationships, preserves his humility in this one. He knew, as a later observer remarked, "the dangers that lurk in iotas." There were days when callers, whatever their importance, were turned away with the explanation that the President was at work: which meant writing.

A series of such days came in November, and the occasion was the preparation of a message to Congress, which would convene December 1. Lincoln saw already what would later become obvious, but was by no means obvious yet: that the war had ended one phase and was about to enter another. This message was intended to signal that event, bidding farewell to the old phase and setting a course for the new. Basically it was dedicatory, for there was need for dedication. The fury of Perryville, the blood that had stained the Antietam and sluiced the ridge in front of Sharpsburg, had reëmphasized the fact disclosed on a smaller scale at First Bull Run and Wilson's Creek, then augmented at Shiloh and the Seven Days, that both armies were capable of inflicting and withstanding terrible wounds. Though it was incredible that the ratio of increase would be maintained, there would be other Shilohs, other Sharpsburgs, other terrors. Men in their thousands now alive would presently be dead; homes so far untouched by sorrow would know tears; new widows and new orphans, some as yet unmarried or unborn, would be made — all, as Lincoln saw it, that the nation might continue and that men now in bondage might have freedom. In issuing the Preliminary Emancipation Proclamation he had made certain that there would be no peace except by conquest. He had weighed the odds and made his choice, foreseeing the South's reaction. "A restitution of the Union has been rendered forever impossible," Davis said. Lincoln had known he would say it; the fact was, he had been saying it all along. What he meant, and what Lincoln knew he meant, was that the issue was one which could only be settled by arms, and that the war was therefore a war for survival — survival of the South, as Davis saw it: survival of the Union, as Lincoln saw it — with the added paradox that, while neither of the two leaders believed victory for his side meant extinction for the other, each insisted that the reverse was true.

On the face of it, Davis had rather the better of his opponent in this contention, since the immediate and admitted result of a southern defeat would be that the South would go out of existence as a nation, however well it might survive in the sense that Lincoln intended to convey. The threat of national extinction was a sharper goad than any the northern leader could apply in attempting the unification he saw was necessary; therefore he determined to try for something other than sharpness. It was here that his particular talent, though so far it had gone unrecognized in general, could most effectively be brought to bear. As he had done against Douglas in the old days, so now in his long-range contest with Davis he shifted the argument onto a higher plane. Douglas had wanted to talk about "popular sovereignty," the right of the people of a region to decide for themselves the laws and customs under which they would live, but Lincoln had made slavery the issue, to the Little Giant's unavoidable discomfort. Similarly, in the present debate, while Davis spoke of self-government, Lincoln — without ever dropping the pretense that Davis was invisible, was in fact not there at all — appealed to "the mystic chords of memory" and "the chorus of the Union," then presently moved on to slavery and freedom, which Davis could no more avoid than Douglas had been able to do. Lincoln tarred them both with the same brush, doing it so effectively in the present case that the tar would never wear off, and managed also to redefine the Davis concept of self-government as destructive of world democracy, which was shown to depend on survival of the Union with the South as part of the whole. In thus discounting the claims of his opponent, he rallied not only his own people behind him, but also those of other lands where freedom was cherished as a possession or a goal, and thus assured nonintervention. Davis in time, like other men before and since, found what it meant to become involved with an adversary whose various talents included those of a craftsman in the use of words.

A case in point was this December message. It was a long one, nearly fifty thousand words, and it covered a host of subjects, all of them connected directly or indirectly with the war. "Fellow-Citizens of the Senate and House of Representatives," it opened. "Since your last annual assembling another year of health and bountiful harvest has passed, and while it has not pleased the Almighty to bless us with a return of peace, we can but press on, guided by the best light he gives us, trusting that in his own good time and wise way all will yet be well. . . . The civil war, which has so radically changed, for the moment, the occupations and habits of the American people, has necessarily disturbed the social condition and affected very deeply the prosperity of the nations with which we have carried on a commerce that has been steadily increasing throughout a period of half a century. It has at the same time excited political ambitions and apprehensions which have produced a profound agitation throughout the civilized world. . . . We have attempted no propagandism and acknowledged no revolution; but we have left to every nation the exclusive conduct and management of its own affairs. Our struggle has been, of course, contemplated by foreign nations with reference less to its own merits than to its supposed and often exaggerated effects and consequences resulting to those nations themselves. Nevertheless, complaint on the part of this government, even if it were just, would certainly be unwise."

After this rather mild and dry beginning, he passed at once — or the clerk did, for Lincoln did not deliver the message in person — to matters drier still. A new commercial treaty had been arranged with the Sultan of Turkey, while similar arrangements with Liberia and Haiti were pending. Financially, he was pleased to report, the country was quite sound. Treasury receipts for the July-through-June fiscal year were \$583,885,247.06, and disbursements totaling \$570,841,700.25 had left a balance of \$13,043,546.81 to be carried over. Restlessness among the frontier tribes perhaps indicated that the Indian system needed to be remodeled. The Pacific Railway was being pushed toward completion. A Department of Agriculture had been established.... The clerk droned on, advising the squirming congressmen that these details "will claim your most diligent consideration," though this could hardly have been easy, comprising as they did nearly half of the long document. By now, the assembled politicians were nearly as restless as the red men on the frontier. Presently, however, approaching its mid-point, the message changed its tone.

"A nation may be said to consist of its territory, its people, and its laws. The territory is the only part which is of certain durability. 'One generation passeth away, and another generation cometh: but the earth abideth forever.' It is of the first importance to duly consider and estimate this ever-enduring part. That portion of the earth's surface which is owned and inhabited by the people of the United States is well adapted to be the home of one national family, and it is not well adapted for two or more.... There is no line, straight or crooked, suitable for a national boundary upon which to divide. Trace through, from east to west, upon the line between the free and slave country, and we shall find a little more than one-third of its length are rivers, easy to be crossed, and populated, or soon to be populated, thickly upon both sides; while nearly all its remaining length are merely surveyors' lines, over which people may walk back and forth without any consciousness of their presence."

Such an argument might have been advanced in support of the unification of Europe or the annexation of Canada, but presently the listeners saw what Lincoln was getting at. He was talking to the inhabitants of the region to which he himself was native, "the great interior region, bounded east by the Alleghenies, north by the British dominions, west by the Rocky Mountains, and south by the line along which the culture of corn and cotton meets.... Ascertain from the statistics the small proportion of the region which has as yet been brought into cultivation, and also the large and rapidly increasing amount of its products, and we shall be overwhelmed with the magnitude of the prospect presented. And yet this region has no seacoast, touches no ocean anywhere. As part of the nation, its people now find, and may forever find, their way to Europe by New York, to South America and Africa by New Orleans, and to Asia by San Francisco.... These outlets, east, west, and south, are indispensable to the well-being of the people inhabiting, and to inhabit, this vast interior region. Which of the three may be the best is no proper question. All are better than either, and all of right belong to that people and to their successors forever. True to themselves, they will not ask where a line of separation shall be, but will vow rather that there shall be no such line." After a pause, he added: "Our national strife springs not from our permanent part, not from the land we inhabit, not from our national homestead. . . . Our strife pertains to ourselves — to the passing generations of men; and it can without convulsion be hushed forever with the passing of one generation."

This brought him at last to what he considered the nub of the issue. "Without slavery the rebellion could never have existed; without slavery it could not continue." So far, he had not mentioned the Preliminary Emancipation Proclamation except to note that it had been issued; nor did he return to it now. What he returned to, instead, was his old plan for compensated emancipation, the one way he saw for bringing the war to an end "without convulsion." His plan, as expanded here, would leave to each state the choice of when to act on the matter, "now, or at the end of the century, or at any intermediary time." The federal government was to have no voice in the action, but it would bear the total expense by issuing long-term bonds as payment to loyal masters. To those critics who would complain that the expense was too heavy, Lincoln replied beforehand that it was cheaper to pay in bonds than in blood, as the country was doing now. Besides, even in dollars and cents the cost would be less. "Certainly it is not so easy to pay something as it is to pay nothing; but it is easier to pay a large sum than it is to pay a larger one. And it is easier to pay any sum when we are able, than it is to pay it before we are able. The war requires large sums, and requires them at once. The aggregate sum necessary for compensated emancipation of course would be large. But it would require no ready cash, nor the bonds even, any faster than the emancipation progresses. This might not, and probably would not, come before the end of the thirty-seven years."

At this point, apparently — at any rate, somewhere along the line — the President had done some ciphering. By 1900, he predicted, "we shall probably have 100,000,000 of people to share the burden, instead of 31,000,000 as now." This was no wild guess on Lincoln's part; or as he put it, "I do not state this inconsiderately. At the same ratio of increase which we have maintained, on an average, from our first national census of 1790 until that of 1860, we should in 1900 have a population of 103,208,415. And why may we not continue that ratio far beyond that period? Our abundant room — our broad national homestead — is our ample resource." The past seventy years had shown an average decennial increase of 34.6 percent. Applying this to the coming seventy years, he calculated the 1930 population at 251,680,914. "And we will reach this, too," he added, "if we do not ourselves relinquish the chance by the folly and evils of disunion, or by long and exhausting war springing from the only great element of national discord among us."

Descending from these rather giddy mathematical heights, Lincoln continued his plea for gradual emancipation, not only for the sake of the people here represented, but also for the sake of the Negroes, whom it would spare "the vagrant destitution which must largely attend immediate emancipation in localities where their numbers are very great." Whatever objections might be raised, he wanted one thing kept in mind: "If there ever could be a proper time for mere catch arguments, that time surely is not now. In times like the present, men should utter nothing for which they would not willingly be responsible through time and in eternity." And having thus admonished the assembly, after forcing it to accompany him on an excursion into the field of applied mathematics, he thought perhaps some note of apology — if not of retraction — was in order. "I do not forget the gravity which should characterize a paper addressed to the Congress of the nation by the Chief Magistrate of the nation. Nor do I forget that some of you are my seniors, nor that many of you have more experience than I in the conduct of public affairs. Yet I trust that in view of the great responsibility resting upon me, you will perceive no want of respect to yourselves in any undue earnestness I may seem to display." Apparently, however, this was intended not only to make amends for what had gone before, but also to brace them for what was to come. Nor was it long in coming. Hard on the heels of this apology for "undue earnestness," he threw a cluster of knotty, rhetorical questions full in their faces:

"Is it doubted, then, that the plan I propose, if adopted, would shorten the war, and thus lessen its expenditure of money and of blood? Is it doubted that it would restore the national authority and national prosperity, and perpetuate both indefinitely? Is it doubted that we here — Congress and Executive — can secure its adoption? Will not the good people respond to a united and earnest appeal from us? Can we, can they, by any other means so certainly or so speedily assure these vital objects? We can succeed only by concert. It is not 'Can any of us imagine better?' but 'Can we all do better?' Object whatsoever is possible, still the question recurs, 'Can we do better?' "

As the long message approached its end, Lincoln asked that question: "Can we do better?" Oratory was not enough. "The North responds ... sufficiently in breath," he had said of the reaction to the September proclamation; "but breath alone kills no rebels." He knew as well as Sherman the need for the nation to be "born again," and he would also have agreed with the New England major who this month wrote home that he sometimes felt like changing the old soldier's prayer into "O God, if there be a God, save my country, if my country is worth saving." A majority of 100,000 voters in Lincoln's own state, fearing the backwash of liberated slaves that would result from Grant's advance, had approved in November the adoption of a new article into the Illinois constitution prohibiting the immigration of Negroes into the state. He knew, too, the reaction of most of the lawmakers to the proposal he was now advancing — including that of Senator Orville Browning, his fellow

Illinoisan and confidant, who would write in his diary of his friend's plea when he went home tonight: "It surprised me by its singular reticence in regard to the war, and some other subjects which I expected discussed, and by the hallucination the President seems to be laboring under that Congress can suppress the rebellion by adopting his plan of compensated emancipation." Yet according to Lincoln it was not he, but they, who were hallucinated and enthralled, and he told them so as the long message wore on toward a close: "The dogmas of the quiet past are inadequate to the stormy present. The occasion is piled high with difficulty, and we must rise with the occasion. As our case is new, so we must think anew and act anew. We must disenthrall ourselves, and then we shall save our country."

Then came the end, the turn of a page that opened a new chapter. And now, through the droning voice of the clerk, the Lincoln music sounded in what would someday be known as its full glory: "Fellow-citizens, we cannot escape history. We of this Congress and this Administration will be remembered in spite of ourselves. No personal significance or insignificance can spare one or another of us. The fiery trial through which we pass will light us down, in honor or dishonor, to the latest generation. We say we are for the Union. The world will not forget that we say this. We know how to save the Union. The world knows we do know how to save it. We — even we here — hold the power and bear the responsibility. In giving freedom to the slave, we assure freedom to the free — honorable alike in what we give and what we preserve. We shall nobly save or meanly lose the last, best hope of earth. Other means may succeed; this could not fail. The way is plain, peaceful, generous, just — a way which, if followed, the world will forever applaud, and God must forever bless."

LIST OF MAPS

Maps drawn by George Annand, of Darien, Connecticut, from originals by the author. All are oriented north.

BIBLIOGRAPHICAL NOTE

Many books by many men, predominantly military experts or professional historians, went into the making of this one book by one man
who is neither, and of these the most useful, as well as the largest, were
the 128-volume *War of the Rebellion: a Compilation of the Official
Records of the Union and Confederate Armies* and the 30-volume
*Official Records of the Union and Confederate Navies in the War of
the Rebellion,* issued by the government in 1880-1901 and 1897-1927
respectively. There you hear the live men speak — there and in their
diaries and letters, their newspapers and periodicals — although not always as they spoke in later life, when they got around to writing their
memoirs, regimental histories, and a host of articles such as the ones
collected in four large volumes and published in 1887 under the title
Battles and Leaders of the Civil War. Early or late, taken in conjunction with the diplomatic correspondence and the congressional tran-
scripts, these complete the first-hand testimony by soldiers and civilians,
some of high rank, some of low rank, some of no rank at all. The evidence is in. All else is speculation or sifting, an attempt to reconcile
differences and bring order out of multiplicity by sorting the fruits
that have poured from this horn of plenty.

Biographies of the participants and studies of the war itself, in
part or as a whole, make up the secondary sources. These are not only
interesting and rewarding in their own right, filling in and deepening
the over-all impression, but they also serve as a guide through the
labyrinth. I found them invaluable on both counts: so much so, indeed,
that while this narrative is based throughout on the original material
referred to above, my obligations are equally heavy on this side of the
line where it leaves off. The present is the first of three intended volumes — *Fort Sumter to Perryville, Fredericksburg to Meridian, Red
River to Appomattox* — and though the last will include a complete

bibliography, I want to state here at the outset my chief debts, particularly to those works still available in bookstores. These include the following biographies, of and by the following men: of Lee by Douglas Southall Freeman, Scribner's, 1934-35: of McClellan by Warren W. Hassler, LSU Press, 1957: of Beauregard by T. Harry Williams, LSU Press, 1954: of Sherman by Lloyd Lewis, Harcourt, Brace, 1932: of Joe Johnston by G. E. Govan and J. W. Livingood, Bobbs-Merrill, 1956: of Sheridan by Richard O'Connor, Bobbs-Merrill, 1953: of Jackson by Burke Davis, Rinehart, 1954: of Kirby Smith by Joseph H. Parks, LSU Press, 1954: of Davis by William E. Dodd, Jacobs, 1907, and Hudson Strode, Harcourt, Brace, 1955: of Lincoln by Carl Sandburg, Harcourt, Brace, 1939; J. G. Randall, Dodd, Meade, 1945-55; and Benjamin P. Thomas, Knopf, 1952.

Among the more general works, my chief debts are to the following: *Lincoln Finds a General* by Kenneth P. Williams, Macmillan, 1949-56: *Lee's Lieutenants* by Douglas Southall Freeman, Scribner's, 1942-44: *The Army of Tennessee* by Stanley F. Horn, Bobbs-Merrill, 1941: *Civil War on the Western Border* by Jay Monaghan, Little, Brown, 1955: *Mr. Lincoln's Army* and *This Hallowed Ground* by Bruce Catton, Doubleday, 1951 and 1956: *Guns on the Western Waters* by H. Allen Gosnell, LSU Press, 1949: *Lincoln and His Generals* by T. Harry Williams, Knopf, 1952: *Statesmen of the Lost Cause* and *Lincoln's War Cabinet* by Burton J. Hendrick, Little, Brown, 1939 and 1946: *The North Reports the Civil War* by J. Cutler Andrews, University of Pittsburgh Press, 1955: *The Railroads of the Confederacy* by Robert C. Black, UNC Press, 1952: *The Life of Johnny Reb* and *The Life of Billy Yank* by Bell Irvin Wiley, Bobbs-Merrill, 1943 and 1952: *Reveille in Washington* by Margaret Leech, Harper, 1941: *The Beleaguered City* by Alfred Hoyt Bill, Knopf, 1946: *Experiment in Rebellion* by Clifford Dowdey, Doubleday, 1946: *The Civil War and Reconstruction* by J. G. Randall, Heath, 1937: *The Story of the Confederacy* by Robert S. Henry, Bobbs-Merrill, 1931: *The American Civil War* by Carl Russell Fish, Longmans, Green, 1937: *The Confederate States of America* by E. Merton Coulter, LSU Press, 1950. There were others but these were the main ones, and to each I owe much.

Other obligations, of a more personal nature, I also incurred during the five years that went into the writing of this first volume: to the John Simon Guggenheim Memorial Foundation, for an extended fellowship which made possible the buying of books and bread: to the superintendents, historians, and guides of the National Park Service, for unfailing industry and courtesy in helping me to get the look and feel of the various battlefields: to Robert N. Linscott and Robert D. Loomis of Random House, for combining enthusiasm and patience: to Mrs. O. B. Crittenden of the William Alexander Percy Memorial Library, Greenville, Mississippi, for the continuing loan of that institution's set of the *Official Records*. To all these I am grateful, as well as to friends in Memphis who had the out-of-hours grace to refrain from mentioning the Civil War.

A word I suppose is in order as to the use I made of these materials, original and secondary, not only because it is customary but also because it appears to be necessary, at least in certain eyes. One of the best of the latter-day authorities, in the course of his carefully documented exegesis, cautions against accepting the testimony of Lew Wallace as to what took place at a council of war preceding the march on Donelson. "Recollections of events long past are always to be suspected," he explains, "and especially when set down by a writer of fiction." Wallace then was doubly suspect. He had waited, and he had written *The Fair God* and *Ben-Hur*. He was a novelist.

Well, I am a novelist, and what is more I agree with D. H. Lawrence's estimate of the novel as "the one bright book of life." I might also agree with the professor quoted above, but only by considering each witness on his merit, his devotion as a writer to what should be his main concern. The point I would make is that the novelist and the historian are seeking the same thing: the truth — not a different truth: the same truth — only they reach it, or try to reach it, by different routes. Whether the event took place in a world now gone to dust, preserved by documents and evaluated by scholarship, or in the imagination, preserved by memory and distilled by the creative process, they both want to tell us *how it was:* to re-create it, by their separate methods, and make it live again in the world around them.

This has been my aim, as well, only I have combined the two. Accepting the historian's standards without his paraphernalia, I have employed the novelist's methods without his license. Instead of inventing characters and incidents, I searched them out — and having found them, I took them as they were. Nothing is included here, either within or outside quotation marks, without the authority of documentary evidence which I consider sound. Although I have left out footnotes, believing that they would detract from the book's narrative quality by intermittently shattering the illusion that the observer is not so much reading a book as sharing an experience, I have thought it proper to employ the three dots of elision to signify the omission of interior matter from quotations. In all respects, the book is as accurate as care and hard work could make it. Partly I have done this for my own satisfaction; for in writing a history, I would no more be false to a fact dug out of a valid document than I would be false to a "fact" dug out of my head in writing a novel. Also, I have tried for accuracy because I have never known a modern historical instance where the truth was not superior to distortion, by any standard and in every way. Wherever the choice lay between soundness and "color," soundness had it every time. Many problems were encountered in the course of all this study, but lack of color in the original materials was never one of them. In fact, there was the rub. Such heartbreak as was here involved came not from trying to decide what to include, but rather from trying to decide what to omit, and in the end the omissions far outnumbered the inclusions.

One word more perhaps will not be out of place. I am a Mississippian. Though the veterans I knew are all dead now, down to the final home guard drummer boy of my childhood, the remembrance of them is still with me. However, being nearly as far removed from them in time as most of them were removed from combat when they died, I hope I have recovered the respect they had for their opponents until Reconstruction lessened and finally killed it. Biased is the last thing I would be; I yield to no one in my admiration for heroism and ability, no matter which side of the line a man was born or fought on when the war broke out, fourscore and seventeen years ago. If pride in the resistance my forebears made against the odds has leaned me to any degree in their direction, I hope it will be seen to amount to no more, in the end, than the average American's normal sympathy for the underdog in a fight.

—S.F.

Index

COMPREHENSIVE TABLE OF CONTENTS

The Civil War: A Narrative
Volume II, *Fredericksburg to Meridian*

"Gettysburg...is described with such meticulous attention to action, terrain, time, and the characters of the various commanders that I understand, at last, what happened in that battle. ...Mr. Foote has an acute sense of the relative importance of events and a novelist's skill in directing the reader's attention to the men and the episodes that will influence the course of the whole war, without omitting items which are of momentary interest. His organization of facts could hardly be bettered." —*Atlantic*

"Though the events of this middle year of the Civil War have been recounted hundreds of times, they have rarely been re-created with such vigor and such picturesque detail as in Mr. Foote's 'Civil War: A Narrative.' " —*New York Times Book Review*

"The lucidity of the battle narratives, the vigor of the prose, the strong feeling for the men from generals to privates who did the fighting are all controlled by a constant sense of how it happened and what it was all about. Foote has the novelist's feeling for character and situation, without losing the historian's scrupulous regard for recorded fact. *The Civil War* is likely to stand unequaled." —Walter Mills

The Civil War: A Narrative
Volume III, *Red River to Appomattox*

"Foote is a novelist who temporarily abandoned fiction to apply the novelist's shaping hand to history: his model is not Thucydides but *The Iliad* and his story, innocent of notes and formal bibliography, has a literary design. Not by accident...but for cathartic effect is so much space given to the war's unwinding, its final shudders and convulsions....To read this chronicle is an awesome and moving experience. History and literature are rarely so thoroughly combined as here; one finishes this volume convinced that no one need undertake this particular enterprise again." —*Newsweek*

"I have never read a better, more vivid, more understandable account of the savage battling between Grant's and Lee's armies....Foote stays with the human strife and suffering, and unlike most Southern commentators, he does not take sides. In objectivity, in range, in mastery of detail, in beauty of language and feeling for the people involved, this work surpasses anything else on the subject. Written in the tradition of the great historian-artists—Gibbon, Prescott, Napier, Freeman—it stands alongside the work of the best of them." —*New Republic*

"The most written-about war in history has, with this completion of Shelby Foote's trilogy, been given the epic treatment it deserves." —*Providence Journal*

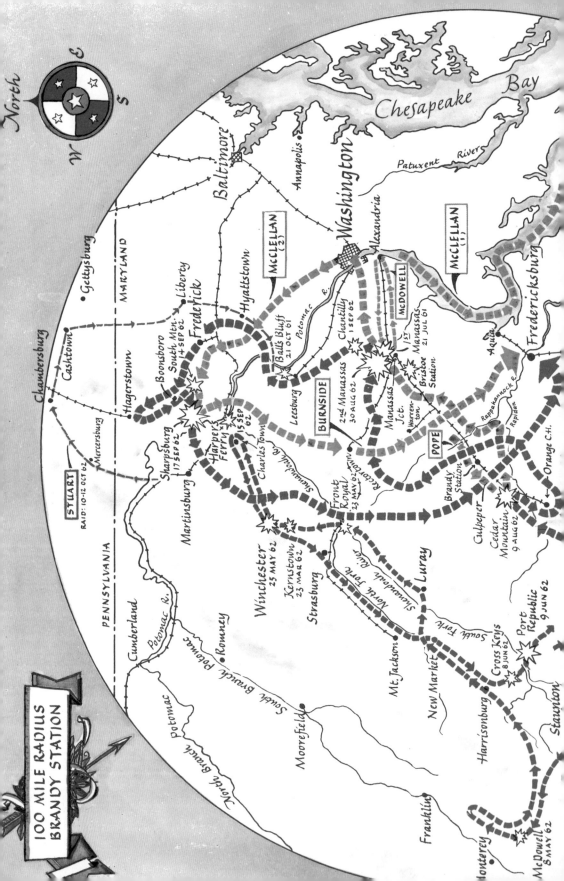

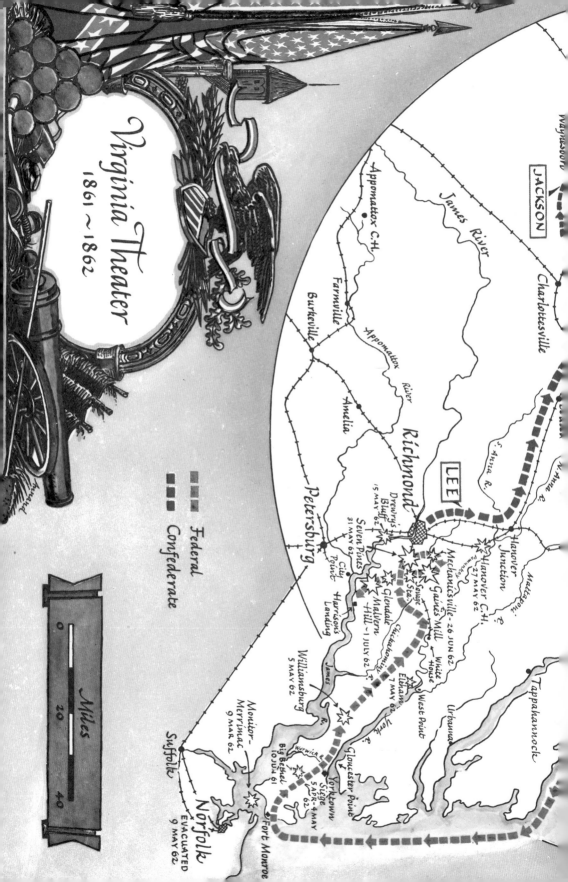

Virginia Theater
1861 ~ 1862

Federal
Confederate

Miles
0   20   40

JACKSON

Waynesboro

James River

Appomattox C.H.

Charlottesville

Farmville

Burkeville

Appomattox River

S. Anna R.

N. Anna R.

LEE

Amelia

Richmond

Hanover Junction

Mattaponi

Petersburg

Drewry's Bluff
15 May 62

Seven Pines
31 May 62

Hanover C.H.
27 May 62

Mechanicsville ~ 26 JUN 62

City Point

Savage

Gaines Mill

White House

Tappahannock

Harrison's Landing

Glendale

Star

Malvern

Chickahominy

Hill ~ 1 JULY 62

Eltham
7 May 62

York R.

West Point

Urbanna

James R.

Williamsburg
5 MAY 62

Monitor–
Merrimac
9 MAR 62

Gloucester Point

Suffolk

Big Bethel
10 JUN 61

Warwick R.

Yorktown
Siege
APR 4–MAY
62

Norfolk
EVACUATED
9 MAY 62

Fort Monroe